ENCYCLOPEDIA C

ENCYCLOPEDIA C

Robert A. Radcliffe

SYBEX®

SAN FRANCISCO • PARIS • DÜSSELDORF • SOEST

Acquisitions Editor: Dianne King
Developmental Editor: James A. Compton
Copy Editors: Kathleen Hummel, Kayla Sussell
Technical Editor: Byron Dazey
Assistant Editor: Janna Hecker
Word Processors: Scott Campbell, Deborah Maizels, Winnie Kelly, Lisa Mitchell
Book Designer: Thomas Ingalls + Associates
Layout Artist: Suzanne Albertson
Technical Art: Delia Brown
Screen Graphics: Cuong Le
Typesetter: Bob Myren
Proofreader: Sylvia Townsend
Indexer: Ted Laux
Cover Designer: Archer Design
Cover Photographer: David Bishop
Screen reproductions produced by XenoFont.

XenoFont is a trademark of XenoSoft.

SYBEX is a registered trademark of SYBEX, Inc.

TRADEMARKS: SYBEX has attempted throughout this book to distinguish proprietary trademarks from descriptive terms by following the capitalization style used by the manufacturer.

SYBEX is not affiliated with any manufacturer.

Every effort has been made to supply complete and accurate information. However, SYBEX assumes no responsibility for its use, nor for any infringement of the intellectual property rights of third parties which would result from such use.

The text of this book is printed on recycled paper.

Library of Congress Card Number: 90-70873

ISBN: 0-89588-655-3

Manufactured in the United States of America
10 9 8 7 6 5 4 3 2 1

Acknowledgments

Although forewarned about tackling a project of this size and scope, I wish to thank Dr. Rudolph Langer and Ms. Dianne King for their confidence in my ability to complete this work, and to make a contribution to the field; and yes, to confirm that everything they said was true.

I must credit P.J. Plauger and Rex Jaeschke, whose books and articles I have studied over the years, for their insights that enabled me to progress from K&R to ANSI C and beyond. I have tried to add another perspective to C, not as an implementor, but rather as a teacher of the next generation of C and C++ programmers.

To Directors of Continuing Education, Deborah Hitchcock and Barbara Fenton, and to my past Intro and Advanced C students at Penn State University, my thanks for the opportunity to develop and experiment with the materials that formed the basis of this book.

Special thanks to Kerry Carter for her support and understanding during this 14-month project that at times seemed as if it would never end (and yes those other times too); and to my family and friends who by now must understand that I am just wired differently: Dad and Dot, Dennis and Jane, Aunt Helen, Tom and Hyunki, Dr. B., Phil and Dan, Terry and Linda, Kursat and Linda, Steven, Janet and Kate, and you know who you are—see you soon.

To those at SYBEX behind the scenes, who have shaped this manuscript into publishable form: My special thanks to Jim Compton, editor, for doing an excellent job and being a helpful silent partner, and Kathy Hummel, copy editor, for meeting the challenge of this complex document and being such a pleasure to work with throughout. For assisting with some fine copy editing and manuscript proofing, my thanks to Kayla Sussell, Janna Hecker, Barbara Gordon, and Brendan Fletcher; credit to Bob Campbell for his valuable technical advice; thanks for Scott Campbell, Deborah Maizels, Lisa Mitchell, and Winnie Kelly's word processing, and to Martha Barrera, Carolina Montilla, and Chris Mockel for handling the scheduling and traffic; hats off to Bob Myren for typesetting—especially the tables—and to Sylvia Townsend for proofreading, and Suzanne Albertson, layout artist.

It is obvious to anyone familiar with publishing that this book was difficult to produce. Everyone at SYBEX made the production of this book possible, not me. Take pride in the satisfaction of a job well done. Again, my heartfelt thanks to all of you!

R.A.R.

Table of Contents

Introduction

Encyclopedia C is a complete desktop reference guide to the recently standardized ANSI C language for programmers working with Microsoft's QuickC (Version 2.5) and Optimizing C (Version 6.0) compilers, the DOS operating system (3.0 and later versions), and the following complement of Microsoft tools: LIB, QLINK, LINK, ILINK, EXEHDR, NMAKE, CVPACK, CV, and QH. It explains the proper use of Microsoft's development tools, and offers techniques and recommendations for writing C programs that conform with Standard C, emphasizing in particular how to write performance-oriented code, and provides complete documentation of the Run-Time Library.

In the years since Kernighan and Ritchie (K&R) first defined C, it has emerged as the software-development language of choice, because of its power and flexibility. As C's popularity grew, the language developed a number of incompatible "dialects," or implementations, making it difficult to write portable source code. The adoption of an ANSI standard for C will curtail the proliferation of other C "dialects" in the future. Throughout this book, all Standard (■) and non-Standard (□) features are clearly portrayed.

Any discussion that attempts to address the practical concerns of working C programmers must be grounded in a particular compiler implementation and host operating system. The Microsoft C compilers and DOS presently dominate the marketplace, and it appears they will continue to do so through the 1990s as well. Microsoft's compilers conform with Standard C and offer both a powerful set of program-development tools and Run-Time Library functions.

Encyclopedia C explains how to use Microsoft's C compilers for DOS and embodies the materials developed by the author to teach Introductory and Advanced C Professional Development courses at Penn State University, representing the equivalent of over 60 classroom hours of instruction.

This book is designed to address the needs of a broad spectrum of C programmers, from beginners approaching C as a second language to experienced professionals. It assumes some familiarity with at least one other high-level language, inasmuch as C is not usually learned as a first language. A complete, authoritative reference, *Encyclopedia C* brings together materials that would otherwise require the purchase of dozens of separate books and hundreds of periodicals (see Appendix A).

As a desktop reference guide, *Encyclopedia C* is meant to be consulted whenever you need quick answers about specific aspects of using Microsoft C with DOS. You do not need to read each chapter in succession to get the most out this book. Extensive cross-referencing makes it easy to find all the discussions that touch upon a particular topic. Several of the books listed in the Bibliography (Appendix A) offer a more tutorial approach to learning the language, particularly Stan Kelly-Bootle's *Mastering QuickC* (Sybex, 1989).

Encyclopedia C presents a complete explanation of the ANSI C programming language and comprehensive documentation of the Microsoft C Run-Time Library. It is written exclusively from an application programmer's point of view, with over 200 complete example programs, pointed explanations, and proven techniques that can be put to use immediately.

Themes Bridge the Gap

Encyclopedia C bridges the gap between C language syntax-intensive books, and bland function-library documentation. The concepts and principles upon which Microsoft's tools have been developed are carefully explained. Alternate coding styles and techniques are evaluated from a performance viewpoint throughout. The important concepts that underlie the development of the C Run-Time Library, which are usually overlooked, are finally explained. Recommended approaches and strategies for the solution of real problems are presented in source code examples that show sample output and are also available on disk to encourage further independent study. (Refer to the Order Form in the back of the book.)

A uniform C coding philosophy underlies the discussions, explanations, and recommendations found throughout this book:

- Establish portability, requirement, and performance objectives before writing any C code.
- Always write Standard C conforming source code, unless impossible to do so.
- When available, use Standard C Run-Time Library functions, not their non-Standard (Microsoft) counterparts.
- To perform tasks not supported by the C Run-Time Library, purchase commercial libraries of functions in source code form, if available.
- Lastly, resort to writing functions in C from scratch, and resort to Assembly language programming only to satisfy unique requirement and performance objectives.

Tables have been used extensively throughout this book to simplify the use and understanding of the subject material. Clearly this reference is intended to represent more than just a consolidation of Microsoft's documentation. *Encyclopedia C* blends experience, recommendations, and solutions throughout that will help you to exploit fully the power of Microsoft C's programming tools.

Organization

Encyclopedia C is divided into eight parts, containing a total of 29 chapters. Part 1, "Getting Started with Microsoft C," comprises Chapters 1-4 and describes the software products provided by Microsoft that, in a coordinated way, enable you to write and develop programs in C. You'll find information about configuring DOS for C (Chapter 1), selecting a C compiler (Chapter 2), using Microsoft's software-development utilities (Chapter 3), and guidelines for writing Standard C programs (Chapter 4).

Parts 2–5 provide a complete review of the features incorporated into the recently standardized ANSI C language. Part 2, "Using the Preprocessor," contains an explanation of the compiler to preprocessor directives (Chapter 5) and a summary of C header files and function prototypes (Chapter 6). Part 3, "Representing Data in C," discusses data types and qualifiers (Chapter 7), arrays and strings (Chapter 8), structures and unions (Chapter 9), addressing and pointers (Chapter 10), and working with bits (Chapter 11). Part 4, "Expressing Logic in C," reviews operators, including precedence and associativity (Chapter 12), and the rules and syntax of constructing expressions and statements (Chapter 13). Part 5, "Writing Functions in C," focuses upon the building blocks of C, function subprograms (Chapter 14), and the memory mapping and other characteristics of special function `main()` (Chapter 15).

Parts 6 and 7 provide a complete summary of all Standard C and Microsoft functions available in the Run-Time Library (except graphics). Part 6, "Using the C Run-Time Library I/O Services," covers those functions used for directory and file management (Chapter 16), stream I/O (Chapter 17), low-level I/O (Chapter 18), and console and port I/O (Chapter 19). Part 7, "Using the C Run-Time Library's Other Services," covers the remaining run-time services for character and data conversion (Chapter 20), date and time management (Chapter 21), DOS/BIOS system calls (Chapter 22), math functions (Chapter 23), memory management (Chapter 24), process control (Chapter 25), string-handling (Chapter 26) and all other services (Chapter 27). Each of these chapters begins with a discussion of the programming issues involved in using the functions and concludes with a series of reference entries in a common format that notes a function's compatibility, header files and prototype, and arguments and return values; it also presents an example or refers you to an entry containing one, and provides comments about the function and example program.

Finally, Part 8, "Extending Microsoft C," explains how to write inline assembly code (Chapter 28), and presents a comprehensive approach to debugging C programs that involves defensive programming techniques, the use of interactive debugging tools, and the purchase of third-party debugging utilities (Chapter 29).

Each chapter provides complete coverage of the language feature at hand. You'll see how to accomplish related programming tasks with C and learn which of the available techniques is preferred (and why). Tables have been carefully prepared to summarize important information and make it easy both to find and to understand that information.

Command summaries of the Microsoft tools covered in this book—the OptimizingC (PWB and CL) and QuickC (QC and QCL) compilers and the LIB, QLINK, LINK, ILINK, EXEHDR, NMAKE, CV, CVPACK, and QH utilities—are found on the inside front cover. Appendices supplement the tables presented in the book with related, but more detailed information. The Index is exhaustive and is supplemented by a special Run-Time Library Quick Index found on the inside covers of the book. Together, these indices will help you quickly find the answer to any question you may have.

The 200+ source code programs found in this book, together with a special master alphabetic list of over 1000 identifiers used by Standard C, Microsoft C and C++, are also available on diskette. Refer to the Order Form in the back of the book.

What's Not in This Book

Certain topics have specifically been excluded from *Encyclopedia C*: editors and editing; freestanding or embedded C programming; the use of Microsoft C with OS/2, UNIX, and Xenix; using graphics library functions; windows; and C++ object-oriented programming.

Editors and editing seemed too elementary; embedded C too hardware-specific; multiple operating system discussions too general; and graphics library programming too non-Standard. The compatibility of each DOS run-time library function with its equivalent provided for OS/2, UNIX and Xenix is, however, noted in the reference entries in Parts 6 and 7 of this book. C++ has been discussed to the extent of its impact upon the formulation of ANSI Standard C. No additional discussion of C++ is provided because it represents a distinct language, or at least the hybridization of C, transforming it from a language that currently facilitates top-down, structured design, to one that provides for bottom-up, object-oriented design.

Finally, everything you really need to write C programs in a Microsoft environment has been integrated by *Encyclopedia C* in a format that supports you, the software developer.

PART

1

Getting Started with Microsoft C

Before you begin C programming, take a moment to ask yourself the following set of questions:

Are you confident that you have DOS optimally configured for working with Microsoft C?

DOS is the host environment that ultimately controls how well the Microsoft C compilers and related utilities operate and perform. All C source code development and program execution rely entirely upon the command-line and directory management services of DOS to access all project source code and data files. The DOS commands that are placed in CONFIG.SYS and AUTOEXEC.BAT are crucial if DOS is to provide these needed services in the most efficient manner. It is folly to bother writing C code using Microsoft's OptimizingC compiler if DOS is not optimally configured as well. Confirm that you have DOS optimized for C by reviewing Chapter 1.

Are you confident that you fully understand the options and limitations of the Microsoft C compiler you are using?

You certainly know that there are two separate Microsoft compilers from which to choose: QuickC, which is usable either in an integrated (QC) or command line (QCL) form; and OptimizingC, which is now available in an integrated form, referred to as the Programmer's Work-Bench (PWB) or command line (CL) form. A comparison of the features and tradeoffs of using each compiler in an integrated or stand-alone manner is provided. Confirm your understanding of the features and limitations of the Microsoft C compiler you intend to use by reviewing Chapter 2.

Are you confident that you fully understand how the LIB, QLINK, LINK, ILINK, EXEHDR, and NMAKE utilities can improve your C programming productivity?

While LIB and LINK are certainly familiar, QLINK, ILINK, EXEHDR, and NMAKE are probably new to you. Each of these utilities can shorten the development cycle time and improve the performance of your programs as well. Confirm your understanding of the options and capabilities provided for each utility by reviewing Chapter 3.

Are you familiar with the major ANSI issues and overall coding guidelines that will help you avoid naming conflicts as Standard C and C++ continue to evolve in the 1990's?

Standard C is something very new. The recent ANSI (American National Standards Institute) sanctioning of the C programming language "codifies existing practice" and establishes the future direction for the C programming language. Chapter 4 will bring you up to date on Standard C.

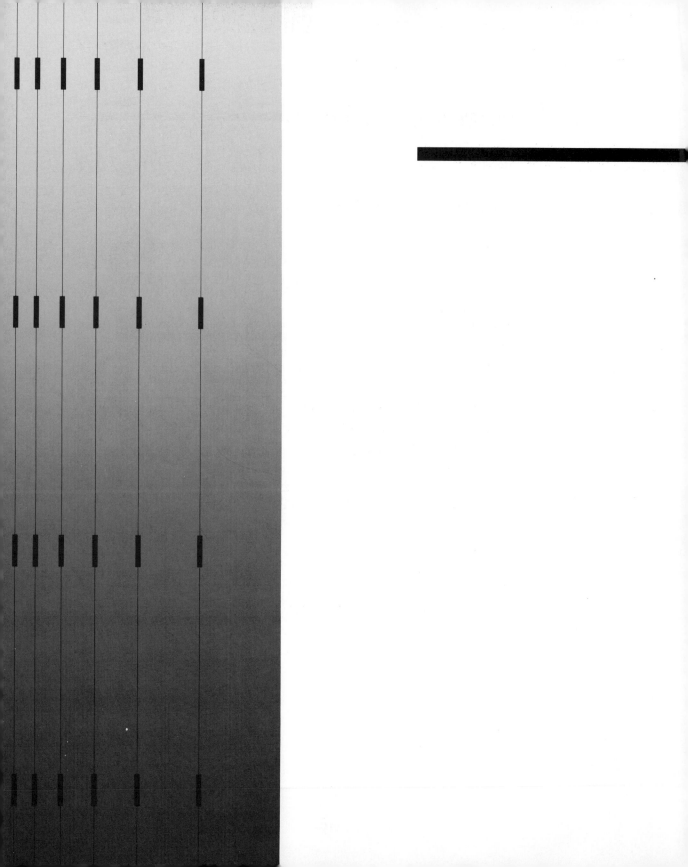

Configuring DOS for C

Configuring DOS for C

■■■■■■ The DOS operating system provides for the startup, execution, and termination processing of all programs running under its control. To realize optimum performance, you must configure DOS to accommodate and complement the needs of the Microsoft C compiler—QuickC Integrated (QC); QuickC Command Line (QCL); OptimizingC Integrated or Programmer's WorkBench (PWB); or OptimizingC Command Line (CL)—the supporting C utilities (ILINK, QLINK, LINK, LIB, NMAKE, EXEHDR, CVPACK, CV, and QH), and the C application programs to be run by DOS. The importance of configuring DOS is often trivialized or overlooked in the software development cycle, and the resulting performance problems and run-time errors that can occur in application programs are often difficult to pinpoint and generally embarrassing when found. So take a moment to review the information presented in this chapter, and verify that DOS is optimally configured for your programming environment. If you need additional information about DOS, consult the references cited in the Bibliography (Appendix A).

Together, DOS and the new ANSI Standard C will enable you to write programs that are more portable and capable of accommodating international use. Use the CONFIG.SYS, AUTOEXEC.BAT, and international DOS batch command sections of this chapter as checklists to review the adequacy of the DOS commands you are presently using. Remember that both of these DOS control files may contain only ASCII characters. When using a word processing program to edit these files, or in fact any C source code file, always specify nondocument mode (ASCII only, high-order bit always off).

CONFIG.SYS: THE SYSTEM CONFIGURATION COMMAND FILE

The CONFIG.SYS file must be located in the root (\) directory of the boot volume. The commands in \CONFIG.SYS are activated when you start DOS, either by hard-booting (powering-up) or soft-booting the computer (pressing Ctrl-Alt-Del). If a command is omitted from CONFIG.SYS, its default value is assumed. Table 1.1 presents the DOS configuration commands of particular importance and their default values.

TABLE 1.1: DOS Configuration Commands

COMMAND	DEFAULT	COMMENT
BREAK	OFF	Use **BREAK=ON**. This allows for the interruption of C compilations, links, and tests. Also a DOS batch command.
BUFFERS	2	Use **BUFFERS=20**; reduce this number only to save memory. The buffer size is 528 bytes, and the maximum number is 99.
COUNTRY	001, 437, or \COUNTRY.SYS	Use **COUNTRY=001**. Make an entry as your default and comment (REM) it as USA (see Table 1.2).
DEVICE	None	Use only if nonstandard device drivers are required for enhanced facility, hardware, or international use (see Table 1.3).
FILES	8	Use **FILES=20**. Assign the maximum number of open file handles permitted per process (program).
LASTDRIVE	E	Normally set to the highest drive specifier physically attached to your computer, but may be lower to logically disable drive specifiers. Available only in DOS 3.3 and later.
REM	None	Use remarks for documentation purposes. Available only in DOS 4.0 and later.
SHELL	\COMMAND.COM or /E:160	Use /P to establish a permanent command processor with a /E:*xxxxx* environment *xxxxx* bytes long. Maximum *xxxxx* is 32,768. Available in DOS 3.2 and later.
NOTE: All configuration commands ignore case.		

Except for BREAK and REM, the configuration commands shown in Table 1.1 may be used only in CONFIG.SYS, and are not recognized as DOS batch commands. If an improper command is specified, DOS displays the message *Unrecognized command in CONFIG.SYS*, ignores the command, and continues processing the file.

BREAK

SYNTAX

BREAK= [OFF | ON]

USAGE

This command controls whether DOS recognizes the Break (Ctrl-Scroll Lock) key combination at all times or only during standard input and output operations. Use **BREAK=ON** to allow for the interruption of programs producing few or no standard device operations, such as C compilations, links, and test programs that become trapped in an endless loop. Without Break recognition, your only recourse is to wait until a standard I/O device operation occurs or to reboot the system. In an integrated programming environment, like QuickC or Programmer's Work-Bench, rebooting will cause the loss of any unsaved source code file in memory. You should include the command

```
BREAK=ON
```

in CONFIG.SYS during program development; however, when you release a program for production use, either specify

```
BREAK=OFF
```

or omit the BREAK command and assume the default value (off). BREAK is also accepted as a batch command. Generally a user should *not* be able to Break from an application program, because open buffered files may not be flushed (see Chapter 16), allocated memory may not be freed (see Chapter 24), `atexit()`/`onexit()` functions may not be performed (see Chapter 25), and normal exit termination operations may be skipped (see Chapter 15).

BUFFERS

SYNTAX

```
BUFFERS=x
```

USAGE

This command determines how many file buffers DOS allocates to enhance the I/O throughput of DOS files (see the reference entry for FILES, later in this chapter). You may specify up to 99 BUFFERS, each of which takes 528 bytes of memory. Typically an *x* value between 10 and 25 provides the best performance. Include the following BUFFERS command in CONFIG.SYS:

```
BUFFERS=20
```

Using more buffers markedly improves the performance of application programs that process data files randomly, but not that of programs that process data files sequentially. Typically, if larger values of x are specified, I/O throughput may actually decrease because of the time necessary to search the available buffers to see whether the data block requested currently resides in memory.

The compiler, librarian, linker, and make facilities used by both the integrated and command-line versions of Microsoft's C compilers all perform file I/O intensively. Thus, failing to specify **BUFFERS**=x, which results in the default value shown in Table 1.1, markedly increases the elapsed time of each compilation-link-test cycle you perform.

COUNTRY

SYNTAX

COUNTRY=*cc*[,[*cp*][,[*FileSpec*]]]

USAGE

This command selects the character set and controls how DOS by default will display its date, time, currency symbol, and decimal separator fields. The *cc* parameter represents the standard three-digit country code, the same code used when dialing overseas long-distance telephone numbers. Table 1.2 lists the *cc* (country) codes currently implemented for DOS.

The optional *cp* parameter specifies a code page (character set) to be activated. If *cp* is omitted, the corresponding *cc* primary code page is defaulted. Table 1.2 lists the *cp* codes intended for each country. A further explanation of code pages appears in the section "Keyboard and Code-Page Translation Tables" later in this chapter.

TABLE 1.2: DOS Country and Keyboard Codes

COUNTRY	COUNTRY CODE	KEYBOARD CODE/KID[1]	PRIMARY CODE PAGE[2]	SECONDARY CODE PAGE[2]
Arabic (speaking)	785	None	865	850
Australia	061	US/103	437	850
Belgium	032	BE/120	850	437
Canada (Eng.)	001	US/103	437	850

TABLE 1.2: DOS Country and Keyboard Codes (continued)

COUNTRY	COUNTRY CODE	KEYBOARD CODE/KID[1]	PRIMARY CODE PAGE[2]	SECONDARY CODE PAGE[2]
Canada (Fr.)	002	CF/058	863	850
Chinese (simplif.)	086	None	936[3]	437
Chinese (tradit.)	088	None	938[3]	437
Denmark	045	DK/159	850	865
Finland	358	SU/153	850	437
France	033	FR/120,189	437	850
Germany	049	GR/129	437	850
Hebrew (speaking)	972	None	862[3]	850
Italy	039	IT/141,142	437	850
Japan	081	None	932[3]	437
Korea	082	None	934[3]	437
Latin America	003	LA/171	437	850
Netherlands	031	NL/143	437	850
Norway	047	NO/155	850	865
Portugal	351	PO/163	850	860
Spain	034	SP/172	437	850
Sweden	046	SV/153	437	850
Switzerland (Fr.)	041	SF/150	850	437
Switzerland (Ger.)	041	SG/000	850	437
United Kingdom	044	UK/168,166	437	850
United States	001	US/103	437	850

NOTES:

1. Up to two Keyboard IDs (KID) are supported per country.
2. There are five standard code pages:

United States	437
Multilingual	850
Portuguese	860
Canadian French	863
Norwegian and Danish	865

3. Special, nonstandard code pages.

The optional *FileSpec* parameter indicates where the DOS control file COUNTRY.SYS can be found. If *FileSpec* is omitted, the root directory of the boot drive is assumed. If COUNTRY.SYS is not available, the COUNTRY command cannot be performed.

The country code may be set only by the COUNTRY configuration command, not from the DOS command line. Once DOS is booted, the country code either is set to an explicit value as shown above or assumes the default values shown in Table 1.1. The normal display conventions of the specified country are then used for the input and output of all DOS date, time, currency, and decimal separator fields. For example, when COUNTRY=001 (United States) is chosen, the familiar date, time, and currency formatting conventions are used:

```
mm-dd-yyyy
hh:mm:ss
$1,000.00
```

If COUNTRY=033 (France) is chosen, the corresponding data-entry and display conventions apply:

```
dd/mm/yyyy
hh:mm:ss,hs
1000,00 F
```

Because the country code may be set only by the COUNTRY command in CONFIG.SYS, to switch between country codes, you must, in effect, switch between versions of CONFIG.SYS in use. To do this, reboot from alternate floppy disks, each containing a CONFIG.SYS file configured for a particular country; or, if your hard disk drive has been partitioned using the DOS command FDISK, each partitioned volume may be a system (bootable) volume that contains its own CONFIG.SYS file. Any system partition may be designated as the volume to be used on startup and from which a CONFIG.SYS file is read to configure DOS and set the country code.

Because there are no standard DOS commands for accessing the data structure DOS creates to retain the current COUNTRY information, a non-Standard C example program that uses the **intdos()** function and DOS interrupt 0x38 both to set and to access the DOS country code structure appears in Chapter 22. Using this model, you can write C programs that reflect the field editing standards established by the DOS country code in effect.

EXAMPLE

The command

```
COUNTRY=033,850
```

places the COUNTRY.SYS control file in the root directory of the default drive and assigns France as the country, using the multilingual code page.

DEVICE

SYNTAX

```
DEVICE=FileSpec [Params]
```

USAGE

The DEVICE command instructs DOS to load additional device drivers that complement or extend the features of the standard device drivers automatically installed by DOS. Such drivers can also provide for essential input, output, printer, diskette, fixed disk, and clock services. DEVICE configuration commands may be entered in CONFIG.SYS for each service that you require. The general format of these commands consists of a .SYS file specification followed by a series of optional parameters.

Device drivers (.SYS files) are hardware-dependent. When a new peripheral device not compatible with any existing device driver is to be attached to a computer, you must add another DEVICE command to configure DOS for the new driver.

The device drivers most commonly used to install IBM and compatible peripheral equipment are described below and demonstrate the use of the DEVICE command. Because of the system programming capabilities of the C language, C programs are often written for nonstandard peripheral devices. Installing a device driver for this purpose is certainly the easiest solution to this type of problem; using the port I/O routines described in Chapter 19 is considerably more difficult.

Table 1.3 lists all the standard DOS device names, some of which are referred to in the following sections.

ANSI.SYS

SYNTAX

```
DEVICE=ANSI.SYS
```

TABLE 1.3: Standard DOS Device Names

RESERVED NAME	DESCRIPTION	C EQUIVALENT
AUX	First serial/parallel adapter port	`stdaux`
COM1	Synonym for AUX	`stdaux`
COM2	Second serial/parallel adapter port	None
CON	Console keyboard/screen[1]	`stdin`, `stdout`, `stderr`
LPT1	Synonym for PRN	`stdprn`
LPT2	Second parallel printer	None
LPT3	Third parallel printer	None
NUL	Nonexistent (dummy) device[1]	None
PRN	First parallel printer	`stdprn`
A:	First floppy disk drive	None
B:	Second floppy disk drive	None
C:	First hard disk drive	None
D:	Second hard disk drive	None
E:	Third hard disk drive	None
F:..Z:	Normally, subsequent floppy, hard, virtual, or logically partitioned devices. Refer to the FDISK command entry in this chapter. If more than E: devices are attached, refer to the LASTDRIVE command entry in this chapter.	None

NOTES:
1. Both CON and NUL can be used as either input or output devices. Using CON for input, you can generate an end-of-file (EOF) mark by pressing F6 or Ctrl-Z and then Return. Using NUL as an input device generates an immediate EOF; when it's used as an output device, no data is written. Working with these device files is an important aspect of C programming.
2. All DOS device names are case insensitive.
3. Drive designators must be suffixed with a colon (:).

USAGE

ANSI.SYS is a replacement for the standard default CON (keyboard and screen) device driver loaded by DOS. This driver provides for extended keyboard and screen features such as the redefinition of key values, reassignment of function keys, control of cursor position, and setting of screen colors. These features are controlled by the PROMPT batch command, discussed later in this chapter.

EXAMPLE

The configuration command

```
DEVICE=C:\DOS\ANSI.SYS
```

locates a device driver in the ANSI.SYS file, located in the DOS directory of drive C, and tells DOS to configure itself to include that driver.

DISPLAY.SYS

SYNTAX

```
DEVICE=DISPLAY.SYS CON=(dtype, [bicp], count)
```

USAGE

This DOS 4.0 driver augments either the standard default CON used by DOS, or the ANSI.SYS CON driver described above, with code-page switching to support the use of different country symbol tables. The details of code pages are explained in the section "Keyboard and Code-Page Translation Tables" later in this chapter.

The *dtype* parameter identifies the type of display screen attached to your computer. These are the allowed values:

LCD   Liquid Crystal Display
EGA   Enhanced Graphics Adaptor

DOS does not support code-page switching for monochrome or CGA (color graphics adaptor) displays. Each *dtype* has a corresponding .CPI (code-page information) file associated with it; hence, LCD.CPI and EGA.CPI.

The *bicp* parameter is the built-in code page of the device. Include it for documentation purposes if known; otherwise, you can omit it.

The *count* parameter specifies the number of additional code pages to use with a device. Allowed values range from 1 through 12.

EXAMPLE

The command

```
DEVICE=DISPLAY.SYS CON=(EGA,,4)
```

locates the device driver DISPLAY.SYS in the root directory of the default drive, extends the device CON to support an EGA display with an unknown built-in code page, and provides for the support of four additional code pages (to be specified via the MODE command).

PRINTER.SYS

SYNTAX

```
DEVICE=PRINTER.SYS LPTx=(ptype, [bicp], count)
```

USAGE

This DOS 4.0 driver augments the standard default LPT*x* driver loaded by DOS with code-page switching. The details of code pages are fully explained in the section "Keyboard and Code-Page Translation Tables."

The LPT*x* parameter allows for the selection of either LPT1 (same as PRN), LPT2, or LPT3 (see Table 1.3).

The *ptype* parameter identifies the type of printer attached to your computer. These are the allowed values:

4201	IBM 4201/4202 Proprinter
4208	IBM 4207/4208 Proprinter XL24
5202	IBM 5202 QuietWriter III

Not all printers support code-page switching, and some do so in a slightly different manner. The PRINTER.SYS device driver is configured for a specific model of IBM/PS2 printer based upon the *ptype* code specified.

The *bicp* and *count* parameters are described above for DISPLAY.SYS. Again, each *ptype* that supports code-page switching has a corresponding .CPI file associated with it, hence: 4201.CPI, 4208.CPI and 5202.CPI.

EXAMPLE

The command

```
DEVICE=D:\PRINTER.SYS LPT1=(5202,437,1)
```

locates the device driver PRINTER.SYS in the root directory of the D: drive, extends the device LPT1 to support an IBM 5202 QuietWriter printer with a built-in United States code page, and allows the user to specify one additional code page (via the MODE command).

FILES

SYNTAX

`FILES=x`

USAGE

This command establishes the maximum number of file handles that can be opened concurrently by DOS, including all active foreground, background, and network processes. The overall limit for DOS is 20. This value also establishes the maximum number of file handles allowed for any single process (program). All C programs are automatically provided five DOS predefined files (**stdin**, **stdout**, **stderr**, **stdaux**, and **stdprn**, defined as object-like macros in the **<stdio.h>** header file), thereby reducing the maximum number of available file handles to 15 (see Chapter 17). Each file handle specified beyond the default of **FILES=8** increases the resident size of DOS by 48 bytes. Include the command

`FILES=20`

in CONFIG.SYS when working in a C programming environment. As stated earlier, the C tools (compiler, linker, and so on) need to perform disk (file) I/O operations constantly. Always close files opened in C as soon as all I/O is complete so that each file's handle becomes free and available for immediate reuse. After all available file handles have been allocated, further attempts to open files will result in one of several related DOS error messages, to the effect that too many files are open. See Chapter 16 for more information about opening and closing DOS files.

LASTDRIVE

SYNTAX

`LASTDRIVE=drive`

USAGE

This command sets the last or highest drive specifier to which DOS shall have access. Parameter *drive* is a letter from A to Z. The default assumed by DOS is E.

Normally you would not want to restrict access to installed drives. Disk space always seems to be at a premium, even with the large and relatively inexpensive drives that are becoming available. When you have many logical drives created using the FDISK batch command on one hard disk drive, however, or multiple hard disk drives on-line, you may wish to exclude drives used for backup purposes, so that they will not be inadvertently overwritten. The LASTDRIVE command makes DOS responsible for refusing any requests for access beyond the drive letter you specify, so that you don't have to rely upon your programming or operations personnel.

Since the LASTDRIVE configuration command, like the COUNTRY command, can be specified only at system boot-time, the switching techniques discussed in the COUNTRY reference entry apply to LASTDRIVE as well. Regardless of the technique used, when you need to access those disk drives beyond the current limit imposed by a LASTDRIVE command, the system must be rebooted. This is a small penalty to pay, however, for the peace of mind you'll have knowing that DOS is restricting access to critical backup drives containing program source code and production backup data files.

EXAMPLE

A typical LASTDRIVE command would appear in CONFIG.SYS as

```
LASTDRIVE=C
```

REM

SYNTAX

```
REM [comment]
```

USAGE

This feature, introduced in DOS 4.0, extends to CONFIG.SYS the standard remark feature permitted in batch files. If any special DOS symbols (such as <, >, >>, or |) are used in comments, they must be surrounded by double quotation marks (for example, **A "<" B**). REM is treated as a command line, and therefore is limited to 127 characters. Documentation of your CONFIG.SYS and AUTOEXEC.BAT files becomes particularly important when using international DOS commands, because of the many codes involved.

EXAMPLE

A typical REM command in AUTOEXEC.BAT (or CONFIG.SYS for DOS 4.0) would appear as follows:

```
REM (blank REM lines add white space for readability)
REM
REM Select Denmark=045, primary code page=865 !!
COUNTRY=045,865
REM
```

SHELL

SYNTAX

SHELL=*FileSpec* [/P][/MSG][/E:*xxxx*][/C*string*]

USAGE

This command specifies the command processor to be loaded by DOS. The *FileSpec* parameter indicates a complete DOS filename specification containing the processor program. The other parameters, all optional, are the same as would be specified in an equivalent COMMAND batch command for the command processor.

/P indicates that the command processor being loaded is to be permanent rather than secondary. Secondary command processors increase the memory space requirement and recognize the DOS command EXIT to return to the permanent command processor.

/MSG instructs DOS to retain in memory certain error messages that it would otherwise need to read from the disk each time it displays them.

/E:*xxxxx* specifies the desired environment table size in bytes. The environment table of a secondary command processor may be a different size than that of the permanent command processor. Normally a minimum of 160 bytes is allocated. When a large number of environment strings is required (see the SET reference entry), it is not uncommon for the allotted environment space to be exhausted and the DOS error message *Out of environment space* to be displayed. To offset this problem, invoke the SHELL command with an /E:*xxxxx* parameter specified to override the default environment space allocated. You can specify up to 32KB of environment space if necessary. The SHELL command can be invoked only from within CONFIG.SYS and establishes the environment table size available to all programs subsequently initiated by the default command processor.

/Cstring specifies a batch command line to be executed upon invocation of the processor. If */Cstring* is omitted, no commands are performed by the command processor before displaying the user prompt.

Another method of configuring a permanent or secondary command processor is to use the COMMAND batch command. Neither COMMAND nor SHELL affects the environment string setting of COMSPEC, which specifies the default command processor to be loaded whenever the system is booted. Unlike COMMAND, however, the SHELL command does not support the /C parameter, and it always invokes AUTOEXEC.BAT. (See the section "AUTOEXEC.BAT: The Automatic Startup Command File" for more information about COMMAND and SET COMSPEC.)

EXAMPLE

The command

```
SHELL=C:\COMMAND.COM /P /E:1024
```

locates the DOS command processor COMMAND.COM in the root directory of the C: drive, makes it permanent, and creates a 1KB environment table.

DOS COMMAND-LINE PROCESSING

For anyone using DOS 3.3 and earlier, and perhaps for some DOS 4.0 users, the DOS prompt and blinking cursor are the notorious trademarks of the operating system. They mark the *command line,*through which the user enters all instructions to the system. Ironically, the command line is displayed not by DOS itself, but by a special application program called the *command processor.* As we've seen in the discussion of the CONFIG.SYS file and its SHELL command, the default command processor is a file called COMMAND.COM, which begins executing immediately after CONFIG.SYS. We've also seen that it's possible to replace the default command processor by specifying another, either with SHELL or with the COMMAND or SET COMSPEC batch-file commands (discussed later in this chapter).

The proliferation of graphic user interfaces such as the one available with DOS 4.0, which supports a mouse to complement normal keyboarding operations, is part of a trend in the industry towards the development of "friendlier" command-processing programs. But regardless of the presentation techniques employed, all command processors are required to accept user commands, perform them if possible, and keep the user informed with appropriate messages. First we'll see how to write and edit a command line so that the command processor can interpret it correctly.

Working with the Command Line

A character string entered by the user is considered complete when the Return key is pressed. Because command-line strings sometimes exceed 80 characters (the width of most monitors), when entering a longer command line, just keep typing and line-wrap the command. Do not press Return, because that will be interpreted as the end of the command line. Long command lines may also be entered in batch command (.BAT) and automatic response files (@files).

As you enter command lines, the command processor temporarily saves the last command in a buffer. Pressing F3 retrieves this line to the screen, where you can either press Return to accept it verbatim or edit it using the special command-line editing keystrokes summarized in Table 1.4. You will probably find F1, F3, Del, ←, and Esc particularly handy when editing the DOS command line.

Tokens

The command processor reserves certain command-line characters for the purpose of separating the string of characters into *tokens*. The space, comma, semicolon, equal sign, and tab characters are the standard

TABLE 1.4: DOS Command-Line Editing Keys

KEY	DESCRIPTION
F1	Display one character from the buffer.
→	Display one character from the buffer.
F2	Display all characters from the buffer up to the character specified.
F3	Display all characters from the buffer.
F4	Delete all characters from the buffer up to the character specified.
F5	Make this edited line the buffer.
F6	Insert an EOF (Ctrl-Z) character.
Ins	Insert a character at the cursor position.
Del	Delete a character at the cursor position.
←	Delete a character to the left of the cursor.
Esc	Skip the present command and begin another.

command-line delimiters. They separate tokens. Tokens represent portions (substrings) of the command line itself. They identify the command (program) to be executed, and any options necessary for the command processor to set up the command (program) for processing. For example, the DOS command line

```
RENAME SAMPLE.DOC SAM.DOC
```

consists of three tokens: RENAME, SAMPLE.DOC, and SAM.DOC. In this case the space character serves as the delimiter. The first token is interpreted as a DOS internal command, and the next two tokens are the filename arguments required by the RENAME command. Other command-line characters are reserved to signify redirection and piping, and also serve as delimiters when command-line tokens are formed. See "Interpreting the Command Line" for more information about tokens.

Redirection, Piping, and the Command Line

Redirection is the rerouting of a program's standard input and output (I/O) without its knowledge. Since the filter program neither knows nor cares what files or devices are associated with its I/O file names, such rerouting is said to be *transparent.*The < character redirects the standard input. The > and >> characters redirect the standard output. Use >> if the output is to be appended to an existing file, and > if the output file is new. *Piping* allows the standard output from one program to be used as standard input to another program. The | character signifies piping.

Table 1.3, earlier in this chapter, lists the standard DOS device names commonly used to implement redirection and piping when disk filenames are not desired.

In C programming, the standard input file and output files are associated with the stream pointers **stdin** and **stdout** (see Chapter 17), and the file handles 0 and 1 (see Chapter 18), respectively. By default, standard input and output are associated with the DOS device CON, or the console. Although other predefined files are available to all C programs (**stderr**, **stdaux**, and **stdprn**), only standard input and output may be redirected or piped from the DOS command line without requiring that the C source-code program be changed and the program relinked. A common use of DOS command-line redirection and piping invokes the DIR list command to "pipe" its output to the SORT command to provide a printed directory listing in alphabetical order by filename:

```
DIR | SORT > PRN
```

For more on redirection and piping, see the section "Filter Programs."

It is important to understand that because redirection and piping are intended to be transparent to an application program, the command processor automatically strips these special characters and their associated parameters from the command line as entered by the user. Once these tokens (substrings) are removed, they are not passed to the executable command or program in the 127-character command-line space provided by the program segment prefix (PSP). Remember that although the command-line delimiting-character standards may vary between command processors, the underlying DOS PSP command-line length restriction remains. For more about the PSP, see the section that follows, "Interpreting the Command Line."

The command line also recognizes the use of *wildcards* in DOS filename and pathname arguments. The question mark (?) character represents any single character in that filename position, and the asterisk (*) represents any series of characters. DOS 4.0 has added a tilde (~) wildcard, which means "not matching" and is always entered preceding the filename expression. For example, the DOS directory command

```
DIR ~*.C
```

would produce a list of all files in the current directory that do *not* have a file extension of .C.

Interpreting the Command Line

Once the command line has been entered, initially scanned into tokens using the delimiters described above, and stripped of any redirection and piping tokens, the command processor's real work begins.

The first (leftmost) token on the command line is interpreted to represent either an internal DOS command name, an executable filename (external DOS command or application program), or a batch filename, in that order, based upon whether a partial or a complete file specification is provided.

If an incomplete pathname is given, DOS first checks whether the token matches an internal DOS command name. If not, it then searches the current path for an executable file ending in .COM, .EXE, or .BAT. Finally, it searches the set of possible drives and directories specified in a PATH command for a matching .COM, .EXE, or .BAT file. If it finds no matching filename, the command processor then displays the message *Bad command or filename*, followed by the familiar DOS prompt. (You can substitute your own prompt; see the PROMPT reference entry in this chapter.) If a complete pathname is specified, either the file is present and DOS processes it, or it is not present and DOS displays *Bad command or filename*, followed again by the DOS prompt.

Internal DOS Commands

Internal or resident DOS commands are loaded into memory when the operating system is booted. The first command-line token is interpreted as an internal DOS command if it is not a drive, directory, or filename, and the token matches one of the names listed in Table 1.5.

The remaining command-line tokens are used to fulfill the required command parameters. Any additional command-line tokens are ignored. Avoid naming executable files that inadvertently conflict with these names, because unless a complete pathname is provided, the command processor will always interpret these names as internal DOS commands. Upon completing the command, DOS redisplays its prompt.

Executable Files

External (transient) DOS commands and C application programs reside on disk storage as executable files (.COM or .EXE) and must be loaded into memory to be run. If the first command-line token is not prefaced with a drive and directory designator, and is not an internal DOS command, then a search for a corresponding filename with either a .COM, .EXE, or .BAT suffix is first made in the default drive and directory, followed by the sequence of paths specified by the PATH environment string. If no matching directory entry is found, the message *Bad command or filename* is displayed, followed by the DOS prompt in effect.

The Program Segment Prefix (PSP)   The DOS program segment prefix (PSP) controls how DOS handles all program setup, execution, and termination. If the DOS command processor finds a matching directory filename entry that ends in .COM or .EXE, it then prepares the program for execution in a

TABLE 1.5: Internal DOS Commands

BREAK	DATE	MD	RENAME
CALL	DEL	MKDIR	RMDIR
CD	DIR	PATH	SET
CHCP	ECHO	PAUSE	SHIFT
CHDIR	ERASE	PROMPT	TIME
CLS	FOR	RD	TYPE
COPY	GOTO	REM	VERIFY
drive:	IF	REN	

standard manner, whether the file is a DOS external command or a C application program.

A standard 256-byte (0–255 or 0x00–0xFF) PSP is constructed and appended to the beginning of the program file that is loaded into memory (RAM). The fixed layout of the PSP is shown in Table 1.6.

Several byte-offset field entries in the PSP are of particular interest. Bytes 44–45 (0x2C–0x2D) hold the starting address of the environment table (SEG:0000) whose size is established by the /E:*xxxx* configuration parameter specified for the primary or secondary command processor in use, and whose string entries are created using the DOS SET command.

Bytes 128–255 (0x80–0xFF) contain the DOS command-line characters that remain after all redirection and piping characters and related tokens have been removed. This 127-byte (0x81–0xFF) space in the PSP is what

TABLE 1.6: The Contents of the Program Segment Prefix (PSP)

BYTE	DESCRIPTION
0–1	Interrupt 0x20. Archaic, use interrupt 0x21 function 0x4C.
2–3	Top of Memory. Segment address above program's allocated memory.
4–5	Reserved.
6–9	Available memory. Bytes free within the segment for a .COM program (Tiny memory model).
10–13	Normal program termination address (CS:IP). Copy of the interrupt 0x22 vector.
14–17	Ctrl-Break or Ctrl-C termination address (CS:IP). Copy of the interrupt 0x23 vector.
18–21	Critical error exit address (CS:IP). Copy of the interrupt 0x24 vector.
22–23	Parent program PSP segment (SEG:0000).
24–43	File handle table. 20 single-byte assigned file handle numbers.
44–45	Program environment table segment address (SEG:0000).
46–49	Reserved.
50–51	File handle count. Default is 20 (maximum).
52–79	Reserved.
80–81	Interrupt 0x21 function dispatcher.
82–91	Reserved.
92–107	Unopened standard File Control Block 1. Archaic, use file handles.
108–123	Unopened standard File Control Block 2. Archaic, use file handles.
124–127	Reserved.
128–128	Byte length of the DOS command line with all redirection effects removed.
129–255	Copy of the DOS command line.

establishes the length restriction of the DOS command line, regardless of which command processor is in use, or whether the command was entered from the keyboard, a batch command file, or other redirected input device. Clearly, when more than 127 characters are entered at the DOS command line, they are ignored (truncated), because there is no way to pass them to the program executed by DOS. The C startup code (Chapter 15) sets up the **argc** and **argv** arguments of function **main()** from the command-line field of the PSP. The use of these standard arguments is preferred over the direct interrogation of the PSP, because the structure of the PSP is not standardized between operating systems.

Three different termination addresses are stored in the PSP to ensure that every program loaded for execution by DOS can be terminated in some manner, regardless of whether the addresses in the interrupt vector table (0000:0000–0000:0400) become corrupted. Bytes 10–13 (0x0A–0x0D) of the PSP contain a program's normal termination address (CS:IP); bytes 14–17 (0x0E–0x11) contain the program's Ctrl-Break address (CS:IP); and bytes 18–21 (0x12–0x15) contain the program's critical error address (CS:IP). See Chapters 22 and 27 for more about these interrupts.

Access to the PSP associated with every C application program is provided by the global variable **_psp** (see Appendix C). This variable holds the segment address of the PSP, with an implied offset component of 0x0000. Each field of the PSP can be accessed by simply constructing a memory address using the **_psp** segment and a byte-offset shown in Table 1.6, casting that address to point to an appropriate type object, and then using pointer indirection.

External DOS Commands   The command processor cannot distinguish between a DOS external command and an executable C application program. Table 1.7 lists the valid DOS external command names.

Avoid using DOS external (or internal) command names as your C application program filenames. If such filename conflicts exist, the first matching directory filename found by the standard searching technique (PATH=*string*) will be executed when incomplete filenames are specified on the command line.

Filter Programs   A *filter* is any program that reads data from a standard input device, modifies the data, and then writes the result to a standard output device. Filter programs are written to exploit the redirection and piping features of the DOS command line. DOS provides three filter

TABLE 1.7: External DOS Commands

APPEND	DISKCOPY	KEYB	REPLACE
ASSIGN	EDLIN	LABEL	RESTORE
ATTRIB	FASTOPEN	MEM	SHARE
BACKUP	FIND	MODE	SORT
CHDSK	FORMAT	MORE	SUBST
COMMAND	GRAFTABL	NLSFUNC	SYS
COMP	GRAPHICS	PRINT	TREE
DISKCOMP	JOIN	RECOVER	XCOPY

programs—FIND, MORE, and SORT. Consider the following command line, which combines the use of redirection, piping, and filters:

```
C:\TEST\MYFILTER < MY.DAT | SORT >> YOUR.DAT
```

The C program MYFILTER.EXE, located on drive C in the \TEST directory, is executed by DOS with its standard input coming from file MY.DAT, which is found on the default drive and directory. The standard output from MYFILTER is piped to the DOS filter SORT, which in turn sorts the file starting in column 1 (the default) and appends its standard output to a file called YOUR.DAT, located in the current drive and directory.

You are also free to create other C filter programs by simply conforming to the standard input and output filter design conventions. A C program written in this fashion can then have its input and output redirected by the DOS command line, thereby extending the utility of the program to any combination of input and output disk- and device-based files (see Chapter 16). Consider the sample filter program shown in Figure 1.1.

This routine processes input from the standard input stream (**stdin**) one character at a time until the end-of-file character is encountered. Each character read is transformed to ASCII (by turning high-order bit 7 off) and written to standard output (**stdout**). For each C newline character (0x0A), the program writes another newline character, effectively double-spacing the output file.

This program (**ch1e1.exe**) can be executed from the DOS command line using any number of possible combinations of disk- and device-based file I/O, such as the following:

```
CH1E1 <ch1e1.c >ch1e1.dup

CH1E1 >prn

CH1E1 <ch1e1.c >nul
```

```
/* FILE: ch1e1.c    */

#include <stdio.h>

#include <io.h>

#include <fcntl.h>

main()

{

int ch;

setmode(fileno(stdin),O_BINARY);

setmode(fileno(stdout),O_BINARY);

while ((ch = getchar()) != EOF) {

    ch &= 0x7F;

    putchar(ch);

    if (ch == '\n') putchar('\n');

    }

fclose(stdin);

fclose(stdout);

exit(0);

}
```

FIGURE 1.1: The sample program ch1e1.c demonstrates the standard input and output filter design conventions.

In the first example, the input is accepted from disk file **ch1e1.c**, and the output is directed to a new disk file called **ch1e1.dup**. In the second example, the input comes from the keyboard (default device CON), and the output goes to the printer. In the last example, the input comes from disk file **ch1e1.c**, and the output goes to device NUL (the "bit bucket"). Device NUL can be helpful in debugging input end-of-file (EOF) detection problems; it can also be used to eliminate unwanted output during testing.

Batch Files

Batch files (ending in .BAT) are the last possibility the command processor considers in interpreting the first token on the command line, after internal DOS commands and executable files. Once a matching .BAT file is located, the command processor's standard input is redirected to that file and processing continues. Characters are read from the batch file as if they were entered from the command line. Special accommodations are made to handle parameter passing to batch files and return conventions (consult your DOS documentation for details); however, normally after all commands from the batch file have been processed, the DOS prompt is again displayed.

AUTOEXEC.BAT: THE AUTOMATIC STARTUP COMMAND FILE

The special batch command file named AUTOEXEC.BAT, if located in the root directory of the boot volume, will be processed by DOS after CONFIG.SYS and before giving the user control. The DOS command processor (shell), specified by the SHELL configuration command or SET COMSPEC= environment string, is invoked by DOS and automatically performs the commands found in AUTOEXEC.BAT whenever DOS is hard- or soft-booted. Any DOS batch command placed into AUTO-EXEC.BAT will be performed at every system boot or upon performing the DOS batch filename AUTOEXEC. If no AUTOEXEC.BAT file is provided, no commands are automatically performed.

For example, the SET command must be used to define the Microsoft-specific environment strings such as

```
SET INIT=base\INIT
SET PATH=base\BIN;base\...
SET INCLUDE=base\INCLUDE
SET HELPFILES=base\HELP\*.HLP
SET TMP=base\TMP
```

among others (see Table 1.9), if the Microsoft C compilers and supporting utility programs are to function properly. Normally, such commands are included in AUTOEXEC.BAT. Application-specific environment strings may also be added and subsequently interrogated by using the C run-time library functions **getenv()** and **putenv()** (see Chapters 15 and 25).

You can also perform DOS commands and batch files from within a C program by using the standard C run-time function **system()**, discussed in Chapter 25.

The following DOS batch commands are particularly important when working with Microsoft's C compilers and supporting utilities: COM-MAND, DATE, FASTOPEN, PATH, PROMPT, SET, and TIME. Each is discussed in the sections that follow.

COMMAND

SYNTAX

COMMAND=*drive*:\[*dir*][/P][/MSG][/E:*xxxx*][/C*string*]

USAGE

This command offers an alternative method of establishing a new primary or secondary DOS command processor. The *drive*:\[*dir*] parameter designates where the command processor can be found if not in the current drive and directory.

The optional parameters are described under the SHELL configuration command. With COMMAND, the AUTOEXEC.BAT file is not automatically processed unless explicitly specified using the /C parameter. If both /P and /C*string* are specified, the /P parameter is ignored.

EXAMPLE

The batch command

COMMAND=C:\DIAGS\COMMAND.COM /P /Cmy.bat

would place a new permanent DOS command processor in the \DIAGS directory of drive C and perform the MY.BAT batch file, located either in the current default drive and directory or in the set of search paths specified by the environment string PATH.

DATE

SYNTAX

DATE [*date*]

USAGE

This command displays the current date in a format controlled by the COUNTRY command specified in CONFIG.SYS, permits you to alter the date if incorrect, and resets the internal clock accordingly. If you do not have a permanent clock, DOS assumes a date of January 1, 1980 when booted. The valid range of dates is January 1, 1980, through December 31,

2099. Always use the current date for the time zone in which you are located.

DOS uses the current date to record the date that each file was either created or last modified. Always include the DATE command in AUTO-EXEC.BAT to ensure that the correct date is set each time you boot the system:

```
DATE
```

The AUTOEXEC.BAT file will pause and display something like the following for the United States country code (**COUNTRY=001**):

```
Current date is Tue  1-01-1980
Enter new date (mm-dd-yy): 32-55-908
Invalid date
Enter new date (mm-dd-yy): 2-18-91
```

The format in which dates are displayed and accepted for input is controlled by the COUNTRY setting in CONFIG.SYS. Valid formats include the following:

mm-dd-yy	United States
dd-mm-yy	European
yy-mm-dd	Japanese

Even if you have a real-time clock with a battery backup, include the DATE command to verify that the battery has not gone dead or weakened. The NMAKE, incremental compilation (/Gi), and incremental linking (ILINK or /Li) utilities rely upon the accuracy of the recorded directory date and time entries (see Chapter 16) to test whether a target is out-of-date relative to its dependents. An incorrect sequence of file dates and times can result in more compilation and link steps being performed than necessary.

Using an incorrect date will invalidate the results of the universal date and time functions discussed in Chapter 21. See that chapter for a complete discussion of the relationship between the various available DOS and C date and time formats.

FASTOPEN

SYNTAX

```
FASTOPEN drive:=size
```

USAGE

This command reduces disk access time by maintaining a memory list of the most recently used directories and filenames. You must issue a separate command for each disk drive or virtual disk for which a buffer should be maintained.

The *size* parameter establishes the length of the memory-resident list. Each list entry consumes 35 bytes of memory. To be most effective, *size* should be set equal to the number of files found in the longest chain of subdirectories on a given drive.

FASTOPEN is particularly useful during the software development cycle, when you are successively compiling and linking a large number of C source code files. Because it is common to place each C function in its own source code file, a large number of directory entries are created. On the other hand, since most application programs work with a limited number of open files, and memory space is at a premium, the FASTOPEN command should generally not be used once a program is actually in use.

EXAMPLE

The command

```
C:\DOS\FASTOPEN A:=200
```

locates the FASTOPEN command in the \DOS directory of drive C and establishes a 200-file list for diskette drive A; this list will consume 7000 bytes of memory. Additional FASTOPEN commands can be issued for other available drives.

PATH

SYNTAX

```
PATH=[[d:]path[[;[d:]path]...]]
```

USAGE

This command sets the search directory. It establishes a chain of additional drives and directories beyond the current path, where DOS can look to find an executable (.COM, .EXE, or .BAT) file that has been entered on the command line. After exhausting this list, DOS displays the message *Bad command or filename.*

EXAMPLE

The command

```
PATH=C:\;C:\DOS;C:\QC2.5\BIN;C:\C600\BIN
```

instructs DOS, after unsuccessfully searching for an executable file in the current path, to search the C:\, C:\DOS, C:\QC2.5\BIN, and C:\C600\BIN directories.

PROMPT

SYNTAX

```
PROMPT [String]
```

This command sets the system prompt. It controls what DOS displays at the start of a command line. The *String* parameter may be constructed of any sequence of the meta-strings shown in Table 1.8. Notice in the table that some meta-strings are influenced by the COUNTRY configuration command in effect.

TABLE 1.8: Meta-Strings for the PROMPT Command

META-STRING	DOS PROMPT DISPLAY
$b	| symbol
$d	Date (for COUNTRY=*cc*)
$e	ESC character (0x1B or 27)
$g	> symbol
$h	Destructive backspace
$l	< symbol
$n	Default drive
$p	Current directory
$q	== symbol
$t	Time (for COUNTRY=*cc*)
$v	DOS version number
$_	CR/LF (Newline)
$$	Currency symbol (for COUNTRY=*cc*)
NOTE: All DOS meta-string characters ignore case.	

When DOS is booted, the default prompt is ng, or *drive>*; however, no PROMPT=*string* entry is created in the environment. When a PROMPT command is issued, a copy of the string is inserted or replaced in the environment table and remains in effect until changed. Issue the PROMPT command without a string if you want DOS to delete any environment string specified in a previous PROMPT command and revert to the default. If **DEVICE=ANSI.SYS** is included in CONFIG.SYS, you can use an additional set of PROMPT escape sequences in the *string* parameter for further control of both the screen and the keyboard. The basic format of the escape sequences is

`$e[ParamsCommands`

where *Params* are numeric and *Commands* are alphabetic control characters. With these control characters, you can position the cursor, erase text from the screen, alter the screen mode, and redefine the meaning of keyboard keys. These extended capabilities are fully described in the DOS *Technical Reference* (see Appendix A: Bibliography).

EXAMPLE

The following PROMPT command, included in AUTOEXEC.BAT, displays a user prompt in the form *Drive\Directory>*:

`PROMPT $p$g`

SET

SYNTAX

`SET [Sname=String]`

USAGE

The SET command edits the command processor's environment table. To see all strings currently stored in the environment table, issue the command SET without any parameters. To remove a string entry from the environment, issue the command

`SET Sname=`

without a *String* parameter. To insert or replace a string entry into the environment, issue the complete command:

`SET Sname=String`

The environment table is simply a reserved portion of memory containing a series of named character strings. It serves as a generic DOS mechanism for passing global information to programs. As discussed in the section "Executable Files," the program segment prefix (PSP) contains the address in memory of the environment table; each program has its own table. When a program executes another program (via the **spawnxxx()** or **execxxx()** library functions), the environment table is copied for the new program. Each program can then modify its environment variable settings without affecting any other program.

Environment strings may be interrogated (or revised) by any program running under DOS control: Microsoft compilers and utilities, any C application program (the **main()** function), or any subsequent process initiated by another program. The size of the environment table is controlled by the /E:*xxxxx* parameter in either the SHELL command in CONFIG.SYS or the COMMAND command in AUTOEXEC.BAT. (The overall limit to the number of characters that an environment string may contain is 32K.) Herein lies the power of the environment table. Environment strings can be used to evade the command-line limit of 127 characters when additional information must be passed to a program.

It is important to note that although conventions exist for *Sname* strings among Microsoft's products, no standards exist for naming environment strings. You are also free to create your own strings for use by your application programs. It is important to understand the Microsoft environment string-naming conventions that are used by its various program components, so that inadvertent naming conflicts do not arise. Table 1.9 summarizes these Microsoft environment strings, where they are used, and their meanings.

Most of these environment strings are created by the Microsoft product installation procedures. Microsoft's NMAKE utility, for instance, automatically treats every environment string as a macro definition. Normally, you can create or modify any environment string as necessary by inserting the necessary SET batch commands into AUTOEXEC.BAT, or by issuing a SET command at the DOS prompt. The SET commands

```
SET
SET PATH=
SET PATH=C:\
```

would first display the entire contents of the environment table (SET), then delete the existing entry (if any) for PATH, and finally create or replace the PATH string with the value C:\.

You can also access the environment table by writing a C **main()** program that uses the global variables **envp** and **environ**, calls the **getenv()**, **putenv()**, and **_searchenv()** C run-time functions, or

TABLE 1.9: Microsoft Environment Strings

STRING NAME	REFERENCING PROGRAM	DESCRIPTION
CL=	CL, QCL, ILINK, QLINK, and LINK	Since the DOS command line is limited to 127 characters by the PSP, and the C compiler and linker programs have a large number of possible options, use the command **SET CL=[[*op-tion*]..[*file*]..]..[/*link*[*link-libinfo*]]** to establish fixed option settings that supplement those entered on the DOS command line. Options that use an assignment (=) or * wildcard are not permitted. There is no default setting for CL.
COMSPEC=	DOS	The DOS command processor to be used when DOS is hard- or soft-booted. SET COMSPEC=\COMMAND.COM is normally the default.
_C_FILE_INFO=	C **main()** startup code	Used by DOS to pass open file information when **_fileinfo** is TRUE (see Appendix C for information about the global variables). All open file handles, except those flagged as **O_NOINHERIT** (see Chapter 16), are passed to a process (program) when either an **execxxx()** or **spawnxxx()** run-time library function is called. The information passed is in binary form, interpreted by the C startup code (**ctr0.asm** and **crt0dat.asm**), limited by the size of the environment table, and deleted from the environment table immediately after being processed.
HELPFILES=	CV, PWB, QC, and QH	Extends the search path of .HLP files when on-line help or the (Quick Help) utility is invoked. The typical installation default is **SET HELPFILES=***base* **\HELP*.HLP** Several standard .HLP help files are supplied by Microsoft, and other custom files may be developed using the HELPMAKE utility.
INCLUDE=	CL, NMAKE, PWB, QC, and QCL	Specifies the directory where any included .H or .MAK files can be found. The typical installation default is **SET IN-CLUDE=***base***\INCLUDE**.
INIT=	CV, NMAKE, and PWB	Specifies the directory where the control file TOOLS.INI can be found. The typical installation default is **SET INIT=***base***\INIT**.
LIB=	CL, ILINK, LIB, QLINK, LINK, PWB, QC, and QCL	Instructs DOS to start file searches in the current directory, then proceed to the command line or library line specifications, and finally instructs the LIB environment variable to find object-code modules (.OBJ/.LIB). The typical installation default is **SET LIB=***base***\LIB**.
LINK=	CL, QCL, ILINK, QLINK, and LINK	Same as CL except that only linker options may be specified, not compile options. There is no default setting for LINK.
NO87=	CL, ILINK, QLINK, LINK, PWB, QC, and QCL	Compile and link with floating-point emulation, implying that no coprocessor is present. The string specified may be a message or blank space, for example: **SET NO87=COPROCESSOR SUP-PRESSED**.

TABLE 1.9: Microsoft Environment Strings (continued)

STRING NAME	REFERENCING PROGRAM	DESCRIPTION
PATH=	DOS	Specifies the directories DOS is to search for .COM, .EXE, and .BAT files after looking in the current directory. The typical installation default is SET PATH=base\BIN; . . . .
PROMPT=	DOS	The present (default) PROMPT command meta-string and escape parameters in effect. The installation default is ng
TMP=	CL, ILINK, QLINK, LINK, PWB, QC, and QCL	Indicates the directory to be used to store temporary files. The typical installation default is SET TMP=base\TMP. but the TMP directory may also be allocated to a virtual disk. Only one directory may be specified.
TZ=	C main()	The C run-time global variables daylight, timezone, and tzname are controlled by the value of TZ and are set when C function tzset() is called. If TZ is not set, the default is understood to be TZ=PST8PDT, where PST is the Pacific Standard Time zone, 8 the number of hours west of Greenwich, and PDT the Pacific Daylight-savings Time designation. Other C run-time time functions rely upon the TZ setting (see Chapter 21 for information about date and time management).

NOTE: All environment string names are in uppercase, but their associated string values are case-sensitive. Treat both the string names and strings as case-sensitive in C programs.

that calls the **system()** function (see Chapter 15). The number and size of the strings placed in the environment table determine the size that must be specified by the SHELL= and COMMAND= commands. If the environment table is not large enough, the DOS error message *Out of environment space* will be displayed, and all subsequent attempts to add string entries in the table will be ignored. When this occurs, the only recourse is to alter the SHELL= or COMMAND= /E:*xxxx* parameter and reboot the system.

TIME

SYNTAX

```
TIME [hh:mm[:ss[.hs]]]
```

USAGE

This command displays the current time in a format controlled by the COUNTRY command specified in CONFIG.SYS, permits you to alter the time if incorrect, and resets the internal clock accordingly. If you do not have a permanent clock, DOS assumes a time of 00:00:00 when booted. DOS uses the current time to record the time that each file was either created or last modified.

The valid range of time values is 00:00:00 through 23:59:59. Always use your current local time (standard or daylight savings), and set the TZ environment variable to correspond with your time zone. For example, to set Eastern Standard Time, use **TZ=EST5**. To set Eastern Daylight Time, use **TZ=EST5EDT**.

If either the internal clock time or the TZ setting is incorrect, the results of the universal date and time functions discussed in Chapter 21 will also be incorrect. (Chapter 21 also discusses the relationship between the various DOS and C date and time formats available.)

Always include the TIME command in AUTOEXEC.BAT to ensure that the correct time is set whenever you boot the system:

```
TIME
```

The AUTOEXEC.BAT file will pause and perhaps display the following for the French country code (COUNTRY=033):

```
Current time is 4:47:09,30
Enter new time: 3x00.00
Invalid time
Enter new time: 14:50
```

Even if you have a real-time clock with a battery backup, include the TIME command to verify that the battery has not gone dead or weakened. The NMAKE, incremental compile (/Gi), and incremental link (ILINK or /Li) utilities rely upon the accuracy of the recorded directory date and time entries (see Chapter 16) to test whether a target is out-of-date relative to its dependents. An incorrect sequence of file dates and times can result in more compilation and link steps being performed than necessary.

KEYBOARD AND CODE-PAGE TRANSLATION TABLES

The system of country codes, keyboard codes, ASCII codes, primary and secondary code pages, and so on, outwardly seems to be one of the most confusing aspects of working with DOS. But before getting lost in the welter of similar-sounding terminology, remember that all computer codes are simply tables that translate between symbolic and binary representations of information. History and culture have shaped the symbols used in the world today, not computers. Man communicates best in symbolic, not binary form. The principal problem to overcome when computer systems (hardware and software) are used to share information electronically between different countries is essentially one of reconciling man's many forms of symbolic communication.

To enable a computer to accept symbolic input, perform work in binary, and produce symbolic output, a scheme of input and output translation tables was devised. Input devices always translate symbols into binary code, and output devices translate binary code into symbols. It would seem that one global code table could solve this problem. Unfortunately, the computer industry is hamstrung by its one-character, one-byte birthright. Only 256 symbols can be represented in eight bits or one byte, and man uses more than 256 symbols world-wide. Even in the United States, only 128 of the 256 possible codes are standardized in the ASCII character set.

Keyboard codes have been devised to handle the interchanging of keyboard devices, and code pages have been devised to handle the translation of all input and output symbols to and from binary. The input side of the problem is greatly simplified because combinations of keystrokes can be assigned to individual symbols, yielding a virtually unlimited number of symbols, and because the assignment of symbols to keys is independent of the key location. Keystrokes generate codes that are mapped to the appropriate symbols using the code-page translation table that is active.

The output side of the problem is complicated, however, by the one-byte limitation that traditionally applies to character-set representation. Limiting the number of symbols to 256 per code page introduces a degree of redundancy in the coding system. Since the first 128 symbols in each code page are standardized by ASCII, only the remaining 128 codes are available to be reused. Code pages have been constructed following this overall design, whereby the last 128 symbols differ, to some degree, for each code page. (Table 1.2, earlier in this chapter, lists code pages and associated keyboard codes.)

Consider an example: The US keyboard sequence representing a cent symbol is Alt-155. When this keystroke combination is interpreted by the United States code page 437, a binary value of 155 (0x9B) is generated, and as a result the cent symbol is displayed. Any computer using code page 437 can reliably display this cent symbol if it is included in a document. From Table 1.2 it is clear that a number of countries use a primary code page of 437.

What code value would be generated by the same US keyboard sequence (Alt-155) when used with the multilingual code page 850? Not 155 (0x9B) as expected, but rather 189 (0xBD). This also generates a cent symbol when code page 850 is used. The same symbol (¢) is represented by different code values in different code pages. This exemplifies the redundancy inherent in the code-page translation scheme. Non-ASCII symbols may have different binary values on different code pages.

When you edit a document file using a given keyboard and code-page translation table, it is easy to change the keyboard and continue editing the document. The key or key sequence used to represent the symbols may change, but the binary codes remain the same. Hence, the need for keyboard codes.

If, on the other hand, a document must be transferred from a computer using code page *xxx* to another using code page *yyy*, the document must deliberately be created using the *yyy* code-page character set. Hence, the need for code-page switching.

Beyond the need to configure a software system for use in a particular country—with a specific keyboard and code-page character set—situations will arise in the 1990s that require the use of the international DOS commands: the proliferation of portable computers, international file transfers of documents, and personnel reassignment because of business mergers and acquisitions.

We have already been exposed to the COUNTRY configuration command, used in CONFIG.SYS. When DOS is installed or configured, a country code and optional code page may be specified. For example, in the United States, once **COUNTRY=001** is specified, we can see in Table 1.2 that the US keyboard (Keyboard ID 103) and the United States code-page (437) translation table are in effect.

Use the commands that follow when you need to override the keyboard and code-page default values specified in CONFIG.SYS. These international DOS commands may be placed in AUTOEXEC.BAT or any other .BAT file, performed from the DOS prompt, or executed from a C program using the run-time **system()** function to modify the present keyboard and code-page translation tables being used. The national language support command, NLSFUNC, must be issued before using any of the other commands described in the sections that follow.

NLSFUNC

SYNTAX

```
NLSFUNC=FileSpec
```

USAGE

This command locates and loads the control file COUNTRY.SYS (*File-Spec*), which contains tables of information needed by other commands supporting internationalization. It must be performed before any of the other commands that follow.

EXAMPLE

The batch command

```
C:\DOS\NLSFUNC=COUNTRY.SYS
```

locates the NLSFUNC command in the \DOS directory of drive C and loads the COUNTRY.SYS control file from the current default drive and directory.

KEYB

SYNTAX

```
KEYB=kc[,[cp][,[FileSpec]]][ /ID:KID]
```

USAGE

This command permits you to specify a keyboard to attach or simulate on a computer. The *kc* parameter specifies the two-letter keyboard code, *cp* designates the code page for the keyboard console, *FileSpec* designates where the DOS file KEYBOARD.SYS can be found, and *KID* is one of the two alternate keyboards that may be associated with each *kc*.

When a code page other than US is activated, you can switch to the US keyboard by pressing Ctrl-Alt-F1 and return to the foreign keyboard with Ctrl-Alt-F2. Also, certain foreign keyboards rely upon dead-key sequences to accommodate the need for accenting characters.

EXAMPLE

The following command assigns the alternate French keyboard (Keyboard ID 189, not 120), with code page 850, and instructs DOS to find the KEYBOARD.SYS control file in the default drive root directory:

```
KEYB=FR,850,\KEYBOARD.SYS /ID:189
```

MODE

SYNTAX

```
MODE Device CODEPAGE PREPARE=((cp[,cp,cp..]) FileSpec.CPI)
MODE Device CODEPAGE SELECT=cp
```

The MODE command is normally used for setting up asynchronous communications and redirecting printer output to serial ports, but you can also use it to prepare devices for code-page switching. Typically the DOS devices CON, PRN, and LPT*x* support code-page switching (refer to Table 1.3).

For each device on which you will use code-page switching, you must issue two MODE commands, first with the PREPARE parameter and then with the SELECT parameter. PREPARE designates a maximum of five code pages to be associated with a device and indicates the location of the corresponding code-page information (*FileSpec*.CPI) control file. SELECT activates one of the designated code pages.

EXAMPLE

The commands

```
MODE CON CODEPAGE PREPARE=((437,850) \EGA.CPI)
MODE CON CODEPAGE SELECT=437
```

prepare the US and International code pages for use with an EGA-compatible console and then select the US code page. See the DEVICE configuration command for a discussion of the possible .CPI filenames. Refer to Table 1.2 for the possible code-page identifiers.

CHCP

SYNTAX

```
CHCP=cp
```

USAGE

This command permits you to reassign the active code page for all output devices, if they have been prepared properly using the MODE command described above.

EXAMPLE

The batch command

```
CHCP=850
```

would change the active code page for all output devices to the multilingual character set.

STANDARD C INTERNATIONAL FEATURES

Just as international commands were added to DOS as the operating system matured, so have international features been added to the C Language. The recent ANSI Standard introduced three separate such features:

1. Trigraphs to overcome the lack of certain C language punctuation (graphic) symbols that are missing on many foreign keyboards.

2. A generic structure declaration **struct lconv** (see Appendix E) and the standard run-time library functions **setlocale()** and **localeconv()**, which establish regional or cultural field display conventions similar to those controlled by the DOS COUNTRY command.

3. Multibyte or wide character sets, which circumvent the one-byte, one-character computer industry character set limitation and provide standard run-time function support for conversion between symbols (wide characters) and their corresponding binary representation (multibyte), and standard support for the declaration of wide-character constants (**L'*w*'**) and strings (**L"*wide character string*"**), together with the I/O support of the **scanf()** and **printf()** family of functions.

Although the QuickC and OptimizingC compilers support the trigraph and locale features, presently the multibyte/wide-character set concept is not implemented and represents the only significant Standard C feature that is unsupported by Microsoft.

The trigraph character sequences that are recognized by Standard C all begin with two question mark symbols (??) and include the following characters:

TRIGRAPH	CHARACTER
??(	[
??/	\

TRIGRAPH	CHARACTER
??)	]
??'	
??<	{
??!	|
??>	}
??-	~
??=	#

The inability of certain foreign character sets to represent the above characters is rooted in the fact that the ISO 646 Invariant Code Set (international counterpart to ASCII) does not agree with ASCII and, therefore, does not contain the characters noted above; however, the C source character set requires these symbols.

Standard C has also implemented the concept of locale to accommodate cultural and regional formatting conventions, similar to the effects that the COUNTRY configuration command has upon the display of date, time, and currency fields for instance. A data structure similar to that used by DOS is now supported by Standard C, so that there will be operating system independent means to enable a software program to be written that can "configure" itself, so to speak, and be portable for use in different countries and cultures (see Chapter 27).

The basic multibyte/wide-character set concept is to permit character sets to be designed which may use more than 1 byte to represent each character; hence the name multibyte or wide characters. Consider that if a 2-byte character table were defined, it could contain 2^{16} or 65,536 unique symbols rather than the familiar 2^8 or 256 unique symbol limitation. In response to international pressures (ISO approval), the C language for the first time offers standard language declaration and library function support for such character sets (see Chapters 7, 8, and 17).

The maturity of both DOS and Standard C has begun to provide the elementary tools that are necessary to develop C application programs that are both portable across different computing platforms and international as well. Each of these features is explored in greater detail in the chapter references noted above. While certainly still in their infant stage of development, better software tools and techniques will continue to emerge that help address the international computing needs of the 1990s and beyond.

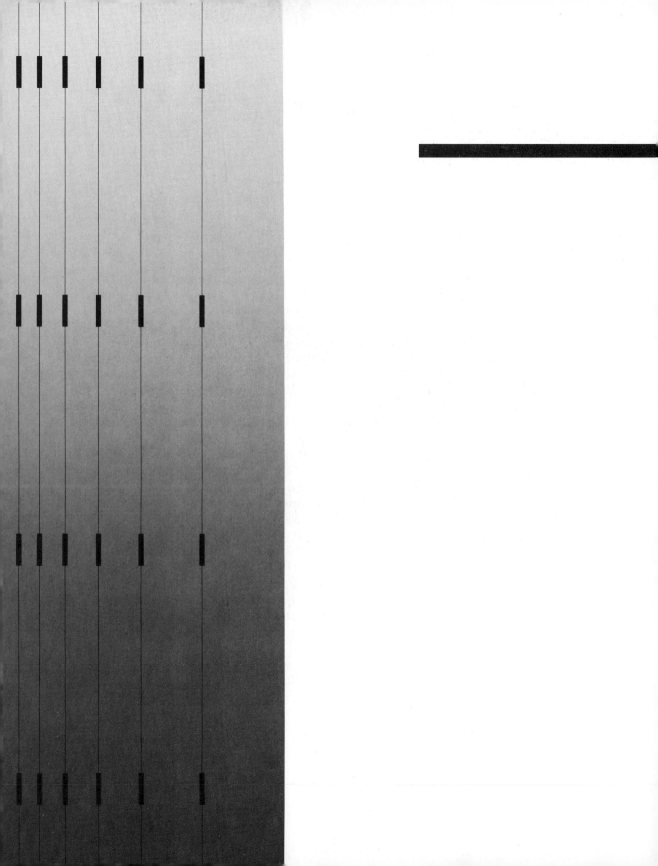

Selecting a C Compiler

Selecting a C Compiler

In selecting a Microsoft C compiler to use, we must match the requirements of a specific software development project with the most appropriate set of software tools.

Microsoft now markets two C compilers: QuickC and the C Professional Development System (OptimizingC). Each of these products is packaged to work in two modes of operation: *integrated* or *command-line*. The integrated mode provides a graphical, menu-driven interface that provides for program editing, compilation, linking, testing, and debugging without encountering the DOS command processor (discussed in Chapter 1) and optionally supports the use of a mouse. Command-line versions require that each such utility program, together with its necessary command-line options, be executed from the DOS command line.

The following identifiers are used throughout this book to distinguish each compiler product, mode of operation, and its DOS executable filename:

QC	QuickC Integrated
QCL	QuickC Command Line
PWB	OptimizingC Integrated (Programmer's WorkBench)
CL	OptimizingC Command Line

Each C compiler offers a distinct set of features from which to choose. This chapter will simplify your decision by contrasting the features of each compiler.

Once you've selected a compiler, you must also decide which of the six possible memory models to install: Tiny, Small, Medium, Compact, Large, or Huge. Memory models restrict the amount of code and data your program may address. This chapter also compares the characteristics of each memory model. You'll also see how math (floating-point) coprocessors ($80x87$) are accommodated by compiler options that control how a C program's floating-point operations are performed at run-time.

Finally, this chapter reviews the process of installing both the QuickC and OptimizingC compilers and presents a summary of corresponding disk storage requirements.

FEATURE COMPARISON

The four compiler alternatives available from Microsoft permit you to select one that best suits your programming needs. The greatest strength of Microsoft's compiler offerings is their compatibility. All compilers now use compatible header files and run-time libraries. You can therefore begin developing source code with the QC integrated compiler or the QCL command-line compiler, and later fully optimize it using either the PWB integrated or CL command-line compiler.

Table 2.1 compares the features that are supported by each of the available Microsoft compilers. The features highlighted in Table 2.1 are ordered to parallel the steps involved in writing a typical C application program:

Editing creates a C (or other) language source-code file.

Browsing performs automated searching and cross-referencing of source-code variables and function calls to facilitate program revision and editing.

Compiling translates a C (or other compiled language) source-code file (.C) into a binary, processor-dependent object module (.OBJ).

Assembling translates an assembly language source-code file (.ASM) to object module (.OBJ) form.

Library-making collects independent object module (.OBJ) files into a single library (.LIB) file to speed up the linking step, while eliminating the need to retain an (.OBJ) file for every (.C) file that is compiled.

Linking collects independent object module (.OBJ) files to produce a single executable file (either .COM or .EXE).

Making performs automated compilation, library-making, and linking of files based upon a set of rules that only compiles those (.C) files which are "out-of-date" relative to their corresponding (.OBJ) files.

Running executes a (.COM or .EXE) file with or without command-line arguments, piping, and redirection.

Debugging removes errors from the source code of an application program, which is automated by the use of interactive utilities that can selectively display the contents of variables and registers while a program is running.

Helping makes available online, context-sensitive documentation in an integrated environment (QC or PWB), or makes accessible such information from the DOS command line using a separate utility such as QuickHelp (QH).

TABLE 2.1: Features of Microsoft Compilers

FEATURE	QuickC INTEGRATED QC (2.5)	QuickC COMMAND LINE QCL (2.5)	OptimizingC INTEGRATED PWB (6.0)	OptimizingC COMMAND LINE CL (6.0)
Editor	Built-in or custom	None; use custom	Built-in or custom	None; use custom
Browser	None	None	Built-in	None
Compilation	Subset of PWB and CL options plus incremental	Subset of PWB and CL options plus incremental	All options plus incremental	All options plus incremental
Assembly	In-line subset of MASM options	In-line subset of MASM options	In-line subset of MASM options	In-line subset of MASM options
Library Facility	None; use LIB	None; use LIB	None; use LIB	None; use LIB
Linker	Subset of LINK options plus incremental	Subset of LINK options plus incremental	All LINK options plus incremental	All LINK options plus incremental
Make Facility	Subset of NMAKE options	None; use NMAKE	All NMAKE options	None; use NMAKE
Run	Full command line	Full command line	Full command line	Full command line
Debugger	Subset of CV (CodeView) options	None; use CV (CodeView)	All CV (CodeView) options	None; use CV (CodeView)
On-Line Help	Yes	None	Yes	None; use QH (Quick Help)

In Table 2.1, the term *incremental* refers to special techniques that are available for compiling and linking a C program. Both incremental compilation and incremental linking can potentially shorten the time it takes to complete the compile-link step that is so frequently performed when developing software.

An incremental compilation compiles only those .C source-code files for which corresponding .OBJ files do not exist, or that have a DOS directory entry whose date and time fields are more recent than in its corresponding .OBJ file. In other words, compilation is performed only when an .OBJ file is "out-of-date" relative to its corresponding .C source file. To use this feature with QuickC or OptimizingC, use the **/Gi** option.

Similarly, when an incremental link is performed, only those .OBJ object-code files that have a DOS directory entry whose date and time fields are more recent than an existing .EXE file are replaced. Incremental linking (ILINK) is predicated upon initially performing a complete LINK step that "pads" additional unused space in the code and data segments of an .EXE file. This "padding" provides the space that is later reclaimed when subsequent .OBJ modules are selectively updated in the executable file being relinked. This feature (compiler option **/Li**; Linker options /INC, /PADC, and /PADD) may be used with either QuickC or OptimizingC for all except the Tiny memory model. It saves the most time with programs compiled using the Large or Huge memory models, and for which only small source-code changes have been made. See Chapter 3 for information about linking.

As their names imply, QuickC is designed to hasten writing initial prototype code, and the Professional Development System (called OptimizingC in this book) is for fine-tuning release (production) code. Since both products are now available in an integrated form with extensive online help, they are both easy to use. Each compiler and mode of operation will be helpful on large projects. If your interest is in learning C programming, use QuickC because it is less expensive, consumes less disk storage space when installed, and provides a faster compile-link-test cycle time. When a fine-tuned production-quality or product version of software is necessary, use OptimizingC because it is then appropriate to exploit the additional optimizing options that are provided.

QuickC Integrated (QC)

The QC compiler's strength is expediting initial program development. It provides a menu-oriented editing, compiling, linking, making, testing, and debugging facility with extensive online help. The major disadvantage is that the compile, link, make, and debug facilities are subsets of those features supported by the PWB and CL compilers. After proper installation (discussed later in this chapter), the QuickC Integrated compiler may be activated by entering the following DOS command:

```
QC [/?] [/b] [/g] [/h] [/k:keyfile] [/nohi] [srcfile]
```

The optional parameters have the following meanings:

/?	For only display of available options
/b	For black-and-white monitors
/g	For AT-compatibles that refresh the monitor at a nonstandard rate
/h	For monitors with more than 25 lines
/k:*keyfile*	For customizing the keystroke function conventions understood by QuickC (**/k:qc.key**)
/nohi	For monitors not supporting high-intensity

srcfile   If omitted, a new UNTITLED.C file is assumed; otherwise, enter a complete filename, or a filename with no suffix, in which case .C will be appended

Note that you can use a dash (-) to replace any forward slash (/) shown above. Also, option names are case-sensitive. A quick-reference summary of QC command-line syntax can be found on the inside front cover of this book.

EXAMPLE

The following DOS command line would invoke the Integrated QuickC compiler for a portable computer with a monochrome LCD display that does not support high-intensity, and would prepare to edit a file called MY.C:

```
QC /b -nohi MY
```

QuickC Keyboard Conventions

Because QC provides extensive online help and an easy-to-use pull-down menu system, this book does not present a step-by-step discussion of the user interface. For our purposes it is sufficient to summarize a few basic keyboard conventions:

Alt: Toggles the top menu bar. Use the left- and right-arrow keys to select a menu title, then press Return to pull down the menu; use the up- and down-arrow keys to choose a command, then press the Return key to activate the command. Instead of using the arrow keys to make a selection, you can press any highlighted letters that appear.

Alt-F4: Exits QC and returns to the DOS command processor.

Ctrl-F10: Maximizes the size of the current active window.

Esc: Closes the current menu, help window, or dialog box; interrupts the compiler and linker.

F1: Invokes online help for the word located by the current cursor position.

F4: Toggles the video display between the QC environment and the DOS command processor.

F5: Compiles, links, and runs the C source-code program in the source-code window.

F6: Selects which visible window should become active and contain the cursor.

Tab: Moves the cursor to the next option field of a command window.

For information about installing and using a mouse with QuickC, refer to your QuickC installation instructions. If you need more information about using the pull-down menu system, consult *Mastering QuickC,* by Stan Kelly-Bootle (SYBEX, 1989).

QC Compiler and Linker Options

In selecting a compiler for programming, we are particularly interested in the compiler and linker options supported by QC. Once in the integrated environment, you can use the Options menu to alter the default values shown. Only a subset of the options available to PWB and CL are available with QC. Compiler options may be specified on the QC command line as they may be for QCL and CL.

To select the available QC compiler and linker options, pull down the Options Menu (Alt-O). Full menus must be enabled. If it is not, press F. You can then select Environment (E), as shown in Figure 2.1.

Selecting Environment displays the Environment menu shown in Figure 2.2.

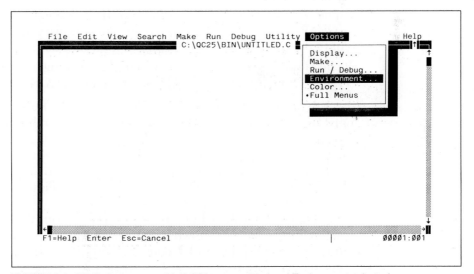

FIGURE 2.1: QC Options menu with Full Menus enabled and Environment selected.

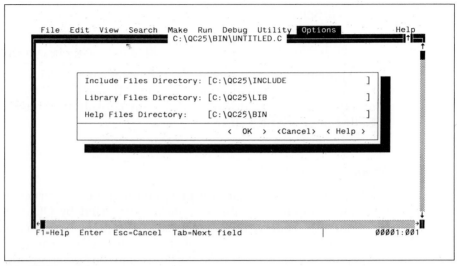

```
      File  Edit  View  Search  Make  Run  Debug  Utility  Options          Help
                              C:\QC25\BIN\UNTITLED.C


        ┌──────────────────────────────────────────────────────────┐
        │  Include Files Directory: [C:\QC25\INCLUDE            ]    │
        │                                                           │
        │  Library Files Directory: [C:\QC25\LIB               ]    │
        │                                                           │
        │  Help Files Directory:    [C:\QC25\BIN               ]    │
        │                                                           │
        │                    <  OK  >  <Cancel>  < Help >           │
        └──────────────────────────────────────────────────────────┘




      F1=Help   Enter   Esc=Cancel   Tab=Next field              00001:001
```

FIGURE 2.2: QC Environment menu.

The Environment menu permits you to set the following components of the DOS environment:

- The Include Files Directory search path for locating any C header files (.h)
- The Library Files Directory search path for locating the C run-time libraries (SLIBCE, SLIBC7, and so on), any graphics libraries (GRAPHICS, PGCHART, and so on), any libraries that you may have purchased, or any libraries you may have developed using LIB
- The Help Files Directory search path for locating any online help (.HLP) files (QC, QCENV, QAGRAPHICS, ERRORS, and so on)

Use the Tab key to step through these menu choices. Refer to Chapter 1 for more information about the DOS environment table and environment strings (Table 1.9).

Pulling down the Options menu (Alt-O) and selecting the Make command (M) as shown in Figure 2.3 displays the Make menu, shown in Figure 2.4.

If you select the <Compiler Flags> option shown in Figure 2.4, you'll see the available compiler options shown in Figure 2.5.

If you instead select the <Linker Flags> option from the Make menu, the available linker options shown in Figure 2.6 will appear.

To modify the compiler and linker options shown in Figures 2.5 and 2.6, press Tab to move to the item and toggle the setting using the up- or down-arrow keys. After making a change, move the cursor to the < OK > option and press Return; press Esc if you want the previous settings to

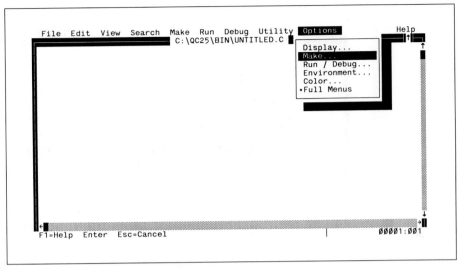

FIGURE 2.3: QC Options Menu with Make selected.

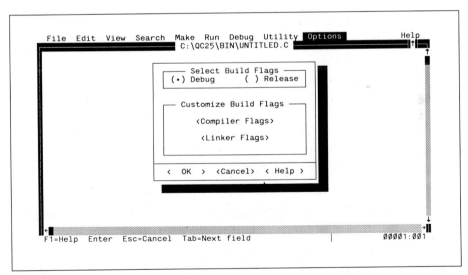

FIGURE 2.4: QC Make menu.

remain in effect. Notice that all other available QuickC compiler and linker options may now be entered at the Global: entry line of the CUSTOM FLAGS section as shown above. This new QC feature makes QC completely compatible with QCL. For a complete inventory and comparison of available compiler options, see Table 2.2 in the "Compiler Options" section, or refer

```
   File  Edit  View  Search  Make  Run  Debug  Utility  █Options█        Help
                        ┌───────── GLOBAL FLAGS ─────────┐
        ┌──── Memory Model ────┐  ┌───── C Language ──────┐
        │ (•) Small   ( ) Medium │  │ ( ) ANSI Compatibility │
        │ ( ) Compact ( ) Large  │  │ (•) MS Extensions      │
        │ ( ) Tiny    ( ) Huge   │  └───────────────────────┘
        └───────────────────────┘      Warning Level: [1 ]

        ┌──── DEBUG FLAGS ────┐    ┌──── RELEASE FLAGS ────┐
        │ [ ] Full CodeView    │    │      Optimizations      │
        │ [X] Pointer Check    │    │ (•) On ( ) Off ( ) Full │
        │ [ ] Incremental Compile│   └─────────────────────────┘
        └────────────────────┘          [X] Stack Check

                        ┌──── CUSTOM FLAGS ─────┐
        Global: [                                    ]
        Debug:  [/Od           ]  Release: [/DNDEBUG   ]

        Defines: [                                     ]

                            <  OK  >  <Cancel>  < Help >

   F1=Help  Enter  Esc=Cancel  Tab=Next field              ØØØØ1:ØØ1
```

FIGURE 2.5: QC <Compiler Flags> menu.

```
   File  Edit  View  Search  Make  Run  Debug  Utility  █Options█        Help
                       C:\QC25\BIN\UNTITLED.C

        ┌───── GLOBAL FLAGS ─────┐    ┌───── DEBUG FLAGS ─────┐
        │ [ ] Ignore Case         │    │ [ ] CodeView          │
        │ [ ] Extended Dictionary │    │ [ ] Map File          │
        │ [ ] Generate .COM File  │    │ [ ] Incremental Link  │
        │ (•) C   ( ) Asm         │    └───────────────────────┘
        │                         │
        │ Memory Needs: [ØxØFFF ] │     -- NO RELEASE FLAGS --
        │ Stack Size: [2Ø48    ]  │
        └─────────────────────────┘

                       ┌──── CUSTOM FLAGS ─────┐
        Global: [                                  ]
        Debug:  [              ]  Release: [         ]

                           <  OK  >  <Cancel>  < Help >

   F1=Help  Enter  Esc=Cancel  Tab=Next field              ØØØØ1:ØØ1
```

FIGURE 2.6: QC <Linker Flags> menu.

to the alphabetic option in Appendix F. Refer to Chapter 3, Table 3.2 for a summary of available linker options.

Once you have specified the compiler and link options that you require, simply edit a source code file using the QC Editor and then press F5 to compile, link, and run a single source-code file program; or pull down the Make menu, create a program list of source-code files, and then press F5.

QuickC Command Line (QCL)

The QCL command-line compiler's strength relative to the integrated QC compiler is its faster compile and link times. Both QCL and QC use the same compiler and have an identical complement of compiler and linker options; however, because QCL does not have the overhead associated with preserving the integrity of the entire integrated environment, it is faster; however, you must work with QCL from the DOS command line, rather than from a series of menus, and it does not offer online Help. When editing, library, making, or debugging services are required, you must use a separate editor, LIB, NMAKE, and CODEVIEW (or third-party equivalent) program from the DOS command line. After proper installation (discussed later in this chapter), the Command Line QuickC compiler may be activated by entering the following DOS command:

```
QCL [compileoption..] srcfile.. [objfile..] [libfile..] [/link
    [libfile..] linkoption..]
```

The parameters have the following meanings:

[compileoption..]	Optional; compiler options as described in Table 2.2.
[srcfile..]	Required; name(s) of source file(s) to compile. QC requires a complete filename.
[objfile..]	Optional; name(s) of object file(s) to link.
[libfile..]	Optional; name(s) of library file(s) to link.
[/link]	Optional; designator for the start of parameters used for the link step of QCL.
[linkoption..]	Optional; linker options as described in Table 3.2.

Note that a dash (−) may be used to replace any forward slash (/) shown above. A summary of QCL command-line syntax can be found on the inside front cover of this book.

EXAMPLE

The following DOS command line would invoke the QuickC Command Line compiler for a source-code file called MY.C with the Large memory model and maximum optimization compiler options.

```
QCL /AL /Ox MY.C /link /ST:1024
```

It would also link the program with the default libraries but override the default stack size of 2048 bytes with a value of 1024 bytes.

Unlike the integrated QC environment, QCL requires that all desired compile and link options be specified on the DOS command line. For a complete inventory and comparison of available compiler options, see Table 2.2, or refer to the alphabetic option list in Appendix F. Also, refer to Chapter 1, Table 1.9, for a summary of the SET environment strings used by the QCL compiler.

OptimizingC Integrated (PWB)

The PWB (Programmer's WorkBench) compiler parallels the features described for QC, but it provides access to all software tool options and adds the unique capabilities of a source-code "browser" to let you easily review all project source-code files. PWB provides a menu-oriented editing, browsing, compiling, linking, making, testing, and debugging facility with extensive on-line help. Everything that can be performed using the CL compiler and all other related Microsoft utility programs individually can be performed using PWB. After proper installation, the OptimizingC Integrated compiler may be activated by entering the following DOS command:

```
PWB [/?] [/D] [/DS] [/DT] [/DP] [/ecmdstr] [/mmark] [/r] [/tfile]
    [srcfile]
```

The optional parameters have the following meanings:

/?: Displays an initial help screen for PWB command-line syntax.

/D: Instructs PWB to ignore the TOOLS.INI and CURRENT.STS control files found in the C:\C600\INIT directory.

/DS: Instructs PWB to ignore the CURRENT.STS file containing the control settings in effect the last time PWB was invoked; therefore implying option **/DP**.

/DT: Instructs PWB to ignore the TOOLS.INI file containing the default setup commands for PWB.

/DP: Instructs PWB to ignore the current program list.

/e*cmdstr*: Instructs PWB to execute the PWB macro command string *cmdstr* upon startup.

/m*mark*: Instructs PWB to start at a specified location indicated by *mark*.

/r: Invokes PWB in read/only mode, so that no files accessed will inadvertently be modified.

/t*file* . .: Invokes PWB and loads *file* as a temporary file, so that when the PWB "exit" function is issued, the file is closed, and the next file specified is automatically opened.

srcfile: If omitted, a new UNTITLED.C file is assumed; otherwise, enter a complete filename, or a filename with a suffix, in which case .C will be appended.

Note that a dash (−) may be used to replace any forward slash (/) shown above. Option names are case-sensitive. A summary of PWB command-line syntax can be found on the inside front cover of this book.

EXAMPLE

The following DOS command line would invoke the Integrated OptimizingC compiler in read/only mode first with file THIS.C, and then, upon exiting, with file NEXT.C:

```
PWB /r /t THIS.C /t NEXT.C
```

PWB Keyboard Conventions

Because PWB, like QC, provides extensive online help and an easy-to-use pull-down menu system, for the purpose of this book it is again sufficient to review the basic keyboarding conventions. They parallel those used with QC, with some minor differences:

Alt: Toggles the top menu bar. Use the left- and right-arrow keys to select a menu title, then press Return to pull down the menu; use the up- and down-arrow keys to choose a command, then press the Return key to activate the command. Instead of using the arrow keys to make a selection, you can press any highlighted letters that appear.

Alt-F4: Exits PWB and returns to the DOS command processor.

Ctrl-F4: Closes the current active window.

Ctrl-F10: Maximizes the size of the current active window.

Esc: Closes the current menu, help window, or dialog box; interrupts the compiler and linker.

F1: Invokes online help for the word located by the current cursor position.

F4: Used with the PWB Search Menu (Alt-S); differs from QC. Does not toggle between PWB and the DOS command processor.

F5: Unassigned in PWB; differs from QC. Does not compile, link, and run the C source-code program in the source-code window.

F6: Selects a visible window to become active.

Tab: Moves the cursor to the next option field of a command window.

For information about installing and using a mouse with PWB (which is highly recommended), refer to your C Professional Development installation instructions.

PWB Compiler and Linker Options

In selecting a compiler for programming, we are particularly interested in the compiler and linker options, and the new Browse utility incorporated into PWB. Once in the PWB integrated environment, you can use the Options menu to alter or set any compiler or related-utility option values.

Since the Environment command parallels that demonstrated in Figure 2.2 for QC, let's begin by examining the default PWB compiler options. Pull down the Options menu (Alt-O), as shown in Figure 2.7.

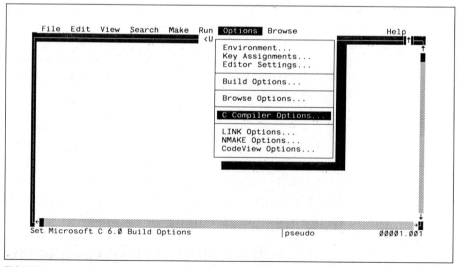

FIGURE 2.7: PWB Options menu with C Compiler Options selected.

Next, select the C Compiler Options command by using the up- and down-arrow keys, and press Return (⏎); the screen shown in Figure 2.8 should appear.

Notice the similarities with the QC options shown in Figure 2.5; PWB, however, gives you complete control over compiler options by selecting <Set Debug Options> using the Tab key. Figure 2.9 shows the default values assumed if <Set Debug Options> rather than <Set Release Options> is chosen from the Compiler Options menu. Those compiler options not expressly highlighted can be specified on the Additional Options field of the Compiler Debug Options menu.

If the LINK Options menu had been selected from Figure 2.7, the screen in Figure 2.10 would have been displayed, showing the default LINK options in effect.

Again, notice the similarities with the QC LINK options shown in Figure 2.6. Once again, however, PWB gives you complete control over compiler options, by selecting <Set Debug Options>. Figure 2.11 shows the default values assumed if <Set Debug Options> rather than <Set Release Options> is chosen from Figure 2.10. Those compiler options not expressly highlighted can be specified on the Additional Options field of the Link Debug Options menu.

To modify the compiler and linker options shown in Figures 2.8 through 2.11, move the cursor to the item and toggle the setting using the up- or down-arrow keys. After making a change, move to the <OK> option and press Return (⏎); press Esc if you want the previous setting to remain in effect.

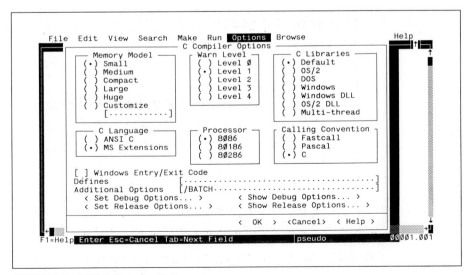

FIGURE 2.8: PWB C Compiler Options menu.

```
    File   Edit   View   Search   Make   Run  Options  Browse                    Help
    ──────────────────── C Compiler Options ─────────────────────
    ──────────────── C Compiler Debug Options ───────────────────
      [X] Stack Checking              [X] Incremental Compile
      [X] Quick Compile               [X] Check Null Pointers
      ───────── Optimization ─────────      ─── Floating Point ───
      [ ] Optimize for Time           (•) Inline Emulation
      [ ] Optimize for Space          ( ) Inline 80x87
                                              Instructions
      [ ] Loop Code Optimization      ( ) Fast Alternate Math
      [ ] Global Code Optimization    ( ) Emulation Calls
      [ ] Improve Float Consistency   ( ) 80x87 Calls
      [ ] Global Register Allocation
      [ ] Generate Intrinsic Functions  ─── Debug Information ───
                                        ( ) None
      [ ] Assume No Aliasing          ( ) Line Numbers Only
      [ ] Aliasing Only Across Calls  (•) CodeView

      Defines:           [.............................................]
      Additional Options [.............................................]
      < Show Options... >

                                      <  OK  >  <Cancel>  < Help >

    F1=Help Enter Esc=Cancel Tab=Next Field            |pseudo         00001.001
```

FIGURE 2.9: PWB C Compiler Debug Options menu.

```
    File   Edit   View   Search   Make   Run  Options  Browse                    Help
    ──────────────────────── <UNTITLED> ─────────────────────────
    ──────────────────────── LINK Options ───────────────────────

      [_] BIND Executable File

      [X] No Ignore Case
      [ ] No Extended Dictionary
      [ ] No Default Library Search

      Stack Size: [2048···] bytes

      Additional Libraries [·································]

      Additional Options   [ /BATCH··························]

        < Set Debug Options... >      < Show Debug Options... >
        < Set Release Options... >    < Show Release Options... >

                                      <  OK  >  <Cancel>  < Help >

    F1=Help Enter Esc=Cancel Tab=Next Field            |pseudo         00001.001
```

FIGURE 2.10: PWB LINK Options menu.

For a complete inventory and comparison of available compiler options, see Table 2.2, or refer to the alphabetic option list in Appendix F. Also, refer to Chapter 1, Table 1.9, for a summary of the SET environment strings utilized by the PWB compiler.

Once you have specified the compiler and link options that you require, simply edit a source-code file using Edit, and then select the Make

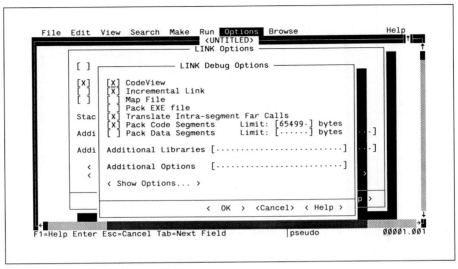

```
    File  Edit  View  Search  Make  Run  Options  Browse              Help
                            ┌───── <UNTITLED> ──────┐
                      ┌──────── LINK Options ────────┐
          ┌─────┐        ┌────────── LINK Debug Options ──────────┐
          [ ]             [X] CodeView
          [X]             [X] Incremental Link
          [ ]             [ ] Map File
          [ ]             [ ] Pack EXE file
          Stac            [X] Translate Intra-segment Far Calls
                          [X] Pack Code Segments    Limit: [65499·] bytes    ···]
          Addi            [ ] Pack Data Segments    Limit: [······] bytes
          Addi      Additional Libraries [···························]         ···]

           <        Additional Options   [···························]
           <
                    < Show Options... >

                                                                    p >
                              <  OK  >   <Cancel>  < Help >
    F1=Help Enter Esc=Cancel Tab=Next Field            |pseudo         00001.001
```

FIGURE 2.11: PWB LINK Debug Options menu.

menu (Alt-M). From that menu, select Build to compile, link, and run a
single source-code file program, or create a program list of source-code
files using the Set Program List option, and then select Rebuild All.

The PWB Browser

A unique feature of PWB is the source-code Browser, which is handy for
reviewing the structure of a C program that is typically composed of a
large number of DOS .C files. To turn the Browser facility on, select the
Options menu (Alt-O) as shown in Figure 2.12 and select the Browse Options menu to display the screen shown in Figure 2.13.

Selecting Generate Browse Information instructs PWB to create additional files (.SBR), upon which the Browser depends, whenever a C program is compiled and linked.

Figures 2.14 through 2.18 illustrate the use of the Browser in testing a
source-code file named COUNTRY.C. This example should give you a good
idea of how the Browser can be helpful in developing C programs.

In Figure 2.14, the Browser has been turned on and its pull-down menu
is displayed. The first thing we want to see is a list of references to various
types of identifiers, so we select List References. This option displays the
pull-down menu shown in Figure 2.15, which allows us to select functions,
variables, types, or macros for cross-referencing. Here, we've selected all
four options. The resulting display is shown in Figure 2.16. With this information, we can locate occurrences of and see improper references to the

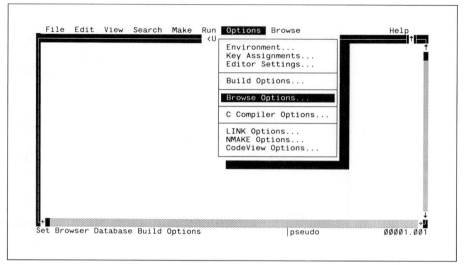

FIGURE 2.12: PWB Options menu with Browse Options selected.

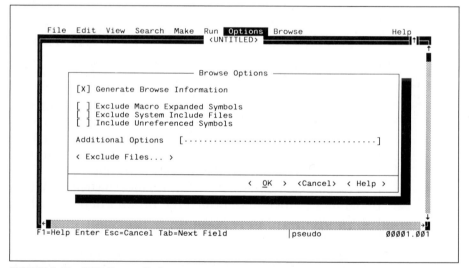

FIGURE 2.13: PWB Browse Options menu.

functions, variables, types, and macros without the visual clutter of looking at C source code.

When we return to the Browser menu and select the Outline option, the resulting menu (Figure 2.17) presents a list of all files called by the source-code file being browsed (including the file itself) and again allows us to select any combination of functions, variables, types, and macros for

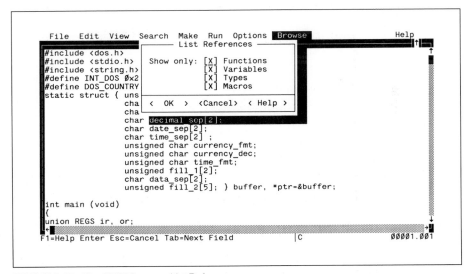

FIGURE 2.14: The PWB Browser menu with List References selected.

FIGURE 2.15: The PWB Browser List References menu.

outlining. Figure 2.18 shows the output, an alphabetical outline of identifiers (all types, as selected in the previous step) in COUNTRY.C. With this information, we can both locate and avoid the inadvertent reuse of a variable name, find an improperly used name (extra leading underscore, for instance), and avoid identifier naming conflicts (see Chapter 4).

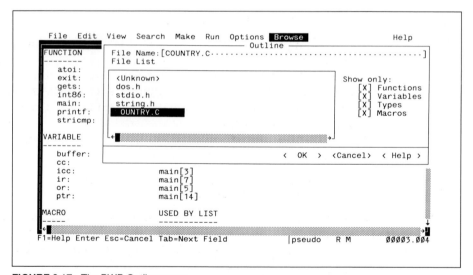

```
    File  Edit  View  Search  Make  Run  Options  Browse                Help
                              <browse>                                       ↑↓
  FUNCTION                CALLED BY LIST                                     ↑
  --------                --------------                                     ▓
    atoi:                 main                                               ▓
    exit:                 main                                               ▓
    gets:                 main                                               ▓
    int86:                main[2]                                            ▓
    main:                                                                    ▓
    printf:               main[16]                                           ▓
    stricmp:              main                                               ▓
                                                                             ▓
  VARIABLE                USED BY LIST                                       ▓
  --------                ------------                                       ▓
    buffer:               (ptr)                                             ▓
    cc:                   main[4]                                            ▓
    icc:                  main[3]                                            ▓
    ir:                   main[7]                                            ▓
    or:                   main[5]                                            ▓
    ptr:                  main[14]                                           ▓
                                                                             ▓
  MACRO                   USED BY LIST                                       ▓
  -----                   ------------                                      ↓
  <General Help> <F1=Help> <Alt=Menu>              |pseudo   R M   ØØØ3.ØØ4
```

FIGURE 2.16: Output from the PWB Browser List References command, as specified in Figure 2.15.

```
    File  Edit  View  Search  Make  Run  Options  ▐Browse▌             Help
                                      ──── Outline ────
  FUNCTION          File Name:[COUNTRY.C·······································]
  --------          File List
    atoi:
    exit:          ┌─────────────────────────────┐  Show only:
    gets:          │ <Unknown>                   │    [X] Functions
    int86:         │ dos.h                       │    [X] Variables
    main:          │ stdio.h                     │    [X] Types
    printf:        │ string.h                    │    [X] Macros
    stricmp:       │ ▐OUNTRY.C▌                   │
                   │                             │
  VARIABLE         └◄▓▓▓▓▓▓▓▓▓▓▓▓▓▓▓▓▓▓▓▓▓▓▓▓▓►┘
  --------
    buffer:                               <  OK  >  <Cancel>  < Help >
    cc:
    icc:                   main[3]
    ir:                    main[7]
    or:                    main[5]
    ptr:                   main[14]
  MACRO                    USED BY LIST
  -----                    ------------
  F1=Help Enter Esc=Cancel Tab=Next Field          |pseudo   R M   ØØØ3.ØØ4
```

FIGURE 2.17: The PWB Outline menu.

In short, the Browser brings to the source-code management process what the CodeView interactive debugger brings to the object-code debugging process: a better tool than is otherwise available.

```
      File  Edit  View  Search  Make  Run  Options  Browse          Help
                                <browse>
COUNTRY.C
   buffer                   (variable:static)
   cc                       (variable:local)
   DOS_COUNTRY              (constant)
   icc                      (variable:local)
   INT_DOS                 (constant)
   ir                       (variable:local)
   main                     (function:public)
   or                       (variable:local)
   ptr                      (variable:static)




<General Help> <F1=Help> <Alt=Menu>              |pseudo   R M        0002.004
```

FIGURE 2.18: Output from the PWB Browser Outline command, as specified in Figure 2.17.

OptimizingC Command Line (CL)

The CL compiler, although it lacks online help, offers access to the complete complement of compilation and linking options. Other necessary editing, library, making, and debugging services must be performed by the separate use of an editor program, along with the LIB, NMAKE, and CODEVIEW utilities or their third-party equivalents, executed from the DOS command line.

After installing the OptimizingC compiler, you can activate it by entering the following DOS command:

```
CL [compileoption..] srcfile.. [objfile..] [libfile..]
   [/link [libfile..] linkoption..]
```

The parameters of the CL command line are the same as those described above for QCL. A summary of CL command-line syntax can be found on the inside front cover of this book. A sample CL command line such as

```
CL /AS /Ox /F0x400 MY.C
```

would invoke the OptimizingC compiler for the same options that were described for the QuickC Command Line example above. Like the Command Line QCL compiler, CL requires you to specify all desired compilation and linking options on the DOS command line. For a complete inventory and comparison of available compiler options, see Table 2.2, or refer to the alphabetic option list in Appendix F. Like PWB, CL offers the full complement of available compilation and linking options. Also refer to Table 1.9 for a summary of the SET environment strings utilized by the CL compiler.

Compiler Options

Table 2.1 broadly summarized the differences in the features offered by the Microsoft compilers. The most important differences lie in the compilation feature, that is, in the set of compiler options each offers. As noted in the table, the QC and QCL compilers offer only a subset of the options available with the flagship PWB and CL compilers. Table 2.2 provides a detailed comparison of the options offered by each compiler.

TABLE 2.2: Options of the Microsoft Compilers

CATEGORY	OPTION	DESCRIPTION	QuickC	OptimizingC
Code Generation	/G0	8086 instructions (default)	Y	Y
	/G1	80186 instructions	Y	Y
	/G2	80286 instructions	Y	Y
	/Gc	_fortran or _pascal calling conventions	Y	Y
	/Gd	_cdecl calling convention	Y	Y
	/Ge	Enable stack checking (default)	Y	Y
	/Gi	Incremental compilation (implies /Li)	Y	Y
	/Gr	_fastcall calling convention	N	Y
	/Gs	No stack checking	Y	Y
	/Gt*number*	Data size threshold	Y	Y
	/Gw	Entry/exit code for Windows/DLL	N	N
Floating Point	/FPa	Calls with altmath library	N	Y
	/FPc	Calls with emulator library	N	Y
	/FPc87	Calls with 80x87 library	N	Y
	/FPi	Inline with emulator (default)	Y	Y
	/FPi87	Inline 80x87 code	Y	Y
Language	/Za	Disable Microsoft extensions	Y	Y
	/Zc	_pascal without regard to case	N	Y
	/Zd	Prepare for SYMDEB debugging	Y	Y

TABLE 2.2: Options of the Microsoft Compilers (continued)

CATEGORY	OPTION	DESCRIPTION	QuickC	OptimizingC
Language (cont.)	`/Ze`	Enable Microsoft extensions (default)	Y	Y
	`/Zg`	Generate function prototypes	N	Y
	`/Zi`	Prepare for CODEVIEW debugging	Y	Y
	`/Zl`	Remove default library information	Y	Y
	`/Zp`	Same as `/Zp1`	Y	Y
	`/Zp1`	Pack structures on 1-byte boundary	Y	Y
	`/Zp2`	Pack structures on 2-byte boundary	Y	Y
	`/Zp4`	Pack structures on 4-byte boundary	Y	Y
	`/Zr`	Enable pointer checking	Y	Y
	`/Zsrcfiles`	Syntax check only	Y	Y
Linking	`/F bytes`	Stack size	Y	Y
	`/Hnumber`	External name length	N	Y
	`/Lc`	Link compatibility mode executable (OS/2)	N	Y
	`/Libyte`	Incremental link decimal boundary	Y	Y
	`Ln`	Use for compiles with QLINK	Y	N
	`/link`	Linker/Options	Y	Y
	`/Lp`	Link protect mode executable (OS/2)	N	N
	`/Lr`	Link real mode executable (OS/2)	N	N
	`/MD`	Link C run-time as DLL (OS/2)	N	N
	`/ML`	Static link C run-time as DLL (OS/2)	N	N
	`/MT`	Link multithread C run-time as DLL (OS/2)	N	N
	`/NDname`	Set data segment name	Y	Y
	`/NMname`	Set the `module_TEXT` segment name	N	Y
	`/NTname`	Set the code segment name	Y	Y
	`/Vstring`	Set version string in .OBJ	Y	Y
Memory Model	`/AC`	Compact model (same as `/Asfd`)	Y	Y
	`/AH`	Huge model (same as `/Alhd`)	Y	Y
	`/AL`	Large model (same as `/Alfd`)	Y	Y
	`/AM`	Medium model (same as `/Alnd`)	Y	Y
	`/AS`	Small model (same as `/Asnd`)	Y	Y
	`/AT`	Tiny model (same as `/Asnd`)	Y	Y

TABLE 2.2: Options of the Microsoft Compilers (continued)

CATEGORY	OPTION	DESCRIPTION	QuickC	OptimizingC
Memory Model (cont.)	/Ad	Set SS equal to DS (memory model default)	Y	Y
	/Af	_far data pointers	Y	Y
	/Ah	_huge data pointers	Y	Y
	/Al	_far code pointers	Y	Y
	/An	_near data pointers	Y	Y
	/As	_near code pointers	Y	Y
	/Au	Set SS not equal to DS; DS loaded at func-entry	Y	Y
	/Aw	Set SS not equal to DS; DS not loaded at func-entry	Y	Y
Optimization	/O	Same as /Ot	Y	Y
	/Oa	Ignore aliasing	N	Y
	/Oc	Enable block common subexpressions	N	Y
	/Od	Disable optimizations	Y	Y
	/Oe	Enable global register allocation	N	Y
	/Og	Global and common subexpressions	N	Y
	/Oi	Enable intrinsic functions	N	Y
	/Ol	Enable loop optimizations	Y	Y
	/On	Disable "unsafe" optimizations	N	Y
	/Op	Enable 8087 register truncation	N	Y
	/Or	disable in_line return	N	Y
	/Os	Optimize for space	N	Y
	/Ot	Optimize for speed (same as /O)	Y	Y
	/Ow	No aliases except across function calls	N	Y
	/Ox	Maximum optimization (/O???? /Gs)	Y	Y
	/Oz	Maximum loop and global register allocation	N	Y
Output Files	/Fa	Assembly listing file .ASM	N	Y
	/Fb	Bound executable file .EXE; OS/2 only	N	N
	/Fc	Mixed source/object listing file .COD	N	Y
	/Feexefile	Rename.EXE file	Y	Y
	/Fl	Object listing file .COD	N	Y

TABLE 2.2: Options of the Microsoft Compilers (continued)

CATEGORY	OPTION	DESCRIPTION	QuickC	OptimizingC
Output Files (cont.)	/Fm	Linker map file .MAP	Y	Y
	/Foobfile file	Rename .OBJ	Y	Y
	/FR	Extended info .SBR browse file	N	Y
	/Fr	Standard info .SBR browse file	N	Y
	/Fs	list file; default: .LST	N	Y
	/Fx	xref file; default: .CRF	N	Y
Preprocessor	/C	Preserve comments	Y	Y
	/D<name>[=text]	Define macro	Y	Y
	/E	Preprocess to stdout with #line	Y	Y
	/EP	Same as /E but without #line	Y	Y
	/I<name>	Add #include path	Y	Y
	/P	Preprocess to file (.I)	Y	Y
	/U<name>	Undefine predefined macro	Y	Y
	/u	Undefine all predefined macros	Y	Y
	/X	Ignore Environment INCLUDE=	Y	Y
Source Listing	/Slcolumns	Set line width (79-255; def 79)	N	Y
	/Splines	Set page length (15-255; def 63)	N	Y
	/Ssstring	Set subtitle string	N	Y
	/Ststring	Set title string	N	Y
Miscellaneous	/B1path	Large-model preprocessor	N	Y
	/B2path	Large-model compiler pass 2	N	Y
	/B3path	Large-model compiler pass 3	N	Y
	/batch	For .BAT files, no prompts	Y	Y
	/c	Compile only, no link	Y	Y
	/HELP	Full QH help if available, or /?	Y	Y
	/help	Full QH help if available, or /?	Y	Y
	/J	Default char type is unsigned	N	Y
	/MA	MASM options	N	Y
	/nologo	Suppress banner display	Y	Y
	/qc	Faster compile (not QC but /Li /Gi /Zr)	N	Y
	/Taasmfile	Assemble file without .ASM	Y	Y
	/Tcsrcfile	Compile file without .C	Y	Y

TABLE 2.2: Options of the Microsoft Compilers (continued)

CATEGORY	OPTION	DESCRIPTION	QuickC	OptimizingC
Miscellaneous (cont.)	/W	Same as /W1 (default)	Y	Y
	/W0	No warnings	Y	Y
	/W1	Severe warning messages only	Y	Y
	/W2	Intermediate messages + /W1	Y	Y
	/W3	Function calls without prototype	Y	Y
	/W4	LINT-like ANSI detailed messages	Y	Y
	/W5	All warnings are fatal (no .OBJ)	N	Y
	/WX	Same as /W5	Y	Y
	/w	Same as /W0	Y	Y
	/?	Command-line syntax help only	Y	Y

NOTES:
A dash (–) may be substituted for the slash (/) shown above to designate the start of an option.
All options are case-sensitive.
See Appendix G.

Of the option categories shown in Table 2.2, Optimization and Output Files merit additional comment. The Optimization options most clearly distinguish the capabilities of OptimizingC from those of QuickC, while from a programmer's point-of-view, the Output Files options available with OptimizingC may actually be more important.

The Optimization options (**/O**) alter the object code produced by the compiler, effectively "changing" the source-code expression of the language to produce a program that is either faster or smaller. Each option selected permits the compiler to implement a specific optimization technique, which at times can be counter-productive (or incompatible). Use the **/Od** option to turn off optimization. Some of the commonly used techniques are briefly described in the Option summaries that follow.

The Output Files options (**/F**) instruct the compiler to produce various kinds of output from the assembly and object code generated by a compilation. The programmer can review and possibly alter these files before assembling the code with MASM to produce a .OBJ file, instead of revising the C source code itself, and recompiling with a C compiler.

Some of the individual options from Table 2.2 that significantly impact program size and performance are summarized below. The floating-point (**/FPxx**) options are discussed in the "Math Coprocessors" section of this chapter.

/c: Compile-only; prevents the automatic initiation of the LINK step. Useful when constructing NMAKE commands.

/F *number*: Overrides the default stack size setting of 2048 (2KB) bytes. Larger stack sizes may be needed for programs using recursion, smaller stack sizes can save unused memory space. You can express the *Number* of bytes in decimal, octal, (prefaced with 0), or hexadecimal (prefaced with 0x) notation. For example, 2KB is 2048 bytes in decimal, or 04000 in octal, or 0x800 in hexadecimal. For a discussion of the stack, refer to Chapter 15.

/Fa: Available only with PWB and CL, and useful for looking at the assembly code generated by a C program to find inefficiencies or bugs. It allows you to compare alternate C coding schemes at the machine level.

/Fc: Produces a combined source- and object-code listing that shows the assembly (object code) generated by each C source-code statement in your program.

/Gi: Using **/Gi** can speed the recompilation process. Use of **/Gi** normally implies the use of **/Li** (incremental linking).

/Gr: Invokes the use of register-function calling conventions (see keyword **_fastcall**); of no benefit with QuickC, but improves the performance of programs compiled with OptimizingC (refer to Chapter 14 for more details).

/Gs: Removes stack checking to reduce program size and improve performance. It may be overridden by using a directive **#pragma check_stack()**.

/Gt *size*: Useful for Compact, Large, and Huge memory models to force the allocation of all data items above *size* outside the default data segment.

/Li: Specifies incremental linking. Using **/Li** invokes the ILINK linker, not LINK, and can speed the relinking process. For a complete discussion of linking, see Chapter 3.

/link: Compiler-only; designates all subsequent options on the command line as linker, not compiler options. The linker options are summarized in Chapter 3, Table 3.2.

/O: Default; implies that some optimization is being performed by all compilers. Use the [**/O...**] series of options to further control the optimization process. The PWB and CL compilers provide the full complement of these options.

/Oa: No aliasing; tells the compiler that for all memory locations, except variables qualified as volatile, the compiler ensures that no program pointers reference variables that are used directly, and pointer-only referenced memory locations are not accessed by other pointers. These restrictions enable the compiler to place more variables and pointers in registers to speed program execution.

/Oc: This option enables common subexpression elimination by the compiler to minimize the repetition of calculations in a single arithmetic statement.

/Od: Disable optimization; use when debugging a program with the QuickC Debug utility or CODEVIEW Debugger. Disabling optimization guarantees an exact correspondence between the source code you wrote and the object code generated. Even the default optimization, which combines common subexpressions, eliminates "dead storage" variables, and avoids propagation of identical constants, is disabled.

/Oe: Instructs the compiler to ignore all explicit register and **_fastcall** keyword program use, and to assign register use in a more effective manner.

/Og: Instructs the compiler to eliminate common subexpressions; this minimizes the repetition of calculations across all statements in a function (see **/Oc**).

/Oi: Used only with PWB and CL; generates intrinsic (inline) code for a number of C run-time functions. This will increase program size but improve program speed. Run-time library functions for which intrinsic forms are available are noted as such in Parts VI and VII of this book.

/Ol: Instructs the compiler to examine all repetition statements to see if any do not need to be recomputed each time through the loop.

/On: Eliminates those optimizations introduced by **/Ol** that may possibly have harmful side-effects.

/Op: Used only with CL and a math coprocessor. Since floating-point registers are 80 bits wide and larger than the IEEE float (32-bit) and double (64-bit) representations used by C, but equal to the new long double real number, truncation can occur when results are transferred from the coprocessor to a variable storage location in memory. With this option selected, precision is always set by the variable, not the register width. This loss of precision will allow you to better control rounding.

/Os: Used only with PWB and CL; optimizes for program space rather than speed.

/Ow: Similar to using **/Oa**, but requires that pointer variables be reloaded from memory after any function call.

/Ox: Used with all compilers; provides the combined effects of several options for speed optimization and [**/Gs**] for the removal of stack checking. The options enabled by **/Ox** differ between Quick-C and OptimizingC.

/P: Not used by QC, but useful for testing and debugging how the preprocessor actually translates the compiler **#directive** commands encountered in your source code. The "unit-of-translation" file produced is the base name of the source code with a (.I) suffix. Refer to Chapter 5 for more information.

/Wn: The default warning level is **/W1**; however, the following settings ofer a more detailed look at compiler warning and error messages:

/W0	No warnings
/W1	Severe warning messages only
/W2	Intermediate message + **/W1**
/W3	Function calls without prototype + **/W2**
/W4	LINT-like ANSI detailed messages
/W5	Any warnings are considered fatal (no .OBJ)

/Za: Disables Microsoft extensions; allows you to compile and check whether you are coding in conformance with the ANSI standard or not.

/Zg: PWB and CL; generates prototype declarations for all functions defined in the source-code file. This is helpful when developing your own library of routines.

/Zi: Necessary for any QC, QCL, PWB, or CL program file (.EXE) to be interactively debugged.

/Zl: QCL, PWB, and CL; eliminates the default library name normally stored with each module. When using the LIB utility, this can save disk space.

/Zs: Instructs the compiler to check only syntax to speed the initial compilation of source code before attempting to compile the source-code program completely.

Compiler Limitations

Table 2.3 summarizes the limits that apply to any source-code program compiled with a Microsoft C compiler. Although these maximum and minimum values are rarely encountered, large or particularly complex applications may approach them. Such limitations generally go unnoticed until they are encountered, because they are typically buried in the error-message sections of the documentation provided by Microsoft. Acquaint yourself with these limitations, so that you may plan your software development effort to avoid these unyielding constraints.

TABLE 2.3: Limits Imposed by the Microsoft Compilers

FEATURE	LIMITATION
Preprocessor	Maximum number of macros: 1024
	Maximum number of macro definitions in `/D` options: 30
	Maximum number of formal parameters: `31`
	Maximum length of a macro argument: 256 bytes
	Maximum levels of nesting for `#if`, `#ifdef` and `#ifndef`: 32
	Maximum levels of nesting include files counting the main program: 10
	Maximum number of search paths for include files: 20
Identifiers	Maximum internal length: 31 characters; excess ignored
	Minimum number of unique characters for external identifiers: 6
Constants	Maximum value of a constant: determined by its type; see `float.h` and `limits.h`
Declarations	Maximum levels of nesting for structure/union definitions: 10
	Maximum size of an array, structure or union: 4GB
	Maximum length of a null terminated string: 4KB
	Maximum number of enumeration constants allowed in a single enumeration: 128
Initializers	Maximum levels of nesting: 10 to 15, depending upon the combination of types involved
Statements	Number of case labels permitted in a switch statement: unlimited
Functions	Maximum storage space for parameters to a function: 32KB
	Maximum storage space for local variables in a function: 32KB

TABLE 2.3: Limits Imposed by the Microsoft Compilers (continued)

FEATURE	LIMITATION
Memory	Maximum size of code modules: 64KB
	Maximum size of data arrays: 64KB (unless working with the Huge memory model)
	Maximum size of data array elements: 64KB
Linker	Maximum number of options and object files: 128
	Maximum number of segments: 128
	Maximum number of libraries: 32
	Maximum number of overlays: 63
Run-time	Maximum file size: 4GB
	Maximum number of open files: 20
	Maximum size of _psp command line: 127 characters
	Maximum environment table size: 32KB; default is 160 bytes
	Maximum stack size: 64KB; default is 2KB

MEMORY MANAGEMENT AND MEMORY MODELS

Regardless of the compiler you decide to use, you must also choose a memory model to install. Microsoft offers six memory models; the next section discusses each one in turn and shows how to select the model that best matches the addressing needs of your application program and the amount of memory installed. (You can install more than one model, but doing so significantly increases the disk storage space required for the associated run-time library files.) To understand why choosing a memory model is necessary, you should first become familiar with the segmented memory-addressing system used by the Intel 80*x*86 microprocessor chips.

Memory Management in the 80x86 Microprocessors

The familiar Intel 80*x*86 microprocessors, described in Table 2.4, were each designed to provide a specific range of allowable memory addresses.

A physical memory address is an ordinal number (unsigned, zero origin) that uniquely references a byte (8 bits) in memory. This ordinal number represents the starting (lowest) address of a data object type, which can be determined using the address-of (**&**) C operator, but which should not be confused with the value represented by the type of object located at the address, which can also be determined using (*****) pointer indirection. For example, if the integer variable **ival**, at memory address 0178:00BB (in segment:offset notation), contains the value of 125, then

&ival	equals 0178:00BB, the address of the **int** object
ival	equals 125, the **int** value at address 0178:00BB
*(&ival)	equals 125, the **int** value at address 0178:00BB

You can see in Table 2.4 that the address size required exceeds the register size available for the 8086 and 80286 chips. Because all address arithmetic is performed in the 16-bit registers of these chips, a segmented-addressing scheme was needed to compute physical memory addresses. The register size also limits the range of possible offsets within a segment to 64KB (2^{16}). A segment, then, can address only a 64KB contiguous range of memory.

The following 80x86 machine registers are used to store current segment (16-bit) addresses:

SS	Stack Segment Register
DS	Data Segment Register
CS	Code Segment Register

The new **_segment** data object type (see Chapter 7 for information about data types) can also be used to store the segment component of an address.

Offsets can be recorded by your program in any **_near** pointer variable, or other machine registers such as the SP (Stack Pointer, offset from SS) and the BP (Base Pointer, offset from SS).

Complete segment:offset addresses are always represented by pointer types qualified as **_far** or **_huge** or may now be constructed using the new **:>** operator for combining the segment and offset components of all **_based** type pointers (see Chapter 12).

TABLE 2.4: Intel 80x86 Microprocessor Specifications

CHIP	YEAR	COPROCESSOR CHIP	DESIGN MEMORY	LIMIT	REQUIRED ADDRESS SIZE	AVAILABLE REGISTER SIZE
8086	1978	8087	1MB	2^{20}	20 bits	16 bits
80286	1982	80287	16MB	2^{24}	24 bits	16 bits
80386	1985	80387	4GB	2^{32}	32 bits	32 bits
80486	1989	Built-in	4GB	2^{32}	32 bits	32 bits

Consider this 8086 example of how a typical segment:offset address, such as 0178:00BB (base 16), would be translated into a physical memory address:

1. Extend the segment by a 0 hexadecimal digit (4 bits) to yield 1780 (base 16).

2. Add the offset (16 bits) to this extended address: 1780 + 00BB. This yields a physical memory address located at 183B (base 16) or 6203 (base 10).

Note that this segment:offset scheme uses two 16–bit register operations to derive a 20-bit address (4 bits + 16 bits).

The 80286, 80386, and 80486 all have alternate addressing schemes (protected vs. real) that utilize local and global *descriptor* tables and provide for memory protection and virtual memory, while retaining the segment:offset scheme that is particularly well-suited to handling multiuser environments. With the 80*x*86 processors, the 8086 segment:offset addressing scheme is modified to yield a 24-bit segmented address (8 bits + 16 bits) that maintains downward compatibility, even though with 32-bit registers, segmented addressing would not otherwise be required.

In protected mode, the 80286 treats all 16-bit segment addresses as an index to a descriptor table of memory addresses (local or global) that contains a 24-bit base address of the actual segment to which the offset is added to calculate a physical address. Consider this 80286 example of how a typical segment:offset address, such as 0001:FFFF (base 16), would be translated into a physical memory address:

1. Interpret the segment (0001:) as an index to the descriptor table, which for the largest possible address segment would return a base segment address in 24 bits as FF0000 (base 16).

2. Adding the :FFFF offset (16 bits) to this base address (FF0000 + FFFF) yields a maximum physical memory address located at FFFFFF (base 16) or 16MB, the design memory limit for the 80286 described in Table 2.4.

The descriptor table mechanism enables the 80*x*86 processors to facilitate memory swapping and enforce memory protection, thereby ensuring that programs access only those memory locations to which access privilege has been granted. For more information about addressing, see Chapter 10, which discusses pointers.

Selecting a Memory Model

The six memory models offered by Microsoft for its compilers are designed to match the segmented addressing scheme just described with the requirements of particular application programs and hardware installations. Table 2.5 shows the size limit imposed on the code segment, the data segment, and the complete program. Note that since the overall limit for the Tiny model is 64KB, each segment must actually be smaller than that limit.

With this table, you can match the size requirements of your program's code and data segments with the ranges of memory addresses supported by a particular model. By selecting the most appropriate memory model, you can minimize the total program size generated by the compiler and its corresponding execution time. Using larger addressing schemes entails a proportionate increase in storage space for pointers (variables containing addresses) and processing time to perform address arithmetic. All models assume that the maximum code space for a single module may not exceed 64KB (one segment), and except for the special Huge model, no single data object may exceed 64KB (one segment).

All of the memory models are based on the allocation of memory illustrated in Figure 2.19, which shows how DOS uses the 1MB range of addresses it can manage. In this system, all executable C programs under DOS consist of the same fundamental components, mapped from high- to low-memory addresses as follows:

High Memory

Heap: Dynamically allocated program memory

Stack: Program stack segment (2KB default, fixed size)

_DATA: Program data segment(s)

_TEXT: Program code segment(s)

_psp: Program segment prefix (256 bytes)

Low Memory

TABLE 2.5: C Compiler Memory Models

MEMORY MODEL	CODE LIMIT	DATA LIMIT	PROGRAM LIMIT
Tiny	64KB	64KB	64KB
Small	64KB	64KB	128KB
Medium	None	64KB	Unlimited code/64KB data
Compact	64KB	None	64KB code/unlimited data
Large	None	None	Unlimited code/unlimited data; arrays may not exceed 64KB
Huge	None	None	Unlimited code/unlimited data; arrays may exceed 64KB

The maps for individual memory models, presented in Figures 2.20 through 2.25, each represent an executable program loaded into the Application Programs section of the map shown in Figure 2.19.

Before studying the memory models and their maps, however, you should be familiar with the following terminology, presented here in the same high-to-low order embodied in the memory maps:

High memory: Addresses approaching the largest available DOS memory address F000:FFFF (1MB).

Far heap: Memory available for the dynamic allocation of data by the non-Standard run-time library functions **_fmalloc()** and

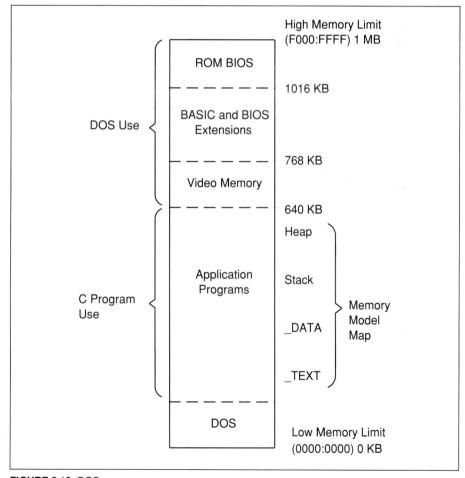

FIGURE 2.19: DOS memory map.

_fcalloc() in a Tiny, Small, or Medium memory model program. See Chapter 24 for more information about memory management.

Heap: Memory available for dynamic allocation by the Standard run-time library functions **malloc()** and **calloc()** in a Tiny, Small, Medium, Compact, or Large memory model program. The non-Standard **halloc()** function must be used in a Huge memory model, and may allocate arrays of data that span segments (greater than 64KB). See Chapter 24.

Near heap: Memory available for the dynamic allocation of data by the non-Standard run-time library functions **_nmalloc()** and **_ncalloc()** in a Compact, Large, or Huge memory model program. See Chapter 24.

Stack: A dynamically shrinking and expanding memory area for the allocation of auto storage class data. This LIFO (last-in, first-out) storage mechanism is limited by default to a maximum size of 2KB. You can override the stack size by using either compiler option **/F** or the linker option /STACK to reduce or extend the stack to a maximum of 64KB. STACK is a separate data segment for all except the Tiny memory model. See Chapter 15.

_BSS: The data segment containing (DS:OFF) addressed uninitialized global and static data (except **_far**, **_based**, or **_huge**).

CONST: The data segment containing (DS:OFF) addressed read-only data created by the C data object qualifier **const**, string literals, and floating-point constants.

_DATA: The default data segment (DS:OFF) containing initialized global and static data (except **_far**, **_based**, or **_huge**).

NULL: A code segment that checks for erroneous null pointer assignment, often caused by improper dynamic memory allocation function operations.

data_Segment: Additional initialized and uninitialized global and static **_far**, **_based**, and **_huge** data segments.

module_TEXT: One **_far** code segment per module for the Medium, Large, or Huge memory models.

_TEXT: The default code segment (CS:OFF) for all memory models (except **_far**, **_based**, or **_huge**).

_psp: The program segment prefix (256 bytes), containing the address of the environment table for the process (program) and a copy of the DOS command line. See Chapter 1.

Low Memory: Addresses beginning at 0000:0000 and increasing thereafter.

An executable (.COM or .EXE) file produced by the linker consists of the segment components shown in Figure 2.19 (except for the Far heap, Near heap, heap, and PSP), with all addresses relative to zero (0x0). To see the relative address ranges of any program, use the **/MAP** Linker option to generate a .MAP file (see Chapter 3 for more information about the Linker utility).

The DOS 0x4B interrupt function constructs the **_PSP** (program segment prefix), loads the executable file, adjusts all relative addresses by the actual starting address, and relinquishes program control (see Chapter 22 for information about DOS/BIOS system calls). All Far heap, Near heap, and heap space is allocated as requested by the program during execution. Program control returns to the parent (calling) process, or the DOS command processor, upon termination. Refer to the discussion of the **_PSP** found in Chapter 1.

The Tiny Model

The Tiny memory model (option /AT) limits a program to a maximum of 64KB (one segment) of code and data combined. By default, all code and data addresses are understood to be near addresses. This model is the only one that generates executable files with the extension .COM, not .EXE. There is no separate stack segment, since for all .COM files, the stack segment (SS) register is set equal to the data segment (DS), and the stack pointer (SP or SS:offset) is simply set above **_BSS**, as shown, by the stack size specified (2KB default). Any remaining memory space (heap) is available for dynamic memory allocation using the Standard C run-time library functions **calloc()** and **malloc()**. Figure 2.20 depicts how the Tiny memory model is mapped into memory.

The Small Model

The Small memory model (option /AS) limits a program to 64KB (one segment) of code and 64KB (one segment) of data. By default, all code and data addresses are understood to be near addresses. The Small model is normally the default option for all compilers. The available heap space, which you can access using the Standard C **calloc()** and **malloc()** functions, is limited to the space remaining above the stack in the 64KB data segment. Figure 2.21 depicts how the Small model is mapped into memory.

The Medium Model

The Medium memory model (option /AM) limits a program to 64KB (one segment) of data and an unlimited number of 64KB code segments (one module per segment). By default, all data is near-addressed, and all code is far-addressed. The available heap space, which you can access using the Standard C **calloc()** and **malloc()** functions, is limited to the space remaining above the stack in the 64KB data segment. Figure 2.22 depicts how the Medium model is mapped into memory.

The Compact Model

The Compact memory model (option /AC) limits a program to 64KB (one segment) of code and an unlimited number of 64KB data segments (maximum data item is one segment). By default, all code is near-addressed, and all data is far-addressed. The available heap space, which you can access using the Standard C **calloc()** and **malloc()** functions, is limited only by the amount of High Memory remaining above the Near heap. Figure 2.23 depicts how the Compact model is mapped into memory.

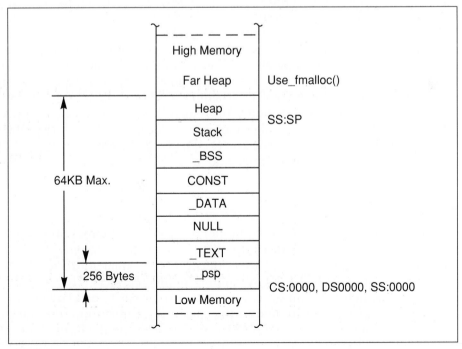

FIGURE 2.20: Tiny memory model map.

The Large Model

The Large memory model (option /AL) places no limits on the number of code and data segments, except that no data item or program module may exceed 64KB (one segment). By default, all code and data is far-addressed. The available heap space, which may be accessed using the Standard C **calloc()** and **malloc()** functions, is limited only by the amount of High Memory remaining above the Near heap. Figure 2.24 depicts how the Large model is mapped into memory.

The Huge Model

The Huge memory model (option **/AH**) places no limits on the number of code and data segments, except that no data array element or program module may exceed 64KB (one segment). By default, all code is far-addressed, and all data is huge-addressed. This model is used by programs for which arrays of data must exceed 64KB. The available heap space, which must be accessed using the non-Standard C **halloc()** function, is limited only by the amount of High Memory remaining above the Near heap. Figure 2.25 depicts how the Huge model is mapped into memory.

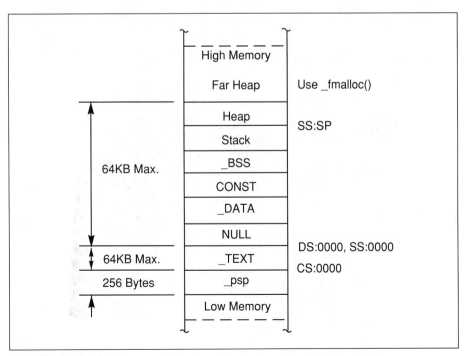

FIGURE 2.21: Small memory model map.

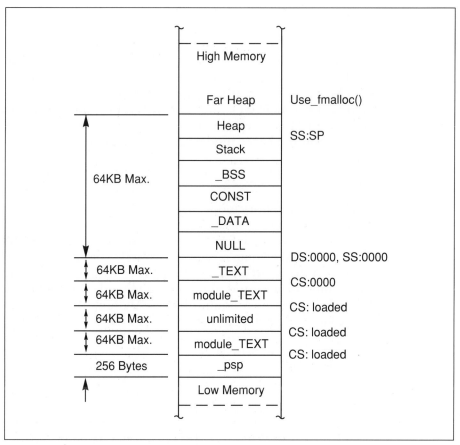

FIGURE 2.22: Medium memory model map.

Overriding a Memory Model

Your program can override the implicit code and data segment addressing limitations associated with each memory model described above by using the non-Standard C keywords **_near**, **_far**, **_huge**, and **_based**, described in Table 2.6.

Use of these non-Standard C keywords will significantly limit the portability of your source code, but in specific situations where the default addressing scheme imposed by a memory model must be overridden, these keywords provide a welcome escape. For a thorough discussion of their use, refer to Chapters 7 and 10.

A Tiny, Small, or Medium memory model program may access the otherwise unused Far heap shown in Figures 2.20, 2.21, or 2.22, respectively, by

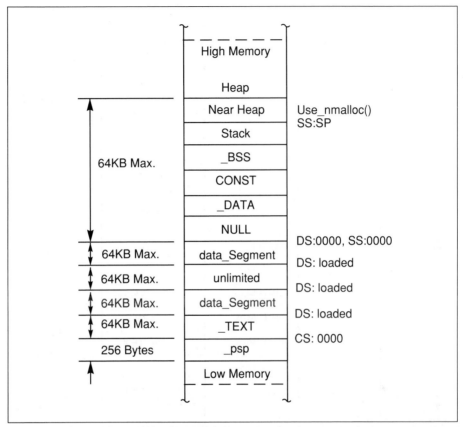

FIGURE 2.23: Compact memory model map.

declaring a **_far** pointer variable and calling one of the non-Standard Far heap memory allocation functions, **_fmalloc()** or **_fcalloc()**. For example, the following statements allocate an array of 1000 characters:

```
char _far *ptr;
ptr = _fmalloc(1000 * sizeof(char));
```

A program using the Compact, Large, or Huge memory model may access the otherwise unused Near heap shown in Figures 2.23, 2.24, or 2.25, respectively, by declaring a **_near** pointer variable and calling one of the Near heap memory allocation functions, **_nmalloc()** or **_ncalloc()**. For example, the following statements allocate an array of 1000 long doubles initialized to zero:

```
long double _near *ptr;
ptr = _ncalloc(1000 * sizeof(long double));
```

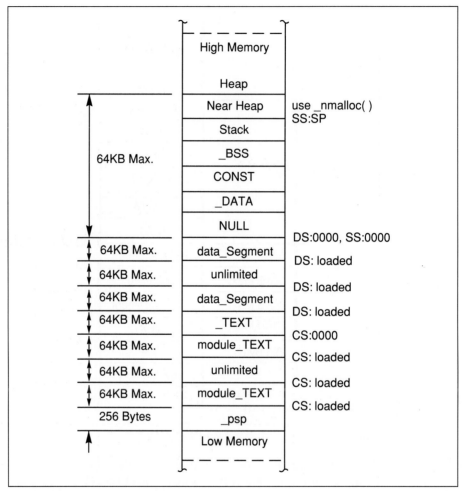

FIGURE 2.24: Large memory model map.

For a complete discussion, with program examples, of the use of the C run-time memory allocation functions, see Chapter 24.

MATH COPROCESSORS

Glancing back at Table 2.4 earlier in this chapter, you can see that in the future (80486 and later chips), a discussion of coprocessors will be unnecessary—they will be built into the chips. However, since we will be dealing with 80*x*86 microprocessors and their corresponding 80*x*87 math

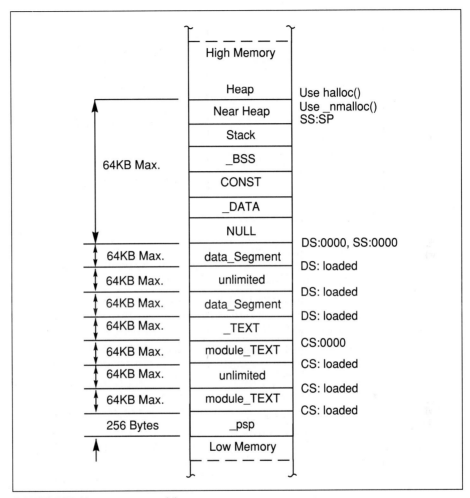

FIGURE 2.25: Huge memory model map.

coprocessors throughout the 1990s, let's understand why coprocessors were created, and how C programs should accommodate them.

Coprocessors (8087, 80287, and 80387) were created because no machine instructions or registers for floating-point arithmetic operations were designed into the corresponding 8086, 80286, and 80386 chips' instruction sets. All floating-point arithmetic therefore had to be emulated, or performed by software instead of hardware. Since most common spreadsheet, database, graphics, and CAD/CAM packages in use rely heavily upon floating-point arithmetic to represent dollar fields and coordinate systems, coprocessors were developed to minimize the resulting

TABLE 2.6: Non-Standard C Addressing Keywords

KEYWORD	CODE ADDRESSING	DATA ADDRESSING	ADDRESS ARITHMETIC
`_near`	In default code segment (CS); 16-bit; CS:OFF	In default data segment (DS); 16-bit; DS:OFF	16-bit
`_far`	In any code segment; 32-bit; SEG:OFF	In any data segment 32-bit SEG:OFF	16-bit
`_based(..)`	Not applicable	In any data or code segment; 32-bit; SEG:OFF	16-bit
`_huge`	Not applicable	In any data segment; arrays may exceed 64KB; 32-bit; SEG:OFF	32-bit

performance problems. Coprocessors can improve the speed of such applications by a factor of 5–10 over emulation.

We must be able to write software that performs floating-point arithmetic on computers either with or without a coprocessor (see Chapter 23). Coordinated use of compiler options, linker options, and the environment string NO87 allows us to do this. Let's consider three separate C programming alternatives: 1) for emulation only, 2) for a coprocessor only, and 3) for either emulation or a coprocessor.

Emulation Only

Writing C programs that will always use emulation for floating-point arithmetic, regardless of whether a coprocessor is present at run-time, maximizes portability but sacrifices efficiency when the program is run with a coprocessor available.

With QuickC (QC and QCL) use compiler option **/FPi** and issue the following DOS command:

```
SET NO87=any message
```

With OptimizingC (PWB and CL), for the fastest emulation and some loss of accuracy, use compiler option **/FPa** and issue the DOS command

```
SET NO87=
```

to remove the NO87 environment string definition; otherwise, for the best accuracy, use compiler option **/FPi** and issue the SET NO87 command with any message. For example,

```
SET NO87=TRUE
```

Coprocessor Only

You can also write C programs that will always require a coprocessor for floating-point arithmetic and will display an error message like *floating point not loaded* if a coprocessor is not present at run-time. Of course, doing so sacrifices portability to speed.

With both QuickC (QC and QCL) and OptimizingC (PWB and CL), use compiler option **/FPi87** and issue the DOS command

`SET NO87=`

to remove the NO87 environment string definition.

Either Emulation or Coprocessor

The approach that best balances portability and speed is to write C programs that will either use a coprocessor if installed or revert to floating-point emulation. The error message *floating point not loaded* will never be encountered.

With QuickC (QC and QCL), use the compiler option **/FPi** and issue the DOS command

`SET NO87=`

to remove the NO87 environment string definition.

With OptimizingC (PWB and CL), for best accuracy, use **/FPi** and issue the **SET NO87=** DOS command to remove the NO87 environment string definition. For more speed, use compiler option **/FPc**, link with the Alternate math library, and issue the **SET NO87=** DOS command.

COMPILER INSTALLATION

Microsoft sells the QuickC (list price $99) and OptimizingC (list price $495) compilers as separate products. It should not be surprising that when you purchase QuickC you are getting a subset of the tools available with OptimizingC. Table 2.7 summarizes the software components provided with each compiler.

The installation process creates directories and copies files from the install disks to your system hard (or floppy) disk. The amount of disk space required depends upon the installation options selected. Use Figure 2.26 to estimate the disk space required for the installation of a specific compiler configuration.

Notice that the standard library names reflect the memory model and math coprocessor selections made. The first character signifies the

TABLE 2.7: A Comparison of the Products Packaged with QuickC and OptimizingC

QuickC 2.0	OptimizingC 6.0	DESCRIPTION
QC		QuickC Integrated Compiler
QCL		QuickC Command Line Compiler
QLINK	LINK	Linker
ILINK	ILINK	Incremental Linker
LIB	LIB	Librarian
NMAKE	NMAKE	Make utility
	PWB	OptimizingC Integrated Compiler
	CL	OptimizingC Command Line Compiler
	EXEHDR	Executable File Utility
	CVPACK	CodeView Pack Utility
	CV	CodeView Debugger
	(QH +)	Quick Help plus other utilities

memory model; both the Large and Huge models generate one library beginning with the letter L. The last character (E, 7, or A) signifies whether floating-point emulation, an $80x87$ math coprocessor, or the Alternate math library was chosen.

The amounts shown in Figure 2.26 are estimated minimum installation values. Although QuickC can be installed to operate on a diskette-based system, a recommended minimum equipment configuration would consist of the following:

> IBM/XT or compatible
>
> 512 KB memory; one 5¼" floppy disk; one 10 MB hard-disk
>
> DOS V3.0+

If you intend to use OptimizingC, a recommended minimum equipment configuration would consist of

> IBM/AT or compatible
>
> 640 KB memory; one 3½" floppy disk; one 20 MB hard-disk
>
> DOS V3.0+

Using the compilers with these configurations will provide an acceptable installation and software development platform for C training and for the completion of small- to medium-sized software development projects. For larger projects, more hard disk space, a mouse, and a faster processor will be necessary for optimum efficiency.

```
Quick C Compiler (QC and QCL)

    Default Components
        \Bin (control, compiler and utility files)          2058
        \INCLUDE (all header files)                          121
        \LIB: (default is SLIBCE, Small Model FP Emulation)  483
        \Samples:                                            145
                                                            -----
        Estimated Minimum Space Required                     2807 KB

    Other Possible \LIB Selections
        SLIBC7 (Small Model w/8087)                          231
        MLIBCE (Medium Model FP Emulation                    246
        MLIBC7 (Medium Model w/8087)                         231
        CLIBCE (Compace Model FP Emulation)                  250
        CLIBC7 (Compact Model w/8087)                        237
        LLIBCE (Large/Huge FP Emulation)                     253
        LLIBC7 (Large/Huge w/8087)                           240
        GRAPHICS (incl PGCHART)                              278
                                                            -----
        Subtotal (add to minimum above)                     1966 KB

OptimizingC Compiler (PWB and CL)

    Default Components
        \BIN (control and compiler files)                    2186
        \BINB (utility files)                                1045
        \INCLUDE (all header files)                          121
        \LIB (default is SLIBCE, Small Model FP Emulation)   483
        \INIT (initialization control files)                4
        \HELP (on-line help files)                           1918
        \SOURCE (startup and documentation)                  307
                                                            -----
        Estimated Minimum Space Required                     6064 KB

    Other Possible \LIB Selections:
        SLIBC7 (Small Model w/8087)                          231
        SCLICA (Small Model w/Alt FP)                        216
        MLIBCE (Medium Model FP Emulation)                   246
        MLIBC7 (Medium Model w/8087)                         231
        MLIBCA (Medium Model w/A1 FP)                        216
        CLIBCE (Compact Model FP Emulation)                  250
        CLIBC7 (Compact Model w/8087)                        237
        CLIBCA (Compact Model w/Alt FP)                      223
        LLIBCE (Large/Huge FP Emulation)                     253
        LLIBC7 (Large/Huge w/8087)                           240
        LLIBCA (Large/Huge w/Alt FP)                         235
        GRAPHICS (including PGCHART)                          278
                                                            -----
        Subtotal (add to minimum above)                     2856 KB
```

FIGURE 2.26: Microsoft product disk storage requirements (in KB).

Installing QuickC

To begin installing QuickC, make A: your default DOS drive, insert the SETUP installation disk, enter the following command at the DOS command line, and press Return (↵):

`SETUP [/?] [/COPY] [/HELP] [/LIB] [/NOFREE] [/NOHELP]`

The optional parameters have the following meanings:

[/?]: Displays an initial SETUP command-line syntax help screen.

[/COPY]: Allows individual files to be loaded from the installation disks. This is necessary because all installation files are in compressed format.

[/HELP]: Same as **/?** noted above.

[/LIB]: Once OptimizingC is installed, use this option to build additional combined libraries, without repeating the entire installation process.

[/NOFREE]: Instructs the SETUP program not to check whether there is sufficient disk space before copying the installation files to your disk.

[/NOHELP]: Instructs the SETUP program not to display help text with each of the three installation screens.

The following prompts are then displayed in a series of three screens (shown in Figures 2.27, 2.28, and 2.29) to which you respond **Y** or **N**, or press Return (↵) to select the default value shown.

The installation choices shown are reflected in the minimum estimated disk storage space required to install the QuickC compiler shown in Figure 2.26. If you have sufficient disk space to load the configuration specified, prompts will follow instructing you to insert various QuickC installation diskettes. If other choices are selected, additional space will be required.

```
Microsoft (R) QuickC (R) Setup Program, Version 2.50

Source of installation disks [A:]: A:
Math options:  Emulator [Y]: Y   8087 [N]: N
Memory models:  Small [Y]: Y  Medium [N]: N  Compact [N]: N  Large [N]: N
Delete the component libraries when finished [Y]: Y
Include in combined libraries: GRAPHICS.LIB [N]: N   PGCHART.LIB [N]: N




Do you want to change any of the above options? [Y]: N
```

FIGURE 2.27: QuickC installation screen 1.

```
Microsoft (R) QuickC (R) Setup Program, Version 2.5Ø

Copy Microsoft Mouse [Y]: N
Copy documentation files [Y]: Y
Copy the DOS patch files [N]: N
Copy sample C programs [N]: N
Copy the QuickC (R) tutorial files [N]: N




Do you want to change any of the above options? [Y]: N
```

FIGURE 2.28: QuickC installation screen 2.

```
Microsoft (R) QuickC (R) Setup Program, Version 2.5Ø

Directory for Executable files [C:\QC25\BIN]: C:\QC25\BIN
Directory for Libraries [C:\QC25\LIB]: C:\QC25\LIB
Directory for Include files [C:\QC25\INCLUDE]: C:\QC25\INCLUDE
Directory for Sample files [C:\QC25\SAMPLES]: C:\QC25\SAMPLES




Do you want to change any of the above options? [Y]: N
```

FIGURE 2.29: QuickC installation screen 3.

When installation is complete, two additional files are generated called NEW-CONF.SYS and NEW-VARS.BAT. NEW-CONF.SYS contains recommended DOS installation commands that should be placed in your CONFIG.SYS file as described in Chapter 1; similarly, NEW-VARS.BAT contains recommended DOS batch commands that should be contained in your

AUTOEXEC.BAT file. Use these files to confirm that you have configured these DOS files accordingly.

Installing OptimizingC

To begin installing OptimizingC, make A: your default DOS drive, insert the SETUP installation disk, enter the following command at the DOS command line, and press Return (↵):

```
SETUP [/?] [/COPY] [/HELP] [/LIB] [/NOFREE] [/NOHELP]
```

(Refer to the "Installing QuickC" section for the meanings of the optional parameters.)

The following prompts are then displayed in a series of three screens to which you respond **Y** or **N**, or press Return (↵) to select the default value shown in Figures 2.30, 2.31, and 2.32.

The installation choices shown are reflected in the minimum estimated disk storage space required to install the OptimizingC compiler shown in Figure 2.26. If you have sufficient disk space to load the configuration specified, prompts will follow instructing you to insert various Optimizing-C installation diskettes. If other choices are selected, additional space will be required. When installation is complete, you should inspect the NEW-CONF.SYS and NEW-VARS.BAT files generated to confirm that you have configured DOS to contain these commands.

```
Microsoft (R) C Setup Program, Version 6.00

Source of installation disks [A:]: A:
Host Operating Mode: OS/2 Protect Mode [N]: N  OS/2 Real Mode and DOS [Y]: Y
Target Operating Mode: OS/2 Protect Mode [N]: N  OS/2 Real Mode and DOS [Y]: Y
Build combined libraries [Y]: Y
Math options:  Emulator [Y]: Y    8087 [N]: N    Alt Math [N]: N
Memory models:  Small [Y]: Y  Medium [N]: N  Compact [N]: N  Large [N]: N
Use default name for DOS Libraries [Y]: Y
Delete the component libraries when finished [Y]: Y
Include in combined libraries: GRAPHICS.LIB [N]: N    PGCHART.LIB [N]: N



Do you want to change any of the above options? [Y]: N
```

FIGURE 2.30: OptimizingC installation screen 1.

```
Microsoft (R) C Setup Program, Version 6.ØØ

Install Microsoft Programmers WorkBench  [Y]: Y
Install Brief compatibility [N]: N
Install Microsoft Mouse [Y]: N
Copy documentation files [Y]: Y
Copy the DOS 3.2 patch files [N]: N
Copy sample programs [N]: N
Copy C start up sources [N]: N




Do you want to change any of the above options? [Y]: N
```

FIGURE 2.31: OptimizingC installation screen 2.

```
Microsoft (R) C Setup Program, Version 6.ØØ

Directory for Bound executable files [C:\C6ØØ\BINB]: C:\C6ØØ\BINB
Directory for Real Mode (DOS) executable files [C:\C6ØØ\BIN]: C:\C6ØØ\BIN
Directory for Libraries [C:\C6ØØ\LIB]: C:\C6ØØ\LIB
Directory for Include files [C:\C6ØØ\INCLUDE]: C:\C6ØØ\INCLUDE
Directory for Initialization files [C:\C6ØØ\INIT]: C:\C6ØØ\INIT
Directory for Help files [C:\C6ØØ\HELP]: C:\C6ØØ\HELP
Directory for Source files [C:\C6ØØ\SOURCE]: C:\C6ØØ\SOURCE




Do you want to change any of the above options? [Y]: N
```

FIGURE 2.32: OptimizingC installation screen 3.

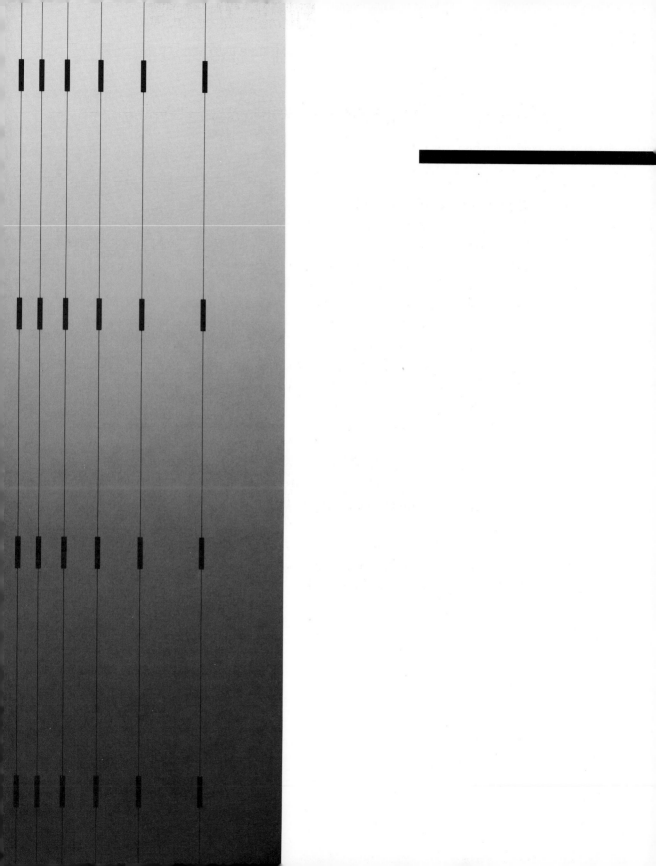

# CHAPTER 3

Using the Program-Development Utilities

Using the Program-Development Utilities

This chapter explains the independent use of Microsoft's LIB, QLINK, LINK, ILINK, NMAKE, and EXEHDR utilities, which support C program development and are supplied when you purchase either the QuickC or OptimizingC compiler. Normally the compiler options you select control whether QLINK, LINK, ILINK, and NMAKE are automatically invoked to create executable files; however, they can also be invoked independently.

The QuickC QLINK and the OptimizingC LINK utilities typically collect hundreds of object modules each time they create an executable file (.EXE or .COM); they rely on the LIB utility to consolidate object files into libraries and thereby provide a faster search mechanism than the standard DOS directory access method. The incremental ILINK utility supplements LINK and, for .EXE files under specific conditions, can reduce the time needed to produce an updated executable file. The NMAKE utility is a C source-code management tool designed to automate the use of other Microsoft tools and executable files. The EXEHDR utility permits you to revise certain parameters within .EXE files without complete relinking.

Along with the details of independently using each of these utilities, you'll find examples that show how to make the most effective use of each of these essential software development tools.

LIB: OBJECT MODULE LIBRARY MANAGER

The object module librarian, LIB, collects any object files that conform to Microsoft's standard object module format (OMF) to create one consolidated object module library file (.LIB) containing the otherwise distinct object (.OBJ) files. Once you've created a library, you can delete the separate object files, thus eliminating the duplication of disk space that necessarily results from using LIB. Any such .OBJ file may, however, subsequently be retrieved from a .LIB file by using a standard LIB utility extract command designed for that purpose.

Libraries provide a convenient means of aggregating object modules to make the QLINK and LINK processes (described later in this chapter) easier to specify and faster to complete. A library is best thought of as a file of files that has a built-in indexing system to quickly locate its component modules. If a library consisted of 100 .OBJ modules, only one filename for the library would appear in the DOS volume directory to identify the location of all 100 modules. Without an object-module library manager such as LIB, 100 separate DOS filenames would be required to store the object files, thereby extending the search time to locate each .OBJ file when needed.

Let's examine the syntax and parameters of the DOS command line used to execute the Object Module Librarian.

SYNTAX

```
LIB oldlibfile [liboption..] [libcommand..]
[,[liblist] [,[newlibfile]]] [;]
```

PARAMETERS

oldlibfile	For this required library parameter, a default .LIB file extension is assumed if omitted. Enter a base filename if located in the current directory; otherwise, enter a complete file specification.
[*liboption..*]	Table 3.1 describes the options recognized by LIB.
[*libcommand..*]	By default, no commands are performed. LIB commands prefix either .OBJ or .LIB filenames. The file extension .OBJ is the default. Table 3.2 describes the commands recognized by LIB.
[,[*liblist*]]	The default is the DOS device NUL. No default file extension is assumed. To produce a cross-reference listing consisting of an alphabetic symbol list by name and within module, enter a *liblist.ext* filename if located in the current directory; otherwise, enter a complete file specification.
[,[*newlibfile*]]	By default, *oldlibfile* becomes *oldlibfile*.BAK and *newlibfile* becomes *oldlibfile*.LIB; otherwise, follow the rules for *oldlibfile* described above.

[;]   If typed after *oldlibfile*, instructs LIB to per-
                                 form only a consistency check to verify that
                                 all object modules are in usable form; if
                                 typed after any other command-line
                                 parameter, defaults the remaining parameters;
                                 otherwise, the commas shown must be
                                 entered to serve as parameter placeholders.

A quick-reference summary of LIB command-line syntax can be found
on the inside front cover of this book. To terminate LIB processing and
return to the DOS command line, press Ctrl-C or Ctrl-Break.

The following observations clarify the options presented in Table 3.1:

- Libraries typically are not case-sensitive because most languages
  used are case-insensitive (Cobol, Fortran, Pascal, BASIC). C language libraries, on the other hand, are typically case-sensitive.

TABLE 3.1: LIB Options

OPTION	DESCRIPTION
/H	Invokes QH (Quick Help) if available, or simply displays command-line syntax help (/?).
/I	The default; instructs LIB to ignore case when comparing identifiers. The resulting library will not be case-sensitive.
/NOE	Instructs LIB not to generate the extended dictionary part of the library that normally helps the linker process *newlibfile* faster.
/NOI	Instructs LIB not to ignore case when comparing names; the opposite effect of /I. The /NOI option should be used because C is a case-sensitive language.
/NOL	Suppress the standard product banner that is normally displayed when LIB is invoked.
/PA:*number*	Page size; controls how LIB aligns modules in the library. The default *number* for *newlibfile* is the page size of *oldlibfile*; otherwise, a page size of 16 bytes is assumed. *Number* can range from 16 to 32,768 in integral powers of 2.
/?	Displays command-line syntax help only.

NOTES:
1. A dash (–) character *may not* be substituted for the slash (/) character shown above to designate the start of an option.
2. The LIB options are case-insensitive.

- Libraries are normally created with an extended dictionary built in. This speeds linker module access, at the expense of requiring some additional library disk storage space.
- The default page size is 16 bytes, which permits each library to be up to 1MB in size ($16 \times 65,536 = 2^{20}$). A maximum of 65,536 .OBJ modules may reside in a single .LIB file. By increasing the *number,* you can create larger libraries, but more disk space may be wasted because each module stored in a library begins on a page-size boundary. For example, if *number* were 1024, the maximum library size would be 64MB ($1024 \times 65,536 = 2^{26}$).

Note that the LIB commands * and –* shown in Table 3.2 permit you to retrieve an .OBJ file from a library, either making a copy only using *, or copying and deleting the module from the library using –*.

Also recall from Chapter 1, Table 1.9, that LIB does not make use of environment table strings, so you can't specify a default directory path for it to search. All *oldlibfile, liblist,* and *newlibfile* filename entries must either be in the current directory or represent a complete file specification. Also note that if LIB itself is not in the current directory, nor in the environment table's PATH= list of drives and directories for DOS to search, you must also explicitly specify where LIB is located. Consider the following sample DOS command line:

```
C:\MYLIB\LIB LIB1 /NOI /PA:32 -module1 +LIB2.LIB, MY.LST;
```

TABLE 3.2: LIB Commands

COMMAND	DESCRIPTION
+	Adds a module to those in *oldlibfile* and creates *newlibfile*.
–	Deletes a module from *oldlibfile* and creates *newlibfile*.
–+	Replaces a module in *oldlibfile* and creates *newlibfile*; same effect as – followed by +.
*	Copies a module from *oldlibfile* and creates a file called *module*.OBJ in the current directory.
–*	Copies a module from *oldlibfile* and creates a file called *module*.OBJ in the current directory, then deletes the module from *oldlibfile* and creates *newlibfile*. Same effect as – followed by *.

NOTES:
1. By default, no LIB commands are performed.
2. LIB commands prefix either .OBJ or .LIB filenames.

This would invoke the object module library manager LIB, which is found in the C:\MYLIB directory, not the current directory. *Oldlibfile* becomes LIB1.LIB; the resulting LIB1.LIB will be case-sensitive; the maximum size of the library will become 2MB because of the 32-byte page size specified; module1 will be deleted; all of the modules contained in library LIB2, found in the current directory, will be added; a cross-reference list file called MY.LST will be created in the current directory; and *newlibfile* will be defaulted to LIB1.LIB because the semicolon is present and *newlibfile* was not specified.

You can also invoke LIB by using either prompts or an automatic-response file. These methods permit you to overcome the DOS command-line limit of 127 characters in an interactive (prompt) or batch (automatic response file) manner. Select the mode of invoking LIB that best fulfills your requirements.

LIB Prompt Mode

To invoke LIB in a prompt mode, simply enter LIB at the DOS prompt, without any of the parameters described above for the command-line mode, as shown below:

```
LIB
```

The following prompt should appear:

```
Library name:
```

LIB is waiting for you to enter *oldlibfile* followed by any options as described in Table 3.1. At any time hereafter, you may press Ctrl-C or Ctrl-Break to terminate the session and return to the DOS prompt or enter a semicolon to default the remaining prompts that would normally appear. Next, the following prompt will appear:

```
Operations:
```

LIB is waiting for you to enter a series of commands as described in Table 3.2. Simply press Return to default the response; no comma is necessary. To enter further commands, place an ampersand (&) after a module or library name and press Return. The prompt will be repeated. Next, the following prompt will appear:

```
List file:
```

LIB is waiting for you to enter *liblist*, as described above. Simply press Return to default the response; no comma is necessary. Next, if any command operation was entered at the *Operations* prompt, the following prompt will appear:

```
Output library:
```

Press Return to default this to *oldlibfile*, or enter a *newlibfile*.

LIB @Response Mode

To invoke LIB in an automatic-response file mode, simply enter **LIB** *@responsefile* at the DOS prompt as shown.

SYNTAX

```
LIB @responsefile
```

PARAMETERS

@   Required symbol designating that an automatic response filename follows.

responsefile   No file extension is assumed. Assumed to be in current directory unless a complete file specification is given. If no file is found, LIB will display *Cannot open response file* and exit to DOS.

The edited *@responsefile* should contain an identical series of keystrokes that would simulate the LIB prompt mode described above. The *@responsefile* behaves like a DOS batch command file in the sense that the keyboard is redirected to the *@responsefile* for its input. If an insufficient number of responses are included in *@responsefile*, the remaining parameters are defaulted.

QLINK AND LINK: THE QUICKC AND OPTIMIZINGC OVERLAY LINKERS

QLINK is designed for use with QuickC and DOS and offers only a subset of the features provided by LINK, which is designed for use with OptimizingC, DOS, OS/2, and Windows. However, both QLINK and LINK construct executable (.EXE and .COM) files from any object modules that conform with Microsoft's standard object module format (OMF). For this reason, QLINK and LINK are not unique to the C programming environment. In a stand-alone fashion they can collect object modules produced from a variety of language compilers and assemblers. The different requirements of these languages are accommodated by the options supported by these linkers.

Beyond providing a different range of compiler options, the Microsoft C compilers also endeavor to provide a seamless interface between the compilation and link phases of computer program development. This process is called *building* or *making*. You can override the integral packaging of the link step by QC, QCL, PWB, and CL by using the compiler option /c (compile only), or by selecting the Make menu's Compile File option with QC and PWB. When the linker is automatically invoked, all of the linker options explicitly chosen, or assumed by default, are passed to QLINK or LINK (or ILINK).

When you work with QLINK or LINK in a stand-alone fashion, be certain that you specify the exact set of linker options you want. For example, in the integrated environment, if you selected compiler option /zi, the linker option /co is automatically assured; and the linker option /NOI is in effect by default, even though in a stand-alone fashion, QLINK and LINK, by default, are case-insensitive. Just remember to double-check your linker option selections when using QLINK or LINK in a stand-alone manner.

SYNTAX

The object module overlay linkers may be activated by entering the following DOS commands:

```
QLINK [linkoption..] objfile.. [,[exefile] [,[maplist] [,[libfile]]]] [;]
LINK [linkoption..] objfile.. [,[exefile] [,[maplist] [,[libfile]]]] ;
```

PARAMETERS

linkoption.. When the QuickC compiler (QC/QCL) is used, QLINK is automatically invoked; when the OptimizingC compiler (PWB/CL) is used, LINK is automatically invoked. Only the options flagged as Y(es) as shown in Table 3.3 are supported for use with QLINK and LINK.

objfile.. For this required parameter, a default .OBJ file extension is assumed if omitted. Either .OBJ or .LIB files may be specified. Enter a base filename if located in the current directory; otherwise, enter a complete file specification. If a .LIB file is specified, all modules from the library are linked.

[, [*exefile*]]	A default file extension of .EXE is assumed, unless the /**T** option is specified, in which case a Tiny memory model .COM file is produced. If no *exefile* is specified, the suffix .EXE is appended to the name of the first object file encountered. Enter a base filename if located in the current directory; otherwise, enter a complete file specification.
[, [*maplist*]]	This optional parameter assumes a default file extension of .MAP. Enter *maplist* if located in the current directory; otherwise, enter a complete file specification. If no name is specified, the base name of *exefile* is used together with the extension .MAP. If you do not want a public symbol and address map, enter the DOS device NUL.
[, [*libfile*]]	This optional parameter assumes a file extension of .LIB. These libraries are used to resolve external references only. Enter a filename and extension if in the current directory; otherwise, enter a complete file specification.
;	If typed after *objfile* or any other command-line parameter, it defaults the remaining parameters; otherwise, the commas must be entered as shown to serve as placeholders. The terminating semicolon is optional with QLINK, but required for use with DOS when LINK is used because additional [, [*mdeffile*]] command-line arguments are supported that are only relevant to OS/2 and Windows.

A quick-reference summary of the QLINK and LINK command-line syntax can be found on the inside front cover of this book. To terminate QLINK or LINK processing and return to the DOS command line, press Ctrl-C or Ctrl-Break.

QLINK and LINK Options

The options supported by QLINK and LINK are shown in Table 3.3. Just as we had found that the compiler options shown in Table 2.2 differentiated the capabilities of the QC/QCL and PWB/CL compilers, so do the linker options differentiate the Microsoft compilers. The QuickC compiler (QC/QCL) has a limited selection of possible linker options, whereas OptimizingC (PWB/CL) can exploit all available options. Some of the options significantly impact program size and performance, as described below.

[/CO]   Necessary if either the QC debugger or CV (CodeView) debugger will be used (see Chapter 29 for information about debugging strategies). The object modules should have been compiled using the **/zi** Compiler

TABLE 3.3: QLINK and LINK Options

OPTIONS	DESCRIPTION	QuickC	OptimizingC
/A:*bytes*	Alignment and size of segment (default 512)	N	Y
/BA	Batch mode; do not prompt	Y	Y
/CO	Codeview debugging preparation	Y	Y
/CP:*bytes*	Maximum allocation of paragraphs	Y	Y
/DO	DOS segment ordering (default)	Y	Y
/DS	Allocate data to high memory	Y	Y
/E	Exepack; removes debugging information	Y	Y
/F	_Far call translation to _near calls	Y	Y
/HE	Help; QH help if available, /? if not	Y	Y
/HI	Place program in high memory (assembly)	Y	Y
/INC	Incremental linking	Y	Y
/INF	Information displayed while linking	Y	Y
/LI	Line numbers displayed in map file	Y	Y
/M	Map file display of global symbols	Y	Y
/NOD:*filename*	No default library search	Y	Y
/NOE	No extended dictionary search, which slows the linker	Y	Y
/NOF	No _far call translation; toggle for /F	Y	Y
/NOG	No group association; linker compatibility	Y	Y
/NOI	Don't ignore upper/lowercase	Y	Y
/NOL	No logo; suppresses banner display	Y	Y
/NON	No null DOS segment; removes null padding	Y	Y

TABLE 3.3: QLINK and LINK Options (continued)

OPTIONS	DESCRIPTION	QuickC	OptimizingC
/NOP	Don't pack code; toggle for /PACKC	Y	Y
/O:*number*	Overlay interrupt; avoids conflicts	Y	Y
/PACKC:*bytes*	Amount of padding in code segments	Y	Y
/PACKD:*bytes*	Amount of padding in data segments	Y	Y
/PADC	Pad code segment; toggle for /PACKC	Y	Y
/PADD	Pad data segment; toggle for /PACKD	Y	Y
/PAU	Pause for swapping diskettes	Y	Y
/PM:*type*	OS/2, Windows (PM, VIO, NOVIO)	N	Y
/Q	Quick library; create .QLB files	N	Y
/SE:*number*	Maximum number of segments	Y	Y
/ST:*bytes*	Stack size (default 2048)	Y	Y
/T	Create a Tiny memory model .COM file	Y	Y
/W	Print warning to fix up unresolved identifiers	N	Y
/?	Command-line syntax help only	Y	Y

NOTES:
1. Only the options flagged as Y(es) apply. QLINK is used with QC/QCL, and LINK is used with PWB/CL.
2. A dash (–) character may be substituted for the slash (/) character shown above to designate the start of a QLINK or LINK option.
3. The QLINK and LINK options are case-insensitive.

option. This increases the size of the resulting executable (.EXE) file by adding symbolic data and line number information. This information may later be removed by relinking with the /E option.

[/CP:number] Controls setting the maximum program size in paragraphs (units of 16 bytes). Unless specified, QLINK and LINK will default *number* to the maximum amount of memory available, leaving no memory available to run another program from the program being linked. The

utility EXEHDR can subsequently be used to alter this value in an existing .EXE file (see the "EXEHDR" section in this chapter).

[/E]   Should not be used if you specify /co because it removes all debugging information. This option will generally create an .EXE file that requires less disk space and loads faster when executed. A message will be generated, however, should the resulting packed file be larger than the unpacked file.

[/F]   Can improve the speed and reduce the size of programs compiled with the Medium, Large, and Huge memory models. **_far** calls to functions that reside in the same segment are reduced to **_near** calls. Typically this option is coordinated with /PACKC. If /F is specified, the use of overlays will not be possible.

[/INC]   This incremental linking option applies to QC and QCL, and it invokes the incremental linker ILINK, not the QLINK or LINK utility.

[/MAP]   This option overrides the *maplist* command-line option, if defaulted, to create a corresponding .MAP listing cross-reference file. A map listing appears under the "Example" heading in this section.

[/NOE]   Prevents the linker from searching library extended dictionaries if they exist. Such dictionaries speed the search for symbols and modules within .LIB files.

[/NOI]   Instructs the linker not to ignore upper- and lowercase for comparisons of module and public symbol names. C libraries are normally case-sensitive.

[/PACKC:bytes]   Used in concert with /F; packs the code segments of Medium, Large, and Huge memory models into segments sized to *bytes*, which by default is 65,536 (64KB), thereby producing a smaller program by eliminating paragraph (16-byte) padding.

[/PACKD:bytes]   Like /PACKC except that it packs data, not code segments.

[/PADC:bytes]   Necessary with incremental linking to provide the "pad" space needed to accommodate small increases in the code size due to changes in the source code. A default *bytes* value of 40 is assumed (2½ paragraphs).

[/PADD:bytes]   Like /PADC except that it pads data, not code segments.

[/ST:bytes]   Allows you to override the default 2KB stack size with any value up to 64KB. The number of bytes specified may be expressed either in decimal (with no prefix), octal (with a 0 prefix), or hexadecimal (with a 0x prefix). The utility EXEHDR can alter this option setting. For more about the stack, see Chapter 15.

[/T]   Necessary if a Tiny memory model program (.COM) is to be produced. When this is specified, be sure to include the CRTCOM.LIB file. This option is incompatible with the /CO, /E, /F, /INC, /PACKC, /PACKD, /PADC, and /PADD options.

Recall that QLINK and LINK make use of the environment table strings presented in Table 1.9. Use of these strings effectively extends the 127-character limit of the DOS command line. Remember that if QLINK or LINK itself is not in the current directory, nor in the environment table's PATH= list of drives and directories for DOS to search, you must explicitly specify where QLINK or LINK is located.

EXAMPLE

The following DOS command-line mode invokes LINK, but could be used with QLINK as well:

```
LINK /E /F /MAP MAIN+MOD1+MOD2+MOD3+MOD4+MOD5,,,MYLIB;
```

This invokes the LINK utility and produces by default a packed executable file MAIN.EXE. It calls for far call optimization and the creation of a .MAP cross-reference file; the object modules specified may be found in the current directory or a library called MYLIB.LIB.

A sample LINK .MAP file for a Large memory model program would resemble Figure 3.1. Compare this .MAP file with the Large memory model map depicted in Figure 2.24. Notice that the program entry relative address is

$$0008{:}001E \rightarrow 0080 + 001E = 009E \text{ (relative)}$$

This confirms that the CS register originates at the **_TEXT** segment, as shown in Figure 2.25. Also note that the DGROUP (Data GROUP of segments) originates at

```
1E86:0000 → 1E860 + 0000 = 1E860 (relative)
```

which also confirms that the DS register originates at the NULL segment, as shown in Figure 2.24. Similarly, by using Figure 2.25 and the .MAP output shown above, we can determine the amount of Near heap space available to this Large memory model program:

```
Near HEAP = DS:0000 + 64KB - SS:SP
```

or

```
Near HEAP = 1E860 + 10000 - 1F6DF
```

or

```
Near HEAP = 2E860 - 1F6DF = F181 = 61,825 bytes
```

Besides the DOS command-line method described above, you can also invoke LINK or QLINK by using either prompts or an automatic-response file. These methods permit you to overcome the DOS command-line limit of 127 characters in an interactive (prompt) or batch (automatic response file) manner. Select the mode of invoking QLINK and LINK that best fulfills your requirements.

QLINK and LINK Prompt Mode

To invoke QLINK or LINK in prompt mode, simply enter **QLINK** or **LINK** at the DOS prompt, without any of the parameters described above for the command-line mode. The following prompt should appear:

```
Object Modules [.OBJ]:
```

The linker is waiting for you to enter one or more *objfiles*. To enter further filenames, place a plus (+) after a module or library name and press Return. The prompt will be repeated. A file extension of .OBJ is assumed. When specifying a complete library of object files to include, specify the complete library .LIB filename. At any time hereafter, you may press Ctrl-C or Ctrl-Break to terminate the session and return to the DOS command

```
Start      Stop       Length     Name              Class
00000H     0004BH     0004CH     MAIN_TEXT         CODE
0004CH     00061H     00016H     FN1_TEXT          CODE
00062H     00077H     00016H     FN2_TEXT          CODE
00078H     0008DH     00016H     FN3_TEXT          CODE
0008EH     01383H     012F6H     _TEXT             CODE
01390H     01391H     00002H     EMULATOR_TEXT     CODE
01392H     01392H     00000H     C_ETEXT           ENDCODE
013A0H     0AFDFH     09C40H     FN15_DATA         FAR_DATA
0AFE0H     14C1FH     09C40H     FN25_DATA         FAR_DATA
14C20H     1E85FH     09C40H     FN35_DATA         FAR_DATA
1E860H     1E860H     00000H     EMULATOR_DATA     FAR_DATA
1E860H     1E8A1H     00042H     NULL              BEGDATA
1E8A2H     1EBD5H     00334H     _DATA             DATA
1EBD6H     1EBD7H     00002H     XIQC              DATA
1EBD8H     1EBE5H     0000EH     DBDATA            DATA
1EBE6H     1EBF3H     0000EH     CDATA             DATA
1EBF4H     1EBF4H     00000H     XIFB              DATA
1EBF4H     1EBF4H     00000H     XIF               DATA
1EBF4H     1EBF4H     00000H     XIFE              DATA
1EBF4H     1EBF4H     00000H     XIB               DATA
1EBF4H     1EBF4H     00000H     XI                DATA
1EBF4H     1EBF4H     00000H     XIE               DATA
1EBF4H     1EBF4H     00000H     XPB               DATA
1EBF4H     1EBF7H     00004H     XP                DATA
1EBF8H     1EBF8H     00000H     XPE               DATA
1EBF8H     1EBF8H     00000H     XCB               DATA
1EBF8H     1EBF8H     00000H     XC                DATA
1EBF8H     1EBF8H     00000H     XCE               DATA
1EBF8H     1EBF8H     00000H     XCFB              DATA
1EBF8H     1EBF8H     00000H     XCF               DATA
1EBF8H     1EBF8H     00000H     XCFE              DATA
1EBF8H     1EBFDH     00006H     CONST             CONST
1EBFEH     1EC05H     00008H     HDR               MSG
1EC06H     1ECDBH     000D6H     MSG               MSG
1ECDCH     1ECDDH     00002H     PAD               MSG
1ECDEH     1ECDEH     00001H     EPAD              MSG
1ECE0H     1ECE0H     00000H     _BSS              BSS
1ECE0H     1ECE0H     00000H     XOB               BSS
1ECE0H     1ECE0H     00000H     XO                BSS
1ECE0H     1ECE0H     00000H     XOE               BSS
1ECE0H     1EEDFH     00200H     c_common          BSS
1EEE0H     1F6DFH     00800H     STACK             STACK

Origin  Group
1E86:0  DGROUP

Program entry point at 0008:001E
```

FIGURE 3.1: Sample LINK .MAP file for a Large memory model program.

line or enter a semicolon to default the remaining prompts that would normally appear.

Next, the following prompt will appear:

`Run file [basename.EXE]:`

The linker is waiting for you to enter *exefile* as described above. Simply press Return to default the response; no comma is necessary.

`List File [NUL.MAP]:`

The linker is waiting for you to enter *maplist* as described above. Simply press return to default the response; no comma is necessary. Next, the following prompt will appear if at least one *command* operation was entered above:

```
Libraries [.LIB]:
```

Press Return to accept the default libraries encoded in the object modules themselves, or enter a *libfile*. Next, the following prompt will appear only for LINK unless a semicolon was entered above:

```
Definitions File [NUL.DEF]:
```

This is required for OS/2 and Windows only, so simply press the Return key to omit the module definitions file.

QLINK and LINK @Response Mode

To invoke QLINK or LINK in an automatic-response file mode, simply enter **LINK @***responsefile* (or **QLINK @***responsefile*) at the DOS prompt.

SYNTAX

```
QLINK @responsefile
LINK @responsefile
```

PARAMETERS

@	Required symbol designating that an automatic response filename follows.
responsefile	No file extension is assumed. It is assumed to be a filename in the current directory unless a complete file specification is given. If no file is found, QLINK and LINK will display *Cannot open reponse file* and exit to DOS.

The edited *@responsefile* should contain an identical series of keystrokes that would simulate the QLINK or LINK prompt mode described above. The *@responsefile* behaves like a DOS batch file in the sense that the keyboard is redirected to the *@responsefile* for its input. If an insufficient number of responses are included in the *@responsefile*, the remaining parameters are defaulted.

QLINK and LINK Overlays

An overlay is a group of modules that reside on disk in an executable file (.EXE) and whose code portion is swapped into memory only as needed. Only code is overlaid, not data. Using overlays reduces the memory required to execute a program, but increases its run-time because of the added disk I/O necessary.

QLINK and LINK can be instructed to create overlays and to group certain modules together into separate transient (swapped) overlays by the use of parentheses and to group the remaining modules into what we will call the root or memory-resident group. The net effect of specifying overlays is to reduce a program's memory size by an amount equal to the sum of the size of all module code minus the sum of its resident code size and the code size of the largest overlay specified.

From this description of overlays, it should be apparent that:

- All modules cannot be placed into overlays. A resident group (root) is needed to start a program.
- At least two overlays (transients), in addition to the root, are required to effect any memory savings at all.
- Each overlay group should have approximately the same code size, or multiples thereof, to maximize memory savings.
- Software design should anticipate the use of overlays and minimize critical program modules from calling modules in other overlays. This will minimize the time-consuming thrashing of overlays that can result.

Certain limitations also apply when constructing overlays:

- Modules may be used only once. They may not be specified to exist in more than one overlay.
- Modules to be overlaid must conform to the standard function-calling conventions (32-bit segment:offset). Modules using the **_near** (16-bit) convention or those calling other modules using a **_near** calling convention must reside in the root. Use of the linker **/F** option will therefore preclude the use of overlays.
- Modules that use the <**setjmp.h**> functions **setjmp()** and **longjmp()** cannot be overlaid. All modules using these function-to-function unconditional branching functions must be located in the root.
- Modules that are called indirectly using function pointers must be in the same overlay, or in the root.
- A maximum of 63 overlays may be created.

EXAMPLE

Either LINK or QLINK may be used to construct overlays.

```
LINK MAIN + (MOD1+MOD2) + (MOD3) + (MOD4+MOD5);
```

This creates MAIN.EXE in the current directory with no command-line linker options, with overlays consisting of MAIN.OBJ in the root, and three transient overlays consisting of (MOD1.OBJ + MOD2.OBJ), (MOD3.OBJ), and (MOD4.OBJ + MOD5.OBJ). *Maplist* is defaulted to `NULL`, and no additional libraries are searched to resolve external references.

Overlays may be specified for QLINK and LINK in either the command line, prompt, or automatic-response file mode. Overlays may only be specified by the QCL or CL command-line compilers, but not from the integrated QC or PWB compilers.

ILINK: THE QUICKC AND OPTIMIZINGC INCREMENTAL LINKER

Typically the ILINK utility is invoked by the QC and PWB compilers based upon a default incremental compile (`/Gi`) or link (`/Li`) option chosen; however, ILINK may also be run directly from the DOS command line. To be effective, the incremental linker, ILINK, must be coordinated with the use of the overlay linkers, QLINK and LINK. ILINK is strictly intended for use during the software development cycle, and not for preparing release software.

QLINK or LINK must be used at least once before ILINK can be used at all, because ILINK presumes that an executable .EXE (not .COM) file exists and that the linker options `/INC`, `/PADC`, and `/PADD` have already been specified. The `/INC` option generates .SYM and .ILK files needed by ILINK, and `/PADD` and `/PADC` provide the size of the module data and code segment "padding" that later permits ILINK to replace out-of-date .OBJ modules in an .EXE file. In this manner, small program changes can occur in perhaps just a few of the many .OBJ modules referenced, and ILINK can then "fix up" the .EXE file without performing an entire link operation—hence the name *incremental*. If any major program changes are made, such as adding a new .OBJ module, changing an .OBJ module's size significantly, redefining symbols that are shared between modules, or including an additional .LIB file, ILINK will fail, and a complete link will have to be performed using QLINK or LINK.

Let's examine how to invoke ILINK from the DOS command line.

SYNTAX

```
ILINK [ilinkoption..] exefile [objfile..]
```

PARAMETERS

[*ilinkoption..*]	Table 3.4 describes the options recognized by ILINK.
exefile	An existing .EXE file that has been prepared for incremental linking by QLINK or LINK using the /INC, /PADC, and /PADD options. Both the *exefile* and its associated *exefile*.SYM and *exefile*.ILK files produced by QLINK or LINK should be in the current directory. If a file extension is omitted from *exefile*, .EXE is assumed.
[*objfile..*]	An optional list of module names, without the .OBJ extension, separated by spaces. If provided, instructs ILINK to replace only those modules in *exefile*. If no *objfiles* are provided, each *exefile* .OBJ module is checked for outdatedness relative to the *exefile*. Only those .OBJ modules whose date and time fields in the DOS directory are more recent than the .EXE directory entry are replaced.

A quick-reference summary of ILINK command-line syntax can be found on the inside front cover of this book. To terminate ILINK processing and return to the DOS command line, press Ctrl-C or Ctrl-Break. No prompt or @*responsefile* modes of running ILINK are available.

ILINK Options

The command-line options recognized by ILINK are summarized in Table 3.4. Notice that specifying the /A option has the same effect as not providing any *objfile* entries at the DOS command line. The /E option permits you to initiate another command should ILINK fail. Normally this is an instruction to perform a complete link step. Unlike QLINK or LINK, ILINK cannot produce a .MAP file, it can only report the module names that were updated in *exefile*, if the /V option is used.

TABLE 3.4: ILINK Options

OPTION	DESCRIPTION
/A	Instructs ILINK to update all .OBJ's that are out-of-date.
/C	Instructs DOS that all public symbols are to be considered case-sensitive.
/E	Introduces a list of DOS commands enclosed in double quotes as "command ; command ; .." that are to executed if ILINK fails; otherwise, the LINK utility is invoked, unless /I is specified. The commands must be separated by spaces and semicolons as shown.
/H	Invokes QH (Quick Help) if available, or simply displays command-line syntax help (/?).
/I	Instructs DOS to perform ILINK only and not to invoke LINK if an incremental link violation occurs.
/NOL	No logo; suppresses the standard product banner that is normally displayed when LIB is invoked.
/V	Verbose mode; lists all .OBJ modules that were updated in .EXE to standard output.
/X	Disables ILINK's use of expanded memory, if it is available. By default, ILINK attempts to use expanded memory.
/?	Displays command-line syntax help only.

NOTES:
1. A dash (–) character may be substituted for the slash (/) character shown above to designate the start of an option.
2. The ILINK options are case-insensitive.

ILINK Error Conditions

It should not be surprising that ILINK may not always be able to correctly update an .EXE file. By its very design, ILINK represents an attempt to improve programming productivity, by shortening the time it takes to perform the so commonly performed link step. To benefit from using ILINK, you must use it strategically. Understanding the conditions that cause ILINK to fail will give you insight into making choices when its use is merited.

Real errors, such as undefined symbols and invalid .OBJ modules, will obviously cause ILINK to fail, just as QLINK or LINK also would fail. Another class of errors, called incremental violations, will cause ILINK to fail and will necessitate the use of QLINK or LINK. There are several types of incremental violations:

1. Changing libraries: any change in the .LIB files used for linking.

2. Exceeding code/data padding: whenever the incremental change in code or data size required by just one module exceeds the available "padding" that remains since the last full link.

3. Moving/deleting data symbols: only **extern** and **static** storage class variables, not **auto** or **register**, create violations. Always add new such symbols to the end of those already specified in your source code. Any moving or deleting of symbols causes a violation.

4. Deleting code symbols: code symbols are understood to be function names (addresses). These may be moved or added within a module, but not deleted. A violation occurs if a function is moved between modules (more than one function defined in a source-code file).

5. Changing segment definitions: adding, changing, or deleting code or data modules. See the memory model maps in Chapter 2.

6. Adding debugger information: ILINK is compatible with Code-View (CV) if /co was specified at the last full link; however, subsequently specifying compiler option /zi for a module that has last been linked without option /co will cause a violation.

NMAKE: PROGRAM MAINTENANCE UTILITY

Although Microsoft calls NMAKE a program maintenance utility, it is more appropriately regarded as a DOS command-generating utility. With experience, you will find that NMAKE is useful for performing much more than just program maintenance. For now, however, let's concentrate on mastering the use of NMAKE for program maintenance.

NMAKE (or New MAKE) supersedes Microsoft's predecessor product MAKE, which was patterned after the UNIX operating system's make utility. NMAKE will become the cornerstone of C development tools used by those working with Microsoft's products.

C's reliance on header files and functions dictates the need for an automated way of ensuring that each executable file (.EXE) created has incorporated the latest header (.H) files, compiled the most recent C source-code (.C) program changes, and located the most current object (.OBJ) modules. Otherwise, the executable file generated by QLINK, LINK, or ILINK may not reflect the most recent version of the source code. NMAKE excels at detecting these (.H), (.C), (.OBJ), and (.EXE) dependencies and assuring that program currency is maintained.

Two new concepts, dependency and inference, are coupled with the familiar C preprocessor concepts of macros and directives (see Chapter 5) to form the design basis of NMAKE.

Dependency defines the explicit relationships that exist between files and the commands necessary to maintain program currency. For example, the presence of **MAIN.EXE : MAIN.OBJ** in a make control file expresses that MAIN.EXE is dependent upon MAIN.OBJ. If the target file MAIN.EXE were out-of-date relative to the dependent file MAIN.OBJ, MAIN.EXE would have to be relinked. NMAKE relies upon the current date and time stamp recorded by DOS for each file or the nonexistence of a file to know whether an out-of-date condition exists. For these reasons, when working with NMAKE, it is important to maintain an accurate DOS date and time (see Chapter 1). Dependency will be discussed at greater length in a section that follows.

Inference defines implicit dependency and commands that are to apply when specific file relationships are not defined in a make control file. Inference rules apply either when no commands are declared for a description block, or if dependent files do not exist. (Description blocks are discussed under "Make Control Files.") In either case, inference rules rely upon a base filename and a set of associated file extensions. Inference rules help to reduce the unnecessary repetition of commands in separate description blocks. Inference will be fully explained in a section that follows.

Macros, like C preprocessor `#define` directives, are understood to represent string substitutions; and directives, like C preprocessor #directives, provide for conditional branching within make control files. Both macros and directives are covered in sections that follow.

The make (or description) control file is edited to contain text describing target:dependency description blocks of commands, comments, macros, directives, and inference rules that NMAKE is to perform. Before delving further into the details of constructing a make control file, let's look at how the program maintenance utility NMAKE is activated from the DOS command line.

SYNTAX

```
NMAKE [makeoption.. /F makefile /X errfile] [macro..] [target..]
```

PARAMETERS

[*makeoption..*]   Table 3.5 describes the options recognized by NMAKE.

/F *makefile*	Although an *option*, /F is shown individually here to recommend its use; otherwise, a default make control file, MAKEFILE, is assumed to exist in the current directory. (See Table 3.5.)
/X *errfile*	Although an *option*, /X is shown individually here to recommend its use; otherwise, the DOS device CON is assumed. (See Table 3.5.)
macro..	An optional but convenient method of substituting a string of text in the description file. Macros are fully described in a section that follows.
[*target..*]	Optional name of one or more targets to build in the make control file. If omitted, only the first target encountered in the make control file is built.

A quick-reference summary of NMAKE command-line syntax can be found on the inside front cover of this book. To terminate NMAKE processing and return to the DOS command line, press Ctrl-C or Ctrl-Break.

NMAKE *Options*

The command-line options recognized by NMAKE are summarized in Table 3.5. The options chosen on the command line remain in effect until NMAKE terminates processing, unless the options are modified using a !CMDSWITCHES directive, the predefined pseudotargets .IGNORE: or .SILENT:, or the command modifiers (−) and (@) (see Table 3.7). Remember that if NMAKE itself is not in the current directory, nor in the environment table PATH= list of drives and directories for DOS to search, you must explicitly specify where NMAKE is located.

EXAMPLE

```
NMAKE /F SAMPLE.MAK /P /N CC=CL NDEBUG= TGROUP >PRN
```

This command line would first try to perform the [NMAKE] portion of the control file called TOOLS.INI (see Figure 3.2 and the following section). Next the make control file SAMPLE.MAK will be performed if located in the current directory. With NMAKE option /P turned on, all macros, inference rules, target descriptions, and command lines generated will be displayed. With NMAKE option /N turned on, command execution will only be simulated. The command-line macro string definitions for CC and NDEBUG will redefine those defined in TOOLS.INI from a debugging to release mode. The target called TGROUP is to be performed from those targets specified in SAMPLE.MAK, and all standard output is to be redirected to the DOS device PRN or printer. The results generated by this NMAKE command will be fully examined in the "NMAKE Comprehensive Example" section.

TABLE 3.5: NMAKE Options

CATEGORY	OPTION	DESCRIPTION
Input	/F *filename*	The preferred method of designating the make control file to use containing NMAKE instructions; enter a complete file specification or a dash (–) to redirect input from DOS device CON.
Execution	/A	Builds all targets even if they are not out-of-date; the equivalent of a complete system rebuild.
	/E	Overrides macro definitions within description files with environment table strings.
	/I	Ignores error codes returned by programs called from a description file.
	/N	Simulates and displays the commands performed by a description file; helpful debugging tool (use with /F).
	/Q	Helpful when NMAKE is invoked from within a batch file; NMAKE returns status code equals 0 when a target is up-to-date; otherwise, status code ! = 0.
	/R	Instructs ILINK to ignore inference rules and macros contained in TOOLS.INI.
	/T	Does not modify the contents, but changes the modification dates of all out-of-date files to the current date (updating the DOS directory date and time fields is commonly referred to as *touching* a file).
	/Z	For internal use by PWB only.
Output	/C	Suppresses display of all copyright, nonfatal errors, and warning messages.
	/D	Displays the modification date of each file when date checked.
	/H	Invokes QH (Quick Help) if available, or simply displays command-line syntax help (/?).
	/N	No logo; suppresses the standard product banner that is normally displayed when NMAKE is invoked.

TABLE 3.5: NMAKE Options (continued)

CATEGORY	OPTION	DESCRIPTION
Output (cont.)	/P	Prints all macro definitions and target descriptions; a helpful .MAK control file debugging tool (use with /N).
	/S	Instructs ILINK not to display commands as they are performed.
	/X *stderrfile*	Redirects all error output from the standard error device CON; enter a complete file specification or another DOS device.
	/?	Displays command-line syntax help only.

NOTES:
1. A dash (–) may be substituted for the slash (/) shown above to designate the start of an option.
2. The MAKE options are case-insensitive.

Make Control Files (.MAK)

Make control files (called description or build files in Microsoft parlance) are, by convention, text files with the suffix (.MAK) that contain NMAKE instructions. There are six basic NMAKE instruction types: comments, description blocks, commands, macros, directives, and inference rules. Each is described in the sections that follow. Use any text editor or word processor in nondocument mode to construct a .MAK control file. Notice that instructions are required to begin either in column one, or at least one space or tab position in from column one. Instructions are understood to be contained on one logical line of input terminated with a newline (Return key) character. If an instruction must be continued beyond one physical line, the backslash-newline sequence may be keyed (see special symbols below). If no *target* is specified on the command line when NMAKE is invoked, only the first target description block encountered in the make control file specified is performed. If *target* is specified, only those description blocks are performed.

Comments

Use the # symbol to introduce comments documenting your make control files. Except for the command section of a description block, in which the # delimiter must begin in the first column, comments may begin at any column position and are understood to continue until a new line is encountered. The characters following a comment # delimiter are ignored, not treated as a string, and do not require double quotations. The special NMAKE characters ^ # ( ) $ \ { } ! @ - may therefore be used as well. If quotations are used, they will simply appear in the text description. The backslash cannot be used to make a comment span a line. Consider the following example:

```
# this comment extends from the # to newline
```

The # may appear at column 1 or more in make control files.

Description Blocks

The description block is a critical component of any make control file. It defines target-dependency relationships, without which NMAKE cannot conditionally initiate and perform DOS commands based upon whether the target is out-of-date relative to any of its dependents.

SYNTAX

```
target.. : {path;..}[dependent..] [;command] [#comment] [command]
[#comment]
[#comment]|[command]
   ...
   ...
target.. : [dependent..] ...
```

COMPONENTS

target	Required filename describing the object to be built. If more than one target, separate with at least one blank space. Targets may also be either user-defined or predefined pseudotargets. See below for discussion of pseudotargets. Targets must begin in column 1.
:	Required separator. A space must appear on either side.
{*path;..*}	An optional list of paths (*dr:\dir,...*) separated by semicolons where the *dependent* files may be found if not in the current directory. Braces shown must be coded.
[*dependent..*]	A list of one or more files upon which the target depends, separated by blank spaces. Must begin at least one space or tab in from column 1.

[*command*]	Optional command. See "Command" section that follows. If no commands are provided, a suitable inference rule (matching .ext of target: dependent) is used.
[#*comment*]	Optional comment. See the "Comments" section.

Two types of pseudotargets are possible: user-defined and predefined. When pseudotargets are specified, the dependent files are always understood to be out-of-date. Pseudotargets are not files but consist of any tag or name that does not qualify as a valid filename and terminates with a colon (:). User-defined pseudotargets simply serve as a handle for a group of dependent files upon which commands may operate using the special dependent file macros (see Table 3.6 under the heading "Macros"). For user-defined pseudotargets to be performed in a make control file, they must be specified as targets on the NMAKE command line. HEADERS on the target : dependency line shown below is an example of a user-defined pseudotarget:

```
HEADERS : $(**).C
    [command]
```

NMAKE predefines certain pseudotargets. No commands may be specified with a description block using one of them. Predefined pseudotargets are associated with implied actions. If present in a make control file, they are processed as encountered and not required to be explicitly specified on the NMAKE command line. The predefined pseudotargets in NMAKE are the following:

.IGNORE:	Ignores command exit codes. Same effect as NMAKE option /i.
.SILENT:	Does not display commands as they are performed. Same as NMAKE option /s.
.SUFFIXES:*list...*	Constructs possible filename using the target base name when a target is specified for which no dependents exist. The extensions .OBJ, .EXE, .C, and .ASM are by default associated with .SUFFIXES: To remove the default suffix list, enter .SUFFIXES: only; to append additional extensions, enter .SUFFIXES: .ext ...

.PRECIOUS:*target...*   Instructs NMAKE not to delete *target...* if the commands being built are interrupted in any way. This overrides the NMAKE default assumption.

If you define more than one description block within a make control file, separate them by a blank line. Normally, targets may be specified only once in a make control file. Multiple description blocks referencing the same target may be specified, but the normal target:dependent syntax must be replaced with the syntax target:dependent.

Commands

Command-line instructions are components of description blocks and of inference rules that update a target. A command is any valid expression that can be performed from the DOS prompt, which includes DOS internal and external commands and any executable (.COM, .EXE) or .BAT filename. You can direct commands either at target or dependent files by using the special predefined NMAKE macros. You may also call NMAKE recursively from within a make control file that issues a command with the special macros $(MAKE) and $(MAKEFLAGS) followed by any other [*makeoption..*], [*macro..*], or [*target..*]. This compatibility of NMAKE with DOS commands extends its range of possible uses well beyond program maintenance.

Commands normally must be indented one space or tab position and contained on one logical line of input. The backslash may be used to permit a command to span several physical lines of input. Blank lines or comments may be intermixed with commands. If a command is placed on the same line as the target : dependency statement, it must be preceded by a semicolon (;). To improve the readability and facilitate the maintenance of make control files, refrain from putting commands on the target:dependency line. Commands may be omitted from a target:dependency block, but are required with inference rules.

Three special command modifiers, which may optionally be used to prefix any command, are recognized by NMAKE. One or more of the following modifiers, with no intervening blank spaces, may precede any command:

    –   Hyphen, minus, or dash; turns off error checking for the command. NMAKE continues processing and does not halt. Has the same effect as the NMAKE option /i, but applies only to a particular command, not to all commands in a make control file.

    @   Prevents NMAKE from displaying the command as it executes. Has the same affect as the NMAKE option /s, but applies only to a particular command, not to all commands in a make control file.

    !   Causes the command to be repeated for each dependent file if the command uses either of the special macros $(?) or $(**). (See Table 3.6.)

Some typical commands directed at target and dependent files would be:

```
# target file processing example
    LINK $(LFLAGS) $(**F), $(@);

# dependent file processing example
    !$(CC) $(CFLAGS) /c $(*).C
```

Note that commands must be indented at least one space or tab in from column #1. Comments with commands are required to be in column #1.

Macros

Macros provide a string substitution facility that, when coupled with directives, adds flexibility and power beyond that normally provided by commands alone in a make control file. Macros are either user-defined or predefined, and may be introduced either on the NMAKE command line, in a make control file, in the tools-initialization file TOOLS.INI, in any referenced !INCLUDE file, or by referencing environment table strings (which are treated as macro definitions by NMAKE). Macros are understood either to be defined or undefined by their presence or absence in a symbol table. Once defined, a macro is redefined by simply reassigning its replacement string. To delete or undefine a macro definition, you must use the !UNDEF directive. A macro may assume the value of a null string, but it is still understood to be defined.

SYNTAX

`macroname=string`

COMPONENTS

macroname Any contiguous string of from one to 127 characters. Only upper/lowercase alphabetic, numeric, and the underscore characters may be used. This conforms with the rules for forming C identifiers. When macros are invoked using $(*macroname*), the name is always transformed to uppercase.

= Use no intervening spaces.

string The replacement character string associated with *macroname* may consist of from zero to 512 characters. If *string* contains a blank, enclose in double quotation marks only when *macroname* is defined on the NMAKE command line. If any of the special NMAKE symbols ^ # ( ) $ \ { } ! @ or - is used, it must be preceded by the caret (^) escape symbol. No character transformations of *string* are performed. A zero-length or null string is a valid string declaration and defines a macro. To remove a macro definition, use the !UNDEF directive.

Once a macro is defined, you can invoke the string substitution by using the NMAKE construction

```
$(macroname)
```

You can create and reference user-defined macros as necessary, but the special predefined macros shown in Table 3.6 provide access to target, dependent, and program filenames that is essential to preparing powerful make control files.

Because macros may be defined in more than one place, NMAKE assigns macro string definitions to the first definition encountered, giving highest precedence to the command line, then the current make control or !INCLUDE file, then a DOS SET environment table variable, then the automatic startup TOOLS.INI file, and finally any special predefined program macros. These precedence rules can be overridden only by using the NMAKE option /E to cause the environment table variables to take precedence over macros defined in description or !INCLUDE files.

Another interesting feature provided by NMAKE is macro substitution, which allows for the substitution of text within the macro itself. For example, if you defined the macro LFLAGS in a make control file as

```
LFLAGS=/link /CO /NOI
```

TABLE 3.6: NMAKE Predefined Macros

CATEGORY	MACRO	MEANING
For target filenames	$(*)	The target name without an extension .ext.
	$(@)	The complete target name of the current target.
	$($@).	The target currently being evaluated; a dynamic macro used only with dependents.
For depend-ent filenames	$(**)	The complete list of dependent files.
	$(<)	The dependent file that is out-of-date with respect to the target; evaluated for inference rules.
	$(?)	The complete list of dependent files that are out-of-date with respect to the target.
For pro-gram names	$(CC)	The command used to invoke a Microsoft C compiler; by default CC = CL or OptimizingC (reassign to QCL if necessary).
	$(AS)	The command used to invoke the Microsoft Macro As-sembler; by default AS = MASM (reassign as needed).
	$(MAKE)	The name used to recursively invoke NMAKE; by default MAKE = NMAKE (reassign to execute another program).
	$(MAKEDIR)	The directory from which NMAKE is invoked.
	$(MAKEFLAGS)	The NMAKE options currently in effect; to invoke NMAKE recursively, use **$(MAKE) $(MAKEFLAGS)** (cannot be reassigned).

NOTES:
1. For macro definition consistency, use the syntax shown above instead of the $*, $@, $$@, $**, $<, and $? normally documented. This helps .MAK control files appear more readable and minimizes confusion with the DOS wildcard symbols * and ?.
2. All macro names are coerced to uppercase for evaluation and substitution purposes. This con-forms with the handling of all environment string names in uppercase.
3. For the macros above, the following suffix characters may be added to alter their meanings:
   - D   The directory part of the file only.
   - F   The filename only (file.ext).
   - B   The base name of the file.
   - R   The complete filename without .ext. For example, if $(@) = C:\QC25\BIN\PI.OBJ, then:
     $(@D) = C:\QC25\BIN
     $(@F) = PI.OBJ
     $(@B) = PI
     $(@R) = C:\QC25\BIN\PI

and wished to delete the /co option when the string was substituted, you could invoke the LFLAGS macro in the following manner:

```
$(LFLAGS:/CO=)
```

This would replace every occurrence of /co with a null. The syntax of macro substitutions is as follows:

```
$(macroname:string1=string2)
```

In the example above, string1 was /co and string2 was null. If we had wanted to replace all forward slashes (/) with a dash (–), we could have used $(LFLAGS:/=–). See the TOOLS.INI and example sections below for additional examples of macro usage.

Directives

Directives provide for the conditional performance of description blocks and commands within a make control file, as well as providing for error message display, the inclusion of other files, and the altering of NMAKE option settings.

SYNTAX

```
!directivename ...
```

COMPONENTS

!directivename Any of the directives described in Table 3.7. All directives must begin with an exclamation point in column one and continue in column two or greater, with intervening blanks allowed.

The use of directives parallels the compiler directives used by the C preprocessor (see Chapter 5) and DOS conditional commands used in batch (.BAT) files.

Note that conditional branching within a make control file can be based upon a string comparison (**!IF** (*constantexpression*)), the presence of a macro definition (**!IFDEF** *macroname*), or the exit code returned by a command (**!IF** [*program invocation*]). The use of (==) and (!=) for string comparisons is not supported in Standard C. See the comprehensive example section below for additional examples of directive usage.

TABLE 3.7: NMAKE Directives

DIRECTIVE	DESCRIPTION
!IF *constantexpression*	If *constantexpression* is true, the statements between !IF and the next !ELSE or !ENDIF are executed.
!ELSE	If the corresponding !IF *constantexpression* is false, the statements between !ELSE and !ENDIF are executed.
!ENDIF	Marks the end of an !IF, !IFDEF, or !IFNDEF block of statements.
!IFDEF *macroname*	If *macroname* is defined, the statements between the next !ELSE or !ENDIF are executed.
!IFNDEF *macroname*	If *macroname* is not defined, the statements between the next !ELSE or !ENDIF are executed.
!UNDEF *macroname*	Marks *macroname* as undefined.
!ERROR *text*	Causes *text* to be displayed and stops NMAKE execution.
!INCLUDE *filename*	Reads and evaluates *filename* before continuing with the current make control file.
!CMDSWITCHES +|−*option*	Turns on (+) or off (−) a subset of the NMAKE options in Table 3.5 (only D, I, N, or S). Specify only one *option* per !CMDSWITCHES directive. A blank space is required before the plus or minus sign, which must immediately precede an option letter.

NOTES:

constantexpression   A logical expression using either integer or string contants and the standard C operators discussed in Chapter 12.

Note that NMAKE permits the use of (==) and (!=) to compare strings! This feature is not supported by Standard C. The string constant comparison `$(CC) == "CL"` would yield true if the current CC macro value was "CL" or the OptimizingC compiler; otherwise, false.

Group expressions by using parentheses (...); or use brackets [...] to enclose program invocations. Program return codes conform to the convention of returning zero (false) if OK; otherwise, nonzero (true). The program invocation `![LIB OLD.LIB $(LIBFLAGS) −+$(@F);]` uses the C NOT (!) operator to reverse the sense of the program return value to conform with the C language convention that (false) is zero, and anything else is considered (true). If LIB terminated normally (value of zero), the program invocation expression would yield true; otherwise false.

macroname   Any name, coerced to uppercase, that may or may not be currently defined as a macro in the make control file.

text   Any text message. Double quotation marks not required; if used, they will appear.

filename   If in the current directory, simply enter a filename with extension; otherwise enter a complete file specification. If <filename> is used, the environment table INCLUDE= string is searched.

Inference Rules

Inference rules establish a default set of commands to be used when either dependent files are missing or commands have not been specified for a description block. Inference rules work only when there is an orderly relationship between a set of suffixes (.SUFFIXES:) and a fixed base filename. For example, in program development the names MY.EXE, MY.OBJ, and MY.C would be used. The base name MY is related by the suffixes .EXE, .OBJ, and .C. Inference rules do not apply to the Standard C header files (.H) because their names do not fit into this naming scheme. The syntax of an inference rule is similar to that of a description block.

SYNTAX

```
{frompath}.fromext{topath}.toext:
    command
    [command]
    . . .
```

COMPONENTS

{frompath}	An optional path that may be specified to locate *.fromext*. Must be column #1 in make control file. The braces { } must be used, and only one path may be specified. Omit if *.fromext* is in the current path.
.fromext	A required file extension that would be analogous to a dependent file specification. See *command* below.
{topath}	An optional path for *.toext* as described above for *{frompath}*.
.toext:	A required file extension that would be analogous to a target file specification. See *command* below.
command	At least one command is required which converts a base file ending in *.fromext* to one ending in *.toext*. Must be at least one space or tab in from column #1. Follow the rules that apply to commands.

Inference rules are either user-defined or predefined by NMAKE. User-defined inference rules may be specified in any make control file,

!INCLUDED file, or in the automatic TOOLS.INI file. The predefined rules are defined as follows:

.c.obj	$(CC) $(CFLAGS) /c $*.c
.c.exe	$(CC) $(CFLAGS) $*.c
.asm.obj	$(AS) $(AFLAGS) $*;

Because inference rules may be defined in more than one place, NMAKE uses the first applicable rule encountered, giving highest precedence to the current description or !INCLUDE file, then to the automatic startup TOOLS.INI file, and finally to the predefined inference rules. This order of precedence permits the predefined rules to be redefined in either a make control file or TOOLS.INI. Refer to Figures 3.2 and 3.3 to see how TOOLS.INI and SAMPLE.MAK were used to redefine .c.obj and .c.exe.

Inline Files

You can embed automatic-response files, like those used with NMAKE's command-line mode of operation (See "NMAKE @Response Mode" below), in a .MAK control file. Using inline files is helpful when a long list of arguments might otherwise exceed the 127-character limit of a DOS command being expressed.

Inline files may be included anywhere within a .MAK control file. They must conform to the following syntax:

SYNTAX

```
<<[filename]
inlinetext..
..inlinetext
<<[KEEP|NOKEEP]
```

COMPONENTS

[*filename*]   Optional filename into which inline text is placed by NMAKE before the .MAK file is processed. If no *filename* is given, a temporary filename is created in the default directory or in the environment string TMP= directory.

[KEEP|NOKEEP]   Optional indicator of KEEP or NOKEEP for the temporary or [*filename*] created by NMAKE. If omitted, NOKEEP is assumed.

The doubled angle brackets define the extent of the inline file information. For example:

```
target.EXE : dependent.OBJ
    LINK @<<target.LNK
target+obj1+obj2+....OBJn,,,;
<<KEEP
```

This code creates a permanent file called TARGET.LNK that contains all of the statements for use as a DOS command-line response file.

Special Symbols

A new line is understood to result when the Return key is pressed, and it is normally represented by the two-character hexadecimal ASCII control sequence 0D-0A (carriage-return/line-feed).

Use the backslash (\) symbol, immediately followed by a newline character, to enter a target : dependent list, command, or macro that must span a line of input. The backslash-newline combination is then interpreted by NMAKE as a blank space.

You can use the asterisk (*) and question-mark (?) DOS wildcard symbols when specifying target and dependent filenames for NMAKE. The (*) in a base filename or extension implies that any character can occupy all remaining positions in the filename or extension; the (?) in a base filename or extension implies that any character can occupy that particular position.

The caret (^) symbol is used to override the special meanings attributed by NMAKE to the following symbols:

^	Escape symbol
#	Comment
(	Start of multicharacter macro
)	End of multicharacter macro
$	Start of macro
\	Line continuation
{	Start of path list
}	End of path list
!	Command modifier

@   Command modifier

–   Command modifier

When a caret prefixes the symbols above, the literal meaning of the symbols is retained, and no special meaning is implied. Carets within double quotes are never treated as an escape character. If the caret is used to prefix any character other than those listed above, it is simply ignored. Use of the caret is helpful when you need to include any of the special symbols shown above in a filename or macro string definition, for example:

FILE^–1.OBJ	yields	FILE–1.OBJ
TEST=^$.^$^$	yields	TEST=$.$$
TEST="^$.^$^$"	yields	TEST=^$.^$^$
DF.EXE ^: DF.C	yields	DF.EXE : DF.C

Another special dependent file character sequence takes the form:

`%|(parts)F`

where (*parts*) specify

d	Drive
e	File extension
f	File base name
p	Path
s	Complete name

These codes give access to information about the first dependent file that is unavailable using the macros described in Table 3.6. For example, if the first dependent file were described by

`C:\QC25\BIN\PI.OBJ`

then the following special character sequences, used individually or expressed in multiples, would be interpreted as shown:

%|dF	C:
%|eF	OBJ
%|fF	PI
%|pF	C:\QC25\BIN
%|sF	C:\QC25\BIN\PI.OBJ

Automatic-Startup Make File (TOOLS.INI)

The special file named TOOLS.INI serves NMAKE in the same way as AUTOEXEC.BAT serves DOS. NMAKE treats TOOLS.INI as an automatic-startup make control file. Each time NMAKE is executed, it looks for the file TOOLS.INI first in the current directory, then in the path specified by the environment table string INIT= if defined.

If TOOLS.INI is found, NMAKE performs the instructions associated with the [NMAKE] tag in that file, then proceeds to perform the instructions found in the /F make file specified on the command line. TOOLS.INI may contain any valid make control instructions. Normally TOOLS.INI contains comments, macros, directives, and inference rules that are common to all subsequent (.MAK) files to be performed; however, if description blocks and commands are included, only the first block encountered will be performed.

If TOOLS.INI is not found by NMAKE, or an [NMAKE] tag is not defined, NMAKE simply begins processing the /F make file. It appears that Microsoft intends to aggregate initialization commands for a number of utilities in TOOLS.INI by defining separate tag names.

Just as it is helpful to insert batch command files in AUTOEXEC.BAT, it is also wise to place make control file instructions in TOOLS.INI and avoid the need to repeat such instructions in each subsequent project's make control file. Consider the sample TOOLS.INI file shown in Figure 3.2.

Notice that the NMAKE command-line option /D is turned on; that the macro $(CC) had to be redefined to overide the default setting of CL (OptimizingC) with the preferred QCL (QuickC); that the compiler $(CFLAGS) and linker $(LFLAGS) macros have been redefined to reflect project standards, with emphasis upon debugging, not optimization; that NMAKE's predefined inference rules have been overridden; and that $(LIBFLAGS), a set of project default LIB options, has been defined.

Remember that blank macro strings that are defined in make control files do not require double quotation marks. Only such strings defined on the command line require double quotes. The !$(CC) macro is used instead of $(CC) to eliminate the possibility that the command-line size generated by NMAKE would exceed 127 characters.

NMAKE Comprehensive Example

The NMAKE command-line example (described earlier in this chapter)

```
NMAKE /F SAMPLE.MAK /P /N CC=CL NDEBUG= TGROUP >PRN
```

along with the supporting TOOLS.INI file shown in Figure 3.2 and the SAMPLE.MAK file shown in Figure 3.3 form the basis of a comprehensive example that uses NMAKE for C program maintenance.

The make initialization file, TOOLS.INI, has been constructed to establish a default debugging mode for NMAKE. The compiler and linker options disable optimization and enable interactive debugging. Because of the precedence rules for processing macros, the macros defined in TOOLS.INI may subsequently be overridden by definitions in SAMPLE.MAK and again by any macros defined on the NMAKE command line. This example relies heavily upon macro precedence.

A close look at SAMPLE.MAK, shown in Figure 3.3, reveals the use of most make control file instruction types. The #comments included in SAMPLE.MAK offer insight and suggestions to consider when creating a master project make control file.

This control file has been designed to be conditionally modified by specifying either the CC or the NDEBUG macro. The default CC setting in TOOLS.INI is the QuickC compiler QCL. To invoke the OptimizingC compiler, specify **CC=CL** on the NMAKE command line. The NDEBUG macro is not defined in TOOLS.INI and may optionally be specified as

```
# FILE: ch3e1.ini

[NMAKE]

# override possible NMAKE options (D I N or S)
# turn on the modification date display switch
!CMDSWITCHES +D

# redefine the predefined macro CC from the
# default CL (OptimizingC) to QCL (QuickC)
CC=QCL

# set up project Compiler Options macro for debugging
CFLAGS=/Od /Zi

# set up project Linker Options macro for debugging
LFLAGS=/CO /NOI

# redefine CC default inference rules to project standards
# permit AS default inference rules to stand
.c.obj:
     !$(CC) $(CFLAGS) /c $(*).C

.c.exe:
     !$(CC) $(CFLAGS) $(*).C /link $(LFLAGS)

# setup project LIB option macro
LIBFLAGS=/NOI
```

FIGURE 3.2: The sample program ch3e1.ini demonstrates a typical TOOLS.INI file entry for the [NMAKE] utility.

```
# FILE: ch3e2.mak

# sample.mak

# this make control file assumes that the TOOLS.INI
# file shown in Figure 3.2 has been processed by NMAKE.

# test whether the special C compiler macro NDEBUG=
# was defined on the NMAKE command line. NDEBUG= is
# used to turn off any <assert.h> assertions used for
# debugging purposes. See Chapter 29.

!IFDEF NDEBUG

DEBUG=/DNDEBUG
.c.obj:
    !$(CC) $(CFLAGS) $(DEBUG) /c $(*).C
.c.exe:
    !$(CC) $(CFLAGS) $(DEBUG)    $(*).C /link $(LFLAGS)

!ELSE

DEBUG=

!ENDIF

# test which compiler environment is specified, either
# the QCL QuickC project "debugging" compiler or
# the CL OptimizingC project compiler

!IF ( "$(CC)" != "QCL" )         # "debugging" defaulted
!IF ( "$(CC)" == "CL"  )         # setup "optimizing"

DEBUG=/DNDEBUG
CFLAGS=/Ox
LFLAGS=/E /NOI
.c.obj:
    !$(CC) $(CFLAGS) $(DEBUG) /c $(*).C
.c.exe:
    !$(CC) $(CFLAGS) $(DEBUG)    $(*).C /link $(LFLAGS)

!ELSE

!ERROR  $(CC) macro incorrect: neither QCL nor CL

!ENDIF
!ENDIF

# header file naming does not fit into the NMAKE file
# dependency scheme of .c -> .obj -> .exe; when a header
# file changes, recompile all or keep track of which
# source files include the altered header files

HEADERS : *.C
    !$(CC) $(CFLAGS) $(DEBUG) /c $(**)

# establish pseudotargets for each project group
# to support complete recompilation, libing, linking
# and running of their source code. With pseudotargets,
# dependents are always understood to be out-of-date.
# If possible, use a file naming scheme that permits
# using DOS wildcards to segregate project group
# source code, for example:
```

FIGURE 3.3: The sample program Ch3e2.mak demonstrates a typical C programming .MAK control file.

```
TGROUP :: TS*.C
    !$(CC) $(CFLAGS) $(DEBUG) /c $(**)

TGROUP :: TS*.C
    !LIB PROJECT $(LIBFLAGS) -+$(**B);

TGROUP :: TS*.C
    LINK $(LFLAGS) PROJECT.LIB, $(@B).EXE;
    $(@B)

# using ! above prevents the compiler command
# line generated from exceeding 127 characters; but
# invokes a separate command line for each .C file
```

FIGURE 3.3: The sample program Ch3e2.mak demonstrates a typical C programming .MAK control file (continued).

NDEBUG= on the NMAKE command line. NDEBUG= is a null string, but defines the macro for testing with !IFDEF. NDEBUG is the defined item name upon which all **<assert.h>** C preprocessor assertions rely. If NDEBUG is defined, any coded assertions are removed; otherwise, they remain in effect. NDEBUG affects compiling only with the QCL compiler. Since the CL compiler is for optimization, in this example, the compiler option /DNDEBUG is used regardless of whether it has been defined on the NMAKE command line. If **NDEBUG=** is defined, the inference rules defined in TOOLS.INI must be redefined to reflect the altered $(DEBUG) compiler option.

Should CC be set to neither QCL or CL, an !ERROR message is displayed, and the NMAKE control file terminates. If CC equals CL, the DEBUG, CFLAGS, and LFLAGS macros must be redefined to reflect appropriate optimizing, not debugging, options; and in turn, the inference rules must again be redefined. Note the use of (==) and (!=) when comparing macro strings. String comparisons in Standard C may not be made in this fashion, rather, run-time library functions must be used (see Chapter 26).

Two targets are defined in SAMPLE.MAK, HEADERS and TGROUP. Since HEADERS is the first description block in the make control file, if no targets are specified on the NMAKE command line, it will be performed to recompile all source-code files in the current directory ending with (.C). Multiple description blocks referencing TGROUP using :: are shown. All of the commands associated with TGROUP will be performed in the order encountered, and could have been consolidated under one **TARGET : TS*.C** instruction. TS*.C is a DOS wildcard specification to identify any file in the current directory that starts with TS and has a (.C) suffix. The command lines shown for target TGROUP compile, library, link, and execute a program called TGROUP.EXE. Note how the current macro definitions are substituted to supply compile, link, and library command-line options. The last entry, **$(@B)**, instructs DOS to execute the program called TGROUP.

Since this NMAKE example has been run with the option /N, the commands that would normally be processed are only simulated. A look at the output from running NMAKE in this manner is shown in Figure 3.4.

Notice that all of the current environment table variables created using the DOS SET= command are treated as macro definitions and are automatically available for use in any make control file. When developing new make control files or modifying existing ones, test and debug them using the /N and /P options and redirecting standard output to the printer. Once you are certain a make control file is correct, resubmit the NMAKE command line without /N and /P. For example, enter

```
NMAKE /F SAMPLE.MAK CC=CL NDEBUG= TGROUP
```

either with or without >PRN redirection to perform the commands generated.

NMAKE @Response Mode

Besides using the DOS command-line method described above, you can also invoke NMAKE by using an automatic-response file; however, a prompt mode of operation is not available. This alternate method of invoking NMAKE permits you to overcome the 127-character command-line limitation in a batch (response file) manner. Select the mode of invoking NMAKE that best fulfills your requirements. To invoke NMAKE in an automatic-response file mode, simply enter **NMAKE @***responsefile* at the DOS prompt.

SYNTAX

```
NMAKE @responsefile
```

PARAMETERS

@	Required symbol designating that an automatic-response filename follows.
responsefile	No file extension is assumed. Assumed to be in current directory unless a complete file specification is given. If no file is found, NMAKE will message *Cannot open reponse file* and exit to DOS.

The edited *@responsefile* should contain an identical series of keystrokes that would simulate the NMAKE command-line mode described above.

```
MACROS:

        INCLUDE = C:\QC25\INCLUDE
       LIBFLAGS = /NOI
             CC = CL
                  cl
        COMSPEC = C:\COMMAND.COM
      MAKEFLAGS = N
             AS = masm
            LIB = C:\QC25\LIB
           MAKE = NMAKE
         PROMPT = $P$G
          DEBUG = /DNDEBUG

           PATH = C:\QC25\BIN;C:\;C:\DOS
         CFLAGS = /Ox
                  /Od /Zi
           INIT = c:\qc2\book
         LFLAGS = /E /NOI
                  /CO /NOI

INFERENCE RULES:

    .c.exe        :
        commands :        !$(CC) $(CFLAGS) $(DEBUG) $(*).C /link $(LFLAGS)

    .c.obj        :
        commands :        !$(CC) $(CFLAGS) $(DEBUG) /c $(*).C

    .asm.obj      :
        commands :        $(AS) $(AFLAGS) $*;

    .SUFFIXES     :        .obj .exe .c .asm

TARGETS:

TGROUP ::
        flags:   -d -n
        dependents : TSYSTEM.C TSIZE.C
        commands :    !$(CC) $(CFLAGS) $(DEBUG) /c $(**)

        flags:   -d -n
        dependents : TSYSTEM.C TSIZE.C
        commands :    !LIB PROJECT $(LIBFLAGS) -+$(**B);

        flags:   -d -n
        dependents : TSYSTEM.C TSIZE.C
        commands :    LINK $(LFLAGS) PROJECT.LIB, $(@B).EXE;
                      TGROUP

HEADERS :
        flags:   -d -n
        dependents : TSYSTEM.C TENVIR.C TSIZE.C
        commands :    !$(CC) $(CFLAGS) $(DEBUG) /c $(**)


  TGROUP              target does not exist
    TSYSTEM.C                   Sat Jun 03 10:56:32 1989
** TSYSTEM.C newer than TGROUP
    TSIZE.C                     Sat Jun 03 15:42:42 1989
** TSIZE.C newer than TGROUP

        CL /Ox /DNDEBUG /c TSYSTEM.C
        CL /Ox /DNDEBUG /c TSIZE.C
```

FIGURE 3.4: Output from the NMAKE comprehensive example.

```
     TSYSTEM.C                      Sat Jun 03 10:56:32 1989
**  TSYSTEM.C newer than TGROUP                            '
     TSIZE.C                        Sat Jun 03 15:42:42 1989
**  TSIZE.C newer than TGROUP

      LIB PROJECT /NOI -+TSYSTEM;
      LIB PROJECT /NOI -+TSIZE;

     TSYSTEM.C                      Sat Jun 03 10:56:32 1989
**  TSYSTEM.C newer than TGROUP
     TSIZE.C                        Sat Jun 03 15:42:42 1989
**  TSIZE.C newer than TGROUP

      LINK /E /NOI PROJECT.LIB, TGROUP.EXE;
     | TGROUP
```

FIGURE 3.4: Output from the NMAKE comprehensive example (continued).

The *@responsefile* behaves like a DOS batch command file in the sense that the keyboard is redirected to the *@responsefile* for its input.

QuickC (QC) Make Menu

The QuickC Integrated Compiler (QC) provides an NMAKE-like facility that is not available with either the QCL or CL compilers. Simple make control files (.MAK) are created by QC but offer only a subset of the capabilities provided by NMAKE. Consequently, .MAK files generated by QC can be processed by NMAKE, but normally not vice-versa.

Let's take a quick look at how to exploit this feature when working with the QuickC Integrated Compiler. Pull down the QC Make menu and select the Set Program List option as shown in Figure 3.5.

The menu shown in Figure 3.6 then appears. Notice that no other .MAK files exist in the default directory, and that we wish to create a new make control file called NEXT.MAK. Entering NEXT.MAK as shown and pressing the Return key (and not one of the existing .MAK files that may appear) brings up the dialog box shown in Figure 3.7.

If we respond <Yes>, the make control file NEXT.MAK can then be edited as shown in Figure 3.8 to include a list of related (.C), (.OBJ), and (.LIB) files.

When using QC, build simple make control files by listing all related files, and rely upon QuickC's MAKE facility and incremental compilation linking features to speed prototype program development.

For additional information, use the online help feature of QC. Simply press F1 when at a menu, or position the cursor and press F1 to get context-sensitive help.

OptimizingC (PWB) Make Menu

The OptimizingC Integrated Compiler (PWB) also provides an NMAKE facility that, unlike QC's, supports all of the available NMAKE options and .MAK control file commands. Since the make facility with PWB

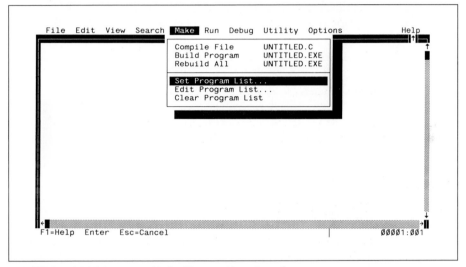

FIGURE 3.5: QC Make menu with Set Program List selected.

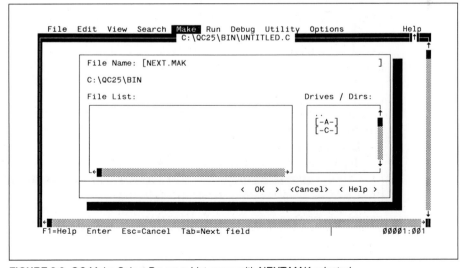

FIGURE 3.6: QC Make Select Program List menu with NEXT.MAK selected.

is more comprehensive, before initiating the creation of a .MAK control file, you can establish NMAKE command-line options by pulling down the Options menu (Alt-O), selecting the NMAKE menu, and pressing Return. The NMAKE Options menu shown in Figure 3.9 should appear. Use this menu to enter any NMAKE command-line options that you may require. To initiate the creation of a .MAK control file, repeat the sequence of steps described above for the QC compiler. The screens and options that will appear are almost identical for both QC and PWB.

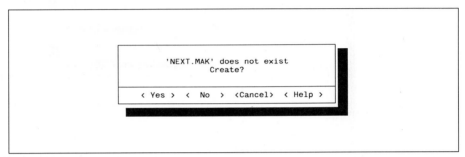

FIGURE 3.7: QC Make dialog box to create NEXT.MAK.

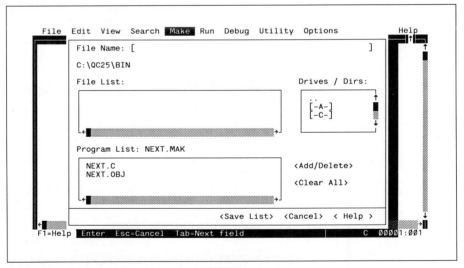

FIGURE 3.8: QC Make editing screen for NEXT.MAK.

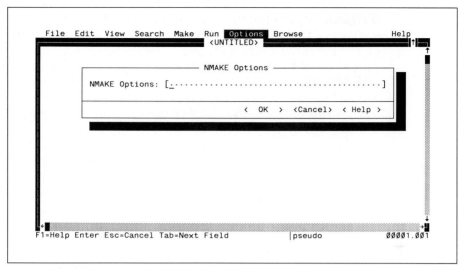

```
    File  Edit  View  Search  Make  Run  Options  Browse            Help
                              <UNTITLED>
          ┌───────────────────── NMAKE Options ─────────────────────┐
          │ NMAKE Options: [.........................................]│
          │                                                         │
          │                   <  OK  >  <Cancel>  < Help >          │
          └─────────────────────────────────────────────────────────┘



    F1=Help Enter Esc=Cancel Tab=Next Field        |pseudo       ØØØØ1.ØØ1
```

FIGURE 3.9: PWB NMAKE Options menu.

When using QC, build simple make control files by listing all related files, and rely upon QuickC's MAKE facility and incremental compilation linking features to speed prototype program development.

For additional information, use the online help feature of QC. Simply press F1 when at a menu, or position the cursor and press F1 to get context-sensitive help.

EXEHDR: EXE File Header Utility

This DOS/OS2 utility program is designed to modify the minimum and maximum program memory allocation and stack size settings of .EXE programs. With this utility, you can avoid relinking .EXE files in three situations: when these parameters must be adjusted, thereby saving development time; when experimentation is needed to adjust the stack; or when you need to make room in memory for the execution of another program (ISR, see Chapter 27). The .EXE program header area created by QLINK or LINK (or ILINK) is used by DOS interrupt 0x4B (EXEC) to subsequently create the program segment prefix, allocate the required memory space, and load a program for execution.

Let's first consider the syntax of the DOS command-line mode of activating EXEHDR.

SYNTAX

```
EXEHDR [hdroption..] exefile
```

PARAMETERS

hdroption..   Table 3.8 describes the options recognized by EXEHDR.

exefile   For this required parameter, a default .EXE file extension is assumed if omitted. Enter a filename with extension if located in the current directory; otherwise, enter a complete file specification.

TABLE 3.8: EXEHDR Options

OPTION	DESCRIPTION
/HEA:*hex number*	Local heap size for Windows; 0x0000– 0xFFFF.
/HEL	Invokes QH (Quick Help) if available, or simply displays command-line syntax help (/?).
/MA:*hex number*	Same effect as LINK Option /CP; establishes the maximum program allocation size in paragraphs (16 bytes each); values may range from /MIN through 0xFFFF.
/MI:*hex number*	Companion to /MAX; establishes the minimum program size in paragraphs.
/NE	New files; OS/2 only; indicates that long filenames are to be supported.
/NO	No logo; suppresses the standard product banner that is normally displayed when EXEHDR is invoked.
/P:*type*	OS/2 and Windows only; enter a type of either PM, VIO, or NOVIO that corresponds to link name statement application type: WINDOWAPI, WINDOWCOMPAT, NOTWINDOWCOMPAT.
/R	Reset error; OS/2 only; clears any Windows link errors.
/S:*hex number*	Same effect as LINK Option /ST; establishes the fixed program stack size with a value from 0x0000–0xFFFF.
/V	OS/2 only; lists complete ("verbose") .EXE header information that includes code and data segment allocations.
/?	Displays command-line syntax help only.

A quick-reference summary of EXEHDR command-line syntax can be found on the inside front cover of this book. To terminate EXEHDR processing and return to the DOS command line, press Ctrl-C or Ctrl-Break. There are no alternate prompt or response file modes of initiating EXEHDR.

If EXEHDR is not in the current directory, nor in the environment table string PATH= list of drives and directories for DOS to search, you must explicitly specify where EXEHDR is located. Note that if no options are provided, a report of the .EXE header is provided, and no alterations to the header are made.

EXAMPLE

If the DOS command line

```
EXEHDR COUNTRY.EXE >PRN
```

were issued, the following output would be redirected for display to the system printer:

```
Microsoft (R) EXE File Header Utility Version 2.01
Copyright (C) Microsoft Corp 1985-1990. All rights reserved.

.EXE size (bytes)          1d41
Magic number:              5a4d
Bytes on last page:        0141
Pages in file:             000f
Relocations:               0005
Paragraphs in header:      0020
Extra paragraphs needed:   00a3
Extra paragraphs wanted:   ffff
Initial stack location:    01d7:0800
Word checksum:             b7f9
Entry point:               0000:01d8
Relocation table address:  001e
Memory needed:             10K
```

In this example, both the EXEHDR utility and the executable file COUNTRY.EXE were located in the current directory. We can see that only a maximum of 0x00A3 extra paragraphs are required for this program, yet 0xFFFF are requested, and the initial stack size is 0x0800 or 2048 bytes (2KB). Issuing the DOS command

```
EXEHDR /MAX:0x00A3 /S:0x0400 COUNTRY.EXE >prn
```

makes the following revisions to the COUNTRY.EXE file:

```
Microsoft (R) EXE File Header Utility Version 2.01
Copyright (C) Microsoft Corp 1985-1990. All rights reserved.

.EXE size (bytes)          1d41
Magic number:              5a4d
Bytes on last page:        0141
Pages in file:             000f
Relocations:               0005
Paragraphs in header:      0020
Extra paragraphs needed:   00a3
Extra paragraphs wanted:   00a3
Initial stack location:    01d7:0400
Word checksum:             b7f9
Entry point:               0000:01d8
Relocation table address:  001e
Memory needed:             10K
```

The result is to free up memory and reduce the stack allocation to 0x0400 or 1024 bytes (1KB). When the EXEHDR utility is used for an OS2/Windows-compatible .EXE file with the /Verbose option selected, an expanded report format is produced.

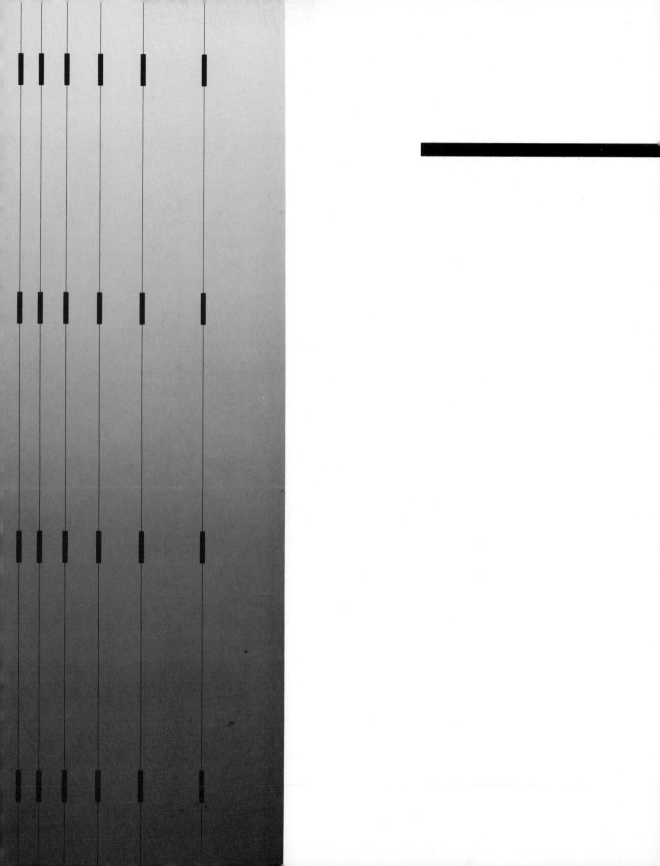

Writing Standard C Programs

Writing Standard C Programs

Now that you've seen how to configure DOS for C (Chapter 1), select and install a Microsoft C compiler (Chapter 2), and use the LIB, QLINK, LINK, and NMAKE utilities (Chapter 3), it is time to discuss writing Standard C programs and to see how each Microsoft software tool supports this process.

C's growing popularity is rooted in its ability to provide portability, power, and performance. In this triad, program power and performance needs typically conflict with the need for portability. It is the programmer's responsibility when using C to balance the degree of program portability required against the competing needs for power and performance. Standard C bolsters this triad by advocating portability, adding powerful new language features, and improving overall program performance.

For those new to C programming, the differences between traditional Kernighan and Ritchie (K&R) C and the new ANSI Standard C will be of particular importance if existing C programs are going to be maintained. For those familiar with K&R C and its variants, some of the new Standard C features may already be familiar. Remember that Standard C evolved from "common existing practice" for the benefit of both the users and implementors of C compilers. It was not the charter of the ANSI X3J11 Standards Committee to create a new language, but rather to clarify the specification of the C language itself.

For most application programmers familiar with the C language, adapting to Standard C will be like using a new version of a familiar software product. Some totally new features have been added, but most changes represent either language fixes, refinements, or extensions. Many of the subtle changes in Standard C are transparent to application programmers, but they significantly impact system programmers responsible for updating existing C compilers to maintain conformance with Standard C. However, this book will focus only on those features of Standard C that affect application programmers. For the system programming details of Standard C, study the ANSI Programming Language C Specification itself (see Appendix A: Bibliography).

The concepts that are crucial to the understanding of C itself will be highlighted in this chapter to provide a checklist of key topics for those new to the C language. Unlike most other high-level languages, C makes it easy "not to see the forest for the trees." Without an adequate understanding of certain key concepts, C will be difficult, if not impossible, to master. Brush up on these concepts before thinking about tackling C++. Review using the C preprocessor, Chapters 5–6; representing data, Chapters 7–11; expressing logic, Chapters 12–13; and writing functions, Chapters 14–15.

C is not commonly taught as an introductory programming language. For this reason, C is presented here as if it were being learned as a second language. C coding techniques will be contrasted with comparable techniques used in BASIC, Fortran, and Pascal. Learning a new computer language involves discarding certain old habits. This is particularly true of learning C. To master C programming, it will be important to let go of some old habits and accept a few new concepts. This chapter will try to help you bridge the gap between the language concepts with which you are familiar and those new C concepts that must be understood, while flagging some obsolete coding habits that should be abandoned along the way. Information about assembly language (MASM) programming with C can be found in Chapter 28.

In closing, this chapter offers a series of practical guidelines for writing Standard C programs. If you are comfortable with languages that are highly structured, you may not whole-heartedly welcome the "free-format" nature of C. Hopefully, the editing, variable naming, and source-code construction guidelines provided will help you get started writing C by summarizing some commonly used C programming conventions.

Emphasis will also be placed upon the use of C coding techniques that improve program performance. The performance measurement macros **START()** and **STOP**, developed in Chapter 5, are introduced to demonstrate an easy but effective technique for evaluating the merits of alternative coding techniques. With the standardization of C and the concurrent development of C++, it is important to adopt macro-, variable-, and function-naming standards that do not conflict with either Standard C or C++. The continued refinement of C and C++ cannot be ignored if programs written today are to remain operational in the future.

USING MICROSOFT'S TOOLS

The software tools highlighted in this book are packaged with the QuickC and OptimizingC compilers. Table 2.7 shows which tools are supplied with each compiler. Except for the debugging tools CV (CodeView) and CVPACK (discussed in Chapter 29), each of these utilities has been discussed in one of the first three chapters. Table 4.1 summarizes how each tool is used in writing Standard C programs.

This table parallels Table 2.1, which compared the features of the Microsoft C compilers (QC, QCL, PWB, and CL). Competing third-party software tools that replicate the functionality of Microsoft's tools are available for each software development stage. The detailed Microsoft product descriptions included in this book should help you evaluate the merits of competing products.

If you accept the premise that computers are simply machines for managing time and space, most application programming problems are ultimately reduced to a subset of problems involving disk-storage space, memory space, and processing time. From this perspective, Table 4.2 has been prepared to summarize which Microsoft software tools and their associated options address these common needs.

TABLE 4.1: Overview of Microsoft Tools

STAGE	SOFTWARE TOOLS	DESCRIPTION
Edit source code.	Custom editor, QC Edit, PWB Edit, and PWB Browser	Use any editor or word processing package in nondocument mode to create .C source-code files.
Compile source code.	QC, QCL, PWB, CL, and InLine Assembler	Use QuickC or OptimizingC and associated command-line options and preprocessor directives to compile .C files and produce .OBJ, .I, .ASM, .COD, .LST, and .SBR browser files.
Maintain object module libraries.	LIB	Use LIB and command-line options to manage .OBJ modules and create .LIB files.
Create and alter executable files.	QLINK, LINK, ILINK, and EXEHDR	Use QLINK, LINK, or ILINK and command-line options to create .COM, .EXE, and .MAP files and compress .EXE files; alter settings in .EXE files with EXEHDR.
Execute program files.	DOS command line	Run DOS commands and .COM, .EXE, and .BAT files with optional arguments, redirection, and piping.
Test and debug source code.	QC Debug, PWB Debug, CV (CodeView), and CVPACK	Interactive debugging and the compression of .EXE files to enable larger programs to be debugged with CV.
Automate the compile, LIB, Link, and run stages.	NMAKE, QC Make, and PWB Make	Use .MAK control files to automate the stages described above.
Get online help.	QH (Quick Help), QC Help, and PWB Help	Use the command-line QH or context-sensitive (F1) help of QC and PWB at any stage of program development.

TABLE 4.2: Common Needs Addressed by Microsoft Tools

OBJECTIVE	TOOL	OPTION
Less disk space	DOS	PATH, redirect I/O
	QC/QCL	A.., C, E.., Fm, Gt, HELP, Li, P, Z..
	PWB/CL	A.., B.., C, E.., F.., Gt, H.., Li, O.., P, qc, Z..
	LIB	NOE, PA
	QLINK/LINK	A, CO, E, F, INC, LI, M, NOF, P.., T
	ILINK	(Requires additional files)
	NMAKE	A, N, X
	EXEHDR	(No effect)
	CVPACK	P
	CV	D
Less memory space	DOS	BUFFERS, DEVICES, FILES, SHELL, COMMAND, FASTOPEN, SET
	QC/QCL	A.., FPi87, G.., Li, O.., Z..
	PWB/CL	A.., B.., FP.., G.., H, Li, O.., qc, Z..
	LIB	NOE, PA
	QLINK/LINK	A, CO, CP, E, F, INC, LI, NOE, NOF, P.., T
	ILINK	X
	NMAKE	(No effect)
	EXEHDR	MA, S
	CVPACK	P
	CV	E, X
Less processing time	DOS	BUFFERS, FASTOPEN
	QC/QCL	A., c, FP.., G.., O.., W.., Z..
	PWB/CL	A.., B.., c, FP.., G.., Li, O.., qc, W.., Z..
	LIB	NOE
	QLINK/LINK	F, INC, NOD, NOE, NOF, T
	ILINK	A, I, V
	NMAKE	A, N, T
	EXEHDR	(No effect)
	CVPACK	P
	CV	D, E, X

OVERVIEW OF K&R VERSUS STANDARD C

To fully appreciate the implementation details of Standard C requires prior working knowledge of a K&R-conforming compiler. The ANSI Standard uses Kernighan and Ritchie's book *The C Programming Language* as a base reference document (see Appendix A: Bibliography). Table 4.3 highlights those features, important to application programmers, that have been either removed from or added to the K&R specification to create the new Standard C.

TABLE 4.3: Changes from K & R to ANSI Standard C

CATEGORY	FEATURE
General	**Obsolete**
	External name (6 characters, case-insensitive) is retained, but yields to new internal name (31 characters, case-sensitive).
	New
	Trigraph sequences for characters #, [,], {, }, \, |, ~, and ^ introduced as ??=, ??(, ??), ??<, ??>, ??/, ??!, ??–, and ??', respectively.
	Additional keywords: `const`, `enum`, `signed`, `void`, `volatile`.
	Ellipsis punctuator ... introduced for functions that have a variable number of arguments.
	Now OK to separate tokens with the \ `new-line` character for continuation.
	Predefined macros `__DATE__`, `__LINE__`, `__TIME__`, `__FILE__`, and `__STDC__` introduced.
	Extensive number of reserved implementation identifiers have been specified; see Table 4.8.
Preprocessor	**New**
	# Null directive.
	# "Stringizing" directive.
	## "Tokenizing" directive.
	The "defined" preprocessing operator.
	`#pragma` directives.
Data	**Obsolete**
	`long float` for `double` is no longer valid.
	Octal digits 8 and 9 are no longer valid.
	New
	Added types: `signed char`, `unsigned char`, `long double`, `unsigned long`, `unsigned short`, `void *`, `void`.

TABLE 4.3: Changes from K & R to ANSI Standard C (continued)

CATEGORY	FEATURE
Data (cont.)	Implied types: `short` is `signed short`; `int` is `signed int`; `long` is `signed long`.
	Hexadecimal constants \x or \X introduced.
	Escape sequences \a alert and \v vertical tab.
	Other lowercase \escape characters are reserved.
	Wide characters prefixed by L introduced.
	Multibyte characters introduced to overcome the traditional 1 byte = 1 char assumption of C; \0 reserved for NULL.
	String literals "...." are no longer modifiable.
	Adjacent string literals separated only by white space are now concatenated.
	unsigned integers (suffix u, U) introduced.
	Floating point constants default to type `double`, unless suffixed by f, F for `float` or l, L for `long double`.
Logic	**Obsolete**
	Old style =op operators are no longer valid.
	New
	Promotion of types: value preserving over unsigned preserving is adopted.
	Floating-point type promotion to integer with truncation towards zero.
	Floating-point promotion from `double` to `float` now permits truncation and controlled rounding (`FLT_ROUNDS` macro).
	Use of parentheses, as in other high-level languages, now controls order of evaluation.
	Structure and union expressions (assignment) permitted.
	Unnamed structures and unions permitted as members.
	Now permitted to initialize the first union member.
	Unary (+) operator is now accepted.
	(`void`) cast is now supported.
	`switch` statement with type `long` now supported, rather than just with type `int`.
Functions	**Obsolete**
	Old-style function prototypes retained, but yield to new prototype specifications.
	Code dependent upon old-style argument-type promotion rules may yield different results when used with new-style prototypes.

TABLE 4.3: Changes from K & R to ANSI Standard C (continued)

CATEGORY	FEATURE
Functions (cont.)	New
	If no prototype is specified, or an old-style prototype is given, K&R rules still apply—default type of `int`, arguments promote to type `double`, etc.
	Function prototypes, with and without identifiers for documentation purposes, are acceptable.
Run-time	**New**
	Function prototypes for all run-time functions are now required in header files.
	Math functions suffixed with (f, l) are reserved for future use (see Table 4.8).
	New control characters for `scanf( )`: %p for pointers, %i to get radix from data, %n for number of characters read.
	New control characters for `printf( )`: %L for `long double`, %lx or %Lx for `long` integer, %p for pointers, and %n for the number of characters written.
	Lowercase characters are reserved for future use by `scanf( )` and `printf()` (see Table 4.8).
	Names reserved for future use (see Table 4.8).

Of course, this table by no means eliminates the need to review the ANSI Standard document itself, but it should help to focus your further study of Standard C. Features described as obsolete were defined by K&R but are being eliminated in Standard C; new features were not defined by K&R and have been added to the language.

As a point of interest, many of the new features have been derived from C++. Although the two- to five-year ANSI standardization process has just begun for C++, and C++ is not yet in common use, it will undoubtedly influence Standard C in the future (ANSI will review the standard every five to ten years). Herein lies the dilemma of C++. It will remain nonstandard, much as K&R C originally did, but the work by Stroustrup and others will eventually result in the development of future ANSI C and C++ language standards. This assumption explains why C++ keywords have been included in Appendix B.

Having compared the major features of Standard and K&R C, this book will henceforth refer only to ANSI Standard C. Standard C has formally replaced K&R.

Portability

As mentioned earlier, Standard C *promotes* program portability (along with power and performance) but does not *mandate* it. Four compliance (portability) terms are defined in Standard C: a strictly conforming program, a conforming hosted implementation (compiler), a conforming freestanding implementation (compiler), and a conforming program.

Strictly Conforming Programs

A strictly conforming program uses only those features of the language and library in the standard and is considered *maximally portable* by Standard C. It does not produce output dependent upon any unspecified, undefined, or implementation-defined behavior, nor does it exceed any minimum implementation limits imposed by Standard C. In summary, this implies the following:

- Only Standard C keywords may be used (no Microsoft extensions).
- Internal identifiers (names) used may not conflict with Standard C keywords or any reserved Standard C hidden identifiers (see Table 4.8).
- External identifiers (names) used must be unique within six characters (case insensitive) and not conflict with any present or reserved Standard C library function names.

Conforming Hosted Implementations

A conforming hosted implementation (compiler) adheres to Standard C's rules for hidden variable naming and diagnostic error messaging, and accepts any strictly conforming program. It may have extensions, such as additional keywords and library functions, provided they do not alter the behavior of strictly conforming programs. Microsoft C presently conforms with all ANSI specifications except the following:

1. It lacks multibyte characters, wide characters and string constants, and the related header file types and run-time library functions.
2. It includes a few naming-class violations (keywords lacking the expected underscore prefix), some non-ANSI macros and types in certain header files, and a few extended library functions such as **read()** and **write()**.

Multibyte character sets will eventually be implemented as the demand for such facilities surfaces, while the other discrepancies will probably remain for some time to provide compatibility with Microsoft's prior compiler versions (which existed before Standard C).

Conforming Freestanding Implementations

A conforming freestanding implementation (compiler) adheres to Standard C's rules for hidden variable naming and diagnostic error messaging, and accepts any strictly conforming program that uses only the features of `<float.h>`, `<limits.h>`, `<stdarg.h>`, and `<stddef.h>`. Again it may have extensions, provided they do not alter the behavior of strictly conforming programs. This category is intended to cover ROM-based (embedded) applications.

Conforming Programs

A conforming program is defined as one that is acceptable to any conforming implementation. A conforming program is therefore less portable than a strictly conforming program. Standard C recognizes that portability is not always the primary objective in writing a computer program. Standard C encourages and promotes the writing of source code that is portable, but defines portability in relative, not absolute terms. Standard C adheres to the basic tenets of the language expounded by K&R by permitting nonstandard performance considerations to prevail at times. The degree to which a program is portable then is dictated by programming needs and discipline, not Standard C itself.

Every effort has been made throughout this book to draw clear distinctions between Standard and non-Standard features of the Microsoft C language compilers so that all decisions to adopt non-Standard features are made deliberately and not inadvertently. In Parts VI and VII of this book, a clear distinction is drawn between those run-time library functions that conform with Standard C and those that are Microsoft-specific.

Benefits of Standard C

The standardization of C has been a controversial process and continues to be debated. While the discussion about which features have been adopted as standard will surely remain controversial, there is relative consensus about the overall benefits of standardizing C:

- A more precise definition of C than that provided by K&R has been attained.

- Both vendors (implementors) and users (programmers) derive savings (time, money) that would otherwise remain unachievable.
- Certain language barriers that prevented vendors from implementing compiler optimization techniques have been overcome. These include the need for the type qualifiers **const** and **volatile**, the necessary distinction of **float**, **double**, and **long double**, and the need for grouping parentheses.
- Improvements to the preprocessor and run-time library specification, essential to promoting portability, were made; and function prototyping, necessary for debugging C programs more quickly, was added.

Future Directions of Standard C

Standardization alone will not ensure the success of C. The marketplace will control whether C succeeds or fails. Standard C, however, is now subject to an ongoing formal review process. Continued ANSI sanction dictates that a formal review (including public review, comments, and so on) must begin again within five years to reassert, amend, or revoke Standard C. The future of C is now in the public forum and will probably evolve much as Fortran-66 (1966) led to Fortran-77 (1977) and Fortran-9x (199x). As those who have been following the ANSI Standard review of Fortran are aware, it has been quite a contested event, and is still ongoing. The precedent has been set for C-9x (199x). If you have any comments or suggestions in the future regarding Standard C, or wish to know more about Standard C, direct your correspondence in the United States to:

X3/JTC1 Secretariat CBEMA

311 First Street, N.W.

Suite 500

Washington, DC 20001-2178

Now that the original work of the ANSI X3J11 Standards Committee is complete, ISO/IEC will become the forum for future discussion and debate. CBEMA (Computer and Business Equipment Manufacturers Asssociation) acts as the Secretariat for both X3 (American National Standard Institute accredited standards committee for Information Processing Systems) and ISO/IEC's (International Standards Organization / International Electrotechnical Commission) JTC1 (Joint Technical Committee 1).

Brief mention of C++ is made in the ANSI Standard C Rationale Document, but no mention at all is made in the ANSI Standard itself. That is not to diminish the effects that C++ development has had upon the present Standard, nor to hide the impacts that will be felt in the years to come. With the broader acceptance of object-oriented, bottom-up design methodology in the 1990s (as opposed to the predominant structured, top-down methodology used in common practice), C++ will compete in the marketplace with other object-oriented languages. If C++ is successful, Standard C will reflect this acceptance in the future and emerge as a "hybrid" language offering features that support both the structured and object-oriented design methodologies.

Major new developments in C may emerge from ISO, or the international community of users. It would seem that additional features will be needed as experience is gained in the overseas market. The concepts of locale, wide character sets, and trigraphs represent ANSI (USA) concessions to ISO (overseas) interests in C. The ability to construct a locale definition in a standard manner that provides for cultural or regional-specific character handling and collation, monetary and numeric formatting, and date and time display is essential for international use of a computer language. Multibyte character set definitions are essential to accommodate languages that require more than 256 symbols—a limitation imposed by the single-byte character conventions presently observed by most computer languages. Multibyte characters permit characters to be defined by more than a single byte; wide characters are those symbols defined to correspond with any multibyte character coding scheme that is devised. Trigraphs (??*x*) represent a concession to certain foreign keyboard and coding schemes in use that do not conform with ASCII and, therefore, lack the ability to represent certain symbols that are defined for use by the C language itself. The expansion of C internationally and the growth of C into the C++ arena should provide sufficient impetus to fuel the standards process through the 1990s.

Other influences upon C reflect underlying trends in the industry, although we can only speculate about how quickly they will be accepted in the marketplace. Topics such as parallel processing, networking, embedded systems, RISC, graphics, and artificial intelligence abound in the literature today. Standard C now represents but one frame of a documentary motion picture depicting the development of language software.

IMPORTANT C CONCEPTS

Structured methodologies solve problems by identifying logical operations that operate upon data structures. Object-oriented methodologies extend the concept of data to include a set of methods (or logic). Object-oriented programs issue messages that direct the data to operate upon itself.

Regardless of which programming paradigm is adopted, data represents objects upon which operations are performed.

Like other programming languages, C provides features that support the declaration of data and development of algorithms; however, it does so with different objectives in mind. C has a robust complement of operators and qualified data types. Understanding the concepts that these features of C were designed to implement will help you avoid (or at least minimize) the initial frustration that many programmers experience when coming to C. The same could be said for those who migrate from writing structured C to object-oriented C++ programs. The principal underlying concepts and assumptions of C are highlighted in the sections below and fully explained in the chapters that follow.

Terminology

Beyond the Standard C compliance terms introduced earlier, certain key terms have been summarized in Table 4.4. You may notice that some are wholly unfamiliar while others convey a slightly different meaning than for other languages.

TABLE 4.4: Key C Terminology

TERM	DEFINITION
Address	The unique location of a byte in memory. The first (lowest) byte of a multibyte object. Invalid for bits, bit-fields, and register-types.
Array	The fixed repetition of an object placed contiguously in memory.
Bit	A unit of memory that can represent one of two values but is not addressable.
Bit-field	A bit or bit-aggregate reference in a structure or union.
Block	A segment of source code found between a matching pair of braces { ... }.
Byte	An implementation-defined number of contiguous bits that can hold at a minimum any member of the basic character set and is addressable.
Cast	A parenthesized (type) preceding an expression that converts the value of the expression to the type.
Declaration	A statement that specifies the interpretation and attributes of a set of identifiers, but no storage (memory) is allocated.
Definition	A declaration that also causes storage (memory) to be reserved for an object or function.
Enumerated type	A set of named integer constant values.

TABLE 4.4: Key C Terminology (continued)

TERM	DEFINITION
Escape sequence	A character-set value expressed as \nnn where nnn is an octal or hexadecimal constant.
Expression	A sequence of operations (operators) upon operands that specify the computation of a value, designate an object or function, generate a side effect, or perform a combination thereof.
External	Describes an identifier whose definition (storage allocation) has been provided elsewhere. The keyword **extern** is used for this purpose.
Function	The smallest unit or program-block in C. Consists of a header with preprocessor directives and the function name with arguments; and the body, with declarations, statements, and function calls.
Header file	A standardized text file of declarations such as global variables, type definitions, structure tags, object- and function-like macros, and function prototypes.
Identifier	A name constructed to begin with a letter or underscore character followed by other letters, digits, or underscores.
Indirection	Accessing the value of an object using an address or pointer of a conforming type.
Lifetime (duration)	The time during which an object is held in storage: either **static** (for the duration of the program) or **auto** (only for each instantiation of a block).
Line	A logical, contiguous string of characters that is terminated by the newline character. Edited lines may be logically continued by using the backslash-newline character sequence.
Linkage	The process by which an identifier declared in different scopes (or multiply referenced in the same scope) is resolved to refer to the same object.
Locale	Program behavior that depends upon local conventions of nationality, culture, and language.
Lvalue (modifiable)	An object-type that is not type **void**, an array type, a **const** qualified type, or a structure or union containing a **const** qualified type. Traditionally the left side of an assigment statement.
Macro	A preprocessor text-substitution feature that may either be object-like (without arguments) or function-like (with arguments).
Newline	Either the escape sequence '\n' or the result of pressing the Return key.
null	A Standard C character value of zero, generally expressed as '\0'.
NULL	The absence of a valid memory address (pointer value); with QuickC version 2.5 and OptimizingC version 6.0 defined as the cast of the integer value of zero as a pointer to type **void**; no Standard C definition is specified—may vary from vendor to vendor.
Object	A contiguous sequence of one or more bytes representing a value(s) that is (are) addressable and of a particular type.

TABLE 4.4: Key C Terminology (continued)

TERM	DEFINITION
Pointer	A data object containing the address of another object (data, function, or incomplete type).
Precedence	In the absence of specific grouping, the order in which operators will be evaluated in expressions. Each operator has a relative order of precedence from 1 (highest) to 15 (lowest).
Preprocessing	The first step in source-code translation; creates a unit of translation from a source-code file by implementing all preprocessor (#) directives.
Prototype	A declaration of the name, return type, and argument types of a function; used to validate any subsequent references to the function.
Recursion	The property exhibited when a function invokes itself.
Run-time	The Standard C and Microsoft functions packaged for use in a standard library installed with the compiler.
R-value	The value of an expression. Traditionally the right side of an assignment statement.
Statement	An instruction that specifies an action to be performed (;).
Stream	A logical input and output file of text or binary data with uniform properties.
String	A null-terminated array of characters.
Structure	The aggregation of like or dissimilar objects placed contiguously in memory that are subsequently referenced as members of the structure.
Tag	A label or name of an incomplete-type declaration that may later be used to define an object.
Token	Keywords, identifiers, constants, string literals, operators, and punctuators.
Trigraph	A special reserved character sequence ??*x* used to represent nine characters not defined in the ISO-646 Invariant Code Set.
Type	The meaning of the value stored in an object: `char`, `int`, `long`, `float`, `double`, `void`, `_segment`. Either describing object-, function-, or incomplete-types (lacking information to determine object size).
Type-Qualifier	A set of keyword attributes that further refine the representation of a fundamental (base) C type.
Union	A structure-like object in which the members are not placed into memory contiguously but, instead, all originate at the beginning of the union, and overlap memory addresses.
Visibility (scope)	The accessibility of an identifier; limited to the extent of the file, block, function, or function prototype in which it is defined.
White space	Any space, horizontal tab, line feed, carriage return, form feed, vertical tab, newline, or comment found in the source code; used to separate tokens.

Preprocessor

The concept of preprocessing is handled in a manner unlike most other computer languages. C incorporates a formal preprocessing stage of language translation that is available for general use by the programmer. Preprocessor directives (prefixed with the # symbol) control the translation of (.c) source-code files into an (.i) intermediate, or unit-of-translation file. Directives are available to control the inclusion of header files and perform macro substitution, conditional compilation, and other useful services. The preprocessor is a powerful tool that can facilitate the development of highly portable source code. The C preprocessor is fully discussed in Chapters 5 and 6.

Data Object Types

The concept of data object types is fundamental to understanding the C language. Objects are abstractions in C that are declared to represent a type of value and to be of a fixed size, and they are typically addressable. Objects are implemented in aggregates of bytes, which in turn are composed of bits. The unqualified or fundamental types are the Standard C keywords **char**, **int**, **enum**, **float**, **double**, and **void**, in addition to the non-Standard keyword **_segment**. Missing from C's base complement of data object types are a boolean or logical type, a string type, and a complex type. Instead, C simply relies upon the convention that zero represents false, and all other values represent true. Strings are by convention null-terminated arrays of characters. Complex numbers are handled as structures (see Appendix E). Both Standard and Microsoft (extension) type qualifiers may be used to modify these implied representations (see "Type Qualifiers" below). The data object types available in C are fully described in Chapter 7.

Type Qualifiers

The concept of type qualifiers is used to extend and refine the meaning and representation of value conveyed by the base data types defined by C. Type qualifiers (adjectives) modify the meaning of the fundamental types (nouns) defined in C. Qualifiers alter the meaning conveyed by the data object types in the following ways:

- The lifetime and visibility of an object can be controlled using the Standard keywords **auto**, **register**, **static**, and **extern**.

- The modifiability of an object can be controlled using the Standard keywords **const** and **volatile**.
- The range of value represented by an object can be controlled using the Standard keywords **short**, **long**, **unsigned**, and **signed**.
- The language convention of representing objects can be altered using the non-Standard keywords **_cdecl**, **_fortran**, and **_pascal**.
- The addressability of an object can be controlled using the Standard keyword **register**, the non-Standard keywords **_based**, **_far**, **_huge**, and **_near**, and the ***** indirection operator.
- The aggregation of objects can be controlled using the keywords **struct** and **union**, and the **[]** subscripting operator.

Meaningful combinations of type qualifiers are used to alter the representation of a data object in C. The type qualifiers available in C are fully described in Chapter 7.

Arrays

In C as in other languages, an array is an ordered repetition of objects. Any data object type, fundamental or qualified, may be expressed as an array using the suffix operator **[..]**. Multiple subscripting is supported using the form **[i][j]..[z]**. All subscript references begin at zero, not one. C permits array elements to be referenced using indirection, since all arrays are treated as pointers. An array name is equivalent to the address of element **[0]**. Multidimensioned arrays are mapped to memory in row-major order (last subscript varies fastest). Unlike structures, arrays may not contain pad bytes. From this regular patterning of objects in memory, the address of any object can easily be derived to produce a storage map equation applicable to any level of subscripting. Pascal and C store arrays in row-major order; however, BASIC and Fortran store arrays in column-major order. Arrays in C are fully described in Chapter 8.

Strings

Strings in C are defined by the presence of a null terminating character (expressed as the escape sequence **\0**) to delimit the end of an array of type **char** objects. All normal operations with strings must be performed using run-time library functions, because the string is not a fundamental type in the C language. Since strings are arrays of type **char**, string names are therefore pointers, which means strings can be treated as subscripted arrays or addressed by using the indirection (*****) operator. The string concept has been extended by Standard C to permit the representation of "wide" or "multibyte" characters. This accommodation to ISO introduces a new wrinkle to the familiar concept of strings; however, Microsoft C does not currently support this Standard C feature. Strings in C are fully described in Chapter 8.

Structures and Unions

Structures allow the aggregation of objects, arrays, other structures and unions, and pointers of dissimilar data types. A structure object is composed of members that may be referenced using the (**.**) member operator or the (**−>**) pointer-to member operator. Structure objects may also be repeated by using the subscripting operator **[..]** in single or multiple dimensions. The alignment of dissimilar objects in a structure may result in the introduction of pad bytes. The size of a structure is the sum of the sizes of all member objects plus the total number of pad bytes. Control over the padding of structure members can be exercised using compiler option **/Zp** or the directive **#pragma pack()**. Structures are analogous to Pascal records.

The concept of unions permits objects to share the same memory addresses. Like structures, unions may comprise an aggregation of dissimilar type objects, arrays, other structures and unions, and pointers. Like structures, union objects may be referenced as (**.**) members or as (**−>**) pointers to members. Union objects may be repeated using subscripting **[..]** in single or multiple dimensions. The size of a union (unlike that of structures) is the size of the largest individual member plus any necessary pad bytes. Unions are analogous to the use of the Fortran EQUI-VALENCE statement. Structures and unions in C are fully described in Chapter 9.

Addressing and Pointers

The concepts of addressing and pointers are interrelated and unavoidable when working with the C language. These concepts are often the hardest to grasp, but they are essential because C implements them with a full complement of operators that offer indirect access to data object types, arrays, strings, structures, unions, other pointers, and functions themselves. The address of any data object is found by simply using the unary operator **&** (address-of). The smallest unit of addressable memory in C is the byte. Pointer variables are declared using the ***** indirection operator. Multiple levels of indirection are supported in C, together with arrays, structures, and unions of pointers. Functions may accept and return pointers. Functions themselves may be treated as pointers. Arrays, structures, and unions of function pointers are possible. Without question, addressing and pointers are the common thread that unites virtually every feature of the C language. Addressing and pointers in C are initially described in Chapter 10 and are discussed as needed throughout this book.

Bits

C offers a full complement of operators to manipulate bit patterns efficiently. This facility, which is normally restricted to assembly-language programming, permits C to act as a portable, structured assembly language, satisfying most systems programming needs. The UNIX operating system was developed in C, as were many of the broadly used microcomputer software packages marketed today. Bit-fields are also supported; they permit members of structures to be subdivided into bits, not bytes, and subsequently treated as if they were integer program variables. Bits and bit-fields are not addressable. Bits and bit-fields in C are fully described in Chapter 11.

Precedence of Operators

The concept of operator precedence is not unique to C but takes on particular importance given the robust set of operators in C and the resulting complexity of expressions that can be constructed. Fifteen levels of precedence by operator type exist in C. From highest to lowest precedence, the order of operators is: Primary, Unary, Multiplicative, Additive, Shift, Inequality, Equality, Bitwise AND, Bitwise XOR, Bitwise OR, Logical AND, Logical OR, Conditional, Assignment, and Sequential. Within each of these categories of operators, either left→right or right←left associativity controls. Despite the large number of operators, Fortran programmers will notice that (**) exponentiation is missing. Also, prior to Standard C, parentheses did not ensure the order of evaluation of expressions, and calculations were never performed in data type **float** but were always promoted to type **double**. Operator precedence and associativity in C are fully described in Chapters 12 and 13.

Functions

Unlike other languages, which tend to distinguish between main programs, subroutines or procedures (return no value by name), and functions (return a value by name), C treats all program units as functions. The main program equivalent in C is a function called **main()**. All C functions potentially pass arguments by value (including pointers) and potentially return a value (including pointers) by the function name itself. If no arguments are desired, an argument of type **void** is declared; if no return value is desired, a function return object of type **void** is declared. C relies heavily upon the run-time library of functions to perform all operations not handled by its complement of keywords and operators (all I/O, memory allocation, string manipulation, and so on). There are no intrinsic or built-in procedures and functions with C, only keywords. Functions may not be declared within other functions, but they may be called recursively. Functions in C are fully described in Chapters 14 and 15, and the run-time library functions are discussed individually in Parts VI and VII.

Handling I/O

In C, all I/O is performed by the run-time library. The language has no intrinsic input or output keywords. The most commonly used functions for character input are named **fgetc()** and **getchar()** and for character output **fputc()** and **putchar()**. The most commonly used functions for handling file input are the **scanf()** family of functions, and for file output, the **printf()** family of functions. Many other I/O run-time functions are provided and are categorized as stream I/O, low-level I/O, and console and port I/O functions. The handling of all I/O in C is fully described in Part VI.

The Run-Time Library

Every C program written uses the C run-time library. As we have seen, all I/O services are provided by functions in the run-time library. The Microsoft run-time library represents a collection of about 540 functions, of which 426 are documented in this book. The remainder have deliberately been omitted because they are graphics-related. The run-time library is supplied when you purchase a C compiler and provides commonly needed services that either conform with Standard C or are non-Standard (Microsoft-specific). C relies heavily upon the run-time library because the language has been kept "small" by not incorporating the run-time services into the language, thereby eliminating the need for additional C keywords and operators. Any service you require that is not available as a C keyword or operator is fulfilled either by using an available run-time function, by purchasing a library that provides such a function, or by writing the function yourself. A strictly conforming C program may use only Standard C functions from the run-time library. A conforming C program may use Microsoft C functions, but only if they do not affect the way strictly conforming programs operate. Software development in C relies heavily upon the development, maintenance, and reuse of libraries of functions. The complete run-time library of Standard C and Microsoft functions, exclusive of graphics, is fully described in Parts VI and VII.

C AS A SECOND LANGUAGE

This book assumes that any reader approaching C for the first time has a working familiarity with at least one other programming language. For the benefit of new C programmers (as well as anyone returning to C after working extensively in another language), this section presents a series of tables comparing the major features of BASIC, Fortran, and Pascal with their equivalents in C; however, the tables do *not* identify features of C that have no equivalent in these languages.

Programmers new to C should use these tables to see how familiar programming techniques are implemented in C and to identify areas for further study. Those returning to C should use the tables to reorient themselves to the language and identify coding habits that should now be discarded. Anyone considering which of the four languages to use for a particular project can use these tables for comparison.

Each comparative table follows a common format. Features of BASIC, Fortran, and Pascal are grouped in the following categories and present a summary of how each feature is equivalently implemented in the C language:

- Editing conventions
- Identifiers
- Data types
- Expressing constants
- Variables
- Aggregated data types
- Operators
- Conversion

- Repetition
- Conditional branching
- Unconditional branching
- Subprograms
- Input/output
- Library

BASIC and C

Table 4.5 summarizes how the major features of BASIC are implemented in C. Note that four specific features of BASIC have been identified that do not have equivalent implementations in C:

- Implicit typing of variables in a program using the statements DEFDBL, DEFINT, DEFSNG, and DEFSTR
- The exponentiation operator ^
- The logical operator XOR (exclusive-or)
- The logical operator IMP (implication)

TABLE 4.5: A Comparison of BASIC and C

CATEGORY	FEATURE	BASIC	C EQUIVALENT
Editing Conventions	Comments	REM statement or single quote at end of line	`/* ... */`
	Compound statement	Line numbers	`{ .. }`
	Continuation	255-char line	No limit
	Format	Interpreted (free)	Free with functions
		Indirect (line #)	
	Main program	Only END required	`main()` `{ ... }`
	Null statement	REM #	`;`
	Simple statement	No termination character required, : may be used	Terminated by `;`
	Spacing	Blanks, tabs	White space
	Statement numbers	0–65,529 or AUTO command	Label:

TABLE 4.5: A Comparison of BASIC and C (continued)

CATEGORY	FEATURE	BASIC	C EQUIVALENT
Identifiers	Default values	Arithmetics zero, strings null	`auto` unknown, `static` zero
	Handling case	Insensitive	Sensitive
	Implicit	DEFDBL, .INT, .SNG, .STR [A–Z]	NO EQUIVALENT
	Length of:		
	Internal	40-char	31-char minimum
	External	Varies	6-char or more; becoming 31-char
	Naming:		
	First character	Letter [A–Z]	`_`, `[a-z]`, `[A-Z]`
	Subsequent	[A–Z], [0–9], decimal point, or suffixes %, !, #	`_`, `[a-z]`, `[A-Z]`, `[0-9]`
	Predefined names	Statements, commands, variables, and functions	Keywords, macros, globals, tags, types, run-time functions, and reserved identifiers
Data Types	Characters, character strings	DEFSTR or var$	`char`, (`signed`, `unsigned`), `literals`, array of `char`, null-terminated
	Floating point:		
	Single-precision	DEFSNG or var!	`float`
	Double-precision	DEFDBL or var#	`double`, `long double`
	Integers	DEFINT or var%	`int`, (`short`, `long`, `signed`, `unsigned`)
	Logical	DEFINT or var%	`int`
	Scope of	Local or global COMMON statement	File, function, block, or prototype
Expressing Constants	Character and string literals	"_", "STRING" or DATA statement	`'_'`, escape sequences, "string"
	Logicals	0 (false), –1 (true)	0 (false), 1 (true, nonzero)
	Number system	base 8 (&nnn), base 10 (nnn), base 16 (&Hnnn)	base 8 (0nnn), base 10 (nnn), base 16 (0xnnn)
	Numerics	Explicit value or DATA statement	Explicit value or `const` type qualifier

TABLE 4.5: A Comparison of BASIC and C (continued)

CATEGORY	FEATURE	BASIC	C EQUIVALENT
Variables	Initialization	By assignment or CLEAR command	When declared or by assignment
	Declaration	DEF*xxx* or simply use without defining	`type var, ..;`
Aggregated Data Types	Arrays	DIM var(0..x, 0..y,) OPTION BASE *n*	`var[0..x-1][0..y-1]..`
	Records	FIELD statement, LSET and RSET	Structures
Operators	Addition	+	`+, +=, ++`
	Assignment	LET var = val	`=`
	Bit manipulation:	Integers	Integers, fields
	Complement	NOT	`~`
	Conjunction	AND	`&, &=`
	Disjunction	OR	`|, |=`
	Exclusive-or	XOR	`^, ^=`
	Concatenation	+	`"..." "..."` or by run-time function
	Division:		
	Divisor	\	`div()`
	Floating point	/	`/, /=`
	Integer	\	`/, /=`
	Remainder	MOD	`%, %=, div()`
	Exponentiation	^	NO EQUIVALENT, use functions
	Logical:		
	Complement	NOT	`!`
	Conjunction	AND	`&&`
	Disjunction	OR	`||`
	Equivalence	EQV	`==`
	Exclusive-or	XOR	NO EQUIVALENT
	Implication	IMP	NO EQUIVALENT
	Multiplication	*	`*, *=`
	Relational:		
	Equal	=	`==`
	Greater than	>	`>`

TABLE 4.5: A Comparison of BASIC and C (continued)

CATEGORY	FEATURE	BASIC	C EQUIVALENT
Operators (cont.)	Greater than/equal	>= or =>	>=
	Less than	<	<
	Less than/equal	<= or =<	<=
	Not equal	<> or ><	!=
	Subtraction	–	–, –=, ––
Conversion	Char to integer	ASC()	Promoted
	Integer to char	CHR$()	Promoted
	Integer to real	CSNG(), CDBL()	=, (cast)
	Real to integer	INT()	=, (cast)
	To string	MKI$(), MKS$(), MKD$(), STR$()	`printf()` or run-time function
	String to numeric	VAL()	Run-time function
Repetition	Fixed increment	Default +1 or STEP	0 (zero) default or any expression
	Fixed iteration	FOR VAR=*first*	`for (var=first;`
		TO last STEP 1 or –1	`val <= last;`
		.. NEXT	`var++ or var––)` `stmt;`
	Pre-test	WHILE (test)... WEND	`while (test) stmt;`
Conditional Branching	Computed goto	`ON (val) GOTO` `#,..,  on (val)` `GOSUB #,  ..`	switch statement
	Conditional test	Parentheses optional	Parentheses required
	False	0 (zero)	0 (zero)
	If (simple)	IF test THEN stmt	`if (test) stmt;` or use ?: operator
	If..else	IF test THEN stmt ELSE stmt	`if (test) stmt;` `else stmt;`
	If..else..if	IF test THEN stmt ELSE IF test THEN ELSE stmt	`if (test) stmt;` `else if (test)` `stmt;` `else;` or `else stmt;`
	True	–1	1 (nonzero)

TABLE 4.5: A Comparison of BASIC and C (continued)

CATEGORY	FEATURE	BASIC	C EQUIVALENT
Unconditional Branching	End of a loop	IF test THEN number:NEXT	`continue;`
	Exit a loop	GOTO *number*	`break;`
	Labels	Statement numbers	`label:`
	Local branch	GOTO *number*	`goto label;`
	Nonlocal branch	RETURN *number*	`setjmp()`, `longjmp()`
	Terminate subroutine	RETURN	`return(val)`
	Terminate program	STOP	`exit()`, `atexit()`, `return` from `main()`
Subprograms	Invoking	FUNCTIONS by name, GOSUB #, ON-GOSUB #, ..	Functions by name or pointer
	Module-like	Subroutines	Function
	Parameters	None	By value (also pointers)
	Recursion	Not supported	Supported
	Return values	Globals altered	Return by value
	Statement functions	See variable-like	Preprocessor macros
	Variable-like	Functions (FN...)	Function
Input/Output	Binary files	Byte I/O not var$	`open` mode `"b"`
	Detect end of file	EOF()	`EOF`, `feof()`
	File input	GET #f, rec#	`fscanf(fv,...);`
	File output	PUT #f, rec#	`fprintf(fv,...);`
	Implementation technique	Keyword statements	Run-time library
	Standard input	INPUT #f, var$_list or READ from DATA	`scanf("ctrl", &var_list);`
	Standard output	WRITE #f, var$_list	`printf("ctrl", var_list);`
	Text files	OPEN *name* FOR *mode* AS #fLEN=recl	Default `open` mode
Library	Built-in services	Keywords, commands, functions	Only keywords

Fortran and C

Table 4.6 summarizes how the major features of Fortran are equivalently implemented in C. Note that four specific features of Fortran do not have equivalent implementations in C:

- Implicit typing of variables in a program using the IMPLICIT statement or default (I-N) as INTEGER otherwise REAL convention
- The base data type COMPLEX, upon which normal Fortran operations are performed
- The base data type LOGICAL, upon which normal Fortran operations are performed
- The exponentiation operator **

TABLE 4.6: A Comparison of Fortran and C

CATEGORY	FEATURE	FORTRAN	C EQUIVALENT
Editing Conventions	Comments	C or * in col 1	`/* ... */`
	Compound statement	No special punctuation	`{ .. }`
	Continuation	Use column 6	No limit
	Format	Column aligned	Free with functions
	Main program	Only END required	`main()`
			`{ ... }`
	Null statement	CONTINUE	`;`
	Simple statement	No termination character; limited by continuation	Terminated by `;`
	Spacing	Blanks, tabs, newlines	White space
	Statement numbers	Column 2–5	Label:
Identifiers	Default values	Undefined	`auto` unknown, `static` zero
	Handling case	Insensitive	Sensitive
	Implicit	(I–N) integer, (A–H, O–Z) real	NO EQUIVALENT
	Length of:		
	Internal	6-char standard	31-char minimum
	External	6-char	6-char or more; becoming 31-char

TABLE 4.6: A Comparison of Fortran and C (continued)

CATEGORY	FEATURE	FORTRAN	C EQUIVALENT
Identifiers (cont.)	Naming:		
	First character	[A–Z]	`_`, `[a-z]`, `[A-Z]`
	Subsequent	[A–Z], [0–9], blanks ignored	`_`, `[a-z]`, `[A-Z]`, `[0-9]`
	Predefined names	Keywords, functions, procedures	Keywords, macros, globals, tags, types, run-time functions, and reserved identifiers
Data Types	Characters	CHARACTER	`char`, (`signed`, `unsigned`)
	Character strings	CHARACTER*n	literals, array of `char`, null terminated
	Complex	COMPLEX*n	NO EQUIVALENT, structure tag
	Floating point	REAL*n, DOUBLE PRECISION	`float`, `double`, `long double`
	Integers	INTEGER*n	`int`, (`short`, `long`, `signed`, `unsigned`)
	Logical	LOGICAL*n	NO EQUIVALENT, use `int`
	Scope of	Local, COMMON (BLANK or NAMED)	File, function, block, or prototype
Expressing Constants	Character	'_'	'_', escape sequences
	Complex	(a, bi) form or CMPLX(a,b)	`.mbr` or `->mbr` form
	Logicals	.FALSE., .TRUE.	0 (false), 1 (true, nonzero)
	Number system	Base 10 (nnn)	base 8 (0nnn), base 10 (nnn), base 16 (0xnnn)
	PARAMETER statement	Variable names	Explicit value or `const` type qualifier
	String literals	'STRING'	`"string"`
Variables	Initialization	By assignment, DATA statements, BLOCK data	When declared or by assignment
	Declaration	*type var,..* or implicit	`type var, ..;`

TABLE 4.6: A Comparison of Fortran and C (continued)

CATEGORY	FEATURE	FORTRAN	C EQUIVALENT
Aggregated Data Types	Arrays	var(1..x,1..y,...) or DIMENSION	`var[0..x-1][0..y-1]..`
	Equivalence	EQUIVALENCE	Unions
Operators	Addition	+	`+, +=, ++`
	Assignment	=	`=`
	Concatenation	//	`"..." "..."` or by run-time function
	Division:	/	`/, /=`
	Divisor	Integer assignment	`div()`
	Remainder	MOD()	`%, %=, div()`
	Exponentiation	**	NO EQUIVALENT, use functions
	Logical:		
	Complement	.NOT.	`!`
	Conjunction	.AND.	`&&`
	Disjunction	.OR.	`||`
	Equivalence	.EQV., .NEQV.	`==, !=`
	Multiplication	*	`*, *=`
	Relational:		
	Equal	.EQ.	`==`
	Greater than	.GT.	`>`
	Greater than/equal	.GE.	`>=`
	Less than	.LT.	`<`
	Less than/equal	.LE.	`<=`
	Not equal	.NE.	`!=`
	Subtraction	–	`-, -=, --`
Conversion	Char to integer	ICHAR()	Promoted
	Integer to char	CHAR()	Promoted
	Integer to real	FLOAT(), REAL(), =, auto promotion	=, (cast)
	Real to integer	INT(), =, auto promotion	=, (cast)
Repetition	Fixed increment	Default +1	0 (zero) default or any expression

TABLE 4.6: A Comparison of Fortran and C (continued)

CATEGORY	FEATURE	FORTRAN	C EQUIVALENT
Repetition (cont.)	Fixed iteration	# CONTINUE	
	Pre-test	WHILE *test* DO... ENDWHILE	`while (test)` `stmt;`
	Post-test	LOOP... UNTIL *test*	`do { stmt }` `while (test);`
Conditional Branching	Conditional test	Parentheses optional	Parentheses required
	False	.FALSE.	0 (zero)
	If (simple)	IF *test* THEN *stmt* ENDIF	`if (test) stmt;` or use `?:` operator

	If..else	IF *test* THEN *stmt*
		
		ELSE *stmt* ENDIF
			`if (test) stmt;`
			
			`else stmt;`

	If..else..if	IF *test* THEN *stmt*
		
		ELSE IF *test* THEN
		
		stmt ENDIF
		or
		ELSE *stmt* ENDIF
			`if (test) stmt;`
			
			`else if (test)`
			`stmt;`
			
			`else;`
			or
			`else stmt;`

	Multiple alternatives	SELECT (var) FROM
		CASE val1
		stmt
		CASE val2
		stmt OTHERWISE
		 stmt
		END SELECT
			`switch (var) {`
			`case val1: stmt;`
			`break;`
			`case val2: stmt;`
			`break;`
			`default: stmt;`
			`}`

	True	.TRUE.	1 (nonzero)
Unconditional Branching	End of a loop	GO TO #	`continue;`
	Exit a loop	GOTO # or QUIT	`break;`
	Labels	Statement numbers	`label:`
	Local branch	GO TO #	`goto label;`
	Nonlocal branch	ENTRY, RETURN(s)	`setjmp(),` `longjmp()`

TABLE 4.6: A Comparison of Fortran and C (continued)

CATEGORY	FEATURE	FORTRAN	C EQUIVALENT
Unconditional Branching (cont.)	Terminate function or subroutine	RETURN END	`return(val);`
	Terminate program	END or STOP	`exit()`, `atexit()`, return from `main()`
Subprograms	Invoking	FUNCTIONS by name	Functions by name or pointer
		CALL SUBROUTINES	
		EXECUTE REMOTE BLOCKS	
	Module-like	SUBROUTINES	Function
	Parameters	By value	By value
		No pointers	(Also pointers)
	Passing values:		
	Arrays	By name	By pointer
	Functions	As INTRINSIC or EXTERN	By value or pointer
	Recursion	Not supported	Supported
	Return values	By value	Return by value
	Statement functions	Supported	Preprocessor macros
	Variable-like	FUNCTIONS	Function
Input/Output	Binary files	File open mode, FORM=UNFORMATTED	`open mode "b"`
	Detect end of file	File open mode, END=#	`EOF`, `feof()`
	File input	READ(UNIT=,FILE=,..)	`fscanf(fv,...);`
	File output	WRITE(UNIT=,FILE=,..)	`fprintf(fv,...);`
	Implementation technique	Keywords	Run-time library
	Standard input	READ*(var_list) READ(UNIT=,FMT=#,) FORMAT stmt "ctrl"	`scanf("ctrl", &var_list);`
	Standard output	WRITE*(var_list)	`printf("ctrl", var_list);`
		WRITE(UNIT=,FMT=#,)	

TABLE 4.6: A Comparison of Fortran and C (continued)

CATEGORY	FEATURE	FORTRAN	C EQUIVALENT
Input/Output (cont.)		FORMAT stmt "ctrl"	
	Text files	File open mode, FORM=FORMATTED	Default open mode
Library	Built-in services	Keywords, functions, procedures	Keywords

Pascal and C

Table 4.7 summarizes how the major features of Pascal are equivalently implemented in C. Note that six specific features of Pascal have been identified that do not have equivalent implementations in C:

- The base data type BOOLEAN, upon which normal Pascal operations are performed
- The PACKED array concept
- The WITH construct for simplifying the identification of record members
- The SET OF concept
- The logical operator XOR (exclusive-or)
- The set operator IN

For additional insight into writing C programs that utilize the nonstandard, inline assembly language (MASM) programming feature of Microsoft C, refer to Chapter 28.

Potential Coding Pitfalls

Now let's examine certain coding techniques that either may generate unexpected results in C or should be modified to accommodate C techniques that produce faster code. The code-timing measurements in this section will use the macros **START()** and **STOP**, developed in Chapter 5, as simple, objective measurement tools to help you readily test, and discover for yourself, which C coding techniques are preferable.

TABLE 4.7: A Comparison of Pascal and C

CATEGORY	FEATURE	PASCAL	C EQUIVALENT
Editing Conventions	Comments	{ .. }	`/* ... */`
	Compound statement	Begin..end;	`{ .. }`
	Format	Free with sections	Free with functions
	Main program	Program..	`main()`
		Begin..end.	`{ ... }`
	Null statement	;	;
	Simple statement	terminated by ;	terminated by ;
	Spacing	Blanks, tabs, newlines	White space
Identifiers	Default values	Undefined	`auto` unknown, `static` zero
	Handling case	Insensitive	Sensitive
	Length of:		
	Internal	Varies	31-char minimum
	External	Varies	6-char or more; becoming 31-char
	Naming:		
	First character	_ or [a–z]	`_, [a-z], [A-Z]`
	Subsequent	_, [a–z], [0–9]	`_, [a-z], [A-Z], [0-9]`
	Predefined names	Keywords, functions, procedures	Keywords, macros, globals, tags, types, run-time functions, and reserved identifiers
Data Types	Characters	Char	`char, (signed, unsigned)`
	Character strings	String	Literals, array of `char`, null-terminated
	Floating point	Real, extended	`float, double, long double`
	Integers	Integer	`int, (short, long, signed, unsigned)`
	Logical	Boolean	NO EQUIVALENT, use `int`
	Scope of	Local, global	File, function, block, or prototype
	Synonymns	TYPE section	`typedef`

TABLE 4.7: A Comparison of Pascal and C (continued)

CATEGORY	FEATURE	PASCAL	C EQUIVALENT
Expressing Constants	Character	' _ '	' _ ', escape sequences
	CONST section	Variable names	Explicit value or `const` type qualifier
	Logicals	False, true	0 (false), 1 (true, nonzero)
	Number system	Base10 (nnn)	Base 8 (0*nnn*), base 10 (*nnn*), base 16 (0x*nnn*)
	Pointers	Nil	`NULL`
	String literals	'string'	`"string"`
Variables	Initialization	By assignment	When declared or by assignment
	Declaration	Var,.. : type	`type var, ..;`
Aggregated Data Types	Arrays:	var(1..x,1..y,...)	`var[0..x-1]` `[0..y-1]..`
	Packed	Packed keyword	NO EQUIVALENT
	Enumerations	var = (enum_list);	`enum var` `{enum_list};`
	Members	With..do statement .mbr references	NO EQUIVALENT .mbr or ->mbr
	Records	Name = record... end;	`struct name {` `... };`
	Sets	Set of set_list	NO EQUIVALENT
	Variants	Name = record... case var of... end;	`union name { ...` `};`
Operators	Addition	+	`+, +=, ++`
	Assignment	:=	`=`
	Bit manipulation:		
	Complement	not	`~`
	Conjunction	and	`&, &=`
	Disjunction	or	`|, |=`
	Exclusive-or	xor	`^, ^=`
	Shift left	shl	`<<, <<=`
	Shift right	shr	`>>, >>=`
	Concatenation	+	"..." "..." or by run-time function

TABLE 4.7: A Comparison of Pascal and C (continued)

CATEGORY	FEATURE	PASCAL	C EQUIVALENT
Operators (cont.)	Division:	/	`/, /=`
	Divisor	div	`div()`
	Remainder	mod	`%, %=, div()`
	Logical:		
	Complement	not	`!`
	Conjunction	and	`&&`
	Disjunction	or	`||`
	Exclusive-or	xor	NO EQUIVALENT
	Multiplication	*	`*, *=`
	Pointers:		
	Allocation	var = ^type;	`type *var`
	Referencing	var^	`*var`
	Relational:		
	Equal	=	`==`
	Greater than/equal	>=	`>=`
	Greater than	>	`>`
	Less than	<	`<`
	Less than/equal	<=	`<=`
	Not equal	<>	`!=`
	Sets	in	NO EQUIVALENT
	Subtraction	–	`–, –=, – –`
Conversion	Char to integer	ord()	Promoted
	Integer to char	chr()	Promoted
	Integer to real	real()	=, (cast)
	Real to integer	trunc()	=, (cast)
Repetition	Fixed increment	1 (one)	0 (zero) default or any expression
	Fixed iteration	`for var := first to last do stmt;` or `for var := last downto first do`	`for (var=first; val <= last; var++) stmt;` or `for (var=first; val <= last; var--) stmt;`

TABLE 4.7: A Comparison of Pascal and C (continued)

CATEGORY	FEATURE	PASCAL	C EQUIVALENT
Repetition (cont.)	Pre-test	While test do stmt;	`while (test)` `stmt;`
	Post-test	Repeat stmt Until test	`do { stmt }` `while (test);`
Conditional Branching	Conditional test	Parentheses optional	Parentheses required
	False	false	0 (zero)
	If (simple)	if test then stmt;	`if (test) stmt;` or use ?: operator
	If..else	If test then stmt else stmt;	`if (test) stmt;` `else stmt;`
	If..else..if	if test then stmt else if test then stmt; or else stmt;	`if (test) stmt;` `else if (test)` `stmt; else; else` `stmt;`
	Multiple alternatives	Case (var) of val1: stmt; val2: stmt; otherwise stmt; end;	`switch (var) {` `case val1: stmt;` `break;` `case val2: stmt;` `break;` `default: stmt;` `}`
	True	true	1 (nonzero)
Unconditional Branching	End of a loop	goto label;	`continue;`
	Exit a loop	goto label;	`break;`
	Labels	LABEL section	label:
	Local branch	goto label;	`goto` label;
	Terminate function or subroutine	Begin..end;	return(val);
	Terminate program	goto label;	`exit()`, `atexit()`, return from `main()`
Subprograms	Invoking	By name	Functions by name or pointer
	Module-like	Procedure	Function

TABLE 4.7: A Comparison of Pascal and C (continued)

CATEGORY	FEATURE	PASCAL	C EQUIVALENT
Subprograms (cont.)	Parameters	By value and address	By value (also pointers)
	Passing values:		
	Arrays	VAR var type;	By pointer
	Functions	Value only	By value or pointer
	Records	VAR var type;	Structures by pointer
	Return values	By value	Return by value
	Variable-like	Function	Function
Input/Output	Binary files	Type FILE OF	open mode "b"
	Detect end of file	eof(fv)	`EOF`, `feof()`
	File input	readln(fv,..);	`fscanf(fv, ...);`
	File output	writeln(fv,..);	`fprintf(fv, ...);`
	Implementation technique	Intrinsic functions and procedures	Run-time library
	Standard input	readln(var_list);	`scanf("ctrl", &var_list);`
	Standard output	writeln(var_list)	`printf("ctrl", var_list);`
	Text files	Type TEXT	Default open mode
Library	Built-in services	Functions, procedures	Keywords
	Dynamic memory:		
	Allocation	New	`calloc()`, `malloc()`
	Disposal	Dispose	`free()`

Base Data Type Characteristics

As you begin to work with C, develop a sensitivity to the memory space and performance associated with each fundamental data type available to you. Do this by running a C program, like the one listed in Figure 4.1, which simply uses the **sizeof** operator and the **printf()** run-time library function. The size of each base data type controls the allowable range of values that can be represented.

```
/* FILE: ch4e1. */
#include <stdio.h>
int main(void)
{
printf("\nchar  =  %2d  ptr = %d\
    \nshort int  =  %2d         ptr = %d\
    \nint        =  %2d         ptr = %d\
    \nenum       =  %2d         ptr = %d\
    \nlong int   =  %2d         ptr = %d\
    \nfloat      =  %2d         ptr = %d\
    \ndouble     =  %2d         ptr = %d\
    \nlong double =  %2d        ptr = %d\
    \n_segment   =  %2d  ptr = %d",
    sizeof(char),             sizeof(char *),
    sizeof(short int),  sizeof(short int *),
    sizeof(int),          sizeof(int *),
    sizeof(enum tag),   sizeof(enum tag *),
    sizeof(long int),    sizeof(long int *),
    sizeof(float),        sizeof(float *),
    sizeof(double),       sizeof(double *),
    sizeof(long double),  sizeof(long double *),
    sizeof(_segment),    sizeof(_segment *) );
exit(0);
}
```

FIGURE 4.1: The sample program ch4e1.c displays the size (in bytes) of each C fundamental data type.

Compiled for the Small memory model, this produces the following result on an Intel 80286-based computer:

```
char        = 1    ptr = 2
short int   = 2    ptr = 2
int         = 2    ptr = 2
enum        = 2    ptr = 2
long int    = 4    ptr = 2
float       = 4    ptr = 2
double      = 8    ptr = 2
long double = 10   ptr = 2
_segment    = 2    ptr = 2
```

Notice that the size of each type is expressed by the **sizeof** operator in bytes. Also, it should not be a surprise that pointer variables to each of these types would all be of the same size. The Small memory model implements **_near** pointer variables that contain the (16-bit) offset portion of an address of another data object in memory.

Next consider the basic arithmetic performance characteristics of each fundamental data type (**char**, **int**, **long int**, **float**, **double**, and **long double**). The program listed in Figure 4.2 uses the **START()** and **STOP** timing macros. It generates the following output for an Intel 80286-based computer without a math coprocessor, with the CL compiler, using options /qc /Od:

```
for  : int math
time : 0.11 sec
```

```
for  : long int math
time : 0.22 sec

for  : float math
time : 8.35 sec

for  : double math
time : 8.84 sec

for  : long double math
time : 10.61 sec
```

```
/* FILE: ch4e2.c */
#define TIMER
#include "timer.h"
#define NTIMES 30000
int main(void)
{
START(int math);
    {
    int i, val=1;
    for (i=0; i<NTIMES; i++) val+=1;
    }
STOP;

START(long int math);
    {
    int i;
    long val=1L;
    for (i=0; i<NTIMES; i++) val+=1L;
    }
STOP;

START(float math);
    {
    int i;
    float val=1.0F;
    for (i=0; i<NTIMES; i++) val+=1.0F;
    }
STOP;

START(double math);
    {
    int i;
    double val=1.0;
    for (i=0; i<NTIMES; i++) val+=1.0;
    }
STOP;

START(long double math);
    {
    int i;
    long double val=1.0L;
    for (i=0; i<NTIMES; i++) val+=1.0;
    }
STOP;

exit(0);
}
```

FIGURE 4.2: The sample program ch4e2.c measures the performance characteristics of some commonly used data types.

From the previous examples, you can conclude that, in the worst case, **long int** variables take 100 percent more storage space and are approximately 100 percent slower than **int** variables; and **double** variables take 100 percent more storage space and are approximately 6 percent slower than **float** variables; while **long doubles** take 150 percent more storage space and are approximately 27 percent slower than **float** variables. All type **char** variables are promoted to type **int** for mathematic purposes.

Coding Incrementors and Decrementors

Probably the most common coding line found in BASIC, Fortran, and Pascal programs is the simple incrementing or decrementing statement such as these, for BASIC, Fortran, and Pascal, respectively:

```
LET X = X + 1
X = X + 1
X := X + 1;
```

Three techniques are available in C to express such an incrementor (or decrementor) statement: i++; i+=; and i=i+1. The program listed in Figure 4.3 reveals the relative merits of using these three different C coding techniques to express simple increment and decrement operations.

This program produces the following output:

```
for  : for loop i++
time : 2.47 sec

for  : for loop i+=
time : 2.47 sec

for  : for loop i=i+1
time : 4.12 sec
```

As you can see, using the familiar expression (or variation) **i = i + 1** is obsolete with C and can represent a 66 percent performance penalty.

Coding Sign Changes

Another common habit is to rely upon multiplication instead of the unary minus (−) operator to change the sign of a value in C. The program example shown in Figure 4.4 yields the following performance measurement results:

```
for  : int by unary −
time : 0.17 sec
for  : int by multiplication
```

```
time : 0.22 sec
.
.
for  : float by unary -
time : 4.88 sec
for  : float by multiplication
time : 9.07 sec
```

Clearly, it is preferable to use the properties of unary minus. The continued use of multiplication for sign changes can result in a 29 percent performance penalty for **int** variables, and an 85 percent penalty for **float** variables.

Confusing the Assignment and Equality Operators

One of the most common coding techniques that causes unexpected results in C is inadvertent use of (**=**) assignment instead of (**==**) logical equality. The equality operator (**==**) only yields a result of 0 (zero, false) or 1

```
/* FILE: ch4e3.c */
#define TIMER
#include "timer.h"
#define NTIMES 500000L
int main(void)
{
START(for loop i++);
    {
    long i;
    for (i=0; i<NTIMES; i++);
    }
STOP;

START(for loop i+=);
    {
    long i;
    for (i=0; i<NTIMES; i+=1L);
    }
STOP;

START(for loop i=i+1);
    {
    long i;
    for (i=0; i<NTIMES; i=i+1);
    }
STOP;
exit(0);
}
```

FIGURE 4.3: The sample program ch4e3.c evaluates the performance differences that can result when coding a simple increment in C.

```
/* FILE: ch4e4.c */
#define TIMER
#include "timer.h"
#define NTIMES 30000
int main(void)
{
START(int by unary -);
    {
    int i, j=1;
    for (i=0; i<NTIMES; i++) j = (-j);
    }
STOP;

START(int by multiplication);
    {
    int i, j=1;
    for (i=0; i<NTIMES; i++) j = (-1)*j;
    }
STOP;

START(float by unary -);
    {
    int i;
    float j=1.0F;
    for (i=0; i<NTIMES; i++) j = (-j);
    }
STOP;

START(float by multiplication);
    {
    int i;
    float j=1.0F;
    for (i=0; i<NTIMES; i++) j = (-1.0F)*j;
    }
STOP;
exit(0);
}
```

FIGURE 4.4: The sample program ch4e4.c measures the performance of several sign change coding techniques.

(one or nonzero, true). The following incorrect code fragment example was intended to add and display the sum of all integers between −5 and +10:

```
static i,j;
for (i==(-5); i=10; i++) j+=i;
printf("\nj = %d",j);
```

This results in an endless loop. The **for** statement has the syntax

```
for (initializer; test; incrementor) statement;
```

and the following components:

initializer	Expression to be performed once.
test	Logical expression evaluated next. If true, *statement* is performed. If false, the **for** statement ends.
incrementor	Expression evaluated after *statement*. Loop control returns to *test*.

The *test* logical expression has used the assignment operator (**=**), not logical equality (**==**). This always yields a value of 10 (nonzero), which is understood by C to be true, setting up the endless loop. Altering this code to

```
for (i==(-5); i==10; i++) j+=i;
```

produces a program that terminates normally, but yields the incorrect result **j = 0**. Upon closer examination, it appears that the *test* expression **i==10** yields an initial result of false since the variable i was set to (−5) by the *initializer.* Constructing an appropriate *test* and rerunning should resolve this problem:

```
for (i==(-5); i<=10; i++) j+=i;
```

But again, the incorrect result **j = 55** is produced. The correct answer is 40. Taking another look at the *initializer* **i== (−5)**, and recognizing that all variables declared to be type-qualified as static are initialized at zero, reveals that the *initializer* is a logical expression yielding false (0), and needs to be an assignment statement. Revising the **for** statement to

```
for (i=(-5); i<=10; i++) j+=i;
```

correctly solves the problem. Note that the initializer was expressed as **i=(−5)** and not **i=−5** because the **=op** form of compound assignment is not permitted in Standard C.

Characters, Character Strings, and Arrays of Characters

Characters in C are normally allocated one byte (unless designated a wide or multibyte character) and may be treated as either signed or unsigned integer numbers. Some valid examples of ways in which individual characters may be assigned values are shown below:

```
#include <ctype.h>
.

.
char chA, cha;       /* char-type variables chA and cha */
ch = 'A';            /* any printable character */
ch = '\071';         /* octal 71 (base 8) */
ch = '\x41';         /* hexadecimal 41 (base 16) */
ch = 65;             /* decimal 65 assignment */
ch = tolower(ch);    /* transform upper- to lowercase */
ch = '\n';           /* any standard C escape sequence */
```

Single-character strings differ from characters in that all strings are null-terminated (\0) and designated using double quotation marks (" "), not single quotation marks (' '). Arrays of **char** are sequences of contiguous bytes in memory. Arrays are only null-terminated when initialized as strings. The program example in Figure 4.5 illustrates two ways of declaring strings.

It produces the following results:

```
sizeof str1 = 2
lengthof str1 = 1
str1 = A
str1[0] = 65
str1[1] = 0

sizeof str2 = 3
lengthof str2 = 1
str2 = A
str2[0] = 65
str2[1] = 0
str2[2] = 0
```

Notice that all strings are null-terminated and that the size of a string is the array size itself, while the length of a string yielded by the run-time library function **strlen()** is the number of characters exclusive of the null-terminating byte. Strings, then, are a special case of arrays of **char** that conform to the null-terminated convention. We will see in Part III that array names are constant character pointers and strings are just consecutive sequences of bytes that are logically terminated by the first occurrence of a null character. If an array of characters were not deliberately null-terminated, using the run-time output function **printf()** would produce unpredictable output for the cases where %s (string) is specified, because the null character is missing.

In Figure 4.5, the type-qualifier **static** was chosen to initialize all memory locations to zero (\0) in the absence of an initializer list, as shown in the code fragment above. If dynamic memory allocation is used to allocate

```
/* FILE: ch4e5.c */
int main(void)
{
static char str1[] = "A";
static char str2[3] = { 'A', '\0');

printf("\nsizeof str1 = %d\nlengthof str1 = %d\nstr1 = %s\
    \nstr1[0] = %d\nstr1[1] = %d\n\
    \nsizeof str2 = %d\nlengthof str2 = %d\nstr2 = %s\
    \nstr2[0] = %d\nstr2[1] = %d\
    \nstr2[2] = %d",\
    sizeof(str1), strlen(str1), str1,\
    str1[0], str1[1],\
    sizeof(str2), strlen(str2), str2,\
    str2[0], str2[1], str2[2]);
exit(0);
}
```

FIGURE 4.5: The sample program ch4e5.c contrasts the differences between characters and strings.

the storage for a string, use **calloc()**, not **malloc()**, for the same reasoning.

Subscripting Anomalies

The array subscripting habits familiar with BASIC, Fortran, and Pascal, whereby either (x,y,..) or [x,y,..] is used, must be abandoned in C. The proper syntax in C isolates each subscript in enclosing brackets, **[x] [y] [..]**, and all subscripts are understood to begin at **[0]**. Should you inadvertently use the Pascal-like syntax [x,y,..] instead, as in the program example shown in Figure 4.6, no compilation errors are detected, but unexpected results are generated!

```
ary[0,0] = 66
ary[0,1] = 70
ary[1,0] = 66
ary[1,1] = 70
ary[1,0] = 66
ary[1,1] = 70

ary[0]   = 66
ary[1]   = 70
ary[2]   = 74
ary[3]   = 78
ary[4]   = 82
ary[5]   = 86
```

This could be dismissed as "garbage," but there is a pattern in the numbers displayed. They represent addresses (segment offsets) in memory. Notice that the values shown always differ by four. When subscripts are

```
/* FILE: ch4e6.c */
int main(void)
{
static int ary[3][2] = { {0, 1}, {10, 11}, {20, 21} };
printf("\nary[0,0] = %d\nary[0,1] = %d\
        \nary[1,0] = %d\nary[1,1] = %d\
        \nary[1,0] = %d\nary[1,1] = %d\n\
        \nary[0]   = %d\nary[1]    = %d\
        \nary[2]   = %d\nary[3]    = %d\
        \nary[4]   = %d\nary[5]    = %d",\
        ary[0,0], ary[0,1],\
        ary[1,0], ary[1,1],\
        ary[2,0], ary[2,1],\
        ary[0], ary[1], ary[2], ary[3], ary[4], ary[5]);
exit(0);
}
```

FIGURE 4.6: The sample program ch4e6.c demonstrates the effects of improperly subscripting arrays in C.

incorrectly expressed as **ary[x,y]**, the compiler treats the comma as an operator and evaluates **ary[x]** first, followed by **ary[y]**; however, **ary[y]** in this instance represents the address of a row of objects in array **ary**. For this reason, all values shown above represent the offset component of a memory address of the first element of each row in array **ary**, which consists of two integers; hence the address difference of four bytes (two integers at two bytes each).

By modifying Figure 4.6 to introduce the indirection (*****) operator, we can display the true values pointed to by these segment addresses.

```
*ary[0,0], *ary[0,1],
*ary[1,0], *ary[1,1],\
*ary[2,0], *ary[2,1],\
*ary[0], *ary[1], *ary[2], *ary[3], *ary[4], *ary[5]);
```

The following output is now produced:

```
ary[0,0] = 0        /* actually [0][0] */
ary[0,1] = 10       /* actually [1][0] */
ary[1,0] = 0        /* actually [0][0] */
ary[1,1] = 10       /* actually [1][0] */
ary[1,0] = 0        /* actually [0][0] */
ary[1,1] = 10       /* actually [1][0] */

ary[0] = 0          /* actually [0][0] */
ary[1] = 10         /* actually [1][0] */
ary[2] = 20         /* actually [2][0] */
ary[3] = -1         /* actually [3][0] out-of-bounds */
ary[4] = 582        /* actually [4][0] out-of-bounds */
ary[5] = 3397       /* actually [5][0] out-of-bounds */
```

The incorrect two-dimensional subscripts are again interpreted in C as two consecutive subscript evaluations (left, then right) separated by the comma operator; hence, the effect in each case above is to locate the subscripts noted in the adjacent comments.

The incorrect one-dimensional references are also interpreted as noted above in the adjacent comments. Clearly, subscripts 3–5 are out-of-bounds.

Several conclusions can be drawn from this series of examples. First, C is very forgiving at the compilation stage when it comes to array subscripting, because it considers subscript values to be offset multipliers. That is, the subscript number is multiplied by the size of the array's data type, and the result is offset from a starting address defined by the array name itself. In the example above, **ary** is interpreted as **&(ary[0][0])**. This also helps explain why no out-of-bounds subscript detection is performed in C. With the erroneous introduction of negative subscripts, out-of-bounds can be visualized to extend beyond both the valid starting and ending memory addresses allocated for any array. If subscripts are inadvertently referenced as shown above, calculations will continue and work with memory addresses, not array element values!

Misleading Results with `printf()`

Most computer languages exhibit what is referred to as strict type-checking. This property of a language is intended to protect the programmer from him/herself. Although the concept of type is fundamental to understanding how the C language works, C is not a strongly typed language. The freedom to cast types is evidence of this fact. The recent introduction of function prototypes, on the other hand, attempts to impose stronger type checking.

The lack of strong typing is particularly noticeable with the widely used `printf()` output functions. If an incorrect correlation between the data type of an object being displayed and the corresponding format designator in the `printf()` statement is used, a program may appear to be operating incorrectly even if it is not. This situation is particularly troubling when such an error is made during the display of intermediate results while debugging. Your suspicions of source-code logic errors are then masked and further compounded by the display of incorrect variable values. Consider the source-code program shown in Figure 4.7.

It generates the following output:

```
L1: FEDCBA
L2: FEDCBA
L3: 70 68 66 0
L4: 4325446 4325446
L5: 0.000000 0.000000
L6: 0.000000
```

In this example, what superficially began as an array of characters was both correctly and incorrectly displayed as characters (`%c`), a string (`%s`), integers (`%d`), long integers (`%ld`), float (`%f`), and double (`%lf`). With the myriad of type-qualifiers available in C, and the extensive features supported by `printf()`, it is easy for your output to be misleading. Double-check the correspondence and appropriateness of the variable object-type and `printf()` control characters used when displaying results.

The examples just presented are not intended to illustrate all of the potential pitfalls, but simply to demonstrate the need to reconsider the relevance of coding techniques rooted in the features of other languages.

```
/* FILE: ch4e7.c */
int main(void)
{
double dval = 1.0;
static char ary[8] = { 70, 69, 68, 67, 66, 65 };
printf("\nL1: %c%c%c%c%c%c%c%c\
        \nL2: %s\
        \nL3: %d %d %d %d\
        \nL4  %ld %ld\
        \nL5: %f %f\
        \nL6: %lf",\
        ary[0], ary[1], ary[2], ary[3],\
        ary[4], ary[5], ary[6], ary[7],\
        ary,\
        ary[0], ary[2], ary[4], ary[6],\
        ary[0], ary[4],\
        ary[0], ary[4],\
        ary[0]);
exit(0);
}
```

FIGURE 4.7: The sample program ch4e7.c demonstrates how easy it is to create misleading results with the run-time function printf().

C CODING GUIDELINES

Before beginning a development project, always formulate a concise statement that communicates your project design priorities and objectives. Are these project values shared by all project members? If not, then how are the day-to-day coding decisions being made? Following is a statement that tries to embody the spirit of C, reaffirm the commandment not to "reinvent the wheel," and challenge the prevalent NIH (Not Invented Here) syndrome:

- Establish portability and performance requirements before writing any C code.
- Always write source code that conforms to Standard C unless it is impossible to do so.
- When available, use Standard C run-time library functions, not their non-Standard Microsoft counterparts.
- To perform tasks not supported by the C run-time library, purchase commercial libraries of functions in source-code form, if available.
- Lastly, resort to writing functions in C from scratch.
- Only resort to assembly language programming to satisfy unique requirement and performance objectives.

The decision hierarchy summarized above may not be applicable to all projects, but it merits consideration. Express your beliefs clearly, communicate them effectively, and reaffirm them periodically. All sub-sequent software project decisions that are made should both support and refine the intent of your overall project design philosophy.

Editing Conventions

C is a free-formatted language, and as such, requires self-imposed editing standards. Only white space (blank, tabs, newline, carriage return, line feed, form feed, and comments) is used to separate tokens in C. Formatting is therefore controlled by the selective use of white space. Tabs are preferred over blanks because they take less space in the source-code file. Set your tab columns at a minimum of four columns, and use comments for source-code documentation purposes, not formatting.

Since functions are the building blocks of every C program, edit only one function (of type **extern**) per file, and give the edited file the name *function*.C. C permits source-code files to contain many function definitions, but coding in this manner makes it difficult to locate and correct source-code files. Only deviate from this guideline when functions of type **static** are declared. The visibility of static objects is restricted to the file in which they are declared.

Since the function **main()** is special (the standard execution entry name; only one per executable file), collect and place all data definitions global to the project (true **extern**s) and initializer lists at the beginning of the file containing **main()**. Do not distribute project-global definitions throughout function source-code files. Standard C now requires that only one unit of translation may contain the external definition of an object. Refer to such objects elsewhere with an **extern** type-qualifier.

Preferably, create one project-specific header file (.h) that contains all necessary variable declarations, type definitions, structure tags, object-like macros, function-like macros, and project function prototypes. This project header should always be included by all project source-code files. This technique will ensure that the compiler enforces the appropriate argument and return type-checking for all function calls made, and also centrally documents this crucial project information.

Next, devise a standardized file "look" that is easily read, uniform in nature, complete, and appropriate for the size and complexity of the project being undertaken:

- Begin each file with a prologue description block.
- Include any necessary preprocessor #directives.
- Enter the function source code itself.

- Code only one statement per line of input, terminated by a semi-colon (;).
- End each file with an epilogue description block.

The prologue should be restricted to provide information necessary for the immediate use of the function. Consider the sample prologue listed in Figure 4.8.

When coding C statements in the body of a function, avoid placing more than one semicolon-terminated statement per line of input, such as this:

```
ival = 10 * j; if (ival < 100) break; else continue;
```

When the CodeView (CV) debugger is used, it will be unable to point to an accurate line number of the C source-code statement in error. If interactive debugging is not an issue, however, this form of expression is acceptable.

The epilogue should reflect any supporting documentation concerning the function, as well as maintain a chronology of updates and revisions. A sample epilogue appears in Figure 4.9.

```
/************************************************************
** NAME
**        funcname: brief one-line description
**
** PROTOTYPE
**        type funcname (type arg1name, type arg2name, ...)
**        arg1name              description
**        arg2name              description
**        :                     :
**        argNname              description
**
** DESCRIPTION
**        text description of funcname()...
**        :
**        :
**        as needed
**
** RETURN
**        brief one-line description
**
** RETURN CODES (if any)
**        ERC_OK     successful return
**        :
**        :          itemize as necessary
**
** LIMITATIONS (if any)
**        compilers, memory models, etc.
**        :
**
** MACROS (if any)
**        NDEBUG     if defined, removes assertions
**        FLAG       if == 1, .....
**        :
**
************************************************************/
```

FIGURE 4.8: A sample prologue.

```
/***********************************************************
** REFERENCES (if any)
**        citations, articles, books etc.
**          :
**
** CHRONOLOGY
**        date, version, notation, author, ...
**          :
**        make one entry for each change
**
***********************************************************/
```

FIGURE 4.9: A sample epilogue.

The overall process of developing a C coding strategy should be starting to crystallize. Let's begin to look at some editing details that merit notice.

Follow the guidelines discussed in Chapter 5 when editing any compiler directives that are interpreted by the preprocessor and eliminated entirely from the intermediate (.i) unit of translation that is actually passed to the C compiler being used. They are summarized below:

- Place the # sign in column 1.
- Use only blank characters or horizontal tabs to indent the directive name for clarity.
- Except in defining macro strings, where you may often need to wrap around long lines by using the \ newline character, restrict the logical length of a line to the physical width of the page.
- Place comments only after the last parameter.
- Terminate each line with a newline.

Next, begin entering the function source code itself. Use blank lines for added visual clarity wherever necessary. Begin by editing all declarations, one per line, followed by a comment. This may seem assembler-like, but it facilitates the copying, moving, reordering, and documentation of declarations, without concern for any subsequent editing side effects. For example:

```
int i;              /* miscellaneous counter */
int j;              /* miscellaneous counter */
int maxsize;        /* maximum size */
```

Consider alphabetizing your declarations for additional clarity.

When making a full-line comment, rather than editing it as

```
/* this is a full-line comment */
```

block the comment as follows:

```
/*
** this is a full-line blocked comment
*/
```

This makes the comment stand out visually, makes adding lines easier (**), and also helps prevent inadvertently nesting or mismatching comments.

When coding either macro or function formal and actual argument lists, always place a blank after each punctuating comma. For example, rather than editing the function prototype as

```
int f(int a1,int a2,int a3,int a4, ...);
```

edit an equivalent prototype as

```
int f(int a1, int a2, int a3, int a4, ...);
```

Note the use of the ellipsis (...), denoting that a variable number of arguments may follow.

Also use blanks to separate operators and tokens in expressions and statements. For example, rather than editing

```
while((*s++=*t++)!='\0');
```

edit this string copy statement as

```
while ((*s++ = *t++) != '\0')
    ;
```

and note that the null statement (;) has been moved to its own line for emphasis because it is generally not your intent to initiate a loop that does nothing.

Parentheses now control the order of evaluation of expressions, as has been customary in most other high-level languages. This is particularly important with scientific and engineering-oriented programs involving complex equations. For example, to express the quadratic equation

$$y = ax^2 + bx + c$$

write

```
y = (a * pow(x,2.0)) + (b * x) + c;
```

as shown, *not*

```
y=a*pow(x,2.0)+b*x+c;
```

even though in this instance, because of the precedence of operators, both forms yield the same result.

When forced to express lengthy string literals (**scanf()** and **printf()** control strings, for example), take advantage of the \ new-line continuation sequence, in concert with Standard C's convention of concatenating adjacent string literals that are separated only by white space. For example, instead of coding

```
fprintf(stdout,"\ncode-1 = %c\ncode-2 = %c"\n ...... );
```

use the following convention:

```
fprintf (stdout,"\ncode-1 = %c"\
    "\ncode-2 = %c"\
    .
    .
    "\ncode-n = %c"\, ...... );
```

Probably the most widely debated editing issue concerns the convention of designating blocks with braces. The K&R precedent, set by the examples in *The C Programming Language,* is widely used in practice. A function conforming to the K&R convention would look like this:

```
int function (argument)
argument declaration;
{
    while (test-1) {
    .
    .
        if (test-2) {
        .
        .
            if (test-3) {
            .
            .
            } /* end of (test-3) */
        .
        .
        } /* end of (test-2) */
    .
    .
    } /* end of (test-1) */
.
.
} /* end of function */
```

In this convention, an opening brace for blocks (compound statements) that follow conditional branching or repetition statements is placed after the test statement, while the closing brace is on its own line, indented to align with the initiating statement. In all other block situations, the opening and closing braces are placed on their own line and are both indented to the start of the previous statement.

Obviously, a myriad of combinations exist for beginning and ending braces. Consider the K&R approach, but feel free to adopt your own standard. Either way, stay with one approach to minimize the distraction of reading other project members' source-coding style.

Identifier Naming

Now that an overall structure and format for your C source-code files has been presented, we can address the important issue of identifier naming, which is more complex in C than most other languages. Among the causes are C's case-sensitivity, its heavy reliance upon the run-time library, and the new reserved-naming policy of Standard C. In any case, it is important to develop a methodology for constructing project identifier names.

There are four separate identifier-naming classes in C:

- Enumerations, formal parameters, functions, macros, typedefs, and variables
- Labels (function scope only)
- Members (structure or union scope)
- Tags (for structures, unions, and enumerations)

Identifiers within a naming class must be unique but may be replicated in other naming classes.

All C identifiers must begin with either a letter or underscore character and may subsequently be followed by any series of letters, digits, or underscores. Identifiers may not begin with a digit; otherwise, they could not be distinguished from arithmetic constants. Identifiers may not conflict with keywords (see Appendix B) and should not replicate any Standard C run-time library function name or any of the reserved names listed in Table 4.8.

Notice that although identifiers must be named starting either with a letter or underscore character, Standard C reserves those names beginning with a single or double underscore sequence.

Within each naming class, the uniqueness of an identifier is understood to be within *scope*. Scope reflects the extent to which the file (.C source-code file), block (within a set of braces {..}), function, or function prototype in which the identifier is declared is visible. An identifier's visibility is controlled by where it is defined and what storage class it is assigned. All identifiers are understood to be defined either externally (outside of braces) or internally (inside of braces).

Externally defined identifiers may have only *file* visibility (**static** storage class), or *global* visibility (**extern** storage class). Global identifiers in C are simply defined at an external level without using the **extern** keyword. Other files or blocks may access such identifiers (or gain their visibility) only by declaring them using the **extern** keyword, implying that the storage for such objects is defined elsewhere. Because functions may not be declared internally in C, function identifiers always have

TABLE 4.8: Standard C Reserved Names

CATEGORY	NAME	SOURCE
Ranges of Reserved Names	`__`...	Hidden
	`_`...	Hidden
	`_[A-Z]`...	Hidden
	`E[A-Z]`...	`<errno.h>`
	`E[0-9]`...	`<errno.h>`
	`is[a-z]`...	`<ctype.h>`
	`LC_[A-Z]`...	`<locale.h>`
	`mem[a-z]`...	`<string.h>`
	`SIG_`...	`<signal.h>`
	`SIG[A-Z]`...	`<signal.h>`
	`str[a-z]`...	`<stdlib.h>`
	`str[a-z]`...	`<string.h>`
	`to[a-z]`...	`<ctype.h>`
	`wcs[a-z]`...	`<string.h>`
Math Function Reserved Names	`acosf`	`<math.h>`
	`asinf`	`<math.h>`
	`atanf`	`<math.h>`
	`atan2f`	`<math.h>`
	`ceilf`	`<math.h>`
	`cosf`	`<math.h>`
	`coshf`	`<math.h>`
	`expf`	`<math.h>`
	`fabsf`	`<math.h>`
	`floorf`	`<math.h>`
	`fmodf`	`<math.h>`
	`frexpf`	`<math.h>`
	`ldexpf`	`<math.h>`
	`logf`	`<math.h>`
	`log10f`	`<math.h>`
	`modff`	`<math.h>`
	`powf`	`<math.h>`
	`sinf`	`<math.h>`
	`sinhf`	`<math.h>`

TABLE 4.8: Standard C Reserved Names (continued)

CATEGORY	NAME	SOURCE
Math Function Reserved Names (cont.)	`sqrtf`	`<math.h>`
	`tanf`	`<math.h>`
	`tanhf`	`<math.h>`

global visibility, unless specifically declared to have a **static** storage class, in which case their identifier visibility is restricted to file scope.

Internally defined identifiers may have only file visibility (**static** storage class) or block visibility (**auto** or **register** storage class). Each nested block (defined by a set of braces) creates an opportunity to initiate another unique occurrence (instance) of an identifier without regard for the potential of confusion with an existing identifier name.

Standard C dictates that internal names be unique to a length of at least 31 case-sensitive characters. External names, however, are implementation-defined and may be restricted to a minimum of six case-insensitive characters. The retention of this six-character external limit represents a concession to existing compiler and linker implementations, but has been flagged as becoming obsolete by Standard C. It is intended that external identifier naming become compatible with the internal name minimum standard of at least 31 case-sensitive characters.

From a project perspective, the creation of internal identifier names does not present a particular problem. Such identifiers have only block scope. Even external identifiers that only have file scope (**static** storage class) present no real problems, as long as you avoid using a conflicting C keyword or predefined macro definition.

The real problem in naming identifiers arises when globally visible identifiers (**extern** storage class) are created. For this reason, it is recommended that you adopt a standard project-naming prefix (suffixes may be truncated!) to minimize the risk of external name conflict. Also note that Microsoft compiler and linker options may be useful. Compiler option /H truncates all external names at a fixed maximum size, and QLINK or LINK option /NOI instructs the linker not to ignore the case differences of names. The default /H setting is <31>, and by default, QLINK and LINK ignore case differences.

Clearly, identifier naming in C is challenging, but at the same time significantly more powerful than that allowed by the traditional six-character global Fortran and eight-character local and global Pascal case-insensitive naming standards.

2

Using the Preprocessor

Hardly a C program is written that does not use the #directive services of the preprocessor. For many, only limited use of the preprocessor is made to **#include** a header file, or to occasionally **#define** a macro. The preprocessor is typically underutilized when source code portability is not a priority. The preprocessor is however one of the primary tools for implementing portability in a C programming environment.

If you have been avoiding the preprocessor, or feel it is not that important, reconsider the importance of program portability, and review the preprocessor directives explained in Chapter 5. Historically, implementations of the preprocessor itself have varied considerably because of the imprecise definition provided by K&R C. With Standard C however, a more uniform behavior can be expected from comforming C compilers. With the proliferation of predefined and reserved identifiers in Standard C, it is now, more than ever, important to understand the power of the preprocessor. Chapter 5 will help you to become a more effective preprocessor directive programmer and to program for greater portability and better overall performance. The start and stop timing macros used throughout this book to evaluate alternative coding techniques are developed in Chapter 5.

If C's failure to provide adequate function argument checking has always bothered you, then brush up on the expanded role that both function prototypes and macros play in Standard C by reviewing the Standard C and Microsoft header files described in Chapter 6. Locating which header file to use, and where particular identifiers, macros, and function prototypes are defined is an easy matter when Chapter 6 is used. Separate appendices are also provided that detail global variables (Appendix C), type definitions (Appendix D), and structure and union tags (Appendix E).

The drudgery of fingering through Microsoft's many indexes, or the time-consuming process of searching through the myriad of help screens to pinpoint what you are looking for is finally over. A master list of alphabetic identifiers is available on diskette. See the Order Form in the back of the book.

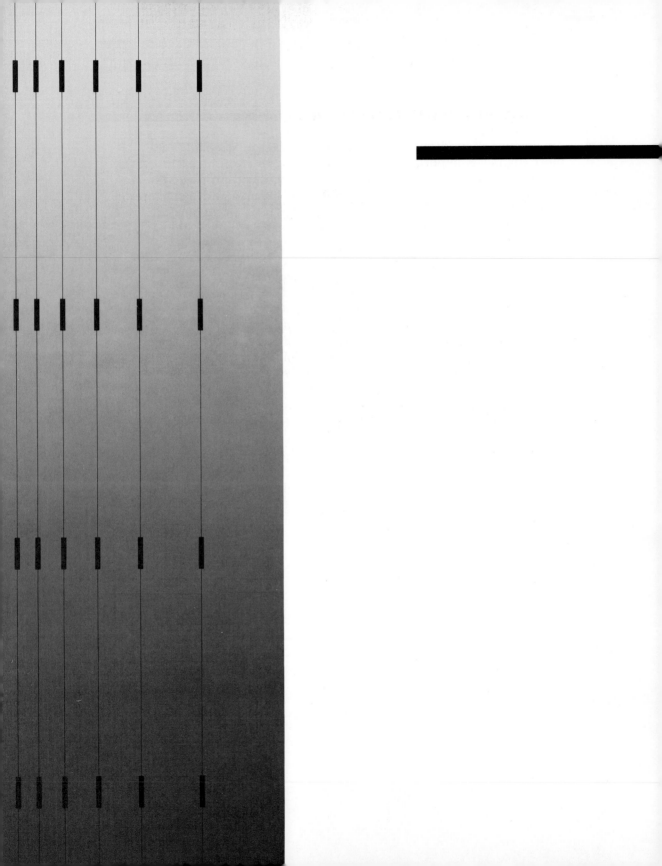

Preprocessor Directives

Preprocessor Directives

All language compilers use stages of translation to convert text files of source code into object code targeted for a particular computer's instruction set. Unlike most languages, however, C provides a distinct source-code preprocessing stage called the *preprocessor.* The commands for the preprocessor are inserted in C source-code (.C) files and called compiler directives. Each compiler directive is prefixed by a pound sign (#). Every C compilation begins by preprocessing each source-code file (.C) and performing any preprocessor directives specified to produce a corresponding intermediate file (.I) devoid of all directives. Unlike a source-code file, the intermediate file becomes a completed C text file, or what is formally termed a *unit of translation.*

Do not confuse preprocessing with actual compilation. Preprocessing does not produce any object code, only a source-code unit of translation that is then subject to compilation.

Before the ANSI standardization of C, preprocessor design varied tremendously, because the original specification provided by Kernighan and Ritchie (K&R) was incomplete. With Standard C, preprocessor implementations will become more compatible. When you need to convert between compilers, operating systems, or hardware, consider passing .I files instead of .C files to remove any side effects caused by incompatible C preprocessors.

SPECIFYING DIRECTIVES

The preprocessor directives that may optionally be used are shown in Table 5.1 and grouped for discussion purposes into the following categories:

- Simple
- File
- Macro
- Conditional
- Operators

The sections that follow will discuss the directives in each of these categories in detail; however, the syntax of all preprocessor directives adheres to a common set of rules.

TABLE 5.1: C Preprocessor Directives

CATEGORY	DIRECTIVE	DESCRIPTION
Simple Directives	#	The null directive. Alternate to a blank line with or without a comment.
	#error *message*	Prints the message if encountered, and terminates the compilation.
	#line *linenbr filename*	Used to update the current source-code line number and file name of predefined macros __LINE__ and __FILE__.
	#pragma *name*..	Implementation-specific compiler controls. See Table 5.2 for Microsoft #pragma names.
File Directive	#include *filename*	Used to include the contents of another file of source code. Normally header files are included. Only one filename may be specified.
Macro Directives	#define *macro string*	Used to create a macro or string substitution command. By K&R convention, macro names are in uppercase and are case-sensitive. A macro is defined in the macro symbol table.
	#undef *macro*	Removes a macro definition from the macro symbol table. A macro is then no longer defined, unless redefined.
Conditional Directives	#if *constant-expr*	Conforms to the C convention that false equals zero and true is nonzero. If true, include the lines that follow until the next #if, #ifdef, #elif, #else, or #endif.
	#elif *constant-expr*	Conforms to the C convention that false equals zero and ture is nonzero. If true, include the lines that follow until the next #elif, #else, or #endif.
	#else	Only one permitted per #if..#endif block. Handles the false or otherwise condition if present.
	#endif	Provided to correspond with each prior #if or #ifdef.
	#ifdef *macro*	Tests whether a macro is defined. True if defined, false otherwise.
	#ifndef *macro*	Tests whether a macro is undefined. True if not defined, false otherwise.

TABLE 5.1: C Preprocessor Directives (continued)

CATEGORY	DIRECTIVE	DESCRIPTION
Directive-Only Operators	#	This string-forming operator is used only with function-like macro definitions (with arguments). Treats a formal argument as a string literal when substituted.
	##	This token-pasting operator is used with both object- and function-like macros to join adjacent tokens.
	#@	This Microsoft-specific character-forming operator is used only with function-like macro definitions (arguments). Treats a formal argument as a character constant when substituted.
	defined(*macro*)	The **defined** operator is used to test whether *macro* is defined (true) or not (false).

NOTE: All preprocessor directives are case-sensitive.

All preprocessor directives are line-oriented, like the NMAKE instructions discussed in Chapter 3. Unlike NMAKE, the C preprocessor does not require that its directives always begin in column one; both the # and the directive name that follow may be preceded by horizontal white space. The syntax of a preprocessor directive is as follows:

```
#directivename [parameter..]
```

The components of a preprocessor directive are described as follows:

directivename A required directive identifier, except for the null directive. Since C is case-sensitive, **include** is correct; **INCLUDE** and **Include** are not. Only one directive name per line may be specified.

[*parameter..*] Optional parameters as required by each directive.

White space in C source code may consist of horizontal white space, designated by the space (' ') or horizontal tab ('\t') characters and comments (/* comment */); vertical white space, designated by the form feed ('\f') or vertical tab ('\v') characters; and an end of line designated either with a newline ('\n') character or carriage return ('\r') and line feed

('\n'). Only horizontal white space may be used to express a compiler directive. If comments are used, they may span lines but may not be nested.

For maximum program portability place the # in column one, use space and horizontal tabs only to indent the directive name as necessary for program clarity and to separate parameters, use the backslash for logical line continuation only in macro definitions, place comments only after the last parameter, and terminate each directive with a new line. The following examples demonstrate these recommendations:

```
#                         /* null directive */
#if !defined(NDEBUG)      /* test for NDEBUG macro */
#   define NDEBUG         /* define NDEBUG macro */
#else
#   undef NDEBUG          /* remove NDEBUG macro */
#endif
#                         /* null directive */
```

Microsoft's implementation of the Standard C compiler places the following restrictions on the preprocessor:

Size of macro: 1024 bytes.

Number of macro definitions in /D options: 30.

Number of function-like macro arguments: 31.

Length of an actual macro argument: 256 bytes.

Level of nesting for **#if**, **#ifdef**, and **#ifndef**: 32.

Levels of nested **#include** files: 10.

Number of **/I** paths for include files: 20.

These preprocessor limitations present no programming hardships in normal practice. We will now examine, by the categories shown in Table 5.1, each compiler directive in detail.

Simple Directives

The **#** or null directive can serve as a blank line within a group of preprocessor directives but is more commonly found in source code generated by a program. Do not confuse the # null directive with the **#** string-forming directive *operator*, which never appears in the first column position. Sample null directives are included in the example above.

The **#error** directive prevents conditional program compilation from proceeding if an abnormal condition is detected during an **#if** conditional block of tests. If encountered, *message* is displayed, and the compilation is terminated at that point. Because *message* is treated as a series of tokens, and not a string, it does not require double quotes. If double quotes are used, they will simply be displayed. An example of an **#error** directive would be:

```
#if !defined(MSDOS)
#error MSDOS undefined: see compiler option /u or /U<name>
#endif
```

The **#line** directive is often used by program generators to make sure that subsequent compiler error messages in generated source code will refer to the original source-code line numbers and filenames. The **__LINE__** and **__FILE__** predefined macros are updated by the **#line** *linenbr filename* directive. The line number is required and must be an integer number in the range 1 to 32,767. The filename may be omitted, in which case the current **__FILE__** is maintained; otherwise enter *filename* as a string in double quotes to update **__FILE__**, or use a macro name that defines a valid DOS filename. If you intend to include a directory specification (\) in *filename*, remember that (\) is a C escape character. Therefore, in order to express *filename* for the DOS file C:\QC25\BOOK\SAMPLE.MAK, the following **#line** directive must be issued:

```
#line 256 "C:\\QC25\\BOOK\\SAMPLE.MAK"
```

The **#pragma** directive allows compiler vendors to provide access to machine-specific features while remaining compatible with the C language itself. The number and names of **#pragma** directives therefore vary somewhat between implementations. Table 5.2 lists the **#pragma** directives defined by Microsoft. Note that QuickC offers only a subset of those available with OptimizingC.

TABLE 5.2: Microsoft #pragma Names

CATEGORY	#pragma NAME	DESCRIPTION	QuickC	OptimizingC
Listing Control	linesize([*chars*])	Sets the number of characters per line in the source-code listing. Default value is 79.	N	Y
	message("*message*")	Sends message to standard output.	Y	Y
	page([*pages*])	Skips specified number of pages in the source-code listing where the #pragma appears. Default value is 0.	N	Y

TABLE 5.2: Microsoft #pragma Names (continued)

CATEGORY	#pragma NAME	DESCRIPTION	QuickC	OptimizingC
Listing Control (cont.)	pagesize([*lines*])	Sets number of lines per page in the source-code listing. Default value is 63.	N	Y
	skip([*lines*])	Skips the number of lines and generates a new line in the source-code listing. Default value is 0.	N	Y
	subtitle("*name*")	Sets a subtitle in the source-code listing.	N	Y
	title("*name*")	Sets the title for a source-code listing that appears in the upper-left corner of each page.	N	Y
Program Control	alloc_text(*segm*, *fn1*[, *fn2*])	Specifies the modules (*fn1*..) to be grouped into a specified code segment (*segm*).	N	Y
	check_pointer([on|off])	Turns null pointer checking on or off. Requires compiler option /Zr. Default value reverts to compiler option.	Y	N
	check_stack([on|off])	Turns stack checking on or off. Default value reverts to compiler option.	Y	Y
	comment(*type*[, "*string*"])	Places comment "*string*" record in an .OBJ file of *type* compiler, exestr, lib, or user.	N	Y
	function(*fn1*[, *fn2*])	Specifies functions that are compiled as standard function calls rather than intrinsics. See Table 5.3 and compiler option /Oi.	N	Y
	intrinsic(*fn1*[, *fn2*])	Specifies functions that are compiled as intrinsic functions rather than standard function calls. See Table 5.3 and compiler option /Oi.	N	Y

TABLE 5.2: Microsoft #pragma Names (continued)

CATEGORY	#pragma NAME	DESCRIPTION	QuickC	OptimizingC
Program Control (cont.)	`loop_opt([on|off])`	Turns loop optimization on or off. Default reverts to compiler option.	N	Y
	`optimize("[ostr]"on|off)`	Enables or disables one or more compiler /O optimization codes (a, c, e, g, l, n, p, t, or w). If "*ostr*" is omitted, the present compiler option may be toggled on or off.	N	Y
	`pack([1|2|4])`	Specifies packing alignment for structures in bytes. See option /Zp. Default value is 2.	Y	Y
	`same_seg(var1[,var2])`	Specifies external **_far** variables to be grouped into the same data segment. See option /ND.	N	Y
NOTE: Pragma names and arguments are case-sensitive.				

Pragmas are often designed to permit command-line compiler options to be overridden for portions of a source-code file. Compiler options remain in effect for the entire unit of translation. Vendors make **#pragma** directives available that can change or toggle the effects of certain command-line options.

Assume that compiler option **/Ge** (enable stack checking) was specified, and that you desire to disable stack checking for just one of a number of static function definitions within the source-code file. Toggle the effect of the command-line option by surrounding the source code for a function as follows:

```
.
.
#pragma check_stack(on)
static void func(int arg1, char *arg2)
{
    .
    .
    .
}
#pragma check_stack(off)
.
.
```

Another performance-oriented use of **#pragma** directives with OptimizingC involves the selective use of **#pragma intrinsic()** and **#pragma function()** with compiler option **/Oi** to control whether individual functions in Table 5.3 are generated as inline code (intrinsic) or simply treated as normal function calls.

TABLE 5.3: Microsoft Intrinsic Functions

CATEGORY	FUNCTION
Console and Port I/O (Ch. 19)	`inp(NS)`, `inpw(NS)`, `outp(NS)`, `outpw(NS)`
Character and Data Conversion (Ch. 20)	`_lrotl(NS)`, `_lrotr(NS)`, `_rotl(NS)`, `_rotr(NS)`
Math (Ch. 23)	`abs()`, `acos()`, `acosl()`, `asin()`, `asinl()`, `atan()`, `atanl()`, `atan2()`, `atan2l()`, `ceil()`, `ceill()`, `cos()`, `cosl()`, `cosh()`, `coshl()`, `exp()`, `expl()`, `fabs()`, `floor()`, `floorl()`, `fmod()`, `fmodl()`, `labs()`, `log()`, `logl()`, `log10()`, `log10l()`, `pow()`, `powl()`, `sin()`, `sinl()`, `sinh()`, `sinhl()`, `sqrt()`, `sqrtl()`, `tan()`, `tanl()`, `tanh()`, `tanhl()`
Memory Management (Ch. 24)	`memcmp()`, `memcpy()`, `memset()`
String Handling (Ch. 26)	`strcat()`, `strcmp()`, `strcpy()`, `strset(NS)`, `strlen()`
Miscellaneous (Ch. 27)	`_enable(NS)`, `_disable(NS)`

NOTES:
1. Intrinsics are only available with OptimizingC (PWB/CL).
2. (NS) Non-Standard, Microsoft function.

If the compiler option **/Oi** is specified, any function referenced from the list in Table 5.3 will be treated as intrinsic and expanded to inline code. With or without compiler option **/Oi**, either of the following forms may be used to specify how individual functions from Table 5.3 are to be treated:

```
#pragma intrinsic (function-list)
#pragma function  (function-list)
```

Note that for the math functions shown, inline code is not generated, but rather the function arguments will be passed directly to the floating-point coprocessor, if one is present; otherwise, normal function-calling conventions are utilized.

File Directives

The **#include** directive instructs the preprocessor to copy the contents of *filename* into the source-code file in which the **#include** directive appears. Included filenames may be nested or, in turn, include other filenames. This directive is typically used to include header (.H) files. The syntax used to specify *filename*, along with the related compiler options **/I** and **/X**, control the search path used to locate *filename* when an incomplete file specification is used.

The *current path* is the path associated with the file containing the **#include** directive itself. The **standard path** is specified during compiler installation and locates the Standard C header files. The standard path is defined by the current value of the environment table variable INCLUDE.

The **/X** compiler option instructs the preprocessor to disregard the standard path altogether. If the **/I** *command-path* compiler option is used, the preprocessor searches for *filename* in *command-path* before searching the standard path. Multiple **/I** *command-path* options define a sequence of command paths to search. Up to twenty such options may be specified. The command-line example that follows demonstrates the use of the **/X** and multiple **/I** compiler options:

```
QCL /X /IC:\QC25\INCLUDE /IC:\QC25\SRC /c myprog.c
```

Here the QuickC command-line compiler is invoked to compile-only a source-code file named **MYPROG.C**. The **/X** option instructs the compiler to disregard the environment table variable INCLUDE and search for any **#include** files first in the path **C:\QC25\INCLUDE** and then in **C:\QC25\SRC**.

Let's consider the three alternative ways of specifying an **#include** **filename** directive. If a complete **filename** syntax such as

```
#include "c:\include\stdio.h"
```

is specified, only the specified path will be searched. Double backslashes (\\) are not needed, because all **#include** directives are processed before the backslash (\) is recognized as an escape sequence by the compiler. If an incomplete **"filename"** syntax such as

```
#include "stdio.h"
```

is specified, the current path will be searched, followed by any command-line paths, and then the standard path. If a complete **<filename>** syntax such as

```
#include <c:\include\stdio.h>
```

is used, only **<*filename*>** will be searched. If an incomplete **<*filename*>** syntax such as

```
#include <stdio.h>
```

is specified, the command-line paths are searched, followed by the standard path. The current path is not searched at all. If the alternative syntax that uses a macro definition such as

```
#include MYFILE
```

is specified, either the **"*filename*"** or **<*filename*>** syntax may be used to define the macro called MYFILE, which may have been created as an object-like or command-line macro (see the "Macro Directives" section).

If a filename cannot be found, the DOS error message *Cannot open include file {filename}* results and the compilation is terminated. To remedy this problem, take the following steps: check the filename specification; check the standard path in INCLUDE using the SET command; increase the FILES command setting in CONFIG.SYS and reboot; try compiling with **/Od** (all debugging options turned off); and try freeing up additional memory by removing any installed TSR (Terminate-and-Stay-Resident) programs.

It is recommended that the **<*filename*>** syntax be used for all Standard C header files, and the **"*filename*"** syntax be used for project-specific header files (see Figure 5.1 later in this chapter). This practice will ensure that the proper header files are included, even if duplicate header file names exist. It also encourages the placement of project-specific headers in the current path, not the standard path, so that subsequent reinstallation of the compiler does not destroy any project-specific headers.

Macro Directives

The **#define** directive is the source-code mechanism for providing string substitution by the preprocessor. Each macro name follows the rules for the formation of any C identifier: only letters, digits, or the underscore character may be used to construct a unique name up to 31 characters in length. By convention, macros normally appear in uppercase to distinguish them from the lowercase program variables and function names normally used. The *string* substitution associated with each occurrence of a *macro* may be comprised of any valid character-set symbols.

Macros defined by preprocessor directives comprise two categories: object-like and function-like. The latter allow formal arguments; the former do not. Moreover, object-like macros may be specified from the DOS command line (or equivalent QC and PWB menus); and the Microsoft compilers have predefined a set of object-like macros. These categories are addressed in separate subsections of this discussion.

Once a macro is defined, it remains defined until an **#undef** *macro* directive or the end of the unit of translation is encountered. The instructions specified by *string* remain in effect until redefined. The string associated with a macro may be changed by issuing another **#define** *macro string* directive, as long as it is of a compatible type. Object-like macros may only be redefined as other object-like macros; a function-like macro may only be redefined as another function-like macro with the same number and spelling of formal arguments. Normally, macro definitions convey constant meaning and should not be redefined. Command-line macro definitions take initial precedence; then source code and included header file macro definitions may subsequently define, redefine, or undefine macros.

Object-Like Macros

Object-like macros may be used to define constants, expressions, or statements. A direct character string substitution is made for all subsequent occurrences of the macro until the end of the unit of translation. The following examples suggest the range of possible uses for object-like macros:

```
#define TRUE 1              /* define a simple constant */
#define MASK 0x2000         /* define a bit mask */
#define void int            /* redefine a C keyword */
#define memcpy memmove      /* replace a function call */
#define register            /* blank-out source code */
#define TOP {printf("\f");} /* issue a form feed */
```

"Function-Like Macros" shows examples of further uses for **#define** macros. You may also use macros to implement inline assembly code as discussed in Chapter 28.

Use the backslash (\) character to extend macro definitions over more than one physical line. Do not enclose strings that contain blank characters in double quotes. For example:

```
#define ST1 test string     /* test string with blanks */
#define ST2 "test string"   /* "test string" with quotes */
```

Macro ST1 expands to "test string" without double quotation marks, whereas macro ST2 expands to "test string" with double quotes. Later in this discussion you'll see how the ST1 and ST2 macros would be defined if they were specified at the command line. It is important to express precisely the strings that you want the preprocessor to substitute; otherwise, the unit of translation that is produced will be incorrect but will not always result in the generation of a compilation error.

If macro strings perform arithmetic, take care to use parentheses to ensure that the proper order of evaluation results:

```
#define TAX     1.06
#define COST1   100.00
#define COST2   200.00

#define SUM1    COST1 + COST2
printf("SALE1 = %f\n",SUM1 * TAX);        /* 312.00 error   */

#define SUM2    (COST1 + COST2)
printf("SALE2 = %f\n",SUM2 * TAX);        /* 318.00 correct */
```

Clearly, without the parentheses surrounding COST1 + COST2, an incorrect answer is generated by the precedence of operators established for the C language, in which multiplication (*****) has precedence over addition (**+**). As we will see in Chapter 12, the topic of operator precedence in C is extremely important because of the many operators available in C.

The **#undef** directive undefines or removes a macro entry altogether from the current table of macros. The **#undef** directive may be issued for a macro that does not exist, and no error is generated. Certain predefined macros cannot be undefined.

A standard use of the **#undef** directive is to force the compiler to use run-time function calls and skip any corresponding macro definitions. The non-Standard functions **toupper()** and **tolower()** are in the C run-time library and also defined as macros in the standard header file **ctype.h**. If your source-code file has an **#include <ctype.h>** directive, the macro definitions will be used unless you issue the following directives to remove the macro definitions from the macro symbol table and leave all source-code references intact in the resulting unit of translation:

```
#undef toupper
#undef tolower
```

When using **#undef** on object- or function-like macros, simply use the syntax **#undef** *macro* without any parentheses or list of formal arguments. To ensure that the proper arguments and return values are used when the functions are invoked, the directives shown above should be accompanied by the following conditional function prototype declarations:

```
#ifndef toupper
    int toupper(int);
#endif

#ifndef tolower
    int tolower(int);
#endif
```

The compiler interprets any calls to these functions as external references to be resolved by the linker. The linker in turn searches the C run-time library to find an entry for the corresponding function names.

Command-Line Macros Although macros are normally defined in either C source code or Standard C or project-specific header files, Microsoft C also supports the definition of object-like macros from the DOS command line when the compiler is invoked. (The integrated compilers use menus for this purpose.) For CL and QCL, the command-line syntax is as follows:

```
/Dname[=string]
```

Specifying a macro name without a string (with or without the equal sign) simply defines a macro to exist and replaces any occurrence with a null string. This is useful in replacing any instance of a macro from a source-code file. A string with embedded blanks must be enclosed in double quotes. You can specify up to 30 **/D** compiler options.

The following QCL or CL command-line options define macros representing an integer constant, a character constant, a string without embedded blanks, and strings with embedded blanks:

```
/DIVAL=1                /* IVAL=1 integer constant */
/DCVAL='A'              /* CVAL='A' character constant */
/DSTR=string            /* STR=string without blanks */
/DST1="test string"     /* ST1=test string with blanks */
/DST2="\"test string\"" /* ST2="test string" with quotes */
```

In the example that follows, the ST2 macro must be used, not ST1, because a compiler error, *Unknown identifier 'string'*, would result for macro ST1 when the white space is encountered:

```
printf("%s\n",ST1);     /* compiler error */
printf("%s\n",ST2);     /* OK */
```

With QC you specify macros from the <Compiler Flags> menu (select the Make Bar from the Options menu) using the Defines field as illustrated here:

```
Defines: ST1="test string" ST2="\"test string""
```

With PWB, use the Defines field of the C Compiler Options menu:

```
Defines [ST1="test string" ST2="\"test string\""]
```

Notice that with both integrated compilers the **/D** prefix is not required.

Predefined Macros   Standard C requires that all conforming compiler implementations provide the following predefined macros, which are understood to be available for use without including any Standard C header files:

__DATE__ represents the date of compilation of the current C source-code file as a string in the form *mmm dd yyyy*, for example, Jul 30 1989.

__FILE__ represents the assumed filename of the current C source-code file as a string in the form *filename.ext*, for example, **macro.c**. The string represented by **__FILE__** may be changed using the **#line** directive.

__LINE__ represents the current line number of the current C source-code file as an integer (decimal) value in the range 1–32767. The decimal value represented by **__LINE__** may be changed using the **#line** directive.

__STDC__ represents a decimal value of 1 (true) or 0 (false), indicating whether the C compiler being used is a Standard C conforming compiler.

__TIME__ represents the date of compilation of the current C source-code file as a string in military time format *hh:mm:ss*; for example, 17:24:44 is 5:24 PM.

You cannot use **#define** or **#undef** directives to alter the definition of any predefined macros. All except **__FILE__** and **__LINE__** remain constant throughout the unit of translation. Table 5.4 lists non-Standard predefined macros provided by Microsoft C.

Other macros are defined by Standard C and Microsoft, but are only defined if the appropriate Standard C header files are included by a source-code file. Chapter 6 provides a complete description of the macros available with each header file.

Function-Like Macros

Function-like macros extend the power of object-like macros by permitting you to define formal arguments as you would a function. Arguments make the string substitution dynamic instead of static, as it normally is for object-like macros. The string to be substituted by the preprocessor may now depend on the formal arguments specified when the macro is invoked. These macros appear identical to function calls, with the difference that function-like macros simply generate inline text substitution.

The choice between a function call or a function-like macro depends on a number of factors. Function-like macros cannot be called from

TABLE 5.4: Microsoft Non-Standard Predefined Macros

IDENTIFIER	DESCRIPTION
_CHAR_UNSIGNED	Indicates that type **char** is unsigned. Compiler option **/J** was specified.
_CODE	The default code segment (CS) name for use with **_segname("..")**.
_CONST	The default constant segment name for use with **_segname("..")**.
_DATA	The default data segment (DS) name for use with **_segname("..")**.
M_I286	Identifies target machine as Intel 80286; compiler option **/G2**.
M_I8086	Identifies target machine as Intel 8086; default, or invoked with compiler option **/G0**.
M_I86	Identifies target machine in Intel family.
M_I86*m*M	Identifies the memory model as Tiny, Small, Medium, Compact, Large, or Huge.
_MSC_VER	Integer representation of the compiler version number. For 5.1, the macro is defined as 510; for 6.0+, the macro is defined as at least 600.
MSDOS	Identifies DOS as the target operating system; **!defined(MSDOS)** implies another operating system.
NO_EXT_KEYS	Microsoft-specific language extension and keywords are disabled. Compiler option **/Za** was specified. Also see compiler option **/Ze**.
_QC	Identifies compiler as QuickC; **!defined(_QC)** implies OptimizingC.
_STACK	The default stack segment (SS) name for use with **_segname("..")**.
__TIMESTAMP__	A string containing the last modification date of a file in the form Ddd Mmm NN HH:MM:SS YYYY, for example, Sun Dec 30 21:36:07 1990.

NOTE: All predefined macros are case-sensitive.

another program as functions can; they cannot be addressed using pointers as functions can; and they have problems dealing with arguments for which the increment (**++**) and decrement (**−−**) operators create side effects (discussed later in this chapter). Beyond these concerns is the issue of program performance (time). Is it faster to use function call and return protocols or repeatedly substitute inline a body of source code? Generally, if a body of logic is repetitively used within a series of loops, a function-like macro would be faster; but if many separate references to a body of logic are made, a library function would be preferred. Function-like macros always make your source code larger, but not necessarily slower. The only sure way to know which is better is to time a section of program logic. A pair of timing macros is presented in the "Preprocessor Programming" section of this chapter.

is equivalent to

```
#if !defined(FLAG)
. C Source code ..
#endif
```

Another simple but effective use of conditional directives is for temporarily commenting out a section of C source code. For example, the following block would instruct the preprocessor to remove all C code between the **#if** and **#endif** directives:

```
#if 0
.. C source code ..
#endif
```

This is a more effective method of removing source code than introducing a comment, because comments cannot be nested.

Restricted Constant Expressions

An integral constant expression in C must evaluate to an integer constant. Integral constant expressions acceptable to the C compiler permit integer, character, floating-point, and enumerated data objects; type casts; **sizeof** expressions; and all C unary, binary, and ternary operators (see Chapter 12) except assignment, increment, decrement, function call, the comma, and in most situations, address-of.

The C preprocessor, however, accepts only restricted integral constant expressions and further eliminates floating-point constants, enumeration constants, type casts, and **sizeof** expressions, but it permits the preprocessor **defined** operator (discussed in the section that follows). Explicitly identify **long** integer constants with the **l** or **L** suffix and **unsigned** integers with **u** or **U**. The defaults are **signed** and type **int**. Also remember that decimal, octal, and hexadecimal numbers may be used. For details refer to Chapter 7. When working with bit operators, it is preferable to use **unsigned** numbers.

Essentially, preprocessor-restricted constant expressions may contain only integer and character constants, the **defined** operator, and all C operators except assignment, increment, decrement, function call, comma, and the address-of operators.

These restrictions are necessary because the preprocessor is only substituting source-code text and cannot rely upon any expression that depends upon compilation and run-time evaluation. Similarly, identifier names utilized in such expressions must be macros. If an identifier used is not a defined macro, the preprocessor assumes an integer value of zero (false). Test for the presence of all macro references, and avoid relying upon this default assigment to zero. If we assume the following macro definitions:

```
#define IFLAG 7U       /* or (unsigned int) 7 */
#define MAXVAL 40000L  /* or (unsigned long) 40000 */
#define CFLAG 'D'
```

then the following restricted constant expressions would be evaluated as shown:

```
ZZZZZ == 1                  /* yields 0 no defn */
IFLAG != 7u                 /* yields 0 or false */
IFLAG % 3 == 1              /* yields 1 or true */
(MAXVAL * 2) > 32000L       /* yields 1 or true */
((IFLAG & 0x05) == 5u)      /* yields 1 or true */
((CFLAG & 0x20) >> 5 == 1u) /* yields 0 or false */
```

Note that parentheses may be freely used to control the order of evaluation of expressions involving multiple operators. The first three examples demonstrate a simple comparison, modulus arithmetic, and a **long** data type. The last two examples use the bit operators **&** (bitwise AND, not address-of) and **>>** (bit shift right). The first bit example above tests whether bit 0 and bit 2 are on; the second tests whether an alphabetic character is lower- or uppercase. Unlike the NMAKE utility, C constant expressions cannot use the equality (==) and inequality (!=) operators to compare strings ("string1" == "string2"). In spite of these restrictions, we can still construct constant expressions for the C preprocessor that are both powerful and complex.

Directive-Only Operators

The directive operators are used with and understood by the preprocessor only and are not among the Standard C operators discussed in Chapter 12.

The **#** "string-forming" operator is used only in preprocessor function-like macro expressions (with arguments), and substitutes a string literal for a formal argument by constructing a corresponding string using double quotes ("*formal argument*"). Consider the following example using the **system()** function to produce a directory listing of all files in the current path ending in **ext** with **stdout** redirected to **dev**:

```
#define DIR(ext,dev)   system("DIR *" #ext " >" #dev)

DIR(.obj,dir.lst);  /* system("DIR *.obj >dir.lst"); */
DIR(.c,PRN);        /* system("DIR *.c >PRN"); */
DIR(.ext,dev.lst);  /* system("DIR *.ext >dev.lst"); */
```

Formal arguments appearing in string literals and character constants are never substituted, but are instead treated literally. The example

```
DIR(.ext,"dev");     /* system("DIR *.ext >"dev");    */
```

would literally be expanded as shown and result in a DOS *file creation error,* because the double quotes are not permitted in DOS filenames. Note that in each example above, the **#** operator is also responsible for combining adjacent string literals if separated by white space.

For another example of the use of the **#** operator, see the **assert()** macro in Chapter 29 or examine the **<assert.h>** header file.

The **##** "token-pasting" operator is used with preprocessor object-like and function-like macro expressions to combine adjacent tokens before macro substitution occurs. The following example demonstrates how "token-pasting," formal argument substitution, and "string-forming" are performed:

```
#define one _1
#define two _2
#define _1_2 Twelve
#define _2_1 Twenty-One

#define P4(y) #y
#define P3(x) printf("%s\n",P4(x))
#define P2(word1,word2) P3(word1 ## word2)
#define PRINTF(word1,word2) P2(word1,word2)

PRINTF(one,two);    /* prints Twelve */
PRINTF(two,one);    /* prints Twenty-One */
```

The macro substitution and expansion is performed as follows:

```
PRINTF(two,one);

→ P2(_2,_1);
→ P3(_2_1);
→ printf("%s\n",P4(_2_1));
→ printf("%s\n","Twenty-One");
→ Twenty-One
```

Note that had the macro **_2_1** been defined as **Twenty-one**, and not **Twenty-One**, macro substitution would have made the final result **Twenty-_1**.

The non-Standard, Microsoft-specific **#@** "character-forming" operator is a companion to the **#** operator; rather than forming a string from a function-like actual argument, it forms a character constant. For example, the function-like macro definition shown below:

```
#define charit(x)  #@x
```

if used in the following manner:

```
char ch = charit(\n);
```

would produce this substitution:

```
char ch = '\n';
```

The **defined** operator is used only to create preprocessor-restricted constant expressions that test whether a macro exists or not. This operator supplements the **#ifdef** and **#ifndef** directives by permitting macro testing in the restricted constant expressions used by **#if** and **#elif**. For example, if **macro** were currently defined, the following tests would have the effects noted:

```
#if  defined(macro)        /* yields 1 or true */
#if !defined(macro)        /* yields 0 or false */
#ifdef  macro              /* yields 1 or true */
#ifndef macro              /* yields 0 or false */
```

Otherwise, if **macro** were not currently defined, the results would be as follows:

```
#if  defined(macro)        /* yields 0 or false */
#if !defined(macro)        /* yields 1 or true */
#ifdef  macro              /* yields 0 or false */
#ifndef macro              /* yields 1 or true */
```

The **defined(macro)** syntax shown above may also be expressed as **defined macro** without the parentheses.

Unlike **#ifdef** and **#ifndef**, the **defined** operator may be used in compound expressions involving the logical operators **&&** (AND) and **||** (OR) to combine macro testing and integer expressions. In the example

```
#if defined NDEBUG && ( (T3 == 'Y') || (T3 == 'N') )
#    if (T3 == 'Y')
     .
     .
     .
#    else
     .
     .
     .
#    endif
#else
#    error NDEBUG or T3 macro invalid
#endif
```

note that macro **T3** should have been defined as a character constant either from the command line or with a **#define** directive such as:

```
/DT3='Y'        /* command-line macro definition  */
#define T3 'Y'   /* directive macro definition     */
```

With the C preprocessor, character constant comparisons are permitted because they are compatible with data type **unsigned int**; however, string constants may not be compared using the **==** (equality) or **!=** (inequality) operators, as permitted with the NMAKE utility. Strings in C may only be compared using the appropriate run-time library functions.

PREPROCESSOR PROGRAMMING EXAMPLES

This section of the chapter is intended to augment the explanation and examples shown thus far and to highlight certain key topics concerning the use of the preprocessor. We will examine the compiler options that control intermediate (.I) file production, the issue of null pointers, and the questions of portability and the use of the predefined macros and identifiers available with Microsoft's compilers.

Lastly, a powerful set of code-timing macros will be developed. You can use **START()** and **STOP** to evaluate alternative coding schemes. They have been used to derive the performance comparisons and coding recommendations found throughout this book.

Intermediate (.I) Files

The preprocessor intermediate file is controlled by using compiler options available to the QC, QCL, PWB, and CL compilers. Intermediate files are useful for debugging preprocessor directive programming and for porting C source code. Four compiler options control the preprocessor:

/E	Direct (.I) to STDOUT with **#line** directives.
/P	Direct (.I) to FILE.I for source code FILE.C; no **#line** directives.
/EP	Direct (.I) to STDOUT and FILE.I with **#line** directives; combines the effects of **/E** and **/P**.
/C	Preserve comments; only valid with **/E**, **/P**, and **/EP**.

Each option suppresses compilation and creates no object (.OBJ) or listing (.LST) files. It is not necessary then to use the compiler option **/c** (compile only, no link) when these preprocessor options are specified.

The **/E** option preserves the line number references to the original C source-code file in any subsequent compiler warnings or errors. This is helpful for debugging.

When porting .I files, it is best to use only options **/C** and **/P**, since the source-code file should appear intact and unencumbered with any prior source-code **#line** directive references.

Remember that if the **/E** option is used, command-line redirection (**>** or **>>**) can be used to reroute **STDOUT** to a printer, or perhaps another file whose name does not have to conform with the corresponding FILE.I naming convention used by option **/P**.

NULL *Pointer Example*

The topic of null pointers is most closely linked with the issue of compiler memory model selection and the dynamic allocation of memory using the **malloc()** family of C run-time library functions. By convention, a null pointer represents a memory address that is reserved for use as the sentinel value of an invalid memory address. Standard C permits a null pointer value to be implementation-defined but defines the macro **NULL** as the standard representation of a null pointer. A null pointer memory location, although addressable, should therefore logically never be assigned value or accessed using indirection.

Microsoft has chosen to implement null pointers by introducing a **NULL** segment at the lowest assignable data memory address. This reserved area of memory is therefore not available for assignment to a program variable. Figures 2.21 through 2.26 depict the location of the **NULL** segment.

The **NULL** segment is initialized to zero at the start of every C program, and if compiler option **/Zr** is used, immediate detection of assignment to this memory location is made and the program is terminated; otherwise, such assignments are only detected when a program terminates. It should be clear that address references to **NULL** are unwanted outside the normal address bounds of all programs, and although programs may operate with **NULL** pointer references and assignments, such conditions are normally indicative of a programming error.

Standard C defines **NULL** in the following C header files: **locale.h**, **stddef.h**, **stdio.h**, **stdlib.h**, and **time.h**. A typical definition is as follows:

```
#ifndef NULL
#if (_MSC_VER >= 600)
#define NULL ((void *)0)
#if (defined M_I86SM || defined M_I86MM)
#    define   NULL          0
#elif (defined M_I86CM || defined M_I86LM || defined M_I86HM)
#    define   NULL          0L
#endif
#endif
```

The predefined macro **_MSC_VER** (see Table 5.4) differentiates how **NULL** is defined for C compiler versions 6.0 and later. Now, **NULL** is uniformly defined

```
#define NULL ((void *)0)
```

as a cast of the zero (octal) to a pointer to type **void**; for older Microsoft compilers (5.1 and earlier), **NULL** was defined differently depending upon the memory model employed. The predefined Microsoft identifiers in the **M_I86mM** family (see Table 5.4) reflect the corresponding memory model compiler option in effect (/AT, /AS, /AM, /AC, /AL, and /AH). The Small and Medium models define **NULL** as

```
#define NULL 0
```

which is an integer constant of data type **int** corresponding to 16 bits, or a **_near** address or pointer. The Compact, Large, and Huge models define **NULL** as

```
#define NULL 0L
```

which is an integer constant of data type **long** corresponding to 32 bits, or a **_far** or **_huge** pointer.

With the introduction of **_based** pointer types with Microsoft version 6.0, two additional macros are defined in **<malloc.h>** that establish a null segment address, **_NULLSEG**, and the maximum **_based** pointer off-set value, **_NULLOFF** as follows:

```
#if (_MSC_VER >= 600)
#define _NULLSEG  ((_segment)0)
#define _NULLOFF  ((void _based(void) *)0xffff)
#endif
```

All functions in the C run-time library that dynamically allocate memory to the Near or Far heap rely upon the convention of returning a **NULL** pointer, rather than a valid starting memory address for the allocation, if the memory allocation attempt failed. The program must then test whether a **NULL** pointer has been returned and handle the error condition appropriately. For example:

```
#include <stdlib.h>
 .
 .
 .
#define NDBL 1000
 .
 .
 .
double *dptr;
 .
 .
```

```
/* allocate NDBL doubles */
dptr = (double *) malloc(NDBL*sizeof(double));
if (dptr == NULL)
    printf("Out of memory\n");
    exit(1); /* terminate this process */
else
    printf("NDBL doubles allocated OK\n");
```

A failure to provide the level of checking and error handling shown above for **dptr** is what generally leads to the generation of NULL pointer assignments and the inadvertent use of a NULL pointer.

Other run-time functions besides **malloc()** utilize a return value of null. For example, the common task of opening a stream file variable for I/O returns a **NULL** pointer if the **fopen()** request failed.

```
#include <stdio.h>
.
.
.
FILE *myfile;
.
.
.
if ((myfile = fopen("myfile.c","w")) == NULL)
    printf("myfile.c open failed\n");
    /* display message, but do not terminate */
else
    printf("myfile.c open for writing\n");
```

Subsequent use of the **FILE** pointer **myfile** would attempt to write to the **NULL** segment.

Additional complexity arises when mixed-memory model programming is employed using a compiler earlier than 6.0. In these versions the non-Standard Microsoft keywords **_near**, **_far**, and **_huge** are used to access memory addresses from incompatible memory model types. In such situations, extreme care must be taken, because the memory model in effect controls the macro assignment of **NULL**. The keyword **_near** must be used with a **#define NULL 0** directive, while keywords **_far** and **_huge** require the directive **#define NULL 0L**. For more details about **NULL** pointers, see Chapter 10.

Portability Example

The preprocessor is an invaluable tool for creating programs which are portable or capable of being easily moved to another hardware configuration, operating system, or compiler environment. In the **NULL** pointer example above, the predefined identifiers in the family M_I86*m*M were tested to establish which representation of **NULL** should be used based upon the memory model employed.

The standard header files (.H) make heavy use of other predefined identifiers, such as those listed in Table 5.4. For example, **NO_EXT_KEYS** is commonly used as follows to introduce the Microsoft keywords **_cdecl** and **_near** or to eliminate them by defining them as null strings:

```
#ifndef NO_EXT_KEYS        /* extensions enabled  */
#       define _CDECL _cdecl
#       define _NEAR  _near
#else                      /* extensions disabled */
#       define _CDECL
#       define _NEAR
#endif
```

The **_CHAR_UNSIGNED** identifier is also used to define data type limits:

```
#ifndef _CHAR_UNSIGNED     /* signed characters */
#       define CHAR_MAX  127
#       define CHAR_MIN -127
#else                      /* unsigned characters */
#       define CHAR_MAX  255
#       define CHAR_MIN  0
#endif
```

All the predefined identifiers shown in Table 5.4 may be removed by either using the **/U***name* or **/u** compiler options. These macros may not be removed using the **#undef** directive.

When creating project-specific header files, or simply trying to write source programs that keep nonportable code isolated, use the conditional compilation features of the preprocessor. Construct appropriate restricted constant expression tests based upon predefined macros or project-specific macros you create to conditionally include, exclude, or redefine the nonportable portions of your source code.

Timing Source-Code Example

We are inundated daily with software advertising that claims to solve every software developer's performance problem. Whether it be expressed in MHz, KB, MB, GB, or nanoseconds, the message is loud and clear—buy the solution to your performance problems. The battleground today has moved from hardware to software. What for years were simply "compilers" are now "optimizing compilers"; what was once "intelligence" is now "artificial intelligence."

The underlying message being conveyed is that productive programmers should spend less time trying to write efficient code and should instead rely upon hardware and software products to recoup any resulting program inefficiency. That is not necessarily the case.

This section presents a simple tool for measuring source-code performance using the preprocessor. Granted, this measurement tool is only accurate within about 0.05 sec (about 18.5 clock ticks/second), but only relative accuracy is of concern here. The tool is intended only to compare alternative C source-coding techniques and to measure which alternative is faster. As you will see throughout this book, even a simple measurement tool such as this will permit us to draw some interesting conclusions. Set aside high-tech for a moment, and put a simple stopwatch to work.

For starters, the project-specific header file **"timer.h"** was created to encapsulate everything needed by our **START(description)** and **STOP** macros. Source code developed using these two macros will generate the timing source code if the object-like macro **TIMER** is defined and the **"timer.h"** header file is included; otherwise, the source-code references will be eliminated. Figure 5.1 lists the complete contents of the **"timer.h"** header file.

All timing relies upon the nonstandard DOS header file **<time.h>** and run-time function **clock()**, which returns a measure of elapsed time in clock-ticks. All messages are directed to **stdout** so that command-line redirection can be used to reroute the timing messages. Also note the use of the backslash (\) continuation character.

A typical C source-code file called **ch5e2.c**, which utilizes the **START(description)** and **STOP** macros, is shown in Figure 5.2.

```
/* FILE: ch5e1.h */
/* "timer.h"  DOS project specific header file for using the
**            macros START(desc); STOP;
*/
#if !defined(TIMER_DEFINED)
    #if defined(TIMER)
        #include <stdio.h>
        #include <time.h>
        clock_t  stop_tick, start_tick;
        #define START(desc) fprintf(stdout,"\n\nfor  : %s",#desc);\
            start_tick = clock()
        #define TICKS   (stop_tick - start_tick)
        #define STOP    stop_tick  = clock();\
            fprintf(stdout,"\nstop : %ld\nstart: %ld",\
            stop_tick, start_tick);\
            fprintf(stdout,"\ntime : %7.2lf sec\n",\
            (double)TICKS/(double)CLOCKS_PER_SEC)
        #define TIMER_DEFINED
    #else
        #define START(desc)
        #define STOP
    #endif
#endif
```

FIGURE 5.1: The sample program Ch5e1.h defines the START() and STOP timing macros used throughout this book.

Note that the **(description)** argument of **START** need not be enclosed in double quotes, since it is made into a string by the **#** directive operator in **"timer.h"**. To use this measurement tool, simply surround any section of source code with the macros **START** and **STOP**. Next, control the conditional compilation of a program by invoking any Microsoft compiler with the command-line macro **TIMER**, defined thus:

```
QCL /DTIMER ch5e2.c
```

If the object-like macro **TIMER** is not defined on the command line, all source-code references to **START** and **STOP** will be removed from the source-code file **ch5e2.c**. Look at the unit of translation created both with and without the command-line definition of **TIMER** by using compiler options **/E** and then **/P**.

After **ch5e2.c** was compiled with the Small memory model using options **/qc /Od** on an Intel 80286-based computer, the following printed output resulted when the program was executed as follows from the DOS command line:

```
CH5E2 >PRN

for  : simple loop
stop : 110
start: 0
time : 0.11 sec
for  : register loop
stop : 170
start: 110
time : 0.06 sec
```

```
/* FILE: ch5e2.c        */
#include "timer.h"
int main( void)
{
int i;
register int j;

START(simple loop);
    for (i=0;i<32000;i++);
STOP;

START(register loop);
    for (j=0;j<32000;j++);
STOP;
exit(0);
}
```

FIGURE 5.2: The sample program ch5e2.c. uses the timing macros to evaluate the performance differences that can result by the use of auto and register storage class index variables.

Note that simply changing the definition of an index variable from **int** to **register int** improves the performance of a program like this approximately 45 percent.

We will use this tool for assessing alternative coding techniques throughout this book. You can use it to develop coding techniques that measurably improve the performance of your C programs. You will find that better coding techniques can improve the performance of your programs beyond what faster equipment and optimizing compilers now provide.

Function-Like Macro Side Effects

Finally, consider the devastating *side-effect* weakness of macros in general. Side effects are created when the (**++**) increment or (−−) decrement C operators are used in conjunction with a formal macro argument that is evaluated more than once within the function-like macro expression. When this occurs, the effects of **++** and −− are doubled. Unlike function arguments which are passed by value, function-like macro arguments are substituted as strings. This problem may occur both in project-specific macros and in some macros defined in the Standard C header files (.H). The macro **toupper** is defined in header file **<ctype.h>**, but is also defined as a function in the C run-time library.

Figure 5.3 shows a source-code file called **ch5e3.c**.

Issue the DOS command line

```
QCL ch5e3.c
```

and then execute the program with the DOS command

```
CH5E3 >prn
```

```
/* FILE: ch5e3.c        */
#include <stdio.h>
#include <ctype.h>
#ifdef UNDEF
#    undef toupper
     int _CDECL toupper(int);
#endif

static char str[] = "abcdefghijklmnopqrstuvwxyz";
int main( void)
{
char *ptr = str;
int i, size = sizeof(str);
fprintf(stdout,"before: %s\n",str);
for (i=0; i<size; i++) str[i] = toupper(*ptr++);
fprintf(stdout,"after : %s\n",str);
}
```

FIGURE 5.3: The macro side-effects example ch5e3.c demonstrates the undesirable side-effects that can result from the improper use of function-like macros.

to produce the following output:

```
before: abcdefghijklmnopqrstuvwxyz
after : BDFHJLNPRTVXZ
```

Obviously, this was not the intended result. By recompiling **ch5e3.c** using a command-line macro definition for UNDEF, we can remove the macro definition for **toupper** and effectively replace it with a function call to **toupper()** from the C run-time library. Using the DOS command line

```
QCL /DUNDEF macro.c
```

to compile **ch5e3.c** in this fashion and executing the program with the DOS command

```
MACRO >prn
```

produced the following output:

```
before: abcdefghijklmnopqrstuvwxyz
after : ABCDEFGHIJKLMNOPQRSTUVWXYZ
```

This is the output originally intended.

This side-effect problem with **toupper** is typical of many function-like macros. The following statements in **<ctype.h>** were responsible for generating the incorrect results:

```
#define toupper(_c)   ((islower(_c)) ? _toupper(_c) : (_c))
#define islower(_c)   ((_ctype+1)[_c] & _LOWER)
#define _LOWER        0x2
#define _toupper(_c)  ((_c)-'a'+'A' )
```

In the statements above, each reference to **(_c)** is replaced by the argument ***p++**. C assigns the indirection operator (*****) higher precedence than incrementation (**++**). This expression can be interpreted to mean "Use the contents of the address pointed to by **p**, then increment the address **p** by one."

The macro **toupper** is expanded by the preprocessor to

```
((islower(*p++)) ? _toupper(*p++) : (*p++))
```

and then to

```
((((_ctype+1)[*p++] & 0x2)) ? ((*p++)-'a'+'A') : (*p++))
```

The ternary expression (**?:**) evaluates **((_ctype+1)[*p++] & 0x2)** first, which yields a value of true (1), but **p** now points to letter 'b' at position [1]. Because the result is true, the expression **((*p++)-'a'+'A')** must be evaluated to complete the macro. ***p** is now the character b; this is transformed to B, and the address of **p** is again incremented to point to position [3]. Repeating the macro call for **toupper** in the next **for** loop sets up the result D, then F as shown above. The **after :** string is terminated normally, because the last character processed is \0 or null, which is not a lowercase letter, therefore the ternary operator (***p++**) is performed, which assigns the null character to position [13].

Simply put, do not use the side-effect increment and decrement unary operators with formal macro arguments. If these operators must be used, be certain that the corresponding macro performs only one substitution or use an **#undef** statement to force the use of a C function instead.

Header Files

Header Files

Little mention of either header files or macros is made in Kernighan and Ritchie's (K&R) *The C Programming Language* (1978); however, a review of the present ANSI Standard C specification reveals a lengthy discussion of both header files and macro definitions. Clearly the standardization committee, in "codifying common existing practice," has documented the evolution of C since K&R. Where no header files were formally specified by K&R, today Standard C has adopted 15 standard headers. Where only the macros **EOF**, **FILE**, and **NULL** were mentioned by K&R, provision for hundreds of macros and reserved identifiers is made today.

With the proliferation of global variables, type definitions, structure and union tags, object- and function-like macros, and function prototypes in C, it is more important than ever to understand the purpose and content of each header file. The Microsoft C compiler installation procedures (described in Chapter 2) copy both Standard C and Microsoft-specific header files into a standard path defined by the environment variable INCLUDE. The non-Standard Microsoft headers supplement the Standard C headers and support the use of Microsoft's DOS.

The sections that follow examine the format common to all header files, discuss old- and new-style function prototype descriptions, examine each Standard C and Microsoft header file, and offer suggestions for developing project-specific headers.

CONSTRUCTING HEADER FILES

Since K&R, certain conventions have emerged in common practice regarding header-file construction:

- Header filenames have been restricted to six characters or less for maximum operating system, compiler, and linker compatibility.
- Header files normally do not include other header files.
- They declare objects but normally do not define (allocate storage for) them.
- Object-like macro names are declared in uppercase to make them visually distinct in source-code listings.
- Programmers have tried to avoid repeating declarations found in other header files.

These header-file conventions have not been formalized in Standard C, but remain as guidelines. However, Standard C does now mandate that all run-time library functions be declared in header files to support the expanded role of function prototyping. Function prototypes are new to Standard C and are included to provide a form of argument checking. Prototype declarations now permit the C compiler to check that the proper number and type of arguments are supplied whenever a function is invoked (see the "Function Prototypes" section that follows).

Standard C also endorses the concept of *idempotence,* in which header files may be included many times and in any order without causing any harmful side-effects. Both the Standard and Microsoft header files embody this concept, and user-defined files should, also. The use of conditional compilation preprocessor directives for this purpose is strongly encouraged (see **timer.h** in Chapter 5.)

Standard C also now mandates that run-time library function names be reserved, together with the other external (global) name categories described earlier in Table 4.8. This practice is necessary to minimize the potential for future naming conflicts that may arise between the C compiler software itself and other libraries of C functions, and C application programs that you develop. In short, to remain in conformance with Standard C, project-specific headers and your C source code must now be constructed more carefully.

The contents of each header file can be grouped into the following six categories, as you'll see in the tables that form the greater part of this chapter: global variables, type definitions, structure and union declarations, object-like macros, function-like macros, and function prototypes.

A typical Standard C and non-Standard Microsoft global variable declaration (see Appendix C) would appear as

```
extern volatile int errno;        /* Standard */
extern long double _LHUGE;        /* non-Standard */
```

A typical Standard C and non-Standard Microsoft type definition (see Appendix D) would appear as

```
typedef unsigned int size_t;      /* Standard */
typedef int (* onexit_t)();       /* non-Standard */
```

A typical Standard C and non-Standard Microsoft structure and union declaration (see Appendix E) would appear as

```
typedef struct _div_t {           /* Standard */
    int quot;
    int rem;
    } div_t;
```

```
struct utimbuf {                    /* non-Standard */
    time_t actime;
    time_t modtime;
    };
```

A typical Standard C and non-Standard Microsoft object-like macro declaration would appear as

```
#define EOF (-1)          /* Standard */
#define _NFILE 20         /* non-Standard */
```

A typical Standard C and non-Standard Microsoft function-like macro declaration would appear as

```
#define feof(_stream)   ((_stream)->_flag & _IOEOF) /* Standard */

#define FP_SEG(fp)       (*((unsigned _far *)&(fp)+1)) /*non-Standard */
```

A typical Standard C and non-Standard Microsoft function prototype declaration would appear as

```
int printf(const char *, ...);     /* Standard */
FILE * _fsopen(const char *, ...); /* non-Standard */
```

You will notice that sometimes both function-like macros and function prototypes are defined within the same header file. For example, **<stdio.h>** contains both of these:

```
/* function-like macro */
#define fileno(_stream)   ((int)(unsigned char)(_stream)->_file)
/* function prototype */
int fileno( FILE *);
```

Every run-time library function that has an equivalent macro is so noted in the reference entries in Parts 6 and 7. Recall from Chapter 5 that, for the example just noted, unless you explicitly issue the directive **#undef fileno** the preprocessor will substitute whatever string is specified in the function-like macro, thereby preventing the run-time library function from being invoked. Also recall that when function-like macros are used, care must be taken not to use the side-effect auto-increment and decrement operators with the arguments of function-like macros that are multiply substituted.

FUNCTION PROTOTYPES

Standard C now requires that prototypes be declared for all functions. Functions that are designed to pass and return no values use the new data type **void**; all argument and return types are passed as declared and not automatically promoted, as in the past, to type **int** and **double**; and functions with a variable number of arguments now use the new ellipsis (...) punctuator. For a complete discussion of function prototypes, refer to Chapter 14.

The older K&R-style function declarations are still supported but have been designated as obsolete in Standard C and will eventually be eliminated. This style provided no formal way to declare that a function had no arguments or return values, to declare how many arguments or the data type of each argument, or to handle functions with a variable number of arguments. Function declarations simply declared the return type of the function as follows:

```
long function1();      /* long return type */
int * function2();     /* pointer to int return type */
char * function3();    /* pointer to char return type */
```

K&R style also relied upon the *widening* concept for arguments, whereby all **float** arguments were promoted to **double**, and all **char** arguments were promoted to **int**. Return values were understood to be **int**, unless otherwise specified, and if **float** or **char** return values were used, they in turn were widened to **double** and **int**, respectively.

For the function prototypes declared in the Standard C and Microsoft-specific header files, see the chapters noted in the tables that follow. The run-time library index that appears on the inside back cover will also direct you to specific functions.

STANDARD C HEADER FILES

Standard C has formally adopted the following 15 header files. These headers and the Standard C (not Microsoft) declarations contained therein will be provided by all conforming compilers in the future.

<assert.h>	Table 6.1	**assert** debugging macro
<ctype.h>	Table 6.2	Character classification
<errno.h>	Table 6.3	**errno** variable definitions
<float.h>	Table 6.4	Constants for math functions
<limits.h>	Table 6.5	Properties of **char** and **int** types
<locale.h>	Table 6.6	Regional and cultural conventions
<math.h>	Table 6.7	Common mathematical functions

`<setjmp.h>`	Table 6.8	Nonlocal **goto** between functions
`<signal.h>`	Table 6.9	Asynchronous interrupt handling
`<stdarg.h>`	Table 6.10	Variable length argument lists
`<stddef.h>`	Table 6.11	Common data types and values
`<stdio.h>`	Table 6.12	Standard input and output
`<stdlib.h>`	Table 6.13	Allocation, sort, search
`<string.h>`	Table 6.14	Manipulating characters and strings
`<time.h>`	Table 6.15	Time and date management

For maximum portability, use the standard headers defined above and only the Standard C items defined within them. Avoid duplicating the definition of items in these headers when you construct project-specific headers, and avoid modifying the contents of standard header files altogether.

`<assert.h>`

Complete examples and discussion of the **assert()** function-like macro and the **_assert()** run-time library function can be found in Chapter 29. Note that the **NDEBUG** object-like macro is to be user-defined and is not defined in the **<assert.h>** header file.

The declaration of the **NDEBUG** (no debugging) macro disables the effect of any C source code assertions. Every assertion (test) must represent integral constant expressions (discussed in Chapter 5). If an assertion is found to be false, the **assert()** macro sends an error message to standard error output (**stderr**), not standard output (**stdout**), and then calls function **abort()**. For example, the source-code fragment

```
i = 1000;
assert(i <= 100);
```

would result in an assertion error causing the following **stderr** output to be generated:

```
Assertion failed: i <= 100, file xxxxx.c, line nn
Abnormal program termination
```

where file *xxxxx*.c is the name of the source-code file containing the error and *nn* is the associated line number. Remember that run-time function **abort()** actually displays the message *Abnormal program termination*, calls process function **raise(SIGABRT)**, and then returns to the parent process or operating system. Unlike function **exit()**, **abort()** does not flush stream buffers or perform **atexit()** or **onexit()** processing (see Chapters 15 and 25). Redirection of **stderr** output cannot be performed using DOS command-line redirection, but can be accomplished using the **dup2()** function described in Chapter 18.

Table 6.1 lists the contents of this file.

TABLE 6.1: <assert.h>

PURPOSE: This Standard C header file defines the **assert** function-like macro, which is helpful in debugging source-code logic. Defining the **NDEBUG** macro (usually on the command-line) instructs the preprocessor to remove all assertion logic from the source code.

CATEGORY	IDENTIFIER	M/S*	DESCRIPTION
Object-like Macros	NDEBUG	S	User-defined; define to turn off assertions.
Function-like Macro	*assert(test)*	S	Assertion debugging macro.
Function Prototypes	See Ch. 25.		

* M = Microsoft-specific (☐ ANSI); S = Standard C (■ ANSI)

<ctype.h>

The character testing (**isxx()**) and conversion (**toxx()**) function-like macros and function prototypes found in **<ctype.h>** rely upon a non-Standard Microsoft global character array called **_ctype[]**. Using the object-like macro bit masks and the bit operators **&** (bitwise AND) and **|** (bitwise OR) included in **<ctype.h>**, the **isxx()** routines return a value of either 0 (false) or 1 (true). The **toxx()** routines either perform the desired character conversion or do nothing. Standard C reserves the identifiers beginning with **is[a-z]** and **to[a-z]** for possible future use. Do not create project-specific macros or functions that begin with these character sequences.

A typical use of an **isxx()** routine is shown in the following source-code fragment:

```
#include <ctype.h>
char ch = 'h';
if (!isxdigit(ch)) exit(99);
```

The routine **isxdigit()** tests whether **ch** is a valid hexadecimal character (0–9, a–f, or A–F). Obviously, the return value of **isxdigit()** is 0 (false). The sense of this IF-test is reversed by the **!** (NOT) operator to yield true (1). The call to the run-time function **exit()** terminates the program normally, then returns status code 99 to the parent process (calling program or operating system).

A typical use of a *toxx()* routine is shown in the following source-code fragment:

```
#include <stdio.h>
#include <ctype.h>
char ch = 'h';
printf("\nch = %c",toupper(ch));
```

The routine **toupper()** in this case would convert the lowercase h character to uppercase H. The standard **printf()** run-time output function would display the message *"ch = H"* to **stdout** on a new line. Note that the **<stdio.h>** header file is included to provide the proper function prototype for **printf()**, which accommodates a variable number of arguments (see **<stdarg.h>** later in this chapter). Note that all **<ctype.h>** routines are applicable regardless of the particular locale that may be in effect. For complete coverage of the functions found in **<ctype.h>**, see Chapter 20.

Table 6.2 lists the contents of this file.

<errno.h>

This header file was created for Standard C. System error codes historically have begun with **E**, and Standard C has reserved names beginning either with **E[A–Z]** and **E[0–9]** for possible future use. Only **EDOM** and **ERANGE** are required by Standard C; however, avoid creating any project-specific identifiers that conflict with these reserved names.

The global variable **errno** reflects the value last assigned by a run-time library function. It is best to set **errno** to **EZERO** (or 0), call one run-time function, and immediately test the value of **errno** again. The standard run-time function **perror()** can be used to display the appropriate text message associated with the **errno** error code value. For a complete example of using **<errno.h>**, refer to Chapter 29.

Table 6.3 lists the contents of this file.

TABLE 6.2: <ctype.h>

PURPOSE: This Standard C header file declares macros and functions that are useful in classifying and mapping characters of the target character set.

CATEGORY	IDENTIFIER	M/S*	DESCRIPTION
Global Variables	_ctype[]	M	Character set control array; does not contain characters.
Object-like Macros	_BLANK	M	Mask _ctype for space char.
	_CONTROL	M	Mask _ctype for control.
	_DIGIT	M	Mask _ctype for digit[0-9].
	_HEX	M	Mask _ctype for hexadecimal.
	_LOWER	M	Mask _ctype for lowercase.
	_PUNCT	M	Mask _ctype for punctuation.
	_SPACE	M	Mask _ctype for white space.
	_UPPER	M	Mask _ctype for uppercase.
Function-like Macros	isalnum(ch)	S	Alphanumeric?
	isalpha(ch)	S	Alphabetic?
	isascii(ch)	M	ASCII (0x00–0x7f)?
	iscntrl(ch)	S	Control (0x00–0x1f or 0x7f)?
	iscsym(ch)	M	isalnum() or underscore?
	iscsymf(ch)	M	isalpha() or underscore?
	isdigit(ch)	S	Numeric?
	isgraph(ch)	S	Printable (0x21–0x7E)?
	islower(ch)	S	Lowercase?
	isprint(ch)	S	Printable (0x20–0x7E)?
	ispunct(ch)	S	Punctuation?
	isspace(ch)	S	White space (0x09–0x0d or 0x20)?
	isupper(ch)	S	Uppercase?
	isxdigit(ch)	S	Hexadecimal digit?
	toascii(ch)	M	Convert to ASCII.
	tolower(ch)	S	Convert to lowercase if OK.
	_tolower(ch)	M	Convert to lowercase.
	toupper(ch)	S	Convert to uppercase if OK.
	_toupper(ch)	M	Convert to uppercase.
Function Prototypes	See Ch. 20.		

* M = Microsoft-specific (☐ ANSI); S = Standard C (■ ANSI)

TABLE 6.3: <errno.h>

PURPOSE: This Standard C header file contains a set of error codes (E...) that may be used to test whether a library function has assigned the value of variable **errno**.

CATEGORY	IDENTIFIER	M/S*	DESCRIPTION
Global Variables	errno	S	Current system error number.
Object-like Macros	EACCES	M	Permission denied.
	EAGAIN	M	No more processes.
	EBADF	M	Bad file number.
	EBUSY	M	Mount device busy.
	ECHILD	M	No children.
	EDEADLOCK	M	Resource deadlock would occur.
	EDOM	S	Math argument.
	EEXIST	M	File exists.
	EFAULT	M	Bad address.
	EFBIG	M	File too large.
	EINTR	M	Interrupted system call.
	EINVAL	M	Invalid argument.
	EIO	M	I/O error.
	EISDIR	M	Is a directory.
	EMFILE	M	Too many open files.
	EMLINK	M	Too many links.
	ENFILE	M	Too many open files.
	ENODEV	M	No such device.
	ENOENT	M	No such file or directory.
	ENOEXEC	M	Exec format error.
	ENOMEM	M	Not enough memory.
	ENOSPC	M	No space left on device.
	ENOTBLK	M	Block device required.
	ENOTDIR	M	Not a directory.
	ENOTTY	M	Not a typewriter.
	ENXIO	M	No such device or address.
	EPERM	M	Not owner.
	EPIPE	M	Broken pipe.
	ERANGE	S	Result too large.
	EROFS	M	Read-only file system.
	ESPIPE	M	Illegal seek.

TABLE 6.3: <errno.h> (continued)

CATEGORY	IDENTIFIER	M/S*	DESCRIPTION
Object-like Macros (cont.)	ESRCH	M	No such process.
	ETXTBSY	M	Text file busy.
	EUCLEAN	M	Error 35.
	EXDEV	M	Cross-device link.
	EZERO	M	Error 0.
	E2BIG	M	Argument list too long.
* M = Microsoft-specific (☐ ANSI); S = Standard C (■ ANSI)			

`<float.h>`

This header file was created for Standard C as an aide in writing restricted constant expressions, and hence more portable source code, with the preprocessor. Object-like macros prefixed with **FLT_** correspond with data type **float**, **DBL_** with type **double**, and **LDBL_** with **long double**. The Microsoft compilers provide an extensive set of floating-point coprocessor macros, but they are not a part of Standard C.

Standard C also defines a set of allowable constants for the object-like macros **DBL_ROUNDS**, **FLT_ROUNDS**, and **LDBL_ROUNDS** which control rounding:

−1	indeterminable
0	round toward zero
1	round to nearest (default value)
2	round toward positive infinity
3	round toward negative infinity

Only floating-point representations are covered by **`<float.h>`**. Integer representations are covered in header file **`<limits.h>`**. Also refer to the related **`<math.h>`** header file, which makes extensive use of the **float**, **double**, and **long double** data types.

Table 6.4 lists the contents of this file.

`<limits.h>`

This header file was also created for Standard C to help programmers write restricted constant expressions, and thereby use directive features of the preprocessor to write portable source code.

TABLE 6.4: <float.h>

PURPOSE: This Standard C header file establishes the properties of floating-point type representations and the various 80*x*87 coprocessor control and return values.

CATEGORY	IDENTIFIER	M/S*	DESCRIPTION
Object-Like Macros	CW_DEFAULT	M	80*x*87 default control word.
	DBL_DIG	S	Decimal digits of precision.
	DBL_EPSILON	S	1.0 + DBL_EPSILON != 1.0.
	DBL_MANT_DIG	S	Bits in mantissa.
	DBL_MAX	S	Maximum value.
	DBL_MAX_10_EXP	S	Maximum decimal exponent.
	DBL_MAX_EXP	S	Maximum binary exponent.
	DBL_MIN	S	Minimum positive value.
	DBL_MIN_10_EXP	S	Minimum decimal exponent.
	DBL_MIN_EXP	S	Minimum binary exponent.
	DBL_RADIX	M	Exponent radix.
	DBL_ROUNDS	M	Addition rounding: near.
	EM_DENORMAL	M	80*x*87 denormal exception mask.
	EM_INEXACT	M	80*x*87 inexact exception mask.
	EM_INVALID	M	80*x*87 invalid exception mask.
	EM_OVERFLOW	M	80*x*87 overflow exception mask.
	EM_UNDERFLOW	M	80*x*87 underflow exception mask.
	EM_ZERODIVIDE	M	80*x*87 zero divide exception mask.
	FLT_DIG	S	Decimal digits of precision.
	FLT_EPSILON	S	1.0 + FLT_EPSILON != 1.0.
	FLT_GUARD	M	Undocumented.
	FLT_MANT_DIG	S	Bits in mantissa.
	FLT_MAX	S	Maximum value.
	FLT_MAX_10_EXP	S	Maximum decimal exponent.
	FLT_MAX_EXP	S	Maximum binary exponent.
	FLT_MIN	S	Minimum positive value.
	FLT_MIN_10_EXP	S	Minimum decimal exponent.
	FLT_MIN_EXP	S	Minimum binary exponent.

TABLE 6.4: <float.h> (continued)

CATEGORY	IDENTIFIER	M/S*	DESCRIPTION
Object-Like Macros (cont.)	FLT_NORMALIZE	M	Undocumented.
	FLT_RADIX	S	Exponent radix.
	FLT_ROUNDS	S	Addition rounding: near.
	FPE_DENORMAL	M	80x87 denormal exception.
	FPE_EXPLICITGEN	M	80x87 raise(SIGFPE) exception.
	FPE_INEXACT	M	80x87 inexact exception.
	FPE_INVALID	M	80x87 invalid exception.
	FPE_OVERFLOW	M	80x87 overflow exception.
	FPE_SQRTNEG	M	80x87 negative square root exception.
	FPE_STACKOVERFLOW	M	80x87 stack overflow exception.
	FPE_STACKUNDERFLOW	M	80x87 stack underflow exception.
	FPE_UNDERFLOW	M	80x87 underflow exception.
	FPE_UNEMULATED	M	80x87 unemulated exception.
	FPE_ZERODIVIDE	M	80x87 zero divide exception.
	IC_AFFINE	M	80x87 affine infinity control.
	IC_PROJECTIVE	M	80x87 projective infinity control.
	LDBL_DIG	S	Decimal digits of precision.
	LDBL_EPSILON	S	1.0 + LDBL_EPSILON != 1.0.
	LDBL_MANT_DIG	S	Bits in mantissa.
	LDBL_MAX	S	Maximum value.
	LDBL_MAX_10_EXP	S	Maximum decimal exponent.
	LDBL_MAX_EXP	S	Maximum binary exponent.
	LDBL_MIN	S	Minimum positive value.
	LDBL_MIN_10_EXP	S	Minimum decimal exponent.
	LDBL_MIN_EXP	S	Minimum binary exponent.
	LDBL_RADIX	M	Exponent radix.
	LDBL_ROUNDS	M	Addition rounding: near.
	MCW_IC	M	80x87 infinity control.
	MCW_EM	M	80x87 exception mask.
	MCW_PC	M	80x87 precision control.

TABLE 6.4: <float.h> (continued)

CATEGORY	IDENTIFIER	M/S*	DESCRIPTION
Object-Like Macros (cont.)	MCW_RC	M	80x87 rounding control.
	PC_24	M	80x87 24-bit precision control.
	PC_53	M	80x87 53-bit precision control.
	PC_64	M	80x87 64-bit precision control.
	RC_CHOP	M	80x87 chop rounding control.
	RC_DOWN	M	80x87 down rounding control.
	RC_NEAR	M	80x87 near rounding control.
	RC_UP	M	80x87 up rounding control.
	SW_DENORMAL	M	80x87 denormal status word.
	SW_INEXACT	M	80x87 inexact precision status word.
	SW_INVALID	M	80x87 invalid status word.
	SW_OVERFLOW	M	80x87 overflow status word.
	SW_SQRTNEG	M	80x87 negative square root status word.
	SW_STACKOVERFLOW	M	80x87 stack overflow status word.
	SW_STACKUNDERFLOW	M	80x87 stack underflow status word.
	SW_UNDERFLOW	M	80x87 underflow status word.
	SW_UNEMULATED	M	80x87 unemulated status word.
	SW_ZERODIVIDE	M	80x87 zero divide status word.
Function Prototypes	See Ch. 23.		

* M = Microsoft-specific (☐ ANSI); S = Standard C (■ ANSI)

The object-like macro **MB_LEN_MAX** defines the size in bytes of a wide or multibyte character supported by any locale (see **<locale.h>**). The default value of **MB_LEN_MAX** is 1, indicating that the historic one-byte-to-one-character relationship is still maintained. This is necessary until Microsoft elects to adopt the multibyte/wide-character features promulgated by Standard C. At that time **MB_LEN_MAX** will be set to reflect the maximum size of a multibyte character.

Table 6.5 lists the contents of this file.

<locale.h>

This header file was created for Standard C to augment the DOS configuration command COUNTRY, discussed in Chapter 1, which controls the display of DOS-related fields involving dates, times, the currency symbol, and the decimal separator. While the COUNTRY command can only

TABLE 6.5: <limits.h>

PURPOSE: This Standard C header file establishes the properties of integral data-type representations.

CATEGORY	IDENTIFIER	M/S*	DESCRIPTION
Object-like Macros	CHAR_BIT	S	Number of bits in a **char**.
	CHAR_MAX	S	Maximum **char** value.
	CHAR_MIN	S	Minimum **char** value.
	INT_MAX	S	Maximum **signed int** value.
	INT_MIN	S	Minimum **signed int** value.
	LONG_MAX	S	Maximum **signed long** value.
	LONG_MIN	S	Minimum **signed long** value.
	MB_LEN_MAX	S	Characters in a multibyte **char**.
	SCHAR_MAX	S	Maximum **signed char** value.
	SCHAR_MIN	S	Minimum **signed char** value.
	SHRT_MAX	S	Maximum **signed short** value.
	SHRT_MIN	S	Minimum **signed short** value.
	UCHAR_MAX	S	Maximum **unsigned char** value.
	UINT_MAX	S	Maximum **unsigned int** value.
	ULONG_MAX	S	Maximum **unsigned long** value.
	USHRT_MAX	S	Maximum **unsigned short** value.

* M = Microsoft-specific (□ ANSI); S = Standard C (■ ANSI)

be updated by rebooting DOS, the **<locale.h>** functions can be configured at run-time. The member components of the structure **lconv** (see Appendix E) can be updated and interrogated to provide for the format and display of data that conforms with locale-specific standards. Both of these facilities contribute to adapting DOS and C to an increasingly international marketplace.

Macro names beginning with **LC_[A–Z]** have been reserved for future use by Standard C. The object-like macros **LC_..** permit the modification of the structure **lconv** in total (**LC_ALL**) or in sub-categories (**LC_TIME**, **LC_[subcategory]**, and so on). Microsoft now supports the locale feature of Standard C, but only to a limited extent (see Chapter 27).

Table 6.6 lists the contents of this file.

<math.h>

Historically, **<math.h>** dealt only with mathematical functions in **double** precision. This has been revised with Standard C to include new

TABLE 6.6: <locale.h>

PURPOSE: This Standard C header file permits the alteration or access of current locale information. The locale concept attempts to provide for cultural and language data representation in terms other than ASCII. Only the C locale is implemented in Microsoft C 6.0.

CATEGORY	IDENTIFIER	M/S*	DESCRIPTION
Structure and Union Declarations	lconv	S	Control for formatting numerics.
Object-like Macros	LC_ALL	S	Category argument affecting all.
	LC_COLLATE	S	Collation argument.
	LC_CTYPE	S	Character and multibyte handling.
	LC_MAX	M	LC_TIME
	LC_MIN	M	LC_ALL
	LC_MONETARY	S	Monetary information.
	LC_NUMERIC	S	Decimal point information.
	LC_TIME	S	Time conversion argument.
	NULL	S	Valid **null** pointer constant.
Function Prototypes	See Ch. 27.		

* Microsoft-specific (□ ANSI); S = Standard C (■ ANSI)

math-related functions that are also of type **float** (reserved names ending in **f**) and **long double** (reserved names ending in **l**). There are now three floating-point type representations from which to choose:

float	4-byte IEEE format
double	8-byte IEEE format
long double	10-byte IEEE format

For more about these and other data types, see Chapter 7 and Chapter 11.

Math function errors are handled in two ways. Either the global variable **errno** is tested against the macros **EDOM** and **ERANGE**, or the non-Standard functions **matherr()** or **_matherrl()** are used. Both of these methods are fully described in Chapter 23. **matherr()** and **_matherrl()** rely upon the structure tag (see Appendix E) and the other object-like macros defined in **<math.h>**.

Table 6.7 lists the contents of this file.

<setjmp.h>

The non-Standard object-like macro **_JBLEN** defines the size of the integer array **jmp_buf[_JBLEN]**, which is designed to hold the processor's

TABLE 6.7: <math.h>

PURPOSE: This Standard C header file provides error return codes and function prototypes for common mathematical operations.

CATEGORY	IDENTIFIER	M/S*	DESCRIPTION
Global Variables	HUGE	M	**double** error return value.
	_LHUGE	M	**long double** error return value.
Structure and Union Declarations	complex	M	**cabs()** argument error structure.
	_complexl	M	**cabsl()** argument error structure.
	exception	M	**double** error structure.
	_exceptionl	M	**long double** error structure.
Object-like Macros	DOMAIN	M	Argument domain error.
	EDOM	S	Math argument error.
	ERANGE	S	Result too large error.
	HUGE_VAL	S	**double** error return.

TABLE 6.7: <math.h> (continued)

CATEGORY	IDENTIFIER	M/S*	DESCRIPTION
Object-like Macros (cont.)	_LHUGE_VAL	M	long double error return.
	OVERFLOW	M	Overflow range error.
	PLOSS	M	Partial loss of significance.
	SING	M	Argument singularity.
	TLOSS	M	Total loss of significance.
	UNDERFLOW	M	Underflow range error.
Function Prototypes	See Ch. 20 and 23.		
* M = Microsoft-specific (□ ANSI); S = Standard (■ ANSI)			

current register settings. For DOS, **_JBLEN** has a value of 9, which permits **jmp_buf** to hold 18 bytes as follows:

bp	base pointer	4 bytes
di	destination index	2 bytes
si	stack index	2 bytes
sp	stack pointer	4 bytes
ret addr	return address	4 bytes
ds	data segment	2 bytes

A function call to **setjmp()** saves a return address and corresponding machine context in **jmp_buf**; in so doing, it effectively labels a point in a function to which you can later return from another function by calling **longjmp()** with **jmp_buf**. This nonlocal mechanism is useful for overcoming the requirement that labels unconditionally branched to by **goto** must be located in the same function. Generally **setjmp()** and **longjmp()** are reserved for unique error and interrupt (signal) process-handling situations and may not be used to branch between functions that reside in separate overlays (see Chapter 3). For more on the use of these nonlocal jump functions, see Chapter 25.

Table 6.8 lists the contents of this file.

<signal.h>

In addition to the object-like macros defined in **<signal.h>**, Standard C has also reserved all names beginning with **SIG_** and **SIG[A-Z]** for future use. Complete examples and discussion of using the **raise()** and **signal()** functions are found in Chapter 25. Signal processing is often accompanied by the use of the functions found in **<setjmp.h>**.

Table 6.9 lists the contents of this file.

<stdarg.h>

This header file was created for Standard C and modeled after the UNIX header **<varargs.h>**. Although **<varargs.h>** is supplied with Microsoft C for UNIX compatibility, only the DOS header **<stdargs.h>** should otherwise be used to comply with Standard C. Complete examples and discussion of using the function-like macros **va_arg()**, **va_start()**, and **va_end()** are found in Chapter 14.

Table 6.10 lists the contents of this file.

<stddef.h>

This header file was created for Standard C and provides the function-like macro **offsetof()**, which locates the byte offset (relative to zero) of a structure member. Members of structures are padded to align the data objects (according to their type) and the ending boundary of a structure itself. Remember that only bytes, not bits, are addressable in the C language. The address of bit-fields within structures is undefined. The relative addresses (offsets) of members of structures can be affected by the use of compiler option **/Zp<n>**, the directive **#pragma pack()**, linker option **/FAR**, and the data-register size of the computer you are using.

TABLE 6.8: <setjmp.h>

PURPOSE: This Standard C header file handles program transfer of control that bypasses normal function-calling and return protocols and permits unconditional branching between functions by saving the return state of the computer in **jmp_buf** before a branch occurs.

CATEGORY	IDENTIFIER	M/S*	DESCRIPTION
Type Definitions	jmp_buf	M	Array of size **_JBLEN** for holding state information (bp, di, si, sp, ret addr, ds).
Object-like Macros	_JBLEN	M	Array size of **jmp_buf**
Function Prototypes	See Ch. 25.		

* M = Microsoft-specific (☐ ANSI); S = Standard C (■ ANSI)

TABLE 6.9: <signal.h>

PURPOSE: This Standard C header file specifies how a program is to handle signal processing when it executes. Signals are used to detect exceptional program behavior such as division by zero or other asynchronous events (e.g., a user hitting Ctrl-Break).

CATEGORY	IDENTIFIER	M/S*	DESCRIPTION
Type Definitions	sig_atomic_t	S	Data objects whose value is never suspended while partially completed.
Object-like Macros	NSIG	M	Maximum signal number + 1.
	SIGABRT	S	Abnormal termination signal.
	SIG_ACK	M	Signal acknowledgment handler.
	SIGBREAK	M	Ctrl-Break signal.
	SIG_DFL	S	System default signal handler.
	SIG_ERR	S	Ignore signal handler.
	SIGFPE	S	Floating point exception signal.
	SIG_IGN	S	Ignore signal handler.
	SIGILL	S	Illegal instruction signal.
	SIGINT	S	Ctrl-C signal (int 0x23).
	SIGSEGV	S	Illegal storage access signal.
	SIG_SGE	M	Signal gets error handler.
	SIGTERM	S	Termination signal.
	SIGUSR1	M	OS/2 user defined signal A.
	SIGUSR2	M	OS/2 user defined signal B.
	SIGUSR3	M	OS/2 user defined signal C.
Function Prototypes	See Ch. 25.		

* M = Microsoft-specific (□ ANSI); S = Standard C (■ ANSI)

If it is important to know where a member actually resides at run-time, perhaps to specify a sort-key offset, use the macro **offsetof()**. For example, assuming compiler option **/Zp1** and the structure tag **lconv** shown in Appendix E from **<locale.h>**, the program shown in Figure 6.1 would produce the following output if compiled with the Small memory model:

```
offset of mbr = 21 in str
```

TABLE 6.10: <stdarg.h>

PURPOSE: This Standard C header file accommodates the need to define and retrieve a variable number of function arguments. These function-like macros complement function prototype declarations in the general form `int fn(int a, ...)`, using the ellipsis (...) punctuator.

CATEGORY	IDENTIFIER	M/S*	DESCRIPTION
Type Definitions	`va_list`	S	Data object type of all arguments. This technique requires that all arguments be of the type `va_list`.
Function-like Macros	`va_arg(ap,t)`	S	Get the next argument.
	`va_end(ap)`	S	Reinitialize the list.
	`va_start(ap,v)`	S	Setup for argument retrieval.

* M = Microsoft-specific (□ ANSI); S = Standard C (■ ANSI)

```
/* FILE: ch6e1.c */
#include <locale.h>
#include <stddef.h>
#include <stdio.h>
int main(void)
{
size_t off;
off = offsetof(struct lconv, frac_digits);
printf("\noffset of mbr = %u in str",off);
exit(0);
}
```

FIGURE 6.1: The sample program ch6e1.c demonstrates the use of the Standard C offset of (s,m) function-like macro.

See Chapter 9 for more about the use of the **offsetof()** function-like macro and a complete explanation of how structures and unions are padded to maintain preferred data object alignment.

Table 6.11 lists the contents of this file.

<stdio.h>

Although **<stdio.h>** is probably the most common Standard C header file, it is one of the least standardized. Most directory and file parameters are operating-system specific and, therefore, cannot be standardized. It is for this reason that C traditionally adopted the generic stream I/O approach, which can be accommodated by all operating systems. With DOS, **<stdio.h>** relies upon the global array structure **_iob[]**, whose size is set by the DOS configuration command FILES in CONFIG.SYS, to manage all stream I/O. If the maximum value of FILES=20 is set, **_iob[20]** is then allocated, thereafter limiting the maximum number of concurrently opened files for a program (or process, see Chapter 25). Microsoft C automatically opens five standard I/O streams:

```
stdin  _iob[0]
stdout _iob[1]
stderr _iob[2]
stdaux _iob[3]
stdprn _iob[4]
```

Thus, only 15 user-defined files remain available to be opened (up to **_iob[19]**).

A number of object-like macros are defined to establish limits for the size of file naming components. The function-like macros that use either *_stream*, *FILE*, or *_c* as arguments all return values by name. For example, the following source-code fragment copies the characters from stream **in** to stream **out**:

```
#include <stdio.h>
#undef getc
```

TABLE 6.11: <stddef.h>

PURPOSE: This Standard C header file defines types and macros that are of general use by C programs.

CATEGORY	IDENTIFIER	M/S*	DESCRIPTION
Global Variables	`errno`	S	Current system error number.
Type Definitions	`ptrdiff_t`	S	Stores the result of subtracting two pointers.
	`size_t`	S	Stores the result of the `sizeof` operator.
	`wchar_t`	S	Unavailable/unsupported.
Object-like Macros	`NULL`	S	Valid null-pointer constant.
Function-like Macros	`offsetof(str,mbr)`	S	Yields the offset in bytes of member `mbr` of structure `str`.

* M = Microsoft-specific (□ ANSI); S = Standard C (■ ANSI)

```
#undef putc
.
.
.
FILE *in, *out;
int ch;
while ((ch = getc(in)) != EOF) putc(out,ch);
```

Obviously stream **in** must first be opened in the appropriate mode using **fopen()**, and finally both streams must be closed. Remember that function-like macro arguments are normally unsafe to use with side-effect unary operators. In this example, the run-time functions, not the function-like macros, for **getc()** and **putc()** are used because both of these function-like macro names have been undefined using the **#undef** compiler directive as shown.

Table 6.12 lists the contents of this file.

TABLE 6.12: <stdio.h>

PURPOSE: This Standard C header file supports file and stream input and output operations.

CATEGORY	IDENTIFIER	M/S*	DESCRIPTION
Global Variables	`_iob[]`	M	Array of `_iobuf`; maximum size is the smaller of `_NFILE` or the FILES=x command in CONFIG.SYS.
Type Definitions	`fpos_t`	S	File position type.
	`size_t`	S	Stores the result of the `sizeof` operator.
	`va_list`	M	Data-object type of all variable length function arguments.
Structure and Union Declarations	`_iobuf`	M	Internal I/O structure definition.
Object-like Macros	`BUFSIZ`	S	Size of all stream buffers.
	`EOF`	S	Designates end-of-file.
	`FILE`	S	Control object for stream files.
	`FILENAME_MAX`	S	Maximum filename length.
	`FOPEN_MAX`	S	Maximum number of open files.

TABLE 6.12: <stdio.h> (continued)

CATEGORY	IDENTIFIER	M/S*	DESCRIPTION
Global Variables (cont.)	_IOEOF	M	I/O end of file.
	_IOERR	M	I/O error.
	_IOFBF	S	**setvbuf()** file buffering argument.
	_IOLBF	S	**setvbuf()** line buffering argument.
	_IOMYBUF	M	Non-standard file buffer.
	_IONBF	S	**setvbuf()** no buffering argument.
	_IOREAD	M	I/O read-only.
	_IORW	M	I/O read/write.
	_IOSTRG	M	Undocumented.
	_IOWRT	M	I/O write-only.
	L_tmpnam	S	Name length of **P_tmpdir**.
	_NFILE	M	Same as **FOPEN_MAX**.
	NULL	S	Valid null-pointer constant.
	P_tmpdir	M	Directory for temporary files.
	SEEK_CUR	S	**fseek()** relative to current.
	SEEK_END	S	**fseek()** relative to end.
	SEEK_SET	S	**fseek()** relative to beginning.
	stdaux	M	Standard auxiliary file variable.
	stderr	S	Standard error file variable.
	stdin	S	Standard input file variable.
	stdout	S	Standard output file variable.
	stdprn	M	Standard printer file variable.
	SYS_OPEN	M	Same as **FOPEN_MAX**.
	TMP_MAX	S	Minimum number of files created by function **tmpnam()**.
Function-like Macros	feof(_stream)	S	Return true at **_stream** EOF.
	ferror(_stream)	S	Return true if **_stream** error.
	fileno(_stream)	M	Get file handle for **_stream** pointer.

TABLE 6.12: <stdio.h> (continued)

CATEGORY	IDENTIFIER	M/S*	DESCRIPTION
Function-like Macros (cont.)	`getc(_stream)`	S	Get a character from `_stream`.
	`getchar()`	S	Get a character from `stdin`.
	`putc(_c,_stream)`	S	Put character `_c` to `_stream`.
	`putchar(_c)`	S	Put character `_c` to `stdout`.
Function Prototypes	See Ch. 16, 17, and 20.		
* M = Microsoft-specific (□ ANSI); S = Standard C (■ ANSI)			

`<stdlib.h>`

This header file was created for Standard C and provides for the declaration of an assortment of commonly used DOS-specific global variables, type definitions, structure and union tags, object- and function-like macros, and run-time library function prototypes. Standard C also reserves all names starting with `str[a-z]` for future use.

Table 6.13 lists the contents of this file.

`<string.h>`

This header file was created for Standard C and provides a header for all string and memory management run-time library functions. It now includes the function prototype declarations for a complete set of non-Standard Microsoft functions that are independent of the memory model (all beginning with `_f`). Standard C also reserves all names beginning with `mem[a-z]`, `str[a-z]`, and `wcs[a-z]` for future use. For more on the use of these functions, see Chapter 26.

Table 6.14 lists the contents of this file.

`<time.h>`

This header file provides prototypes for run-time functions that provide for DOS-specific clock and calendar time measurements. Calendar measurements are normally accurate to seconds (see Appendix E), while clock measurements are normally accurate to hundredths of a second. The source-code timing example (**START()** and **STOP** macros) developed in Chapter 5 relies upon the service of the **clock()** run-time library function. For more on the use of these clock and calendar services, see Chapter 21.

Table 6.15 lists the contents of this file.

TABLE 6.13: <stdlib.h>

PURPOSE: This Standard C header file provides an assortment of commonly used macros and functions from the run-time library.

CATEGORY	IDENTIFIER	M/S*	DESCRIPTION
Global Variables	_doserrno	M	MS-DOS system error number.
	environ	M	Pointer to environment table.
	errno	S	Current system error number.
	_fileinfo	M	File inheritance mode for child processes.
	_fmode	M	Default file translation mode.
	_osmajor	M	DOS 3.3x _osmajor is 3.
	_osminor	M	DOS 3.3x _osminor is .3x.
	_osmode	M	DOS address mode, real/protected.
	_psp	M	Program segment prefix segment address.
	sys_errlist[]	M	perror() error message table.
	sys_nerr	M	Number of entries in sys_errlist.
Type Definitions	div_t	S	The return value of div().
	ldiv_t	S	The return value of ldiv().
	onexit_t	M	Function pointer for onexit().
	size_t	S	The return value of sizeof.
	wchar_t	S	Unavailable/unsupported.
Structure and Union Declarations	_div_t	M	Type div_t structure.
	_ldiv_t	M	Type ldiv_t structure.
Object-like Macros	DOS_MODE	M	Real address mode.
	EXIT_FAILURE	S	Unsuccessful termination code.

TABLE 6.13: <stdlib.h> (continued)

CATEGORY	IDENTIFIER	M/S*	DESCRIPTION
Object-like Macros (cont.)	`EXIT_SUCCESS`	S	Successful termination code.
	`_MAX_DIR`	M	Max length of path component.
	`_MAX_DRIVE`	M	Max length of drive component.
	`_MAX_EXT`	M	Max length of extension component.
	`_MAX_FNAME`	M	Max length of filename component.
	`_MAX_PATH`	M	Max length of full pathname.
	`MB_CUR_MAX`	S	Maximum characters in a multibyte `char`.
	`NULL`	S	Valid null-pointer constant.
	`OS2_MODE`	M	Protected address mode.
	`RAND_MAX`	S	Maximum `rand()` return value.
Function-like Macros	`max(a,b)`	M	Return maximum of (a,b).
	`min(a,b)`	M	Return minimum of (a,b).
Function Prototypes	See Ch. 16, 17, 20, 23, 24, 25, and 27.		
* M = Microsoft-specific (☐ ANSI); S = Standard C (■ ANSI)			

TABLE 6.14: <string.h>

PURPOSE: This Standard C header file supports working with strings and arrays of characters.

CATEGORY	IDENTIFIER	M/S*	DESCRIPTION
Type Definitions	`size_t`	S	The return value of `sizeof`.
Function Prototypes	See Ch. 24 and 26.		
* M = Microsoft-specific (☐ ANSI); S = Standard C (■ ANSI)			

TABLE 6.15: <time.h>

PURPOSE: This Standard C header file supports various methods of working with the DOS system time functions.

CATEGORY	IDENTIFIER	M/S*	DESCRIPTION
Global Variables	`daylight`	M	Nonzero if daylight savings time is used.
	`timezone`	M	Difference in seconds between GMT and local time.
	`tzname[]`	M	Standard/daylight savings time zone names.
Type Definitions	`clock_t`	S	Elapsed processor time value.
	`size_t`	S	Return value of `sizeof` operator.
	`time_t`	S	Calendar time value.
Structure and Union Declarations	`tm`	S	Calendar time structure.
Object-like Macros	`CLK_TCK`	M	Same as `CLOCKS_PER_SEC`.
	`CLOCKS_PER_SEC`	S	Number of clock ticks per second returned by `clock()`.
	`NULL`	S	Valid null-pointer constant.
Function Prototypes	See Ch. 21.		

* M = Microsoft-specific (□ ANSI); S = Standard C (■ ANSI)

MICROSOFT HEADER FILES

Microsoft supplies additional header files that supplement the Standard C headers and provide access to various DOS/BIOS services. These headers and the declarations contained therein are not a part of Standard C and, therefore, are subject to change by the vendor in the future. These files are copied, along with the Standard C header files described above, when you install a Microsoft compiler (see Chapter 2). All header files are compatible for use by both the QuickC and OptimizingC compilers.

`<bios.h>`	Table 6.16	BIOS service functions
`<conio.h>`		Console and port I/O

`<direct.h>`	Table 6.17	Directory control
`<dos.h>`	Table 6.18	DOS interface services
`<fcntl.h>`	Table 6.19	**open()** and **sopen()** flags
`<io.h>`	Table 6.20	File handling and low-level I/O
`<malloc.h>`	Table 6.21	Dynamic memory allocation
`<memory.h>`	Table 6.22	Buffer manipulation routines
`<process.h>`	Table 6.23	Process control
`<search.h>`	Table 6.24	Searching and sorting
`<share.h>`	Table 6.25	**sopen()** file sharing flags
`<sys\locking.h>`	Table 6.26	**locking()** file locking flags
`<sys\stat.h>`	Table 6.27	File status information
`<sys\timeb.h>`	Table 6.28	Time functions
`<sys\types.h>`	Table 6.29	File status and time types
`<sys\utime.h>`	Table 6.30	**utime()** file last-modified date

Use the Microsoft headers defined above when you reference any non-Standard run-time library function or use a DOS-specific service. Recognize that your source-code portability is restricted to other DOS machines once you rely upon the declarations and function prototypes defined in these Microsoft headers.

Three Microsoft header files are not discussed here: **<varargs.h>**, **<graph.h>**, and **<pgchart.h>**. You should not use the UNIX-style **<varargs.h>** header with DOS, but rather use the Standard C header **<stdargs.h>**. Both **<graph.h>** and **<pgchart.h>** relate to the Microsoft graphics library routines, which are not covered in this book.

`<bios.h>`

This header file provides a complete complement of structure and union declarations and object-like macros that are necessary to properly control the available BIOS services. Table 6.16 lists the contents of this file. For examples of these BIOS service functions, refer to Chapter 22.

TABLE 6.16: <bios.h>

PURPOSE: This Microsoft header file supports access to all BIOS service functions and interrupts.

CATEGORY	IDENTIFIER	M/S*	DESCRIPTION
Structure and Union Declarations	`BYTEREGS`	M	Byte registers.
	`diskinfo_t`	M	Send/receive information to/from the BIOS disk services.
	`REGS`	M	General purpose registers union.
	`SREGS`	M	Segment registers.
	`WORDREGS`	M	Word registers.
Object-like Macros	`_COM_INIT`	M	Init serial port.
	`_COM_SEND`	M	Send serial port character.
	`_COM_RECEIVE`	M	Receive serial port character.
	`_COM_STATUS`	M	Get serial port status.
	`_COM_CHR7`	M	Initialize serial port to 7-bit character.
	`_COM_CHR8`	M	Initialize serial port to 8-bit character.
	`_COM_STOP1`	M	Initialize serial port to 1 stop bit.
	`_COM_STOP2`	M	Initialize serial port to 2 stop bits.
	`_COM_NOPARITY`	M	Initialize serial port to no parity.
	`_COM_ODDPARITY`	M	Initialize serial port to odd parity.
	`_COM_EVENPARITY`	M	Initialize serial port to even parity.
	`_COM_110`	M	Initialize serial port to 110 baud.
	`_COM_150`	M	Initialize serial port to 150 baud.
	`_COM_300`	M	Initialize serial port to 300 baud.
	`_COM_600`	M	Initialize serial port to 600 baud.

TABLE 6.16: <bios.h> (continued)

CATEGORY	IDENTIFIER	M/S*	DESCRIPTION
Object-like Macros (cont.)	_COM_1200	M	Initialize serial port to 1200 baud.
	_COM_2400	M	Initialize serial port to 2400 baud.
	_COM_4800	M	Initialize serial port to 4800 baud.
	_COM_9600	M	Initialize serial port to 9600 baud.
	_DISK_RESET	M	Reset disk controller.
	_DISK_STATUS	M	Get disk status.
	_DISK_READ	M	Read disk sectors.
	_DISK_WRITE	M	Write disk sectors.
	_DISK_VERIFY	M	Verify disk sectors.
	_DISK_FORMAT	M	Format disk track.
	_KEYBRD_READ	M	Read next character from keyboard.
	_KEYBRD_READY	M	Check for keyboard keystroke.
	_KEYBRD_SHIFTSTATUS	M	Keyboard current shift key status.
	_NKEYBRD_READ	M	Read next character from enhanced keyboard.
	_NKEYBRD_READY	M	Check for enhanced keyboard keystroke.
	_NKEYBRD_SHIFTSTATUS	M	Enhanced keyboard current shift key status.
	_PRINTER_WRITE	M	Write character to printer.
	_PRINTER_INIT	M	Intialize printer.
	_PRINTER_STATUS	M	Get printer status.
	_TIME_GETCLOCK	M	Get current clock count.
	_TIME_SETCLOCK	M	Set current clock count.
Function Prototypes	See Ch. 19, 21, 22, and 24.		

* M = Microsoft-specific (☐ ANSI); S = Standard (■ ANSI)

<conio.h>

This file provides Microsoft-specific function prototypes to support all console and port I/O services. For prototypes and complete examples of these DOS services, refer to Chapter 19.

<direct.h>

This file defines the **size_t** type and provides function prototypes for all directory-management operations. Table 6.17 lists its contents. For examples of these DOS services, refer to Chapter 16.

<dos.h>

This header defines the key object-like macros and structure and union tags (see Appendix E) required to access all run-time library **_dos_xx** functions directly and to use the **int86()**, **int86x()**, **intdos()**, and **intdosx()** functions that provide access to all resident BIOS and DOS interrupt services. The function-like macros **FP_SEG()** and **FP_OFF** can be used to split **_far** addresses into their segment and offset components, if it is not desirable to use the new non-Standard **_based** pointer type. For complete examples of using these DOS services, refer to Chapter 22.

Table 6.18 lists the contents of this file.

<fcntl.h>

This header should be included to define the file creation, access, translation, and inheritance mode macro definitions, and whenever header file **<io.h>** is included. Table 6.19 lists the contents of this file. For a complete description of these file characteristics, refer to Chapter 16.

TABLE 6.17: <direct.h>

PURPOSE: This Microsoft header file supports all directory-management operations.

CATEGORY	IDENTIFIER	M/S*	DESCRIPTION
Type Definitions	size_t	M	Return type of sizeof operator.
Function Prototypes	See Ch. 16.		

* M = Microsoft-specific (□ ANSI); S = Standard (■ ANSI)

TABLE 6.18: <dos.h>

PURPOSE: This Microsoft header file supports all DOS service functions and interrupts.

CATEGORY	IDENTIFIER	M/S*	DESCRIPTION
Global Variables	_osversion	M	Complete DOS version number.
Structure and Union Declarations	BYTEREGS	M	Byte registers.
	dosdate_t	M	DOS system date values.
	diskfree_t	M	_dos_getdiskfree() return value.
	DOSERROR	M	dosexterr() structure.
	dostime_t	M	DOS system time values.
	find_t	M	DOS directory file information.
	REGS	M	General purpose registers union.
	SREGS	M	Segment registers.
	WORDREGS	M	Word registers.
Object-like Macros	_A_ARCH	M	Archive (used by backup/restore).
	_A_HIDDEN	M	Hidden (omitted by DIR command).
	_A_NORMAL	M	Read/write (normal file).
	_A_RDONLY	M	Read-only file.
	_A_SUBDIR	M	Subdirectory.
	_A_SYSTEM	M	System file (omitted by DIR command).
	_A_VOLID	M	Volume ID file (only root directory).
	_HARDERR_ABORT	M	Abort program issuing Int 0x23.
	_HARDERR_IGNORE	M	Ignore the error.
	_HARDERR_FAIL	M	Fail the system call in progress.
	_HARDERR_RETRY	M	Retry the operation.
Function-like Macros	FP_SEG(fp)	M	Segment component of _far pointer fp.
	FP_OFF(fp)	M	Offset component of _far pointer fp.
Function Prototypes	See Ch. 16, 18, 21, 22, 24, 25 and 27.		

* M = Microsoft-specific (□ ANSI); S = Standard (■ ANSI)

TABLE 6.19: <fcntl.h>

PURPOSE: This Microsoft header file provides the flags used with the file control functions `_dos_open()`, `open()`, and `sopen()`.

CATEGORY	IDENTIFIER	M/S*	DESCRIPTION
Object-like Macros	O_APPEND	M	Writes always done at EOF.
	O_BINARY	M	File mode is binary (untranslated).
	O_CREAT	M	Create and open file.
	O_EXCL	M	Open only if new.
	O_NOINHERIT	M	Child process does not inherit file.
	O_RAW	M	File mode is binary (untranslated).
	Q_RDONLY	M	Open for reading only.
	O_RDWR	M	Open for reading and writing.
	O_TEXT	M	File mode is text (translated).
	O_TRUNC	M	Open and truncate.
	O_WRONLY	M	Open for writing only.
* M = Microsoft-specific (□ ANSI); S = Standard C (■ANSI)			

<io.h>

This file supports file-handling and low-level I/O operations. For complete examples of the run-time library functions described in this header file, refer to Chapters 16 and 18.

<malloc.h>

This header file supplements standard header **<stdlib.h>** and provides the complete complement of dynamic memory allocation functions available for DOS. Three categories of routines are available:

Near heap	**_n...**
Heap	**calloc()**, **malloc()**, **halloc()** used by the default memory model selected.
Far heap	**_f...**

These routines provide the ability to access the Near heap, heap, and Far heap described in Chapter 2. For complete examples of using the run-time library functions described in this header file, refer to Chapter 24.

Table 6.20 lists the contents of this file.

TABLE 6.20: <malloc.h>

PURPOSE: This Microsoft header file supports all dynamic run-time memory allocation operations to the Near heap, heap, and Far heap (see the memory model maps presented in Chapter 2).

CATEGORY	IDENTIFIER	M/S*	DESCRIPTION
Global Variables	`_amblksiz`	M	Unit of heap allocation.
Type Definitions	`_HEAPINFO`	M	heap control structure.
	`size_t`	M	Return type of `sizeof` operator.
Structure and Union Declarations	`_heapinfo`	M	heap control structure.
Object-like Macros	`_FREEENTRY`	M	`_useflag` member for `_heapwalk()`.
	`_HEAPBADBEGIN`	M	`_heapwalk()` return bad header.
	`_HEAPBADNODE`	M	`_heapwalk()` return bad node.
	`_HEAPBADPTR`	M	`_heapwalk()` return bad pointer.
	`_HEAPEMPTY`	M	`_heapwalk()` return no heap init.
	`_HEAPEND`	M	`_heapwalk()` return at end OK.
	`_HEAP_MAXREQ`	M	Maximum heap allocation permitted.
	`_HEAPOK`	M	`_heapwalk()` return OK.
	`_NULLOFF`	M	`_based` heap null offset.
	`_NULLSEG`	M	`_based` heap null segment.
	`_USEDENTRY`	M	`_useflag` member for `_heapwalk()`.
Function Prototypes	See Ch. 24.		
* M = Microsoft-specific (☐ ANSI); S = Standard (■ ANSI)			

<memory.h>

This header file supplements the standard header **<stdlib.h>** and now provides a memory-model-independent set of buffer manipulation functions that are named to begin with **_f**. Table 6.21 lists the contents of this file. For complete examples of using the run-time library functions described in this header file, refer to Chapter 24.

`<process.h>`

Note that DOS only supports the use of the **P_WAIT** and **P_OVERLAY** object-like macros. Table 6.22 lists the contents of this file. For complete

TABLE 6.21: <memory.h>

PURPOSE: This Microsoft header file supports all memory (buffer) manipulation routines.

CATEGORY	IDENTIFIER	M/S*	DESCRIPTION
Type Definitions	`size_t`	M	Return type of `sizeof` operator.
Function Prototypes	See Ch. 24.		

* M = Microsoft-specific (□ ANSI); S = Standard C (■ ANSI)

TABLE 6.22: <process.h>

PURPOSE: This Microsoft header file supports all process-related run-time services.

CATEGORY	IDENTIFIER	M/S*	DESCRIPTION
Global Variables	`_p_overlay`	M	Same as **P_OVERLAY**.
Object-like Macros	`P_WAIT`	M	**spawn..()** DOS mode flag; suspend parent until child is complete.
	`P_NOWAIT`	M	**spawn..()** OS/2 mode flag; concurrent parent and child processes.
	`P_NOWAITO`	M	**spawn..()** OS/2 mode flag.
	`P_OVERLAY`	M	**spawn..()** DOS mode flag; overlay parent with child.
	`OLD_P_OVERLAY`	M	**spawn..()** mode flag.
	`WAIT_CHILD`	M	Child wait OS/2 mode flag.
	`WAIT_GRANDCHILD`	M	Grandchild wait OS/2 mode flag.
Function Prototypes	See Ch. 25.		

* M = Microsoft-specific (□ ANSI); S = Standard C (■ ANSI)

examples of using the run-time library functions described in this header file, refer to Chapters 15 and 25.

<search.h>

Table 6.23 lists the contents of this file, which supports the searching and sorting run-time library functions. For complete examples of using the functions described in this header file, refer to Chapter 27.

<share.h>

Table 6.24 lists the contents of this file. For a complete description of file-sharing, refer to Chapter 16 and to examples detailing the use of functions **_dos_open()** and **sopen()** in Chapter 18.

TABLE 6.23: <search.h>

PURPOSE: This Microsoft header file supports the searching and sorting run-time functions.

CATEGORY	IDENTIFIER	M/S*	DESCRIPTION
Type Definitions	`size_t`	M	Return type of `sizeof` operator.
Function Prototypes	See Ch. 27.		

* M = Microsoft-specific (□ ANSI); S = Standard C (■ ANSI)

TABLE 6.24: <share.h>

PURPOSE: This Microsoft header file supports the file-sharing argument of the `_dos_open()`, `_fsopen()`, and `sopen()` run-time functions.

CATEGORY	IDENTIFIER	M/S*	DESCRIPTION
Object-like Macros	`SH_COMPAT`	M	Compatibility mode.
	`SH_DENYRW`	M	Deny read/write mode.
	`SH_DENYWR`	M	Deny write mode.
	`SH_DENYRD`	M	Deny read mode.
	`SH_DENYNO`	M	Deny no modes.

* M = Microsoft-specific (□ ANSI); S = Standard C (■ ANSI)

`<sys\locking.h>`

Table 6.25 lists the contents of this file. For a complete description of record-locking, refer to the examples detailing the use of the **`locking()`** function in Chapter 16.

`<sys\stat.h>`

Table 6.26 lists the contents of this file. For complete examples of using the file-status run-time library functions **`fstat()`** and **`stat()`**, refer to Chapter 16.

`<sys\timeb.h>`

Table 6.27 lists the contents of this file. For complete examples of using the run-time library function described in this header file, refer to Chapter 21.

`<sys\types.h>`

This header file should be included whenever a program includes the header file **`<sys\stat.h>`**, **`<sys\utime.h>`**, or **`<sys\timeb.h>`**. Table 6.28 lists the contents of this file. For complete examples of using the run-time library functions supported by the type definitions described in this header file, refer to Chapters 16 and 21.

TABLE 6.25: `<sys\locking.h>`

PURPOSE: This Microsoft header file supports the mode argument of the `locking()` run-time function.

CATEGORY	IDENTIFIER	M/S*	DESCRIPTION
Object-like Macros	`LK_LOCK`	M	Lock the file region; 10 tries.
	`LK_NBLCK`	M	Nonblocking `LK_LOCK`; 1 try.
	`LK_NBRLCK`	M	Nonblocking `LK_RLCK`; 1 try.
	`LK_RLCK`	M	Lock the file region; 10 tries.
	`LK_UNLCK`	M	Unlock range of locked bytes.

* M = Microsoft-specific (☐ ANSI); S = Standard C (■ ANSI)

TABLE 6.26: <sys\stat.h>

PURPOSE: This Microsoft header file supports the file status run-time functions **fstat()** and **stat()**.

CATEGORY	IDENTIFIER	M/S*	DESCRIPTION
Type Definitions	time_t	M	Calendar time value.
Structure and Union Declarations	stat	M	Return file-status information.
Object-like Macros	S_IEXEC	M	Execute/search permission, owner.
	S_IFCHR	M	Character special (device, not file).
	S_IFDIR	M	Directory.
	S_IFMT	M	File-type mask.
	S_IFREG	M	Regular.
	S_IREAD	M	Read-only permission, owner.
	S_IWRITE	M	Read/write permission, owner.
Function Prototypes	See Ch. 16.		

* M = Microsoft-specific (□ ANSI); S = Standard C (■ ANSI)

TABLE 6.27: <sys\timeb.h>

PURPOSE: This Microsoft header file supports the run-time library time function **ftime()**.

CATEGORY	IDENTIFIER	M/S*	DESCRIPTION
Type Definitions	time_t	M	Calendar time value.
Structure and Union Declarations	timeb	M	Returned by **ftime()** system call.
Function Prototypes	See Ch. 21.		

* M = Microsoft-specific (□ ANSI); S = Standard C (■ ANSI)

`<sys\utime.h>`

Table 6.29 lists the contents of this file. For complete examples of using the run-time library function described in this header file, refer to Chapter 16.

TABLE 6.28: <sys\types.h>

PURPOSE: This Microsoft header file defines types required by run-time library file-status and time functions.

CATEGORY	IDENTIFIER	M/S*	DESCRIPTION
Type Definitions	`dev_t`	M	Device code.
	`ino_t`	M	I-node number (not used by DOS).
	`off_t`	M	File offset value.
	`time_t`	M	Calendar time value.

* M = Microsoft-specific; S = Standard C (■ ANSI)

TABLE 6.29: <sys\utime.h>

PURPOSE: This Microsoft header file supports the `utime()` run-time function for altering the last modification date associated with each DOS file.

CATEGORY	IDENTIFIER	M/S*	DESCRIPTION
Type Definitions	`time_t`	M	Calendar time value.
Structure and Union Declarations	`utimbuf`	M	Returned by `utime()`.
Function Prototypes	See Ch. 16.		

* M = Microsoft-specific (□ ANSI); S = Standard C (■ ANSI)

PROJECT-SPECIFIC HEADER FILES

Before creating a project-specific header file, be certain that any needed global variables, type definitions, structure or union tags, macros, and function prototypes have not already been defined in an existing Standard C or Microsoft header file. Avoid duplicating identical declarations.

Give the project header a unique name, one that does not conflict with an existing header file name. Conform to a six-character file name if possible. Store project headers in the current project path, and use the suggested **#include "xxx.h"** syntax. Do not store project header files in the standard installation path, and do not use the syntax **<xxx.h>**. Source code containing the syntax **#include "xxx.h"** is a visual reminder that project-specific headers are being referenced and are to be found in the default directory.

Avoid the temptation to modify either Standard C or Microsoft distribution header files. Confusion will result when updating to a newer compiler version or porting your software to another environment. Try to hold to the guidelines discussed in this chapter for header file construction. Most importantly, adhere to the idempotence concept, and provide function prototypes for all project-specific functions.

Use conditional directives to make your project headers idempotent. It should be possible to include a project header file at any time and in any order without harmful side effects. The following example demonstrates this technique:

```
#if !defined(THIS_MACRO)
#
# define MACRO value
# define ...
# define THIS_MACRO
#endif
```

THIS_MACRO is a "dummy" macro name used only to test whether **MACRO** has been defined yet. Preprocessor programming such as this will prevent redundant declarations and stop the proliferation of such side effects as the redefinition of an object-like macro constant. For other examples of this technique, refer to the **"timer.h"** header file described in Chapter 5 or the header files described in this chapter.

Remember to include project-specific function prototype declarations as well to ensure that argument checking is actually performed upon every reference to a project-specific function found in your source code. Rely on the compiler to warn you of any argument-type mismatches by specifying compiler warning level **/W3** or greater. Working in this fashion does require some discipline; far more work, however, is involved in debugging source code that has elusive function argument-calling errors.

A simple technique for generating the function prototypes for project-specific functions is to use the C compiler option **/Zg**. When this option is used, no compilation or linking takes place; rather, a function prototype is generated for each function definition found in the C source-code files to be compiled. For example:

```
QCL /Zg MY.C > MY.PRO
```

This DOS command will invoke the QuickC command-line compiler and produce function prototype descriptions for all function definitions found in the source-code file **MY.C**. Note the use of command-line redirection (**>**) above. Without redirection, the standard output from this command would only be displayed on the screen and not saved in the file MY.PRO. The contents of MY.PRO may then be copied into a project-specific header file together with other project-specific declarations.

It is recommended that all project-specific function prototypes be aggregated into one common project header file or subdivided into separate functional header-file categories. This will serve a dual role of documenting all project function calling and return conventions and providing a foolproof way to ensure that project function prototypes are always used.

3

Representing Data in C

All value representation in C involves type specification. In fact, the type concept is integral to everything represented in the C language: data, logic, and functions. The fact that every data object and function declaration is typed, and that a void data type even exists, would suggest that C is strongly typed. However, the flexibility that exists to coerce objects from one type to another using casts, coupled with the degree to which every type can be accessed using indirection, makes C a less strongly typed language.

In a way, C has a dual personality. One facade superficially looks and feels like most other high-level languages with familiar constructs and syntax, while another less apparent, but powerful facade, mirrors each familiar feature using indirection. Arrays, strings, structures, unions, pointers, and even functions may be handled in a traditional manner, while at the same time referenced indirectly using pointers. This dual nature of C cleverly allows its strongly typed syntax to behave less strongly typed whenever necessary.

Chapter 7 describes the fundamental C data type objects, together with an explanation of the many qualifiers (adjectives) that may be used to refine the meaning of each fundamental type (noun). A straightforward tabular method of constructing valid declarations of the fundamental data (and pointer) object types is presented, which overcomes the otherwise confusing terminology and rules that are typically used to describe the data declaration process.

Chapters 8 and 9 discuss how these fundamental data types may be aggregated to accommodate the need for familiar data structures that replicate the occurrence of similar (arrays) and dissimilar (structures) data object types and allocate types that share memory locations (unions). Emphasis is placed upon understanding storage (memory) allocation, object padding and alignment, and the performance tradeoffs of using subscripting and pointers to reference elements of arrays and members of structures and unions.

Chapter 10 discusses the declaration of pointers and the use of indirection with all fundamental and aggregated data object and incomplete types. It is probably not an understatement to say that to master C one must master using pointers. The segmented addressing notation used by DOS with the INTEL 80x86-family of precessors (8086, 80186, 80286 etc) is fully explained for the four address types supported by Microsoft's compiler memory models. Complete coverage is provided for all aspects of pointer declaration, operator manipulation, and the related topics of multiple levels of indirection, arrays of pointers, and structures and unions of pointers.

Chapter 11 describes C's powerful features for declaring and manipulating bits. Unlike most other compiled languages, C provides operators, not intrinsic or run-time library routines, for bit manipulation. Although bits are not addressable in C, a full complement of bit operators provides for the manipulation of integral bit types, and the flexible aggregation of bits within structures and unions, called bit-fields.

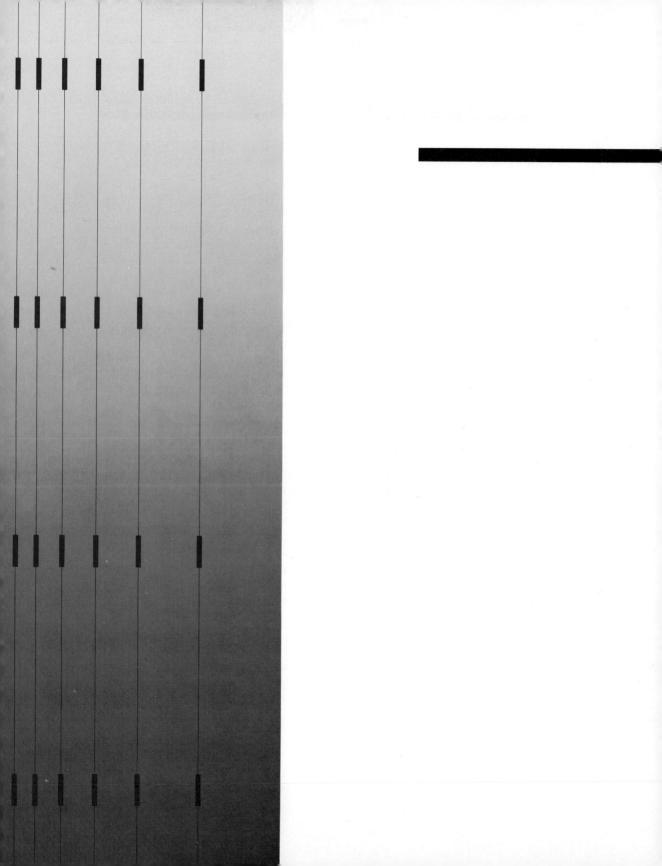

Data Types and Qualifiers

Data Types and Qualifiers

The concept of type is fundamental to the formation of all expressions in the C language. Type conveys the meaning of the value stored in an object. The concept of type is not unique to C, only the degree to which types have been integrated into the language. There are three broad categories of type in C: data-object types, function types, and incomplete types. This chapter explains data-object types. Data-object types (**char**, **int**, **enum**, **float**, **double**, **void**, and **_segment**) are the fundamental building blocks of data representation, which we aggregate to produce arrays, structures, and unions, and from which we derive pointers and develop function prototypes. The **enum** and **void** types did not exist in Kernighan and Ritchie (K&R) C, and have been added to the language by Standard C; the **_segment** type is Microsoft-specific, created for version 6.0 to support the use of the new **_based** pointer type.

Function types, including the topics of function pointers, function prototypes, and function argument and return values, are completely described in Chapters 14 and 15.

Incomplete types describe arrays of unspecified size, structure and union tags, and function prototypes, for which additional information must be provided before storage space is allocated and actual value represented. Although type **void** is technically an incomplete C type, for our purposes it is presented as a special "null" fundamental type. Additional discussion of incomplete types can be found in Chapters 8, 9, and 14.

Chapters 8 and 9 also discuss the aggregate data types, arrays, structures, and unions, which build upon the fundamental types discussed in this chapter. For more about fundamental pointer types refer to Chapter 10. For more about bits, which are derived from integral fundamental types, and bit-fields, derived from structures and unions, refer to Chapter 11. For more about functions and function pointer types, see Chapter 14.

FUNDAMENTAL DATA OBJECT TYPES

For the sake of simplicity, we can consider **char**, **int**, **enum**, **float**, **double**, **void**, and **_segment** to be the fundamental data types in C. Other publications are technically correct in including **signed**, **unsigned**, **short**, **long**, and **long double** as fundamental types, but this book will treat them as modifiers of the fundamental types. Thinking of them in this way provides a logical, structured method of declaring data and function type objects, as you'll see in this and the following chapters.

The fundamental data types belong to various categories, whose hierarchy (from less to more inclusive) is shown in Figure 7.1. You'll encounter this terminology throughout Part III.

Table 7.1 shows the minimum properties required by Standard C for each fundamental data object type. It is important to understand that Standard C mandates only the minimum properties of C data type objects. This gives C implementors (vendors) the flexibility of conforming with the ANSI Standard while exploiting the instruction set characteristics of a particular target machine's architecture. The data-object type properties presented in this chapter are those implemented for Microsoft C using the DOS operating system on Intel's 80x86-based (8086, 80186, 80286, and so on) microprocessors.

The derived types shown in Table 7.1 describe other valid type descriptions and their corresponding properties. Note that when no fundamental

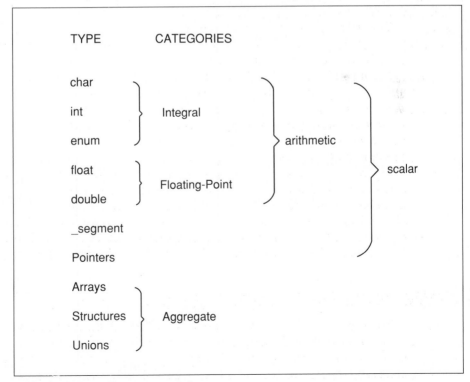

FIGURE 7.1: Data-object type categories.

TABLE 7.1: Standard C Data-Object Type Requirements

FUNDAMENTAL TYPE	DERIVED TYPES	DESCRIPTION	MINIMUM RANGE
char		Minimum of 8 bits	0 to 127
	signed char		−127 to 127
	unsigned char		0 to 255
int		Minimum of 16 bits	−32,767 to 32,767
	signed		Same
	signed int		Same
	(default)		Same
	unsigned		0 to 65,535
	unsigned int		0 to 65,535
short		Minimum of 16 bits	−32,767 to 32,767
	signed short		Same
	short int		Same
	signed short int		Same
	unsigned short		0 to 65,535
	unsigned short int		0 to 65,535
long		Minimum of 32 bits	−2,147,483,647 to 2,147,483,647
	signed long		Same
	long int		Same
	signed long int		Same
	unsigned long		0 to 4,294,967,295
	unsigned long int		0 to 4,294,967,295
enum		Minimum of 16 bit int	−32,767 to 32,767
float		Minimum of 6 decimal digits precision	-10^{38} to 10^{-38}, 0, 10^{-38} to 10^{38}
double		Minimum of 10 decimal digits precision	-10^{38} to -10^{-38}, 0, 10^{-38} to 10^{38}
	long double		Same
void		Always incomplete	No value, no storage

type is specified, the implied type is understood to be type **int**. For example, the program shown in Figure 7.2 would by default define each of the variables shown as type **int** except for the declaration **int_internal**;, which will produce a compilation error.

Because each compiler vendor may satisfy the minimum ANSI Standard requirements differently, resulting in different ranges of value for certain fundamental types, Table 7.2 summarizes Microsoft C's actual type properties.

Notice that the Microsoft **char**, **double**, and **long double** type implementations differ from the minimums established by the ANSI Standard. Also note that no standard exists for type **_segment**, which is Microsoft-specific. Again, Standard C does not dictate how each type is to be implemented, rather it only establishes the minimum acceptable range of value representation.

Take, for example, the type **signed long int**. Signed integral types are represented in two's complement notation (see Chapter 11). With 32 bits, allocating 1 bit for the sign leaves 31 bits, which can yield 2^{31} or 2,147,483,648 unique bit combinations. Recognizing that zero (0) uses one of the available combinations, the value range is −2,147,483,648 through 2,147,483,647, inclusive. Similarly, for the type **unsigned long int**, no sign bit is required, and so 2^{32} or 4,294,967,296 unique bit combinations are possible, yielding an actual value range of 0 through 4,294,967,295, inclusive.

The Standard IEEE representation of type **float**, although four bytes in size like a **long int**, makes an entirely different use of the same number of bits to provide for the actual value ranges shown in Table 7.2.

It is interesting to note the absence of certain fundamental types common to other languages, namely the Boolean (or LOGICAL*n) type,

```
/*FILE: ch7e1.c */
#include <stdio.h>
int_external;    /* OK! */
extern int_external_extern;
static int_external_static;

main()
{
auto int_internal_auto;
register int_internal_register;
static int_internal_static;
extern int_internal_extern;
int_internal;    /* ERROR! */
}
```

FIGURE 7.2: Sample program ch7e1.c.

TABLE 7.2: Microsoft Data-Object Type Implementations

FUNDAMENTAL TYPE	DERIVED TYPE	SIZE	VALUE RANGE
char		1 byte, 8 bits	−128 to 127
	signed char		Same
	unsigned char		0 to 255
int		2 bytes, 16 bits	−32,768 to 32,767
	default		Same
	signed		Same
	signed int		Same
	unsigned		0 to 65,535
	unsigned int		0 to 65,535
short		2 bytes, 16 bits	−32,768 to 32,767
	signed short		Same
	short int		Same
	signed short int		Same
	unsigned short		0 to 65,535
	unsigned short int		0 to 65,535
long		4 bytes, 32 bits	−2,147,483,648 to 2,147,483,647
	signed long		Same
	long int		Same
	signed long int		Same
	unsigned long		0 to 4,294,967,295
	unsigned long int		0 to 4,294,967,295
enum		2 bytes, 16 bits	−32,768 to 32,767
float		4 bytes, 32 bits, IEEE format	-10^{38} to -10^{-38}, 0, 10^{-38} to 10^{38}
double		8 bytes, 64 bits, IEEE format	-10^{-308} to -10^{308}, 0, 10^{-308} to 10^{308}

TABLE 7.2: Microsoft Data-Object Type Implementations (continued)

FUNDAMENTAL TYPE	DERIVED TYPE	SIZE	VALUE RANGE
`long double`		10 bytes, 80 bits, IEEE format	-10^{4932} to -10^{-4932}, 0, 10^{-4932} to 10^{4932}
`void`		0 bytes, 0 bits	No value
`_segment`		2 bytes, 16 bits	0x0000–0xF000
NOTE: Value ranges from Microsoft `<float.h>` and `<limits.h>` are understood to be inclusive.			

string (or CHARACTER*n) type, and COMPLEX*n types, familiar to Pascal and Fortran.

C relies upon a simple convention that expressions which evaluate to zero (0) represent false, and all other values are taken to represent true. All negative and nonzero expression values represent the logical result true.

There is no string data type or intrinsic ability to handle string operations in C. A string in C is simply an array of characters that is logically terminated by a null (\0) character (see Chapter 8). All string handling must be performed by C run-time library functions or custom-written routines (see Chapter 26 for a discussion of string handling).

The *complex* data type, which allows Fortran programs to use standard arithmetic operators to perform complex arithmetic, is not provided by the C language; rather, a structure (see Appendix E) is used to represent complex numbers in the form *(a + bi)*, and C run-time library functions must be used to perform all necessary math operations (see Chapter 23).

STANDARD C TYPE QUALIFIERS

If you think of the fundamental types as "nouns," then type qualifiers may be thought of as "adjectives" that individually or in combination modify the meaning of the fundamental types themselves. Two broad categories of type qualifiers exist in C, namely Standard and non-Standard (Microsoft-extension) qualifiers. Table 7.3 presents the Standard C qualifiers, or "adjectives," that may be used to control the lifetime and visibility, modifiability, and range of value (sign and size) of the fundamental types `char`, `int`, `enum`, `float`, `double`, `void`, and `_segment`. The precise meaning and effect of using these Standard C type qualifiers are described in the sections that follow.

Lifetime and Visibility

The C keywords, **auto**, **register**, **static**, and **extern**, are commonly referred to as storage classes. They may only be used individually as qualifiers and convey two properties, lifetime and visibility. Every type object in C (data object, function, or incomplete) has a storage-class qualifier associated with it.

An object's *lifetime*, or *duration*, is said to be *global* if the object has allocated storage space and an assigned value throughout the execution of a program. It is said to be *local* if storage is allocated and value assigned each

TABLE 7.3: Standard C Type Qualifiers

CATEGORY	NAME	TYPES USED WITH	DESCRIPTION
Lifetime and Visibility	auto	char, int, enum, float, double, _segment, pointers	Temporary variables
	register	char, int, enum, _segment, _near pointers	Provide fastest data access
	static	char, int, enum, float, double, _segment, pointers	Permanent initialized storage with visibility constraints
	extern	char, int, enum, float, double, _segment, pointers	Permanent initialized storage
Modifiability	const	char, int, enum, float, double, _segment, all pointer types except void	Cannot be modified by program
	volatile	char, int, enum float, double, _segment, all pointer types except void	May be modified by factors outside of the program
Sign	signed	char, int	+ or −
	unsigned	char, int	+ only
Size	short	int	16-bit
	long	int	32-bit
		double	Implementation defined

time execution passes control through the block (defined by braces) in which the object is defined; otherwise, no meaningful storage or value may be assumed to exist.

Visibility, or *scope,* is a measure of the extent to which an object name or identifier may be referenced. A data object's visibility is controlled by where it is initially defined. *External* object definitions are those declared outside of braces {..} and exhibit global lifetime and file visibility, while internal object definitions are those declared within braces {..} and typically exhibit local lifetime and block visibility.

The exact meaning of each storage-class qualifier for data objects then depends upon whether the declaration of that data object occurs externally or internally. In the following C source-code file example, the variables **i_ext** (outside of function **print()**) and **j_ext** (outside of function **main()**) are declared at the external level, while variables **i_int** and **j_int** are declared at the internal level:

```
#include <stdio.h>

int i_ext;
void print(void)
{
int i_int=0;
printf("\ni_ext = %d\nj_ext = %d",i_ext,j_ext);
}

int j_ext;
main()
{
int j_int=0;
print();
}
```

External Level Definitions

Data objects declared at the external (outside of braces) level may use only the optional storage-class qualifiers **static** and **extern**, and are understood to have global lifetime. All external declarations that define data objects (allocate storage) without the use of the qualifiers **static** and **extern** may be defined only once as such across all source-code files. Such data objects will automatically be initialized to zero (0) and such pointer objects to NULL, but for documentation purposes it is still recommended that an initial value be provided. It is recommended that all such definitions be collected and placed into the source-code file containing the **main()** function for a given program application (see Chapter 4). For example, in the following code fragment the variables **ui_val**,

li_val, and **f_val** are external definitions of variables with global life-time and visibility that may extend across all source-code files for a program:

```
#include ..
unsigned int ui_val = -1u;
long int li_val = 128L;
float f_val = 0.0F;
.

.

int main(void)
```

Note the use of the suffixes **u** or **U** for **unsigned**, **l** or **L** for **long int**, and **f** or **F** for **float** for the constants shown above.

If the **static** qualifier is used, the visibility of each external data object is restricted to the source-code file in which it is defined. Such data objects will automatically be initialized to zero (0) and such pointer objects to **NULL**, but again it is recommended that an initial value be provided for documentation purposes. For example, if we modify the previous source-code fragment, the variables **ui_val**, **li_val**, and **f_val** are still external definitions of variables with global lifetime, but the visibility is now restricted to the source-code file shown:

```
#include ..
static unsigned int ui_val;
static long int li_val = 128L;
static float f_val = 0.0F;
.

.

int main(int argc, char *argv[])
```

In this case the variable **ui_val** is initialized to zero (0) by default. Notice that the special function **main()** has been passed arguments from the DOS command line, which are accessed using the function arguments **argc** and **argv** (see Chapter 15 for a discussion of special function **main()**).

If the **extern** qualifier is explicitly used, the storage and initialization of the data object referenced are assumed to have been performed in another source-code file as described earlier in this section. The lifetime of such a data object is global. No initialization of a data object may be specified if the qualifier **extern** is used. For example, in the following source-code fragment the variables **ui_val**, **li_val**, and **f_val** are still external declarations of variables with global lifetime, but they are declared assuming that the storage space and initialization has been provided elsewhere (perhaps in the **main()** source-code file described above):

```
#include ..
extern unsigned int ui_val;
extern long int li_val;
```

```
extern float f_val;
  .
  .
void func1(void){..
```

For additional examples of using the keyword **extern**, refer to Appendix C, which lists the Standard and non-Standard global data objects defined by the Microsoft compiler itself.

Tables 7.4 and 7.5 summarize the lifetime, visibility, and initialization properties of data objects defined using the storage-class qualifiers available for internal and external declarations.

Internal Level Definitions

Data objects declared at the internal level (inside of braces) may optionally use the storage-class qualifiers **auto**, **register**, **static**, or **extern**. If no qualifier is used, the default storage class is understood to be **auto**. If the qualifier **auto** or **register** is used, the lifetime is understood to be local; if **static** or **extern** is used, the lifetime is global.

The visibility of a data object (identifier) declared at the internal level (within braces) is understood to extend from its point of declaration to the end of the block or function in which it is defined.

TABLE 7.4: Lifetime and Visibility of Data-Object Storage Classes

	EXTERNAL		INTERNAL			
	static	extern	auto	register	static	extern
Lifetime	Global	Global	Local	Local	Global	Global
Retain storage?	Yes	Yes	No	No	Yes	Yes
Retain value?	Yes	Yes	No	No	Yes	Yes
Visibility						
To calling function	Within current file only	To all files	Within block	Within block	Within block	To all files
To other functions	Within current file only	To all files	No	No	No	To all files

TABLE 7.5: Initialization of Data-Object Storage Classes

	EXTERNAL		INTERNAL			
INITIALIZATION	`static`	`extern`	`auto`	`register`	`static`	**extern**
Automatic						
To zero	Yes	Yes	No	No	Yes	Yes
Nonzero	No	No	No	No	No	No
Explicit[1]						
Fundamental types	Yes	No[2]	Yes	Yes	Yes	No
Arrays	Yes	No[2]	Yes	No	Yes	No
Structures	Yes	No[2]	Yes	No	Yes	No
Unions (1st member only)	Yes	No[2]	Yes	No	Yes	No

NOTES:
1. For externally declared storage classes, explicit initialization applies to any constant expression. For internally declared storage classes, it applies to any rvalue expression.
2. If defined with the EXTERN qualifier; otherwise Yes.

Storage Class `auto` If the `auto` qualifier is used or implied by default, the visibility is limited to the function or block in which the data object is defined or to any nested blocks that may be present. Unless you explicitly specify an initial value, none may be assumed. Storage is allocated each time the function or block of which it is a part is encountered during the execution of a program. In the following source-code fragment, variables `i_val` and `j_val` are internally defined to have local lifetime (`auto` by default), and their visibility extends to the end of the function block. A nested block defines another identifier called `i_val`, which is also an internal definition with local lifetime (`auto`), and whose visibility extends to the `printf(..)` statement shown. Both identifiers `int i_val` and `float i_val` exist as distinct data objects, but the initial value for `int i_val` is unknown, while `float i_val` is specified to be 1.0F.

```
int func1(void)
{
int i_val, j_val=0;
    {
    float i_val=1.0F;
    printf("\ni = %e\nj = %d",i_val,j_val);
    }
return(0);
}
```

The output produced by this function yields

```
i = 1.000000e+000
j = 0
```

Notice that the scope of **j_val** extends to the nested block and that the **i_val** identifier of type **float** overrides the scope of **i_val** of type **int**; each is properly displayed as shown above. The storage for **int i_val**, **int j_val**, and **float i_val** is allocated only when they are encountered, and it is released upon the return (0) of function **func1()**. All **auto** variables are allocated memory on the stack (see Chapter 15).

Storage Class **register**   If the **register** qualifier had been used in the previous source-code fragment, the lifetime and visibility would be the same, but the variables **int i_val** and **int j_val** would become candidates for allocation to a computer's register, not storage (memory):

```
register int i_val=0, j_val=0;
```

The use of the **register** qualifier does not mandate that registers be used but only flags those variables as register candidates to the C compiler. Recognize that all computers have a limited number of general registers available for program use, and that some data object types (**float** and **double**) are not appropriate to put into a register. With the Intel 80*x*86 chips, only the **DI** and **SI** registers are normally used for **register** variable allocation. If more than two variables are declared to be of storage class **register**, it is implementation (vendor) defined which variables are placed into registers and which revert to storage class **auto**.

It must also be remembered that **register** variables may not subsequently be used in expressions involving addressing or indirection, because only memory locations, not registers, have addresses in computers. Variables are placed into registers at the compiler's discretion; if a data object is specified as storage class **register** and cannot be placed there, it reverts to storage class **auto**. The **register** storage class should be thought of as a special case of the **auto** class. Both classes of variables are allocated storage (and initialized if so specified) each time they are encountered.

Use of the **register** qualifier can yield significant improvements in performance, however. Typically, variables that act as simple loop-counters (incrementors and decrementors) are chosen because of the memory fetch and store operations that can be saved for each cycle through the loop. In Chapter 5, the "Timing Source-Code Example" used the timing macros **START()** and **STOP** in a simple loop structure with and without declaring the index variable as **register**. Using the qualifier **register** produced a 45 percent improvement in overall performance.

Storage Class **static** If the **static** qualifier is used, the lifetime of the data object is global, but its visibility is limited to the file, function, or block within which it is defined or to any nested blocks that may be present. If specific initialization is omitted, a value of zero (0) or NULL may be assumed; however, it is recommended that all **static** variables be appropriately initialized. Such variables are initialized once and not reinitialized each time execution passes to the function or block in which they are declared, as for storage classes **auto** and **register**. Because the lifetime is global for **static** variables, subsequent reentry to a function or block containing a variable declared as **static** will find that it has retained the last value assigned to it. Consider the following code fragment example:

```
register int i, j;
static long int sum;
for (i=0;i<LIMIT;i++) {
    for(j=0;j<LIMIT;j++) {
        sum += 10;
        }
    }
```

Here, efficiencies are gained by appropriately specifying variables **i** and **j** as **register**. No matter how many times this function or block is encountered, the **static** variable **sum** will continue to accumulate and will never be reset to zero (0).

Storage Class **extern** If the **extern** qualifier is used, the storage and initialization of the data object referenced is assumed to have been performed elsewhere; no initialization of a data object may be specified. Instead of specifying **extern** variables at an internal level, specify them all at the external level in the corresponding source-code file. There is no difference in the behavior (lifetime or visibility) of variables specified as **extern** at the external and internal levels.

Modifiability

The new Standard C keyword **const** designates a fundamental type representation as a constant value that, subsequent to its initialization, may not be modified during the object's lifetime. A sample type declaration using the keyword **const** might appear in a C program as follows:

```
const char a_ch = 'A';
const int *ptr_int;
unsigned int * const ptr_uint;
const double * const ptr_dbl;
```

This defines the variable **a_ch** to be of type **char** and assigns it the constant value of the character A, variable **ptr_int** to be a pointer to an object of type **const int**, variable **ptr_uint** to be a **const** pointer to an object of type **unsigned int**, and variable **ptr_dbl** to be a **const** pointer to an object of type **const double**.

The new Standard C keyword **volatile** designates a fundamental type representation that is subject to modification by factors outside of the current program. Data object types modified by this keyword are typically reserved for use by signal handlers, concurrently executing programs, and interfaces to special equipment. A typical declaration using the keyword **volatile** might appear as

```
extern const volatile unsigned int v_uint;
```

This declares the variable **v_unit** to be an **unsigned int** whose storage is declared elsewhere (**extern**) and whose value may not be altered by the current program (**const**) but may otherwise be modified (**volatile**). Note that the qualifiers **const** and **volatile** may be used both individually and in combination to modify a fundamental type.

Sign

The C keywords **signed** and **unsigned** are used to control the value ranges assignable to objects of the fundamental types **char** and **int** by controlling whether a sign-bit is used. Sample type declarations using these keywords might appear in a C program as follows:

```
signed char a_ch;
signed int b_int;
unsigned long int c_ulint;
```

These define the variable **a_ch** as type **signed char**, variable **b_int** as type **signed int**, and variable **c_ulint** as type **unsigned long int**. The qualifiers **signed** and **unsigned** may not be combined to modify a fundamental type.

Size

The C keyword, **short**, in the case of Microsoft's implementation, does not alter the representation of the fundamental type **int**. **Int** is implemented as 16 bits, and **short** is defined by the ANSI Standard to be 16 bits at a minimum. However, another vendor's implementation of C for a machine with a different architecture could well have defined an **int** to be 32 bits, and a **short int** would then have 16 bits. A sample type declaration using the keyword **short** might appear in a C program as

```
short int i_sint;
```

and define the variable **i_sint** as type **short int**.

The C keyword **long**, in the case of Microsoft's implementation, does alter the representation of the fundamental type **int**, and with the version 6.0 compilers also alters the representation of type **double**. The use of the qualifier **long** with the fundamental type **int** results in a 32-bit representation. The use of **long** with the fundamental type **double** results in an 80-bit representation, not the 64 bits specified by IEEE. As in the case of **short int** and **int**, **double** and **long double** both conform with the ANSI Standard minimum type requirements. The **long double** offers additional precision and takes advantage of the Intel 80*x*87 floating-point coprocessors' 80-bit representation format.

Sample type declarations using the keyword **long** might appear in a C program as

```
long int i_lint;
long double a_ldbl, b_ldbl;
```

and define the variable **i_lint** as type **long int**, and the variables **a_ldbl** and **b_ldbl** as type **long double**. When the qualifiers **short** and **long** are used, they may not be combined to modify a fundamental type.

NON-STANDARD C (MICROSOFT) TYPE QUALIFIERS

The other category of fundamental data type qualifiers is non-Standard Microsoft extensions to C. Table 7.6 presents the non-Standard C qualifiers, or "adjectives," you can use to alter the meaning and representation of data object types in C related to mixed-language interfaces and addressing. The precise meaning and effect of using these non-Standard C type qualifiers are described in the sections that follow.

Mixed Languages

The non-Standard C keywords **_cdecl**, **_fortran**, and **_pascal** accommodate the intermingled use of data objects and functions in the C (**_cdecl**), Fortran (**_fortran**), and Pascal (**_pascal**) languages. Note however that these keywords may not be used to qualify the declaration of pointers (see Table 7.8 in the "Pointer Types" section). The predominant use of these keywords relates to the development of function prototypes and definitions, a discussion of which is provided in Chapter 14.

However, these non-Standard C keywords may also be used to control how the C compiler treats data object identifiers. If the keyword **_cdecl** is used, normal C identifier naming and translation standards apply:

TABLE 7.6: Non-Standard C (Microsoft) Type Qualifiers

CATEGORY	NON-STANDARD	DESCRIPTION	APPLICABLE TO
Mixed Languages	_cdecl	C-compatible data elements and functions	C language interface, except pointers
	_export	Microsoft-specific C-compatible functions	Dynamic-link libraries (DLL)
	_fastcall	Microsoft-specific C-compatible functions	Performance-oriented, register specific
	_fortran	Fortran-compatible data elements and functions	Fortran language interface, except pointers
	_pascal	Pascal-compatible data elements and functions	Pascal language interface, except pointers
Addressing	_near	16-bit offset	Code and Data pointers
	_far	32-bit segment:offset	Code and Data pointers
	_huge	32-bit segment:offset, using high-order 4 bits of 20-bit address	Only Data pointers (for > 64KB)
	_based	16-bit offset, any segment may be specified	Only Data pointers

upper-/lowercase sensitivity is observed and an underscore character is prefix-appended. If the keyword **_fortran** or **_pascal** is used, the C compiler generates uppercase identifiers only, and no underscore character is prefix-appended. Whether used for data object or function type qualification, the keywords **_fortran** and **_pascal** have an equivalent effect. Their individual use serves to self-document the source code. In the source-code fragment

```
int _cdecl i_val;
extern char _fortran c_val;
extern int _pascal i_val;
```

the variable **i_val** is an **int** type data object with Standard C naming conventions; **c_val** is a **char** type data object defined elsewhere with Fortran naming standards; and, similarly, **i_val** is an **int** type data object defined elsewhere with Pascal naming standards.

When the qualifiers **_cdecl**, **_fortran**, and **_pascal** are used, they may not be combined to modify a fundamental type. It is understandable why these keywords were not included in the ANSI Standard. To include **_fortran** and **_pascal** opens the door to an endless progression of language keywords, none of which were found by the X3J11 Standards Committee to be in common use, nor certainly are they considered portable.

By default, the Microsoft compilers recognize the non-Standard keywords (option **/Ze**) shown in Table 7.6. By using the **/Za** option, the **_cdecl**, **_fortran**, and **_pascal** keywords will be ignored by the compiler, but all occurrences of these keywords in the source code will be treated as ordinary identifiers.

To entirely remove the presence of these keywords from a source-code file, use the following compiler directives:

```
#define _cdecl
#define _fortran
#define _pascal
```

The effect of these **#define** directives is to replace each occurrence of the keywords with no string (null).

Addressing

The non-Standard C keywords **_near**, **_far**, **_huge**, and **_based(..)** are used to override the default addressing mode associated with the memory model of the compiler being employed.

If, for example, the Tiny, Small, or Medium memory model is being used, the default addressing mode is **_near** or 16-bit; if the Compact or Large memory model is being used, the default mode is **_far** or 32-bit;

if the Huge memory model is being used, the default mode is **_huge** or 32-bit with special handling of all address arithmetic.

Thus, if you are working with the Tiny, Small, or Medium memory model and wish to interface with a data object created using the Compact or Large memory model, the non-Standard keyword qualifier **_far** is used; and for interfacing with the Huge memory model, **_huge** is used.

Similarly, if you are working with the Compact or Large memory model and you wish to interface with a data object created using the Tiny, Small, or Medium memory model, the non-Standard keyword qualifier **_near** is used; for interfacing with the Huge memory model **_huge** is used.

If you are working with the Huge memory model and you wish to interface with a data object created using the Tiny, Small, or Medium memory model, the non-Standard keyword qualifier **_near** is used; for interfacing with the Compact or Large memory model **_far** is used.

The new **_based(..)** qualifier is independent of particular memory models and supports the construction of memory addresses from separate segment (**_segment** type or equivalent) and offset (any unsigned integer value 0–65,535) components using the new version 6.0 operator **:>** (see Chapter 12).

The qualifiers **_near**, **_far**, **_huge**, and **_based(..)** may not be combined to modify a fundamental type. The following source-code fragment defines four pointer variables: **c_nvar** is a **char** object that is **near** addressed; **i_fvar** is an **int** object that is **_far** addressed; **d_hvar** is a **double** object that is **_huge** addressed; and **ld_var** is a **long double** object whose addressing is **_based** on the current **DS** register value.

```
char _near c_nvar;
int _far i_fvar;
double _huge d_hvar;
long double _based(_segment(_"DATA")) ld_var
```

You can see why these keywords were not included in the ANSI Standard. They are an outgrowth of the segmented addressing architecture used by some, but not all, computers. By default, only 80x86 compilers recognize these non-Standard keywords (option **/Ze**). By using the **/Za** option, the **_near**, **_far**, **_huge**, and **_based(..)** keywords will be ignored by the compiler, and all occurrences in the source code will be treated as ordinary identifiers.

To remove occurrences of these keywords altogether, use the **#define** directive approach described above in the section entitled "Mixed Languages" as follows:

```
#define _near
#define _far
#define _huge
#define _based
```

For a complete discussion of memory models and addressing, see Chapters 2 and 10.

DATA-OBJECT DECLARATION

From the preceding discussions of the fundamental data object types and the Standard and non-Standard type qualifiers, a systematic approach for developing valid data-object type declarations involving these components now emerges. Table 7.7 has been prepared to facilitate writing the definitions for the fundamental types presented in Tables 7.1 and 7.2.

Every fundamental type declaration written in C is developed by optionally combining the qualifiers shown in each column of the table. Notice that no relevant choices are available for the column "Modifiable Pointer." For each base type, the default or implied modifiers are shown in square brackets. For example, a data object named **i_val** may be defined to be of type **int** in a Small memory model program:

```
int i_val;
```

We can see in the table that, depending upon whether this declaration occurs at the external or internal level (outside or inside braces), either

```
[extern][none][signed][none] int [_cdecl][memory model][none] i_val;
```

or

```
[auto][none][signed][none] int [_cdecl][memory model][none] i_val;
```

would result, which in turn can be interpreted as

```
[extern] signed int _cdecl _near i_val;
```

or

```
auto signed int _cdecl _near i_val;
```

It is clear that the variable **i_val**, understood to be of storage class **extern** or **auto** depending upon where it is declared, represents a signed integer data object that is **_near** addressed, and conforms with the C language naming conventions (case-sensitive and prefixed with underscore).

Only one qualifier from among those shown under each column (category of qualifiers, or "adjectives") may be chosen except for the column titled "Modifiability" (see note 2). For example, from Table 7.7 another valid **int** type definition might be expressed as

```
static const unsigned long int _fortran _far i_val;
```

defining the variable **i_val** to be a **static**, **constant**, **unsigned long int** that is **_far** addressed and conforms to the Fortran, not C, naming conventions (case-insensitive and no leading underscore).

If type declarations at the external level (outside {..} braces) omit the base type, notice that type **int** is assumed; however, at the internal level (within {..} braces), a compilation error results if a base type is omitted.

Notice that the qualifiers that can be used with fundamental type **enum**, although implemented as type **int**, do not include the sign or size qualifiers. Also, with **enum** the data object identifier may be omitted (see the "Enumerated (**enum**) Type" section below).

Notice that the storage class (lifetime and visibility) for types **float** and **double** does not include the keyword **register**. Floating-point types are not candidates for **register** allocation because of their size and dependence upon the presence of a floating-point coprocessor.

The fundamental type **void** may not be used to allocate data objects at all, and in a way, **void** is the antithesis of type. Type **void** is used to define the absence of type (and hence storage) and represents a new type with Standard C.

With K&R C, the lack of a **void** type object required that a default object type of **int** always be assumed. Type **void** is widely used to declare the absence of function prototype arguments and return types, and for the declaration of pointer variables that are compatible with all other pointer types, but which must be cast to point to a type object before being dereferenced using the indirection operator (*****).

The new non-Standard type **_segment**, introduced with version 6.0, is implemented as type **int** but, like **enum**, does not permit the use of the sign and size qualifiers. A **_segment** type variable contains the segment portion of a memory address.

Enumerated (*enum*) Type

Type **enum** requires a somewhat different declaration syntax than other fundamental types. Three forms are possible:

```
enum {list};                /* format #1 */
enum {list} varname;
enum tag {list};            /* format #2 */
enum tag {list} varname;
enum tag varname;           /* format #3 */
```

Before examining the differences between these formats, let's look at the meaning of {*list*}. From 1 to 128 enumerated or named integer values may

TABLE 7.7A: Syntax of Fundamental Type Declarations

LIFETIME AND VISIBILITY [1]	MODIFIABLE TYPE[2]	SIGN	SIZE	BASE TYPE[3]
[auto/extern] register static	[none] const volatile	[signed] unsigned	[none]	char
[auto/extern] register static	[none] const volatile	[signed] unsigned	[none] short long	int [none]
[auto/extern] register static	[none] const volatile	[none]	[none]	enum *tag* *{list}* enum *tag*
[auto/extern] static	[none] const volatile	[none]	[none]	float
[auto/extern] static	[none] const volatile	[none]	[none] long	double
[none]	[none]	[none]	[none]	void
[auto/extern] register static	[none] const volatile	[none]	[none]	_segment

NOTES:
1. Lifetime and visibility (storage-class) qualifier must appear first with Standard C. [auto] assumed if defined within braces (internal); otherwise, [extern] assumed.
2. Both choices may be specified for modifiable type. All other qualifier columns permit only one selection to be made.

TABLE 7.7B Syntax of Fundamental Type Declarations (continued)

BASE TYPE[3]	MIXED LANGUAGE	ADDRESSING[4]	MODIFIABLE POINTER	DATA OBJECT IDENTIFIER
char	[_cdecl] _fortran _pascal	[*memory model*] _near _far _huge _based(..)	[none]	varname;
int [none]	[_cdecl] _fortran _pascal	[*memory model*] _near **_far** _huge **_based(..)**	[none]	varname;
enum *tag {list}* enum *tag*	[_cdecl] _fortran _pascal	[*memory model*] _near _far **_huge** **_based(..)**	[none]	[none] varname;
float	[_cdecl] _fortran _pascal	[*memory model*] _near _far **_huge** **_based(..)**	[none]	varname;
double	[_cdecl] _fortran _pascal	[*memory model*] **_near** **_far** _huge **_based(..)**	[none]	varname;
void	[none]	[none]	[none]	[none]
_segment	[_cdecl] _fortran _pascal	[*memory model*] _near _far **_huge** **_based(..)**	[none]	varname;

NOTES (cont.):

3. Type **enum** is implemented as type **int** by Microsoft. The syntax **enum tab {list}** implies a comma-separated list of identifiers within braces. Type **_segment** is a non-Standard type implemented as type **int** by Microsoft.

4. **_huge** may be specified only with storage classes **static** and **extern**, not **auto** or **register**. The syntax **_based(..)** denotes that a segment reference must be provided in parentheses. The segment references **void** and **_self** may not be used with **_based(..)** for fundamental type declarations.

be specified within the braces of an enumeration list. Consider the following example:

```
{ false, true, zero=0, one, two }
```

The first variable (identifier) in the list by default always assumes the value of 0, and subsequent identifiers are assigned values incremented by one unless reset by use of **=n**. In the example above, the named identifiers (variables) are assigned the following values:

VARIABLE	VALUE
false	0
true	1
zero	0
one	1
two	2

If the =0 had not been specified for the variable zero, the following values would have been assigned:

VARIABLE	VALUE
false	0
true	1
zero	2
one	3
two	4

The storage class specified for an enumerated type controls the lifetime and visibility of the variables named in an enumeration list.

Format 1, described above, does not require that a data object identifier be provided. The only variables created may be those within the enumeration list. If, however, a pointer is to be declared, then a data-object identifier must be included (see Table 7.8 in the next section).

Format 2, described above, behaves identically to format 1, but in the process declares a *tag* name that is subsequently associated with that enumeration list. Like the tag names created for structures and unions (see Chapter 9), they may later be referenced to simplify the declaration process for other variables or pointers.

Format 3, described above, relies upon the prior declaration of a *tag* (by format 2) to allocate subsequent variables and pointers having the characteristics of that tag enumeration list. The variables within the referenced tag enumeration list are not reallocated!

A common use for enumerated types is the naming of constants that will later serve as index values to multidimension arrays.

Pointer Types

The syntax for declaring pointers to fundamental data object types, shown in Table 7.8, parallels that shown in Table 7.7 for defining objects of the fundamental types. Pointers are data-object types that represent memory addresses. A complete discussion of pointers appears in Chapter 10; here we simply present a method for defining pointers to the fundamental types.

Every fundamental pointer type declaration written in C is developed by optionally combining the qualifiers shown in each column of Table 7.8. By comparing the column heads in the two tables, you'll see that pointer declaration may include a modifiable pointer qualifier but not a mixed languages qualifier. For each base type, the implied or default qualifier in effect is shown in square brackets. For example, when a pointer data object named **j_val** is defined to be of type **int** as in

```
int *j_val;
```

(using the Small memory model) depending upon whether **j_val** was declared at the external or internal level, one of the following would result from the base type **int** line of Table 7.8:

```
[extern][none][signed][none] int [none][memory model]*[none] j_val;
```

or

```
[auto][none][signed][none] int [none][memory model]*[none] j_val;
```

In turn, these declarations can be interpreted as

```
[extern] signed int _near *j_val;
```

or

```
auto signed int _near *j_val;
```

It is clear that the pointer variable **j_val** is understood to be of storage class **extern** or **auto**, depending upon where it is declared, and contains the **_near** memory address (in the default Small memory model mode) of a type object representing a signed integer. Again, only one qualifier from among those shown under each column (category of qualifiers, or "adjectives") may be chosen, except for the columns "Modifiable Type" and "Modifiable Pointer" (see note 2).

TABLE 7.8A: Syntax of Fundamental Pointer Type Declarations

LIFETIME AND VISIBILITY[1]	MODIFIABLE TYPE[2]	SIGN	SIZE	BASE TYPE[3]
[auto/extern] register static	[none] const volatile	[signed] unsigned	[none]	char
[auto/extern] register static	[none] const volatile	[signed] unsigned	[none] short long	int [none]
[auto/extern] register static	[none] const volatile	[none]	[none]	enum *tag* {*list*} enum *tag*
[auto/extern] register static	[none] const volatile	[none]	[none]	float
[auto/extern] register static	[none] const volatile	[none]	[none] long	double
[auto/extern] register static	[none]	[none]	[none]	void
[auto/extern] register static	[none] const volatile	[none]	[none]	_segment

NOTES:
1. Lifetime and visibility (storage-class) qualifier must appear first with Standard C. [auto] assumed if defined within braces (internal); otherwise, [extern] assumed.
2. Both choices may be specified for modifiable type and modifiable pointer. All other qualifier columns permit only one selection to be made.

TABLE 7.8B Syntax of Fundamental Pointer Type Declarations (continued)

BASE TYPE[3]	MIXED LANGUAGE	ADDRESSING[4]	MODIFIABLE POINTER[2]	DATA OBJECT IDENTIFIER

`char`	[none]	[*memory model*] `*`
		`_near *`
		`_far *`
		`_huge *`
		`_based (..) *`
			[none]
			`const`
			`volatile`
				`varname;`

`int`
[none]
	[none]	[*memory model*] `*`
		`_near *`
		`_far *`
		`_huge *`
		`_based (..) *`
			[none]
			`const`
			`volatile`
				`varname;`

`enum tag {list}`
`enum tag`
	[none]	[*memory model*] `*`
		`_near *`
		`_far *`
		`_huge *`
		`_based (..) *`
			[none]
			`const`
			`volatile`
				`varname;`

`float`	[none]	[*memory model*] `*`
		`_near *`
		`_far *`
		`_huge *`
		`_based (..) *`
			[none]
			`const`
			`volatile`
				`varname;`

`double`	[none]	[*memory model*] `*`
		`_near *`
		`_far *`
		`_huge *`
		`_based (..) *`
			[none]
			`const`
			`volatile`
				`varname;`

`void`	[none]	[*memory model*] `*`
		`_near *`
		`_far *`
		`_huge *`
		`_based (..) *`
			[none]
			`const`
			`volatile`
				`varname;`

`_segment`	[none]	[*memory model*] `*`
		`_near *`
		`_far *`
		`_huge *`
		`_based (..) *`
			[none]
			`const`
			`volatile`
				`varname;`

NOTES (cont.):

3. Type `enum` is implemented as type `int` by Microsoft. The syntax `enum tag {list}` implies a comma-separated list of identifiers within braces. Type `_segment` is a non-Standard type implemented as type int by Microsoft.

4. `_huge` may be specified only with storage classes `static` and `extern`, not `auto` or `register`. The syntax `_based(..)` denotes that a segment reference must be provided in parentheses.

For example, from Table 7.8, another valid **int** type pointer declaration might be expressed as

```
static const unsigned long int _far * const j_val;
```

defining the constant **_far** pointer variable **j_val** to be of storage class **static**, which contains the memory address of a type object representing a constant **unsigned long int**.

Notice that the qualifiers that can be used with fundamental type **enum** do not permit the sign or size qualifiers to be specified, even though type **enum** is implemented as type **int**.

Notice that, unlike **float** and **double** fundamental type declarations, such pointer declarations may be specified as storage class (lifetime and visibility) **register**. Storage class is associated with the pointer data object itself, not the object type pointed to.

Also, pointers to fundamental type **void** may be used to allocate a generic pointer data object with the lifetime and visibility, modifiable pointer, and addressing qualifiers that define a pointer to **void**. Type pointer-to **void** may subsequently be cast to represent a pointer to any other qualified data-object type.

Although type **_segment** itself contains the segment portion of a memory address, pointers to such data objects may be declared to support indirect access to such objects.

Microsoft's Physical Storage of Data Object Types

Now that the methodology for declaring fundamental data object types has been established, refer to Table 7.2, which defines the physical storage (memory) space, in bytes, used by Microsoft to implement each of the possible qualified fundamental types. Data object definition, in contrast to declaration, allocates storage (memory) while establishing an associated data object identifier. It is helpful to visualize the space (memory storage in bytes) that each data object type is allocated and its associated starting memory address (byte). Remember that although every byte of storage has a unique physical memory address, only the first byte of a data object is used to define the object's memory. Figure 7.3 helps you to visualize the storage and memory addressing associated with each fundamental and pointer-type data object.

Once you can visualize the fundamental data-object types, together with the aggregated array, structure, and union types, then the groundwork is established to understand the inseparability of the type and pointer concepts in the C language. To identify bits, the lowest level of object visualization, refer to Chapter 11 and Figure 11.1.

Figure 7.3 also shows that pointer data objects occupy the storage required to represent either a **_near**, **_far**, **_huge**, or **_based(..)** memory address. This fact was first demonstrated in Chapter 4, section "Base Data Type Characteristics," which found that, within the Small memory model, objects of the fundamental types and pointers to such objects had the following sizes:

```
char         =  1    ptr = 2
short int    =  2    ptr = 2
int          =  2    ptr = 2
long int     =  4    ptr = 2
float        =  4    ptr = 2
double       =  8    ptr = 2
long double  = 10    ptr = 2
_segment     =  2    ptr = 2
```

Had the Compact, Large, or Huge memory model been used, the pointers to the fundamental types shown would all have been four bytes, not two bytes, in size.

Multibyte (Wide) Character Type

The implementation of multibyte (wide) character sets in the C language is a new Standard C feature and represents an accommodation of the interests of the international community of C users (as represented by the ISO). Unfortunately, Microsoft C version 6.0 presently does not implement this feature.

For source code, Standard C specifies a minimal character set consisting of 96 symbols: 26 uppercase letters, 26 lowercase letters, 10 decimal digits, 29 graphic characters, 1 space character, and 4 control characters (horizontal tab, vertical tab, form feed, and newline). These characters are all contained in the ASCII character set, but a few of them are not contained in the related ISO-646 Invariant Code Set (a subset of ASCII). To make these characters available for C source code on machines that do not otherwise support them, Standard C has introduced *trigraphs*, three-character sequences in the form **??*x***. Each trigraph is interpreted to represent one of the missing characters. DOS machines, of course, support the full ASCII character set, so trigraphs are not needed in Microsoft C.

The same need to keep Standard C independent of ASCII is reflected in the introduction of multibyte characters. Using one byte to define a character allows ASCII to represent only 256 characters. Languages such as Japanese and Chinese, however, require thousands of ideograms (symbols, not sounds) to convey meaning.

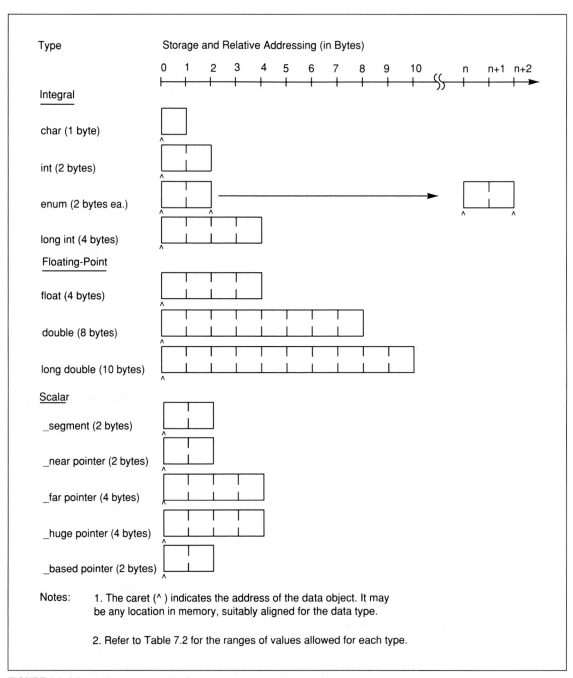

FIGURE 7.3: Microsoft type representations.

As you can see, the need for extended code sets is related to the new Standard C concept of locale (see the header file **<locale.h>**). Each multibyte character sequence is associated with a unique internal integer representation referred to as its corresponding wide character code. The Standard C type definition **wchar_t** (see Appendix D) defines the integer form of representation that in turn establishes a maximum number of unique symbols that may be represented. If **wchar_t** is defined as **int**, for example, 16 bits could be used to represent 2^{16} or 65,536 symbols.

When supported, multibyte characters may be present in the source character set within comments, character constants, string literals, or filenames. Null-terminated multibyte character strings may also utilize the C run-time library functions for string handling, character and string I/O using **scanf()** and **printf()**, for example, and other new multibyte to wide-character code translation functions.

The declaration of wide character constants will be discussed in the section "Type Constants" that follows. Wide character strings will be discussed in Chapter 8. Wide character and multibyte conversions, string handling, and I/O are not discussed in Parts VI and VII because these run-time functions are not yet available with Microsoft C.

Typedef *Type Definitions*

The Standard C keyword **typedef** allows the programmer to create additional type *synonyms* that subsequently may be used to define objects of any data, function, or incomplete type. **Typedef**s do not create new types, only synonyms for existing fundamental and qualified fundamental types, and are analogous to using the TYPE section of a Pascal program. **Typedef**s are useful in promoting program portability while at the same time simplifying the readability of complex type definitions.

Some commonly used **typedef**s (summarized in Appendix D) are defined when the corresponding header files are included by a source-code file. Notice that the entries are grouped as either Standard or non-Standard (Microsoft) C type definitions (**typedef**). The Standard C types are widely used throughout all header files and should be used to define such types in programs that you write. Use of these Standard **typedef**s in your programs will prevent an inappropriate type from being inadvertently specified. Although Standard and non-Standard **typedef**s are available, you are free to define additional **typedef**s as needed.

Let's examine the rules for declaring **typedef**s. Refer to Tables 7.7, 7.8, 9.1, and 9.2. To declare a **typedef**, substitute the keyword **typedef** for the lifetime and visibility storage-class qualifiers **auto**, **register**,

static, or **extern**. No other storage-class qualifier may be specified for a **typedef**. Choices may be made from all other columns in these tables. Note that the data object identifier column is interpreted as a **typedef** *synonym,* not a program variable.

Consider the following **typedef** for the lengthy definition for the variables **i_val** and **j_val** presented earlier:

```
static const unsigned long int i_val, *j_val;
```

or

```
typedef const unsigned long int CULI;
static CULI i_val;
static CULI *j_val;
```

Although capitalization is normally reserved for preprocessor macro identifiers, it is sometimes useful to highlight **typedef**s in your source code this way as well. Obviously this is simply a matter of programming style, but remember that C is upper-/lowercase-sensitive. The examples above define a variable **i_val** to be of type **CULI**, which is a synonym for type **const unsigned long int**. Notice that the keyword **static** is used to further qualify the **typedef CULI**. Variable **j_val** becomes a static pointer to a data object of type **CULI**.

Only the sign and size qualifiers (**signed**, **unsigned**, **short**, **long**) may not be used to further modify defined **typedef**s. For example, the **i_val** and **j_val** variables could also be defined as

```
extern volatile CULI _fortran i_val;
static CULI _near * const j_val;
```

which would define **i_val** as a volatile constant **unsigned long int** of storage class **extern** conforming to Fortran naming conventions, and **j_val** as a constant **_near** pointer to a constant **unsigned long int** of storage class **static**.

Complete examples of more complex **typedef**s will be included in the remaining chapters of Part III, involving arrays, strings, structures, unions, pointers, and bits. Also see Chapter 14 for examples of using **typedef**s to simplify the formation of complex function pointer declarations.

TYPE CONSTANTS

Constants are differentiated from identifiers (variables) in C source code by the fact that all identifiers must begin with a letter and may subsequently be followed by a letter, digit, or underscore character. Consequently, constants never begin with a letter, except for the new multibyte (wide) character and string prefix character **L (L'_' and L"_")**.

Table 7.9 summarizes the rules for expressing constants in the various types discussed in this chapter. Table 7.10 includes C escape sequences allowed as character constants. Integer constants are always assumed to be **signed** and of the type appropriate to the size of the value expressed unless octal or hexadecimal expressions are used, in which case **unsigned** is assumed. Under K&R standards, all floating-point constants were of type **double**. With Standard C, such constants are still of type **double** by default, but may be represented as type **float** by using the suffix **f** or **F**, or type **long double** by using the suffix **l** or **L**.

Using the guidelines in Table 7.9, let's look at some valid, and some unique invalid, examples of constants. The brackets [].[] shown are only used to indicate selection options; they are not a part of the constant specification itself, nor do they represent the subscript (array) operator.

For the type **char or signed char**, consider the valid constants for the source character A:

```
'A'
'\101'
'\[x or X]41'           /* '\x41' */
```

Also notice the following null character constants:

```
''         /* invalid null character */
'\0'       /* standard expression */
'\x0'      /* OK, but rarely used */
```

For the type **unsigned char**, consider the following character constants for the USA keyboard cent symbol, or decimal 155:

```
'\233'
'\[x or X]9[b or B]'    /* '\x9B' */
```

For more about string literals (string character constants), see Chapter 8.

For the type multibyte (wide) **char**, consider the valid constants for the source character A:

```
L'A'
L'\101'
L'\[x or X]41'          /* L'\x41'      */
```

Again, the multibyte (wide) null character would be specified as follows:

```
L''        /* invalid null character */
L'\0'      /* standard expression */
L'\x0'     /* OK, but rarely used */
```

For more about multibyte (wide) string literals (string character constants), refer to Chapter 8.

TABLE 7.9: Type Constants

TYPE	VALID CONSTANTS
`char`	`signed`: (default) actual range of value supported is –128 through 127. Any source-code character enclosed in single quotes, except the single quote, backslash, and newline characters. The adjacent use of single quotation marks to represent a null character is not permitted. Any octal (base 8) number, in the actual range, of the form '*n*' where *n* is up to three octal digits 0–7. All decimal (base 10) constants are understood to represent type `int` unless assigned or explicitly cast to type `char`. Any hexadecimal (base 16) number, in the actual range, of the form '\\x*n*' or '\\X*n*' where *n* is up to two hexadecimal digits 0–9, a–f, or A–F. One of the specially designated C escape sequences shown in Table 7.10. All other lowercase escape sequence characters are reserved for future use by Standard C. Negative values specify the unary – operator before the constant expression described above. `unsigned`: actual range of value supported is 0 through 255. Each `unsigned char` may be represented in the actual range as described above for `signed char`. `multibyte (wide)`: Microsoft presently does not support this Standard C feature whereby each wide character may be represented as described above for `signed char`, except that the prefix character `L` is appended. `strings (array of char)`: Additional support of null-terminated strings is provided by enclosing a character or sequence of characters in double quote marks. The adjacent use of double quotes is permitted to represent a null character. String constants may be up to 4KB characters long. See Chapter 8. Microsoft presently does not support the Standard C feature whereby a wide character string may be represented as a character string, except that the prefix character `L` is appended.
`int`	signed: (default) actual range of value supported is –32,768 through 32,767. Any octal (base 8) number in the appropriate range of the form *n..n* or 0*n..n* where *n* is any octal digit 0–7. Octal numbers are always prefixed with a leading 0 digit. Any decimal (base 10) number in the appropriate range of the form *n..n* where *n* is any decimal digit 0–9, except that no leading 0 digits are permitted.

TABLE 7.9: Type Constants (continued)

TYPE	VALID CONSTANTS
`int` (cont.)	Any hexadecimal (base 16) number in the appropriate range of the form 0x*n..n* or 0X*n..n* where *n* is any hexadecimal digit 0–9, a–f, or A–F. Hexadecimal numbers are always prefixed with a leading 0x or 0X. Negative values specify the unary − operator before the constant expression described above. `unsigned`: actual range of value supported is 0 through 65,535. Any of the methods described above for `signed int` may be used to establish a value in the actual range, except that the suffix character `u` or `U` is appended.
`short`	Implemented as type `signed int` above.
`long`	Actual range of value supported is −2,147,483,648 through 2,147,483,647. Any of the methods described above for `signed int` may be used to establish a value in the actual range, except that the suffix character `l` or `L` is appended. `unsigned long`: Actual range of value supported is 0 through 4,294,967,295. Any of the methods described above for `long int` may be used to establish a value in the actual range, except that the suffix characters `u` or `U`, and `l` or `L`, in any order, are appended.

`enum`	Implemented as `signed int` above. Enumerated constants are named constants that are initialized to an implied or specified value. For example:
	
	`enum { RED, GREEN, BLUE };`
	
	`enum { TRUE=1, FALSE=0 };`
	
	The enumerated constants `RED`, `GREEN`, and `BLUE` by default assume the values 0, 1, and 2 respectively.
	
	Up to 128 enumerated constants may be expressed by one enumeration type declaration.

`float`	Actual range of value supported is [−10^{38} through −10^{-38}], [0], [10^{-38} through 10^{38}] in IEEE 4-byte binary floating-point format.
	
	Any decimal (base 10) number in the form of
	
	`[whole].[fraction]{f or F}`
	
	`[whole][.][fraction][e or E][+ or −]`
	`[n..n]{f or F}`

TABLE 7.9: Type Constants (continued)

TYPE	VALID CONSTANTS

`float` (cont.)	where [whole] and [fraction] are any digits, [e or E] is scientific notation, [+ or –] is the power or inverse power of the exponent [n..n], and the {f or F} is a required suffix character.
	
	    Negative values specify the unary – operator before the constant expression described above.
	
	    No octal (base 8) or hexadecimal (base 16) forms of representation are permitted.

`double`	(Default) Actual range of value supported is $[-10^{308}$ through $-10^{-308}]$, [0], $[10^{-308}$ through $10^{308}]$ in IEEE 8-byte binary floating-point format.
	
	    Any decimal (base 10) number in the form of
	
	        `[whole].[fraction]`
	
	        `[whole][.][fraction][e or E][+ or –][n..n]`
	
	where [whole] and [fraction] are any digits, [e or E] is scientific notation, and [+ or –] is the power or inverse power of the exponent [n..n]. When no suffix character is specified as shown, the default type is `double`.
	
	    Negative values specify the unary – operator before the constant expression described above.
	
	    No octal (base 8) or hexadecimal (base16) forms of representation are permitted.
	
	    `long double`: Actual range of value supported is $[-10^{4932}$ through $-10^{-4932}]$, [0], $[10^{-4932}$ through $10^{4932}]$ in IEEE 10-byte binary floating-point format.
	
	    Any decimal (base 10) number in the form of
	
	        `[whole].[fraction]{l or L}`
	
	        `[whole][.][fraction][e or E][+ or –][n..n]{l or L}`
	
	where [whole] and [fraction] are any digits, [e or E] is scientific notation, [+ or –] is the power or inverse power of the exponent [n..n], and the {l or L} is a required suffix character.
	
	    Negative values specify the unary – operator before the constant expression described above.
	
	    No octal (base 8) or hexadecimal (base 16) forms of representation are permitted.

`void`	Since no storage is allocated for type `void`, it is inappropriate to express constants with type `void`. Pointers to type `void`, however, may be expressed as constants (see `_near`, `_far`, `_huge`, and `_based` pointers below).

TABLE 7.9: Type Constants (continued)

TYPE	VALID CONSTANTS
`_segment`	The segment: (16-bit) portion only of a memory address. `_segment` types are used to establish the segment portion of a `_based(..)` pointer that is combined with the offset using the `:>` operator (see Chapter 12) to construct a memory address. Constants that represent any valid paragraph (16-byte multiple) from 0x0000 through 0xF000 may be specified. The keyword `_segname("..")` can be used to transform predefined segment names (`_CODE`, `_DATA`, `_CONST`, and `_STACK`) or other valid code or data segment names to `_segment` values. The macro `_NULLSEG` defines a null segment, and `_NULLOFF` defines a null offset.
`_near pointer`	The offset (16-bit) portion only of a memory address. The CS or DS register is assumed to contain the segment component used to construct a memory address that uses only the offset (16 bits) to perform address arithmetic, thereby limiting the size of an object to one segment or 64KB. The macro `NULL` is used to define a `_near NULL` pointer.
`_far pointer`	A complete segment offset (32-bit) representation of a memory address that uses only the offset (16 bits) to perform address arithmetic, thereby limiting the size of an object to one segment or 64KB. The macro `NULL` is used to define a `_far NULL` pointer.
`_huge pointer`	A complete segment offset (32-bit) representation of a memory address that uses the complete memory address (20 bits) to perform all address arithmetic, thereby permitting the size of an object to span segments and exceed 64KB. The macro `NULL` is used to define a `_huge NULL` pointer.
`_based pointer`	The offset (16-bit) portion only of a memory address. The segment can be set to any valid (16-byte) paragraph address value and uses only the offset (16 bits) to perform address arithmetic, thereby limiting the size of an object to one segment or 64KB. See the discussion for `_segment` above.

For the type **int**, **signed**, **signed int**, **short**, **short int**, **signed short**, or **signed short int**, consider the constants for the decimal number −128:

```
-128
0177600
0[x or X][f or F][f or F]80        /* 0xFF80 */
```

TABLE 7.10: C Escape Sequences Allowed As Character Constants

SEQUENCE	DESCRIPTION	DEC	OCT	HEX
'\a'	Alert	7	\07	\x7
'\b'	Backspace	8	\010	\x8
'\f'	Form feed	12	\014	\xC
'\n'	Newline	10	\012	\xA
'\r'	Carriage return	13	\015	\xD
'\t'	Horizontal tab	9	\011	\x9
'\v'	Vertical tab	11	\013	\xB
'\''	Single quote	39	\047	\x27
'\"'	Double quote	34	\042	\x22
'\?'	Question mark	63	\077	\x3F
'\\'	Backslash	92	\0134	\x5C

For the type **unsigned int**, **unsigned**, **unsigned short**, or **unsigned short int**, consider the constants for the decimal number 128:

```
128
128[u or U]              /* 128u */
0200
0200[u or U]            /* 0200u */
0[x or X]80              /* 0x80 */
0[x or X]80[u or U]      /* 0x80u */
```

For the type **long int**, **long**, **signed long int**, or **signed long**, consider the constants for the decimal number 128:

```
128[l or L]              /* 128L */
0200[l or L]            /* 0200L */
0[x or X]100[l or L]     /* 0x100L */
```

For the type **unsigned long int** or **unsigned long**, consider the constants for the decimal number 128:

```
128[u or U][l or L]         /* 128ul */
0200[u or U][l or L]        /* 0200ul */
0[x or X]100[u or U][l or L] /* 0x100ul */
```

For the type **enum**, implemented as **int** by Microsoft, consider the constants zero=0, one=1, and so forth:

```
enum { zero, one, two, three, minus=-1 };
enum digits { three=3, two=2, one=1, zero=0, minus=-1 };
```

For the type **float**, consider the constants for the number −186,000.0:

```
-186000[e or E]0[f or F]       /* -186000e0f */
-186000[e or E]+0[f or F]      /* -186000E+0F */
-1.86[e or E]5[f or F]         /* -1.86E5F */
-1.86[e or E]+5[f or F]        /* -1.86E+5F */
```

For the type **double**, consider the constants for −186,000.0:

```
-186000[e or E]0       /* -186000e0 */
-186000[e or E]+0      /* -186000E+0 */
-1.86[e or E]5         /* -1.86E5 */
-1.86[e or E]+5        /* -1.86E+5 */
```

For the type **long double**, consider the constants for −186,000.0:

```
-186000[e or E]0[l or L]       /* -186000e0l */
-186000[e or E]+0[l or L]      /* -186000E+0L */
-1.86[e or E]5[l or L]         /* -1.86E5L */
-1.86[e or E]+5[l or L]        /* -1.86E+5L */
```

DATA OBJECT INITIALIZATION

Remember that the complete specification of a type definition essentially establishes a unique identifier (name), allocates the storage (memory or register) for a data object in bytes, restricts the objects to the operations permitted for that type (see Chapter 12), and establishes a valid range of value representation for the data object.

The matter of placing value or initial bit-representation in the allotted storage is called *initialization*. Initialization of **extern** and **static** variables to constant expressions can be performed at compile time, whereas dynamic expressions must be evaluated at run-time. Obviously, compile-time initialization is preferred. Otherwise, variable initialization must be handled during program execution by assignment or by using I/O run-time library routines (refer to Part VI). Standard C does not mandate the manner or timing of initialization and leaves it to the implementor's discretion.

The only automatic initialization is provided by the storage-class qualifiers **static** and **extern**. Remember that every data object definition is assigned a storage-class qualifier. Any variable of the storage class **static** or **extern** can be assumed to be initialized to zero (0), but it is still recommended that initialization be provided. Initialization is always necessary for storage classes **auto** and **register**. Any **auto** or **register** storage-class variable that has not been initialized cannot safely be assumed to have any certain value, zero or otherwise.

To initialize the types discussed in this chapter, except for pointers, is a simple matter of incorporating the assignment operator (the equal sign) in the definition itself, followed by a compatible constant or dynamic expression. The following examples demonstrate initialization:

```
char cval = 'A';
wchar_t wval = L'A';
int  ival = -128;
long lval = 128L;
enum {false, true} no=false, yes=true;
float fval = 1.86E5F;
double dval = 1.86e5;
long double ldval= 1.86e5L;
```

The initialization of enumerated types (**enum**) involves the definition of the associated set of integer constants and, optionally, other variables or pointers of that type. Note that enumerated types may only declare type **int** data objects, which may not be qualified further by use of the keywords **signed**, **unsigned**, **short**, or **long**. As indicated in the previous section, "Enumerated (**enum**) Type," only values in the value range of an **int** -32,768 through 32,767 may be assigned. For a complete description of initializing pointer variables, refer to Chapter 10.

TYPE CASTS

Casting is the temporary conversion of a data object from one type to another. The topic is fully described in Chapter 12, but we can briefly consider it here. Earlier, mention was made of the fact that C is a less strongly typed language than Pascal, for example. The cast feature of C facilitates retyping data object, function, and incomplete types. Consider this data-object type casting example, which uses the cast **(double)** to convert the **int** variable **i_val** and the **long int** variable **l_val** to type **double** before performing the calculation and assignment shown:

```
int i_val=30000;
long int l_val=1000000L;
double d_val;
d_val = (double)i_val / (double)l_val;
```

Otherwise the calculations would have been performed in integral **long** format, thereby truncating any fractional part and assuring that **d_val** resulted in a value of 0.0.

Casts utilize any parenthesized scalar type (or **typedef**) to convert the representation of the object that the cast immediately precedes. Note that only the scalar types **char**, **int**, **enum**, **float**, **double**, **_segment**, and pointers may be used with casts (see Figure 7.1). The aggregate types involving arrays, structures, and unions may not be used with casts.

Obviously, care must be exercised so that significant value representation is not lost when cast operations are performed. For more about this refer to Chapter 13.

Casts are particularly useful when working with pointers. The concept that a pointer variable contains the address of another object, whose value may be retrieved using indirection (*****), is predicated on the fact that a pointer variable is not just an address, but it also points to a particular type of data representation. Just as normal variables may be cast (retyped) to alter the form of representation, pointer variables may be cast (retyped) to alter the interpretation of the object type being pointed to. A complete discussion of using casts with pointers is deferred to Chapter 10.

TYPE PERFORMANCE CONSIDERATIONS

All variables (identifiers) used within a C program must be defined before they may be assigned value. The declaration methodology presented in this chapter for the qualified fundamental types and pointer-type data objects assure that a data object is created by the compiler and that it has a consistent set of characteristics.

Data objects must be chosen carefully to optimize the storage and performance characteristics of the resulting computer program. Table 7.11 presents a graphic reminder of the comparative storage and performance characteristics of the **int**, **long**, **float**, **double**, and **long double** fundamental types. Use this storage relationships table to evaluate the impact of selecting a different data-object type. For example, if you were going to change from type **double** to type **int**, the storage requirement factor would be 0.25, meaning that **int** takes only one-quarter of the storage space required by **double**. Conversely, to go from **int** to **double**, the storage factor would be 4.0, or four times the storage space. For individual data objects, these results may seem trivial; however, when working with structures and multidimensional arrays, storage trade-offs become a significant program design consideration.

The table will also help you evaluate the impact of selecting a different data object type. The relative times associated with performing **int**, **long**, **float**, **double**, and **long double** additions have been summarized assuming that floating-point emulation (not the coprocessor) was used. To go from using a **double** to an **int** the math factor is 0.036; that is, integer addition takes one twenty-eighth of the time required by **double**. Conversely, to go from **int** to **double** the math factor would be 28.1, or over 28 times as long for **double** addition. These differences are considerably more significant than the storage factors discussed above.

TABLE 7.11: Type Storage and Performance Characteristics

Type Storage Relationships					
TO:	`int`	`long`	`float`	`double`	`long double`
FROM:					
`int`	×1.0	×2.0	×2.0	×4.0	×5.0
`long`	×0.5	×1.0	×1.0	×2.0	×2.5
`float`	×0.5	×1.0	×1.0	×2.0	×2.5
`double`	×0.25	×0.5	×0.5	×1.0	×1.25
`long double`	×0.2	×0.4	×0.4	×0.8	×1.0
Type Arithmetic (+) Relationships (CL with FP Emulation)					
TO:	`int`	`long`	`float`	`double`	`long double`
FROM:					
`int`	×1.00	×1.13	×26.6	×28.1	×30.5
`long`	×0.88	×1.00	×23.8	×25.0	×27.1
`float`	×0.038	×0.042	×1.00	×1.05	×1.14
`double`	×0.036	×0.040	×0.95	×1.00	×1.09
`long double`	×0.032	×0.036	×0.87	×0.92	×1.00

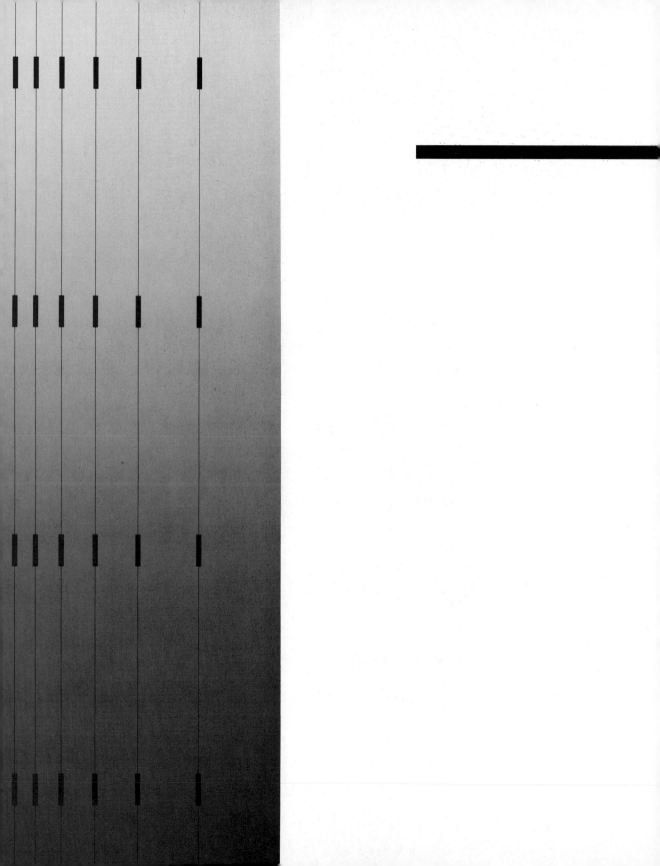

Arrays and Strings

Arrays and Strings

An *array* is a distinct data-object type in C that encapsulates the allocation of a fixed number of objects belonging to another fundamental, pointer, or aggregate type in such a manner that the individual elements may subsequently be referenced by using only the declared array name and an appropriate index value.

The bracket **[]** postfix operator is used to specify the number of objects that are consecutively allocated in memory. A one-dimensional array of ten **int**-type objects declared as

```
int int_array[10];
```

would permit the first element to be referenced as **int_array[0]**, and the last element as **int_array[9]**. When more than one set of brackets is specified, an array is said to be multiply dimensioned, and a corresponding number of indexes must be specified to correctly identify an individual array element.

This chapter explains the precise manner in which array elements are allocated to memory and develops a series of memory-mapping equations that describe the interrelationships between arrays, addressing, and pointers in the C language. By understanding arrays from this perspective, you can avoid the confusion commonly associated with the use of arrays, pointers, address arithmetic, and indirection in C code.

Strings are discussed in this chapter because they represent a special case of arrays of type **char** objects. Strings are not a fundamental type in C, as they are in other languages, but rather represent a special case of an array of type **char**. For this reason, all string-handling operations must be performed using run-time functions, not Standard C operators. By convention, the null character (**'\0'**) serves as a sentinel to indicate the end of a string.

For both arrays and strings, we will explain the impact of the new Standard C multibyte and wide-character sets; show how to declare incomplete arrays; review valid operations; discuss initialization; and assess the impact of various coding techniques.

ARRAYS

The basic syntax used to specify an array in C is as follows:

```
type  array_id [d1]..[dn];
```

The components of an array are the following:

type	Any type specifier, except type **void**, a bit-field, or function, that establishes the type of each element in the array.
array_id	Any valid identifier that becomes the array name and is equivalent to its starting (lowest) memory address.
[d1]	The number of elements associated with the first dimension.
..**[dn]**	An optional number of succeeding dimensions.

The total number of elements allocated for an array always equals the product of the dimensions specified ($d1 \times d2 \times .. dn$). Because all index (subscript) values originate at 0 for C, the largest valid subscript values are represented by $[d1-1].. [dn-1]$.

The lifetime and visibility of an array-type object are controlled by the storage class that is specified; however, **register** storage class is not appropriate for use with arrays, and if specified will automatically revert to **auto** storage class.

Arrays are most commonly used to allocate the fundamental types described in Table 7.7 (except type **void**). For example, the following statements:

```
int i_val[10];              /* 1-dimensional array */
float f_val[10][10];        /* 2-dimensional array */
double d_val[10][10][10];   /* 3-dimensional array */

char c1_val[];              /* incomplete 1-dim array type */
char c2_val[][10];          /* incomplete 2-dim array type */
enum tag varname[][10][10]  /* incomplete 3-dim array type */
```

define array **i_val**, consisting of 10 type **int** data objects; array **f_val**, consisting of 100 ($[10] \times [10]$) type **float** data objects; and array **d_val**, consisting of 1000 ($[10] \times [10] \times [10]$) type **double** data objects. Of the incomplete array types shown, **c1_val** is a one-dimensional character array, **c2_val** is a two-dimensional character array, and **varname** is a three-dimensional enumerated array.

Array notation using the bracket **[]** postfix operator may also be used to replicate objects of other types as well. For instance, all of the following may be treated as arrays: the pointer-type objects described in Table 7.8 and in Chapter 10, the data objects described by structures and unions (see Chapter 9), and function pointers (see Chapter 14).

Noticeably absent from the objects that can be subscripted are bits and bit-fields (see Chapter 11), because bits are not addressable, and arrays of functions themselves (see Chapter 14).

It is important to note that, while C identifies each element of **array[n]** with the bracketed subscripts **[0..n−1]**, other high-level languages have different conventions. For example, BASIC uses parenthesized subscripts $(0..n)$, Fortran uses parenthesized subscripts $(1..n)$, and Pascal uses any equivalent user-defined range of bracketed subscript values such as $[(k+1)..(k+n)]$, where k is any signed constant value. The effects of confusing the expression of subscripts in C with that of other language conventions were demonstrated in Chapter 4.

In the sections that follow, the row-major order in which the data objects of a C array are placed into storage is fully explained, together with array initialization. C handles array allocation in row-major (last subscript varies fastest) order like Pascal, while Fortran and BASIC use a column-major (first subscript varies fastest) memory-allocation algorithm.

To understand the concept of size related to arrays, consider the source-code fragment

```
double d_array[10][10];
printf("\nelement size = %d",sizeof(d_array[0][0]));
printf("\nrow size     = %d",sizeof(d_array[0]));
printf("\narray size   = %d",sizeof(d_array));
```

which produces the following results measured in bytes:

```
element size = 8
row size     = 80
array size   = 800
```

The array named **d_array** is defined to consist of the repetition of 100 ($[10] \times [10]$) type **double** objects. The first **printf()** statement above uses the **sizeof** operator to determine and display the size of one element, **d_array[0][0]**. The size is correctly shown as eight bytes, which is the representation of **sizeof(double)** used by Microsoft. Every element of an array is always of the same size.

The second **printf()** statement above determines the size of the first row of **double** type data objects. The expression **sizeof(d_array[0])** correctly displays the result of 80 bytes, or [10] objects × 8 bytes each. Multiply dimensioned arrays, designated by the successive declaration of the **[]** postfix operator, are interpreted from left to right, according to the precedence of operators established in Chapter 12. Therefore, **d_array[0]** expands to another array of [10] elements in this case, thereby confirming the size of **d_array[0]** as 80 bytes.

Consider if **d_array** had been dimensioned as **d_array[5][10][15]**. **d_array[0]** would then expand to a two-dimensional array of [10] × [15] elements, and **d_array[0][0]** would expand to a one-dimensional array of [15] elements. This view of C arrays is appropriate to *n* dimensions and explains, as we will discover later, how each level of subscripting adds a level of pointer indirection.

The third **printf()** statement determines the size of the array data object **d_array** itself and correctly displays the result of 800 bytes (or 100 data objects × 8 bytes each). Notice that an array data object is always exactly the size of the sum of the sizes of its elements. For this reason, as we will see in Chapter 9, structure and unions types are always padded to an appropriate boundary, so that they may in turn be treated as the base type of an array. Arrays themselves never contain pad bytes, but individual array elements may contain padding.

It is also important to understand the limitations imposed upon sizing array definitions. The maximum size of an array type object in bytes is not limited by Standard C, but rather becomes an implementation constraint. Two factors come into play: the segmented-addressing architecture of the 80*x*86 family of processors, and the storage class (lifetime and visibility) of the array object itself.

Because of the segmented architecture used with Microsoft C for DOS (refer to Chapter 2), all memory models except Huge limit array data objects to one data segment of 64KB (or less). Recall that 64KB is 64 × 1024 or 65,536 bytes. Only the Huge memory model permits array data objects to span 64KB boundaries up to the amount of available memory. Refer to Chapter 10 for complete details about pointers and addressing.

The size of arrays is further limited if they are of storage class **auto** rather than **extern** or **static**. All **auto** variables are allocated to the stack (**_STACK** segment); however, the stack is always fixed in size (default is normally 2KB). Recall the compiler (Chapter 2) and linker (Chapter 3) options for controlling stack size. Also refer to Chapter 15 for a discussion of how to size the stack.

Once an array object has been allocated storage, initialization of the memory space must be considered. Arrays of storage class **extern** or **static** are automatically initialized to zero, but it is still recommended that they be explicitly initialized. Remember that only external definitions without the keyword **extern** may be initialized, not subsequent declarations explicitly using **extern**. Also recall that external (**static** and **extern**) initialization may only use constant expressions because they must be evaluated at compile time (see Table 7.5).

Arrays of storage class **auto** (**register** reverts to **auto** for arrays) must always be initialized because they assume no reliable value by default. Initial values for storage classes **auto** and **register** are not restricted to constant expressions (as for **extern** and **static**) and may be any rvalue expression because they are evaluated at run-time. Complete details for the specification of initializer lists with arrays are provided in the following sections that describe array dimensioning alternatives.

Multibyte Character Arrays

The new Standard C concept of multibyte (wide) characters was introduced in Chapter 7 but is more fully explained in this chapter. The **typedef wchar_t** (see Appendix D) is implementation-defined and establishes the fundamental type representation of each wide-character constant. Remember that the objective of multibyte (wide) characters is to overcome the one-byte-equals-one-character barrier and its associated 256-character code limitation, inherent in the commonly used ASCII code set.

All of the array concepts discussed in this chapter may be directly applied to multibyte character data objects of type **wchar_t**. For example, the statement

```
wchar_t wide[5];
```

would define an array of five occurrences of a data object of type **wchar_t**. Each element of array **wide** would be referenced using subscripts **wide[0]** through **wide[4]**, inclusive.

The elements of array **wide** could have been initialized when defined if the statement above had been expressed as

```
wchar_t wide[5] = { L'a', L'b', L'c', L'd', L'e' };
```

where the character-constant prefix character L designates each character constant to be a wide-character type (refer to Chapter 7).

It is best to think of multibyte (wide) characters as a derived type (**typedef**) that defines a data object used to internally represent a unique wide-character code (integer) that subsequently may be encoded from a multibyte character representation and decoded to a multibyte character. The symbolic representation of these multibyte character strings is implementation defined and representative of a locale character-set extension to the basic C character set (see Chapter 6).

We will discuss in sections that follow how Standard C now supports arrays of **wchar_t**-type data objects. Multibyte (wide) characters then simply become **wchar_t** and array-of-**wchar_t** data objects that are special because they are logically treated as type **char** objects, but their interpretation follows a different encoding and decoding algorithm than the ASCII Character Set.

Arrays as Pointers

Once the storage (memory) space has been allocated by an array definition using the bracket **[]** postfix operators, C then permits array elements to be referenced either by using subscripts (originating at zero) or without subscripts by using pointer indirection and address arithmetic.

C treats array names as constant pointers to a data object of array type. This can be expressed as

```
array  =  &array[0]      /* Eq #1 */
```

which can then be recast to state the following:

```
*array =  array[0]      /* Eq #2 */
```

This expression can be recast as

```
array[0] = *(array + 0)   /* Eq #3 */
```

which can in turn be extrapolated to represent the **[i]** or **i-th** element as follows:

```
array[i] = *(array + i)   /* Eq #4 */
```

The expression on the right, (**array + i**), represents address arithmetic, since by substituting Eq #1 we get

```
array[i] = *(&array[0] + i)    /* Eq #5 */
```

In this case, with the expression (**&array[0] + i**) we are adding an address to a byte-offset. The term **i** represents the offset in bytes from the starting array address of element **i** of the array. Since all array elements are, by definition, of the same type (and thus size), it is implied therefore that all index (subscript) values are automatically scaled before address arithmetic is performed in C programs. The index value, **i**, on the right-hand side of Eq #5 is therefore automatically scaled as follows:

```
i = i * sizeof(array[0])        /* Eq #6 */
```

We find that

```
array[i] = *( &array[0] + i * sizeof(array[0]) )   /* Eq #7 */
```

which forms the basis of all array storage mapping equations, and as we will see, explains why all subscripts originate at zero, array elements are allocated in ascending address order, and no subscript bounds-checking is provided in C.

From Eq #7 we can see that when subscript **i** equals zero, the computed address becomes **&array[0]**, or the starting address of the array. All arrays in C are therefore assumed to originate from subscript **[0]**.

Similarly, we can conclude from Eq #7 that the elements of an array are placed into memory in ascending order. Successively larger index values result in successively higher memory address values.

Eq #7 also confirms why no array bounds-checking is performed in C. An expression such as

```
array[-10]
```

is perfectly acceptable in C as long as a valid memory address results when the expression

```
&array[0] - 10 * sizeof(array[0])
```

is evaluated.

Although BASIC, Fortran, and Pascal normally generate out-of-bounds subscripting compiler or run-time errors, unless an invalid address is generated, C provides no such protection.

Another interesting conclusion can be drawn from the equivalence of array names and addressing. As we will see in Chapter 10, any pointer (variable containing an address of a type object) may be treated as a one-dimensional array, even though it was not defined as such. For example, a simple pointer defined as

```
double *ptr;
```

may subsequently use subscript notation

```
ptr[i] = -12.0;
```

or

```
*(ptr+i) = -12.0;
```

Knowing the starting address (array name) and the type of object, everything necessary is then known to reference any array element using address arithmetic.

It should be apparent that this and other pointer-related features of C are fraught with danger. Such features were not designed into C by accident or oversight, however, but reflect K&R's original design philosophy to "trust the programmer" and "not prevent the programmer from doing what must be done." Although Standard C has taken steps (function prototypes) in some ways "to protect the programmer," K&R's basic design philosophy has been preserved by Standard C.

Complete examples of using indirection to reference the array elements using the storage mapping equations developed for multidimensioned arrays are provided in the sections that follow. Since arrays of multibyte (wide) characters are simply arrays of type **wchar_t**, pointers may also be used to reference each array element (wide-character code).

The special case of arrays of character strings is discussed in the "Arrays of Strings" section of this chapter. Their behavior is not to be confused with the manner in which an array of pointers to strings is used by DOS to pass command-line arguments to the C **main()** function using **main(argc, *argv[])**, which is discussed in Chapter 15.

One-Dimensional Arrays

One-dimensional arrays are defined using one set of bracket postfix operators (**[d1]**) appended to any valid data object type description. The following statements represent valid one-dimensional array definitions:

```
char char_array[2];
static const signed char _cdecl char_array[2];
wchar_t wchar_array[2];

int int_array[2];
extern unsigned short int int_array[2];

enum {one=1, two, three} enum_array[2];
static enum {one=1, two, three} _cdecl enum_array[2];

float float_array[2];
extern const float _fortran float_array[2];

double double_array[2];
auto long double double_array[2];

_segment seg_array[2];
extern _segment _based(_segname("_DATA")) seg_array[2];
```

Every array definition described above allocates two of the qualified fundamental type objects described in Table 7.7 except type **void**, which may not be subscripted.

To establish a uniform basis upon which multidimensional array storage-mapping and hence addressing can be explained, visualize the array data object allocated to storage by the statement **int array[2]** shown in Figure 8.1.

The elements of any one-dimensional array, **array[d1]**, are correctly referenced by using subscripting as **array[0]** through **array[d1-1]**, or, by using pointer indirection, as ***(array+0)** through ***(array+i)**.

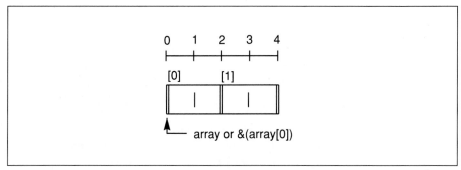

FIGURE 8.1: Storage-mapping and relative addressing (in bytes) of int array[2].

The expression **sizeof(array)** for the array in Figure 8.1 yields 4 bytes; **sizeof(array[0])** yields 2 bytes; the relative address **&(array+0)** is 0, and **&(array+1)** is 2.

The storage-mapping address equation that describes how C maps one-dimensional array elements can be evaluated as follows:

```
&(array[i]) = &(array[0]) + (i * sizeof(array[0]))
```

From Figure 8.1 for example, the address of the second array element can be computed using the formula

$$\&(array[1]) = 0 + (1 * 2) = 2$$

to yield the correct relative memory address for **array[1]**.

The program example shown in Figure 8.2 demonstrates three different array-element referencing techniques: subscripting, pointer indirection, and compact pointer expressions.

Compact pointer expressions involve the combined use of indirection (*****), autoincrement (**++**), and autodecrement (**--**) operators. Because the instruction set characteristics of the 80x86 microprocessors (and others) accommodate these combined operations, smaller and faster machine code is usually generated by the Microsoft compilers if this method is used. The "Array Performance Issues" section below quantifies the performance differences of one-, two-, and three-dimensional arrays. For more on the **++** and -- operators see Chapter 12.

To initialize a one-dimensional array when it is defined, an initializer list is specified. The following examples correctly initialize the elements of **array[2]** shown in Figure 8.1 to the values of −1:

```
int array[2] = { -1, -1 };
int array[2] = { {-1},
                 {-1} };
```

```
/* FILE: ch8e1.c */
#define TIMER
#include "timer.h"
#define SIZE 15625

int one[SIZE];                          /* 1-dim array */
int i;                                  /* index */
int *beg_addr = &one[0];                /* beg address */
int *end_addr = &one[(SIZE-1)];         /* end address */

int main( void)
{
START(1-dim subscripting);
   for(i=0; i<SIZE; i++) one[i]=0;
STOP;

START(1-dim pointer subscripting);
   for(i=0; i<SIZE; i++) *(one+i)=0;
STOP;

START(1-dim compact pointer subscripting);
   while(beg_addr <= end_addr) *beg_addr++=0;
STOP;

exit(0);
}
```

FIGURE 8.2: One-dimensional array subscripting.

The number of initializer values must not exceed the total number of array elements. If fewer initial values than the total number of array elements are provided, the remaining values are set to zero (0). All initial values are separated by commas. To initialize a complete array to zero, specify at least one element initializer.

Two-Dimensional Arrays

Two-dimensional arrays are defined using two sets of bracket postfix operators (**[d1][d2]**) appended to any valid data object type description. The following statements represent valid two-dimensional array definitions:

```
char char_array[2][2];
static const signed char _cdecl char_array[2][2];
wchar_t wchar_array[2][2];

int int_array[2][2];
extern unsigned short int int_array[2][2];

enum {one=1, two, three} enum_array[2][2];
static enum {one=1, two, three} _cdecl enum_array[2][2];

float float_array[2][2];
extern const float _fortran float_array[2][2];
```

```
double double_array[2][2];
auto long double double_array[2][2];

_segment seg_array[2][2];
extern _segment _based(_segname("_DATA")) seg_array[2][2];
```

Every array definition described above allocates four of the qualified fundamental type objects described in Table 7.7, except type **void**.

To establish a uniform basis upon which multidimensional array storage-mapping and hence addressing can be explained, visualize the array data object allocated to storage by the statement **int array[2][2]** shown in Figure 8.3.

The elements of every two-dimensional array, **array[d1][d2]**, are correctly referenced as **array[i][j]**, beginning with **array[0][0]** through **array[d1–1][d2–1]** or using pointer indirection as ***(*(array+0)+0)** through ***(*(array+i)+j)**. The expression **sizeof(array)** for the array shown in Figure 8.3 yields 8 bytes; the size of row 0 in the array is 4 bytes; the size of **array[0][0]** is 2 bytes; the range of relative addresses for **&(array[0][0])** through **&(array[1][1])** is 0 through 6.

The storage-mapping address equation that describes how C maps two-dimensional array elements can be evaluated as

```
&(array[i][j]) = &(array[0][0]) + (i * sizeof(array[0]))
                               + (j * sizeof(array[0][0]))
```

From Figure 8.3 for example, the address of the fourth array element can be computed using the formula

$$\texttt{\&(array[1][1])} = 0 + (1 * 4) + (1 * 2) = 6$$

to yield the correct relative memory address for **array[1][1]**.

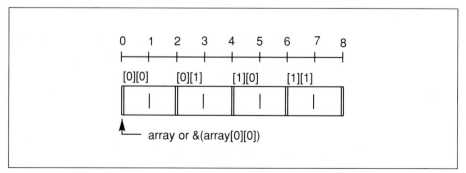

FIGURE 8.3: Storage-mapping and relative addressing (in bytes) of int **array[2][2]**.

The program example shown in Figure 8.4 demonstrates three different array-element referencing techniques: subscripting, pointer indirection, and compact pointer expressions. Again, compact pointer expressions involve the combined use of indirection (*****), autoincrement (**++**), and autodecrement (**−−**) operators and generally result in more compact code generation and better program performance (see the "Array Performance Issues" section below and Chapter 12).

To initialize a two-dimensional array when it is defined, specify an initializer list. The following examples correctly initialize the elements of **array[2][2]** shown in Figure 8.3 to the values of −1:

```
int array[2][2] = { -1, -1, -1, -1  };
int array[2][2] = { {-1, -1 },
                    {-1, -1 } };
```

The number of initializer values must not exceed the total number of array elements. If fewer initial values than the total number of array elements are provided, the remaining values are set to zero (0). The use of nested braces groups initial values into rows. All initial values are separated by commas. To initialize a complete array to zero, specify at least one element initializer.

```
/*FILE: ch8e2.c */
#define TIMER
#include "timer.h"
#define SIZE 125

int two[SIZE][SIZE];                    /* 2-dim array */
int i, j;                               /* indexes */
int *beg_addr = &two[0][0];             /* beg address */
int *end_addr = &two[(SIZE-1)][(SIZE-1)]; /* end address */

int main( void)
{
START(2-dim subscripting);
   for(i=0; i<SIZE; i++) for(j=0; j<SIZE; j++) two[i][j]=0;
STOP;

START(2-dim pointer subscripting);
   for(i=0; i<SIZE; i++) for(j=0; j<SIZE; j++) *(*(two+i)+j)=0;
STOP;

START(2-dim compact pointer subscripting);
   while(beg_addr <= end_addr) *beg_addr++=0;
STOP;

exit(0);
}
```

FIGURE 8.4: Two-dimensional array subscripting.

Three-Dimensional Arrays

Three-dimensional arrays are defined using three sets of bracket postfix operators (`[d1][d2][d3]`) appended to any valid data-object type description. The following statements represent valid three-dimensional array definitions:

```
char char_array[2][2][2];
static const signed char _cdecl char_array[2][2][2];
wchar_t wchar_array[2][2][2];

int int_array[2][2][2];
extern unsigned short int int_array[2][2][2];

enum {one=1, two, three} enum_array[2][2][2];
static enum {one=1, two, three} _cdecl enum_array[2][2][2];

float float_array[2][2][2];
extern const float _fortran float_array[2][2][2];

double double_array[2][2][2];
auto long double double_array[2][2][2];

_segment seg_array[2][2][2];
extern _segment _based(_segname("_DATA")) seg_array[2][2][2];
```

Every array definition described above allocates eight replications of the qualified fundamental type objects described in Table 7.7 except type **void**.

To establish a uniform basis upon which multidimensional array storage-mapping and hence addressing can be explained, visualize the array data object allocated to storage by the statement **int array[2][2][2]** shown in Figure 8.5. The elements of every three-dimensional array, **array[d1][d2][d3]**, are correctly referenced as elements **array[0][0][0]** through **array[d1-1][d2-1][d3-1]** or, using pointer indirection, as elements ***(*(*(array+0)+0)+0)** through ***(*(*(array+i)+j)+k)**. For the array shown in Figure 8.5, **sizeof(array)** yields 16 bytes; **sizeof(array[0])** yields 8 bytes; **sizeof(array[0][0])** yields 4 bytes; and **sizeof(array[0][0][0])** yields 2 bytes. The relative address **&(array[0][0][0])** is 0, and the range of relative addresses for elements **&(array[0][0][1])** through **&(array[1][1][1])** is 2 through 14.

The storage mapping address equation that describes how C maps three-dimensional array elements can be evaluated is

```
&(array[i][j][k]) = &(array[0][0][0]) +
                    (i * sizeof(array[0])) +
                    (j * sizeof(array[0][0])) +
                    (k * sizeof(array[0][0][0]))
```

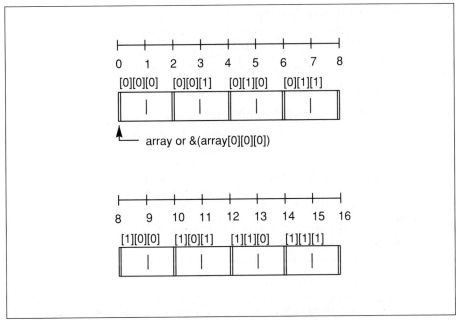

FIGURE 8.5: Storage-mapping and relative addressing (in bytes) of int array[2][2][2].

From Figure 8.5 for example, the address of the eighth array element can be computed using the formula

$$\texttt{\&(array[1][1][1])} = 0 + (1 * 8) + (1 * 4) + (1 * 2) = 14$$

to yield the correct relative memory address for **array[1][1][1]**.

The program example shown in Figure 8.6 demonstrates three different array-element referencing techniques: subscripting, pointer indirection, and compact pointer expressions. Again, compact pointer expressions involve the combined use of the indirection (*****), autoincrement (**++**), and autodecrement (**−−**) operators and generally result in more compact code generation and better program performance (see the "Array Performance Issues" section below and Chapter 12).

To initialize a three-dimensional array when it is defined, specify an initializer list. The following examples correctly initialize the elements of **array[2][2][2]**, shown in Figure 8.5, to the values of −1:

```
int array[2][2][2] = { −1, −1, −1, −1, −1, −1, −1, −1 };
int array[2][2][2] = { {−1, −1, −1, −1 },
                        {−1, −1, −1, −1 } };
```

The number of initializer values must not exceed the total number of array elements. If fewer initial values than the total number of array elements are provided, the remaining values are set to zero (0). The use of nested braces above groups initial values into rows. All initial values are separated by commas. To initialize a complete array to zero, specify at least one element initializer.

N-Dimensional Arrays

Unlike other common languages, C imposes no limit to the number of dimensions that may be used to define arrays. Obviously, the data and stack segment-related limits discussed above do control the total number of bytes based upon the memory addressing model being utilized. For example, the declaration of an **auto** storage class array as small as **double[20][20]** requires 3200 bytes, which exceeds the default stack size of 2048 bytes. *N*-dimensional arrays are treated in the same manner as multidimensional arrays discussed above.

```
/*FILE: ch8e3.c */
#define TIMER
#include "timer.h"
#define SIZE 25

int three[SIZE][SIZE][SIZE];                    /* 3-dim array */
int i, j, k;                                    /* indexes */
int *beg_addr = &three[0][0][0];                /* beg address */
int *end_addr = &three[(SIZE-1)][(SIZE-1)][(SIZE-1)]; /* end address */

int main( void)
{
START(3-dim subscripting);
  for(i=0; i<SIZE; i++)
  for(j=0; j<SIZE; j++)
     for (k=0; k<SIZE; k++)
        three[i][j][k]=0;
STOP;

START(3-dim pointer subscripting);
  for(i=0; i<SIZE; i++)
    for (j=0; j<SIZE; j++)
      for (k=0; k<SIZE; k++)
       *(*(*(three+i)+j)+k)=0;
STOP;

START(3-dim compact pointer subscripting);
  {
  while(beg_addr <= end_addr)
    *beg_addr++=0;
  }
STOP;

exit(0);
}
```

FIGURE 8.6: Three-dimensional array subscripting.

The storage-mapping address equation that describes how C maps n-dimensional array elements can be logically extended from the three-dimensional equation stated above as

```
&(array[i][j][k]..[n]) = &(array[0][0][0]..[0]) +
                          (i * sizeof(array[0])) +
                          (j * sizeof(array[0][0])) +
                          (k * sizeof(array[0][0][0])) +
                          .

                          .
                          (n * sizeof(array[0][0][0]..[0]))
```

Array initialization in n dimensions follows the same row-major structure described above for two- and three-dimensional arrays.

Incomplete Array Types

The declaration of an incomplete array type in C uses sets of bracket operators that specify all but the first dimensional size (row), such as

```
char one_array[];            /* incomplete 1-dim array */
int two_array[][5];          /* incomplete 2-dim array */
double three_array[][5][10]; /* incomplete 3-dim array */
_segment n_array[][5]..[10]; /* incomplete n-dim array */
```

All incomplete arrays have the common property that no storage allocation is made unless an initializer list is provided or the declaration appears elsewhere or is repeated in complete form. An array declaration of this form technically has been declared but not defined.

Initializer lists are commonly used with incomplete array types, which permits the compiler to size the missing array (row) accordingly. In the example

```
char one_array[] = { 'a', 'b', 'c', 'd' };
wchar_t wc_array[] = { L'a', L'b', L'c', L'd', L'e' };

int two_array[][4] = { {0, 1, 2, 3 },
                       {0, 1, 2, 3 } };
double three_array[][1][2] = { {0.0, 1.0 },
                               {0.0, 1.0 },
                               {0.0, 1.0 } };
```

one_array is declared as a one-dimensional array of **char** type objects and defined as **one_array[4]** by the initializer list; **wc_array** is declared as a one-dimensional array of **wchar_t** (wide-character) type objects and defined as **wc_array[5]** by the initializer list; **two_array** is declared as a two-dimensional array of **int** type objects and defined as **two_array[2][4]** by the initializer list; and **three_array** is declared as a three-dimensional array of **double** type objects and defined as **three_array[3][1][2]** by the initializer list.

Another common use of incomplete array types is for referencing externally defined data objects, such as

```
extern char *sys_errlist[];
```

which can be found in Appendix C. The **extern** qualifier indicates that the storage and initialization of this array of system error messages has been performed elsewhere. In the "Array Operations" section that follows, we will see how to determine the dimensioned sizes used with any array declared in this fashion.

Incomplete array types can later be redeclared to form a complete array data object definition. For example, the array

```
double d_array[][10];
```

could subsequently be completed if redeclared within the same visibility (scope) as

```
double d_array[10][10];
```

Array Operations

Since array objects are aggregate, not scalar, types (see Figure 7.1), the operations that can be performed upon an entire array object are limited. For a complete summary of the operations that may be performed upon array names and elements, refer to the Tables presented in Chapter 12.

Even the seemingly simple assignment of arrays is not permitted. For example, the source-code fragment

```
int x[4], y[] = { 1, 2, 3, 4 };
x = y;    /* error ! */
```

is incorrect when it tries to assign array **y** to array **x**. Only individual array elements may be assigned and manipulated by C operators, not the array data object itself.

We will find in Chapter 9 that C permits the assignment of compatible structure and unions types. Let's examine this apparent inconsistency. Recall that array names are actual constant pointers. Thus the assignment statement above is actually trying to treat a constant object (x) as a modifiable lvalue. This is not permitted. Because of the interrelationship of array names and pointers, it is impossible to express the syntax of array assignment without violating the syntax of C.

On the other hand, structure and union names are not equivalent to pointers unless subscripted, so they may be assigned, but only to compatible types. The assignment of scalar types relies upon the automatic casting of incompatible types. By contrast, casts may not be used upon aggregate types; hence the need for structures and unions to be compatible if they are to be assigned.

The only way to bypass this restriction is to define an array within a structure or union, which in turn can be assigned to other compatible structures or unions containing the array.

Another common problem when working with arrays is to determine the number of object type repetitions so that loops may be established to manipulate individual array elements. It is common to use macro preprocessor **#define** directives; however, as we will see, it is possible to dynamically calculate all dimensioned array sizes at run-time.

The following equations will always yield the total number of type objects in an array, N, where N is defined as type **size_t** (see Appendix D).

```
N = sizeof(array) / sizeof(array[0]);        /* 1-dim */
N = sizeof(array) / sizeof(array[0][0]);     /* 2-dim */
N = sizeof(array) / sizeof(array[0][0][0]);  /* 3-dim */
```

This basic equation is confirmed by the **sizeof** values revealed for the one-, two-, and three-dimensional array cases discussed above.

Similarly, the exact size of each subscript for multidimensioned arrays can be derived using variations of this basic equation. The first dimension, **d1**, defined to be of type **size_t**, of any n-dimensional array can be determined from the equation

```
d1 = sizeof(array) / sizeof(array([0]);
```

The second dimension, **d2**, defined to be of type **size_t**, of any n-dimensional array can be determined from the equation

```
d2 = sizeof(array[0]) / sizeof(array[0][0]);
```

The third dimension, **d3**, defined to be of type **size_t**, of any n-dimensional array can be determined from the equation

```
d3 = sizeof(array[0][0]) / sizeof(array[0][0][0]);
```

A formula for the general case of n dimensions, **dn**, can be inferred from the examples shown above. These equations exploit the manner in which multiply dimensioned array declarations are expanded to successive arrays of objects until the type object size itself is repeated as discussed in section "*N*-Dimensional Arrays" above.

The use of **typedef**s with arrays is an extension of the basic concept developed in Chapter 7 to include the postfix operator **[]**. Consider the array declaration

```
static const long int l_val[5][5][5];
```

which could correctly be declared with **typedef**s as follows:

```
typedef long int L3[5][5][5];
typedef long int L2[5][5];
typedef long int L1[5];

static const L3 l_val;              /* l_val[5][5][5] */
static const L2 l_val[5];           /* l_val[5][5][5] */
static const L1 l_val[5][5];        /* l_val[5][5][5] */
```

Recall that storage class qualifiers (**auto**, **register**, **static**, **extern**) cannot be included in a **typedef** and that all qualifier adjectives except the sign and size columns from Tables 7.7 and 7.8 may subsequently be used to qualify a **typedef** declaration of an object.

From the example noted above, **typedef L3** represents the typical use of a **typedef** for defining a three-dimensional array. Note that **typedef L2** can achieve the same result, but **l_val** must then be defined as **l_val[5]** to add another level of subscripting to the **L2** definition. Notice that **typedef L1** can also achieve the same effect.

It is also possible to use **typedef**s to declare incomplete array types; for example

```
typedef char STRING[];
```

which can correctly be defined and initialized as

```
STRING ch_array = "string";    /* ch_array[7] */
```

Array Performance Issues

In the one-, two-, three-, and *n*-dimensional array discussions above, three distinct element referencing techniques were described: subscripting, pointer indirection, and compact pointer expressions. The compilation and execution of the sample programs shown in Figures 8.2, 8.4, and 8.6, which use the **START()** and **STOP** timing macros developed in Chapter 5, yielded the following results when compiled with the Small memory model and executed on an 8086-based computer:

```
for  : 1-dim subscripting
time : 0.61 sec
for  : 1-dim pointer subscripting
time : 0.61 sec
```

```
for  : 1-dim compact pointer subscripting
time : 0.61 sec

for  : 2-dim subscripting
time : 1.21 sec
for  : 2-dim pointer subscripting
time : 1.21 sec
for  : 2-dim compact pointer subscripting
time : 0.61 sec

for  : 3-dim subscripting
time : 1.81 sec
for  : 3-dim pointer subscripting
time : 1.81 sec
for  : 3-dim compact pointer subscripting
time : 0.61 sec
```

Several important conclusions can be drawn from these results. First of all, regardless of the array dimensioning involved, there is no performance difference between subscripting and pointer subscripting. Whether you choose to code using the **array[i]** or ***(array+i)** form of subscripting, the resulting program performance will be the same. In essence, both forms are identical.

A second conclusion that can be drawn is that the performance of compact pointer subscripting is independent of the form of dimensional array representation chosen and only dependent upon the total number of elements in a given array. Whenever possible, use the compact pointer subscripting form to reference elements of an array.

Another conclusion that can be inferred from these results is that a linear relationship exists between the performance and dimensionality of an array. This is explained by the characteristics of the storage-mapping equations developed for each dimensional form. Multiple subscripting involves, by necessity, the fixed overhead of additional arithmetic address calculations. Whenever possible, avoid using multiply-dimensioned arrays.

Finally, it is important to note that by introducing **register** storage class variables in the programs shown in Figures 8.2, 8.4, and 8.6, the performance measurements shown would all be reduced by a factor of approximately 35 percent in absolute terms, but the relative differences between the subscripting methods would remain the same.

STRINGS

Strings in C are best thought of as a special case of character arrays. Normal character arrays represent the fixed repetition of a **char** data object. The maximum number of stored characters is established by the dimensioned size of a one-dimensional array of **char** elements. The following statement defines an array named **ch_array** to contain five characters referenced as **ch_array[0]** through **ch_array[4]**:

```
char ch_array[5] = { 'a', 'b' 'c', 'd', 'e' };
```

With the initialization shown above, element **ch_array[0]** equals **'a'**, **ch_array[1]** equals **'b'**, and so on.

Strings, however, although normally stored in arrays of type **char**, by convention are terminated by the first occurrence of a null (**\0**) character. Their length is established by the presence of this character, not the dimensioned size of the array itself.

Because strings are null-terminated, normal array subscripting is less useful than using pointers and compact pointer subscripting. Whereas heavy use of **for**-loops is made with arrays when the dimensioned limits are known, strings require **while**-loops because the location of the terminating null character is unknown.

The tedious initialization of arrays of **char** using character constants also gives way to the prevalent use of string constants to initialize strings. For example, the preferred way to store a string of characters in **ch_array** would be to assign the string literal constant "abcd":

```
char ch_array[5] = { "abcd" };
```

or

```
char ch_array[5]="abcd";
```

or

```
char ch_array[]="abcd";
```

which initializes **ch_array** in a manner identical to this:

```
char ch_array[5] = { 'a', 'b' 'c', 'd', '\0' };
```

Notice that the terminating null character takes one array element storage position! It is common in C to express the null (all bits off) character as **'\0'**, or octal zero; however, **'\x0'**, or hexadecimal zero, would also be appropriate but unnecessarily requires another keystroke. Interestingly, the null character is simply treated as a delimiter and not considered a part of the string length itself, but is actually stored as a character in the array.

It is important to make a clear distinction between the use of the operator **sizeof** in C and the function **strlen()**. The **sizeof** operator, as we have seen, concerns itself only with the storage and storage mapping characteristics of data-object types, not with the individual values assigned to array elements. In the example above, **sizeof(ch_array)** would yield five bytes, and **sizeof(ch_array[0])** would yield one byte.

To determine the string length of the character values stored in **ch_array**, the Standard C run-time library function **strlen()** is normally used. For example, **strlen(ch_array)** would return an integer value of 4, representing the number of **char** data objects in the string, exclusive of the null terminating character. Remember that the dimensioned size of an array of **char**, intended to represent strings, must reserve one element of the array for the null terminating character itself.

Should the null character be missing, almost assuredly other storage locations in memory will inadvertently be accessed or *clobbered*, because C does not provide for array bounds-checking!

Multibyte Character Strings

Multibyte (wide) character strings are a special case of arrays of **wchar_t** data type objects. (As discussed in Chapter 7, this data type is defined by Standard C but not yet implemented in Microsoft C.) An array of multibyte characters can be defined as

```
wchar_t wide[5] = L"abcd" ;
```

where the character-constant prefix character **L** designates each character of the string literal to be a wide-character type.

It is best to think of multibyte (wide) characters as a derived type that defines a data object used to internally represent a unique wide-character code (integer) that subsequently may be encoded from a multibyte character string representation and decoded to a multibyte character string. The symbolic representation of these multibyte character strings is implementation-defined and representative of a locale character set extension (see Chapter 6) to the basic C character set. Multibyte (wide) strings are simply handled by C as a special case of array of **wchar_t** type data objects, much as normal character strings are handled as a special case of array of **char** type objects.

All of the string concepts discussed in this chapter may be directly applied to strings of multibyte characters. For example, the declaration

```
wchar_t wide[5] = { L'a', L'b', L'c', L'd', L'\0' };
```

would initialize the array **wide** in the same manner as described above.

The null-terminated characteristic of strings is maintained in any multibyte (wide) code set, because '**\0**' or zero must be reserved to represent the null character. The preservation of this concept permits normal string handling and permits I/O run-time library functions to work transparently with wide-character extended code sets in the C language. For more information about these functions, refer to "String Operations" below.

Strings as Pointers

Again because of the array/pointer equivalence in C, a string begins with character ***array** (or in fact at any address) and is defined to extend thereafter as ***(array+1)**, ***(array+2)**, and so on, using address arithmetic, until the first null (**'\0'**) character is encountered.

Whether normal **char** or **wchar_t** type data objects are utilized, the pointer concepts developed earlier for referencing array elements still apply. For the character array definitions

```
char ch_array[5];
wchar_t wide[5];
```

the characters of either may be referenced as ***(ch_array+i)** and ***(wide+i)** respectively. The address arithmetic performed upon **+i** in these expressions is automatically scaled to **i*sizeof(char)** and **i*sizeof(wchar_t)** respectively to accommodate the data object type sizes involved.

There is a curious but powerful relationship between the conventions in C that:

- Strings are null- (zero-) terminated.
- True is equivalent to nonzero (!0).
- False is equivalent to zero (0).

These conventions, coupled with the dependence of the **while** statement upon a conditional test yielding true for looping to continue, create a dependent but powerful partnership between strings, the null character, and the **while** statement in C. Consider the source-code program shown in Figure 8.7, which involves four different techniques for copying string **t[]** to **s[]** using functions **strcpy1()**, **strcpy2()**, **strcpy3()**, and **strcpy4()**.

The functions **strcpy1r()**, **strcpy2r()**, **strcpy3r()**, and **strcpy4r()** identically implement the four alternative methods but introduce the use of **register** storage class variables for performance reasons. Refer to the section "String Performance Issues" for a comparison of these techniques.

Function **strcpy1()** uses traditional subscripting to assign **t[i]** to **s[i]** and compare the resulting value with **NCH**, a macro definition for the null terminating character constant. Notice that the **while** conditional

```
/*FILE: ch8e4.c */
#include <stdlib.h>
#define TIMER
#include "timer.h"
#define NCH '\0'
#define NTIMES for(i=0;i<5000;i++)

static void strcpy1 (char *s, char *t)
{
  int i = 0;
  while ((s[i] = t[i]) != NCH) i++;
}

static void strcpy1r (register char *s, register char *t)
{
  register int i = 0;
  while ((s[i] = t[i]) != NCH) i++;
}

static void strcpy2 (char *s, char *t)
{
  while ((*s = *t) != NCH) { s++; t++; }
}

static void strcpy2r (register char *s, register char *t)
{
  while ((*s = *t) != NCH) { s++; t++; }
}

static void strcpy3 (char *s, char *t)
{
  while ((*s++ = *t++) != NCH) ;
}

static void strcpy3r (register char *s, register char *t)
{
  while ((*s++ = *t++) != NCH) ;
}

static void strcpy4 (char *s, char *t)
{
  while (*s++ = *t++) ;
}

static void strcpy4r (register char *s, register char *t)
{
  while (*s++ = *t++) ;
}

int main( void)
{
  char s[80], t[] = "stringstringstringstring";

int i;

START(strcpy ver1); NTIMES strcpy1(s,t); STOP;
START(register strcpy ver1r); NTIMES strcpy1r(s,t); STOP;

START(strcpy ver2); NTIMES strcpy2(s,t); STOP;
START(register strcpy ver2r); NTIMES strcpy2r(s,t); STOP;

START(strcpy ver3); NTIMES strcpy3(s,t); STOP;
START(register strcpy ver3r); NTIMES strcpy3r(s,t); STOP;

START(strcpy ver4); NTIMES strcpy4(s,t); STOP;
START(register strcpy ver4r); NTIMES strcpy4r(s,t); STOP;
exit(0);
}
```

FIGURE 8.7: Classic string copy function alternatives.

test remains true (nonzero) until after the null character itself has been copied from **t[i]** to **s[i]**.

Function **strcpy2()** uses pointer indirection, instead of normal subscripting, and address arithmetic (**s++**, **t++**) to achieve the same result.

Function **strcpy3()** uses compact pointer subscripting by combining the indirection and autoincrement operators (***s++**, ***t++**) to have the **while** statement drive a null statement loop.

Function **strcpy4()** represents the most elegant expression of a string copy operation by eliminating the logical operation (**!= NCH**) from the conditional test to rely upon the fact that when the null terminating character is copied, the conditional expression evaluated by the **while** statement evaluates to zero (false) and ends. Any character copied, except null, results in a true (nonzero) test result to continue the loop.

As you'll see in the "String Performance Issues" section, however, the most concise source-code expression of the string-copy function **strcpy4()** is not necessarily the fastest.

Arrays of Strings

Multidimensioned arrays of strings behave identically to any multi-dimensioned array of **char** (or **wchar_t**), described earlier in this chapter. Consider the program in Figure 8.8. It produces the following results:

```
test[ 6][10]
This is an array of strings
This is an array of strings
```

Notice the inclusion of header file **<stddef.h>** to pick up the type definition **size_t** appropriate for use with the **sizeof** operator in C. The first dimension (**d1**) of the two-dimensional array is set to [6] by the initialization list provided. Each string is specified to have a maximum of 10 characters, including the terminating null character. Note that the run-time determination of array dimensions uses the formulas developed earlier in this chapter. The embedded **while** loop takes advantage of the fact that the only character value of zero is the terminating null character of a string. Each string is displayed, character-by-character, using the **printf()** character (**%c**) format control, while the second **printf()** relies upon the string (**%s**) format control to display characters starting at row **test[i]** and thereafter, until a null character is encountered.

It is important not to confuse arrays of strings with arrays of pointers to strings, which are used to handle the passing of DOS command line arguments to the C **main()** function using **argc** and ***argv[]** (or ****argv**).

```
/* FILE: ch8e5.c */
#include <stddef.h>
int main(void)
{
char test[][10] = {("This"),
                    ("is"),
                    ("an"),
                    ("array"),
                    ("of"),
                    ("strings")};

size_t d1 = sizeof(test)/sizeof(test[0]);
size_t d2 = sizeof(test[0])/sizeof(test[0][0]);
int i, j;

printf("\ntest[%2d][%2d]\n\n",d1,d2);
for (i=0; i < d1; i++) {
  j=0;
  while (test[i][j]) printf("%c",test[i][j++]);
  printf("%c",' ');
  }
printf("\n\n");
for (i=0; i < d1; i++) printf("%s ",test[i]);
exit(0);
}
```

FIGURE 8.8: Two-dimensional array of strings.

Arrays of strings, as in the example above, tend to make inefficient use of space. For example, the array **test[6][10]** allocates a total of 60 bytes, of which only 28 bytes (characters) were actually used. Arrays of pointers to strings, on the other hand, normally rely upon dynamic memory allocation (the **malloc()** family of functions, see Chapter 24) to allocate the exact size of a string, and then save the pointers to each string in an array. In this example, such a technique would have used 28 bytes plus 6 pointers (2 bytes each), or a total of 40 bytes. Obviously, as the number of strings involved increases, savings increase as well with this method. For more on arrays of pointers to strings, see Chapter 10.

String Constants (Literals)

There are two categories of string constants, normal and multibyte (wide) character. In contrast to normal character constants, which are enclosed in single quotes, normal string constants are enclosed in double quotes and referred to as string literals. Multibyte (wide) character and string constants follow the same syntax, except both wide character and string literals are prefixed with an L. For example, the following normal character strings are equivalent:

```
""              { '\0' }

"a"             { 'a', '\0' }
```

```
"abc"          {  'a',  'b',  'c',  '\0'  }
"ab"           {  'a',  'b',  'c',  '\0'  }
"c"
"x=%d"         {  'x',  '=',  '%',  'd',  '\0'  }
```

Likewise the following wide character strings:

```
L""            {  L'\0'  }
L"a"           {  L'a',  L'\0'  }
L"abc"         {  L'a',  L'b',  L'c',  L'\0'  }
L"ab"          {  L'a',  L'b',  L'c',  L'\0'  }
L"c"
```

Notice that unlike character constants, which cannot use adjacent single quotes to designate a null character, string constants are permitted to have adjacent double quotes to designate a null string. There is a significant difference between a single-character null constant (one byte), and a single-character null string literal (two bytes). A new feature of Standard C supports adjacent string literal declarations as shown above. If separated only by white space, adjacent string literals are automatically concatenated.

Escape sequence characters may also be embedded in strings; however, remember that if the single quote, double quote, question mark, or backslash is to be included in a string, it must be preceded by a backslash because these characters are considered special escape sequences themselves:

```
\'        single quote
\"        double quote
\?        question mark
\\        backslash
```

See Chapters 5 and 7 for examples of using double quotes and backslash characters in strings defining DOS file names with directories.

The following examples demonstrate normal and wide string literals that include the single quote and question mark characters:

```
"\'a\'"        {  '\'',  'a',  '\'',  '\0'  }
"\?a\?"        {  '\?',  'a',  '\?',  '\0'  }
L"\'\'"        {  L'\'',  L'\'',  L'\0'  }
L"\?\?"        {  L'\?',  L'\?',  L'\0'  }
```

String Initialization

String initialization follows the rules established for initializing one-, two-, three-, and *n*-dimensional arrays of type **char**. The row-major element storage algorithm used by C dictates the interpretation of the initializer lists that you provide in defining an array data object.

The following examples demonstrate the initialization of one-, two-, and three-dimensional arrays of normal and multibyte (wide) character strings:

```
char d1_array[20]        = {   "string[0..19]"          };
char d2_array[2][20]     = { { "string[0][0..19]" },
                             { "string[1][0..19]" }     };
char d3_array[2][2][20] = { { "string[0][0][0..19]",
                               "string[0][1][0..19]" },
                             { "string[1][0][0..19]",
                               "string[1][1][0..19]" } };

wchar_t d1_array[20]        = {   L"string[0..19]"          };
wchar_t d2_array[2][20]     = { { L"string[0][0..19]" },
                                { L"string[1][0..19]" }     };
wchar_t d3_array[2][2][20] = { { L"string[0][0][0..19]",
                                 L"string[0][1][0..19]" },
                               { L"string[1][0][0..19]",
                                 L"string[1][1][0..19]" } };
```

Compared with arrays of other data types, arrays of **char** may seem confusing. Remember that the product of the subscript sizes identifies the total number of (**char** or **wchar_t**) array elements. The **d1_array** above allocates 20 characters, **d2_array** allocates 40 characters, and **d3_array** allocates 80 characters. The subscripts used thereafter to reference a group of 20 characters (string) simply identify an address within the total number of type **char** repetitions that were allocated.

Incomplete String Types

Because strings are a special case of array of type **char**, the same rules apply that were discussed in the section above entitled "Incomplete Array Types." The examples included in the "String Initialization" section above represent complete array definitions because the size of each dimension is given.

Incomplete array type definitions could have been expressed for each of these cases by eliminating the first array dimension and letting the compiler size the array from the initializer list provided. The following partial example demonstrates this for the normal character strings shown above:

```
char d1_array[]        =  {"string[0..19]        "};
char d2_array[][20]    =  {{"string[0][0..19]    "},
                           {"string[1][0..19]    "}};
char d3_array[][2][20] =  {{"string[0][0][0..19]",
                            "string[0][1][0..19]"},
                           {"string[1][0][0..19]",
                            "string[1][1][0..19]"}};
```

which would define each array as **d1_array[20]**, **d2_array[2][20]**, and **d3_array[2][2][20]**. Notice that to maintain complete similarity, the string literal for the **d1_array** above had to be padded with blank characters to have exactly 20 characters, including the null terminating character. The same technique would apply for multibyte (wide) character strings as well.

String Operations

The discussion in the section above entitled "Array Operations" applies to strings because strings are not a fundamental type in C, but rather a derived, aggregate array type. Strings may not be assigned, copied, concatenated, subdivided, truncated, or moved without invoking a run-time function. Normal C operators do not apply to strings because array objects themselves are not considered modifiable lvalues. Most necessary normal string-handling operations are now provided by the C run-time library. Microsoft C 6.0 presently does not provide run-time library functions for multibyte character manipulation, however.

Header file **<string.h>** includes the function prototypes for all normal string-handling library functions and reserves the function names beginning with **mem[a-z]** and **str[a-z]** for future normal string-handling and **wcs[a-z]** for the future handling of wide-character string operations.

Header file **<stdlib.h>** includes the definition of object-like macro **MB_CUR_MAX**, which is the maximum length of a multibyte sequence for the current locale function prototype definitions for handling multibyte and wide character conversion operations, and reserves the function names beginning with **str[a-z]** for future string handling use.

Header file **<locale.h>** defines the macro **LC_CTYPE**, a category argument value to **setlocale()**, which affects the behavior of all character-handling and multibyte functions for a given locale. Remember that multibyte code sets were introduced by Standard C to accommodate cultural and regional symbolic representation needs (see Chapter 27).

Header file **<limits.h>** defines the macro **MB_LEN_MAX** as the maximum length of of a multibyte sequence for all defined locales. For additional header file details, refer to Chapter 6.

Presently Standard C defines the run-time library functions **mblen()**, **mbstowcs()**, **mbtowc()**, **wcstombs()**, and **wctomb()** for determining the length of multibyte and wide characters and strings and for converting between them; however, Microsoft has not yet implemented these functions. Refer to Chapter 26 for details on using the available string-handling functions.

String Performance Issues

In the section "Strings as Pointers" above, Figure 8.7 demonstrated four alternative coding techniques for copying **string t[]** to **string s[]**. Using the **START()** and **STOP** function-like macros developed in Chapter 5, we can compare the efficiency of these techniques.

Normally, concise or "elegant" source coding techniques are adopted because they generally result in fewer machine operations. A comparison of the four techniques reveals that in this case the most elegant style is not the best performer.

The compilation and execution of the source code shown in Figure 8.7 yields the following results using the QCL compiler on an 8086-based computer, and the Small memory model.

```
for  : strcpy ver1
time : 6.54 sec
for  : register strcpy ver1r
time : 5.71 sec

for  : strcpy ver2
time : 5.76 sec
for  : register strcpy ver2r
time : 3.52 sec

for  : strcpy ver3
time : 5.93 sec
for  : register strcpy ver3r
time : 3.96 sec

for  : strcpy ver4
time : 5.93 sec
for  : register strcpy ver4r
time : 3.96 sec
```

Several important conclusions can be drawn from these results. First, regardless of whether time-saving **register** storage class variables are used, **strcpy ver1** (**strcpy1** and **strcpy1r**) is the slowest, **strcpy ver2** (**strcpy2** and **strcpy2r**) is the fastest, and the **strcpy ver3** (**strcpy3** and **strcpy3r**) and **ver4** (**strcpy4** and **strcpy4r**) results are identical but slower than **strcpy ver2**.

Although it appeared that **strcpy ver4** would yield the best performance, it did not in this instance, but probably would on other microprocessors. The important lesson here is that the techniques you use to express the C language do have a significant impact upon the resulting program performance. Remember that the most elegant code isn't always the fastest, and that Microsoft's optimizing compiler will not necessarily produce a program that performs the best, as evidenced by the fact that the use of **register** storage-class variables is found to reduce measured performance times by up to 38 percent.

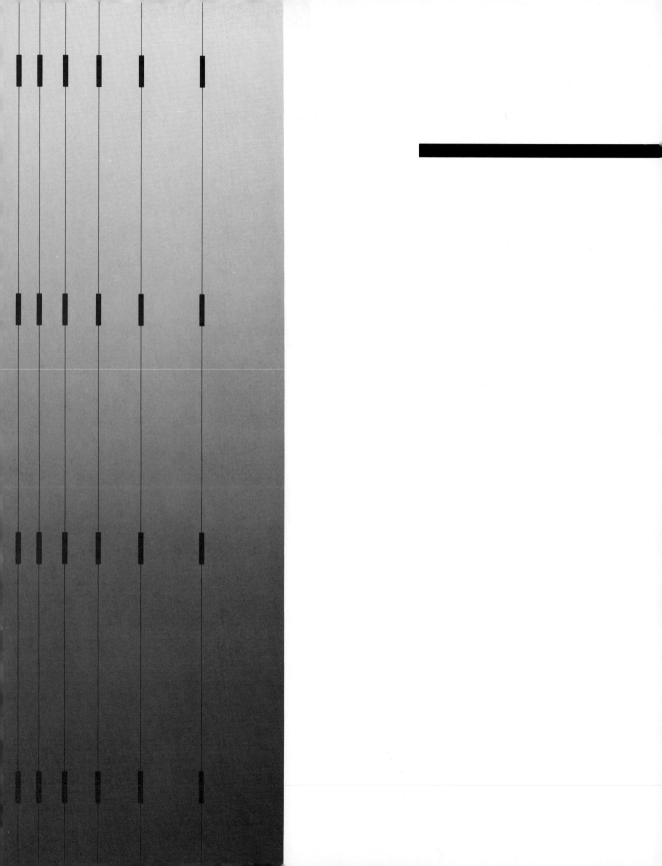

# CHAPTER 9

Structures and Unions

Structures and Unions

███████████ Structures and unions represent distinct data-object types in C that are used to encapsulate other dissimilar fundamental, pointer, bit-field (see Chapter 11), and aggregate types, in such a manner that individual members may be referenced by using only the declared structure or union name and a unique identifier constructed with the member operator (.). Structures are used to define fixed records in C and are analogous to the *record* type in Pascal, while unions are useful in defining variant records in C and are analogous to the *equivalence* statement in Fortran.

The term *member,* instead of *element,* is normally used to describe the components of a structure or union, because structure and union objects may themselves be treated as arrays. Structures and unions are unlike arrays in that arrays may only replicate one data object type, and arrays never introduce pad bytes. Structures and unions themselves differ in the manner in which their members are allocated to memory.

This chapter explains how structure and union members are allocated to memory and aligned (padded) to maintain the appropriate boundary alignment of each member object. By understanding the concept of alignment and pad bytes, you will then be able to create record designs that save both memory and disk space, and exploit the unique addressing properties of structures and unions.

For both structures and unions we will explain how to declare complete and incomplete types, how to work with arrays of the objects, how to declare and work with complex record formats, and how to initialize and operate upon these objects. We will also assess the relative performance tradeoffs of the various possible coding techniques.

STRUCTURES

The naming of structure variables (complete types) and structure tags (incomplete types) conforms to the rules for identifier naming discussed in Chapter 4. Structure names are identifiers that have a lifetime and visibility, like other program variables, determined by their storage class and whether they are defined externally (outside of braces) or internally (inside of braces). Structure member names, however, are unique within, and have scope limited to, the structure { . . } in which they are declared.

The following complete structure declaration defines a structure tag called **tag_struct** (see the section "Incomplete Structure Types and Definitions" below); a structure variable **struct_name**, having three members named **a_val**, **b_val**, and **c_val**; and a pointer to a structure named **ptr_struct_name** that may contain the address of a structure compatible with the tag **tag_struct**:

```
struct tag_struct {char a_val;
    int b_val;
    char c_val;} struct_name, *ptr_struct_name;
```

Note that a semicolon is required after the last member declaration of every structure. The members of **struct_name** may correctly be referenced using the (.) member operator as follows:

```
struct_name.a_val
struct_name.b_val
struct_name.c_val
```

If the structure pointer **ptr_struct_name** is initialized properly, they may also be referenced as:

```
ptr_struct_name->a_val
ptr_struct_name->b_val
ptr_struct_name->c_val
```

In this example, no structure initialization (see "Structure Initialization" below), no array members (see "Arrays of Structures" below), no structure or union members (see "Structures of Structures and Unions" below), nor any bit-fields (see Chapter 11) have been declared by structure **struct_name**.

Remember that any of the qualified fundamental types described in Tables 7.7 and 7.8 may be declared as structure members, but the storage-class (lifetime and visibility) qualifier for all members must be omitted. A structure is a distinct data object type having its own storage class and qualifiers as shown in Table 9.1. The qualifiers of a structure control those of its members. As in other declaration tables presented in this book, the default qualifiers for each group appear in brackets.

Use Table 9.1 as a guide for developing structure declarations. Notice that storage class **register** is not an appropriate qualifier for structures. For example, in the definition of the structure variable **struct_name** above, the table shows that we can assume either

```
[extern] [none] struct tag_struct {..}
    [_cdecl] [memory model] [none] struct_name;
```

TABLE 9.1: Structure and Union Type Declarations

LIFETIME AND VISIBILITY[1]	MODIFIABLE TYPE[2]	BASE TYPE[3]	MIXED LANGUAGE	ADDRESSING[4]	MODIFIABLE POINTER	DATA OBJECT IDENTIFIER
[auto/extern]	[none]	struct tag {..}	[_cdecl]	[memory model]	[none]	varname;
static	const	struct tag	_fortran	_near		[none];
	volatile		_pascal	_far		
				_huge		
				_based (..)		
[auto/extern]	[none]	union tag {..}	[_cdecl]	[memory model]	[none]	varname;
static	const	union tag	_fortran	_near		[none];
	volatile		_pascal	_far		
				_based (..)		

NOTES:

1. Lifetime and visibility (storage-class) qualifier must appear first with Standard C. [auto] assumed if defined within braces (internal); otherwise [extern] is assumed.

2. Both choices may be specified for modifiable type. All other qualifier columns only permit one selection to be made.

3. The syntax struct tag {..} and union tag {..} implies a semicolon-separated list of members within braces. The tag is optional when defining a complete type.

4. _huge may be specified only with storage classes static and extern, not auto. The syntax _based (..) denotes that a segment reference must be provided in parentheses. The segment references void and self may not be used with _based (..) for structure and union type declarations.

or

```
[auto] [none] struct tag_struct {..}
    [_cdecl] [memory model] [none] struct_name;
```

depending on whether this declaration occurs at the external (outside of braces) or internal (inside of braces) level. These definitions can in turn be interpreted, for the Small memory model, as either

```
[extern] struct tag_struct {..} _cdecl _near struct_name;
```

or

```
auto struct tag_struct {..} _cdecl _near struct_name;
```

Another possible alternative declaration of variable **struct_name** might have been expressed as

```
[static][const] struct {..} [_fortran][_far][none] struct_name;
```

or

```
static const struct {..} _fortran _far struct_name;
```

defining a variable, **struct_name**, to be a static, constant structure without a tag name that conforms to Fortran, not C, naming conventions and has **_far** addressing (no assumed DS register segment).

The expression **sizeof(struct_name)** yields the size of the structure object in bytes and represents the sum of the sizes of each member plus any required pad bytes.

Pointers to a structure data object may be expressed using Table 9.2 as a template. Again, the default qualifier for each base type appears in brackets.

Notice that **register** storage class is acceptable for pointer variables, but that no mixed language keywords may be used. For example, the definition of the structure-pointer variable **ptr_struct_name** in the example above can be interpreted according to the table (using the Small memory model) as either

```
[extern] [none] struct tag_struct {..} [none]
    [memory model] * [none] ptr_struct_name;
```

or

```
[extern] struct tag_struct {..} _near *ptr_struct_name;
```

It is clear that structure-pointer variable **ptr_struct_name** is understood to be of storage class **extern** and represents a **_near** address (offset to assumed segment DS register). Another possible alternative declaration of **ptr_struct_name** might have been

TABLE 9.2: Structure and Union Pointer Type Declarations

LIFETIME AND VISIBILITY[1]	MODIFIABLE TYPE[2]	BASE TYPE[3]	MIXED LANGUAGE	ADDRESSING[4]	MODIFIABLE POINTER[2]	DATA OBJECT IDENTIFIER
[auto/extern] register static	[none] const volatile	struct tag {..} struct tag	[none]	[memory model] * _near * _far * _huge * _based (..) *	[none] const volatile	varname;
[auto/extern] register static	[none] const volatile	union tag {..} union tag	[none]	[memory model] * _near* _far* _huge* _based (..) *	[none] const volatile	varname;

NOTES:

1. Lifetime and visibility (storage-class) qualifier must appear first with Standard C. [auto] assumed if defined within braces (internal); otherwise [extern] is assumed.
2. Both choices may be specified for modifiable type and modifiable pointer. All other qualifier columns permit only one selection to be made.
3. The syntax struct tag {..} and union tag {..} implies a semicolon-separated list of members within braces. The tag is optional when defining a complete type.
4. _huge may be specified only with storage classes static and extern, not auto. The syntax _based (..) denotes that a segment reference must be provided in parentheses.

```
[static] [const] struct {..} [none]
    [_far] * [none] ptr_struct_name;
```

or

```
static const struct {..} _far *ptr_struct_name;
```

This defines a pointer variable, **ptr_struct_name**, to be a static pointer to a constant structure without a tag name, representing a **_far** address (no assumed DS register segment addressing).

Pointers to structures are simply pointer variables whose size is not **sizeof(struct_name)** but **sizeof(ptr_struct_name)**, which is always either two bytes (**_near**, **_based**) or four bytes (**_far**, **_huge**), depending upon the compiler memory-addressing model being used.

If the structure-pointer variable **ptr_struct_name**, defined above, were assigned an address value using the (**&**) address-of operator as

```
ptr_struct_name = &struct_name;
```

then the members of **struct_name** could alternatively be referenced using the pointer to a member operator (**->**), as follows:

```
ptr_struct_name->a_val
ptr_struct_name->b_val
ptr_struct_name->c_val
```

Standard C mandates that structure members be data object types, not incomplete or function types. This precludes any structure (or union) from including itself as a member; however, members may represent pointers to either incomplete or function types, thus opening the possibility of having a structure contain a pointer reference to itself. This is the basis of implementing singly and doubly linked lists (refer to Chapter 10). Pointers to incomplete and function types may be included in structures (or unions) because the storage for a pointer may be allocated, and a value (actual address) may be initialized when the pointer member is defined or later assigned at run-time. Although Microsoft has extended the C language to support the definition of an incomplete array type as the last member of a structure (see Chapter 29), use of this non-Standard feature is not recommended.

The performance characteristics of the member (**.**) and pointer-to-a-member (**->**) operators are compared in the "Structure and Union Performance Issues" section below.

Structure Alignment and Size

The default alignment of structure members and structures themselves is controlled by the following rules:

1. Members of type **char** are byte-aligned.
2. All other members are word-aligned. For Intel 8086, 80186, and 80286, two bytes per word; and for Intel 80386 and 80486, four bytes per word.
3. Structures (or unions) themselves are word-aligned and padded after their last member descriptions if necessary.

The use of compiler option **/G0**, **/G1**, and **/G2** establishes the default word sizes noted above. If the default alignment (no compiler option **/Zp<1|2|4>** or **#pragma pack(1|2|4)** specified) is used with an Intel 8086 microcomputer to compile and execute the program shown in Figure 9.1, then a word size of two bytes is assumed, and the following output is generated:

```
sizeof struct_name  6
sizeof member a_val 1
sizeof member b_val 2
sizeof member c_val 1
```

Notice that two pad bytes were introduced in the output example above. Pad bytes do not have an identifier or any reliably assigned value, nor do they alter the storage characteristics of adjacent members. A structure itself must be aligned to establish a proper boundary so that it may subsequently be replicated using the array **[]** postfix operator. Remember that arrays never introduce pad bytes!

Table 9.3 summarizes the effects of the Intel chip (**/Gn**) and compiler option (**/Zp<n>**) upon structure and member sizes, using the

```
/* FILE: ch9e1.c */
#include <stdio.h>
int main(void)
{
struct tag_struct {char a_val;
                   int b_val;
                   char c_val;} struct_name;
printf("\nsizeof struct_name  %d",sizeof(struct_name));
printf("\nsizeof member a_val %d",sizeof(struct_name.a_val));
printf("\nsizeof member b_val %d",sizeof(struct_name.b_val));
printf("\nsizeof member c_val %d",sizeof(struct_name.c_val));
exit(0);
}
```

FIGURE 9.1: The sample program ch9e1.c displays the size (in bytes) of the members of a structure.

struct_name structure described above (see Chapter 2). Notice that any padding introduced to satisfy the alignment requirements of members or structures themselves affects only the overall size of a structure, not the size of any member.

It is sometimes important, for sorting and other record-handling purposes, to know the exact offset (from the structure address itself) of a structure member. Standard C has added the function-like macro definition **offsetof(s,m)**, defined in header file **<stddef.h>**, which returns the zero-origin offset in bytes of member *m* in structure (or union) **s**. The program listed in Figure 9.2 demonstrates the use of the new **offsetof(s,m)** macro with the Small memory model on an 8086-based computer and produces the following output:

```
offsetof a_val 0
offsetof b_val 2
offsetof c_val 4
```

We will see in Chapter 10 how these offset values may in turn be used as an alternative method of determining the address of a structure member.

Figure 9.3 will help you visualize Table 9.3, confirm the results produced by Figure 9.2, and demonstrate the use of the **offsetof(s,m)** macro. Notice that pad bytes affect the offsets of members within a structure but not the member properties themselves. All pad bytes shown in Figure 9.3 at the end of each structure are necessary to maintain structure, not member, alignment.

TABLE 9.3: Structure and Member Sizes

INTEL CHIP	COMPILER OPTION	struct_name	a_val	b_val	c_val
8086 (/G0), 80186 (/G1), or 80286 (/G2) (word=2)	/Zp1	4	1	2	1
	/Zp2	6	1	2	1
	/Zp4	6	1	2	1
80386 or 80486 (word=4)	/Zp1	4	1	2	1
	/Zp2	6	1	2	1
	/Zp4	12	1	2	1

NOTES:
- /Zp1 same as #pragma pack(1); /Zp2 same as pack(2); /Zp4 same as pack(4).
- If just Zp is specified, /Zp1 is assumed.
- If /Zpn exceeds the word size of the chip, then /Zpword is assumed.

From Figure 9.3, notice that for the **struct_name** example presented earlier (Intel 8086, **/Zp<2>**), one pad byte is located immediately following member **a_val** to start member **b_val** on a proper **<word=2>** boundary, and the second pad byte is located immediately following member **c_val** to align the structure itself on a proper **<word=2>** boundary.

Incomplete Structure Types and Definitions

Incomplete structure types have the property of declaring a structure template, assigning a structure tag name for subsequent reference, and allocating no storage space for a structure variable itself. (See Appendix E for a complete list of Standard and Microsoft C incomplete structure types.) Incomplete structure types (tags) are used to facilitate the subsequent definition of commonly used structure types. Every incomplete structure type has the following basic format:

```
struct tag_struct {..};
```

In this format **struct** is a C keyword, **tag_struct** is any valid tag name, and **{..}** indicates a structure member declaration list. No qualifiers are used with incomplete structure types, because no storage is being allocated; only a template definition is being created. Unlike incomplete array types, no initializer lists may be specified with an incomplete structure type.

Once a structure tag name is created, it may subsequently be referenced, if within scope (visible), to define a complete structure variable and therefore allocate storage space:

```
[qualifier..] struct tag_struct [qualifier..] u_struct_name;
```

```
/* FILE: ch9e2.c */
#include <stdio.h>
#include <stddef.h>
int main(void)
{
struct tag_struct {char a_val;
                   int b_val;
                   char c_val;} struct_name;
printf("\noffsetof a_val %d",offsetof(struct tag_struct,a_val));
printf("\noffsetof b_val %d",offsetof(struct tag_struct,b_val));
printf("\noffsetof c_val %d",offsetof(struct tag_struct,c_val));
exit(0);
}
```

FIGURE 9.2: The sample program ch9e2.c displays the offsets (in bytes) of the members of a structure.

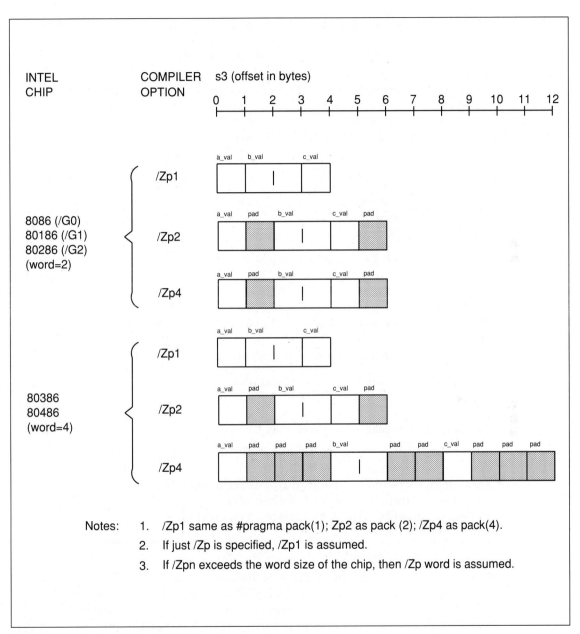

INTEL CHIP   COMPILER OPTION   s3 (offset in bytes)

8086 (/G0)
80186 (/G1)
80286 (/G2)
(word=2)

/Zp1
/Zp2
/Zp4

80386
80486
(word=4)

/Zp1
/Zp2
/Zp4

Notes: 1.   /Zp1 same as #pragma pack(1); Zp2 as pack (2); /Zp4 as pack(4).
2.   If just /Zp is specified, /Zp1 is assumed.
3.   If /Zpn exceeds the word size of the chip, then /Zp word is assumed.

FIGURE 9.3: Structure member offsets.

or

```
[qualifier..] struct tag_struct [qualifier..] i_struct_name
    = {initializer list};
```

Once **tag_struct** has been declared, an uninitialized structure variable **u_struct_name** and an initialized structure variable **i_struct_name** could be defined as shown above. Notice that **[qualifier..]** is shown to indicate that the type qualifiers shown in Table 9.1 may be included. For more on structure initializer lists, see "Structure Initialization" below.

Two other formats for complete, combined structure declarations are possible. In the following two examples, the structure variables **u_struct_name** and **i_struct_name** are allocated storage for a **{..}** structure member declaration list; and at the same time, a tag name, **tag_struct**, is created for future use:

```
struct tag_struct {..} u_struct_name;
```

```
struct tag_struct {..} i_struct_name = {initializer list};
```

Notice that tag names are optional when a complete structure definition is made; however, they are required when an incomplete structure type is declared.

In a similar fashion, pointers to structures may be specified as

```
[qualifier..] struct tag_struct [qualifier..] *ptr_struct_name;
```

or

```
[qualifier..] struct {..} [qualifier..] *ptr_struct_name;
```

using a reference to either an incomplete or a complete structure type declaration. Storage for pointers to structures may be allocated even though an incomplete structure type is referenced. Pointers to structures may also be initialized if appropriate reference is made to a previously defined compatible structure variable. For example:

```
[qualifier..] struct tag_struct [qualifier..] *ptr_struct_name
    = &(struct_name);
```

It is the ability to define pointers to incomplete structure types (and arrays, unions, and functions) that permits structures to contain pointer references to incomplete types and supports the creation of linked lists. For more on pointer members of structures and unions, see Chapter 10.

Arrays of Structures

Because the complete definition of a structure data type object always allocates an appropriately padded structure object, every structure variable is a candidate to be treated as an array of structure objects using the postfix array operator **[]** discussed in Chapter 8.

Arrays of structure type objects follow all of the rules and conventions established for arrays in general. Only the methods of referencing array elements and structure members need further clarification.

A structure variable array, like any other array, can be expressed in *n* dimensions. For example, arrays of **tag_struct** objects can be defined as follows:

```
#define D1 2
#define D2 3
#define D3 4

struct tag_struct {char a_val;
    int b_val;
    char c_val;} struct_name;

struct tag_struct d1_struct_name[D1];
struct tag_struct d2_struct_name[D1][D2];
struct tag_struct d3_struct_name[D1][D2][D3];
```

Remember that the size of the basic structure object, **struct_name**, is controlled by the compiler option **/Zpn**, compiler directive **#pragma pack(n)**, and the associated word size (**/Gn** option) in effect. The **struct_name** object above, which is **sizeof(struct_name)** bytes long, is repeated by the array dimensions specified. In the example above, **d1_struct_name** allocates two, **d2_struct_name** allocates six, and **d3_struct_name** allocates 24 **struct_name** type objects.

Care must be taken when defining arrays of structures. If the storage class is **auto**, an array of structures will be allocated to the stack (default size is 2KB). If the stack size is exceeded, a run-time error results (see compiler option **/F<n>** in Chapter 2; linker option **/ST:<n>** or **EXEHDR** option **/S<n>** in Chapter 3; and sizing the stack, discussed in Chapter 15).

If the storage class is **static** or **external**, the default DS register data segment for the Tiny, Small, and Medium memory models is used and may contain only up to 64KB; however, for the Compact, Large, and Huge memory models, separate 64KB segments may be allocated (see Figures 2.21 through 2.26). Only the Huge memory model supports data objects that are larger than 64KB. Data segment memory and stack restrictions are always a factor to consider with arrays, and even more so with arrays of structures, whose elements are typically larger in size than individual fundamental data object types.

The **c_val** member of the *last* array element in each of the above arrays may be referenced using the (.) member operator as follows:

```
d1_struct_name[1].c_val
d2_struct_name[1][2].c_val
d3_struct_name[1][2][3].c_val
```

We may also use pointer indirection and the –> pointer-to-a-member operator to reference the members described above. The pointer variable **ptr_struct_name** could be defined and assigned the address of the corresponding array element to permit the members of the *last* structure object to be referenced as follows:

```
struct tag_struct *ptr_struct_name;

ptr_struct_name = &(d1_struct_name[1]);
ptr_struct_name->c_val

ptr_struct_name = &(d2_struct_name[1][2]);
ptr_struct_name->c_val

ptr_struct_name = &(d3_struct_name[1][2][3]);
ptr_struct_name->c_val
```

The examples presented so far demonstrate the typical use of the member (.) and pointer-to-a-member (–>) operators with arrays of structures. However, since arrays may be referenced using normal subscripting (**[]..[]**), or by using pointer indirection (*****), other valid forms of expression may be used to reference the members of an array of structures.

In the fundamental relationship between array subscripting and pointer indirection, **array[i]** is equivalent to ***(array+i)**. Instead of using the subscript operators **[]..[]**, as discussed in Chapter 8, we can use the pointer indirection operator (*****) with both the (.) member and (–>) pointer-to-a-member operators.

Let's first examine how to recast the expression of subscripted arrays of structures to use indirection with the member operator. As we will discover in Chapter 12, the member operator has a higher precedence than the indirection operator. We must therefore use parentheses to override the default order of operator precedence. The following structure member references are patterned after the expressions developed in Chapter 8 for array elements and are equivalent to those developed using subscripts **[]..[]** and the structure member (.) operators shown above:

```
(*(d1_struct_name+1)).c_val
(*(*(d2_struct_name+1)+2)).c_val
(*(*(*(d3_struct_name+1)+2)+3)).c_val
```

Now consider how subscripted arrays of structures may be recast to use indirection with the —> operator. The fact that any array name is equivalent to `&(array[0])` in C permits us to eliminate the introduction of the pointer variable **ptr_struct_name** altogether:

```
d1_struct_name = &(d1_struct_name[0])
d2_struct_name = &(d2_struct_name[0][0])
d3_struct_name = &(d3_struct_name[0][0][0])
```

Also, since the —> operator has a higher precedence than both the indirection and addition operators, we must again use parentheses to override the default order of operator precedence. The following examples are equivalent to those developed earlier using subscripts `[]..[]` and the —> operator, and are patterned after the expressions developed in Chapter 8 for array elements:

```
(d1_struct_name+1)->c_val
(*(d2_struct_name+1)+2)->c_val
(*(*(d3_struct_name+1)+2)+3)->c_val
```

The merits of using the alternative member referencing techniques described in this section, together with another composite form (compact pointer addressing), are compared from a performance point of view in the "Structure and Union Performance Issues" section below.

Before ending the discussion of arrays of structures, let's clarify the case where a member of an array of structures is an array itself. Consider the revised structure template **rev_tag_struct** shown below:

```
struct rev_tag_struct {char a_val;
    int b_val[10];
    char c_val;} struct_name;
```

In this case, member **b_val** is itself an array of type **int** data objects. Consider the following valid references to the last element of member **b_val**, **b_val[9]**, for the last element of each array of structures, using the four alternative member referencing techniques described earlier:

```
d1_struct_name[1].b_val[9]
d2_struct_name[1][2].b_val[9]
d3_struct_name[1][2][3].b_val[9]

ptr_struct_name = &(d1_struct_name[1]);
ptr_struct_name->b_val[9]
ptr_struct_name = &(d2_struct_name[1][2]);
ptr_struct_name->b_val[9]
ptr_struct_name = &(d3_struct_name[1][2][3]);
ptr_struct_name->b_val[9]
```

```
(*(d1_struct_name+1)).b_val[9]
(*(*(d2_struct_name+1)+2)).b_val[9]
(*(*(*(d3_struct_name+1)+2)+3)).b_val[9]

(d1_struct_name+1)->b_val[9]
(*(d2_struct_name+1)+2)->b_val[9]
(*(*(d3_struct_name+1)+2)+3)->b_val[9]
```

The syntax requirements of Standard C dictate that structure member names must always be explicitly specified. This prevents structure members that are structures, unions, or arrays themselves from being expressed without subscripts, as shown above. Member **b_val[]** above may not be equivalently expressed using the fundamental array relationship **array[i]** = ***(array+i)**.

Structures of Structures and Unions

Since structures are designed to aggregate dissimilar data object types, there is nothing to prevent us from defining a structure that contains other structures or unions. The only constraint upon the Standard declaration of structure and union members is the rule that they may not contain incomplete or function types. This prevents structures from containing a direct self-reference because, at the point in a structure where such a member is declared, the structure itself is incomplete. For example, the following definition is *incorrect* because the member reference to the **tag_struct** template is still incomplete when the member reference for **d_val** is encountered.

```
struct tag_struct {char a_val;
    int b_val;
    char c_val;
    struct tag_struct d_val;} struct_name;
```

We will find in Chapter 10 that incomplete types may be referenced only by structure members that are referenced using pointers. The following structure declaration is *correct* and demonstrates this point:

```
struct tag_struct {char a_val;
    int b_val;
    char c_val;
    struct tag_struct *d_val;} struct_name;
```

Here, **d_val** is declared as a pointer to an incomplete structure template defined by **tag_struct**. Structures also may not contain direct member references to function types, but as we will see in Chapter 14, structure members may be declared as pointers to function types.

Let's first examine a structure containing a member that is a structure, to understand how such a member is referenced and to see the layout of the record that results. Consider the program listed in Figure 9.4.

This example defines a structure named **s3**, which is composed of members **ch** and **ival**, and another structure named **s2**, also with members **ch** and **ival**. Header files **<stdio.h>** and **<stddef.h>** are included to define the function-like macro **offsetof(s,m)** and the function prototype for the run-time library functions **printf()** and **exit()**. Figure 9.5 helps you visualize the layout of structure **s3**.

```
/* FILE: ch9e3.c */
#include <stdio.h>
#include <stddef.h>
main()
{
struct ts1 {char ch; int ival;} s1;
struct ts2 {char ch; int ival; struct ts1 s2;};
struct ts2 s3;                  /* structure s3 */

printf("\nsize s1        = %d",sizeof(s1));
printf("\nsize s3.ch     = %d",sizeof(s3.ch));
printf("\nsize s3.ival   = %d",sizeof(s3.ival));
printf("\nsize s3.s2     = %d",sizeof(s3.s2));
printf("\nsize s3.s2.ch  = %d",sizeof(s3.s2.ch));
printf("\nsize s3.s2.ival = %d",sizeof(s3.s2.ival));
printf("\nsize s3        = %d",sizeof(s3));

printf("\noffset s3.ch     = %d",offsetof(struct ts2,ch));
printf("\noffset s3.ival   = %d",offsetof(struct ts2,ival));
printf("\noffset s3.s2     = %d",offsetof(struct ts2,s2.ch));
printf("\noffset s3.s2.ch  = %d",offsetof(struct ts2,s2.ch));
printf("\noffset s3.s2.ival = %d",offsetof(struct ts2,s2.ival));
exit(0);
}
```

FIGURE 9.4: The sample program ch9e3.c displays the size and offset (in bytes) of each member of a structure to reveal the location of any "pad" bytes.

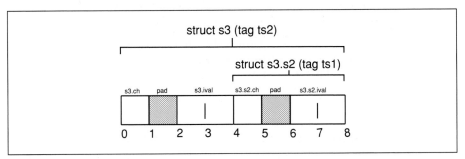

FIGURE 9.5: Structure of structures.

Structure member **s3.s2** is the entire member object (bytes 4–7), **s3.s2.ch** is the **ch** member of the structure tag **ts1** (byte 4), and **s3.s2.ival** is the **ival** member of the structure tag **ts1** (bytes 6 and 7). To identify structure members within structures, repeat the (.) member operator to the level of nesting required to reflect a scalar member's unique identification.

This example also demonstrates the scope declaration properties of the members of a structure. The identical member names **ch** and **ival**, declared for both structure tags **ts1** and **ts2**, are not in conflict because the visibility (scope) of a member's declaration is limited to the structure in which it is defined.

The following output, produced by this sample program, confirms the structure template and member offsets described in Figure 9.5:

```
size s1          = 4
size s3.ch       = 1
size s3.ival     = 2
size s3.s2       = 4
size s3.s2.ch    = 1
size s3.s2.ival  = 2
size s3          = 8

offset s3.ch       = 0
offset s3.ival     = 2
offset s3.s2       = 4
offset s3.s2.ch    = 4
offset s3.s2.ival  = 6
```

Microsoft also supports the non-Standard practice of permitting "nameless" structures to be included as members of other structures and unions when member name space conflicts do not arise. For example, the structure declarations in Figure 9.4 could have been revised and expressed as

```
struct ts1 {char cch; int iival;} s1;
struct ts2 {char ch; int ival; struct ts1;};
struct ts2 s3;
```

thereby eliminating the reference to member **s2** of structure tag **ts2** altogether and resolving the name conflicts by introducing members **cch** and **iival**. The correct member references in structure **s3** would then be

```
s3.ch
s3.ival
s3.cch
s3.iival
```

Now let's examine a structure containing a member that is a union, to understand how such a member is referenced and to see the layout of the structure that results. Such a data structure could be used to implement what in Pascal would be referred to as a variant record. Consider the program example listed in Figure 9.6.

This defines a structure named **s4**, which is composed of members **ch** and **ival**; another structure named **s2**, with members **ch** and **ival**; and a union named **u2**, with members **ch** and **cval**. Again, header files **<stdio.h>** and **<stddef.h>** are included to define the function-like macro **offsetof()** and the function prototype for the run-time library function **printf()** and **exit()**. Figure 9.7 helps you visualize the layout of structure **s4**.

Union member **s4.u2** is the entire member object, **s4.u2.ch** is the **ch** member of union tag **tu1**, and **s4.u2.cval** is the **cval** member of union tag **tu1**. To identify union members within structures, repeat the (.) member operator to the level of nesting required to reflect a scalar member's unique identification.

This example again demonstrates the scope declaration properties of members of structures and unions. The identical member name **ch** (declared for structure tags **ts1** and **ts2**) and union tag **tu1** are not in

```
/* FILE: ch9e4.c */
#include <stdio.h>
#include <stddef.h>
main()
{
union  tu1 {unsigned char ch; signed char cval;} u1;
struct ts1 {char ch; int ival;} s1;
struct ts2 {char ch; int ival; struct ts1 s2; union tu1 u2;};
struct ts2 s4;              /* structure s4 */

printf("\nsize u1        = %d",sizeof(u1));
printf("\nsize s1        = %d",sizeof(s1));
printf("\nsize s4.ch     = %d",sizeof(s4.ch));
printf("\nsize s4.ival   = %d",sizeof(s4.ival));
printf("\nsize s4.s2     = %d",sizeof(s4.s2));
printf("\nsize s4.s2.ch  = %d",sizeof(s4.s2.ch));
printf("\nsize s4.s2.ival = %d",sizeof(s4.s2.ival));
printf("\nsize s4.u2     = %d",sizeof(s4.u2));
printf("\nsize s4.u2.ch  = %d",sizeof(s4.u2.ch));
printf("\nsize s4.u2.cval = %d",sizeof(s4.u2.cval));
printf("\nsize s4        = %d",sizeof(s4));

printf("\noffset s4.ch      = %d",offsetof(struct ts2,ch));
printf("\noffset s4.ival    = %d",offsetof(struct ts2,ival));
printf("\noffset s4.s2      = %d",offsetof(struct ts2,s2.ch));
printf("\noffset s4.s2.ch   = %d",offsetof(struct ts2,s2.ch));
printf("\noffset s4.s2.ival = %d",offsetof(struct ts2,s2.ival));
printf("\noffset s4.u2      = %d",offsetof(struct ts2,u2.ch));
printf("\noffset s4.u2.c    = %d",offsetof(struct ts2,u2.ch));
printf("\noffset s4.u2.cval = %d",offsetof(struct ts2,u2.cval));
exit(0);
}
```

FIGURE 9.6: The sample program ch9e4.c displays the size and offset (in bytes) of the members of a structure for which one member is a union.

conflict because the visibility (scope) of a member's declaration is limited to the structure of which it is a part.

Also note in Figure 9.7 that a pad byte is added at the end of structure **s4** to satisfy the alignment requirements of that structure so that it may subsequently be treated as an array.

The following output produced by this sample program confirms the structure template and member offsets described in Figure 9.7 above:

```
size u1           = 1
size s1           = 4
size s4.ch        = 1
size s4.ival      = 2
size s4.s2        = 4
size s4.s2.ch     = 1
size s4.s2.ival   = 2
size s4.u2        = 1
size s4.u2.ch     = 1
size s4.u2.cval   = 1
size s4           = 10
offset s4.ch      = 0
offset s4.ival    = 2
offset s4.s2      = 4
offset s4.s2.ch   = 4
offset s4.s2.ival = 6
offset s4.u2      = 8
offset s4.u2.ch   = 8
offset s4.u2.cval = 8
```

Notice that the size of union member **s4.u2** is only one byte. Because the union members are all of type **char**, union **u2** is properly aligned

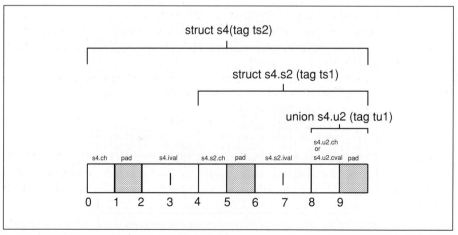

FIGURE 9.7: Structure of unions.

at one byte. Notice also that both the union **s4.u2** and its members **s4.u2.ch** and **s4.u2.cval** are offset in structure **s4** to the same address. For the explanation of this, see the "Unions" section of this chapter.

Structure Initialization

Structure initialization follows the same syntax rules and techniques presented for initializing arrays in Chapter 8. Remember that **external** or **static** storage class structures may use only constant initializers, because they are evaluated at compile time, whereas storage class **auto** structures may use any rvalue expression that can be evaluated dynamically and assigned at run-time. Remember that incomplete initializer lists cause any nonspecified elements to be set to zero (all bits off).

The simple structure variable **struct_name** could have been initialized when defined using the following expression, which sets member **struct_name.a_val** equal to the lowercase letter a, sets member **struct_name.b_val** equal to the signed integer value of 0, and sets member **struct_name.c_val** to the uppercase letter A:

```
struct tag_struct {char a_val;
    int b_val;
    char c_val;} struct_name = {'a', 0, 'A'};
```

The array-of-structures variable **d1_struct_name** could have been initialized when defined using the following expressions:

```
struct tag_struct d1_struct_name[D1] =
    {{'a', 0, 'A'},
     {'b', 1, 'B'}};
```

The initialization list for **d1_struct_name** sets each element of the array and every member of the structure to the values shown. Each nested brace encloses the corresponding structure member values for a row of the array [0] through [1].

The array-of-structures variable **d2_struct_name** could have been initialized when defined using the following expressions:

```
struct tag_struct d2_struct_name[D1][D2] =
    {{'a', 0, 'A', 'b', 1, 'B', 'c', 2, 'C'}};
```

The initialization list for **d2_struct_name** sets the first row of structure elements, [0][0], [0][1], and [0][2], to the corresponding values shown. The remaining elements of this two-dimensional array are then defaulted to an appropriate null value ([1][0], [1][1], [1][2]).

The array-of-structures variable **d3_struct_name** could have been initialized when defined using the following expressions:

```
struct tag_struct d3_struct_name[D1][D2][D3] =
    {{'a', 0, 'A'},
     {'b', 1, 'B'}};
```

The initialization list for **d3_struct_name** sets only the first column elements of each row of structure elements, [0][0][0] and [1][0][0], to the corresponding values shown. The remaining 22 elements of this three-dimensional array are then defaulted to a null value.

The structure-of-structures variable **s3** in Figure 9.4 could have been initialized when defined using the following expressions:

```
struct ts1 {char ch; int ival;} s1;
struct ts2 {char ch; int ival; struct ts1 s2;};

struct ts2 s3 = {'a', 0, 'A', 0};
```

Notice that the type and number of initializers match identically with the layout of the structure shown in Figure 9.5. Always use a record template to sequence the list of initializers you provide.

The structure-of-unions variable **s4** in Figure 9.6 could have been initialized when defined using the following expressions:

```
union  tu1 {unsigned char ch; signed char cval;} u1;
struct ts1 {char ch; int ival;} s1;
struct ts2 {char ch; int ival; struct ts1 s2; union tu1 u2;};

struct ts2 s4 = {'a', 0, 'A', 0, '\xff'};
```

Notice that the type and number of initializers match identically with the layout of the structure shown in Figure 9.7. In this case, and with the initialization of any union, only the first declared member of a union may be initialized. Therefore, union member **S4.u2.ch** above is an **unsigned char** and controls the type of the initializer that was specified.

Let these examples serve as a guideline for the expression of initializer lists for complex structure definitions involving nested structures and unions. If you have questions about the order of initializers, prepare a structure (record) diagram, like the ones shown in Figures 9.3, 9.5, and 9.7, to help visualize the structure template. Use this record template to check the list of initializers you provide, and remember that all structure members may be initialized, but only the first member of a union may be initialized.

Structure Operations

Standard C has incorporated a new feature that permits compatibly defined structures to be assigned using the simple assignment operator (**=**). This is the only arithmetic operator that may be used to act upon an entire structure. Note that compatible structures may be assigned, regardless of the types of member declarations they contain; however, arrays of structures may be assigned only element by element. Recall that arrays are not directly assignable because an array name is considered a constant pointer.

If, however, you define an array as a member of a structure, you may assign it indirectly by assigning that structure. The following examples demonstrate the assignment of structures using the structure definitions developed earlier in this chapter. The structure variable **struct_name** could be assigned to another structure variable, **struct_name_2**, as follows:

```
struct tag_struct {char a_val;
    int b_val;
    char c_val;};

struct tag_struct struct_name = {'a', 99, 'A'}, struct_name_2;

struct_name_2 = struct_name;
```

The array-of-structures variable **d1_struct_name[D1]** could be assigned to structure variables **d1_struct_name_2[D1]** and **d1_struct_name_3** an array element at a time, as follows:

```
struct tag_struct {char a_val;
    int b_val;
    char c_val;};

struct tag_struct d1_struct_name[D1] = {{'a', 0, 'A'}};
struct tag_struct d1_struct_name_2[D1], d1_struct_name_3;

for (i=0; i<D1; i++) d1_struct_name_2[i] = d1_struct_name[i];
d1_struct_name_3 = d1_struct_name[0];
```

Multidimensional arrays of structures are treated in a similar fashion. The structure-of-structures variable **s3** could be assigned to another structure variable, **s3_2**, as follows:

```
struct ts1 {char ch; int ival;} s1;
struct ts2 {char ch; int ival; struct ts1 s2;};

struct ts2 s3 = {'a', 0, 'A', 0}, s3_2;
s3_2 = s3;
```

The structure-of-unions variable **s4** could be assigned to another structure variable, **s4_2**, as follows:

```
union  tu1 {unsigned char ch; signed char cval;} u1;
struct ts1 {char ch; int ival;} s1;
struct ts2 {char ch; int ival; struct ts1 s2; union tu1 u2;};

struct ts2 s4 = {'a', 0, 'A', 0, '\xff'}, s4_2;
s4_2 = s4;
```

It might seem logical to assume that if structures can be assigned, it must be possible to compare structures using the equality (**==**) operator. That is not the case! Ironically, the reason is rooted in the pad bytes that may exist in a structure. No specific value (bit pattern) can be assumed to exist for a pad byte, and Standard C does not mandate a pad-byte bit pattern. Unlike the byte-by-byte copy performed for the assignment of structures, a corresponding byte-by-byte comparison of structures (or unions) by the (**==**) operator could potentially mismatch if unequal pad-byte representations were present.

It is therefore necessary to compare structures member by member. Even if a structure is known not to contain pad bytes, avoid the temptation of using the run-time library function **memcmp()** (see Chapter 24) to compare two structures. The introduction of pad bytes is a function of the microprocessor and compiler options being used, and a valid comparison using **memcmp()** for a particular microprocessor and set of compiler options may not result for all such combinations.

The best way to compare structures is demonstrated below, using the structure variables **struct_name** and **struct_name_2** defined above:

```
if (struct_name.a_val == struct_name_2.a_val &&
    struct_name.b_val == struct_name_2.b_val &&
    struct_name.c_val == struct_name_2.c_val) ...
```

This test expression will produce a value of 0 or false if any structure members are unequal, and 1 or true if all structure members are equal. Note that because the precedence of the operator **&&** (logical AND) is lower than the operator **==** (equality), no use of parentheses is necessary to override the default order of processing (see Chapter 12). All other operations except assignment must therefore be performed upon individual scalar members of structures as demonstrated by this example.

You've seen that the **offsetof(s,m)** function-like macro determines the exact location of members in a structure when it is unknown where pad bytes may have been introduced. An alternative way of calculating such member offsets involves the use of the address-of (**&**) operator and a simple pointer-to-a-character cast (**char ***). Consider the program example listed in Figure 9.8.

The variable definition of **byte_offset** is of type **ptrdiff_t**, which is defined in header file **<stddef.h>** and used for correctly defining a type to store the result of subtracting two pointers (addresses). The casting of the addresses for both data objects (**s4.u2** and **s4**) to a pointer to a character (**char   ***) resolves any compiler warnings otherwise generated regarding different levels of pointer indirection. In this case, the following correct result is produced:

```
member s4.u2 offset = 8
```

More about the operations that may be performed using pointers (addresses) will be explained in Chapters 10 and 12.

As we discovered for arrays, casts are not permitted with structures because they are aggregate, not scalar, types. Pointers to structures, however, may be cast to other pointer types.

The use of **typedef**s with structures is possible and can serve to provide a short-hand method of variable definition, but it is more common to use the tag name approach to develop templates for structures that are commonly used. This is evidenced by the principal use of structure tags and not **typedef**s in Appendix E.

Let's compare the use of **typedef**s and structure tags for structure object definition. Consider the Standard C type **div_t** and an equivalent structure tag **_div_t**:

```
typedef struct {int quot;
    int rem;} div_t;

struct  _div_t  {int quot;
    int rem;};
```

```
/* FILE: ch9e5.c */
#include <stdio.h>
#include <stddef.h>
int main(void)
{
union  tu1 {unsigned char ch; signed char ival;} u1;
struct ts1 {char ch; int ival;} s1;
struct ts3 {char ch; int ival; struct ts1 s2; union tu1 u2;};
struct ts3 s4;      /* structure s4 */

ptrdiff_t byte_offset = (char *)&(s4.u2) - (char *)&(s4);
printf("\nmember s4.u2 offset = %d",byte_offset);
exit(0);
}
```

FIGURE 9.8: The sample program ch9e5.c demonstrates how structure member offsets can be computed by using address arithmetic.

A structure variable, **dt_struct**, could be defined as

```
div_t dt_struct;          /* typedef declaration */

struct _div_t dt_struct;  /* structure tag declaration */
```

Interestingly, it is possible to declare a structure tag within a **typedef**. For example, had the **typedef div_t** above been defined as

```
typedef struct _div_t {int quot;
    int rem;} div_t;
```

it would then have alone supported the declaration of structure variable **dt_struct** shown above.

There is no distinct advantage or disadvantage in using **typedef**s over structure tags to declare structure objects, because **typedef**s, once defined, can be further qualified as the other structure and structure pointer declarations shown in Tables 9.1 and 9.2.

In the prior examples, had we wished to define a one-dimensional array of **div_t** structure objects, the **typedef** principles described for arrays in Chapter 8 would have directly applied. For example:

```
div_t dt_struct[5];          /* typedef declaration */

struct _div_t dt_struct[5];  /* structure tag declaration */
```

UNIONS

The remaining material presented in this chapter concerning unions supplements the material presented thus far for structures, as unions are really a special case of structures. Most, but not all, structure conventions apply to unions.

The naming and scope (visibility) of union variables (complete types) and union tags conform to the rules discussed for structures. The complete union declaration

```
union tag_union {char a_val;
    int b_val;
    char c_val;} union_name, *ptr_union_name;
```

defines a union tag called **tag_union** (see the section "Incomplete Union Types and Definitions" below); the union variable **union_name**, having three members named **a_val**, **b_val**, and **c_val**; and a pointer to a union named **ptr_union_name**, which may contain the address of a union compatibly defined with the tag **tag_union**. Note that a semicolon is required after the last member declaration of every union. The members of **union_name** may be correctly referenced using the (.) member operator as

```
union_name.a_val
union_name.b_val
union_name.c_val
```

respectively, and if the pointer **ptr_union_name** is properly initialized, alternatively as

```
ptr_union_name->a_val
ptr_union_name->b_val
ptr_union_name->c_val
```

In the example above, no union initialization (see "Union Initialization" below), no array members (see "Arrays of Unions" below), no structure or union members (see "Unions of Structures and Unions" below), nor any bit fields (see Chapter 11) have been declared for union **union_name**.

Remember that any of the qualified fundamental types described in Chapter 7 may be declared as union members, but the storage class lifetime and visibility qualifier for individual members must be omitted. Like structures, unions in Standard C may not contain incomplete types or function types; however, pointers to incomplete and function types are permitted.

A union is a distinct type of data object, having its own storage-class and qualifiers as shown in Table 9.1. The qualifiers of a union control those of its members. Use Table 9.1 as a guide for developing union declarations. For example, by following the default (bracketed) qualifiers for base type **union**, we can express the definition of union variable **union_name** as either

```
[extern] [none] union tag_union {..}
    [_cdecl] [memory model] [none] union_name;
```

or

```
[auto] [none] union tag_union {..}
    [_cdecl] [memory model] [none] union_name;
```

depending upon whether this declaration was made externally (outside of braces) or internally (inside of braces). It would be interpreted for the Small memory model as either

```
[extern] union tag_union {..} _cdecl _near union_name;
```

or

```
auto union tag_union {..} _cdecl _near union_name;
```

Similarly, pointers to unions may be expressed using Table 9.2 as a guideline. For example, by following the default qualifiers for base type **union**, the definition of union pointer variable **ptr_union_name** can be expressed (for the Small memory model) as either

```
[static] [none] union tag_union {..}
    [none] [memory model] * [none] ptr_union_name;
```

or

```
static union tag_union {..} _near *ptr_union_name;
```

It is clear that union pointer variable **ptr_union_name** is understood to be of storage class **static** and to represent a **_near** (assumed DS register segment) address.

Pointers to unions are simply pointer variables whose size is not **sizeof(union_name)** but **sizeof(ptr_union_name)**, which is always either two or four bytes, depending upon the memory address qualifier being used.

If the union pointer variable **ptr_union_name**, defined above, were assigned an address value using the (**&**) address-of operator, as follows:

```
ptr_union_name = &union_name;
```

then the members of **union_name** could alternatively be referenced using the –> operator as

```
ptr_union_name->a_val
ptr_union_name->b_val
ptr_union_name->c_val
```

Remember that union member declarations cannot contain incomplete or function types. This precludes any union from including itself as a member; however, members may represent pointers to either incomplete or function types, thus opening the possibility of having a union contain a pointer reference to itself. Refer to Chapter 10 for more on unions that contain pointers. Pointers to incomplete and function types may be included in unions because the storage for a pointer may be allocated and a value (actual address) initialized when the pointer member is defined or later assigned at run-time.

A summary of the performance characteristics of using the member and pointer-to-a-member operators with union members is deferred to the "Structure and Union Performance Issues" section below.

Union Alignment and Size

Since each member of a union originates at the starting address (offset) of the union itself, every union data object is the size of its largest member. If a union is composed of members that are fundamental types, no pad bytes are involved or required. Pad bytes are only a factor in the sizing of unions that contain structure members. Remember that the compiler option **/Zp<n>** and directive **#pragma pack(n)** control only alignment of structures and structure members, not that of unions and union members. Unions that contain structures, either directly or indirectly, are subject to the alignment of each structure member itself, since unions, like structures, may subsequently be replicated using the array **[]** postfix operator. For more on these topics, refer to the "Unions of Structures and Unions" and "Arrays of Unions" sections below.

In the union example listed in Figure 9.9, which does not contain a structure member, no pad or alignment bytes are necessary, and the union data object simply becomes the size of the largest union member, **union_name.b_val**.

The program's output demonstrates this size and alignment.

```
sizeof union_name    2
sizeof member a_val 1
sizeof member b_val 2
sizeof member c_val 1
```

Since members of all data object types originate at offset zero (0) within a union, the exact offset of a union member needs to be determined only when a union contains a structure member (refer to the "Unions of Structures and Unions" section below).

```
/* FILE: ch9e6.c */
#include <stdio.h>
int main(void)
{
union tag_union {char a_val;
                int b_val;
                char c_val;} union_name;
printf("\nsizeof union_name   %d",sizeof(union_name));
printf("\nsizeof member a_val %d",sizeof(union_name.a_val));
printf("\nsizeof member b_val %d",sizeof(union_name.b_val));
printf("\nsizeof member c_val %d",sizeof(union_name.c_val));
exit(0);
}
```

FIGURE 9.9: The sample program ch9e6.c demonstrates that the size of a union is always that of its largest member.

Incomplete Union Types and Definitions

Incomplete union types behave identically to those described for structure types. They declare a union template, assign a union tag name for subsequent reference, and allocate no storage space for a union variable. Appendix E lists all the Standard and Microsoft C incomplete types. The important **REGS** union is an incomplete type that supports access to DOS and BIOS services (see Chapter 22) by several run-time library functions and is completely explained in the "Unions of Structures and Unions" section that follows. Every incomplete union type has the basic format

```
union tag_union {..};
```

where union is a C keyword, **tag_union** is any valid tag name, and **{..}** indicates a union member declaration list. No qualifiers are used with incomplete union types because no storage is being allocated and only a template definition is being created. Unlike incomplete array types, no initializer lists may be specified with an incomplete union type.

Once a union tag name is created, it may subsequently be referenced, if within scope (visible), to define a complete union variable and therefore allocate storage space. For example:

```
[qualifier..] union tag_union [qualifier..] u_union_name;
```

or

```
[qualifier..] union tag_union [qualifier..] i_union_name
    = {initializer list};
```

Once **tag_union** has been declared, the uninitialized union variable **u_union_name** and the initialized union variable **i_union_name** could be defined as shown above. Notice that the union data-object type-qualifiers shown in Table 9.1 may be included. For more on union initializer lists, see the "Union Initialization" section below.

Two other complete combined declaration formats are possible. In the example

```
union tag_union {..} u_union_name;

union tag_union {..} i_union_name = {initializer list};
```

the union variables **u_union_name** and **i_union_name** are allocated storage for a **{..}** union member declaration list, and at the same time, the tag name **tag_union** is created for future use. Notice that tag names may optionally be specified when a complete union definition is made; however, tag names are required when an incomplete union type is declared.

In a similar fashion, pointers to unions may be specified by using a reference to either an incomplete or complete union type declaration, as shown below:

```
[qualifier..] union tag_union [qualifier..] *ptr_union_name;
```

or

```
[qualifier..] union {..} [qualifier..] *ptr_union_name;
```

Storage for pointers to unions may be allocated, even though an incomplete union type is referenced. Pointers to unions may also be initialized if appropriate reference is made to the address of a previously defined union variable.

It is the ability to define pointers to incomplete union types (and arrays, structures, and functions) that permits unions to contain pointer references to themselves. For more on pointer members of unions, see Chapter 10.

Arrays of Unions

Since the complete definition of a union is always appropriately aligned, each union variable can be treated as an array of union objects, using the subscript operator **[]** discussed in Chapter 8. Arrays of union type objects follow all of the rules and conventions established for arrays in general, and arrays of structures in particular.

A union variable array, like any other array, can be expressed in n dimensions. For example, arrays of **tag_union** objects can be defined as follows:

```
#define D1 2
#define D2 3
#define D3 4

union tag_union {char a_val;
    int b_val;
    char c_val;} union_name;

union tag_union d1_union_name[D1];
union tag_union d2_union_name[D1][D2];
union tag_union d3_union_name[D1][D2][D3];
```

Remember that the size of the basic union object **union_name** is the size of the largest union member. The **union_name** object above is **sizeof(union_name)**, or two bytes long, multiplied by the array dimensions specified. In the example above, **d1_union_name** allocates two, **d2_union_name** allocates six, and **d3_union_name** allocates 24 **union_name** type objects.

As we found for arrays of structures, when declaring arrays of unions, remember that **auto** storage-class variables are allocated to the stack (2KB default), and **static** or externally defined variables are limited to 64KB, unless the Huge memory addressing model is used.

The **c_val** member of the last array elements in each of the above arrays may be referenced using the (**.**) member operator as follows:

```
d1_union_name[1].c_val
d2_union_name[1][2].c_val
d3_union_name[1][2][3].c_val
```

We may also use pointer indirection and the (—>) pointer-to-a-member operator to reference the members shown above. A pointer variable, **ptr_union_name**, could be defined and assigned the address of the corresponding array element to permit the members of that union object to be referenced. For example:

```
union tag_union *ptr_union_name;

ptr_union_name = &(d1_union_name[1]);
ptr_union_name->c_val

ptr_union_name = &(d2_union_name[1][2]);
ptr_union_name->c_val

ptr_union_name = &(d3_union_name[1][2][3]);
ptr_union_name->c_val
```

The examples presented thus far demonstrate the typical use of the union (**.**) member and pointer indirection (—>) operators with arrays of unions. However, since arrays may be referenced using normal subscripting (**[]..[]**) as shown or by using (*****) pointer indirection, other valid ways of expressing the member references shown above are possible.

In the fundamental relationship between array subscripting and pointer indirection, **array[i]** is equivalent to ***(array+i)**. Instead of using the subscript operators as discussed in Chapter 8, we can use the pointer indirection operator (*****) with both the (**.**) member and (—>) pointer-to-a-member operators.

Subscripted arrays of unions may be recast to use indirection (*****) with the (**.**) union member operator, just as we did for arrays of structures. For example:

```
(*(d1_union_name+1)).c_val
(*(*(d2_union_name+1)+2)).c_val
(*(*(*(d3_union_name+1)+2)+3)).c_val
```

Subscripted arrays of unions may also be recast to use indirection (*****) with the **−>** operator, as we did for arrays of structures. For example:

```
(d1_union_name+1)->c_val
(*(d2_union_name+1)+2)->c_val
(*(*(d3_union_name+1)+2)+3)->c_val
```

The merits of using the alternative member referencing techniques described in this section, together with another composite form (compact pointer addressing), are compared in the "Structure and Union Performance Issues" section below.

Before ending the discussion of arrays of unions, let's clarify the case where a member of an array of unions is an array itself. Consider the revised union template **rev_tag_union**, shown below:

```
union rev_tag_union {char a_val;
    int b_val[10];
    char c_val;} union_name;
```

In this case, member **b_val** is itself an array of type **int** data objects. Consider the following valid references to the last element of member **b_val**, **b_val[9]**, for the last element of each array of unions, using the four alternative member referencing techniques described earlier:

```
d1_union_name[1].b_val[9]
d2_union_name[1][2].b_val[9]
d3_union_name[1][2][3].b_val[9]

ptr_union_name = &(d1_union_name[1]);
ptr_union_name->b_val[9]
ptr_union_name = &(d2_union_name[1][2]);
ptr_union_name->b_val[9]
ptr_union_name = &(d3_union_name[1][2][3]);
ptr_union_name->b_val[9]

(*(d1_union_name+1)).b_val[9]
(*(*(d2_union_name+1)+2)).b_val[9]
(*(*(*(d3_union_name+1)+2)+3)).b_val[9]

(d1_union_name+1)->b_val[9]
(*(d2_union_name+1)+2)->b_val[9]
(*(*(d3_union_name+1)+2)+3)->b_val[9]
```

Union member names in C must always be explicitly specified. This prevents union members that are structures, unions, or arrays themselves from being expressed other than with subscripts, as shown above. Member **b_val[]** above may not equivalently be expressed using the fundamental array relationship **array[i] = *(array+i)**.

Unions of Structures and Unions

If a union contains a structure member, then pad bytes may be introduced to align both the members of the structure object and the union object itself. The factors controlling the padding of structures, discussed in the section "Structure Alignment and Size" above, may then control how a union is sized. The **/Zp<n>**, **#pragma pack(n)**, and Intel chip word size factors only apply to structures, not unions. When structures are members of unions, if a padded structure member is the largest member of the union, it then becomes the size of the union object itself. For example, consider the program listed in Figure 9.10.

When the default alignment (no compiler option **/Zp<1|2|4>** or **#pragma pack**(1|2|4) specified) is used with an Intel 8086 microcomputer to compile and execute the program, a word size of two bytes is assumed, and the following output is generated:

```
sizeof struct_name   6
sizeof member a_val  1
sizeof member b_val  2
sizeof member c_val  1
sizeof u1.s1         6
sizeof u1.s1.a_val   1
sizeof u1.s1.b_bal   2
sizeof u1.s1.c_val   1
sizeof u1            6
```

```
/* FILE: ch9e7.c */
#include <stdio.h>
int main(void)
{
struct ts1 {char a_val;
            int b_val;
            char c_val;} struct_name;
union tu1 {char a_val; int b_val; char c_val;
           struct ts1 s1;} u1;

printf("\nsizeof struct_name   %d",sizeof(struct_name));
printf("\nsizeof member a_val %d",sizeof(u1.a_val));
printf("\nsizeof member b_val %d",sizeof(u1.b_val));
printf("\nsizeof member c_val %d",sizeof(u1.c_val));
printf("\nsizeof u1.s1        %d",sizeof(u1.s1));
printf("\nsizeof u1.s1.a_val  %d",sizeof(u1.s1.a_val));
printf("\nsizeof u1.s1.b_bal  %d",sizeof(u1.s1.b_val));
printf("\nsizeof u1.s1.c_val  %d",sizeof(u1.s1.c_val));
printf("\nsizeof u1           %d",sizeof(u1));
exit(0);
}
```

FIGURE 9.10: The sample program ch9e7.c demonstrates that structures and unions themselves are "padded" to permit their subsequent use as elements of an array.

Notice that two pad bytes were introduced for the **s1** structure member of union **u1**, and in turn control the resulting size of union **u1**. Recall that unions themselves must be aligned to establish a proper boundary for the union data object, so that it may subsequently be replicated using the array postfix operators **[ ] . . [ ]**.

Table 9.4 summarizes the effects of the Intel chip and compiler option **/Zp<n>** upon union and member sizes, using the **u1** union described above. Notice that any padding introduced to satisfy the alignment requirements of structure members may ultimately determine the size of a union.

It is sometimes important, for sorting and other record-handling purposes, to know the exact offset (from the union address itself) of a structure member. Standard C has added the function-like macro definition **offsetof(s,m)**, defined in header file **<stddef.h>**, that returns the zero-origin offset, in bytes, of member **m** in structure **s**. Figure 9.11 demonstrates the proper use of the **offsetof(s,m)** macro when a union contains a structure member.

This program produces the following output:

```
offset u1.s1.a_val   0
offset u1.s1.b_val   2
offset u1.s1.c_val   4
```

Figure 9.12 helps you visualize the effects that the Intel chip and compiler option **/Zp<n>** or **#pragma pack(n)** have upon the offsets of structure members within unions, using the union **u1** described above.

TABLE 9.4: Union and Member Sizes

INTEL CHIP	COMPILER OPTION	u1	a_val	b_val	c_val	s1
8086 (/G0), 80186 (/G1), 80286 (/G2), or (word=2)	/Zp1	4	1	2	1	4
	/Zp2	6	1	2	1	6
	/Zp4	6	1	2	1	6
80386, 80486, or (word=4)	/Zp1	4	1	2	1	4
	/Zp2	6	1	2	1	6
	/Zp4	12	1	2	1	12

NOTES:
- /Zp1 same as **#pragma pack(1)**; /Zp2 same as **pack(2)**; /Zp4 same as **pack(4)**.
- If just **Zp** is specified, /Zp1 is assumed.
- If /**Zp*n*** exceeds the word size of the chip, then /**Zp*word*** is assumed.

All pad bytes shown in Figure 9.12 at the end of each union are necessary to maintain structure and hence union alignment so they may subsequently be subscripted **[]..[]** and treated as an array.

The union **REGS**, described in Appendix E, is a classic example of a union of structures. **REGS** is a union of two structures, **BYTEREGS** and **WORDREGS**, also described in Appendix E. The **REGS**, or register union, overlays a structure containing the 8086/8088 8-bit (**BYTEREGS**) and 16-bit (**WORDREGS**) registers.

Figure 9.13 depicts how the union **REGS** permits either 8-bit or 16-bit register values to be referenced when working with the run-time library functions **int86()**, **int86x()**, **intdos()**, **intdosx()**, and others that require **REGS** and provide access to DOS and BIOS services (see Chapter 22).

Unions may also contain members that describe other unions. Let's see how a series of variant record descriptions could be specified that occupy the same buffer (memory) space. Consider the following partial program example, which demonstrates how four different record types ('A', 'B', 'C', and 'D') could contain different fields that could assume a variety of code and value record formats:

```
#include <stdio.h>
#include <stddef.h>
main()
{
union codes  {char cc; int ic; long int lc;};
union values {char cv; int iv; float fv;};
struct rec1  {char type; union codes code;};
struct rec2  {char type; union values value;};
struct rec3  {char type; union codes code; union values value;};
```

```
/* FILE: ch9e8.c */
#include <stdio.h>
#include <stddef.h>
int main(void)
{
struct ts1 {char a_val;
            int b_val;
            char c_val;} struct_name;
union tu1 {char a_val; int b_val; char c_val;
           struct ts1 s1;} u1;

printf("\noffset u1.s1.a_val %d",offsetof(union tu1,s1.a_val));
printf("\noffset u1.s1.b_val %d",offsetof(union tu1,s1.b_val));
printf("\noffset u1.s1.c_val %d",offsetof(union tu1,s1.c_val));
exit(0);
}
```

FIGURE 9.11: The sample program ch9e8.c demonstrates the proper use of the offsetof (s,m) macro when a union contains a structure member.

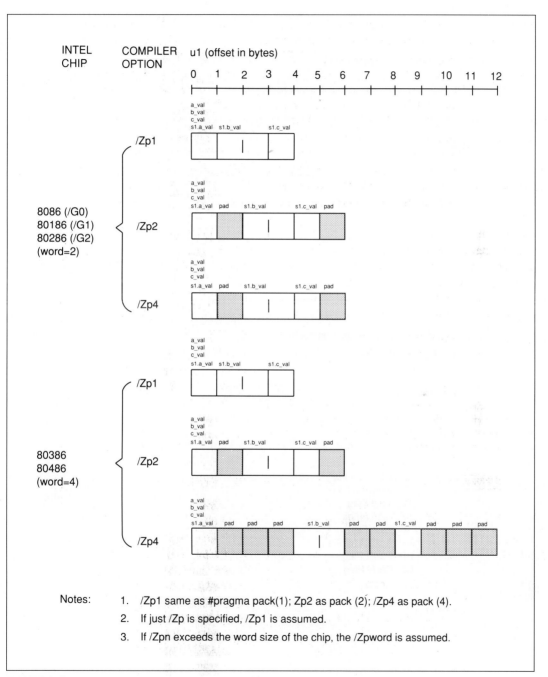

FIGURE 9.12: Union member offsets.

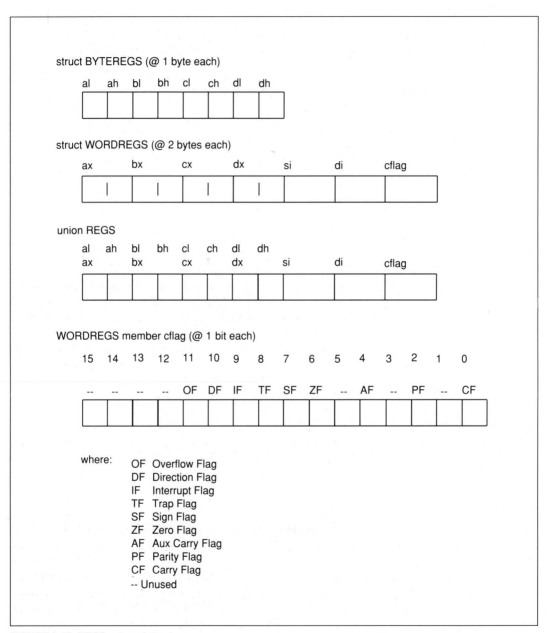

FIGURE 9.13: REGS union of structures.

```
struct rec4  {char type; union values value; union codes code;};
union recs   {char type; struct rec1 reca; struct rec2 recb;
     struct rec3 recc; struct rec4 recd;} record;

if (record.type == 'A') {
   record.reca.code.cc = '1';
   }
if (record.type == 'B') {
   record.recb.value.iv = 1;
   }
if (record.type == 'C') {
   record.recc.code.lc = 2L;
   record.recc.value.fv = 10.0F;
   }
if (record.type == 'D') {
   record.recd.value.cv = '*';
   record.recd.code.cc = 'X';
   }
}
```

Figure 9.14 helps you visualize the union named **record** that results. Remember that unions of unions tend to standardize variable naming in a program while minimizing the memory space allocated for buffers that hold a large variety of record layouts.

Microsoft also supports the non-Standard practice of permitting nameless unions to be included as members of other structures and unions when member-name space conflicts do not arise. For example:

```
union ts1 {char cch; int iival;};
struct ts2 {char ch; int ival; union ts1;} s3;
```

The correct member references in structure **s3** would then be **s3.ch**, **s3.ival**, **s3.cch**, and **s3.iival**.

Union Initialization

Union initialization parallels the syntax and techniques developed for initializing arrays in Chapter 8, but is simplified by the fact that only the very first member described for a union may be initialized. External or **static** storage-class unions may still use only constant initializers because they are evaluated at compile-time, whereas storage class **auto** unions may use any rvalue expressions that can be dynamically evaluated and assigned at run-time. Incomplete initializer lists for arrays of unions still cause any nonspecified elements to be set to zero (all bits off).

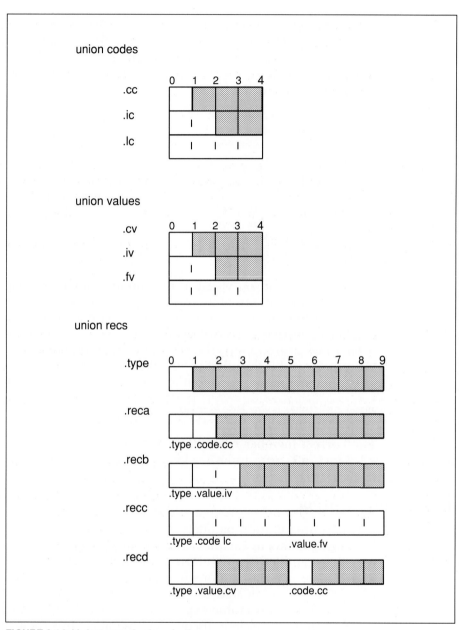

FIGURE 9.14: Variant record union of unions.

We will demonstrate how to initialize each of the four union type examples (simple unions, arrays of unions, unions of structures, and unions of unions) that were presented in this chapter.

The simple union variable **union_name** could have been initialized when defined using the expression

```
union tag_union {char a_val;
    int b_val;
    char c_val;} union_name = {'a'};
```

which sets member **union_name.a_val** equal to the lowercase letter a. Since members **union_name.b_val** and **union_name.c_val** share the same memory location (offset), only the first member can be initialized to a meaningful value. Unions retain the value of the last member type assigned.

The array-of-unions variable **d1_union_name** could have been initialized when defined using the following expressions:

```
union tag_union d1_union_name[D1] =
    {{'a'},
     {'b'}};
```

The initialization list for **d1_union_name** sets each element of the array and the first member of the union to the values shown. Each nested brace encloses the first union member value for a row of the array [0] through [1].

The array-of-unions variable **d2_union_name** could have been initialized when defined using the following expression:

```
union tag_union d2_union_name[D1][D2] = {{'a', 'b', 'c'}};
```

The initialization list for **d2_union_name** sets the first row of union elements to the corresponding values shown for the array **[0][0]**, **[0][1]**, and **[0][2]**. The remaining elements of this two-dimensional array are then defaulted to an appropriate null value (**[1][0]**, **[1][1]**, **[1][2]**).

The array-of-unions variable **d3_union_name** could have been initialized when defined using the following expressions:

```
union tag_union d3_union_name[D1][D2][D3] =
    {{'a'},
     {'b'}};
```

The initialization list for **d3_union_name** sets only the first column elements of each row of union elements to the corresponding values shown for the array **[0][0][0]** and **[1][0][0]**. The remaining 22 elements of this three-dimensional array are then defaulted to an appropriate null value.

The union-of-structures variable **u1** in Figure 9.10 could have been initialized when defined using the following expressions:

```
struct ts1 {char a_val; int b_val; char c_val;}struct_name;
union tu1  {char a_val; int b_val; char c_val;
    struct ts1 s1;};

union tu1 u1 = {'a'};
```

Notice that only an initializer of a type corresponding to **char** (member **a_val**) may be specified because it was declared as the first member.

The union-of-unions variable **record**, defined above, could have been initialized when defined using the expressions

```
union recs    {char type;
    struct rec1 reca;
    struct rec2 recb;
    struct rec3 recc;
    struct rec4 recd;} record = {'A'};
```

which would have placed the character constant 'A' into **record.type**. Let these examples serve as a reminder that only the first declared member of a union may be initialized!

Union Operations

Standard C has incorporated a new feature that permits compatibly defined unions to be assigned using the simple assignment operator (**=**). This is the only operator that may be used to act upon an entire union. Note that such unions may be assigned, regardless of the types of member declarations they contain; however, arrays of unions may be assigned only element by element. Recall that arrays are not directly assignable. Since an array of union elements is just another array of data objects, arrays of unions may be assigned only an element at a time.

If, however, you define an array as a member of a union, you may assign it indirectly by assigning that union. The following example demonstrates the assignment of unions using a union definition developed earlier in this chapter. The union variable **union_name** could be assigned to another union variable, **union_name_2**, as follows:

```
union tag_union {char a_val;
    int b_val;
    char c_val;};
```

```
union tag_union union_name = {'a'}, union_name_2;

union_name_2 = union_name;
```

The other examples (array of unions, union of structures, and union of unions) parallel those shown earlier in the chapter for structures.

It might seem logical to assume that if unions can be assigned, it must be possible to compare unions using the equality (**==**) operator. However, as for structures, this is not the case! Mismatches for unions could be rooted in the pad bytes described for structure members and in the fact that a union often has unassigned bytes that do not represent any reliable value for other than the last member type assigned. It is only appropriate to compare unions against the corresponding, and most recently assigned, members. All other operations except union assignment (**=**) must therefore be performed upon individual (scalar) members of unions.

It is important to recognize that no promotion or casting of member values occur within a union. In the union **union_name**, declared earlier in this chapter, member **char a_val** occupies one byte (offset 0) and member **int b_val** occupies two bytes (offset 0). If the character constant 'A' were assigned to **union_name.a_val**, and the value of **union_name.b_val** were then used for calculation or display, no reliable value would result. When working with union members, visualize the sequence of operations taking place to determine whether member value has been appropriately assigned. Only the last member assigned may reliably be retrieved.

The **offsetof(s,m)** function-like macro introduced earlier may be used to determine the exact location of structure members within a union but otherwise is of no use with unions whose members all originate at offset zero.

As we discovered for arrays, casts are not permitted with unions because unions are aggregate, not scalar, types. Pointers to unions, however, may be cast to other pointer types, as we will see in Chapter 10.

The use of **typedef**s with unions is completely analogous to the use of **typedef**s for structures. Refer to the "Structure Operations" section of this chapter for explanation and examples.

STRUCTURE AND UNION PERFORMANCE ISSUES

Although the source-code timing examples presented in this section feature the use of structures, the examples could easily be recast to feature the use of unions. Regardless of whether structure or union examples are used, the conclusions and recommendations presented in this section are applicable to the referencing of both structure and union members and array elements.

Each program example has been prepared using the **START()** and **STOP** timing macros developed in Chapter 5 to compare the relative performance advantages of alternative techniques for coding references to the members and array elements of structures and unions. All test programs were compiled using the QC compiler and the Small memory model with no math co-processor on an 8086-based computer.

The program shown in Figure 9.15 was designed to determine the performance characteristics of using the (.) member and (—>) pointer-to-a-member operators with normal structures (or unions). The test program produced the following results:

```
for  : 0-dim .
time : 0.33 sec
for  : 0-dim ->
time : 0.61 sec
```

Clearly, when working with normal (nonarray) structures, the . operator is 50 percent faster than the —> operator.

```
/* FILE: ch9e9.c */
#define TIMER
#include "timer.h"
#define NTIMES for(n=0;n<2;n++)
#define LIMIT 4096

struct tag_struct {char a_val;
                   int  b_val;
                   char c_val;} struct_name;
struct tag_struct *ptr_struct = &struct_name;
int i, n;

int main(void)
{
START(0-dim .);
NTIMES  for(i=0; i<LIMIT; i++) {
                struct_name.a_val = 'a';
                struct_name.b_val = 99;
                struct_name.c_val = 'A';});
STOP;

START(0-dim ->);
NTIMES  for(i=0; i<LIMIT; i++) {
                ptr_struct->a_val = 'a';
                ptr_struct->b_val = 99;
                ptr_struct->c_val = 'A';});
STOP;
exit(0);
}
```

FIGURE 9.15: The sample program ch9e9.c demonstrates the relative performance difference that exists between the (.) member and (->) pointer to a member operator.

The next three comparisons evaluate five alternative methods of referencing members of one-, two-, and three-dimensional arrays of structures (or unions).

1. **[ ] .** notation: normal subscript **[ ] . . [ ]** and member (**.**)
2. **–>** notation: pointer to a member (**–>**)
3. *** .** notation: pointer indirection (*****) instead of normal subscripting **[ ] . . [ ]** and member (**.**)
4. ***–>** notation: pointer indirection (*****) instead of normal subscripting **[ ] . . [ ]** and pointer to a member (**–>**)
5. Compact notation: combined use of the address arithmetic and autoincrementation (**++**)

The program shown in Figure 9.16 was designed to determine the performance characteristics of using the five alternative member referencing techniques with a one-dimensional array of structures.

The test program produced the following results:

```
for  : 1-dim [].
time : 1.27 sec

for  : 1-dim ->
time : 0.82 sec

for  : 1-dim *.
time : 1.27 sec

for  : 1-dim *->
time : 1.27 sec

for  : 1-dim compact
time : 0.49 sec
```

Clearly, in support of the conclusions drawn for arrays in Chapter 8, it is always best to use compact pointer addressing, if appropriate. The (–>) pointer-to-a-member technique is then preferred (by a factor of 35 percent) over the remaining techniques, which all perform equivalently.

The program shown in Figure 9.17 was designed to determine the performance characteristics of using the five alternative member-referencing techniques with a two-dimensional array of structures.

The test program produced the following results:

```
for  : 2-dim [].
time : 2.14 sec

for  : 2-dim ->
time : 1.10 sec
```

```
/* FILE: ch9e10.c */
#define TIMER
#include "timer.h"
#define D1 4096
#define NTIMES for(n=0;n<2;n++)

struct tag_struct {char a_val;
                   int  b_val;
                   char c_val;} struct_name;
struct tag_struct *ptr_struct;
struct tag_struct *beg_addr;
struct tag_struct *end_addr;
struct tag_struct d1_struct_name[D1];
int i, n;

main()
{
START(1-dim [].);
NTIMES for(i=0;i<D1;i++) {
        d1_struct_name[i].a_val = 'a';
        d1_struct_name[i].b_val = 99;
        d1_struct_name[i].c_val = 'A';};
STOP;

START(1-dim ->);
NTIMES for(i=0;i<D1;i++) {
        ptr_struct = &(d1_struct_name[i]);
        ptr_struct->a_val = 'a';
        ptr_struct->b_val = 99;
        ptr_struct->c_val = 'A';};
STOP;

START(1-dim *.);
NTIMES for(i=0;i<D1;i++) {
        (*(d1_struct_name+i)).a_val = 'a';
        (*(d1_struct_name+i)).b_val = 99;
        (*(d1_struct_name+i)).c_val = 'A';};
STOP;

START(1-dim *->);
NTIMES for(i=0;i<D1;i++) {
        (d1_struct_name+i)->a_val = 'a';
        (d1_struct_name+i)->b_val = 99;
        (d1_struct_name+i)->c_val = 'A';};
STOP;

START(1-dim compact);
NTIMES  {beg_addr = &(d1_struct_name[0]);
         end_addr = &(d1_struct_name[D1-1]);
         while (beg_addr <= end_addr) {
             beg_addr->a_val = 'a';
             beg_addr->b_val = 99;
             beg_addr->c_val = 'A';
             beg_addr++; } };
STOP;
exit(0);
}
```

FIGURE 9.16: The sample program ch9e10.c evaluates the performance characteristics of using five alternative member-referencing techniques with a one-dimensional array of structures.

```
/* FILE: ch9e11.c */
#define TIMER
#include "timer.h"
#define D2 64
#define NTIMES for(n=0;n<2;n++)

struct tag_struct {char a_val;
int  b_val;
char c_val;} struct_name;
struct tag_struct *ptr_struct;
struct tag_struct *beg_addr;
struct tag_struct *end_addr;
struct tag_struct d2_struct_name[D2][D2];
int i, j, n;

main()
{
START(2-dim [].);
NTIMES for(i=0;i<D2;i++) for(j=0;j<D2;j++) {
        d2_struct_name[i][j].a_val = 'a';
        d2_struct_name[i][j].b_val = 99;
        d2_struct_name[i][j].c_val = 'A';);
STOP;

START(2-dim ->);
NTIMES for(i=0;i<D2;i++) for(j=0;j<D2;j++) {
        ptr_struct = &(d2_struct_name[i][j]);
        ptr_struct->a_val = 'a';
        ptr_struct->b_val = 99;
        ptr_struct->c_val = 'A';);
STOP;

START(2-dim *.);
NTIMES for(i=0;i<D2;i++) for(j=0;j<D2;j++) {
        (*(*(d2_struct_name+i)+j)).a_val = 'a';
        (*(*(d2_struct_name+i)+j)).b_val = 99;
        (*(*(d2_struct_name+i)+j)).c_val = 'A';);
STOP;

START(2-dim *->);
NTIMES for(i=0;i<D2;i++) for(j=0;j<D2;j++) {
        (*(d2_struct_name+i)+j)->a_val = 'a';
        (*(d2_struct_name+i)+j)->b_val = 99;
        (*(d2_struct_name+i)+j)->c_val = 'A';);
STOP;

START(2-dim compact);
NTIMES  {beg_addr = &(d2_struct_name[0][0]);
            end_addr = &(d2_struct_name[D2-1][D2-1]);
            while (beg_addr <= end_addr) {
                    beg_addr->a_val = 'a';
                    beg_addr->b_val = 99;
                    beg_addr->c_val = 'A';
                    beg_addr++; } };
STOP;
exit(0);
}
```

FIGURE 9.17: The sample program ch9e11.c evaluates the performance characteristics of using five alternative member referencing techniques with a two-dimensional array of structures.

```
for  : 2-dim *.
time : 2.14 sec

for  : 2-dim *->
time : 2.14 sec

for  : 2-dim compact
time : 0.49 sec
```

Again, the results support the conclusions drawn for arrays in Chapter 8. It is always best to use compact pointer addressing, if appropriate, followed by the (->) pointer-to-a-member technique. The remaining techniques perform equivalently and offer no distinct coding advantage over one another.

The program shown in Figure 9.18 was designed to determine the performance characteristics of using the five alternative member referencing techniques with a three-dimensional array of structures.

The test program produced the following results:

```
for  : 3-dim [].
time : 3.02 sec

for  : 3-dim ->
time : 1.43 sec

for  : 3-dim *.
time : 3.02 sec

for  : 3-dim *->
time : 3.02 sec

for  : 3-dim compact
time : 0.49 sec
```

Again the results support the conclusions drawn for arrays in Chapter 8. It is always best to use compact pointer addressing, if appropriate, followed by the (->) pointer-to-a-member technique. The remaining techniques perform equivalently and offer no distinct coding advantage over one another.

You may have noticed in each of the above examples that an identical number of structure elements (2 × 4096) and members (three) were operated upon. For an equivalent number of structure member operations, nonarray structures (or unions) are referenced more quickly than arrays of structures (or unions); a linear relationship exists between the performance

```
/* FILE: ch9e12.c */
#define TIMER
#include "timer.h"
#define D3 16
#define NTIMES for(n=0;n<2;n++)

struct tag_struct {char a_val;
                                        int  b_val;
                                        char c_val;} struct_name;
struct tag_struct *ptr_struct;
struct tag_struct *beg_addr;
struct tag_struct *end_addr;
struct tag_struct d3_struct_name[D3][D3][D3];
int i, j, k, n;

main()
{
START(3-dim [].);
NTIMES for(i=0;i<D3;i++) for(j=0;j<D3;j++) for(k=0;k<D3;k++) {
        d3_struct_name[i][j][k].a_val = 'a';
        d3_struct_name[i][j][k].b_val = 99;
        d3_struct_name[i][j][k].c_val = 'A';});
STOP;

START(3-dim ->);
NTIMES for(i=0;i<D3;i++) for(j=0;j<D3;j++) for(k=0;k<D3;k++) {
        ptr_struct = &(d3_struct_name[i][j][k]);
        ptr_struct->a_val = 'a';
        ptr_struct->b_val = 99;
        ptr_struct->c_val = 'A';});
STOP;

START(3-dim *.);
NTIMES for(i=0;i<D3;i++) for(j=0;j<D3;j++) for(k=0;k<D3;k++) {
        (*(*(*(d3_struct_name+i)+j)+k)).a_val = 'a';
        (*(*(*(d3_struct_name+i)+j)+k)).b_val = 99;
        (*(*(*(d3_struct_name+i)+j)+k)).c_val = 'A';});
STOP;

START(3-dim *->);
NTIMES for(i=0;i<D3;i++) for(j=0;j<D3;j++) for(k=0;k<D3;k++) {
        (*(*(d3_struct_name+i)+j)+k)->a_val = 'a';
        (*(*(d3_struct_name+i)+j)+k)->b_val = 99;
        (*(*(d3_struct_name+i)+j)+k)->c_val = 'A';});
STOP;

START(3-dim compact);
NTIMES  {beg_addr = &(d3_struct_name[0][0][0]);
                end_addr = &(d3_struct_name[D3-1][D3-1][D3-1]);
                while (beg_addr <= end_addr) {
                        beg_addr->a_val = 'a';
                        beg_addr->b_val = 99;
                        beg_addr->c_val = 'A';
                        beg_addr++; } );
STOP;
exit(0);
}
```

FIGURE 9.18: The sample program ch9e12.c evaluates the performance characteristics of using five alternative member referencing techniques with a three-dimensional array of structures.

and dimensionality of an array; compact pointer notation performance is independent of the form of dimensional array representation chosen; and there is no performance difference between using the **[] .**, *** .**, or ***->** forms of notation.

As would be expected, these results for arrays of structures (or unions) confirm the conclusions presented earlier for arrays in Chapter 8. A structure (or union) is simply an aligned data object that may in turn be repeated by the subscript **[] . . []** operators.

Again it is important to recall that by introducing **register** storage-class variables in the programs shown in Figure 9.15 through Figure 9.18, the performance measurements shown would be uniformly reduced by a factor of approximately 35 percent, but the results on a comparative basis remain the same.

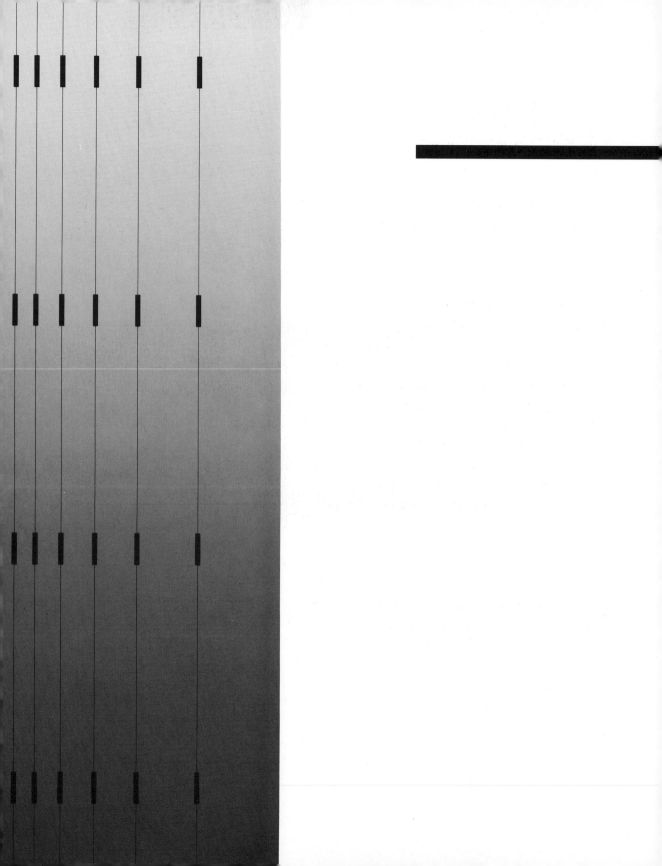

Pointers

Pointers

This chapter explains the fundamental concepts of pointers, which support the indirect access and manipulation of all byte-addressable objects in the C language. It is important to remember that pointers are simply another type of data object in C. The values represented by pointer variables are memory addresses. Recall from Chapter 2 that all DOS memory addresses are expressed by two components in segment:offset notation. This address format is dictated by the architecture of the 80*x*86 family of processors. Pointer variables become data objects whose size is determined by the default memory model being used (Tiny, Small, Medium, Compact, Large, or Huge), unless overridden by the non-Standard Microsoft C keywords, **_near**, **_far**, **_huge**, or **_based** (see Appendix B). The choice of a memory model establishes a default mode of allocating code and data pointers within a unit of translation, while use of the keywords **_near**, **_far**, **_huge**, or **_based** permits these default pointer types to be selectively overridden.

Some applications of pointers are discussed elsewhere in this book. For example, the treatment of arrays as pointers can be found in Chapter 8, the use of pointers with structures and unions can be found in Chapter 9, and the entire explanation of function-type pointers and use of pointers as function arguments and return values has been deferred to Chapters 14 and 15.

AN OVERVIEW OF POINTERS IN C

Pointers may contain the address of any memory resident byte-addressable data-object type, function type, or incomplete type possible in the C language. Since pointers themselves are a data-object type, they also may contain the addresses of other pointer variables. Such pointers are said to define multiple levels of indirection. Although there is no limit to the number of levels of indirection in Standard C, it is uncommon in practice to use more than three levels of indirection.

Pointer variable declarations define the type of address value representation (**_near**, **_far**, **_huge**, **_based**) and the particular data (or function) object types with which it is associated. If the pointer was defined to contain the address of a character, the bit settings of the byte located by that address are interpreted as ASCII characters; if defined to contain the address of an integer, the bit settings within the next two bytes located by the address are interpreted as a 16-bit **signed** integer; if defined to contain the address of a **double**, the bit settings within the next eight bytes are interpreted according to the eight-byte IEEE extended precision binary floating-point format; and so on.

Pointers (addresses) are meaningless unless currently associated with a data-object type that they were defined to locate in memory. Given a pointer (address), you can locate a particular memory (byte) location. However, the interpretation of the bits within that byte (and successive bytes) is controlled by the type declaration associated with that pointer, because the address of any object type in C represents only the lowest starting address, regardless of the object's overall size.

Because array names in C are defined to represent the address of element **array[0]**, the array name itself is also a constant pointer variable (see Chapter 8). Because there is no way to distinguish between an array name which is a pointer variable and any other pointer variable, all pointers may be treated as if they had been declared as one-dimensional (not multidimensional) arrays. This conclusion is supported by the one-dimensional array identity

> array = **&array[0]**

developed for arrays in Chapter 8. By substituting the identity

> **array[0]** = type object

we find that

> array = **&**type object

By substituting the identity

> **&**type object = pointer

we find that

> array = pointer

which supports the conclusion that there is no difference between a one-dimensional array name in C and a pointer variable. Therefore, you can treat any pointer variable as a one-dimensional array and alternatively use subscripting **[]** or address arithmetic ***(ptr+i)** to access the value pointed to.

Because of pointers, every *direct* mode of referencing data- and function-type objects in C using identifiers has an *indirect* counterpart using indirection. The implementation of pointers in C is supported by two principal C operators: the address-of operator (**&**), which yields the address of any byte-addressable data- (or function-) type object (identifier) in C, and the indirection operator (*****), which yields the value of the object pointed to by an address.

The type concepts introduced in Chapter 7 and the pointer concepts introduced in this chapter provide the mechanisms by which values are represented and subsequently manipulated. Without type encoding and decoding, and addressing for storage and retrieval, the reusable switches (bits) of a computer's memory could not be exploited. Errors still can occur, however, when pointers and the objects to which they point are not consistent; for example, when variables and control string parameters are mismatched using the **scanf()** and **printf()** I/O functions (see Chapter 4), or when function argument and return types are inadvertently mismatched.

Since pointers contain the address values of data- and function-type objects in memory, both the pointer address and object pointed to must be current in memory if subsequent use of these values is to be valid. For example, addresses only identify byte locations in memory; therefore, **register** storage-class variables, bits and bit-fields, and **longjmp()** branches to functions in overlays (disk storage) are not permitted. Neither registers nor overlays are currently resident in memory, and neither bits nor bit-fields are byte-addressable. For more information about the **register** storage class, see Chapter 7; for more about bits and bit-fields, see Chapter 11; and for more on the nonlocal branching functions **setjmp()** and **longjmp()**, see Chapter 25.

The data object pointed to must also be current. For example, uninitialized pointers, improperly cast pointers, pointers containing addresses to dynamically assigned memory that has already been freed, and functions incorrectly returning pointers to **auto** storage-class variables all represent situations where the object pointed to is not current with an associated pointer. For more about function-type pointers and function argument and return values, see Chapters 14 and 15. For more about run-time library routines that dynamically handle memory allocation, refer to Chapter 24.

Microsoft C supports the development of mixed memory model programs, either by using the default code and data addressing modes provided when a memory model is selected or by qualifying individual pointers with the non-Standard keywords **_near**, **_far**, **_huge**, and **_based**. However, keep in mind that not all chips use segment:offset notation to develop memory addresses, and that the addressing keywords are non-Standard. Use these features only if portability will not be an important consideration. Generally, it is best to avoid using the non-Standard C keywords and to rely upon the default pointer types associated with a memory model being used. The consistent use of the default pointer types associated with a selected memory model permits Standard C code to be written and allows a different memory model to be chosen later during the software development cycle, without modifying any existing source code.

This flexibility permits you to optimize the code and data size characteristics of your program, while minimizing the porting problems involved with transferring a software product to another target machine environment. The importance of choosing the most appropriate memory model for a particular application program also highlights the design philosophy presented throughout this book—you cannot assume that the selection of an appropriate combination of compiler options will compensate for poor programming practices. The inappropriate choice of a memory model, which establishes the size used for all pointers and temporary address variables within a program environment, cannot be fixed by the selection of optimizing (**/O***n*) compiler options.

The selective use of the non-Standard keywords **_near**, **_far**, **_huge**, and **_based** in addressing situations that do not complement the available memory model selections, however, can significantly improve program performance. See the "Pointer Performance Issues" section in this chapter.

SEGMENTED ADDRESSING NOTATION

The topic of addressing was introduced in Chapter 2. Since all pointer variables represent address values, consider how DOS (for the 80*x*86 family of processors) and therefore C handle the representation of address values.

The 20-bit segment:offset scheme addresses up to 1MB of memory, of which 640KB is available for program use, while the remainder is reserved for video, BASIC, and BIOS extensions, and the ROM BIOS (see Figure 2.20). The 20-bit segmented addressing notation is demonstrated as follows:

SEGMENT:OFFSET	HEXADECIMAL ADDRESS	DECIMAL ADDRESS
0000:0000	00000	0
0000:FFFF	0FFFF	65,535
0001:0000	00010	16
0001:FFFF	1000F	65,551

SEGMENT:OFFSET	HEXADECIMAL ADDRESS	DECIMAL ADDRESS
0002:0000	00020	32
0002:FFFF	1001F	65,567
.		
.		
EFFF:0000	EFFF0	983,024
EFFF:FFFF	FFFEF	1,048,559
F000:0000	F0000	983,040
F000:FFFF	FFFFF	1,048,575

From this table and the discussion provided in Chapter 2, it is clear that with this segmented addressing scheme, represented by five hexadecimal digits (5×4 bits each = 20 bits), the range of physical memory addresses that can be developed is 0 through 1,048,575. This is equivalent to 1024KB (1,048,576/1024 bytes) or 1MB (1024KB/1024 bytes).

Notice that each segment begins at a paragraph (16-byte boundary), which represents one hexadecimal digit or the high-order four-bit portion of segment address. Each segment can be offset by 0x0000 through 0xFFFF (0–$65,535$ or 2^{16}) to physically address a 64KB range of memory addresses. Although each segment can address a 64KB range, segments originate at 16-byte (paragraph), not 64KB, boundaries. Note that most physical memory locations can be addressed by up to 4,096 (65,536/16) different possible segment:offset combinations.

Pointer variables and address constants (address-of temporary variables) are allocated data object storage in units of either two bytes (**_near**, **_based**; **unsigned int**) or four bytes (**_far**, **_huge**; **unsigned long int**) depending upon the memory model and keyword modifiers being used. Pointers are all represented by integral scalar types, which support the address arithmetic needed to locate elements of arrays and members of structures and unions. Recall that the address of any data object is always its lowest or starting byte address, regardless of its size. Elements of arrays and members of structures and unions simply represent an offset (in bytes) from the address of the object of which they are a part.

A reexamination of Tables 2.5 and 2.6 permits the categorization of pointer types used by default with each of the Microsoft compiler memory models, as shown in Table 10.1. It should be clear that without the use of the non-Standard keywords **_near**, **_far**, **_huge**, and **_based**, the Medium, Compact, and Huge memory models incorporate mixed memory addressing for pointers to code and data. This fact is also confirmed by Figures 2.20 through 2.25.

_near *Pointers*

All _near addresses within a program assume that only one segment is required for addressing either code or data. The code segment is defaulted to the CS register value and the data segment to the DS register value; therefore, only the offset address component must be allocated for all code and data _near pointers. _near addresses (16-bit; **unsigned int**) can represent an address range of 0000 through FFFF, or 65,536 bytes.

For example, the Small memory model uses _near addresses and separate segments for its code and data; hence the maximum program size is 64KB of code and 64KB of data, or 128KB. Obviously, any function or data-type object addressed with a _near pointer cannot exceed 64KB in size. Address arithmetic for _near pointers is performed for an array defined as

```
char _near array[25];
```

in the following manner, assuming the address of **array[0]** is at offset 0012 and the DS register value is set to 2FA3. The address 2FA3:0012 defines a data object named **array** and represents the following physical address:

$$2FA3:0012 = 2FA30 + 0012 = 2FA42 \text{ (base 16)} = 195138 \text{ (base 10)}$$

Then, recalling the properties of arrays from Chapter 8, the address of **array[i]**, for a one-dimensional array, would be developed as

```
&array[i] = &array[0] + i * sizeof(array[0])
```

TABLE 10.1: Memory Model Pointer Types

MEMORY MODEL	CODE POINTERS	DATA POINTERS
/AT Tiny	_near	_near
/AS Small	_near	_near
/AM Medium	_far	_near
/AC Compact	_near	_far
/AL Large	_far	_far
/AH Huge	_far	_huge

and, for example, **&array[10]** would equal

    &array[10] = 195138 + 10 * 1 = 195148 (base10)

                                       2FA4C (base16)

Recall that **array[10]** is actually element eleven of **array[25]** because all subscripts originate at **array[0]**.

With the Tiny, Small, and Medium memory models, **_near** data-object pointers are returned by the **malloc()** and **calloc()** dynamic memory allocation routines. These Standard C functions are also used by the compiler to allocate data objects to the unused portion of the data segment (DS) called the heap, which is 64KB less the fixed size of the stack (2KB default) and all of the program's static and global data items (see Figures 2.20 through 2.22). The non-Standard C function **_fmalloc()** can be used to access the remaining unused portion of memory referred to as the Far heap (see Chapter 24).

_far *Pointers*

All **_far** addresses within a program assume that more than one segment may be required to address either its code or data; therefore, both the segment and offset (32 bits) of all pointers must be preserved, since a default segment value such as the CS or DS register value cannot be assumed. However, the largest function- and data-type objects are still restricted to less than 64KB each with all memory models except **/AH** Huge, because **_far** address arithmetic (like **_near** and **_based**) involves only the offset component of the address. An example of the address arithmetic associated with **_far** pointers would parallel that described above for **_near** pointers.

With the Compact and Large memory models, **_far** data object pointers are returned by the Standard C **malloc()** and **calloc()** dynamic memory allocation routines. These functions are used to allocate data objects to the heap. Additional segments are allocated until all unused memory outside of the DS segment (the Near heap) is allocated. The Near heap is 64KB less the stack size (2KB default) and all static and global data items (see Figures 2.23 through 2.25) for the Compact, Large, and Huge memory models. A non-Standard C function, **_nmalloc()**, can be used to access the remaining unused portion of memory referred to as the Near heap (see Chapter 24).

When more than 64KB of initialized static or global data must be allocated, the compiler option **/Gt[*size*]** should be used. The option **/Gt** establishes a threshold size against which memory allocation requests are compared. If the request is greater than or equal to **[*size*]**, the data objects are allocated to a new data segment, not DS. The following **/Gt** compiler option specifications are correct:

```
/Gt
/Gt1024
```

When no **/Gt** option is specified, a default size of 32,767 is assumed; when **/Gt** is specified without a **[size]** value, a default size of **[256]** is assumed; otherwise, the **/Gt[size]** value (up to a maximum of 65,535) becomes the threshold value.

_huge *Pointers*

All **_huge** addresses, like the **_far** addresses described above, require that both the segment and offset (32 bits) components of each pointer be preserved. The largest function- (code-) type object may still not exceed 64KB; however, aggregate data-type objects are permitted to be larger than 64KB. While the address arithmetic used with code pointers for a Huge memory model program is identical to that used with **_far** pointers, the address arithmetic used with data pointers now involves both the segment and offset address components (20 bits), because the offset component alone (16 bits) can only address up to 64KB.

Although **_huge** pointers can address more than 64KB of data, there are still restrictions imposed upon the Huge memory model. The largest individual object (array element) that can be allocated using **malloc()** and **calloc()** is still limited to 64KB. This limitation is reflected in the C type definition of **size_t** (see Appendix D) defined in header file **<stddef.h>** as

```
typedef unsigned int size_t;
```

which is used by the **malloc**-related run-time library routines (see Chapter 24), and in turn by the compiler itself, to dynamically allocate the memory space for all data objects. Each of these memory allocation function prototypes defines the individual element size argument to be of type **size_t**. This effectively restricts the largest single data object to 64KB (**unsigned int** = 16 bits = 2^{16} = 65,536). For instance, the following definitions are incorrect because each data object exceeds 64KB:

```
char cv1[1000000];      /* incorrect */
char cv3[100][100][100]; /* incorrect */
```

When it is necessary to allocate more than 64KB of data space in the aggregate, use the run-time function **halloc()**, which returns a **_huge** pointer to an individual data-object type. For example, to correctly allocate the array of **doubles** noted above as **double dv[10000]**, the **halloc()** function would be used as shown in Figure 10.1. This sample program defines a **_huge** pointer to a data object of type **double** called **ptr**; uses **halloc()** to allocate the memory space for $10,000 \times 8 = 80,000$ bytes of storage; and casts the **_huge** pointer to **void** returned by **halloc()** to be a **_huge** pointer to a **double**. Remember that the **_huge** pointer variable **ptr** may also be treated as if it were a one-dimensional array of **double** object types. All 10,000 **doubles** can subsequently be referenced as shown in Figure 10.1 by Example 1 using address arithmetic, or by Example 2 as a one-dimensional (not multidimensional) array using subscripts.

   _huge pointers are therefore only necessary when the total contiguous data space allocation exceeds 64KB, because the addresses for elements of the data object will exceed the address range of one segment. In Figure 10.1, the **doubles** allocated by **halloc()** and defined by ***(ptr+i)** or **ptr[i]** are effectively an array of **doubles** equivalent to **ptr[10000]**. Because the consecutive space for the elements of the array **ptr** exceed 64KB, only the first 8,192 elements ($8,192 \times 8 = 65,536$ bytes) can be addressed by one segment. The remaining 1,808 elements must be addressed using another segment. The output produced by the program in Figure 10.1 for Example 3 looked like this:

```
element     0  addr = 1D74:0000

element  8190  addr = 1D74:FFF0
element  8191  addr = 1D74:FFF8
```

```
/* FILE: ch10e1.c */
#include <stdio.h>
#include <stddef.h>
#include <malloc.h>
int main(void)
{
int i;
double _huge *ptr;
ptr = (double _huge *) halloc(10000L,sizeof(double));
/* Example 1 of using pointer variable, ptr */
for (i=0;i<10000;i++) *(ptr+i) = 0.0;
/* Example 2 of using pointer variable, ptr */
for (i=0;i<10000;i++) ptr[i] = 0.0;
/* Example 3 array element addressing */
printf("\nelement %5d  addr = %lp\n",0,ptr);
for (i=8190;i<8196;i++)
    printf("\nelement %5d  addr = %lp",i,(ptr+i));
printf("\n\nelement %5d  addr = %lp",9999,(ptr+9999));
exit(0);
}
```

FIGURE 10.1: The sample program ch10e1.c demonstrates how _huge arrays of objects can exceed 64KB in size and span segment boundaries.

```
element   8192   addr = 2D74:0000
element   8193   addr = 2D74:0008

element   9999   addr = 2D74:3878
```

Notice that each address is incremented by eight bytes (the size of a **double**), and that a new segment was introduced after element 8,191 was allocated by **halloc()**. Figure 10.2 depicts the memory allocation for this **ptr[10000]** array of **doubles**.

The address of **ptr[0]** is 1D74:0000. As described for the **_near** pointer example earlier, the starting address would be determined as follows:

$$1D74:0000 = 1D740 + 0000 = 1D740 \text{ (base 16)} = 120,640 \text{ (base 10)}$$

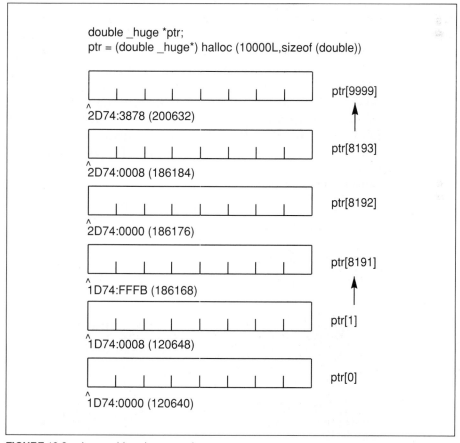

FIGURE 10.2: _huge addressing example.

and the last array element [8191] in segment 1D74 should fall at offset :FFF8 (or :FFFF − (**sizeof**(**double**)−1)):

$$1D74:FFF8 = 1D740 + FFF8 = 2D738 \text{ (base 16)} = 186,168 \text{ (base 10)}$$

To verify that 65,536 bytes have been allocated to segment 1D74, perform the following address arithmetic:

$$186,168 − 120,640 + 1 = 65,529 + 7 = 65,536 \text{ bytes } (8,192 \text{ elements} \times 8)$$

Clearly (80,000 − 65,536) or 14,464 bytes (or 14,464/8 = 1,808 elements) remain to be addressed using another base segment. As shown, segment 2D74 was used to address array elements [8192] (2D74:0000) through [9999] (2D74:3878), or

$$2D74:0000 = 2D740 + 0000 = 2D740 \text{ (base 16)} = 186,176 \text{ (base 10)}$$

through

$$2D74:3878 = 2D740 + 3878 = 30FB8 \text{ (base 16)} = 200,632 \text{ (base 10)}$$

Looking at the starting (1D74:0000) and ending (2D74:3878) addresses, it should be apparent that address arithmetic involving **_huge** pointers must involve the segment and offset portions of the address to preserve the four-bit portion of the segment, which may be nonzero when **_huge** pointer arithmetic and comparisons are made. For example, to determine the number of **double** elements in **ptr[10000]** from the starting and ending element addresses, we must subtract both the segment and offset portions as follows:

Ending Address	(2D74:3878)	30FB8
Starting Address	(1D74:0000)	−1D740
		13878
		+ 00008 (last element)
Bytes Allocated		13880 (base 16) = 80,000 (base 10)
Doubles Allocated (/8)		2710 (base 16) = 10,000 (base 10)

Notice that the effect of using multiple data segments results in a high-order hexadecimal digit from 0 through F.

Since the **sizeof** operator overflows when **size_t** (**unsigned int**) is exceeded, use the following expression when working with arrays larger than 64KB:

```
(unsigned long) sizeof(huge_array)
```

Similarly, calculated pointer differences with **_huge** addresses, **ptrdiff_t** (see Appendix D), defined in the **<stddef.h>** header file as

```
typedef int ptrdiff_t;
```

may overflow when pointers differ by more than 32,767, so use the following expression:

```
(long) (huge_ptr_2 - huge_ptr_1)
```

to yield the correct result.

Another restriction to be aware of when using **halloc()** is that for an allocation less that 128KB, array elements may vary from a size of one through 64KB, while for an allocation greater than 128KB, the array element size must be an even power of two up to 64KB.

The compiler option **/Gt**, discussed in the "**_far** Pointers" section above, still applies to the Huge memory model. The Huge model differs from the Compact or Large models only in the support of full 32-bit address arithmetic for all data pointers. Static and global declaration and heap-memory allocation performed using **malloc()** and **calloc()** are still limited to objects up to 64KB. These functions may be used to allocate data objects to the heap. Additional segments are allocated until all unused memory outside of the DS segment (Near heap) is allocated. The Near heap is 64KB less the stack size (2KB default) and all static and global data items (see Figure 2.25) for the Huge memory models. A non-Standard C function, **_nmalloc()**, can be used to access the Near heap (see Chapter 24).

_based *Pointers*

The concept of **_based** pointers has been introduced by Microsoft with the version 6.0 C compiler. Like **_huge** pointers, **_based** pointers are restricted for use with data types (fundamental, pointer, and derived types), and may not be used with function types (see Chapter 14). Unlike **_near**, **_far**, and **_huge** pointers, a **_based** pointer type cannot be implemented by selecting a memory model, although **_based** pointers provide complete control over both the segment and offset components of a memory address. Each **_based** pointer variable occupies two bytes but has the power and flexibility associated with a four-byte **_far** pointer. All address arithmetic with **_based** pointers conforms to that used with **_near** and **_far** pointers, and limits the range of addressing to 64KB.

To implement **_based** pointers, Microsoft has introduced a number of additional non-Standard keywords (see Appendix B):

_based(..)	Pointer type like **_near**, **_far**, and **_huge**.
_segment	Fundamental segment type.
_segname("..")	Convert segment name to value; use predefined macros below, compiler options **/ND /NM /NT**, or create a new segment.
_self	Uses the pointer's own segment as the base.

It has also introduced the following object-like macros:

MACRO	LOCATION	DESCRIPTION
_CODE	Predefined	Default code segment
_DATA	Predefined	Default data segment
_CONST	Predefined	Constant segment
_STACK	Predefined	Stack segment
_NULLSEG	**<malloc.h>**	**((_segment)0)**
_NULLOFF	**<malloc.h>**	**((void _based(void) *) 0xFFFF)**

and a new operator (see Chapter 12)

:>   **Based operator**   **SEGment>:OFFset**

which is used to combine a segment with an offset to compute an effective memory address. In this section we will explain how these new keywords, macros, and operators complement the use of **_based** pointers.

In the subsections that follow, we will present five different techniques for declaring pointers which are **_based** upon a segment that is defined as one of the following: segment constant, segment variable, pointer, **void**, or **_self**. Let's examine each of these **_based** pointer declaration techniques in detail.

_based *(Segment Constant)*

The segment component of a **_based** pointer may be expressed using the **_segname** keyword to substitute the segment name specified by its corresponding segment address. The syntax **_segname("..")** requires that a quoted string always be included as an argument. The sample program in Figure 10.3 demonstrates this technique. When this program is compiled using the Small memory model, output similar to the following is produced:

```
i_ptr1 = 133A:0000      ← Stack
i_ptr2 = 133A:0000      ← Const
i_ptr3 = 133A:0000      ← Data
i_ptr4 = 1339:0000      ← MYSEG
i_ptr5 = 1220:0000      ← Code
```

Notice that the segment addresses confirm the relative ordering of the segments shown in Figure 2.21. The data, const, and stack segments all originate at the data segment (DS).

Notice that when a pointer is **_based** on a **_segname("MYSEG")** that has not been created using the compiler **/ND /NM /NT** options, a new segment is introduced. In this instance, the segement is introduced as if the Small memory model program were actually written for the Compact memory model (see Figure 2.23). **MYSEG** is introduced between the code and data segments.

_based *(Segment Variable)*

The new Microsoft version 6.0 non-Standard fundamental-type keyword **_segment** can be used to declare (cast) a variable that contains the value of a segment address component. The program example shown in Figure 10.4 demonstrates how a **_segment** variable can be used to specify the segment component of a **_based** memory address.

```
/* FILE: ch10e2.c */
#include <stdio.h>
int main(void)
{
static int _based(_segname("_STACK")) *i_ptr1;
static int _based(_segname("_CONST")) *i_ptr2;
static int _based(_segname("_DATA")) *i_ptr3;
static int _based(_segname("MYSEG")) *i_ptr4;
static int _based(_segname("_CODE")) *i_ptr5;
printf("\ni_ptr1 = %lp", (int _far *)i_ptr1);
printf("\ni_ptr2 = %lp", (int _far *)i_ptr2);
printf("\ni_ptr3 = %lp", (int _far *)i_ptr3);
printf("\ni_ptr4 = %lp", (int _far *)i_ptr4);
printf("\ni_ptr5 = %lp", (int _far *)i_ptr5);
exit(0);
}
```

FIGURE 10.3: The sample program ch10e2.c demonstrates the use of pointers which are _based upon a segment constant.

```
/* FILE: ch10e3.c */
#include <stdio.h>
int main(void)
{
_segment segval = _segname("_DATA");
_segment _based(segval) *ptr_aseg = (_segment _based(void) *)&segval;
printf("\nsegval   = %hp",segval);
printf("\n&segval  = %hp",&segval);
printf("\nptr_aseg = %lp",(void _far *)ptr_aseg);
printf("\n&ptr_aseg= %lp",(void _far *)&ptr_aseg);
printf("\n*ptr_aseg= %hp",*ptr_aseg);
exit(0);
}
```

FIGURE 10.4: The sample program ch10e3.c demonstrates the use of pointers which are _based upon a sequence variable.

When the program is compiled using the Small memory model, the following output is produced:

```
segval      = 133A
&segval     = 0DB2
ptr_aseg    = 133A:0DB2
&ptr_aseg   = 133A:0DB0
*ptr_aseg   = 133A
```

Notice that the variables **segval** and **ptr_aseg** are both **auto** storage class and are pushed onto the stack in the order specified within the body of function **main()**, as confirmed by the addresses noted above (see Chapter 15). In this instance, the **_DATA** segment is requested for use by the **_based** pointer; however, any segment (16-byte; paragraph-aligned) can be specified.

_based *(Pointer)*

The ability to specify a pointer variable as the base of a **_based** pointer is a particularly useful and powerful technique. When a pointer variable is specified, that pseudo-segment address is simply added to the offset, rather than treated as a true segment, which would be shifted left four bits and then added to the offset. Because of this, changing the address in the pointer offsets all references to the dependent **_based** pointer from a new base address.

The example program in Figure 10.5 has been constructed to simulate how dynamically allocated blocks of memory can be selectively used to transfer up to 64KB blocks of memory to other memory locations or another peripheral device.

```
/* FILE: ch10e4.c */
#include <stdio.h>
static char buffer1[0x80];
static char buffer2[0x100];
static char buffer3[0x1000];
static char *base;
static double _based(base) *dptr;
static char *addr[] = {buffer1,
                         buffer2,
                         buffer3};
static int size[] = {sizeof(buffer1)/sizeof(double),
                     sizeof(buffer2)/sizeof(double),
                     sizeof(buffer3)/sizeof(double)};
static int nbuf = sizeof(size)/sizeof(int);
int main(void)
{
int i, ibuf, nelem, avelem;
while (1) {
  /* get number of elements from user */
  printf("\n\nEnter number of doubles to allocate: ");
  scanf("%d",&nelem);
  ibuf = nbuf;
  for (i=0; i<nbuf; i++) {
    if (size[i] < nelem) continue;
    else {
      ibuf = i;
      base = addr[ibuf];
      printf("\nUsing buffer%1d...",ibuf+1);
      break;
      }
    }
  if (ibuf == nbuf) {
    printf("\nNo buffer available...");
    exit(99);
    }
  for (i=0; i<nelem; i++) dptr[i] = i * 10;
  printf("\n#elements  = %d", nelem);
  printf("\n#available = %d", size[ibuf]);
  }
exit(0);
}
```

FIGURE 10.5: The sample program ch10e4.c demonstrates the use of pointers which are _based upon another pointer variable.

The sample program creates three character buffers, used to store type **double** variables according to space needs. Some typical output is shown below:

```
Enter number of doubles to allocate: 1
Using buffer1...
#elements  = 1
#available = 16

Enter number of doubles to allocate: 17
Using buffer2...
#elements  = 17
#available = 32
```

```
Enter number of doubles to allocate: 512
Using buffer3...
#elements  = 512
#available = 512

Enter number of doubles to allocate: 513
No buffer available...
```

Notice that the subscripting used is all relative to the starting address of the appropriate character buffer space: buffer1, buffer2, or buffer3. Simply reassigning an address to the pointer variable **base** causes a different range of memory addresses to be used when the **_based** pointer variable, **dptr**, is subscripted.

_based(void)

When a pointer is declared as **_based(void)**, the segment component must be specified and the new base operator (**:>**) used to compute an effective memory address. The sample program shown in Figure 10.6 uses this technique to directly address DOS video memory, using the **_based(void)** pointer variable, **vp**.

Notice how a **_segment** variable is used to define a starting segment address, and the variable **vp** is used to vary the offset so that the expression ***(segvar:>vp)** can use the indirection operator to retrieve the

```
/* FILE: ch10e5.c */
#include <stdio.h>
int main(void)
{
/* color monitor DOS SEGment */
/* use 0xB800 for color; 0xB000 for mono */
_segment segvar = 0xB800;
static int _based(void) *vp;
int cvp;
int i, j;
for (i=0; i<25; i++) {
    fprintf(stdout,"\n");
    for (j=0; j<80; j++, vp++) {
        cvp = *(segvar:>vp);
        fprintf(stdout,"%c", (char)cvp);
        }
    }
exit(0);
/* run this program with DOS command line
** redirection to your printer, like
** DOS> ch10e5 >prn
** to display the current screen contents
*/
}
```

FIGURE 10.6: The sample program ch10e5.c demonstrates the use of pointers that are _based upon type void and utilize the non-Standard :> operator.

word (**int**), located at the memory address found by using the **:>**
operator. Obviously this technique is powerful when specific memory-
address ranges must be interrogated.

_based(_self)

You can save space and improve performance by directing the compiler to allocate pointers that are **_based** upon the segment in which
they reside. Otherwise, you would have to allocate **_far** pointers. The
example program shown in Figure 10.7 highlights the property of
_based((_segment)_self) pointers.

When compiled using the Small memory model, it produced the following output:

```
data SEGment = 1362
MYSEG1        = 133A
s1.next       = 133A:00D0
MYSEG2        = 1347
s2.next       = 1347:00D0
MYSEGn        = 1354
s3.next       = 1354:00D0
```

Notice that by creating new segments which by design fall on paragraph
boundaries 208/16 = 13, the offsets shown above for the last member of
each structure (.next) are identical. Because they are **_self** based, however, only two bytes are allocated, not four bytes.

```
/* FILE: ch10e6.c */
#include <stdio.h>
struct tag {int member[102];
           struct tag _based((_segment)_self) *prior;
           struct tag _based((_segment)_self) *next;};
int main(void)
{
static struct tag _based(_segname("MYSEG1")) s1;
static struct tag _based(_segname("MYSEG2")) s2;
static struct tag _based(_segname("MYSEGn")) s3;
printf("\nData SEGment = %hp", _segname("_DATA"));
printf("\nMYSEG1       = %hp", (_segment) &s1);
printf("\ns1.next      = %lp", (struct tag _far *) &(s1.next));
printf("\nMYSEG2       = %hp", (_segment) &s2);
printf("\ns2.next      = %lp", (struct tag _far *) &(s2.next));
printf("\nMYSEGn       = %hp", (_segment) &s3);
printf("\ns3.next      = %lp", (struct tag _far *) &(s3.next));
exit(0);
}
```

FIGURE 10.7: The sample program ch10e6.c demonstrates the use of pointers that are _based
upon the keyword _self.

NULL *Pointers*

The object-like macro **NULL** is defined in a number of the Standard C header files and serves as a sentinel address against which the return values of functions (returning pointers) can be compared to test whether the function task was completed successfully.

Standard C requires that a null pointer represent an address that should never be assigned to either code (function type) or data (data-object types). Since all Microsoft C pointers are either two bytes (**_near**, **_based**) or four bytes (**_far**, **_huge**) in mixed memory addressing programs, the definition of a **NULL** pointer may vary.

In compiler versions prior to 6.0, two different **NULL** values were defined in header files, whereas with Microsoft C 6.0, a single definition has been introduced as follows:

```
#ifndef NULL
#if  (_MSC_VER >= 600)
#define NULL ((void *)0)
#elif (defined(M_I86SM) || defined(M_I86MM)
#define NULL 0
#else
#define NULL 0L
#endif
#endif
```

This technique utilizes the memory model predefined object-like macros **M_I86xM**.

It is important to be consistent when comparing pointer values against the **NULL** pointer definition. In compiler versions prior to 6.0, it was necessary to distinguish between **_near** pointer comparisons and those used with **_far** and **_huge** pointers in mixed memory model programs.

Other C compiler vendors may use a different representation of value for a **NULL** pointer other than zero, so long as it is a memory address normally not assigned to either code or data. This topic was discussed in Chapter 5. Earlier mention of the **NULL** segment was made in Chapter 2.

The program example listed in Figure 10.8 shows how the inadvertent assignment of an rvalue to the memory location pointed to by a **NULL** (segment) address is detected.

When compiled without using the compiler option **/Zr** (or by inserting the statement **#pragma check_pointer(off)** at the start of the program example) and then executed, this program produced the following output:

```
ch   = 027E:0DE4
NULL = 027E:0000
0 0 0 0 0 0 0
```

```
41 0 0 0 0 0 0 0
run-time error R6001
- null pointer assignment
```

Recompiling the same example with the compiler option **/Zr** (or by inserting the statement **#pragma check_pointer(on)** at the start of the program example above) and then executing, produced the following output:

```
ch   = 027E:0DE4
NULL = 027E:0000
run-time error R6012
- illegal near pointer use
```

Clearly, in the first case, execution proceeded to completion, and a run-time error message R6001 resulted; however, no indication is provided about where the error(s) occurred. Microsoft apparently uses an initialized area (the **null** segment) of 16 bytes (large enough for the largest fundamental data type, **double**), which is checked just prior to program completion to detect whether anything was overwritten. In this case, the ASCII character 'A' (0x41) was written as shown, and the R6001 message results. Program execution was not interrupted, and certainly more than one **NULL** pointer assignment could have been made.

But when the compiler option **/Zr** or directive **#pragma check _pointer(on)** is used, the program terminated at the first violation of the **NULL** pointer address, and the run-time error R6012 results. In either case, the inadvertent use of **NULL** pointers or reference to addresses outside of the bounds of a program's data- or code-segment addresses is not advisable and should be resolved.

```
/* FILE: ch10e7.c */
#include <stdio.h>
#define NEWLINE printf("\n");
#define REPEAT for(i=0;i<8;i++)
int main(void)
{
char ch, *ptr = NULL;
int i;
printf("\nch   = %lp",&ch);
printf("\nNULL = %lp",ptr);
NEWLINE REPEAT printf("%0x ",*ptr);     /* or ptr[0] */
*ptr = 'A';     /* or ptr[0] */
NEWLINE REPEAT printf("%0x ",*ptr);     /* or ptr[0] */
exit(0);
}
```

FIGURE 10.8: The sample program ch10e7.c demonstrates the effect of a NULL pointer assignment when the compiler pointer-checking options are disabled and enabled.

FUNDAMENTAL POINTER-TYPE DECLARATION

A methodology for defining pointers to the fundamental types (**char**, **int**, **enum**, **float**, **double**, **void**, and **_segment**) was introduced in Chapter 7 and summarized in Table 7.8. Recall that pointers are allocated storage based either upon the default code or data-pointer types established by the compiler memory model being used (see Table 2.5 and Table 10.1), or upon the non-Standard keywords **_near**, **_far**, **_huge**, and **_based** (see Table 2.6), which override these defaults when specified.

Obviously pointers can be defined, as any other data-object types are, at either an external (outside braces) or internal level (inside braces), and accordingly assume the lifetime (duration) and visibility (scope) characteristics of the storage classes **auto**, **register**, **static**, or **extern** as summarized in Table 7.4.

Let's examine more closely some of the characteristics that result when pointers to fundamental types are defined using the methodology presented in Chapter 7. The pointer definitions described in Table 7.8 are said to exhibit one level of indirection, since only one indirection operator (*****) is specified. Multiple levels of indirection are discussed in the next section "Pointers to Other Pointers."

Although we were able to use the mixed-language qualifiers for defining fundamental types in Table 7.7, Microsoft does not permit these non-Standard keywords to be used to define fundamental pointer data types.

Let's first focus upon the significance of using the Table 7.8 columns "Modifiable Type," "Addressing," and "Modifiable Pointer." The latter two qualifiers shape the characteristics of the pointer variable **varname** itself, while the first modifies the property of the data-object type pointed to. Consider the following sample declarations for each fundamental pointer type:

```
/* char pointer examples */
/* Example 1 */
char *ptr_ex1a;
auto char * const ptr_ex1b;
register const char *ptr_ex1c;
static const char * const ptr_ex1d;
extern volatile const char * const ptr_ex1e;

/* int pointer examples */
int _near *ptr_ex2a;
/* Example 2 */
auto int _near * const ptr_ex2b;
register const int _near *ptr_ex2c;
static const int _near * const ptr_ex2d;
extern volatile const int _near * const ptr_ex2e;
```

```
/* enum pointer examples */
enum {false1, true1} _near *ptr_ex3a;
auto enum {false2, true2} _near * const ptr_ex3b;
/* Example 3 */
register const enum {false3, true3} _near *ptr_ex3c;
static const enum {false4, true4} _near * const ptr_ex3d;
extern volatile const enum {false5, true5} _near * const ptr_ex3e;

/* float pointer examples */
float _far *ptr_ex4a;
auto float _far * const ptr_ex4b;
register const float _far *ptr_ex4c;
/* Example 4 */
static const float _far * const ptr_ex4d;
extern volatile const float _far * const ptr_ex4e;

/* double pointer examples */
double _huge *ptr_ex5a;
auto double _huge * const ptr_ex5b;
register const double _huge *ptr_ex5c;
static const double _huge * const ptr_ex5d;
/* Example 5 */
extern volatile const double _huge * const ptr_ex5e;

/* void pointer examples */
void *ptr_avoid;
auto void _near * const ptr_bvoid;
register void _far *ptr_cvoid;          /* no volatile void */
static void _huge * const ptr_dvoid;    /* no const void    */
extern void volatile _based(void) * const ptr_evoid;

/* _segment pointer examples */
_segment _based(void) *ptr_aseg;
auto _segment _based(void) * const ptr_bseg;
register const _segment _based(void) *ptr_cseg;
static const _segment _based(void) * const ptr_dseg;
extern volatile const _segment _based(void) * const ptr_eseg;
```

The first five pointer variables above employ a naming convention with a numeric and alphabetic suffix (1a, 1b, .., 5d, 5e). The numeric suffix identifies the "Base Type" and "Addressing" column choices selected as follows: 1=[**char**, memory model], 2=[**int**, **_near**], 3=[**enum**, **_near**], 4=[**float**, **_far**], and 5=[**double**, **_huge**]; and the alphabetic suffix identifies the "Lifetime and Visibility," "Modifiable Type," and "Modifiable Pointer" column choices selected as follows: a=[none, none, none], b=[**auto**, none, **const**], c=[**register**, **const**, none], d=[**static**, **const**, **const**], and e=[**extern**, **volatile const**, **const**]. Examples 1 through 5 above are described below.

Pointer variable **ptr_ex1a** in Example 1 defines a default data-type pointer, based upon the memory model selected, to a character-type object of storage class **auto** or **[extern]**, depending upon whether it is defined internally (inside of {..} braces) or externally (outside of {..} braces). **sizeof**(**char**) is one byte, and **sizeof**(**ptr_ex1a**) is either two bytes (Tiny, Small, or Medium model) or four bytes (Compact, Large, or Huge). It is implicit that the pointer itself, **ptr_ex1a**, and the object pointed to, a character, are not constants and are modifiable.

Pointer variable **ptr_ex2b** in Example 2 defines a constant **_near** pointer of storage class **auto**, regardless of the memory model employed, to an integer-type object. **sizeof**(**int**) and **sizeof**(**ptr_ex2b**) are both two bytes. It is explicit that the pointer variable **ptr_ex2b** is a constant which may only be assigned to a constant expression, while the integer data object pointed to is implicitly not a constant, and its value is modifiable.

Pointer variable **ptr_ex3c** in Example 3 defines a **_near** pointer of storage class **register**, regardless of the memory model employed, to a constant enumerated type object. **sizeof**(**false**) is two bytes, and **sizeof**(**ptr_ex3c**) is two bytes. It is implicit that the pointer **ptr_ex3c** is modifiable, while the object pointed to is constant and may not be changed.

Pointer variable **ptr_ex4d** in Example 4 defines a constant **_far** pointer of storage class **static**, regardless of the memory model employed, to a constant **float** object. **sizeof**(**float**) and **sizeof**(**ptr_ex4d**) are both four bytes. It is explicit that the pointer itself, **ptr_ex4d**, and the object pointed to, a **float**, are constants, and may be assigned only to constant expressions.

Pointer variable **ptr_ex5e** in Example 5 defines a constant **_huge** pointer of storage class **extern**, regardless of the memory model employed, to a volatile constant **double** type object. **sizeof**(**double**) is eight bytes, and **sizeof**(**ptr_ex5e**) is four bytes. It is explicit that both the pointer itself, **ptr_ex5e**, and the **double** data object pointed to are constants and may only be assigned to constant expressions; however, the object pointed to is also qualified as volatile, which means it can also be assigned to a constant expression outside of the present program environment.

Figure 10.9 has been prepared to help visualize Examples 1 through 5 described above.

Fundamental type **void** is the only incomplete (no storage) type in C that may never be completed (assigned storage). This explains why there are no choices available in the columns "Modifiable Type," "Sign," and "Size" in Table 7.8. However, because we are allocating a pointer to type **void**, the pointer variable itself may be allocated storage, and hence the

char *ptr_ex1a = &c_val;

/AT /AS /AM	ptr_ex1a	c_val
(_near)	000x	
	^DS:000n	^DS:000x

/AC /AL	ptr_ex1a	c_val
(_far)	000x SEGx	
	^SEGn:000n	^SEGx:000x

/AH	ptr_ex1a	c_val
(_huge)	000x SEGx	
	^SEGn:000n	^SEGx:000x

auto int _near * const ptr _ex2b = &i_val;

/AT /AS /AM /AC /AL /AH	ptr_ex2b	i_val
(_near)	000x	
	^DS:000n	^DS:000x

register const enum {false3, true3] _near *ptr_ex3c =&false3;

/AT /AS /AM /AC /AL /AH	ptr _ex3c	false3
(_near)	000x	
	^(none: register)	^DS:000x

FIGURE 10.9: Simple pointer indirection.

static const float _far * const ptr _ex4d = &f_val;

/AT /AS /AM
/AC /AL /AH
(_far)

ptr_ex4a

| 000x | SEGx |

^
SEGn:000n

f_val

^
SEGx:000x

extern volatile const double _huge * const ptr _ex5e = &d_val;

/AT /AS /AM
/AC /AL /AH
(_huge)

ptr _ex5e

| 000x | SEGx |

^
SEGn:000n

d_val

^
SEGx:000x

void *ptr_avoid + &c_val:

/AT /AS /AM
(_near)

ptr _avoid

| 000x |

^
DS:000n

c_val

^
DS:000x

/AC /AL
(_far)

ptr _avoid

| 000x | SEGx |

^
SEGn:000n

c_val

^
SEGx:000x

/AH
(_huge)

ptr _avoid

| 000x | SEGx |

^
SEGn:000n

c_val

^
SEGx:000x

_segment_based (SEGx)*ptr_aseg = &segval;

/AT /AS /AM
/AC /AL /AH
(_based)

ptr _aseg

| 000x |

^
SEGn:000n

segval

^
SEGx:000x

Notes: 1. Caret (^) denotes address of data object.

2. DS denotes data segment register value.

FIGURE 10.9: Simple pointer indirection (continued).

storage class ("Lifetime and Visibility") qualifiers are relevant, together with the "Addressing" and "Modifiable Pointer" qualifiers.

Pointers to **void** may never be "dereferenced" with the indirection operator (*****) without first having been cast to a complete type (data object or function type). Attempts to do so will result in the compiler error *illegal indirection*. For more about pointers to type **void**, refer to the "Pointers to Incomplete Types" section below.

The new non-Standard fundamental type **_segment**, introduced by Microsoft with version 6.0, may contain any valid segment portion of a memory address. **sizeof(_segment)** is always two bytes (16-bit:offset), and **sizeof(ptr_xseg)** is always two bytes for the new **_based** pointer type. For more about type **_segment** and pointer type **_based**, see the "**_based** Pointers" section above.

Pointers to Other Pointers

Since a pointer is itself a data-object type, we can define pointers that point to other pointers. Such pointers are said to exhibit multiple levels of indirection. Whereas a simple pointer (one level of indirection) is declared using one indirection operator (*****) as shown in Table 7.8, a pointer exhibiting two levels of indirection uses two indirection operators (******), one exhibiting three levels uses three operators (*******), and so on. There is no limit in Standard C to the number of levels of indirection; however, rarely are more than three levels necessary.

When pointers exhibiting multiple levels of indirection are to be defined, remember that each pointer in the sequence may have its own qualifiers. In the simplest case, all pointers in the sequence have the same qualifiers. In the example

```
char **ptr_char;
```

if the Small memory model was used, **ptr_char** would represent a **_near** pointer to a **_near** pointer to a **char** type object; if the Large memory model were used, **ptr_char** would then represent a **_far** pointer to a **_far** pointer to a **char** type object.

Since the default (memory model) address representations can be overridden by using the keywords **_near**, **_far**, **_huge**, and **_based**, it is possible, and sometimes necessary, to define pointers exhibiting multiple levels of indirection in the following manner:

```
char _far * *ptr_char;
static int _huge * *ptr_int;
```

If the Small memory model were used, **ptr_char** would represent a **_near** pointer to a **_far** pointer to a **char**; if the Large model were used, **ptr_int** would represent a **static _far** pointer to a **_huge** pointer to an **int** type object. Notice that the addressing qualifiers **_near**, **_far**, **_huge**, and **_based** always precede the data, pointer, or function object that they qualify.

In the case where no reliance is placed upon the default pointer types, explicit definitions can be made:

```
char _far * _near *ptr_char;
static int _huge * _far *ptr_int;
```

These would replicate the previous example and be totally independent of the memory model that might be employed.

This declaration format can be extended to three or more levels of indirection or expanded to include the additional pointer qualifier categories from the columns of Table 7.8. Consider this example:

```
static const unsigned char _far * const _near * const ptr_char;
```

The pointer variable **ptr_char** would represent a **static** constant **_near** pointer to a constant **_far** pointer to a constant **unsigned char** type object. For more about the use of type **void** with multiple levels of indirection, see the section "Pointers to Incomplete Types."

Figure 10.10 helps you to visualize pointers involving multiple indirection.

The classic example of using an array of pointers exhibiting two levels of indirection is the method by which DOS command-line arguments are passed to function **main()** by using **argc**, an integer count of arguments, and either ****argv** or ***argv[]**, as an array of pointers to type **char** objects.

```
int main(int argc, char **argv) { .. }
```

or

```
int main(int argc, char *argv[]) { .. }
```

These techniques are fully described in Chapter 15.

Pointers to Incomplete Types

Pointers to incomplete types are possible because pointers may be defined (allocated storage), although the object to which they point is incomplete or yet to be defined. This section will center upon the declaration of pointers to incomplete fundamental type **void**. For more about pointers to incomplete array types, refer to Chapter 8; for more about pointers to incomplete structure and union types, refer to Chapter 9 and also the section in this chapter

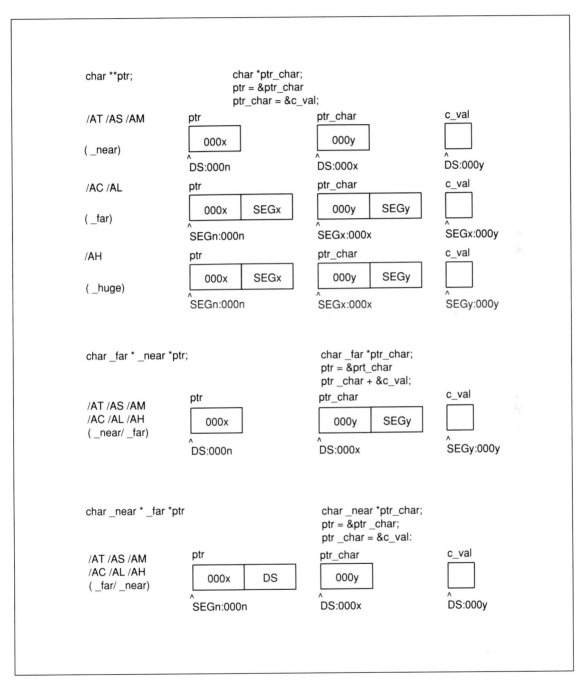

FIGURE 10.10: Multiple pointer indirection.

```
char * _based (SEGx) *ptr;                char *ptr_char;
                                          ptr + &ptr_char;
                                          ptr_char + &c_val;
```

	ptr	ptr_char	c_val
/AT /AS /Am			
(_near)	000x	000y	
	^ DS:000n	^ SEGx:000x	^ DS:000y
/AC /AL	ptr	ptr_char	c_val
(_far)	000x	000y SEGy	
	^ SEGn:000n	^ SEGx:000x	^ SEGy:000y
/AH	ptr	ptr_char	c_val
(_huge)	000x	000y SEGy	
	^ SEGn:000n	^ SEGx:000x	^ SEGy:000y

Notes: 1. Caret (^) denotes address of data object
        2. DS denotes data segment register value.

FIGURE 10.10: Multiple pointer indirection (continued).

entitled "Structures and Unions of Pointers," which demonstrates how linked lists are developed using structure members that are pointers to incomplete structure types.

The most common pointer declaration to an incomplete type involves the fundamental type **void**. **void** is the only incomplete type that can never be completed, which confirms the fact that storage is never allocated for type **void**. The declaration of pointers to type **void** were introduced in Chapter 7 (see Table 7.8). The only qualifiers available from Table 7.8 for base type **void** are from the columns "Lifetime and Visibility," "Addressing," and "Modifiable Pointer." Consider the following pointer to **void** declarations, which are memory model-dependent, presented earlier in this chapter:

```
/* void pointer examples */
void *ptr_avoid;
auto void * const ptr_bvoid;
register void *ptr_cvoid;                /* no volatile void */
static void * const ptr_dvoid;           /* no const void */
extern void * const volatile ptr_evoid;/* no volatile const void */
```

In the example above, **ptr_avoid**, of storage class **[extern]** or **auto**, is a pointer to a **void** object; **ptr_bvoid**, of storage class **auto**, is a constant pointer to a **void** object; **ptr_cvoid**, of storage class **register**, is a pointer to a **void** object; **ptr_dvoid**, of storage class **static**, is a constant pointer to a **void** type object; and **ptr_evoid**, of storage class **extern**, is a constant **volatile** pointer to a **void** object.

Each pointer to type **void** above must be cast to a data-object type before indirection (*****) can be used. The use of indirection upon a pointer to **void** results in compiler error C2100: *illegal indirection*, because **void** has no associated storage with which to represent value, and hence it can never be dereferenced. Consider the following valid examples of casting the pointer-to-**void** variable **ptr**.

```
void *ptr;
(char *) ptr         /* cast ptr to pointer to char */
(double *) ptr       /* cast ptr to pointer to double */
(struct st *) ptr    /* cast ptr to pointer to struct
                        incomplete type st (tag) */
```

A pointer to **void** is compatible with pointers to any other data-object type, and therefore is particularly useful when pointer variables must be declared in multiple levels of indirection. Consider the program example listed in Figure 10.11.

If compiled with the Small memory model, it produces the following output:

```
sizeof(ptr_dv)= 2        ← _near (default)
sizeof(*ptr_dv)= 4       ← _far; ptr2 object
sizeof(**ptr_dv)= 2      ← _near (default); ptr3 object
sizeof(***ptr_dv)= 8     ← double (dv) object
***ptr_i= 9.9e+009       ← dv value
```

```
/* FILE: ch10e8.c */
#include <stdio.h>
main()
{
double dv=9.9e9;

double * _far * *ptr_dv;
void _far * ptr2;
double * ptr3;

ptr_dv = &ptr2;
ptr2 = (void _far *) &ptr3;
ptr3 = &dv;

printf("\nsizeof(ptr_dv)= %d",sizeof(ptr_dv));
printf("\nsizeof(*ptr_dv)= %d",sizeof(*ptr_dv));
printf("\nsizeof(**ptr_dv)= %d",sizeof(**ptr_dv));
printf("\nsizeof(***ptr_dv)= %d",sizeof(***ptr_dv));
printf("\n***ptr_i= %g",***ptr_dv);
exit(0);
}
```

FIGURE 10.11: The sample program ch10e8.c demonstrates the characteristics of pointers that exhibit multiple levels of indirection.

Notice how the pointer involved in the intermediate levels of indirection, **ptr2**, was declared above as type **void**; otherwise, the compiler warning message *different levels of indirection* would result. Since the Small memory model was used, **&ptr3**, which was optionally cast using (**void _far***), would be a **_near** address by default. The assignment operator would have correctly cast **&ptr3** from pointer type **_near *** to **_far ***, had this cast been omitted.

Many run-time library functions return pointers to **void**; however, this return value must be cast to an appropriate data-object type before subsequently being dereferenced. The **malloc()** family of functions for dynamic memory allocation all return **void *** or **char ***. For prototype definitions of each run-time library function, see Parts VI and VII.

Pointers to Function Types

The ability in C to treat function names as pointers (similar to how array names are treated as pointers) is a most powerful feature of the language, and fundamental to the extension of C into object-oriented design and the implementation of C++ (dynamic binding, inheritance).

Function-type pointers and arrays of function pointers represent a logical extension of the concept of indirection. Whereas a data-pointer declaration describes the data type of the object pointed to, a function pointer declaration must describe the function object pointed to, including its object return value and any formal parameters (arguments).

The subject of pointers to function types is deferred to Chapter 14.

Typedefs *for Fundamental Pointers*

The use of **typedef**s for fundamental pointer-types was introduced in Chapter 7. This section will expand upon declaring **typedef**s for pointers exhibiting multiple levels of indirection.

Typedefs declared for pointer types parallel those described for array types in Chapter 8, in the sense that once a **typedef** is defined, it may subsequently be further qualified. In the case of arrays, additional **[]** subscripting operators could be specified when variables were defined using a **typedef** to add additional levels of subscripting (indirection).

Additional indirection operators may be specified when pointer variables are defined using a **typedef** to add additional levels of indirection. For example, just as the fundamental **typedef**, **INT**, defined as

```
typedef int INT;
```

could be used to define an integer data type object named **i_val** by declaring

```
INT i_val;
```

the following pointer variables could also be defined using the **typedef INT**:

```
INT *i_ptr1, **i_ptr2, ***i_ptr3;
```

i_ptr1 exhibits one level of indirection, **i_ptr2** exhibits two levels of indirection, and so on.

In a similar fashion, had the **typedef** been defined as **IPTR** as follows:

```
typedef int *IPTR;
```

the previously defined pointer variables, **i_ptr1**, **i_ptr2**, and **i_ptr3** could be defined in an equivalent manner as

```
IPTR i_ptr1, *i_ptr2, **i_ptr3;
```

In the case where the chain of pointers involves a mixture of qualified **_near**, **_far**, **_huge**, and **_based** pointers, as described in the section "Pointers to Other Pointers" above, alternate declarations using **typedef INT** with the Small memory model may be used:

```
INT _near *i_ptr1, _far * const *i_ptr2,
              * _huge * volatile *i_ptr3;
```

Similarly, you can use **IPTR** to define **i_ptr1** as a **_near** pointer to an integer, **i_ptr2** as a **_near** pointer to a constant **_far** pointer to an integer, and **i_ptr3** as a **_near** pointer to a volatile **_huge** pointer to a **_near** pointer to an integer.

```
IPTR _near i_ptr, _far * const i_ptr2,
              * _huge * volatile i_ptr3;
```

For more about using **typedef**s with arrays of pointers, see the section "Arrays of Pointers," and for using **typedef**s with structures and unions, see "Structures and Unions of Pointers" below.

POINTER INITIALIZATION

Since pointer variables are simply a data-type object that represents memory address values, all of the normal rules established for initializing data-type objects in Chapter 7 still apply. Each pointer, like all type objects in C, has an associated storage class (**auto**, **register**, **static**, or **extern**) that conveys the lifetime and visibility properties of that object.

Recall that **static** and **extern** storage class data objects can be initialized only with constant expressions because they are evaluated at compile-time, allocated storage, and initialized only once. **auto** and **register** storage-class objects, however, may be initialized using any rvalue expression because they are evaluated at run-time, allocated storage, and initialized each time execution passes control through the block (set of braces) in which they are defined.

Since all pointer variables represent memory address values, the assignment of value to a pointer variable usually employs the address-of operator (**&**). For example, if the following pointer variables were declared at the external level (outside braces), they may only be assigned to the address of fixed or constant memory locations.

```
oval = 99;                    /* extern int type */
int ival = 99;                /* extern global */
extern int eval;              /* defined elsewhere */
static int sval;              /* =0; file visibility */

*ptr_oval = &oval;            /* (int *) by default */
int *ptr_ival = &ival;        /* global variable */
extern *ptr_eval = &eval;     /* error, extern */
static int *ptr_sval = &sval; /* file visibility */
```

Consider the following pointer variables, declared at an internal level (inside braces):

```
auto int a_ival = 0;
register int r_ival = 0;
static int s_ival;            /* =0; file visibility */
extern int e_ival;            /* defined elsewhere */

/* auto storage class pointer variables */
int *ptr_a_ival1 = &a_ival;
int *ptr_r_ival1 = &r_ival;   /* error, register */
int *ptr_s_ival1 = &s_ival;
int *ptr_e_ival1 = &e_ival;

/* register storage class pointer variables */
register int *ptr_a_ival2 = &a_ival;
register int *ptr_r_ival2 = &r_ival;  /* error, register */
register int *ptr_s_ival2 = &s_ival;
register int *ptr_e_ival2 = &e_ival;

/* static storage class pointer variables */
static int *ptr_a_ival3 = &a_ival;  /* error, auto */
static int *ptr_r_ival3 = &r_ival;  /* error, register */
static int *ptr_s_ival3 = &s_ival;
static int *ptr_e_ival3 = &e_ival;
```

```
/* extern storage class pointer variables */
extern int *ptr_a_ival4 = &a_ival;   /* error, extern */
extern int *ptr_r_ival4 = &r_ival;   /* error, register/extern */
extern int *ptr_s_ival4 = &s_ival;   /* error, extern */
extern int *ptr_e_ival4 = &e_ival;   /* error, extern */
```

Notice the errors. Although pointer variables may be placed into registers, because **register** storage-class variables are not located in memory, neither the address-of (**&**) nor indirection operators (*****) may be used with them. Normally **register** storage class is used when intermediate address arithmetic calculations are to be performed.

Also note that storage-class variables **static** and **extern** cannot be initialized with the addresses of **auto** storage-class variables since they are dynamically allocated at run-time and not known at compile-time. Even though it is generally not recommended to declare storage-class **extern** variables internally, it is permitted, but initialization may never occur.

Any pointer variable can be initialized to its corresponding null value using the **NULL** macros defined in header file **<stddef.h>** and others, but care must be taken to ensure that when a program uses a mixture of **_near**, **_far**, **_huge**, and **_based** pointers, the appropriate **NULL** macro is within scope. Refer to the earlier section titled "**NULL** Pointers" and to Chapter 5.

Another common way to initialize pointers is to assign them to another pointer variable. If pointers are being assigned which are not of the same size (**_near**, **_based** = 2 bytes; **_far**, **_huge** = 4 bytes), a compiler warning message *conversion of long address to short address* will result to remind you that perhaps the segment address has been lost.

For example, consider the following possible assignment combinations:

```
char ch = 'A';
char _near *n_ptra = &ch, _near *n_ptrb;
char _far *f_ptrc  = &ch, _far *f_ptrd;
char _huge *h_ptre = &ch, _huge *h_ptrf;
char _based(void) *b_ptrg = &ch, _based(void) *b_ptrh;

n_ptrb = n_ptra;    /* _near to _near OK */
n_ptrb = f_ptrc;    /* _far to _near WARNING */
n_ptrb = h_ptre;    /* _huge to _near WARNING */
n_ptrb = b_ptrg;    /* _based to _near WARNING */

f_ptrd = n_ptra;    /* _near to _far OK */
f_ptrd = f_ptrc;    /* _far to _far OK */
f_ptrd = h_ptre;    /* _huge to _far OK */
f_ptrd = b_ptrg;    /* _based to _far WARNING */
```

```
h_ptrf = n_ptra;      /* _near to _huge OK */
h_ptrf = h_ptre;      /* _huge to _huge OK */
h_ptrf = f_ptrc;      /* _far to _huge OK */
h_ptrf = b_ptrg;      /* _based to _huge WARNING */

b_ptrh = n_ptra;      /* _near to _based WARNING */
b_ptrh = h_ptre;      /* _huge to _based WARNING */
b_ptrh = f_ptrc;      /* _far to _based WARNING */
b_ptrh = b_ptrg;      /* _based to _based WARNING */
```

Since array (and function) names are constant pointers, they may be assigned to another pointer variable as follows:

```
int array[10], *ptr;
ptr = array;
```

However, the opposite is never true. Since array names are **const** pointers, they may never be used as lvalues. For example:

```
int array1[10], array2[10], *ptr;
ptr = array1;                  /* OK */
ptr = array2;                  /* OK */
array1 = ptr;                  /* error */
array2 = ptr;                  /* error */
array1 = array2;               /* error */
array2 = array1;               /* error */
```

For more on how pointer values may be directly assigned using decimal, octal, and hexadecimal integer constants representing the segment and offset components of a memory address, and the use of the **scanf()** family of routines for inputting address values in segment:offset notation, refer to the following section.

POINTER OPERATIONS

This section examines each relevant C operation that may be performed using pointers. From what has been described thus far, the role that the **sizeof**, address-of (**&**), indirection (*****), additive (**+**, **−**, **++**, **−−**), and cast operators play when working with pointers should be clear. The **sizeof** keyword returns the size of a pointer in bytes; the address-of operator (**&**) returns the lowest (starting) address of any data object; the indirection operator (*****) returns the value of the object pointed to by a pointer; all address arithmetic is implemented using the **+**, **−**, **++**, and **−−** operators; and casts may be used to alter the description of the objects pointed to.

The other operations that can be performed upon pointers are grouped for convenience into the "Nonallowable Operators," "Allowable Operators," "Run-time I/O Services," and "Other Run-time Services" sections that follow. Subscripting is described in the section "Arrays of Pointers," and the structure and union member operators are described later in the "Structures and Unions of Pointers" section. For a complete discussion of individual C operators, refer to Chapter 12.

Nonallowable Operators

Pointers (memory addresses) may not be used in expressions involving the following arithmetic operators:

OPERATOR	DESCRIPTION	EXAMPLE
−	Unary minus	−Pointer
*	Multiplication	Pointer * 2
/	Division	Pointer / 2
%	Modulus	Pointer % 2

nor any of the bit operators:

OPERATOR	DESCRIPTION	EXAMPLE
~	Complement	~Pointer
|	Inclusive OR	Pointer | 0x0f
^	Exclusive XOR	Pointer ^ 0x11
&	AND	Pointer & 0x00
<<	Shift left	Pointer << 2
>>	Shift right	Pointer >> 2

nor any of the above operators used in compound assignment form:

OPERATOR	EXAMPLE
*=	Pointer *= 2;
/=	Pointer /= 2;
%=	Pointer %= 2;
|=	Pointer |= 0x0f;
^=	Pointer ^= 0x11;
&=	Pointer &= 0x00;
<<=	Pointer <<= 2;
>>=	Pointer >>= 2;

Use of these operators will generate the compiler error message *bad operand*. For a complete description of these operators, see Chapter 12.

Allowable Operators

Three categories of allowable operators will be discussed in this section: assignment, arithmetic, and relational. The initialization of pointers was introduced in the section "Pointer Initialization" above.

How can an address be assigned to a pointer without relying upon either the address-of operator (**&**) or the **scanf("%p",..)** I/O function? Two different approaches are needed because two different pointer-storage formats are possible (two bytes or four bytes).

POINTER	DESCRIPTION
CS:OFF	2 bytes unsigned int _near code
DS:OFF	2 bytes unsigned int _near data
SEG:OFF	4 bytes unsigned long int _far code or data
SEG:OFF	4 bytes unsigned long int _huge data
XXX:OFF	2 bytes unsigned int _based(XXX) data

_near pointers rely upon the CS or DS register to contain the segment associated with the offset of a memory location. For example, if the offset from the DS register is known, then a simple assignment of the **_near** pointer to the offset value expressed in decimal, octal, or hexadecimal notation would work. For example, a **_near** pointer at offset 0x0100 could be assigned using

```
char _near *ptr;
ptr = 0x0100;      /* hexadecimal */
ptr = 0400;        /* octal */
ptr = 256;         /* decimal */
```

_far and **_huge** pointers are identically represented, but **_huge** pointers can address only data, not code, and all **_huge** address math operations utilize 20 bits (segment:offset), not just 16 bits (:offset). Initializing **_far** or **_huge** pointers presents somewhat of a challenge, because no run-time library function is provided to permit separate segment and offset values to be joined to represent a complete memory address.

Although every address is represented as an **unsigned long int**, the segment (high order) and offset (low order) components are treated as two separate **unsigned int** values. To visualize this, refer to Figure 11.2. If the pointer were represented by L0, then the segment would be located at I1 (high order), and the offset located at I0 (low order). However, the address of the pointer object itself is located at L0-Bit-0.

The following non-Standard **_far** or **_huge** pointer function-like macros, provided by Microsoft in header file **<dos.h>**, provide the ability to get or set the segment (**FP_SEG()**) or offset (**FP_OFF()**) component of any **_far** or **_huge** pointer.

```
#define FP_SEG(fp)  (*((unsigned *)&fp) + 1))
#define FP_OFF(fp)  (*((unsigned *)&fp)))
```

The use of (+1) in each segment function-like macro above correctly locates the **unsigned int I1**, which is offset from **I0** by the size of one (+1) **unsigned int** type object.

In the following example, ptr2 is assigned to the initialized memory address of ptr1, using the **FP_SEG()** and **FP_OFF()** function-like macros.

```
#include <dos.h>
char ch;
char _far *ptr1=(char _far *)&ch;
char _far *ptr2;

FP_SEG(ptr2) = FP_SEG(ptr1);
FP_OFF(ptr2) = FP_OFF(ptr1);
```

These function-like macros can also be used as follows to initialize a **_far** or **_huge** pointer with constant segment and offset values. The example

```
static _far *ptr;
FP_SEG(ptr,0x1234);
FP_OFF(ptr,0x5678);
printf("\nptr = %lp",ptr);
```

would produce the following output:

```
ptr = 1234:5678
```

It should be apparent that the new **_based** pointer type accomplishes exactly what the non-Standard **FP_SEG()** and **FP_OFF()** macros are intended to do—provide the ability to construct memory addresses from distinct segment and offset components (see "**_based** Pointers" above).

The use of the arithmetic operators (**+**, **−**, **++**, **−−**) and their associated compound assignment (**OP=**) forms are demonstrated in the sections describing address arithmetic and compact pointer notation in Chapters 8 and 9. In the discussion of structures and unions (Chapter 9), the **offsetof(s,m)** macro was introduced for locating the exact offset of structure members within structures and unions, given the probability that pad bytes will be introduced to properly align each member. An alternate method of determining the addresses of member objects, given these offsets, is demonstrated by the program example listed in Figure 10.12.

This program produces the following, correct output:

```
cv = Z
iv = -99
lv = 12345678
```

Notice that **<stddef.h>** was included to pick up the **offsetof(s,m)** function-like macro definition, and that the pointer, **pstr**, in each case was cast to (**char ***) so that, when the offset (in bytes) was added, **pstr** was correctly factored by **sizeof(char)** instead of **sizeof(str)**. Remember that all address arithmetic using pointers automatically factors offsets (integral values) by the size of the object pointed to.

Another common arithmetic use of pointers is to determine the number of array objects between a given range of addresses, as illustrated in Figure 10.13.

This program produces the following, correct output:

```
elements = 25
```

Notice that when pointers are subtracted, the number of type objects results, not the address difference in bytes. Recall that **ptrdiff_t** is a

```
/* FILE: ch10e9.c */
#include <stdio.h>
#include <stddef.h>
int main(void)
{
static struct st (char cv; int iv; long lv;) str =
                ('Z', -99, 12345678);
struct st *pstr = &str;
void *ptr;
char *ptr_cv;
int *ptr_iv;
long *ptr_lv;

ptr = (char *)pstr + offsetof(struct st,cv);
ptr_cv = ptr;
printf("\ncv = %c", *ptr_cv);

ptr = (char *)pstr + offsetof(struct st,iv);
ptr_iv = ptr;
printf("\niv = %d", *ptr_iv);

ptr = (char *)pstr + offsetof(struct st,lv);
ptr_lv = ptr;
printf("\nlv = %ld", *ptr_lv);
exit(0);
}
```

FIGURE 10.12: The sample program ch10e9.c demonstrates a method of determining the address of a structure member by using the offsetof (s,m) macro.

Standard C type definition (See Appendix D) that is defined to support pointer arithmetic.

Lastly, recall that pointers are scalar values (see Figure 7.1) and therefore can be used within relational and logical expressions. Because use of the negation operator (!) is supported with pointers, a simple null-pointer test can be expressed as shown in Figure 10.14.

This program correctly produces the following result:

```
1st ptr is NULL
2nd ptr is not NULL
```

Rather than testing the return value of the **malloc()** dynamic memory allocation run-time function as follows:

```
char *ptr;
ptr = malloc(100);
if (ptr == NULL) { .. }
```

use the following construct instead:

```
if (!malloc(100)) { .. }
```

```
/* FILE: ch10e10.c */
#include <stdio.h>
#include <stddef.h>
int main(void)
{
int array[25];
int *ptr_beg = &array[0];
int *ptr_end = &array[24];
ptrdiff_t elements = ptr_end - ptr_beg + 1;
printf("\nelements = %d",elements);
exit(0);
}
```

FIGURE 10.13: The sample program ch10e10.c demonstrates the use of address arithmetic to determine the number of elements in an array.

```
/* FILE: ch10e11.c */
#include <stdio.h>
int main(void)
{
int *ptr = NULL;
if (!ptr) printf("\n1st ptr is NULL");
ptr = (int *)&ptr;
if (!ptr) printf("\n2nd ptr is NULL");
else
printf("\n2nd ptr is not NULL");
exit(0);
}
```

FIGURE 10.14: The sample program ch10e11.c demonstrates the use of the negation operator (!) with pointer variables.

This will avoid the potential problems that can arise when testing for **NULL** pointers in mixed-memory-model programs. For a complete description of pointer operators, see Chapter 12.

Run-Time I/O Services

Standard C now provides the **"%p"** control string for accepting pointer values with the **scanf()** and **printf()** family of run-time library functions (see Chapter 17). Microsoft C provides the additional non-Standard control characters **N** and **F** and the Standard qualifiers **h** and **l** to specify the data entry and display of segmented memory addresses in the format segment:offset.

The display of a pointer (memory address) can show either the offset portion only, by using the control string **"hp"**, or both the segment and offset, using **"%lp"**. The control characters **h** and **l** depict the size of the pointer itself. Think of the character **h** as "half," or two bytes (offset only), and the character **l** as "long," or four bytes (segment:offset). The use of these **printf()** control strings can correctly display the following:

```
"%hp"     /* offset only of _near, _far, _huge, or _based */
"%lp"     /* segment:offset of _far or _huge */
```

The data entry of a pointer (memory address) is complicated somewhat by the need to designate the size of the pointer itself, using the control characters **h** and **l**, and by the question of whether the pointer is located relative to the DS register (**_near**), using **N**, or in another segment (**_far**), using **F**. The use of these **scanf()** control strings can correctly enter the following:

```
"%Nhp"    /* offset of _near or _based pointer in DS segment */
"%Fhp"    /* offset of _near or _based pointer in non-DS segment */
"%Nlp/"   /* segment:offset of _far or _huge pointer in DS segment */
"%Flp"    /* segment:offset of _far or _huge pointer in non-DS segment */
```

The program example listed in Figure 10.15 demonstrates the use of these control strings for a **_far** pointer in the DS segment using the Small memory model.

When executed, this program produces the following results:

```
&array[0] = 3786:0042

Enter xSEG:xOFF of [0] = 3786:0042
    element [0] = 100

Enter xSEG:xOFF of [1] = 3786:0044
    element [1] = 200
```

```
Enter xSEG:xOFF of [2] = 3786:0046
   element [2] = 300
```

Notice that the addresses entered were derived from the starting array address displayed by the program, and from the knowledge that arrays represent the consecutive, ascending repetition of a type object. In this case, the **int** type object is two bytes in size; hence the address increment (in bytes) of 0x0002 as shown above.

Other Run-Time Services

When working with mixed memory models, it may be necessary to query the machine registers containing the current segment values for the CS (code segment), DS (data segment), ES (extra segment), and SS (stack segment). The function **segread()** uses the **SREGS** structure defined in header file **<dos.h>** to return the current CS, DS, ES, and SS register values. These segment values may in turn be used to construct pointers using the **FP_SEG()** and **FP_OFF()** macros described earlier in the "Allowable Operators" section.

An alternative approach would be to utilize the new (version 6.0) predefined segment-name object-like macros **_CODE**, **_DATA**, **_STACK**, and **_CONST**, which can be used with **_segname** as follows:

```
_segname("_CODE")
_segment("_DATA")
_segment("_STACK")
_segment("_CONST")
```

This will yield the 16-byte segment address of each of these program memory-map components. In fact, with **_segment(..)**, any segment name that was created using compiler options **/ND /NM /NT** can be referenced.

```
/* FILE: ch10e12.c */
#include <stdio.h>
int main(void)
{
static int array[3] = {100,200,300};
int _far *ptr = array;
int i;
printf("\n&array[0] = %lp",ptr);
for(i=0;i<3;i++) {
    printf("\n\nEnter xSEG:xOFF of [%ld] = ", i);
    scanf("%Nlp",&ptr);
    printf("              element [%ld] = %d", i,*ptr);
    }
exit(0);
}
```

FIGURE 10.15: The sample program ch10e12.c demonstrates the use of the non-Standard scanf() and printf() control string argument qualifiers with pointer variables.

Another approach that can be used to access register values involves writing inline assembly code. For complete details, see Chapter 28.

The dynamic memory allocation **malloc** family of routines merits additional description. Each function, if successful, returns a pointer to type **void**; otherwise a **NULL** pointer value is returned. This pointer must be cast to an appropriate type that is consistent with the data object(s) allocated. The routines are intended to be used to control where storage is allocated, regardless of which memory model is employed.

malloc()	Memory model-dependent heap allocation
_nmalloc()	Allocate to Near heap
_fmalloc()	Allocate to Far heap
halloc()	Allocate to heap (**_huge**)
_bmalloc()	Allocate to based heap

Refer to Figure 2.20 through Figure 2.25 and Table 2.6 for additional information. Memory space that is allocated may be released (freed) by using the corresponding memory release functions:

free()	Memory-model-dependent heap
_nfree()	Free Near heap space
_ffree()	Free Far heap space
	Free heap space (**_huge**)
hfree()	
_bfree()	Free based heap space

Just as the pointer returned by a memory-allocation function is of type **void**, the pointer argument used with each memory-release function should be cast to a pointer to **void**.

ARRAYS OF POINTERS

Since pointers are distinct data-object types, there is no reason that pointers may not be treated as arrays, as described in Chapter 8. For example, to define one-, two-, and three-dimensional arrays of pointers to the fundamental data-object types, simply write

```
int *ptr1a[3], *ptr2a[3][3], *ptr3a[3][3][3];
int _near *ptr1b[3];
int _far *ptr2c[3][3];
int _huge *ptr3d[3][3][3];
int _based(void) ptr4e[3]..[3];  /* n-dimensions */
```

In the example above, the identifiers that end in the character **'a'** are pointers whose size is memory-model-dependent. Those ending in **'b'** are **_near** pointers, regardless of the memory model employed; those ending in **'c'** are always **_far** pointers; those ending in **'d'** are always **_huge** pointers; and those ending in **'e'** are always **_based** pointers.

Figure 10.16 helps you to visualize arrays of pointers to each fundamental data-object type. Obviously, since pointers may represent the addresses of other pointers, incomplete types (**void**, structures and unions), and functions, arrays of pointers may be constructed that point to any data object, function, or incomplete type in the C language.

Since array names are equivalent to **&array[0]**, each pointer within the arrays described above for each fundamental type could be alternately referenced as follows, when assigned an address value:

```
/* int _near *ptr1b[3]; [i] elements */
ptr1b[0]              ptr1b[1]              ptr1b[2]
*(ptr1b+0)            *(ptr1b+1)            *(ptr1b+2)

/* int _far *ptr2c[3][3]; [1][i] elements only */
ptr2c[1][0]           ptr2c[1][1]           ptr2c[1][2]
*(ptr2c+1)[0]         *(ptr2c+1)[1]         *(ptr2c+1)[2]
*(*(ptr2c+1)+0)       *(*(ptr2c+1)+1)       *(*(ptr2c+1)+2)

/* int _huge *ptr3d[3][3][3]; [1][1][i] elements only */
ptr3d[1][1][0]        ptr3d[1][1][1]        ptr3d[1][1][2]
*(ptr3d+1)[1][0]      *(ptr3d+1)[1][1]      *(ptr3d+1)[1][2]
*(*(ptr3d+1)+1)[0]    *(*(ptr3d+1)+1)[1]    *(*(ptr3d+1)+1)[2]
*(*(*ptr3d+1)+1)+0)   *(*(*ptr3d+1)+1)+1)   *(*(*ptr3d+1)+1)+2)
```

Notice that each element of the pointer arrays described above contains a memory address value either in **_near** or **_based** :offset notation or in **_far** or **_huge** segment:offset notation. For each array of pointers above, to access the value of the integer object pointed to by each element of the pointer array as shown, one additional level of indirection would be necessary to dereference the pointer (address) values stored in the array. For example

```
*(ptr1b[0]) ..
*(*(ptr1b+0)) ..

*(ptr2c[1][0]) ..
*(*(ptr2c+1)[0]) ..
*(*(*(ptr2c+1)+0)) ..

*(ptr3d[1][1][0]) ..
*(*(ptr3d+1)[1][0]) ..
*(*(*(ptr3d+1)+1)[0]) ..
*(*(*(*ptr3d+1)+1)+0)) ..
```

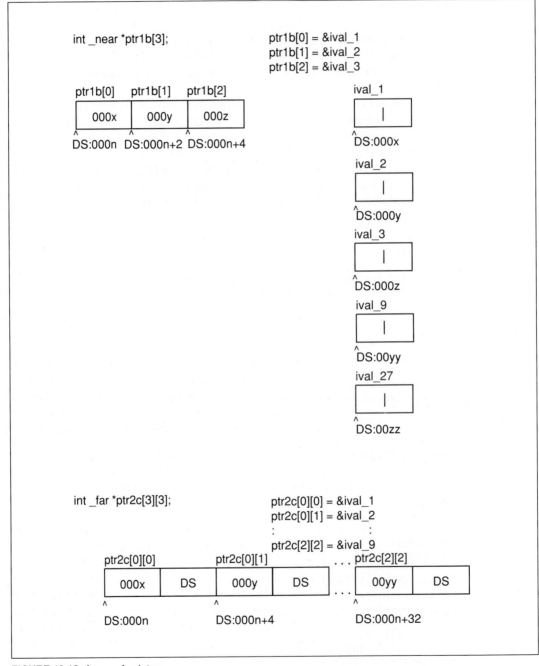

FIGURE 10.16: Arrays of pointers.

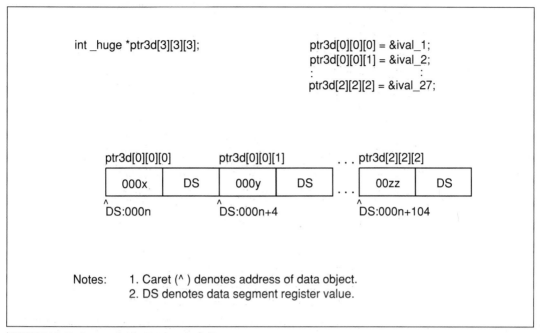

FIGURE 10.16: Arrays of pointers (continued).

Remember that every pointer object within an array of pointers must be of the same size because arrays only replicate one data-object type; therefore, **_far** and **_huge** pointers cannot be intermingled with **_near** or **_based** pointers in the same array, though it would be possible to intermingle **_near** and **_based** or **_far** and **_huge** pointers. In either case, individual elements of a pointer array may be cast to alter the characteristics of the object pointed to.

Arrays of Pointers to Strings

Arrays of strings merit special attention. Not only are strings used in virtually every program, in C they are not a fundamental data type but derived type objects (arrays of **char**), and are null-terminated by convention.

In Chapter 8 you saw that space was wasted when arrays of strings were treated simply as two-dimensional arrays of characters, because the size, or length, of each string is determined by the presence of a null character ('\0'), not the dimensioned size of the array of characters itself. Figure 10.17 recasts the example program from Figure 8.8 to represent an array of pointers to string literals.

It now produces the following output:

```
test[ 6] = 12 bytes

This is an array of strings
```

Notice that Version 1 in Figure 10.17 allocates a one-dimensional array of **_near** pointers (at two bytes each) to six string literals (constants) and relies upon computing the number of array elements to establish a **for**-loop to print out the strings to which each array element points.

Another common technique that is used when working with arrays of pointers is demonstrated by modifying Version 1 as shown in Figure 10.18.

This produces the following output:

```
test[ 7] = 14 bytes

This is an array of strings
```

Version 2 initializes the **NULL** pointer as the last element value and later uses this sentinel as a test for the **while**-loop to print out the strings to which each array element points. Remember that this technique will only work properly if the very last element is set to **NULL**; otherwise, the first **NULL** pointer encountered terminates the **while**-loop. This is analogous to the null character ' **\0** ' termination of a string.

In both examples above, considerable space is saved over the original example shown in Figure 8.8. Whereas the program in Figure 8.8 allocated a test array of (6×10), or 60 bytes, Version 1 allocated 12 bytes for the pointers plus the actual size of the string literals themselves $(5 + 3 + 3 + 6 + 3 + 8)$, or 28 bytes, totaling 40 bytes. Version 2 allocated 14 bytes plus 28 bytes, or 42 bytes, to achieve the same results.

```
/* FILE: ch10e13.c */
#include <stddef.h>
int main(void)              /* Version 1 */
{
char _near *test[] = { {"This"},
                       {"is"},
                       {"an"},
                       {"array"},
                       {"of"},
                       {"strings"}};

size_t d1 = sizeof(test)/sizeof(test[0]);
int i;
printf("\ntest[%2d] = %2d-bytes\n\n",d1,sizeof(test));
for (i=0; i < d1; i++) printf("%s ",test[i]);
exit(0);
}
```

FIGURE 10.17: The sample program ch10e13.c demonstrates the typical declaration and use of an array of pointers to strings.

For more on passing and returning arrays of pointers as function arguments and return values, and using arrays of function pointers, see Chapter 14. The classic example of an array of pointers to strings is the representation of the DOS command-line arguments **argc** and **argv**, passed to the **main()** function (see Chapter 15).

Typedefs for Arrays of Pointers

Typedefs may be defined for arrays of pointers by combining the techniques discussed in the section above, "**Typedef**s for Fundamental Pointers," and in the "Array Operations" section in Chapter 8. For example, a one-dimensional array of pointers named "test," as shown in the examples in Figures 8.8, 10.17, and 10.18, could have been defined as

```
typedef int INT;
INT *test[];
```

or

```
typedef int *INT;
INT test[];
```

or

```
typedef int INT[];
INT *test;
```
or

```
typedef int *INT[];
INT test;
```

```
/* FILE: ch10e14.c */
#include <stddef.h>
int main(void)              /* Version 2 */
{
char _near *test[] = { ("This"),
                       ("is"),
                       ("an"),
                       ("array"),
                       ("of"),
                       ("strings"),
                       (NULL )};
size_t d1 = sizeof(test)/sizeof(test[0]);
int i=0;
printf("\ntest[%2d] = %2d-bytes\n\n",d1,sizeof(test));
while (test[i]) printf("%s ",test[i++]);
exit(0);
}
```

FIGURE 10.18: The sample program ch10e14.c demonstrates the added utility of declaring a NULL-terminated array of pointers.

Recall that **typedef**s do not create new types, only synonyms for existing types in the C language and, once declared, they may subsequently be "modified" as noted in the example above.

STRUCTURES AND UNIONS OF POINTERS

Again, since pointers are distinct data-object types, they may be incorporated as members within structures and unions. The curious ability to define a pointer to an incomplete type permits pointer members of structures to reference themselves. Recall that all members of structures and unions must be complete types. Pointers are always complete types (allocated storage) and represent the address (value) of any data object, function, or incomplete type in C.

The most common application of this feature involves supporting the declaration and implementation of complex data structures involving singly- and doubly-linked lists used for database management. We will use a doubly-linked list to demonstrate how pointers may be incorporated in simple structures (and unions). Although linked lists can be implemented as arrays of structures, records are normally allocated as needed using the dynamic memory allocation **malloc** family of run-time functions, and pointers are used to link structure records together to form a list. This overcomes the inherent need to size arrays, which usually wastes storage (memory) space when elements go unused.

Consider the following structure declarations, which will be used in a doubly-linked list program example:

```
struct dbl_link { char field_n;
                  struct dbl_link *prev;
                  struct dbl_link *next; };

typedef struct dbl_link *PTR_RECORD;

ptr_RECORD my_ptr, ptr;
struct list { PTR_RECORD first;
              PTR_RECORD last; } my_list;
```

Notice that structure members ***prev** and ***next** are pointers to the incomplete structure tag **dbl_link**. This is correct because a pointer is a complete type and can be allocated storage even though structure tag **dbl_link** is yet incomplete. The member **field_n** in this case is simply a character field but represents any definable set of member descriptions.

The **typedef PTR_RECORD** has been declared as a pointer to a structure of type (tag) **dbl_link**. This **typedef** defines pointers to the structure type **dbl_link**, **my_ptr**, and **ptr**. The members of structure **my_list** define and store pointers to the first and last records in the doubly-linked list to be developed by dynamically allocating records one at a time. Consider the complete program example shown in Figure 10.19. It produces the following output:

ABCDEF

FEDCBA

```c
#include <stdio.h>
#include <malloc.h>
int main(void)
{
struct dbl_link {char field_n;
                 struct dbl_link *prev;
                 struct dbl_link *next;};
typedef struct dbl_link *PTR_RECORD;
PTR_RECORD my_ptr, ptr;
struct list {PTR_RECORD first;
                      PTR_RECORD last;} my_list;

int i;

/* allocate 1st record */
my_ptr = (PTR_RECORD) malloc(sizeof(struct dbl_link));
if (!my_ptr) exit(1);                    /* exit if NULL */
my_list.first = my_ptr;
my_list.last = my_ptr;
my_ptr->field_n = 'A';
my_ptr->prev = my_list.first;
my_ptr->next = my_list.last;

/* allocate record 2->6 to end of my_list */
for (i=2;i<=6;i++) {
        my_ptr = (PTR_RECORD)malloc(sizeof(struct dbl_link));
        if(!my_ptr) exit(i);             /* exit if NULL */
        ptr = my_list.last;              /* get last record */
        my_list.last = my_ptr;           /* update root */
        my_list.first->prev=my_ptr;      /* update first */
        ptr->next = my_ptr;              /* update last */
        my_ptr->field_n = ptr->field_n+1;  /* increment alphabetic */
        my_ptr->prev = ptr;              /* update current */
        my_ptr->next = my_list.first;    /* update current */
        }

/* display first -> last */
ptr = my_list.first;
printf("\n\n");
do {
    printf("%c",ptr->field_n);
    ptr = ptr->next;
    } while (ptr != my_list.first);      /* circular list */

/* display last -> first */
ptr = my_list.last;
printf("\n\n");
do {
    printf("%c",ptr->field_n);
    ptr = ptr->prev;
    } while (ptr != my_list.last);       /* circular list */
exit(0);
}
```

FIGURE 10.19: The sample program ch10e15.c demonstrates the power of using pointers as structure members to support the development of dynamically allocated linked lists.

Notice that the function **malloc()** allocates an object of size **sizeof(struct dbl_link)** and returns a pointer to type **void**, which must be cast as shown to represent a pointer to a structure of type (tag) **dbl_link**. The pointer returned by **malloc()** is the address of the object and, if **NULL**, indicates that the allocation could not be performed.

The first record allocated has the member **field_n** initialized to the character **'A'**. Subsequent records update their fields by incrementing this character field by one unit or alphabetic character. This example simply adds successive records to the end of the list and updates the pointers of the first and last records, as well as the root structure, which maintains the first and last record addresses in memory.

When it is necessary to create a sorted list of records, no physical sorting of the records ever occurs; rather, each record is logically inserted into the list after it is allocated by rearranging the connecting pointers. To simplify the program example above, we have created an unsorted list.

Notice that the display technique utilizes the fact that this list exhibits circular behavior; that is, the first and last records point to each other, while the addresses of the first and last records are maintained in a separate structure named **my_list**.

Figure 10.20 helps you visualize the allocation of the structure records used in this program.

The incorporation of pointers in structures (and unions) and arrays of structures (and unions) complements the use of dynamic memory allocation routines and facilitates the development of complex data structures in C. For more about the use of the **malloc()** family of functions, see Chapter 24.

POINTER PERFORMANCE ISSUES

Given the differences in both the size and address arithmetic performed with the **_near**, **_far**, **_huge**, and **_based** address types available with Microsoft C, it should not be surprising that performance differences do exist between these pointer types. Figure 10.21 presents a program, developed using the familiar **START()** and **STOP** timing macros discussed in Chapter 5, which measures the relative performance characteristics of the **_near**, **_far**, **_huge**, and **_based** pointer types.

The following output was produced using the Small memory model on an 80286-based computer:

```
for  : _near-ptr loop
time : 1.81 sec
```

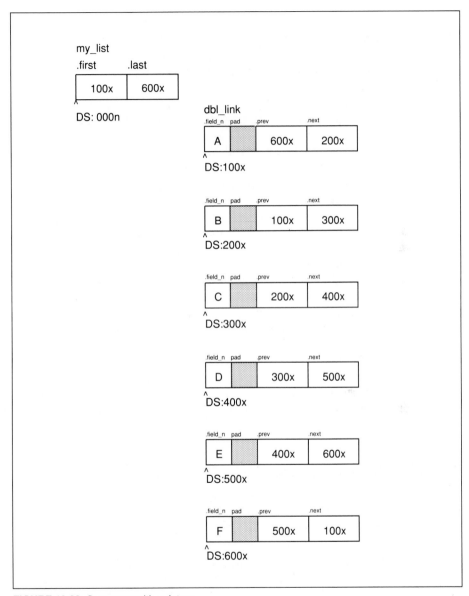

FIGURE 10.20: Structures with pointers.

```
/* FILE: ch10e16.c */
#define TIMER
#include "timer.h"
#define REPEAT for(i=0;i<100;i++)
#define NTIMES for(j=1;j<1000;j++)
main()
{
int i, j;
static char _near *n_array[1000] = ((char _near *)n_array);
static char _far  *f_array[1000] = ((char _far *)f_array);
static char _huge *h_array[1000] = ((char _huge *)h_array);
static char _based(_segname("_DATA")) *b_array[1000] =
            ((char _based(void) *)b_array);

START(_near-ptr loop);
REPEAT NTIMES n_array[j] = *(n_array+j-1);
REPEAT NTIMES n_array[j] = n_array[j] + (n_array[j] - n_array[0]);
STOP;

START(_far-ptr loop);
REPEAT NTIMES f_array[j] = *(f_array+j-1);
REPEAT NTIMES f_array[j] = f_array[j] + (f_array[j] - f_array[0]);
STOP;

START(_huge-ptr loop);
REPEAT NTIMES h_array[j] = *(h_array+j-1);
REPEAT NTIMES h_array[j] = h_array[j] + (h_array[j] - h_array[0]);
STOP;

START(_based-ptr-loop);
REPEAT NTIMES b_array[j] = *(b_array+j-1);
REPEAT NTIMES b_array[j] = b_array[j] + (b_array[j] - b_array[0]);
STOP;

exit(0);
}
```

FIGURE 10.21: The sample program ch10e16.c determines the relative performance characteristics of using _near, _far, _huge, and _based pointers.

```
for  : _far-ptr loop
time : 2.48 sec

for  : _huge-ptr loop
time : 3.79 sec

for  : _based-ptr loop
time : 2.03 sec
```

These results should confirm your intuitive feeling that **_near** pointers should outperform **_far** pointers, which in turn should outperform **_huge** pointers:

$$\textbf{\_far} \text{ pointer speed} = 1.37 \times \textbf{\_near} \text{ pointer speed}$$

$$\textbf{\_huge} \text{ pointer speed} = 1.52 \times \textbf{\_far} \text{ pointer speed}$$

$$\textbf{\_huge} \text{ pointer speed} = 2.09 \times \textbf{\_near} \text{ pointer speed}$$

Interestingly, **_based** pointers fall between **_near** and **_far** pointers in performance:

_based pointer speed = 1.12 × **_near** pointer speed

_far pointer speed   = 1.22 × **_based** pointer speed

Obviously, from both a space (**_near** = 2 bytes, **_based** = 2 bytes, **_far** = 4 bytes, **_huge** = 4 bytes) and performance (**_near** = 1.00, **_based** = 1.12, **_far** = 1.33, **_huge** = 2.07) point of view, **_near** pointers should be used whenever possible, followed by **_based** pointers, **_far** pointers, and finally **_huge** pointers.

These results also confirm the importance of selecting a compiler memory model (Tiny **/AT**, Small **/AS**, Medium **/AM**, Compact **/AC**, Large **/AL**, Huge **/AH**) that appropriately matches the code and data pointer addressing requirements of the program being developed; otherwise, a performance penalty will necessarily result when address arithmetic is performed.

Further refinement of the performance of a given memory model program can therefore be achieved by the selective use of the non-Standard keywords **_near**, **_far**, **_huge**, and **_based** to override the default pointer types when they are inappropriate.

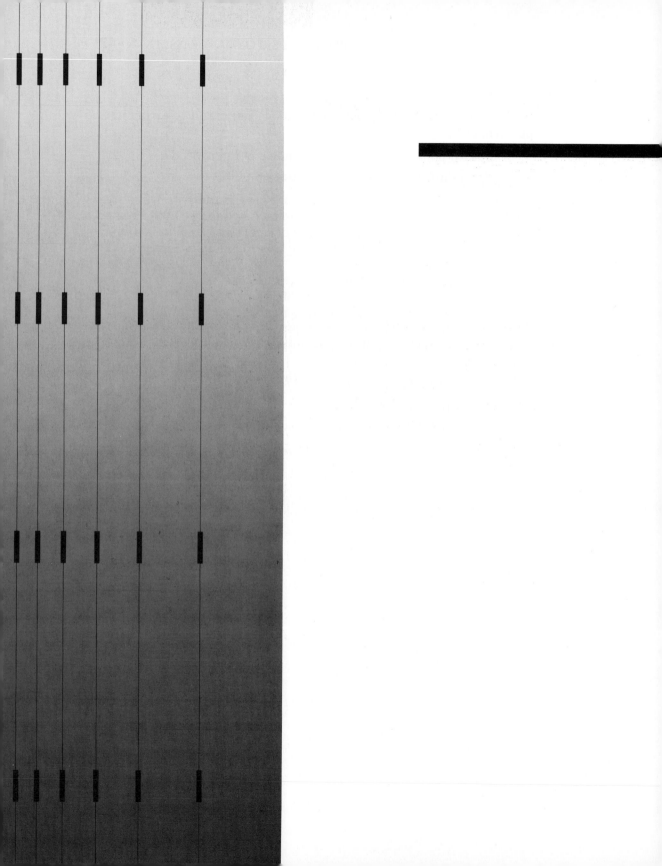

# CHAPTER 11

Working with Bits in C

Working with Bits in C

This chapter presents the features of C that support the declaration and individual manipulation of bits. Although all data are expressed in bit (binary digit) patterns, we have so far worked only with the declaration and manipulation of data type objects comprised of multiples of bytes (eight bits each). We will now explore working with bits individually and in aggregates of bits called bit-fields.

Most other languages offer bit operations couched in calls to library routines; however, C offers a full complement of operators that work directly upon bits declared in two different ways. Bits may be manipulated within any integral data-object type (**char**, **int**, **long**, or **enum**; see Figure 7.1), or alternatively declared and manipulated as bit-fields within structures and unions. Whereas integral bit definitions may only be operated upon using the bitwise operators (**~**, **&**, **|**, **^**, **<<**, and **>>**), bit-fields may involve the bitwise operators and any other C operator except **&** (address of), **[]** (subscripting), ***** (indirection), and **sizeof**. As structure (or union) members, each bit-field has an identifier that permits subsequent references in normal integral arithmetic and logical expressions.

This chapter will also review the concepts supporting bit representation, including base number systems and conversion, two's complement notation for the representation of negative integral types, and the widely used IEEE binary floating-point notation used with floating types. The syntax for the definition of integral and bit-field types will be presented, and the differences between the *logical* identification and *physical* ordering of bits within integral, bit-field, and floating-point type definitions will be clarified.

Finally, the chapter will explain bit constants, initialization, and operations, and present the performance trade-offs encountered when electing to use integral versus bit-field type definitions.

BIT CONCEPTS

Standard C defines a bit, or binary digit, as a unit of data storage large enough to "hold an object that may have one of two values." The unit of data storage (integral type object) may be addressable, but individual bits (objects) are not addressable in C. The physical analogy to the implementation of a bit is a switch. Storage (memory) may then be thought of as a sequential bank of switches that are by convention byte-addressable (every eight bits). Bytes in turn become the fundamental units or building blocks of all other data-object types in C, as discussed in Chapter 7 and described in Table 7.2 and Figure 7.3.

By convention, a bit (switch) that is *off* has a value of zero (0), and a bit (switch) that is *on* has a value of one (1). These two values in turn become the digits (symbols) used by the binary (base 2) number system. Recall that the base of any number system signifies the number of constituent symbols that represent digits or units of value. The base 8 (octal) number system uses eight digits (symbols 0 through 7), the base 10 (decimal) system uses ten digits (symbols 0 through 9), the base 16 (hexadecimal) number system uses sixteen digits (symbols 0 through 9, and A through F representing 10 through 15 units).

When bits are aggregated into groups, each bit is *logically* identified beginning with the rightmost, or least significant, bit-0 to the leftmost, or most significant, bit-*n*. Although we logically identify bit-0 through bit-*n*, the *physical* ordering of bits within bytes or other data type objects is not dictated by Standard C, and does vary between different C compilers and microprocessors.

Figure 11.1 summarizes the logical bit layouts that Microsoft uses to represent the unique data-object types in C: **char**, **int**, **enum**, **float**, **double**, **long double**, and **_segment**. In studying these layouts, you'll find it helpful to refer to Figure 7.3 and Table 7.2. Note that Standard C does not dictate how either integral (whole number) or floating-point (fractional number) value is represented, only the minimum standards for the ranges of value that will be represented (refer to Table 7.1); thus, it does not mandate the bit layouts shown in Figure 11.1. They are specific to Microsoft.

Notice that fundamental type **void** has been omitted from Figure 11.1. It has no associated storage and hence no bit representation of value. The (byte) numbering (B0 through B7) is shown to correlate with Figure 11.2 (discussed below). All integral type bit constants and masks are expressed using the logical bit patterns shown in Figure 11.1. For example, the following masks would be appropriate for isolating the sign bit of each integral type as shown:

```
char cmask    = 0x7F;       /* 0111 1111 */
int  imask    = 0x7FFF;     /* 0111 1111 1111 1111 */
long lmask    = 0x7FFFFFFF; /* 0111 1111 1111 1111
                               1111 1111 1111 1111 */
```

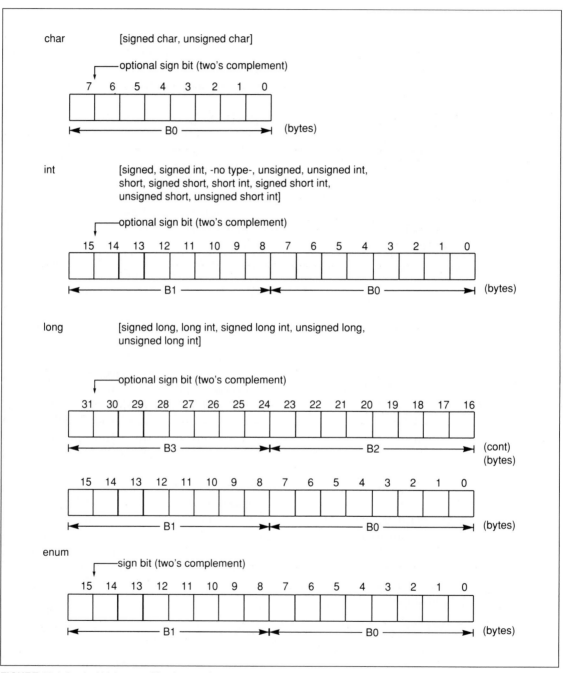

FIGURE 11.1: Logical bit layout of fundamental types.

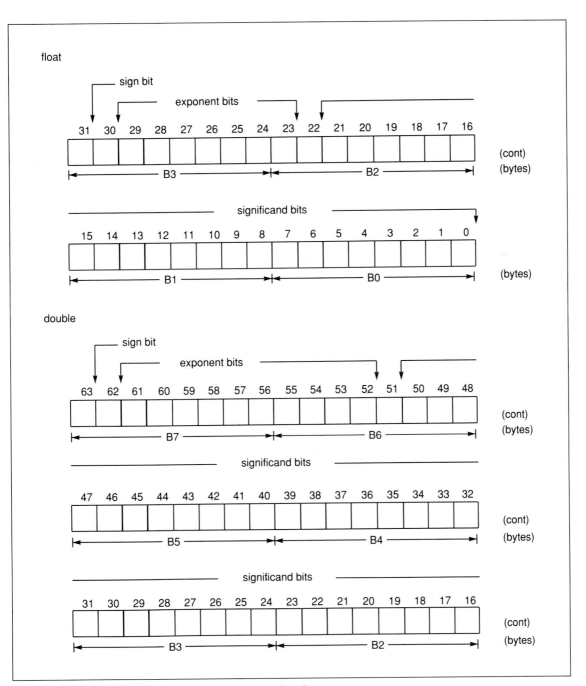

FIGURE 11.1: Logical bit layout of fundamental types (continued).

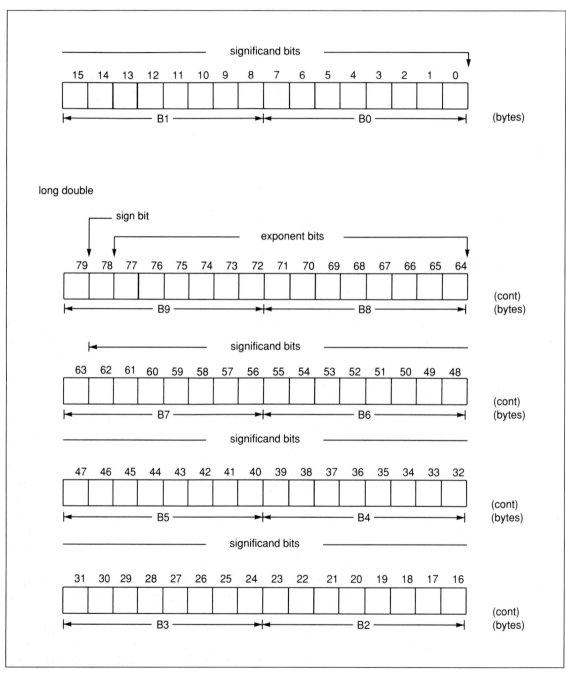

FIGURE 11.1: Logical bit layout of fundamental types (continued).

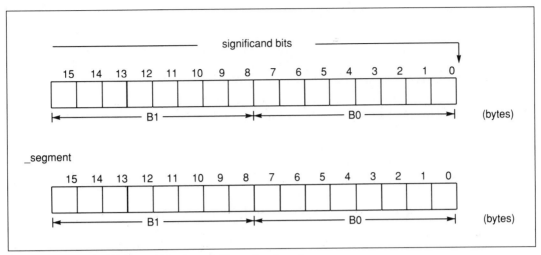

FIGURE 11.1: Logical bit layout of fundamental types (continued).

In the case of a **char** (one-byte representation), we identify bit-0 as the rightmost or least significant, and bit-7 as the leftmost or most significant bit. For a **signed char** (or **char**), sign bit and 2^7 significand bit combinations yield a range of value representation from −128 through +127. For an **unsigned char**, 2^8 significant bit combinations yield a range of value representation from 0 through 255.

The integer (**int**) data type uses two bytes for value representation. The bits are identified as bit-0 (rightmost, least significant) through bit-15 (leftmost, most significant). The **signed int** (or **int**) range of value (2^{15}) becomes −32,768 through +32,767, and the **unsigned int** range of value (2^{16}) becomes 0 through 65,535.

The **long** integer (**long int**) data type uses four bytes for value representation. The bits are identified as bit-0 (rightmost, least significant) through bit-31 (leftmost, most significant). The **signed long int** value range (2^{31}) becomes −2,147,483,648 through 2,147,483,647, and the **unsigned** range of value (2^{32}) becomes 0 through 4,294,967,295.

The **enum** data type is implemented by Microsoft as a **signed int**. Refer to the discussion of type **int** above.

The **float**, **double**, and **long double** types are not integral types, but floating-point types. The standards used for the representation of value are entirely different from integral types. Whole and fractional value is represented in IEEE binary floating-point format by the sign, exponent, and significand bits shown. More details about the IEEE binary floating-point format are provided in the section below entitled "IEEE Floating-Point Notation."

The new **_segment** type is an **unsigned int** and is used to represent the segment component of a memory address (segment:offset). **_segment** is a scalar, not an aggregate type, because it can only represent one value at a time; but not an arithmetic type, because the memory address segment values they represent cannot be meaningfully manipulated by the full complement of C arithmetic operators.

The bit layouts shown in Figure 11.1 permit us to work logically with bits; however, the order of neither bytes nor bits within data object types is dictated by Standard C. Figure 11.2 has been prepared to present a corresponding physical view of the bit layouts for each fundamental type presented in Figure 11.1. For example, when Microsoft upgraded its version 3.0 C compiler to version 4.0, it reversed the bit-ordering convention that had previously been adopted. Vendors (implementors) are free to logically order bits from the right or left. The order of bytes within other C data types also varies depending upon whether the microprocessor is either *big-* or *little-endian* in design.

Big-endian processors (Motorola 680x0) always store the most significant byte at the lowest memory address, whereas little-endian processors (Intel 80x86) always store the least significant byte at the lowest memory address.

Consider the following example. In Figure 11.1 notice that for type **long** the most significant byte is labeled as B3, and the least significant byte as B0. Notice in Figure 11.2 the physical (Intel 80x86; little-endian) ordering of the bytes (B0 through B3) in type **long** (L0), confirming that the lowest memory address is associated with the least significant byte because the address of the L0 object is at B0.

These physical byte- and bit-ordering considerations are of concern when it is necessary to do any of the following:

1. *Map* bytes or bits to an externally defined data structure.
2. *Overlay* different data types within a union.
3. *Isolate* the logical bits shown in Figure 11.1 for a given data-object type using bit-fields.

Examples of the techniques used with the **float** and **double** data-object types are included in the sections entitled "Bit-Field Types" and "**&** Bitwise AND (Conjunction)" below.

Base Number Systems

For the integral types (**char**, **int**, **long**, and **enum**) shown in Figure 11.1, the identifier associated with each bit represents its corresponding power-of-two multiplier. Figure 11.3 illustrates this arithmetic for the binary

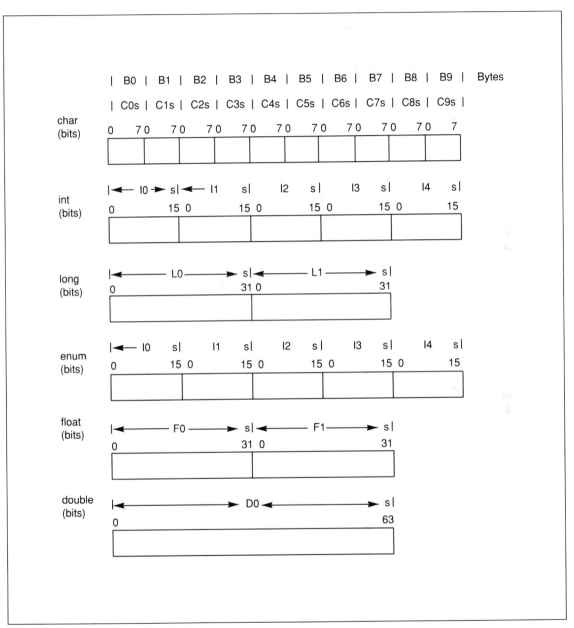

FIGURE 11.2: Physical bit layout of fundamental types.

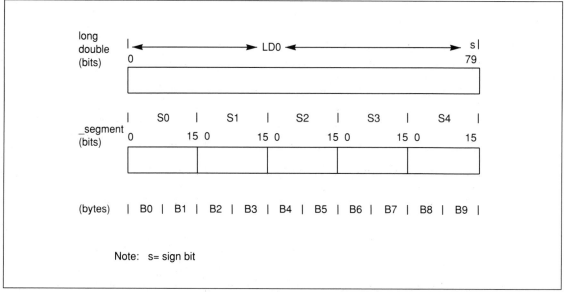

FIGURE 11.2: Physical bit layout of fundamental types (continued).

number 10101 (decimal 21) and shows how the octal and hexadecimal expressions of the same value are converted to decimal.

C does not provide a facility for the expression of integral constants in binary (base 2), only octal (base 8), decimal (base 10), and hexadecimal (base 16), as discussed in Chapter 7. Floating-type constants may be expressed only in decimal or scientific notation, not binary, octal, or hexadecimal. The programmer needs to make these conversions manually before writing source code. It is important when working with bits and bit-fields in C to be able to express integral (whole) numbers in these commonly used base number systems.

The examples in Figure 11.3 provide the mechanism for the conversion of base n numbers to their equivalent representation in base 10 (decimal). Figure 11.4 illustrates the technique for converting from base 10 to any base n number system, again using the decimal number 21 and the base 16, base 8, and base 2 number systems. Essentially, the method of conversion is to divide any base 10 number by the n of the desired base n number and record the remainders, until the divisor is zero.

One technique for the conversion between base 2, base 8, and base 16 is a two-step process that first converts the number to base 10 and then to the desired base, using both techniques described above. For example, to go from base 2 to base 16, convert the base 2 number to base 10, and then convert the base 10 number to base 16.

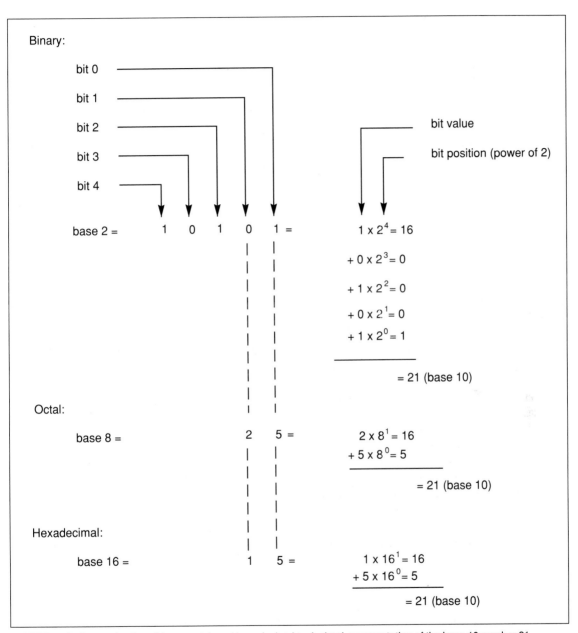

FIGURE 11.3: Conversion from binary, octal, and hexadecimal to decimal representation of the base 10 number 21.

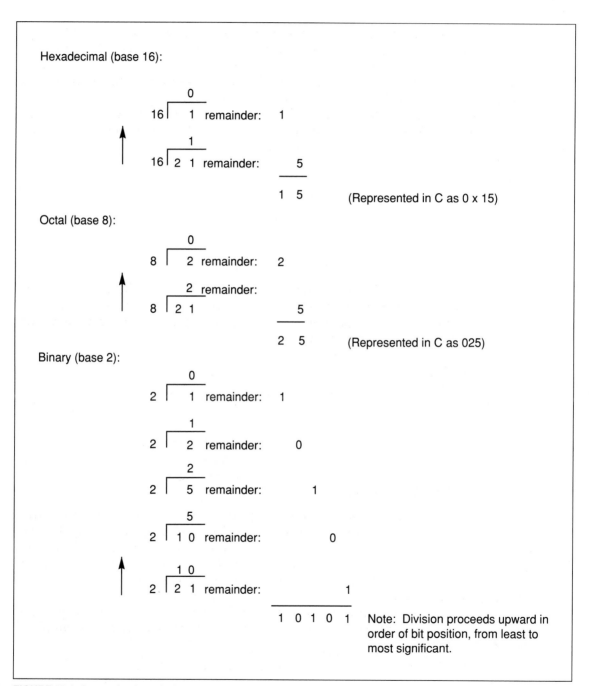

FIGURE 11.4: Conversion from decimal to hexadecimal, octal, and binary representations of the base 10 number 21.

Another technique that is easier to use for base 2, base 8, and base 16 number conversions is to rely upon the fact that a base 8 digit is always represented by three binary digits (8 octal digits represented by 2^3 binary digits), and a base 16 digit is always represented by four binary digits (16 hexadecimal digits represented by 2^4 binary digits).

To go from base 8 to base 2, express each octal digit as three equivalent binary digits; and to go from base 16 to base 2, express each hexadecimal digit as four equivalent binary digits. For example:

```
025 (base 8)   =    2    5

                   010  101   = 10101 (base 2)
```

or

```
0x15 (base 16) =    1    5

                   0001 0101  = 10101 (base 2)
```

This technique can be used in a reverse fashion to convert any binary number to either base 8 or base 16 by simply taking groups of either three or four binary digits and expressing them as an equivalent octal or hexadecimal digit, respectively. For example:

```
                    2    5  = 025 (base 8)

10101 (base 2)    = 010  101
```

or

```
                    1    5  = 0x15 (base 16)

10101 (base 2)   = 0001 0101
```

Two's Complement Notation

The techniques noted above handle the representation of positive (**unsigned**) integral (whole) numbers. Negative (**signed**) integral numbers employed are represented in two's complement notation. From the preceding examples, if the binary number 10101 represents 21 units in base 10, how then do we represent −21 (base 10) in binary (base 2)?

Negative numbers are represented in two's complement form, which is defined as the one's complement (switch all 0's and 1's) of the bit pattern for the corresponding positive number, then add one unit. For example:

```
+21 (base 10) =   00010101 (base 2)
                  11101010 (base 2)   ←one's complement
              +          1            ←add one unit

−21 (base 10) =   11101011 (base 2)   ←two's complement
```

The subsequent addition of +21 and −21 should yield zero (all bits off). All subsequent math operations with negative numbers proceed normally. For example, if you add +21 to −21 as shown below:

```
+21 (base 10)  =  00010101 (base 2)
-21 (base 10)  =  11101011 (base 2)
                  _____
  0 (base 10)  =  01000000 (base 2)
```

the correct answer of zero (0) results. Consider another example that adds +2 (base 10) to −1 (base 10), which should yield +1:

```
+2 (base 10)  =  00000010 (base 2)
-1 (base 10)  =  11111111 (base 2)
                 _____
+1 (base 10)  =  00000001 (base 2)
```

Subtraction, then, simply represents the addition of negative numbers represented in two's complement form. This principle even holds true for **unsigned** integral types. **unsigned** types do not prevent subtraction from taking place; however, only the interpretation of the result ignores the two's complement form (sign bit) and treats it as an **unsigned** number. For example, consider the subtraction of two **unsigned** integer numbers $(5 - 10) = (5 + (-10))$, which yields an answer of 65531, not −5.

```
 10  =  0000 0000 0000 1010
~10  =  1111 1111 1111 0101
 +1  =  0000 0000 0000 0001
        _____
-10  =  1111 1111 1111 0110
 +5  =  0000 0000 0000 0101
        _____
     =  1111 1111 1111 1011 = 65531 (unsigned)
```

If this bit pattern is treated as if it were a signed value, then because the high-order bit is on, a conversion from two's complement form must take place, which subtracts one unit and then reverses all bits.

```
65,531    =    1111 1111 1111 1011
   -1     =    1111 1111 1111 1111
               _____
65,530         1111 1111 1111 1010
~65,530   =    0000 0000 0000 0101  = -5
```

The bit pattern that results from the use of two's complement arithmetic establishes the ranges of value associated with each qualified integral type, and likewise controls the underflow and overflow properties exhibited by the integral types.

Consider the following overflow example of type **signed char**:

```
127  =     0111 1111
 +1  =     0000 0001
           _____
           1000 0000   (two's complement)
 -1  =     1111 1111

127  =     0111 1111
~127 =     1000 0000   = -128
```

When one unit is added to a signed char value of 127, the value of −128 results, demonstrating the wrap-around characteristics of a **signed char** overflow.

Consider this parallel example of a type **unsigned char** underflow.

```
  0  =     0000 0000
 -1  =     1111 1111
           _____
           1111 1111   = 255 (unsigned)
```

When one unit is subtracted from the **unsigned char** value of 0, the value of 255 results, demonstrating the wrap-around characteristic of an **unsigned char** underflow.

IEEE Floating-Point Notation

Historically, C has been a strong systems programming language, but less useful for scientific applications. Standard C has taken steps to strengthen the scientific (or floating-point) features inherent in the K&R definition of C. For instance, **float** type arguments were always promoted to type **double** for function calls and return values. Floating-point constants were always understood to be of type **double**. Mixed floating expressions were always evaluated as **double**, and the use of parentheses did not necessarily control the order of evaluation. The data storage and processing time for scientific programs were inflated, because the smaller and faster type **float** variables (four bytes) were constantly being cast to type **double** (eight bytes) for all calculations and when passed as function arguments. The uncertainty surrounding the interpretation of grouping parentheses, so often used in the expression of complex equations, also diminished C's attractiveness as a scientific programming language compared to Fortran.

These K&R deficiencies have been resolved in Standard C. Now, type **float** is distinct from type **double** and **long double**, and parentheses do control the order of evaluation of expressions. With these changes however, Standard C still does not mandate a binary floating-point standard of representation. A separate IEEE standard for floating-point representation does, however, exist. The logical bit layouts for the floating types, **float**, **double**, and **long double**, shown in Figure 11.1, represent Microsoft's implementation of this standard. Floating-point formats other than the IEEE standard do exist. For example, refer to the nonStandard run-time library functions **fieeetomsbin()**, **fmsbintoieee()**, **dieeetomsbin()**, and **dmsbintoieee()**, described in Chapter 20, for information about Microsoft's floating-point representation format, which is used with Microsoft's BASIC language.

It is important to notice that the manner in which bits are utilized to represent value for floating types (**float**, **double**, **long double**) is entirely different from that used for integral types. Floating types have a "true" sign-bit (not two's-complement notation). If the sign-bit is *on*, it indicates a negative number; otherwise, if *off*, a positive number, and the representation of the whole and fractional parts is implemented by assigning a range of bits for use as either the exponent or significand.

The fundamental type **float** has a binary exponent (eight bits), which is biased or offset by 0x7F, controlling the location of the "implied" binary decimal point within the significand bits (23 bits). The significand bits control the number of available significant digits that may be represented (2^{22} or 0 through 4,194,304), which can only represent six–seven significant digits. Together these **float** type components (sign, exponent, and significand) support the representation of a range of value from 8.43×10^{-37} through 3.37×10^{38}.

The fundamental type **double** has a binary exponent (11 bits), which is biased or offset by 0x3FF, controlling the location of the "implied" binary decimal point within the significand bits (52 bits). The significand bits control the number of available significant digits that may be represented (2^{51} or 0 through 2,251,799,813,685,248), which can only represent 15–16 significant digits. Together these **double** type components (sign, exponent, and significand) support the representation of a range of value from 4.19×10^{-307} through 1.67×10^{308}.

With the Microsoft version 6.0 compiler, a distinct type, **long double**, has been introduced, which complies with the 80-bit "normalized" $80x87$ coprocessor internal form of representation. The fundamental type **long double** has a binary exponent (15 bits), which is biased or offset by 0x3FFF, controlling the location of the "implied" binary decimal point within the significand bits (64 bits). The significand bits control the number of available significant digits that may be represented (2^{63} or 0 through 9,223,372,036,854,775,808), which can only represent 19 significant digits. Together these **double** type components (sign, exponent, and significand) support the representation of a range of values from 3.36×10^{-4932} through 1.19×10^{4932}.

For more about the details of **float** and **double** types, refer to *Data Handling Utilities in Microsoft C,* by Radcliffe/Raab, Sybex 1988.

Since all bitwise operators in C are restricted to working with integral, not floating types, several examples are presented in the section "**&** Bitwise AND (Conjunction)" below, which utilize a union of integral and floating types to demonstrate the indirect manipulation of bits within floating types. In the section that follows entitled "Bit-Field Types," examples are also presented that utilize a union of bit-fields and the floating types for bit manipulation and interrogation.

INTEGRAL BIT TYPES

Integral bit types are understood to represent individual bits within an integral fundamental type object (**char**, **int**, **long**, **enum**), upon which the bitwise operators in Standard C are restricted to operate. Recall that the enumeration data type in Standard C is implemented as type **int**. The following bitwise operators may be used to manipulate the bits within any integral data type object.

OPERATOR	DESCRIPTION	ASSIGNMENT	TYPE
~	Complement	=	Unary
&	AND	&=	Binary
|	Inclusive OR	|=	Binary
^	Exclusive XOR	^=	Binary
<<	Shift left	<<=	Binary
>>	Shift right	>>=	Binary

Examples of using each of the bitwise operators described above are found in the "Bit Operations" section below. The Assignment column lists the compound assignment operators for all except the ~ (complement) operator, which is a unary type operator. Unary prefix operators act upon one operand immediately following; binary operators (infix), on the other hand, require two operands, one immediately preceding and one following. For more on operators, see Chapter 12.

Notice that these operators may not directly be used with floating types (**float**, **double**, **long double**), only the integral types described above. We will discover however, in the "**&** Bitwise AND (Conjunction)" section below, that the bits of floating types may be indirectly operated upon by using a union of floating and integral types, and in the "Bit-Field Type" section, that a union of width :1 bit-fields may also be used to manipulate bits within floating types.

Any variable declared to be of an integral type may subsequently act as a unit of data storage, containing objects that may have one of two values. Individual bits within integral types are not "named" or identified as bit-field types are, and neither types are addressable in C.

BIT-FIELD TYPES

C provides an alternative to integral bit types that are commonly referred to as bit-fields. The subject of bit-fields properly belongs with structures and unions but was deferred from Chapter 9 to be presented in this chapter.

Bit-fields are members of structures (or unions) that contain individual bits or groups of bits that, once defined, may subsequently be operated upon with the bitwise operators normally used with integral types, and all other C operators except **&**, **[]**, *****, and **sizeof**. The ability to define bit-fields within unions is a new feature incorporated by Standard C.

Bit-fields are declared as members of structures (or unions) in the following form:

```
struct {...; type var : n; ...;}
```

or

```
union  {...; type var : n; ...;}
```

The components of the form are as follows:

type	Any **signed** or **unsigned** integral type.
var	Any valid member identifier.
:	(Colon) punctuator required with bit-fields.
n	Non-negative width of bit-fields in bits; no larger than the "word" size of the microprocessor; if (0) specified, align next bit-field on a word boundary; otherwise align adjacent to predecessor bit-field, if space remaining to the next "word" boundary is sufficient.

Bit-fields defined as such are commonly referred to as being either plain, **unsigned**, or **signed**. Plain bit-fields, which are declared without an explicit **signed** or **unsigned** qualifier, are understood to be **signed** (Microsoft); otherwise, explicit use of the qualifiers **signed** or **unsigned** establishes the bit-field arithmetic characteristics.

Bit-fields are defined as members of a structure (or union) and behave as normal variables with **signed** or **unsigned** integral type behavior.

They have a custom width of *n* bits, and are not restricted to the one-, two-, or four-byte aggregates normally associated with the **char**, **int**, **long**, and **enum** types. Bit-fields may be intermingled with other fundamental types and simply behave as structure (or union) members.

Consider the following incomplete structure declaration:

```
struct bits {unsigned sign_bit   : 1;
             unsigned            : 0;
             unsigned other_bits : 15;};
```

This could subsequently serve as a template for the definition of a structure variable with initialization, as in the program example shown in Figure 11.5.

This routine initializes member **sign_bit** to zero and aligns member **other_bits** to a new word boundary, assigning it the octal constant 077777. Because member **other_bits** is composed of 15 bits, it was cleaner to specify five octal digits (at three bits each) to turn all 15 bits on and represent 2^{15}, or 32,767, units, which is correctly shown by the output that is produced:

```
sign= 0
othr= 32767
size= 4
```

Had the unnamed alignment bit-field (: 0) not been specified, the **sizeof**(**int_bits**) would have been two bytes, not four bytes, as shown above. The **sizeof** operator cannot be used on bit-fields. Notice that each bit-field is treated as a normal member of a given type, in this case **unsigned** (**int**), and is treated as a normal variable, with its unique overflow and underflow properties.

```
/* FILE: ch11e1.c */
#include <stdio.h>
int main(void)
{
struct bits {unsigned sign_bit   : 1;
             unsigned            : 0;
             unsigned other_bits : 15;};
struct bits int_bits;
int_bits.sign_bit = 0;
int_bits.other_bits = 077777;

printf("\nsign= %u",int_bits.sign_bit);
printf("\nothr= %u",int_bits.other_bits);
printf("\nsize= %d",sizeof(int_bits));
exit(0);
}
```

FIGURE 11.5: Sample program ch11e1.c demonstrates the alignment properties of bit-field members within a structure.

As we will see, it is preferable to use integral data types and bitwise operators over bit-fields from a performance point of view (see the "Bit Performance Issues" section below).

Let's examine using a union of single-bit bit-fields with an integral **char** type data object and a floating type **float** data object. Figure 11.6 illustrates such a union. Remember, however, to use compiler option **/Od** (disable optimization) when using unions in this fashion. With optimization on, value assignment and retrieval in this manner may be mistakenly omitted.

This program produces the following output:

```
ch = 0100 0001
float = 1011 1111 1100 0000 0000 0000 0000 0000
```

Notice that the physical bit order is used to map single-bit bit-fields within the fundamental data types, as shown in Figure 11.2. The correct result appears for the uppercase letter A as the ASCII binary equivalent of 0100 0001. The individual bits of other **int** and **long int** types can be displayed by simply modifying this program.

The **float** result hints at how the IEEE format uses the sign, exponent, and significand components of a **float**. The sign bit is on, thereby correctly signifying a negative number (−1.5). The next eight bits (0111 1111) represent a biased exponent. By removing the exponent bias of 0x7F or adding a −0x7F as follows:

```
 0x7F 0111 1111
~0x7F 1000 0000
   +1 0000 0001
      ─────────
−0x7F 1000 0001
+     0111 1111
      ─────────
      0000 0000 (actual exponent—locates binary point)
```

we find that the "implied" binary point is located to the immediate left of the first significand bit (zero shift right), with an implied leading bit always assumed. **float** is then interpreted as −1.5, as shown in Figure 11.7.

Notice that significand bits to the right of the implied binary point are evaluated as inverse powers of two $(1/(2^n))$, while those to the left are treated in a normal fashion as (2^n).

The type **double** (and **long double**) can be displayed bit-for-bit by simply modifying this program. For more on working with the bits within floating types, see the section "**&** Bitwise AND (Conjunction)" below.

```
/* FILE: ch11e2.c */
#include <stdio.h>
int main(void)
{
struct cvt {unsigned bit0 : 1;  unsigned bit1 : 1;
    unsigned bit2 : 1;  unsigned bit3 : 1;
    unsigned bit4 : 1;  unsigned bit5 : 1;
    unsigned bit6 : 1;  unsigned bit7 : 1;};

union {char cv; struct cvt cvs;} cvu = {'A'};

struct fvt {unsigned bit0  : 1; unsigned bit1  : 1;
    unsigned bit2  : 1; unsigned bit3  : 1;
    unsigned bit4  : 1; unsigned bit5  : 1;
    unsigned bit6  : 1; unsigned bit7  : 1;
    unsigned bit8  : 1; unsigned bit9  : 1;
    unsigned bit10 : 1; unsigned bit11 : 1;
    unsigned bit12 : 1; unsigned bit13 : 1;
    unsigned bit14 : 1; unsigned bit15 : 1;
    unsigned bit16 : 1; unsigned bit17 : 1;
    unsigned bit18 : 1; unsigned bit19 : 1;
    unsigned bit20 : 1; unsigned bit21 : 1;
    unsigned bit22 : 1; unsigned bit23 : 1;
    unsigned bit24 : 1; unsigned bit25 : 1;
    unsigned bit26 : 1; unsigned bit27 : 1;
    unsigned bit28 : 1; unsigned bit29 : 1;
    unsigned bit30 : 1; unsigned bit31 : 1;};

union {float fv; struct fvt fvs;} fvu = {-1.5};

printf("\n\nch = %1d",cvu.cvs.bit7);
printf("%1d",cvu.cvs.bit6);
printf("%1d",cvu.cvs.bit5);
printf("%1d",cvu.cvs.bit4);
printf(" %1d",cvu.cvs.bit3);
printf("%1d",cvu.cvs.bit2);
printf("%1d",cvu.cvs.bit1);
printf("%1d",cvu.cvs.bit0);

printf("\n\nfloat = %1d",fvu.fvs.bit31);
printf("%1d",fvu.fvs.bit30);
printf("%1d",fvu.fvs.bit29);
printf("%1d",fvu.fvs.bit28);
printf(" %1d",fvu.fvs.bit27);
printf("%1d",fvu.fvs.bit26);
printf("%1d",fvu.fvs.bit25);
printf("%1d",fvu.fvs.bit24);
printf(" %1d",fvu.fvs.bit23);
printf("%1d",fvu.fvs.bit22);
printf("%1d",fvu.fvs.bit21);
printf("%1d",fvu.fvs.bit20);
printf(" %1d",fvu.fvs.bit19);
printf("%1d",fvu.fvs.bit18);
printf("%1d",fvu.fvs.bit17);
printf("%1d",fvu.fvs.bit16);
printf(" %1d",fvu.fvs.bit15);
printf("%1d",fvu.fvs.bit14);
printf("%1d",fvu.fvs.bit13);
printf("%1d",fvu.fvs.bit12);
printf(" %1d",fvu.fvs.bit11);
printf("%1d",fvu.fvs.bit10);
printf("%1d",fvu.fvs.bit9);
printf("%1d",fvu.fvs.bit8);
```

FIGURE 11.6: Sample program ch11e2.c demonstrates the use of unions to overlay a bit-field with a floating-point type.

```
printf(" %1d",fvu.fvs.bit7);
printf("%1d",fvu.fvs.bit6);
printf("%1d",fvu.fvs.bit5);
printf("%1d",fvu.fvs.bit4);
printf(" %1d",fvu.fvs.bit3);
printf("%1d",fvu.fvs.bit2);
printf("%1d",fvu.fvs.bit1);
printf("%1d",fvu.fvs.bit0);
exit(0);
}
```

FIGURE 11.6: Sample program ch11e2.c demonstrates the use of unions to overlay a bit-field with a floating-point type (continued).

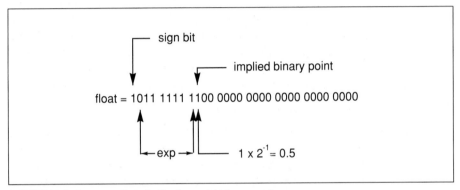

FIGURE 11.7: Interpretation of a floating-point binary number.

BIT CONSTANTS AND INITIALIZATION

Since bits are integral by definition, bit constants include all forms of integral constants described in Chapter 7 for data object types **char**, **int**, and **enum**.

Character constants may be expressed as an individual character enclosed in single quotes (`'A'`), as an octal (`'\37'`) or hexadecimal (`'\xFF'`) sequence of digits, or as one of a number of special escape sequences (`'\n'`) defined in C. Each establishes a logical bit pattern of value representation described in Figure 11.1.

Integer constants may be expressed as either decimal (21), octal (025), or hexadecimal (0x15). There is no provision in C for expressing a number directly in binary.

Since any number of units (whole, integral) may be expressed equivalently in any base n number system of digits, any equivalent form may be used to initialize the bits of either integral bit types or bit-field types.

Integral type initialization can be performed when a variable is defined, or as a constant that subsequently is used as a mask, or as a bit pattern that is used as an operand with any bitwise operator. The following examples initialize a **char**, **int**, or **long int** integral bit type.

```
char cv  = '\377';      /* octal character constant */
int  iv  = -1;          /* decimal integer constant */
long lv  = 0xFFFFFFFF;   /* hexadecimal integer constant */
```

In each case, all bits of the integral type object are set On. Notice that the octal character constant represents the binary equivalent 011 111 111, or eight bits On.

Bit-field type initialization follows the rules established for structure and union initialization in Chapter 9. Because bit-fields are **signed** or **unsigned** integral types, regardless of the fact that the number of bits may range from one to the word size, they are simply initialized with a character or integer constant that corresponds to an acceptable range of values for the number of bits comprising the bit-field member. To set all of the bits of the following structure members On, a hexadecimal character constant and octal and decimal constants were specified.

```
struct {char cv; int iv; long lv;} bits = {'\xFF', 0177777, -1L};
```

Notice that the octal integer constant consists of the following binary equivalent 001 111 111 111 111 111, or 16 bits On.

Since only the first member of a union may be initialized, to accomplish the same effect as the previous two examples, the **long** member would have to be declared first and initialized as follows:

```
union {long lv; char cv; int iv;} bits = {-1L};
```

because member **lv** is the "widest" member (32 bits versus 16 bits and eight bits).

BIT OPERATIONS

The address-of operator (**&**) cannot be used upon individual bits within integral types or upon bit-field members. Since array names are defined to be equivalent to the address of **array[0]**, bit-fields may not be subscripted, since use of the address-of (**&**) operator is implied. Similarly, since the address-of (**&**) operator may not be used, using the indirection (*****) operator is not permitted. Also, since the **sizeof** operator returns a data object's size in bytes, it may not be used to determine the width of bit-fields. The macro **offsetof(s,m)**, described in Chapter 9, is not permitted with bit-field types because of its reliance upon addressing and indirection, and because its offset is measured in bytes, not bits.

The following sections highlight the principal bitwise operators that may be used to directly manipulate bits within either integral or bit-field type definitions. Refer to Chapter 12 for more about the operators available in C.

~ *One's Complement (Negation)*

The unary bitwise NOT (one's complement) operator (**~**) reverses the sense of every bit in an integral or bit-field type. Every Off (0) bit is set On (1), and every On (1) bit is set Off (0). This supports the conversion to and from the two's complement form used to represent negative integral numbers, as demonstrated in the following example:

```
int ival = 21;
ival = ~ival + 1;
printf("\nneg 21 = %d",ival);
ival = ~(ival-1);
printf("\npos 21 = %d",ival);
```

This example produces the following results:

```
neg 21 = -21
pos 21 =  21
```

The **int** variable **ival** is assigned the decimal value of 21, yielding

$$\mathbf{ival} = 21 \rightarrow \ 0000\ 0000\ 0001\ 0101 \ \ \text{(bits)}$$

Next, we take the one's complement and add one unit, with the expression $\mathbf{ival} = \mathbf{\sim ival} + 1$

```
ival = ~ival → 1111 1111 1110 1010
 + 1                             1
            _____
            1111 1111 1110 1011  = -21 (base 10)
```

The reverse of this algorithm is performed next with the statement, $\mathbf{ival} = \mathbf{\sim(ival}-1)$

```
ival = -21 → 1111 1111 1110 1011
       + (-1)1111 1111 1111 1111
            _____
            1111 1111 1110 1010
~(ival-1)   0000 0000 0001 0101 = 21 (base 10)
```

& *Bitwise AND (Conjunction)*

The binary bitwise conjunction (AND) operator is described by the "truth table" shown below.

&	0	1
0	0	0
1	0	1

The resulting bit setting from an AND operation is Off (0) for all cases except when both bits are On (1), in which case an On (1) bit setting results. The bitwise AND operator is a single ampersand (**&**). Don't confuse it with the logical AND operator, two consecutive ampersands (**&&**). The bitwise AND operator is useful for setting bits off.

The conversion of ASCII lowercase alphabetics to uppercase can be accomplished using the **&** AND operator. Consider the ASCII symbols a and A.

```
bit 5 = 2  = 32 (base 10)
```
$$\text{bit } 5 = 2^5 = 32 \text{ (base 10)}$$

```
a = 97 (base 10) = 0x61 = 0110 0001 (bits)
A = 65 (base 10) = 0x41 = 0100 0001 (bits)
```

This example highlights the fact that all upper- and lowercase alphabetics differ by 32, or 2^5. Turning off bit 5 of any lowercase character transforms it to the equivalent uppercase alphabetic ASCII character.

```
char ch = 'a';
ch &= 0xDF;
```

The AND compound operator (**&=**) combines the character constant **'a'** with the mask **0xDF**. When expanded, the compound statement **ch &= 0xDF** becomes **ch = ch & 0xDF**. The following bit operations are performed:

```
'a'   =   0110 0001
0xDF  =   1101 1111

AND   =   0100 0001

          4    1 = 0x41 (base 16) = 'A'
```

These effectively turn off bit 5 and transform the lowercase ASCII alphabetic character **'a'** to its equivalent uppercase character, **'A'**.

In a similar fashion, the sign bit of a **float** or **double** can be masked and turned off using a union to effectively perform an absolute value operation. The example shown in Figure 11.8 exploits the relationships between the *physical* byte/bit order shown in Figure 11.2 and the *logical* byte/bit order shown in Figure 11.1. Again, remember to use compiler option **/Od** to disable optimization.

The program produces the following output:

```
abs(float-ch)   = 1.000000
abs(float-int)  = 1.000000
abs(float-long) = 1.000000

abs(double-ch)   = 9.9e099
abs(double-int)  = 9.9e099
abs(double-long) = 9.9e099
```

```
/* FILE: ch11e3.c */
#include <stdio.h>
int main(void)
{
struct tsc {char c0; char c1; char c2; char c3;
            char c4; char c5; char c6; char c7;};
struct tsi {int i0; int i1; int i2; int i3;};
struct tsl {long l0; long l1;};
struct tsf {float f0; float f1;};
union {struct tsc sc;
       struct tsi si;
       struct tsl sl;
       struct tsf sf;
       double d0;} ud;

ud.sf.f0 = -1.0f;
ud.sc.c3 &= 0x7f;
printf("\nabs(float-ch)   = %f",ud.sf.f0);

ud.sf.f0 = -1.0F;
ud.si.i1 &= 0x7fff;
printf("\nabs(float-int)  = %f",ud.sf.f0);

ud.sf.f0 = -1.0F;
ud.sl.l0 &= 0x7fffffff;
printf("\nabs(float-long) = %f",ud.sf.f0);

ud.d0 = -9.9e99;
ud.sc.c7 &= 0x7f;
printf("\nabs(double-ch)   = %g",ud.d0);

ud.d0 = -9.9e99;
ud.si.i3 &= 0x7fff;
printf("\nabs(double-int)  = %g",ud.d0);

ud.d0 = -9.9e99;
ud.sl.l1 &= 0x7fffffff;
printf("\nabs(double-long) = %g",ud.d0);
exit(0);
}
```

FIGURE 11.8: Sample program ch11e3.c demonstrates the use of unions to overlay the base data types.

which demonstrates in each instance that the sign bit of the corresponding **float** or **double** was turned off (positive, not negative).

The use of the following masks established a bit pattern with all bits on except the logical leftmost sign bit as follows:

```
0x7F       = 0111 1111
0x7FFF     = 0111 1111 1111 1111
0x7FFFFFFF = 0111 1111 1111 1111 1111 1111 1111 1111
```

The use of the **&** (AND) operator will preserve all bit settings that are on in the **long int** (**float**) or (half **double**) bit positions except the sign bit, which will always be set off to reflect a positive (+), not a negative (−) value.

The apparent complexity of logically locating the correct sign bit position within the **float** four-byte, **double** eight-byte, and **long double** 10-byte object is rooted in the physical ordering of the bytes in **int**, **long int**, **float**, and **double** type objects. Notice in Figure 11.2 that the sign bit of **float F0** aligns exactly in the union with the sign bits for **char C3**, **int I1**, and **long L0**. The program code above reflects this fact and demonstrates that when either of these integral type sign bits is turned off, the sign bit of the **float F0** is effectively turned off or made positive (absolute value). Similarly, notice that the sign bits of **char C7**, **int I3**, and **long L1** coincide with the sign bit for **double D0**. Again, this fact is demonstrated in the example above.

| *Bitwise Inclusive OR (Disjunction)*

The binary bitwise inclusive (OR), or disjunction, operator is described by the "truth table" shown below.

|	0	1
0	0	1
1	1	1

The resulting bit setting from an OR operation is On (1) for all cases when either of the corresponding bits is On (1). Only in the case where both bits are Off (0) is the resulting bit set Off (0). The OR operator is a single vertical bar (**|**), not two consecutive vertical bars (**| |**), which is a logical, not a bitwise OR, operator. The bitwise OR operator is useful for setting bits On.

The conversion of lowercase ASCII alphabetics to uppercase (as described for **&** AND operator above) cannot readily be accomplished using the **|** OR operator, but rather the ^ exclusive OR operator described in the section that follows. The | inclusive OR operator is particularly useful, however, for building up the effects of several bit masks. The following example:

```
unsigned int ival=0;
ival |= 0x0001 | 0x0002 | 0x0004 | 0x0008;
ival |= 0x00F0 | 0x0F00 | 0xF000;
printf("\ninclusive OR = %d",ival);
```

correctly produces the following output:

```
inclusive OR = -1
```

Let's examine the bit settings that produced this result.

```
ival = 0 → 0000 0000 0000 0000   (bits)
      OR   0000 0000 0000 0001
      OR   0000 0000 0000 0010
      OR   0000 0000 0000 0100
      OR   0000 0000 0000 1000

  ival = 0000 0000 0000 1111   (bits)
    OR   0000 0000 1111 0000
    OR   0000 1111 0000 0000
    OR   1111 0000 0000 0000

  ival = 1111 1111 1111 1111   (bits)
```

Notice how the | OR operator was used to turn on all the bits of variable **ival**. How can an **unsigned int** produce a result of −1? Notice that the **printf()** control string used the **%d** format, which tells **printf()** to treat the two-byte integer, **ival**, as if it were **signed**! With bit 15 On, a negative number is signified, so **printf()** produces a minus sign (−) and then displays the positive number equivalent (1) in character form as follows:

```
ival =          1111 1111 1111 1111   ←two's complement assumed
      + (-1)    1111 1111 1111 1111   ←two's complement of -1

                1111 1111 1111 1110
        ~       0000 0000 0000 0001   îone's complement is +1
```

Hence the result, **inclusive OR = −1**, is produced. Had the **printf()** control string correctly used **%u**, the result **inclusive OR = 65535** would have been produced.

For more examples of using the | OR operator, refer to header file **<ctype.h>** discussed in Chapter 6, which makes extensive use of the | OR operator to develop the variety of masks necessary to perform the many **isxx()** character-testing operations defined as function-like macros.

^ *Bitwise Exclusive XOR*

The binary bitwise exclusive (XOR) operator is described by the "truth table" shown below.

^	0	1
0	0	1
1	1	0

The resulting bit setting from an XOR operation is Off (0) for all cases except when both bits are Off (0) and both bits are On (1). The XOR operator is a single caret (^) and is a unary, not a binary, operator. The XOR operator is useful for setting bits Off or On.

The conversion of lowercase ASCII alphabetics to uppercase (as described for **&** AND operator above) can also be accomplished using the **^** XOR operator as follows:

```
char ch = 'a';
ch ^= 0x20;
```

Notice that you perform the XOR operation on the character constant **'a'** with the mask **0x20**, using the compound operator **^=**. When expanded, the compound statement **ch ^= 0x20** becomes **ch = ch ^ 0x20**.

```
'a'    =   0110 0001
0x20   =   0010 0000
           _____
XOR    =   0100 0001
           _____
            4    1 = 0x41 (base 16) = 'A'
```

This effectively turns off bit 5 and transforms the lowercase ASCII alphabetic character **'a'** to its equivalent uppercase character, **'A'**.

In a similar fashion, the embedded control characters in word processing files can be removed using the XOR operator. Such characters utilize eight bits of a **char**, which is beyond the seven-bit ASCII standard (bit 7 always Off). To transform these codes in a document file, use the **^** XOR operator as follows:

```
char ch = '\xCF';
ch ^= 0x80;
printf("\n^= %#x",ch);
```

or use an equivalent **&** AND operation with a mask of **0x7F** to transform the character:

```
^= 0x4F
```

Notice that the XOR operation was performed on the hexadecimal character constant `'\xCF'` with the mask 0x80 as follows:

```
'\xCF' =  1100 1111
0x80   =  1000 0000
          ─────────
XOR    =  0100 1111
          ─────────
          4     F = 4F  (base 16)
```

This effectively turns off bit 7 and forces the otherwise non-Standard control character into the value range associated with Standard ASCII characters.

<< *Shift Left*

The binary bitwise shift-left **<<** operator may be used in the following manner with both **signed** and **unsigned** integral types:

```
int iv = -1;
unsigned int uv = 1;
printf("\niv = %d",iv << 2);
printf("\nuv = %u",uv << 2);
```

This shifts the bits represented by each integral type to the left by two bit positions and fills all vacated bits with the binary digit 0. The preceding example produces the following output:

```
iv = -4
uv =  4
```

Let's examine how this was performed:

```
-1   =  1111 1111 1111 1111
<< 2 =  1111 1111 1111 1100   = -4
```

and

```
1    =  0000 0000 0000 0001
<< 2 =  0000 0000 0000 0100   =  4
```

The shift-left operator is two consecutive less than symbols (**<<**), not one (**<**), which is a relational operator. If the bit-shift value is greater than the size of the left operand or a negative number, Standard C states that the results are implementation-defined. For the case of a shift value that is too large, the result becomes zero (0), as might be expected; when the shift value is negative, the left operand remains unchanged.

Again, remember that the bitwise **<<** operator may only be used with integral types and would be no value if used to indirectly operate upon floating types, because of the way in which bits within floating types are utilized.

Notice that each bit shift to the left effectively multiplies the left operand by another power of two. The "Bit Performance Issues" section includes a comparison of left bit-shift and multiplication for this operation.

>> *Shift Right*

The binary bitwise shift-right **>>** operator may be used in the following manner with both **signed** and **unsigned** integral types:

```
int iv = -4;
unsigned int uv = 4;
printf("\nneg iv = %d",iv >> 2);
iv = 4;
printf("\npos iv = %d",iv >> 2);

printf("\nuv1 = %u",uv >> 2);
uv = 0xFFFF;
printf("\nuv2 = %u",uv >> 2);
```

This shifts the bits represented by each integral type to the right by two bit positions and fills all vacated bits with the initial high-order bit for **signed** types and the binary digit (0) zero for **unsigned** types. The preceding example produces the following output:

```
neg iv = -1
pos iv =  1

uv1 =  1
uv2 =  16383
```

Let's examine how this was performed.

```
-4   =  1111 1111 1111 1100
>> 2 =  1111 1111 1111 1111   = -1 (sign bit extended)

 4   =  0000 0000 0000 0100
>> 2 =  0000 0000 0000 0001   =  1 (sign bit extended)
```

and

```
 4     =  0000 0000 0000 0100
>> 2   =  0000 0000 0000 0001 =  1

0xFFFF =  1111 1111 1111 1111
>> 2   =  0011 1111 1111 1111 =  16383
```

The shift-right operator is two consecutive greater-than symbols (**>>**), not one (**>**), which is a relational operator. If the bit-shift value is greater than the size of the left operand or is a negative number, Standard C states that the results are implementation-defined. For a shift value that is too large, the result becomes zero (0) for positive **signed** and **unsigned** types, and (−1) for negative **signed** types; when the shift value is negative, the left operand remains unchanged.

Again, remember that the bitwise **>>** operator may only be used with integral types and would be of no value if used to operate indirectly upon floating types because of how the bits within floating types are utilized.

Notice that each bit shift to the right effectively divides the left operand by another power of two. A comparison is presented in the "Bit Performance Issues" section of using a right bit shift instead of division for integral power of 2^n division.

Run-Time Library Functions

Four additional bit-related, non-Standard run-time library functions are available in Chapter 20 for the rotation of bits within either **unsigned int** or **unsigned long int** type objects.

_rotl()	**unsigned int rotate left**
_rotr()	**unsigned int rotate right**
_lrotl()	**unsigned long int rotate left**
_lrotr()	**unsigned long int rotate right**

Unlike a shift-left **<<** or shift-right **>>** operation, which "loses" bits at the boundaries of the data objects, these functions preserve all bits by rotating them from one boundary to the other. For example, the **unsigned int** **uv** bit pattern established by the mask

uv = **0x1248** = 0001 0010 0100 1000 (base 2)

would produce the following bit pattern if rotated to the left by four bit positions:

uv = 0010 0100 1000 0001 (base 2) = **0x2481**

or would produce the following bit pattern if rotated to the right by four bit positions:

uv = 1000 0001 0010 0100 (base 2) = **0x8124**

For more details on these assembler-like functions, refer to Chapter 20.

Typedefs and Casts

Since integral bit types are derived from the fundamental types **char**, **int**, and **enum**, and bit-field types are derived from structures and unions, bits in turn derive their **typedef** and cast properties from those types. **Typedef**s are typically used to define structures and unions that contains bit-field members.

Although bit-fields can only be defined as **signed** or **unsigned** integral types, there is no reason that such members could not in turn be cast to data type **float** or **double**. Bit-fields may be considered structure (or union) members, except for their inability to use the **&**, **[]**, *****, and **sizeof** operators.

Refer to Chapter 9 for more about using **typedef**s and casts when bit-fields are defined as members.

BIT PERFORMANCE ISSUES

The ability to manipulate bits using either integral type objects with the bitwise operators, or by using bit-fields within structures raises the interesting question of which way is better (faster). After reviewing Chapter 9 and understanding the "overhead" associated with addressing members of structures and unions, it would seem that integral types should outperform bit-fields, hands down. This is the case; however, bit-fields do tend to provide source code that is intuitively easier to understand.

The performance evaluation program listed in Figure 11.9 again uses the **START()** and **STOP** macros developed in Chapter 5, and is designed to compare the relative performance differences between using integral and bit-field members of a structure (or union).

It produces the following output:

```
for  : integral-1
time : 0.88 sec

for  : integral-2
time : 1.04 sec

for  : bit-field-1
time : 0.88 sec

for  : bit-field-2
time : 2.25 sec

for  : bit-field-3
time : 1.04 sec

for  : bit-field-4
time : 2.47 sec
```

```
/* FILE: ch11e4.c */
#define TIMER
#include "timer.h"
#define NTIMES  for(i=0;i<30000;i++)

int main(void)
{
int i;
unsigned int ityp;
struct {unsigned int it;
        unsigned int bf : 5;} bits = {1, 1};

START(integral-1);
ityp=0;
NTIMES ityp++;
STOP;

START(integral-2);
ityp=0;
NTIMES ityp &= ~ityp;
STOP;

START(bit-field-1);
bits.it=0;
NTIMES bits.it++;
STOP;

START(bit-field-2);
bits.bf=0;
NTIMES bits.bf++;
STOP;

START(bit-field-3);
bits.it=0;
NTIMES bits.it &= ~bits.it;
STOP;

START(bit-field-4);
bits.bf=0;
NTIMES bits.bf &= ~bits.bf;
STOP;

exit(0);
}
```

FIGURE 11.9: Sample program ch11e4.c demonstrates the performance characteristics of integral and bit-field types.

This performance comparison is intended to contrast integral and bit-field types and also to look at the relative efficiency of performing similar operations upon integral and bit-field members of a structure.

Notice that the integral variable **ityp** and the structure member **bits.it** are 16 bits wide, while the bit-field member **bits.bf** is only five bits wide. It might seem that bit-field operations should then be faster; however, the results are to the contrary.

The simple autoincrement operations performed show that the integral members were 60 percent faster (0.88 seconds versus 2.26 seconds) than the bit-field member. A comparable result (1.04 seconds versus 2.47 seconds) was produced when the more complex AND and complement operations were performed. Notice that integral variables and structure members perform comparably, while bit-fields are consistently slower.

Another interesting comparison involves weighing the merit of using left and right bit-shift operations instead of multiplication and division when integral powers of two are involved. The program listed in Figure 11.10 evaluates this scenario.

It produces the following results:

```
for  : multiply & divide
time : 3.13 sec

for  : shift left & right
time : 2.14 sec
```

From this it can be concluded that shift operations are faster than comparable multiplication and division by about 70 percent when integral powers of two are involved.

```
/* FILE: ch11e5.c */
#define TIMER
#include "timer.h"
#define NTIMES for(i=0;i<2000;i++)
#define WORD for(j=0;j<15;j++)

int main(void)
{
int i, j;
unsigned int uv;

uv=1;
START(multiply & divide);
NTIMES {WORD uv*=2; WORD uv/=2;};
STOP;

uv=1;
START(shift left & right);
NTIMES {WORD uv<<=1; WORD uv>>=1;};
STOP;
exit(0);
}
```

FIGURE 11.10: Sample program ch11e5.c demonstrates the performance advantage of using shift operators for certain arithmetic operations.

4

Expressing Logic in C

Part IV will complete the explanation of the C keywords that have not yet been discussed, individually review which operators may be used with the data-object types presented in Part III, and discuss the rules that govern the construction, evaluation, and performance of all C expressions and statements.

Chapter 12, "Operators," presents a coherent picture of all operators, as well as a detailed explanation of each individual operator, and identifies which operators may be used with each data-object type presented in Part III.

Chapter 13, "Expressions and Statements," explains why expressions are the building blocks of the C language, and how expressions are used to convey value and to construct statements that direct actions. The rules for formulating expressions are explained from an application programmer's viewpoint using *terms*, and not from a compiler-construction viewpoint using *tokens*. The manner in which terms are promoted to form expressions, then balanced and grouped for evaluation, and finally typecast and assigned is clearly described. To complete the progression, the way in which expressions are then combined with keywords to form statements, which unlike expressions can alter the flow of program execution, is also explained.

By the end of Part IV, it will be clear that C must rely heavily upon run-time library and custom-developed functions to perform tasks that are normally built into other high-level languages. For instance, noticeably absent from C are keywords that support basic input and output (I/O). On the other hand, C has a broad complement of operators that are not ordinarily found in other high-level languages. To remain a compact, portable, performance-oriented language, C does not incorporate any services that are typically performed by a host operating system, such as DOS or UNIX, or which can be derived from the C keywords and operators of the C language itself.

Whenever tasks cannot be accomplished using constructs of the C language itself, they must be fulfilled by writing a function or calling one that exists. The entire topic of function development is covered in Part V, while the use of existing run-time library functions is found in Parts VI and VII.

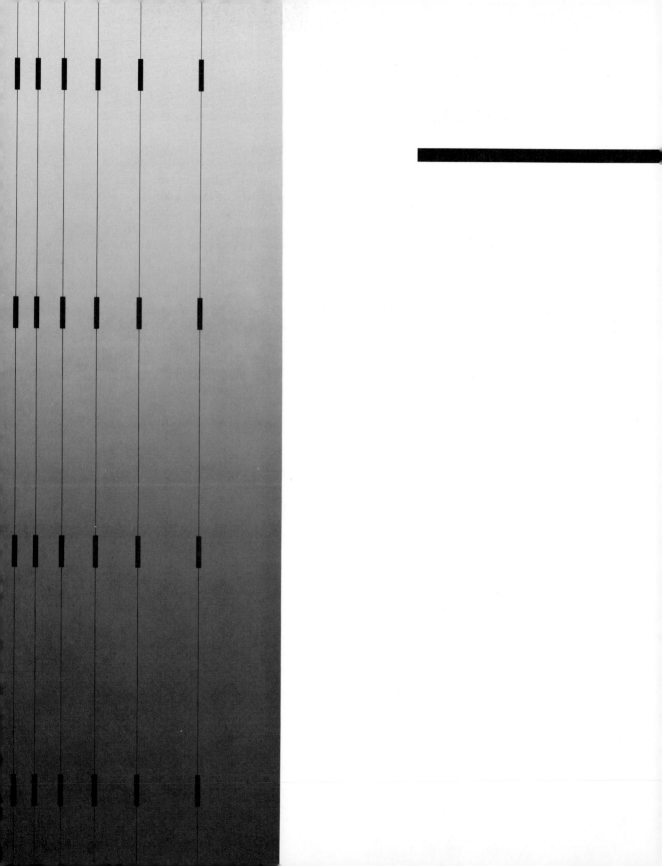

Operators

Operators

C has a robust complement of operators in comparison to most other computer languages. The symbols used to define the operators are interpreted both individually and in multicharacter groups, according to context, to manipulate type objects used to represent value in C.

To present a coherent view of the individual properties of C operators and the relationships among them, this chapter discusses three ways of categorizing operators: by precedence, by the number and placement of operands they work with, and by purpose.

The first of these, precedence, is defined by Standard C. It determines the relative importance of operators when they are combined in expressions. Table 12.1 summarizes this hierarchy. As you can see, there are 15 levels of precedence, corresponding to types of operations. This table is discussed further in the "Operator Precedence" section of this chapter.

TABLE 12.1: Operator Precedence

PRECEDENCE	OPERATOR TYPE	ASSOCIATIVITY (GROUPING)	OPERATOR (NOTATION)	OPERATOR DESCRIPTION
1	Primary (postfix)	L → R	X++	Postincrement
			X--	Postdecrement
			X[Y]	Array subscript
			X(Y)	Function call
			X.Y	Select member
			X->Y	Point to member
			X:>Y	_based(void) operator
2	Unary (prefix)	R → L	sizeof X	Size of expression
			sizeof (type)	Size of type cast
			++X	Preincrement
			--X	Predecrement
			&X	Address of
			*X	Indirection

TABLE 12.1: Operator Precedence (continued)

PRECEDENCE	OPERATOR TYPE	ASSOCIATIVITY (GROUPING)	OPERATOR (NOTATION)	OPERATOR DESCRIPTION
2 (cont.)			`+X`	Plus
			`-X`	Minus
			`~X`	Bitwise NOT
			`!X`	Logical NOT
			`(type)X`	Type cast
3	Multiplicative	L → R	`X*Y`	Multiply
			`X/Y`	Divide
			`X%Y`	Remainder
4	Additive	L → R	`X+Y`	Add
			`X-Y`	Subtract
5	Shift	L → R	`X<<Y`	Left shift
			`X>>Y`	Right shift
6	Inequality	L → R	`X<Y`	Less than
			`X<=Y`	Less than or equal
			`X>Y`	Greater than
			`X>=Y`	Greater than or equal
7	Equality	L → R	`X==Y`	Equal
			`X!=Y`	Not equal
8	Bitwise AND	L → R	`X&Y`	Bitwise AND
9	Bitwise XOR	L → R	`X^Y`	Bitwise XOR
10	Bitwise OR	L → R	`X|Y`	Bitwise OR
11	Logical AND	L → R	`X&&Y`	Logical AND
12	Logical OR	L → R	`X||Y`	Logical OR
13	Conditional (ternary)	R → L	`Z?X:Y`	Conditional
14	Assignment	R → L	`X=Y`	Assignment
			`X*=Y`	Multiply assign
			`X/=Y`	Divide assign

TABLE 12.1: Operator Precedence (continued)

PRECEDENCE	OPERATOR TYPE	ASSOCIATIVITY (GROUPING)	OPERATOR (NOTATION)	OPERATOR DESCRIPTION
14 (cont.)			X%=Y	Remainder assign
			X+=Y	Add assign
			X−=Y	Subtract assign
			X<<=Y	Left shift assign
			X>>=Y	Right shift assign
			X&=Y	Bitwise AND assign
			X^=Y	Bitwise XOR assign
			X|=Y	Bitwise OR assign
15	Sequential	L → R	X, Y	Comma

NOTE: The :> operator is non-Standard (Microsoft).

Before considering the effects of combining operators, you should be familiar with their individual properties. Notice in the table that each operator has either one, two, or three operands (X, Y, or Z type objects). Operators that work with one operand are described as unary, those with two operands as binary, and the one with three operands (Z?X:Y) as ternary.

Unary operators are further classified as being either prefix (preceding, level 1) or postfix (succeeding, level 2). Notice that the unary operator **sizeof** is the only operator that is implemented as a C keyword (see Appendix B: C Keywords).

Binary or infix operators are surrounded by operands and describe those operators of precedence levels 3 through 12, 14, and 15. Certain operators are considered to be unary or binary based upon their context or placement in a source-code file. For example, the unary operators

+X	Plus
−X	Minus
*X	Indirection
&X	Address of

may also be interpreted as binary operators, and convey the following meanings:

X+Y	Addition
X−Y	Subtraction

X*Y	Multiplication
X&Y	Bitwise AND

In a similar manner, the auto-increment and decrement operators assume different meanings, depending upon whether they precede or succeed the associated operand:

++X	Add one unit then use X.
X++	Use X then add one unit.
––X	Subtract one unit then use X.
X––	Use X then subtract one unit.

The parenthesized type-cast operator **(type) X** is differentiated from **X()**, the function-call operator, by the relative placement of parentheses, which may also be treated simply as a punctuator, along with

[]	Incomplete array
*	Pointer declaration
=	Initialization
,	Argument and initialization list separator

These symbols have independent syntactic and semantic meanings but, as punctuators, never specify that an operation is to be performed.

A third categorization of operators, shown in Table 12.2, regroups the operators shown in Table 12.1 into related, functional categories.

The sections that follow discuss each of these categories. For each functional category, a table summarizes the operands or data-object types with which those operators may be used. For more information about these data types, see the chapters listed below:

TYPE	DESCRIPTION	REFERENCE
Arithmetic	**char**, **int**, **enum**, **float**, **double**	Ch. 7
	Integral and bit-field types	Ch. 11
Scalar	**_segment**, pointers	Ch. 10
Aggregate	Array names and elements	Ch. 8
	Structure and union names and members	Ch. 9

The indications (Yes, No, N.A.) used in these operator-use tables specify whether an operator is appropriate, inappropriate, or not applicable with that data-object type, respectively. The tables categorize each data-object

TABLE 12.2: Functional Categories of Operators

CATEGORY	OPERATOR (NOTATION)	PRECEDENCE	ASSOCIATIVITY	OPERATOR TYPE
Data access	`X[Y], X.Y, X->Y, X:>Y`	1	L → R	Primary
	`&X, *X`	2	R → L	Unary
Arithmetic	`X++, X--`	1	L → R	Primary
	`++X, --X, +X, -X`	2	R → L	Unary
	`X*Y, X/Y, X%Y`	3	L → R	Multiplicative
	`X+Y, X-Y`	4	L → R	Additive
	`X=Y, X*=Y, X/=Y, X%=Y, X+=Y, X-=Y`	14	R → L	Assignment
Bitwise	`~X`	2	R → L	Unary
	`X<<Y, X>>Y`	5	L → R	Shift
	`X&Y`	8	L → R	Bitwise AND
	`X^Y`	9	L → R	Bitwise XOR
	`X|Y`	10	L → R	Bitwise OR
	`X<<=Y, X>>=Y, X&=Y, X^=Y, X|=Y`	14	R → L	Assignment
Logical	`!X`	2	R → L	Unary
	`X<Y, X<=Y, X>Y, X>=Y`	6	L → R	Inequality
	`X==Y, X!=Y`	7	L → R	Equality
	`X&&Y`	11	L → R	Logical AND
	`X||Y`	12	L → R	Logical OR
	`Z?X:Y`	13	R → L	Conditional
Miscellaneous	`X(Y)`	1	L → R	Primary
	`sizeof X, sizeof(type), (type) X`	2	R → L	Unary
	`X,Y`	15	L → R	Sequential

NOTE: The `:>` operator is non-Standard (Microsoft).

type as being either arithmetic, scalar, or aggregate, according to the classification first presented in Figure 7.1.

Once the individual properties of each operator are understood, together with the object-type operand(s) with which they may be used and their individual performance characteristics, we will resume the discussion of operator precedence. Precedence controls how operators "behave" when combined with other operators.

Let's begin by examining each functional category of operators established by Table 12.2.

DATA ACCESS OPERATORS

The data access operators listed in Table 12.2 locate data objects in memory. They can be summarized as follows:

OPERATOR	DESCRIPTION
X[Y]	Element **Y** of array named **X**.
X.Y	Member **Y** of structure or union named **X**.
X->Y	Member **Y** of a structure or union pointed to by **X**.
X:>Y	Forms an effective memory address from an **X** segment and **Y** offset value (non-Standard).
&X	Memory address of object **X** (**_near**, **_far**, **_huge**, **_based**).
*X	Value of the object pointed to by address **X**.

No alteration of the object values is made by these operators unless they are combined with others to form simple and compound expressions or statements (see Chapter 13).

The operands, or data-object type **X** or **Y**, upon which these data access operators may act, are summarized in Tables 12.3A and 12.3B.

Notes 1 to 10 qualify the applicability of the operators shown in Tables 12.3A and 12.3B. The declarations shown below are used by the code examples that follow to illustrate each note in the tables above. For instance, Note 1 ("Pointers are equivalent to a one-dimensional array") is clarified below by the example **ptr[0]**, indicating that although the variable **ptr** is declared as ***ptr**, it can also be accessed as **ptr[0]**.

```
int ival, *ptr = &ival, *ptr_d1[3], _based(void) bptr;
_segment segval = _segname("_CONST");
int ival_d1[3], ival_d2[3][3], ival_d3[3][3][3];
struct s1 {int i1;
```

TABLE 12.3A: Using Data Access Operators with Arithmetic and Scalar Data

| OPERATOR | ARITHMETIC/SCALAR | | | | | | | SCALAR | |
| | INTEGRAL | | | FLOATING-POINT | | BITS | | | |
	char	int	enum	float	double	Integral	Fields	_segment	Pointers
X[Y]	No	No	No	No	No	No	No	No	Yes[1]
X.Y	No	No	No	No	No	No	Yes	No	No
X->Y	No	No	No	No	No	No	Yes	No	No[2]
X:>Y	No	No	No	No	No	No	No	Yes	Yes[3]
&X	Yes	Yes	Yes	Yes	Yes	No	No	Yes	Yes
*X	No	No	No	No	No	No	No	No	Yes

NOTES:
1. Pointers are equivalent to a one-dimensional array.
2. Unless a pointer to a structure or union.
3. For **_based(void)** pointers only.

```
        float f1[3];
        double *d1;} str1, *pstr1 = &str1;
struct {int i2;
        float f2[3];
        double *d2;
        struct s1 str1;} str2[3], *pstr2 = &str2[2];
```

EXAMPLES

Note 1

`ptr[0]`

Note 2

`pstr1->i1`   `pstr2->d2`

Note 3

`segval:>bptr`

Note 4

`ival_d2[2][2]`   `ival_d3[2][2][2]`

Note 5

`str1.f1[2]`   `str2[2].f2[2]`

TABLE 12.3B: Using Data Access Operators with Aggregate Data

	ARRAY		STRUCTURE/UNION	
OPERATOR	**Names**	**Elements**	**Names**	**Members**
`X[Y]`	Yes	Yes[4]	No[6]	No[5]
`X.Y`	No[5]	No[6]	No[7]	Yes
`X->Y`	No[6]	No	No[7]	Yes
`X:>Y`	No[3]	No[3]	No[3]	No[3]
`&X`	No	Yes	Yes	Yes
`*X`	Yes[8]	No[9]	No	No[10]

NOTES:
3. For **_based(void)** pointers only.
4. For multidimensional arrays, elements expand to arrays.
5. Unless an array member of a structure or union.
6. Unless an array of structures or unions.
7. Unless itself a structure or union member.
8. Array names are equivalent to a pointer.
9. Unless an array of pointers.
10. Unless itself a pointer member.

Note 6

```
str2[2].i2          str2[2].d2
```

Note 7

```
str2[2].str1.i1     pstr2->str1.d1
```

Note 8

```
*ival_d1            *(ival_d1 + 2)
```

Note 9

```
*ptr_d1[2]          *(*(ptr_d1 + 2))
```

Note 10

```
*str1.d1            *pstr1->d1
```

Performance and Data Access Operators

X[Y]   For a complete discussion of the performance characteristics of subscripted variables, refer to Chapter 8. Because of the address arithmetic necessary to evaluate the storage-mapping equations involved with multi-dimensional arrays, every level of subscripting contributes to decreased program performance. Multiple-dimensioned arrays should be avoided if at all possible, subscript and pointer indirection with arrays perform identically, and compact pointer notation consistently performs the best.

X.Y *and* **X->Y**   For a complete discussion of the performance characteristics of structure and union member operators, refer to Chapter 9. For nonsubscripted structures and unions, the member operator always outperforms the pointer-to-a-member operator. When single and multiple-dimensioned arrays of structures and unions are involved, however, the pointer-to-a-member operator is preferred, second only to compact pointer notation. All other data access forms of expression perform identically.

X:>Y   For a comparison of **_near**, **_far**, **_huge**, and **_based** pointers, refer to Chapter 10. The **_based** pointer type is faster than **_far** and **_huge**, and somewhat slower than **_near**, yet it has the flexibility of **_far** pointers and can address any 64KB range of memory.

&X *and* ***X**   The relative performance characteristics of the address-of and indirection operators can be evaluated using the program listed in Figure 12.1.

The performance measures from this program are summarized in Table 12.4. The factors shown are relative, not absolute, measures of performance. The fastest time is represented by a factor or multiplier of 1.0.

It must be noted that the **&X** operator factors shown in Table 12.4 are correct only for constant expressions that can be evaluated at compile time. Obviously, expressions involving subscripting or explicit address arithmetic are dynamic in nature, will be evaluated at run-time, and will always be slower (see Chapter 8). However, the indirection operator will always be slower than the address-of operator because of the data-object type representation and retrieval or assignment involved.

Notice the performance improvement that was recorded when using the OptimizingC compiler with the **/qc**, quick compile (limited optimization) versus the default optimization /O that otherwise is assumed.

```
/* FILE: ch12e1.c */
#define TIMER
#include "timer.h"
#define NTIMES for(i=0;i<100000;i++)

long i;
char        cval,  *cptr;
int         ival,  *iptr;
long        lval,  *lptr;
float       fval,  *fptr;
double      dval,  *dptr;
long double ldval, *ldptr;

void time_char(void)
{
START(&char variable);      NTIMES cptr = &cval;        STOP;
START(char variable);       NTIMES cval = 'A';          STOP;
START(*char variable);      NTIMES *cptr = 'A';         STOP;
}

void time_int()
{
START(&int variable);       NTIMES iptr = &ival;        STOP;
START(int variable);        NTIMES ival = 65;           STOP;
START(*int variable);       NTIMES *iptr = 65;          STOP;
}

void time_long()
{
START(&long variable);      NTIMES lptr = &lval;        STOP;
START(long variable);       NTIMES lval = 65L;          STOP;
START(*long variable);      NTIMES *lptr = 65L;         STOP;
}

void time_float()
{
START(&float variable);     NTIMES fptr = &fval;        STOP;
START(float variable);      NTIMES fval = 65.0F;        STOP;
START(*float variable);     NTIMES *fptr = 65.0F;       STOP;
}

void time_double()
{
START(&double variable);    NTIMES dptr = &dval;        STOP;
START(double variable);     NTIMES dval = 65.0;         STOP;
START(*double variable);    NTIMES *dptr = 65.0;        STOP;
}

void time_ldouble()
{
START(&ldouble variable);   NTIMES ldptr = &ldval;      STOP;
START(ldouble variable);    NTIMES ldval = 65.0L;       STOP;
START(*ldouble variable);   NTIMES *ldptr = 65.0L;      STOP;
}

int main(void)
{
time_char();
time_int();
time_long();
time_float();
time_double();
time_ldouble();
}
```

FIGURE 12.1: Sample program ch12e1.c evaluates the performance characteristics of using the address-of (&) and indirection (*) operators.

TABLE 12.4: Relative Performance of Data Access Operators

COMPILER COMMAND	OPERATOR	DATA-OBJECT TYPE						
		char[a]	int	enum[b]	long	float	double	long double
CL /qc ch12e1.c	&	1.0	1.0	1.0	1.0	1.0	1.0	1.0
	*	1.1	1.1	1.1	1.2	17.4	18.9	16.8
CL ch12e1.c	&	1.0	1.0	1.0	1.0	1.0	1.0	1.0
	*	1.1	1.1	1.1	1.2	1.4	1.6	1.6

NOTES:
All entries shown are factors relative to the fastest times measured using the **START ()** and **STOP** macros.
a. Type **char** promotes to type **int**.
b. Type **enum** is implemented as type **int**.

ARITHMETIC OPERATORS

The arithmetic operators listed in Table 12.2 perform fundamental arithmetic and assignment operations upon data-object values, or they may be used alone or combined with other operators to construct expression statements with side effects. They can be summarized as follows:

OPERATOR	DESCRIPTION
X++	Use the value of object **X**, then increment the value of object **X** by 1.
X––	Use the value of object **X**, then decrement the value of object **X** by 1.
++X	Increment the value of object **X** by 1, then use the value of object **X**.
––X	Decrement the value of object **X** by 1, then use the value of object **X**.
+X	Affirm that the value of object **X** is unchanged.
–X	Negate the value of object **X**.
X*Y	Find the product of multiplying the values of objects **X** and **Y**.
X/Y	Find the divisor resulting from the division of the value of object **X** by the value of object **Y**.

OPERATOR	DESCRIPTION
X%Y	Find the remainder resulting from the division of the value of object **X** by the value of object **Y**.
X+Y	Find the sum of adding the value of object **Y** to the value of object **X**.
X–Y	Find the difference of subtracting the value of object **Y** from the value of object **X**.
X=Y	Assign the value of object **Y** to object **X**.
X*=Y	Assign the value of object **X** the product of multiplying the values of objects **X** and **Y**.
X/=Y	Assign the value of object **X** the divisor resulting from the division of the value of object **X** by the value of object **Y**.
X%=Y	Assign the value of object **X** the remainder resulting from the division of the value of object **X** by the value of object **Y**.
X+=Y	Assign the value of object **X** the sum of adding the value of object **Y** to the value of object **X**.
X–=Y	Assign the value of object **X** the difference of subtracting the value of object **Y** from the value of object **X**.

In this chapter, like operands are assumed for all binary operators. When dissimilar operand types are involved, type promotion and balancing occurs as explained in Chapter 13. The operands, or data-object type **X** or **Y** upon which these arithmetic operators may act, are summarized in Tables 12.5A and 12.5B.

Notes 1 to 5 qualify the applicability of the operators shown in Table 12.5B. The declarations shown below are used by the code examples that follow to illustrate each note in the tables above. For instance, Note 2 ("Except array names as lvalues") is clarified below by the example **ival_d1 = ptr**, indicating that it is incorrect to make an assignment of value to an array name which, although a pointer, is constant and cannot be modified.

```
int *ptr;
int ival_d1[3], jval_d1[3];
float fval[3];
struct s1 {int i1;
    float f1[3];
    double *d1;} str1;
struct {int i2;
    float f2[3];
    double *d2;
    struct s1 str1;} str2[3];
```

TABLE 12.5A: Using Arithmetic Operators with Arithmetic and Scalar Data

| OPERATOR | ARITHMETIC/SCALAR | | | | | | | SCALAR | |
| | INTEGRAL | | | FLOATING-POINT BITS | | | | | |
	char	int	enum	float	double	Integral	Fields	_segment	Pointers
X++	Yes	Yes	Yes	Yes	Yes	No	Yes	Yes	Yes
X--	Yes	Yes	Yes	Yes	Yes	No	Yes	Yes	Yes
++X	Yes	Yes	Yes	Yes	Yes	No	Yes	Yes	Yes
--X	Yes	Yes	Yes	Yes	Yes	No	Yes	Yes	Yes
+X	Yes	Yes	Yes	Yes	Yes	No	Yes	No	Yes
-X	Yes	Yes	Yes	Yes	Yes	No	Yes	No	No
X*Y	Yes	Yes	Yes	Yes	Yes	No	Yes	No	No
X/Y	Yes	Yes	Yes	Yes	Yes	No	Yes	No	No
X%Y	Yes	Yes	Yes	No*	No*	No	Yes	No	No
X+Y	Yes	Yes	Yes	Yes	Yes	No	Yes	Yes	Yes
X-Y	Yes	Yes	Yes	Yes	Yes	No	Yes	Yes	Yes
X=Y	Yes	Yes	Yes	Yes	Yes	No	Yes	Yes	Yes
X*=Y	Yes	Yes	Yes	Yes	Yes	No	Yes	No	No
X/=Y	Yes	Yes	Yes	Yes	Yes	No	Yes	No	No
X%=Y	Yes	Yes	Yes	No*	No*	No	Yes	No	No
X+=Y	Yes	Yes	Yes	Yes	Yes	No	Yes	Yes	Yes
X-=Y	Yes	Yes	Yes	Yes	Yes	No	Yes	Yes	Yes

* Run-time library function `fmod()` must be used instead.

EXAMPLES

Note 1

```
*ival_d1++        *jval_d1--
*++ival_d1        *--jval_d1
+ival_d1          +jval_d1
ival_d1+1         jval_d1-1
```

TABLE 12.5B: Using Arithmetic Operators with Aggregate Data

OPERATOR	ARRAY		STRUCTURE/UNION	
	Names	**Elements**	**Names**	**Members**
X++	Yes[1]	Yes[3]	No[4]	Yes[5]
X--	Yes[1]	Yes[3]	No[4]	Yes[5]
++X	Yes[1]	Yes[3]	No[4]	Yes[5]
--X	Yes[1]	Yes[3]	No[4]	Yes[5]
+X	Yes	Yes[3]	No[4]	Yes[5]
-X	No	Yes[3]	No	Yes[5]
X*Y	No	Yes[3]	No	Yes[5]
X/Y	No	Yes[3]	No	Yes[5]
X%Y	No	Yes[3]	No	Yes[5]
X+Y	Yes[1]	Yes[3]	No[4]	Yes[5]
X-Y	Yes[1]	Yes[3]	No[4]	Yes[5]
X=Y	Yes[2,1]	Yes[3]	Yes[4]	Yes[5]
X*=Y	No	Yes[3]	No	Yes[5]
X/=Y	No	Yes[3]	No	Yes[5]
X%=Y	No	Yes[3]	No	Yes[5]
X+=Y	Yes[2,1]	Yes[3]	No[4]	Yes[5]
X-=Y	Yes[2,1]	Yes[3]	No[4]	Yes[5]

NOTES:
1. Since array names are pointers; for address arithmetic.
2. Except array names as lvalues.
3. Unless the element type does not support the operator.
4. Unless an array of structures or unions.
5. Unless the member type does not support the operator.

Note 2

```
ptr = ival_d1;       ptr = jval_d1;
ival_d1 = ptr;       jval_d1 = ival_d1;    /* error */
ptr += ival_d1;      ptr -= jval_d1;
ival_d1 += ptr;      jval_d1 -= ptr;       /* error */
```

Note 3

```
fval[0]%2          fval[0]%=2;            /* error */
-str2[2]           str2[2]*=2;            /* error */
```

Note 4

```
*str2++ = str2[0];
str2+1 = str2;
str2[2] = str2[0];
str2[2].str1 = str2[1].str1;
```

Note 5

```
str1.f1[0]%2       *(str2[2].str1.d1)%10    /* error */
```

Performance and Arithmetic Operators

X++, X−−, ++X, *and* **−−X**   For a complete discussion of these pre- and postincrement and decrement operators, refer to Chapter 4, section "Coding Incrementors and Decrementors." These operators are equivalent to the **+=** and **−=** compound operators but always outperform such equivalent statements as **X=X+1** and **X=X−1**. They are also instrumental in the formation of efficient compact pointer expressions such as ***X++, *X−−, *++X,** and ***−−X**.

+X   The unary plus operator is implemented syntactically, but not semantically, in the language and merely affirms that a data-object value remains unchanged. There is no performance cost associated with its use.

−X   The unary minus operator does alter the value of a data object and is the preferred form over such equivalent expressions as **X=(−1)*X**, as demonstrated in Chapter 4, section "Coding Sign Changes."

X*Y, X/Y, X%Y, X+Y, *and* **X−Y**   The relative performance characteristics of these arithmetic operations were evaluated for each basic operator using a program patterned after the example listed in Figure 12.2.

The performance measures from this program are summarized in Table 12.6. The factors shown are relative, not absolute, measures of performance. The fastest times are represented by a factor or multiplier of 1.0.

```
/* FILE: ch12e2.c */
#define TIMER
#include "timer.h"
#include <limits.h>
#include <float.h>
#include <math.h>
#define REPEAT for(i=0;i<100000;i++)

int main(void)     /* replicate for -, *, /, and % operators */
{
START(char + math);
{
long i;
char j=1;
REPEAT j+=1;
}
STOP;

START(char * math);
{
long i;
char j=1;
REPEAT j*=2;
}
STOP;

START(char / math);
{
long i;
char j=SCHAR_MAX;
REPEAT j/=2;
}
STOP;

START(char % math);
{
long i;
char j=SCHAR_MAX;
REPEAT j%=2;
}
STOP;

START(int + math);
{
long i;
int j=1;
REPEAT j+=1;
}
STOP;

START(long int + math);
{
long i;
long j=1L;
REPEAT j+=1L;
}
STOP;

START(long int / math);
{
long i;
long j=LONG_MAX;
REPEAT j/=2L;
}
STOP;
```

FIGURE 12.2: Sample program ch12e2.c evaluates the performance characteristics of using the C arithmetic operators.

```
START(float + math);
{
long i;
float fval=1.0F;
REPEAT fval+=1.0F;
}
STOP;

START(float * math);
{
long i;
float fval=1.0F;
REPEAT fval*=1.00001F;
}
STOP;

START(float / math);
{
long i;
float fval=FLT_MAX;
REPEAT fval/=1.00001F;
}
STOP;

START(double + math);
{
long i;
double dval=1.0;
REPEAT dval+=1.0;
}
STOP;

START(long double + math);
{
long i;
long double dval=1.0L;
REPEAT dval+=1.0L;
}
STOP;

START(float % math);        /* special case, fmod() with float */
{
long i;
float fval=1.0;
REPEAT fval+=fmod(fval,1.0);
}
STOP;

START(double % math);     /* special case, fmod() with double */
{
long i;
double dval=1.0;
REPEAT dval+=fmod(dval,1.0);
}
STOP;

START(long double % math);     /* special case, fmodl() with double */
{
long i;
double ldval=1.0;
REPEAT ldval+=fmodl(ldval,1.0);
}
STOP;
}
```

FIGURE 12.2: Sample program ch12e2.c evaluates the performance characteristics of using the C arithmetic operators (continued).

TABLE 12.6: Relative Performance of Arithmetic Operators

COMPILER COMMAND	OPERATOR	DATA-OBJECT TYPE						
		char[a]	int	enum[a]	long	float	double	long double
CL /qc ch12e2.c	+	1.0	1.0	1.0	1.1	38.7	41.2	38.3
	−	1.0	1.0	1.0	1.1	38.7	41.2	38.3
	*	1.1	1.1	1.1	1.8	45.3	51.8	48.4
	/	1.3	1.3	1.3	4.4	53.7	57.0	53.3
	%	1.2	1.2	1.2	4.1	171.4[b]	137.5[b]	137.5[b]
CL ch12e2.c	+	1.0	1.0	1.0	1.2	32.9	34.7	37.7
	−	1.0	1.0	1.0	1.2	32.9	34.7	37.7
	*	1.0	1.0	1.0	1.2	39.9	46.5	48.3
	/	1.3	1.3	1.3	5.3	39.9	46.5	48.3
	%	1.3	1.3	1.3	5.1	135.2[b]	118.2[b]	118.2[b]

NOTES:
All calculations reflect the use of an 80286-based computer with floating-point emulation only.
All entries shown are factors relative to the fastest times measured using the **START()** and **STOP** macros.
  a. Fundamental types **char** and **enum** are both integral types.
  b. The **%** operator may not be used with floating types; the **fmod()** function as used.

Notice the performance improvement that was recorded when using the OptimizingC compiler with the **/qc**, quick compile (limited optimization) versus the default optimization **/O** that otherwise is assumed. Also note that significant performance penalties are imposed by repetitive function calls to **fmod()**. Performance can be improved in this instance by introducing the compiler directive

```
#pragma intrinsic(fmod)
```

as described in Chapter 5, or by selecting compiler option **/Oi**, to further reduce the factors to the following values:

OPERATOR	float	double	long double
%	95.6	98.3	98.3

For a complete discussion of the relative performance of using function-like macros, intrinsic functions, **register** storage class function arguments, **_fastcall** functions, and normal functions, see Chapters 14 and 15.

Note that these findings are based upon floating-point emulation. Significantly greater improvement ($5-10x$) can be achieved by using a floating-point coprocessor $80x87$ chip.

X=Y, X*=Y, X/=Y, X%=Y, X+=Y, *and* **X–=Y**   The compound operators **+=** and **-=** perform in a manner equivalent to the **++** and **--** operators and are always preferred over the statements **X=X+1** and **X=X–1**. Although the other forms offer no distinct advantage, they should be used to establish a coding style that can be exploited if software is to be ported to other processors and optimizing compilers.

BITWISE OPERATORS

The bitwise operators listed in Table 12.2 perform bit and assignment operations upon either integral or bit-field type data-object values. They may be used alone or combined with other operators to construct expression statements with side effects (see Chapter 13). They can be summarized as follows:

~X   Performs the bitwise NOT, or complement (exchange all bit settings), of the value of object **X**.

X<<Y   Shifts the value of object **X** to the left by **Y** bit positions, zerofilling the vacated bit positions.

X>>Y   Shifts the value of object **X** to the right by **Y** bit positions, sign-extending the vacated bit positions.

X&Y   Performs the bitwise AND by setting each bit of the result On if the corresponding bits in object **X** and object **Y** are On.

X^Y   Performs the bitwise XOR by setting each bit of the result On if the corresponding bits in object **X** and object **Y** differ.

X|Y   Performs the bitwise OR by setting each bit of the result On if either of the corresponding bits in object **X** and object **Y** are On.

X<<=Y   Assigns the value of object **X** the result found by shifting the value of object **X** to the left by **Y** bit positions, zero-filling the vacated bit positions.

X>>=Y   Assigns the value of object **X** the result found by shifting the value of object **X** to the right by **Y** bit positions, sign-extending the vacated bit positions.

X&=Y   Assigns the value of object **X** the result found by performing the bitwise AND, by setting each bit of the result On if the corresponding bits in both object **X** and object **Y** are On.

X^=Y   Assigns the value of object **X** the result found by performing the bitwise XOR, by setting each bit of the result On if the corresponding bits in object **X** and object **Y** differ.

X|=Y   Assigns the value of object **X** the result found by performing the bitwise OR, by setting each bit of the result On if either of the corresponding bits in object **X** and object **Y** are On.

The operands, or data-object type **X** or **Y**, upon which these bitwise operators may act, are summarized in Tables 12.7A and 12.7B.

Notes 1 and 2 qualify the applicability of the operators shown in Table 12.7B. The declarations shown below are used by the code examples that follow to illustrate each note in the tables above. For instance, Note 1 ("Unless the element type does not support the operator") is clarified below by the example **fval[0] ^ 0xffffffff**, indicating that it is incorrect to use the bitwise XOR operator with a floating-point type object.

```
float fval[3];
struct s1 {int i1;
    float f1[3];
    double *d1;} str1;
```

EXAMPLES

Note 1

```
fval[0] ^ 0xffffffff              /* error */
```

Note 2

```
*(str1.d1) | 0x00000000ffffffff   /* error */
```

Performance and Bitwise Operators

For a complete discussion of using the bitwise operators, see Chapter 11. The individual performance differences between these operators are insignificant; however, always use integral over bit-field types, and consider

TABLE 12.7A: Using Bitwise Operators with Arithmetic and Scalar Data

| OPERATOR | ARITHMETIC/SCALAR | | | | | | | SCALAR | |
| | INTEGRAL | | | FLOATING-POINT | | BITS | | | |
	char	int	enum	float	double	Integral	Fields	_segment	Pointers
~X	Yes	Yes	Yes	No*	No*	Yes	Yes	No	No
X<<Y	Yes	Yes	Yes	No*	No*	Yes	Yes	No	No
X>>Y	Yes	Yes	Yes	No*	No*	Yes	Yes	No	No
X&Y	Yes	Yes	Yes	No*	No*	Yes	Yes	No	No
X^Y	Yes	Yes	Yes	No*	No*	Yes	Yes	No	No
X|Y	Yes	Yes	Yes	No*	No*	Yes	Yes	No	No
X<<=Y	Yes	Yes	Yes	No*	No*	Yes	Yes	No	No
X>>=Y	Yes	Yes	Yes	No*	No*	Yes	Yes	No	No
X&=Y	Yes	Yes	Yes	No*	No*	Yes	Yes	No	No
X^=Y	Yes	Yes	Yes	No*	No*	Yes	Yes	No	No
X|=Y	Yes	Yes	Yes	No*	No*	Yes	Yes	No	No

* Unless in a union with bit-field types; see Chapter 11, section "Bit-Field Types."

left or right shifting over multiplication or division when integral powers of two are involved. Again, the compound-operator form of assignment is preferred for portability and optimization reasons, although it presently offers no distinct performance advantage with Microsoft C.

LOGICAL OPERATORS

The logical operators listed in Table 12.2 perform logical tests upon data-object values used by the repetition and conditional branching statements described in Chapter 13. They can be summarized as follows:

!X   Performs a logical NOT by yielding a value of one (true) if the value of object **X** is zero (false); otherwise (if object **X** is nonzero), yields a result of zero (false).

TABLE 12.7B: Using Bitwise Operators with Aggregate Data

OPERATOR	ARRAY		STRUCTURE	
	Names	Elements	Names	Members
~X	No	Yes[1]	No	Yes[2]
X<<Y	No	Yes[1]	No	Yes[2]
X>>Y	No	Yes[1]	No	Yes[2]
X&Y	No	Yes[1]	No	Yes[2]
X^Y	No	Yes[1]	No	Yes[2]
X|Y	No	Yes[1]	No	Yes[2]
X<<=Y	No	Yes[1]	No	Yes[2]
X>>=Y	No	Yes[1]	No	Yes[2]
X&=Y	No	Yes[1]	No	Yes[2]
X^=Y	No	Yes[1]	No	Yes[2]
X|=Y	No	Yes[1]	No	Yes[2]

NOTES:
1. Unless the element type does not support the operator.
2. Unless the member type does not support the operator.

X<Y Tests whether the value of object **X** is less than the value of object **Y**, and yields a result of zero if false or one if true.

X<=Y Tests whether the value of object **X** is less than or equal to the value of object **Y** and yields a result of zero if false or one if true.

X>Y Tests whether the value of object **X** is greater than the value of object **Y** and yields a result of zero if false or one if true.

X>=Y Tests whether the value of object **X** is greater than or equal to the value of object **Y** and yields a result of zero if false or one if true.

X==Y Tests whether the value of object **X** is equal to the value of object **Y** and yields a result of zero if false or one if true.

X!=Y   Tests whether the value of object **X** is not equal to the value of object **Y** and yields a result of zero if false or one if true.

X&&Y   Tests whether both of the values of objects **X** and **Y** are nonzero (true) and yields a result of zero if false or one if true.

X||Y   Tests whether either of the values of objects **X** or **Y** are nonzero (true) and yields a result of zero if false or one if true.

Z?X:Y   If the value of object **Z** is nonzero (true), yields a result of the value of object **X**; otherwise (if object **Z** is zero) yields a result of the value of object **Y**.

For the sake of discussion in this chapter, like operands are assumed. When dissimilar operand types are involved, type promotion and balancing occurs as explained in Chapter 13.

The operands, or data-object type **X** or **Y**, upon which these logical operators may act are summarized in Tables 12.8A and 12.8B.

Notes 1 to 3 qualify the applicability of the operators shown in Table 12.8B. The declarations shown below are used by the code examples that follow to illustrate each note in the tables above. For instance, Note 3 ("Unless the member is a structure or union") is clarified below by the example **!str2[2].str1**, indicating that it is incorrect to use the logical NOT operator upon a structure member that is itself a structure name.

```
int ival_d1[3], jval_d1[3];
struct s1 {int i1;
    float f1[3];
    double *d1;} str1, *pstr1 = &str1;
struct {int i2;
    float f2[3];
    double *d2;
    struct s1 str1;} str2[3], *pstr2 = &str2[2];
```

EXAMPLES

Note 1

```
!ival_d1
ival_d1 <= jval_d1
!ival_d1 && !jval_d1
ival_d1 < jval_d1 ? ival_d1 : jval_d1;
```

TABLE 12.8A: Using Logical Operators with Arithmetic and Scalar Data

| OPERATOR | ARITHMETIC/SCALAR | | | | | | | SCALAR | |
| | INTEGRAL | | | FLOATING-POINT | | BITS | | | |
	char	int	enum	float	double	Integral	Fields	_segment	Pointers
!X	Yes	Yes	Yes	Yes	Yes	No	Yes	No	Yes
X<Y	Yes	Yes	Yes	Yes	Yes	No	Yes	Yes	Yes
X<=Y	Yes	Yes	Yes	Yes	Yes	No	Yes	Yes	Yes
X>Y	Yes	Yes	Yes	Yes	Yes	No	Yes	Yes	Yes
X>=Y	Yes	Yes	Yes	Yes	Yes	No	Yes	Yes	Yes
X==Y	Yes	Yes	Yes	Yes	Yes	No	Yes	Yes	Yes
X!=Y	Yes	Yes	Yes	Yes	Yes	No	Yes	Yes	Yes
X&&Y	Yes	Yes	Yes	Yes	Yes	No	Yes	Yes	Yes
X||Y	Yes	Yes	Yes	Yes	Yes	No	Yes	Yes	Yes
Z?X:Y	Yes	Yes	Yes	Yes	Yes	No	Yes	Yes	Yes

Note 2

```
!str2[2]
str2[0] <= str2[2]
!str2[0] && pstr1
str2 == NULL ? pstr1 : str2
```

Note 3

```
!str2[2].str1                          /* error */
str2->str1 <= pstr2->str1              /* error */
(str2+2)->str1 && pstr2->str1          /* error */
str2[0].str1 < pstr2->str1 ? str2 : pstr2;   /* error */
```

Performance and Logical Operators

The only relative performance differences that exist in expressions using logical operators involve the use of the compound operators **&&** and **||**. For example, to form an expression that tests whether variable **ival** is less than or equal to 10, the following expressions perform identically:

```
ival <= 10
!(ival > 10)
```

TABLE 12.8B: Using Logical Operators with Aggregate Data

OPERATOR	ARRAY		STRUCTURE/UNION	
	Names	Elements	Names	Members
`!X`	Yes[1]	Yes[2]	No[2]	Yes[3]
`X<Y`	Yes[1]	Yes[2]	No[2]	Yes[3]
`X<=Y`	Yes[1]	Yes[2]	No[2]	Yes[3]
`X>Y`	Yes[1]	Yes[2]	No[2]	Yes[3]
`X>=Y`	Yes[1]	Yes[2]	No[2]	Yes[3]
`X==Y`	Yes[1]	Yes[2]	No[2]	Yes[3]
`X!=Y`	Yes[1]	Yes[2]	No[2]	Yes[3]
`X&&Y`	Yes[1]	Yes[2]	No[2]	Yes[3]
`X||Y`	Yes[1]	Yes[2]	No[2]	Yes[3]
`Z?X:Y`	Yes[1]	Yes[2]	No[2]	Yes[3]

NOTES:
1. Since array names are pointers.
2. Unless an array of structures or unions.
3. Unless the member is a structure or union.

However, the following expression is slower:

```
ival<10 || ival==10
```

Using the conditional operator as follows:

```
i<0 ? (i=0) : (i=i)
```

instead of

```
if (i<0) i=0; else i=i;
```

is only a matter of style, because both forms of expression perform identically.

MISCELLANEOUS OPERATORS

The miscellaneous operators listed in Table 12.2, which provide the often-needed size of a data object in bytes, type value representation conversion, and the sequencing of operations, include the following:

OPERATOR	DESCRIPTION
X(Y)	Initiates a call to a function named **X** with the argument value of the object **Y** and yields a result equal to the return value of function **X**. This is not a data-object type operator. Refer to Part V for complete details.
sizeof X	Yields a result equal to the size of the object or expression **X** in bytes **(size_t)**.
sizeof(type)	Yields a result equal to the size of a **(type)** cast expression in bytes **(size_t)**.
(type) X	Yields a result that converts the value of object **X** to object type **(type)**.
X,Y	Evaluates the value of expression **X**, then evaluates the value of expression **Y**.

These operators are generally combined with other operators to form compound expressions and statements.

The operands, or data-object type **X** or **Y**, upon which these miscellaneous operators may act, are summarized in Tables 12.9A and 12.9B.

Notes 1 to 5 qualify the applicability of the operators shown in Table 12.9B. The declarations shown below are used by the code examples that follow to illustrate each note in the tables above. For instance, Note 2 ("Unless an array of structures and unions") is clarified below by the example **(double) str2[0]**, indicating that it is incorrect to use a cast operation upon an element of an array that itself is a structure or union.

```
int *ptr;
int ival_d1[3];
struct s1 {int i1;
    float f1[3];
    double *d1;} str1;
struct {int i2;
    float f2[3];
    double *d2;
    struct s1 str1;} str2[3];
```

EXAMPLES

Note 1

```
(char *)ival_d1
```

TABLE 12.9A: Using Miscellaneous Operators with Arithmetic and Scalar Data

| OPERATOR | ARITHMETIC/SCALAR | | | | | | | SCALAR | |
| | INTEGRAL | | | FLOATING-POINT | | BITS | | | |
	char	int	enum	float	double	Integral	Fields	_segment	Pointers
X(Y)	N.A.	N.A.	N.A.	N.A.	N.A.	N.A.	N.A.	N.A.	N.A.
sizeof X	Yes	Yes	Yes	Yes	Yes	No	No	Yes	Yes
sizeof(type)	Yes	Yes	Yes	Yes	Yes	No	No	Yes	Yes
(type) X	Yes	Yes	Yes	Yes	Yes	No	Yes	Yes	Yes
X, Y	Yes	Yes	Yes	Yes	Yes	Yes	Yes	Yes	Yes

N.A. indicates not applicable to data-object types, only function types; see Chapter 14.

Note 2

```
(double) str2[0].f2[0]
(double) str2[0]               /* error */
```

Note 3

```
(double) str2[0].str1.f1[0]
(double) str2[0].str1          /* error */
```

Note 4

```
str2++, ptr = (void *) str2
```

Note 5

```
str1.i1 = 0, str2[0].i2 = 0;
```

Performance and Miscellaneous Operators

The overhead associated with function calls (versus intrinsic) was demonstrated in the section "Performance and Arithmetic Operators" above and will be further examined in Chapter 14.

The explicit use of type casting may replicate the operations already performed when expressions are evaluated. For example:

```
int ival;
double dval;
dval = ival;
dval = (double)ival;
```

TABLE 12.9B: Using Miscellaneous Operators with Aggregate Data

OPERATOR	ARRAY		STRUCTURE/UNION	
	Names	Elements	Names	Members
`X(Y)`	N.A.	N.A.	N.A.	N.A.
`sizeof X`	Yes	Yes	Yes	Yes
`sizeof(type)`	Yes	Yes	Yes	Yes
`(type) X`	Yes[1]	Yes[2]	No	Yes[3]
`X,Y`	Yes[1]	Yes[2,4]	Yes[4]	Yes[5]

NOTES:
N.A. indicates not applicable to data-object types, only function types; see Chapter 14.
1. Since array names are pointers; for address arithmetic.
2. Unless an array of structures or unions.
3. Unless the member is a structure or union.
4. For all valid structure and union name operations.
5. For all valid member operations.

Both **dval** assignment statements perform identically, although the second assignment statement is self-documenting. For more information about the assignment and automatic casting of expressions, see Chapter 13.

The comma operator is useful to control the order in which two or more expressions must be evaluated in contexts where only one expression is permitted. For example:

```
char array[i,j,k]
```

The classic inappropriate use of the comma operator within a subscript yields a subscript value equaling the value of k in this instance, because the comma operator associates left to right. For additional discussion, see Chapter 4, section "Subscripting Anomalies."

The comma operator is also commonly used within a **for** statement in which more than one expression is used to express the initializer and incrementor steps, as described in Chapter 13.

```
for (i=0, j=100; j>5; i+=3, j--) { .. }
```

OPERATOR PRECEDENCE

Operator precedence controls how C compilers interpret expressions and statements involving the use of multiple operators. Operators may be combined with keywords, identifiers, punctuators, and other operators to develop expressions in C. Expressions are formed using operators that act upon data-object and function types to effectively locate, modify, test, or report on type objects. As we will see in Chapter 13, expressions always yield values, while statements direct actions in the C language.

Recall that there are three categories of type in C: data-object, function, and incomplete. This chapter has focused upon using operators with data-object type operands. Part V will focus upon the use of operators with function types. The discussion of using operators with incomplete types was introduced in Part III for pointers, arrays, structures, and unions, and will be continued in Part V for the development of function prototypes.

We will restrict the discussion of operator precedence to the development of simple and compound expressions involving two or more operators. For example, in the following statements operator precedence controls the values that result and the actions that are performed:

```
char c_ary[] = {'A','B','C'}, *ptr=c_ary;        /* Stmt #1 */
*++ptr = *(c_ary+2);                             /* Stmt #2 */
printf("\n%c %c %c",c_ary[0],c_ary[1],c_ary[2]); /* Stmt #3 */
```

This example produces the following output:

```
A C C
```

The rules of operator precedence explain why. Every C operator has an assigned level of precedence, (1) being first or highest and (15) being last or lowest (see Table 12.1). Operators assigned the same level of precedence are associated with each other either left-to-right or right-to-left, thereby defining a set of rules that control the order in which expression values are computed and statement actions are performed.

For example, Stmt #1 above instructs the compiler to allocate data-object storage (keyword **char**) and perform initialization (braces **{..}** punctuator). Although the comma operator is of the lowest precedence (15), it establishes the fact that the expression

```
char c_ary[] = {'A','B','C'}
```

is performed before

```
char *ptr=c_ary
```

because the comma operator associates left to right. If the comma operator associated right to left, we would not be able to initialize pointer variable **ptr** with the address of **c_ary**, because **c_ary** would not yet have been allocated storage. Likewise, the assignment operators in both cases associate right to left, and so the value of the expression on the right-hand side is evaluated before being assigned to the object identified (located) by the left-hand side.

The complex expression

```
*++ptr = *(c_ary+2);
```

demonstrated above by Stmt #2 demands that operator precedence be understood to both write and understand its effects. The assignment operator associates right to left, therefore the expression

```
*(c_ary+2)
```

is evaluated first. The parentheses in this case are neither a function call nor type cast, but are treated as a punctuator and used for grouping operations. Although the indirection (*****, level 2) operator has a higher precedence than addition (**+**, level 4), the address arithmetic (**c_ary+2**) is performed first because of the punctuator. The indirection operator is then applied to the result, in this case yielding the letter **'C'**. Next, the expression ***++ptr** is evaluated. Since both the indirection (*****, level 2) and preincrement (**++**, level 2) operators are of the same precedence level, the right-to-left associativity controls the order of evaluation. The address represented by pointer **ptr[0]** is incremented by the size of one **char** data object, and then indirection is applied to locate the lvalue, **ptr[1]**, or **c_ary[1]**. Finally, the letter value of **'C'** is assigned or placed in the memory location identified by **c_ary[1]** (same as **ptr[1]**), thereby yielding the result displayed by Stmt #3 above.

Had Stmt #2 been expressed as

```
++*ptr = *(c_ary+2);
```

a compiler error would have resulted, *left operand must be lvalue*. Again, the preincrement (**++**, level 2) and indirection (*****, level 2) operators are of the same precedence level; therefore, the right-to-left associativity controls the evaluation. The expression ***ptr** yields the character **'A'**, and **++'A'** yields an rvalue of the integer value of 66, or the character equivalent of the letter **'B'**. However, rvalues may not be used on the left-hand side of an assignment statement, hence the compiler error.

The expression of an equation in the form

```
a = b + c * d;        /* Stmt #4 */
```

would be interpreted as

```
a = b + (c * d);
```

because the precedence of multiplication (*****) is higher than that of addition (**+**); however, had Stmt #4 above been expressed as

```
a = (b + c) * d;     /* Stmt #5 */
```

the use of the parentheses as a punctuator would have overridden the default order of precedence. Expressions grouped with parentheses always override the precedence of operators. This is a new feature of Standard C that was not always true with K&R C.

Common logical expressions involving simple and compound logical expressions, such as

```
a == b || c == d
```

expressed without punctuators, would be interpreted as follows:

```
(a == b) || (c == d)
```

because the equality operators have a higher precedence (7) than the logical **OR** operator (12). Also, because the **||** operator associates left to right, if the expression **(a==b)** were true, then the expression **(c==d)** would not have to be evaluated at all.

The right-to-left associativity of the assignment operators also permits expressions such as

```
x = y = z = 2;
```

to be constructed and to properly perform variable initialization.

The most complex expressions involving operator precedence are usually associated with declarations of function types. This topic is thoroughly explained in Chapter 14.

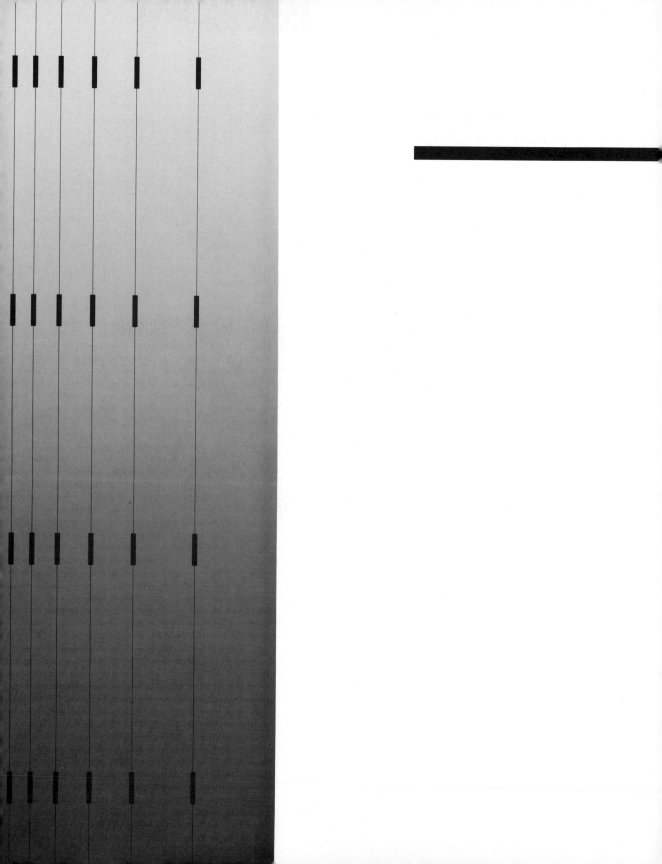

# CHAPTER 13

Expressions and Statements

Expressions and Statements

A major purpose of the many tables presented in this book is to bridge the gap that exists between a systems and an application programmer's view of the C language. Recall from Chapter 4 that the ANSI Standards Committee included more implementors than users. If you have ventured to read the *ANSI Programming Language C* document itself, or the excellent Plauger/Brodie *Standard C* guide to ANSI C, it is obvious that a "compiler construction" bias prevails (see Appendix A). In fact, most books tend to present the C language from a systems programming perspective. Does this imply that you should not begin writing C language programs until you understand the language from a compiler's point of view? Certainly not.

Just as some liberties were taken to introduce data types and qualifiers (Chapter 7), certain liberties will be taken in this chapter to discuss the formation of expressions, which are the building blocks of the C language. No mention will be made of phases of translation, preprocessor tokens, C tokens, sequence points, and the like. This has been done not to minimize the importance of C compiler construction, but to provide an alternate perspective on the C language, using terminology and techniques that are more familiar and of more immediate use to application programmers. Total mastery of the C language does mandate that an implementor's viewpoint of the language be adopted; however, few, it would seem, are earmarked to attain that distinction.

It will become clear that expressions are the building blocks of the C language when you see that expressions may be used throughout a source-code file to convey program properties, express compile-time initializers, and perform all run-time calculations. Because expressions convey value, they always have specific type and storage-class properties. Statements, on the other hand, are restricted for use in the body **{ . . }** of a function and orchestrate the evaluation of expressions under the direction of C keywords (see Appendix B).

It is also helpful to understand that every expression is composed of *terms*. The concept of terms supports the discussion of the C language from an *application* rather than a *compiler construction* point of view. Each term is recognized easily and has a well-defined type and storage class. Simple expressions are formed from one term, or from one term in combination with one or more unary operators. Compound expressions, on the other hand, involve two or more terms combined with one or more unary, binary, or ternary operators (see Chapter 12). For the value of simple and compound expressions to be determined, the rules by which terms are promoted and balanced, expressions are grouped and evaluated, and values are cast and assigned, must be well understood.

Once terms and expressions are understood, either expression or keyword statements may be formed. Three categories of keyword statements (repetition, conditional branching, and unconditional branching) will be used to present the available Standard C statement types. Each statement type will be explained in detail. Also, guidelines will be presented for deciding which repetition and conditional branching statement types to use.

EXPRESSIONS

Since both simple and compound expressions are composed of terms, let's first gain an understanding of what constitutes a term in the C language. Table 13.1 presents seven categories of possible C terms: identifiers, character constants, string literals, integer constants, floating constants, the **sizeof()** operator, and the parentheses **()** punctuator. A complete description of each term type, including examples, is provided in Table 13.1 to simplify the process of forming and interpreting C expressions.

Terms are the source code elements from which all expressions, and hence statements, are formed in C. Note that each term always has a well-defined type and storage class and, therefore, value associated with it. Since individual terms always represent value, expressions composed of terms always represent value. To understand how value is determined for all expressions requires an understanding of how individual terms are promoted, then balanced and grouped, and cast to convert between data-object types. Promotion involves the rules by which data-type objects are progressively widened to transform the representation of value assigned to types **char**, **int**, and **long**. Balancing involves the promotion of two dissimilar terms so that their forms of representation are compatible. Casting is used to transform between the many forms of type representation, and typically involves the promotion of a type object to a broader form of representation, or the demotion of a type object to a narrower form of representation.

We will first examine simple expressions consisting of one term with or without accompanying unary operators and next look at compound expressions consisting of two or more terms joined by one or more operators. We will see that expression statements, consisting of a simple or compound expression terminated by a semicolon, may be used for their

TABLE 13.1: C TERMS

CATEGORY Subcategory	DESCRIPTION	TYPE	EXAMPLE
IDENTIFIERS	Alphabetic/underscore character, then any alphanumeric/underscore sequence		
Function	If within scope	return type	`pow(2.0,10.0)`
	If not within scope	`int` by default	`myfunc()`
Data Object	Any complete or incomplete data type	Object type	`ival` or `array[]`
Enumeration	Any named constant	Always `int`	`enum` (false, true)
Type Cast	Any (type) expression	As defined	`(double)ival`
CHARACTER CONSTANTS	normal `char` (or `int`) type, unless an L-prefixed wide character		
No Prefix		`int`	`'A' '\07' '\ff' '\n'`
L-Prefix		`wchar_t`	`L'A' L'\0'`
STRING LITERALS	Number of characters plus a null establishes the size, unless an L-prefixed wide character.		
No Prefix		`char[7]`	"string"
L-Prefix		`wchar_t[7]`	L"string"
INTEGER CONSTANTS	Value, base, and suffix establish the type.		
(Base 10) No Suffix		`int, long, unsigned long`	−23, 52550, 4000000000
u or U Suffix		`unsigned int, unsigned long`	23U, 52550U
l or L Suffix		`long, unsigned long`	−23L, 4000000000L
Any UL Suffix		`unsigned long`	−23UL
(Base 8) No Suffix		`int, unsigned int, long, unsigned long`	017, 0177777, 0277777, 037777777777
u or U Suffix		`unsigned int, unsigned long`	017U, 0277777U

TABLE 13.1: C TERMS (continued)

CATEGORY Subcategory	DESCRIPTION	TYPE	EXAMPLE
l or L Suffix Any UL Suffix		`long, unsigned long` `unsigned long`	017L, 037777777777L 017UL

(Base 16) No
Suffix
u or U Suffix
 	
l or L Suffix
 	
Any UL Suffix
		`int, unsigned int,`
		`long, unsigned long`
		`unsigned int,`
		`unsigned long`
		`long, unsigned long`
		`unsigned long`
			0xFF, 0xFFFF, 0x1FFFF,
			0xFFFFFFFF
			0xFFu, 0x1FFFFu
			
			0xFFl, 0xFFFFFFFFl
			0xFFul

**FLOATING
CONSTANTS**
No Suffix
f or F Suffix
l or L Suffix
	The suffix establishes
	the type.
		`double`
		`float`
		`long double`
			−1.0
			−1.0F
			−1.0L

`sizeof()`	Size in bytes of type or object	`size_t`	`sizeof(int)`
`(...)` `PUNCTUATOR`	Grouping to override operator precedence	Type of expression value	(a + b)

"side effects." As you may recall from Chapters 4 and 12, side effects involve the alteration of an assigned value, which can occur intentionally or unintentionally. For example, when a function is called that simply displays information or returns a value that is ignored, there are no side effects; however, when a function return value is captured, or the prefix and postfix operators **++** and **−−** are used, there are side effects—data-type object values are altered. We will also see that keyword statements always involve the use of keywords and expressions and are solely responsible for altering the default order (top to bottom, left to right) in which statements are performed.

Promoting Simple Expressions

A simple expression is formed using one term, or one term combined with one or more unary operators, from the possible terms described in Table 13.1. Four categories of simple expressions are described in Table 13.2: function, lvalue, rvalue, and **void**.

TABLE 13.2: Simple Expressions

CATEGORY Subcategory	DESCRIPTION	TYPE	EXAMPLE

FUNCTION	Any function name
	
	Any name assigning a function pointer
		Function return type
		
		`_near` or `_far` pointer type
			`pi = acos(-1.0)`
			
			`ptr = myfunc`

LVALUE	A data object expression that accesses a stored value, alters a stored value, or determines the address of a data object		

Accessible	Any data-object type other than an array type	Object type	`static int ival,`
			`*ptr=&ival;`
			`ival = 0`

Modifiable	Any data-object type other than an array type or a `const` type	Object type	`ival++`
Array	Any complete or incomplete array type	Array type	`int a_ival[] =` `{0,1};`
		Element type	`a_ival[0] = 2`
Incomplete Non-Array	Any incomplete type other than array type (`void`, structure, union)	Type `struct str`	`struct str { int` `i j; };`
RVALUE	Any value (expression) that has a data-object type other than array type for specifying a value for the preprocessor, to initialize a value prior to execution, or to compute a value at run-time		
`#if` expression	Restricted constant expression only (see Chapter 5)	`int` type only	`#elif __STDC__`
Integer Constant	Any integer-type expression that can be evaluated where they occur in a program	`int` type only	`100`
Arithmetic Constant	Any arithmetic-type (`char`, `int`, `enum`, `float`, `double`) expression that can be evaluated prior to program startup	Object type	`22.0/7.0`
Address Constant	Any pointer-type expression that can be evaluated prior to program startup	`_near`, `_far`, `_huge`, or `_based` pointer type	`&ival`
void	Any `void` type expression that only produces side effects	Always type `void`	`void func(a,b);`

For a value to be determined for a simple expression (term), the concept of type promotion must be understood. When integral arithmetic types (**char**, **int**, **enum**, bit-field) must be evaluated, automatic type promotion is always involved because they are considered rvalue expressions. Therefore all **char** and bit-field types are always promoted to **signed** or **unsigned int** for value determination, whereas floating-point and scalar types are promoted only to balance dissimilar types in compound expressions.

The concept of type promotion is now governed by the new Standard C philosophy that value should be preserved if possible. This value-preserving philosophy has superceded the earlier K&R **unsigned**-preserving approach. The net effect of this change is to favor the promotion to types **int** and **long**, thus preserving the sign bit and only promoting to type **unsigned int** or **unsigned long** if necessary to preserve original value representation. Figure 13.1 summarizes the value-preserving promotion sequence, with the understanding that only at times will **unsigned int** (16 bits) be favored over **signed int** (15 bits) and **unsigned long** (32 bits) favored over **signed long** (31 bits) to preserve original value.

These default rules apply when explicit type casting is not provided in the source code. Frequently, this occurs when rvalue expressions must be evaluated and when dissimilar terms must be balanced in compound expressions. Casts, however, may always be explicitly written to control the manner in which terms are promoted.

Neither the new value-preserving nor the original unsigned-preserving approach by itself guarantees correct results. The value-preserving approach, however, tends to minimize the "questionably signed" ambiguitites that arise when **unsigned** and **signed int** terms must be promoted and balanced. The examples shown in Table 13.3 and found in the "Grouping and Evaluating Expressions" section that follows, demonstrate the new value-preserving approach. It remains the programmer's responsibility to avoid the detrimental effects that arise when **signed** and **unsigned** integral terms are intermixed by the judicious use of grouping parentheses and explicit type cast operations.

Balancing Compound Expressions

A compound expression is defined to be composed of two or more terms, or simple expressions, combined with one or more operators. Consider the following compound expressions, which are based upon the type declarations shown.

```
char cval = 'a';
int ival  = 10;
long lval = 100;
fval = 1.0F;
dval = -1.0;
```

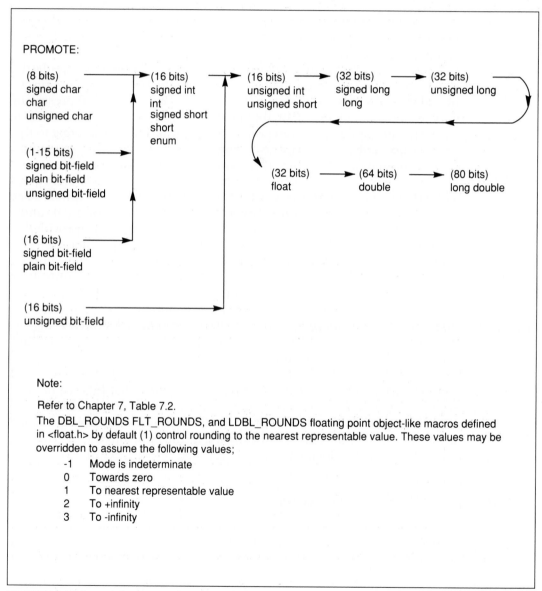

FIGURE 13.1: Microsoft C type promotion and balancing.

TABLE 13.3A: Microsoft C Arithmetic Type Casting

TO ——————→ ↓ FROM	signed char	unsigned char	signed int	unsigned int
signed char (65) (0x41)	OK (65) (0x41)	PB (65) (0x41)	OK,SE (65) (0x0041)	SE (65) (0x0041)
unsigned char (255) (0xff)	PB (−1) (0xff)	OK (255) (0xff)	OK,ZE (255) (0x00ff)	OK,ZE (255) (0x00ff)
signed int (−1) (0xffff)	TH (−1) (0xff)	TH (255) (0xff)	OK (−1) (0xffff)	PB (65535) (0xffff)
unsigned int (65535) (0xffff)	TH (−1) (0xff)	TH (255) (0xff)	PB (−1) (0xffff)	OK (65535) (0xffff)
signed long (−65535) (0xffff0001)	TH (1) (0x01)	TH (1) (0x01)	TH (1) (0x0001)	TH (1) (0x0001)
unsigned long (4294967295) (0xffffffff)	TH (−1) (0xff)	TH (255) (0xff)	TH (−1) (0xffff)	TH (65535) (0xffff)
float (−1.0)	FI,TH (−1) (0xff)	FI,TH (255) (0xff)	FI,TH (−1) (0xffff)	FI,TH (65535) (0xffff)
double (−4294967295.0)	FI,TH (1) (0x01)	FI,TH (1) (0x01)	FI,TH (1) (0x0001)	FI,TH (1) (0x0001)

NOTES:

FI   Floating to integral conversion: [**double** → **float** → **long** → **unsigned long** →]
LS   Loss of significance (possible)
OK   Value always preserved
PB   Preserve binary

TABLE 13.3B: Microsoft C Arithmetic Type Casting (continued)

TO ⟶ ⬇ FROM	signed long	unsigned long	float	double
signed char (65) (0x41)	OK,SE (65) (0x00000041)	SE (65) (0x00000041)	OK (65.0)	OK (65.0)
unsigned char (255) (0xff)	OK,ZE (255) (0x000000ff)	OK,ZE (255) (0x000000ff)	OK (255.0)	OK (255.0)
signed int (−1) (0xffff)	OK,SE (−1) (0xffffffff)	SE (4294967295) (0xffffffff)	OK (−1.0)	OK (−1.0)
unsigned int (65535) (0xffff)	OK,ZE (65535) (0x0000ffff)	OK,ZE (65535) (0x0000ffff)	OK (65535.0)	OK (65535.0)
signed long (−65535) (0xffff0001)	OK (−65535) (0xffff0001)	PB (4294901761) (0xffff0001)	LS (−65535.0)	OK (−65535.0)
unsigned long (4294967295) (0xffffffff)	PB (−1) (0xffffffff)	OK (4294967295) (0xffffffff)	LS (4294967296.0)	OK (4294967295.0)
float (−1.0)	FI (−1) (0xffffffff)	FI,PB (4294967295) (0xffffffff)	OK (−1.0)	OK (−1.0)
double (−4294967295.0)	FI (1) (0x00000001)	FI,PB (1) (0x00000001)	LS (−4294967296.0)	OK (−4294967295.0)

NOTES (cont.):
SE   Sign extend (left)
TH   Truncate high-order bits (left)
ZE   Zero extend (left)

1. `cval –'a'`
2. `ival – 10`
3. `++cval + lval`
4. `cval + fval`
5. `ival + dval`

Notice that compound expressions, like simple expressions, always result in a value and, therefore, have a type and storage class. Unlike simple expressions that may involve type promotion, however, compound expressions often require type balancing. Balancing is performed in compound expressions to resolve computations involving terms that are of dissimilar type. As shown in Figure 13.1, terms are progressively *widened* to preserve value and hence to establish the final type of the expression involved. The adage "always compare apples with apples" applies.

In the compound expression examples labeled above, example 1 depicts two like terms of type **char**, which are both promoted to type **int** to form an expression of type **int**. Example 2 depicts two like terms of type **int**, which yield an expression of type **int** without any type promotion. Example 3 depicts two unlike terms for which term **cval** must be promoted (widened) from type **char** to **int** and then to **long** to yield an expression of type **long**. Example 4 depicts two unlike terms for which term **cval** must be promoted from type **char** to **int** to **long** and then to **float** to yield an expression of type **float**. Example 5 depicts two unlike terms for which term **ival** must be promoted from type **int** to **long** to **float** and then to **double** to yield an expression of type **double**.

Grouping and Evaluating Expressions

The effects that operators have upon term values within an expression are controlled by two factors: the effect that the parentheses punctuator has upon the grouping or order in which terms of an expression are evaluated, and the default precedence of operators (see Chapter 12).

Without the use of parentheses, the precedence of operators depicted in Tables 12.1 and 12.2 controls the order in which operators are applied to terms in an expression (see Chapter 12). The effect that parentheses have upon the grouping of terms in Standard C is guaranteed, whereas with K&R C it was not. This was particularly troublesome when complex equations were written in K&R C, and even more so as an obstacle to implementing compiler optimization techniques.

For example, parentheses can play an important role in the formation of more readable, and hence understandable, compact pointer expressions. Consider this array declaration:

```
int i[]= {99, 199, 299, 399, 499, 599}, *ptr=i;
```

In the following examples, note the different effects that grouping parentheses orchestrate:

EXAMPLE	EXPRESSION	VALUE	SIDE EFFECTS
1(a)	`*ptr++`	99	`ptr= &i[1]`
1(b)	`*(ptr++)`	199	`ptr= &i[2]`
1(c)	`(*ptr)++`	299	`i[2]= 300`
2(a)	`++*ptr++`	301	`i[2]=301,` `ptr= &i[3]`
2(b)	`++(*ptr++)`	400	`i[3]=400,` `ptr= &i[4]`
2(c)	`++*(ptr++)`	500	`i[4]=500,` `ptr= &i[5]`

The expression and side-effect values shown assume the initial values shown for **array i[]** and the effects of processing the expressions shown consecutively, to yield these values:

```
int i[]= {99, 199, 301, 400, 500, 599}
```

Examples 1(a) and 1(b) have the identical effect of using the value of the object pointed to, and postincrementing the pointer itself.

Example 1(c), because of the parentheses, postincrements the value of the object pointed to.

In Examples 2(a), 2(b), and 2(c), identical effects are achieved, whereby the object value pointed to is preincremented, and the pointer itself is postincremented.

Standard C now mandates that parentheses always control the order in which terms of an expression are evaluated, and they override the default order of operator precedence. When this new feature is coupled with the ability to override the automatic K&R promotion of all floating-point types to type **double** in Standard C, and thus handle **float**, **double**, and **long double** data-type constants and objects separately, C finally overcomes the barriers that have deterred its expanded use in the scientific community.

Casting and Assigning Expressions

The topics of type casting and assignment are inseparable. Casts are used to alter the form of representation of a value from one type object to another. All C assignment statements will automatically cast the value of the expression on the right-hand side (rvalue) of an assignment statement to the type of the object on the left-hand side (lvalue). Essentially, this process is an implicit cast operation. When it is necessary for term promotion (widening), or to balance or assign an expression, automatic casting occurs; however, anywhere that casts are explicitly coded, they are performed (unless subsequently overridden by compiler optimization techniques).

When either assignment or casting occurs, the rules governing the manner in which value representation (type) conversions are performed control the value of the result. Two tables have been prepared that summarize the effects that assignment or casting have when performed upon data-object and function types. Recall that the three broad categories of data-object types—arithmetic, scalar, and aggregate—were repeatedly used in Chapter 12 to summarize which operators could be used with each data-object type. Scalar types represent one value, while aggregate types can represent several different values. Recall that arithmetic types (**char**, **int**, **enum**, **bit**, **float**, and **double**) represent a subset of scalar types and can be operated upon by the full complement of arithmetic operators. The remaining scalars (**_segment** and **pointer**) can be meaningfully operated upon only by a subset of the available arithmetic operators. The cast operator was found to be valid for use with arithmetic and scalar types, but not with aggregate type objects.

Table 13.3 examines the rules that govern the automatic (promotion, assignment) and explicit casting of arithmetic type objects.

Note that for each entry there is an example shown both in decimal (base 10) and hexadecimal (base 16) to clarify the effects that PB (preserve binary), SE (sign extend), TH (truncate high-order bits), and ZE (zero extend) have upon the value-preserving cast operation. Because fewer than half of the table entries shown guarantee the preservation of value, all casting and assignment of dissimilar types in C should be monitored carefully. Notice that all floating to integral type conversions (FI) enforce the new ANSI value-preserving philosophy (to **signed**, then **unsigned**). Also note the loss of significance (LS) that occurs when conversion is made between type **unsigned long** and **float**, and between type **double** and **float**.

Table 13.4 examines the rules that govern the automatic (balancing, assignment) and explicit casting between scalar (pointer) and arithmetic type objects.

TABLE 13.4: Microsoft C Scalar Type Casting

TO ———————▶ ▼ FROM	ARITHMETIC TYPE	DATA POINTER	FUNCTION POINTER
ARITHMETIC TYPE	OK, refer to Table 13.3	From `int` or `_segment` only; OK for `_near` and `_based`, not `_far` or `_huge`	From `int` only; OK for `_near`, not `_far`
DATA POINTER	To `int` or `_segment` only; OK for `_near` and `_based`, not `_far` or `_huge`	OK	Not recommended (non-Standard)
FUNCTION POINTER	To `int` only; OK for `_near`, not `_far`	Not recommended (non-Standard)	OK

Note that casting between pointer and integer types may occur for **`_near`** and **`_based`** pointers, but not **`_far`** or **`_huge`** pointers. This is explained by the fact that **`_far`** and **`_huge`** pointers store both the segment and offset address components, whereas **`_near`** and **`_based`** pointers do not (see Chapter 10, section "Pointer Operations"). Casting (conversion) is not recommended between data- and function-type pointers (addresses) because it would provide a convenient and undesirable means of dynamically modifying the logic of a program; however, with **`_based`** pointers it is now possible to allocate data-objects to a code segment. Standard C does not permit the casting between data and function pointers; however, because Microsoft C supports this non-Standard language extension feature (see Chapter 29), the indication "Not Recommended" is shown in Table 13.4.

STATEMENTS

Statements are always found in the body **{ .. }** of a function (see Chapter 14) and are commonly classified by the number of discrete actions they perform.

NUMBER OF ACTIONS	STATEMENT	SYNTAX
Zero	Null (**void**)	**;** (Semicolon only)
One	Simple	Expression; or keyword statement;

NUMBER OF ACTIONS	STATEMENT	SYNTAX
Zero or more	Compound (block)	**{** (Nothing or null) **;** (Semicolon) Expression; .. Statement; .. **}**

Null statements perform no actions and may be expressed by a semicolon or an empty set of braces **{ }**. Simple statements perform one action, are always semicolon terminated, and may represent either an expression statement (simple or compound) or any repetition, conditional branching, or unconditional branching statement described in the sections that follow. Compound statements (blocks) perform the actions of a group of null, simple, or other block statements, and are designated by surrounding a set of statements with braces **{..}**. When a statement block is specified, it is not semicolon terminated.

It is clear from this classification scheme that statements are capable of performing from zero to n-actions and, because expression statements do not involve the use of keywords, they cannot alter the default top-to-bottom processing of statements as keyword statements do.

Any expression that is semicolon terminated becomes an expression statement. Such statements direct the compiler to perform a computation (action) since all expressions represent value. Expression statements are described either as having side effects or as "valid, but not meaningful." For example:

```
int ival = 10;

ival++;         /* side effect, ival = 11 */
ival+=1;        /* side effect, ival = 11 */
ival < 10;      /* valid, but not meaningful */
ival - 10;      /* valid, but not meaningful */
```

Keyword statements utilize expressions that either yield a value, perform a test, or produce only side effects. For example:

```
ival - 10       /* yields a value of 0 */
ival < 10       /* performs a test, false (0) or true (1) */
ival++          /* side effect, ival = 11 */
```

The statements that involve the use of Standard C keywords will be discussed in the sections that follow, and have been grouped into three broad categories: repetition statements (looping), conditional branching (testing), and unconditional branching (jumping). Each of these statement types is used to alter the default top-to-bottom order of processing statements in C and provides the logic that controls the order in which the statements of a program are performed.

Repetition

Repetition statement types are used to repeat the execution of other statements (null, simple, or block). Repetition may be introduced using three different keywords that parallel other high-level languages and are commonly referred to as a fixed-iteration (**for**), a pretest (**while**), or a posttest (**do..while**) loop. Although care must always be taken to avoid the inadvertent construction of an infinite pretest or posttest loop condition, it is even possible in C, unlike other languages, to construct an infinite loop with the fixed-iteration **for**-loop. Let's examine the syntax and behavior of each of these repetition statement types.

for

The **for**-loop statement in C facilitates the construction of fixed-iteration loops, but in reality it represents a hybrid of a fixed and pretest type construct. Because of its pretest structure, the statement or statement block of a **for**-loop may be performed from *zero* to *n* times. The syntax and behavior of a **for**-loop is depicted in Figure 13.2.

Note that expr1 is an initializer and as such is performed first and only once. Expr2 represents a pretest or relational expression that is performed after expr1 and before each iteration of the loop. If the result of expr2 is false (0), the loop ends; otherwise the statement or statement block is performed, followed by expr3, which is an incrementor that typically is responsible for varying a term of expr2, the test expression. When expr3 is completed, expr2 is repeated to either terminate or continue the next iteration of the loop. The parentheses surrounding expr1, expr2, and expr3 are required. Consider the following examples:

```
int i, j=0;

for (i=0; i<10000; i++,j++) ;          /* null statement */

for (i=0,j=0; i<10000; i++) j++;       /* simple statement */

for (i=0,j=0; i<10000) {               /* block statement */
    i++;
    j++;
    }
```

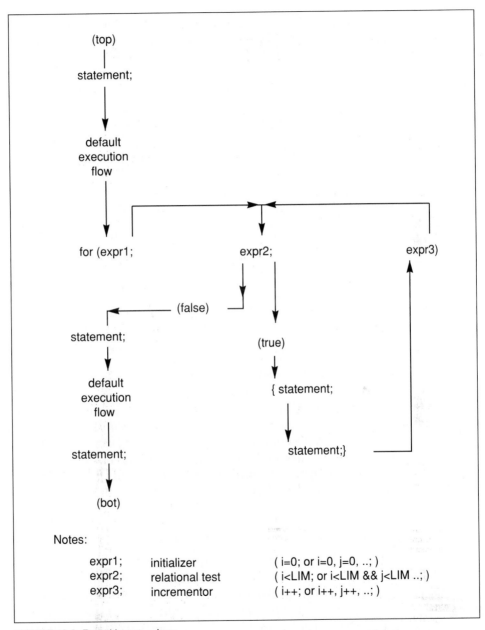

FIGURE 13.2: Repetition: `for`-loop.

All three examples above perform the identical task of incrementing the operator (see Chapter 12) may be used to replace the single expressions (expr1, expr2, and expr3) with more than one expression, and by virtue of the comma operator's associativity, the expressions are evaluated left to right.

The expr1, expr2, and expr3 components of the **for**-loop may also be omitted. The following example would accomplish the same result as the examples shown above:

```
int i=0, j=0;

for (;i<10000;) {
    i++;
    j++;
    }
```

In this case, both the initializer (expr1) and the incrementor (expr3) are treated as null statements.

It is also possible to construct an infinite **for**-loop that accomplishes the same result.

```
int i=0, j=0;

for (;;) {
    i++;
    j++;
    if (i>=10000) break;
    }
```

Notice that when the relational test (expr2) is omitted, the test is always considered true (nonzero) and therefore establishes an infinite loop that can be terminated only if a **break**, **goto**, **return**, or nonreturning function statement (**abort()**, **execxxx()**, **exit()**, **setjmp()/longjmp()**, **raise()/signal()**, **spawnxxx()**, or certain DOS/BIOS systems calls) is encountered in the statement block.

while

The **while**-loop statement in C facilitates the construction of pretest type loops, which permit the associated statement or statement block to be performed from *zero* to *n* times. The syntax and behavior of a **while**-loop is patterned after a **for**-loop, without the initializer and incrementor expressions. A relational expression (test) must evaluate true (nonzero) for the statement or statement block to be performed; otherwise, statement processing continues with the statement immediately following the

while-loop itself. Consider the following examples:

```
int i=0;

while (i<10000) i++;      /* simple statement */

while (i<10000) {         /* block statement */
    i++;
    }
```

Unlike a **for**-loop, the relational expression (test) must always be specified and enclosed in parentheses as shown. All necessary variable initialization must occur before the **while**-loop is encountered, and all incrementation must be performed within the statement block itself.

To construct an infinite loop, simply use a relational expression (test) or constant value that is always considered to be true (nonzero). For example:

```
while (1)  ..
while (!0) ..
while (~0) ..
while (-1) ..
```

As in the case of infinite **for**-loops, infinite **while**-loops can be terminated only if a **break**, **goto**, **return**, or nonreturning function statement (**abort()**, **execxxx()**, **exit()**, **setjmp()/longjmp()**, **raise()/signal()**, **spawnxxx()**, or certain DOS/BIOS systems calls) is encountered in the statement block.

do..while

The **do..while**-loop statement in C facilitates the construction of posttest type loops, which permit the associated statement or statement block to be performed from *one* to *n* times. The syntax and behavior of a **do..while**-loop parallels that of a **while**-loop but places the relational expression (test) at the end of the loop, thereby always performing the associated statement at least one time. The relational expression (test) must evaluate true (nonzero) for the statement or statement block to be repeated; otherwise, statement processing continues with the statement immediately following the **while**-loop itself. Consider the following examples:

```
int i=0;

do i++;
while (i<10000);     /* simple statement */

do  {
    i++;
} while (i<10000);  /* block statement */
```

As in the **while**-loop, the relational expression (test) in a **do..while**-loop must always be specified and enclosed in parentheses as shown. Notice that a semicolon is always needed to terminate a **do..while**-loop. All necessary variable initialization must occur before the **do..while**-loop is encountered, and all incrementation must be performed within the statement block itself.

To construct an infinite loop, simply use a relational expression (test) or constant value that is always considered to be true (nonzero), as presented for the **while**-loop above. For example

```
do .. while (1);
do .. while (!0);
do .. while (~0);
do .. while (-1);
```

As in the case of infinite **for**- and **while**-loops, infinite **do..while**-loops can be terminated only if a **break, goto, return**, or nonreturning function statement (**abort()**, **execxxx()**, **exit()**, **setjmp()/longjmp()**, **raise()/signal()**, **spawnxxx()**, or certain DOS/BIOS systems calls) is encountered in the statement block.

Conditional Branching

Conditional branching statements are used to skip the execution of other statements (null, simple, or block). Conditional branching enables decision points to be introduced in the logic of a program in the form of relational expressions (tests yielding true or false), which can be used to implement the processing of from *one* to *n* different alternatives. Four different constructs are available in C, which parallel other high-level languages to differentiate between one alternative (**if..stmt**), two alternatives (**if..stmt1..else..stmt2**), or multiple alternatives (**if..stmt1..else..if..stmt***n*.. or **switch..stmt***n*). Let's examine the syntax and behavior of each of these conditional branching statement types.

if..stmt

The **if..stmt** statement in C facilitates the implementation of a simple one-way test. If the relational expression (test) is true (nonzero), the associated statement (null, simple, or block) is performed; otherwise, statement processing continues with the statement immediately following

if..stmt. Consider the following examples:

```
int i=0, j=0;

if (i>0) ;          /* null statement */

if (i<=0) i++;      /* simple statement */

if (i==0) {         /* block statement */
    i++;
    j++;
    }
```

The relational expression (test) must always be specified and be enclosed in parentheses as shown.

It is also possible for the statement (**stmt**) to be another **if** statement, such as

```
if (i>=0) if (i<=3) i++;
```

This could be expressed equivalently using a compound relational expression:

```
if (i>=0 && i<=3) i++;
```

thus eliminating the need to introduce another **if..stmt**.

if..stmt1..else..stmt2

The **if..stmt1..else..stmt2** statement in C facilitates the implementation of a simple two-way test. If the relational expression (test) is true (nonzero), the associated statement (null, simple, or block), **stmt1**, is performed; otherwise, statement **stmt2** is performed. Consider the following examples:

```
int i=0, j=0;

if (i<=0) ;         /* null statement */
else i++;           /* simple statement */

if (i<=0) {         /* null block statement */
    }
else {              /* block statement */
    i++;
    j++;
    }
```

The relational expression (test) must always be specified and enclosed in parentheses as shown. Any combination of statement types (null, simple, block) may be used to represent **stmt1** and **stmt2**. As we will discover in

"Performance Considerations" below, the `if..stmt1..else..stmt2` construct is favored when a simple two-way test is needed.

if..stmt1..else..if..stmtn..

The `if..stmt1..else..if..stmtn..` statement in C facilitates the implementation of multiway tests. If the first relational expression (test1) is true (nonzero), the associated statement (null, simple, or block), `stmt1`, is performed, and a branch occurs to the statement following this construction; otherwise, if the nth relational expression (test$n$) is true (nonzero), then statement `stmtn` is performed. Consider the following examples:

```
int i=0, j=0;

if (i<0) ;                  /* null statement */
else if (i==0) i++;         /* simple statement */
else if (i>0) { i++;
   j++; }                   /* block statement */
```

The relational expression (test) must always be specified and enclosed in parentheses as shown. Any combination of statement types (null, simple, block) may be used to represent `stmt1` through `stmtn`. When a true (nonzero) test is encountered, the associated nth statement is performed, and processing continues with the statement immediately following the complete `if..stmt1..else..if..stmtn`. As we will discover in "Performance Considerations" below, however, the `switch..stmtn` construct is favored when a multiway test is needed.

switch..stmtn

The switch statement in C facilitates the implementation of multiway tests and is also recommended over the alternate construct `if..stmt1..else..if..stmtn..` when it is applicable. The switch statement in C parallels the CASE..END statement available in Pascal and the SELECT..ENDSELECT statement available in Fortran. The syntax of the switch statement is depicted in Figure 13.3.

Note that unlike the syntax of the other conditional branching constructs in C, expression `iexpr` is not a relational expression (test), but rather is an integral (qualified type `int` or `long`) expression, yielding a value against which the `case` integer constant expressions `ival1` through `ivaln` are compared. `ival1` through `ivaln` expressions must not be duplicated.

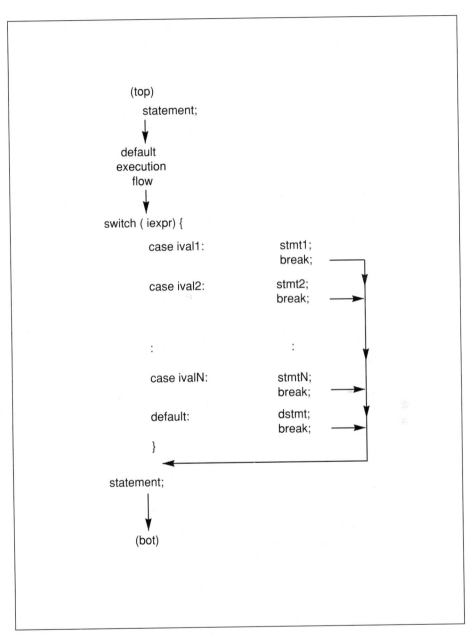

FIGURE 13.3: Conditional branching: switch.

Notes:

iexpr	Any qualified type int or long expression
case	C keyword; unlimited number of case statements
ival1 :	Integer constant expressions only
ival2 :	No duplicate values permitted
ivalN :	Cast to type iexpr for comparison
default:	No-match case; optional; only one permitted
break	Optional; transfer control outside of switch; if not specified, all succeeding statements encountered are performed.

FIGURE 13.3: Conditional branching: switch. (continued)

Since the value of **iexpr** is compared against each **ival1** through **ivaln** in the default top-to-bottom order, arrange the test values from most probable to least probable to improve the performance of a **switch** statement. When a match occurs, the corresponding statement(s) are performed, and if a **break** statement is included as shown, control immediately transfers to the statement following the **switch** statement itself. If the **break** statement is omitted, all succeeding statements are performed in the order encountered! Clearly, each case **ivaln** expression simply becomes a label to which control is transferred when a match (equality) is encountered.

If none of the case **ivaln** values match the value of **iexpr**, control passes to the **default:** label, if it is included, and **dstmt(s)**, are performed as shown in Figure 13.3. If no **default:** label is included, control passes to the statement immediately following the **switch** statement itself, and no **case** statements are performed at all. The **case** and **default** keywords in C represent reserved labels (see the "**goto** label:" section). Consider the following example:

```
int ch = 'A';

switch (ch) {
   case 'A': break;
   case 'B': ch = 'A';
             break;
   case 'C': ch = 'A';
             break;
   case 'D': ch = 'A';
             break;
   default:  ch = '\0';
             break;
   }
```

In the preceding example all uppercase symbols (**'A'**, **'B'**, **'C'**, and **'D'**) are converted to uppercase symbol **A**, while all other **ch**-values are set equal to the null character because the **default:** label is present.

Note that all **ival1** through **ivaln** expressions are single values and never represent multiples or ranges of value. To accomplish this effect, which would have been useful in the preceding example, consider the following revision:

```
switch (ch) {
    case 'A':
    case 'B':
    case 'C':
    case 'D': ch = 'A';
              break;
    default:  ch = '\0';
              break;
    }
```

The preceding example associates the labels **case 'A':**, **case 'B':**, **case 'C':**, and **case 'D':** with the same statement to be performed.

Unconditional Branching

Unconditional branching statement types are used to transfer program control. Unconditional branching is not based upon a condition test, but provides another means of altering the normal logic (top to bottom, repetition, or conditional branching) that can be expressed in C. Four different keywords are available in C that provide the ability to transfer control or jump: the **break**, **continue**, **goto**, and **return** statements. Run-time library functions (see Part VII) supplement these keywords and provide other means to transfer control (**abort()**, **execxxx()**, **exit()**, **setjmp()/longjmp()**, **raise()/signal()**, **spawnxxx()**, and certain DOS/BIOS systems calls). Let's examine the syntax and behavior of each of the keyword unconditional branching statement types.

break

The **break** statement may be used only within a **for**-loop, **while**-loop, **do**-loop, or **switch** statement and provides a mechanism for immediate transfer of control to the statement following the block { .. } containing the **break** statement itself. The **break** statement may transfer control only from one level of nesting. Other high-level languages sometimes provide the ability to "break *n*," or to transfer control from *n*-levels of nesting. In C, the **goto** statement must be used to accomplish *n*-level transfers of control (see the "**goto** label:" section).

In the "Repetition" section above, the **break** statement was used to terminate an infinite loop, and in the "Conditional Branching" section above, the **break** statement supported the need to exit the **switch** statement after performing the statements associated with a particular **case** label.

continue

The **continue** statement may be used only within a **for**-loop, **while**-loop, or **do**-loop and immediately initiates the next iteration of the looping structure containing the **continue** statement itself.

If a **continue** statement is encountered within a **for**-loop of the form

```
for (expr1; expr2; expr3) {
    statement1;
    continue;
    statementN; }
```

then statement 1 is performed, and control is immediately transferred to incrementor expression, expr3. The relational test expression, expr2, is then evaluated to determine whether another iteration of the loop is to be performed. In this example, **statementN** is not performed.

If a **continue** statement is encountered within a **while**-loop of the form

```
while (expr) {
    statement1;
    continue;
    statementN; }
```

then control is immediately transferred to the relational expression (expr) which is evaluated to determine whether another iteration of the loop is to be performed. **StatementN** is not performed.

If a **continue** statement is encountered within a **do**-loop of the form

```
do { statement1;
    continue;
    statementN;
} while (expr);
```

then control is immediately transferred to the relational expression (expr) which is evaluated to determine whether another iteration of the loop is to be performed. **StatementN** is not performed.

goto *Label:*

The **goto** statement may transfer control only to a label within the same function. Recall from Chapter 4 that labels represent one of four distinct categories of identifiers in the C language. The **goto** statement is characterized as a local transfer of control mechanism because all labels have a scope (visibility) that is restricted to the function in which they are defined. That is, they begin with a letter or underscore, are followed by a letter, digit, or the underscore character, and provide up to 31 characters of uniqueness. Labels are terminated with a colon (:), and always precede a statement. The labels

```
label_1: ;                /* null statement label */
label_2: statement;       /* simple statement label */
label_3: { statement(s); }  /* block statement label */
```

may be *jumped* to within a function simply by issuing a **goto** statement to the label name, as follows:

```
goto label_1;
goto label_2;
goto label_3;
```

Notice that a **goto** statement uses the label name, which does not include the colon (:). The colon punctuator differentiates label identifiers from all other identifier types. The **goto** statement itself is semicolon terminated. Note, however, that the labels **case** and **default**, used within a **switch** statement may not be used by a **goto** statement.

Since the **goto** statement can be used to transfer control from one statement block to another (*n* levels of nesting) within a function, such jumps can affect how data objects are initialized. Recall that whenever a block { .. } is introduced, data objects may be declared. Every object that is declared has a storage class (lifetime and visibility) associated with it. Objects of storage class **extern** or **static** have the lifetime or duration of the program itself and are allocated storage and initialized at compile-time, whereas **auto** and **register** storage-class objects have a lifetime or duration typically less than that of the program itself and are dynamically allocated storage and initialized at run-time.

The use of **goto** statements does not affect how **extern** or **static** storage-class objects are initialized but may affect the initialization of **auto** or **register** storage-class objects.

When blocks that allocate **auto** or **register** storage-class objects are entered in a normal fashion (from top to bottom), data-object allocation and initialization proceed normally. When such blocks are entered by a transfer of control (**goto**) to a label within the block, data-object storage is performed normally, but no data initialization occurs! Consider the following partial function example:

```
int isw=0;
goto label_5;
label_4:
{
    int ival = 10;
    label_5: printf("\nival = %d",++ival);
    ival=0;
    if (isw) break;
    else { isw++;
        goto label_4; }
}
```

The first entry to the block is abnormal, by a **goto** jump to **label_5**; therefore, the printed value of **++ival** would be questionable because, although the storage for object **ival** was allocated, it was not initialized to the value of ten. However, when the **goto label_4** statement is encountered, the block is entered in a normal fashion, and object **ival** is allocated and properly initialized, producing the predictable value 11.

The run-time library functions **setjmp()** and **longjmp()** provide for the ability to perform *nonlocal* jumps, or unconditional branches between functions, which is not permitted with the **goto** statement. For more about nonlocal jumps, see Chapter 25.

Note that local and nonlocal jumps should be used sparingly because they tend to subvert the design objectives embodied in the structured programming paradigm.

return

The **return** statement immediately terminates the execution of a function, transfers control to the expression that called the function, and optionally returns an expression value that is compatible with the declared function return type. **return** statements may be used only from within the body of a function (see Chapter 14).

If a function is declared to have a **return** type of **void**, such as

```
void myfunc()
{
statement(s);
}
```

then no **return** statement may be specified; otherwise a compiler error will result.

If a function is declared to have any **return** type other than **void**, such as

EXAMPLE A

```
int myfunc()
{
statement(s);
/* Error—no return
statement */
}
```

EXAMPLE B

```
int myfunc()
{
statement(s);
return; /* Error—no return
value */
}
```

and no **return** statement is provided as shown above in Example A, or no **return** expression is included as shown in Example B, then the integer **return** value is undefined. The function **return** statements should be corrected in such instances.

If a function is declared to have a **return** type other than **void**, such as

EXAMPLE C

```
int myfunc()
{
statement(s);
return expr;
}
```

EXAMPLE D

```
int myfunc()
{
statement(s);
return (expr);
}
```

and return statements are provided, then expr should be assignment-compatible with the declared **return** type **int**. As shown in Example C, enclosing parentheses may be omitted, or included as shown in Example D. If expr were not of type **int**, then expr would be promoted or cast, as if assignment of the expression had occurred.

When a function is called that returns a value, the **return** value may be either captured or ignored. For example:

```
int ival;
ival = myfunc();     /* capture return value */
myfunc();            /* ignore return value */
```

Table 13.5 has been prepared to summarize all of the possible value types that may be used in the expression of a return statement. Notice that all types described in Part III and used in Chapter 12 are identified in Table 13.5. For a description of the mechanism by which values are returned by functions, refer to Chapter 15.

All functions in C may utilize the **return** statement. However, since a **return** from function **main()** actually is a **return** to the host operating

TABLE 13.5: Allowable `return` Types

OBJECT	RETURN OBJECT?	RETURN OBJECT POINTER?
`char`	Yes	Yes
`int`	Yes	Yes
`enum`	Yes	Yes
`float`	Yes	Yes
`double`	Yes	Yes
`void`	No	Yes
Integral bit	No[1]	No[2]
Bit-field	No	No
`_segment`	Yes	Yes
Pointer	Yes	Yes
Array	No[3]	Yes[4]
Array element	Yes[5]	Yes
Structure	Yes[5]	Yes
Structure member	Yes[5]	Yes
Union	Yes[5]	Yes
Union member	Yes[5]	Yes
Function	No	Yes

NOTES:
1. Only the object of which it is a part.
2. Only a pointer to the object of which it is a part.
3. Since an array name is a pointer.
4. Using only the array name.
5. Unless itself an array.

system DOS, the **return** statement should not be used with **main()**; use an **exit()** function call instead. For more on function **main()**, see Chapter 15.

PERFORMANCE CONSIDERATIONS

Given the fact that three comparable statement types are available that perform repetition (**for**-loop, **while**-loop, **do..while**-loop), it would seem that one method might offer a performance advantage over the others. For example, does the apparent complexity of the **for**-loop make it slower? To resolve this question and any others you may have about

```
/* FILE: ch13e1.c */
#define TIMER
#include "timer.h"
#define LIM 30000

int main(void)
{
long i, j;

START(for-loop);
j=0;
for(i=1;i<=LIM;i++)j+=i;
STOP;
printf("\ni=%ld   j=%ld",i,j);

START(while-loop);
j=0;
i=1;
while(i<=LIM) { j+=i; i+=1; }
STOP;
printf("\ni=%ld   j=%ld",i,j);

START(do-while-loop);
j=0;
i=1;
do { j+=i; i+=1; } while (i<=LIM);
STOP;
printf("\ni=%ld   j=%ld",i,j);
exit(0);
}
```

FIGURE 13.4: The sample program ch13e1.c evaluates the performance characteristics of the for-loop, while-loop, and do-while-loop repetition statements.

selecting a repetition statement type in C, consider the program listed in Figure 13.4. It measures the relative performance of each statement type, using the preprocessor timing macros, **START()** and **STOP**, developed in Chapter 5.

The following output was produced using the QC compiler with the Small memory model on an $80x86$ computer with floating-point emulation. As you can see, all three repetition statement types perform identically.

```
for  : for-loop
time : 2.20 sec
i=30001   j=450015000

for  : while-loop
time : 2.20 sec
i=30001   j=450015000

for  : do-while-loop
time : 2.20 sec
i=30001   j=450015000
```

The three statement types also perform identically for constructing an infinite loop.

We have taken a similar approach to examine the relative merits of using the four comparable statement types that are available to perform conditional branching: the `if..stmt`, `if..stmt1..else..stmt2`, `if stmt1..else..if..stmtn..`, and `switch..stmtn` statements. Again, it would seem that one statement type might offer a performance advantage over the others. Does the apparent complexity of the switch statement make it slower? To resolve this question and any others you may have about selecting a conditional branching statement type in C, consider the program listed in Figure 13.5, which measures the relative performance of each statement type, again using the preprocessor timing macros, **START()** and **STOP**, developed in Chapter 5.

The following output was produced using the same configuration as for Figure 13.4. It can be concluded that each conditional branching statement type is preferred under different circumstances:

```
for  : if stmts #1            /* if..stmt is the best */
time : 2.42 sec               /* for one-way tests */
for  : if else stmt #1
time : 2.42 sec
for  : switch stmt #1
time : 2.70 sec

for  : if stmts #2
time : 3.96 sec
for  : if else stmt #2        /* if..stmt1..else..stmt2 */
time : 2.53 sec               /* is best for two-way tests */
for  : switch stmt #2
time : 2.96 sec

for  : if stmts #3
time : 5.55 sec
for  : if else stmt #3
time : 3.57 sec
for  : switch stmt #3         /* switch..stmtn is best */
time : 3.02 sec               /* for multi-way tests */
```

Note that the `if..stmt` statement type is preferred when performing a test for one alternative, the `if..stmt1..else..stmt2` statement type is preferred when performing a test for two alternatives, and the `switch..stmtn` statement type is preferred when performing a test for multiple alternatives.

```
/* FILE: ch13e2.c */
#define TIMER
#include "timer.h"
#define LIM 30000
#define REPEAT for(i=0;i<LIM;i++)

int main(void)
{
int i, j;

START(if stmts #1);
REPEAT { if (i%2==0) j=0; }    STOP;

START(if else stmt #1);
REPEAT { if (i%2==0) j=0;
         else; }               STOP;

START(switch stmt #1);
REPEAT switch (i%2)
       { case 0: j=0; }         STOP;

START(if stmts #2);
REPEAT { if (i%2==0) j=0;
         if (i%2==1) j=1; }    STOP;

START(if else stmt #2);
REPEAT { if (i%2==0) j=0;
         else j=1; }            STOP;

START(switch stmt #2);
REPEAT switch (i%2)
       { case 0: j=0;
                 break;
         case 1: j=1; }         STOP;

START(if stmts #3);
REPEAT { if (i%3==0) j=0;
         if (i%3==1) j=1;
         if (i%3==2) j=2; }    STOP;

START(if else stmt #3);
REPEAT { if (i%3==0) j=0;
         else if (i%3==1) j=1;
         else j=2; }            STOP;

START(switch stmt #3);
REPEAT switch (i%3)
       { case 0: j=0;
                 break;
         case 1: j=1;
                 break;
         case 2: j=2; }         STOP;
exit(0);
}
```

FIGURE 13.5: The sample program ch13e2.c evaluates the performance characteristics of the if...stmt, if...else...stmt, and switch...stmt conditional branching statements.

PART

5

Writing Functions in C

Just as we discovered in Part IV that expressions are the building blocks of the C language, we will now find that functions are the building blocks of C programs, because they contain the actions that a program is to perform.

All C functions have an identical template, composed of a unique name, a return type, argument(s), and a body. Function names, like array names in C, are the only identifiers that are treated as pointers without explicitly being declared as such. The return type of a function is understood to represent its value. Functions may optionally be declared to accept arguments. A function body contains expression and keyword statements that control the actions that are to be performed.

Since function names are pointers, you must understand how to declare not only function prototypes, but function pointers as well. Such declarations are considered complex because they involve more than one array `[]`, indirection (`*`), grouping parentheses `(..)`, or function `()` postfix operator and they are, by far, the most difficult expressions both to construct and interpret in the C language. To do so requires an understanding of the so-called "right-left" rule.

Chapter 14 explains the declaration of functions, function pointers, and function prototypes in a manner that parallels the tabular-declaration approach first introduced in Part III to simplify the expression and interpretation of data declarations. The use of function pointers as function argument and return value is also presented and function prototypes are reexamined to supplement the discussion introduced in Chapter 6.

Chapter 15 examines the unique characteristics of function `main()`, which is the interface to the DOS operating system. The function arguments passed to `main()` are those from the DOS command line, and any return values from `main()` are treated by DOS as exit `<status>` codes. The roles that the C startup code, stack, and heap play during program execution are also clarified, including an explanation of how stack frames are used to implement function calls, and how registers are used to return values. Finally, the `execxxx()`, `spawnxxx()`, and `system()` functions are introduced, which also can be used to initiate the execution of a C program.

The material presented in Parts I through V completes the explanation of the Standard C Language itself. Part V provides the missing function ingredient that integrates the use of C's keywords, operators, and statement types; provides the component necessary to begin the development of project-specific function libraries; and explains the properties common to all C run-time library functions described in Parts VI and VII.

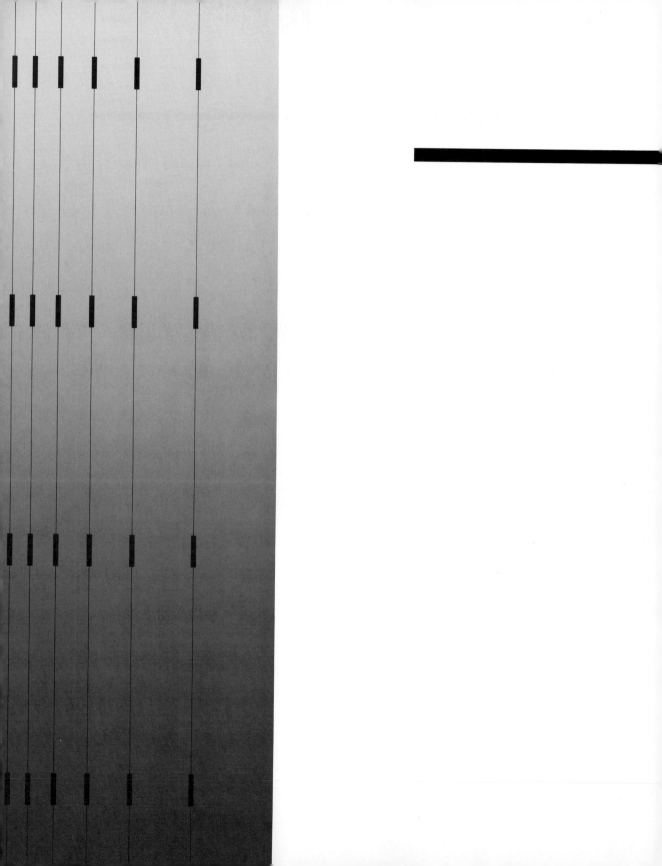

Function Subprograms

Function Subprograms

Part III introduced the concept of type and described the data object and incomplete forms of value representation, but deferred the discussion of function types to Chapters 14 and 15. As we will discover, function-type objects represent value, as data-object types do, but they also control the flow of program execution.

Every C function has a common template or structure composed of a name, return type, argument(s), and a body. The value representation of the function type is its return type, while the flow of execution is expressed by the statements contained within the body.

Unlike BASIC, Fortran, and Pascal, C does not make a distinction between the main program, subroutines, procedures, and functions; rather, the basic program building block is simply the function type. C is not a completely block-structured language like Pascal, because a C function may not be declared within another function; however, C does support recursion, which permits a function to invoke itself.

Function declarations are complex because the components of a function may be qualified to refine their type descriptions. A function declaration that describes the function object itself, its arguments, and return type, but omits the body, is called a prototype; however, the storage space for a function is allocated only when the description of the function body is also provided.

This chapter will simplify the process of expressing function declarations by using the tabular-declaration approach first introduced in Part III, and by clarifying the so-called "right-left" rule used to interpret and construct complex descriptions that involve the use of the subscripting []..[], indirection *, grouping parentheses (), and the function postfix operator ().

Once the basic technique for declaring functions that have a fixed or variable number of arguments is understood, then techniques for the declaration of function pointer objects will be examined to permit functions to be used as function argument and return values, as elements of an array, as members of structures and unions, and as **typedef**s and casts.

The new and expanded role that function prototyping plays with Standard C is explored, together with an explanation of the interrelationships that exist between the continued use of the old-style K&R function return type declarations, and the new-style Standard C and C++ function argument and return type declarations.

Finally, some techniques that can improve overall program performance dramatically, including the use of register storage-class function arguments, function-like macros, and intrinsic functions are examined.

FUNCTION DECLARATIONS

All function declarations describe the function, argument, and return types of function objects. Objects of type function occupy storage (memory) and are allocated only when they are defined **{ .. }**, not simply declared (**;**). The object definition concept introduced in Part III applies to functions as well. Every function in C, whether included in the C runtime library or in one you've purchased or custom-developed, has a common template or structure that it follows. Table 14.1 summarizes the four components of every function in the C language: return type, function name, argument(s), and function body.

The return and argument component declarations always represent types and hence value: data-object, incomplete, or function types. Each of these object types in turn may be qualified to refine the properties attributed to it. The function name identifies the entire function object, which has a storage class and can be described further by the use of non-Standard qualifiers that convey mixed language, register handling, and function addressing properties.

Since all function identifiers (names) must be externally defined (outside of braces), they are considered external definitions and, as such, may be assigned only storage class **extern** or **static**, thereby establishing the function's visibility as either global or file-only, respectively.

Every function in C (even function **main()**, discussed in Chapter 15) follows this function definition template. This simplifies and promotes the development of modular, reusable C code. The use of any function, once tested and reliable, becomes a simple matter: Provide an **#include** statement for the header file that contains the function's prototype declaration, then invoke it with the appropriate type and number of arguments, and finally capture or ignore its return value. Because each function-type object represents a value, functions may be used within the C programming environment wherever the return-type value (or cast value) is appropriate. Let's examine the qualifiers that may be used to define the properties of a function and its return and argument types.

Function-Type Qualifiers

Since all functions are types, and types represent value in C, all functions become objects that occupy storage (memory). Any C type object in memory has an associated storage class and, except for bit objects, is

TABLE 14.1: Function Definition Template

TEMPLATE
| ```
return-type function-name (argument declaration(s))
        {
            function body
        }
``` |

COMPONENT	DESCRIPTION
Return-Type	Any qualified data object or incomplete type, except arrays and functions; however, pointers to arrays and functions are permitted. If omitted, type **int** is assumed. (See Tables 14.4, 14.5, and 14.7.) In the example below, the return type is **unsigned int**.
Function-Name	Any valid qualified identifier within scope (**static** or **extern**); up to 31 symbols, the first of which is a letter or underscore character, and subsequent symbols being either a letter, digit, or an underscore. (See Tables 14.2 and 14.3.) In the example below, **myfunc** is the function name.
Argument Declaration	Formal parameter declarations (like return-type above). Include a variable name if other than type **void**, are separated by commas, and are of storage class **auto** by default or **register** if specified. Either no arguments (**void**), a fixed number of arguments, or a variable number of arguments (ellipsis . . .) may be specified. (See Table 14.6.) In the example below, the arguments are **int ival** and **int modulus;**.
Function Body	A block or compound statement optionally containing declarations followed by statements (null, simple, block), and containing a return statement if the return type is other than type **void**.

EXAMPLE
| ```
unsigned myfunc ( int ival, int modulus )
        {
            unsigned int temp;
            temp = ival % modulus;
            return (temp);
        }
``` |

addressable. Recall that Standard C establishes minimum requirements that must be met for an implementation of the compiler to meet the ANSI Standard. However, nothing prevents a vendor's implementation from exceeding these minimum requirements. Microsoft C provides additional non-Standard keywords that qualify the properties of function-type objects. Table 14.2 summarizes these Microsoft keywords.

Each of the keywords, except those categorized as register handling, was introduced earlier in Tables 7.4 and 7.6.

The mixed language qualifiers **_cdecl**, **_fortran**, and **_pascal** are used to convey both function naming (upper/lowercase, and length) and stack argument ordering properties, and are applicable for use with both data and function types; however, the keywords **_export** and **_fastcall** are for use only with function types.

The **_export** keyword should be used to create functions that will reside in a dynamic-link library (DLL), or be used by Microsoft's Windows, Presentation Manager, or OS/2 products. The **_export** keyword may be specified with **_cdecl**, **_fortran**, and **_pascal**, but not **_fastcall**.

The **_fastcall** keyword causes the function arguments to be passed in registers, rather than on the stack as described in Chapter 15. There is no performance advantage gained by the use of **_fastcall** with

TABLE 14.2: Function-Type Qualifiers

LIFETIME AND VISIBILITY[1]	MIXED LANGUAGE[2]	REGISTER HANDLING[3]	FUNCTION ADDRESSING[4]
[extern]	[_cdecl]	[none]	[memory model]
static	_cdecl	_interrupt	_near
extern	_export	_loadds	_far
	_fastcall	_saveregs	
	_pascal _fortran		

NOTES:
1. Lifetime and Visibility (storage-class) qualifier must appear first with Standard C. **[extern]** assumed if **static** and **extern** omitted.
2. **_fastcall** is incompatible with **_cdecl**, **_export**, **_fortran**, **_pascal**, **_interrupt**, and **_saveregs**. See Tables 7.4 and 14.3; **_export** is compatible with **_cdecl**, **_fortran**, and **_pascal**, but restricted for use with DLL (Dynamic Link Libraries) used with OS/2.
3. More than one choice is permitted; however, **_saveregs** and **_interrupt** are mutually exclusive, and **_interrupt** must always be specified with **_cdecl** and **_far**. See Table 14.3.
4. Function addressing may never be **_huge** or **_based**.

QuickC; however, gains will be realized when using OptimizingC. Use of compiler option **/Gr** enables **_fastcall** for all functions, while the **_fastcall** keyword enables this feature on a function-by-function basis. Note, however, that the use of **_fastcall** is incompatible with functions for which **_cdecl**, **_export**, **_fortran**, **_pascal**, **_interrupt**, or **_saveregs** are specified, for functions that have a variable number of arguments, or for functions using inline assembly (see Chapter 28).

The register handling qualifiers, **_interrupt**, **_loadds**, and **_saveregs**, described in Table 14.3, are used to override the normal function calling and return register conventions that are used with the 80x86 processors.

The **_interrupt** keyword indicates that the function is an interrupt handler and causes the compiler to generate the appropriate entry and exit sequences necessary to save and restore all registers and execute an assembly language IRET, (rather than RET) instruction to return (see Chapter 27). The **_interrupt** keyword must be specified together with **_cdecl** and **_far**, and never with **_saveregs**.

The **_loadds** keyword causes a specific segment value to be loaded into the DS register upon entry to the function, and the previous DS register value to be restored upon exiting the function. Either the segment value specified with compiler option **/ND** is loaded, or the DGROUP (Data Group) segment is loaded. Use of compiler option **/Au** enables **_loadds** for all functions, while the **_loadds** keyword enables this feature on a function-by-function basis.

The **_saveregs** keyword saves all register values upon function entry, and restores all register values upon returning, except those used to return the function type (see Table 15.2). The use of **_saveregs** is incompatible with **_interrupt**.

Notice that the function addressing qualifiers shown do not include the keywords **_huge** and **_based**, which are data-object, not function

TABLE 14.3: Register-Handling Type Qualifiers

QUALIFIER	DESCRIPTION	USE ONLY WITH
_interrupt	Function interrupt handling designator	Interrupt functions; always with **_cdecl** and **_far**; never with **_saveregs** (see Chapter 27).
_loadds	Control DS register loading on function entry	**_far** and **_huge** data segments only.
_saveregs	Automatic save and restore of registers on function entry/exit	Inline assembly and mixed-language interfaces; never with **_interrupt**; (see Chapter 28).

(code)- object qualifiers. Since function names, like array names, are themselves pointers, they may be addressed using either **_near** (representing a 16-bit offset to the default code segment register) or **_far** (representing a complete 32-bit segment:offset memory address).

The use of these function-type qualifiers is demonstrated by the examples accompanying Tables 14.4 and 14.5, which follow. Let's now examine the possible type objects that may be returned by a function and represent the value of the function-type object itself.

Return Types

Functions always return a type object, because the return-type of a function represents the value of the function object itself. In Chapter 13 the return statement was described as the mechanism by which functions return their declared return type (value). Table 13.5 summarized the "allowable return types" and hence the set of possible function return type declarations that may be specified.

Note from Table 13.5 that all object types, except **void**, bits, arrays, and functions, may be returned as objects. Functions may be declared as type **void**, but in that case, no **return** value may be specified by the **return** statement. A function may then be defined to return nothing by declaring a return type of **void**. Notice that unlike arrays and functions, entire structure and union-type objects may be returned. For a description of the actual mechanism used to return values, refer to Chapter 15.

Data Objects

Table 14.4 summarizes, in the tabular-declaration format first introduced in Chapter 7, the syntax and default qualifiers that may be used to declare (and define) functions that return the data-object types described in Table 13.5 (except pointer, array, and function-type objects, which will be described in sections that follow). Notice that any function declaration that does not specify a return base type is assumed to represent type **int**. This is consistent with the fundamental data-object declaration conventions described in Chapter 7.

Each function and return type declaration (without argument declarations) is developed by optionally combining the qualifiers shown in Table 14.4 by the following column categories:

- Lifetime and Visibility (function)
- Modifiable Type (return)
- Sign (return)

TABLE 14.4A: Syntax of Functions Returning Data-Object Types

LIFETIME AND VISIBILITY[1]	MODIFIABLE TYPE[2]	SIGN	SIZE	RETURN BASE TYPE[3]
[extern] static	[none] const volatile	[signed] unsigned	[none]	char
[extern] static	[none] const volatile	[signed] unsigned	[none] short long	int [none]
[extern] static	[none] const volatile	[none]	[none]	enum tag {..} enum tag
[extern] static	[none] const volatile	[none]	[none]	float
[extern] static	[none] const volatile	[none]	[none] long	double
[extern] static	[none]	[none]	[none]	void
[extern] static	[none] const volatile	[none]	[none]	_segment
[extern] static	[none] const volatile	[none]	[none]	union tag {..} union tag struct tag {..} struct tag

NOTES:
1. Storage-class [Lifetime and Visibility] qualifier must appear first with Standard C.
   [extern] assumed if **static** and **extern** omitted.
2. Both choices may be specified for Modifiable Type.
3. Type **enum** is implemented as type **int** by Microsoft.
   The syntax **enum tag {..}** implies a comma separated list of identifiers within braces.
   Type **_segment** is a non-Standard type implemented as type **int** by Microsoft.
   The syntax **union tag {..}** and **struct tag {..}** implies that a semicolon separated corresponding list of members within braces.

TABLE 14.4B: Syntax of Functions Returning Data-Object Types (continued)

RETURN BASE TYPE[3]	MIXED LANGUAGE[4]	REGISTER HANDLING[5]	FUNCTION ADDRESSING[6]	FUNCTION IDENTIFIER

`char`	`[_cdecl]`
	`_export`
	`_fastcall`
	`_fortran`
	`_pascal`
		`[none]`
		`_interrupt`
		`_loadds`
		`_saveregs`
			`[memory model]`
			`_near`
			`_far`
				`fn(args) {}`
				`fn(args);`

`int`
`[none]`
	`[_cdecl]`
	`_export`
	`_fastcall`
	`_fortran`
	`_pascal`
		`[none]`
		`_interrupt`
		`_loadds`
		`_saveregs`
			`[memory model]`
			`_near`
			`_far`
				`fn(args) {}`
				`fn(args);`

`enum tag {..}`
`enum tag`
	`[_cdecl]`
	`_export`
	`_fastcall`
	`_fortran`
	`_pascal`
		`[none]`
		`_interrupt`
		`_loadds`
		`_saveregs`
			`[memory model]`
			`_near`
			`_far`
				`fn(args) {}`
				`fn(args);`

`float`	`[_cdecl]`
	`_export`
	`_fastcall`
	`_fortran`
	`_pascal`
		`[none]`
		`_interrupt`
		`_loadds`
		`_saveregs`
			`[memory model]`
			`_near`
			`_far`
				`fn(args) {}`
				`fn(args);`

`double`	`[_cdecl]`
	`_export`
	`_fastcall`
	`_fortran`
	`_pascal`
		`[none]`
		`_interrupt`
		`_loadds`
		`_saveregs`
			`[memory model]`
			`_near`
			`_far`
				`fn(args) {}`
				`fn(args);`

`void`	`[_cdecl]`
	`_export`
	`_fastcall`
	`_fortran`
	`_pascal`
		`[none]`
		`_interrupt`
		`_loadds`
		`_saveregs`
			`[memory model]`
			`_near`
			`_far`
				`fn(args) {}`
				`fn(args);`

`_segment`	`[_cdecl]`
	`_export`
	`_fastcall`
	`_fortran`
	`_pascal`
		`[none]`
		`_interrupt`
		`_loadds`
		`_saveregs`
			`[memory model]`
			`_near`
			`_far`
				`fn(args) {}`
				`fn(args);`

`union tag {..}`
`union tag`
`struct tag {..}`
`struct tag`
	`[_cdecl]`
	`_export`
	`_fastcall`
	`_fortran`
	`_pascal`
		`[none]`
		`_interrupt`
		`_loadds`
		`_saveregs`
			`[memory model]`
			`_near`
			`_far`
				`fn(args) {}`
				`fn(args);`

NOTES (cont.):

4. `_fastcall` is incompatible with `_cdecl`, `_fortran`, `_pascal`, `_interrupt`, and `_saveregs`. `_export` is compatible with `_cdecl`, `_fortran`, and `_pascal`, but restricted for use with DLL (Dynamic Link Libraries).

5. More than one choice is permitted; however, `_saveregs` and `_interrupt` are mutually exclusive, and `_interrupt` must always be specified with `_cdecl` and `_far`.

6. Function addressing may never be `_huge` or `_based`.

- Size (return)
- RETURN BASE TYPE (return)
- Mixed Language (function)
- Register Handling (function)
- Function Addressing (function)
- Function Identifier (function)

For each base type (**char**, **int**, **enum**, **float**, **double**, **void**, **_seg-ment**, and **struct/union**), the implied or default qualifiers in effect appear in brackets. For example, when a function object named **fn(void)** is declared with **return** type **double**, the following default qualifiers result:

```
[extern][none][none][none] double
    [_cdecl][none][memory-model] fn(void);
```

This declaration in turn can be interpreted as

```
extern double _cdecl _near fn(void);
```

if the Tiny, Small, or Compact memory model is employed; or as

```
extern double _cdecl _far fn(void);
```

if the Medium, Large, or Huge memory model is employed. In either form, the statement declares a function called **fn()** with global lifetime and visibility, conforming with C language naming and calling conventions, located at the [memory model] address, and returning a **double** data-object type. The notes to Table 14.4 comment on some restrictions that apply when formulating function declarations.

Pointer Objects

Table 14.5 summarizes, in tabular declaration format, the syntax and default qualifiers that may be used to declare (and define) functions that return pointers to the objects described in Table 13.5 (except other pointer, multidimensioned array, and function-type objects themselves, which are described later in the chapter).

Notice that all types of objects except bits may be returned by the use of pointers. A pointer to **void** is considered to represent any data-object type pointer, which may later be cast as necessary to another data type, but not to a function type. Recall from Table 13.4 that it is not recommended that pointers be cast between data- and function-type objects.

Each function and return type declaration (without argument declarations) is developed again by optionally grouping the qualifiers into the column categories shown in Table 14.5. For each base type (**char**, **int**, **enum**, **float**, **double**, **void**, **_segment**, and **struct/union**), the implied or default qualifiers in effect appear in brackets. For example, when a function object named **fn(void)** is declared with return type **void ***, the following default qualifiers result:

```
[extern][none][none][none] void [memory-model] * [none]
    [_cdecl][none][memory-model] fn(void);
```

This declaration in turn can be interpreted as

```
extern void _near * _cdecl _near fn(void);
```

if the Tiny or Small memory model is employed; or as

```
extern void _near * _cdecl _far fn(void);
```

if the Medium memory model is employed; or as

```
extern void _far * _cdecl _near fn(void);
```

if the Compact memory model is employed; or as

```
extern void _far * _cdecl _far fn(void);
```

if the Large or Huge memory model is employed. The statement declares a function called **fn()** with global lifetime and visibility, conforming with C language naming and calling conventions, located at a [memory model] address, and returning a [memory model] address to a data-object of type **void**. The notes to Table 14.5 comment on some restrictions that apply when formulating function declarations.

The method of declaring functions that return pointers to pointers (ad infinitum) is patterned after the material presented in Chapter 10. For example, the function definition

```
int * * fn(char cv) { .. }
```

returns a pointer to a pointer to an **int** type object. Recall that each pointer in the chain of pointers becomes a candidate to be qualified by the keywords **_near**, **_far**, **_huge**, or **_based**, which immediately precede the object they modify, together with keywords **const** and **volatile**, which now with Standard C must immediately follow the pointer object they modify.

Another equivalent way of defining this function would be

```
int (* fn(char cv))[] { .. }
```

TABLE 14.5A: Syntax of Functions Returning Pointers to Data-Object Types

LIFETIME AND VISIBILITY[1]	MODIFIABLE TYPE[2]	SIGN	SIZE	RETURN BASE TYPE[3]	POINTER ADDRESSING[4]
[extern] static	[none] const volatile	[signed] unsigned	[none]	char	[memory model]* _near * _far * _huge * _based (..) *
[extern] static	[none] const volatile	[signed] unsigned	[none] short long	int [none]	[memory model] * _near * _far * _huge * _based (..) *
[extern] static	[none] const volatile	[none]	[none]	enum tag {..} enum tag	[memory model] * _near * _far * _huge * _based (..) *
[extern] static	[none] const volatile	[none]	[none]	float	[memory model] * near * far * huge * based (..) *
static [extern]	[none] const volatile	[none]	[none] long	double	[memory model] * _near * _far * _huge * _based (..) *
[extern] static	[none]	[none]	[none]	void	[memory model] * _near * _far * _huge * _based (..) *
static [extern]	[none] const volatile	[none]	[none]	_segment	[memory model] * _near * _far * _huge * _based (..) *
[extern] static	[none] const volatile	[none]	[none]	union tag {..} union tag struct tag {..} struct tag	[memory model] * _near * _far * _huge * _based (..) *

NOTES:
1. Storage-class [Lifetime and Visibility] qualifier must appear first with Standard C.
   [extern] assumed if **static** and **extern** omitted.
2. Both choices may be specified.
3. Type **enum** is implemented as type **int** by Microsoft.
   The syntax **enum tag {..}** implies a comma separated list of identifiers within braces.
   Type **_segment** is a non-Standard type implemented as type **int** by Microsoft.
   The syntax **union tag {..}** and **struct tag {..}** implies that a semicolon separated corresponding list of members within braces.

TABLE 14.5B: Syntax of Functions Returning Pointers to Data-Object Types (continued)

POINTER ADDRESSING[4]	MODIFIABLE POINTER[2]	MIXED LANGUAGE[5]	REGISTER HANDLING[6]	FUNCTION ADDRESSING[7]	FUNCTION IDENTIFIER
[memory model]* _near * _far * _huge * _based (..) *	[none] const volatile	[_cdecl] _export _fastcall _fortran _pascal	[none] _interrupt _loadds _saveregs	[memory model] _near _far	fn(args) {} fn(args);
[memory model] * _near * _far * _huge * _based (..) *	[none] const volatile	[_cdecl] _export _fastcall _fortran _pascal	[none] _interrupt _loadds _saveregs	[memory model] _near _far	fn(args) {} fn(args);
[memory model] * _near * _far * _huge * _based (..) *	[none] const volatile	[_cdecl] _export _fastcall _fortran _pascal	[none] _interrupt _loadds _saveregs	[memory model] _near _far	fn(args) {} fn(args);
[memory model] * near * far * huge * based (..) *	[none] const volatile	[_cdecl] _export _fastcall _fortran _pascal	[none] _interrupt _loadds _saveregs	[memory model] _near _far	fn(args) {} fn(args);
[memory model] * _near * _far * _huge * _based (..) *	[none] const volatile	[_cdecl] _export _fastcall _fortran _pascal	[none] _interrupt _loadds _saveregs	[memory model] _near _far	fn(args) {} fn(args);
[memory model] * _near * _far * _huge * _based (..) *	[none] const volatile	[_cdecl] _export _fastcall _fortran _pascal	[none] _interrupt _loadds _saveregs	[memory model] _near _far	fn(args) {} fn(args);
[memory model] * _near * _far * _huge * _based (..) *	[none] const volatile	[_cdecl] _export _fastcall _fortran _pascal	[none] _interrupt _loadds _saveregs	[memory model] _near _far	fn(args) {} fn(args);
[memory model] * _near * _far * _huge * _based (..) *	[none] const volatile	[_cdecl] _export _fastcall _fortran _pascal	[none] _interrupt _loadds _saveregs	[memory model] _near _far	fn(args) {} fn(args):

NOTES (cont.)

4. The syntax **_based(..)** denotes that a segment reference must be provided in parentheses.
5. **_fastcall** is incompatible with **_cdecl**, **_fortran**, **_pascal**, **_interrupt**, and **_saveregs**. **_export** is compatible with **_cdecl**, **_fortran**, and **_pascal**, but restricted for use with DLL (Dynamic Link Libraries).
6. More than one choice is permitted; however, **_saveregs** and **_interrupt** are mutually exclusive, and **_interrupt** must always be specified with **_cdecl** and **_far**.
7. Function addressing may never be **_huge** or **_based**.

Even though there is an equivalence between ***** and **[]**, and ***** ***** and **[] []**, it is not possible to express function **fn** as

```
int fn(char cv)[][] { .. }     /* incorrect */
```

because a function may not return an array of objects, only a pointer to an object or array of objects.

The technique used to declare functions that return arrays of all object types except function types relies upon the inherent equivalence of pointers and one-dimensional arrays of objects in the C language. Any one-dimensional array of objects is simply returned as a pointer to array element **[0]**.

Given a pointer to (starting address of) a one-dimensional array, and knowing the elemental object type, either subscripting or indirection and address arithmetic may be used to access any element of the array. Recall from Chapter 10 that any address can be treated as if it were the starting point of an array of objects because there is no array subscript bounds-checking enforced in C!

Finally, let's examine the possible argument types that may be declared as the last component of a complete function declaration or definition.

Argument Types

Functions may be declared to accept no arguments, a single argument, or a fixed or variable number of them. Every argument's type, regardless of whether it is a pointer type, is always passed by value. Arguments always represent copies of values (types) that exhibit either **auto** or **register** storage class. **auto** arguments are copied to the stack and represent the default storage class if none is specified. **register** arguments are placed in a machine register if possible, otherwise they revert to storage class **auto**. Notice that function arguments may never be declared to be storage class **extern** or **static**.

The possible combinations of arguments that may be declared for a function are portrayed in Table 14.6. Two categories of arguments are presented: fixed and variable. Each of these categories will be discussed in detail in the sections that follow. Notice that type **void** may be specified only when no arguments are to be defined; that for all argument declarations, storage class **auto** may be omitted but is considered the default storage class if **register** is not specified; and that storage class **register** may not be specified for the argument that is required to precede the variable argument punctuator (**, . . .**).

TABLE 14.6: Function Arguments

	TYPE	LIFETIME AND VISIBILITY[1]	1ST ARG BASE TYPE	NTH ARG BASE TYPE	NTH+1 ARG BASE TYPE
Fixed	`F-0`	[none]	`void`	[none]	[none[none]
	`F-1`	[auto] `register`	Any valid data-object type[2]	[none]	[none]
	`F-N`	[auto] `register`	Any valid data-object type[2]	, Any valid data-object type[2]	Any nth arg base type
Variable	`V-1`	[auto]	Any valid data-object type[2]	(ellipsis) , ...[3]	[none]
	`V-N`	[auto] `register`	Any valid data-object type[2]	, Any valid data-object type[2]	Any nth arg base type

NOTES:
1. Each argument has an associated storage class.
2. Except `void`, bits, arrays, or function-type objects; although pointers to `void`, arrays, and function-types are permitted. If subscripts `[]..[]` are specified, they are accepted but understood as `*..*`.
3. One argument must immediately preceed `( ,... )`, represents the count of variable arguments that follows, and may not be of storage class `register` nor be a type that may be automatically promoted by the compiler if its function prototype is out-of-scope.

Unlike C++, Standard C does not permit function arguments to be initialized. For example:

```
int fn(int ival=0, double dval=1.0) { }      /* incorrect */
```

Each argument may only be of storage class **auto** or **register**, but in each case, the formal arguments may not specify an initial value as shown (this is permitted with C++).

As discussed in Chapter 15, Microsoft C provides a way to process DOS wildcard characters automatically within filenames that occur as arguments to special function **main()**. For other functions, however, no such facility exists. If such wildcard argument processing is required, the code must be developed but could be patterned after a Microsoft C sample program called **wild.c**. For a description of the "stack frame" and register conventions used to pass argument values, refer to Chapter 15.

Fixed Number

Any function whose arguments list does not include the ellipsis (. . .) punctuator, or in a non-Standard fashion is terminated with a comma (see Language Extensions, Chapter 29), is considered to have a fixed number of arguments. Consider the following examples which parallel those types designated in Table 14.6.

```
F-0a      fname(void);                          /* declaration */

F-0b      fname(void) { }                       /* definition */

F-1a      fname(int);                           /* declaration */
          or
          fname(register int);

F-1b      fname(int iv) { }                     /* definition */
          or
          fname(register int iv) { }

          fname(iv)                             /* alternate */
          int iv; or register int iv;           /* "obsolete" */
          {  }                                  /* definition */

F-Na      fname(int *, char);                   /* declaration */
          or
          fname(register int *, register char);

F-Nb      fname(int *iv, char cv) { }           /* definition */
          or
          fname(register int *iv, register char cv) { }

          fname(iv, cv)                         /* alternate */
          int *iv; or register int *iv;         /* "obsolete" */
          char cv; or register char cv;         /* definition */
          {  }
```

The letter suffix (a) above is used to identify function declarations, and the letter (b) to identify function definitions (storage allocation). Form (a) or (b) may be used to declare arguments, while form (b) must be used to define arguments. The forms labeled "alternate" may still be used for function definitions, but they have been designated as "obsolete" and will not be supported in future versions of the ANSI Standard. They are being made obsolete by the adoption of C++ style function prototype definitions. See the "Function Prototypes" section below.

When a function has no arguments, only the **void** type may be specified as shown for **F-0a** and **F-0b** above. Such a function might rely solely upon global variables, or simply display a fixed report heading. When a function is declared as such, it must be called (or invoked) as shown:

```
fname()
```

Notice that an empty set of parentheses must be specified for function **fname** to be performed properly, even though it is declared not to have any arguments.

When a function has from one (**F-1a** and **F-1b**) to *N* (**F-Na** and **F-Nb**) fixed arguments, each argument has its own storage class, and each argument declaration or definition is separated by a comma as shown.

Actual function arguments, which replace the formal declared function arguments, may satisfy the number and type of arguments with any appropriate expression. Each argument expression is evaluated first to yield a value of an appropriate type before it is promoted, if necessary, and then passed (copied) to the function itself. For example:

```
static void fname(int iv, double dv) { .. };

int int_arg = 10;
double double_arg = -1.0;

fname(2*5, -1.0F);
fname(int_arg, double_arg);
```

Both calls to function **fname()** above pass identical actual arguments for the formal arguments **iv** and **dv**, declared when function **fname()** was defined as shown.

Although it is a simple matter to define functions with a fixed number of formal arguments and to reference these identifiers as needed within the body of a function definition, when a function has a variable number of arguments, references to the variable arguments themselves are more complicated, as we will see in the following section.

Variable Number

Any function that has one or more arguments followed by the ellipsis (**...**) punctuator is considered to have a variable number of arguments. Consider the following examples which parallel those types described in Table 14.6.

```
V-1a        fname(int, ... );                    /* declaration */

V-1b        fname(int iv, ... ) { }              /* definition */

            fname (iv, ... )                     /* alternate */
```

```
          int iv;                               /* obsolete */
          { }                                   /* definition */

V-Na      fname(char, int, ... );               /* declaration */
          or
          fname(register char, int, ... );

V-Nb      fname(char cv, int iv, ... ) { }      /* definition */
          or
          fname(register char cv, int iv, ... ) { }

          fname(cv, iv, ... )                    /* alternate */
          char cv; or register char cv;         /* obsolete */
          int iv;                               /* definition */
          {  }
```

Again the letter suffix is used to identify (a) declarations, and (b) definitions. Either form may be used to declare arguments, although only (b) may be used to define arguments. Again, the alternate forms may be used only for function definitions, but have been designated as obsolete and will not be supported in future versions of the ANSI Standard. These are being made obsolete by the adoption of C++ style function prototype definitions. See the "Function Prototypes" section below.

Examples V-1a and V-1b highlight the fact that if a function is to be defined that has a variable number of arguments (, ...), then at least one preceding argument must be defined, which may not be of type **void** nor of storage class **register**. Clearly, it is incorrect to declare a function as follows:

```
fname( ... );          /* incorrect */
```

Examples V-Na and V-Nb demonstrate that each argument has its own storage class and that any number of arguments may precede the ellipsis punctuator, which indicates that a variable number of arguments follow. Also note that for this case, an argument of type **void** may never be specified, and the argument that precedes (, ...) may not be of storage class **register**.

Just as the fixed argument that immediately precedes the set of variable arguments may not be of storage class **register**, when the ellipsis punctuator, or a trailing comma (non-Standard, language extension, see Chapter 29) is specified, the variable arguments are always placed on the stack, not in registers. To better understand why certain restrictions apply when declaring functions with a variable number of arguments, we must examine the function-like macros **va_start()**, **va_arg()**, and **va_end()**, declared in Standard header file **<stdarg.h>**.

```
typedef char *va_list;
#define va_start(ap,v) ap = (va_list)&v + sizeof(v)
```

```
#define va_arg(ap,t) ((t *)(ap += sizeof(t)))[-1]
#define va_end(ap) ap = NULL
```

typedef va_list is used to allocate a character pointer, **ap**, that will hold the stack memory address of the first variable argument when **va_start(ap, v)** is called, and **v** is the name of the fixed variable that precedes the ellipsis (, . . .) and successively holds the addresses of each subsequent variable argument of type **t** when **va_arg(ap, t)** is invoked. Macro **va_end()** reinitializes pointer **ap** if it is necessary to reprocess the variable arguments from the stack.

Notice the address-of operator prefixed to argument **v** of the macro **va_start()**. Use of this operator requires that **v**, the fixed argument immediately preceding the ellipsis, be in memory (addressable, on the stack), and not in a register as noted in Table 14.6.

This function-like macro also illustrates why at least one fixed argument must precede the ellipsis in a function prototype. Its argument, **ap**, is successively incremented by macro **va_arg(ap, t)**, which yields the value (not the address, by virtue of [-1]) of the next variable argument of type **t**. If an argument must be retrieved more than once, call **va_end(ap)**, then reissue a **va_start(ap,v)** and retrieve the arguments in sequence again. This is possible since the contents of the **auto** variables remain on the stack until the function returns. As we will see in Chapter 15, it is the **_cdecl** convention of placing function arguments on the stack in a rightmost to leftmost order that enables C (unlike BASIC, Fortran, and Pascal) to have functions with a variable number of arguments. The **_cdecl** placement of arguments on the stack is exploited by the **va_start()**, **va_arg()**, and **va_end()** macros described above.

The program example in Figure 14.1 demonstrates the use of these macros to retrieve the variable argument values from the stack. Function **bit_mask** constructs an **unsigned** integer mask by using the logical OR operator to combine a series of integral bit representations.

Note that header file **<stdarg.h>** should be used with DOS, not the alternate non-Standard header file **<varargs.h>**, which is also distributed by Microsoft for UNIX/XENIX compatibility. Notice that the fixed argument immediately preceding the start of the variable argument list is treated as a count of arguments that follow. The preceding example produced the following results:

```
or_mask = 8888
or_mask = FFFF
or_mask = FFF5
```

Refer to Chapter 11 or Table 13.3 if you are having difficulty confirming these results.

```
/* FILE: ch14e1.c */
#include <stdio.h>
#include <stdarg.h>        /* not XENIX/UNIX <varargs.h> */

unsigned bit_mask(int n_args, ...)
{
va_list args;
unsigned i, mask = 0x0000;
va_start(args, n_args);
for (i=0; i<n_args; i++) mask |= (unsigned) va_arg(args, unsigned);
va_end(args);
return(mask);
}

int main(void)
{
printf("\n or_mask = %04X", bit_mask(4, 32768u, 2048, 128, 8));
printf("\n or_mask = %04X", bit_mask(4, ~2, ~1, 1, 2));
printf("\n or_mask = %04X", bit_mask(2, -15, 4));
exit(0);
}
```

FIGURE 14.1: Sample program ch14e1.c demonstrates the technique for writing a function that has a variable number of function arguments.

FUNCTION POINTER DECLARATIONS

We will now examine how pointers to function-type objects (code) are declared so that functions and arrays of function pointers may be used as function argument and return types. Recall that functions may not directly use arrays or functions as argument and return values; pointers to those object types must be declared instead. Also, because functions cannot be subscripted, a pointer to an array of function pointers must be used to enable arrays of functions to be used as function argument and return types.

Function-type pointers contain the address (**_near** or **_far** only, not **_huge** or **_based**) of a function-type object. Since function-type objects represent code and not data, function pointers are segregated from data-object type pointers, and as we discovered in Chapter 13, casting is not recommended between function and data-object type pointers.

When a function pointer is declared, a pointer-type object of either two bytes (**_near**, default code segment (CS) register, offset address component only) or four bytes (**_far**, both segments:offset address components) of storage is allocated. Function pointers then are always either two or four bytes, while function-type objects vary in size and represent the machine language instructions translated from the C statements found within the body of a function definition.

Because both a function and function pointer declaration represent the composite declaration of a function-type object together with its return and argument-type objects, such declarations are by far the most complex of all declarations possible in the C language.

Function pointer declarations involve the use of the `[]` .. `[]` arrays, indirection (`*`), grouping parentheses `()`, and the function postfix operator `()`. Because of the restrictions associated with the handling of arrays and functions, it is necessary to understand operator precedence and to employ what we will refer to as the "Right-Left" rule to properly construct and interpret function pointer declarations.

Right-Left Rule

The "Right-Left" rule is rooted in the precedence relationship of the operators used to construct complex function declarations. Recall from Table 12.1 that the function `()` and array `[]` postfix operators associate to the right and have precedence over indirection `*` which associates to the left; hence the origin of the so-called "Right-Left" rule.

`X(Y)`	function call	primary postfix	L → R
`X[Y]`	array subscript	primary postfix	L → R
`*X`	indirection	unary prefix	R → L

Also note that the following operations are never permitted:

`() []`	Function returning array—incorrect
`[] ()`	Array of functions—incorrect
`() ()`	Function returning a function—incorrect

The adjacent use of such operators must always be separated by grouping parentheses that override the default associativity of operators if valid declarations are to be expressed, as follows:

`(*()) []`	Function returning a pointer to an array—correct
`(*[]) ()`	Array of pointers to functions—correct
`(*()) ()`	Function that returns a pointer to a function—correct

All function and function pointer declarations are interpreted using the Right-Left rule by working from the inside out and following these steps:

Step 1: Locate the function identifier (not the return or argument declarations) and look to the right for any brackets `[]` or function `()` operators.

Step 2: Interpret these bracket **[ ]** or function **( )** operators, and then look to the left and interpret any indirection ***** operators.

Step 3: If a right grouping parentheses **)** is encountered, immediately repeat steps 1 and 2 for everything within the parentheses.

Consider the following function definition:

```
int * fn(char ch, double *pdbl) { .. }
^    ^ ^ ^
4    3 1 2
```

It allocates a function-type object called **fn**, which accepts two arguments, the first of type **char** called **ch**, and the second a pointer to type **double** called **pdbl**, and returns a pointer to type **int**.

By modifying this expression, we can define a function pointer, **pfn**, as follows:

```
int * (* pfn)(char, double *);
^     ^ ^ ^   ^
5     4 2 1   3
```

This allocates a pointer called **pfn**, which points to a function that accepts two arguments, the first of type **char** and the second a pointer to type **double**, and returns a pointer to type **int**.

With another modification of this expression, we can define an array of function pointers as follows:

```
int * (* pfn[6])(char, double *);
^     ^ ^ ^  ^   ^
6     5 3 1  2   4
```

This allocates an array of six pointers to functions that accept two arguments, the first of type **char** and the second a pointer to type **double**, and returns a pointer to type **int**.

The ^ indicator and associated numbers shown in the examples above parallel the sequence of steps that demonstrate how the "Right-Left" rule is used to interpret complex function declarations.

COMPLEX FUNCTION DECLARATIONS

Now that we understand how to declare function pointer variables, consider Tables 14.7 A–E, which demonstrate how to declare functions that utilize complex declarations of the following argument and return types:

1. Data objects
2. Pointers to data objects

3. Arrays of pointers to data objects
4. Pointers to functions
5. Arrays of pointers to functions

Notice that arrays of data-object types are properly declared using (2) above, but that (4) cannot be used for arrays of function types because arrays of functions are not permitted; (5) must be used instead.

The ^ indicator and associated numbers shown in Tables 14.7 A–E also parallel the sequence of steps to demonstrate how the "Right-Left" rule is used to interpret complex function declarations. To assist you in

TABLE 14.7A: Complex Function Declarations—Argument: Nonpointer Data Object

RETURN TYPE	DECLARATION FORMAT
Data-Object Type Nonpointer	```void f11(int);``` ^ ^ ^ 3 1 2
Data-Object Type Pointer[a]	```struct stag * f21(void);``` ^ ^ ^ ^ 4 3 1 2
Array of Data-Object Type Pointers	```double * * f31(char);``` ^ ^ ^ ^ ^ 5 4 3 1 2
Function-Type Pointer[b]	```int (* f41(long)) (float);``` ^ ^ ^ ^ ^ 5 3 1 2 4
Array of Function-Type Pointers	```char (* * f51(enum etag)) (int);``` ^ ^ ^ ^ ^ ^ 6 4 3 1 2 5

NOTES:
^ Indicator to interpret the Right-Left rule
* Pointer
* * Pointer to an array of pointers
a. Use this form to return a pointer to the first element of an array of data-object types, since functions cannot return arrays, only a pointer to an array.
b. Although function names are pointers, unlike array names, functions may not be subscripted.

understanding this rule, Table 14.8 interprets the 25 function declaration combinations (**f11** through **f55**) shown in Tables 14.7 A–E.

In Part VII we will find that several run-time library functions utilize function pointers as argument and return values.

FUNCTION	HEADER FILE	CHAPTER
atexit()	**<stdlib.h>**	25: Process Control
bsearch()	**<stdlib.h>**	27: Miscellaneous
_chain_intr()	**<dos.h>**	27: Miscellaneous
_dos_getvect()	**<dos.h>**	27: Miscellaneous

TABLE 14.7B: Complex Function Declarations—Argument: Pointer to Data Object

RETURN TYPE	DECLARATION FORMAT

Data-Object Type Nonpointer	```void f12(int *);```
	``` ^ ^ ^```
	``` 3 1 2```

Data-Object Type Pointer[a]	```struct stag * f22(void *);```
	``` ^ ^ ^ ^```
	``` 4 3 1 2```

Array of Data-Object Type Pointers	```double * * f32(char *);```
	``` ^ ^ ^ ^ ^```
	``` 5 4 3 1 2```

Function-Type Pointer[b]	```int (* f42(long *)) (float);```
	``` ^ ^ ^ ^ ^```
	``` 5 3 1 2 4```

Array of Function-Type Pointers	```char (* * f52(enum etag *)) (int);```
	``` ^ ^ ^ ^ ^ ^```
	``` 6 4 3 1 2 5```

NOTES:
^ Indicator to interpret the Right-Left rule
* Pointer
* * Pointer to an array of pointers
a. Use this form to return a pointer to the first element of an array of data-object types, since functions cannot return arrays, only a pointer to an array.
b. Although function names are pointers, unlike array names, functions may not be subscripted.

FUNCTION	HEADER FILE	CHAPTER
`_dos_setvect()`	`<dos.h>`	27: Miscellaneous
`_harderr()`	`<dos.h>`	27: Miscellaneous
`lsearch()`	`<search.h>`	27: Miscellaneous
`lfind()`	`<search.h>`	27: Miscellaneous
`onexit()`	`<stdlib.h>`	25: Process Control
`qsort()`	`<stdlib.h>`	27: Miscellaneous
`signal()`	`<signal.h>`	25: Process Control

TABLE 14.7C: Complex Function Declarations—Argument: Array of Pointers to Data Objects

RETURN TYPE	DECLARATION FORMAT

Data-Object Type Nonpointer	`void f13(int * *);`
	
	`  ^      ^ ^`
	`  3      1 2`

Data-Object Type Pointer[a]	`struct stag * f23(void * *);`
	
	`  ^              ^ ^ ^`
	`  4              3 1 2`

Array of Data-Object Type Pointers	`double * * f33(char * *);`
	
	`  ^      ^ ^ ^`
	`  5      4 3 1 2`

Function-Type Pointer[b]	`int (* f43(long * *)) (float);`
	
	`  ^    ^ ^  ^           ^`
	`  5    3 1  2           4`

Array of Function-Type Pointers	`char (* * f53(enum etag * *)) (int);`
	
	`  ^    ^ ^ ^      ^ ^           ^`
	`  6    4 3 1      2             5`

NOTES:
^ Indicator to interpret the Right-Left rule
* Pointer
* * Pointer to an array of pointers
a. Use this form to return a pointer to the first element of an array of data-object types, since functions cannot return arrays, only a pointer to an array.
b. Although function names are pointers, unlike array names, functions may not be subscripted.

For example programs that demonstrate the use of these functions, refer to the chapters noted above in Part VII.

Now that we understand how to declare and interpret functions and function pointers, it should be clear that in addition to using function pointers as function argument and return values, we also can utilize them as casts and as members of structures and unions (see "Function-Related Operations" section below).

FUNCTION PROTOTYPES

The topic of function prototypes was first introduced in Chapter 6 to explain the important role that Standard and non-Standard (Microsoft)

TABLE 14.7D: Complex Function Declarations—Argument: Pointer to Function

RETURN TYPE	DECLARATION FORMAT

Data-Object Type Nonpointer	`void f14( int (*) (void) );`
	` ^    ^     ^    ^    ^`
	` 5    1     4    2    3`

Data-Object Type Pointer[a]	`struct stag * f24( void (*) (void) );`
	` ^            ^ ^    ^    ^    ^`
	` 6            5 1    4    2    3`

Array of Data-Object Type Pointers	`double * * f34( char (*) (void) );`
	` ^       ^ ^ ^    ^    ^    ^`
	` 7       6 5 1    4    2    3`

Function-Type Pointer[b]	`int (* f44( long (*) (void) )) (float);`
	` ^    ^ ^    ^    ^   ^           ^`
	` 7    5 1    4    2   3           6`

Array of Function-Type Pointers	`char (* * f54( enum etag (*) (void) )) (int);`
	` ^    ^ ^ ^    ^           ^   ^        ^`
	` 8    6 5 1    4           2   3        7`

NOTES:
^ Indicator to interpret the Right-Left rule
* Pointer
* * Pointer to an array of pointers
a. Use this form to return a pointer to the first element of an array of data-object types, since functions cannot return arrays, only a pointer to an array.
b. Although function names are pointers, unlike array names, functions may not be subscripted.

header files play in providing the prototype declarations of all C run-time library functions. Function prototypes did not exist with K&R C. They have been adopted as a new feature by Standard C and, in truth, represent a feature that has been copied from the still to be standardized C++ language specification.

Typically, new language features are easy to explain; however, in this instance, because Standard C has chosen to accommodate both the old style K&R and new style C++ forms of function declaration, the explanation is more complex. Although the old style of function declaration has been earmarked as obsolete by Standard C, until the old style is completely dropped by a future version of Standard C, both forms are accommodated.

TABLE 14.7E: Complex Function Declarations—Argument: Array of Pointers to Functions

RETURN TYPE	DECLARATION FORMAT

Data-Object Type Nonpointer	`void f15( int (* *) (char) );`
	`^    ^     ^     ^ ^   ^`
	`6    1     5     3 2   4`

Data-Object Type Pointer[a]	`struct stag * f25( void (* *) (char) );`
	`^              ^ ^    ^      ^ ^   ^`
	`7              6 1    5      3 2   4`

Array of Data-Object Type Pointers	`double * * f35( char (* *) (char) );`
	`^        ^ ^ ^        ^      ^ ^   ^`
	`8        7 6 1        5      3 2   4`

Function-Type Pointer[b]	`int (* f45( long (* *) (char) )) (float);`
	`^    ^ ^    ^      ^ ^   ^           ^`
	`8    6 1    5      3 2   4           7`

Array of Function-Type Pointers	`char (* * f55( enum etag (* *) (char) )) (int);`
	`^     ^ ^ ^          ^          ^ ^   ^            ^`
	`9     7 6 1          5          3 2   4            8`

NOTES:

^ Indicator to interpret the Right-Left rule

* Pointer

* * Pointer to an array of pointers

a. Use this form to return a pointer to the first element of an array of data-object types, since functions cannot return arrays, only a pointer to an array.

b. Although function names are pointers, unlike array names, functions may not be subscripted.

TABLE 14.8: Interpreting Complex Declarations

FUNCTION	DESCRIPTION
f11	Accepts one `int` type argument and returns type `void`.
f12	Accepts one pointer to an `int` type argument and returns type `void`.
f13	Accepts one pointer to an array of pointers to type `int` argument and returns type `void`.
f14	Accepts one pointer to a function argument, which accepts no arguments and return type `int`, and returns type `void`.
f15	Accepts one pointer to an array of pointers to a function type argument, which accept one argument of type `char` and return type `int`, and returns type `void`.
f21	Accepts no arguments and returns a pointer to a structure of type `stag`.
f22	Accepts one pointer to a `void` type argument and returns a pointer to a structure of type `stag`.
f23	Accepts one pointer to an array of pointers to type `void` argument and returns a pointer to a structure of type `stag`.
f24	Accepts one pointer to a function argument, which accepts no arguments and returns type `void`, and returns a pointer to a structure of type `stag`.
f25	Accepts one pointer to an array of pointers to a function type argument, which accepts an argument of type `char` and returns type `void`, and returns a pointer to a structure of type `stag`.
f31	Accepts one `char` type argument and returns a pointer to array of pointers to type `double`.
f32	Accepts one pointer to a `char` type argument and returns a pointer to an array of pointers to type `double`.
f33	Accepts one pointer to an array of pointers to type `char` argument and returns a pointer to an array of pointers to type `double`.
f34	Accepts one pointer to a function type argument, which accepts no arguments and returns type `char`, and returns a pointer to an array of pointers to type `double`.
f35	Accepts one pointer to an array of pointers to a function type argument, which accept one argument of type `char` and return type `char`, and returns a pointer to an array of pointers to type `double`.
f41	Accepts one `long` type argument and returns a pointer to a function type, which accepts one `float` type argument and returns type `int`.
f42	Accepts one pointer to a `long` type argument, and returns a pointer to a function type, which accepts one `float` type argument and returns type `int`.
f43	Accepts one pointer to an array of pointers to type `long` argument and returns a pointer to a function type, which accepts one `float` type argument and returns type `int`.

TABLE 14.8: Interpreting Complex Declarations (continued)

FUNCTION	DESCRIPTION
f44	Accepts one pointer to a function type argument, which accepts no arguments and returns type **long**, and returns a pointer to a function type that accepts one **float** type argument and returns type **int**.
f45	Accepts one pointer to an array of pointers to a function type argument, which accept one argument of type **char** and return type **long**, and returns a pointer to a function type that accepts one **float** type argument and returns type **int**.
f51	Accepts one enumerated type **etag** argument and returns a pointer to an array of pointers to a function type, which accept one **int** type argument and return type **char**.
f52	Accepts one pointer to an enumerated type **etag** argument, and returns a pointer to an array of pointers to a function type, which accept one **int** type argument and return type **char**.
f53	Accepts one pointer to an array of pointers to an enumerated type **etag** argument, and returns a pointer to an array of pointers to a function type, which accept one **int** type argument and return type **char**.
f54	Accepts one pointer to a function type argument, which accepts no arguments and returns an enumerated **etag** type, and returns a pointer to an array of pointers to a function type, which accept one **int** type argument and return type **char**.
f55	Accepts one pointer to an array of pointers to a function type argument, which accepts one **char** type argument and returns an enumerated **etag** type, and returns a pointer to an array of pointers to a function type, which accept one **int** type argument and return type **char**.

NOTE: All pointers default to the [memory model] of the compiler being employed, unless individually qualified by the non-Standard Microsoft keywords **_near**, **_far**, **_huge**, or **_based**.

Before beginning to unravel this accommodation in Standard C, you must understand that any new source-code development should adopt the C++/Standard C style of function prototypes; and, if existing (K&R style) source code is to remain in conformance with Standard C, over time it should be modified to incorporate the use of function prototypes as well. In the meantime, however, both forms may coexist but they convey significantly different meanings.

To unravel this issue, let's first explain the old K&R style, look at the new C++ style, and finally summarize how these two styles presently coexist under Standard C.

K&R Style

Function prototypes, as we will come to know them, did not exist in the K&R specification of the C programming language. What did exist was a simple mechanism for the declaration of the return type of a function. Header files were relied upon in K&R C for the declarations of functions in the C run-time library. There was no means of declaring the number or type of function arguments, nor was there any way to indicate that a variable number (...) of or no (**void**) arguments were intended. If a function declaration was not within scope (visibility), a return type of **int** was assumed.

For example, some familiar run-time library declarations would have been specified with K&R C as

```
int printf();        /* standard output */
char * strcpy();     /* string copy */
double fabs();       /* real absolute value */
char * malloc();     /* memory allocation */
```

Because formal argument declarations were never provided, all integral-type actual arguments were automatically promoted to type **int**, and all floating-point types were automatically promoted to type **double**.

C++ Style

Since the development of C++ paralleled the work of the ANSI X3J11 Standards Committee, certain features from C++ were adopted by the new Standard in an effort to fix some of the major shortcomings of K&R C. One significant feature that was adopted from C++ was that of function prototype declarations, which describe not only the return but also the argument types of each function and introduce the new type, **void**, and the ellipsis (...) notation to signify a variable number of arguments.

For example, the run-time library declarations shown above for K&R C would be declared as follows with C++:

```
int printf(const char *, ...);          /* standard output */
char * strcpy(char *, const char *);    /* string copy */
double fabs(double);                     /* real absolute value */
void * malloc(size_t);                   /* memory allocation */
```

Because formal argument declarations must be provided, all actual arguments are automatically promoted to their corresponding formal declared type. No longer are all integral types automatically promoted to type **int** and floating-point types to type **double**. Compiler error and warning messages are provided when the number of actual function arguments differs from the prototype template declaration (compiler warning level **/W3**). Type **int** default return values may be assumed when prototypes are declared, but every function must have a prototype declaration within scope (visibility) when used with C++.

Standard C Style

Since Standard C has chosen to accommodate both the old style K&R and new style C++ function declarations, it becomes somewhat complicated how Standard C interprets and prioritizes the presence of both K&R and C++ style function declarations.

If the prototype is not visible (not within scope), the C compiler will assume a function return type of **int** and permit any number or type of arguments to be specified. Each actual argument will be *widened* to type **int** or **double** as appropriate, in conformance with K&R style function declarations.

When a function prototype is visible (within scope) to a function call, then both the number and corresponding type of actual arguments must be compatible with the formal arguments declared by the prototype; otherwise, a compiler warning or error message will result. Each actual argument will, if necessary, be cast to the type specified by the prototype in conformance with C++ style function declarations. If a function prototype with an ellipsis (...) punctuator is not visible (within scope) to a function expression statement, then variable arguments may not be retrieved reliably.

Some confusion does arise when more than one function declaration is within scope. Declarations that have the identical name and return the same type are said to be compatible; otherwise a compiler warning or error is generated.

Next, Standard C accommodates the interpretation of compatible function declarations that have dissimilar argument declarations in the following two ways.

First, in the case where the two function declarations for function **f1** are encountered:

```
int f1();              /* K*R style */
int f1(char, float);   /* C++ style */
```

Standard C interprets function **f1** as if it were declared in C++ style:

```
int f1(int, double);
```

or in essence, as if K&R style argument promotions were made.

Second, in the case where the two function declarations for function **f2** are encountered as follows:

```
int f2()                 /* K&R "obsolete" */
char cv;                 /* style */
float fv;
{ .. }

int f2(char cv, float fv);     /* C++ style */
```

Standard C interprets function **f2** as if it were declared in C++ style:

```
int f2(char cv, float fv);
```

or in essence, as if the C++ style argument promotions were made.

Because of the unreliable effects of mixing K&R and C++ style function prototypes, avoid intermingling and duplicating function prototype declarations unnecessarily.

Prototype Generation

Since all C run-time and other purchased libraries provide header files that include a prototype declaration for each function, function prototypes need to be written only for custom-developed functions. Normally a project-specific **"project.h"** header file is created to describe all such custom functions. The prototype declarations may be generated automatically by the Microsoft C compiler from the function definitions found in C source code files. Figure 14.2 demonstrates how the use of compiler option **/Zg** can be used for this purpose.

By simply invoking the Microsoft C Compiler with the **/Zg** option at the DOS prompt as follows:

```
CL /Zg ch14e2.c >prn
```

a printer list of function prototype declarations that correspond to those shown for functions **f11** through **f55** described in Tables 14.7 A–E and 14.8 will be produced.

Simply by redirecting the output of this command from DOS device **>prn** to a disk header file name, such as **>project.h**, a header file can be created and edited later as necessary.

```
/* FILE: ch14e2.c
** Use the CL (Optimizing Compiler) to generate the
** function prototypes shown in Tables 14.7A-E by entering
** the following DOS Command "CL /Zg ch14e2.c >prn"
*/

void f11(int iv) { }
void f12(int piv[]) { }
void f13(int * piv[]) { }
void f14(int (*pf) (void)) { }
void f15(int (* *pf) (char)) { }

struct stag {int iv;};

struct stag * f21(void) { }
struct stag * f22(void * pv) { }
struct stag * f23(void * pv[]) { }
struct stag * f24(void (*pf) (void)) { }
struct stag * f25(void (* *pf) (char)) { }

double * *f31(char cv) { }
double * *f32(char pcv[]) { }
double * *f33(char * pcv[]) { }
double * *f34(char (*pf) (void)) { }
double * *f35(char (* *pf) (char)) { }

int (*f41(long lv)) (float) { }
int (*f42(long lv[])) (float) { }
int (*f43(long * lv[])) (float) { }
int (*f44(long (*pf) (void))) (float) { }
int (*f45(long (* *pf) (char))) (float) { }

enum etag {false, true};

char (* *f51(enum etag ev)) (int) { }
char (* *f52(enum etag ev[])) (int) { }
char (* *f53(enum etag * ev[])) (int) { }
char (* *f54(enum etag (*fn) (void))) (int) { }
char (* *f55(enum etag (* *fn) (char))) (int) { }

int main(void)
{
}
```

FIGURE 14.2: Sample Program ch14e2.c generates the function declarations for functions f11()
through f55() found in Tables 14.7A through 14.7E.

FUNCTION TYPEDEFS

As we discovered throughout Part III, **typedef**s provide a mechanism by
which the declaration and definition of data-object types can be simplified,
made more readable, and used to promote program portability.

Given the complexity of function declarations, it is desirable to
use **typedef**s when declaring functions; however, unlike data-object
types, **typedef**s may not be used to define functions. Let's first consider

how **typedef**s may be used to simplify the declaration of functions that have the complex argument and return types highlighted earlier in Tables 14.7 A–E. Consider function declaration **f11** for example:

```
void f11(int);
```

We could replicate this declaration in the following manner:

```
typedef void F11(int);
static F11 f11;
```

We could also use **typedef F11** to define a **_far** function pointer, **pf11**, as follows:

```
F11 _far *pf11;
```

As we will see in the examples that follow for functions **f44** and **f55** from Table 14.7 A–E, the usefulness of **typedef**s increases in proportion to the complexity of the function declaration itself.

First consider the function declaration of **f44**:

```
int (* f44( long (*) (void) )) (float);
```

We could replicate this declaration in the following manner:

```
typedef long (* F44_arg1) (void);
typedef int (* F44_ret1) (float);
F44_ret1 f44( F44_arg1);
```

Now consider the function declaration of **f55**:

```
char (* * f55( enum etag (* *) (char) )) (int);
```

which can be simplified in the following manner:

```
typedef enum etag (* * F55_arg3) (char);
typedef char (* * F55_ret3) (int);
F55_ret3 f55(F55_arg3);
```

Rather than shy away from working with complex function declarations, introduce **typedef**s to simplify the declaration and understanding of the intended argument and return values, as demonstrated above.

FUNCTION-RELATED OPERATIONS

In Chapter 12 a series of tables was presented that summarized which operators could be used for each arithmetic, scalar, and aggregate data-object type in C. Only the function **()** operator, shown in Table 12.9, "Using Miscellaneous Operators," was omitted. In this section we will summarize how the function postfix operator **()** performs when functions and function pointers are encountered in expressions and statements.

Let's first consider the effect of the function operator upon a function name.

```
#include <stdio.h>
#include <math.h>
printf( "\nsin(90-deg) = %f", sin(acos(-1.0)/2.0) );
```

In this example, one statement involves the following three function operators:

```
int printf(..)
double sin(..)         /* argument to printf(..) */
double acos(..)        /* argument to sin(..) */
```

Because all functions are type objects, their value is represented by the return type declared by their function prototype found in the header files **<stdio.h>** and **<math.h>** as shown above.

The return values of these functions could have been captured as follows:

```
double val_sin, val_acos;
val_acos = acos(-1.0);
val_sin = sin(val_cos/2.0);
printf( "\nsin(90-deg) = %f", val_sin );
```

However, this is not necessary, unless those values must be retained for future use. Wherever function expressions are encountered, program control passes to the function located by its name (address), and any arguments are passed (by register or stack). When the function returns, it becomes an rvalue representing its return type, and program execution continues with the next expression or statement to be evaluated or performed. The return type of a function therefore controls which operators may be used with expressions involving functions. (Refer to Chapter 12, Tables 12.3, 12.5, 12.7, 12.8, and 12.9).

Although functions may not be declared within the body of another function, any function may invoke itself and exhibit what is referred to as *recursion*. Recursion represents an alternate method of coding *iterative* (looping) problem solutions. The program example shown in Figure 14.3 demonstrates how to compute a factorial using both iteration and recursion.

Both solutions yield the following identical results:

```
iteration = 3628800.000000
recursion = 3628800.000000
```

However, the recursive solution relies upon multiple function calls and a heavy use of the stack to pass argument values and to subsequently allocate

```
/* FILE: ch14e3.c */
double i_nfact(int n)
{
int i;
double nfact = 1.0;
for (i=1; i<=n; i++) nfact *= i;
return(nfact);
}

double r_nfact(int n)
{
double nfact = 1.0;

if (n > 1) nfact = n * r_nfact (n-1);
return (nfact );
}

#include <stdio.h>
int main(void)
{
printf("\niteration = %lf",i_nfact(10));
printf("\nrecursion = %lf",r_nfact(10));
exit(0);
}
```

FIGURE 14.3: Sample program ch14e3.c demonstrates the technique for writing a recursive function.

any **auto** storage-class variables. For more discussion on the caveats of using recursion, see the discussion about the stack provided in Chapter 15.

Pointers

Now let's consider the effect of the function operator upon a function pointer. For example, we could have performed the preceding trigonometric example in an equivalent manner, shown in Figure 14.4, by defining two function pointers, assigning them, and using the indirection operator to locate and pass control to the function-type object in memory.

Figure 14.4 produces the following result:

`sin(90°) = 1.000000`

Obviously, there is little advantage to using function pointers where functions suffice. Function pointers become essential, however, when it is necessary to pass a function as an argument or return value, because only function pointers, not functions, may then be used.

It is important to remember that since functions may be specified at link-time to be placed in an overlay, it is not appropriate to use function pointers to such objects, for they may not be located in memory when program control is transferred. Recall that only code (functions), not data, may be placed in overlays. When function names, not function pointers, are used, the overlay manager automatically retrieves and loads the overlay segment containing the required code to memory. Whenever function pointers are

```
/* FILE: ch14e4.c */
#include <stdio.h>
#include <math.h>
int main(void)
{
double (*math_ptr)();          /* function pointer */
int (*print_ptr)();            /* function pointer */
double val_sin, val_acos;

math_ptr = acos;
val_acos = (*math_ptr)(-1.0);
math_ptr = sin;
val_sin = (*math_ptr)(val_acos/2.0);
print_ptr = printf;
(*print_ptr)("\nsin(90-deg) = %f", val_sin);
}
```

FIGURE 14.4: Sample program ch14e4.c demonstrates the use of function pointers.

used as function argument and return values however, the overlay manager is circumvented; and if the function object pointed to is not in memory (addressable), it is not automatically loaded into memory, and a run-time error will most certainly result.

Since function pointers are themselves scalar data-object types, pointers control which operators may be used with expressions involving function pointers. Refer to Chapter 12, Tables 12.3, 12.5, 12.7, 12.8, and 12.9 for the operators that may be used with pointers.

Casting

Recall that the only operation that is restricted when working with pointers involves casting between data-object and function-type pointers (see Table 13.4).

Consider the example in Figure 14.5, which demonstrates function pointer cast operations and reveals the close relationship between casting function pointers and function prototype declarations. Notice that the generic function pointer declaration provides no information (K&R style) about any arguments and declares that type **void** is returned. The function prototype in **<math.h>** for function **fabs** is

```
double fabs (double);
```

Although **(*fptr) (−1.0)** is correctly invoked for **ABS1**, a compilation error results because a type **void** object that cannot be displayed is returned.

Examples **ABS2**, **ABS3**, and **ABS4** demonstrate the proper technique for expressing a function pointer cast operation against **fptr** as

```
(double (*) ()) fptr
```

This properly adjusts **fptr** to return type **double** and maintains agreement between the function types of ***fptr** and **fabs** but again provides no information (K&R style) about the type **double** argument anticipated by function **fabs**. Because of this, arithmetic-type actual arguments (in the case of K&R style function declarations) are promoted to either type **int** or **double**. The example program in Figure 14.5 produces the following output:

```
ABS2 = 0.000000
ABS3 = 0.000000
ABS4 = 99.000000
ABS5 = 99.000000
```

Examples **ABS2** (type **int** argument) and **ABS3** (type **long** argument) therefore yield incorrect results because the actual parameters passed were not type **double** as anticipated.

Example **ABS4** (type **float** argument) works correctly because type **float** was promoted to type **double** as expected by function **fabs**. Example **ABS5** demonstrates a C++ or Standard C function pointer declaration style, whereby both the return and argument types are declared. Even though example **ABS5** is called with an **int** type argument, the cast operation promotes the **int** type argument to type **double** to ensure that the correct argument type is pushed to the stack.

It is convenient to declare a generic function pointer variable as we have done in this example because a pointer to type **void** is compatible with any cast operation. Simply remember to cast the generic function pointer with a C++ or Standard C prototype declaration that specifies the appropriate corresponding return and argument types before dereferencing the pointer with the indirection operator.

```c
/* FILE: ch14e5.c */
#include <stdio.h>
#include <math.h>
int main(void)
{
void (*fptr)() = fabs;    /* generic function pointer */
/*
printf("\nABS1 = %lf", (*fptr)(-1.0));
*/
printf("\nABS2 = %lf", (* (double (*)())fptr ) (-99));
printf("\nABS3 = %lf", (* (double (*)())fptr ) (-99L));
printf("\nABS4 = %lf", (* (double (*)())fptr ) (-99.0F));
printf("\nABS5 = %lf", (* (double (*)(double))fptr ) (-99));
exit(0);
}
```

FIGURE 14.5: Sample program ch14e5.c demonstrates the pitfalls of intermingling the use of K&R style and C++ style function prototypes in Standard C.

Arrays

Just as we can declare an array of pointers to data objects, we can also declare an array of pointers to functions, as shown in the following example:

```
int *ptr[10];        /* ptr is an array of ten pointers to type int */

int (*fptr[10]) ()   /* fptr is an array of ten pointers to
                         functions returning type int */
```

Both arrays above require the same storage space when the Tiny, Small, Large, and Huge memory models are used (see Table 10.1), and contain memory addresses, but they point to objects of vastly different types. For the sake of this discussion we will work with one-dimensional arrays, but certainly two-, three- and n-dimensional arrays of function pointers can be declared (refer to Chapter 10).

Consider the program example listed in Figure 14.6. It uses an array of function pointers and demonstrates a number of other interesting coding techniques. Notice that the array of function pointers is initialized with a series of compatible function names (return type **double**, argument type **double**) from **<math.h>**, and is later treated as a **NULL**-terminated list.

The controlling **while**-loop demonstrates the use of the comma operator, which associates left-to-right so that variable **i** is reinitialized to zero, and then the **scanf** function is invoked. Its return value is compared with EOF, which is defined as (−1) in **<stdio.h>**, to end the program.

To generate an EOF from the keyboard, either press Ctrl-Z ↵ or, using the numeric keypad, press Alt-26 ↵. The Ctrl-Z sequence generates an 0x1A

```
/* FILE: ch14e6.c */
#include <stdio.h>
#include <math.h>
#define PI (acos(-1.0))
int main(void)
{
double (*fp[])(double) = {sin, cos, tan, sinh,\
                          cosh, tanh, NULL};
double angle, radians;
int i;
printf("\nEnter Angle in degrees = ");
while (i=0, scanf("%lf",&angle) != EOF) {
    printf("\n");
    radians = PI * (angle/180.0);
    while (fp[i]) printf("%8.4e ", (*fp[i++])(radians));
        printf("\n\nEnter Angle in degrees = ");
        }
exit(0);
}
```

FIGURE 14.6: Sample program ch14e6.c demonstrates the use of an array of function pointers often referred to as a dispatch table.

(decimal 26), which is treated as an end-of-file character by DOS. The Alt-26 technique permits any decimal character code value to be entered from the keyboard, not just the symbols included on your particular keyboard.

The various trigonometric function values are displayed for the angle (in degrees) entered by using a **while**-loop that tests for a **NULL** pointer value to end. For example

```
Enter Angle in degrees = 90.0
1.0000e+000 6.1257e-017 1.6325e_016 ... 9.1715e-001
Enter Angle in degrees = ^Z
```

Because **NULL** is equivalent to zero, it is logically false; otherwise, each pointer value is considered to be nonzero or logically true. The subscript variable **i** is postincremented with the expression that initiates the performance of the functions using the pointers in the array **fp**.

Structure and Union Members

Function pointers may also be declared as members of structures and unions, and as members of dynamically allocated (using the **malloc()** family of functions) structure objects which support the implementation of complex data structures, such as lists and trees.

Consider the following structure declaration, rec, which consists of three members: **rec.raw_pt_number**, **rec.raw_pt_value**, and **rec.ptr_scale_fn**, a function pointer.

```
structure stag { unsigned raw_pt_number;
    double raw_pt_value;
    double (*ptr_scale_fn) (double); }
structure stag rec, *ptr = &rec;

double scaled_value;
```

Assuming that the structure members have been initialized, to invoke a scaling function for the **raw_pt_value** use **ptr_scale_fn** and the member operator (.) as shown:

```
scaled_value = (*rec.ptr_scale_fn) (rec.raw_pt_value)
```

Or use the pointer to a member operator (–>) as follows:

```
scaled_value = (*ptr->ptr_scale_fn) (ptr->raw_pt_value)
```

Function pointers that are members of structures (or unions) behave in the same way as data-object type pointer members, which were discussed in Chapters 9 and 10.

Error Handling

Most functions in C are designed to return an error value in the event that they cannot perform their assigned task successfully. By capturing and testing a function's return value, appropriate actions can then be taken.

When a function has no return value (**void**), it is not possible to return a unique error value and the global variable **errno** is sometimes employed (see Appendix C and Chapter 6). Since this variable is potentially reset whenever a function is called, the following coding technique is recommended:

1. **#include <stdlib.h>** to provide the **extern** description of global variable **errno**.
2. Immediately preceding such a function call, set the value of **errno** either to zero or the object-like macro **EZERO**.
3. Invoke the function that utilizes global variable **errno** to set an error condition.
4. Immediately following the function call, test whether the value of **errno** has changed from zero or **EZERO**.
5. If an error condition is indicated, use the run-time library function **perror()** or **strerror()** to display an appropriate message that is associated with the object-like macro error codes defined in **<errno.h>**, and branch accordingly to accommodate the failure of the function call.

Use of this technique is employed in many of the sample programs found in Parts VI and VII of this book.

All DOS system calls (see Chapter 22) support the use of the run-time library function **dosexterr()**, which can be used to retrieve extended error information in the structure **DOSERROR**, defined in header file **<dos.h>** (see Appendix E). For more about this technique, see Chapter 22 and Chapter 29.

Another technique is also available with the floating-point math run-time library functions found in Chapter 23. When a floating-point error (domain, singularity, range, or precision) occurs, the run-time function **matherr()** may be used to retrieve extended error information in the **exception** and **_exceptionl** structures defined in header file **<math.h>** (see Appendix E). For more about this technique, see Chapters 23 and 29.

Clearly, because we rely upon functions in C to perform all program actions, we must be vigilant to ensure that every function performs as intended and anticipate that an error may occur.

PERFORMANCE CONSIDERATIONS

Declaring the storage class of function arguments to be **register** will significantly improve program performance. Recall from Figure 8.7, "Classic String Copy Function Alternatives," that the use of **register** storage class for both of two function arguments improved overall performance by up to 38 percent. When the number of arguments exceeds the two or three registers normally available, designate only those arguments as **register** that will most significantly impact overall performance. Recall that if registers are not available, the storage class automatically reverts to **auto** (on the stack). Another approach is to use compiler option **/Gr** or the qualifier **_fastcall** to instruct the compiler to select the arguments to be passed in registers rather than on the stack.

When developing custom functions or using the C run-time library functions, another key consideration is whether an equivalent function-like macro or an intrinsic function can be used instead of the function call itself.

There are several ways to control whether certain C run-time library functions are to be treated as functions, intrinsic functions, or function-like macros. The progression from functions to intrinsics to macros normally improves overall program performance, but at the expense of increased program size. First we'll consider the use of function-like macros.

Function-Like Macros

All function-like macros generate inline code because they represent simple text substitution. It is generally preferable to use a function-like macro when the logic of the intended function is simple and the number of function occurrences is small, but the number of invocations is high—for example, a single function call within a loop that is performed many times. However, as the number of function occurrences increases, using function-like macros increases the size of the source code itself, which may be counterproductive.

As we discovered in Chapter 5, certain run-time library functions are also declared as macros within header files. To have the function-like macro substitution performed by the preprocessor, include the appropriate header file. To have the run-time function invoked, **#include** the appropriate header file and then use a **#undef** directive to undefine the function-like macros that you wish to disable, so that the text substitution is not performed, and the run-time library function is invoked instead.

Intrinsic Functions

By using the **#intrinsic** directive, certain of the C run-time library functions (listed in Table 5.3) may be designated not to be be treated in the Standard C calling convention (see Chapter 15) using the stack (or select register arguments), but rather to use only registers for argument and return value handling. Intrinsics are not function-like macros, but object-code that is interfaced in this special manner. Intrinsic function may be invoked using compiler option **/Oi** or by specifying the individual functions to be used from Table 5.3, using the **#pragma intrinsic** directive.

The performance advantage of using intrinsics was demonstrated in Figure 12.6 when the use of function **fmod()** was compared with the use of the intrinsic version of **fmod()**. The relative performance measures of using the **fmod()** function and its corresponding intrinsic form are summarized below, and indicate a minimum improvement of from 30 to 40 percent.

ARGUMENT →	float	double	long double
function fmod()	171.4	137.5	137.5
	135.2	118.2	118.3
intrinsic fmod()	95.6	98.3	98.3

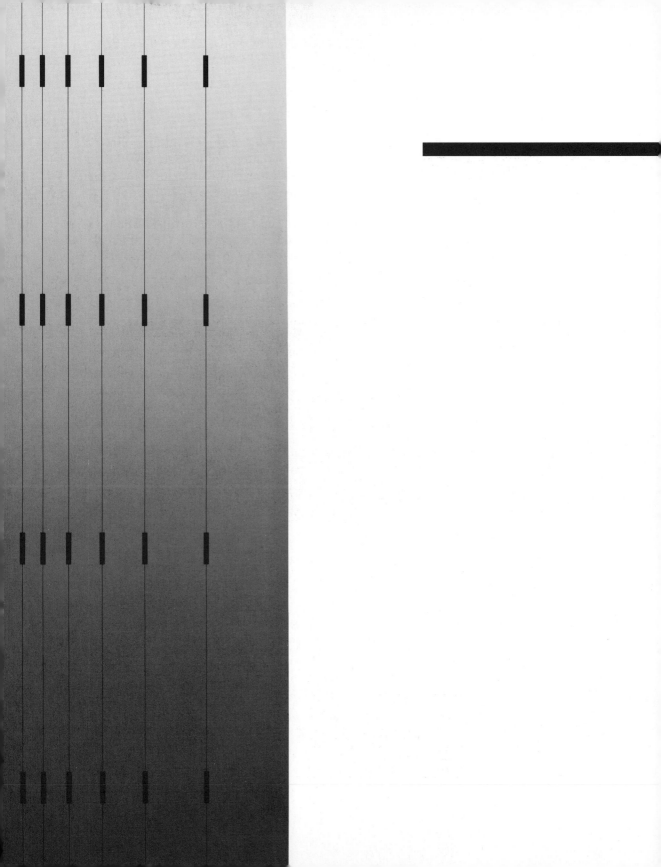

# CHAPTER 15

Special Function **main()**

Special Function `main()`

As discussed in Chapter 14, all functions in C have a common template. Although function `main()` adheres to that template, it is treated differently because it serves as both the entry point from and exit point to the host operating system DOS.

Unlike all other run-time library functions, function `main()` is not prototyped in any header file; rather, it is the programmer's responsibility to provide one, and only one, function `main()` when the linker constructs an executable program (.COM or .EXE). Failure to provide a function called `main()` results in a _main: *unresolved external* linker error message; and the inclusion of duplicate `main()` functions (or in fact any duplicate symbol) results in the linker error message _main: *symbol multiply defined.* Because of its unique status, function `main()` is often described as the program driver from which all other function calls originate. In Chapter 29 function `main()` is also referred to as an "embedded test driver."

The sections that follow explain the special function, argument, and return value declaration conventions that apply to `main()`, as well as how `main()` returns `<status>` codes. The DOS startup code (`crt0.asm`), which establishes the Standard C run-time environment consisting of code (text), data, the stack, and heap, is also examined.

The operations that can be performed upon `main()` functions, including the transfer of control to other `main()` programs using the run-time library family of `spawnxxx()` and `execxxx()` functions and recursion, are explored. This chapter also examines the `system()` function, which invokes the DOS command processor, which in turn is used to execute internal DOS commands, .BAT batch command files, and other external DOS commands and programs suffixed by .COM and .EXE.

Techniques for improving the performance of function `main()`, including the deliberate elimination of the standard environment arguments (`argc`, `argv`, and `envp`) and special handling of the stack and heap, are then explained.

`main()` FUNCTION TYPE QUALIFIERS

Only two alternate declarations of function **main()** conform with Standard C:

```
extern int main(void) { .. }
```

or

```
extern int main(int argc, char * argv[]) { .. }
```

Although variations of these prototypes are acceptable, by and large they are nonconforming. Let's examine the special manner in which function **main()** is handled.

The function-type qualifiers that may be used with **main()** represent a subset of those presented in Table 14.2. Only the [default] entries shown in Table 14.2 may be specified for function **main()**.

Storage-class keyword **static** is inappropriate because the associated file scope would hide the required symbol, **_main**, from the linker. Mixed language keywords **_fastcall**, **_fortran**, and **_pascal** are inappropriate because the external symbol **_main**, not **_MAIN**, is expected, and the order in which the arguments (**argc**, **argv**, **envp**) would be retrieved from the stack frame would be incorrect (see the "Stack Frame" section below). The register handling keywords **_interrupt**, **_loadds**, and **_saveregs** inappropriately describe function **main()**, and the function addressing keywords **_near** and **_far** are unnecessary because function **main()** is initiated by an assembly-language call statement which automatically accommodates whether **_main()** requires **_near** or **_far** addressing.

In summary, function **main()** is appropriately described by specifying no type qualifiers at all, or if qualifiers are specified, only use of keywords **extern** and **_cdecl** is appropriate.

RETURN TYPES

The correct declaration of the return type for function **main()** is simply type **int**. Although some books indicate that a return type of **void** is correct, a closer look at the DOS startup code for **main()**, contained in file **crt0.asm**, indicates that the exit status of **main()** is always interpreted as the contents of byte AL (8 bits) of register AX (16 bits), regardless of how function **main()** was declared or terminated. Therefore, a return type of **int** more appropriately describes the return value (register AX) of **main()** as a signed integer, even though a restricted range of value from −128 through 127 (8 bits) is imposed. Typically zero (0) is understood to indicate normal termination, while nonzero values are understood to indicate abnormal return values.

Although the normal function convention of using the return statement may be used with function **main()**, it is recommended that a run-time library function from Table 15.1 be used. Each function shown performs additional operations prior to relinquishing program control to the DOS command processor (COMMAND.COM) or another calling program (process). Table 15.1 describes in a logical sequence, from the first (left) to the last (right) column, the operations that are performed by the run-time library functions available to **main()**.

The column "**raise(SIGABRT)**" describes whether an abnormal termination signal is generated or not. For more on signal processing, see Chapter 25. The columns "Flush Buffers" and "Close Files" apply to both permanent and temporary files that may be open when the termination routines are encountered.

The column "**atexit()/onexit()**" refers to the functions that establish a LIFO (last in/first out) list of function pointers to be performed. Each function pointer must be a function that has no arguments and returns type **void**.

```
void (*fp) (void);
```

Up to 32 such function pointers may be stacked to sequence a series of function termination operations. Use function **atexit()** for conformance with Standard C, rather than function **onexit()**. For an example of using function **atexit()**, see the example stack sizing program shown in Figure 15.12, later in this chapter.

If a return statement is used that specifies a value such as **return (0);** it is understood to be equivalent to **exit(0);**. However, when a return statement is used that specifies no value, such as **return;**, then it is understood to be equivalent to **exit();**. The value returned is uncertain and simply represents the last value contained in the AL byte of register AX.

If no return statement is specified, and function **main()** ends by encountering the closing brace **}** (by dropping out of a function), it is equivalent to having coded

```
return;
```

or

```
exit();
```

TABLE 15.1: main() Termination Options

RUN-TIME FUNCTION	raise (SIGABRT)	PRINT MESSAGE	FLUSH BUFFERS	CLOSE FILES	atexit() onexit()	TERMINATE PROCESS	RETURN TO CALLER	RETURN TO DOS	RETURN <status>
abort (void)	Yes	Yes	No	No	No	Yes	No	Yes	Yes[3]
_cexit (void)	No	No	Yes	Yes	Yes	No	Yes	No	No
_c_exit (void)	No	No	No	No	No	No	Yes	No	No
exit (int)	No	No	Yes	Yes	Yes	Yes	No	Yes	Yes
_exit (int)	No	No	No	No	No	Yes	No	Yes	Yes
return[1]	No	No	Yes	Yes	Yes	Yes	No	Yes	Yes
[none][2]	No	No	Yes	Yes	Yes	Yes	No	Yes	No

NOTES:
1. C keyword, not a function; not recommended.
2. Not recommended.
3. Always returns <status> of <3>.

Do not rely upon the return statement in function **main()** or dropping out; rather, always terminate **main()** with a function call to one of the run-time library functions shown in Table 15.1.

For examples of using each of the functions featured in Table 15.1, refer to Chapter 25.

Using Exit Codes

When function **main()** returns to DOS, an **IF** batch file command may be used to test whether the exit **<status>** code **(ERRORLEVEL)** is equal to or greater than a stated value. For example

```
IF ERRORLEVEL 1 command          true if ERRORLEVEL >= 1
```

or

```
IF NOT ERRORLEVEL 1 command      true if ERRORLEVEL < 1
```

When function **main()** does not return to DOS, but rather serves as a child process, the parent process can interrogate the return value of one of the family of run-time library functions called **spawnxxx()** using an **if..else..** statement as follows:

```
if (!spawnxxx(...))  spawnxxx(...);
else printf("\nmessage ..");
```

For more about using the **spawnxxx()** family of functions, see the "Process Initiation" section below and Chapter 25.

ARGUMENT TYPES

Standard C supports a declaration of function **main()** that either has no arguments

```
int main(void);
```

or a fixed number of arguments, declared either as

```
main(int argc, char * argv[])
```

or

```
main (int argc, char * * argv)
```

where **argc** is the number of arguments, and **argv** is an array of pointers to characters or equivalently a pointer to a pointer to a character. Recall that one level of subscripting is equivalent to one level of indirection.

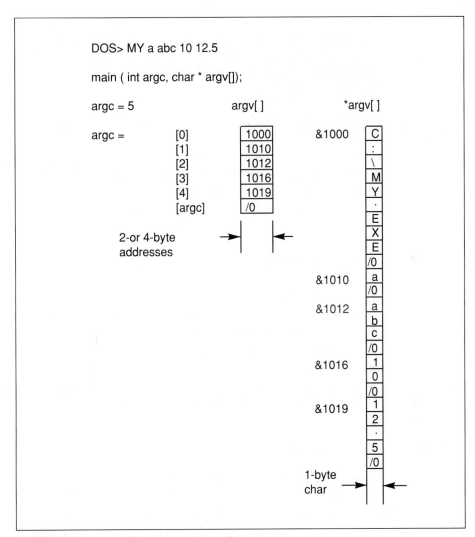

FIGURE 15.1: Command line arguments argc & argv.

Figure 15.1 demonstrates how **argc** and **argv** are passed to function **main()** from the DOS command line.

Notice that **argc** always includes the complete program filename as **argv[0]**, and that **argv[argc]** is always a **NULL** pointer. Each command-line argument is passed as a character string! The linked program example, **MY.EXE**, shown in Figure 15.2, demonstrates how these strings can be converted to their intended data types using the run-time library family of **atox()** functions described in Chapter 20.

```
/* FILE: ch15e1.c */
#include <stdio.h>
#include <stdlib.h>
int main(int argc, char * argv[])
{
int i = 0;
char arg1, arg2[5];
int arg3;
double arg4;
while (argv[i]) {
    printf("\narg[%1d] = %s",i,argv[i]);
    switch (i) {
        case 1:   arg1 = *argv[i];
                  break;
        case 2:   strcpy(arg2,argv[i]);
                  break;
        case 3:   arg3 = atoi(argv[i]);
                  break;
        case 4:   arg4 = atof(argv[i]);
                  break;
        }
    i++;
    }
printf("\n\narg1 = %c\
    \narg2 = %s\
    \narg3 = %d\
    \narg4 = %lf",arg1, arg2, arg3, arg4);
exit(0);
}
```

FIGURE 15.2: Sample program ch15e1.c demonstrates the proper use of the Standard arguments, argc and argv, of special function main().

The sample program in Figure 15.2 produces the following output:

```
arg[0] = C:\MY.EXE
arg[1] = a
arg[2] = abc
arg[3] = 10
arg[4] = 12.5

arg1 = a
arg2 = abc
arg3 = 10
arg4 = 12.500000
```

It is also interesting to note that the formal arguments of function **main()** need not always be named **argc** and **argv**, but can be given any names. It is by K&R convention that these names are used. For example, the program shown in Figure 15.3 parallels the example above, and confirms the addressing noted in Figure 15.1.

It generates the following output:

```
arg[0] = 1000   *arg[0] = C   string = C:\MY.EXE
arg[1] = 1010   *arg[1] = a   string = a
arg[2] = 1012   *arg[2] = a   string = abc
arg[3] = 1016   *arg[3] = 1   string = 10
arg[4] = 1019   *arg[4] = 1   string = 12.5
```

```
/* FILE: ch15e2.c */
#include <stdio.h>
int main(int cnt, char * ary[])
{
int i = 0;
while (ary[i]) {
    printf("\narg[%1d] = %Np  *arg[%1d] = %c   string = %s",
           i, ary[i], i, *ary[i], ary[i]);
    i++;
    }
exit(0);
}
```

FIGURE 15.3: Sample program ch15e2.c demonstrates that any names may be used to identify the arguments to special function main ().

Notice that formal arguments **argc** and **argv** were replaced by the identifiers **cnt** and **ary**, respectively, and that the addresses generated when you compile and execute this program may differ but demonstrate the concept depicted in Figure 15.1.

Handling Wildcard Arguments

Microsoft C provides a technique to accommodate the expansion of command-line arguments that represent DOS filenames containing the special ***** and **?** wildcard characters (see Chapter 1, "Redirection, Piping, and the Command Line"). The object module **setargv.obj**, included in the run-time library by default, ignores all such wildcards and constructs argument **argv** literally without expanding such characters.

A special object module with the same name (**setargv.obj**), which performs the expansion of any filename wildcards when argument **argv** is constructed, is provided on the C Compiler installation diskettes.

To override the default use of **setargv.obj** from the run-time library, simply include the special **setargv.obj** version in the build list and specify option **/NOE** to the linker, or use the LIB command (see Chapter 3) to replace the default module in the run-time library. When this special object module is included, all wildcards (***** and **?**) will be expanded from the command line, unless specifically included in double quotation marks or if no wildcard matches are found to exist. Refer to the sample program in Figure 15.4.

If this sample program were compiled and linked without the special **setargv.obj** module and then executed from the DOS command line as

```
C:\> ch15e3  i*.doc i*.doc
```

the following output would result:

```
arg[1] = i*.doc
arg[2] = i*.doc
```

```
/* FILE: ch15e3.c */
#include <stdio.h>
int main(int argc, char * argv[])
{
int i = 1;
while (argv[i]) {
    printf("\narg[%1d] = %s",i,argv[i]);
    i++;
    }
exit(0);
}
```

FIGURE 15.4: Sample program ch15e3.c demonstrates the fact that Standard C mandates that argv[argc] is always a NULL pointer.

Whereas, if the same program were compiled and linked using the special **setargv.obj** module and the **/NOE** option and executed from the DOS command line as shown above, then the following might be generated:

```
arg[1] = INTRO-BK.DOC
arg[2] = INTRO-P1.DOC
arg[3] = INTRO-P2.DOC
arg[4] = INTRO-P3.DOC
arg[5] = INTRO-P4.DOC
arg[6] = INTRO-P5.DOC
arg[7] = i*.doc
```

If no wildcard matches were found, the following output would have been generated:

```
arg[1] = i*.doc
arg[2] = i*.doc
```

Accessing the Environment Table

Microsoft C provides another non-Standard argument called **envp**, which is declared in a fashion similar to **argv** as follows:

```
int main( int argc, char * argv[], char * envp[])
```

or

```
int main( int argc, char * * argv, char * * envp)
```

It contains the environment strings that are created and displayed using the DOS SET command (see Chapter 1). Refer to the example program in Figure 15.5.

If you compiled and executed the example program shown in Figure 15.5 and issued the DOS SET commands

```
C:\>SET COMSPEC=C:\COMMAND.COM
C:\>SET PROMPT=$P$G
```

```
/* FILE: ch15e4.c */
#include <stdio.h>
int main(int argc, char * argv[], char * envp[])
{
int i = 0;
while (envp[i]) {
     printf("\nenvp[%1d] = %s",i,envp[i]);
     i++;
     }
exit(0);
}
```

FIGURE 15.5: Sample program ch15e4.c demonstrates the use of the non-Standard argument envp with special function main().

```
C:\>SET PATH=C:\QC2\BIN;C:\;C:\DOS
C:\>SET LIB=C:\QC2\LIB
C:\>SET INCLUDE=C:\QC2\INCLUDE
```

the following output would be generated:

```
envp[0] = COMSPEC=C:\COMMAND.COM
envp[1] = PROMPT=$P$G
envp[2] = PATH=C:\QC2\BIN;C:\;C:\DOS
envp[3] = LIB=C:\QC2\LIB
envp[4] = INCLUDE=C:\QC2\INCLUDE
```

Notice that when the **envp** argument is declared, it must follow the declarations of **argc** and **argv** as shown above. Also note that, like **argv** (Figure 15.1), **envp** is a **NULL**-terminated pointer array. This feature supports the use of the **while**-loop, as shown in Figure 15.5. Notice that the strings constructed for **envp** contain the environment variable name, followed by an equal sign (**=**) and the string associated with the variable.

Standard C provides an alternate technique that uses the run-time library function **getenv()**, not the non-Standard **envp** approach, to retrieve the strings associated with a given environment variable. For example, the program shown in Figure 15.6 uses function **getenv()**, whose prototype is declared in header file **<stdlib.h>**.

The program produces the following output:

```
COMSPEC = C:\COMMAND.COM
PROMPT = $P$G
PATH = C:\QC2\BIN;C:\;C:\DOS
LIB = C:\QC2\LIB
TMP = (null)
INCLUDE = C:\QC2\INCLUDE
```

Notice that function **getenv()** returns a pointer to a **char** and also returns a **NULL** if no match is found. The spelling and capitalization of the SET environment variables must exactly agree if a match is to be found.

```
/* FILE: ch15e5.c */
#include <stdio.h>
#include <stdlib.h>
int main(void)
{
int i = 0;
char * names[] = { "COMSPEC",
                   "PROMPT",
                   "PATH",
                   "LIB",
                   "TMP",
                   "INCLUDE",
                   NULL };
while (names[i]) {
    printf("\n%s = %s",names[i],getenv(names[i]));
    i++;
    }
exit(0);
}
```

FIGURE 15.6: Sample program ch15e5.c demonstrates the use of the Standard run-time function, getenv(), to retrieve strings from the environment table.

For example, had **comspec** been declared instead of **COMSPEC**, a **NULL** would have been displayed. Also note that variable TMP was not SET, and therefore a **NULL** (null) was returned.

Another non-Standard technique that can be employed to access environment strings is the use of the global variable **environ**, declared in **<stdlib.h>** and described in Appendix C as

```
extern char * * environ;
```

or

```
extern char * environ[];
```

This supports access to the environment variables without resorting to the use of the **envp** argument. Refer to Figure 15.7 for an example program.

This program displays the current environment strings as follows:

```
environ[0] = COMSPEC=C:\COMMAND.COM
environ[1] = PROMPT=$P$G
environ[2] = PATH=C:\QC2\BIN;C:\;C:\DOS
environ[3] = LIB=C:\QC2\LIB
environ[4] = INCLUDE=C:\QC2\INCLUDE
```

It is also possible to add, remove, or modify environment strings using the non-Standard run-time library function **putenv()**, rather than the DOS SET command. Recall from Chapter 1 that a copy of the environment is passed to each program by a pointer in its PSP (program segment prefix). When it is necessary to alter the environment, another version of this environment may be created, which represents a relocated copy of the original environment strings.

```
/* FILE: ch15e6.c */
#include <stdio.h>
extern char * * environ;
int main()
{
int i = 0;
while (environ[i]) {
     printf("\nenviron[%ld] = %s",i,environ[i]);
     i++;
     }
exit(0);
}
```

FIGURE 15.7: Sample program ch15e6.c demonstrates the use of the non-Standard global variable, environ, to retrieve strings from the environment table.

The use of **getenv()**, **environ**, and **putenv()** can assure the integrity of the information in a program's environment if it has been changed, whereas the **envp** argument simply reflects the initial location of the environment strings. The example program in Figure 15.8 deletes, modifies, and adds environment strings.

It displays the following output using both the **envp** and **environ** arrays to demonstrate a before and after scenario.

```
envp[0] = COMSPEC=C:\COMMAND.COM
envp[1] = PROMPT=$P$G
envp[2] = PATH=C:\QC2\BIN;C:\;C:\DOS
envp[3] = LIB=C:\QC2\LIB
envp[4] = INCLUDE=C:\QC2\INCLUDE

environ[0] = COMSPEC=C:\COMMAND.COM
environ[1] = PROMPT=
environ[2] = PATH=C:\QC2\BIN;C:\;C:\DOS
environ[3] = LIB=C:\QC2\LIB;C:\MSCV5\LIB;C:\C600\LIB;
environ[4] = INCLUDE=C:\QC2\INCLUDE
environ[5] = TMP=C:\QC2\TMP
environ[6] = MYSTRING=a custom application specific string

envp[0] = COMSPEC=C:\COMMAND.COM
envp[1] = PROMPT=
envp[2] = PATH=C:\QC2\BIN;C:\;C:\DOS
envp[3] = LIB=C:\QC2\LIB;C:\MSCV5\LIB;C:\C600\LIB;
envp[4] = INCLUDE=C:\QC2\INCLUDE
```

Notice that after the alteration of the environment string values, the use of **environ** displayed the proper result; however, the subsequent use of **envp** (function **dis_envp()**) did not.

```
/* FILE: ch15e7.c */
#include <stdio.h>
#include <stdlib.h>
extern char * * environ;

void dis_envp(char * envp[])
{
int i = 0;
printf("\n");
while (envp[i]) {
    printf("\nenvp[%1d] = %s",i,envp[i]);
    i++;
    }
}

int main( int argc, char * argv[], char * envp[])
{
int i = 0;
dis_envp(envp);          /* display "initial" values */

putenv("PROMPT=");
putenv("LIB=C:\\QC2\\LIB;C:\\MSCV5\\LIB;C:\\C600\\LIB;");
putenv("TMP=C:\\QC2\\TMP");
putenv("MYSTRING=a custom application specific string");
printf("\n");
while (environ[i]) {
    printf("\nenviron[%1d] = %s",i,environ[i]);
    i++;
    }

dis_envp(envp);          /* display "modified" values */
exit(0);
}
```

FIGURE 15.8: Sample program ch15e7.c demonstrates that if the environment table is altered, it may be copied and relocated to a new address in memory.

Modifying Arguments `argc` and `argv`

Standard C mandates that the arguments to function **main()** may be modified. This feature is demonstrated by the sample program in Figure 15.9, which modifies argument **argv** and also demonstrates that function **main()** can, like any other function, be called recursively. Rather than performing a program iteratively, this example relies upon the integer value of **argv[1]** to indicate how many more repetitions must be performed, and recursively calls **main()** until the number of iterations of the job is completed.

If we issue the following DOS command:

`C:\> ch15e8  0005`

the program produces the following result:

```
cnt = 1
cnt = 2
cnt = 3
cnt = 4
cnt = 5
```

```
/* FILE: ch15e8.c */
#include <stdio.h>
#include <stdlib.h>
int main(int argc, char * argv[])
{
static cnt = 1;
int ntimes;
if (argc != 2) exit(-1);
ntimes = atoi(argv[1]);
if (ntimes > 0) {
    /* begin code to be repeated */

    printf("\ncnt = %d",cnt);
    cnt++;

    /* end code to be repeated */

    /* setup for next iteration */
    sprintf(argv[1],"%4d",ntimes-1);
    main(2,argv);
    }
else exit(0);
}
```

FIGURE 15.9: Sample program ch15e8.c demonstrates that special function main() may also be called recursively.

Notice that the contents of **argv[1]** are altered by function **sprintf()** each time function **main()** is performed. Care is taken that the **sprintf()** function does not clobber anything in **argv** except **argv[1]**. Note that successive calls to **main()** do not reinvoke the startup (**crt0.asm**, entry point named **_astart**) code; rather, after **_astart** relinquishes control, **main()** behaves as any other function, except that it returns to DOS when it terminates.

OPERATIONS

The operations that may be performed with function **main()** are restricted because **main()** returns a type **int** value (8-bit AL of register AX) that behaves more like a **signed char** than an integer, and when **main()** terminates, it typically returns to DOS or another parent process. However, when **main()**'s properties are coupled with the **spawn*xxx*()** and **exec*xxx*()** families of run-time library functions, some new and interesting possibilities emerge.

We will first examine the run-time environment that every **main()** function inherits from the **crt0.asm** startup code when a C program is initiated by DOS from the command line (COMMAND.COM). Then we will examine how **main()** can be initiated by a process other than COMMAND.COM. Any parent process (DOS program) can initiate **main()** using the **spawn*xxx*()** or **exec*xxx*()** family of run-time library functions.

Finally, we will see how the **system()** function may be used to invoke COMMAND.COM itself.

Let's begin by examining the default DOS startup code typically used to initiate every Microsoft C program.

Startup Code

Although we think of function **main()** as the function to which the operating system passes control when a C program is initiated from the DOS command line, DOS actually passes control to an assembly language label called **_astart**, which is included in every C **main()** program (.COM and .EXE file) produced by the linker. The object module named **crt0.obj** represents the assembled startup **crt0.asm** module.

Although the assembly language source code (**crt0.asm**) for the Standard C program startup is provided with the C compiler installation diskettes so that it can be modified, normally the default object module version (**crt0.obj**) found in each C run-time library is used. This code is responsible for establishing the run-time environment (initial register values) that is assumed to exist by every C program.

Recall from the memory model diagrams presented in Chapter 2 (Figures 2.21 through 2.26) that every C program consists of an ordered set of segments (64KB addressable areas of memory). For discussion purposes, these memory model diagrams can be generalized as shown in Figure 15.10.

Notice that the Code, Data, Stack, and Heap segments are ordered from low to high memory addresses. The arrows shown indicate the direction in which growth occurs within each category. Recall that the stack has a fixed default size of 2KB, but can be adjusted up to 64KB if necessary. Notice that the stack grows towards low memory. The top-of-stack address is always recorded by the stack pointer (SP), and the bottom-of-stack address is located by the **_end** symbol defined in **crt0.asm**.

In the "Stack" section that follows, a program example uses the **_end** symbol defined in **crt0.asm** as the bottom-of-stack to demonstrate a technique for determining the amount of unused stack space over the duration of a program's execution. In the "Performance Considerations" section that follows, the role that **xvarstck.obj** plays in permitting the unused Stack space to be shared with the Heap is explained.

The **crt0.asm** startup code performs a number of key steps (among others) that are necessary to establish the C run-time environment depicted in Figure 15.10 and are specifically implemented for each memory model depicted in Figures 2.20 through 2.25.

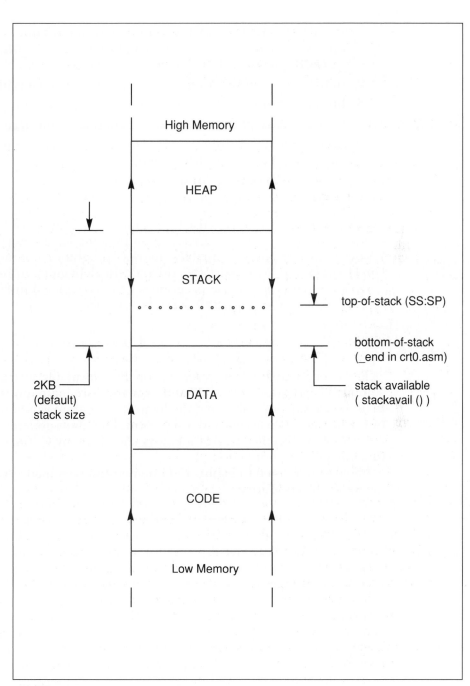

FIGURE 15.10: C run-time environment.

1. Initialize the registers with appropriate segment values, based upon the memory model being employed (**_CODE**, **_DATA**, **_STACK**, **_CONST**, etc.).

2. Initialize the uninitialized static data (**_BSS**) to all bits off (zero).

3. Invoke **setenvp()** to establish the environment array.

4. Invoke **setargv()** to establish the command-line argument array.

5. Accommodate any inherited files from the environment string **_C_FILE_INFO=** (see Chapter 16).

6. Invoke **main(argc, argv, envp)**.

7. Return to DOS with **<status>** code.

Of the preceding steps, effective C programming demands a clear understanding of step 1 to aid in the selection of compiler memory models to properly declare pointer variables, to avert program run-time errors related to stack and heap overflow, and to devise debugging strategies.

Let's examine each of the program segments depicted in Figure 15.10 that are initialized by the **crt0.asm** startup code.

Code

The code or text area is reserved for the executable instructions of a compiled C program. The code and data areas are maintained separately to minimize the possibility that the logic of a program would be modified by inadvertent data access and assignment. Functions generate code, and the only access to this area of memory should be by C function calls or function pointer indirection.

The program listed in Figure 15.11 demonstrates an inadvertent attempt to modify the code area:

```
/* FILE: ch15e9.c */
#include <stdio.h>

void fn()
{
printf("\nending fn()");
}

int main(void)
{
strcpy(fn,"clobber bytes");
fn();
printf("\nending main()");
}
```

FIGURE 15.11: Sample program ch15e9.c demonstrates an inadvertent attempt to write data to a code segment in memory.

Notice that the string copy function, **strcpy()**, attempts to copy the character string "clobber bytes" to the address designated by **fn**, the address of function **fn()**. The following output resulted:

```
ending fn()
ending main()
run-time error R6001
- null pointer assignment
```

Obviously, the **strcpy()** operation was not performed, and attempts to modify code are not desirable; rather, to modify code, alter your C source code and recompile your program! With the introduction of **_based(..)** pointers, it is now possible to allocate data to code segment(s). This technique is generally not recommended, but might be useful, for example with the Small memory model, to extend the usable data space beyond 64KB by allocating data to the unused portion of the allowable 64KB code space, without resorting to using the Compact memory model, which would increase the size of all data pointers from **_near** to **_far**.

Data

The data area consists only of **extern** and **static** storage class variables, not **auto** variables, which are always allocated in the stack area. The data area is subdivided into initialized and uninitialized segments, depending upon how the data is declared by a program. All such data is characterized as load-time, not run-time, data. Initialized segments such as CONST contain initialized data when loaded into memory, whereas the uninitialized segments such as BSS (block started by symbol) are set to binary zero (all bits off) by step 2 of the **crt0.asm** startup code noted above. This explains why all **extern** and **static** variables are automatically initialized to zero and retain those values, unless altered, for the entire duration of a program.

Stack

The stack area has a maximum size that is set either at compile-time (default = 2KB; maximum = 64KB), by the linker, or by the EXEHDR utility. The stack is used to temporarily store the following in a LIFO (last-in, first-out) fashion, much like a spring-loaded stack of cafeteria trays.

1. Function actual arguments.
2. Function return addresses.

3. Auto variables.

4. Temporary values during expression evaluation.

5. Recursion: repeat 1–4 above.

Notice that the stack is the only memory area of a program that grows towards low memory. The current top-of-stack address is always held in the stack pointer (SP). Fundamentally, two assembly language instructions control the operation of the stack: PUSH and POP. PUSH decrements the address in SP by a word (two or four bytes), and places the value of a word at that address, whereas POP removes a word from address SP, then increments SP by either two or four bytes. Variations of these instructions exist for different machine architectures, but these two operations essentially describe how the stack is manipulated.

Before describing how the stack is used, let's understand how to determine the best size of the stack, given the fact that its maximum size is fixed and may not be altered at run-time.

Sizing the Stack The problem of appropriately sizing the stack is seldom addressed; rather, programmers often rely on the compiler to generate run-time error messages when the stack overflows (is too small). Ideally, the stack size should be set large enough to permit a program to run until completion without overflowing the stack; however, there is no Microsoft or Standard C facility that reports the maximum amount of stack space utilized or, conversely, the amount of excess stack allocated. The sample program in Figure 15.12 finally solves this problem.

Compile program ch15e10.c using one of the following DOS command lines:

```
QCL /DNDEBUG ch15e10.c
```

or

```
CL  /DNDEBUG ch15e10.c
```

If function **markstack()** is included as the first executable statement in **main()** as shown in Figure 15.12, then when **main()** terminates, a one-line message will be displayed that reveals the amount of unused stack space in bytes over the entire duration of a program's execution. Knowing this piece of information, you can intelligently size the stack and minimize any wasted space.

Figure 15.10 and the **crt0.asm** startup code hold the keys to understanding how **markstack()** works. Global symbol **_end** is defined in **crt0.asm** to locate the bottom-of-stack. C run-time library function **stackavail()** (see Chapter 24) returns the approximate amount

```
/* FILE: ch15e10.c */
/* mark_stack(): reports the amount of unused stack space
   over the duration of a program's execution; useful for
   adjusting the /STACK smaller to save memory or deciding to
   use the special module xvarstck.obj; also see The C Gazette,
   Autumn 1989, "Measuring Stack Usage" by John Rex
   (see Appendix A: Bibliography)
*/
#include <stdio.h>
#include <malloc.h>

extern char end;                       /* stack bottom in crt0.asm */

static char * stack_bot = (char *) &end;
static char mark = 0xff;                /* clean stack footprint */
static char * ptr;

static void report_stack(void)         /* atexit style function */
{
static unsigned unused;
unused = 0;
ptr = stack_bot;
while (*ptr++ == mark) unused++;    /* look for footprints */
printf("\n\nUnused Stack = %u Bytes\n\n",unused);
}

void mark_stack(void)
{
static char * stack_top;
stack_top = stack_bot + stackavail();   /* OK within 256-bytes */
ptr = stack_bot;
do {                             /* paint the stack */
   *ptr++ = mark;
   } while (ptr < stack_top);
atexit(report_stack);            /* log function ptr with atexit */
}

#ifdef NDEBUG                     /* conditional compile */
int main (void)
{
mark_stack();                    /* ENTER ONCE AS 1ST STMT */
exit(0);                         /* report_stack() upon exit */
}
#endif
```

FIGURE 15.12: Sample program ch15e10.c provides a function that determines the amount of unused stack space over the duration of a program's execution.

(within 256 bytes) of unused stack. Function **markstack()** simply "paints" the unused stack space with variable **mark**, a known stack footprint. Function pointer **report_stack** is registered with function **atexit()** to be performed when **main()** terminates normally. When **main()** terminates, function **report_stack()** is performed, which looks at the "painted" stack from the bottom-of-stack until a "non-footprint" is found, thereby determining the amount of unused stack space.

With this information, either the stack size can be reduced to free up additional heap space, or a decision can be made to use the special **xvarstck.obj** module and permit the heap to use any available stack space. Now that the stack has been appropriately sized, let's examine how functions use the stack.

Stack Frames Unless **register** storage class is specified for function arguments or the **_fastcall** keyword is employed, all C function arguments are passed using the stack and a technique known as creating function stack frames. The term *stack frame* is an assembly language convention that describes the items that are placed on the stack to enable a function to be called and to return correctly. Figure 15.13 depicts the sequence of events surrounding the formation and use of a stack frame.

All functions in C, even function **main()**, are called using the technique shown in Figure 15.13. Although the schematic may look confusing, consider that it represents a snapshot of the stack and portrays a sequence of three function calls as described below.

pfn()   Prior function that called **cnf()**.

cfn()   Current function that calls **nfn()**, then returns to **pfn()**.

nfn()   Next function that returns to **cfn()**.

The boxed items represent the stack frames for these functions. Each function in C has a stack frame associated with it each time it is invoked. Notice the numbering scheme, whereby the suffixes **(p)**, **(c)**, and **(n)** correspond to functions **pfn()**, **cfn()**, and **nfn()**, respectively, and are responsible for creating that stack frame item. The assembly and C language mixture of instructions shown is necessary to identify the hidden steps involved in calling and returning from a C function.

Every stack frame is created in part by the calling and called functions involved. To call a function, the calling function must first place the arguments of the called function on the stack (items 1 and 2) and then actually call the function (item 3), which places the calling function's return address IP (instruction pointer) on the stack and resets the IP to the address of the function being called.

When the function qualifier **_cdecl** is used, arguments are placed in the stack, rightmost to leftmost, whereas if the keywords **_fortran** or **_pascal** are used, the arguments are placed on the stack leftmost to rightmost. Because of this order, the Standard C (**_cdecl**) calling convention readily supports functions with a variable number of arguments (**. . .** punctuator); the Fortran, Pascal, and BASIC calling conventions do not.

Then the called function must immediately save the base pointer (BP) of the calling program on the stack (item 4) and reset the BP = SP (stack pointer) for the called function. The base pointer (BP) remains constant for a function's stack frame, unless otherwise altered by that function, while the stack pointer always points to the top-of-stack. Since the BP is

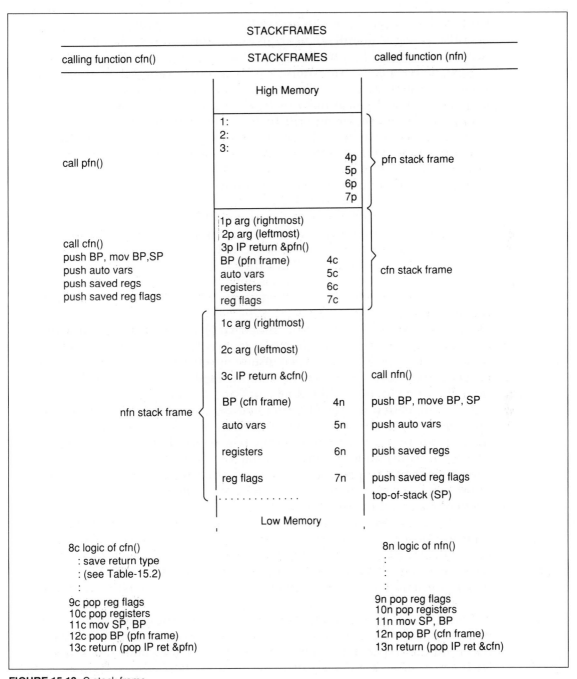

FIGURE 15.13: C stack frame.

fixed, any function arguments are addressed relative to BP using positive (+) offsets, and as we will see next, all **auto** storage class variables are addressed relative to BP by negative (−) offsets.

Next the called function must push any **auto** variables to the stack (item 5), save any registers that may be changed by the function (item 6), and save any register flags that may be changed by the function (item 7).

Items 1c, 2c, 3c, 4n, 5n, 6n, and 7n depict a typical stack frame construction sequence. Once items 4n, 5n, 6n, and 7n are completed, the called function **nfn()** performs its logic (item 8n) and then begins the return process.

When a function returns, the stack frame construction sequence must be reversed. First any register flags are popped (restored) from the stack (item 9n), followed by any registers (item 10n). Next, rather than popping off the **auto** variables, SP is simply set equal to BP (item 11n), which always points to the BP on the stack, thereby skipping any **auto** variables that were allocated. Then the BP of the calling function is popped from the stack (item 12n), and the return is initiated (item 13n), which pops the instruction pointer (IP) of the calling function from the stack to complete function **nfn()**.

At this point, we are again processing **cfn()** (item 8c), which either ignores or retrieves the return function type. All **_cdecl** function return values are handled by a standard register convention, based on the type of the data object involved. The conventions used by **_cdecl** type C functions are summarized in Table 15.2.

The compilation of **cfn()** generated the assembly language instructions necessary at the **nfn()** return address to either ignore or save the return value from **nfn()** placed in the registers as shown in Figure 15.10. The return conventions differ somewhat for functions declared as having either **_fortran** or **_pascal** calling conventions, for which some return values are placed on the stack and therefore require that stack space be allotted by the calling program.

Next, function **cfn()** continues with its logic and begins to repeat the return sequence (items 9c through 13c) because **cfn()** becomes the called function, and **pfn()** the calling function. The stack frame for **cfn()** is depicted above the stack frame for **nfn()** and, like that for **nfn()**, is composed of seven items, three of which were performed by **pfn()**, and the remaining four items by **cfn()**.

Notice that as functions are called in a nested fashion, the stack grows larger; otherwise, stack frames are created, then relinquished, and again overwritten when created, since the stack pointer (SP) always locates the current top-of-stack address.

This stack frame mechanism explains why recursion may result in a stack overflow, as well as how a large number of **auto** variables or structures and unions passed by value and not by reference (pointer) may overflow the stack.

TABLE 15.2: _cdecl Function Return Conventions

RETURN Type	MECHANISM
`char`	AL byte of register AX
`int`	AX register
`enum`	Same as `int`
`long`	DX (high), AX (low)
`float`	Copy to global `_fac`
`double`	Copy to global `_fac`
`long double`	On the stack (80x87 stack if present)
`_segment`	Same as `int`
`_near *`	AX `register` (:OFF)
`_far *`	DX `register` (SEG:), AX register (:OFF)
`_huge *`	Same as `_far *`
`_based(..) *`	Same as `_far *`
`arrays`	Only as `_near *`, `_far *`, `_huge *`, `_based(..) *`
`structures`	Copy structure to a global variable, then return the `&` (global variable) as `_near *`, `_far *`, `_huge *`, `_based(..) *`; or simply as `_near *`, `_far *`, `_huge *`, `_based(..) *`
`unions`	Same as structures
`functions`	Only as `_near *` or `_far *`

Heap

The heap area is used for all dynamic or run-time memory allocation of data. The size of the heap is limited only by the amount of actual unused memory, unless the special **xvarstck.obj** module is used (see the "Performance Considerations" section below), which permits the heap to also allocate data to the unused portion (stack available) of the stack.

All dynamic memory allocations from a C program utilize the **xmalloc()** family of run-time functions, **malloc()**, **nmalloc()**, and **fmalloc()** (see Chapter 24). Data objects are allocated memory that matches their respective size and type requirements (alignment) and must be freed to release heap space for subsequent reuse. As shown in the Chapter 2 memory model diagrams (Figures 2.20 through 2.25), heap space is classified as either heap, Near heap, or Far heap space. Regardless of the memory model employed, the **malloc()** function allocates memory to the area labeled "heap" on Figures 2.20 through 2.25. The Near heap is always accessed using the function **_nmalloc()** and is available when the Compact, Large, or Huge memory model is employed. The Far heap is always accessed using the function **_fmalloc()** and is available when the Tiny, Small, or Medium memory model is employed.

Process Initiation

When programming for the single-tasking operating system DOS, only one program (process) may be executed at a time, and it is common to interchangeably use the terms *program* and *process*. Technically speaking, a program only represents the contents of a .COM or .EXE file, whereas a process represents the entity created when all of the resources it requires (memory, I/O, etc.) are allocated to it by the operating system. The term *process*, however, is preferred because it conforms with the terminology that is necessarily used by such multitasking operating systems as OS/2 and UNIX, which are capable of executing more than one process at a time. For a complete description of the process entity, see Chapter 25. Under DOS, normally all processes are executed by the command-line processor; however, certain C run-time library functions are available that permit processes to instruct DOS to execute other processes or to invoke the DOS command-line processor itself.

By using the **spawn*xxx*()** or **exec*xxx*()** family of C run-time library functions (see Chapter 25), any C program can initiate other executable programs by simply issuing one of these function calls. By using the **system()** function, a C program can invoke COMMAND.COM itself, which in turn executes a command (DOS, .BAT, .COM, .EXE). Let's examine how these functions work and how they differ from one another.

spawn*xxx*()

The **spawn*xxx*()** family of functions permits a DOS-hosted C program to either relinquish control to another program, which in turn is loaded into memory where the calling program resides (**P_OVERLAY**), or to load another program into free memory space and resume execution when the called program returns control (**P_WAIT**).

Various versions of **spawn*xxx*()** exist that accommodate locating the program to be executed and control how command-line arguments and environment strings are passed. The following function name suffixes are available:

p	Use PATH environment string to locate program.
l	Itemize arguments separately.
v	Array of pointers to arguments.
e	Array of pointers to environment strings.

When **p** is omitted, the program name given describes the complete filename or an incomplete name relative to the current directory. When **e** is omitted, the program inherits the environment of the calling program.

This naming scheme yields the following run-time library functions:

spawnl()	No PATH	**args** separate	Inherit **envp**
spawnlp()	PATH	**args** separate	Inherit **envp**
spawnle()	No PATH	**args** separate	**envp** pointer
spawnlpe()	PATH	**args** separate	**envp** pointer
spawnv()	No PATH	**argv** pointer	Inherit **envp**
spawnvp()	PATH	**argv** pointer	Inherit **envp**
spawnve()	No PATH	**argv** pointer	**envp** pointer
spawnvpe()	PATH	**argv** pointer	**envp** pointer

The example program shown in Figure 15.14 demonstrates the use of the **spawn*xxx*()** family of run-time library functions.

This example prompts for the type of **spawn*xxx*()** call to make (**P_WAIT**, **P_OVERLAY**, and an unsupported **P_NOWAIT**), and then asks for a program name (**prog**). The return codes from each **spawn*xxx*()** function call are interrogated using the convention that −1 indicates an error condition that is recorded by the global variable **errno** (see Appendix C) and interpreted by the run-time library function **perror()**. The argument to **perror()** is a string that is concatenated with the error message from global variable **sys_errlist[]**.

Successive calls to (1), **P_WAIT**, with the name of this program, will eventually exhaust available memory. When such a series of **P_WAIT** calls is ended, successive (0) END responses will have to be made to finally exit to DOS. The effect of using **spawn*xxx*()** in this fashion is to create a series of recursively called programs that reside in available memory as separate program images.

```
/* FILE: ch15e11.c */
#include <stdio.h>
#include <process.h>
#include <errno.h>
#include <string.h>

int main(int argc, char * argv[], char *envp[])
{
int opt, erc;
char prog[20];
while (1) {
    printf("\n\nSelect END (0), P_WAIT (1) or P_OVERLAY (2)? ");
    scanf("%d", &opt);
    if (opt) {
        printf("\nEnter Program Name: ");
        scanf("%s", prog);
        }
    switch (opt) {
        case 0:  exit(0);
        case 1:  erc = spawnl(P_WAIT, prog, NULL);
                 if (erc == -1) perror(strcat(prog, "/P_WAIT >>"));
                 break;
        case 2:  erc = spawnle(P_OVERLAY, prog, NULL, envp);
                 if (erc == -1) perror(strcat(prog, "/P_OVERLAY >>"));
                 break;
        default: erc = spawnl(P_NOWAIT, prog, NULL);
                 if (erc == -1) perror(strcat(prog, "/P_NOWAIT >>"));
                 break;

        }
    }
}
```

FIGURE 15.14: Sample program ch15e11.c demonstrates the use of the spawn*xxx*() family of functions (also see Chapter 25).

exec*xxx*()

The **exec*xxx*()** functions permit a DOS-hosted C program to relinquish control to another program, which in turn is loaded into memory where the calling program resides. This will occur unless an error is encountered before the program is loaded. In that situation an error code of −1 will be returned. The **exec*xxx*()** family of functions is identical to using a **spawn*xxx*()** function in a **P_OVERLAY** mode.

Various versions of **exec*xxx*()** exist that accommodate locating the program to be executed and control how command-line arguments and environment strings are passed. The **exec*xxx*()** function name suffixes parallel those available for **spawn*xxx*()** in the section above.

From this naming scheme, the following run-time library functions are possible, with the characteristics as indicated:

execl()	No PATH	**args** separate	Inherit **envp**
execlp()	PATH	**args** separate	Inherit **envp**
execle()	No PATH	**args** separate	**envp** pointer

execlpe()	PATH	**args** separate	**envp** pointer
execv()	No PATH	**argv** pointer	Inherit **envp**
execvp()	PATH	**argv** pointer	Inherit **envp**
execve()	No PATH	**argv** pointer	**envp** pointer
execvpe()	PATH	**argv** pointer	**envp** pointer

The example program shown in Figure 15.15 demonstrates the use of the **execxxx()** family of run-time library functions.

Unlike the **spawnxxx()** family of functions described above, **execxxx()** functions always relinquish control, unless an error is detected. Again, the **perror()** function is used to conveniently report on any error conditions that may arise.

system()

The **system()** function enables any program to initiate the DOS command-line processor (COMMAND.COM) and to pass a string representing a DOS command line. Issuing the **system()** function is comparable to issuing a **spawnxxx()** function with **P_WAIT** and passing along command-line arguments. The example program in Figure 15.16 demonstrates the use of the **system()** function.

```
/* FILE: ch15e12.c */
#include <stdio.h>
#include <process.h>
#include <errno.h>

int main(int argc, char * argv[], char *envp[])
{
int opt, erc, i=0;
char prog[20];
while (1) {
    printf("\n\nSelect END (0), Continue(1)? ");
    scanf("%d", &opt);
    if (opt) {
        printf("\nEnter Program Name: ");
        scanf("%s", prog);
        }
    switch (opt) {
        case 0:  exit(0);
        case 1:  erc = execl(prog, NULL);
                 if (erc == -1) perror(prog);
                 break;
        default: erc = execl(NULL, NULL);
                 if (erc == -1) perror(NULL);
                 break;
        }
    }
}
```

FIGURE 15.15: Sample program ch15e12.c demonstrates the use of the execxxx() family of functions (also see Chapter 25).

```
/* FILE: ch15e13.c */
#include <stdio.h>
#include <process.h>
#include <errno.h>

int main(void)
{
int opt, erc, i=0;
char line[80];
while (1) {
    printf("\n\nSelect END (0), Continue(1)? ");
    scanf("%d", &opt);
    if (opt) {
        printf("\nEnter Command Line: ");
        fflush(stdin);
        gets(line);
        }
    switch (opt) {
        case 0: exit(0);
        case 1: erc = system(line);
                if (erc == -1) perror(line);
        }
    }
}
```

FIGURE 15.16: Sample program ch15e13.c demonstrates the use of the system() function (also see Chapter 25).

Again, if an error is encountered, **perror()** is used to report on the error condition. Notice that the keyboard input (**stdin**) is cleared using function **fflush()** before issuing function **gets()** to ensure that no unwanted characters remain in the keyboard buffer.

The command-line string argument can represent any valid DOS command (internal or external), a batch file (.BAT) name, and any executable file name (.COM or .EXE). The redirection and piping command-line features are also supported (see Chapter 1).

PERFORMANCE CONSIDERATIONS

The startup code **crt0.asm**, (described in the "Operations" section above), which precedes the execution of every C program, includes calls to functions **setargv()** and **setenvp()**, which set up **main()** arguments **argv** and **envp**, respectively (see "Startup Code" section above). When no main arguments are needed, we declare function **main()** as

```
int main(void);
```

However, the startup code still prepares the **argv** and **envp** arrays. Just as we were able to substitute a wildcard version of function **setargv()**, we are also able to substitute null versions of **setargv()** and **setenvp()**, which do nothing. Both of these functions must exist because they are always called by **crt0.asm**; however, if we define them as

```
void setargv(void) { }
void setenvp(void) { }
```

compile them, and provide these null object modules at build or LINK time with option **/NOE**, the default modules found in the C run-time library will not be included when the executable (.COM or .EXE) file is generated, thereby eliminating the processing time and space necessary to perform these operations.

Another object module that may be substituted affects how the stack and heap interact. Module **xvarstck.obj** is provided with the C compiler installation diskettes and permits the heap to use any unused stack space. The *x* in the module name indicates the associated memory model (s=Small, m=Medium, c=Compact, or l=Large/Huge).

The stack is normally a fixed size, and the heap consists of the available remaining memory space. The memory models also support the use of the default **xvarstck.obj** module in the C run-time library. When **xvarstck.obj** is used (refer to Figure 15.10), the heap can allocate space beginning at **_end** (bottom-of-stack) up to current top-of-stack (SP), thus temporarily reducing the amount of available stack space as shown. To activate this available stack space-sharing model, simply LINK the special version of **xvarstck.obj** with your program.

This method of allocating the heap and stack may be more appropriate for an application that predictably uses the stack when memory allocation (the **malloc()** family of functions) is not being used. This feature can optimize the use of memory space, and possibly avert the problem of running out of heap space and encountering a **NULL** return value from a **malloc()** run-time library function.

PART 6

Using the C Run-Time Library's I/O Services

Standard C provides no keywords or operators for the expression of input/output (I/O); all such services are provided as run-time library functions. This approach has kept C a compact, portable language, and enabled implementors to tailor I/O services to exploit the power of a particular processor, set of peripherals, and operating system.

Part VI presents the I/O functions provided with the Microsoft C run-time library that are required in most application programs and are commonly provided by other programming languages.

While some run-time I/O functions are defined by Standard C, most are Microsoft-specific. The unique directory and file management conventions of host operating systems defy standardization.

Chapter 16, Directory- and File-Management Functions, begins with a complete description of the DOS directory structure and related concepts and conventions, including file-naming, device-buffering, positioning, sharing, locking, and inheritance. This discussion is an extended introduction to all of Chapters 16–18. The rest of the chapter presents the functions used with all files, whether subsequently opened using stream or low-level I/O conventions.

Chapter 17, Stream I/O Functions, presents the functions used with buffered and formatted files; Chapter 18, Low-Level I/O Functions, presents those used with unbuffered, unformatted files.

Chapter 19, Console and Port I/O Functions, discusses console (keyboard and display) and port (unsupported peripheral devices) services independent of the functions described in Chapters 16–18. These functions work with devices, rather than files, and provide no buffering of data.

The format used to present each run-time library function in Parts VI and VII provides the following information:

Compatibility: Either ☐ not compatible or ■ compatible with ANSI (Standard C) or with C compiler implementations for OS/2, UNIX, or XENIX.

See Also: Related run-time functions.

Specification: The preprocessor **#include** directives required to use the function properly, and the common form of the prototype definition found in the associated header **<.h>** file.

Arguments: A description of each function argument.

Return Value: A description of the function's possible return values.

Example: Either a complete program example or a reference to another function example in the chapter.

Output: Included whenever a program example is provided.

Comments: Important reminders about the features of the function and its use in the program example.

# CHAPTER 16

Directory and File Management Functions

Directory and File Management Functions

This chapter presents the run-time library functions that perform DOS directory and file-management operations. These tasks must normally precede and supplement those operations performed by the stream and low-level I/O functions described in Chapters 17 and 18, respectively. The chapter first reviews the underlying DOS directory and file concepts that any C programmer must understand to use the run-time library functions featured in Chapters 16–18 correctly. Take a moment to review these fundamental DOS concepts before attempting to put these library services to work.

Among the tables presented in this chapter are two designed to help you quickly find the functions available for a given directory- or file-management task. Table 16.2 appears in the section "The DOS Directory" and groups the directory-management functions into categories by task; Table 16.6 appears in "The DOS File" and categorizes the file management functions. For example, if you need to create a unique filename, Table 16.2 reveals that you have a choice of using function **tmpnam()**, which conforms with Standard C, or functions **tempnam()** and **mktemp()**, which are Microsoft-specific. To maintain program portability, use functions conforming with Standard C (■ANSI) whenever they are available.

The rest of the chapter consists of an alphabetical series of reference entries for the functions listed in Tables 16.2 and 16.6. The same entry format is used for each function in the run-time library. A complete alphabetic, page-numbered index of all run-time library functions is also provided on the inside back cover of this book.

Let's begin by reviewing the DOS directory and file conventions upon which each function of this chapter and the next two depend to implement the services they perform.

THE DOS DIRECTORY

A DOS directory is an index to a group of files stored on a (removable) diskette or (fixed) hard disk. It is stored permanently on the disk (until deliberately deleted) and contains a unique record for each filename in the group. This record consists of information about the status of the file, independent of the data in the file itself.

As you probably know, the DOS directory system is a tree-like hierarchy that begins with a single directory embracing all the files on the diskette or in the partition. (For the sake of convenience, this discussion will henceforth refer to a diskette or partition as a *volume.*) This directory is known as the *root,* and DOS creates it when you format the volume using the FORMAT command. DOS then relies on the presence of this directory to identify a volume as compatible. DOS can recognize and work only with volumes formatted with its FORMAT command.

To begin formatting a volume, DOS queries the user to identify the drive (device) that contains the volume. DOS uses a standard naming convention for drives (devices), consisting of an alphabetic character followed by a colon (:). For example,

DRIVE LETTER	DEVICE	DRIVE NUMBER
A:	1st diskette drive	0 or 1
B:	2nd diskette drive	1 or 2
C:	1st hard disk drive	2 or 3
D:	2nd hard disk drive	3 or 4
E:	3rd hard disk drive	4 or 5

and so on, through drive Z.

Although all DOS commands require us to use the drive letter in specifying a volume's current or permanent location, some run-time library functions refer to disk drives by number. Unfortunately, drive numbers originate at either 0 or 1, depending on the function being used. Be careful when specifying drive numbers that are passed and returned by run-time library functions and data structures.

The FORMAT command creates a root directory (\) for a volume. The number of directory entries DOS allows for a root directory depends upon the type of disk storage device:

STORAGE DEVICE	MAXIMUM ENTRIES
(SS) Single-sided diskette 5.25" (160KB/180KB)	64
(DS) Double-sided diskette 5.25" (320KB/360KB)	112
(HD) High-density diskette 5.25" (1.2MB) or 3.5" (720KB/1.44MB)	224
(FD) Fixed (Hard) Disk	512 (per partition)

Once a volume is formatted, the number of available root (\) directory entries is thereafter fixed. To overcome this limitation, DOS allows us to create subdirectories. The number of available directory entries for subdirectories is limited only by the amount of disk storage space that remains on the volume. The root directory is therefore the only DOS directory that has a fixed limit on the number of entries it may contain. When you copy a large number of files on to a diskette (for backup or distribution), be sure to place all files in a subdirectory to avoid exceeding the number of files permitted in the root directory, even if you do not otherwise need to group them.

Two FORMAT command options are worth noting here: the /V switch allows you to assign a volume label; and the /S switch copies into the volume the system files that DOS uses to boot itself. These are COMMAND.COM, IBMBIO.COM (in PC-DOS) or IO.SYS (in MS-DOS), and IBMDOS.COM (in PC-DOS) or MSDOS.SYS (in MS-DOS).

It's a good idea to label each volume, but only for your own documentation purposes. Unlike other operating systems, DOS cannot use a label to locate a volume; it can only use an identifier (letter or number). Use the /S switch for any program diskette or primary partition from which you intend to start the system. You cannot boot from an extended DOS partition.

Once a volume has been formatted, its root directory has been initialized for use. Let's examine the information that DOS stores about each file when a file directory entry is created or updated, and understand how DOS implements volume label, sub-directory, system, and hidden files.

The Directory Entry

DOS recognizes files to exist only if they have a valid directory entry. Each DOS directory entry consists of a 32-byte record, containing the fields of information summarized in the following paragraphs. Bytes 12–21 are reserved by DOS.

Bytes 0–7: The Filename Field

A valid DOS filename consists of from one to eight ASCII characters, except the following: " + , (comma) . (period) / ; < > = [\ ] and |.

Filenames may not contain DOS device names (listed in Table 1.3). The use of AUX, COM1, COM2, CON, LPT1, LPT2, LPT3, NUL, and PRN is not permitted (in either upper- or lowercase). Although DOS devices are addressed as files, they cannot appear as filenames in a DOS directory. DOS and the run-time library functions always interpret such names as DOS device names. Note that when you use such device names with the run-time library functions, the colon (:) suffix required on the DOS command line is not permitted.

DOS also assigns the following meanings to the first character of the Filename field of a directory entry:

FIRST CHARACTER	MEANING
0x00	Filename never used; this flags unused entries at the end of a directory to terminate searches and improve performance.
0x05	The first filename character is 0xE5.
0x2E	Directory name (.); two consecutive 0x2E characters (..) point to the parent directory; use the DOS commands **CD ..**, **CD ..\..**, and so on, to "back out" of a subdirectory.
0xE5	Filename was used, but the file has been erased; basis of file recovery operations until the entry is reused.

Bytes 8–10: The Filename Extension Field

A valid DOS filename extension consists of from one to three ASCII characters, excluding those not permitted for filenames.

Byte 11: The File Access Attribute Field

This byte describes the accessibility of a file, using a bit pattern you can develop with the object-like macros defined in **<dos.h>** (see "Notes on Directories"). The unused bits in this field must be zero (logically turned off).

Bytes 22 and 23: The Time Field

These two bytes represent the time when the file was created or last updated. The value is stored in DOS time format as follows:

BITS	FIELD
0–4	Two-second increments (0–29)
5–10	Minutes (0–59)
11–15	Hours (0–23)

This field is not meaningful for directories. As discussed in Chapter 21, the run-time library functions for date and time management represent time values in several different ways.

Bytes 24 and 25: The Date Field

These two bytes represent the date when the file was created or last updated. The value is stored in DOS date format as follows:

BITS	FIELD
0–4	Day (1–31)
5–8	Month (1–12)
9–15	Year (1980–2099; 1980 = 0)

This field is not meaningful for directories. As discussed in Chapter 21, the run-time library functions for date and time management represent date values in several different ways.

Bytes 26 and 27: The File Starting Cluster Number Field

This field represents the disk sector containing the first data byte of the file. (Use the File Allocation Table (FAT) to convert physical cluster numbers to logical sector numbers.)

Bytes 28–31: The Size Field

This field represents the total size in bytes of the data contained in the file, usually excluding any logical EOF (0x1A) markers. This field is not meaningful for directories.

Notes on Directory Entries

From the directory entry record structure it is clear that volume and directory names conform to those of filenames (11 characters maximum, including filename and extension), because they are also stored in the Filename and Extension fields of a directory entry and are interpreted according to the File Access Attribute field setting for that directory entry. For example, DOS allows directory names that include an extension (with a period separator) such as these:

```
MSC.600
XXXXXXXX.XXX
```

You may not, however, enter volume names that contain a period. Normally the extension is omitted when naming directories, to avoid confusing them with filename extensions. To create a directory, use the DOS command MKDIR, or the run-time library function **mkdir()**; to change the volume ID, use the DOS command LABEL.

When a directory or file is deleted, only the first character of its directory Filename entry is overwritten with a 0xE5 character. File deletion does not imply erasure of the directory entry and its data, only the overwriting of the first character of the Filename directory entry, and the release of the associated sectors to the pool of unused (free) sectors on that volume. The DOS command RECOVER and various commercial file-recovery utilities rely upon the fact that the directory entry of a deleted file still exists (except for the first character of its filename field), and that the File Starting Cluster Number field still contains the starting cluster (sector) of the data that was associated with that file. A file may be fully recovered only if its directory Filename entry and its associated data sectors have not yet been reused (overwritten). For this reason, file recovery is reliable only if initiated immediately after a file has been deleted.

We can also see that a DOS file's Attribute field may designate read-only or read/write I/O access. It is not possible to have a DOS file that is write-only. Do not confuse the *access* attribute, assigned when a file is created, with the *permission* mode requested when a file is subsequently opened for use. For example, a file that has read/write access may be restricted to write-only permission when the file is opened, even though DOS files cannot have write-only access.

You can create a "composite" value for the File Access Attribute field by combining, with OR, the object-like macros defined in **<dos.h>**, which appear in Table 16.1.

The directory record structure also explains why, for example, newly created files must first be closed before they may subsequently be renamed or deleted. DOS files are understood to exist only when they have a directory entry, and DOS directory entries are created or updated only when files are closed. Closing a file empties all buffers and creates or updates the directory entry associated with the file. Do not confuse the effects of "closing" a file with "flushing" it. Flushing only forces any buffered data of a file to be transferred but does not update the directory entry itself. (The **close()**, **_dos_close()**, **fclose()**, **fcloseall()**, **fflush()**, and **flushall()** functions, discussed in Chapter 17, can carry out these operations in Microsoft C programs.)

TABLE 16.1: Object-Like Macros for the File Access Attribute Field

MACRO	BIT PATTERN	MEANING
_A_NORMAL	0x00	Designates this file as having read/write access.
_A_RDONLY	0x01	Designates this file as having read-only access.
_A_HIDDEN	0x02	Designates a directory or file as hidden (normally skipped by DOS command DIR and others); hidden files are always recognized by the run-time library functions.
_A_SYSTEM	0x04	A directory or file that is designated to contain DOS-specific information; used to identify those files copied by the DOS commands FORMAT and SYS; system files are normally skipped by DIR and other DOS commands.
_A_VOLID	0x08	Reserved for use by the root directory (\) whose Filename entry is understood to be the volume label; created by the DOS commands FORMAT and LABEL.
_A_SUBDIR	0x10	Any directory entry except the root; directories always have read/write access but may be hidden.
_A_ARCHIVE	0x20	Set for any file that has been written to and closed; used by the DOS commands BACKUP and RESTORE.

Directory Tasks

The C run-time library provides a number of functions that perform directory management services. They are summarized in Table 16.2. Because the C language relies entirely upon functions to perform all I/O operations, I/O services must be implemented in ways specific to particular operating systems. This explains why only the **rename()** function conforms with Standard C (■ANSI) and all others are Microsoft-specific (☐ANSI).

Recall that every DOS file on a volume is identified by a unique pathname that consists of a drive, directory, filename, and extension component. The functions in Table 16.2 support the manipulation of the drive and directory components of a DOS pathname specification. Table 16.2

TABLE 16.2: Directory Management Functions

TASK		FUNCTION	
		STANDARD C ■ **ANSI**	**MICROSOFT C □** **ANSI**

Control Drive
Path Component:
	Get the current drive
	number
			`_dos_getdrive()`
			`fstat()`
			`_getdrive()`
			`stat()`

	Change the current drive number		`_chdrive()` `_dos_setdrive()`
Control Directory **Path Component:**	Change current directory on any drive		`chdir()`
	Make new directory on current drive		`mkdir()`
	Remove directory on current drive		`rmdir()`
	Rename directory on current drive	`rename()`	

Locate Directory:	Test/search for a
	directory
			`access()`
			`_dos_findfirst()`
			`_dos_findnext()`

	Get current directory on current drive		`getcwd()`
	Get current directory on any drive		`_getdcwd()`

Control Directory
Characteristics:
	Get directory attributes		`access()`
			`_dos_findfirst()`
			`_dos_findnext()`
			`_dos_getfileattr()`
			`stat()`

	Set directory attributes		`_dos_setfileattr()`

summarizes the run-time functions available in the following task-related categories:

- Control Drive Path Component
- Control Directory Path Component
- Locate Directory
- Control Directory Characteristics

The **_dos_getdrive()** and **_getdrive()** functions get the current or default drive, while **fstat()** and **stat()** return the drive associated with a particular file, together with other file-related information.

The current or default drive may be reset from within a C program, without using the DOS command processor, by issuing function calls to **_chdrive()** or **_dos_setdrive()**.

Similar services are provided to change, make, remove, and rename the directory component, exclusive of the drive component, using functions **chdir()**, **mkdir()**, **rmdir()**, and **rename()**, respectively.

To test whether a directory exists, use one of the functions **access()**, **_dos_findfirst()**, or **_dos_findnext()**. To get the default directory associated with a particular drive, use functions **getcwd()** or **_getdcwd()**.

Since directories are recorded in the DOS directory structure, they may have attributes associated with them; for example, they may be *system* or *hidden*. To get the current attributes associated with a directory use the **access()**, **_dos_findfirst()**, **_dos_findnext()**, **_dos_getfileattr()**, or **stat()** functions. Likewise, to set or change a directory attribute, use the function **_dos_setfileattr()**.

None of the functions described in Table 16.2 are available either as function-like macros or in an intrinsic (**#pragma**) form; however, several of the tasks they perform may be accomplished using a DOS command initiated either from the DOS command line or by using the **system()** function (see Chapter 25) from the run-time library.

THE DOS FILE

We've seen that DOS recognizes the existence of a disk-based filename only if it has a valid directory entry. Any discussion of DOS files must also take into account the following complications: DOS recognizes and treats certain devices as files (refer to Table 1.3 for the standard DOS device names); every Microsoft C program is automatically provided with five predefined files that are by default associated with standard DOS devices;

and the DOS command line supports the redirection and piping of **stdin** and **stdout** (see Chapter 1).

All DOS files, whether disk- or device-based, are logically treated in the same manner—as either a transmitter (input) or receiver (output) of bytes to or from the central processing unit. In this chapter we are interested in creating a clear understanding of the overall DOS file and device concepts that establish the framework within which the run-time library functions of Part VI are designed to operate.

All DOS files must first be *opened*, either to establish a logical connection between your software program and an existing permanent file resource or to *create* a new temporary or permanent file resource. The process of opening a file establishes all of the conventions that will be followed when that file is subsequently used to transmit or receive data. No I/O may be performed upon a file that is not open. Once all I/O has been completed, the file must be *closed*, to break the logical connection established when the file was opened, and to save the file again, with any changes that may have been made.

Since the details of how DOS files are opened, I/O is performed, and files are closed all differ depending upon whether stream I/O (Chapter 17) or low-level I/O (Chapter 18) conventions are employed, this chapter focuses upon the concepts that are common to both approaches. Let's begin by examining how DOS files are initially created. Note that since file creation is a part of the file-opening process, the issues discussed in the section "Opening DOS Files" apply to the creation of files as well.

Creating Files

Only disk-based files must be initially created by a program. Device-based files simply represent the complement of standard peripheral devices installed on a particular computer and recognized by DOS. They use the standard DOS device names listed in Table 1.3.

You create a disk-based file by opening a filename that does not already exist in a particular directory, providing an acceptable File Access Attribute description, writing 0 to n bytes of data to the file, and closing the file to permanently record the data and create a valid directory entry. Each step in this overall process can be accomplished using run-time library functions. You'll find program examples in the reference entries throughout Part VI.

The Contents of a Directory Entry

First let's examine how each field of a directory entry is determined when a disk-based file is initially created.

Filename.Extension: A valid nondevice name must be specified when the run-time **xxopen** function is issued.

File Access Attribute: Depending upon the **xxopen** function used, object-like macros are individually specified, or combined using the OR (|) operator, to reflect the desired access characteristics of that file. Apart from the archive bit, the File Access Attribute is not altered by the subsequent opening and closing of a file once created. It can be altered only by using a function call designed for that purpose. The following constants are used by DOS to establish the settings of the File Access Attribute field:

	STREAM I/O	LOW-LEVEL I/O
Read-Only	Explicit function call only!	**_A_RDONLY**
		S_IREAD
Read/Write	"w" family of modes	**_A_NORMAL**
	"a" family of modes	**S_IREAD|S_IWRITE**
		S_IWRITE

Although you cannot create a read-only file using stream I/O, once you have created the file in read/write mode, you can use either **chmod()** or **_dos_setfileattr()** to set its File Access Attribute to read-only. Also, when low-level I/O is used to create a read/write file, **S_IWRITE** is understood to be equivalent to **S_IREAD|S_IWRITE** because DOS does not permit write/only files. See "Access Mode," later in this chapter, for more information.

Time   Automatically "timestamped" by DOS using the current system clock. Always maintain an accurate clock setting.

Date   Automatically "datestamped" by DOS using the current system clock. Always maintain an accurate clock setting.

Cluster Number   Automatically assigned by DOS when data is written to the file.

Size   Automatically determined by DOS when the file is closed. The maximum file size permitted is limited only by the amount of available volume storage space, or the maximum value that can be represented by this directory field (2^{31}).

Opening Files

All disk-based and device-based files (except the predefined files listed in Table 16.3, which are automatically opened and available for either stream or low-level I/O to any Microsoft C program) must be opened before any I/O may be performed.

As shown in the table, each predefined file is device-based unless reassigned to a disk-based file either by using redirection and piping from the DOS command line (see Chapter 1) or by calling a run-time library function such as **freopen()** or **dup2()**.

DOS files are typically opened for exclusive use by the program being written, with no intent that they be available for concurrent or shared use by other programs (see the Sharing section). When DOS files are opened they may be treated as either stream (Chapter 17) or low-level (Chapter 18) files, as indicated in Table 16.6 later in this chapter.

Stream I/O files are normally identified by a file pointer, are buffered, utilize Standard C run-time library functions, and are opened using one of the following functions: **fopen()**, **fdopen()**, or **freopen()**.

Low-level I/O files are always identified by a file handle, are unbuffered, utilize non-Standard C run-time library functions, and are opened using one of these functions: **creat()**, **_dos_creat()**, **_dos_creatnew()**, or **_dos_open()**.

TABLE 16.3: Predefined Filenames for I/O Operations

STREAM POINTER	LOW-LEVEL HANDLE	DOS DEVICE NAME
`stdin`	0	CON
`stdout`	1	CON
`stderr`	2	CON
`stdaux`	3	AUX or COM1
`stdprn`	4	PRN or LPT1

DOS permits a maximum of 20 files to be concurrently opened for each process (program). The actual number for each DOS installation is established by the FILES=*xx* command in the DOS system configuration command file, CONFIG.SYS (see Chapter 1). Because the five predefined device files listed in Table 16.3 are automatically opened, only 15 files may be opened by an application program.

For this reason, it is recommended that each file be closed when all its I/O is completed. Once a file is closed, its stream pointer or file handle becomes available to be reused. Normal program termination procedures close all open files, but it is a better practice to explicitly close each file that has been opened before exiting.

Characteristics of Files

The next sections explore the various characteristics by which we classify all DOS files: whether the file is disk- or device-based; its access *mode;* its access *permission;* the *position* within an open file at which the next I/O operation will take place; whether the file is *shared* between programs; and, if so, whether it is *locked;* whether it is *buffered* by default; and whether I/O operations *translate* it as text or leave it unaltered as binary data.

Disk or Device-Based?

Every open DOS file is described as either disk- or device-based. The distinction is important because many run-time functions produce unpredictable results if the file is device- rather than disk-based. Because files can be redirected from the command line and reassigned by run-time library functions, at any point in time, a file may be associated with either a disk file or device. To test whether a file is currently device-based, use the function **isatty()**, which returns a nonzero value (true) for a device-based file and zero (false) for a disk-based file.

When a file is device-based, the directory management tasks described in Table 16.2 are not applicable, and only the following file management tasks described in Table 16.6 can be performed:

- Open a stream file.
- Empty stream file buffers.
- Close a stream file.
- Close a low-level file.
- Duplicate file handles.
- Set file translation mode.

Chapters 17 and 18 further detail which run-time library functions apply when working with device- or disk-based files.

Access Mode

As discussed earlier, in "Notes on Directory Entries," a file has both an *access mode* and a *permission status*. Both specify whether the file may be opened for reading, writing, both, or neither. The difference is that the access mode is assigned (via the File Access Attribute field) when the file is initially created; permission is granted when the file is subsequently opened for use.

We also saw earlier that a file's access mode may be assigned only as read/write or read-only, not as write-only. The File Access Attribute field is initialized when a file is created but subsequently may be changed by using the run-time library functions **chmod()** or **_dos_setfileattr()**. The read-only or read/write access setting for a file is used to control whether access permission will be granted when subsequent requests are made to open the file. Your C programs can use the **access()** function to determine a file's access attribute.

If a file is device-based, it has no directory entry and therefore no File Access Attribute field. The access characteristic of a DOS device is implicitly established by the I/O properties of the device itself, as listed in Table 16.4. We can see in this table that files associated with printer ports are write-only, while those associated with two-way communication ports are read/write.

TABLE 16.4: Implicit Access Attributes of DOS Device Files

DEVICE	ACCESS ATTRIBUTE
AUX	Read/write
COM1	Read/write
COM2	Read/write
CON	Read/write
LPT1	Write only
LPT2	Write only
LPT3	Write only
NUL	Read/write
PRN	Write only

Access Permission

The **xxopen()** run-time library functions (listed in Tables 16.2 and 16.6 and presented in depth in Chapters 17 and 18) each request permission to open an existing file in a specific mode: read-only, write-only, or read/write. DOS either grants or denies permission to open the file according to its access setting. As discussed in the preceding section, this setting is specified explicitly in the File Access Attribute field of a disk file; it is established implicitly by the I/O properties of a device file.

Permission to open a read/write disk file in any mode is always granted. Permission to open a read-only disk file in read/write or write-only mode is always denied.

Permission to open read/write and read-only device files is granted or denied in the same way as for disk files. Permission to open a write-only device file in read-only or read/write mode is always denied.

As discussed in "Notes on Directory Entries," the permission status under which a file is opened can temporarily override the file's permanent access setting—if the permission is more restrictive. That is, if a file with read/write access is opened with write-only permission, it cannot be read from until closed and reopened. Similarly, a read/write file cannot be written to while opened with read-only permission.

Translation Mode

Each file has a translation mode, either text or binary. This characteristic specifies how I/O operations are to handle carriage-return/linefeed and end-of-file (Ctrl-Z) characters. A text file will have those characters translated as outlined below; a binary file will leave them unaltered. The default translation modes of the predefined files were summarized in Table 16.4. All other files, whether disk- or device-based, are assigned a translation mode controlled by the current value of the global variable **_fmode** (see Appendix C). The default value of **_fmode** is text. The object-like macros **O_TEXT**, **O_BINARY**, and **O_RAW**, defined in **<fcntl.h>**, are used to assign the translation mode of a file. These macros convey the following meanings:

O_TEXT	Text mode (translated).
	Input: When a <cr><lf> is encountered, it is converted to <lf>; when a Ctrl-Z is encountered, it is interpreted as EOF.
	Output: Each <lf> encountered is converted to a <cr><lf>.

O_TEXT	Text mode (translated).
O_BINARY	Binary mode (untranslated).
	Input: Each byte is transferred without alteration.
	Output: Each byte is transferred without alteration.
O_RAW	Binary mode (same as **O_BINARY**).

The following references (used above) are understood to represent the accompanying character code values:

REFERENCE	**CHARACTER TYPE**	**VALUE**
\<cr>	**'\r'**	0x0D
\<lf>	**'\n'**	0x0A
Ctrl-Z	None	0x1A
EOF	None	(−1) **\<stdio.h>**

DOS and Microsoft C offer several ways to establish the translation mode of a file. The most common is to specify the desired translation mode explicitly when the file is opened. The techniques for doing this differ for stream I/O (Chapter 17) and low-level I/O (Chapter 18). Refer to these chapters for details.

Another method is to assign the global variable **_fmode** the value of **O_TEXT** or **O_BINARY**, and then open files without explicitly specifying a translation mode. Whenever a file is opened for which a translation mode is not explicitly specified, the C compilers assume the default value of **_fmode**; otherwise, the explicitly specified value is always used.

Finally, your program can assign or reassign the translation mode of a file at any time by calling the run-time library function **setmode()** with the desired setting. See the **setmode()** reference entry in this chapter for an example.

Buffering

Buffering is a software technique designed to make I/O operations more efficient. A buffer is a data area in memory (RAM) allocated by the program that opens the file. Buffers improve I/O performance by reducing the number of physical data transfers between the program and the peripheral device (disk or otherwise) with which the file is associated; access to all such devices is significantly slower than access to RAM. Each byte logically read from or written to an unbuffered file is physically transferred when requested. But when a file is buffered, all logical I/O requests are serviced from the buffer, and the physical data transfers are made in multiples of the buffer size.

Each buffered file is normally allocated a separate buffer whose default size is 512 bytes. This size is determined by the value of the object-like macro **BUFSIZ**, defined in **<stdio.h>**.

Table 16.3, earlier in this chapter, listed the default buffering status of each predefined device file. All other files, whether disk- or device-based, are buffered if opened for stream I/O and unbuffered if opened for low-level I/O.

Stream I/O functions can process both buffered and unbuffered files, while low-level I/O functions can process only unbuffered files. Any file that is to be processed simultaneously using both types of functions must be unbuffered if the functions are to work correctly.

You can change the buffer characteristics of an open file using the runtime library functions **setbuf()** and **setvbuf()**, presented in Chapter 17. These functions enable you to convert a file from buffered to unbuffered and vice-versa, and to specify a buffer size other than the value of **BUFSIZ**.

Care must also be taken when working with buffered files that are being both read from and written to. You can remove extraneous characters in the keyboard buffer (**stdin**) by flushing it. Each time the I/O access mode of a file is about to be changed, care must be taken to flush the buffer and reposition the file pointer before proceeding. This is particularly true when a file is granted read/write permission in append mode. Data written to a file opened in append mode is always written to the end of the file, regardless of the file pointer's position when a write to the file is initiated.

Similar precautions apply to files that are buffered and associated with more than one stream pointer or file handle in the same program (process). Since each buffered file is allocated a separate buffer and maintains a separate location "pointer," the sequence of I/O operations, including the emptying of buffers, can yield unpredictable results when files are shared. This explains why only unbuffered files should be used when files are to be granted shared access by other programs.

Positioning

The concept of file *position* applies only to disk-based files, not to device-based files. Once a disk file is opened, and until it is closed, the system keeps track of the position within the file where the next I/O access will occur. Each byte in a file is referenced relatively as an offset in bytes from the beginning of the file, which is understood to be byte 0. The location of this *pointer* is automatically incremented after each I/O operation to indicate the next available byte. The run-time library provides functions that you can use to assign this pointer by specifying offsets (in bytes) from the location identified by the following object-like macros found in **<stdio.h>**:

SEEK_SET	Beginning of file
SEEK_CUR	Current location
SEEK_END	End of file

Data is always read from and written to a file starting at the current pointer location, unless the file is opened in append mode, which forces data to be written at **SEEK_END**. When a file is opened, the file pointer is positioned at **SEEK_SET**. Consecutive read or write file operations automatically increment the file pointer location. If you need access to a file at some specific, nonconsecutive position, use one of the run-time functions **fseek()** or **fsetpos()** discussed in Chapter 17 or **lseek()** discussed in Chapter 18, to position the file pointer before beginning the I/O operation.

The data structure that C uses to maintain the file position is not standardized and varies between manufacturers. C programs never use the data structure directly but, instead, use the function calls that interface to the data structure. For that reason, this book does not attempt to document Microsoft's data structure.

Sharing

Disk files that can be opened by more than one program on the same machine at the same time (for example, when the run-time library function **spawn()** has been used) are said to be *shared.*The concepts of file access and permission, discussed earlier in this chapter, become somewhat more complicated with file sharing.

For file sharing to be implemented, an *arbiter* or third party must be introduced to interrogate all requests to open files and to grant or deny permission for shared file access. The arbiter is the DOS command SHARE, available beginning with version 3.0, which you must install to permanently establish it as a TSR (Terminate-and-Stay-Ready) program. Once SHARE is installed, you can use a special set of run-time library function calls (**_dos_open**, **_fsopen**, **sopen**) to control file sharing. As discussed in Chapters 17 and 18, these functions take an additional argument, which consists of one of the following object-like macros found in **<share.h>**:

SH_COMPAT	Compatibility mode
SH_DENYRD	Deny other read accesses

SH_DENYWR	Deny other write accesses
SH_DENYNO	Do not deny any accesses
SH_DENYRW	Deny other read/write accesses

When the DOS command SHARE has not been installed, no file-sharing services are enforced, and nothing prevents another program (process) from opening any file for which normal access permission is granted. If the file-sharing **xxopen** functions are used, their file-sharing parameters are simply ignored, and they function as if a normal run-time library **xxopen** (**fopen()**, **fdopen()**, or **freopen()**) function had been used.

On the other hand, when SHARE is installed, all run-time library **xxopen** functions, normal or shared, are "interrogated" by SHARE. When a normal **xxopen** function is used, no file-sharing parameters can be specified, and a sharing mode of **SH_COMPAT** is assumed. With this parameter in effect, subsequent requests by the current process to open the file in any mode (read-only, write-only, or read/write) are granted, and subsequent requests by any other process to open the file are denied. **SH_COMPAT** was introduced along with the DOS command SHARE to maintain compatibility with files created using earlier DOS versions. With SHARE installed, a file opened using **SH_COMPAT** behaves just as DOS files traditionally did. Thus, when SHARE is installed, you should open a file with **fopen()**, **fdopen()**, or **freopen()** only if no other process will need to access that file before you close it. Specifying the other file-sharing parameters in a given program's **xxopen()** function has the following effects:

SH_DENYRD: Allows the current process to open the file subsequently in any mode; allows any other process to open the file only for writing.

SH_DENYWR: Allows the current process to open the file subsequently in any mode; allows any other process to open the file only for reading.

SH_DENYNO: Allows both the current process and any other to open the file subsequently in any mode.

SH_DENYRW: Denies both the current process and any other permission to open the file subsequently in any mode.

Subsequent requests to open a file by the process that first opened it will fail in only three circumstances:

1. When that process has opened the file with **SH_DENYRW**.
2. When another process has opened the file with either **SH_COMPAT** or **SH_DENYRW**.

3. When another process has opened the file with **SH_DENYRD** and the request is to open the file for reading, or with **SH_DENYWR** if the request is to write to the file.

Table 16.5 summarizes the effect of the **SH_xx** parameters on subsequent requests to access a file.

Clearly, when a process uses one of the shared **xxopen()** functions, it anticipates that another process may request access and acknowledges that such access should be permissible under certain circumstances. Sharing privileges are granted by a given process to itself and to other processes. The enforcement of these privileges is entirely the responsibility of the SHARE arbiter, not the process requesting file access.

Locking

Whereas file sharing intends to restrict access to entire shared files, *locking* intends to restrict shared access to ranges of bytes within a file. Only a file that has been opened using a file-sharing function (**_dos_open**, **_fsopen**, or **sopen**) while the DOS command SHARE is installed can be locked. Any range of bytes (such as a record) within a shared file may be locked, or withheld access from other processes (programs), by using the run-time library function **locking()** with one of the following object-like macros, found in **<sys\locking.h>**, as a parameter:

LK_LOCK	Lock range of bytes; 10 tries
LK_RLCK	Lock range of bytes; 10 tries

TABLE 16.5: The Effect of SHARE Parameters on Subsequent Access Requests

FIRST PROCESS SHARE PARAMETER	ACCESS SUBSEQUENTLY REQUESTED BY FIRST PROCESS			ACCESS SUBSEQUENTLY REQUESTED BY OTHER PROCESS		
	Read-only	Write-only	Read/Write	Read-only	Write-only	Read/Write
SH_DENYRW	Denied	Denied	Denied	Denied	Denied	Denied
SH_DENYWR	Granted	Denied	Denied	Granted	Denied	Denied
SH_DENYRD	Denied	Granted	Denied	Denied	Granted	Denied
SH_DENYNO	Granted	Granted	Granted	Granted	Granted	Granted
SH_COMPAT	Granted	Granted	Granted	Denied	Denied	Denied

LK_NBLCK	Nonblocking **LK_LOCK**; 1 try
LK_NBRLCK	Nonblocking **LK_RLCK**; 1 try
LK_UNLCK	Unlock range of previously locked bytes

Blocking and the number of *tries* refer to the behavior of the SHARE arbiter in evaluating the function call. The nonblocking parameters (**LK_NBLCK** and **LK_NBRLK**) instruct the arbiter simply to test whether the indicated range of bytes is currently locked. Only one attempt is made, no bytes are locked or unlocked, and no request to lock a range of bytes is queued up. The **LK_LOCK** and **LK_RLCK** parameters instruct SHARE to queue up the locking request, which at some (software-defined) interval will make ten attempts to lock the range of bytes. This instruction temporarily blocks other **LK_LOCK** and **LK_RLCK** requests (by sending them to the end of the queue), but allows **LK_NBLCK**, **LK_NBRLK**, and **LK_RLCK** requests to be evaluated during the interval when the arbiter is waiting to make another try.

To use the **locking()** function, you first actively request that a lock be placed on a range of bytes that you intend to use immediately; then alter the locked range of bytes as intended; and, finally, release the lock on the range of bytes. Assuming that others may need access to that record, your program should carry out the procedure as quickly as possible. It is not reliable to assume that if a range of bytes has been locked, any attempt to read those bytes will generate an error message! Every process that might encounter locked bytes within a shared file should always first attempt to lock the range of bytes it wishes to control. If such a request fails, then it is certain that another process has locked that range of bytes.

Although this methodology may seem unnecessary or redundant, it mirrors the design philosophy of the DOS interrupts on which the Microsoft C run-time functions for opening and locking shared files rely. To operate correctly, these functions require that a positive request for control be issued before control is assumed. The SHARE arbiter must first be asked permission for what is subsequently intended to be done.

Inheritance

Inheritance describes whether files that have been opened by a parent process are to be automatically passed along to (inherited by) a child process created using one of the **execxxx()** or **spawnxxx()** functions.

Whether inheritance actually occurs is controlled first by the global variable **_fileinfo** (see Appendix C) and then by the object-like macro **O_NOINHERIT**. By default, **_fileinfo** is set equal to 0 (false), and file inheritance never occurs, regardless of whether **O_NOINHERIT** has been specified as the **xxopen()** function parameter. To enable file inheritance to occur, include the following statements in your C program before calling any **execxxx()** or **spawnxxx()** run-time library function:

```
#include <stdlib.h>
_fileinfo = 1;
```

With **_fileinfo** set to 1 (true), all open files in the parent process that have been opened without the **O_NOINHERIT** parameter will automatically be inherited by a child process.

To prevent an individual open file within the parent process from being passed along to a child process, specify the **O_NOINHERIT** macro, defined in **<fcntl.h>**, when the file is opened. Note that not all of the run-time library **xxopen** functions support the use of the **O_NOINHERIT** parameter.

To implement file inheritance, the parent process must set the **_C_FILE_INFO** environment string (see Chapter 1 for information about the DOS command SET), and the C startup code of the child process must subsequently process this binary information (see Chapter 15 for information about the special function **main()**). Obviously, this mechanism requires that the environment table be sized large enough to hold this binary string of file information. Also, because the **_C_FILE_INFO** string information is not in ASCII character form, its format is implementation defined and cannot be user-specified with a DOS SET command. See Chapter 25 for an example demonstrating the use of **_C_FILE_INFO**.

Recall that DOS restricts each process (program) to a maximum of 20 open files, only 15 of which are available to the program. When file inheritance in enabled (**_fileinfo** set equal to 1) and open files in the parent process are designated as **O_NOINHERIT**, the child process begins with more file handles available to it than if **O_NOINHERIT** had not been specified.

Observations on File Management

At this point it may be useful to summarize briefly the most important file management considerations.

Files are permanently created when a directory entry is made. Until that time they are temporary and not recognized by any DOS operation that is predicated upon the existence of a volume directory entry. To change the name of or delete a file, only the directory entry itself is altered, not the data file of bytes (cluster) with which it is associated.

DOS provides several levels of file security and access protection. In the most fundamental way, files can simply be "hidden" from view and not easily located using normal DOS commands. Next, files can be designated permanently as read-only, thereby permitting access but preventing any data modification.

When a file is to be accessed by only one program (process) at a time, you can use file **xxopen** functions to restrict its access level to read-only or write-only and to ensure that it is not inherited by any child process that may be generated.

When files are intended for access by more than one program (process) at a time, the file-sharing open functions (**_dos_open**, **_fsopen**, and **sopen**) can restrict access by other programs (processes) and, if necessary, restrict their own access. Any program can further restrict access to specific contents of a file by using the **locking()** function to keep another program (process) from either reading or writing a selected range of bytes within the file.

File Tasks

The C run-time library provides a number of functions that perform file management services. They are summarized in Table 16.6. Because the C language relies entirely upon functions to perform all I/O operations, and I/O services are implemented in ways specific to particular operating systems, few of the run-time library functions conform with Standard C (■ANSI), and most therefore are Microsoft-specific (☐ANSI, non-Standard).

Since DOS requires every file to have a Filename and Extension entry in the directory, it is essential that C provide services to manipulate these pathname components, along with the drive and directory pathname components discussed earlier. Table 16.6 summarizes the run-time functions available in the following task-related categories:

Create Filenames and Pathnames

Perform File operations

Control File Characteristics

The following functions supplement those presented in Table 16.2 for dissecting and constructing complete DOS pathnames: **_makepath()**, **_splitpath()**, **_fullpath()**, **tempnam()**, **tmpnam()**, and **mktemp()**.

To rename or delete a file, use functions **rename()** or **remove()** and **unlink()**. To create a temporary file, one that exists only for the duration of a program (no directory entry), use **tmpfile()**; to delete one, use **rmtmp()**.

TABLE 16.6: File Management Functions

TASK		FUNCTION	
		STANDARD C ■ ANSI	**MICROSOFT C** □ ANSI
Create Filenames and Pathnames:	Create pathname from components		`_makepath`
	Split pathname into components		`_splitpath`
	Create a complete path		`_fullpath`
	Create a unique filename	`tmpnam`	`tempnam`
	Create a filename from a template		`mktemp`

Perform File Operations:	Search for a filename		`_dos_findfirst`
			
			`_dos_findnext`
			`_searchenv`

	Rename a perm-anent file	`rename`	
	Delete a permanent file	`remove`	`unlink`
	Create a temporary file	`tmpfile`	
	Delete temporary files		`rmtmp`
	Open a stream file	`fopen` (Chapter 17)	`fdopen` (Chapter 17)
		`freopen` (Chapter 17)	`_fsopen` (Chapter 17)
	Empty stream file buffers	`fflush` (Chapter 17)	`flushall` (Chapter 17)
	Close a stream file	`fclose` (Chapter 17)	`fcloseall` (Chapter 17)

	Open a low-level file		`creat` (Chapter 18)
			`_dos_creat`
			(Chapter 18)
			`_dos_creatnew`
			(Chapter 18)
			`_dos_open` (Chapter 18)
			`sopen` (Chapter 18)

	Close a low-level file		`close` (Chapter 18)

TABLE 16.6: Implicit Access Attributes of DOS Device Files (continued)

TASK		FUNCTION	
		STANDARD C ■ ANSI	MICROSOFT C □ ANSI
Perform File Operations: (cont.)	Get file handle number		fileno
			_dos_close (Chapter 18)
	Duplicate file handles		dup (Chapter 18)
			dup2 (Chapter 18)
	Get file length		_dos_findfirst
			_dos_findnext
			filelength
			fstat
			stat
	Set file length		chsize
	Lock bytes of a file		locking
Control File Characteristics:	Check if file is a DOS device		isatty
			fstat
			stat
	Set file translation mode		setmode
	Get file attribute		_dos_findfirst
			_dos_findnext
			_dos_getfileattr
			fstat
			stat
	Set file attributes		_dos_setfileattr
	Test for file access mode		access
			_dos_findfirst
			_dos_findnext
			_dos_getfileattr
	Set file access mode		chmod
			_dos_setfileattr

TABLE 16.6: Implicit Access Attributes of DOS Device Files (continued)

TASK		FUNCTION	
		STANDARD C ■ **ANSI**	**MICROSOFT C** ☐ **ANSI**

Control File Characteristics: (cont.)	Get last date/time file modified		`umask`
			
			`_dos_findfirst`
			
			`_dos_findnext`
			`_dos_getftime`
			`fstat`
			`stat`

	Set last date/time file modified		`_dos_setftime` `utime`

To open a stream I/O file for exclusive use, use **fopen()**, **freopen()**, or **fdopen()**. For a low-level I/O file, use **creat()**, **_dos_creat()**, **_dos_creatnew()**, or **_dos_open()**.

To open a file for shared use by other programs (processes), use **_fsopen()** for stream and **_sopen()** for low-level I/O files. To lock ranges of bytes within shared files, use the **locking()** function.

Since only stream I/O files have buffers, the **fflush()** and **flush-all()** buffer-emptying functions may not be used with low-level I/O files that are always unbuffered.

To close a stream I/O file, use **fclose()** or **fcloseall()**; use **close()** or **_dos_close()** for low-level I/O files.

Because it is sometimes necessary to duplicate the assignment of files using the functions **dup()** and **dup2()**, the function **fileno()** is needed to return the file handle number associated with a stream I/O file. All C files have file handles, but only stream I/O files have file pointers.

When it is necessary to know the length of a file, use **_dos_find-first()**, **_dos_findnext()**, **filelength()**, **fstat()**, or **stat()**; to change the length of a file, use **chsize()**.

Whether a file is device or disk-based can be determined using function **isatty()**, **fstat()**, or **stat()**.

The attributes associated with DOS files that have been discussed in this chapter may be interrogated using **_dos_findfirst()**, **_dos_findnext()**, **_dos_getfileattr()**, **fstat()**, or **stat()**.

Likewise, file attributes may be set or changed using **_dos_setfileat-tr()**, **chmod()**, or **umask()**.

The last modified date and time recorded for a file may be interrogated using **_dos_findfirst()**, **_dos_findnext()**, **_dos_getftime()**, **fstat()**, or **stat()**. Likewise, these directory date and time stamps may be altered using **_dos_setftime()** or **utime()**.

Of the functions described in Table 16.6, only **fileno()** is available as a **#define** function-like macro, and none of the functions are available in an intrinsic (**#pragma**) form; however, some of the tasks they perform may be accomplished using a DOS command, initiated either from the DOS command line or by using the **system()** function (see Chapter 25) from the run-time library.

Recall from Chapter 5 that, although function-like macros generally outperform their function counterparts, when arguments that have side-effects (−−, ++) are used, only functions, not macros, will definitely work as intended. For example, to ensure that the function **putchar()**, which is also defined as a macro in **<stdio.h>**, is used, insert an **#undef** directive as shown below:

```
#include <stdio.h>
#undef putchar
```

Otherwise, the macro version will be employed.

RUN-TIME LIBRARY FUNCTIONS FOR DIRECTORY AND FILE MANAGEMENT

This section provides detailed information about each function listed in Tables 16.2 and 16.6, arranged alphabetically by function name. The standard presentation format used in Parts VI and VII of this book make it easy to find the following information:

- The function's compatibility with Standard C and with other operating systems.
- Related run-time functions and programming techniques.
- The preprocessor (#) directives required when using the function.
- A complete function prototype, with a description of each argument.
- The function's return value, if any.
- A program example demonstrating correct use of the function, along with sample output. (Some examples demonstrate the use of more than one function; cross-references will guide you to these.)
- Comments on the function or the program example.

Note that any example program identified with the comment

```
/* FILE: chxxeyy.c */
```

is available on the *Encyclopedia C* program disk that may be purchased separately (see the order form in the back of the book). Each program is uniquely identified by the *xx* chapter number and *yy* example number within that chapter. Over 200 program files are available to facilitate your use, testing, and understanding of material presented in this book.

access ( )   *Test or get directory and file attributes*

Compatibility   □ANSI   ■OS/2   ■UNIX   ■XENIX

See Also

_dos_findfirst(), _dos_findnext(), _dos_getfileattr(), stat()

Specification

```
#include <io.h>
#include <errno.h>
int access(const char *pathname, int mode);
```

Arguments

pathname: directory or file pathname string.

mode: 00 (exist), 02 (write), 04 (read), or 06 (read/write).

Return Value

0 if successful

−1 if unsuccessful

errno set to **EACCES**, **ENOENT**

Example   See also: **chmod()**, **chsize()**, **_dos_setftime()**, **locking()**.

```
/* FILE: ch16e1.c*/
#include <io.h>
#include <errno.h>
#include <stdio.h>
#include <string.h>
int main(void)
{
char pathname[FILENAME_MAX] = "c:\\ibmbio.com", *ptr;
int mode, erc, error;
while (strcmpi(pathname, "END")) {
    for (mode=0; mode<=6; mode+=2) {
```

```
        errno = 0;
        erc = access(pathname, mode);
        error = errno;
        ptr = strerror(error);
        printf("\npathname=%s mode=%d erc=%d errno=%d <%s>",\
        pathname, mode, erc, error, ptr);
        }
    printf("\n\nEnter a directory or file path: ");
    gets(pathname);
    }
    exit(0);
    }
```

Output

```
pathname=c:\ibmbio.com mode=0 erc=0 errno=0 <Error 0>
pathname=c:\ibmbio.com mode=2 erc=-1 errno=13 <Permission denied>
pathname=c:\ibmbio.com mode=4 erc=0 errno=0 <Error 0>
pathname=c:\ibmbio.com mode=6 erc=-1 errno=13 <Permission denied>

Enter a directory or file path: c:\
pathname=c:\ mode=0 erc=0 errno=0 <Error 0>
pathname=c:\ mode=2 erc=-1 errno=13 <Permission denied>
pathname=c:\ mode=4 erc=0 errno=0 <Error 0>
pathname=c:\ mode=6 erc=-1 errno=13 <Permission denied>

Enter a directory or file path: end
```

Comments   Except for the root directory, all DOS directories have a read/write at-tribute. DOS files have either a read-only or read/write attribute.

Although the *mode* constants are shown as octal digits, identical decimal values may be used without error because all are less than 7.

chdir()   *Change current directory on any drive*

Compatibility   ☐ANSI   ■OS/2   ■UNIX   ■XENIX

See Also

```
mkdir(), rename(), system()
```

Specification

```
#include <direct.h>
#include <errno.h>
int chdir(const char *dirname);
```

Arguments

dirname: Directory pathname string.

Return Value

0 if successful

−1 if unsuccessful

errno set to **ENOENT**

Example

```
/* FILE: ch16e2.c        */
#include <direct.h>
#include <errno.h>
#include <stdio.h>
#include <string.h>
int main(void)
{
char dirname[FILENAME_MAX], *ptr;
int erc, error;
strcpy(dirname,getcwd(dirname,FILENAME_MAX));
while (strcmpi(dirname,"END")) {
    errno = 0;
    erc = chdir(dirname);
    error = errno;
    ptr = strerror(error);
    printf("\ndirname=%s erc=%d errno=%d <%s>",\
        dirname, erc, error, ptr);
    printf("\n\nEnter a drive:\directory path: ");
    gets(dirname);
    }
exit(0);
}
```

Output

```
dirname=C:\QC2\BOOK erc=0 errno=0 <Error 0>

Enter a drive:directory path: c:\xxx
dirname=c:\xxx erc=-1 errno=2 <No such file or directory>

Enter a drive:directory path: end
```

Comments   Identical to the DOS command CD (or CHDIR). The current directory can be changed for any drive, even though a drive itself may not be current.

_chdrive ()   *Change the current drive number*

Compatibility   ☐ ANSI   ■ OS/2   ☐ UNIX   ☐ XENIX

See Also

```
_dos_setdrive(), system()
```

Specification

```
#include <direct.h>
int _chdrive(int drive);
```

Arguments

drive: Drive number 0 = current drive, 1 = A:, 2 = B:, and so on.

Return Value

0 if successful

−1 if unsuccessful

Example

```
/* FILE: ch16e3.c      */
#include <direct.h>
#include <errno.h>
#include <stdio.h>
int main(void)
{
int drive=0, erc=0;
char dirname[FILENAME_MAX];
while (drive >= 0) {
    drive = _getdrive();
    getcwd(dirname,FILENAME_MAX);
    printf("\nerc=%d  current drive=%d  current directory=%s",\
        erc, drive, dirname);
    printf("\n\nSelect a drive number (-1 to quit): ");
    scanf("%d",&drive);
    erc = _chdrive(drive);
    }
exit(0);
}
```

Output

```
erc=0  current drive=3  current directory=C:\QC2\BOOK

Select a drive number (-1 to quit): 1
erc=0  current drive=1  current directory=A:\

Select a drive number (-1 to quit): 0
erc=-1  current drive=1  current directory=A:\

Select a drive number (-1 to quit): -1
```

Comments   Identical to issuing the series of DOS commands A:↵, B:↵, C:↵, and so on. For this function, the drive numbers originate at 1.

chmod ()   *Set file access mode*

Compatibility   □ ANSI   ■ OS/2   ■ UNIX   ■ XENIX

See Also
```
_dos_setfileattr(), system(), umask()
```

Specification
```
#include <sys\types.h>
#include <sys\stat.h>
#include <io.h>
#include <errno.h>
int chmod(const char *filename, int pmode);
```

Arguments

filename: File pathname string.

pmode: Valid permission modes: **S_IREAD** (read-only); **S_IWRITE** (read/write); **S_IREAD|S_IWRITE** (read/write).

Return Value

0 if successful

−1 if unsuccessful

errno set to **ENOENT**

Example
```
/* FILE: ch16e4.c      */
#include <sys\types.h>
#include <sys\stat.h>
#include <io.h>
#include <errno.h>
#include <stdio.h>
#include <string.h>
int main(void)
{
char filename[FILENAME_MAX] = "c:\\ibmbio.com", *ptr;
int pmode = S_IREAD | S_IWRITE;
char pmodestr[3];
int erc, error;
char rbuf[]="/READ ", wbuf[]="/WRITE";
while (strcmpi(filename,"END")) {
    printf("\nbefore: ");
    if (!access(filename,04)) printf(rbuf);
    if (!access(filename,02)) printf(wbuf);
    errno = 0;
    erc = chmod(filename,pmode);
    error = errno;
```

```
    ptr = strerror(error);
    printf("\nfilename=%s pmode=%o erc=%d errno=%d <%s>",\
           filename, pmode, erc, error, ptr);
    if (!error) {
        printf("\nafter : ");
        if (!access(filename,04)) printf(rbuf);
        if (!access(filename,02)) printf(wbuf);
        }
    printf("\n\nEnter file pathname: ");
    gets(filename);
    printf("\n\nEnter pmode as R, W, or RW: ");
    gets(pmodestr);
    pmode = S_IREAD;
    if (!strcmpi(pmodestr,"W")) pmode |= S_IWRITE;
    if (!strcmpi(pmodestr,"RW")) pmode |= S_IWRITE;
    }
exit(0);
}
```

Output

```
before: /READ
filename=c:\ibmbio.com pmode=600 erc=0 errno=0 <Error 0>
after : /READ /WRITE


Enter file pathname: c:\ibmbio.com
Enter pmode as R, W, or RW: r
before: /READ /WRITE
filename=c:\ibmbio.com pmode=400 erc=0 errno=0 <Error 0>
after : /READ


Enter file pathname: c:\dos
Enter pmode as R, W, or RW: w
before: /READ /WRITE
filename=c:\dos pmode=600 erc=-1 errno=13 <Permission denied>

Enter file pathname: end
Enter pmode as R, W, or RW:
```

Comments   Similar to DOS command ATTRIB.

It is not possible to make a DOS directory or file write-only, and all directories except the root must be read/write.

chsize()   *Set length of any unbuffered/unformatted file*

Compatibility   ☐ ANSI   ■ OS/2   ■ UNIX   ■ XENIX

Specification

```
#include <io.h>
#include <errno.h>
int chsize(int handle, long size);
```

Arguments

handle: Open file number.

size: File length in bytes.

Return Value

0 if successful

−1 if unsuccessful

errno set to **EACCES**, **EBADF**, **ENOSPC**

Example

```
/* FILE: ch16e5.c        */
#include <io.h>
#include <errno.h>
#include <stdio.h>
#include <string.h>
#include <sys\types.h>
#include <sys\stat.h>
#include <fcntl.h>
int main(void)
{
char filename[FILENAME_MAX], *ptr;
int handle, erc, error;
long size;
while (1) {
    printf("\n\nEnter file pathname: ");
    fflush(stdin);
    gets(filename);
    if (!strcmpi(filename,"END")) break;
    if (!access(filename,00)) printf("\tWarning! existing file\n");
    handle = open(filename, O_CREAT|O_RDWR, S_IREAD|S_IWRITE);
    printf("\tfilename=%s  handle=%d  initial size=%ld",\
        filename, handle, filelength(handle));
    write(handle, filename, 10u);
    size=filelength(handle);
    printf("\n\tafter write size=%ld",size);
    printf("\n\tEnter desired size in bytes: ");
    scanf("%ld", &size);
    errno = 0;
    erc = chsize(handle, size);
    error = errno;
    ptr = strerror(error);
    printf("\terc=%d desired size=%ld errno=%d <%s>",\
        erc, filelength(handle), error, ptr);
```

```
        close(handle);
        }
    exit(0);
    }
```

Output

```
Enter file pathname: test.xxx
    filename=test.xxx  handle=5  initial size=0
    after write size=10
    Enter desired size in bytes: 15
    erc=0 desired size=15 errno=0 <Error 0>

Enter file pathname: test.xxx      Warning! existing file
    filename=test.xxx  handle=5  initial size=15
    after write size=15
    Enter desired size in bytes: 0
    erc=0 desired size=0 errno=0 <Error 0>

Enter file pathname: end
```

Comments   May be used to truncate or extend the file size. While a file handle is open, only those write operations that extend the original file size are reflected in its file length. When the file is closed, the directory entry is updated.

_dos_findfirst()   *Search for directories or files*

Compatibility   ☐ANSI   ☐OS/2   ☐UNIX   ☐XENIX

See Also

```
access(), _dos_findnext(), _searchenv()
```

Specification

```
#include <dos.h>
#include <errno.h>
unsigned _dos_findfirst(const char *filename,
    unsigned attrib, struct find_t *fileinfo);
```

Arguments

filename: File pathname string.

attrib: **_A_NORMAL** (read/write); **_A_RDONLY** (read-only); **_A_HIDDEN** (hidden); **_A_SYSTEM** (system); **_A_VOLID** (volume ID); **_A_SUBDIR** (subdirectory); **_A_ARCH** (archive). These object-like macros may be combined using OR (|).

fileinfo: Pointer to type **find_t** structure buffer (see Appendix E).

Return Value

0 if successful

ENOENT if unsuccessful

Example

```
/* FILE ch16e6.c  */
#include <dos.h>
#include <errno.h>
#include <stdio.h>
#include <string.h>
int main(void)
{
char filename[FILENAME_MAX], yorn[5], *ptr;
unsigned attrib, erc;
struct find_t fileinfo;
char * attrnames[] = { "_A_RDONLY", "_A_HIDDEN", "_A_SYSTEM",
    "_A_VOLID ", "_A_SUBDIR", "_A_ARCH  " };
int i, error, nbrattr = sizeof attrnames/ sizeof(attrnames[0]);
while (1) {
    printf("\n\nEnter a file-search pathname: ");
    fflush(stdin);
    gets(filename);
    if (!strcmpi(filename,"END")) break;
    attrib = _A_NORMAL;
    printf("\nSelect attributes Y<cr>:");
    for(i=0; i<nbrattr;i++) {
    printf("\n\t%s \?: ",attrnames[i]);
    gets(yorn);
    if (strcmpi(yorn,"Y")) continue;
    switch (i) {
        case 0: attrib |= _A_RDONLY; break;
        case 1: attrib |= _A_HIDDEN; break;
        case 2: attrib |= _A_SYSTEM; break;
        case 3: attrib |= _A_VOLID;  break;
        case 4: attrib |= _A_SUBDIR; break;
        case 5: attrib |= _A_ARCH;   break;
        }
    }
    errno=0;
    erc = _dos_findfirst(filename, attrib, &fileinfo);
    error = errno;
    ptr = strerror(error);
    printf("\nsearchpath=%s attrib=%#04x erc =%d errno=%d <%s>",\
        filename, attrib, erc, error, ptr);
    if (!error) do {
    printf("\nfilename=%s attrib=%#04x time=%#0x date=%#0x size=%ld",\
        fileinfo.name, fileinfo.attrib, fileinfo.wr_time,\
        fileinfo.wr_date, fileinfo.size);
    } while (!_dos_findnext(&fileinfo));
    }
exit(0);
}
```

Output

```
Enter a file-search pathname: c:\*
Select attributes Y<cr>:
   _A_RDONLY ?: n
   _A_HIDDEN ?: n
   _A_SYSTEM ?: n
   _A_VOLID  ?: y
   _A_SUBDIR ?: n
   _A_ARCH   ?: n
searchpath=c:\* attrib=0x08 erc =0 errno=0 <Error 0>
filename=RRMASTER attrib=0x28 time=0x5904 date=0x142C size=0

Enter a file-search pathname: c:\ibm*.com
Select attributes Y<cr>:
   _A_RDONLY ?: n
   _A_HIDDEN ?: y
   _A_SYSTEM ?: y
   _A_VOLID  ?: n
   _A_SUBDIR ?: n
   _A_ARCH   ?: n
searchpath=c:\ibm*.com attrib=0x06 erc =0 errno=0 <Error 0>
filename=IBMBIO.COM attrib=0x27 time=0x6d60 date=0xA67 size=9564
filename=IBMDOS.COM attrib=0x27 time=0x6d60 date=0xA67 size=27760

Enter a file-search pathname: end
```

Comments   This example illustrates the use of OR (|) to combine file attributes
(_A_xxxx).

The DOS wildcards ? and * may be used to define the search path.

The date and time fields returned are in DOS (bit-field) format, and are therefore displayed as hexadecimal values. See **_dos_setftime()**.

_dos_findnext ()   *Search for directories or files*

Compatibility   □ANSI   □OS/2   □UNIX   □XENIX

See Also

```
access(), _dos_findfirst(), _searchenv()
```

Specification

```
#include <dos.h>
#include <errno.h>
unsigned _dos_findnext(struct find_t *fileinfo);
```

Arguments

fileinfo: Pointer to type **find_t** structure buffer (see Appendix E).

Return Value

0 if successful

ENOENT if unsuccessful

Example   See: `_dos_findfirst()`.

Comments   You must call function `_dos_findfirst()` with a given attribute (**attrib** = **_A_xxx**) before subsequently calling `_dos_findnext()`. The `_dos_findfirst()` program example uses a **do..while** loop for this purpose.

_dos_getdrive()   *Get the current drive number*

Compatibility   ☐ANSI   ☐OS/2   ☐UNIX   ☐XENIX

See Also

```
fstat(), _getdrive(), stat()
```

Specification

```
#include <dos.h>
void _dos_getdrive(unsigned *drive);
```

Arguments

drive: Pointer to drive number buffer, (1 = A:), (2 = B:), and so on.

Return Value   None

Example   See: `_dos_setdrive()`.

Comments   The drive numbers for this function originate at 1.

_dos_getfileattr()   *Get directory and file attributes*

Compatibility   ☐ANSI   ☐OS/2   ☐UNIX   ☐XENIX

See Also

```
access(), _dos_findfirst(), _dos_findnext(), fstat(), stat()
```

Specification

```
#include <dos>
#include <errno.h>
unsigned _dos_getfileattr(const char *pathname, unsigned *attrib);
```

Arguments

pathname: Directory or file pathname string

attrib: Pointer to attribute buffer

Return Value

0 if successful

ENOENT if unsuccessful

Example

```
/* FILE: ch16e7.c       */
#include <dos.h>
#include <errno.h>
#include <io.h>
#include <stdio.h>
#include <string.h>

static void dispattr(char *pathname)
{
unsigned attrib, erc;
int error;
char *ptr;
errno = 0;
erc = _dos_getfileattr(pathname, &attrib);
error = errno;
ptr = strerror(error);
printf("\npathname=%s erc=%u attrib=%X errno=%d <%s>\n",\
       pathname, erc, attrib, error, ptr);
if (!error) {
    if (attrib & _A_RDONLY) printf("READ/ WRITE/ ");
    if (attrib & _A_RDONLY) printf("READ ONLY/ ");
    if (attrib & _A_HIDDEN) printf("HIDDEN/ ");
    if (attrib & _A_SYSTEM) printf("SYSTEM/ ");
    if (attrib & _A_VOLID ) printf("VOLID/ ");
    if (attrib & _A_SUBDIR) printf("DIR/ ");
    if (attrib & _A_ARCH  ) printf("ARCHIVE ");
    }
}

int main(void)
{
char pathname[FILENAME_MAX], yorn[5], *ptr;
unsigned attrib, erc;
int i, error;
char * attrnames[] = {"_A_RDONLY", "_A_HIDDEN", "_A_SYSTEM",
      "_A_VOLID ", "_A_SUBDIR", "_A_ARCH  "};
while (1) {
    printf("\n\nEnter a directory or file path: ");
    gets(pathname);
    if (!strcmpi(pathname,"END")) break;
    printf("\nbefore:");
```

```
        dispattr(pathname);
        attrib = _A_NORMAL;
        printf("\n\nSelect desired attributes Y<cr>:");
        for (i=0;i<6;i++) {
            printf("\n\t%s \?: ",attrnames[i]);
            gets(yorn);
            if (strcmpi(yorn,"Y")) continue;
            switch (i) {
                case 0: attrib |= _A_RDONLY;  break;
                case 1: attrib |= _A_HIDDEN;  break;
                case 2: attrib |= _A_SYSTEM;  break;
                case 3: attrib |= _A_VOLID;   break;
                case 4: attrib |= _A_SUBDIR;  break;
                case 5: attrib |= _A_ARCH;    break;
                }
            }
        errno = 0;
        erc = _dos_setfileattr(pathname, attrib);
        error = errno;
        ptr = strerror(error);
        printf("\nset:");
        printf("\npathname=%s erc=%u attrib=%X errno=%d <%s>\n",\
                pathname, erc, attrib, error, ptr);
        printf("\nafter:");
        dispattr(pathname);
        }
    exit(0);
    }
```

Output

```
Enter a directory or file path: test.xxx

before:     pathname=test.xxx erc=0 attrib=20 errno=0 <Error 0>
READ/ WRITE/ ARCHIVE
Select desired attributes Y<cr>:
    _A_RDONLY ?: y
    _A_HIDDEN ?: y
    _A_SYSTEM ?: n
    _A_VOLID  ?: n
    _A_SUBDIR ?: n
    _A_ARCH   ?: y
set:        pathname=test.xxx erc=0 attrib=23 errno=0 <Error 0>
after:      pathname=test.xxx erc=0 attrib=23 errno=0 <Error 0>
READ ONLY/ HIDDEN/ ARCHIVE

Enter a directory or file path: end
```

Comments Bit 0 of the attribute is shared by **_A_NORMAL** and **_A_RDONLY**; therefore, a file is only considered read-only if bit 0 is ON. Otherwise it is considered read/write. This explains why no DOS directories and files may be designated write-only.

_dos_getftime ()   *Get last date/time file written*

Compatibility ☐ANSI   ☐OS/2   ☐UNIX   ☐XENIX

See Also

```
_dos_findfirst(), _dos_findnext(), fstat(), stat()
```

Specification

```
#include <dos.h>
#include <errno.h>
unsigned _dos_getftime(int handle, unsigned *date, unsigned *time);
```

Arguments

handle: Open file number.

date: Pointer to DOS date buffer.

time: Pointer to DOS time buffer.

Return Value

0 if successful

EBADF if unsuccessful

Example   See: **_dos_setftime ().**

Comments   The arguments *date* and *time* are in DOS (bit-field) date and time format, not the type representations discussed in Chapter 21.

_dos_setdrive ()   *Change the current drive number*

Compatibility ☐ANSI   ☐OS/2   ☐UNIX   ☐XENIX

See Also

```
_chdrive(), system()
```

Specification

```
#include <dos.h>
void _dos_setdrive(unsigned drive, unsigned *ndrives);
```

Arguments

drive: Drive number (0 = current drive, 1 = A:, 2 = B:, and so on).

ndrives: Pointer to buffer representing total number of drives.

Return Value   None

Example

```
/* FILE: ch16e8.c      */
#include <dos.h>
#include <direct.h>
#include <errno.h>
#include <stdio.h>
int main(void)
{
int drive=0, ndrives;
char dirname[FILENAME_MAX], *ptr;
while (drive >= 0) {
    _dos_getdrive(&drive);
    ptr = _getdcwd(drive, dirname, FILENAME_MAX);
    printf("\ncurrent drive=%d  current-dir=%s  current-dir=%s",\
          drive, dirname, ptr);
    printf("\n\nSelect a drive number (-1 to quit): ");
    scanf("%d",&drive);
    _dos_setdrive(drive, &ndrives);
    printf("\ntotal drives=%d",ndrives);
    }
exit(0);
}
```

Output

```
current drive=3  current-dir=C:\QC2\BOOK  current-dir=C:\QC2\BOOK

Select a drive number (-1 to quit): 0
total drives=5
current drive=3  current-dir=C:\QC2\BOOK  current-dir=C:\QC2\BOOK

Select a drive number (-1 to quit): 1
total drives=5
current drive=1  current-dir=A:\  current-dir=A:\

Select a drive number (-1 to quit): -1
total drives=5
```

Comments   The drive number for this function originates at 1.

The maximum drive number (5) is the minimum value returned by DOS (two floppy drives, three hard drives). This corresponds to drive E:, the default value assumed for the LASTDRIVE command in CONFIG.SYS (see Chapter 1).

_dos_setfileattr()   *Set directory and file attributes*

Compatibility   ☐ANSI   ☐OS/2   ☐UNIX   ☐XENIX

See Also

```
chmod(), system(), umask()
```

Specification

```
#include <dos.h>
#include <errno.h>
unsigned _dos_setfileattr(const char *pathname, unsigned attrib);
```

Arguments

pathname: Directory or file pathname string.

attrib: **_A_NORMAL** (read/write); **_A_RDONLY** (read-only); **_A_HIDDEN** (hidden); **_A_SYSTEM** (system); **_A_VOLID** (volume ID); **_A_SUBDIR** (subdirectory); **_A_ARCH** (archive). These object-like macros may be combined using OR (|).

Return Value

0 if successful

EACCES or **ENOENT** if unsuccessful

Example   See: **_dos_getfileattr()**.

Comments   Attribute values occupy the low-order byte of the attribute word. Similar to using the DOS command ATTRIB.

_dos_setftime()   *Set last date/time file written*

Compatibility   ☐ANSI   ☐OS/2   ☐UNIX   ☐XENIX

See Also

```
utime()
```

Specification

```
#include <dos.h>
#include <errno.h>
unsigned _dos_setftime(int handle, unsigned date, unsigned time);
```

Arguments

handle: Open file number.

date: DOS modification date.

time: DOS modification time.

Return Value

0 if successful

EBADF if unsuccessful

Example

```
/* FILE: ch16e9.c */
#include <dos.h>
#include <errno.h>
#include <io.h>
#include <fcntl.h>
#include <sys\types.h>
#include <sys\stat.h>
#include <sys\utime.h>
#include <stdio.h>
#include <string.h>

static struct dos_date { unsigned day : 5;
                         unsigned month : 4;
                         unsigned year80 : 7; };
 static struct dos_time { unsigned sec2 : 5;
                         unsigned minutes : 6;
                         unsigned hours : 5; };
 static union { struct dos_date d_date;
              unsigned date; } u1;
 static union { struct dos_time d_time;
              unsigned time; } u2;
 static void dfdatetime (int handle)
{
int erc, error;
char *ptr;
errno = 0;
erc = _dos_getftime (handle, &u1.date, &u2.time); /* DOS format */
error = errno;
ptr = strerror(error);
printf("\n_dos_getftime: date=%u/%u/%u  time=%u:%u:%u"\
     " erc=%d errno=%d <%s>",\
     u1.d_date.month, u1.d_date.day, (u1.d_date.year80 + 1980),\
     u2.d_time.hours, u2.d_time.minutes, (u2.d_time.sec2 * 2),\
     erc, error, ptr);
}

int main(void)
{
char filename[FILENAME_MAX]={NULL}, *ptr;
int handle, erc, error;
while (strcmpi(filename,"END")) {
    printf("\n\nEnter a file pathname: ");
    gets(filename);
    if (access(filename,00)) continue;
    handle = open(filename,O_RDWR);
    dfdatetime(handle);   /* current file date/time */
```

```
        /* set file date/time with utime &utimbuf==NULL   */
        errno = 0;
        erc = utime(filename, NULL);
        error = errno;
        ptr = strerror(error);
        printf("\n==>utime set current time erc=%d errno=%d <%s>",\
               erc, error, ptr);
        close(handle);
        handle = open(filename,O_RDWR);
        dfdatetime(handle);    /* current file date/time */

        /* set file date/time with _dos_setftime */
        u1.d_date.year80 = (1990-1980);
        u1.d_date.month  = 1;
        u1.d_date.day = 1;      /* setting Jan 1, 1990 */
        u2.d_time.hours = 23;
        u2.d_time.minutes = 59;
        u2.d_time.sec2 = (58/2);   /* setting max 23:59:58 */
        errno = 0;
        erc = _dos_setftime(handle, u1.date, u2.time);
        error = errno;
        ptr=strerror(error);
        printf("\n==>_dos_setftime  erc=%d errno=%d <%s>",\
               erc, error, ptr);
        close(handle);
        handle = open(filename,O_RDWR);
        dfdatetime(handle);    /* latest file date/time */
        }
    exit(0);
    }
```

Output

```
Enter a file pathname: test.xxx
_dos_getftime: date=12/30/1989 time=6:21:34 erc=0 errno=0 <Error 0>
==>utime set current time erc=0 errno=0 <Error 0>
_dos_getftime: date=2/6/1990 time=10:14:40 erc=0 errno=0 <Error 0>
==>_dos_setftime  erc=0 errno=0 <Error 0>
_dos_getftime: date=1/1/1990 time=23:59:58 erc=0 errno=0 <Error 0>

Enter a file pathname: end
```

Comments   The date and time fields are in DOS (bit-field) format, and not in the other type formats discussed in Chapter 21.

The **close()** function had to be used repeatedly to update the directory record entries; otherwise, **_dos_getftime()** works from the file control buffer in memory.

Using the function **utime(filename, NULL)** with a NULL argument sets both the current time and date. This is equivalent to "touching" a file. (See the NMAKE command-line option /T in Chapter 3.)

`filelength()`   *Get file length*

Compatibility   ☐ ANSI   ■ OS/2   ☐ UNIX   ☐ XENIX

See Also

```
_dos_findfirst(), _dos_findnext(), fstat(), stat()
```

Specification

```
#include <io.h>
#include <errno.h>
long filelength(int handle);
```

Arguments

handle: Open file number.

Return Value

File length in bytes if successful

−1L if unsuccessful

errno set to **EBADF**

Example   See: `chsize()`.

Comments   Remember that `filelength()` returns type `long`!

`fileno()`   *Get file handle number*

Compatibility   ☐ ANSI   ■ OS/2   ■ UNIX   ■ XENIX

Specification

```
#include <stdio.h>
int fileno(FILE *stream);
```

Arguments

stream: Pointer to stream FILE buffer.

Return Value

File handle if successful

Undefined if unsuccessful

Example   See also: **setmode()**.

```
/* FILE: ch16e10.c */
#include <stdio.h>
#include <io.h>
#undef fileno
int main(void)
{
FILE *stream[_NFILE] = {stdin, stdout, stderr, stdaux, stdprn };
int handle[_NFILE];
int i;
for(i=0;i<_NFILE;i++) {
    if (!stream[i]) stream[i] = tmpfile();
    if (!stream[i]) break;
    handle[i] = fileno(stream[i]);
    printf("\nhandle=%d  ",handle[i]);
    if (isatty(handle[i])) printf("file=DEVICE");
    else printf("file=DISK");
    }
printf("\n#temp-files deleted=%d",rmtmp());
exit(0);
}
```

Output

```
handle=0   file=DEVICE
handle=1   file=DISK
handle=2   file=DEVICE
handle=3   file=DEVICE
handle=4   file=DEVICE
handle=5   file=DISK
.

.
handle=19  file=DISK
#temp-files deleted=15
```

Comments   Use either the function or macro version. Notice that by using the directive **#undef fileno** we have invoked the run-time library function **fileno()**, not the function-like macro defined in **<stdio.h>**.

The maximum file number (handle) is controlled by the FILES=n statement in the DOS file CONFIG.SYS, with a limit established by the object-like macro **_NFILE**.

Notice in the sample output that the five predefined file handles are normally DOS devices; however, the sample output was generated by redirecting **stdout** (1) to a disk file (see Table 1.3).

Fifteen temporary files were created and then deleted.

`fstat()`   *Get file characteristics*

Compatibility   ☐ ANSI   ■ OS/2   ■ UNIX   ■ XENIX

See Also

`_dos_getdrive()`, `_dos_getfileattr()`, `_dos_findfirst()`, `_dos_findnext()`, `_dos_getftime()`, `filelength()`, `stat()` `_getdrive()`, `isatty()`

Specification

```
#include <sys\types.h>
#include <sys\stat.h>
#include <errno.h>
int fstat(int handle, struct stat *buffer);
```

Arguments

handle: Open file number.

buffer: Pointer to type **stat** structure buffer (see Appendix E).

Return Value

0 if successful

−1 if unsuccessful

errno set to **EBADF**

Example   See: `stat()`.

Comments   Notice that the drive number returned by this function originates at 0.
Notice also that the time returned by this function is in **time_t** format (see Chapter 21).

`_fullpath()`   *Create complete path from partial path*

Compatibility   ☐ ANSI   ■ OS/2   ☐ UNIX   ☐ XENIX

See Also

`_makepath()`

Specification

```
#include <stdlib.h>
char *_fullpath(char *buffer, const char *pathname, size_t maxlen);
```

Arguments

buffer: Character array containing the pathname.

pathname: Pathname fragment string.

maxlen: Maximum length of **_buffer_**.

Return Value

Address of **_buffer_** if successful

NULL if unsuccessful

Example

```
/* FILE: ch16e11.c  */
#include <stdlib.h>
#include <direct.h>
#include <errno.h>
#include <stdio.h>
#include <string.h>
#define SIZE 0x80
int main(void)
{
char partpath[SIZE], pathname[SIZE]={NULL};
char drive[3], dir[FILENAME_MAX], fname[9], ext[5];
while (strcmpi(partpath,"END")) {
    printf("\n\nEnter a partial path: ");
    gets(partpath);
    if (!_fullpath(pathname, partpath, SIZE)) continue;
    printf("\n_fullpath : %s",pathname);
    _splitpath(pathname, drive, dir, fname, ext);
    printf("\n_splitpath: |%s|%s|%s|%s|",drive, dir, fname, ext);
    _makepath(pathname, drive, dir, fname, ext);
    printf("\n_makepath : %s",pathname);
    }
exit(0);
}
```

Output

```
Enter a partial path: c:
_fullpath : C:\QC2\BOOK
_splitpath: |C:|\QC2\|BOOK||
_makepath : C:\QC2\BOOK

Enter a partial path: c:\
_fullpath : c:\
_splitpath: |c:|\|||
_makepath : c:\

Enter a partial path: c:\qc2\book
_fullpath : c:\qc2\book
_splitpath: |c:|\qc2\|book||
_makepath : c:\qc2\book
```

```
Enter a partial path: c:\qc2\book\test.xxx
_fullpath : c:\qc2\book\test.xxx
_splitpath: |c:|\qc2\book\|test|.xxx|
_makepath : c:\qc2\book\test.xxx

Enter a partial path: end
```

Comments   Notice that partial paths are completed using the current drive and directory settings.

getcwd ()   *Get current directory on current drive*

Compatibility   ☐ ANSI   ■ OS/2   ■ UNIX   ■ XENIX

See Also

```
_getdcwd()
```

Specification

```
#include <direct.h>
#include <errno.h>
char *getcwd(char *buffer, int maxlen);
```

Arguments

buffer: Character array containing the pathname.

maxlen: Maximum length of *buffer*.

Return Value

Pointer to buffer if successful

NULL if unsuccessful

Example   See: **chdir()**, **creat()** (Chapter 18).

Comments   If the buffer used is NULL, **getcwd()** will automatically allocate a buffer using **malloc()**; however, it is your responsibility to **free()** that memory.

_getdcwd ()   *Get current directory on any drive*

Compatibility   ☐ ANSI   ■ OS/2   ☐ UNIX   ☐ XENIX

See Also

```
getcwd()
```

Specification

```
#include <direct.h>
#include <errno.h>
char *_getdcwd(int drive, char *buffer, int maxlen);
```

Arguments

drive: Drive number (0 = current drive, 1 = A:, 2 = B:, and so on).

buffer: Character array containing the current pathname.

maxlen: Maximum length of **buffer** including the terminating null.

Return Value

Pointer to buffer if successful

NULL if unsuccessful

Example   See: **_dos_setdrive()**.

Comments   The drive number used by this function originates at 1. Use of a 0 value assumes the current drive.

If the buffer used is NULL, **getdcwd()** will automatically allocate a buffer using **malloc()**; however, it is your responsibility to **free()** that memory.

_getdrive()   *Get the current drive number*

Compatibility   ☐ANSI   ■OS/2   ☐UNIX   ☐XENIX

See Also

```
_dos_getdrive(), fstat(), stat()
```

Specification

```
#include <direct.h>
int _getdrive(void);
```

Return Value

Drive number: (1 = A:, 2 = B:, and so on)

Example   See: **_chdrive()**.

Comments   The drive number originates at 1 for this function.

`isatty()`   *Check if file is a DOS device*

Compatibility   ☐ ANSI   ■ OS/2   ■ UNIX   ■ XENIX

See Also

```
fstat(), stat()
```

Specification

```
#include <io.h>
int isatty(int handle);
```

Arguments

handle: Open file number.

Return Value

Nonzero (true) if successful

0 (false) if unsuccessful

Example   See: `fileno()`.

Comments   If a file handle is associated with a device, many run-time library functions that expect the file handle to be associated with a disk file will produce unpredictable results.

`locking()`   *Lock bytes in a file*

Compatibility   ☐ ANSI   ■ OS/2   ■ UNIX   ■ XENIX

Specification

```
#include <sys\locking.h>
#include <io.h>
#include <errno.h>
int locking(int handle, int mode, long nbytes);
```

Arguments

handle: Open file number.

mode: **LK_LOCK** (lock range of bytes; 10 tries).

LK_RLCK (lock range of bytes; 10 tries).

LK_NBLCK (nonblocking **LK_LOCK**).

LK_NBRLCK (nonblocking **LK_RLCK**).

LK_UNLCK (unlock range of previously locked bytes).

nbytes: Number of bytes to lock.

Return Value

0 if successful

−1 if unsuccessful

errno set to **EACCES, EBADF, EDEADLOCK, EINVAL**

Example

```
/* FILE: ch16e12.c  */
#include <sys\locking.h>
#include <sys\types.h>
#include <sys\stat.h>
#include <share.h>
#include <io.h>
#include <errno.h>
#include <process.h>
#include <string.h>
#include <fcntl.h>
#include <stdio.h>
#define NBYTES 5

int main(void)
{
static int phandle, chandle, erc, error, process, i;
static char *ptr, pbyte[] = {0x77,0x33}, cbyte[]={0x7f, 0xee};

if(access("ch16e12.xxx",00)) {  /* parent process = 0 */
    process=0;
    system("share");   /* install SHARE */
    phandle = creat("ch16e12.xxx", S_IREAD|S_IWRITE);
    for (i=0;i<NBYTES;i++) write(phandle,&pbyte[0],1u);
    for (i=0;i<NBYTES;i++) write(phandle,&pbyte[1],1u);
    close(phandle);
    errno = 0;
    phandle = sopen("ch16e12.xxx", O_NOINHERIT|O_BINARY|O_RDWR,\
        SH_DENYNO);
    error = errno;
    ptr = strerror(error);
    printf("\n==>parent opening control file: handle=%d"\
        "errno=%d <%s>", phandle, error, ptr);
    }
else { /* child process = 1 */
    process = 1;
    errno = 0;
    chandle = sopen("ch16e12.xxx", O_BINARY|O_RDONLY, SH_DENYNO);
    error = errno;
    ptr = strerror(error);
    printf("\n==>child opening control file:  handle=%d"\
        "errno=%d <%s>", chandle, error, ptr);
    }
```

```
if (!process) { /* parent process */
    errno = 0;
    erc = locking(phandle,LK_NBLCK,(long)(2*NBYTES));
    error = errno;
    ptr = strerror(error);
    printf("\nparent locking 0-9 : erc=%d errno=%d <%s>",\
        erc, error, ptr);

    lseek(phandle,0L,SEEK_SET);
    errno = 0;
    erc = locking(phandle,LK_UNLCK,(long)(2*NBYTES));
    error = errno;
    ptr = strerror(error);
    printf("\nparent unlocking 0-9: erc=%d errno=%d <%s>",\
        erc, error, ptr);

    lseek(phandle,(long)NBYTES,SEEK_SET);
    errno = 0;
    erc = locking(phandle,LK_NBLCK,(long)NBYTES);
    error = errno;
    ptr = strerror(error);
    printf("\nparent locking 5-9: erc=%d errno=%d <%s>",\
        erc, error, ptr);

    printf("\n==>parent initiates child process");
    errno = 0;
    erc = spawnl(P_WAIT,"ch16e12.exe",NULL);
    error = errno;
    ptr = strerror(error);
    printf("\n==>child returns: erc=%d errno=%d <%s>",
        erc, error, ptr);
    printf("\nContinue parent process ...");
    printf("\nRemove outstanding locks ...");
    printf("\nExit appropriately ...");
    remove("ch16e12.xxx");
    exit(0);
    }

else { /* child process */
    lseek(chandle,0L,SEEK_SET);
    errno = 0;
    erc = locking(chandle, LK_LOCK,(long)NBYTES);
    error = errno;
    ptr = strerror(error);
    printf("\nchild locking 0-4: erc=%d errno=%d <%s>",\
        erc, error, ptr);
    if (!error) {
        lseek(chandle,0L,SEEK_SET);
        for (i=0;i<NBYTES;i++) {
            errno = 0;
            erc = read(chandle,cbyte,1u);
            error = errno;
```

```
            ptr = strerror(error);
            printf("\nchild reading: byte=%d value=%X cnt=%d"\
                  "errno=%d <%s>",i, cbyte[0], erc, error, ptr);
            }

      lseek(chandle,0L,SEEK_SET);
      errno = 0;
      erc = locking(chandle, LK_UNLCK, (long)NBYTES);
      error = errno;
      ptr=strerror(error);
      printf("\nchild unlocking 0-4: erc=%d errno=%d <%s>",\
            erc, error, ptr);
      }

      lseek(chandle, (long)NBYTES,SEEK_SET);
      errno = 0;
      erc = locking(chandle, LK_NBLCK,(long)NBYTES);
      error = errno;
      ptr = strerror(error);
      printf("\nchild locking 5-9: erc=%d errno=%d <%s>",\
            erc, error, ptr);
      exit(99);
      }
}
```

Output

```
==>parent opening control file: handle=5  errno=0 <Error 0>
parent locking 0-9 : erc=0 errno=0 <Error 0>
parent unlocking 0-9: erc=0 errno=0 <Error 0>
parent locking 5-9: erc=0 errno=0 <Error 0>
==>parent initiates child process
==>child opening control file:  handle=6  errno=0 <Error 0>
child locking 0-4: erc=0 errno=0 <Error 0>
child reading: byte=0 value=77  cnt=1  errno=0 <Error 0>
child reading: byte=1 value=77  cnt=1  errno=0 <Error 0>
child reading: byte=2 value=77  cnt=1  errno=0 <Error 0>
child reading: byte=3 value=77  cnt=1  errno=0 <Error 0>
child reading: byte=4 value=77  cnt=1  errno=0 <Error 0>
child unlocking 0-4: erc=0 errno=0 <Error 0>
child locking 5-9: erc=-1 errno=13 <Permission denied>
==>child returns: erc=99 errno=0 <Error 0>
Continue parent process ...
Remove outstanding locks ...
Exit appropriately ...
```

Comments The **locking()** function can be used only with DOS version 3.0 or greater, when the DOS command SHARE is installed, and upon a file opened for sharing with **_dos_open()**, **_fsopen()**, or **sopen()**.

The example demonstrates proper use of **locking()**. Always try to lock the area of the file before performing your intended I/O; do not rely upon the I/O to fail because another process has locked the file!

Segmented and overlapping regions of the file may be locked, but they should be unlocked in like fashion before the process terminates.

Think of SHARE as the interceptor and arbiter of all file access when SHARE is installed.

_makepath()   *Create pathname from components*

Compatibility   □ ANSI   ■ OS/2   □ UNIX   □ XENIX

See Also

```
_fullpath(), _splitpath()
```

Specification

```c
#include <stdlib.h>
void _makepath(char *path, const char *drive,
const char *dir, const char *fname,
const char *ext);
```

Arguments

path: Pointer to pathname buffer.

drive: Drive letter string.

dir: Path string.

fname: Filename string.

ext: File extension string.

Example   See: `_fullpath()`.

Comments   The *drive* argument letter may optionally include a trailing colon (:). If the *dir* argument is NULL, no directory or backslash is inserted. If a *dir* string is provided, it should have a leading backslash, but the trailing backslash is optional. The *fname* argument should not contain an extension. The *ext* argument may optionally contain a period.

mkdir()   *Make new directory on current drive*

Compatibility   □ ANSI   ■ OS/2   □ UNIX   □ XENIX

See Also

```
chdir(), rename(), system()
```

Specification

```
#include <direct.h>
#include <errno.h>
int mkdir(const char *dirname);
```

Arguments

dirname: Directory pathname string.

Return Value

0 if successful

−1 if unsuccessful

errno set to **EACCES, ENOENT**

Example

```
/* FILE: ch16e13.c  */
#include <direct.h>
#include <errno.h>
#include <stdio.h>
#include <string.h>
int main(void)
{
char dirname[FILENAME_MAX]={NULL}, *ptr;
int erc, error;
while (1) {
    printf("\n\nCreate directory path: ");
    gets(dirname);
    if (!strcmpi(dirname,"END")) break;
    errno = 0;
    erc = mkdir(dirname);
    error = errno;
    ptr = strerror(error);
    printf("\n\tcreate directory: %s   erc=%d errno=%d <%s>",\
          dirname, erc, error, ptr);
    if (!error) {
        errno = 0;
        erc = rmdir(dirname);
        error = errno;
        ptr = strerror(error);
        printf("\n\tremove directory: %s   erc=%d errno=%d <%s>",\
              dirname, erc, error, ptr);
        }
    else {
        printf("\n\nRemove directory path: ");
        gets(dirname);
        errno = 0;
        erc = rmdir(dirname);
        error = errno;
        ptr = strerror(error);
        printf("\n\tremove directory: %s   erc=%d errno=%d <%s>",\
```

```
                    dirname, erc, error, ptr);
            }
        }
    exit(0);
    }
```

Output

```
Create directory path: c:\xxx
    create directory: c:\xxx  erc=0 errno=0 <Error 0>
    remove directory: c:\xxx  erc=0 errno=0 <Error 0>

Create directory path: xxx
    create directory: xxx  erc=0 errno=0 <Error 0>
    remove directory: xxx  erc=0 errno=0 <Error 0>

Create directory path: end
```

Comments   Identical to the DOS command MD (or MKDIR). If no drive or directory is provided, the current values of those components will be used.

mktemp()   *Create a filename from a template*

Compatibility   ☐ANSI   ■OS/2   ■UNIX   ■XENIX

See Also

```
tempnam(), tmpnam()
```

Specification

```
#include <io.h>
char *mktemp(char *template);
```

Arguments

template: filename "fn*XXXXXX*" string that is no longer than the eight-character maximum for DOS.

Return Value

Pointer to filename if successful

NULL if unsuccessful

Example

```
/* FILE ch16e14.c */
#include <io.h>
#include <sys\types.h>
#include <sys\stat.h>
#include <stdio.h>
```

```
#include <string.h>
#include <malloc.h>
int main(void)
{
char name1[3][L_tmpnam], name2[3][L_tmpnam], name3[3][L_tmpnam];
char template[L_tmpnam], dir[FILENAME_MAX], prefix[L_tmpnam], *ptr;
int i, handle;
while (1) {
    printf("\n\nEnter mktemp 2-char base-template (or end): ");
    gets(template);
    if (!strcmpi(template,"END")) break;
    strcat(template,"XXXXXX");
    printf("\nEnter tempnam existing directory: ");
    gets(dir);
    printf("\nEnter tempnam prefix: ");
    gets(prefix);
    for (i=0;i<3;i++) {
        strcpy(name1[i],template);
        printf("\nmktemp : %s", mktemp(name1[i]) );
        handle = creat(name1[i], S_IREAD|S_IWRITE);
        close(handle);
        ptr = tempnam(dir,prefix);
        strcpy(name2[i],ptr);
        free(ptr);
        printf("\ntempnam: %s", name2[i] );
        strcpy(name3[i],tmpnam(name3[i]));
        printf("\ntmpnam : %s\n", name3[i] );
        }
    remove(name1[0]);
    remove(name1[1]);
    remove(name1[2]);
    }
exit(0);
}
```

Output

```
Enter mktemp 2-char base-template (or end): qq
Enter tempnam existing directory: c:\qc2\book
Enter tempnam prefix: temp

mktemp : qq002995
tempnam: c:\qc2\book\temp2
tmpnam : \2

mktemp : qqa02995
tempnam: c:\qc2\book\temp3
tmpnam : \3

mktemp : qqb02995
tempnam: c:\qc2\book\temp4
tmpnam : \4

Enter mktemp 2-char base-template (or end): end
```

Comments   `mktemp()` expects **template** to contain six uppercase X characters; otherwise, an error results.

Unless the filenames generated by **mktemp()** are created (and saved), the same name will continue to be generated for a process.

remove ()   *Delete a permanent file*

Compatibility   ■ ANSI   ■ OS/2   □ UNIX   □ XENIX

See Also

```
rename(), rmtmp(), system(), unlink()
```

Specification

```
#include <stdio.h>
#include <errno.h>
int remove(const char *filename);
```

Arguments

filename: File pathname string.

Return Value

0 if successful

Nonzero if unsuccessful

errno set to **EACCES**, **ENOENT**

Example   See: **mktemp()**, **rename()**.

Comments   Identical to DOS command DEL or ERASE. Files that have a read-only attribute cannot be removed. They must be changed first to read/write.

rename ()   *Rename a directory or file*

Compatibility   ■ ANSI   ■ OS/2   □ UNIX   □ XENIX

See Also

```
system()
```

Specification

```
#include <stdio.h>
#include <errno.h>
int rename(const char *old, const char *new);
```

Arguments

old: Existing file pathname string.

new: New file pathname string.

Return Value

0 if successful

Nonzero if unsuccessful

`errno` set to **EACCES**, **ENOENT**, **EXDEV**

Example

```
/* FILE: ch16e15.c */
#include <sys\types.h>
#include <sys\stat.h>
#include <io.h>
#include <fcntl.h>
#include <errno.h>
#include <stdio.h>
#include <string.h>
int main(void)
{
char oldpath[FILENAME_MAX], newpath[FILENAME_MAX];
char filename[FILENAME_MAX], *ptr;
int erc, error, handle, flip=0;

while (1) {
    printf("\n\nEnter an existing directory or file path: ");
    gets(oldpath);
    if (!strcmpi(oldpath,"END")) break;
    printf("\nEnter a new pathname: ");
    gets(newpath);
    errno = 0;
    erc = rename(oldpath, newpath);
    error = errno;
    ptr = strerror(error);
    printf("\nrenaming: old=%s new=%s erc=%d errno=%d <%s>",\
        oldpath, newpath, erc, error, ptr);
    tmpnam(filename);
    handle = open(filename,O_CREAT|O_RDWR, S_IREAD|S_IWRITE);
    close(handle);
    if (flip = (!flip)) {
        errno = 0;
        erc = remove(filename);
        error = errno;
        ptr = strerror(error);
        printf("\n\n==>using remove(): ");
        }
    else {
        errno = 0;
        erc = unlink(filename);
```

```
                error = errno;
                ptr = strerror(error);
                printf("\n\n==>using unlink(): ");
                }
           printf("file=%s erc=%d errno=%d <%s>",\
                filename, erc, error, ptr);
            }
    exit(0);
    }
```

Output

```
Enter an existing directory or file path: c:\dos
Enter a new pathname: a:\dos
renaming: old=c:\dos
          new=a:\dos erc=-1 errno=18 <Cross-device link>

==>using remove(): file=\2 erc=0 errno=0 <Error 0>

Enter an existing directory or file path: c:\autoexec.bat
Enter a new pathname: c:\dos\autoexec.bat
renaming: old=c:\autoexec.bat
          new=c:\dos\autoexec.bat erc=0 errno=0 <Error 0>

==>using remove(): file=\4 erc=0 errno=0 <Error 0>

Enter an existing directory or file path: end
```

Comments   Similar to the DOS command REN; however, **rename()** also allows you to rename directories. Files and directories can be renamed only on the same drive. Files can be moved to another directory by renaming, but directories can only be renamed, not moved. A file with a read-only attribute cannot be renamed; it must first be changed to read/write.

rmdir() *Remove directory on current drive*

Compatibility   □ANSI   ■OS/2   □UNIX   □XENIX

See Also

```
chdir(), rename(), system()
```

Specification

```
#include <direct.h>
#include <errno.h>
int rmdir(const char *dirname);
```

Arguments

dirname: Directory pathname string.

Return Value

0 if successful

Nonzero if unsuccessful

`errno` set to **EACCES**, **ENOENT**

Example   See: `mkdir()`.

Comments   Identical to the DOS command RD (or RMDIR). Subdirectories can be removed only if they are empty and not current.

rmtmp()   *Delete temporary files*

Compatibility   ☐ANSI   ■OS/2   ■UNIX   ■XENIX

See Also

`tmpfile()`

Specification

```
#include <stdio.h>
int rmtmp(void);
```

Return Value

Number of files closed and deleted

Example   See: `fileno()`.

Comments   `rmtmp()` removes only those files in the current directory that have been created using `tmpfile()`.

_searchenv()   *Search for a filename using an environment path*

Compatibility   ☐ANSI   ■OS/2   ☐UNIX   ☐XENIX

See Also

`_dos_findfirst()`, `_dos_findnext()`

Specification

```
#include <stdlib.h>
void _searchenv(const char *filename
    const char *varname, char *pathname);
```

Arguments

filename: File pathname string.

varname: Environment string to search.

pathname: Pointer to buffer representing complete pathname.

Example

```
/* FILE: ch16e16.c  */
#include <stdlib.h>
#include <stdio.h>
#include <string.h>
int main(int argc, char *argv[], char *envp[])
{
char pathname[FILENAME_MAX], filename[FILENAME_MAX];
char string[FILENAME_MAX];
int i=-1;
printf("\ncurrent environment strings:\n");
while (envp[++i]) {
    printf("\n\t%s",envp[i]);
    }
while (1) {
    printf("\n\nEnter a filename: ");
    gets(filename);
    if(!strcmpi(filename,"END")) break;
    printf("\nEnter an environment string name: ");
    gets(string);
    _searchenv(filename, string, pathname);
    if (pathname[0]) printf("\n\nfilename=%s",pathname);
    else printf("\n\nCannot find %s",filename);
    }
exit(0);
}
```

Output

```
current environment strings:

    COMSPEC=C:\COMMAND.COM
    PROMPT=$P$G
    PATH=C:\QC2\BIN;C:\;C:\DOS
    LIB=C:\QC2\LIB
    INCLUDE=C:\QC2\INCLUDE

Enter a filename: ibmbio.com
Enter an environment string name: path

Cannot find ibmbio.com

Enter a filename: ibmbio.com
Enter an environment string name: PATH
```

```
filename=C:\ibmbio.com

Enter a filename: end
```

Comments Notice that when matching environment variable names, this function makes case-sensitive comparisons. The search is performed first in the current directory and then in the order of directories specified by the environment variable.

setmode() *Set file translation mode*

Compatibility □ANSI ■OS/2 □UNIX □XENIX

See Also
_fmode (Appendix C)

Specification
```
#include <fcntl.h>
#include <io.h>
#include <errno.h>
int setmode(int handle, int mode);
```

Arguments
handle: Open file number

mode: O_TEXT (translated), O_BINARY (untranslated).

Return Value
Previous mode if successful

−1 if unsuccessful

errno set to **EBADF**, **EINVAL**

Example
```
/* FILE: ch16e17.c  */
#include <fcntl.h>
#include <io.h>
#include <stdio.h>
#include <stdlib.h>
int main(void)
{
int prv;
char message[] = "\n[\ncr\ncr\ncr]";

fprintf(stdout,"\ndefault _fmode translation mode: %x", _fmode);
fprintf(stdout,message);
_fmode = O_TEXT;
fprintf(stdout,"\nsetting _fmode to O_TEXT: %x", _fmode);
```

```
fprintf(stdout,message);
_fmode = O_BINARY;
fprintf(stdout,"\nsetting _fmode to O_BINARY: %x", _fmode);
fprintf(stdout,message);

prv = setmode(fileno(stdout),O_BINARY);
fprintf(stdout,"\r\n\nsetmode to O_BINARY: prior=%x"\
        " current=%x\r\n", prv, _fmode);
fprintf(stdout,message);

prv = setmode(fileno(stdout),O_TEXT);
fprintf(stdout,"\nsetmode to O_TEXT: prior=%X current=%X",\
        prv, _fmode);
fprintf(stdout,message);

exit(0);
}
```

Output

```
default _fmode translation mode: 0
[
cr
cr
cr]
setting _fmode to O_TEXT: 4000
[
cr
cr
cr]
setting _fmode to O_BINARY: 8000
[
cr
cr
cr]

setmode to O_BINARY: prior=4000 current=8000
[
    cr
        cr
            cr]
setmode to O_TEXT: prior=8000 current=4000
[
cr
cr
cr]
```

Comments Notice that setting the value of global variable **_fmode** affects only those files subsequently opened. To change the current translation mode of an open file, you must use function **setmode()**.

_splitpath()   *Split pathname into components*

Compatibility   □ANSI   ■OS/2   □UNIX   □XENIX

See Also

_fullpath(), _makepath()

Specification

```
#include <stdlib.h>
void _splitpath(const char *path, char *drive,
    char *dir, char *fname, char *ext);
```

Arguments

path: Complete pathname string.

drive: Pointer to drive letter buffer.

dir: Pointer to directory buffer.

fname: Pointer to filename buffer.

ext: Pointer to extension buffer.

Example   See: **_fullpath()**

Comments   The **drive** argument will always have a trailing colon (:). The **dir** argument will always have leading and trailing backslashes. The **ext** argument will always have a leading period (.).

stat()   *Get directory and file characteristics*

Compatibility   □ANSI   ■OS/2   ■UNIX   ■XENIX

See Also

_dos_getdrive(), _dos_getfileattr(), _dos_findfirst(), _dos_findnext(),
_dos_getftime(), filelength(), fstat(), _getdrive(), isatty()

Specification

```
#include <sys\types.h>
#include <sys\stat.h>
#include <errno.h>
int stat(char *pathname, struct stat *buffer);
```

Arguments

pathname: Pathname string.

buffer: Pointer to type **stat** structure (see Appendix E).

Return Value

0 if successful

Nonzero if unsuccessful

errno set to **ENOENT**

Example

```c
/* FILE: ch16e18.c  */
#include <sys\types.h>
#include <sys\stat.h>
#include <errno.h>
#include <io.h>
#include <fcntl.h>
#include <stdio.h>
#include <string.h>
int main(void)
{
char pathname[FILENAME_MAX], *ptr;
struct stat buffer;
int handle, flip=1, erc, error;
while (1) {
    printf("\n\nEnter a directory or file path: ");
        gets(pathname);
    if (!strcmpi(pathname,"END")) break;
    if (flip = (!flip)) {
        errno = 0;
        erc = stat(pathname, &buffer);
        error = errno;
        printf("\n==>using stat()");
        }
    else {
        handle = open(pathname, O_BINARY|O_RDONLY);
        errno = 0;
        erc = fstat(handle, &buffer);
        error = errno;
        printf("\n==>using fstat()");
        close(handle);
        }
    ptr = strerror(error);
    printf("\tpathname=%s erc=%d errno=%d <%s>",\
    pathname, erc, error, ptr);
    if (!error) {
        printf("\n\tstat.drive=%d\n\tstat.size =%ld"\
            "\n\tstat.time =%ld\n\tstat.mode =", buffer.st_dev,
            buffer.st_size, buffer.st_atime);
        if ((buffer.st_mode & S_IFMT)   == S_IFMT)   printf("FILE/ ");
        if ((buffer.st_mode & S_IFDIR)  == S_IFDIR)  printf("DIR/ ");
        if ((buffer.st_mode & S_IFCHR)  == S_IFCHR)  printf("DEV/ ");
        if ((buffer.st_mode & S_IFREG)  == S_IFREG)  printf("REG/ ");
        if ((buffer.st_mode & S_IREAD)  == S_IREAD)  printf("READ/ ");
        if ((buffer.st_mode & S_IWRITE) == S_IWRITE) printf("WRITE/ ");
        if ((buffer.st_mode & S_IEXEC)  == S_IEXEC)  printf("EXEC/ ");
```

```
            }
        }
    exit(0);
    }
```

Output

```
Enter a directory or file path: test.xxx
==>using fstat()      pathname=test.xxx erc=0 errno=0 <Error 0>
    stat.drive=2
    stat.size =20
    stat.time =631267198
    stat.mode =REG/ READ/ WRITE/

Enter a directory or file path: end
```

Comments Notice that the drive number returned by this function originates at 0, and that the time returned is in **time_t** format (see Chapter 21).

tempnam() *Create a unique temporary filename*

Compatibility □ANSI   ■OS/2   ■UNIX   ■XENIX

See Also

```
mktemp(), tmpnam()
```

Specification

```
#include <stdio.h>
char *tempnam(char *dir, char *prefix);
```

Arguments

dir: Target directory string if TMP environment string not defined.

prefix: Filename prefix string.

Return Value

Pointer to filename if successful

NULL if unsuccessful

Example   See: **mktemp()**, **creat()** (Chapter 18).

Comments The function attempts to create a file first in the directory specified by environment variable TMP, if defined, then in the *dir* directory, if that exists. Failing those alternatives, it creates the file in the **P_tmpdir** directory, defined in **<stdio.h>**.

tempnam() allocates a buffer for the filename using **malloc()**; the user must free this buffer.

tmpfile()   *Create a temporary file*

Compatibility   ■ ANSI   ■ OS/2   ■ UNIX   ■ XENIX

See Also
```
rmtmp()
```

Specification
```
#include <stdio.h>
FILE *tmpfile(void);
```

Return Value

Pointer to FILE buffer if successful.

NULL if unsuccessful

Example   See: **fileno()**.

Comments   **tmpfile()** creates a temporary file in the current directory. This file is automatically removed when it is closed, when the program terminates normally, or when **rmtmp()** is called.

tmpnam()   *Create a unique temporary filename*

Compatibility   ■ ANSI   ■ OS/2   ■ UNIX   ■ XENIX

See Also
```
mktemp(), tempnam()
```

Specification
```
#include <stdio.h>
char *tmpnam(char *string)
```

Arguments

string. Pointer to temporary filename string, **L_tmpnam** bytes long, in the **P_tmpdir** directory.

Return Value

Pointer to string if successful

NULL if unsuccessful

Example
See: `mktemp()`, `rename()`.

Comments
Creates up to **TMP_MAX** (defined in **<stdio.h>**) unique files in the **P_tmpdir** directory.

If *string* is NULL, a static buffer will automatically be allocated. This buffer is reused, and your program does not have to free it.

umask ()   *Set default process file access mode*

Compatibility   □ANSI   ■OS/2   ■UNIX   ■XENIX

See Also

```
chmod(), _dos_setfileattr()
```

Specification

```
#include <sys\types.h>
#include <sys\stat.h>
#include <io.h>
int umask(int pmode);
```

Arguments

pmode: Valid permission settings: S_IREAD (write-only); S_IWRITE (read-only). These macros may not be combined with OR.

Return Value

Previous **pmode** value if successful

Undefined if unsuccessful

Example

```
/* FILE: ch16e19.c  */
#include <sys\types.h>
#include <sys\stat.h>
#include <io.h>
#include <stdio.h>
int main(void)
{
int i_pmode, p_pmode;
printf("\naccess (pmode) settings: \n\n\tS_IREAD=%o"\
    "\n\tS_IWRITE=%o\n", S_IREAD, S_IWRITE);
```

```
i_pmode = umask(S_IWRITE);
printf("\n\tinitial process pmode=%o", i_pmode);
printf("\nsetting process READ ONLY");

p_pmode = umask(S_IREAD);
printf("\n\tprocess pmode=%o",p_pmode);
printf("\nsetting process WRITE ONLY");

p_pmode = umask(i_pmode);
printf("\n\tprocess pmode=%o", p_pmode);
printf("\nsetting original pmode");

p_pmode = umask(i_pmode);
printf("\n\tfinal process pmode=%o", p_pmode);

exit(0);
}
```

Output

```
access (pmode) settings:

    S_IREAD=400
    S_IWRITE=200

    initial process pmode=0
setting process READ ONLY
    process pmode=200
setting process WRITE ONLY
    process pmode=400
setting original pmode
    final process pmode=0
```

Comments   **umask()** sets the default pmode value for a process. Subsequent files created using **creat()**, **open()**, or **sopen()** will use this default value. Notice that the object-like macros **S_IREAD** and **S_IWRITE** are used by this function in what seems to be the reverse of the way they are used for all other functions.

unlink()   *Delete a permanent file*

Compatibility   □ANSI   ■OS/2   ■UNIX   ■XENIX

See Also

```
remove(), rename(), system()
```

Specification

```
#include <stdio.h>
#include <errno.h>
int unlink(const char *filename);
```

Arguments

filename: File pathname string.

Return Value

0 if successful

−1 if unsuccessful

errno set to **EACCES**, **ENOENT**

Example

See: **rename()**.

Comments

Identical to DOS commands DEL or ERASE. Files that have a read-only attribute cannot be unlinked; they must first be changed to read/write.

utime() *Set last date/time file written*

Compatibility ☐ANSI ■OS/2 ■UNIX ■XENIX

See Also

_dos_setftime()

Specification

```
#include <sys\types.h>
#include <sys\utime.h>
#include <errno.h>
int utime(char *filename, struct utimbuf *times)
```

Arguments

filename: File pathname string

times: Pointer to type **utimbuf** structure buffer (see Appendix E); if NULL, update with current date/time.

Return Value

0 if successful

−1 if unsuccessful

errno set to **EACCES, EINVAL, EMFILE, ENOENT**

Example

See: **_dos_setftime()**.

Comments   The *times* argument is in **time_t** format (see Chapter 21).

Using the function **utime(filename,NULL)** with a NULL argument sets both the current time and date. This is equivalent to "touching" a file. (See the NMAKE command-line option /T in Chapter 3.)

The file must be open for **utime()** to work correctly.

Stream I/O Functions

Stream I/O Functions

This chapter presents the run-time library functions that support the buffered and formatted processing of files in what is referred to in C as stream I/O, and that implement the fundamental DOS file properties described in Chapter 16.

We will first examine how stream I/O implements the DOS conventions governing disk- and device-based files, access and permission modes, translation modes, and buffering, positioning, sharing, locking, and inheritance discussed in Chapter 16. Then we will review how to create stream files and open them for processing, and examine the differences between character, formatted, and direct stream I/O.

If you are uncertain which functions are available to perform a specific stream I/O task, refer to Table 17.5, later in this chapter, which also indicates whether each function conforms with Standard C (■ ANSI) or is Microsoft-specific (□ ANSI).

The rest of the chapter consists of a complete alphabetic list of the functions shown in Table 17.5, presented in the standard run-time library format. For your convenience, a page-number index of all run-time library functions also appears on the inside back cover of this book.

Let's begin by examining the concepts and conventions adopted when the buffered and formatted stream I/O approach is taken to access DOS device- or disk-based files.

STREAM I/O CONVENTIONS

DOS files opened for processing as streams require that a *stream-pointer,* or *file-pointer,* variable be declared. This pointer is subsequently used to identify the file to be processed by any of the functions described in this chapter. For example, stream-pointer variables ***in** and ***out** would be declared in the following manner:

```
#include <stdio.h>
FILE *in, *out;
```

The **<stdio.h>** header file must be included because it defines the **typedef FILE** in the following manner:

```
struct _iobuf { char *_ptr;
    int _cnt;
```

```
    char *_base;
    char _flag;
    char _file; };

typedef struct _iobuf FILE;
 extern FILE _iob[];
```

The stream-pointer declarations described above (**FILE *in, *out**) are assigned the address of an element of the array of structures called **_iob** that is described by the structure template tag **_iobuf**. The **extern** storage class designation for the **_iob[]** array indicates that the storage allocation for **_iob[]** is provided elsewhere.

Actually, **_iob[]** is allocated when DOS is booted. The **_iob[]** array is allocated a number of elements equal to the value of the FILES=xx system configuration command found in CONFIG.SYS (see Chapter 1). The maximum number of elements that may be assigned is limited for DOS to 20, the maximum number of open files for a DOS program (process). If the FILES=xx command is omitted from CONFIG.SYS, a default value of 8 is assumed. Once DOS has allocated this array, you can change it only by altering the FILES value in CONFIG.SYS and then rebooting.

It is important to understand that the structure template **_iobuf** is not described or mandated by Standard C; the ANSI standard requires only that stream I/O be supported and leaves the implementation details up to the vendor (implementor). The structure template utilized varies from vendor to vendor. To maintain compatibility, use only the functions described in this chapter to perform stream I/O, and do not write source code that interrogates or alters the values of the members of the non-Standard array of structures **_iob[]**. The implementation details—how stream I/O files support the properties of associated DOS files—are intended to remain hidden to a program.

Stream-pointer variables contain the memory address (pointer) of an array element of structure **_iob[]**. The corresponding index position of an array element is referred to in C as a *file handle*. The low-level I/O functions described in Chapter 18 always refer to open files using the integer-valued *file handle* index position of the array **_iob[]**. The macro or run-time function **fileno()** returns the file handle value associated with an open stream pointer; hence the equivalence between stream pointers and file handles.

The difference between a file pointer and a file handle can best be demonstrated by an example. Consider the following pointer declarations:

```
FILE *in;
```

The contents of **in** would be displayed as either hhhh (for a near address) or hhhh:hhhh (in segment:offset notation for a far address). By contrast, the file handle for **in** would be simply an integer from 0 to 19. For more about file handles, see Chapter 18.

Thus, your program can access a DOS file using either its stream pointer or its file handle. In fact, a file may be accessed using both techniques in the same program, although typically only one technique or the other is used. When both techniques are employed, the file must specifically be designated as unbuffered with the function **setbuf()** or **setvbuf()**; otherwise, the mixed effect of using stream and low-level I/O will be unpredictable.

OPENING AND CREATING STREAM FILES

As discussed in Chapters 1 and 16, five predefined DOS device files are always automatically opened and available for use by every C program. Table 17.1 shows the stream pointers, access modes, and default buffering status and translation modes of these files.

Any program that includes the **<stdio.h>** header can use the predefined stream-pointer variables **stdin**, **stout**, **stderr**, **stdaux**, and **stdprn**. No variable declarations or **xxopen** functions must be called. The following table lists the stream I/O functions that rely on predefined stream pointers.

POINTER	FUNCTIONS
stdin	**getchar**, **gets**, **scanf**
stdout	**fputchar**, **printf**, **putchar**, **puts**, **vprintf**
stderr	**perror**
staux	None
stdprn	None

TABLE 17.1: Predefined DOS Devices and Stream I/O

DOS DEVICE NAME	STREAM POINTER	ACCESS MODE	DEFAULT BUFFERING	DEFAULT TRANSLATION
CON	**stdin**	Read-only	Yes	Text
CON	**stdout**	Write-only	Yes	Text
CON	**stderr**	Write-only	No	Text
AUX or COM1	**stdaux**	Read-write	No	Binary
PRN or LPT1	**stdprn**	Write-only	Yes	Binary

If any standard DOS device name (see Table 1.3) is specified to be opened for stream I/O without a trailing colon (:), a new stream pointer will be assigned to one of the available remaining **_iob[]** array elements. The existence of predefined DOS device-based files does not prevent an application from opening other DOS devices for use.

If, on the other hand, a disk-based filename is specified to be opened for stream I/O and is found not to exist in the directory of the volume (drive letter) specified, DOS creates a file and directory entry using the parameters specified. All stream I/O **xxopen** functions require that file access requests be expressed using *mode* strings, not the object-like macro definitions used with the low-level I/O **xxopen** functions discussed in Chapter 18. The use of mode strings simplifies the open process, but relinquishes some control over the assignment of file properties. In contrast, using the low-level I/O functions described in Chapter 18 gives your program complete control over the assignment of file properties. Table 17.2 lists the mode string choices supported for stream I/O and summarizes the information each mode conveys about a file.

For example, when a file is created using a stream I/O **xxopen** function with one of the mode strings, the File Access Attribute field of its corresponding directory entry is always set to read/write (**_A_NORMAL**), and all such files can be inherited by child processes (**O_NOINHERIT** cannot be specified). A read-only access file cannot be created by stream **xxopen** functions; your program must make a subsequent call to either **chmod()** or **_dos_setfileattr()** (see Chapter 16).

Although every access permission and translation mode can be expressed using mode strings, stream I/O files are automatically buffered at **BUFSIZ** bytes (see **<stdio.h>** in Chapter 6). If stream files are to be unbuffered, or buffered at other than **BUFSIZ** bytes, a function call to either **setbuf()** or **setvbuf()** must be made after stream files are successfully created and before any I/O is performed. Stream I/O file positioning is controlled independently of the "create" or "open" process. Remember, when switching between reading and writing a file, flush the buffers and reposition the location pointer if necessary. Also, all write operations to files opened in append mode are made at the end-of-file (EOF) regardless of where the location pointer may currently be positioned prior to the write. File sharing and locking of stream I/O files requires the use of function **_fsopen()** or the reassignment of a low-level file handle to an unbuffered stream I/O file using the function **fdopen()**.

TABLE 17.2: Stream I/O Mode Strings

MODE	DESCRIPTION
`"r"`	Existing file read-only; `_fmode mode`; else error
`"rb"`	Existing file read-only; binary mode; else error
`"rt"`	Existing file read-only; text mode; else error
`"r+"`	Existing file read/write; `_fmode mode`; else error
`"r+b"`	Existing file read/write; binary mode; else error
`"r+t"`	Existing file read/write; text mode; else error
`"w"`	New/existing file write-only; `_fmode mode`; destroy contents
`"wb"`	New/existing file write-only; binary mode; destroy contents
`"wt"`	New/existing file write-only; text mode; destroy contents
`"w+"`	New/existing file read/write; `_fmode mode`; destroy contents
`"w+b"`	New/existing file read/write; binary mode; destroy contents
`"w+t"`	New/existing file read/write; text mode; destroy contents
`"a"`	New/existing file write-only; `_fmode mode`; write at EOF
`"ab"`	New/existing file write-only; binary mode; write at EOF
`"at"`	New/existing file write-only; text mode; write at EOF
`"a+"`	New/existing file read/write; `_fmode mode`; write at EOF
`"a+b"`	New/existing file read/write; binary mode; write at EOF
`"a+t"`	New/existing file read/write; text mode; write at EOF

CHARACTER, FORMATTED, AND DIRECT I/O

Once a stream I/O file has been created or opened, input and output may be performed in three ways:

Character   One character or byte at a time; also the basis of string (array or characters) input and output.

Formatted   Upon input or output, internal C data-object types may be converted to equivalent ASCII character string representations, and vice-versa.

Direct   Any C data-object type may be input or output from any file position, without any formatted I/O data conversion.

The popularity of stream I/O rests in its broad support of buffered character and formatted I/O operations. The most familiar of these functions are the families of input functions derived from **scanf()** and of output functions derived from **printf()**.

The **scanf()** family of input functions (**cscanf()**, **fscanf()**, **scanf()**, and **sscanf()**) all use the format-conversion control string parameters described in Table 17.3.

TABLE 17.3: The scanf() Control String Format

FORMAT	
% [*] [Width] [Addr_Mode] [Size] Type	
COMPONENT	**DESCRIPTION**
%	Required.
[*]	Optional. Read, but do not store, the next item.
[Width]	Optional. Maximum number of characters to be read expressed as a whole decimal number.
[Addr_Mode]	Optional, Microsoft-specific. Indicates where the data object is allocated in a mixed memory model program:
	F **_far**; use only in a Tiny, Small, or Medium memory model program.
	N **_near**; use only in a Compact, Large, or Huge memory model program.
[Size]	Optional. Specifies the size of a Type object.
	h For short int with **d**, **i**, **o**, **x**, **X**.
	For unsigned short int with **u**.
	For **_near** pointer with **p**, **s**.
	l For long int with **d**, **i**, **o**, **x**, **X**.
	For unsigned long with **u**.
	For double with **e**, **E**, **f**, **g**, **G**.
	For **_far** pointer with **p**, **s**.
	L For long double with **e**, **E**, **f**, **g**, **G**.
Type	Required. Use one selection to describe the data-object type of the variable being read:
	c Single character, or more if **Width** is greater than 1.
	d Decimal integer.
	e Signed exponent notation, lowercase **e**.
	E Signed exponent notation, uppercase **E**.
	f Signed floating point.
	g Most compact form of **e**, **E**, **f**, lowercase **e**.

TABLE 17.3: The scanf() Control String Format (continued)

FORMAT	
% [*] [*Width*] [*Addr_Mode*] [*Size*] *Type*	

COMPONENT	DESCRIPTION	
Type (cont.)	G	Most compact form of `e`, `E`, `f`, uppercase `E`.
	i	Decimal integer.
	n	Not an output field, but a pointer to an integer (`int *`) into which `printf()` places the number of characters output. The return value of `scanf()` equals the number of items, not the number of characters read.
	o	Unsigned octal integer.
	p	Hexadecimal digits (h).
		If `_near`, hhhh for offset only.
		If `_far`, hhhh:hhhh for segment:offset.
	s	Null-terminated character string.
	[]	Delimiter-terminated character string; either `[c..c]` list of nondelimiters, or `[^c..c]` list of delimiters, which terminate the scan to form a string.
	u	Unsigned decimal short int.
	U	Unsigned decimal long int.
	x	Upper-/lowercase hexadecimal digits without leading 0x.
	X	Non-Standard form of *Type* x above.
	%	To require the reading of a percent sign; any character or sequence of characters not including `scanf()` control characters may be specified, and must match identically.

Each control string item that begins with a percent sign (%) corresponds to the address of a C data-object type variable to be converted from an ASCII character string to its corresponding internal binary representation. Notice that all valid C data-object types, including pointers, can be read in a formatted manner using the **scanf()** family of functions. For more about **scanf()**, see its reference entry later in this chapter.

The **printf()** family of output functions (**cprintf()**, **fprintf()**, **printf()**, **sprintf()**, **vprintf()**, **vfprintf()**, **vsprintf()**) all use the format-conversion control string parameters described in Table 17.4.

TABLE 17.4: The printf() Control String Format

FORMAT
% [*Flags*] [*Width*][*.Precision*] [*Addr_Mode*] [*Size*] *Type*

COMPONENT	DESCRIPTION
%	Required.
[*Flags*]	Optional. Use one of the following:
	– Left-justify the output.
	+ Display a sign with numerical result.
	' ' (Blank) prefixing of numericals.
	# Alternate *Type* format:
	With o, **x**, **X** show 0 prefix.
	With e, **E**, **f** insert decimal point.
	With g, **G** insert decimal; trailing zeroes.
	0 Pad with leading zeroes to [*Width*].
[*Width*]	Optional. Minimum number of characters to display, expressed as a whole decimal number.
[*.Precision*]	Optional. Maximum number of characters to display, expressed in decimal. Decimal point required as shown.
[*Addr_Mode*]	Optional, Microsoft-specific. Specifies the size of a pointer (p) or string (s) Type object.
	F Synonymous with [*Size*] l; a **_far** or 32-bit address.
	N Synonymous with [*Size*] h; a **_near** or 16-bit address.
[*Size*]	Optional. Specifies the size of a *Type* object.
	h For short int with **d**, **i**, **o**, **x**, **X**.
	For unsigned short int with **u**.
	For **_near** pointer with **p**, **s**.
	l For long int with **d**, **i**, **o**, **x**, **X**.
	For unsigned long with **u**.
	For double with **e**, **E**, **f**, **g**, **G**.
	For **_far** pointer with **p**, **s**.
	L For long double with **e**, **E**, **f**, **g**, **G**.
Type	Required. Use one selection to describe the data-object type of the variable being read:
	c Single character.
	d Decimal integer.

TABLE 17.4: The printf() Control String Format (continued)

FORMAT		
% [*Flags*] [*Width*][.*Precision*] [*Addr_Mode*] [*Size*] *Type*		

COMPONENT	DESCRIPTION	
Type (cont.)	e	Signed exponent notation, lowercase **e**.
	E	Signed exponent notation, uppercase **E**.
	f	Signed floating point.
	g	Most compact form of **e**, **E**, **f**, lowercase **e**.
	G	Most compact form of **e**, **E**, **f**, uppercase **E**.
	i	Decimal integer.
	n	Not an output field, but a pointer to an integer (`int *`) into which `printf()` places the number of characters output. The return value of `printf()` also equals the number of characters output.
	o	Unsigned octal integer.
	p	Hexadecimal digits (h). If **_near**, hhhh for offset only. If **_far**, hhhh:hhhh for segment:offset.
	s	Null-terminated character string.
	u	Unsigned decimal short int.
	U	Unsigned decimal long int.
	x	Lowercase hexadecimal digits.
	X	Uppercase hexadecimal digits.
	%	To output a percent sign or any other single character that is not a `printf()` control character.

Each control string item that begins with a percent sign (%) corresponds to a C variable of a data-object type to be converted from an internal binary C type representation to a corresponding ASCII character string. Notice in the table that all valid C data-object types, including pointers, can be written in a formatted manner using the **printf()** family of functions. For more about function **printf()**, see its reference entry later in this chapter.

The use of direct stream I/O provides no data format conversion and mimics the features provided by the low-level I/O functions described in Chapter 18, while providing for the buffering of all data transfers.

Stream I/O functions provide a more robust set of services with a perceived "ease of use" not available with the low-level I/O functions described in Chapter 18; however, they relinquish some functionality and control in doing so. The advantages of using stream over low-level I/O must also be weighed against the increased code size and run times that are necessarily associated with all stream I/O functions.

STREAM I/O TASKS

Table 17.5 describes the tasks performed by the run-time library functions that support stream I/O. As you can see, most stream I/O tasks are performed using functions that conform with Standard C (■ANSI).

TABLE 17.5: Stream Management Functions

TASK		FUNCTION	
		STANDARD C ■ ANSI	**MICROSOFT C** □ ANSI
Stream file access:	Open a stream file	`fopen()` `freopen()`	`fdopen()` `_fsopen()`
	Control stream file buffering	`setbuf()`	`flushall()`
	Empty stream file buffers	`setvbuf()`	dup() (Chapter 18)
	Duplicate file handles	`fflush()`	dup2() (Chapter 18)
	Close a stream file	`fclose()`	`fcloseall()`
Stream file operations:	Get a stream file handle number		`fileno()` (Chapter 16)
	Create a temporary stream file	`tmpfile()` (Chapter 16)	

Stream file positioning:	Test/get the current location	`fgetpos()`
		
		`ftell()`
		`feof()`	

	Set the current location	`fseek()`
		`fsetpos()`
		`rewind()`	

	Test if a DOS device (no positioning)		`isatty()` (Chapter 16)

TABLE 17.5: Stream Management Functions (continued)

TASK		FUNCTION	
		STANDARD C ■ **ANSI**	**MICROSOFT C** ☐ **ANSI**
Character I/O:	Input operations	`fgetc()`	`fgetchar()`
		`fgets()`	
		`getc()`	
		`getchar()`	
		`gets()`	
		`ungetc()`	
	Output operations	`fputc()`	`fputchar()`
		`fputs()`	
		`putc()`	
		`putchar()`	
		`puts()`	
Formatted I/O:	Input operations	`fscanf()`	
		`scanf()`	
	Output operations	`fprintf()`	
		`printf()`	
		`vfprintf()`	
		`vprintf()`	
Direct I/O:	Input operations	`fread()`	`getw()`
	Output operations	`fwrite()`	`putw()`
Error Handling:		`clearerr()`	
		`ferror()`	
		`perror()`	

Several of the functions are available in function-like macro form (**feof**, **ferror**, **getc**, **getchar**, **putc**, and **putchar**), while none are available in an intrinsic (**#pragma**) form or can be accomplished by using either a DOS command or the **system()** run-time library function.

You may recall from Chapter 5 that, although function-like macros generally outperform their function counterparts (see the **getc()** example program), when arguments that have side-effects (−−, ++) are used, only functions, not macros, will definitely work as intended. For example, to ensure that the function **getc()** (defined as a macro in **\<stdio.h\>**) is used, insert the **#undef** directive as shown here:

```
#include <stdio.h>
#undef getc
```

Otherwise, the macro version will be employed.

RUN-TIME LIBRARY FUNCTIONS FOR STREAM I/O

clearerr()   *Reset error and EOF indicators for a stream*

Compatibility ■ANSI   ■OS/2   ■UNIX   ■XENIX

See Also

```
fclose(), fseek(), fsetpos(), rewind()
```

Specification

```
#include <stdio.h>
void clearerr(FILE *stream);
```

Arguments

stream: Pointer to stream FILE buffer.

Example   See: **_fsopen()**.

Comments   Resets the error and end-of-file (EOF) indicators to zero. The error indicator remains set until explicitly cleared using **clearerr()**, by the use of function **rewind()**, or the file is closed. The end-of-file indicator remains set until explicitly cleared using **clearerr()**, by the repositioning of the file location pointer, or when the file is closed.

fclose()   *Close an open stream*

Compatibility ■ANSI   ■OS/2   ■UNIX   ■XENIX

See Also

```
fcloseall()
```

Specification

```
#include <stdio.h>
int fclose(FILE *stream);
```

Arguments

stream: Pointer to stream FILE buffer.

Return Value

0 if successful.

EOF if unsuccessful.

Example

See: **fdopen()**, **setvbuf**.

Comments

Valid for use with any open stream, including the predefined streams.

Closing a file empties all buffers, updates the directory entry, and releases any system-allocated buffer space, but not buffers assigned using **setbuf()** or **setvbuf()**.

Normal program termination has the same effect.

fcloseall()   *Close all open streams*

Compatibility   □ANSI   ■OS/2   □UNIX   □XENIX

See Also

fclose()

Specification

```
#include <stdio.h>
int fcloseall(void);
```

Return Value

Number of streams closed if successful

EOF if unsuccessful

Example

See: **fgetpos**, **fprintf**, **putw**.

Comments

Closes files (including any **tmpfile()** temporary files) except **stdin**, **stdout**, **stderr**, **stdaux**, and **stdprn** (see **fclose()**).

fdopen()   *Associate a stream with a low-level file*

Compatibility   □ANSI   ■OS/2   ■UNIX   ■XENIX

See Also

Chapter 18: **dup2**

Specification

```
#include <stdio.h>
FILE *fdopen(int handle, const char *mode);
```

Arguments

handle: Open file number.

mode: Mode string; see Table 17.2.

Return Value

Stream pointer if successful

NULL if unsuccessful

Example

```
/* FILE: ch17e1.c */
#include <stdio.h>
#include <fcntl.h>
#include <sys\types.h>
#include <sys\stat.h>
#include <io.h>
#include <string.h>
int main(void)
{
char *name;
int handle, dimens, i;
FILE *stream;
char *msg[] = { "string1\n",
    "string2\n",
    "string3\n"
    "string4\n" };
char line[15], *ptr;
dimens = sizeof(msg)/sizeof(msg[0]);
name = tmpnam(NULL);
handle = open(name,O_CREAT|O_RDWR|O_BINARY, S_IWRITE);
for (i=0; i<dimens; i++) write(handle,msg[i],strlen(msg[i]));

stream = fdopen(handle,"r+b");
fseek(stream,0L,SEEK_SET);
ptr = fgets(line,sizeof(line),stream);
while (ptr) {
    printf("%s",ptr);
    ptr = fgets(line,sizeof(line),stream);
    }
if (fclose(stream)) printf("\nfclose(stream) failed!");
if (close(handle)) printf("\nclose(handle) failed!");
remove(name);
exit(0);
}
```

```
string1
string2
string3
string4
```

Comments   Access will be granted only if the permission request is compatible with the existing open file.

Do not use this function to associate a stream with a shared low-level file (with or without locking) unless the stream is unbuffered (see **setbuf()** and **setvbuf()**).

feof()   *Test whether end-of-file (EOF) was encountered*

Compatibility   ■ANSI   ■OS/2   ■UNIX   ■XENIX

Specification

```
#include <stdio.h>
int feof(FILE *stream);
```

Arguments

stream: Pointer to stream FILE buffer.

Return Value

Nonzero (true) if EOF encountered

0 (false) if EOF not encountered

Example   See: **getc()**, **putw()**, **ungetc()**.

Comments   Once the EOF is reached, attempts to read the file return an EOF indicator until **clearerr()** is called, the stream location pointer is changed, or the file is closed.

Use either the function or macro version.

ferror()   *Test for an I/O error on a stream*

Compatibility   ■ANSI   ■OS/2   ■UNIX   ■XENIX

Specification

```
#include <stdio.h>
int ferror(FILE *stream);
```

Arguments

stream: Pointer to stream FILE buffer.

Return Value

Nonzero (true) if error encountered

0 (false) if error not encountered

Example   See: `_fsopen()`.

Comments   Once an error is detected for a stream, the error indicator remains set until the error is cleared using **clearerr()**, function **rewind()** is called, or the file is closed.

Use either the function or macro version.

fflush()   *Empty a stream buffer*

Compatibility   ■ANSI   ■OS/2   ■UNIX   ■XENIX

See Also

flushall()

Specification

```
#include <stdio.h>
int fflush(FILE *stream);
```

Arguments

stream: Pointer to stream FILE buffer.

Return Value

0 if successful, no buffer, or open read-only

EOF if unsuccessful

Example   See: `fgetpos()`, `fprintf()`, `_fsopen()`, `ftell()`, `putw()`, `scanf()`.

Comments   Input buffers are cleared and the effects of **ungetc()** are negated, while output buffers are transferred to the associated device- or disk-based file. If used on unbuffered files, no action is taken, and no error indicators are set.

As an alternative, close the file or terminate the program normally.

`fgetc()` *Read a character from a stream*

Compatibility ■ANSI ■OS/2 ■UNIX ■XENIX

See Also

```
fscanf(), getc()
```

Specification

```
#include <stdio.h>
int fgetc(FILE *stream);
```

Arguments

stream: Pointer to stream FILE buffer.

Return Value

Character if successful

EOF if unsuccessful

Example   See: `setvbuf`.

Comments   Identical to function `getc()`. Since `fgetc()` returns an integer value, EOF should not be relied upon for end-of-file detection; use `feof()` or `ferror()` instead.

`fgetchar()` *Read a character from stream* `stdin`

Compatibility □ANSI ■OS/2 □UNIX □XENIX

See Also

```
fgetc(), fscanf(), getc(), getchar(), scanf()
```

Specification

```
#include <stdio.h>
int fgetchar(void);
```

Return Value

Character if successful

EOF if unsuccessful

Example   See: `fgetpos()`.

Comments   Identical to function `getchar()`; comparable to using `fgets(stdin)`.

`fgetpos()`   *Get the current stream file position (absolute)*

Compatibility   ■ANSI   ■OS/2   □UNIX   □XENIX

See Also

`ftell()`

Specification

```
#include <stdio.h>
#include <errno.h>
int fgetpos(FILE *stream, fpos_t *pos);
```

Arguments

stream: Pointer to stream FILE buffer

pos: Pointer to position indicator; type `fpos_t` defined in `<stdio.h>`

Return Value

0 if successful

Nonzero if unsuccessful (`errno` set to `EBADF`, `EINVAL`)

Example

```
/* FILE: ch17e2.c */
#include <stdio.h>
#include <io.h>
#include <stdlib.h>
#include <string.h>

char string[0x80], *ptr;
fpos_t line[80], pos;
FILE *in, *out;
int nlines;

void redisplay(void)
{
fseek(in, 0L, SEEK_SET);
nlines=0;
printf("\n");
while (1) {
    fgetpos(in,&pos);
    ptr = fgets(string,sizeof(string),in);
    if (!ptr) break;
```

```
        if(line[nlines] == -1) {
            nlines++;
  continue;
 }
        if (ptr) {
            printf("\r\nline[%1d]: %s", nlines, ptr);
            line[nlines++]= pos;
            }
        else line[nlines++]= (-1);
        }
fflush(in);
}

int main(void)
{
int ac, ch, i;
char *pfile = "c:\\config.sys";
char *tfile = "c:\\config.xxx";
in  = fopen(pfile,"a+b");
out = fopen(tfile,"w+b");
printf("\nEDITING c:\\config.sys !!\n");
redisplay();
while (1) {
        printf("\n\n(A)dd (C)hange (D)elete (R)edisplay (E)nd : ");
        ac = 0;
        fflush(stdin);
        switch (ch = toupper(fgetchar())) {
            case 'A':
            case 'C':  ac = 1;
            case 'D':  if (ch != 'A') {
                printf("\nWhich line number ? ");
                fflush(stdin);
                fscanf(stdin,"%d", &nlines);
                line[nlines]= (-1);
                }
            break;
            case 'R':  break;
            }
        if (ch == 'E') break;
        if (ac) {
            printf("\nEnter new line : ");
            fflush(stdin);
            gets(string);
            fputs("\r\n",in);
            fputs(string,in);
            fflush(in);
            }
        redisplay();
        }
for (i=0;i<nlines;i++) {
        if (line[i] == -1) continue;
        fsetpos(in,&line[i]);
        fgets(string,sizeof(string),in);
```

```
        fwrite(string, 1, strlen(string), out);
        }
fcloseall();
remove(pfile);
printf("\nOVERWRITING c:\\config.sys !!");
rename(tfile,pfile);
exit(0);
}
```

Output

```
EDITING c:\config.sys !!

line[0]: files=20
line[1]: buffers=20
line[2]: country=001
line[3]: shell=c:\command.com /P /E:1024

(A)dd (C)hange (D)elete (R)edisplay (E)nd : a
Enter new line : break=off
line[0]: files=20
line[1]: buffers=20
line[2]: country=001
line[3]: shell=c:\command.com /P /E:1024
line[4]:
line[5]: break=off

(A)dd (C)hange (D)elete (R)edisplay (E)nd : d
Which line number ? 4

line[0]: files=20
line[1]: buffers=20
line[2]: country=001
line[3]: shell=c:\command.com /P /E:1024
line[5]: break=off

(A)dd (C)hange (D)elete (R)edisplay (E)nd : d
Which line number ? 5

line[0]: files=20
line[1]: buffers=20
line[2]: country=001
line[3]: shell=c:\command.com /P /E:1024

(A)dd (C)hange (D)elete (R)edisplay (E)nd : e

OVERWRITING c:\config.sys !!
```

Comments   The type representation, **fpos_t**, of the location pointer is compatible with that returned by **ftell()** and used by **fseek()**.

Notice that a pointer to, or address of, the location variable is used to return the current stream pointer location, not the function return type.

Because of the effect that the file translation mode has upon the determination of pointer location, always use **fgetpos()** in conjunction with **fsetpos()**.

fgets() *Read a string from a stream*

Compatibility ■ANSI ■OS/2 ■UNIX ■XENIX

See Also

gets(), fscanf()

Specification

```
#include <stdio.h>
char *fgets(char *string, int n, FILE *stream);
```

Arguments

string: Pointer to a character array buffer.

n: Maximum size of *string* including the trailing \0 character.

stream: Pointer to stream FILE buffer.

Return Value

Pointer to string if successful

NULL if unsuccessful

Example   See: **fdopen()**, **fgetpos()**.

Comments The function reads *string* starting at the current location, up to and including the first '\n' character it encounters, unless it reaches an EOF or has read *n*–1 characters before that point. It then appends a \0 null character.

flushall() *Empty all stream buffers*

Compatibility □ANSI ■OS/2 □UNIX □XENIX

See Also

fflush()

Specification

```
#include <stdio.h>
int flushall(void);
```

Return Value

Number of open streams

Example   See: `getc()`.

Comments   All open files, including the buffered predefined files, are flushed, but remain open.

`fopen()`   *Open a stream file*

Compatibility   ■ANSI   ■OS/2   ■UNIX   ■XENIX

See Also

```
fdopen(), freopen(), _fsopen()
```

Specification

```
#include <stdio.h>
FILE *fopen(const char *filename, const char *mode);
```

Arguments

filename: Filename string.

mode: Mode string; see Table 17.2.

Return Value

Pointer to stream FILE buffer if successful

NULL if unsuccessful

Example   See: `fgetpos()`, `_fsopen()`, `ftell()`, `putw()`, `setvbuf()`, `ungetc()`.

Comments   Streams are created or opened based upon the mode string discussed in the first part of this chapter. Read-only files cannot be created, nor can inheritance be impeded.

Zero-length directory file entries are permitted.

File sharing and locking are not supported using **fopen()**; rather, see **_fsopen()**.

`fprintf()` *Formatted write to a stream*

Compatibility ■ANSI ■OS/2 ■UNIX ■XENIX

See Also
`vfprintf()`

Specification
```
#include <stdio.h>
int fprintf(FILE *stream, const char *format, ...);
```

Arguments

stream: Pointer to stream FILE buffer.

format: Control string; see Table 17.4.

`. . .`: Variable number of arguments.

Return Value

Number of characters printed

Example   See also: `vfprintf()`.

```
/* FILE: ch17e3.c */
#include <stdio.h>
int main(void)
{
fcloseall();
dup2(1,2);  /* stderr == stdout */
dup2(1,3);  /* stdaux == stdout */
dup2(1,4);  /* stdprn == stdout */
printf("\n1) stdin/stdout/stderr/stdaux/stdprn remain open!");
fprintf(stdout,"\n2) all buffers are flushed before closing");
fflush(stdout);
fprintf(stderr,"\n3) tmpfile() files are closed");
fflush(stderr);
fprintf(stdaux,"\n4) system-allocated buffers are freed");
fflush(stdaux);
fprintf(stdprn,"\n5) user-allocated buffers are not freed");
fflush(stdprn);
exit(0);
}
```

Output

```
1) stdin/stdout/stderr/stdaux/stdprn remain open!
2) all buffers are flushed before closing
3) tmpfile() files are closed
4) system-allocated buffers are freed
5) user-allocated buffers are not freed
```

Comments The **printf()** family of functions (**cprintf**, **fprintf**, **printf**, **sprintf**, **vfprintf**, **vprintf**, and **vsprintf**) use the **printf()** control string formats described in Table 17.4.

fputc() *Write a character to a stream*

Compatibility ■ANSI ■OS/2 ■UNIX ■XENIX

See Also

```
fprintf(), putc()
```

Specification

```
#include <stdio.h>
int fputc(int c, FILE *stream);
```

Arguments

c: Character to be written.

stream: Pointer to stream FILE buffer.

Return Value

Character written if successful

EOF if unsuccessful

Example See: **ungetc()**.

Comments Identical to **putc()**. Character *c* is written starting at the current stream location, unless the file is opened in append mode, in which case it is always written at EOF.

fputchar() *Write a character to stream* stdout

Compatibility □ANSI ■OS/2 □UNIX □XENIX

See Also

```
fprintf(), fputc(), printf(), putc(), putchar()
```

Specification

```
#include <stdio.h>
int fputchar(int c);
```

Arguments

c: Character to be written.

Return Value

Character written if successful

EOF if unsuccessful

Example   See: **ungetc()**.

Comments   Identical to **putchar(c)**; comparable to **fputc(c, stdin)**.

Character *c* is written to stream **stdout** at the current location, unless the file is opened in append mode, in which case it is always written at EOF.

fputs()   *Write a string to a stream*

Compatibility   ■ANSI   ■OS/2   ■UNIX   ■XENIX

See Also

puts(), fprintf()

Specification

```
#include <stdio.h>
int fputs(const char *string, FILE *stream);
```

Arguments

string: Pointer to a null-terminated array of characters.

stream: Pointer to stream FILE buffer.

Return Value

Nonnegative value if successful

EOF if unsuccessful

Example   See: **fgetpos()**, **_fsopen()**, **ftell()**.

Comments   Writes ***string*** to ***stream*** starting at the current location, unless the stream is opened in append mode, in which case it is written at EOF.

The null \0 terminating character of the string is *not* written, nor is it replaced by '\n' as it is for **puts()**.

`fread()`   *Direct unformatted read from a stream*

Compatibility   ■ ANSI   ■ OS/2   ■ UNIX   ■ XENIX

See Also

```
getw()
```

Specification

```
#include <stdio.h>
size_t fread(void *buffer, size_t size, size_t count, FILE *stream);
```

Arguments

buffer: Pointer to a type array.

size: Size in bytes of each type object.

count: Number of type objects to read.

stream: Pointer to stream FILE buffer.

Return Value

Number of type objects read

Example   See: **putw()**.

Comments   Performs the unformatted transfer of an array of data-object types, beginning at the current pointer location, in the same way as the low-level I/O functions described in Chapter 18.

`freopen()`   *Reassign a stream file*

Compatibility   ■ ANSI   ■ OS/2   ■ UNIX   ■ XENIX

See Also   Chapter 18: **dup()**, **dup2()**

Specification

```
#include <stdio.h>
FILE *freopen(const char *filename, const char *mode, FILE *stream);
```

Arguments

filename: Filename string.

mode: Mode string; see Table 17.2.

stream: Pointer to stream FILE buffer.

Return Value

New stream pointer if successful

NULL if unsuccessful

Example   See: `getc()`.

Comments
Closes the current stream pointer and reassigns *stream* to another device- or disk-based filename. Typically used to reassign the predefined streams: **stdin**, **stdout**, **stderr**, **stdaux**, and **stdprn**. Notice that DOS device NULL is assigned in the **getc()** example to minimize the amount of output displayed to **stdout**.

fscanf()   *Formatted read from a stream*

Compatibility   ■ANSI   ■OS/2   ■UNIX   ■XENIX

See Also

scanf

Specification

```
#include <stdio.h>
int fscanf(FILE *stream, const char *format, ...);
```

Arguments

stream: Pointer to stream FILE buffer.

format: Control string; see Table 17.3.

. . .: Variable number of arguments.

Return Value

Number of successful field conversions if successful

EOF if unsuccessful

Example   See: `fgetpos()`.

Comments
Whereas **scanf()** is always associated with stream pointer **stdin**, **fscanf()** can read formatted data from any assigned stream.

`fseek()`   *Set position in a stream file (relative)*

Compatibility   ■ANSI   ■OS/2   ■UNIX   ■XENIX

See Also

```
fsetpos()
```

Specification

```
#include <stdio.h>
int fseek(FILE *stream, long offset, int origin);
```

Arguments

stream: Pointer to stream FILE buffer.

offset: Byte offset relative to *origin*.

origin: Object-like macro defined in **<stdio.h>**: **SEEK_CUR** (current position in stream); **SEEK_END** (end of stream); **SEEK_SET** (beginning of stream).

Return Value

0 if successful

Nonzero if unsuccessful

Example   See: **fdopen()**, **fgetpos()**.

Comments   Positions the file location pointer for the next read or write operation, unless the stream is opened in append mode, in which case the next write always occurs at EOF. The desired location is always expressed as an offset (+/−) relative to *origin*.

fseek() does not clear the end-of-file or error indicators.

`fsetpos()`   *Set position in a stream file (absolute)*

Compatibility   ■ANSI   ■OS/2   □UNIX   □XENIX

See Also

```
fseek(), rewind()
```

Specification

```
#include <stdio.h>
#include <errno.h>
int fsetpos(FILE *stream, const fpos_t *pos);
```

Arguments

> **stream**: Pointer to stream FILE buffer.
>
> **pos**: Pointer to storage location value; type **fpos_t** defined in **<stdio.h>**.

Return Value

> 0 if successful
>
> Nonzero if unsuccessful (**errno** set to **EBADF**, **EINVAL**)

Example   See: **fgetpos()**.

Comments   Normally **fsetpos()** is called after function **fgetpos()**, always clears the end-of-file indicator, and negates the effect of any prior **ungetc()**.

The file position set will control where the next read or write occurs, unless the stream is opened in append mode, in which case the next write always occurs at EOF.

_fsopen()   *Open a stream file for file sharing*

Compatibility   □ ANSI   ■ OS/2   □ UNIX   □ XENIX

See Also

> fdopen

Specification

```
#include <stdio.h>
#include <share.h>
FILE *_fsopen(const char *filename, const char *mode, int shflag);
```

Arguments

> **filename**: Filename string.
>
> **mode**: Mode string; see Table 17.2.
>
> **shflag**: File sharing object-like macro defined in **<share.h>**: **SH_COMPAT** (compatibility mode); **SH_DENYRW** (deny read/write access); **SH_DENYWR** (deny write access); **SH_DENYRD** (deny read access); **SH_DENYNO** (permit read/write access).

Return Value

> Pointer to stream FILE buffer if successful.
>
> NULL if unsuccessful.

Example

```
/* FILE: ch17e4.c */
#include <stdio.h>
#include <share.h>
#include <errno.h>
#include <string.h>
int main(void)
{
FILE *stream, *stream2;
char *file = "share.xxx";
char *ptr, string[10];
int erc, error;
dup2(1,2);   /* stderr == stdout */
printf("\nInstalling SHARE!\n");
fflush(stdout);
system("share");   /* install SHARE command */
stream = _fsopen(file, "w", SH_DENYNO);
if (ferror(stream) || !stream) {
    perror("(macro) ferror");
    clearerr(stream);
    stream = fopen(file,"w");
    }
fflush(stderr);
if (!ferror(stream)) printf("\nfile: %s opened r/w!",file);
fflush(stdout);
fprintf(stream,"%s\n",file);
perror("\n(macro) ferror/ stream write ");
fflush(stream);

#undef ferror
stream2 = _fsopen(file, "r", SH_DENYNO);
if (!ferror(stream2)) printf("\nfile: %s opened r/o!",file);
fputs(file, stream2);
if (ferror(stream2)) {
    printf("\n(function) ferror/ write failure!");
    clearerr(stream2);
    }
fgets(string, sizeof(string), stream2);
if (!ferror(stream2)) printf("\n\nfile %s = %s", file, string);
exit(0);
}
```

Output

```
Installing SHARE!
SHARE already installed

file: share.xxx opened r/w!
(macro) ferror/ stream write : Error 0

file: share.xxx opened r/o!
(function) ferror/ write failure!

file share.xxx = share.xxx
```

Comments   The only stream I/O open function that supports file sharing and record locking, unless **fdopen()** is used to associate an open shared low-level file with an unbuffered stream. See Chapter 16 for a discussion of file sharing and locking.

ftell()   *Get the current file position (absolute)*

Compatibility   ■ANSI   ■OS/2   ■UNIX   ■XENIX

See Also

```
fgetpos()
```

Specification

```
#include <stdio.h>
#include <errno.h>
long ftell(FILE *stream);
```

Arguments

stream: Pointer to stream FILE buffer.

Return Value

Current position if successful

−1L if unsuccessful

Example

```
/* FILE: ch17e5.c */
#include <stdio.h>
int main(void)
{
FILE *stream;
char *name, line[80];
long pos[6];
int i;
name = tmpnam(NULL);
stream = fopen(name, "w+");
for (i=0; i<5; i++) {
    pos[i] = ftell(stream);
    printf("\nEnter a string <cr>: ");
    gets(line);
    fputs(line,stream);
    }
pos[i] = ftell(stream);
for (i=0; i<=5; i++) printf("\n[%1d]=%1d",i,pos[i]);
fflush(stream);
```

```
for (i=0; i<5; i++) {
    fseek(stream,pos[i],SEEK_SET);
    fgets(line,pos[i+1]-pos[i]+1,stream);
    printf("\n%s",line);
    }
fclose(stream);
remove(name);
exit(0);
}
```

Output

```
Enter a string <cr>: Robert
Enter a string <cr>: A.
Enter a string <cr>: Radcliffe
Enter a string <cr>: CAE, Inc.
Enter a string <cr>: 555-218-9307
[0]=0
[1]=6
[2]=8
[3]=17
[4]=26
[5]=38
Robert
A.
Radcliffe
CAE, Inc.
555-218-9307
```

Comments   Because of the effect that the translation mode has upon the determination of the pointer location, always use **ftell()** in conjunction with **fseek()**. The byte offsets returned by **ftell()** are compatible with those returned by **fgetpos()**.

fwrite()   *Direct unformatted write to a stream*

Compatibility   ■ ANSI   ■ OS/2   ■ UNIX   ■ XENIX

See Also

```
putw()
```

Specification

```
#include <stdio.h>
size_t fwrite(const void *buffer, size_t size, size_t count, FILE *stream);
```

Arguments

buffer: Pointer to a type array.

size: Size in bytes of each type object.

count: Number of type objects to write.

stream: Pointer to stream FILE buffer.

Return Value

Number of type objects written

Example

See: **fgetpos()**, **putw()**.

Comments

This is the companion function to **fread()**; it performs unformatted data transfers for stream files that normally exhibit formatted behavior. See Chapter 18 for alternatives to this function.

getc() *Read a character from a stream*

Compatibility ■ANSI ■OS/2 ■UNIX ■XENIX

See Also

fgetc(), fscanf()

Specification

```
#include <stdio.h>
int getc(FILE *stream);
```

Arguments

stream: Pointer to stream FILE buffer.

Return Value

Character read if successful

EOF if unsuccessful

Example

```
/* FILE: ch17e6.c */
#include <stdio.h>
#define TIMER
#define LIMIT 100
#define NTIMES for(i=0;i<LIMIT;i++)
#include "timer.h"
int main(void)
{
int ch, i;
freopen("c:\\config.sys","r",stdin);
freopen("nul","w",stderr);
ch = getc(stdin);
```

```
START(macro version feof/getc/putc\n);
NTIMES {
    rewind(stdin);
    while (!feof(stdin)) {
        ch = getc(stdin);
        if (!i) putc(ch,stdout);
        else putc(ch,stderr);
        }
    }
STOP;

START(macro version feof/getchar/putchar/putc\n);
NTIMES {
    rewind(stdin);
    while (!feof(stdin)) {
        ch = getchar();
        if (!i) putchar(ch);
        else putc(ch,stderr);
        }
    }
STOP;

#undef feof
#undef getc
#undef putc
#undef getchar
#undef putchar

START(function version feof/getc/putc\n);
NTIMES {
    rewind(stdin);
    while (!feof(stdin)) {
        ch = getc(stdin);
        if (!i) putc(ch,stdout);
        else putc(ch,stderr);
        }
    }
STOP;

START(function version feof/getchar/putchar/putc\n);
NTIMES {
    rewind(stdin);
    while (!feof(stdin)) {
        ch = getchar();
        if (!i) putchar(ch);
        else putc(ch,stderr);
        }
    }
STOP;

flushall();
exit(0);
}
```

Output

```
for   : macro version feof/getc/putc
files=20
buffers=20
country=001
shell=c:\command.com /P /E:1024

time :   11.04 sec

for   : macro version feof/getchar/putchar/putc
files=20
buffers=20
country=001
shell=c:\command.com /P /E:1024

time :   11.04 sec

for   : function version feof/getc/putc
files=20
buffers=20
country=001
shell=c:\command.com /P /E:1024

time :   11.53 sec

for   : function version feof/getchar/putchar/putc
files=20
buffers=20
country=001
shell=c:\command.com /P /E:1024

time :   11.76 sec
```

Comments   `getc()` is identical to **`fgetc()`** except that it is available in a function-like macro form.

In the example, notice that the macro versions outperform their corresponding function versions. This is normally true because functions must push and pop arguments from the stack. The timing macros **`START()`** and **`STOP`** used in this example are discussed in Chapter 5.

getchar()   *Read a character from stream* stdin

Compatibility   ■ANSI   ■OS/2   ■UNIX   ■XENIX

See Also

```
fgetc(), fgetchar(), fscanf(), getc(), scanf()
```

Specification

```
#include <stdio.h>
int getchar(void);
```

Return Value

Character read if successful

EOF if unsuccessful

Example   See: `getc`.

Comments   `getchar()` is identical to **`fgetchar()`** except that it is available in a function-like macro form; comparable to **`getc(stdin)`**. Macro forms usually outperform equivalent function versions, but may require a greater amount of program code space.

gets()   *Read a string from stream* `stdin`

Compatibility ■ANSI   ■OS/2   ■UNIX   ■XENIX

See Also

```
fgets(), fscanf(), scanf()
```

Specification

```
#include <stdio.h>
char *gets(char *buffer);
```

Arguments

buffer: Pointer to a character array.

Return Value

Pointer to buffer if successful

NULL if unsuccessful

Example   See: `fgetpos`, `ftell`, `putw`, `ungetc`.

Comments   This function is identical to **`fgets()`** except that it always reads from stream **`stdin`**, and if an '\n' character is encountered, the scan is terminated but the '\n' character is not included.

getw() *Read a type int from a stream*

Compatibility ☐ANSI ■OS/2 ■UNIX ■XENIX

See Also

```
fread()
```

Specification

```
#include <stdio.h>
int gets(FILE *stream);
```

Arguments

stream: Pointer to stream FILE buffer.

Return Value

Type **int** value if successfu.

EOF if unsuccessful

Example   See: **putw()**.

Comments   This function has limited utility compared with function **fread()**, and is provided primarily for library compatibility purposes.

getw() does not assume any special alignment of bytes within the type **int** word. See Chapter 18 for alternatives to this function.

perror() *Display an error message to stream* stderr

Compatibility ■ANSI ■OS/2 ■UNIX ■XENIX

See Also   Chapter 26: **strerror()**, **_strerror()**

Specification

```
#include <stdio.h>
void perror(const char *string);
```

Arguments

string: Error message string.

Example   See: **_fsopen()**.

Comments   **perror()** displays the *string* (which can be null), followed by a colon, and the text associated with the error number controlled in the global variable **errno**.

Always call **perror()** immediately after a function returns, since global variable **errno** may otherwise be reassigned and not reflect the desired error condition.

printf()   *Formatted write to stream* stdout

Compatibility   ■ANSI   ■OS/2   ■UNIX   ■XENIX

See Also

```
fprintf, vfprintf, vprintf
```

Specification

```
#include <stdio.h>
int printf(const char *format, ...);
```

Arguments

format: Format control string; see Table 17.4.

. . .: Variable number of arguments.

Return Value

Number of characters written if successful

Negative value if unsuccessful

Example   See: **fprintf**, **scanf**.

Comments   The **printf()** family of functions (**cprintf**, **fprintf**, **sprintf**, **vprintf**, **vfprintf**, and **vsprintf**) rely upon the control string formats described in Table 17.4.

putc()   *Write a character to a stream*

Compatibility   ■ANSI   ■OS/2   ■UNIX   ■XENIX

See Also

```
fprintf(), fputc()
```

Specification

```
#include <stdio.h>
int putc(int c, FILE *stream);
```

Arguments

c: Character to be written.

stream: Pointer to stream FILE buffer.

Return Value

The character written if successful

EOF if unsuccessful

Example   See: `getc()`.

Comments   `putc()` is identical to function `fputc()`, but is available in function-like macro form. Output is directed to the current pointer location unless the stream is opened in append mode, in which case the character *c* is always written at EOF, regardless of the current location.

Since `putc()` returns an integer, do not rely upon EOF to detect end-of-file; rather, use `ferror()` or interrogate global variable **errno**.

putchar()   *Write a character to stream* stdout

Compatibility   ■ANSI   ■OS/2   ■UNIX   ■XENIX

See Also

`fprintf(), fputc(), fputchar(), printf(), putc()`

Specification

```
#include <stdio.h>
int putchar(int c);
```

Arguments

c: Character to be written.

Return Value

The character written if successful

EOF if unsuccessful

Example   See: `getc()`.

Comments   `putchar()` is identical to function `fputchar()`, but is available in function-like macro form; comparable to `putc(c, stdout)`.

Output is directed to the current pointer location unless the stream is opened in append mode, in which case the character *c* will be written at EOF regardless of the current location.

Since **putchar()** returns an integer, do not rely upon EOF to detect end-of-file; rather, use **ferror()** or interrogate global variable **errno**.

puts ()   *Write a string to stream* stdout

Compatibility   ■ANSI   ■OS/2   ■UNIX   ■XENIX

See Also
```
fputs(), fprintf(), printf()
```

Specification
```
#include <stdio.h>
int puts(const char *string);
```

Arguments
string: Pointer to a null-terminated array of characters.

Return Value
Nonnegative value if successful

EOF if unsuccessful

Example   See: **ungetc()**.

Comments   The string is written to stream **stdout** at the current location pointer unless opened in append mode, in which case the string is written at EOF.

Unlike **fputs()**, replaces the string-terminating null '\0' character with a '\n' character.

putw ()   *Write a type* int *value to a stream*

Compatibility   □ANSI   ■OS/2   ■UNIX   ■XENIX

See Also
```
fwrite()
```

Specification
```
#include <stdio.h>
int putw(int binint, FILE *stream);
```

Arguments

binint: Type int value to be written.

stream: Pointer to stream FILE buffer.

Return Value

binint value if successful

EOF if unsuccessful

Example

```
/* FILE: ch17e7.c */
#include <stdio.h>
#include <stdlib.h>
#include <string.h>
int main(void)
{FILE *stream1, *stream2;
char string[80];
char *file1 = "sample.df1";
char *file2 = "sample.df2";
int ival, count=0, ibuf[10];

stream1 = fopen(file1,"w+b");
stream2 = fopen(file2,"w+b");
if (!stream1 || !stream2) {
    printf("\nopen failed!");
    exit(99);
    }

while (1) {
    printf("\n\nEnter an integer or \"end\": ");
    fflush(stdin);
    gets(string);
    if (!string) continue;
    if (!strcmpi(string,"END")) break;
    ival = atoi(string);
    putw(ival, stream1);
    if (++count >= 10) break;
    }

fflush(stream1);
rewind(stream1);
fread(ibuf,sizeof(int),count,stream1);
fwrite(ibuf,sizeof(int),count,stream2);

printf("\nEnd file2 build, start report..\n");
fflush(stream2);
rewind(stream2);
while (1) {
    ival = getw(stream2);
    if (feof(stream2)) break;
    itoa(ival,string,10);
```

```
        puts(string);
        }
fcloseall();
remove(file1);
remove(file2);
exit(0);
}
```

Output

```
Enter an integer or "end": 128
Enter an integer or "end": -23000
Enter an integer or "end": 43
Enter an integer or "end": 256
Enter an integer or "end": end

End file2 build, start report..
128
-23000
43
256
```

Comments   This function has limited utility compared with function **fwrite()**, and is provided primarily for library compatibility purposes.

putw() does not assume any special alignment of bytes within the type **int** word.

rewind()   *Position stream pointer to beginning of file*

Compatibility   ■ ANSI   ■ OS/2   ■ UNIX   ■ XENIX

See Also

```
fseek(), fsetpos()
```

Specification

```
#include <stdio.h>
void rewind(FILE *stream);
```

Arguments

stream: Pointer to stream FILE buffer.

Example   See: **getc()**, **putw()**.

Comments   Issuing the **rewind()** function is equivalent to using **fseek(stream, 0L, SEEK_SET)**, except that the end-of-file and error indicators are cleared.

`scanf()` *Formatted read from stream* `stdin`

Compatibility ■ANSI   ■OS/2   ■UNIX   ■XENIX

See Also

```
fscanf()
```

Specification

```
#include <stdio.h>
int scanf(const char *format, ...);
```

Arguments

format: Control string; see Table 17.3.

. . .: Variable number of arguments.

Return Value

Number of successful field conversions if successful

EOF if unsuccessful

Example

```
/* FILE: ch17e8.c */
#include <stdio.h>
int main(void)
{
char cv, cvs[]= "ABCDEFGHI", string[80];
int niitems, nichars, noitems, nochars;
void *nptr;

printf("\nEnter a single character, then <cr>: ");
scanf("%c", &cv);
printf("\n\tcv= %c %#02x", cv, cv);

printf("\nEnter another single character, then <cr>: ");
niitems = scanf("%c", &cv);
printf("\n\tcv= %#02x", cv);
fflush(stdin);  /* clear the keyboard input buffer */

printf("\nEnter six or more characters, then <cr>: ");
niitems = scanf("%6c%n",cvs, &nichars);
noitems = printf("\tcvs= %s %n niitems=%d nichars=%d",\
cvs, &nochars, niitems, nichars);
printf("\n\tnoitems=%d  nochars=%d", noitems, nochars);
fflush(stdin);
nptr = NULL;
```

```
printf("\nEnter a near pointer as 0000 <cr>: ");
scanf("%p", &nptr);
printf("\tnptr=%p", (void far *) nptr);
fflush(stdin);

printf("\nEnter a string only containing [A-Z,a-z,blank] : ");
scanf("%[A-Z,a-z, ]", string);
printf("\tstring= %s",string);
fflush(stdin);

printf("\nEnter a string containing all except [A-Z,blank] : ");
scanf("%[^A-Z, ]", string);
printf("\tstring= %s",string);
fflush(stdin);

printf("\nCorrectly enter the sequence  A-Z 3<cr> : ");
niitems = scanf("%A-Z %c", &cv);
if (!niitems) printf("\tscanf failed");
else printf("\tniitems= %d cv= %c  %%%!", niitems, cv);
fflush(stdin);

printf("\nIncorrectly enter the sequence  A-Z 3<cr> : ");
niitems = scanf("%A-Z %c", &cv);
if (!niitems) printf("\tscanf failed");
else printf("\tniitems= %d cv= %c  %%%!", niitems, cv);
exit(0);
}
```

Output

```
Enter a single character, then <cr>: f
    cv= f 0x66
Enter another single character, then <cr>: Q
    cv= 0xa
Enter six or more characters, then <cr>: radcliffe
    cvs= radcliGHI  niitems=1 nichars=6
    noitems=36  nochars=16
Enter a near pointer as 0000 <cr>: EFEF
    nptr=EFEF
Enter a string only containing [A-Z,a-z,blank] : abc DEF ghi3
    string= abc DEF ghi
Enter a string containing all except [A-Z,blank] : xyz3487!@#A
    string= xyz3487!@#
Correctly enter the sequence  A-Z 3<cr> : A-Z 3
    niitems= 1 cv= 3  %!
Incorrectly enter the sequence  A-Z 3<cr> : a-z 3
    scanf failed
```

Comments The **scanf()** functions (**cscanf()**, **fscanf()**, **scanf()**, and **sscanf()**) accept formatted input from a stream using the control-string parameters specified in Table 17.3. The example above highlights the use of some of the commonly overlooked and misunderstood control strings (**%c**, **%n**, **%p**, **%[]**).

setbuf() *Assign/disable a standard stream buffer*

Compatibility ■ANSI ■OS/2 ■UNIX ■XENIX

See Also
```
setvbuf
```

Specification
```
#include <stdio.h>
void setbuf(FILE *stream, char *buffer);
```

Arguments
stream: Pointer to stream FILE buffer.

buffer: Pointer to a **BUFSIZ** buffer, or NULL for no buffering.

Example See: **setvbuf()**.

Comments setbuf() must be called after a stream has been opened, but before any I/O has taken place.

To disable buffering of a stream, simply call **setbuf()** with a NULL buffer.
If you do include the *buffer* argument, it must be **BUFSIZ** bytes in size.

setvbuf() *Assign/disable a custom stream buffer*

Compatibility ■ANSI ■OS/2 ■UNIX ■XENIX

See Also
```
setbuf()
```

Specification
```
#include <stdio.h>
int setvbuf(FILE *stream, char *buffer, int mode, size_t size);
```

Arguments
stream: Pointer to stream FILE buffer.

buffer: Pointer to a **BUFSIZ** buffer, or NULL for a system-allocated buffer of *size* bytes.

mode: Object-like macro defined in **<stdio.h>**: **_IOFBF** (file buffering); **_IOLBF** (same as **_IOFBF**); **_IONBF** (no buffering).

size: Size of buffer in bytes.

Return Value

0 if successful

Nonzero if unsuccessful

Example

```
/* FILE: ch17e9.c */
#include <stdio.h>
#include <io.h>
#include <string.h>
int main(void)
{
FILE *myfile;
char *name, mybuf[80]= "";
char *message[] = { "1st stream I/O ",
    "1st low-level I/O ",
    "2nd stream I/O ",
    "2nd low-level I/O",
    "\r\n" };
int handle, ch, i;

name = tmpnam(NULL);
myfile = fopen(name,"w");
setbuf(myfile, NULL); /* unbuffered */
handle = fileno(myfile);
fprintf(myfile, "%s", message[0]);
write(handle, message[1], strlen(message[1]));
write(handle, message[4], 2);
fprintf(myfile, "%s", message[2]);
write(handle, message[3], strlen(message[3]));
write(handle, message[4], 2);
fclose(myfile);

myfile = fopen(name,"r");
handle = fileno(myfile);
setvbuf(myfile, mybuf, _IOFBF, sizeof(mybuf));
fgetc(myfile);
for (i=0;i<80;i++) printf("%c", mybuf[i]);
close(handle);
remove(name);
exit(0);
}
```

Output

```
1st stream I/O 1st low-level I/O
2nd stream I/O 2nd low-level I/O
```

Comments   The example first uses unbuffered I/O to build a file called **name**; it then opens the file using buffered I/O with buffer **mybuf[80]**. Even though only a single character read is issued (**fgetc(myfile)**), the program displays the entire contents of the buffer, because the length of the message is less than the 80-character buffer size.

setvbuf() must be called after a stream has been opened, but before any I/O has taken place.

To disable buffering of a stream, simply specify the **mode** as **_IONBF**.

If *buffer* is NULL, the system will allocate a buffer *size* bytes long.

ungetc()   *Put a character back into a stream*

Compatibility   ■ ANSI   ■ OS/2   ■ UNIX   ■ XENIX

See Also

```
fseek(), fsetpos()
```

Specification

```
#include <stdio.h>
int ungetc(int c, FILE *stream);
```

Arguments

c: Character to replace.

stream: Pointer to stream FILE buffer.

Return Value

Character *c* if successful

EOF if unsuccessful

Example

```
/* FILE: ch17e10.c  */
#include <stdio.h>
#include <ctype.h>
int main(void)
{
char file[80];
FILE *stream;
int ch, line=1;

puts("");
puts("Line-numbered Listing Generator");
while (1) {
    printf("\nEnter a text file pathname: ");
    gets(file);
    stream = fopen(file,"r+b");
    if (!stream) {
        printf("\nfile open failed!");
```

```
            continue;
            }
        else {
            printf("\n[%04d] ",line);
            break;
            }
        }

    while (1) {       /* line-loop */
        while (1) {    /* character-loop */
            ch = getc(stream);
            if (feof(stream)) break;
            if (ch > 0x7f ) ch &= 0x7f;
            if (!iscntrl(ch) ) {
                fputc(ch,stdout);
                continue;
                }
            else {
                while (1) {
                    switch (ch) {
                        case 0x09:  fputchar(0x20);
                                break;
                        case 0x0a:  ++line;
                                printf("\n[%04d] ",line);
                                break;
                        }
                    ch = getc(stream);
                    if (feof(stream)) break;
                    if (iscntrl(ch) ) continue;
                    break;
                    } /* while */
                } /* if..else */
            if (feof(stream)) break;
            ungetc(ch,stream);
            break;
            }
        if (feof(stream)) break;
        }
    exit(0);
    }
```

Output

```
Line-numbered Listing Generator

Enter a text file pathname: ch17e5.c
[0001] /* FILE: ch17e5.c */
[0002] #include <stdio.h>
[0003] int main(void)
[0004] {
  .
  .
[0028] exit(0);
[0029] }
```

Comments   Pushes a character back onto the stream opened for reading, clearing the end-of-file indicator. If successful, adjusts the file location pointer.

The example above can be used to list a file of any type: source code, word processing, and so on.

`vfprintf()`   *Formatted write to a stream*

Compatibility   ■ANSI   ■OS/2   ■UNIX   ■XENIX

See Also

```
vprintf()
```

Specification

```
#include <stdio.h>
#include <stdarg.h>
int vfprintf(FILE *stream, const char *format, va_list argptr);
```

Arguments

stream: Pointer to stream FILE buffer.

format: Control string; see Table 17.4.

argptr: Pointer to argument list.

Return Value

Number of characters written if successful

Negative value if unsuccessful

Example

```
/* FILE: ch17e11.c  */
#include <stdio.h>
#include <stdarg.h>

void print(FILE *stream,  char * control, ...)
{
va_list arg_ptr;
va_start(arg_ptr, control);
if (stream == stdout || stream == NULL) {
    printf("\n\nvprintf==>");
    vprintf(control, arg_ptr);
    }
else {
    fprintf(stream,"\n\nvfprintf==>");
    vfprintf(stream, control, arg_ptr);
    }
va_end(arg_ptr);
}
```

```
int main(void)
{
char cv = 'Q';
int iv = -33;
long lv = 100000L;
float fv = -1.275F;
double dv = 1.25e12;

print(NULL, "\nNULL  : \t%c \n\t\t%d \n\t\t%ld \n\t\t%f \n\t\t%g", \
     cv, iv, lv, fv, dv);
print(stderr, "\nstderr  : \t%g \n\t\t%ld \n\t\t%c", dv, lv, cv);
print(stdout, "\nstdout  : \t%f \n\t\t%d", fv, iv);

exit(0);
}
```

Output

```
vprintf==>
NULL  : Q
     -33
     100000
     -1.275000
     1.25e+012

vfprintf==>
stderr  : 1.25e+012
     100000

vprintf==>
stdout  : -1.275000
     -33
```

Comments   Identical to **vprintf()**, except that output can be directed to any stream using a pointer to a control string that corresponds to a variable number of arguments. See **printf()** and Table 17.4 for the complete list of possible control string parameters.

vprintf()   *Formatted write to stream* stdout

Compatibility   ■ANSI   ■OS/2   ■UNIX   ■XENIX

See Also

vfprintf()

Specification

```
#include <stdio.h>
```

```
#include <stdarg.h>
int vprintf(const char *format, va_list argptr);
```

Arguments

format: Control string; see Table 17.4.

argptr: Pointer to argument list.

Return Value

Number of characters written if successful

Negative value if unsuccessful

Example   See: **vfprintf()**.

Comments   Identical to **vfprintf()**, except that output is always directed to **stdout** using a pointer to a control string that corresponds to a variable number of arguments. See **printf()** and Table 17.4 for the complete list of possible control string parameters.

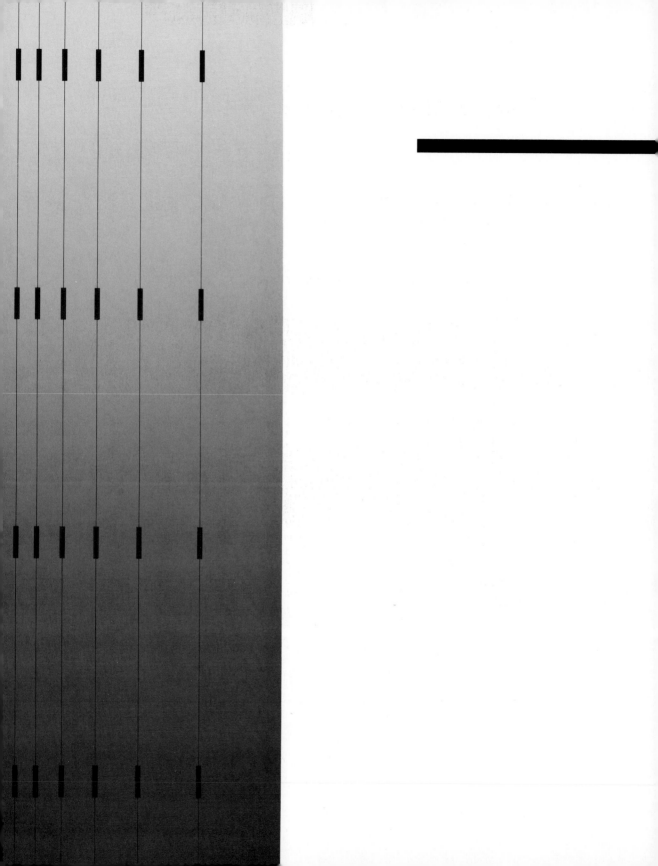

Low-Level I/O Functions

Low-Level I/O Functions

This chapter will highlight the run-time library functions that support the unbuffered and unformatted processing of files in what is referred to in C as low-level I/O.

We will first examine how these low-level I/O functions implement the fundamental DOS file properties described in Chapter 16, which include: disk- and device-based files, access modes and permissions, translation modes, buffering, positioning, sharing, locking, and inheritance. Then we will review how low-level files are created and opened for processing and examine the characteristics of direct I/O.

If you are uncertain which functions are available to perform a specific I/O task, see Table 18.4, further on in this chapter, which groups the available low-level I/O functions by task-performance categories. All of the functions listed in that table and discussed in this chapter are non-Standard (Microsoft-specific).

The rest of the chapter consists of an alphabetic series of the reference entries for the functions featured in this chapter, provided in the standard run-time library presentation format. For your convenience, a page-number index of run-time library functions is also provided on the inside back cover of this book.

Let's begin by examining the concepts and conventions adopted when the unbuffered and unformatted low-level I/O approach is adopted to access a DOS device- or disk-based file.

LOW-LEVEL I/O CONVENTIONS

DOS files that are to be opened for processing as low-level files require that a file-handle integer variable be declared. This handle is subsequently used to identify files to be processed by any of the functions described in this chapter. For example, the handle variables *in* and *out* should be declared in the following manner:

```
#include <sys\types.h>
#include <sys\stat.h>
#include <io.h>
#include <dos.h>
#include <fcntl.h>
```

```
#include <share.h>
#include <errno.h>
.
.
.
int in, out;
```

The entire complement of related low-level header files shown above may be required, depending on which function is selected to open a file. Although the stream pointers described in Chapter 17 were assigned the address of an element in the array of structures called **_iob[]**, low-level I/O file handles are assigned an index position in the **_iob[]** array associated with an open DOS file. The valid range of DOS file handle values ranges from **_iob** index position [0] through [19].

The **_iob[]** array is allocated when DOS is booted. The size of **_iob[]** is equal to the value assigned by the FILES=*xx* command found in CONFIG.SYS (see Chapter 1). The maximum number of elements that may be assigned is limited to 20 for DOS (the maximum number of open files for a DOS program or process). If the FILES=*xx* command is omitted from CONFIG.SYS, a default value of 8 is assumed. Once DOS has allocated the **_iob[]** array, you can change it only by altering the FILES=*xx* command value in CONFIG.SYS and then rebooting.

The low-level I/O functions described in this chapter always identify files using the integer-valued file handle index element position in the array **_iob[]**; hence the equivalence between stream pointers and file handles (see Chapter 17).

Thus, any DOS file may be accessed using either its stream pointer or its file handle. You can use either the macro or run-time function version of **fileno()** to return the file handle value that is associated with an open stream pointer.

In fact, a file may be accessed using both techniques in the same program, although typically only one technique is used. Because file handles do not work correctly with buffered files, when both techniques are employed, a stream pointer must be specifically designated as unbuffered with a function call to **setbuf()** or **setvbuf()** if it is to be used simultaneously to access a file opened for low-level I/O with a file handle.

OPENING AND CREATING LOW-LEVEL FILES

DOS and Microsoft C support five predefined file handles (shown in Table 18.1) that are automatically opened and available for use by every C program and correspond identically with those stream pointers described in Chapter 17 for stream I/O.

TABLE 18.1: Predefined Integer File Handle Values

FILE HANDLE	DOS DEVICE NAME	ACCESS MODE	DEFAULT BUFFERING	DEFAULT TRANSLATION
0	CON	Read-only	No	Text
1	CON	Write-only	No	Text
2	CON	Write-only	No	Text
3	AUX or COM1	Read/write	No	Binary
4	PRN or LPT1	Write-only	No	Binary

The predefined integer file handle values shown in Table 18.1 correspond to stream pointers **stdin**, **stdout**, **stderr**, **stdaux**, and **stdprn**, respectively. No file handle variable declarations or open functions must be called to utilize the predefined low-level files. Note, however, that buffering of the predefined files is not supported. Also, header file **<stdio.h>** need not be included for their use, unless other defined macros (**EOF**, **NULL**, etc.) or function prototype declarations found in **<stdio.h>** are necessary.

If a standard DOS device name (see Table 1.3) is specified to be opened for low-level I/O without a trailing colon (:), a new file handle will be assigned to one of the available remaining **_iob[]** array elements. The existence of predefined DOS device-based files does not preempt an application from opening other DOS devices for use.

If, on the other hand, a disk-based filename is specified to be opened for low-level I/O and is found not to exist in the directory of the volume (drive letter) specified, then a DOS file and its directory entry are created using the specified open parameters. For all low-level I/O open functions (see Table 18.4), you must express file access modes and permission requests using object-like macros, not the mode strings used with the stream I/O open functions described in Chapter 17.

When low-level I/O open functions are utilized, complete control over the assignment of all DOS file properties is maintained using the object-like macros defined by the header files that support the use of low-level I/O. Table 18.2 describes the object-like macros available for use with low-level I/O open functions.

When you create a file using a low-level I/O open function, you can combine one or more of the macro choices shown above, using the | (OR) operator, to express the exact properties that you wish the file access attribute of the file to be assigned when its directory entry is recorded.

Although the use of mode strings simplified the file-opening process for stream I/O, it also relinquished certain control over the assignment of file

TABLE 18.2: Low-Level Open Macros

MACRO	DESCRIPTION	HEADER FILE	OPEN FUNCTIONS
_A_NORMAL	Read/write	`<dos.h>`	`_dos_creat()`, `_dos_creatnew()`
_A_RDONLY	Read-only	`<dos.h>`	`_dos_creat()`, `_dos_creatnew()`
_A_HIDDEN	Hidden file	`<dos.h>`	`_dos_creat()`, `_dos_creatnew()`
_A_SYSTEM	System file	`<dos.h>`	`_dos_creat()`, `_dos_creatnew()`
_A_VOLID	Volume ID	`<dos.h>`	`_dos_creat()`, `_dos_creatnew()`
_A_SUBDIR	Subdirectory	`<dos.h>`	`_dos_creat()`, `_dos_creatnew()`
_A_ARCH	Archive file	`<dos.h>`	`_dos_creat()`, `_dos_creatnew()`
O_RDONLY	Read-only	`<fcntl.h>`	`_dos_open()`, `open()`, `sopen()`
O_WRONLY	Write-only	`<fcntl.h>`	`_dos_open()`, `open()`, `sopen()`
O_RDWR	Read/write	`<fcntl.h>`	`_dos_open()`, `open()`, `sopen()`
O_APPEND	Append	`<fcntl.h>`	`open()`, `sopen()`
O_CREAT	Create	`<fcntl.h>`	`open()`, `sopen()`
O_TRUNC	Truncate	`<fcntl.h>`	`open()`, `sopen()`
O_EXCL	Exclusive	`<fcntl.h>`	`open()`, `sopen()`
O_TEXT	Text mode	`<fcntl.h>`	`open()`, `sopen()`
O_BINARY	Binary mode	`<fcntl.h>`	`open()`, `sopen()`
O_RAW	O_BINARY	`<fcntl.h>`	`open()`, `sopen()`
O_NOINHERIT	No inheritance	`<fcntl.h>`	`_dos_open()`, `open()`, `sopen()`
S_IREAD	Read-only	`<stat.h>`	`creat()`, `open()`, `sopen()`
S_IWRITE	Write-only	`<stat.h>`	`creat()`, `open()`, `sopen()`
SH_COMPAT	Compatibility	`<share.h>`	`_dos_open()`, `sopen()`
SH_DENYRW	Deny read/write	`<share.h>`	`_dos_open()`, `sopen()`
SH_DENYWR	Deny write	`<share.h>`	`_dos_open()`, `sopen()`
SH_DENYRD	Deny read	`<share.h>`	`_dos_open()`, `sopen()`
SH_DENYNO	Deny none	`<share.h>`	`_dos_open()`, `sopen()`

properties (read-only access, inheritance, and so on). Table 18.3 shows stream mode strings described in Chapter 17 and their equivalent low-level macros.

Observe exactly how stream modes are implemented for a better understanding of the restrictions associated with opening stream versus low-level I/O files.

Low-level I/O files are never buffered and functions are not available for that purpose. Low-level I/O file positioning is still controlled independently of the create or open process, and, as for stream I/O, is meaningful only for disk-based, not device-based, files. To test whether a file handle is

TABLE 18.3: Stream Modes and Low-Level Macros

MODE	EQUIVALENT MACROS USING `open()`
`"r"`	`O_RDONLY, SH_COMPAT`
`"rb"`	`O_RDONLY	O_BINARY, SH_COMPAT`
`"rt"`	`O_RDONLY	O_TEXT, SH_COMPAT`
`"r+"`	`O_RDWR, SH_COMPAT`
`"r+b"`	`O_RDWR	O_BINARY, SH_COMPAT`
`"r+t"`	`O_RDWR	O_TEXT, SH_COMPAT`
`"w"`	`O_CREAT	O_WRONLY	O_TRUNC, SH_COMPAT`
`"wb"`	`O_CREAT	O_WRONLY	O_TRUNC	O_BINARY, SH_COMPAT`
`"wt"`	`O_CREAT	O_WRONLY	O_TRUNC	O_TEXT, SH_COMPAT`
`"w+"`	`O_CREAT	O_RDWR	O_TRUNC, SH_COMPAT`
`"w+b"`	`O_CREAT	O_RDWR	O_TRUNC	O_BINARY, SH_COMPAT`
`"w+t"`	`O_CREAT	O_RDWR	O_TRUNC	O_TEXT, SH_COMPAT`
`"a"`	`O_CREAT	O_WRONLY	O_APPEND, SH_COMPAT`
`"ab"`	`O_CREAT	O_WRONLY	O_APPEND	O_BINARY, SH_COMPAT`
`"at"`	`O_CREAT	O_WRONLY	O_APPEND	O_TEXT, SH_COMPAT`
`"a+"`	`O_CREAT	O_RDWR	O_APPEND, SH_COMPAT`
`"a+b"`	`O_CREAT	O_RDWR	O_APPEND	O_BINARY, SH_COMPAT`
`"a+t"`	`O_CREAT	O_RDWR	O_APPEND	O_TEXT, SH_COMPAT`

associated with a device or not, use the run-time function **isatty()**. When switching between reading and writing an unbuffered low-level file, remember to reposition the location pointer as needed. Recall that all write operations to files opened in append mode are made at the end-of-file (EOF), regardless of where the location pointer is positioned prior to the write. File sharing and locking of low-level I/O files requires the use of function **_dos_open()** or **sopen()**, or the reassignment of a low-level file handle to an unbuffered stream I/O file using the function **fdopen()** or **_fsopen()**, described in Chapter 17.

DIRECT I/O

Once a low-level I/O file has been successfully created or opened, all data input and output is performed on an unformatted basis. No formatted translation of bytes will occur, except that characters may be introduced or removed if a file is opened in text rather than binary translation mode. The other characteristic of direct I/O is that the transfer of data can begin at any location within the file. Low-level file positioning functions enable direct I/O to be performed. Simply put, direct I/O implies that bytes of information may be read and written randomly within a file. Low-level I/O performs this in an unbuffered and unformatted manner.

The popularity of stream I/O was found to rest in its adoption and conformance with Standard C, broad support of buffered I/O, support of character, formatted, and direct I/O, and perceived ease of use. Low-level I/O is often preferred, however, when compactness, control, and speed are of utmost concern, and neither portability nor the need for a variety of services is of paramount importance.

LOW-LEVEL I/O TASKS

Table 18.4 describes those run-time library functions that support the processing of DOS files in a low-level I/O manner. Note that all of the low-level I/O tasks are performed by functions that do not conform with Standard C (□ANSI).

Of the functions described above, none are available either in function-like macro or **#pragma intrinsic** form, nor can any of these low-level tasks be accomplished by using either a DOS command or the **system()** run-time library function.

RUN-TIME LIBRARY FUNCTIONS FOR LOW-LEVEL I/O

close()   *Close an open file handle*

Compatibility   □ANSI   ■OS/2   ■UNIX   ■XENIX

See Also
```
_dos_close()
```

Specification
```
#include <io.h>
#include <errno.h>
int close(int handle);
```

Arguments
handle: open file number.

TABLE 18.4: Low-Level I/O Management Functions

TASK		FUNCTION	
		STANDARD C ■ ANSI	MICROSOFT C □ ANSI
Low-Level File Access	Open/create a file		`creat()`
			`_dos_creat()`
			`_dos_creatnew()`
			`_dos_open()`
			`open()`
			`sopen()`
	Duplicate file handles		`dup()`
			`dup2()`
	Close a file		`close()`
			`_dos_close()`
Stream File Positioning	Test/get the current location		`eof()`
			`tell()`
	Set the current location		`lseek()`
	Test if a DOS device (no positioning)		`isatty()` (Chapter 16)
Direct I/O	Input operations		`_dos_read()`
			`read()`
	Output operations		`_dos_write()`
			`write()`

Return Value

0 if successful

−1 if unsuccessful

errno set to **EBADF**

Example   See: `creat()`, `_dos_creat()`, `dup2()`.

Comments   If `close()` is used on the file handle associated with a buffered stream file, buffers are not emptied; therefore, data may be lost.

When either the stream pointer or the file handle associated with a DOS file is closed, the other is no longer open and valid.

creat ()   *Create a new, or truncate an existing file*

Compatibility   ☐ANSI   ■OS/2   ■UNIX   ■XENIX

See Also

_dos_creat(), open(), sopen()

Specification

```
#include <sys\types.h>
#include <sys\stat.h>
#include <io.h>
#include <errno.h>
int creat(const char *filename, int pmode);
```

Arguments

filename: pathname string.

pmode: used only if a file is created; valid permission settings from the object-like macros declared in **<stat.h>**: **S_IREAD** (read-only), **S_IWRITE** (read/write), **S_IREAD** | **S_IWRITE** (read/write).

Return Value

file handle number if successful

−1 if unsuccessful

errno set to **EACCESS**, **EMFILE**, **ENOINT**

Example

```
/* FILE: ch18e1.c */
#include <sys\types.h>
#include <sys\stat.h>
#include <io.h>
#include <direct.h>
#include <errno.h>
#include <stdio.h>
#include <string.h>
#include <malloc.h>
#include <conio.h>
int main(void)
{
char *ptrdir, *ptrfile, ch;
int handle, count;
long length, pos;
do {
if (!(ptrdir = getcwd(NULL,0)) ) printf("\ngetcwd failed!");
else printf("\ndir= %s",ptrdir);
```

```
if (!(ptrfile = tempnam(ptrdir, "xxx")) )
    printf("\ntempnam failed!");
else printf("\nfile= %s",ptrfile);

handle = creat(ptrfile, S_IREAD|S_IWRITE);
if (!handle) printf("\ncreat failed!");
else printf("\nhandle= %d",handle);
count = write(handle, ptrfile, strlen(ptrfile));
length = filelength(handle);
printf("\nwrite count=%d length=%ld", count, length);

if (lseek(handle, 0L, SEEK_SET))
    printf("\nseek to beginning of file failed!");
else printf("\nseek to SEEK_SET OK!");
while (!eof(handle) ) {
    pos = tell(handle);
    if (read(handle, &ch, 1u) != 1 )
        printf("\nread failed at pos= %ld!", pos);
    else printf("\nread ch= %c pos= %ld",ch,pos);
    }
close(handle);

if (remove(ptrfile)) printf("\nremove failed!");
else printf("\nfile deleted!");
free(ptrfile);
free(ptrdir);
printf("\n\nEnter <cr> to Continue; Enter N to Stop: ");

} while (toupper(getche()) != 'N');
exit(0);
}
```

Output

```
dir= C:\QC2\BOOK
file= C:\QC2\BOOK\xxx2
handle= 5
write count=16 length=16
seek to SEEK_SET OK!
read ch= C  pos= 0
read ch= :  pos= 1
read ch= \  pos= 2
read ch= Q  pos= 3
read ch= C  pos= 4
read ch= 2  pos= 5
read ch= \  pos= 6
read ch= B  pos= 7
read ch= O  pos= 8
read ch= O  pos= 9
read ch= K  pos= 10
read ch= \  pos= 11
read ch= x  pos= 12
read ch= x  pos= 13
```

```
read ch= x  pos= 14
read ch= 2  pos= 15
file deleted!

Enter <cr> to Continue; Enter N to Stop: n
```

Comments   Existing files are opened successfully only if their access attribute permits writing; therefore, read-only files cannot be opened using **creat()**.

Existing files that are opened successfully are truncated and opened for writing, and they ignore the **pmode** value specified.

Newly created files are opened for writing and, when closed, are assigned a directory access attribute value that reflects the combined effects of the default process access mode set by function **umask()** (Chapter 16), which is normally defaulted to read/write, and the **pmode** value provided.

It is recommended that function **open()** be used instead of **creat()**.

_dos_close()   *Close an open file handle*

Compatibility   ☐ANSI   ☐OS/2   ☐UNIX   ☐XENIX

See Also

```
close()
```

Specification

```
#include <dos.h>
#include <errno.h>
unsigned _dos_close(int handle);
```

Arguments

handle: open file number.

Return Value

0 if successful

errno if unsuccessful

errno set to EBADF

Example   See: **_dos_creat()**, **_dos_creatnew()**.

Comments   If **_dos_close()** is used on the file handle associated with a buffered stream file, buffers are not emptied; therefore, data may be lost.

When either the stream pointer or file handle associated with a DOS file is closed, the other is no longer open and valid.

`_dos_creat ()`   *Create a new, or truncate an existing file*

Compatibility   ☐ANSI   ☐OS/2   ☐UNIX   ☐XENIX

See Also

```
creat(), open(), sopen()
```

Specification

```
#include <dos.h>
#include <errno.h>
unsigned _dos_creat(const char *filename, unsigned attrib, int *handle);
```

Arguments

filename: pathname string.

attrib: used for created files only; object-like macro declared in **<dos.h>**:
_A_NORMAL (read/write), **_A_RDONLY** (read-only), **_A_HIDDEN** (hidden),
_A_SYSTEM (system), **_A_VOLID** (volume ID), **_A_SUBDIR** (subdirectory),
_A_ARCH (archive). These macros may be combined using | (OR).

handle: address-of handle variable.

Return Value

0 if successful

errno if unsuccessful

errno set to **ENOENT, EMFILE, EACCESS**

Example

```
/* FILE: ch18e4.c */
#include <dos.h>
#include <errno.h>
#include <sys\types.h>
#include <sys\stat.h>
#include <io.h>
#include <fcntl.h>
#include <stdio.h>
#include <string.h>
int main(void)
{
int erc, error, handle, errhandle, nread, i, nwrite;
char *ptr, ch, file[] = "c:\\stderr.lst";
char *errmsg[] = { "stderr cannot be redirected\r\n",
    "on the DOS command line,\r\n",
    "unless your version of DOS\r\n",
    "supports the use of >2&\r\n" };
errno = 0;
erc = _dos_creat(file, _A_NORMAL, &handle);
```

```
    error = errno;
    ptr = strerror(error);
    printf("\n_dos_creat: erc= %d errno= %d <%s>", erc, error, ptr);

    errno = 0;
    errhandle = fileno(stderr);
    erc = dup2(handle, errhandle);
    error = errno;
    ptr = strerror(error);
    printf("\ndup2: erc= %d errno= %d <%s>", erc, error, ptr);
    for (i=0;i<2;i++) write(errhandle, errmsg[i], strlen(errmsg[i]));
    for (i=2;i<4;i++) _dos_write(errhandle, errmsg[i],\
        strlen(errmsg[i]), &nwrite);
    if (!_dos_close(handle) ) printf("\n%s created & closed!",file);

    handle = open(file, O_RDONLY);
    if (handle != -1) printf("\n%s reopened!",file);
    printf("\n");
    lseek(handle, 0L, SEEK_SET);
    while (1) {
        _dos_read(handle,&ch,1u,&nread);
        if (nread) printf("%c",ch);
        else break;
        }
    if (!close(handle)) printf("%s closed again!",file);
    exit(0);
    }
```

Output

```
    _dos_creat: erc= 0 errno= 0 <Error 0>
    dup2: erc= 0 errno= 0 <Error 0>
    c:\stderr.lst created & closed!
    c:\stderr.lst reopened!
    stderr cannot be redirected
    on the DOS command line,
    unless your version of DOS
    supports the use of >2&
    c:\stderr.lst closed again!
```

Comments   Existing files are opened successfully only if their access attribute permits writing; therefore, read-only files cannot be opened using **_dos_creat()**

Existing files that are opened successfully are truncated and opened for writing, and the **attrib** value specified is ignored.

Newly created files are opened for reading and writing and, when closed, assigned the directory access attribute value of **attrib**.

_dos_creatnew()   *Create/open a new file*

Compatibility   ☐ANSI   ☐OS/2   ☐UNIX   ☐XENIX

See Also

```
open(),  sopen()
```

Specification

```
#include <dos.h>
#include <errno.h>
unsigned _dos_creatnew(const char *filename, unsigned attrib, int *handle);
```

Arguments

filename: pathname string.

attrib: object-like macro declared in **<dos.h>**: **_A_NORMAL** (read/write), **_A_RDONLY** (read-only), **_A_HIDDEN** (hidden), **_A_SYSTEM** (system), **_A_VOLID** (volume ID), **_A_SUBDIR** (subdirectory), **_A_ARCH** (archive). These macros may be combined using **|** (OR).

handle: address-of handle variable.

Return Value

0 if successful

errno if unsuccessful

errno set to **ENOENT, EMFILE, EACCESS, EEXIST**

Example

```
/* FILE: ch18e2.c */
#include <dos.h>
#include <errno.h>
#include <fcntl.h>
#include <stdio.h>
#include <string.h>
int main(void)
{
char file[] = "c:\\config.sys", *ptr, ch;
int handle, erc, error, nwrite, nread, i;
if (_dos_creatnew(file, _A_NORMAL | _A_HIDDEN, &handle) ) {
    printf("\n_dos_creatnew failed!");
    if(_dos_open(file, O_RDONLY, &handle) ) {
        printf("\nCannot create or open file!");
        exit(99);
        }
    else printf("\n%s opened!", file);
    }

errno = 0;
erc = _dos_write(handle, file, strlen(file), &nwrite);
error = errno;
ptr = strerror(error);
printf("\n_dos_write: erc=%d errno=%d <%s>", erc, error, ptr);
```

```
for (i=0; i<10;i++) {
    _dos_read(handle, &ch, 1u, &nread);
    if (ch == '\r' || ch == '\n' )
        printf("\nch = %#x nread= %d", ch, nread);
    else printf("\nch= %c nread= %d", ch, nread);
    if (!nread) {
        printf("\nEOF encountered!");
        break;
        }
    }

_dos_close(handle);
errno = 0;
erc = _dos_close(handle);
error = errno;
ptr = strerror(error);
printf("\n2nd _dos_close: erc= %d errno= %d <%s>",\
    erc, error, ptr);
exit(0);
}
```

Output

```
_dos_creatnew failed!
c:\config.sys opened!
_dos_write: erc=5 errno=13 <Permission denied>
ch= f nread= 1
ch= i nread= 1
ch= l nread= 1
ch= e nread= 1
ch= s nread= 1
ch= = nread= 1
ch= 2 nread= 1
ch= 0 nread= 1
ch = 0xd nread= 1
ch = 0xa nread= 1
2nd _dos_close: erc= 6 errno= 9 <Bad file number>
```

Comments Unlike function **_dos_creat()**, this function fails if the filename specified exists.

Newly created files are opened for reading and writing and, when closed, assigned the directory access attribute value of *attrib*.

_dos_open () *Open an existing file*

Compatibility ☐ANSI ☐OS/2 ☐UNIX ☐XENIX

See Also

```
open(), sopen()
```

Specification

```
#include <dos.h>
#include <fcntl.h>
#include <share.h>
#include <errno.h>
unsigned _dos_open(const char *filename, unsigned mode, int *handle);
```

Arguments

filename: pathname string.

mode: object-like macro declared in **<fcntl.h>** and **<share.h>**: **O_RDONLY** (read-only), **O_WRONLY** (write-only), **O_RDWR** (read/write), **O_NOINHERIT** (not passed to child), **SH_COMPAT** (compatibility), **SH_DENYRW** (deny read/write), **SH_DENYWR** (deny write), **SH_DENYRD** (deny read), **SH_DENYNO** (permit read/write).

For this function, only one macro may be specified from each macro category (**O_xxxxxx**, **SH_xxxxx**), except for **O_NOINHERIT**, which may be combined (using OR) with the **O_xxxxxx** macro selected.

handle: address-of handle variable.

Return Value

0 if successful

errno if unsuccessful

errno set to **EINVAL, ENOENT, EMFILE, EACCESS**

Example   See: **_dos_creatnew()**.

Comments   This function is similar to **sopen()** and **_fsopen()**, and supports the opening of shared files and record locking.

If SHARE is not installed, the **SH_xxxxxx** macros specified are ignored.

_dos_read()   *Direct unformatted read of bytes from a file*

Compatibility   □ANSI   □OS/2   □UNIX   □XENIX

See Also

```
read()
```

Specification

```
#include <dos.h>
#include <errno.h>
unsigned _dos_read(int handle, void _far *buffer, unsigned count,
        unsigned *numread);
```

Arguments

handle: open file handle.

buffer: pointer to an array of characters.

count: number of bytes to read.

numread: address-of variable to contain the number of bytes actually read.

Return Value

0 if successful

errno if unsuccessful

errno set to **EACCESS**, **EBADF**

Example   See: **_dos_creat()**, **_dos_creatnew()**.

Comments   If **numread** is zero, then I/O was attempted at EOF.

The value of **numread** may differ from that of **count**, for instance, because DOS stops reading input from a keyboard device when it encounters a **<cr><lf>** character.

_dos_write()   *Direct unformatted write of bytes to a file*

Compatibility   ☐ANSI   ☐OS/2   ☐UNIX   ☐XENIX

See Also

```
write()
```

Specification

```
#include <dos.h>
#include <errno.h>
unsigned _dos_write(int handle, void _far *buffer, unsigned count, unsigned
*numwrt);
```

Arguments

handle: open file handle.

buffer: pointer to an array of characters.

count: number of bytes to write.

numwrt: address-of variable to contain the number of bytes actually written.

Return Value

0 if successful

errno if unsuccessful

errno set to **EACCESS**, **EBADF**

Example

See: **_dos_creat()**, **_dos_creatnew()**.

Comments

If *numwrt* differs from *count*, an error has occurred, perhaps indicating that the volume is out of disk space.

If the file handle is opened in append mode, all writes to the file occur at **EOF** regardless of the current setting of the location pointer.

dup () *Associate a new handle with an open file*

Compatibility □ANSI ■OS/2 ■UNIX ■XENIX

See Also

dup2()

Specification

```
#include <io.h>
#include <errno.h>
int dup(int handle);
```

Arguments

handle: open file number.

Return Value

new handle if successful

−1 if unsuccessful

errno set to **EBADF**, **EMFILE**

Example

See: **dup2()**.

Comments

When you use **dup()**, all of the file properties associated with *handle* are duplicated, and the new file handle is a separate entry in **_iob[]**.

dup2 ()   *Associate a specific handle with an open file*

Compatibility   ☐ANSI   ■OS/2   ■UNIX   ■XENIX

See Also
dup()

Specification
```
#include <io.h>
#include <errno.h>
int dup2(int handle1, int handle2);
```

Arguments
handle1: any open file number.

handle2: any valid handle to associate with the file specified by *handle1*; if *handle2* is open, it is closed and reassigned.

Return Value
0 if successful

−1 if unsuccessful

errno set to **EBADF**, **EMFILE**

Example
```
/* FILE: ch18e3.c */
#include <io.h>
#include <errno.h>
#include <stdio.h>
#include <string.h>
int main(void)
{
int o_handle, e_handle, n_handle;
int erc, error;
char *ptr;
o_handle = fileno(stdout);
e_handle = fileno(stderr);
dup2(o_handle,e_handle);
write(o_handle,"stdout\r\n",8u);
n_handle = dup(fileno(stdout));
if (!close(o_handle)) write(n_handle,"stdout closed\r\n",15u);
errno = 0;
erc = write(o_handle,"stdout err\r\n",12u);
error = errno;
ptr = strerror(error);
fprintf(stderr,"\nstdout write: erc= %d errno= %d <%s>\n",\
     erc, error, ptr);
fflush(stderr);
```

```
if (!close(n_handle)) write(e_handle,"dup stdout closed\r\n",19u);
errno = 0;
erc = write(n_handle,"dup stdout err\r\n",16u);
error = errno;
ptr = strerror(error);
fprintf(stderr,"\ndup stdout write: erc= %d errno= %d <%s>",\
    erc, error, ptr);
fprintf(stderr,"\nclosing stderr!");
exit(0);
}
```

Output

```
stdout
stdout closed
stdout write: erc= -1 errno= 9 <Bad file number>
dup stdout closed
dup stdout write: erc= -1 errno= 9 <Bad file number>
closing stderr!
```

Comments   When you use **dup2()**, all of the file properties associated with *handle1* are duplicated, but *handle2* remains a separate entry in **_iob[]**.

eof()   *Test whether end-of-file (EOF) was encountered*

Compatibility   □ ANSI   ■ OS/2   □ UNIX   □ XENIX

See Also

```
tell()
```

Specification

```
#include <io.h>
#include <errno.h>
int eof(int handle);
```

Arguments

handle: open file handle.

Return Value

1 if current position is at **EOF**;

0 if current position is not at **EOF**

−1 if unsuccessful

errno set to **EBADF**

Example   See: **creat()**.

Comments   Device-based files use Ctrl-Z (0x1A) to signify EOF, but disk-based files logically attempt to read beyond the current length of the file.

lseek()   *Set position in a file (relative)*

Compatibility   ☐ ANSI   ■ OS/2   ■ UNIX   ■ XENIX

Specification

```
#include <io.h>
#include <stdio.h>
#include <errno.h>
long lseek(int handle, long offset, int origin);
```

Arguments

handle: open file handle.

offset: number of bytes from origin.

origin: object-like macro defined in **<stdio.h>**: **SEEK_SET** (beginning of file), **SEEK_CUR** (current position in file), **SEEK_END** (end of file).

Return Value

New position if successful

−**1L** if unsuccessful

errno set to **EBADF**, **EINVAL**

Example   See: **creat()**, **_dos_creat()**.

Comments   The file position is expressed as a (+/−) offset relative to *origin*.
The location pointer cannot be placed before the beginning of the file, but may exceed the current EOF.

open()   *Create a new file, or open an existing one*

Compatibility   ☐ ANSI   ■ OS/2   ■ UNIX   ■ XENIX

See Also

```
_dos_open(), sopen()
```

Specification

```
#include <sys\types.h>
#include <sys\stat.h>
```

```
#include <fcntl.h>
#include <io.h>
#include <errno.h>
int open(const char *filename, int oflag, ...);
```

Arguments

filename: pathname string.

oflag: open characteristics of file using object-like macros declared in **<fcntl.h>**: **O_RDONLY** (read-only), **O_WRONLY** (write-only), **O_RDWR** (read/write), **O_APPEND** (append to EOF), **O_CREAT** (create new file), **O_TRUNC** (truncate existing file), **O_EXCL** (open new file only), **O_TEXT** (open in text mode), **O_BINARY** (open in binary mode), **O_NOINHERIT** (do not pass to child). These macros may be combined using OR (|).

...: Optionally enter a *pmode* argument if *oflag* is **O_CREAT**. These object-like macros are declared in **<stat.h>**: **S_IREAD** (read-only), **S_IWRITE** (read/write), **S_IREAD | S_IWRITE** (read/write).

Return Value

File handle number if successful

−1 if unsuccessful

errno set to **EACCESS**, **EEXIST**, **EINVAL**, **EMFILE**, **ENOENT**

Example

See: **_dos_creat()**.

Comments

This is the most versatile function for opening low-level files, except for **sopen()**, which also supports file sharing.

The optional *pmode* argument is required and used only when a file is created.

Newly created files are opened for writing and, when closed, assigned a directory access attribute value that reflects the combined effects of the default process access mode set by function **umask()** (Chapter 16), which is normally defaulted to read/write, and the *pmode* value provided.

read() *Direct, unformatted read of bytes from a file*

Compatibility ☐ANSI ■OS/2 ■UNIX ■XENIX

See Also

_dos_read()

Specification

```
#include <io.h>
```

```
#include <errno.h>
int read(int handle, void *buffer, unsigned count);
```

Arguments

handle: open file number.

buffer: pointer to an array of characters.

count: number of bytes to read.

Return Value

count of bytes read if successful

−1 if unsuccessful

errno set to **EBADF**

Example   See: **creat()**.

Comments   The number of bytes actually read may differ from **count** if the EOF was encountered, or if the file is in text translation mode, in which case **<cr><lf>** sequences are interpreted as **<lf>**.

A return value of zero means that an attempt was made to begin reading at EOF.

sopen()   *Create a new shared file, or open an existing one*

Compatibility   □ ANSI   ■ OS/2   □ UNIX   □ XENIX

See Also

_dos_open(), **_fsopen()** (Ch. 17)

Specification

```
#include <sys\types.h>
#include <sys\stat.h>
#include <fcntl.h>
#include <share.h>
#include <io.h>
#include <errno.h>
int sopen(const char *filename, int oflag, int shflag, ...);
```

Arguments

filename: pathname string.

oflag: open characteristics of file using object-like macros declared in **<fcntl.h>**: O_RDONLY (read-only), O_WRONLY (write-only), O_RDWR (read/write), O_APPEND (append to EOF), O_CREAT (create new file), O_TRUNC (truncate existing file), O_EXCL (open if no file exists), O_TEXT (open in text mode), **O_BINARY** (open in binary mode), **O_NOINHERIT** (do not pass to child). These macros may be combined using OR (|).

shflag: file sharing characteristics of file using the object-like macros declared in **<share.h>**: **SH_COMPAT** (compatibility), **SH_DENYRW** (deny read/write), **SH_DENYWR** (deny write), **SH_DENYRD** (deny read), **SH_DENYNO** (permit read/write). These macros may be combined using OR (|).

. . .: optionally enter a *pmode* argument if **oflag** is **O_CREAT**. These object-like macros are declared in **<stat.h>**: **S_IREAD** (read-only), **S_IWRITE** (read/write), **S_IREAD | S_IWRITE** (read/write).

Return Value

File handle number if successful

−1 if unsuccessful

errno set to **EACCESS**, **EEXIST**, **EINVAL**, **EMFILE**, **ENOENT**

Example

See: **locking()** (Chapter 16).

Comments

This function is similar to **_dos_open()** and **_fsopen()**. It supports record locking and the opening of shared files.

If SHARE is not installed, the share macros specified are ignored.

The optional **pmode** argument is required and used only when a file is created.

Newly created files are opened for writing and, when closed, assigned a directory access attribute value that reflects the combined effects of the default process access mode set by function **umask()** (Chapter 16), which is normally defaulted to read/write, and the *pmode* value provided.

tell()　*Get the current file position (absolute)*

Compatibility　□ANSI　■OS/2　□UNIX　□XENIX

Specification

```
#include <io.h>
#include <errno.h>
long tell(int handle);
```

Arguments

handle: open file handle.

Return Value

The current position if successful

−**1L** if unsuccessful

errno set to **EBADF**

Example   See: **creat()**.

Comments   The byte positions in a file originate at zero.

The positions determined by **tell()**, **ftell()**, and **fgetpos()** are all compatible for DOS.

write()   *Direct, unformatted write of bytes to a file*

Compatibility   □ANSI   ■OS/2   ■UNIX   ■XENIX

See Also

_dos_write()

Specification

```
#include <io.h>
#include <errno.h>
int write(int handle, void *buffer, unsigned count);
```

Arguments

handle: open file number.

buffer: pointer to an array of characters.

count: number of bytes to write.

Return Value

Count of bytes written if successful

−1 if unsuccessful

errno set to **EBADF**, **ENOSPC**

Example   See: **creat()**, **_dos_creat()**, **dup2()**.

Comments   If the actual number of bytes written differs from *count*, an error has occurred, perhaps indicating that the volume is out of disk space.

If the file handle is opened in append mode, then all writes to the file occur at **EOF** regardless of the current setting of the location pointer.

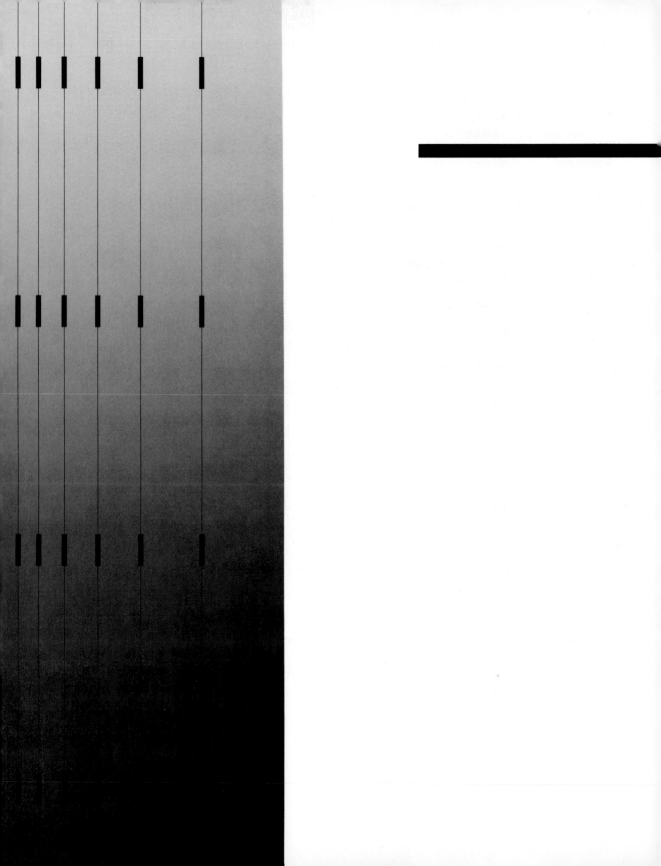

# CHAPTER 19

Console and Port I/O Functions

Console and Port I/O Functions

■■■■■■ This chapter highlights two special types of input and output services: the *console,* which represents both an input keyboard device and an output display device; and *ports,* which enable all peripheral devices to be interfaced with the processor.

Console and port I/O services are available without requiring a device to be opened or closed, and the buffering of I/O is not supported. Console and port I/O are *not* analogous to the predefined DOS device-based files described in Chapters 17 and 18, because console and port I/O devices are never opened or closed—they are simply available if properly installed.

If you are uncertain which functions are available to perform such I/O tasks, see Table 19.1 later in this chapter.

The rest of the chapter consists of an alphabetic series of reference entries for the functions featured in this chapter, provided in the standard run-time library presentation format. For your convenience, a page-number index of run-time library functions is also provided on the inside back cover of this book.

Let's begin by examining the conventions that apply to the console and port I/O functions.

CONSOLE I/O CONVENTIONS

Typically, console keyboard devices are described as either standard or extended, based on the number and configuration of keys, while video display devices typically are classed as either monochrome or color (CGA, EGA, or VGA standard). Because the DOS device CON is by default the predefined standard input (**stdin**) and output (**stdout**) device, all functions described in this chapter, except **_bios_keybrd()**, may be subject to redirection or piping from the DOS command line (see Chapter 1).

Even though console I/O is affected by redirection, the functions in this chapter do not in any way rely upon the **_iob[]** array, stream pointers **stdin** and **stdout**, or file handles [0] and [1] described in Chapters 17 and 18. It is recommended therefore that console I/O not be intermixed with calls to stream or low-level I/O associated with **stdin** and **stdout** or file handles [0] and [1].

The console input functions do not recognize the DOS convention of treating the Ctrl-Z (0x1A) sequence as the end of file (EOF); however, the Ctrl-C (cancel) sequence is detected as a software interrupt (INT 0x23) to terminate the program.

The distinct advantage of the console keystroke functions (**cscanf()**, **getch()**, **getche()**, **kbhit()**) is that, unlike their stream and low-level I/O counterparts, they read keystrokes one at a time, and do not require that a character be followed by a ⏎ key to initiate detection.

PORT I/O CONVENTIONS

Ports represent special I/O addresses that are distinct and separate from memory (RAM). Port I/O services are normally required when the available BIOS (Basic Input/Output System) and DOS interrupt services do not provide support for a peripheral (hardware) device. The BIOS provides access to standard peripheral devices such as the keyboard, video display, floppy disk, hard disk, serial communications, printer, clock, and joystick; while DOS itself provides additional services that supplement the BIOS. For more about BIOS and DOS interrupt services, see Chapter 22.

The classic example of a device for which BIOS/DOS services are unavailable and port I/O functions are therefore necessary is the speaker on the mother board (see the **inp()** example program). Port I/O would also be essential for anyone developing a new insertable PC board so that software could be written to provide the functions for which it was designed.

Each peripheral device type attached to a computer is assigned a range of I/O memory addresses which may vary between configurations and across vendors. For example, the IBM AT (Intel 80286) reserves the following port addresses for the following system board peripherals:

PORT (HEX)	DEVICE
0x000–0x01F	DMA controller 1, 8237A-5
0x020–0x03F	Interrupt controller 1, 8259A, Master
0x040–0x05F	Timer, 8254.2
0x060–0x06F	8042 (Keyboard)
0x070–0x07F	Real-time Clock, NMI mask
0x080–0x09F	DMA page register, 74LS612
0x0A0–0x0BF	Interrupt controller 2, 8259A

PORT (HEX)	DEVICE
0x0C0–0x0DF	DMA controller 2, 8237A-5
0x0F0	Clear Math Coprocessor Busy
0x0F1	Reset Math Coprocessor
0x0F8–0x0FF	Math Coprocessor

The IBM AT also assigns the following port addresses to support other peripheral devices as follows:

PORT (HEX)	DEVICE
0x1F0–0x1F8	Fixed Disk
0x200–0x207	Game I/O
0x278–0x27F	Parallel Printer Port 2
0x2F8–0x2FF	Serial Port 2
0x300–0x31F	Prototype Card
0x360–0x36F	Reserved
0x378–0x37F	Parallel Printer Port 1
0x380–0x38F	SDLC, Bisynchronous 2
0x3A0–0x3AF	Bisynchronous 1
0x3B0–0x3BF	Monochrome Display & Printer Adapter
0x3C0–0x3CF	Reserved
0x3D0–0x3DF	Color/Graphics Monitor Adapter
0x3F0–0x3F7	Diskette Controller
0x3F8–0x3FF	Serial Port 1

The address ranges are treated as either 8-bit (**inp()/outp()**) or 16-bit (**inpw()/outpw()**) registers that are interrogated by the device to which they are assigned. To use port I/O correctly, you need extensive knowledge of the hardware and access to technical documentation that describes the assignment of I/O address registers and the control sequences necessary to instruct a peripheral device to perform a specific task.

CONSOLE AND PORT I/O TASKS

Table 19.1 describes those run-time library functions that provide console and port I/O services. Notice that all of these tasks are performed by functions that do not conform with Standard C (□ ANSI).

Of the functions described above, none are available in function-like macro form; however, several functions (**inp()**, **inpw()**, **outp()**,

outpw()) are available in **#pragma intrinsic** form. None of these services can be accomplished by using either a DOS command or the **system()** run-time library function.

TABLE 19.1: Console and Port I/O Management Functions

TASK		FUNCTION	
		STANDARD C ■ ANSI	MICROSOFT C □ ANSI
Console I/O:	Character Input		_bios_keybrd()
			cgets()
			getch()
			getche()
			kbhit()
			ungetch()
	Character Output		cputs()
			putch()
	Formatted Input		cscanf()
	Formatted Output		cprintf()
Port I/O:	Byte Input		inp()
	Byte Output		outp()
	Word Input		inpw()
	Word Output		outpw()

RUN-TIME LIBRARY FUNCTIONS FOR CONSOLE AND PORT I/O

_bios_keybrd()   *Perform BIOS keyboard services*

Compatibility   □ANSI   □OS/2   □UNIX   □XENIX

See Also

getch(), getche(), kbhit()

Specification

```
#include <bios.h>
unsigned _bios_keybrd(unsigned service);
```

Arguments

service: BIOS object-like macros declared in **<bios.h>** for a normal keyboard: **_KEYBRD_READ** (read next char), **_KEYBRD_READY** (check for keystroke), **_KEYBRD_SHIFTSTATUS** (get shift status). For an enhanced keyboard: **_NKEYBRD_READ** (read next char), **_NKEYBRD_READY** (check for keystroke), **_NKEYBRD_SHIFTSTATUS** (get shift status).

Return Value

An ASCII character value, extended ASCII scan code value, or shift status value (see "Comments" below).

Example

See also: **inp()**.

```
/* FILE: ch19e1.c */
#include <bios.h>
#include <stdio.h>
int main(void)
{
unsigned i, keystroke;
while (_bios_keybrd(_KEYBRD_READY)) _bios_keybrd(_KEYBRD_READ);
do {
    if (!_bios_keybrd(_KEYBRD_READY)) {
        printf("\nPlease enter keystrokes..."\
            "Press Scroll-Lock or End key to stop");
        for(i=0;i<TMP_MAX;i++);
        continue;
        }
    keystroke = _bios_keybrd(_KEYBRD_READ);
    if (keystroke & 0x00FF) {
        printf("\n\tASCII character ==> %c", keystroke & 0x00FF);
        continue;
        }
    else {
        printf("\n\tExtended ASCII Scan Code ==> %u", keystroke >> 8);
        if ((keystroke >> 8) == 79) break;
        }
    } while (!(_bios_keybrd(_KEYBRD_SHIFTSTATUS) & 0x0010));
printf("\n\tScroll-Lock or End key encountered...stopping");
while (_bios_keybrd(_KEYBRD_READY)) _bios_keybrd(_KEYBRD_READ);
exit(0);
}
```

Output

```
Please enter keystrokes...Press Scroll-Lock or End key to stop
Please enter keystrokes...Press Scroll-Lock or End key to stop q
    ASCII character ==> q
Please enter keystrokes...Press Scroll-Lock or End key to stop Alt-W
    Extended ASCII Scan Code ==> 17 (Alt-W)
Please enter keystrokes...Press Scroll-Lock or End key to stop F1
    Extended ASCII Scan Code ==> 59 (F1)
```

```
Please enter keystrokes...Press Scroll-Lock or End key to stop End
   Scroll-Lock or End key encountered...stopping
```

Comments   The example clears the keyboard input buffer of all extraneous characters before prompting the user to begin, and before exiting the program.

The expression **(keystroke & 0x00FF)** tests the low-order byte; similarly, **(keystroke >> 8)** tests the high-order byte.

When **_KEYBRD_READY** is used, this function behaves like **kbhit()**.

The **_KEYBRD_READ** and **_NKEYBRD_READ** services wait to read a character; the low-order byte is nonzero for ASCII characters; otherwise, it is zero, and the high-order byte then contains an extended ASCII or scan code as follows:

3	NUL character
15	Shift-tab
16–25	Alt-Q,W,E,R,T,Y,U,I,O,P
30–38	Alt-Z,X,C,V,B,M,N
59–68	Function keys F1–F10
71	Home
72	Cursor Up
73	Page Up
75	Cursor Left
77	Cursor Right
79	End
80	Cursor Down
81	Page Down
82	Insert
83	Delete
84–93	F11–F20 (Shift F1–F10)
94–103	F21–F30 (Ctrl F1–F10)

The **_KEYBRD_READY** and **_NKEYBRD_READY** services return zero if no character is waiting; otherwise they returnsthe character itself but do not remove the character from the buffer.

The **_KEYBRD_SHIFTSTATUS** and **_NKEYBRD_SHIFTSTATUS** services return a value that can be tested as shown to see if the following keys are pressed:

bit 0 ON: rightmost Shift
bit 1 ON: leftmost Shift
bit 2 ON: Ctrl

bit 3 ON: Alt

bit 4 ON: Scroll Lock

bit 5 ON: Num Lock

bit 6 ON: Caps Lock

bit 7 ON: INSERT mode

cgets ()   *Read a string directly from the console*

Compatibility   ☐ ANSI   ■ OS/2   ☐ UNIX   ☐ XENIX

See Also

cscanf()

Specification

```
#include <conio.h>
char *cgets(char *buffer);
```

Arguments

buffer: address of an array of characters.

Return Value   Pointer to *buffer*

Example

```
/* FILE: ch19e2.c */
#include <conio.h>
#include <stdio.h>
#include <string.h>
int main(void)
{
char buffer[13] = { 11 }, *ptr;
while (1) {
    printf("\nEnter a string (10-char max) or END: ");
    ptr = cgets(buffer);
    if (!strcmpi(ptr,"END")) break;
    printf("\nMaximum =%d Actual=%d\n", buffer[0], buffer[1]);
    cputs(ptr);
    }
    exit(0);
    }
```

Output

```
Enter a string (10-char max) or END: test
Maximum =11  Actual=4
test
```

```
Enter a string (10-char max) or END: large string
Maximum =11  Actual=10
largestrin
Enter a string (10-char max) or END: end
```

Comments   Notice the unconventional manner in which the first two bytes of **buffer[]** are used: **buffer[0]** is the maximum size of the string to be read including a terminating null character; **buffer[1]** contains the count of characters actually read excluding the terminating null.

cgets() does not accept a string that is longer than **buffer[0]**; the input string is read until a **<cr>** character is encountered.

The return value always points to the address of **buffer[2]**.

cprintf()   *Write formatted data directly to the console*

Compatibility   □ANSI   ■OS/2   □UNIX   □XENIX

See Also

```
cputs(), putch()
```

Specification

```
#include <conio.h>
int cprintf(const char *format, ...);
```

Arguments

format: Format control string. See Table 17.4 for the rules of constructing valid output control strings.

...: Variable number of arguments to be displayed.

Return Value   The number of characters written

Example   See: **cscanf()**.

Comments   Unlike the other **xprintf()** output functions, **cprintf()** does not perform character translation. **<lf>** is not expanded to a **<cr><lf>** sequence; hence the use of the '**\r**' '**\n**' sequence in the example.

Output is displayed starting at the current cursor location.

cputs()   *Write a string directly to the console*

Compatibility   □ANSI   ■OS/2   □UNIX   □XENIX

See Also

```
cprintf()
```

Specification

```
#include <conio.h>
int cputs(const char *string);
```

Arguments

string: A null-terminated array of characters.

Return Value

0 if successful

nonzero if unsuccessful

Example   See: `cgets()`.

Comments   `cputs()` does not perform character translation or automatically append a **<cr><lf>** at the beginning or end of the string.

Output is displayed starting at the current cursor location.

cscanf()   *Read formatted data directly from the console*

Compatibility   ☐ ANSI   ■ OS/2   ☐ UNIX   ☐ XENIX

See Also

```
cgets(), getch(), getche()
```

Specification

```
#include <conio.h>
int cscanf(const char *format, ...);
```

Arguments

format: Format control string. See Table 17.3 for the rules of constructing valid input control strings.

. . .: Variable number of argument addresses to be read.

Return Value   The number of fields that were read and assigned (excluding any [*] fields), or EOF if end of file encountered

Example

```
/* FILE: ch19e3.c */
#include <conio.h>
#include <stdio.h>
#include <string.h>
int main(void)
{
char *control[] = { "%s", "%c", "%d", "%f" };
char cv, string[10]= { '\r', '\n' };
int iv;
float fv;
cprintf(control[0], "\nEnter a character: ");
cscanf(control[1], &cv);
strcpy(&string[2], control[1]);
cprintf(string, cv);

cprintf(control[0], "\n\rEnter an integer: ");
cscanf(control[2], &iv);
strcpy(&string[2], control[2]);
cprintf(string, iv);

cprintf(control[0], "\n\rEnter a float: ");
cscanf(control[3], &fv);
strcpy(&string[2], control[3]);
cprintf(string, fv);
exit(0);
}
```

Output

```
Enter a character: q
q
Enter an integer: 125
125
Enter a float: -14.75
-14.750000
```

Comments   Unlike the other **xscanf()** input functions, **cscanf()** does not translate any **<cr><lf>** sequences encountered to **<lf>**.

When consecutive single characters are read, no special care need be taken to allocate a dummy variable to trap the **<lf>** character that normally remains in the keyboard buffer. See **scanf()** (Chapter 17).

getch()   *Read a character from the console without echo*

Compatibility   ☐ ANSI   ■ OS/2   ☐ UNIX   ☐ XENIX

Specification

```
#include <conio.h>
int getch(void);
```

Return Value The ASCII character read, or zero, indicating that a scan code follows (see **_bios_keybrd()**)

Example See: **kbhit()**.

Comments The character read by **getch()** is not displayed to the console.

If zero is returned, then another **getch()** call must be issued to retrieve the scan code; otherwise, the scan code remains in the buffer.

No translation of characters occurs: **<cr><lf>** is not converted to **<lf>**.

getche () *Read a character from the console with echo*

Compatibility ☐ANSI ■OS/2 ☐UNIX ☐XENIX

See Also

```
_bios_keybrd()
```

Specification

```
#include <conio.h>
int getche(void);
```

Return Value The ASCII character read, or zero, indicating that a scan code follows (see **bios_keybrd**)

Example See: **kbhit()**.

Comments The character read by **getch()** is displayed to the console.

If zero is returned, another **getche()** call must be issued to retrieve the scan code; otherwise, the scan code remains in the buffer.

No translation of characters occurs: **<cr><lf>** is not converted to **<lf>**.

inp () *Read a byte from any port*

Compatibility ☐ANSI ■OS/2 ☐UNIX ☐XENIX

Specification

```
#include <conio.h>
int inp(unsigned port);
```

Arguments

port: Processor port number; hardware and vendor specific; values may range between 0x0000 and 0xFFFF, but are hardware specific.

Return Value   The byte read as type `int`

Example   See also: `inpw()`.

```
/* FILE: ch19e4.c */
#include <conio.h>
#include <bios.h>
#include <stdio.h>
#define T_FREQ 1193180LU
#define T_MODE 0x43
#define T_OSCIL 0xB6
#define T_COUNT 0x42
#define PPI_8255 0x61
#define SPEAKER_ON 0x03
#define LO_PPI 100LU
#define HI_PPI 32000LU

int main(void)
{
unsigned freq, ratio, new_ppi, next_ppi, keystroke;
unsigned char orig_ppi;
char *message[] = {"entry", "up-arrow", "dn-arrow",\
                   "pg-up", "pg-down", "underflow",
                   "overflow"};

char *ptr;
orig_ppi = inp(PPI_8255);
outp(T_MODE, T_OSCIL);
new_ppi = T_FREQ/(10UL * LO_PPI);
outp(T_COUNT, new_ppi & 0x00FF);
outp(T_COUNT, (new_ppi >> 8) & 0x00FF);
outp(PPI_8255, (orig_ppi | SPEAKER_ON));
printf("\n\nPress UP-ARROW to raise tone by +25%%");
printf("\nPress DN-ARROW to lower tone by -25%%");
printf("\nPress PG-UP to raise tone by +33%%");
printf("\nPress PG-DN to lower tone by -33%%");
printf("\nPress END key to exit program");
printf("\n\torig_ppi = %u [%s]",new_ppi,message[0]);
while (1) {
  keystroke = _bios_keybrd(_KEYBRD_READ);
  if ((keystroke & 0x00FF)) continue;
  else {
    keystroke >>= 8;
    switch (keystroke) {
      case 72: next_ppi = new_ppi - (new_ppi/4L);
               ptr = message[1];
               break;
```

```
        case 80: next_ppi = new_ppi + (new_ppi/4L);
                 ptr = message[2];
                 break;
        case 73: next_ppi = new_ppi - (new_ppi/3L);
                 ptr = message[3];
                 break;
        case 81: next_ppi = new_ppi + (new_ppi/3L);
                 ptr = message[4];
                 break;
      }
   if (keystroke == 79) break;
   if (next_ppi < LO_PPI) {
     next_ppi = LO_PPI;
     ptr = message[5];
     }
   else if (next_ppi > HI_PPI) {
     next_ppi = HI_PPI;
     ptr = message[6];
     }
   new_ppi = next_ppi;
   printf("\n\tnew_ppi = %u [%s]",new_ppi,ptr);
   outp(T_COUNT, new_ppi & 0x00FF);
   outp(T_COUNT, (new_ppi >> 8) & 0x00FF);
   }
 }
outp(PPI_8255, orig_ppi);
exit(0);
}
```

Output

```
Press UP-ARROW to raise tone by +25%
Press DN-ARROW to lower tone by -25%
Press PG-UP to raise tone by +33%
Press PG-DN to lower tone by -33%
Press END key to exit program

    orig_ppi = 1193 [entry]
    new_ppi = 895 [up-arrow]
    new_ppi = 672 [up-arrow]
    new_ppi = 448 [pg-up]
    new_ppi = 299 [pg-up]
     .

     .
    new_ppi = 100 [underflow]
    new_ppi = 125 [dn-arrow]
    new_ppi = 156 [dn-arrow]
    new_ppi = 195 [dn-arrow]
    new_ppi = 260 [pg-down]
     .

     .
    new_ppi = 24224 [pg-down]
    new_ppi = 32000 [overflow]
```

```
new_ppi = 32000 [overflow]
new_ppi = 24000 [up-arrow]
    .
    .
    .
(until "end" key pressed)
```

Comments   This example varies the tone of the speaker in response to the use of the up-arrow, down-arrow, page-up and page-down keys, until the End key is pressed to terminate the program.

The example uses the Programmable Peripheral Interface (PPI) chip to control the system timer chip and speaker as follows:

1 Save the current PPI register (**orig_ppi**).

2 Set the timer to oscillate (**T_MODE, T_OSCIL**).

3 Factor the timer frequency (**new_ppi**).

4 Set timer **new_ppi** (low-byte, high-byte).

5 Turn the speaker ON.

6 Examine user keystrokes; reset timer.

7 Detect End key; turn speaker off by restoring PPI register (**orig_ppi**).

Notice that the return value is an **int**, not an **unsigned int**, because only eight bits are returned.

Note that you can use either the function or the **#pragma intrinsic** form.

inpw()   *Read a word from any port*

Compatibility   ☐ ANSI   ■ OS/2   ☐ UNIX   ☐ XENIX

Specification

```
#include <conio.h>
unsigned inpw(unsigned port);
```

Arguments

port: Processor port number; hardware and vendor specific; values may range between 0x0000 and 0xFFFF, but are hardware specific.

Return Value   The word read as type **unsigned int**

Example

```
/* FILE: ch19e5.c */
#include <conio.h>
#include <stdio.h>
#define P_8259A_20 0x20u
```

```
#define P_8259A_21 0x21u

int main(void)
{
unsigned PW_20_21;
int PB_20, PB_21;
PW_20_21 = inpw(P_8259A_20);
printf("\nPort 20+21: %#04x", PW_20_21);
PB_20 = inp(P_8259A_20);
PB_21 = inp(P_8259A_21);
printf("\nPort 20: %#02x", PB_20);
printf("\nPort 21: %#02x", PB_21);
outpw(P_8259A_20, PW_20_21);
printf("\nWriting Ports 20+21 with %#04x", PW_20_21);
PB_20 = inp(P_8259A_20);
PB_21 = inp(P_8259A_21);
printf("\nPort 20: %#02x", PB_20);
printf("\nPort 21: %#02x", PB_21);
exit(0);
}
```

Output

```
Port 20+21: 0xbc00
Port 20: 00
Port 21: 0xbc
Writing Ports 20+21 with 0xbc00
Port 20: 00
Port 21: 0xbc
```

Comments   Notice the order in which the **int** (a word) is placed into the port (in bytes). This is characteristic of Intel's $80x86$ "little-endian" chip architecture.
Notice that the return value is **unsigned** to accommodate the return of 16 bits.
Note that you can use either the function or the **#pragma intrinsic** form.

kbhit()   *Test for an unread console keystroke*

Compatibility   ☐ ANSI   ■ OS/2   ☐ UNIX   ☐ XENIX

See Also

    _bios_keybrd()

Specification

```
#include <conio.h>
int kbhit(void);
```

Return Value

Nonzero (true) if keystroke is buffered

0 (false) if keystroke is not buffered

Example

```
/* FILE: ch19e6.c */
#include <conio.h>
#include <stdio.h>
int main(void)
{
int ascii, scan;
while (1) {
  if (!kbhit()) printf("\n\nkbhit() -> press a key or Q to end: ");
  scan = 0;
  ascii = getche();
  if (!ascii) {
     scan = getche();
     printf("\nentered: ascii = %c scan = %d", ascii, scan);
     continue;
     }
     else if (ascii == 'Q' || ascii == 'q') break;
     printf("\nentered: ascii = %c", ascii);
     if (ungetch(ascii) != EOF) printf("\n\t1st ungetch() OK!");
     printf("\n\tputback ungetch() = %c", ascii);
     if (ungetch(ascii) == EOF) printf("\n\t2nd ungetch() failed!");
     ascii = getch();
     printf("\n\tnon-echo getch() + putch() = ");
     if (putch(ascii) == EOF) printf("\n\tputch() failed!");
     }
printf("\nQuitting!");
exit(0);
}
```

Output

```
kbhit() -> press a key or Q to end: (Alt-W)
entered: ascii = 0 scan = 17

kbhit() -> press a key or Q to end: z
entered: ascii = z
    1st ungetch() OK!
    putback ungetch() = z
    2nd ungetch() failed!
    non-echo getch() + putch() = z

kbhit() -> press a key or Q to end: q
Quitting!
```

Comments **kbhit()** detects the presence of both ASCII and Extended ASCII scan codes that may be held in the keyboard hardware buffer.

outp ()   *Write a byte to any port*

Compatibility   □ANSI   ■OS/2   □UNIX   □XENIX

Specification

```
#include <conio.h>
int outp(unsigned port, int byte);
```

Arguments

port: Processor port number; hardware and vendor specific; values may range between 0x0000 and 0xFFFF, but are hardware specific.

byte: The byte to be written.

Return Value   The byte written as type **int**

Example   See: **inp()**.

Comments   When writing individual bytes, rather than words, no byte-ordering considerations ("big-" vs "little-endian") are involved.

Notice that the return value is an **int**, not an **unsigned int**, because only eight bits are returned.

Note that you can use either the function or the **#pragma intrinsic** form.

outpw ()   *Write a word to any port*

Compatibility   □ANSI   ■OS/2   □UNIX   □XENIX

Specification

```
#include <conio.h>
unsigned outpw(unsigned port, unsigned word);
```

Arguments

port: Processor port number; hardware and vendor specific; values may range between 0x0000 and 0xFFFF, but are hardware specific.

word: The word to be written.

Return Value   The word written as type **unsigned int**

Example   See: **inpw()**.

Comments   Notice that the return value is **unsigned** to accommodate the return of 16 bits.

In the **inpw()** example, notice the order in which the **int** (word) is placed into the port (bytes). This is characteristic of Intel's 80x86 "little-endian" chip architecture.

Note that you can use either the function or the **#pragma intrinsic** form.

putch ()   *Write a character to the console*

Compatibility   ☐ ANSI   ■ OS/2   ☐ UNIX   ☐ XENIX

See Also
cprintf()

Specification
```
#include <conio.h>
int putch(int c);
```

Arguments
c: Character to be written.

Return Value
The character written if successful

EOF if unsuccessful

Example   See: **kbhit()**.

Comments   No automatic introduction or translation of **<lf>** to **<cr><lf>** characters occurs.

Output is displayed starting at the current cursor location.

ungetch ()   *Put back a character to the console*

Compatibility   ☐ ANSI   ■ OS/2   ☐ UNIX   ☐ XENIX

Specification
```
#include <conio.h>
int ungetch(int c);
```

Arguments
c: Character to be put back.

Return Value

The character put back if successful

EOF if unsuccessful

Example   See: **kbhit()**.

Comments   After a character is read, only one character may be put back; subsequent attempts will generate an **EOF** error.

No automatic introduction or translation of **<lf>** to **<cr><lf>** characters occurs.

7

Using the C Run-Time Library's Other Services

Part VII highlights the remaining Microsoft C run-time library functions that were not covered in Part VI except for any graphics functions, which are excluded from this book.

Chapter 20, "Character and Data Conversion Functions," features those functions that support the testing and conversion of the fundamental integral and floating C data-object types between character and internal forms of representation.

Chapter 21, "Date and Time Management Functions," reviews the various formats used to support the representation of the system date and time. A complete explanation of how time, and hence date, is measured and recorded can be found in this chapter, together with the related Standard and non-Standard functions available in the run-time library.

Chapter 22, "Functions for DOS/BIOS System Calls," explains the process by which a *software interrupt* may be issued so that a BIOS or DOS function (system call) may be performed. Use of any function described in this chapter is strictly non-Standard and unique to the DOS operating system. The BIOS and DOS services available may vary depending upon the DOS version in use.

Chapter 23, "Math Functions," describes the complement of trigonometric and other common integer and floating-point functions, together with **matherr()** and those functions that control an 80*x*87 coprocessor chip if installed.

Chapter 24, "Memory Management Functions," discusses dynamic memory allocation to the heap, Near heap, and Far heap, together with coverage of the new **_based** heap family of functions and the traditional memory copy, compare, and move facilities.

Chapter 25, "Process Control Functions," demonstrates the use of all *process* (program) related functions that control exiting a process, nonlocal branches (**setjmp** and **longjmp**), and signal processing.

Chapter 26, "String-Handling Functions," highlights all string (null-terminated arrays of type **char**) manipulation functions, including the new memory-model independent **_fstrxx** family of functions.

Finally, Chapter 27, "Miscellaneous Functions," highlights a select group of functions that are otherwise difficult to categorize. Among them are the *search, find,* and *sort* functions, together with a series of *interrupt* processing functions, and the new *locale* specific functions introduced by Standard C.

Character and Data Conversion Functions

Character and Data Conversion Functions

━━━━━━━ This chapter highlights the run-time functions used for converting and testing the type of data objects. Typically, such conversion involves character strings and internal type representations and is associated with I/O operations. The familiar **scanf()** functions encode or accept character strings and produce C data-object type representations, while the **printf()** functions decode or translate C data-object types into character string representations. Given the variety of C data-object types (see Tables 7.7 and 7.8), such conversions must be made frequently.

When a Standard C data object is encoded, different forms of representation may be used. Recall that Standard C does not mandate how floating-point types are represented; rather, it establishes a minimum set of resulting type properties. Normally, the IEEE standard binary floating-point forms of representation are used for types **float**, **double**, and **long double**; however, Microsoft BASIC sometimes uses a different Microsoft format. Thus the need to convert between IEEE and Microsoft encoded **float** and **double** data types occasionally arises, and so Microsoft has provided the **fieeetomsbin()**, **dieeetomsbin()**, **fmsbintoieee()**, and **dmsbintoieee()** functions.

Sometimes, bits, the most elemental form of representation, must be moved rather than just individually tested and set. To meet this need, Microsoft has provided a set of functions for *rotating* bits and *swapping* bytes: **_lrotl()**, **_lrotr()**, **_rotl()**, **_rotr()**, and **swab()**.

Finally, the **sprintf()**, **sscanf()**, and **vsprintf()** functions are highlighted in this chapter, rather than in Part VI, because they are truly generic data-conversion routines, capable of handling most data-object type conversions without performing conventional I/O at all.

The body of this chapter consists of an alphabetic series of reference entries for the functions summarized in Table 20.1, presented in the standard run-time library presentation format. For your convenience, a page-number index of run-time library functions is also provided on the inside back cover of this book.

DATA TESTING AND CONVERSION

Table 20.1 summarizes the run-time library functions that are available to perform character testing and C data-type conversions. It groups the functions described in this chapter by data-object type, while indicating which functions conform with Standard C (■ ANSI) and which ones are Microsoft-specific (□ ANSI).

You will find that many of these functions are available in three forms: macro, function, and **#pragma intrinsic**. If the function form is to be used, you must utilize the preprocessor **#undef** command to undefine any defined macro substitutions that may exist. Also, to invoke an intrinsic

TABLE 20.1: Character and Data Conversion Functions

TASK		FUNCTION	
		STANDARD C ■ **ANSI**	**MICROSOFT C** □ **ANSI**
Character Testing		isalnum()	isascii()
		isalpha()	iscsym()
		iscntrl()	iscsymf()
		isdigit()	
		isgraph()	
		islower()	
		isprint()	
		ispunct()	
		isspace()	
		isupper()	
		isxdigit()	
Data Type Conversion	any	sprintf()	
		sscanf()	
		vsprintf()	
	char	tolower()	toascii()
		toupper()	_tolower()
			_toupper()
	int	atoi()	itoa()
			_rotl()
			_rotr()
			swab()

TABLE 20.1: Character and Data Conversion Functions (continued)

TASK		FUNCTION	
		STANDARD C ■ ANSI	MICROSOFT C ☐ ANSI
Data Type Conversion (cont.)	long	atol() strtol() strtoul()	ltoa() _lrotl() ultoa() _lrotr() fieeetomsbin() fmsbintoieee()
	float		
	double	atof() strtod()	dieeetomsbin() dmsbintoieee() ecvt() fcvt() gcvt()
	long double		_atold() _strtold()
	bit/byte		_lrotl() _lrotr() _rotl() _rotr() swab()

function, either use compiler option **/Oi** or specify the preprocessor **#pragma intrinsic(..)** command; otherwise, either the macro or function form will be employed.

Notice that the **isxx()** functions (such as **isalnum()** and **isascii()**) test any integer value (type **char** promoted to **int**) and return an indication of whether the test result was false (0) or true (1). To understand exactly what each **isxx()** function is designed to test for, carefully examine the output produced by the example program shown in the **isxx()** reference entry.

Don't overlook the **sprintf()** and **sscanf()** functions. These functions perform all of the formatted data-type conversions performed by **printf()** and **scanf()**, described in Chapter 17. They work with a memory buffer and do not perform any standard I/O. Function **vsprintf()** is more complex, but it is handy to use within functions whose prototypes include the ellipsis (...), indicating that a variable number of arguments may be provided when the function is called.

The remaining functions are grouped by C data type. When using these functions, be particularly careful to test for any exceptions that may occur (for example, underflow, overflow, and invalid character string). Each function handles the flagging of such errors in a slightly different manner. Some use the global variable **errno**, while others return zero or a designated maximum or minimum value (see Chapter 6).

RUN-TIME LIBRARY FUNCTIONS FOR CHARACTER AND DATA CONVERSION

atof() *Convert a string to type double*

Compatibility ■ANSI ■OS/2 ■UNIX ■XENIX

See Also

```
_atold(), sscanf(), strtod(), strtold()
```

Specification

```
#include <stdlib.h> or <math.h>
double atof(const char *string);
```

Arguments

string: Character array to be converted, limited to 100 characters.

Return Value

0.0 if error encountered

Undefined if an overflow occurs

Example

```
/*FILE: ch20e1.c*/
#include <stdio.h>
#include <stdlib.h>
#include <string.h>
int main(void)
{
char line[80], buffer[80], *ptr;
int dec, sign;
double dv;
```

```
long double ldv;
while (1) {
    printf("\n\nEnter a number string: ");
    gets(line);
    if (!stricmp(line,"END")) break;

    dv = atof(line);
        printf("\natof-dv    = %g", dv);
    dv = strtod(line, &ptr);
        printf("\nstrtod-dv  = %g", dv);
        printf("\nstopped@= %c", *ptr);
    printf("\necvt-dv    = %s", ecvt(dv, 20, &dec, &sign));
        printf("\ndec@= %d\tsign= %d", dec, sign);
    printf("\nfcvt-dv    = %s", fcvt(dv, 20, &dec, &sign));
        printf("\ndec@= %d\tsign= %d", dec, sign);
    printf("\ngcvt-dv    = %s", gcvt(dv, 20, buffer));

    ldv = _atold(line);
        printf("\n_atold-ldv = %Lg", ldv);
    ldv = _strtold(line, &ptr);
        printf("\n_strtold-ldv= %Lg", ldv);
        printf("\nstopped@= %c", *ptr);
}
exit(0);
}
```

Output

```
Enter a number string: -123.456x
atof-dv     = -123.456
strtod-dv   = -123.456
stopped@= x
ecvt-dv     = 12345600000000000000
dec@= 3    sign= 1
fcvt-dv     = 123456000000000000000000
dec@= 3    sign= 1
gcvt-dv     = -123.456
_atold-ldv  = -123.456
_strtold-ldv= -123.456
stopped@= x

Enter a number string: end
```

Comments   Conversion terminates at the first unrecognizable character, or when a null ('\0') is encountered.

Conversion follows the rules established for the control strings used for floating-point types with the **scanf()** family of functions (see Chapter 17).

`atoi()`   *Convert a string to type* `int`

Compatibility   ■ANSI   ■OS/2   ■UNIX   ■XENIX

See Also

```
atol(), sscanf()
```

Specification

```
#include <stdlib.h>
int atoi(const char *string);
```

Arguments

string: Character array to be converted.

Return Value

0 if error encountered

Undefined if overflow occurs

Example

```
/* FILE: ch20e2.c */
#include <stdio.h>
#include <stdlib.h>
#include <string.h>
int main(void)
{
char line[80], buffer[80], *ptr;
int iv, base;
long int lv;
unsigned long int ulv;

printf("\n\nWhich base-n number system? (2-36): ");
scanf("%d", &base);
fflush(stdin);
base < 2 ? base=2 : base;
base >36 ? base=36 : base;

while (1) {
    printf("\n\nEnter a base number string, or END: ");
    gets(line);
    if (!stricmp(line,"END")) break;

    iv = atoi(line);
        printf("\natoi-iv    = %d", iv);
        printf("\nitoa-iv    = %s", itoa(iv, buffer, base));

    lv = atol(line);
        printf("\natol-lv    = %ld", lv);
        printf("\nltoa-lv    = %s", ltoa(lv, buffer, base));
```

```
    lv = strtol(line, &ptr, base);
        printf("\nstrtol-lv   = %ld", lv);
        printf("\nstopped@    = %c", *ptr);
        printf("\nltoa-lv     = %s", ltoa(lv, buffer, base));

    ulv = strtoul(line, &ptr, base);
        printf("\nstrtoul-ulv = %lu", ulv);
        printf("\nstopped@    = %c", *ptr);
        printf("\nultoa-ulv   = %s", ultoa(ulv, buffer, base));
    }
exit(0);
}
```

Output

```
Which base-n number system? (2-36): 10

Enter a base number string, or END: -1x
atoi-iv     = -1
itoa-iv     = -1
atol-lv     = -1
ltoa-lv     = -1
strtol-lv   = -1
stopped@    = x
ltoa-lv     = -1
strtoul-ulv = 4294967295
stopped@    = x
ultoa-ulv   = 4294967295

Enter a base number string, or END: end
```

Comments   Conversion terminates at the first unrecognizable character, or when a null (`'\0'`) is encountered.

Conversion follows the rules established for the control strings used for integer types with the **scanf()** family of functions (see Chapter 17).

atol()   *Convert a string to type* long int

Compatibility   ■ANSI   ■OS/2   ■UNIX   ■XENIX

See Also

```
sscanf(), strtol(), strtoul()
```

Specification

```
#include <stdlib.h>
long atol(const char *string);
```

Arguments

string: Character array to be converted.

Return Value

0 if error encountered

Undefined if overflow occurs

Example   See: `atoi()`.

Comments   Conversion terminates at the first unrecognizable character, or when a null (`'\0'`) is encountered.

Conversion follows the rules established for the control strings used for integer types with the `scanf()` family of functions (see Chapter 17).

`_atold()`   *Convert a string to type* `long double`

Compatibility   □ANSI   ■OS/2   □UNIX   □XENIX

See Also

```
atof(), sscanf(), _strtold()
```

Specification

```
#include <stdlib.h> or <math.h>
long double _atold(const char *string);
```

Arguments

string: Character array to be converted, limited to 100 characters.

Return Value

0 if error encountered

Undefined if overflow occurs

Example   See: `atof()`.

Comments   Conversion terminates at the first unrecognizable character, or when a null (`'\0'`) is encountered.

Conversion follows the rules established for the control strings used for floating-point types with the `scanf()` family of functions.

dieeetomsbin() *Convert between IEEE and Microsoft type* double *format*

Compatibility ☐ ANSI ■ OS/2 ☐ UNIX ☐ XENIX

See Also

```
dmsbintoieee(), fieeetomsbin()
```

Specification

```
#include <math.h>
int dieeetomsbin(double *ieee, double *msbin);
```

Arguments

ieee: Microsoft C type **double** (IEEE) binary floating-point format (8 bytes).

msbin: Microsoft BASIC **double** binary floating-point type (8 bytes).

Return Value

Nonzero (true) if an error encountered

Zero (false) if conversion successful

Example

```
/* FILE: ch20e3.c */
#include <stdio.h>
#include <math.h>
#define FLT 4
#define DBL 8

union utag{unsigned char ch[8];
    float fv;
    double dv;} uf;

static void printx(const char *label, int bcnt, union utag *ptr)
{
int i;
printf("\n%s ", label);
for (i=0; i<bcnt; i++) printf("%02.2X", ptr->ch[i]);
}

int main(void)
{
float cfloat, ieeefloat, msbinfloat;
double cdouble, ieeedouble, msbindouble;

printf("\nEnter a C float type value: ");
scanf("%f", &cfloat);
printf("\nEnter a C double type value: ");
scanf("%lf", &cdouble);
```

```
fieeetomsbin(&cfloat, &msbinfloat);
fmsbintoieee(&msbinfloat, &ieeefloat);
printf("\n\ncfloat: %f", cfloat);
uf.fv= cfloat;
printx("cfloat:", FLT, &uf);
uf.fv= ieeefloat;
printx(" ieee:", FLT, &uf);
uf.fv= msbinfloat;
printx(" msbin:", FLT, &uf);

dieeetomsbin(&cdouble, &msbindouble);
dmsbintoieee(&msbindouble, &ieeedouble);
printf("\n\ncdouble: %lf", cdouble);
uf.dv= cdouble;
printx("cdouble:", DBL, &uf);
uf.dv= ieeedouble;
printx("   ieee:", DBL, &uf);
uf.dv= msbindouble;
printx("  msbin:", DBL, &uf);
exit(0);
}
```

Output

```
Enter a C float type value: 511.375
Enter a C double type value: 511.375

cfloat: 511.375000
cfloat: 00B0FF43
  ieee: 00B0FF43
 msbin: 00B07F89

cdouble: 511.375000
cdouble: 0000000000F67F40
   ieee: 0000000000F67F40
  msbin: 0000000000B07F89
```

Comments   Does not handle IEEE NAN (not-a-number) and infinity values.

The hexadecimal character strings shown in the example above must be reordered to reflect the logical ordering of bits within types **float** and **double** (see Figures 11.1 and 11.2) as follows:

```
cfloat: 43FFB000
  ieee: 43FFB000
 msbin: 897FB000

cdouble: 407FF60000000000
   ieee: 407FF60000000000
  msbin: 897FB00000000000
```

Notice the bit pattern differences between the IEEE (**ieee**) and Microsoft (**msbin**) binary floating-point formats.

dmsbintoieee ()   *Convert between Microsoft type* double *and IEEE format*

Compatibility   ☐ ANSI   ■ OS/2   ☐ UNIX   ☐ XENIX

See Also

```
dieeetomsbin(), fmsbintoieee()
```

Specification

```
#include <math.h>
int dmsbintoieee(double *msbin, double *ieee);
```

Arguments

msbin: Microsoft's BASIC **double** binary floating-point type (8 bytes).

ieee: Microsoft C type **double** (IEEE) binary floating-point format (8 bytes).

Return Value

Nonzero (true) if an error encountered

Zero (false) if conversion successful

Example   See: **dieeetomsbin()**.

Comments   Does not handle IEEE NAN (not-a-number) and infinity values.

ecvt ()   *Convert type* double *to a string*

Compatibility   ☐ ANSI   ■ OS/2   ■ UNIX   ■ XENIX

See Also

```
fcvt(), gcvt(), printf(), sprintf()
```

Specification

```
#include <stdlib.h>
char *ecvt(double value, int count, int *dec, int *sign);
```

Arguments

value: Type **double** to be converted.

count: Maximum number of digits in the returned string.

dec: Zero or negative, then decimal point lies to the left of the first string character; otherwise, to the right.

sign: If zero, positive; otherwise, negative.

Return Value

A pointer to a null-terminated character string

No error return code

Example   See: `atof()`.

Comments   If the actual number of digits exceeds *count*, the low-order digit is rounded; otherwise the string is padded with zeroes.

Only digits are placed into the string; the *dec* and *sign* arguments complete the floating-point description.

Each call to `ecvt()` destroys the statically allocated string buffer shared by `fcvt()`.

fcvt ()   *Convert type* double *value to a string*

Compatibility   ☐ ANSI   ■ OS/2   ■ UNIX   ■ XENIX

See Also

`ecvt(), gcvt(), printf(), sprintf()`

Specification

```
#include <stdlib.h>
char *fcvt(double value, int count, int *dec, int *sign);
```

Arguments

value: Type **double** to be converted

count: Maximum number of digits in the returned string

dec: Zero or negative, then decimal point lies to the left of the first string character; otherwise, to the right

sign: If zero, positive; otherwise, negative

Return Value

A pointer to a null-terminated character string

No error return code

Example   See: `atof()`.

Comments If the actual number of digits exceeds **count**, the low-order digit is rounded; otherwise the string is padded with zeroes.

Only digits are placed into the string; the **dec** and **sign** arguments complete the floating-point description.

Each call to **fcvt()** destroys the statically allocated string buffer shared with **ecvt()**.

fieeetomsbin()   *Convert between IEEE and Microsoft type* `float` *format*

Compatibility ☐ANSI   ■OS/2   ☐UNIX   ☐XENIX

See Also

```
dieeetomsbin(), fmsbintoieee()
```

Specification

```
#include <math.h>
int fieeetomsbin(float *ieee, float *msbin);
```

Arguments

ieee: Microsoft C type **float** (IEEE) binary floating-point format (4 bytes).

msbin: Microsoft BASIC binary floating-point type **float** (4 bytes).

Return Value

Nonzero (true) if an error encountered

Zero (false) if conversion successful

Example See: **dieeetomsbin()**.

Comments Does not handle IEEE NAN (not-a-number) and infinity values.

fmsbintoieee()   *Convert between Microsoft type* `float` *and IEEE format*

Compatibility ☐ANSI   ■OS/2   ☐UNIX   ☐XENIX

See Also

```
dmsbintoieee(), fieeetomsbin()
```

Specification

```
#include <math.h>
int fmsbintoieee(float *msbin, float *ieee);
```

Arguments

msbin: Microsoft BASIC binary floating-point type **float** format (4 bytes).

ieee: Microsoft C type **float** (IEEE) binary floating-point format (4 bytes).

Return Value

Nonzero (true) if an error encountered

Zero (false) if conversion successful

Example   See: **dieeetomsbin()**.

Comments   Does not handle IEEE NAN (not-a-number) and infinity values.

gcvt ()   *Convert type* double *to a string*

Compatibility ☐ANSI ■OS/2 ■UNIX ■XENIX

See Also

```
ecvt(), fcvt(), printf(), sprintf()
```

Specification

```
#include <stdlib.h>
char *gcvt(double value, int digits, char *buffer);
```

Arguments

value: Type **double** to be converted.

digits: Number of significant digits in the returned string or buffer.

buffer: User-supplied pointer to a character storage array.

Return Value

A pointer to a null-terminated character string, same as **buffer**

No error return code

Example   See: **atof()**.

Comments **buffer** should be large enough to hold the result plus the terminating null character (`'\0'`).

If **buffer** is too small, an exponential form of **value** is placed into **buffer**. Unlike **fcvt()** and **ecvt()**, this function requires the user to supply a **buffer**, and the **buffer** contains both a sign and decimal point.

isxx ()   *Test for specific types of characters*

Compatibility   See individual entries.

Specification

```
#include <ctype.h>
int isxx (int c)
```

Arguments

   c: Integer (character) value.

Return Value

   Zero if false

   Nonzero if true

Example

```
/* FILE: ch20e4.c */
#include <stdio.h>
#include <ctype.h>
int main(void)
{
int ch;
for (ch=0; ch<=0x7F; ch++) {
    printf("%2x ", ch);
    printf(" %s", isalnum(ch)  ? "ALN" : "   ");
    printf(" %s", isalpha(ch)  ? "ALP" : "   ");
    printf(" %s", isascii(ch)  ? "ASC" : "   ");
    printf(" %s", iscntrl(ch)  ? "CNT" : "   ");
    printf(" %s", iscsym(ch)   ? "CSY" : "   ");
    printf(" %s", iscsymf(ch)  ? "CSF" : "   ");
    printf(" %s", isdigit(ch)  ? "DIG" : "   ");
    printf(" %s", isgraph(ch)  ? "GRA" : "   ");
    printf(" %s", islower(ch)  ? "LOW" : "   ");
    printf(" %s", isprint(ch)  ? "PRI" : "   ");
    printf(" %s", ispunct(ch)  ? "PUN" : "   ");
    printf(" %s", isspace(ch)  ? "WSP" : "   ");
    printf(" %s", isupper(ch)  ? "UPR" : "   ");
    printf(" %s", isxdigit(ch) ? "HEX" : "   ");
    printf("\n");
    }
exit(0);
}
```

Output

```
0              ASC CNT
.
.
30  ALN    ASC     YM     DIG GRA     PRI           HEX
.
.
5f         ASC  YM YMF      GRA     PRI PUN
.
.
61  ALN ALP ASC    YM YMF     GRA LOW PRI           HEX
.
.
7f         ASC CNT
```

Comments The ASCII character set is assumed, and the following tests are applied:

isalnum: Is it an alphanumeric character ('A'–'Z', 'a'–'z', '0'–'9')?

isalpha: Is it an alphabetic character ('A'–'Z', 'a'–'z')?

isascii: Is it an ASCII character (0x00–0x7F)?

iscntrl: Is it a control character (0x00–0x1F, 0x7F)?

iscsym: Is it an alphanumeric C identifier, including underscore (0x5F)?

iscsymf: Is it an alphabetic C identifier, including underscore (0x5F)?

isdigit: Is it a numeric character ('0'–'9')?

isgraph: Is it printable, except white space (0x21–0x7E)?

islower: Is it lowercase alphabetic ('a'–'z')?

isprint: Is it printable, including space (0x20–0x7E)?

ispunct: Is it punctuation (0x21–0x2F, 0x3A–0x40, 0x5B–0x60, 0x7B–0x7E)?

isspace: Is it white space (0x09–0x0D, 0x20)?

isupper: Is it uppercase alphabetic ('A'–'Z') isxdigit?

isxdigit: Is it hexadecimal ('A'–'F', 'a'–'f', '0'–'9')?

As an alternative, all functions in this group are also available as function-like macros.

isalnum()   *Is a character value an alphanumeric character?*

Compatibility ■ANSI   ■OS/2   ■UNIX   ■XENIX

See Also

isxx()

Specification

```
#include <ctype.h>
int isalnum(int c);
```

isalpha() *Is a character value an alphabetic character?*

Compatibility ■ANSI ■OS/2 ■UNIX ■XENIX

See Also

isxx()

Specification

```
#include <ctype.h>
int isalpha(int c);
```

isascii() *Is a character value an ASCII character?*

Compatibility □ANSI ■OS/2 ■UNIX ■XENIX

See Also

isxx()

Specification

```
#include <ctype.h>
int isascii(int c);
```

iscntrl() *Is a character value a control character?*

Compatibility ■ANSI ■OS/2 ■UNIX ■XENIX

See Also

isxx()

Specification

```
#include <ctype.h>
int iscntrl(int c);
```

`iscsym()`   *Is a character value an alphanumeric C identifier?*

Compatibility   ☐ ANSI   ■ OS/2   ☐ UNIX   ☐ XENIX

See Also

iszz()

Specification

```
#include <ctype.h>
int iscsym(int c);
```

`iscsymf()`   *Is a character value an alphabetic C identifier?*

Compatibility   ☐ ANSI   ■ OS/2   ☐ UNIX   ☐ XENIX

See Also

iszz()

Specification

```
#include <ctype.h>
int iscsymf(int c);
```

`isdigit()`   *Is a character value a numeric?*

Compatibility   ■ ANSI   ■ OS/2   ■ UNIX   ■ XENIX

See Also

iszz()

Specification

```
#include <ctype.h>
int isdigit(int c);
```

`isgraph()`   *Is a character value printable, except white space?*

Compatibility   ■ ANSI   ■ OS/2   ■ UNIX   ■ XENIX

See Also

iszz()

Specification

```
#include <ctype.h>
int isgraph(int c);
```

islower() *Is a character value a lowercase alphabetic?*

Compatibility ■ANSI ■OS/2 ■UNIX ■XENIX

See Also

```
isxx()
```

Specification

```
#include <ctype.h>
int islower(int c);
```

isprint() *Is a character value printable, including space?*

Compatibility ■ANSI ■OS/2 ■UNIX ■XENIX

See Also

```
isxx()
```

Specification

```
#include <ctype.h>
int isprint (int c);
```

ispunct() *Is a character value punctuation?*

Compatibility ■ANSI ■OS/2 ■UNIX ■XENIX

See Also

```
isxx()
```

Specification

```
#include <ctype.h>
int ispunct(int c);
```

`isspace ()`   *Is a character value C white space?*

Compatibility   ■ANSI   ■OS/2   ■UNIX   ■XENIX

See Also

```
isxx()
```

Specification

```
#include <ctype.h>
int isspace(int c);
```

`isupper ()`   *Is a character value uppercase alphabetic?*

Compatibility   ■ANSI   ■OS/2   ■UNIX   ■XENIX

See Also

```
isxx()
```

Specification

```
#include <ctype.h>
int isupper(int c);
```

`isxdigit ()`   *Is a character value a hexadecimal digit?*

Compatibility   ■ANSI   ■OS/2   ■UNIX   ■XENIX

See Also

```
isxx()
```

Specification

```
#include <ctype.h>
int isxdigit(int c);
```

`itoa ()`   *Convert a type* `int` *value*

Compatibility   □ANSI   ■OS/2   □UNIX   □XENIX

See Also

```
ltoa(), printf(), sprintf(), ultoa()
```

Specification

```
#include <stdlib.h>
char *itoa(int value, char *string, int radix);
```

Arguments

value: Integer value to be converted.

string: Pointer to a character storage array.

radix: The base number system of value, a value from 2–36.

Return Value

A pointer to a null-terminated character string, the same as **string**

No error return code

Example

See: **atoi()**.

Comments

String may contain up to 17 characters, excluding the terminating null ('/0').

Only when **radix** equals 10 will a minus sign be generated if **value** is negative.

_lrotl() *Rotate the bits in a type int value to the left*

Compatibility ☐ANSI ■OS/2 ☐UNIX ☐XENIX

See Also

```
_lrotr(), _rotl
```

Specification

```
#include <stdlib.h>
unsigned long _lrotl(unsigned long value, int shift);
```

Arguments

value: An **unsigned long** type whose bits are to be rotated.

shift: A positive number of bit shifts.

Return Value

The rotated **unsigned long** value

Example

```
/* FILE: ch20e5.c */
#include <stdio.h>
#include <stdlib.h>
```

```
int main(void)
{
unsigned int ival = 0x4F00, tival;
unsigned long lval = 0x004FF400, tlval;

printf("\n ival= %04.4X", ival);
tival = _rotr(ival, 8);
printf("\ntival= %04.4X", tival);
ival = _rotl(tival, 8);
printf("\n ival= %04.4X", ival);
tival= 0x0;
swab( (char *)&ival, (char *)&tival, 4);
printf("\nsival= %04.4X", tival);

printf("\n lval= %08.8lX", lval);
tlval = _lrotl(lval, 16);
printf("\ntlval= %08.8lX", tlval);
lval = _lrotr(tlval, 16);
printf("\n lval= %08.8lX", lval);
tlval=0x0;

swab( (char *)&lval, (char *)&tlval, 8);
printf("\nslval= %08.8lX", tlval);
exit(0);
}
```

Output

```
 ival= 4F00
tival= 004F
 ival= 4F00
sival= 004F
 lval= 004FF400
tlval= F400004F
 lval= 004FF400
slval= 4F0000F4
```

Comments   Bit rotation involves wrapping bits rotated off one end of the byte or word to the other end (see the example).

As an alternative to the function, you can use the **#pragma intrinsic** form.

_lrotr ()   *Rotate the bits in a type* long *value to the right*

Compatibility   ☐ANSI   ■OS/2   ☐UNIX   ☐XENIX

See Also

```
_lrotl(), _rotr()
```

Specification

```
#include <stdlib.h>
unsigned long _lrotr(unsigned long value, int shift);
```

Arguments

value: An unsigned type **long** value whose bits are to be rotated.

shift: A positive number of bit shifts.

Return Value

The rotated **unsigned long** value

Example

See: **_lrotl()**.

Comments

Bit rotation involves wrapping bits rotated off one end to the other end (see the example).

As an alternative to the function, you can use the **#pragma intrinsic** form.

ltoa () *Convert a type int value to a character string*

Compatibility

□ ANSI ■ OS/2 □ UNIX □ XENIX

See Also

```
printf(), sprintf(), ultoa()
```

Specification

```
#include <stdlib.h>
char *ltoa(long value, char *string, int radix);
```

Arguments

value: **long** value to be converted.

string: Pointer to a character storage array.

radix: The base number system of value, a value from 2 to 36.

Return Value

Pointer to a null-terminated character string, same as *string*

No error return code

Example

See: **atoi()**.

Comments

string may contain up to 33 characters, excluding the terminating null ('/0').

Only when the **radix** equals 10 will a minus sign be generated if **value** is negative.

_rotl()   *Rotate the bits in a type* int *value*

Compatibility   ☐ ANSI   ■ OS/2   ☐ UNIX   ☐ XENIX

See Also

```
_lrotl(), _rotr()
```

Specification

```
#include <stdlib.h>
unsigned int _rotl(unsigned int value, int shift);
```

Arguments

value: An **unsigned int** whose bits are to be rotated.

shift: A positive number of bit shifts.

Return Value

The rotated **unsigned int** value

Example   See: **_lrotl()**.

Comments   Bit rotation involves wrapping bits rotated off one end of the byte or word to the other end (see the example).

As an alternative to the function, you can use the **#pragma intrinsic** form.

_rotr()   *Rotate the bits in a type* int *value to the right*

Compatibility   ☐ ANSI   ■ OS/2   ☐ UNIX   ☐ XENIX

See Also

```
_lrotr(), _rotl()
```

Specification

```
#include <stdlib.h>
unsigned int _rotr(unsigned int value, int shift);
```

Arguments

value: An **unsigned int** whose bits are to be rotated.

shift: A positive number of bit shifts.

Return Value

The rotated **unsigned int** value

Example

See: `_lrotl()`.

Comments

Bit rotation involves wrapping bits rotated off one end to the other end (see the example).

As an alternative to the function, you can use the **#pragma intrinsic** form.

`sprintf()` *Formatted write to a string*

Compatibility ■ANSI ■OS/2 ■UNIX ■XENIX

See Also

`printf()`

Specification

```
#include <stdio.h>
int sprintf(char *string, const char *format, ...);
```

Arguments

string: Pointer to a character storage array.

format: Format control string; refer to Table 17.4.

. . .: Variable number of arguments.

Return Value

Number of characters written if successful

Negative value if unsuccessful

Example

```
/* FILE: ch20e6.c */
#include <stdio.h>
#include <stdarg.h>

static void printx(const char *format, ...)
{
char buffer[40];
va_list ptr;
va_start(ptr, format);
vsprintf(buffer, format, ptr);
printf("\nbuffer= %s", buffer);
}
```

```
int main(void)
{
char string1[] = "10 test 100 1.25 2.4e60";
char string2[40], ch[5];
int iv;
long int lv;
float fv;
double dv;

sscanf(string1, "%d%s%ld%f%lf", &iv, ch, &lv, &fv, &dv);
printf("\nch= %s", ch);
printf("\niv= %d\tlv= %ld", iv, lv);
printf("\nfv= %f\tdv= %g", fv, dv);

sprintf(string2, "%g %f %ld %d %s", dv, fv, lv, iv, ch);
printf("\nstring2= %s", string2);
sscanf(string2, "%s%f", ch, &fv);
printf("\nch= %s\nfv= %f", ch, fv);

printx( "%d %s %ld %f %g", iv, "test", lv, fv, dv);
exit(0);
}
```

Output

```
ch= test
iv= 10        lv= 100
fv= 1.250000        dv= 2.4e+060
string2= 2.4e+060 1.250000 100 10 test
ch= 2.4e+060
fv= 1.250000
buffer= 10 test 100 1.250000 2.4e+060
```

Comments All C data-type formats may be converted from internal to character strings using the **printf()** family format control strings described in Table 17.4.

Notice in the example how the order of the values in **string 1[]** was changed in **string2[]**, then interpreted, and finally reconstructed using **printx()**.

sscanf()   *Formatted read from a string*

Compatibility ■ANSI   ■OS/2   ■UNIX   ■XENIX

See Also

```
scanf()
```

Specification

```
#include <stdio.h>
int sscanf(const char *string, const char *format, ...);
```

Arguments

string: Pointer to a character array.

format: Format control string; refer to Table 17.3.

. . .: Variable number of arguments.

Return Value

Number of fields successfully converted and assigned

Zero if no fields were read;

EOF (−1) if end of string encountered

Example   See: `sprintf()`.

Comments   All C data-type formats may be converted from character strings using the `printf()` family format control strings described in Table 17.3.

Notice in the example that each time `sscanf()` is used to read data from string, it begins processing from the beginning of the string.

`strtod()`   *Convert a character string to type* `double`

Compatibility   ■ANSI   ■OS/2   ■UNIX   ■XENIX

See Also

`atof()`, `_atold()`, `scanf()`, `sscanf()`, `_strtold()`

Specification

```
#include <stdlib.h>
double strtod(const char *string, char **end);
```

Arguments

string: Pointer to a character array.

end: If end is not **NULL**, then a pointer to the character that stopped the scan is stored in end.

Return Value

The converted floating-point number

Zero if no conversion or an underflow occurred

+/− HUGE (see **<math.h>**) if overflow occurred.

Example   See: `atof()`.

Comments *string* may contain up to 100 characters, excluding the terminating null (`'/0'`).

If an overflow or underflow occurs, global variable **errno** is set to ERANGE.

Conversion follows the rules established for the control strings used for floating-point types with the **scanf()** family of functions (see Chapter 17).

strtol() *Convert a character string to type* int

Compatibility ■ANSI   ■OS/2   ■UNIX   ■XENIX

See Also

atoi(), atol(), scanf() sscanf(), strtoul()

Specification

```
#include <stdlib.h>
long strtol(const char *string, char **end, int radix);
```

Arguments

string: Pointer to a character array.

end: If end is not **NULL**, then a pointer to the character that stopped the scan is stored in end.

radix: The base number system of value, a value from 2 to 36.

Return Value

The converted **long** or **unsigned long** number

Zero if no conversion occurred

+/− **LONG_MAX** (see **<limits.h>**) if overflow occurred

Example   See: **atoi()**.

Comments *string* may contain up to 33 characters, excluding the terminating null (`'/0'`).

If an overflow or underflow occurs, global variable **errno** is set to ERANGE.

Conversion follows the rules established for the control strings used for integer types with the **scanf()** family of functions (see Chapter 17).

_strtold() *Convert a character string to type* long double

Compatibility □ANSI   ■OS/2   ■UNIX   ■XENIX

See Also

```
atof(), _atold(), sscanf(), scanf(), _strtod()
```

Specification

```
#include <stdlib.h>
long double _strtold(const char *string, char **end);
```

Arguments

string: Pointer to a character array.

end: If end is not **NULL**, then a pointer to the character that stopped the scan is stored in end.

Return Value

The converted floating-point number

Zero if no conversion or an underflow occurred

$+/-$ **_LHUGE** (see **<math.h>**) if overflow occurred

Example   See: **atof()**.

Comments   *string* may contain up to 100 characters, excluding the terminating null (**'/0'**).

If an overflow or underflow occurs, global variable **errno** is set to ERANGE.

Conversion follows the rules established for the control strings used for floating-point types with the **scanf()** family of functions (see Chapter 17).

strtoul ()   *Convert a character string to type* unsigned long

Compatibility   ■ANSI   ■OS/2   □UNIX   □XENIX

See Also

```
atol(), scanf(), sscanf(), strtol()
```

Specification

```
#include <stdlib.h>
unsigned long strtoul(const char *string, char **end, int radix);
```

Arguments

string: Pointer to a character array.

end: If end is not **NULL**, then a pointer to the character that stopped the scan is stored in end.

radix: The base number system of value, a value from 2–36.

Return Value

The converted **long** or **unsigned long** number

Zero if no conversion occurred

ULONG_MAX (see **<limits.h>**) if overflow occurred

Example   See: **atoi()**.

Comments   *string* may contain up to 33 characters, excluding the terminating null (**'/0'**).

If an overflow or underflow occurs, global variable **errno** is set to **ERANGE**.

Conversion follows the rules established for the control strings used for integer types with the **scanf()** family of functions (see Chapter 17).

swab()   *Swaps adjacent memory byte values*

Compatibility   □ANSI   ■OS/2   ■UNIX   ■XENIX

Specification

```
#include <stdlib.h>
void swab(char *source, char *dest, int nbytes);
```

Arguments

source: Pointer to a character array.

dest: Pointer to a destination array.

nbytes: Even number of bytes from source to be swapped and copied to **dest**.

Return Value   None

Example   See: **_lrotl()**.

Comments   This function is usually used to prepare binary data for transfer between big-endian (Motorola 680*x*0) and little-endian (Intel 80*x*86) machines.

As an alternative, you can use a union of **unsigned** character array and a C data-object type.

toxx()   *Convert specific types of characters*

Compatibility   See individual entries.

Specification

```
#include <ctype.h>
int toxx(int c);
```

Arguments

c: Integer (character) value.

Return Value

The converted character value

There are no error codes

Example

```
/* FILE: ch20e7.c */
#include <stdio.h>
#include <ctype.h>
#include <string.h>
int main(void)
{
char string[80], buffer[80];
int i, j, nbr, size;
char *labels[] = {"tolower", "toupper", "toascii",
    "_tolower", "_toupper"};
printf("\nEnter a string: ");
gets(string);
printf("\n\nInput string: %s", string);
size = strlen(string);
nbr= sizeof(labels)/sizeof(labels[0]);
for (i=0, j=0; j<nbr; j++, i=0) {
    printf("\n\nUsing %s:", labels[j]);
    while (string[i]) {
        switch (j) {
            case 0: buffer[i]= tolower(string[i]);
                break;
            case 1: buffer[i]= toupper(string[i]);
                break;
            case 2: buffer[i]= toascii(string[i]);
                break;
            case 3: buffer[i]=_tolower(string[i]);
                break;
            case 4: buffer[i]=_toupper(string[i]);
                break;
            }
        i++;
        }
    buffer[i]='\0';
    printf("\n\t");
    for(i=0; i<size; i++) printf("%c",buffer[i]);
    }
exit(0);
}
```

Output

```
Enter a string: THIS IS a TEST

Input string: THIS IS a TEST

Using tolower:
    this is a test

Using toupper:
    THIS IS A TEST

Using toascii:
    THIS IS A TEST

Using _tolower:
    this@is@a@test

Using _toupper:
    4()3)3A4%34{88
```

Comments   The ASCII character set is assumed, and the following conversions are applied:

toascii: All bits except the low-order 7 bits (bit 0 thru bit 6) are turned off (c &= 0x007F)

tolower: "safe" upper- to lowercase alphabetic conversion

_tolower: C must be uppercase or conversion is undefined

toupper: "safe" lower- to uppercase alphabetic conversion

_toupper: C must be lowercase or conversion is undefined

Notice in the program example the number of invalid conversions that were made. Remember that you can enter any character not directly available on the keyboard by pressing the Alt key, typing the equivalent ASCII value on the numeric keypad, and then releasing the Alt key.

As an alternative, each function is also available in a macro version.

toascii()   *Convert an integer value to ASCII*

Compatibility   ☐ANSI   ■OS/2   ■UNIX   ■XENIX

See Also

toxx()

Specification

```
#include <ctype.h>
int toascii(int c);
```

Comments   As an alternative, this function is available as a macro.

tolower()   *Convert an integer value to lowercase*

Compatibility   ■ANSI   ■OS/2   ■UNIX   ■XENIX

See Also
> to*xx*()

Specification
```
#include <ctype.h>
int tolower(int c);
```

Comments   As an alternative, this function is available as a macro.

_tolower()   *Convert an uppercase character to lowercase*

Compatibility   □ANSI   ■OS/2   ■UNIX   ■XENIX

See Also
> to*xx*()

Specification
```
#include <ctype.h>
int _tolower(int c);
```

Comments   As an alternative, this function is available as a macro.

toupper()   *Convert an integer value to uppercase*

Compatibility   ■ANSI   ■OS/2   ■UNIX   ■XENIX

See Also
> to*xx*()

Specification
```
#include <ctype.h>
int toupper(int c);
```

Comments   As an alternative, this function is available as a macro.

_toupper ()   *Convert a lowercase character to uppercase*

Compatibility   □ANSI   ■OS/2   ■UNIX   ■XENIX

See Also

toxx()

Specification

```
#include <ctype.h>
int _toupper(int c);
```

Comments   As an alternative, this function is available as a macro.

ultoa ()   *Convert an* unsigned long *to a character string*

Compatibility   □ANSI   ■OS/2   □UNIX   □XENIX

See Also

ltoa(), printf(), sprintf()

Specification

```
#include <stdlib.h>
char *ultoa(unsigned long value, char *string, int radix);
```

Arguments

value: unsigned long value to be converted.

string: Pointer to a character storage array.

radix: The base number system of value, a value from 2–36.

Return Value

A pointer to a null-terminated character string, same as string

No error return code

Example   See: atoi().

Comments   *string* may contain up to 33 characters, excluding the terminating null ('/0').

Only for the case where the **radix** equals 10 will a minus sign be generated if value is negative.

Conversion follows the rules established for the control strings used for integer types with the **scanf()** family of functions (see Chapter 17).

vsprintf() *Formatted write to a string*

Compatibility ■ANSI ■OS/2 ■UNIX ■XENIX

See Also

```
printf()
```

Specification

```
#include <stdio.h>
#include <stdarg.h>
int vsprintf(char *string, const char *format, va_list argptr);
```

Arguments

string: Pointer to a character storage array.

format: Format control string; refer to Chapter 17.

argptr: Pointer to a variable length argument list.

Return Value

Number of characters written if successful

Negative value if unsuccessful

Example   See: **sprintf()**.

Comments   Identical to **sprintf()**, except that the argument list specified is a pointer to a variable length argument list, not an argument list.

All C data-type formats may be converted from internal to character strings using the **printf()** family format control strings described in Table 17.4.

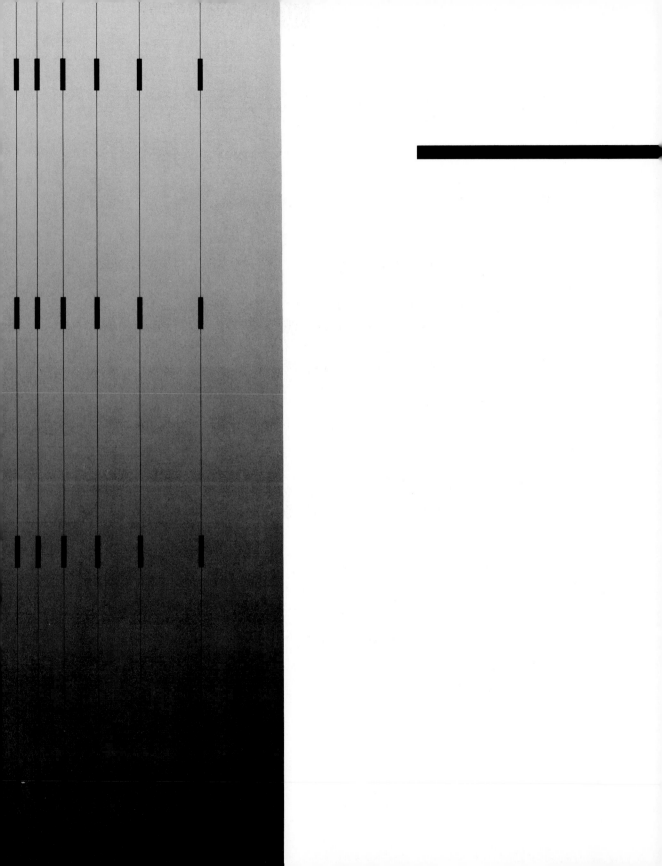

# CHAPTER 21

Date and Time Management Functions

Date and Time Management Functions

As fundamental as dates and times are in our everyday lives, it is somewhat surprising how complicated it is to maintain accurate dates and times with a computer. Even more surprising is the degree to which these fundamental concepts are misunderstood. In this chapter you will find explanations of each run-time library function that supports the capture, conversion, and display of time, from which all date and time measures are derived. Existing documentation of the functions related to universal (GMT) time (`time()`, `localtime()`, `gmtime()`, and `mktime()`) have been notoriously misleading and incorrect over the years. Hopefully, these inaccuracies have finally been put to rest. The example programs provided in this chapter demonstrate the proper use of these functions and detail the relationships that exist between the global variables `daylight`, `timezone`, and `tzname[]`, and environment string TZ=. They also explain how computer, local, and universal times are calculated.

Before proceeding, it is prudent to reemphasize the importance of maintaining correct DOS system date and time settings, as well as the proper string definition for environment variable TZ= (refer to Chapter 1). The DOS system date and time setting should always be set to reflect local time, relative to 00:00:00 (midnight), and the TZ= string should define the corresponding standard time zone location and whether daylight saving time is in effect. It is from the TZ= string definition that the DOS global variables are derived (see Appendix C) and upon which all universal time is dependent.

For example, 5:00 PM in any time zone, whether standard or daylight saving time, should be expressed as 17:00:00 (hh:mm:ss). The values of `daylight` and `timezone` control how a computer's measure of time is adjusted to display local or universal dates and times. Failure to adhere to these DOS conventions invalidates the use of all universal date and time functions discussed in this chapter.

Let's begin by reviewing how a computer measures time in order to understand the fundamental mechanisms that support the recording, translation, and display of date and time.

COMPUTER TIME

All system date and time measures available under DOS are derived from either the 8253 timer (oscillator) chip, or a real-time (battery-supported) clock if one is installed and operating. Although real-time clocks provide additional features beyond those of the 8253 timer (broader range of dates, alarm functions, and alternate timing resolution), each replicates the capabilities of the 8253 chip. The 8253 timer was first discussed in Chapter 19 in the example program for the **inp()** function that used the timer to drive the speaker port to produce sound.

The 8253 timer oscillates at 1,193,180 Hz (cycles/second), or 1.19 MHz (million cycles/second), with a built-in divisor of 65,536, and emits a BIOS interrupt 0x08 (see Chapter 22) 18.2 times per second, or about every 0.055 seconds. Real-time clocks match this rate. BIOS interrupt 0x08 maintains a count of such interrupts, hereafter referred to as timer *ticks,* from the point that a system is powered-on up to an elapsed period of one day, at which time the Carry Flag is set on, and the tick count is reset to zero.

The following table summarizes the tick constants used by the BIOS to measure units of time.

TIME	TICKS	CALCULATION
Second	18	(1,193,180/65,536)
Minute	1092	(1,193,180/65,536) * 60
Hour	65,543	(1,193,180/65,536) * 60 * 60
Day	1,573,040	(1,193,180/65,536) * 60 * 60 * 24

The timer tick count maintained by BIOS interrupt 0x08, whether by the 8253 chip or a real-time clock, is available directly using the **bios_timeofday()** function. Because of the 48-hour limitation (24 hours + overflow flag) of BIOS interrupt 0x08, another mechanism is needed if dates derived from an elapsed time measured in ticks are to be maintained.

DOS DATE AND TIME

A DOS clock device driver or a real-time clock implements these additional services using BIOS interrupt 0x1A. If a real-time clock is not installed, DOS relies on a clock device driver to maintain the current system date and time. The DOS commands DATE and TIME (see Chapter 1) and DOS interrupt 0x21 (see Table 22.4) maintain the following fields of information, based on a combination of user input and the current number of ticks measured by BIOS interrupt 0x08.

FIELD	DESCRIPTION
2 bytes	Days (since 1/1/1980)
1 byte	Hours (0–23)
1 byte	Minutes (0–59)
1 byte	Seconds (0–59)
1 byte	1/100 seconds (0–99)

This data structure represents the DOS system date and time, and is typically initialized by using DOS commands DATE and TIME. These commands alter the clock device driver data structure values, noted above, and the timer tick count, using either DOS interrupt 0x21 timer services (functions 0x2A–0x2D) or the underlying BIOS interrupt 0x1A. This structure enforces the following valid ranges for all dates and times:

Dates: 1/1/1980 through 12/31/2099 (mm/dd/yy)

Times: 00:00:00 through 23:59:59 (hh:mm:ss)

If a real-time clock is installed, the BIOS interrupt 0x1A automatically acquires and sets the DOS structure and provides additional services that read and set the real-time clock date and time. BIOS interrupt 0x50 can be used to set a periodic alarm; BIOS interrupt 0x70, the real-time clock interrupt counterpart of interrupt 0x08, offers tick rates other than 18.2 times/sec.

All date and time functions in the run-time library rely on the DOS clock device driver data structure, described above, to perform their stated tasks. For this reason, it is important to keep the system date and time always set properly and, as we will discover, also the string setting for the TZ= environment variable and the global variables `timezone`, `daylight`, and `tzname[]`. Even the DOS directory date and time fields discussed in Chapter 16 were derived from the DOS clock device driver. Now let's consider how a universal measure of date and time is implemented for DOS.

UNIVERSAL DATE AND TIME

To maintain compatibility with UNIX, several DOS run-time library functions and data structures are available that permit the underlying DOS clock device driver measures of time to support universal (GMT) time as well as standard and daylight saving time.

The concept of Greenwich Mean Time (GMT) assumes that each day begins at 00:00:00 (midnight) relative to the prime meridian (0° longitude) that passes through Greenwich, England. The globe is then divided into 24 hours, where every 15° (360°/24 hours) of longitude represents a distinct time zone and one hour away from the prime meridian. (In practice, of course, time zones are often adjusted to reflect national and provincial boundaries.) Time zones are measured positive from 0° to 180° west longitude, and negative from 0° to 180° east longitude, from the prime meridian. Because the sun is assumed to be at high noon at 12:00:00 at the prime meridian, the International Date Line, which demarcates the meeting point of the west and east longitudes, always begins a day (00:00:00) and ends a day (24:00:00).

The non-Standard DOS-specific global variables (**timezone**, **daylight**, and **tzname[]**) and environment string (TZ=) are used to implement universal GMT-based time and to provide a complement of UNIX-compatible functions within the DOS operating system. Each of the universal time functions relies upon these global variables (see Appendix C) to extrapolate the DOS clock device driver time to a universal measure of time.

These global variables assume default values based on an assumed TZ= string setting of

TZ=PST8PDT

established by the Microsoft Corporation (located in Redmond, WA) to reflect Pacific Daylight Time. Recall that the DOS SET command may be used to create, update, or delete an environment variable string (see Chapter 1), and that the string setting is case-sensitive. TIME is the DOS command always set to local time. Another method of setting the TZ= string would be to use the **putenv()** function introduced in Chapter 15 and described completely in Chapter 25. Several program examples in this chapter utilize function **putenv()**.

By convention, the TZ environment variable consists of three components, which are illustrated in the default example, PST8PDT, as follows:

PST: A three-character standard time zone abbreviation; for the United States the following abbreviations are used:

PST: Pacific standard time (120° west)

MST: Mountain standard time (105° west)

CST: Central standard time (90° west)

EST: Eastern standard time (75° west)

8: The number of whole hours, measured from the prime meridian; a positive value of 0 to 12 if west longitude, and 0 to -12 if east longitude. If it is positive, the plus sign may be omitted; if negative, the negative sign must be specified.

PDT: A three-character abbreviation used to designate daylight saving time is in effect for this time zone; for the United States, the following abbreviations are used:

PDT: Pacific daylight time

MDT: Mountain daylight time

CDT: Central daylight time

EDT: Eastern daylight time

If daylight saving time is not in effect, leave this field entirely blank.

The values for **timezone**, **daylight**, and **tzname[]** are derived as follows from the TZ= string when the run-time library function **tzset()** is called.

timezone: The number of seconds difference between the local time zone (meridian) and the Greenwich meridian, computed from the number of hours specified in the TZ= environment string as follows:

PST	8 hrs	(28,800 sec)
MST	7 hrs	(25,200 sec)
CST	6 hrs	(21,600 sec)
EST	5 hrs	(18,000 sec)

daylight: A flag that is set to zero if daylight saving time is not in effect (the three-character abbreviation was omitted); or 1, if daylight saving time is in effect (the three-character abbreviation was provided).

tzname[0]: Contains the three-character standard time zone descriptive string.

tzname[1]: Contains the three-character daylight saving time descriptive string, or a null string.

The global variables **timezone**, **daylight**, and **tzname[]** are automatically initialized to the following values by DOS, assuming the default TZ=PST8PDT environment variable setting:

timezone	28,800
daylight	1
tzname[0]	PST
tzname[1]	PDT

They may be updated using the run-time function **tzset()**, which interrogates the current TZ= enviroment variable string setting to establish new global variable values.

The universal (GMT) compatible functions are implemented using the DOS clock device driver information and the global variables **timezone**, **daylight**, and **tzname[]**. Each serves in its own way both to control and limit how these functions operate under DOS. For instance, although all universal time measures are recorded relative to January 1, 1970, all DOS dates still begin at January 1, 1980.

DATE AND TIME DATA TYPES

To dispel the confusion that exists surrounding the documentation of the run-time library functions described in this chapter, in the following subsections we will clarify the terminology and forms of data-type representation that are utilized which include:

- the use of hardware-generated ticks
- the Standard C definitions of type **clock_t** and **time_t**, and structure **tm** defined in **<time.h>**
- the Microsoft C definitions of structure **dosdate_t**, **dostime_t** defined in **<dos.h>**, and structure **timeb** defined in a header file **<sys\timeb>**
- the unique bit-oriented definitions of dates and times used by the DOS directory structure

Ticks

Whenever we speak of ticks, we are referring to the count of interrupts that are generated by the 8253 timer chip or real-time clock, and accumulated by the BIOS, as described in the earlier section "Computer Time."

For example, if you had a tick count of 66,733, using the BIOS constants described earlier, the measure of time would be calculated as follows:

1-hour: 66733 − (1 * 65,543) = 1190
1-min : 1190 − (1 * 1092) = 98
5-sec : 98 − (5 * 18) = 8 (8 * 0.055 = 0.42 sec) sec

This would yield a time of 01:01:05.42 in hh:mm:ss.hs format (see function **_bios_timeofday()**).

In a similar fashion, when using the **_bios_timeofday()** function to set the current tick count, the function argument ticks represent a time in seconds converted to ticks. To do this, simply divide the time in seconds by (1,193,180/65,536).

Standard C Time and Date Representations

Standard C defines two data-object types, **clock_t** and **time_t**, for representing data in **<time.h>**, and one data structure, **tm**.

clock_t

The Standard C **clock_t** type is defined as

```
typedef long clock_t;
```

and represents the elapsed process (program) time in seconds multiplied by the object-like macro **CLK_TCK** or **CLOCKS_PER_SEC**, which is set to 1000 for DOS in **<time.h>**.

For example, if you had a **clock_t** type value of 3,665,420, the actual number of seconds would equal

3,665,420/1000 = 3665.420 seconds

1 hour: 3665.420 − (1 * 3600) = 65.420
1 min : 65.420 − (1 * 60) = 5.420
5 sec : 5.420 − (5 * 1) = 0.420

This would yield a time of 01:01:05.42 in hh:mm:ss.hs format (see function **clock()**).

Since **clock_t** is implemented as type **long** for DOS and represents an elapsed time, all **clock_t** values will be positive numbers in the range of value from 0L through 2,147,483,647L. This represents elapsed times up to 2,147,483.647 seconds or, dividing by 86,400 seconds per day, approximately 24.8 days before overflow would occur.

time_t

This is the most widely misunderstood Standard C type. It supports the implementation of universal time and was first discussed in Chapter 16 with functions **fstat()**, **stat()**, and **utime()** and is defined as

```
typedef long time_t;
```

A **time_t** type represents the number of elapsed seconds since 00:00:00 (midnight) relative to 00:00:00 at the prime meridian (GMT) January 1, *1970,* for compatibility with UNIX, whereas all DOS dates are originated at January 1, *1980.* The basic equation that is used by function **time()** is as follows:

time_t = (elapsed time in seconds) + (adjustment)

where

adjustment = (**timezone**) − (**daylight** * 3600)

Global variable **daylight** may assume only a value of zero or 1. Remember that if daylight saving time is in effect (**tzname[1]** != null), one hour, or 3600 seconds, is subtracted to ensure that the actual elapsed time is correct.

Consider the date of April 5, 1990, and the local time of 16:37:04, relative to midnight, expressed in eastern daylight savings time (EDT), for which the environment variable has been set to TZ=EST5EDT and **tzset()** has been used to establish the global variables daylight=1 (hour) and timezone=18,000 (seconds).

To calculate the corresponding **time_t** value, first determine the (elapsed time in seconds) as follows:

years: 1990 − 1970 = 20 @ 365 days/year	=	7300 days
leap years: '72, '76, '80, '84, '88	=	5 days
months: 1990 JAN=31, FEB=28, MAR=31	=	90 days
days: APR 5	=	4 days
TOTAL	=	7399 days

seconds: (7399 days * 86400 sec/day)	=	639,273,600 sec
(16 hours * 3600 sec/hr)	=	57,600 sec
(37 minutes * 60 sec/min)	=	2220 sec
(4 seconds * 1 sec/sec)	=	4 sec
TOTAL	=	639,333,424 sec

Next, compute the adjustment as follows:

adjustment = (**timezone**) − (**daylight** * 3600)

or

adjustment = (18,000) − (1 * 3600) = 14400 sec

Finally complete the **time_t** equation as follows:

time_t = 639,333,424 + 14,400 = 639,347,824 seconds

The output produced by the example program for function **time()** verifies this calculation. Remember that **time_t** type values represent the actual elapsed time in seconds since January 1, 1970, relative to 00:00:00 (midnight) at Greenwich, England (prime meridian 0°).

Local Time Adjustments: Whenever a **time_t** value is displayed using function **ctime()**, the global variable **daylight** must be used to compensate for the effects of daylight saving time in order to display the local date and time properly. In the case of our preceding example, the **time_t** value actually represents

$$\text{time\_t} = 639{,}347{,}824 \text{ sec} = \text{APR-5-1990 } 15{:}37{:}04$$

relative to 00:00:00 GMT January 1, 1970, which represents EST (eastern standard time), not EDT (eastern daylight time). The **time_t** value must be adjusted by function **ctime()** as follows, based on the current value of global variable **daylight**.

$$\text{local } \text{time\_t} = (\text{time\_t}) + (\text{daylight} * 3660)$$

This yields the correct local time display:

$$\text{local } \text{time\_t} = 639{,}347{,}824 + 3600 = 639{,}351{,}424 \text{ sec}$$

or

APR-5-1990 16:37:04

When the **localtime()** function is used to create a **tm** structure, the same daylight saving time correction is applied to the **time_t** timer argument before the **tm** structure members are assigned. The **tm_isdst** member of **tm** structures is set accordingly by function **localtime()**, either to zero if standard time or to 1 if daylight saving time is in effect.

GMT Adjustments: When the **gmtime()** function is used to create a **tm** structure, however, a different adjustment equation is used to alter the **time_t** (timer) argument before the **tm** structure members are assigned.

$$\text{gmt } \text{time\_t} = (\text{time\_t}) + (\text{timezone})$$

This equation yields the correct Greenwich mean time (GMT) display:

$$\text{gmt } \text{time\_t} = 639{,}347{,}824 + 18{,}000 = 639{,}365{,}824 \text{ sec}$$

or

APR-5-1990 20:37:04

The **tm_isdst** member of **tm** structures created by function **gmtime()** is always set equal to zero.

mktime() *Adjustments:*   When the **mktime()** function is used to create a **time_t** type value from a **tm** structure, the structure members are interpreted as if they represent local time, regardless of how the **tm** structure was created—by using **localtime()**, **gmtime()**, or simply by assigning values to the members of a **tm** structure. As we will see, the calculation of a **time_t** value from a **tm** structure parallels the calculation of a **time_t** value from the DOS system date and time described above, but it also differs slightly.

Consider the program example and output included with function **mktime()**, which establishes the local time base as TZ=EST5 (eastern standard time) for the earliest possible valid DOS date, January 1, 1980 00:00:00. The output indicates that the **time_t** value for this date and time is 315,550,800 seconds. Let's verify the computation of this value using the formula developed earlier for **time_t**.

> **time_t** = (elapsed time in seconds) + (adjustment)
>
> where
>
> adjustment = (**timezone**) − (**daylight** * 3600)

First compute the elapsed time in seconds as follows:

years: 1980 − 1970 = 10 @ 365 days/year	=	3650 days
leap years: '72, '76	=	2 days
months: 1980	=	0 days
days: JAN 1	=	0 days
TOTAL	=	3652 days

seconds: (3652 days * 86,400 sec/day)	=	315,532,800 sec
(0 hours * 3600 sec/hr)	=	0 sec
(0 minutes * 60 sec/min)	=	0 sec
(0 seconds * 1 sec/sec)	=	0 sec
TOTAL	=	315,532,800 sec

Next, compute the (adjustment) as follows, with the replacement of the global variable **daylight** with **tm** structure member **tm_isdst** as follows:

> adjustment = (**timezone**) − (**tm_isdst** * 3600)

or

$$\text{adjustment} = (18,000) - (0 * 3600) = 18,000 \text{ sec}$$

Here member **tm_isdst** is only interpreted as zero (false) or 1 (true), based on the value entered, whereas any nonzero value is considered to be true. Now, complete the **time_t** equation as follows:

$$\textbf{time\_t} = 315,532,800 + 18,000 = 315,550,800 \text{ seconds}$$

This confirms the result shown in the program example.

Had the TZ=EST5 setting remained in effect and the **base.tm_isdst** member been set equal to 1, the **tm** structure would have been interpreted by function **mktime()** as if EDT had been used to express the local time values assigned to the **tm** structure-named base in the program example, and an invalid **time_t** value of 315,547,200 would have been calculated.

Had the **base.tm_hour** setting remained at zero, the program example would have exited with a status code value of 99 because a DOS date that preceded January 1, 1980 00:00:00 would have been generated. To overcome this problem, the **base.tm_hour** member would have to be set equal to 1, indicating that the daylight saving time expression of hour 00:00:00 is actually 1:00:00.

From these examples we can see that the **mktime()** function adjusts a **tm** structure local time description by the current **timezone** global variable value, based on the setting of member **tm_isdst**, not the global variable **daylight**.

struct tm

Whenever a **tm** structure is created using either the **localtime()** or **gmtime()** functions, the assigned member values are directly used for display purposes. The template of structure **tm** is defined as

```
struct tm {
    int tm_sec;        /* seconds after the minute - [0,59] */
    int tm_min;        /* minutes after the hour - [0,59]   */
    int tm_hour;       /* hours since midnight - [0,23]     */
    int tm_mday;       /* day of the month - [1,31]         */
    int tm_mon;        /* months since January - [0,11]     */
    int tm_year;       /* years since 1900                  */
    int tm_wday;       /* days since Sunday - [0,6]         */
    int tm_yday;       /* days since January 1 - [0,365]    */
    int tm_isdst; };   /* daylight saving time flag         */
```

in **<time.h>** as shown in Appendix E. Display functions **asctime()** and **strftime()** do not perform adjustments to these member values, although they do verify that all member values fall within their assigned allowable range of values.

If you define a **tm** structure and assign values to its members that are outside of the normal range of value, the member values are first "normalized," or adjusted, so that each member value falls within the allowable range before it is displayed. Although typically the **localtime()** function is used to create a **tm** structure for which select members are altered, in the program example included with the **mktime()** function, a **tm** structure was initialized with values that subsequently were modified with normal and abnormal values.

The value of the **tm_isdst** structure member indicates whether the **tm** structure represents standard or daylight saving time and can be used as an index variable to select the proper element from the **tzname[]** array:

```
printf("\n%s", tzname[xxx.tm_isdst]);
```

Microsoft-Specific Time and Date Representations

Microsoft C defines the **dosdate_t** and **dostime_t** data structures in **<dos.h>**, the **timeb** data structure in **<sys\timeb>**, and still other formats to record last modified dates and times for all of DOS directory file entries.

struct dosdate_t

The non-Standard **dosdate_t** structure type, defined as

```
struct dostime_t {
    unsigned char hour;          /* 0-23 */
    unsigned char minute;        /* 0-59 */
    unsigned char second;        /* 0-59 */
    unsigned char hsecond; };    /* 0-99 */
```

in **<dos.h>**, is used by the **_dos_getdate()** and **_dos_setdate()** functions to retrieve and set the DOS system date. Each member of this structure has restricted ranges of value that must be satisfied, or an error condition is generated.

struct dostime_t

The non-Standard **dostime_t** structure type, defined as

```
struct dosdate_t {
    unsigned char day;                    /* 1-31 */
```

```
unsigned char month;              /* 1-12 */
unsigned int year;                /* 1980-2099 */
unsigned char dayofweek; };       /* 0-6, 0=Sunday */
```

in **<dos.h>**, is used by the **_dos_gettime()** and **_dos_settime()** functions to retrieve and set the DOS system time. Each member of this structure has restricted ranges of value that must be satisfied, or an error condition is generated.

struct timeb

The non-Standard **timeb** structure type, defined as

```
struct timeb {
    time_t time;              /* GMT in seconds */
    unsigned short millitm;/* millisecond fraction */
    short timezone;           /* GMT - Local Time in minutes */
    short dstflag; };         /* =1 if DST in effect   */
```

in **<sys\timeb.h>**, used by function **ftime()**, represents a composite structure that contains a type **time_t** member, a measure of time in milliseconds, and equivalent representations of the global variable values of **timezone** and **daylight**. The flexibility of types **time_t** and **struct tm** now overshadows the use of **struct timeb**, which has been included to maintain UNIX/XENIX compatibility.

The DOS Directory Date and Time Format

Although not utilized by any functions described in this chapter, another DOS date and time bit format is used by the DOS directory structure, defined as

```
struct dos_date {
    unsigned day : 5;
    unsigned month : 4;
    unsigned year80 : 7; };

struct dos_time {
    unsigned sec2 : 5;
    unsigned minutes : 6;
    unsigned hours : 5; }
```

where each member is a bit-field, used by functions **_dos_getftime()** and **_dos_setftime()** described in Chapter 16.

DATE AND TIME TASKS

The available date and time run-time library functions have been broken into two separate categories of date and time functions, DOS and Universal, as shown in Table 21.1. DOS date and time functions do not support the recording of universal time (GMT) as such, nor do they account in any special way for daylight saving time (DST). We will first examine the functions that are DOS-specific, and then examine those functions that implement universal time (GMT) and maintain compatibility with the UNIX operating system.

The function **bios_timeofday()** simply returns the timer tick count using BIOS interrupt 0x1A, which in turn interrogates the tick count maintained by BIOS interrupt 0x08. Note that whenever the timer tick count exceeds 24 hours (1,573,040 ticks), the count is reset to zero.

The **clock()** function, first described in Chapter 5 for the timing macros **START()** and **STOP**, differs from **_bios_timeofday()** in that the tick count returned is adjusted to the starting time of the process (program) being executed and is factored by either object-like macro **CLK_TCK** or **CLOCKS_PER_SEC**, defined in **<time.h>**, to reflect the elapsed time in milliseconds. The function **clock()** was chosen for use over **_bios_timeofday()** and **time()** for the **START()** and **STOP** function-like macros because **clock()** is ANSI-compatible and, unlike the **time()** function, records time to 1/1000 seconds.

The **_dos_get..()** and **_dos_set..()** functions utilize DOS interrupt 0x21 functions 0x2A through 0x2D to get or set the date and time maintained by the clock device driver or real-time clock, if installed. The **_str..()** functions simply convert and display the system date and time. The data structures utilized by these functions, **dosdate_t** and **dostime_t**, are described in Appendix E.

The family of universal time functions are all dependent upon the values assigned to DOS global variables **timezone**, **daylight**, and **tzname[]**. These values are assigned by the function **tzset()** from the TZ= environment variable string setting.

The principal function that supports the implementation of universal time is **time()**, which gets the system date and time and expresses it in the number of seconds relative to January 1, 1970 00:00:00 GMT. Function **ctime()** is used to display a date and time in **time_t** format returned by function **time()**. Function **difftime()** supports the addition and subtraction of **time_t** type values.

Functions **localtime()** and **gmtime()** create the Standard structure **tm** from a **time_t** value created by function **time()**. Structure type **tm** is the mechanism by which universal dates and times are displayed using functions **asctime()** and **strftime()**.

Function **mktime()** provides the ability to create a **time_t** type from a **tm** structure and, in so doing, permits date and time math operations to be performed.

Function **ftime()** returns a less commonly used, non-Standard **timeb** type structure.

TABLE 21.1: Date and Time Management Functions

TASK		FUNCTION	+
		STANDARD C ■ ANSI	**MICROSOFT C** □ ANSI
DOS Date and Time	Timer ticks since power-on		**_bios_timeofday()**
	Elapsed time for a process	**clock()**	
	Get system date (**dosdate_t**)		**_dos_getdate()**
	Set system date (**dosdate_t**)		**_dos_setdate()**
	Get system time (**dostime_t**)		**_dos_gettime()**
	Set system time (**dostime_t**)		**_dos_settime()**
	Display system date (mm/dd/yy)		**_strdate()**
	Display system time (hh:mm:ss)		**_strtime()**
	Last date/time file modified (see Chapter 16)		**_dos_findfirst()**
			_dos_findnext()
			_dos_getftime()
			_dos_setftime()
Universal Date and Time	Set DOS global variables (TZ=)		**tzset()**
	Get system date and time		
	time_t	**time()**	
	struct timeb		**ftime()**
	Convert system date and time		
	time_t to **struct tm**	**gmtime()**, **localtime()**	
	struct tm to **time_t**	**mktime()**	
	time_t	**difftime()**	
	Display system date and time		
	time_t	**ctime()**	
	struct tm	**asctime()**, **strftime()**	
	Last date/time file modified (see Chapter 16)		**fstat()**
			stat()
			utime()

RUN-TIME LIBRARY FUNCTIONS FOR DATE AND TIME MANAGEMENT

`asctime()`   *Convert the Standard `tm` structure to a string*

Compatibility   ■ANSI   ■OS/2   ■UNIX   ■XENIX

See Also

```
strftime()
```

Specification

```
#include <time.h>
char *asctime(const struct tm *pointer);
```

Arguments

pointer: Pointer to the Standard C date and time structure, **tm** (see Appendix E).

Return Value

A pointer to a **static** character string that is always 26 characters and in the format

```
Wed Jan 02 02:03:55 1980\n\0
```

regardless of the **COUNTRY=xxx** command found in CONFIG.SYS (see Chapter 1).

Example   See: `gmtime()`.

Comments   The **tm** structure is created using either **gmtime()** or **localtime()**, or by initializing a **tm** structure.

Function **asctime()** "normalizes" the values stored in structure **tm** and displays the result.

Function **asctime()** shares a **static** buffer also used by functions **ctime()**, **gmtime()**, and **localtime()**.

`bios timeofday()`   *Get/Set the system timer clock ticks (BIOS Interrupt 0x1A)*

Compatibility   □ANSI   □OS/2   □UNIX   □XENIX

See Also

```
clock()
```

Specification

```
#include <bios.h>
unsigned _bios_timeofday(unsigned service, long *ticks);
```

Arguments

service: Use either the **_TIME_GETCLOCK** or **_TIME_SETCLOCK** object-like macros found in **<bios.h>**.

ticks: Pointer to a **long** that is used either to return the clock tick count or to serve as the value to set the clock tick count.

Return Value

When the **_TIME_GETCLOCK** service is used, a value of 0 is returned if midnight has been passed since the last get or set time was performed; otherwise a value of 1 is returned

When **_TIME_SETCLOCK** is used, there is no return value

Example

```c
/* FILE: ch21e1.c */
#include <stdio.h>
#include <bios.h>
#include <time.h>
int main(void)
{
long int bios_start, bios_end;
clock_t clock_start, clock_end;
float elap_bios, elap_clock;

_bios_timeofday(_TIME_GETCLOCK, &bios_start);
clock_start = clock();
printf("\n_bios = %ld\t\tclock = %ld",
    bios_start, clock_start);
clock_end = clock();
_bios_timeofday(_TIME_GETCLOCK, &bios_end);
printf("\n_bios = %ld\t\tclock = %ld",
    bios_end, clock_end);

elap_bios = (bios_end - bios_start)/18.2F;
elap_clock = (clock_end - clock_start)/(float) CLK_TCK;
printf("\nelap_bios = %f sec\nelap_clock = %f sec",
    elap_bios, elap_clock);
exit(0);
}
```

Output

```
_bios = 1082716        clock = 0
_bios = 1082718        clock = 110
elap_bios  = 0.109890 sec
elap_clock = 0.110000 sec
```

Comments Note that in the example above the tick count returned by **_bios_timeofday()** is relative to when the system was powered-on.

clock() *Elapsed process time in* clock_t *format*

Compatibility ■ANSI   ■OS/2   □UNIX   □XENIX

See Also
```
_bios_timeofday()
```

Specification
```
#include <time.h>
clock_t clock(void);
```

Return Value
The product of the time in seconds and the value of the object-like macro **CLOCKS_PER_SEC** (or **CLK_TCK**) found in **<time.h>**

Example See: **_bios_timeofday()**.

See also Chapter 5, Figure 5.1 (**ch5e1.h** or **timer.h**), and the **START()** and **STOP** timing macros.

Comments Notice the difference between ticks and type **clock_t** demonstrated in the program example output. The **clock()** function returns a measure of time in units of 1/1000 seconds.

ctime() *Convert a* time_t *value to represent a local time string*

Compatibility ■ANSI   ■OS/2   ■UNIX   ■XENIX

See Also
```
asctime(), _strdate(), strftime(), _strtime()
```

Specification
```
#include <time.h>
char *ctime(const time_t *timer);
```

Arguments
timer: Pointer to a time value in **time_t** format that was acquired using function **time()**.

Return Value

A pointer to a **static** character string that is always 26 characters and in the format

Wed Jan 02 02:03:55 1980\n\0

regardless of the **COUNTRY=*xxx*** command found in CONFIG.SYS (see Chapter 1); the string reflects either standard time or daylight saving time, based upon the current setting of global variable **daylight**.

A null string is returned if the date is earlier than Jan. 1, 1980.

Example   See: **gmtime()**, **mktime()**, **strftime()**, and **time()**.

Comments   Function **ctime()** shares a **static** buffer also used by functions **asctime()**, **gmtime()**, and **localtime()**.

difftime()   *Subtract two time values in* time_t *format*

Compatibility   ■ANSI   ■OS/2   ■UNIX   ■XENIX

Specification
```
#include <time.h>
double difftime(time_t timer1, time_t timer0);
```

Arguments

timer1: Ending time value.

timer0: Starting time value.

Return Value

Elapsed time difference in whole seconds, may be a positive or negative value

Example   See: **time()**.

Comments   The program example output demonstrates that **time_t** values are not adjusted by function **difftime()**, simply subtracted, because **time_t** values are all relative to the same base (January 1, 1970 00:00:00 [midnight] GMT).
   Subtract as type **long int**.

_dos_getdate()   *Get the system date in* struct dosdate_t *format using DOS interrupt 0x21 function 0x2A*

Compatibility   □ANSI   □OS/2   □UNIX   □XENIX

See Also

_dos_setdate()

Specification

```
#include <dos.h>
void _dos_getdate(struct dosdate_t *date);
```

Arguments

date: Pointer to the non-Standard DOS date structure, **dosdate_t** (see Appendix E)

Example

```
/* FILE: ch21e2.c */
#include <stdio.h>
#include <time.h>
#include <dos.h>

int main(void)
{
char datebuf[9], timebuf[9];
struct dosdate_t o_date, n_date = { 1, 1, 1990 };
struct dostime_t o_time, n_time = { 12, 30, 45 };

printf("\ncurrent date: %s", _strdate(datebuf));
printf("\ncurrent time: %s", _strtime(timebuf));

_dos_getdate(&o_date);
_dos_gettime(&o_time);
if (_dos_setdate(&n_date))
    printf("\n_dos_setdate() failed!");
if (_dos_settime(&n_time))
    printf("\n_dos_settime() failed!");
printf("\ncurrent date: %s", _strdate(datebuf));
printf("\ncurrent time: %s", _strtime(timebuf));

if (_dos_setdate(&o_date))
    printf("\n_dos_setdate() failed!");
if (_dos_settime(&o_time))
    printf("\n_dos_settime() failed!");
printf("\ncurrent date: %s", _strdate(datebuf));
printf("\ncurrent time: %s", _strtime(timebuf));
exit(0);
}
```

Output

```
current date: 04/05/90
current time: 16:32:13
current date: 01/01/90
current time: 12:30:44
```

```
current date: 04/05/90
current time: 16:32:13
```

Comments   Structure **dosdate_t** may contain any date between January 1, 1980 and December 31, 2099, acquired from the DOS clock device driver.

_dos_gettime()   *Get the system time in* struct dostime_t *format using DOS interrupt 0x21 function 0x2C*

Compatibility ☐ANSI   ☐OS/2   ☐UNIX   ☐XENIX

See Also

```
_dos_settime()
```

Specification

```
#include <dos.h>
void _dos_gettime(struct dostime_t * time);
```

Arguments

time: Pointer to the non-Standard DOS time structure **dostime_t** (see Appendix E).

Example   See: **_dos_getdate()**.

Comments   Structure **dostime_t** may contain any time between 00:00:00 and 23:59:59, acquired from the DOS clock device driver.

_dos_setdate()   *Set the system date in* struct dosdate_t *format using DOS interrupt 0x21 function 0x2B*

Compatibility ☐ANSI   ☐OS/2   ☐UNIX   ☐XENIX

See Also

```
_dos_getdate()
```

Specification

```
#include <dos.h>
unsigned _dos_setdate(struct dosdate_t *date);
```

Arguments

date: Pointer to the non-Standard DOS date structure **dosdate_t** (see Appendix E).

Return Value

> If successful, zero (false)
>
> A nonzero value, and global variable **errno** set to **EINVAL**

Example   See: **_dos_getdate()**.

Comments   Any date between January 1, 1980 and December 31, 2099 alters the DOS clock device driver days-elapsed field.

_dos_settime()   *Set the system time in* struct dostime_t *format using DOS interrupt 0x21 function 0x2D*

Compatibility   ☐ ANSI   ☐ OS/2   ☐ UNIX   ☐ XENIX

See Also

> _dos_gettime()

Specification

```
#include <dos.h>
unsigned _dos_settime(struct dostime_t *time);
```

Arguments

> *time*: Pointer to the non-Standard DOS time structure **dostime_t** (see Appendix E).

Return Value

> If successful, zero (false)
>
> Otherwise, a nonzero value, and global variable **errno** set to **EINVAL**

Example   See: **_dos_getdate()**.

Comments   Any time between 00:00:00 and 23:59:59 alters the DOS clock device driver time fields and updates the current clock tick count maintained by BIOS interrupt 0x08.

ftime()   *Get the system time in* struct timeb *format*

Compatibility   ☐ ANSI   ■ OS/2   ■ UNIX   ■ XENIX

See Also

```
gmtime(), localtime()
```

Specification

```
#include <sys\types.h>
#include <sys\timeb.h>
void ftime(struct timeb *timeptr);
```

Arguments

timeptr: Pointer to the non-Standard structure, **timeb** (see Appendix E).

Example   See: **gmtime()**.

Comments   **timeb** structure member **millitm**, although a millisecond fraction, always ends with zero; hence, only 1/100 second accuracy, not 1/1000 second as implied.

Note from the program example output that the **timeb** time zone member is recorded in minutes, not seconds, and should not be confused with the DOS global variable, **timezone**.

gmtime()   *Convert a* time_t *value to universal (GMT) time in Standard structure* tm *format*

Compatibility   ■ANSI   ■OS/2   ■UNIX   ■XENIX

See Also

```
localtime(), mktime()
```

Specification

```
#include <time.h>
struct tm *gmtime(const time_t *timer);
```

Arguments

timer: Acquired type **time_t** value using function **time()**.

Return Value

A pointer to the structure **tm**

Any error condition returns a **NULL** pointer

Example

```
/* FILE: ch21e3.c */
#include <stdio.h>
```

```c
#include <time.h>
#include <stdlib.h>
#include <string.h>
#include <sys\types.h>
#include <sys\timeb.h>

int main(void)
{
time_t any_time;
struct tm *tm_time;
char *tptr, c_date[9], c_time[9];
char tzstr[10], tzsave[13]= "TZ=";
struct timeb bptr;

strcat(tzsave,getenv("TZ"));
while (1) {
    putenv("TZ=PST8PDT");
    tzset();
    printf("\nEnter (TZ=xxxhhyyy or END): ");
    gets(tzstr);
    if (!stricmp(tzstr,"END")) break;

    printf("\ndefault TZ=PST8PDT\
        \ndaylight= %d\ttimezone= %ld\n",
        daylight, timezone);
    if(putenv(tzstr)) {
        printf("\nputenv failed!\n");
        continue;
        }
    else printf("putenv OK!");
    tzset();
    printf("\ndaylight= %d\ttimezone= %ld",
        daylight, timezone);
    ftime(&bptr);
    printf("\n\ntimeb dstflag = %d\
        \ntimeb time = %ld (sec since 1/1/70)\
        \ntimeb millitm = %u (1/1000 sec)\
        \ntimeb timezone = %d (minutes)\n",
        bptr.dstflag, bptr.time,
        bptr.millitm, bptr.timezone);

    printf("\ndate = %s\t\ttime = %s",
        _strdate(c_date), _strtime(c_time));
    time(&any_time);
    printf("\nany_time= %ld\tdesc= %s",
        any_time, ctime(&any_time));

    tm_time = localtime(&any_time);
    tptr = asctime(tm_time);
    printf("\nlocal_time = %stm_isdst = %d",
        tptr, tm_time->tm_isdst);
```

```
tm_time = gmtime(&any_time);
    tptr = asctime(tm_time);
    printf("\ngmt_time = %stm_isdst = %d\n",
        tptr, tm_time->tm_isdst);
    }
putenv(tzsave);
exit(0);
}
```

Output

```
Enter (TZ=xxxhhyyy or END): TZ=EST5
default TZ=PST8PDT
daylight= 1      timezone= 28800
putenv OK!
daylight= 0      timezone= 18000

timeb dstflag  = 0
timeb time     = 639351189 (sec since 1/1/70)
timeb millitm  = 270 (1/1000 sec)
timeb timezone = 300 (minutes)

date = 04/05/90        time = 16:33:09
any_time= 639351189    desc= Thu Apr 05 16:33:09 1990

local_time = Thu Apr 05 16:33:09 1990
tm_isdst = 0
gmt_time = Thu Apr 05 21:33:09 1990
tm_isdst = 0

Enter (TZ=xxxhhyyy or END): TZ=EST5EDT
default TZ=PST8PDT
daylight= 1      timezone= 28800
putenv OK!
daylight= 1      timezone= 18000

timeb dstflag  = 1
timeb time     = 639347599 (sec since 1/1/70)
timeb millitm  = 430 (1/1000 sec)
timeb timezone = 300 (minutes)

date = 04/05/90        time = 16:33:19
any_time= 639347599    desc= Thu Apr 05 16:33:19 1990

local_time = Thu Apr 05 16:33:19 1990
tm_isdst = 1
gmt_time = Thu Apr 05 20:33:19 1990
tm_isdst = 0

Enter (TZ=xxxhhyyy or END): END
```

Comments The current **time_t** (timer) value is always adjusted by function **gmtime()**, by adding the value of global variable **timezone** before structure **tm** is created.

Recall that **timezone** represents the positive (west longitude) or negative (east longitude) number of seconds between the prime meridian and the time zone established by the TZ= string setting in effect by default, or when function **tzset()** is explicitly called.

Function **gmtime()** shares a **static** buffer also used by functions **asctime()**, **ctime()**, and **localtime()**.

localtime() *Convert a* time_t *value to local time in Standard structure* tm *format*

Compatibility ■ANSI ■OS/2 ■UNIX ■XENIX

See Also

```
gmtime(), mktime()
```

Specification

```
#include <time.h>
struct tm *localtime(const time_t *timer);
```

Arguments

timer: Acquired type **time_t** value using function **time()**.

Return Value

A pointer to the structure **tm**

Any error condition returns a **NULL** pointer

Example See: **gmtime()**, **strftime()**.

Comments The current **time_t** (timer) value is always adjusted by function **localtime()** by adding the value of global variable **daylight** times 3600 before structure **tm** is created.

Recall that **daylight** only assumes a value of 0 or 1 and is controlled by the value of the TZ= string. If a three-character daylight-saving-time string is provided, daylight=1; otherwise, daylight=0. A default value of 1 is assumed (TZ=PST8PDT). If the TZ= string is changed using a DOS SET command or function **putenv()**, function **tzset()** must be called to update the global variables **daylight**, **timezone**, and **tzname[]**; otherwise, they remain unchanged.

Function **localtime()** shares a **static** buffer also used by functions **asctime()**, **ctime()**, and **gmtime()**.

mktime() *Convert Standard structure* tm *local time to a* time_t *value*

Compatibility ■ANSI ■OS/2 □UNIX □XENIX

See Also

_dos_setdate, _dos_settime()

Specification

```
#include <time.h>
time_t mktime(struct tm *timeptr);
```

Arguments

timeptr: Pointer to the Standard structure **tm** (see Appendix E).

Return Value

The **time_t** value or −1 if an error occurred

Example

```
/* FILE: ch21e4.c */
#include <stdio.h>
#include <time.h>
#include <stdlib.h>

int main(void)
{
struct tm base, next, *ptr;
time_t b_time, n_time;
int i, tmval;
char *prompt[] = { "tm_year= " , "tm_mon= " ,
    "tm_mday= " , "tm_hour= ",
    "tm_min= " , "tm_sec= ",
    "tm_isdst= " , NULL };
putenv("TZ=EST5");
tzset();

/* set 1/1/1980, 00:00:00 EST */
base.tm_isdst = 0;
base.tm_year = 80;
base.tm_mon = 0;
base.tm_mday = 1;
base.tm_hour = 0;
base.tm_min = 0;
base.tm_sec = 0;
b_time = mktime(&base);
```

```
    if (b_time == (time_t)-1L) exit(99);
    next = base;

    printf("\nEnter a +/- integer offset value"\
        "\nfor the struct tm member prompts"\
        "\nThe values may exceed normal values...\n");

    for(i=0; prompt[i]; i++) {
        if(!i) printf("\nbase: %ld %s", b_time, ctime(&b_time));
        printf("\n%s", prompt[i]);
        scanf("%d", &tmval);
        fflush(stdin);
        switch(i) {
            case 0: next.tm_year += tmval; break;
            case 1: next.tm_mon += tmval; break;
            case 2: next.tm_mday += tmval; break;
            case 3: next.tm_hour += tmval; break;
            case 4: next.tm_min += tmval; break;
            case 5: next.tm_sec += tmval; break;
            case 6: next.tm_isdst += tmval; break;
            }
        n_time = mktime(&next);
        if (n_time == (time_t)-1L) printf("\nError!!! ");
        printf("next: %ld %s", n_time, ctime(&n_time));
        }
    exit(0);
    }
```

Output

```
    Enter a +/- integer offset value
    for the struct tm member prompts
    The values may exceed normal values...

    base: 315550800 Tue Jan 01 00:00:00 1980

    tm_year= 10
    next: 631170000 Mon Jan 01 00:00:00 1990

    tm_mon= 3
    next: 638946000 Sun Apr 01 00:00:00 1990

    tm_mday= 3
    next: 639205200 Wed Apr 04 00:00:00 1990

    tm_hour= 39
    next: 639345600 Thu Apr 05 15:00:00 1990

    tm_min= 37
    next: 639347820 Thu Apr 05 15:37:00 1990

    tm_sec= 4
    next: 639347824 Thu Apr 05 15:37:04 1990
```

```
tm_isdst= 0
next: 639347824 Thu Apr 05 15:37:04 1990
```

Comments Only the **tm_wday** and **tm_yday** members of the **tm** structure are ignored when setting a new date and time.

The program example output demonstrates the calculation of the **time_t** value of January 5, 1990 15:37:04 EST, not EDT (see section **time_t**).

The **mktime()** function assumes that the time described by the **tm** structure is expressed in either standard or daylight saving local time.

The normal allowable ranges of value associated with each **tm** structure member may be exceeded; this facilitates the performance of relative date and time math operations.

All **tm** structure member values are normalized if they exceed the ranges of allowable value.

mktime() uses the value of global variable **timezone** and member **tm_isdst**, not **daylight**, to compute the **time_t** value.

_strdate() *Gets the system date in mm/dd/yy format*

Compatibility □ANSI ■OS/2 □UNIX □XENIX

See Also

```
asctime(), ctime(), strftime()
```

Specification

```
#include <time.h>
char *_strdate(char *string);
```

Arguments

string: The current system date in **mm/dd/yy\0** string format.

Return Value

Pointer to the current system date in *string*

Example See: **_dos_getdate()**, **gmtime()**.

Comments The format is not affected by the COUNTRY=*xxx* command found in CONFIG.SYS (see Chapter 1).

`strftime ()` *Formatted structure `tm` date and time string*

Compatibility   ■ANSI   ■OS/2   ☐UNIX   ☐XENIX

See Also
```
asctime(), ctime(), _strdate(), _strtime()
```

Specification
```
#include <time.h>
size_t strftime(char *string, size_t maxsize,
    const char *format,  const struct tm *timeptr);
```

Arguments
string: Pointer to a character storage array.

maxsize: The maximum number of characters that may be placed into *string*, including the terminating null \0 character.

format: A control string, like those used with the **scanf()** and **printf()** family of functions, that is limited to the control characters shown in Table 21.2.

timeptr: A pointer to the structure **tm**; any error condition returns a **NULL** pointer.

Return Value
If unsuccessful, zero (false)

Otherwise the number of characters placed into *string*, including the terminating null \0

Example
```
/* FILE: ch21e5.c */
#include <stdio.h>
#include <time.h>
#include <locale.h>
#define SIZE 80

int main(void)
{
time_t c_time;
struct tm *t_time;
char string[SIZE], *ptr;

putenv("TZ=EST5EDT");
tzset();
time(&c_time);
t_time = localtime(&c_time);
printf("\n%s", ctime(&c_time));
```

TABLE 21.2: strftime() Control String Format

FORMAT	DESCRIPTION
%a	Abbreviated weekday name
%A	Full weekday name
%b	Abbreviated month name
%B	Full month name
%c	Locale-specific date and time representation
%d	Day of month (01-31)
%H	Hour in 24-hour format (00-23)
%I	Hour in 12-hour format (01-12)
%j	Day of year (001-366)
%m	Month as a number (01-12)
%M	Minute as a number (00-59)
%p	Locale-specific AM/PM indicator
%S	Second as a number (00-59)
%U	Week of the year; Sunday is first day (00-53)
%w	Weekday as a number (0-6, Sunday=0)
%W	Week of the year; Monday is first day (00-53)
%x	Locale-specific date representation
%X	Locale-specific time representation
%y	Year without century as a number (00-99)
%Y	Year with a century as a number
%z	Time zone name or abbreviation; blank if unknown
%%	Percent sign

```
strftime(string, SIZE, "month: %B %b %m", t_time);
printf("\n%s", string);
strftime(string, SIZE, "day: %A %a %d %w %j",
    t_time);
printf("\n%s", string);
strftime(string, SIZE, "year: %Y %y", t_time);
printf("\n%s", string);
strftime(string, SIZE, "week: %U %W", t_time);
printf("\n%s", string);
strftime(string, SIZE, "time: %H %I %M %S %z",
    t_time);
printf("\n%s", string);
strftime(string, SIZE, "locale: %c %p %x %X",
    t_time);
```

```
printf("\n%s", string);
ptr = setlocale(LC_TIME, NULL);
printf("\nLC_TIME: %s", ptr);
exit(0);
}
```

Output

```
Thu Apr 05 16:36:40 1990

month:     April Apr 04
day:       Thursday Thu 05   4 095
year:      1990 90
week:      13 14
time:      16 04 36 40   EDT
locale:    04/05/90 16:36:40 PM   04/05/90 16:36:40
LC_TIME: C
```

Comments This function reflects the current locale **LC_TIME** category of values. Microsoft presently supports only the C locale (refer to Chapter 27).

The formats are not affected by the COUNTRY=*xxx* command found in CONFIG.SYS (see Chapter 1), only by the current locale.

_strtime ()   *Gets the system time in hh:mm:ss format*

Compatibility ☐ANSI ■OS/2 ☐UNIX ☐XENIX

See Also

```
asctime(), ctime(), strftime()
```

Specification

```
#include <time.h>
char *_strtime(char *string);
```

Arguments

string: Buffer to fill with the current system time in **hh/mm/ss\0** string format.

Return Value

Pointer to the current system time in *string*

Example   See: **_dos_getdate()**, **gmtime()**.

Comments The format is not affected by the COUNTRY=*xxx* command found in CONFIG.SYS (see Chapter 1).

`time ()`   *Get the system time in* `time_t` *format*

Compatibility   ■ANSI   ■OS/2   ■UNIX   ■XENIX

See Also

```
_bios_timeofday()
```

Specification

```
#include <time.h>
time_t time(time_t *timer);
```

Arguments

timer: Pointer to a **time_t** type variable that is assigned the number of seconds elapsed since 00:00:00 GMT January 1, 1970.

If **timer** is **NULL** no value is stored.

Return Value

The elapsed time in seconds identical to that placed in **timer** (if **timer** was not **NULL**)

Example   See also: **gmtime()**, **strftime()**.

```
/* FILE: ch21e6.c */
#include <stdio.h>
#include <time.h>
#include <stdlib.h>
int main(void)
{
time_t t0_time, t1_time;
double delta_time;
int i;
char *test[][2] = { { "TZ=EST5"   , "TZ=EST5EDT"   },
    { "TZ=PST8"   , "TZ=PST8PDT"   },
    { "TZ=EST5"   , "TZ=PST8"      },
    { "TZ=EST5"   , "TZ=PST8PDT"   },
    { "TZ=EST5EDT", "TZ=PST8"      },
    { "TZ=EST5EDT", "TZ=PST8PDT"   },
    {   NULL       ,    NULL        } };
for (i=0; test[i][0]; i++) {
    printf("\nCase %1d: %s %s", i, test[i][0], test[i][1]);

    if(putenv(test[i][0])) printf("\nputenv failed!");
    tzset();
    time(&t0_time);
    printf("\ndaylight= %d t0_time= %ld\n%s",
        daylight, t0_time, ctime(&t0_time));
```

```
        if(putenv(test[i][1])) printf("\nputenv failed!");
        tzset();
        time(&t1_time);
        printf("daylight= %d t1_time= %ld\n%s",
            daylight, t1_time, ctime(&t1_time));

        delta_time = difftime(t1_time, t0_time);
        printf("difftime = %lf\n", delta_time);
        }
exit(0);
}
```

Output

```
Case 0: TZ=EST5 TZ=EST5EDT
daylight= 0  t0_time= 639351424
Thu Apr 05 16:37:04 1990
daylight= 1  t1_time= 639347824
Thu Apr 05 16:37:04 1990
difftime = -3600.000000

Case 1: TZ=PST8 TZ=PST8PDT
daylight= 0  t0_time= 639362224
Thu Apr 05 16:37:04 1990
daylight= 1  t1_time= 639358624
Thu Apr 05 16:37:04 1990
difftime = -3600.000000

Case 2: TZ=EST5 TZ=PST8
daylight= 0  t0_time= 639351424
Thu Apr 05 16:37:04 1990
daylight= 0  t1_time= 639362224
Thu Apr 05 16:37:04 1990
difftime = 10800.000000

Case 3: TZ=EST5 TZ=PST8PDT
daylight= 0  t0_time= 639351424
Thu Apr 05 16:37:04 1990
daylight= 1  t1_time= 639358624
Thu Apr 05 16:37:04 1990
difftime = 7200.000000

Case 4: TZ=EST5EDT TZ=PST8
daylight= 1  t0_time= 639347824
Thu Apr 05 16:37:04 1990
daylight= 0  t1_time= 639362224
Thu Apr 05 16:37:04 1990
difftime = 14400.000000

Case 5: TZ=EST5EDT TZ=PST8PDT
daylight= 1  t0_time= 639347824
Thu Apr 05 16:37:04 1990
daylight= 1  t1_time= 639358624
Thu Apr 05 16:37:04 1990
difftime = 10800.000000
```

Comments   The **time_t** (timer) value represents the number of elapsed seconds since January 1, 1970, based upon the current DOS system time setting, which is then adjusted by the setting of **timezone** and **daylight** according to the following formula:

$$\text{time\_t} = (\text{elapsed seconds}) + (\textbf{timezone}) - (\text{daylight} * 3600)$$

If no TZ= environment string exists, a default of PST8PDT is assumed, so that global variable **daylight** equals 1, in which case 3600 seconds (one hour) are subtracted, and **timezone** equals 28,800 seconds, or eight hours.

The **timezone** adjustment reflects the signed number of hours (West= +hr, East= −hr) from GMT to the **timezone** used to express the current DOS system time.

Whenever a daylight-saving-time three-character abbreviation is provided in the TZ= string, the value of global variable **daylight** is 1, and a 3600= second adjustment is made to **time_t** accordingly; otherwise, the **daylight** adjustment is zero.

The environment string TZ= should always be set to accurately reflect whether daylight saving time is in effect or not. Omit the DST string component of TZ= to indicate that standard time is in effect.

The program example output emphasizes how **time_t** values are calculated and how adjustments are made using global variables **daylight** and **timezone** and functions **putenv()** and **tzset()**.

tzset ()   *Set global variables* daylight, timezone, *and* tzname *from the current TZ= environment variable*

Compatibility   □ANSI   ■OS/2   ■UNIX   ■XENIX

Specification

```
#include <time.h>
void tzset(void);
```

Example   See: **gmtime()**, **mktime()**, **strftime()**, **time()**.

Comments   Function **tzset()** must be called after setting environment string TZ= to modify the values of the global variables **daylight**, **timezone**, and **tzname[]**. Refer to Table 1.9 in Chapter 1.

Assume the default TZ=PST8PDT settings of **daylight** = 1, **timezone** = 28,800, **tzname[0]** = PST, and **tzname[1]** = PDT; or issue the DOS SET command or **putenv()** function call, and then call **tzset()**.

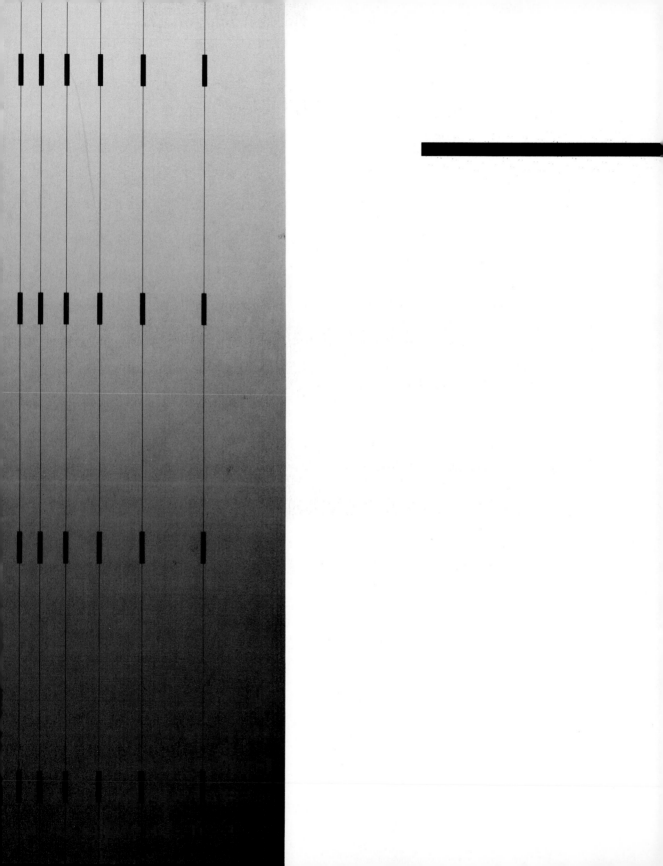

Functions for DOS/BIOS System Calls

Functions for DOS/BIOS System Calls

The DOS Memory Map presented in Chapter 2, Figure 2.19, reveals that DOS application programs occupy only about half of the one megabyte of memory space that is normally addressable. The remainder is occupied by operating system software, providing services categorized as either BIOS (basic input/output services) or DOS.

The ROM BIOS services provide for the direct interface and control of the timer, keyboard, video, external storage (cassette, floppy, hard), serial communications, and printer, while DOS provides additional services such as a file system, memory management, process control, and I/O services. Although the C run-time library provides access to some of these memory resident DOS/BIOS services, many are accessible from a C application program only if software interrupts are used.

Software interrupts permit you to write C programs that exploit the full complement of memory-resident DOS and BIOS services without resorting to the use of assembly language (see Chapter 28). This chapter explains how software interrupts are used to access these DOS and BIOS services. Particular emphasis is placed upon explaining how the run-time functions **bdos()**, **intdos()**, **intdosx()**, **int86()**, and **int86x()** are used to initiate 80*x*86 software interrupts.

Because the run-time library documentation provided in this book has been organized from a "programming task" point of view, you will not find all interrupt-based, run-time functions documented in this chapter. Table 22.1 summarizes the functions that are documented in this chapter.

Although all run-time functions that begin with **_dos..()** or **_bios..()** utilize DOS/BIOS interrupts, other run-time functions not following this naming convention also utilize software interrupts. For example, most of the process control functions documented in Chapter 25 utilize software interrupts, while few of the string handling functions found in Chapter 26 do so.

One particular subset of DOS interrupt functions that has been omitted from this chapter supports the writing and installation of custom-developed C interrupt functions. Interrupt handlers can be written in C and made to replace the standard DOS/BIOS interrupt functions that are loaded for use when a particular version of DOS is booted. The DOS hidden system files, IBMBIO.COM and IBMDOS.COM, must be present when a system volume is booted because they represent programs that configure DOS by loading the current DOS system functions, remedy any DOS/BIOS fixes or upgrades and, as we will discover, load the Interrupt Vector Table with the correct memory addresses of all available DOS/BIOS services. For the details of writing C interrupt handlers and the function descriptions for **_chain_intr()**, **_disable()**, **_dos_getvect()**, **_dos_setvect()**, **_enable()**, **_harderr()**, **_hardresume()**, and **_hardretn()**, see Chapter 27.

Use of the run-time functions **bdos()**, **intdos()**, **intdosx()**, **int86()**, **int86x()**, and any functions named beginning with **_dos_..()** or **_bios_..()** is always non-Standard and is not portable for use with another operating system (OS/2, UNIX, Xenix, etc.). Run-time functions may conform with Standard C, however, even though they are implemented using a DOS-specific software interrupt. Such Standard functions are available with the same prototype declaration in the C run-time library supplied for use with other operating systems.

Although it might seem logical that the memory-resident DOS and BIOS services (functions) could simply be called by name from a C program

TABLE 22.1: BIOS and DOS Interrupt Run-Time Library Functions Presented in Chapter 22

TASK		FUNCTION	
		STANDARD C ■ ANSI	MICROSOFT C □ ANSI
BIOS	Peripheral access		_bios_disk(), _bios_equiplist(), _bios_printer(), _bios_serialcom()
	Interrupt services		int86() int86x() segread()
DOS	Peripheral access		_dos_getdiskfree()
	Interrupt services		bdos() int86() int86x() intdos() intdosx() segread()
	Error Handling		dosexterr()

and their memory addresses resolved by the linker to produce an executable file, access to memory-resident DOS/BIOS services is not handled in this manner. To understand why, let's examine the characteristics of 80x86 interrupts.

HARDWARE AND SOFTWARE INTERRUPTS

The interrupt mechanism is rooted in the need for the 80x86 processor to accommodate asynchronous hardware peripheral requests, whether for the normal sequencing of I/O operations, or to resolve critical errors should they occur. The ROM BIOS (basic input/output services) software represents the layer of operating system software that interfaces directly with the peripheral components of a computer, and that is dependent upon the particular hardware characteristics of installed peripheral devices.

The 8259A chip is responsible for fielding and prioritizing all peripheral interrupt requests for processor resource time. It is the ongoing dialogue between 80x86 and the 8259A chip that is responsible for both the recognition and initiation of a hardware interrupt. When such interrupts occur, the 80x86 must be stopped (interrupted) so that this special external event can be handled, and then it is permitted to continue as if nothing abnormal had occurred. Therefore, the code (function) that is executed when such an interrupt occurs must do so in a manner that permits the 80x86 ultimately to resume processing as if the ongoing flow of execution had not been disrupted.

Interrupt Vector Table

When the 8259A chip interrupts the 80x86 processor, it passes the processor an interrupt number consisting of one byte. Each interrupt number represents an index position in the interrupt vector table. The interrupt vector table is always located in absolute memory addresses 0000:0000 to 0040:0000 (1024 bytes). Each entry in the table is a **_far** pointer (SEG:OFF, four bytes) to an interrupt function. There are a total of 256 (1024/4) available table entries, which correspond to interrupt numbers 0x00 through 0xFF. Since only some of the entries in this table are required to service the processing of hardware interrupts, the remainder are available for general use, or as software interrupts.

The interrupt vector table is essentially an array of function pointers loaded with **_far** addresses when DOS is booted. Each address in this table therefore points to a function that has the same prototype declaration.

The standard prototype declaration format of an interrupt function (**int_fn**) is defined in C as

```
void _cdecl _interrupt _far int_fn
    (unsigned _es,    unsigned _ds,
     unsigned _di,    unsigned _si,
     unsigned _bp,    unsigned _sp,
     unsigned _bx,    unsigned _dx,
     unsigned _cx,    unsigned _ax,
     unsigned _ip,    unsigned _cs,
     unsigned flags);
```

A typical interrupt function, then, returns type **void** and implicitly has the formal register arguments shown above, which correspond to the 80*x*86 register set described in Table 22.2.

The formal argument names described for the interrupt function template **int_fn** above correspond to the register values pushed to the stack just before servicing an interrupt request, and therefore are available for use from within a handler, if necessary.

The interrupt function **int_fn** declaration qualifiers (refer to Chapter 14, Table 14.2) are shown below:

```
.. _cdecl _interrupt _far int_fn ( ..
```

They specify that C interrupt functions use the C language calling convention, which pushes the arguments to the stack, rightmost to leftmost; that function **int_fn** is an interrupt function, and therefore special entry and exit protocols must be followed; and that all interrupt functions are addressed using **_far** pointers because they may be located anywhere in memory.

Interrupt Numbers

Interrupt numbers (intnum), which consist of one byte, are converted to a corresponding physical address in the interrupt vector table for an 80*x*86 using DOS simply by using the following bit operation:

```
intnum << 2
```

This reflects that the size of each entry in the interrupt vector table is four bytes, and the table originates at 0000:0000. This integer value must be cast as follows to reflect that it represents a **_far** (SEG:OFF) pointer:

```
(void _far *) (intnum << 2)
```

TABLE 22.2: DOS Registers

CATEGORY	REGISTER	DESCRIPTION
General	AX	Accumulator (16 bits)
		AH high-order (bit-15 through bit-8)
		AL low-order (bit-7 through bit-0)
	BX	Base (16-bits)
		BH high-order (bit-15 through bit-8)
		BL low-order (bit-7 through bit-0)
	CX	Count (16-bits)
		CH high-order (bit-15 through bit-8)
		CL low-order (bit-7 through bit-0)
	DX	Data (16-bits)
		DH high-order (bit-15 through bit-8)
		DL low-order (bit-7 through bit-0)
Segment	CS	Code Segment (16 bits)
	DS	Data Segment (16 bits)
	SS	Stack Segment (16 bits)
	ES	Extra Segment (16 bits)
Index	DI	Destination Index (16 bits)
	SI	Stack Index (16 bits)
Pointers	SP	Stack Pointer (16 bits)
	BP	Base Pointer (16 bits)
	IP	Instruction Pointer (16 bits)
Flags	OF	Overflow (bit-11)
	DF	Direction (bit-10)
	IF	Interrupt (bit-9)
	TF	Trap (bit-8)
	SF	Sign (bit-7)
	ZF	Zero (bit-6)
	AF	Auxiliary Carry (bit-4)
	PF	Parity (bit-2)
	CF	Carry (bit-0)

A **_far** pointer (SEG:OFF) to an interrupt function is found at this memory address. All unassigned entries assume the value of a **NULL** (0000:0000) pointer.

If the standard interrupt function prototype described above is expressed as a function pointer, **int_fn_ptr**, as follows (refer to Chapter 14)

```
void (_cdecl _interrupt _far *int_fn_ptr) (void);
```

and is assigned the address derived from the interrupt number as shown above, then any interrupt that does not require initializing other registers may be executed as follows:

```
(*int_fn_ptr)();
```

The following sample program demonstrates this for interrupt number 0x05, which is equivalent to pressing Shift-PrtSc on the keyboard to print the current video display.

```
/* FILE: ch22e10.c */
#include <stdio.h>
int main(void)
{
int intnum = 0x05;
void _far * _far *vt_addr;
void (_cdecl _interrupt _far *int_fn_ptr) (void );

vt_addr = (void _far *)(intnum << 2);
int_fn_ptr = *vt_addr;
printf("\n\nTable Address = %lp", vt_addr);
printf("\nFunction Address= %lp", int_fn_ptr);
(*int_fn_ptr)();
exit(0);
}
```

When compiled without Pointer Checking enabled, the program produces the following output and a printout of the current video display:

```
Table Address    = 0000:0014
Function Address = F000:FF54
```

This example confirms the mapping of the interrupt vector table and demonstrates that it represents an array of function pointers originated at 0000:0000.

Interrupt Handlers

Notice that although the Standard C interrupt function prototype described above listed formal function arguments, no actual register argument values are required normally, because these register and flag values are automatically pushed to the stack when the **_interrupt** keyword is used to describe a function or function pointer. The instructions required to push the register and flag arguments to the stack upon function entry, and to pop or restore them upon exiting, are generated by the **_interrupt** keyword qualifier (see Chapter 14).

From this description it is clear that interrupt handlers represent a special class of functions that normally pass no actual arguments and return type **void** (nothing). All arguments to interrupt handlers therefore are normally passed in registers, and not as actual arguments on the stack. For this reason, DOS/BIOS system services are usually invoked using assembly language because this language provides instructions to control the assignment of registers, whereas C and other high-level languages do not. It is the role of the run-time functions **bdos()**, **intdos()**, **intdosx()**, **int86()**, and **int86x()** to provide these essential assembly language, register-handling services for the C programming language.

Also, interrupt functions are normally identified by number, not by name. Interrupt numbers are used to identify the index position to an array of function pointers called the interrupt vector table. Interrupt numbers range in value from 0x00 through 0xFF (one byte), and identify a memory address containing a **_far** pointer to an interrupt function (handler).

Whenever **_interrupt** functions are executed (assembler instruction INT), the present state of the 80x86 processor is automatically pushed to the stack; any arguments required by the handler are then loaded into registers. Upon completion, all return values are copied to a memory buffer area, and all registers are restored (assembler instruction IRET), which permits the 80x86 processor to continue as if never interrupted.

Normal C function-calling conventions are not utilized to directly access DOS/BIOS services, because then a program that had been linked would operate properly only if executed on a DOS machine with the same BIOS and DOS version numbers. Using interrupt numbers and the vector table instead permits Microsoft and IBM to continue improving and expanding DOS and the BIOS, while ensuring that existing application programs (.COM and .EXE) continue to operate without being relinked. It also permits interrupt handler memory address locations to change.

For more details about writing and installing custom interrupt handlers (ISRs) in C, refer to Chapter 27.

AVAILABLE 80X86 INTERRUPTS

Although up to 256 interrupt numbers are supported, to date, far fewer actually have been assigned. Let's examine the BIOS and DOS interrupt numbers that have been assigned and the variety of services performed by each interrupt handler.

The interrupt numbers used to identify which interrupt handler is executed are always expressed in hexadecimal, and range in value from 0x00 through 0xFF. Most BIOS interrupt numbers fall below interrupt 0x20. As we shall see, although DOS reserves interrupt numbers 0x20 through 0x3F, there are no absolute rules controlling the assignment of interrupt numbers. As new hardware devices are designed, new BIOS services are sometimes required, and although most DOS services are handled by interrupt 0x21, others outside of the typical 0x20 through 0x3F range are also considered DOS services.

Some interrupts provide a variety of services, referred to as functions or subfunctions, that are specified when the interrupt handler is invoked by setting specific register values in either AH and/or AL. All arguments are passed to DOS/BIOS interrupt handler functions using registers, not the stack.

The tables included in this section, describing the available BIOS and DOS interrupts and services, present an overview of the available software interrupts. This overview is directed toward explaining what is available and which services can be accessed from C using either the **bdos()**, **intdos()**, **intdosx()**, **int86()**, or **int86x()** run-time functions. Reference must be made to DOS and BIOS technical reference manuals for detailed descriptions of the proper input and output register settings for each interrupt and subfunction service. It is not the intent of this chapter to provide complete BIOS and DOS interrupt service documentation; rather, to explain how software interrupts are invoked from a C program.

BIOS Interrupts and Services

Table 22.3 summarizes the available BIOS interrupt numbers and services. The BIOS services that are available may vary depending on the hardware you are using and the particular BIOS version you have installed. Refer to your BIOS technical reference manual for the exact list of services available for your computer. Note that BIOS services may be accessed only by using **int86()** or **int86x()**. Also note the C run-time functions listed that utilize a BIOS interrupt service. Only those run-time functions named beginning with **_bios_**.. are shown. Other run-time functions may also utilize BIOS services. All interrupt services for which C run-time functions do not exist may be accessed only by using either the **int86()** or **int86x()** run-time functions that are flagged Y(es) in Table 22.3.

TABLE 22.3: BIOS Interrupts and Services

INT hex	AH hex	DESCRIPTION	bdos()	intdos() /intdosx()	int86() /int86x()	RUN-TIME FUNCTION
00		Divide by zero	N	N/N	Y/Y	
01		Single step interrupt	N	N/N	Y/Y	
02		Nonmaskable	N	N/N	Y/Y	
03		Breakpoint interrupt	N	N/N	Y/Y	
04		Arithmetic overflow	N	N/N	Y/Y	
05		Print screen	N	N/N	Y/Y	
08		System timer	N	N/N	Y/Y	
09		Keyboard	N	N/N	Y/Y	
0B		Communications (COM2)	N	N/N	Y/Y	
0C		Communications (COM1)	N	N/N	Y/Y	
0D		Hard disk controller	N	N/N	Y/Y	
0E		Floppy disk	N	N/N	Y/Y	
0F		Printer	N	N/N	Y/Y	
10		Video				
	00	Set CRT mode	N	N/N	Y/Y	
	01	Set cursor type	N	N/N	Y/Y	
	02	Set cursor position	N	N/N	Y/Y	
	03	Read cursor position	N	N/N	Y/Y	
	04	Read light pen position	N	N/N	Y/Y	
	05	Select active page	N	N/N	Y/Y	
	06	Scroll active page up	N	N/N	Y/Y	
	07	Scroll active page down	N	N/N	Y/Y	
	08	Read ch/attr at cursor	N	N/N	Y/Y	
	09	Write ch/attr at cursor	N	N/N	Y/Y	
	0A	Write ch only at cursor	N	N/N	Y/Y	
	0B	Set color palette	N	N/N	Y/Y	
	0C	Write dot	N	N/N	Y/Y	
	0D	Read dot	N	N/N	Y/Y	
	0E	Write tty to active page	N	N/N	Y/Y	
	0F	Get current video state	N	N/N	Y/Y	
	10	Set palette registers	N	N/N	N/Y	
	11	Character generator	N	N/N	N/Y	
	13	Write string	N	N/N	N/Y	

TABLE 22.3: BIOS Interrupts and Services (continued)

INT hex	AH hex	DESCRIPTION	bdos()	intdos() /intdosx()	int86() /int86x()	RUN-TIME FUNCTION
11		Equipment status	N	N/N	Y/Y	_bios_equiplist()
12		Memory size	N	N/N	Y/Y	_bios_memsize()
13		Floppy/Hard disk				_bios_disk()
	00	Reset floppy	N	N/N	Y/Y	
	01	Get floppy status	N	N/N	Y/Y	
	02	Read floppy sectors	N	N/N	N/Y	
	03	Write floppy sectors	N	N/N	N/Y	
	04	Verify floppy sectors	N	N/N	Y/Y	
	05	Format floppy tracks	N	N/N	N/Y	
	08	Return disk parameters	N	N/N	N/Y	
	09	Initialize hard drive	N	N/N	Y/Y	
	0A	Read long sector	N	N/N	N/Y	
	0B	Write long sector	N	N/N	N/Y	
	0C	Seek cylinder	N	N/N	Y/Y	
	0D	Alternate disk reset	N	N/N	Y/Y	
	15	DASD type	N	N/N	Y/Y	
	16	Change line status	N	N/N	Y/Y	
	17	Set DASD format type	N	N/N	Y/Y	
	18	Set media format type	N	N/N	N/Y	
14		Communications				_bios_serialcom()
	00	Initialize port	N	N/N	Y/Y	
	01	Write to port	N	N/N	Y/Y	
	02	Read from port	N	N/N	Y/Y	
	03	Get port status	N	N/N	Y/Y	
	04	PS/2 extended init	N	N/N	Y/Y	
	05	PS/2 extended comm port	N	N/N	Y/Y	
15		Cassette				
	00	Turn motor on	N	N/N	Y/Y	
	01	Turn motor off	N	N/N	Y/Y	
	02	Read data blocks	N	N/N	Y/Y	

TABLE 22.3: BIOS Interrupts and Services (continued)

INT hex	AH hex	DESCRIPTION	bdos()	intdos() /intdosx()	int86() /int86x()	RUN-TIME FUNCTION
15	03	Write data blocks	N	N/N	Y/Y	
	0F	PS/2 format interrupt	N	N/N	Y/Y	
	21	PS/2 self-test log	N	N/N	N/N	
	4F	Keyboard intercept	N	N/N	Y/Y	
	80	Device open (multitask)	N	N/N	Y/Y	
	81	Device close (multitask)	N	N/N	Y/Y	
	82	Program term (multitask)	N	N/N	Y/Y	
	83	Event wait (INT 70)	N	N/N	N/Y	
	84	Joystick support	N	N/N	Y/Y	
	85	System request key	N	N/N	Y/Y	
	86	Wait (INT 70)	N	N/N	N/Y	
	87	Extended memory move	N	N/N	N/Y	
	88	Extended memory size	N	N/N	Y/Y	
	89	Switch protected mode	N	N/N	N/Y	
	C0	System configuration	N	N/N	N/Y	
	C1	Extended BIOS addr	N	N/N	N/Y	
	C2	Pointing Device BIOS	N	N/N	Y/Y	
	C3	PS/2 watchdog timer	N	N/N	Y/Y	
	C4	PS/2 programmable option	N	N/N	Y/Y	
16		Keyboard				`_bios_keybrd()`
	00	Read a character	N	N/N	Y/Y	
	01	Read keyboard status	N	N/N	Y/Y	
	02	Return keyboard flags	N	N/N	Y/Y	
	05	Write keyboard buffer	N	N/N	Y/Y	
	10	Get keystroke	N	N/N	Y/Y	
	11	Check keyboard	N	N/N	Y/Y	
	12	Get keyboard status	N	N/N	Y/Y	
17		Printer				`_bios_printer()`
	00	Write a character	N	N/N	Y/Y	
	01	Initialize printer	N	N/N	Y/Y	
	02	Get printer status	N	N/N	Y/Y	

TABLE 22.3: BIOS Interrupts and Services (continued)

INT hex	AH hex	DESCRIPTION	bdos()	intdos() /intdosx()	int86() /int86x()	RUN-TIME FUNCTION
18		ROM BASIC	N	N/N	Y/Y	
19		Warm Boot	N	N/N	Y/Y	
1A		System Timer				`_bios_timeofday()`
	00	Get clock counter	N	N/N	Y/Y	
	01	Set clock counter	N	N/N	Y/Y	
	02	Read real-time clock	N	N/N	Y/Y	
	03	Set real-time clock	N	N/N	Y/Y	
	04	Read real-time date	N	N/N	Y/Y	
	05	Set real-time date	N	N/N	Y/Y	
	06	Set an alarm	N	N/N	Y/Y	
	07	Reset an alarm	N	N/N	Y/Y	
1B		Ctrl-Break	N	N/N	Y/Y	
1C		Timer tick interrupt	N	N/N	Y/Y	
1D		Video Initialization	N	N/N	Y/Y	
1E		Disk Initialization	N	N/N	Y/Y	
1F		Graphics Bitmap Table	N	N/N	Y/Y	
50		Periodic Alarms	N	N/N	Y/Y	
70		Real-time Clock Interrupt	N	N/N	Y/Y	

DOS Interrupts and Services

Table 22.4 summarizes the DOS interrupt numbers and services that are available. These may vary depending upon the version of DOS you have booted. Refer to your DOS technical reference manual for the exact list of services that are available for your computer.

Note that interrupt number 0x21 provides most DOS services. Unlike BIOS services, DOS services may be accessed using **bdos()**, **intdos()**, and **intdosx()**, as well as **int86()** or **int86x()**. Also note the C run-time functions listed that utilize a DOS interrupt service. Only those run-time functions named beginning with **_dos_..** are shown. Other run-time functions utilize DOS services. Interrupt services for which C run-time functions do not exist may be accessed only by using one of the C run-time software interrupt functions flagged Y(es) in Table 22.4.

TABLE 22.4: DOS Interrupts and Services

INT hex	AH hex	AL hex	DESCRIPTION	bdos()	intdos() /intdosx()	int86() /int86x()	RUN-TIME FUNCTION
20			Terminate Program	N	N /N	N /Y	
21			DOS functions				
	00		Terminate program	N	N /Y	N /Y	
	01		Keyboard input w/echo	Y	Y /Y	Y /Y	
	02		Display output	Y	Y /Y	Y /Y	
	03		Auxiliary input	Y	Y /Y	Y /Y	
	04		Auxiliary output	Y	Y /Y	Y /Y	
	05		Printer output	Y	Y /Y	Y /Y	
	06		Direct console I/O	N	Y /Y	Y /Y	
	07		Direct **stdin** input	Y	Y /Y	Y /Y	
	08		**stdin** input	Y	Y /Y	Y /Y	
	09		Display string	Y*	Y*/Y	Y*/Y	
	0A		Buffered **stdin** input	Y*	Y*/Y	Y*/Y	
	0B		Check **stdin** status	Y	Y /Y	Y /Y	
	0C		Clear buffer and input	Y	Y /Y	Y /Y	
	0D		Reset disk	Y	Y /Y	Y /Y	
	0E		Select disk	Y	Y /Y	Y /Y	`_dos_setdrive()`
	0F		Open file (FCB)	Y*	Y*/Y	Y*/Y	
	10		Close file (FCB)	Y*	Y*/Y	Y*/Y	
	11		Find first entry (FCB)	Y*	Y*/Y	Y*/Y	
	12		Find next entry (FCB)	Y*	Y*/Y	Y*/Y	
	13		Delete file (FCB)	Y*	Y*/Y	Y*/Y	
	14		Read sequential (FCB)	Y*	Y*/Y	Y*/Y	
	15		Write sequential (FCB)	Y*	Y*/Y	Y*/Y	
	16		Create file (FCB)	Y*	Y*/Y	Y*/Y	
	17		Rename file (FCB)	Y*	Y*/Y	Y*/Y	
	19		Get default drive	Y	Y /Y	Y /Y	`_dos_getdrive()`
	1A		Set DTA address	Y*	Y*/Y	Y*/Y	
	1B		Get FAT information	N	Y*/Y	Y*/Y	
	1C		Get drive FAT info	N	Y*/Y	Y*/Y	
	21		Random file read (FCB)	Y*	Y*/Y	Y*/Y	
	22		Random file write (FCB)	Y*	Y*/Y	Y*/Y	
	23		Get file size (FCB)	Y*	Y*/Y	Y*/Y	

TABLE 22.4: DOS Interrupts and Services (continued)

INT hex	AH hex	AL hex	DESCRIPTION	bdos()	intdos() /intdosx()	int86() /int86x()	RUN-TIME FUNCTION
21	24		Set random record (FCB)	Y*	Y*/Y	Y*/Y	
	25		Set interrupt vector	Y*	Y*/Y	Y*/Y	_dos_setvect()
	26		Create PSP	Y	Y /Y	Y /Y	
	27		Random block read (FCB)	N	Y*/Y	Y*/Y	
	28		Random block write (FCB)	N	Y*/Y	Y*/Y	
	29		Parse filename	N	N /Y	N /Y	
	2A		Get system date	N	Y /Y	Y /Y	_dos_getdate()
	2B		Set system date	N	Y /Y	Y /Y	_dos_setdate()
	2C		Get system time	N	Y /Y	Y /Y	_dos_gettime()
	2D		Set system time	N	Y /Y	Y /Y	_dos_settime()
	2E		Set verify flag	Y	Y /Y	Y /Y	
	2F		Get DTA address	N	N /Y	N /Y	
	30		Get DOS version	N	Y /Y	Y /Y	
	31		Terminate/Stay Ready	Y	Y /Y	Y /Y	_dos_keep()
	33		Get/Set system values	Y	Y /Y	Y /Y	
	35		Get interrupt vector	N	N /Y	N /Y	_dos_getvect()
	36		Get free disk space	N	Y /Y	Y /Y	_dos_getdiskfree()
	38		Get/Set country info	N	Y*/Y	Y*/Y	
	39		Create subdirectory	N	Y*/Y	Y*/Y	
	3A		Remove subdirectory	N	Y*/Y	Y*/Y	
	3B		Set directory	N	Y*/Y	Y*/Y	
	3C		Create/Trunc (handle)	N	Y*/Y	Y*/Y	
	3D		Open file (handle)	N	Y*/Y	Y*/Y	_dos_open()
	3E		Close file (handle)	N	Y /Y	Y /Y	_dos_close()
	3F		Read file/dev (handle)	N	Y*/Y	Y*/Y	_dos_read()
	40		Write file/dev (handle)	N	Y*/Y	Y*/Y	_dos_write()
	41		Delete file	N	Y*/Y	Y*/Y	
	42		Move file pointer	N	Y /Y	Y /Y	
	43		Get/Set file attrib	N	Y*/Y	Y*/Y	_dos_getfileattr()
							_dos_setfileattr()
	44		IOCTL				
		00	Get device info	N	Y /Y	Y /Y	

TABLE 22.4: DOS Interrupts and Services (continued)

INT hex	AH hex	AL hex	DESCRIPTION	bdos()	intdos() /intdosx()	int86() /int86x()	RUN-TIME FUNCTION
21		01	Set device info	N	Y /Y	Y /Y	
		02	Character dev read	N	Y*/Y	Y*/Y	
		03	Character dev write	N	Y*/Y	Y*/Y	
		04	Block driver read	N	Y*/Y	Y*/Y	
		05	Block driver write	N	Y*/Y	Y*/Y	
		06	Get input status	N	Y /Y	Y /Y	
		07	Get output status	N	Y /Y	Y /Y	
		08	Block dev removable	N	Y /Y	Y /Y	
		09	Block dev local/remote	N	Y /Y	Y /Y	
		0A	Handle local/remote	N	Y /Y	Y /Y	
		0B	Set sharing retry count	N	Y /Y	Y /Y	
		0C	Generic I/O (handles)	N	Y*/Y	Y*/Y	
		0D	Generic I/O block dev	N	Y*/Y	Y*/Y	
		0E	Get logical drive map	N	Y /Y	Y /Y	
		0F	Set logical drive map	N	Y /Y	Y /Y	
	45		Duplicate handle	N	Y /Y	Y /Y	
	46		Force duplicate handle	N	Y /Y	Y /Y	
	47		Get current directory	N	Y*/Y	Y*/Y	
	48		Allocate memory	N	Y /Y	Y /Y	**_dos_allocmem**()
	49		Release memory	N	N /Y	N /Y	**_dos_freemem**()
	4A		Modify memory alloc	N	N /Y	N /Y	**_dos_setblock**()
	4B	00	Execute program (EXEC)	N	N /Y	N /Y	
		03	Load overlay	N	N /Y	N /Y	
	4C		Terminate w/return code	Y	Y /Y	Y /Y	
	4D		Get return code	Y	Y /Y	Y /Y	
	4E		Search first match	N	Y*/Y	Y*/Y	**_dos_findfirst**()
	4F		Search next match	N	Y /Y	Y /Y	**_dos_findnext**()
	54		Get verify flag	Y	Y /Y	Y /Y	
	56		Rename file	N	N /Y	N /Y	
	57	00	Get file date/time	N	Y /Y	Y /Y	**_dos_getftime**()
		01	Set file date/time	N	Y /Y	Y /Y	**_dos_setftime**()

TABLE 22.4: DOS Interrupts and Services (continued)

INT hex	AH hex	AL hex	DESCRIPTION	bdos()	intdos() /intdosx()	int86() /int86x()	RUN-TIME FUNCTION
21	59		Get extended err info	N	Y /Y	Y /Y	`_dosexterr()`
	5A		Create temporary file	N	Y*/Y	Y*/Y	
	5B		Create file	N	Y*/Y	Y*/Y	`_dos_creat()`
							`_dos_creatnew()`
	5C		Set file access	N	Y /Y	Y /Y	
	5E	00	Get machine name	N	Y*/Y	Y*/Y	
		02	Set printer setup	N	Y*/Y	Y*/Y	
		03	Get printer setup	N	N /Y	N /Y	
	5F	02	Get redirection entry	N	N /Y	N /Y	
		03	Redirect device	N	N /Y	N /Y	
		04	Cancel redirection	N	N /Y	N /Y	
	62		Get PSP address	N	Y /Y	Y /Y	
	63	00	Get lead byte table	N	Y /Y	Y /Y	
		01	Set interim flag	N	Y /Y	Y /Y	
		02	Get interim flag	N	Y /Y	Y /Y	
	65		Get ext. country info	N	N /Y	N /Y	
	66	01	Get global page table	N	Y /Y	Y /Y	
		02	Set global page table	N	Y /Y	Y /Y	
	67		Set handle count	N	Y /Y	Y /Y	
	68		Flush buffer	N	Y /Y	Y /Y	
	6C		Extended open/create	N	Y*/Y	Y*/Y	
22			Terminate Address	N	N /N	Y /Y	
23			Ctrl-C Interrupt	N	N /N	Y /Y	
24			Critical Error Vector	N	N /N	Y /Y	
25			Absolute disk read	N	N /N	Y*/Y	
26			Absolute disk write	N	N /N	Y*/Y	
27			Terminate/Stay Ready	N	N /N	N /Y	

TABLE 22.4: DOS Interrupts and Services (continued)

INT hex	AH hex	AL hex	DESCRIPTION	bdos()	intdos() /intdosx()	int86() /int86x()	RUN-TIME FUNCTION
2F			Print Install Check				
		00	Install status	N	N /N	Y*/Y	
		01	Submit file	N	N /N	Y*/Y	
		02	Remove file	N	N /N	Y*/Y	
		03	Remove all files	N	N /N	Y*/Y	
		04	Hold queue/get status	N	N /N	Y*/Y	
		05	Restart queue	N	N /N	Y*/Y	
33			Microsoft Mouse	N	N /N	Y*/Y	
5C			NetBIOS interface	N	N /N	Y*/Y	
67			Memory management	N	N /N	Y*/Y	

NOTES:
Y* For **_near** pointers only; otherwise, N(o).
  By default interrupt handlers are assigned the **_near** DS register (DGROUP).
  If SREGS is used, then DS is overridden.

INVOKING 80*X*86 INTERRUPTS

There are five C run-time functions that support the initiation of interrupts by number using the current address values found in the interrupt vector table: **bdos()**, **intdos()**, **intdosx()**, **int86()**, and **int86x()**. The following rules govern which interrupts may be initiated by these C run-time functions:

bdos(): Only with interrupt 0x21, and only for functions that are called using the DX and AL registers, and which return values only in the AX register. If the Carry Flag (CF) or any other register is required, this function may not be used.

intdos(): Only with interrupt 0x21, and for all functions except those requiring the use of segment registers (CS, DS, SS, ES); otherwise, this function supports the use of all other registers and flags.

intdosx(): Only with interrupt 0x21, but for all functions, no restrictions.

int86(): With any interrupt number, and for all functions except those requiring the use of segment registers (CS, DS, SS, ES); otherwise, this function supports the use of all other registers and flags.

int86x(): With any interrupt number and all functions, no restrictions apply.

The characteristics of each interrupt handler determine which of these run-time functions may be used. The Y(es)/N(o) indicators shown in Tables 22.3 and 22.4 indicate which of the run-time functions may be used to access each available interrupt service.

Whenever one of these C run-time functions is used to generate a software interrupt (INT assembler instruction), the following sequence of events takes place:

1. The state of the computer is preserved by pushing register values to the stack in the following order: flags, CS, IP, AX, CX, DX, BX, SP, BP, SI, DI, DS, ES. Only the stack segment (SS) register is omitted.

2. The DS register is first set equal to the **_near** data segment of the calling program by default, then the registers are assigned any initial (DX, AL, REGS, or SREGS) values, which should be assigned to conform with the calling convention of the particular interrupt service being requested. All arguments are passed to DOS/BIOS interrupt handlers in registers.

3. The interrupt number specified is used as an index to the interrupt vector table to retrieve a **_far** address to which an immediate jump occurs, marking the start of interrupt processing. Unless the **_enable()** function or the assembly instruction STI is performed, no other interrupts will be acknowledged until the processing of the interrupt is complete (see Chapter 27).

4. All return register and flag values are assigned to REGS and SREGS, prior to initiating the IRET (assembler instruction).

5. The state of the computer is restored by popping the following arguments from the stack in the following order: ES, DS, DI, SI, BP, SP, BX, DX, CX, AX, IP, CS, flags, and the run-time function return value is then placed into the AX register.

By performing Step 5 above, the interrupted function continues from the point that Step 1 was invoked, and the **bdos()**, **intdos()**, **intdosx()**, **int86()**, or **int86x()** function return value is placed into the AX register. Access to other values returned by an interrupt handler is found in the buffer area updated by Step 4.

Two non-Standard data structures REGS and SREGS play a key role in using the **intdos()**, **intdosx()**, **int86()**, and **int86x()** functions described above. For a complete description of REGS and SREGS, refer to header file **<dos.h>** or Appendix E and to Chapter 9, Figure 9.13. The program examples included in this chapter demonstrate the proper use of these structures and unions when calling register arguments is required by an interrupt service, and when return register arguments are provided by an interrupt handler.

DOS/BIOS INTERRUPT TASKS

Although efforts have been made to differentiate BIOS and DOS services, from a C application programming perspective, whether a particular service is BIOS or DOS is unimportant. All DOS/BIOS services are nameless and are accessed in the same manner using the C run-time functions **bdos()**, **intdos()**, **intdosx()**, **int86()**, and **int86x()**.

BIOS services may be accessed only by using either **int86()** or **int86x()**. When **int86x()** is used, function **segread()** is first used to establish current segment register values (CS, DS, SS, ES) in SREGS. Any required calling register values are passed in REGS.

Function **_bios_disk()** is valid for use only with diskette drives, not hard drives. The low-level nature of this function dictates a considerable degree of caution when performing **_DISK_FORMAT** or **_DISK_WRITE** services. Back up any floppy disk that is to be used before testing a program written with this function.

Unlike function **_bios_disk()**, function **_bios_equiplist()** is not dangerous and simply provides a report on the status of the equipment that is presently installed.

Functions **_bios_printer()** and **_bio_serialcom()** provide low-level services for byte-by-byte I/O with these devices. High transmission rates (above 1200 baud) may not be possible using **_bios_serialcom()** because of the overhead (time) associated with the function itself.

The **bdos()** function services a limited number of 0x21 DOS interrupts that require only the use of the DX, AL, and AX registers, and do not require segment registers or the use of the Carry Flag.

The **dosexterr()** function can provide extended error messaging services whenever DOS interrupt 0x21 or 0x24 is employed. Refer to the program example for this function and to Table 22.6 for a complete description of the available extended error messages.

Function **_dos_getdiskfree()** represents one of the **_dos..** family of run-time functions that utilize DOS interrupt 0x21 and retrieves the amount of free disk space on any mounted disk volume.

The **intdos()** and **intdosx()** functions only provide interrupt 0x21 services, and both require the use of the REGS data structure. Function **intdos()** handles all 0x21 subfunctions except those requiring segment registers (SREGS) for which **intdosx()** must be used.

The **int86()** and **int86x()** functions can be used to initiate any 80*x*86 software interrupt. Function **int86()** is limited to those interrupt services that do not utilize segment registers (SREGS) for which **int86x()** must be used.

RUN-TIME LIBRARY FUNCTIONS FOR DOS/BIOS SYSTEM CALLS

bdos()   *Invoke a DOS interrupt 0x21 subfunction that uses only the DX and AL registers*

Compatibility   □ANSI   □OS/2   □UNIX   □XENIX

See Also
```
intdos(), intdosx(), int86(), int86x()
```

Specification
```
#include <dos.h>
int bdos(int dosfunc, unsigned int dosdx, unsigned int dosal);
```

Arguments
dosfunc: DOS subfunction (AH) number; refer to Table 22.4.

dosdx: DX register value; refer to a DOS technical reference manual.

dosal: AL register value; refer to a DOS technical reference manual.

Return Value
value of the AX register

Example
```
/* FILE: ch22e1.c */
#include <stdio.h>
#include <dos.h>
#include <stdlib.h>

int main(void)
{
int ret, drive;
char letter;
```

```
long free;
struct diskfree_t disk;
char msg[] = "\nDefault Drive Number is $";

ret = bdos(0x19, 0, 0);
drive = ret & 0x00FF;
letter = 'A' + drive;
bdos(0x09, (unsigned)msg, (unsigned)0);
printf("%d or %c\n", drive, letter);

system("DIR *.*");

_dos_getdiskfree((unsigned)(drive + 1), &disk);
free = (long) disk.avail_clusters *
    (long) disk.sectors_per_cluster *
    (long) disk.bytes_per_sector;
printf("\nBytes/Sector = %d", disk.bytes_per_sector);
printf("\nComputed Bytes Free = %ld", free);

exit(0);
}
```

Output

```
Default Drive Number is 2
Volume in drive C is RRMASTER
Directory of C:\QC2\BOOK
. <DIR> 5-23-89 9:31a
.. <DIR> 5-23-89 9:31a
OUTLINE  DOC   2432   2-11-90   6:47p
 .
 .
 .
CH-10    DOC 111232   3-15-90   2:40p
     422 File(s) 274432 bytes free
2 or C
Bytes/Sector = 512
Computed Bytes Free = 274432
```

Comments **bdos()** invokes only INT 0x21, and should be used only for DOS functions that have no arguments or arguments that only require the DX (DH, DL) and/or AL registers, and which do not set the Carry Flag (see Figure 9.13) to indicate that an error has occurred.

In the example program, had the $-terminated string **msg** been located in a **_far** data segment beyond the address range of the DS register, then function **bdos()** could not have been used, and either **intdosx()** or **int86x()** would have been required. See the note accompanying Table 22.4.

_bios_disk() _Invoke BIOS Floppy/Hard disk services interrupt 0x13_

Compatibility ☐ANSI ☐OS/2 ☐UNIX ☐XENIX

Specification

```
#include <bios.h>
unsigned _bios_disk(unsigned service, struct diskinfo_t *diskinfo);
```

Arguments

service: One of the following object-like macros found in **<bios.h>**:

_DISK_FORMAT: Format one track specified in the **diskinfo_t** structure.

_DISK_READ: Read one or more sectors specified in the **diskinfo_t** structure. The high-order byte of the return value (AX register) will be set as shown in Table 22.5.

_DISK_RESET: Force the disk controller to perform a hard reset and prepare for I/O. Structure **diskinfo_t** is ignored.

TABLE 22.5: _bios_disk() Return Values for Service Option _DISK_READ

Return Value	Description
0x00**	No error
0x01**	Invalid request
0x02**	Address mark not found
0x04**	Sector not found
0x05**	Reset failed
0x07**	Drive parameter activity failed
0x09**	DMA overrun
0x0A**	Bad sector flag detected
0x10**	Data read (ECC) error
0x11**	Corrected data read (ECC) error
0x20**	Controller failure
0x40**	Seek error
0x80**	Disk timed-out
0xAA**	Drive not ready
0xBB**	Undefined error
0xCC**	Write fault on drive
0xE0**	Status error

_DISK_STATUS: Obtain the status of the last operation. See the error codes listed for **_DISK_READ**. Structure **diskinfo_t** is ignored.

_DISK_VERIFY: Check that the specified sectors described in structure **diskinfo_t** exist and can be read. See the error codes listed for **_DISK_READ**.

_DISK_WRITE: Write one or more sectors specified in the **diskinfo_t** structure. See the error codes listed for **_DISK_READ**.

diskinfo: Pointer to a **diskinfo** type structure; see the structure declaration found in Appendix E.

Return Value

Value of the AX register

Example

```
/* FILE: ch22e2.c */
#include <stdio.h>
#include <bios.h>
#define DR_MAX 3
#define HD_MAX 4
#define TR_MAX 128
#define SE_MAX 32

int main(void)
{
static char buffer[1024];
unsigned heads, tracks, sectors;
void _far *ptr = (char _far *)buffer;
struct diskinfo_t di = {0, 0, 0, 1, 1, ptr};
int dr, hd, tr, se;
unsigned ret;

printf("\nFloppy Drive Report");
for (dr=0; dr<=DR_MAX; dr++) {
    heads = tracks = sectors = 0;
    di.drive = dr;
    _bios_disk(_DISK_RESET, &di);
    ret = _bios_disk(_DISK_READ, &di);
    if (ret &= 0xFF00) {
        printf("\n\nNo Volume/Drive %d <status=%#0x>", dr, ret);
        continue;
        }

    for (hd=0; hd<=HD_MAX; hd++) {
        di.head = hd;
        ret = _bios_disk(_DISK_READ, &di);
        if (ret &= 0xFF00) {
            _bios_disk(_DISK_RESET, &di);
            break;
```

```
            }
        if (hd > heads) heads = hd;
        }

    di.head = 0;
    for (tr=0; tr<=TR_MAX; tr++) {
        di.track = tr;
        ret = _bios_disk(_DISK_READ, &di);
        if (ret &= 0xFF00) {
            _bios_disk(_DISK_RESET, &di);
            break;
            }
        if (tr > tracks) tracks = tr;
        }

    di.track = 0;
    for (se=1; se<=SE_MAX; se++) {
        di.sector = se;
        ret = _bios_disk(_DISK_READ, &di);
        if (ret &= 0xFF00) {
            _bios_disk(_DISK_RESET, &di);
            break;
            }
        if (se > sectors) sectors = se;
        }

    di.sector = 1;
    printf("\n\nDrive %d", dr);
    printf("\nHeads : 0 - %u", heads);
    printf("\nTracks : 0 - %u", tracks);
    printf("\nSectors : 1 - %u", sectors);
    }
exit(0);
}
```

Output

```
Floppy Drive Report

Drive 0
Heads   : 0 - 1
Tracks  : 0 - 39
Sectors : 1 - 9

No Volume/Drive 1 <status=0x6000>

No Volume/Drive 2 <status=0x8000>

No Volume/Drive 3 <status=0x8000>
```

Comments   The nondestructive program example attempts to query floppy disk drives 0–3 and reports the number of heads, tracks, and sectors that exist for each installed drive that has a floppy disk mounted.

Notice that the buffer member of structure type **diskinfo_t** is a **_far** pointer. Error code <status=0x6000> represents the OR combination of error codes 0x20** and 0x40**.

Use the appropriate DOS commands as an alternative to this function.

_bios_equiplist() *Invoke BIOS equipment list services interrupt 0x11*

Compatibility ☐ANSI ☐OS/2 ☐UNIX ☐XENIX

Specification

```
#include <bios.h>
unsigned _bios_equiplist(void);
```

Return Value

unsigned int bit settings of installed equipment as follows:

BIT	DESCRIPTION
0	TRUE if any disk drive installed
1	TRUE if math coprocessor installed
2–3	System RAM in 16KB blocks
4–5	Initial video mode
6–7	Number of floppy disk drives
8	FALSE if DMA chip installed
9–11	Number of RS–232 ports installed
12	TRUE if game adapter installed
13	TRUE if internal modem installed
14–15	Number of printers installed

Example

```
/* FILE: ch22e3.c */
#include <stdio.h>
#include <bios.h>

#define DISKS 0x0001
#define MATH 0x0002
#define SRAM 0x000C
#define VMOD 0x0030
#define FDISK 0x00C0
#define DMA 0x0100
#define RS232 0x0E00
#define GAME 0x1000
```

```c
#define MODEM 0x2000
#define PRINT 0xC000

int main(void)
{
unsigned bits, temp;
bits = _bios_equiplist();
printf("\nbits = %#04x\n", bits);

if (bits & DISKS) printf("\nDisk Drive Installed");
else printf("\nDisk Drive NOT Installed");

if(bits & MATH) printf("\nCoprocessor Installed");
else printf("\nCoprocessor NOT installed");

temp = (bits & SRAM) >> 2;
printf("\nSystem RAM = %dKB", 16 + (temp * 16) );

temp = (bits & VMOD) >> 4;
printf("\nInitial Video Mode = %#0x ", temp);
switch (temp) {
    case 1: printf("(40x25 color)"); break;
    case 2: printf("(80x25 color)"); break;
    case 3: printf("(80x25 mono)"); break;
    }

temp = (bits & FDISK) >> 6;
printf("\nNumber of Floppy Drives = %d", temp+1);

if (bits & DMA) printf("\nDMA Chip NOT Installed");
else printf("\nDMA Chip Installed");

temp = (bits & RS232) >> 9;
printf("\nNumber of RS-232 Ports = %d", temp);

if (bits & GAME) printf("\nGame Adapter Installed");
else printf("\nGame Adapter NOT Installed");

if (bits & MODEM) printf("\nInternal Modem Installed");
else printf("\nInternal Modem NOT Installed");

temp = (bits & PRINT) >> 14;
printf("\nNumber of Printers = %d", temp);
exit(0);
}
```

Output

```
bits = 0x423d

Disk Drive Installed
Coprocessor NOT installed
System RAM = 64KB
Initial Video Mode = 0x3 (80x25 mono)
```

```
Number of Floppy Drives = 1
DMA Chip Installed
Number of RS-232 Ports = 1
Game Adapter NOT Installed
Internal Modem NOT Installed
Number of Printers = 1
```

Comments This function is nondestructive and simply reports on the status of installed devices.

_bios_printer() *Invoke BIOS printer services interrupt 0x17*

Compatibility ☐ANSI ☐OS/2 ☐UNIX ☐XENIX

Specification

```
#include <bios.h>
unsigned _bios_printer(unsigned service, unsigned printer, unsigned data);
```

Arguments

service: One of the following object-like macros found in **<bios.h>**:
_PRINTER_INIT, **_PRINTER_STATUS**, or **_PRINTER_WRITE**

printer: 0=LPT1, 1=LPT2 etc.

data: Low-order byte sent to printer.

Return Value

Value of the AX register

The low-order byte, which reflects the error conditions noted in the program example that follows

Example

```
/* FILE: ch22e4.c */
#include <stdio.h>
#include <bios.h>

static void retmsg(unsigned ret)
{
char *msg[]= {
    "bit-0: printer timed out",
    "bit-1: not used",
    "bit-2: not used",
    "bit-3: I/O error",
    "bit-4: printer selected",
    "bit-5: out of paper",
    "bit-6: acknowledge",
    "bit-7: printer not busy" };
```

```
int i;
unsigned test=0x0001;
if (ret != 0x0000)
    for (i=0; i<8; i++) if (ret & (test << i))
        printf("\n\t>%s<", msg[i]);
}

int main(void)
{
unsigned ret, data = 0;
enum { LPT1, LPT2, LPT3, PRN=0 };

ret = _bios_printer(_PRINTER_STATUS, LPT1, data);
printf("\nPresent Printer <status=%#04x>", ret);
retmsg(ret & 0x00FF);

ret = _bios_printer(_PRINTER_INIT, LPT1, data);
printf("\nInitialized Printer <status=%#04x>", ret);
retmsg(ret & 0x00FF);

data = '\f';
ret = _bios_printer(_PRINTER_WRITE, PRN, data);
printf("\nForm Feed Printer <status=%#04x>", ret);
retmsg(ret & 0x00FF);

exit(0);
}
```

Output

```
Present Printer <status=0x90>
    >bit-4: printer selected<
    >bit-7: printer not busy<
Initialized Printer <status=0000>
Form Feed Printer <status=0000>
```

Comments   The output reflects a normal printer waiting **_PRINTER_STATUS** return value, followed by error free **_PRINTER_INIT** and **_PRINTER_WRITE** operations, which perform a form-feed.

Note the use of the **enum** type declaration that initializes LPT1=0, LPT2=1, LPT3=2 by virtue of the default initialization performed for **enum** types.

As an alternative to **_bios_printer()**, you can use any **stdprn** or redirected **stdout** stream or equivalent low-level I/O function.

_bios_serialcom()   *Invoke BIOS serial communications services*
Interrupt 0x14

Compatibility   ☐ANSI   ☐OS/2   ☐UNIX   ☐XENIX

Specification

```
#include <bios.h>
unsigned _bios_serialcom(unsigned service, unsigned port, unsigned data);
```

Arguments

service: One of the following object-like macros found in **<bios.h>**:
_COM_INIT, _COM_SEND, _COM_RECEIVE, or **_COM_STATUS**

port: 0=COM1, 1=COM2

data: When **_COM_INIT** is specified, the data argument is expressed by an OR combination of the following object-like macros found in **<bios.h>**:
_COM_CHR7, _COM_CHR8, _COM_STOP1, _COM_STOP2, _COM_NOPARITY, _COM_EVENPARITY, _COM_ODDPARITY, _COM_110, _COM_150, _COM_300, _COM_600, _COM_1200, _COM_2400, _COM_4800, and **_COM_9600**.

When **_COM_SEND** is specified, the low-order byte of the data argument is sent to port.

When **_COM_RECEIVE** is specified, the data argument is ignored.

When **_COM_STATUS** is specified, the data argument is ignored.

Return Value

unsigned int bit settings of the status of communications convey the status and error conditions noted in the program example that follows.

When **_COM_INIT** is specified, bit 0 through bit 7 are set.

When **_COM_SEND** is specified, bit 15 is on if data could not be sent.

When **_COM_RECEIVE** is specified, bit 9, bit 10, bit 11, or bit 15 will be set if an error occurs; otherwise, the byte read is returned in bit 0 through bit 7.

When **_COM_STATUS** is specified, bit 0 through bit 7 are set.

Example

```
/* FILE: ch22e5.c */
#include <stdio.h>
#include <bios.h>

static void retmsg(unsigned status, unsigned ret)
{
char *msg[] = {
    "bit-0 : change in clear-to-send status",
    "bit-1 : change in date-set-ready status",
    "bit-2 : trailing-edge ring indicator",
    "bit-3 : change in receive-line signal detected",
    "bit-4 : clear to send",
    "bit-5 : data set ready",
    "bit-6 : ring indicator",
    "bit-7 : receive-line signal detected",
```

```
        "bit-8 : data ready",
        "bit-9 : overrun error",
        "bit-10: parity error",
        "bit-11: framing error",
        "bit-12: break detected",
        "bit-13: transmission-hold register empty",
        "bit-14: transmission-shift register empty",
        "bit-15: timed out",
        "bit-15: data could not be sent" };
    int i;
    unsigned test=0x0001;
    for (i=0; i<16; i++)
        if (ret & (test << i)) switch (status) {
            case _COM_SEND    : if (i==15) i++;
            case _COM_INIT    :
            case _COM_STATUS  : printf("\n\t>%s<", msg[i]);
                break;
            case _COM_RECEIVE : if (i < 8) break;
                printf("\n\t>%s<", msg[i]);
                break;
        }
    }

int main(void)
{
unsigned ret, data = 0;
enum { COM1, COM2, COM3 };

ret = _bios_serialcom(_COM_STATUS, COM1, data);
printf("\nPresent COM1 <status=%#04x>", ret);
retmsg(_COM_STATUS, ret);

data = _COM_1200 | _COM_CHR7 | _COM_STOP2 | _COM_NOPARITY;
ret = _bios_serialcom(_COM_INIT, COM1, data);
printf("\nInitialized COM1 <status=%#04x>", ret);
retmsg(_COM_INIT, ret);

data = 0x20;
ret = _bios_serialcom(_COM_SEND, COM1, data);
printf("\nCOM1 Send <status=%#04x>", ret);
retmsg(_COM_SEND, ret);

exit(0);
}
```

Output

```
Present COM1 <status=0x6010>
    >bit-4 : clear to send<
    >bit-13: transmission-hold register empty<
    >bit-14: transmission-shift register empty<
    .
    .
```

```
COM1 Send <status=0x9020>
    >bit-5 : data set ready<
    >bit-12: break detected<
    >bit-15: data could not be sent<
```

Comments The **msg[]** array of pointers to type **char** in **static** function retmsg() summarizes the status and error bit settings returned by **_bios_serialcom()**.

As an alternative use direct **inp()** and **outp()** programming of the serial-port controllers.

dosexterr() *Invoke DOS interrupt 0x21 extended error subfunction 0x59*

Compatibility □ANSI □OS/2 □UNIX □XENIX

Specification

```
#include <dos.h>
int dosexterr(struct DOSERROR *info);
```

Arguments

info: Pointer to a structure of type **DOSERROR**:

```
struct DOSERROR {int exterror;
    char class;
    char action;
    char locus;};
```

If **NULL** used, then the **DOSERROR** structure is not filled, and the **exterror** field is returned (AX register value).

Table 22.6 summarizes the message codes values and descriptions available for the members of a **DOSERROR** type structure.

Return Value

The value of the **exterror** member of structure type **DOSERROR**

Example See: **intdosx()**.

Comments Whenever DOS interrupt 0x21 or 0x24 is invoked and yields an error condition, the **dosexterr()** function may be called immediately to expand upon the error message that would otherwise result if global variable **errno** were tested and displayed using **strerror()**.

In the program example, when the **intdosx()** function encounters an error condition, the Carry Flag (CF) bit 0 of the **cflag** member of REGS is set On (true), and the extended error messaging is provided.

This function augments the error handling provided by global variables **errno**, **_doserrno**, **sys_errlist[]**, and **sys_nerr**, and run-time functions **perror()**, **strerror()**, and **_strerror()**.

TABLE 22.6: **dosexterr()** Error Codes

STRUCTURE MEMBER	REGISTER	VALUE	DESCRIPTION
exterror	AX	01	Invalid function number
		02	File not found
		03	Path not found
		04	Too many open files
		05	Access denied
		06	Invalid handle
		07	Memory control blocks destroyed
		08	Insufficient memory
		09	Invalid memory block address
		10	Invalid environment
		11	Invalid format
		12	Invalid access code
		13	Invalid data
		15	Invalid drive
		16	Attempt to remove current directory
		17	Not same device
		18	No more files
		19	Write protected diskette
		20	Unknown unit
		21	Drive not ready
		22	Unknown command
		23	Data error (crc)
		24	Bad request structure length
		25	Seek error
		26	Unknown media type
		27	Sector not found

TABLE 22.6: `dosexterr()` Error Codes (continued)

STRUCTURE MEMBER	REGISTER	VALUE	DESCRIPTION
`exterror` (cont.)	AX	28	Printer out of paper
		29	Write fault
		30	Read fault
		31	General failure
		32	Sharing violation
		33	Lock violation
		34	Invalid disk change
		35	FCB unavailable
		36	Sharing buffer overflow
		37–49	*Reserved*
		50	Network request unsupported
		51	Remote computer unavailable
		52	Duplicate network name
		53	Missing network name
		54	Network busy
		55	Network device no longer exists
		56	NetBIOS command limit exceeded
		57	Network adaptor hardware error
		58	Incorrect network response
		59	Unexpected network error
		60	Incompatible network adapter
		61	Print queue full
		62	Out of print file space
		63	Print file deleted
		64	Network name deleted
		65	Access denied
		66	Network device type incorrect
		67	Network name not found
		68	Network name limit exceeded
		69	NetBIOS session limit exceeded
		70	Temporarily paused
		71	Network request rejected
		72	Print or disk redirect paused
		80	File exists

TABLE 22.6: `dosexterr()` Error Codes (continued)

STRUCTURE MEMBER	REGISTER	VALUE	DESCRIPTION
`exterror` (cont.)	AX	82	Directory entry failed
		83	INT 24 failure
		84	Too many redirections
		85	Duplicate redirection
		86	Invalid password
		87	Invalid parameter
		88	Network data fault
`class`	BH	01	Out of resource
		02	Temporary situation
		03	Authorization
		04	Internal error
		05	Hardware failure
		06	System failure
		07	Application program error
		08	Not found
		09	Bad format
		10	Locked
		11	Media
		12	Already exists
		13	Unknown
`action`	BL	01	Retry
		02	Delay retry
		03	User
		04	Abort
		05	Immediate exit
		06	Ignore
		07	Retry after user intervention
`locus`	CH	01	Unknown
		02	Block device
		03	Network
		04	Serial device
		05	Memory

_dos_getdiskfree()   *Invoke DOS interrupt 0x21 disk information subfunction 0x36*

Compatibility   ☐ANSI   ☐OS/2   ☐UNIX   ☐XENIX

Specification

```
#include <dos.h>
#include <errno.h>
unsigned _dos_getdiskfree(unsigned drive, struct diskfree_t *space);
```

Arguments

drive: 0=A, 1=B, 2=C, and so forth.

space: Pointer to a **diskfree_t** type structure defined in Appendix E.

Return Value

If successful, zero (false)

Otherwise, nonzero (true), and global variable **errno** set to **EINVAL**

Example   See: **bdos()**.

Comments   The program example demonstrates the equivalence of using a DOS command or calculating the unused or free disk space from the members of structure type **diskfree_t**.

int86()   *Execute any 80x86 interrupt using REGS*

Compatibility   ☐ANSI   ☐OS/2   ☐UNIX   ☐XENIX

See Also

```
int86x()
```

Specification

```
#include <dos.h>
int int86(int intnum, union REGS *inregs, union REGS *outregs);
```

Arguments

intnum: Any 80x86 interrupt number (hex); refer to Tables 22.3 and 22.4.

inregs: Pointer to a **REGS** type structure containing the calling register argument values required for the BIOS or DOS function being invoked (AX, BX, CX, DX, SI, DI).

outregs: Pointer to a **REGS** type structure containing the return register and flag values of the BIOS or DOS interrupt that was performed (AX, BX, CX, DX, SI, DI, CFLAGS).

Return Value

Value of the AX register

If the **cflag** field of outregs is nonzero, an error has occurred, and global variable **_doserrno** is set accordingly (see function **dosexterr()**)

Example

```
/* FILE: ch22e6.c */
#include <stdio.h>
#include <bios.h>
#include <stdarg.h>
#include <string.h>

#define INT_VIDEO 0x10
#define FN_WRCA 0x09
#define FN_GETDM 0x0F

int aprintf(unsigned char attr, char *format, ... )
{
unsigned char page;
char buffer[80];
va_list ptr;
int ret, i, size;
union REGS ir, or;

va_start(ptr, format);
ret = vsprintf(buffer, format, ptr);
size = strlen(buffer);

/* get active page number */
ir.h.ah = FN_GETDM;
int86(INT_VIDEO, &ir, &or);
page = or.h.bh;

/* write attributes and string */
ir.h.ah = FN_WRCA;
ir.h.al = ' ';
ir.h.bh = page;
ir.h.bl = attr;
ir.x.cx = size;
int86(INT_VIDEO, &ir, &or);
printf("%s", buffer);

/* reset the attribute setting */
ir.h.ah = FN_WRCA;
ir.h.al = ' ';
ir.h.bh = page;
ir.h.bl = 0x07;
```

```
    ir.x.cx = 1;
    int86(INT_VIDEO, &ir, &or);
    printf("%c", ' ');
    return (ret);
    }

    int main(void)
    {
    int retval;
    unsigned attr;

    /* Attribute Byte Bit Settings

        bit-7    Blink Control           (0=OFF,  1=ON)
        bit-6    Background Red-gun       (0=OFF,  1=ON)
        bit-5    Background Green-gun     (0=OFF,  1=ON)
        bit-4    Background Blue-gun      (0=OFF,  1=ON)

        bit-3    Intensity Control       (0=LOW,  1=HIGH)
        bit-2    Foreground Red-gun       (0=OFF,  1=ON)
        bit-1    Foreground Green-gun     (0=OFF,  1=ON)
        bit-0    Foreground Blue-gun      (0=OFF,  1=ON)

        Examples:
             0x00    nondisplay
             0x01    underline display
             0x07    normal display (white on black)
             0x70    reverse video
             0x87    blinking normal display
             0xF0    blinking reverse video display
    */

    while (1) {
        printf("\n\nEnter Attribute (as 0xhh) or 0x00 to END: ");
        scanf("%x", &attr);
        fflush(stdin);
        if (!attr) break;
        retval = aprintf(attr, "%d %f %s", 33, -100.25, "Sample String!");
        printf("\nCharacter written = %d", retval);
        }
    exit(0);
    }
```

Output

```
    Enter Attribute (as 0xhh) or 0x00 to END: 0x07
    33 -100.250000 Sample String!    (normal)
    Character written = 29

    Enter Attribute (as 0xhh) or 0x00 to END: 0x70
    33 -100.250000 Sample String!    (reverse video)
    Character written = 29

    Enter Attribute (as 0xhh) or 0x00 to END: end
```

Comments `int86()` may be used to invoke any 80*x*86 (BIOS or DOS) interrupt provided that it does not require the use of any segment registers (ES, CS, SS, DS) that are normally described in SREGS. The REGS structure is used to pass and return register and flag values (AX, BX, CX, DX, SI, DI, and CFLAGS).

The program example demonstrates the use of `int86()` to perform BIOS interrupt 0x10, for which no C run-time functions are provided.

The example creates a new function called `aprintf()`, which supports all the features of the `printf()` family of functions, in addition to providing attribute control over what is displayed to the video—underlining, reverse video, blinking, intensity control, etc.

Notice that the `int86()` in `aprintf()` just prior to the `printf()` statement is responsible for setting the attribute, and does not move the cursor in doing so. The `printf()` call moves the cursor location.

Refer to Chapter 20 for a description of using the `vsprintf()` function in `aprintf()`.

`int86x()`   *Execute any 80x86 interrupt using* REGS *and* SREGS

Compatibility   □ANSI   □OS/2   □UNIX   □XENIX

Specification
```
#include <dos.h>
int int86x(int intnum, union REGS *inregs,
    union REGS *outregs,
    struct SREGS *segregs);
```

Arguments
inregs: Pointer to a **REGS** type structure containing the calling register argument values required for the BIOS or DOS function being invoked (AX, BX, CX, DX, SI, DI).

outregs: Pointer to a **REGS** type structure containing the return register and flag values of the BIOS or DOS interrupt that was performed (AX, BX, CX, DX, SI, DI, CFLAGS).

segregs: Pointer to an **SREGS** type structure containing the current (ES, CS, SS, CS) register values, derived using function `segread()`, or as derived from a `_far` pointer using the `FP_SEG()` macro defined in `<dos.h>`. As input, only ES and DS registers are used; as output, the function ES and DS values are saved, and DS is restored.

Return Value
Value of the AX register

If the **cflag** field of **outregs** is nonzero, an error has occurred and global variable **_doserrno** is set accordingly (see function **dosexterr()**)

Example

```
/* FILE: ch22e7.c */
#include <stdio.h>
#include <dos.h>
#include <stdlib.h>
#define INT_DOS 0x21
#define FN_REN 0x56

int main(void)
{
char srch_path[40], command_line[80] = "DIR ";
static char oldpath[60], newpath[60];
char _far *optr=oldpath, *nptr=newpath;
union REGS ir, or;
struct SREGS sr;

printf("\nTest Program for Renaming DOS Files\n");
while (1) {
    printf("\n\nEnter a Drive:\Directory or END ");
    gets(srch_path);
    if (!stricmp(srch_path, "END")) break;
    strcpy(&command_line[4], srch_path);
    system(command_line);

    printf("\nEnter a complete oldFile pathname: ");
    gets(oldpath);
    printf("\nEnter a complete newFile pathname: ");
    gets(newpath);

    segread(&sr);
    ir.h.ah = FN_REN;
    sr.es = sr.ds;
    ir.x.di = (unsigned)nptr;
    sr.ds = FP_SEG(optr);
    ir.x.dx = (unsigned) FP_OFF(optr);
    int86x(INT_DOS, &ir, &or, &sr);

    if (or.x.cflag & 0x0001) {
        printf("\nRenaming error: ");
        switch (or.x.ax ) {
            case 0x02: printf("File not found!"); break;
            case 0x03: printf("Path not found!"); break;
            case 0x05: printf("Access denied!"); break;
            case 0x11: printf("Not same device!"); break;
            }
        }
    }
exit(0);
}
```

Output

```
Test Program for Renaming DOS Files

Enter a Drive:Directory or END  C:\

Volume in drive C is RRMASTER
Directory of C:\
COMMAND  COM    23210   3-07-85   1:43p
SHUTDOWN BAT       59   1-01-80  12:11a
.
.
DOS           <DIR>         6-01-85  12:01a
       22 File(s)    249856 bytes free
Enter a complete oldFile pathname: C:\SHUTDOWN.BAT

Enter a complete newFile pathname: C:\SHUTDOWN.SAV
Enter a Drive:Directory or END  C:\
Volume in drive C is RRMASTER
Directory of C:\
COMMAND  COM    23210   3-07-85   1:43p
SHUTDOWN SAV       59   1-01-80  12:11a
.
.
DOS           <DIR>         6-01-85  12:01a
       22 File(s)    249856 bytes free
Enter a complete oldFile pathname: C:\SHUTDOWN
Enter a complete newFile pathname: C:\SHUTDOWN.BAT
Renaming error: File not found!

Enter a Drive:Directory or END  end
```

Comments **int86x()** may be used to invoke any 80*x*86 BIOS or DOS interrupt, because all registers and flags are passed and returned.

The program example demonstrates the correct use of **segread()** and **FP_SEG()** when both **_near** and **_far** pointers are passed using registers.

The DOS 0x21 subfunction 0x56 performs the renaming of files. The files may be in different directories, but must be on the same drive (volume).

As discussed in Chapter 28, using assembly language offers an alternative to this function.

intdos() *Execute a DOS interrupt 0x21 subfunction using* REGS

Compatibility ☐ANSI   ☐OS/2   ☐UNIX   ☐XENIX

See Also

```
bdos(), indosx(), int86(), int86x()
```

Specification

```
#include <dos.h>
int intdos(union REGS *inregs, union REGS *outregs);
```

Arguments

inregs: Pointer to a **REGS** type structure containing the calling register argument values required for the BIOS or DOS function being invoked (AX, BX, CX, DX, SI, DI).

outregs: Pointer to a **REGS** type structure containing the return register and flag values of the BIOS or DOS interrupt that was performed (AX, BX, CX, DX, SI, DI, CFLAGS).

Return Value

Value of the AX register

If the **cflag** field of **outregs** is nonzero, an error has occurred, and global variable **_doserrno** is set accordingly (see function **dosexterr()**)

Example

```
/* FILE: ch22e8.c */
#include <stdio.h>
#include <dos.h>
#define FN_COUNTRY 0x38

static struct {unsigned date;
    char currency_sym[5];
    char thousands_sep[2];
    char decimal_sep[2];
    char date_sep[2];
    char time_sep[2] ;
    unsigned char currency_fmt;
    unsigned char currency_dec;
    unsigned char time_fmt;
    unsigned fill_1[2];
    char data_sep[2];
    unsigned fill_2[5];} buffer, *ptr=&buffer;

int main (void)
{
union REGS ir, or;
char cc[5];
int icc;
ir.h.ah = FN_COUNTRY;
ir.h.al = 0x0;
ir.x.dx = (unsigned) ptr;

intdos(&ir, &or);
```

```
printf("\ncountry code = %03d\n", or.x.bx);
printf("\ndate format = %u ", ptr->date);
    if (ptr->date == 0) printf("mm/dd/yy");
    if (ptr->date == 1) printf("dd/mm/yy");
    if (ptr->date == 2) printf("yy/mm/dd");
printf("\ndate separator = %s\n", ptr->date_sep);
printf("\ntime format = %u ", ptr->time_fmt);
    printf("hh:mm:ss");
printf("\ntime separator = %s\n", ptr->time_sep);
printf("\ncurrency format = %u ", ptr->currency_fmt);
    if(ptr->currency_fmt & 0x01) printf("suffix");
    else printf("prefix");
    if(ptr->currency_fmt & 0x02) printf("/1-space");
    else printf("/0-space");
printf("\ncurrency symbol = %s", ptr->currency_sym);
printf("\nthousands separator = %s", ptr->thousands_sep);
printf("\ndecimal separator = %s", ptr->decimal_sep);
printf("\ncurrency decimal places= %d\n", ptr->currency_dec);
printf("\ndata list separator = %s\n", ptr->data_sep);
exit(0);
}
```

Output

```
country code          = 001

date format           = 0 mm/dd/yy
date separator        = -

time format           = 0 hh:mm:ss
time separator        = :

currency format       = 0 prefix/0-space
currency symbol       = $
thousands separator   = ,
decimal separator     = .
currency decimal places= 2

data list separator   = ,
```

Comments   intdos() may be used to invoke any DOS interrupt 0x21 subfunction provided that it does not require the use of any segment registers (ES, CS, SS, DS) that are normally described in **SREGS**. The **REGS** structure is used to pass and return register and flag values (AX, BX, CX, DX, SI, DI, and CFLAGS).

The program example demonstrates the use of **intdos()** to perform DOS interrupt 0x21 subfunction 0x38, which returns the DOS-specific international date, time, and currency display formats, and characters based upon the CONFIG.SYS, FILES=*xxx* country code setting discussed in Chapter 1.

Microsoft C version 6.0 only supports the C locale with the Standard C functions. When other locale description tables are available, it will no longer be necessary to employ such non-Standard approaches as shown above to accommodate the formation and display of international dates, times, and currency values from an application program.

`intdosx()`   *Execute a DOS interrupt 0x21 subfunction using* REGS *and* SREGS

Compatibility   ☐ANSI   ☐OS/2   ☐UNIX   ☐XENIX

See Also

```
int86x()
```

Specification

```
#include <dos.h>
int intdosx(union REGS *inregs,
    union REGS *outregs,
    struct SREGS *segregs);
```

Arguments

inregs: Pointer to a **REGS** type structure containing the calling register argument values required for the BIOS or DOS function being invoked (AX, BX, CX, DX, SI, DI).

outregs: Pointer to a **REGS** type structure containing the return register and flag values of the BIOS or DOS interrupt that was performed (AX, BX, CX, DX, SI, DI, CFLAGS).

segregs: Pointer to an **SREGS** type structure containing the current (ES, CS, SS, CS) register values, derived using function **segread()**, or as derived from a **_far** pointer using the **FP_SEG()** macro defined in **<dos.h>**. As input, only ES and DS registers are used; as output, the function ES and DS values are saved, and DS is restored.

Return Value

Value of the AX register

If the **cflag** field of **outregs** is nonzero, an error has occurred, and global variable **_doserrno** is set accordingly (see function **dosexterr()**)

Example

```
/* FILE: ch22e9.c */
#include <stdio.h>
#include <dos.h>
#include <stdlib.h>
#define FN_GETINT 0x35

int main(void)
{
```

```
union REGS ir, or;
struct SREGS sr;
struct DOSERROR de;
unsigned char inter;
unsigned long pspaddr, pspkbs, phyaddr, kbs;

pspaddr = (unsigned long)_psp << 4;
pspkbs = pspaddr / 1024ul;
printf("\n\n80x86 interrupt Table\n");
for (inter=0x00; inter<=0x70; inter++) {
    printf("\ninterrupt %#.02x ", inter);
    ir.h.ah = FN_GETINT;
    ir.h.al = inter;
    segread(&sr);
    intdosx(&ir, &or, &sr);
    if (or.x.cflag & 0x0001) {
        dosexterr(&de);
        printf("Error: %d Class: %d Action: %d Locus: %d",
            de.exterror, de.class, de.action, de.locus);
    }
    else {
        printf("Address %04x:%04x = ", sr.es, or.x.bx);
        phyaddr = ((unsigned long)sr.es << 4) +
            (unsigned long) or.x.bx;
        kbs = phyaddr / 1024ul;
        printf("%9lu (%4luKB+)", phyaddr, kbs);
        if (kbs == 0) printf("  N/A");
        else if (kbs < pspkbs) printf("  DOS or PROG");
        else if (kbs >= pspkbs && kbs < 640) printf("  PROG");
        else if (kbs >= 640 && kbs < 768) printf("  VIDEO");
        else if (kbs >= 768 && kbs < 1016) printf("  BIOS EXT");
        else if (kbs >= 1016) printf(" ROM BIOS");
    }
}
printf("\n");
exit(0);
}
```

Output

```
80x86 Interrupt Table

Interrupt 0x00  Address  0bc3:032c  =     48988 (  47KB+)  PROG
Interrupt 0x01  Address  0070:01f0  =      2288 (   2KB+)  DOS or PROG
Interrupt 0x02  Address  f000:f85f  =   1046623 (1022KB+)  ROM BIOS
Interrupt 0x03  Address  0070:01f0  =      2288 (   2KB+)  DOS or PROG
.
.
.
Interrupt 0x40  Address  f000:ec59  =   1043545 (1019KB+)  ROM BIOS
Interrupt 0x41  Address  c800:03e7  =    820199 ( 800KB+)  BIOS EXT
Interrupt 0x42  Address  0000:0000  =         0 (   0KB+)  N/A
.
.
.
Interrupt 0x70  Address  0000:0000  =         0 (   0KB+)  N/A
```

Comments `intdosx()` may be used to invoke any DOS (INT 0x21) interrupt, because all registers and flags may be passed and returned.

The program example utilizes DOS interrupt 0x21 subfunction 0x35 to retrieve the addresses found in the interrupt vector table for interrupts 0x00 through 0x70 (maximum of 0xFF), and displays them in a variety of formats: segment:offset, converted absolute memory addresses, in units of KBs, and depending upon which DOS Memory Map region (see Figure 2.19) the corresponding interrupt function (handler) resides in.

Notice that the **_psp** (program segment prefix) address (**_psp:0000**) was used to establish the lowest memory address associated with the example program being executed.

Execute this program example from the DOS command line, not from within the QC or PWB integrated environment.

segread() *Get the current segment register values (SREGS)*

Compatibility □ANSI ■OS/2 □UNIX □XENIX

Specification

```
#include <dos.h>
void segread(struct SREGS *segregs);
```

Arguments

segregs: Pointer to a **SREGS** type structure to contain the current (ES, CS, SS, CS) register values.

Example See: `int86x()`, `intdosx()`.

Comments Use this function to set up **SREGS** for use with **intdosx()** and **int86x()**. An alternative is to use assembly language, as discussed in Chapter 28.

Math Functions

Math Functions

Because K&R C was originally designed as a system programming language, its use has been overshadowed by Fortran in the scientific computing arena. Now that Standard C has removed a number of the impediments to its use for scientific purposes, however, Standard C may rival Fortran as the language of choice in the future.

The strengths of Fortran are rooted in its exponentiation operator, complex number support, and rich complement of intrinsic math functions, together with its perceived ease of use. Its shortcomings are earmarked by its lack of support for bit operations, pointer types, and recursion, all features at which C excels.

Now, Standard C also boasts separate syntax handling for the **float**, **double**, and **long double** data types; function prototyping to overcome the automatic promotion to types **int** and **double**; and the assurance that grouping parentheses now control the precedence of operations. However, C lacks an exponentiation operator and complex number support like Fortran, and still relies upon the run-time library to perform all needed math functions.

The run-time library functions necessary to perform commonly needed integral and floating-point math operations (normally available with Fortran) are documented in this chapter. Coverage of formatted I/O operations involving floating-point types can be found in Chapter 17 (**fscanf()**, **scanf()**, **fprintf()**, **printf()**, **vfprintf()**, **vprintf()**) and Chapter 19 (**cscanf()**, **cprintf()**), while all data conversion between character and floating-point types is discussed in Chapter 20 (**atof()**, **strtod()**, **ecvt()**, **fcvt()**, **gcvt()**, **_atold()**, **_strtold()**, **sprintf()**, **sscanf()**, **vsprintf()**).

Because the 80x86 processors do not provide register and instructions support for floating-point math operations, all such operations must be performed using software emulation or a companion 80x87 math coprocessor. Recall from Chapter 2 that when a C compiler is installed, if a math coprocessor is not present, the floating-point emulation (**xLIBCE.LIB**) or alternate math run-time library (**xLIBCA.LIB**) must be installed; or if a coprocessor is present, then inline code can be generated using the **xLIBC7.LIB** run-time library. Subsequent use of the **/FPxxx** compiler options and the NO87 environment variable governs which library and whether an 80x87 coprocessor is utilized. Together these choices establish the floating-point math package that is to be used by a particular program.

To maintain compatibility with the available math coprocessors, all emulation libraries mimic the hardware features of the 80*x*87 chip. For this reason, the use of the 80*x*87 control and status word registers is explained in this chapter. As we will see, the control word configures the behavior of the 80*x*87 (or emulation software), while the status word reports any error conditions that may result when an 80*x*87 (or software emulation) instruction is performed.

FLOATING-POINT MATH PACKAGE

Whenever I/O, an expression, or a function is called that uses a floating-point type (**float**, **double**, **long double**), the floating-point math package that was selected for installation with the C compiler establishes how all floating-point math operations are performed by a C program.

Typically, little further thought is given to the floating-point math package once you have installed the compiler and established either the **/Fpxxx** or NO87 settings to designate one of the following:

/Fpa	Calls with alternate math library
/Fpc	Calls with emulator library
/Fpc87	Calls with 80*x*87 library
/Fpi	Inline with emulator
/Fpi87	Inline 80*x*87 code

If an 80*x*87 coprocessor is installed, the control word represents the contents of a hardware register (16 bits), whereas if software emulation is being used instead, the control word is simply a **register** storage-class program variable. Whether you are using software emulation or have an 80*x*87 coprocessor installed, however, the floating-point control word (16 bits) setting directs how all floating-point calculations are actually performed.

Control Word

The default control word setting is established in **<float.h>** by the definition of the macro **CW_DEFAULT**. The bit settings within the control word embody four control components that are located by the following control word masks:

MCW_IC	0x1000	Infinity Control
MCW_RC	0x0C00	Rounding Control

MCW_PC	0x0300	Precision Control
MCW_EM	0x003F	Interrupt (Exception Mask) Control

Each of these components of the control word offers the control options summarized in Table 23.1.

Each time a floating-point instruction is performed, the control word bit settings are interrogated as needed by that machine instruction to establish how infinity, rounding, precision, and interrupt conditions are to be accommodated. The default control word is defined in **<float.h>** from the following combination of components:

```
#define CW_DEFAULT (IC_AFFINE + RC_NEAR + PC_64 +
    EM_DENORMAL + EM_UNDERFLOW + EM_INEXACT)
```

or

```
#define CW_DEFAULT (0x1000 + 0x0000 + 0x0300 +
    0x0002 + 0x0010 + 0x0x20)
```

or

```
#define CW_DEFAULT (0x1332)
```

TABLE 23.1: Floating-Point Control Word

COMPONENT	VALUE	MACRO	DESCRIPTION
Infinity	0x1000	IC_AFFINE	Infinity as either + or −
	0x0000	IC_PROJECTIVE	Infinity always +
Rounding	0x0C00	RC_CHOP	Set fractional part to 0
	0x0800	RC_UP	Round to + infinity
	0x0400	RC_DOWN	Round to − infinity
	0x0000	RC_NEAR	To nearest or even
Precision	0x0300	PC_64	**long double** (10 bytes)
	0x0200	PC_53	**double** (8 bytes)
	0x0000	PC_24	**float** (4 bytes)
Interrupt	0x0020	EM_INEXACT	Result not exactly represented
	0x0010	EM_UNDERFLOW	Result too small to represent
	0x0008	EM_OVERFLOW	Result too large to represent
	0x0004	EM_ZERODIVIDE	Result infinite magnitude
	0x0002	EM_DENORMAL	Biased exponent of 0
	0x0001	EM_INVALID	Any error not otherwise handled

This default control word setting is automatically set whenever the floating-point package is loaded or reinitialized using the run-time function **_fpreset()**. To alter the control word setting, you must use the run-time function **_control87()**.

The first consideration in any C program that uses a floating-point math package should be to assess whether the default control word, **CW_DEFAULT**, is appropriate for use; if it is not, the **_control87()** function should be invoked before any floating-point math operations are performed.

Getting and Setting

To get the current control word setting, call the **_control87()** function with the first argument, **new**, assigned any value, and the second argument, **mask**, assigned a value of 0x0000 as follows:

```
unsigned cw_setting;
cw_setting = _control87(CW_DEFAULT, 0x0000);
```

A new control word is established by modifying the current control word setting using the **_control87()** function. The first argument, **new**, contains a mask of the new bits to be set from the available bits defined by the second argument, **mask**. Normally, only one component (infinity, rounding, precision, interrupt) of the control word must be altered. (See Table 23.1.) For example, to alter **CW_DEFAULT** so that all rounding is performed by chopping (setting the fraction to zero) rather than by rounding in a traditional sense (**RC_NEAR**), the following function call would be issued:

```
old_cw_setting = _control87(RC_CHOP, MCW_RC);
```

MCW_RC defines which subset of control word bits relates to rounding control, and **RC_CHOP** defines which bits within **MCW_RC** are set to reflect chopping (**RC_CHOP**). Whenever **_control87()** is called and the second argument, **mask**, is nonzero, then a new control word is set and the previous control word setting is returned, as shown above.

The bit operation performed by **_control87()** is then correctly described by

```
new_cw_setting = ((old_cw_setting & ~mask) | (new & mask))
```

which for the previous example results in a control word setting of 0x1F32:

```
new_cw_setting = ((0x1332 & ~0x0C00) | (0x0C00 & 0x0C00))
    = ((0x1332 & 0xF3FF) | (0x0C00))
    = ((0x1332) | (0x0C00))
    = (0x1F32)
```

When it is necessary to restore more than one component of the control word at a time, the individual arguments may be combined using OR. For example, to set the infinity control to projective (always positive), and the precision control to 24 bits (float), we issue the following function call:

```
_control87(IC_PROJECTIVE | PC_24, MCW_IC | MCW_PC);
```

To restore the **CW_DEFAULT** setting itself, the following statement would be issued:

```
_control87(CW_DEFAULT, 0xFFFF);
```

Interrupt Component

The significance of altering the **MCW_EM** interrupt component of the control word warrants further explanation. Unless the bit positions of these interrupts in the control word are set on (masked), the floating-point math package generates an external interrupt, which initiates the performance of a standard interrupt handler that displays an error message in the following format:

```
run-time error M61xx: MATH
- floating-point error: Message
```

and then terminates the program abnormally. This means that the present process terminates and returns control to the parent process without flushing file buffers or performing any queued **atexit()**/**onexit()** functions. The following error number and messages conform with the **MCW_EM** family of interrupt masks:

ERROR	MESSAGE	INTERRUPT
M6106	Inexact	**EM_INEXACT** (masked by default)
M6105	Underflow	**EM_UNDERFLOW** (masked by default)
M6104	Overflow	**EM_OVERFLOW**
M6103	Divide by 0	**EM_ZERODIVIDE**
M6102	Denormal	**EM_DENORMAL** (masked by default)
M6101	Invalid	**EM_INVALID**

When the default control word, **CW_DEFAULT**, is used, the **EM_INEXACT**, **EM_UNDERFLOW**, and **EM_DENORMAL** interrupts are masked. When an interrupt is masked, error messaging and program termination does not occur; rather, the following actions are taken by each floating-point exception interrupt type:

EM_INEXACT: Although the true result cannot be exactly represented in the precision format specified (**MCW_PC**), processing simply continues.

EM_UNDERFLOW: Although the true result is too small in magnitude to be represented in the precision format specified (**MCW_PC**), the fraction portion will be shifted right until the exponent is in range.

EM_OVERFLOW: Although the true result is too large in magnitude to be represented in the precision format specified (**MCW_PC**), the encoding for infinity (1.#INF) is assumed.

EM_ZERODIVIDE: When the divisor is zero and the dividend is nonzero and not infinity, the encoding for infinity (1.#INF) is assumed.

EM_DENORMAL: Although the result is denormalized and has the smallest exponent but a nonzero significand, processing continues. The normalized floating-point storage format used to represent nonzero floating-point numbers assumes that the significand portion has a leading bit. Normalization ensures that all leading zeroes have been eliminated and the decimal point location is located within the significand by the floating-point exponent (see Chapter 11).

EM_INVALID: Although a stack overflow, stack underflow, indeterminate form, or a nonnumber (NAN) is encountered, a specific NAN called INDEFINITE is generated and calculation continues to propagate other NANs if necessary.

To prevent the abnormal termination of programs that encounter floating-point interrupts, it is necessary to trap any unmasked interrupts with the run-time library function **signal()**, described in Chapter 25.

The use of the **signal()** function provides a Standard C method of writing and installing an interrupt handler. Discussion of the basic concepts of hardware and software interrupts is provided in Chapter 22. Additional explanation of writing and installing interrupt handlers is provided in Chapter 27. All methods of handling interrupts, except by the use of **signal()**, are non-Standard (not portable). The use of the run-time functions **signal()** and **raise()** provides a Standard C method of "trapping" and "setting" the following DOS interrupts, whose macro definitions appear in `<signal.h>`:

MACRO	DESCRIPTION
SIGINT	Ctrl-C or Ctrl-Break
SIGFPE	Floating-point exception
SIGABRT	Abnormal termination

In the "Math Exception Handling" section of this chapter we will examine trapping interrupt **SIGFPE** with **signal()**. The handling of the other signal interrupts shown above is discussed in Chapter 25. The use of **signal()** as a debugging tool is also demonstrated in Chapter 29.

Status Word

If an $80x87$ coprocessor is installed, the status word represents the contents of a hardware register (16 bits), whereas if software emulation is being used instead, the control word is simply a **register** storage-class program variable. Using OR, the status word is set to reflect the result of the most recently completed floating-point instruction. The allowable status word settings parallel the interrupt component (**MCW_EM**) of the control word (described above) that is detected by the floating-point math package. The basic settings are defined by the following macros in `<float.h>`:

SW_INEXACT	0x0020	Result not exactly represented
SW_UNDERFLOW	0x0010	Result too small to represent
SW_OVERFLOW	0x0008	Result too large to represent
SW_ZERODIVIDE	0x0004	Result infinite magnitude
SW_DENORMAL	0x0002	Biased exponent of 0
SW_INVALID	0x0001	Any other error

If no interrupts are masked by the control word, then all such interrupts will result in abnormal program termination; therefore, a parallel set of status word settings is necessary to trap such interrupt conditions if they are masked by the control word. If **SW_INVALID** is set, then the following additional subconditions are also recorded:

SW_STACKUNDERFLOW	0x0400	FP stack underflow
SW_STACKOVERFLOW	0x0200	FP stack overflow
SW_SQRTNEG	0x0080	Square root of negative
SW_UNEMULATED	0x0040	Unemulated instruction

If it is important to detect whether any masked floating-point interrupts have occurred, the only method for doing so is to interrogate the status word after a suspicious floating-point instruction has been performed.

Getting and Clearing

To get the current status word setting, use the **_status87()** function as follows:

```
unsigned sw_setting;
sw_setting = _status87();
```

To clear (0x0000) the status word setting before a suspicious floating-point operation is performed, use the **_clear87()** function as follows:

```
unsigned sw-setting;
old_sw_setting = _clear87();
```

The status word is also cleared (0x0000) whenever the function **_fpreset()** is called to initialize the floating-point math package.

MATH EXCEPTION HANDLING

Programs that do not use floating-point type data objects or functions do not require the services of a floating-point math package and involve only integer math operations. A limited number of exceptions associated with integer arithmetic occur; namely, overflow, underflow, and division by zero. Likewise, few recovery strategies are necessary to handle integer math exceptions. Note that "exceptions" are not always "errors." They represent conditions that are sometimes OK, and sometimes not OK, depending on what your program is designed to do.

Integral operations that result in overflow (values greater than the maximum allowed for the data type; for **int**, 32,767) and underflow (values below the type's minimum; for **int**, −32,768) "wrap around," reversing the sign of the number as follows:

```
int low = -32768, high = 32767;
low--; /* 32767 */
high++; /* -32768 */
```

No special interrupts are generated, and processing simply continues. When working with integral data types, declare program variables of a type sufficient to represent the anticipated range of assigned value (see Chapter 7).

When an integral division by zero occurs, however, BIOS interrupt 0x00 is generated, and the following standard message is displayed:

```
run-time error R6003- integer divide by 0
```

The program is then terminated abnormally. To trap such exceptions and to prevent abnormal program termination, you can write and install a C interrupt handler to replace interrupt 0x00 in the interrupt vector table (see Chapter 27); however, the ramifications of integer division by zero are sufficiently serious that this strategy is not recommended.

On the other hand, when floating-point arithmetic is involved, a variety of possible exceptions and recovery strategies is possible. The possible exceptions and recovery strategies that can occur are discussed in the following sections.

Floating-Point Math Package Exceptions

An error condition (exception) encountered in any floating-point expression, from a simple assignment statement to a complex function call, causes an interrupt signal to be generated by the floating-point math package in use, whether that be an $80x87$ coprocessor chip or emulation software. Six such interrupts were described in the section "Interrupt Component" above:

Inexact

Underflow

Overflow

Zero Divide

Denormal

Invalid

Regardless of whether these interrupts are masked or not, they occur. The masking of floating-point interrupts with the floating-point control word alters only the action to be taken when such an interrupt occurs. Unmasked floating-point interrupts, for which the corresponding bits in the control word are off (zero), result in the display of an M61xx error message, followed by abnormal program termination. Masked floating-point interrupts, however, for which the corresponding control word bit is on (one), result in the actions described in the section "Interrupt Component."

In each case, the present floating-point status word is updated to reflect any exception conditions that take place. Let's examine what options exist to handle masked and unmasked floating-point interrupts when they occur.

Masked Floating-Point Interrupts

All masked floating-point interrupts, as described in the section "Interrupt Component," perform a specific action and permit processing to continue as if an exception had not occurred. No messaging takes place and no history of the event is recorded. Recall that when the default status word (**CW_DEFAULT**) is used, the inexact (**EM_INEXACT**), underflow (**EM_UNDERFLOW**), and denormal (**EM_DENORMAL**) interrupt conditions are masked, hinting that such exceptions are quite common, but typically innocuous. If it is important for a program to detect whether a masked interrupt has occurred, then it is necessary to interrogate the status word in the following manner:

```
double dv1=10.0, dv2=0.0;
unsigned sw_setting;

/* Step 1) clear the status word—set to 0x0000 */
_clear87();

/* Step 2) perform the floating-point operation */
dv1 /= dv2;

/* Step 3) test the status word */
sw_setting = _status87();
if (sw_setting) { ..exception processing.. };
```

In this example, if the **EM_ZERODIVIDE** interrupt were masked, then additional exception processing could take place only if the status word were tested as shown above.

The **SW_xxx** macros defined in **<float.h>** enable a program to perform a series of tests to determine which status word bits had been set, thereby indicating the exception that had occurred. To test whether a zero divide exception has occurred, use the following C statement:

```
if (sw_setting & SW_ZERODIVIDE) { /* true: divide by 0.0  */ };
```

If an **INVALID** exception were found to occur, then four additional tests can be performed to provide further information:

```
if (sw_setting & SW_INVALID) {
    if (sw_setting & SW_UNEMULATED) { .. };
    if (sw_setting & SW_SQRTNEG) { .. };
    if (sw_setting & SW_STACKOVERFLOW) { .. };
    if (sw_setting & SW_STACKUNDERFLOW) { .. };
    }
```

Now, let's examine the options that are available to you when nonmasked floating-point interrupts occur.

Nonmasked Floating-Point Interrupts

All nonmasked floating-point interrupts will cause the standard M61*xx* error message to display, followed by an abnormal program termination.

When nonmasked interrupts occur, the **raise(SIGFPE)** function call is issued. If the **signal(SIGFPE,..)** function has been called, your program can trap and prevent the normal handling of nonmasked floating-point interrupts. Essentially the **signal()** function permits you to install a custom signal-handling function that behaves like an interrupt handler, without the complexity and loss of portability that comes with installing interrupt handlers under DOS (see Chapter 27). As we will see, however, if processing is to continue after a custom signal handler is called, then the **setjmp()** and **longjmp()** functions must also be used.

The basic outline of the coding technique used to trap a nonmasked floating-point interrupt using the **signal()** function, in concert with the run-time functions **setjmp()** and **longjmp()**, is summarized by the program example listed in Figure 23.1.

This program produces the following output:

```
1st unmasked EM_ZERODIVIDE interrupt
fpe_signal = 83  FPE_ZERODIVIDE
2nd masked EM_ZERODIVIDE interrupt
sw_setting = 4  SW_ZERODIVIDE
```

Notice that unlike the use of **signal()** to detect other DOS interrupts (**SIGABRT** and **SIGINT**), **fpe_handler**, the signal-handler function used with **SIGFPE** (floating-point exceptions), passes a second argument, **num**, which assumes one of the following macro values defined in **<signal.h>**:

FPE_INEXACT	0x86
FPE_UNDERFLOW	0x85
FPE_OVERFLOW	0x84
FPE_ZERODIVIDE	0x83
FPE_DENORMAL	0x82
FPE_INVALID	0x81
FPE_UNEMULATED	0x87
FPE_SQRTNEG	0x88
FPE_STACKOVERFLOW	0x8A
FPE_STACKUNDERFLOW	0x8B
FPE_EXPLICITGEN	0x8C

```
/* FILE: ch23e1.c */
#include <stdio.h>
#include <math.h>
#include <float.h>
#include <signal.h>
#include <setjmp.h>

jmp_buf mark;
int fpe_signal;

void fpe_handler(int sig, int num)
{
fpe_signal = num;              /* save the SIGFPE subcode */
_fpreset();                    /* control word = CW_DEFAULT;
                                  status word = 0x0000 */
longjmp(mark, -1);             /* nonlocal return */
}

int main(void)
{
double dv1 = 10.0, dv2 = 0.0;
int jmpret;
unsigned sw_setting;

signal(SIGFPE, fpe_handler);    /* install exception handler */
_control87(CW_DEFAULT, 0xFFFF); /* set control word */
jmpret = setjmp(mark);          /* establish nonlocal return */
if (jmpret == 0) dv1 /= dv2;    /* perform suspicious calc */
else {
    printf("\n1st unmasked EM_ZERODIVIDE interrupt");
    printf("\nfpe_signal = %x FPE_ZERODIVIDE", fpe_signal);
    }

_control87(MCW_EM, EM_ZERODIVIDE); /* masked EM_ZERODIVIDE */
jmpret = setjmp(mark);          /* establish new nonlocal return */
if (jmpret == 0) dv1/dv2;       /* perform suspicious calc */
else {
    printf("\n2nd unmasked EM_ZERODIVIDE interrupt");
    printf("\nfpe_signal = %x FPE_ZERODIVIDE", fpe_signal);
    }

sw_setting = _status87();       /* get status word */
if (sw_setting) {
    printf("\n2nd masked EM_ZERODIVIDE interrupt");
    printf("\nsw_setting = %x SW_ZERODIVIDE", sw_setting);
    }
exit(0);
}
```

FIGURE 23.1: A sample floating-point exception handler

These macros correspond to the control and status word settings described earlier, with the addition of **FPE_EXPLICITGEN**, which indicates that the **raise(SIGFPE)** call was issued explicitly by an application program, not by the floating-point math package itself.

Clearly, with this technique, any nonmasked floating-point math package interrupts that occur can be trapped by an application program. Rather than abnormally terminating, the application program can, by design, perform either a normal termination sequence or continue processing with or without messaging or logging the exception event.

Like other interrupt handlers (see Chapter 27), C coding restrictions apply to the statements that may be placed in a signal handler such as **fpe_handler**, shown in the example program above.

- No stream (Chapter 17) or low-level (Chapter 18) I/O may be performed.
- No dynamic memory allocation (Chapter 24) or run-time functions that use the **malloc()** family of functions may be used.
- No DOS 0x21 interrupt services may be used.
- Use only the **longjmp()** function with **SIGFPE** signals.
- Do not use any functions that reside in an overlay (Chapter 3).

Floating-Point Function Exceptions

When floating-point calculations are performed by run-time library functions, other exceptions may be encountered in addition to the floating-point math package interrupts. These further exceptions involve the individual or combined use of the global variable **errno** and the run-time functions **matherr()** or **_matherrl()**, which are the programmer's primary tools for detecting erroneous math operations. This section discusses their use.

When the global variable **errno** is used by a function, it is set to one of the following macros defined in **<errno.h>**:

MACRO	DESCRIPTION
EDOM	Domain error
ERANGE	Range error

Domain (**EDOM**) errors reflect function argument values that are outside the range of possible value for a function, whereas range (**ERANGE**) errors reflect either a particular invalid argument value or a singularity (such as **log**(0.0)), or a return value that exhibits overflow, underflow, a total loss of precision, or a partial loss of precision.

The functions utilizing these **errno** global variable settings are documented as such in the function reference entries later in this chapter. The proper technique for using **errno** is summarized by the following partial program example:

```
errno = 0;
runtime_function(..);
if (errno) { ..error processing.. };
```

Remember that **errno** is a continually reused global variable that is not automatically reset. Therefore, as shown above, always reset **errno=0** before calling a function.

Default **matherr()**, **_matherrl()**

Some of the run-time library math functions call function **matherr()** (type **double**) or **_matherrl()** (type **long double**) when an exception is detected. The detected exception conditions that generate calls to these functions are defined by the following macros defined in **<math.h>**:

MACRO	VALUE	DESCRIPTION
DOMAIN	1	Argument domain error
SING	2	Argument singularity error
OVERFLOW	3	Return overflow error
UNDERFLOW	4	Return underflow
TLOSS	5	Return total loss of precision
PLOSS	6	Return partial loss of precision

Only the math run-time library functions summarized in Table 23.2 detect these exception conditions and call the **matherr()** or **_matherrl()** run-time functions. The **atan()**, **atanl()**, **tanh()**, and **tanhl()** functions, which do not generate exceptions and therefore never call **matherr()** or **_matherrl()**, nor set the global variable, **errno**, are noticeably absent from this list.

When the default (run-time library versions) **matherr()** or **_matherrl()** functions are used, all error messages except overflow and underflow are directed to stream file, **stderr**, and processing continues in a normal manner. Unlike floating-point nonmasked interrupts, which abnormally terminate program execution, the default **matherr()** and **_matherrl()** functions do not abnormally terminate program execution.

The program listed in Figure 23.2 demonstrates how the error messages can be directed to the screen as output (illustrated in Figure 23.3).

The run-time **matherr()** functions, however, do not provide complete control over exception handling. For example, the messaging to **stderr** cannot be redirected in a standard fashion from the DOS command line. Such messaging can be done only by using the non-Standard function **dup2()** (see Chapter 18) as shown in Figure 23.2. Moreover, error messages are not displayed when an overflow or underflow occurs. To detect these conditions the global variable **errno** must be independently tested.

TABLE 23.2: Run-Time Functions Using matherr(), _matherrl()

FUNCTION	stderr MESSAGE	errno VALUE
acos(), acosl()	domain	EDOM
asin(), asinl()	domain	EDOM
atan2(), atan2l()	domain	EDOM
y0(), _y0l()	domain	EDOM
y1(), _y1l()	domain	EDOM
yn(), _ynl()	domain	EDOM
cabs(), cabsl()	none	ERANGE
cos(), cosl()	ploss/tloss	ERANGE
cosh(), coshl()	none	ERANGE
exp(), expl()	none	ERANGE
hypot(), hypotl()	none	ERANGE
log(), logl()	domain/sing	EDOM/ERANGE
log10(), log10l()	domain/sing	EDOM/ERANGE
pow(), powl()	domain/none	EDOM/ERANGE
sin(), sinl()	ploss/tloss	ERANGE
sinh(), sinhl()	none	ERANGE
sqrt(), sqrtl()	domain	EDOM
tan(), tanl()	ploss/tloss	ERANGE

When it necessary to assume a greater degree of control over exceptions that are detected by the run-time library functions **matherr()** and **_matherrl()**, replacement functions must be written in C and linked to your application program.

Custom **matherr(), _matherrl()**

Replacement functions can be written in C that conform to the function prototype declarations described for **matherr()** and **_matherrl()** in the alphabetic list of function descriptions included at the end of this chapter. Both functions rely on the non-Standard structure declarations **exception** and **_exceptionl**, found in **<math.h>** and documented in Appendix E, which contain members that describe the following: the exception type, the function name generating the exception, and the function arguments and assigned return value.

```
/* FILE: ch23e2.c */
#include <stdio.h>
#include <math.h>
#include <stdlib.h>
#include <io.h>

unsigned sw_setting;

void print(char *fn, double dv)
{
sw_setting = _status87();    /* get status word */
printf("\tCustMsg=> %s: RET=%g sw_setting=%x errno=%d\n",
    fn, dv, sw_setting, errno);
_clear87();                  /* clear status word */
errno=0;
}

int main(void)
{
struct complex z = { HUGE_VAL, HUGE_VAL };

errno=0;
_clear87();                  /* clear status word */
setbuf(stdout, NULL);    /* unbuffer stdout */
dup2(1,2);                   /* redirect stderr to stdout */

/* generate FP exceptions; see Table 23.2 */
print("acos"    ,acos(2.0));
print("asin"    ,asin(-2.0));
print("atan2"   ,atan2(0.0, 0.0));
print("y0"      ,y0(-1.0));
print("y1"      ,y1(-1.0));
print("yn"      ,yn(1,-1.0));
print("cabs"    ,cabs(z));
print("cos"     ,cos(HUGE_VAL));
print("cosh"    ,cosh(HUGE_VAL));
print("exp"     ,exp(HUGE_VAL));
print("hypot"   ,hypot(HUGE_VAL, HUGE_VAL));
print("log"     ,log(0.0));
print("log10"   ,log10(-10.0));
print("pow"     ,pow(0.0,0.0));
print("pow"     ,pow(2.0,HUGE_VAL1));
print("sin"     ,sin(HUGE_VAL));
print("sinh"    ,sinh(HUGE_VAL));
print("sqrt"    ,sqrt(-1.0));
print("tan"     ,tan(HUGE_VAL));
exit(0);
}
```

FIGURE 23.2: Program ch23e2.c, displaying matherr() messages

The replacement **matherr()** or **_matherrl()** function itself can return either a value of zero (false), indicating that the standard **matherr()** or **_matherrl() stderr** message and **errno** settings are to be made; or a nonzero (true), indicating that no error message is to be displayed and **errno** is to remain unchanged. Typically, when a value of zero is returned by **matherr()** or **_matherrl()**, an error condition is acknowledged to exist; however, if a nonzero value is returned, a successful corrective action has been taken.

```
acos: DOMAIN error
        CustMsg=> acos: RET=0  sw_setting=0  errno=33
asin: DOMAIN error
        CustMsg=> asin: RET=0  sw_setting=0  errno=33
atan2: DOMAIN error
        CustMsg=> atan2: RET=0  sw_setting=0  errno=33
y0: DOMAIN error
        CustMsg=> y0: RET=-1.79769e+308  sw_setting=0  errno=33
y1: DOMAIN error
        CustMsg=> y1: RET=-1.79769e+308  sw_setting=0  errno=33
yn: DOMAIN error
        CustMsg=> yn: RET=-1.79769e+308  sw_setting=0  errno=33
        CustMsg=> cabs: RET=1.79769e+308  sw_setting=28  errno=34
cos: TLOSS error
        CustMsg=> cos: RET=0  sw_setting=0  errno=34
        CustMsg=> cosh: RET=1.79769e+308  sw_setting=20  errno=34
        CustMsg=> exp: RET=1.79769e+308  sw_setting=20  errno=34
        CustMsg=> hypot: RET=1.79769e+308  sw_setting=28  errno=34
log: SING error
        CustMsg=> log: RET=-1.79769e+308  sw_setting=0  errno=34
log10: DOMAIN error
        CustMsg=> log10: RET=-1.79769e+308  sw_setting=0  errno=33
pow: DOMAIN error
        CustMsg=> pow: RET=0  sw_setting=0  errno=33
        CustMsg=> pow: RET=1.79769e+308  sw_setting=0  errno=34
sin: TLOSS error
        CustMsg=> sin: RET=0  sw_setting=0  errno=34
        CustMsg=> sinh: RET=1.79769e+308  sw_setting=20  errno=34
sqrt: DOMAIN error
        CustMsg=> sqrt: RET=0  sw_setting=0  errno=33
tan: TLOSS error
        CustMsg=> tan: RET=0  sw_setting=0  errno=34
```

FIGURE 23.3: Output from program ch23e2.c

Custom **matherr()** and **_matherrl()** functions can take total control over the processing of exceptions that are detected by the run-time library math functions listed in Table 23.2, reassigning function return values if necessary, messaging or logging such events, and even terminating program execution.

When custom **matherr()** and **_matherrl()** functions are used, linker option /NOE (no external dictionary search) must be specified to prevent a linker error from occurring; otherwise, the replacement functions behave like any other C function and, unlike interrupt handlers (Chapter 27) and signal handlers (Chapter 25), there are no restrictions upon the types of statements that may appear within them.

The reference entry for function **matherr()**, presented later in this chapter, shows a complete example of a replacement **matherr()** function.

MATH FUNCTION TASKS

The function-naming conventions introduced with Standard C (see Chapter 4, Table 4.8) have reserved those math function names ending in

`..f()` corresponding to type **float**, as well as those ending in `..l()` included in this chapter, which correpond to type **long double**.

All such `..l()` functions are understood to be ANSI conforming and available with OS/2; however, at present, no such `..l()` functions are available yet in the run-time libraries of UNIX or XENIX. No such `..f()` functions are presently provided by the run-time libraries of either DOS, OS/2, UNIX, or XENIX.

Please note that for all functions included in this chapter that have an alternate `..l()` form available, such as

```
acos(), acosl()
```

the compatibility depicted using the familiar ■ and □ format is modified in this chapter to include the use of an (*) asterisk as follows:

■ ANSI ■ OS/2 ■ $\overset{*}{\text{UNIX}}$ ■ $\overset{*}{\text{XENIX}}$

to indicate that the base function identifier (**acos()** in this instance) is available with UNIX and XENIX, but the `..l()` function identifier (**acosl()** in this instance) is not presently available with UNIX and XENIX.

Recall that with Standard C, floating-point constants are identified by the following notation:

CONSTANT	TYPE	BYTES
1.0f or 1.0F	**float**	4
1.0	**double**	8
1.0l or 1.0L	**long double**	10

Before using the functions documented in this chapter, it may be helpful to refresh your understanding of the storage formats associated with each of these floating-point data types. Refer to Chapter 7, Figure 7.3, and Chapter 11, Figures 11.1 and 11.2.

Another commonly overlooked detail is that all run-time functions in C accepting arguments and returning values of angular measure are in radians, not degrees (as in Fortran). Remember that there are π radians in 180°; however, C does not predefine a constant value for π. When converting between radians and degrees, rather than defining an approximate constant value for π, use a function call such as

```
const double pi = acos(-1.0);
const long double lpi = acosl(-1.0L);
```

The math function run-time library functions documented in this chapter are summarized by task in Table 23.3. Notice that only the **abs()**, **labs()**, **div()**, **ldiv()**, **rand()**, and **srand()** functions are integral types. Recall that no integral type calculations are performed by the floating-point math package. Also note that all ASCII to integer and floating-point type conversion services are documented in Chapter 20, and all related I/O services are documented in Chapters 17 and 19.

TABLE 23.3: Function Tasks

TASK		FUNCTION	
		STANDARD C ■ **ANSI**	**MICROSOFT C** ☐ **ANSI**
Integral Types	Absolute value	`abs()` `labs()`	
	Quotient and remainder	`div()` `ldiv()`	
	Random numbers	`rand()` `srand()`	
Floating-Point Types	Absolute value	`fabs()`, `fabsl()`	`cabs()`, `cabsl()`
	Bessel functions		`j0()`, `_j0l()`
			`j1()`, `_j1l()`
			`jn()`, `_jnl()`
			`y0()`, `_y0l()`
			`y1()`, `_y1l()`
			`yn()`, `_ynl()`
	Complex numbers		`cabs()`, `cabsl()`
	Coprocessor support		`_clear87()`
			`_control87()`
			`_fpreset()`
			`_status87()`
	Error handling		`matherr()`, `_matherrl()`
	Exponentiation	`exp()`, `expl()` `frexp()`, `frexpl()` `ldexp()`, `ldexpl()` `pow()`, `powl()`	`hypot()`, `hypotl()`

TABLE 23.3: Function Tasks (continued)

TASK		FUNCTION	
		STANDARD C ■ ANSI	MICROSOFT C ☐ ANSI
Floating-Point Types (cont.)	Logarithms	`sqrt()`, `sqrtl()` `log()`, `logl()` `log10()`, `log10l()`	
	Quotient and remainder	`fmod()`, `fmodl()` `modf()`, `modfl()`	
	Rounding	`ceil()`, `ceill()` `floor()`, `floorl()`	
	Trig Functions	`acos()`, `acosl()` `asin()`, `asinl()` `atan()`, `atanl()` `atan2()`, `atan2l()` `cos()`, `cosl()` `cosh()`, `coshl()` `sin()`, `sinl()` `sinh()`, `sinhl()` `tan()`, `tanl()` `tanh()`, `tanhl()`	`hypot()`, `hypotl()`
	Type Conversion	See Chapter 20	See Chapter 20

The absolute values of **int** types are determined by **abs()**, and of **long int**, by function **labs()**. Similarly, the quotient and remainder of integer division are returned by **div()** and **ldiv()**, respectively, in the Standard C structure **typedef**s **div_t** and **_div_t**, described in Appendix E.

The only run-time random number function, **rand()**, is of type **int** and can be *seeded* or initialized using function **srand()** to return a value from zero to **RAND_MAX**, which is defined in **<stdlib.h>**.

The other function tasks described in this chapter may be performed upon integer types only if they are first explicitly cast to a floating-point type, or implicitly cast when specified as an actual function argument by a function prototype declaration found in **<math.h>**. The floating-point functions perform either common mathematical operations, or the internal tasks that control the floating-point math package itself.

As we discovered in the "Floating-Point Math Package" section above, complete control over the emulation, coprocessor, or inline math package being used is provided by the coprocessor support functions: **_clear87()**, **_control87()**, **_fpreset()**, and **_status87()**. The **matherr()** and **_matherrl()** functions provide for the default or custom handling of exceptions detected by some of the run-time functions documented in this chapter.

The only complex number support provided by the C language or run-time library is limited to the **cabs()** and **cabsl()** functions for determining the absolute value of a complex number expressed as $(x + yi)$ in the non-Standard structures **complex** and **_complexl**, described in Appendix E.

The absolute values of floating-point types are determined using **fabs()** and **fabsl()**, while the quotient and remainder of floating-point types are determined using **fmod()** or **fmodl()** and **modf()** or **modfl()**.

The ability to raise a floating-point type value to a power is provided in a variety of ways using the **exp()**, **expl()**, **frexp()**, **frexpl()**, **ldexp()**, **ldexpl()**, **pow()**, **powl()**, **sqrt()**, **sqrtl()**, **hypot()**, and **hypotl()** functions.

Logarithms are supported using functions **log()** and **logl()** for natural logarithms, and **log10()** or **log10l()** for base-10 logarithms.

The rounding of floating-point types, beyond the **MCW_RC** control word component, is augmented by the run-time functions **ceil()**, **ceill()**, **floor()**, and **floorl()**.

A complement of trigonometric functions is provided, which includes the following:

arccosine: **acos()**, **acosl()**

arcsine: **asin()**, **asinl()**

arctangent: **atan()**, **atanl()**, **atan2()**, **atan2l()**

cosine: **cos()**, **cosl()**

hyperbolic cosine: **cosh()**, **coshl()**

sine: **sin()**, **sinl()**

hyperbolic sine: **sinh()**, **sinhl()**

tangent: **tan()**, **tanl()**

hyperbolic tangent: **tanh()**, **tanhl()**

Finally, a set of Bessel functions of the First Kind (orders 0, 1, and n: **j0()**, **_j0l()**, **j1()**, **_j1l()**, **jn()**, **_jnl()**) and Bessel functions of the Second Kind (orders 0, 1, and n: **y0()**, **_y0l()**, **y1()**, **_y1l()**, **yn()**, **_ynl()**) are also available.

RUN-TIME LIBRARY FUNCTIONS FOR MATH FUNCTIONS

abs ()   *Calculate the absolute value of an integer number*

Compatibility   ■ANSI   ■OS/2   ■UNIX   ■XENIX

See Also

```
labs()
```

Specification

```
#include <stdlib.h> or <math.h>
int abs(int n);
```

Arguments

n: Any signed integer value.

Return Value

The absolute value of argument *n*

Example

```
/* FILE: ch23e3.c */
#include <stdio.h>
#include <math.h>
int main(void)
{
struct complex z = {2.0, 2.0};
struct _complexl zl = {-2.0L, -2.0L};
double dval = -25.033;
long double dvall = -250.33;
int ival = -100;
long lval = -40000L;
printf("\nsizeof(zl)    = %d", sizeof(zl));
printf("\nsizeof(dvall) = %d", sizeof(dvall));
printf("\ncabs    = %lf", cabs(z));
printf("\ncabsl   = %Lf", cabsl(zl));
printf("\nfabs    = %lf", fabs(dval));
printf("\nfabsl   = %Lf", fabsl(dvall));
printf("\nabs     = %d",  abs(ival));
printf("\nlabs    = %ld", labs(lval));
exit(0);
}
```

Output

```
sizeof(zl)    = 20
sizeof(dvall) = 10
cabs    = 2.828427
```

```
cabsl = 2.828427
fabs  = 25.033000
fabsl = 250.330000
abs   = 100
labs  = 40000
```

Comments As an alternative, you can use the **#pragma intrinsic** form of this function.

Exception handling: no error return values; **errno** not set; integer function types do not follow floating-point exception-handling protocols.

acos(), acosl()   *Calculate the arccosine*

Compatibility ■ANSI   ■OS/2   ■*UNIX   ■*XENIX

Specification

```
#include <math.h>
#include <errno.h>
double acos(double x);
long double acosl(long double x);
```

Arguments

x: A cosine value between −1.0 and 1.0.

Return Value

Angle, between 0 and π radians, whose cosine value is *x*

If a domain error is detected, a value of 0.0 is returned

Example

```
/* FILE: ch23e4.c */
#include <stdio.h>
#include <math.h>
int main(void)
{
const double pifact = acos(-1.0)/180.0;
const long double lpifact = acosl(-1.0L)/180.0L;
double dcos, dsin, dtan, ddeg, drad;
long double dlcos, dlsin, dltan, dldeg, dlrad;

printf("\n\nEnter a cosine (-1.0 to +1.0): ");
scanf("%lf", &dcos);
drad = acos(dcos);
ddeg = drad/pifact;
printf("\ncos= %lf  acosrad= %lf  acosdeg=  %lf",
    dcos, drad, ddeg);
dlcos = dcos;
```

```
dlrad = acosl(dlcos);
dldeg = dlrad/lpifact;
printf("\ncosl= %Lf  acoslrad= %Lf  acosldeg= %Lf",
    dlcos, dlrad, dldeg);

printf("\n\nEnter a sine (-1.0 to +1.0)  : ");
scanf("%lf", &dsin);
drad = asin(dsin);
ddeg = drad/pifact;
printf("\nsin= %lf  asinrad= %lf  asindeg= %lf",
    dsin, drad, ddeg);
dlsin = dsin;
dlrad = asinl(dlsin);
dldeg = dlrad/lpifact;
printf("\nsinl= %Lf  asinlrad= %Lf  asinldeg= %Lf",
    dlsin, dlrad, dldeg);

printf("\n\nEnter a tangent : ");
scanf("%lf", &dtan);
drad = atan(dtan);
ddeg = drad/pifact;
printf("\ntan= %lf  atanrad= %lf  atandeg= %lf",
    dtan, drad, ddeg);
dltan = dtan;
dlrad = atanl(dltan);
dldeg = dlrad/lpifact;
printf("\ntanl= %Lf  atanlrad= %Lf  atanldeg= %Lf",
    dltan, dlrad, dldeg);

drad = atan2(dsin, dcos);
ddeg = drad/pifact;
printf("\n\ny= %lf  x= %lf  atan2rad= %lf  atan2deg= %lf",
    dsin, dcos, drad, ddeg);
dlrad = atan2l(dlsin, dlcos);
dldeg = dlrad/lpifact;
printf("\ny= %Lf  x= %Lf  atan2lrad= %Lf  atan2ldeg= %Lf",
    dlsin, dlcos, dlrad, dldeg);
exit(0);
}
```

Output

```
Enter a cosine (-1.0 to +1.0): 0.5
cos=  0.500000  acosrad=  1.047198  acosdeg=  60.000000
cosl= 0.500000  acoslrad= 1.047198  acosldeg= 60.000000

Enter a sine (-1.0 to +1.0)  : 0.5
sin=  0.500000  asinrad=  0.523599  asindeg=  30.000000
sinl= 0.500000  asinlrad= 0.523599  asinldeg= 30.000000

Enter a tangent            : 1.0
tan=  1.000000  atanrad=  0.785398  atandeg=  45.000000
tanl= 1.000000  atanlrad= 0.785398  atanldeg= 45.000000
```

```
y= 0.500000  x= 0.500000  atan2rad=  0.785398  atan2deg=  45.000000
y= 0.500000  x= 0.500000  atan21rad= 0.785398  atan21deg= 45.000000
```

Comments Exception handling: if argument **x** is not within the range −1.0 to 1.0, a value of 0.0 is returned, **errno** is set to **EDOM**, and **matherr()** or **_matherrl()** is called.

As an alternative, you can use the **#pragma intrinsic** form of this function.

asin(), asinl() *Calculate the arcsine*

Compatibility ■ANSI ■OS/2 ■* UNIX ■* XENIX

Specification
```
#include <math.h>
#include <errno.h>
double asin(double x);
long double asinl(long double x);
```

Arguments

x: A sine value between −1.0 and 1.0.

Return Value

Angle, between between −π/2 and π/2 radians, whose sine value is **x**; if a domain error is detected, a value of 0.0 is returned

Example See: **acos()**.

Comments Exception handling: if argument **x** is not within the range −1.0 to 1.0, a value of 0.0 is returned, **errno** is set to **EDOM**, and **matherr()** or **_matherrl()** is called.

As an alternative, you can use the **#pragma intrinsic** form of this function.

atan(), atanl() *Calculate the arctangent*

Compatibility ■ANSI ■OS/2 ■* UNIX ■* XENIX

See Also
```
atan2(), atan21()
```

Specification

```
#include <math.h>
double atan(double x);
long double atanl(long double x);
```

Arguments

x: Any signed tangent value.

Return Value

Angle, between $-\pi/2$ and $\pi/2$ radians, whose tangent value is *x*

Example   See: `acos()`.

Comments   Exception handling: no error return values; **errno** not set; **math-err()** or **_matherrl()** not called.

As an alternative, you can use the **#pragma intrinsic** form of this function.

atan2(), atan2l()   *Calculate the arctangent of y/x*

Compatibility   ■ANSI   ■OS/2   ■* UNIX   ■* XENIX

See Also

```
atan(), atanl()
```

Specification

```
#include <math.h>
#include <errno.h>
double atan2(double y, double x);
long double atan2l(long double y, long double x);
```

Arguments

x: Any signed value.

y: Any signed value.

Return Value

Angle, between $-\pi$ and π radians, whose tangent value is *y/x*

If a domain error is detected, a value of 0.0 is returned

Example   See: `acos()`.

Comments   Exception handling: if both arguments **x** and **y** are 0.0, a value of 0.0 is returned, **errno** is set to **EDOM**, and **matherr()** or **_matherrl()** is called. As an alternative, you can use the **#pragma intrinsic** form of this function.

Bessel Functions   *Compute Bessel functions*

Compatibility   ☐ANSI   ■OS/2   ■*UNIX   ■*XENIX

Specification

```
#include <math.h>
#include <errno.h>
First Kind Functions:
 double j0(double x);
long double _j0l(long double x);
double j1(double x);
long double _j1l(long double x);
double jn(int n, double x);
long double _jnl(int n, long double x);

Second Kind Functions:
double y0(double x);
long double _y0l(long double x);
double y1(double x);
long double _y1l(long double x);
double yn(int n, double x);
long double _ynl(int n, long double x);
```

Arguments

x: A signed value.

n: Integer order [2,3,...].

Return Value

j0, _j0l, j1, _j1l, jn, _jnl return Bessel functions of the First Kind

y0, _y0l, y1, _y1l, yn, _ynl return Bessel functions of the Second Kind; if a domain error is detected, a value of −(**HUGE_VAL**) or −(**_LHUGE_VAL**) is returned

Example

```
/* FILE: ch23e5.c */
#include <stdio.h>
#include <math.h>
int main(void)
{
int i;
double x;
```

```
long double x l;
printf("\n\nEnter First Kind Bessel (+/-) x      = ");
scanf("%lf", &x);
xl = x;
printf("\nFirst Kind Bessel for x  = %lf", x);
printf("\nOrder j0    = %lf\t_j0l    = %Lf", j0(x), _j0l(xl));
printf("\nOrder j1    = %lf\t_j1l    = %Lf", j1(x), _j1l(xl));
for (i=2; i<5; i++)
    printf("\nOrder jn(%1d) = %lf\t_jnl(%1d) = %Lf",
        i, jn(i,x), i, _jnl(i,xl));
printf("\n\nEnter Second Kind Bessel (+ only) x = ");
scanf("%lf", &x);
xl = x;
printf("\nSecond Kind Bessel for x = %lf", x);
printf("\nOrder y0    = %lf\t_y0l    = %Lf", y0(x), _y0l(xl));
printf("\nOrder y1    = %lf\t_y1l    = %Lf", y1(x), _y1l(xl));
for (i=2; i<5; i++)
    printf("\nOrder yn(%1d) = %lf\t_ynl(%1d) = %Lf",
        i, yn(i,x), i, _ynl(i,xl));
exit(0);
}
```

Output

```
Enter First Kind Bessel (+/-) x      = -1.25
First Kind Bessel for x  = -1.250000
Order j0    = 0.645906    _j0l    = 0.645906
Order j1    = -0.510623   _j1l    = -0.510623
Order jn(2) = 0.171091    _jnl(2) = 0.171091
Order jn(3) = -0.036868   _jnl(3) = -0.036868
Order jn(4) = 0.005877    _jnl(4) = 0.005877

Enter Second Kind Bessel (+ only) x = 1.25
Second Kind Bessel for x = 1.250000
Order y0    = 0.258217    _y0l    = 0.258217
Order y1    = -0.584364   _y1l    = -0.584364
Order yn(2) = -1.193199   _ynl(2) = -1.193199
Order yn(3) = -3.233874   _ynl(3) = -3.233874
Order yn(4) = -14.329395  _ynl(4) = -14.329395
```

Comments   Exception handling: if argument **x** is negative for Second Kind Bessel functions, a value of $-($**HUGE_VAL**$)$ or $-($**_LHUGE_VAL**$)$ is returned, **errno** is set to **EDOM**, and **matherr()** or **_matherrl()** is called.

cabs(), cabsl()   *Calculate the absolute value of a complex number*

Compatibility   ☐ ANSI   ■ OS/2   ■[*] UNIX   ■[*] XENIX

See Also

```
sqrt(), sqrtl(), pow(), powl()
```

Specification

```
#include <math.h>
#include <errno.h>
double cabs(struct complex z);
long double cabsl(struct _complexl z);
```

Arguments

z: See structures **complex** and **_complex** in Appendix E; each contains the real and imaginary components of complex number z in the form $(x + yi)$; member $z.x$, the real component, and member $z.y$, the imaginary component, can assume any signed value.

Return Value

The value computed by the formula $\text{sqrt}(z.x * z.x + z.y * z.y)$

If an overflow error is detected, a value of **HUGE_VAL** or **_LHUGE_VAL** is returned

Example   See: **abs()**.

Comments   Exception handling: if the return value overflows, a value of **HUGE_VAL** or **_LHUGE_VAL** is returned, **errno** is set to **ERANGE**, and **matherr()** or **_matherrl()** is called.

ceil(), ceill()   *Calculate the ceiling of a floating-point value*

Compatibility   ■ANSI   ■OS/2   ■*UNIX   ■*XENIX

See Also

```
floor(), floorl()
```

Specification

```
#include <math.h>
double ceil(double x);
long double ceill(long double x);
```

Arguments

x: Any signed value.

Return Value

The largest whole number that is greater than or equal to x

Example   See: **fmod()**.

Comments   Exception handling: no error return values, **errno** not set, **matherr()** or **_matherrl()** not called.

Notice in the program example how negative values of *x* are handled.

As an alternative, you can use the **#pragma intrinsic** form of this function.

_clear87()   *Gets and clears the floating-point math package status word*

Compatibility   ☐ ANSI   ■ OS/2   ☐ UNIX   ☐ XENIX

See Also
```
_fpreset(), _status87()
```

Specification
```
#include <float.h>
unsigned int _clear87(void);
```

Return Value
The previous floating-point math package status word

Example   See: **_control87()**.

Comments   Exception handling: no error return values; **errno** not set; **matherr()** not called.

Refer to the discussion of the status word in the section "Floating-Point Math Package."

_control87()   *Gets and sets the floating-point math package control word*

Compatibility   ☐ ANSI   ■ OS/2   ☐ UNIX   ☐ XENIX

See Also
```
_fpreset()
```

Specification
```
#include <float.h>
unsigned int _control87(unsigned int new, unsigned int mask);
```

Arguments
new: Individual floating-point control word bit values to be set.

mask: Either the infinity, rounding, precision, or interrupt control word component mask of which ***new*** is a part (see Table 23.1).

Return Value

The existing floating-point math package control word, before modification by the **new** bit settings

Example

```
/* FILE: ch23e6.c */
#include <stdio.h>
#include <math.h>
#include <float.h>
int main(void)
{
double dv1 = 10.0, dv2 = 0.0;
unsigned int cw, sw;

/* get default control word */
cw = _control87(0x0000, 0x0000);
printf("\nDefault 80x87 control word = %x", cw);
/* get default status word */
sw = _status87();
printf("\nDefault 80x87 status word = %x", sw);

/* override default control word */
_control87(MCW_EM, EM_ZERODIVIDE);
cw = _control87(0x0000, 0x0000);
printf("\n\nOverride 80x87 control word = %x", cw);

/* clear the status word */
_clear87();
/* divide by zero */
dv1 /= dv2;
sw = _status87();
printf("\nError 80x87 status word    = %x  SW_ZERODIVIDE", sw);

/* reset the Math Package upon error */
_fpreset();
cw = _control87(0x0000, 0x0000);
printf("\n\n80x87 control word after _fpreset = %x", cw);
sw = _status87();
printf("\n80x87 status word after _fpreset = %x", sw);
exit(0);
}
```

Output

```
Default 80x87 control word = 1332
Default 80x87 status word  = 0

Override 80x87 control word = 1336
Error 80x87 status word     = 4  SW_ZERODIVIDE

80x87 control word after _fpreset = 1332
80x87 status word after _fpreset  = 0
```

Comments   If the *mask* argument is 0x0000, then the function makes no changes to the existing control word; the function only gets the control word.

Exception handling: no error return values; **errno** not set; **matherr()** not called.

Refer to the discussion of the control word in the section "Floating-Point Math Package."

cos(), cosl()   *Calculate the cosine*

Compatibility   ■ANSI   ■OS/2   ■*UNIX   ■*XENIX

Specification

```
#include <math.h>
#include <errno.h>
double cos(double x);
long double cosl(long double x);
```

Arguments

x: Any signed angle value in radians.

Return Value

Cosine, between −1.0 and 1.0, whose angle value is *x*; if a total loss of precision is detected, a value of 0.0 is returned

Example

```
/* FILE: ch23e7.c */
#include <stdio.h>
#include <math.h>
int main(void)
{
const double pifact = acos(-1.0)/180.0;
const long double lpifact = acosl(-1.0L)/180.0L;
double ddeg, drad;
long double dldeg, dlrad;

printf("\n\nEnter an Angle in Degrees (+/-) : ");
scanf("%lf", &ddeg);
drad = ddeg * pifact;
dldeg = ddeg;
dlrad = dldeg * lpifact;

printf("\ncos= %lf cosl= %Lf cosh= %lf coshl= %Lf",
    cos(drad), cosl(dlrad), cosh(drad), coshl(dlrad));
printf("\nsin= %lf sinl= %Lf sinh= %lf sinhl= %Lf",
    sin(drad), sinl(dlrad), sinh(drad), sinhl(dlrad));
```

```
printf("\ntan= %lf tanl= %Lf tanh= %lf tanhl= %Lf",
    tan(drad), tanl(dlrad), tanh(drad), tanhl(dlrad));
exit(0);
}
```

Output

```
Enter an Angle in Degrees (+/-) : 45.0
cos= 0.707107   cosl= 0.707107   cosh= 1.324609   coshl= 1.324609
sin= 0.707107   sinl= 0.707107   sinh= 0.868671   sinhl= 0.868671
tan= 1.000000   tanl= 1.000000   tanh= 0.655794   tanhl= 0.655794
```

Comments   Exception handling: if x is large, a partial or total loss of precision may occur, **errno** is set to **ERANGE**, and **matherr()** or **_matherrl()** is called.

As an alternative, you can use the **#pragma intrinsic** form of this function.

cosh(), coshl()   *Calculate the hyperbolic cosine*

Compatibility   ■ANSI   ■OS/2   ■*UNIX   ■*XENIX

Specification

```
#include <math.h>
#include <errno.h>
double cosh(double x);
long double coshl(long double x);
```

Arguments

x: Any signed angle value in radians.

Return Value

Hyperbolic cosine whose angle value is x

If an overflow is detected, a value of ±**(HUGE_VAL)** or ±**(_LHUGE_VAL)** is returned

Example   See: **cos()**.

Comments   Exception handling: if x is large, an overflow may occur, **errno** is set to **ERANGE**, and **matherr()** or **_matherrl()** is called.

As an alternative, you can use the **#pragma intrinsic** form of this function.

div()   *Calculate an integer quotient and remainder*

Compatibility   ■ANSI   ■OS/2   □UNIX   □XENIX

See Also

```
ldiv()
```

Specification

```
#include <stdlib.h>
div_t div(int numer, int denom);
```

Arguments

numer: Any signed integer value.

denom: Any nonzero, signed integer value.

Return Value

See structure **typedef div_t** in Appendix E, which contains member **quot**, the signed quotient, and member **rem**, the remainder of the integer calculation of (*numer/denom*).

Example   See: **fmod()**.

Comments   As an alternative, use the C modulus operation (**%**).

Exception handling: if argument **denom** is 0, an R6003 −integer divide by 0, run-time error occurs, and the program terminates abnormally (INT 0x00); integer function types do not follow floating-point exception handling protocols.

exp(), expl()   *Calculate the exponential*

Compatibility ■ANSI   ■OS/2   ■* UNIX   ■* XENIX

Specification

```
#include <math.h>
#include <errno.h>
double exp(double x);
long double expl(long double x);
```

Arguments

x: Any signed value.

Return Value

The value of e raised to the *x* power

If an underflow occurs, a value of 0.0 is returned; if an overflow occurs, a value of **HUGE_VAL** or **_LHUGE_VAL** is returned

Example

```
/* FILE: ch23e8.c */
#include <stdio.h>
#include <math.h>
int main(void)
{
int iexp, iexpl;
double x, y, mant;
long double xl, yl, mantl;

printf("\nEnter a positive x = ");
scanf("%lf", &x);
xl = x;
printf("\nEnter a positive y = ");
scanf("%lf", &y);
yl = y;

printf("\n\nexp(x)    = %g  expl(x)    = %Lg",
    exp(x), expl(xl));
printf("\nhypot(x,y)= %g   hypotl(x)  = %Lg",
    hypot(x,y), hypotl(xl,yl));
printf("\npow(x,y)  = %g  powl(x,y)  = %Lg",
    pow(x,y), powl(xl,yl));
printf("\nsqrt(x)    = %g   sqrtl(x)   = %Lg",
    sqrt(x), sqrtl(xl));
mant = frexp(x,&iexp);
printf("\nfrexp(x,exp)  mant =%g exp =%d", mant, iexp);
/* bug in frexpl() at this time: run-time M6111
    mantl = frexpl(xl,&iexl);
    printf("\nfrexpl(x,exp)  mant = %Lg exp =%d", mantl, iexpl);
*/
mantl = mant;
iexpl = iexp;
printf("\nldexp(mant,exp) = %g", ldexp(mant,iexp));
printf("\nldexpl(mant,exp)= %Lg",ldexpl(mantl,iexpl));
exit(0);
}
```

Output

```
Enter a positive x = 16.0
Enter a positive y = 2.0

exp(x)    = 8.88611e+006  expl(x)    = 8.88611e+006
hypot(x,y)= 16.1245   hypotl(x)  = 16.1245
pow(x,y)  = 256 powl(x,y)   = 256
sqrt(x)    = 4 sqrtl(x)      = 4
frexp(x,exp)   mant =0.5 exp =5
ldexp(mant,exp) = 16
ldexpl(mant,exp)= 16
```

Comments   Exception handling: if either an underflow or overflow of the return value is detected, **errno** is set to **ERANGE**, and **matherr()** or **_matherrl()** is called.

As an alternative, you can use the **#pragma intrinsic** form of this function.

`fabs()`, `fabsl()`   *Calculate the absolute value of a floating-point number*

Compatibility   ■ANSI   ■OS/2   ■[*] UNIX   ■[*] XENIX

Specification

```
#include <math.h>
double fabs(double x);
long double fabsl(long double x);
```

Arguments

x: Any signed floating-point value.

Return Value

The absolute value of argument *x*

Example   See: **abs()**.

Comments   Exception handling: no error return values; **errno** not set; **matherrl()** or **_matherrl()** not called.

As an alternative, you can use the **#pragma intrinsic** form of this function.

`floor()`, `floorl()`   *Calculate the floor of a floating-point value*

Compatibility   ■ANSI   ■OS/2   ■[*] UNIX   ■[*] XENIX

See Also

```
ceil(), ceill()
```

Specification

```
#include <math.h>
double floor(double x);
long double floorl(long double x);
```

Arguments

x: Any signed floating-point value.

Return Value

The largest whole number that is less than or equal to **x**

Example

See: **fmod()**.

Comments

Notice in the program example how negative values of **x** are handled. Exception handling: no error return values; **errno** is not set; **matherr()** or **_matherrl()** not called.

As an alternative, you can use the **#pragma intrinsic** form of this function.

fmod(), fmodl()   *Calculates the floating-point remainder*

Compatibility   ■ANSI   ■OS/2   ■*UNIX   ■*XENIX

See Also

```
modf(), modfl()
```

Specification

```
#include <math.h>
double fmod(double x, double y);
long double fmodl(long double x, long double y);
```

Arguments

x: A signed dividend value.

y: A signed divisor value.

Return Value

The signed floating-point remainder value of the calculation *x/y*; if *y* is 0.0, then a value of 0.0 is returned

Example

```
/* FILE: ch23e9.c */
#include <stdio.h>
#include <math.h>
#include <stdlib.h>
int main(void)
{
int ival = 325, iden = 33;
div_t istr;
long lval = 43000L;
ldiv_t lstr;
double dval = 25.25;
```

```
double wdval, fdval, rdval;
long double dlval = -745.275L;
long double wdlval, fdlval, rdlval;

istr = div(ival, iden);
printf("\nint = %d divisor= %d", ival, iden);
printf("\nint quotient = %d", istr.quot);
printf("\nint remainder= %d", istr.rem);

lstr = ldiv(lval, (long)iden);
printf("\n\nlong = %ld divisor= %ld", lval, (long)iden);
printf("\nlong quotient = %ld", lstr.quot);
printf("\nlong remainder= %ld", lstr.rem);

printf("\n\ndouble = %g divisor = %d", dval, iden);
printf("\nceil = %g floor = %g", ceil(dval), floor(dval));
rdval = fmod(dval, (double)iden);
fdval = modf(dval, &wdval);
printf("\nfmod = %g modf: whole = %g fract = %g",
    rdval, wdval, fdval);

printf("\n\nlong double = %Lg divisor = %d", dlval, iden);
printf("\nceill= %Lg floorl = %Lg", ceill(dlval), floorl(dlval));
rdlval = fmodl(dlval, (long double)iden);
fdlval = modfl(dlval, &wdlval);
printf("\nfmodl = %Lg modfl: whole = %Lg fract = %Lg",
    rdlval, wdlval, fdlval);
exit(0);
}
```

Output

```
int = 325   divisor= 33
int quotient = 9
int remainder= 28

long = 43000   divisor= 33
long quotient = 1303
long remainder= 1

double = 25.25   divisor = 33
ceil = 26   floor = 25
fmod = 25.25   modf: whole = 25   fract = 0.25

long double = -745.275   divisor = 33
ceill= -745 floorl = -746
fmodl = -19.275   modfl: whole = -745   fract = -0.275
```

Comments   This function is necessary because the C modulus (%) operator can be used only with integral types.

The return value always has the same sign as argument x, and its absolute value is always less than the absolute value of argument x.

Exception handling: no error return values; **errno** not set; **matherr()** or **_matherrl()** not called.

As an alternative, you can use the **#pragma intrinsic** form of this function.

_fpreset() *Resets the floating-point math package*

Compatibility ☐ANSI ■OS/2 ☐UNIX ☐XENIX

See Also

```
_clear87(), _control87()
```

Specification

```
#include <float.h>
void _fpreset(void);
```

Example   See: **_control87()**.

Comments Use of this function is crucial when an $80x87$ coprocessor is installed, because the state of the $80x87$ may be changed by successively running application programs that generate exceptions; when software emulation is employed, each program execution effectively reinitializes the math package.

Exception handling: no error return values; **errno** not set; **matherr()** not called.

Refer to the discussion in the "Floating-Point Math Package" section of this chapter.

frexp(), frexpl() *Get the mantissa and exponent of a floating-point number*

Compatibility ■ANSI ■OS/2 ■* UNIX ■* XENIX

See Also

```
ldexp(), ldexpl()
```

Specification

```
#include <math.h>
double frexp(double x, int *expptr);
long double frexpl(long double x, int *expptr);
```

Arguments

x: Any signed floating-point value.

expptr: Pointer to the power-of-2 exponent value, *n*, that corresponds to **x**.

Return Value

The signed mantissa value (absolute value between 0.5 and 1.0), m, corresponding to x

If argument x is 0.0, then a mantissa and exponent value of 0.0 result

Example   See: **exp()**.

Comments   Given a floating-point value, x, this function returns m, a mantissa, and n, an exponent, such that the formula $x = m \times 2^n$ is satisfied.

Exception handling: no error return values; **errno** not set; **matherr()** or **_matherrl()** not called.

hypot(), hypotl()   *Calculate the hypotenuse of a right triangle*

Compatibility   □ANSI   ■OS/2   ■* UNIX   ■* XENIX

See Also

sqrt(), sqrtl(), pow(), powl()

Specification

```
#include <math.h>
#include <errno.h>
double hypot(double x, double y);
long double hypotl(long double x, long double y);
```

Arguments

x: The length of side x^l.

y: The length of side y^l.

Return Value

The length of the hypotenuse of a right triangle with sides x^l and y^l

If an overflow error is detected, a value of **HUGE_VAL** or **_LHUGE_VAL** is returned.

Example   See: **exp()**.

Comments   A call to function **hypot()** or **hypotl()** is equivalent to performing the calculation **sqrt(x*x + y*y)**.

Exception handling: if an overflow of the return value occurs, **errno** is set to **ERANGE**, and **matherr()** or **_matherrl()** is called.

j0(), _j0l()   *Compute a First Kind Bessel function, Order 0*

See Bessel Functions.

j1(), _j1l()   *Compute a First Kind Bessel function, Order 1*

See Bessel Functions.

jn(), _jnl()   *Compute a First Kind Bessel function, Order n*

See Bessel Functions.

labs()   *Calculate the absolute value of a long integer number*

Compatibility   ■ANSI   ■OS/2   □UNIX   □XENIX

See Also

abs()

Specification

```
#include <stdlib.h> or <math.h>
long labs(long n);
```

Arguments

n: Any signed **long** integer value.

Return Value

The absolute value of argument *n*

Example   See: **abs()**.

Comments   Exception handling: no error return values; **errno** not set; integer function types do not follow floating-point exception handling protocols.

As an alternative, you can use the **#pragma intrinsic** form of this function.

`ldexp()`, `ldexpl()` *Compute a floating-point number given a mantissa and exponent*

Compatibility ■ANSI   ■OS/2   ■*UNIX   ■*XENIX

See Also
```
pow(), powl(); see: frexp(), frexpl()
```

Specification
```
#include <math.h>
#include <errno.h>
double ldexp(double x, int exp);
long double ldexpl(long double x, int exp);
```

Arguments
x: Any signed floating-point value (usually between 0.5 and 1.0).

exp: Any signed integer exponent.

Return Value
The value calculated by the equation $(x \times 2^{exp})$; if an overflow of the return value is detected, $\pm$ **HUGE_VAL** or $\pm$ **_LHUGE_VAL** is returned.

Example   See: `exp()`.

Comments   Exception handling: if an overflow of the return value is detected, **errno** is set to **ERANGE**, and **matherr()** or **_matherrl()** is called.

`ldiv()` *Compute the quotient and remainder of a* `long` *integer number*

Compatibility ■ANSI   ■OS/2   □UNIX   □XENIX

See Also
```
div()
```

Specification
```
#include <stdlib.h>
ldiv_t ldiv(long int numer, long int denom);
```

Arguments
numer: Any **signed long** integer value.

demon: Any nonzero, **signed long** integer value.

Return Value

See structure **typedef ldiv_t** in Appendix E, which contains member **quot**, the signed quotient, and member **rem**, the remainder of the **long** integer calculation of (*numer/denom*).

Example   See: **fmod()**.

Comments   Exception handling: if argument **denom** is 0L, an R6003 run-time error (integer divide by 0) occurs, and the program terminates abnormally (INT 0x00); integer function types do not follow floating-point exception handling protocols. As an alternative, use the C modulus (**%**) operator.

log(), logl()   *Calculate a natural logarithm*

Compatibility   ■ANSI   ■OS/2   ■*UNIX   ■*XENIX

See Also

```
log10(), log10l()
```

Specification

```
#include <math.h>
#include <errno.h>
double log(double x);
long double logl(long double x);
```

Arguments

x: Any positive, nonzero floating-point value.

Return Value

The natural or base-e logarithm of argument *x*; if argument *x* is either negative or 0.0, then a value of −(**HUGE_VAL**) or −(**_LHUGE_VAL**) is returned

Example

```
/* FILE: ch23e10.c */
#include <stdio.h>
#include <math.h>
int main(void)
{
int i;
double dval;
long double dlval;
```

```
    for (i=0; i<3; i++) {
        printf("\nEnter a positive/nonzero number : ");
        scanf("%lf", &dval);
        dlval = dval;
        printf("\n\nlog = %g logl = %Lg", log(dval), logl(dlval));
        printf("\nlog10= %g log10l= %Lg", log10(dval), log10l(dlval));
        }
    exit(0);
    }
```

Output

```
Enter a positive/nonzero number : 10.0

log = 2.30259  logl = 2.30259
log10= 1  log10l= 1
Enter a positive/nonzero number : 100.0

log = 4.60517  logl  = 4.60517
log10= 2  log10l= 2
Enter a positive/nonzero number : 1000.0

log = 6.90776  logl = 6.90776
log10= 3  log10l= 3
```

Comments Exception handling: if argument **x** is negative, **errno** is set to **EDOM**; if argument **x** is 0.0, **errno** is set to **ERANGE**; in both cases, **matherrl()** or **_matherrl()** is called.

As an alternative, you can use the **#pragma intrinsic** form of this function.

log10(), log10l() *Calculate a base 10 logarithm*

Compatibility ■ANSI ■OS/2 ■[*]UNIX ■[*]XENIX

See Also

```
log(), logl()
```

Specification

```
#include <math.h>
double log10(double x);
long double log10l(long double x);
```

Arguments

x: Any positive, nonzero floating-point value.

Return Value

The base-10 logarithm of argument *x*

If argument *x* is either negative or 0.0, then a value of –(**HUGE_VAL**) or –(**_LHUGE_VAL**) is returned

Example   See: `log()`.

Comments   Exception handling: if argument *x* is negative, **errno** is set to **EDOM**; if argument *x* is 0.0, **errno** is set to **ERANGE**; in both cases, **matherr()** or **_matherrl()** is called.

As an alternative, you can use the **#pragma intrinsic** form of this function.

`matherr(), _matherrl()`   *Math error exception handling*

Compatibility   ☐ANSI   ■OS/2   ■* UNIX   ■* XENIX

Specification

```
#include <math.h>
int matherr(struct exception *except);
int _matherrl(struct _exceptionl *except);
```

Arguments

except: Pointer to error handling structures, **exception** and **_exceptionl**, defined in Appendix E. Each contains a member, **type**, defining the exception type detected (see macros defined in **<math.h>**); a member, **name**, the name of the function where the error occurred; members, **arg1** and **arg2**, the first and second (if any) arguments of function name; and member **retval**, the value returned by the function.

Return Value

Either an integer value of 0 (false), or any nonzero value (true); if a value of 0 is returned, then a message is directed to **stderr**, and **errno** is set to either **EDOM** or **ERANGE**; otherwise, if a nonzero value is returned, then no error mesage is displayed to **stderr**, and **errno** remains unchanged; normally a nonzero value is returned to reflect that a corrective action was taken (**retval** altered), and processing is to continue as if no exception had been detected.

Example

```
/* FILE: ch23e11.c */
#include <stdio.h>
#include <math.h>
#include <stdlib.h>
```

```c
int matherr(struct exception *err)
{
static char *msg[] = { "domain", "singularity",
    "overflow", "underflow",
    "total loss", "partial loss"};
printf("\nMathERR=> %s: %s: a1=%g: a2=%g: RET=%g",
    err->name, msg[err->type-DOMAIN],
    err->arg1, err->arg2, err->retval);
return 1;
}

int main(void)
{
struct complex z = { HUGE_VAL, HUGE_VAL };

/* generate FP exceptions;
    see Table 23.2 and ch23e2.c */

    acos(2.0);
    asin(-2.0);
    atan2(0.0, 0.0);
    y0(-1.0);
    y1(-1.0);
    yn(1,-1.0);
    cabs(z);
    cos(HUGE_VAL);
    cosh(HUGE_VAL);
    exp(HUGE_VAL);
    hypot(HUGE_VAL, HUGE_VAL);
    log(0.0);
    log10(-10.0);
    pow(0.0,0.0);
    pow(2.0,HUGE_VAL);
    sin(HUGE_VAL);
    sinh(HUGE_VAL);
    sqrt(-1.0);
    tan(HUGE_VAL);

exit(0);
}
```

Output

```
MathERR=> acos: domain: a1=2: a2=0: RET=0
MathERR=> asin: domain: a1=-2: a2=0: RET=0
  .

  .
MathERR=> sqrt: domain: a1=-1: a2=1.79769e+308: RET=0
MathERR=> tan: total loss: a1=1.79769e+308: a2=1.79769e+308: RET=0
```

Comments   If a custom **matherr()** or **_matherrl()** function is written in C, it should be linked using the /NOE option.

The behavior of the default **matherr()** and **_matherrl()** functions found in the run-time library are discussed in the "Floating-Point Function Exceptions" section of this chapter (see Table 23.2).

modf(), modfl()   *Split a floating-point value into its whole and fractional parts*

Compatibility   ■ANSI   ■OS/2   ■[*]UNIX   ■[*]XENIX

See Also

```
fmod(), fmodl()
```

Specification

```
#include <math.h>
double modf(double x, double *intptr);
long double modfl(long double x, long double *intptr);
```

Arguments

x: Any signed floating-point value.

intptr: Pointer to a floating-point value that contains the resulting whole part of argument ***x***.

Return Value

The signed fraction part of argument ***x***

Example   See: **fmod()**.

Comments   Exception handling: no error return values; **errno** not set; **matherr()** or **_matherrl()** not called.

pow(), powl()   *Calculate x raised to the power of y*

Compatibility   ■ANSI   ■OS/2   ■[*]UNIX   ■[*]XENIX

See Also

```
exp(), expl(), sqrt(), sqrtl()
```

Specification

```
#include <math.h>
double pow(double x, double y);
long double pow(long double x, long double y);
```

Arguments

x: Any nonzero floating-point value.

y: Any **signed** floating-point power of *x* up to 2^{64}.

Return Value

The value of *x* raised to the *y* power; if both *x* and *y* are 0.0 then 0.0 is returned; if *x* is nonzero and *y* is 0.0, then 1.0 is returned; if *x* is negative and *y* is not integral, then 0.0 is returned; if *x* is 0.0 and *y* is negative, a value of 0.0 is returned; if an overflow is detected, then either $\pm$**(HUGE_VAL)** or $\pm$**(_LHUGE_VAL)** is returned.

Example

See: **exp()**.

Comments

Exception handling: if both *x* and *y* are 0.0, **errno** is set to **EDOM**; if *x* is negative and *y* is not integral, **errno** is set to **EDOM** (because logarithms are used); if *x* is 0.0 and *y* is negative, then **errno** is set to **EDOM**; if an overflow occurs, **errno** is set to **ERANGE**; in all cases **matherr()** or **_matherrl()** is called.

Use either the function or **#pragma intrinsic** form.

rand() *Generate a pseudorandom number*

Compatibility ■ANSI   ■OS/2   ■* UNIX   ■* XENIX

See Also

srand()

Specification

```
#include <stdlib.h>
int rand(void);
```

Return Value

Random number in the range between 0 and **RAND_MAX**

Example

```
/* FILE: ch23e12.c */
#include <stdio.h>
#include <stdlib.h>
#include <time.h>
int main(void)
{
int i;
printf("\nRandom sequence (no seed)");
for (i=0; i<5; i++) printf("\n\t%6d", rand());
```

```
printf("\nRandom sequence (time seed)");
srand((unsigned) time(NULL));
for (i=0; i<5; i++) printf("\n\t%6d", rand());

printf("\nRandom sequence (reset seed)");
srand(1U);
for (i=0; i<5; i++) printf("\n\t%6d", rand());

exit(0);
}
```

Output

```
Random sequence (no seed)
        41
     18467
      6334
     26500
     19169
Random sequence (time seed)
     21124
      7555
     26833
     26165
     25486
Random sequence (reset seed)
        41
     18467
      6334
     26500
     19169
```

Comments   Notice in the example that unless **rand()** is initialized or *seeded* using **srand()**, identical number sequences are generated.

Exception handling: no error return values; **errno** not set; integer function types do not follow floating-point exception handling protocols.

sin(), sinl()   *Calculate the sine*

Compatibility   ■ANSI   ■OS/2   ■* UNIX   ■* XENIX

Specification

```
#include <math.h>
#include <errno.h>
double sin(double x);
long double sinl(long double x);
```

Arguments

x: Any signed angle value in radians.

Return Value

Sine, between -1.0 and 1.0, whose angle value is x; if a total loss of precision is detected, a value of 0.0 is returned

Example   See: `cos()`.

Comments   Exception handling: if x is large, a partial or total loss of precision may occur, **errno** is set to **ERANGE**, and **matherr()** or **_matherrl()** is called.

As an alternative, you can use the **#pragma intrinsic** form of this function.

sinh(), sinhl()   *Calculate the hyperbolic sine*

Compatibility ■ANSI   ■OS/2   ■*UNIX   ■*XENIX

Specification

```
#include <math.h>
#include <errno.h>
double sinh(double x);
long double sinhl(long double x);
```

Arguments

x: Any signed angle value in radians.

Return Value

Hyperbolic sine whose angle value is x

If an overflow is detected, a value of $\pm$(**HUGE_VAL**) or $\pm$(**_LHUGE_VAL**) is returned

Example   See: `cos()`.

Comments   Exception handling: if x is large, an overflow may occur, **errno** is set to **ERANGE**, and **matherr()** or **_matherrl()** is called.

As an alternative, you can use the **#pragma intrinsic** form of this function.

sqrt(), sqrtl()   *Calculate the square root*

Compatibility ■ANSI   ■OS/2   ■*UNIX   ■*XENIX

See Also

```
pow(), powl(), hypot(), hypotl()
```

Specification

```
#include <math.h>
#include <errno.h>
double sqrt(double x);
long double sqrtl(long double x);
```

Arguments

x: Any positive floating-point value.

Return Value

The square root of **x**

If argument *x* is negative, a value of 0 is returned

Example   See: **exp()**.

Comments   Exception handling: if argument *x* is negative, **errno** is set to **EDOM**, and **matherr()** or **_matherrl()** is called.

As an alternative, you can use the **#pragma intrinsic** form of this function.

srand()   *Establish the starting or seed value for* rand()

Compatibility   ■ANSI   ■OS/2   ■UNIX   ■XENIX

See Also

```
rand()
```

Specification

```
#include <stdlib.h>
void srand(unsigned int seed);
```

Arguments

seed: A bit pattern that establishes the starting point of the random numbers generated by function **rand()**.

Example   See: **rand()**.

Comments   Exception handling: **errno** not set; integer function types do not follow floating-point exception handling protocols.

_status87() *Get the floating-point math package status word*

Compatibility ☐ANSI ■OS/2 ☐UNIX ☐XENIX

See Also
```
_clear87(), _fpreset()
```

Specification
```
#include <float.h>
unsigned int _status87(void);
```

Return Value
The present floating-point math package status word

Example   See: _control87().

Comments   Exception handling: no error return values; **errno** not set; **math-err()** not called.

Refer to the discussion of the status word in the section "Floating-Point Math Package."

tan(), tanl() *Calculate the tangent*

Compatibility ■ANSI ■OS/2 ■* UNIX ■* XENIX

Specification
```
#include <math.h>
#include <errno.h>
double tan(double x);
long double tanl(long double x);
```

Arguments
x: Any signed angle value in radians.

Return Value
Tangent whose angle value is x

If a total loss of precision is detected, a value of 0.0 is returned

Example   See: cos().

Comments   Exception handling: if x is large, a partial or total loss of precision may occur, **errno** is set to **ERANGE**, and **matherr()** or **_matherrl()** is called.

As an alternative, you can use the **#pragma intrinsic** form of this function.

`tanh()`, `tanhl()`   *Calculate the hyperbolic tangent*

Compatibility   ■ANSI   ■OS/2   ■*UNIX   ■*XENIX

Specification

```
#include <math.h>
double tanh(double x);
long double tanhl(long double x);
```

Arguments

x: Any signed angle value in radians.

Return Value

Hyperbolic tangent whose angle value is x

Example   See: `cos()`.

Comments   Exception handling: no error return values; **errno** not set; **matherr()** or **_matherrl()** not called.

As an alternative, you can use the **#pragma intrinsic** form of this function.

`y0()`, `_y0l()`   *Compute a Second Kind Bessel Function, Order 0*

See Bessel Functions.

`y1()`, `_y1l()`   *Compute a Second Kind Bessel Function, Order 1*

See Bessel Functions.

`yn()`, `_ynl()`   *Compute a Second Kind Bessel Function, Order n*

See Bessel Functions.

Memory Management Functions

Memory Management Functions

The conventional memory map of DOS portrayed in Figure 2.19 limits all addressing to a maximum of 1MB and the size of any application program to something less than 640KB. These limitations were set by the specifications established for the 8086 chip (see Table 2.4). Even though today most 80286 and 80386-based PCs are furnished with at least 1MB of memory, unless expanded (EMS) or extended memory management is employed, C application programs running under DOS must still adhere to these limitations. Given this fact and the inherent performance advantage of memory over disk-based storage, memory is still a precious computer resource. Over 100 of the Microsoft C run-time library functions are available that provide memory allocation services. This chapter will help you to master the use of these essential run-time library functions.

The terminology surrounding the classification of memory was first introduced in Chapter 2, together with memory maps that depicted the text, data, stack, and heap areas of memory. The naming and placement of these memory areas were found to vary based upon the compiler memory model installed (Figures 2.20 through 2.25).

As discussed in Chapter 15, the text area consists of the machine-language instructions (logic) for the functions that constitute a C program. The data area contains all **static** and **extern** storage-class data objects and constants declared by a program. The stack provides for the allocation of all **auto** storage-class data objects and supports the mechanism (stack frames) by which program control is transferred when functions are called. The heap constitutes any remaining addressable memory exclusive of that assigned to the text, data, and stack areas.

In this chapter we will see how to work with memory buffer areas and how to allocate objects on the stack; more importantly, however, we will explore using the heap. The most attractive characteristic of the heap is that memory allocation is dynamic. The allocation of data objects to the heap is performed at execution-time, and is not predetermined at compile- or link-time, as are the text, data, and stack areas of every program.

Let's begin by examining how memory-buffer areas may be manipulated, review some additional features of the stack, and then explore the broader issues concerning the use of the heap.

BUFFER AREAS

A memory-buffer area represents any contiguous portion of memory that is contained within a single memory segment (64KB). Normally, a buffer is understood to represent a holding area for an array of data objects. Typically, we associate buffers with arrays of type **char**.

All buffer-handling operations are performed byte by byte, regardless of the underlying data type of the objects in the array contained in the buffer area. Initialization assigns a fixed value to each byte in a buffer, either individually or by range. When buffers are copied, individual byte values are replicated and provisions are made to accommodate buffers that overlap or are located in separate segments. Buffers are compared one byte at a time, and the comparison may be either case-sensitive or not. The only restriction on these functions is that buffer areas may not span segment boundaries.

The run-time library buffer-handling functions shown in Table 24.1 are named beginning with **mem..()** or **_fmem..()**. Standard C has reserved all function names beginning with **mem..**, and constructed using any subsequent [a-z] character (see Table 4.8), for future use; therefore, avoid naming any application functions in this manner. The **_fmem** nomenclature used by Microsoft adopts the Standard C guideline to preface all non-Standard identifiers with an underscore character, and by convention has used the prefix **_fmem..()** to depict the memory-model independent versions of the buffer-handling run-time library functions. All **_fmem..()** functions employ **_far** addressing for their arguments, even if the Tiny, Small, or Medium memory model is employed. Also, notice that these buffer-handling, run-time library functions parallel those available for string-handling described in Chapter 26.

MORE ON THE STACK

The only control over the stack involves setting its size, either by using the compiler options (Chapter 2), the linker options (Chapter 3), or the EXEHDR utility (Chapter 3). The stack size set for an executable file (.COM or .EXE) is used by all processes derived from that file. Once a process is loaded into memory, the stack size remains constant and cannot be changed by the executing program. Unlike the code, data, and heap areas of memory, memory allocation to the stack grows from high to low memory addresses (see Figure 15.10).

As noted in the "Performance Considerations" section of Chapter 15, a portion of the stack may optionally be shared with the heap if the xVARSTCK.OBJ module is included when the program is linked. When this technique is used, stack memory is allocated from the top of the stack downward, as usual, and heap memory is allocated from the bottom of the stack upward until the stack space is exhausted and the R6000 run-time error message *stack overflow* results.

The run-time library provides only one non-standard function, **alloca()**, for the allocation of objects directly to the stack. Each object allocated is pushed on the stack, and its lowest (starting) address is returned. Certain restrictions, other than the obvious size limitation of the stack itself, apply to the allocation of objects in this manner (see the documentation of the **alloca()** function).

BASIC HEAP CONCEPTS

Since memory is a critical computer resource, it is managed by the operating system itself. The DOS memory-management services may be accessed directly by issuing non-Standard DOS interrupts as described in Chapter 22; however, to permit C source code to be ported to other operating systems, Standard C defines a mimimal set of functions, **malloc()**, **calloc()**, **realloc()** and **free()**, which manage the heap area of memory.

By using these functions, C source code can be written that is portable, because the run-time libraries of Standard C compilers written for other operating systems are also required to provide these functions. In this manner, all C compiler vendors (implementors) can provide functions that exploit the particular hardware and operating system for which their compiler is designed and marketed, while providing a minimal set of portable memory-management services that maintain the heap.

The C startup code described in Chapter 15 establishes the Near and Far heap boundaries for each process that is loaded for execution (see Figures 2.20 through 2.25). These heap areas are managed using the Standard and non-Standard functions listed in Table 24.1. Each function relies upon a common doubly-linked list data structure that maintains information about each portion of the heap that has been allocated. It is important to understand that this heap data structure is independent of the list maintained by DOS itself to manage the allocation of all available memory.

Microsoft's strategy for minimizing the overhead of this data structure is to keep the DOS memory-block request sizes large relative to the size of the linked-list data structure itself. The heap management functions only request blocks of memory from DOS in increments defined by global variable **_amblksiz** (see Appendix C), which by default is 8KB. This value may be changed at any time. Subsequently, program requests are fulfilled by subdividing the memory controlled by the heap itself, not DOS. Requests to free heap space return used memory blocks to the heap, not DOS, and flag them as free, or available for reuse. Free heap space is returned to DOS only when the **_heapmin()** functions are used. Although each block of memory allocated to the heap is contiguous, there is no assurance that subsequent requests for space will be at an adjacent or higher memory address. Requests are fulfilled in one of two ways: either based upon an algorithm that is responsible only for finding enough contiguous memory space; or by additional requests to DOS in **_amblksiz** increments, which will be provided when insufficient memory is available.

Only one doubly-linked list of heap-segment descriptors that control the heap is maintained. This internal heap structure is subject to change, but is described, together with the C startup code, in a file named HEAP.INC. Each block of memory that is allocated has an associated heap-segment descriptor that fully describes the "state" of that memory block. All heap run-time services represent a coordinated approach to the allocation of memory blocks, which are individually categorized as being in the Near heap, Far heap, or a Based heap. This and other miscellaneous structures represent the "overhead" spoken of when blocks of memory are allocated to the heap, and embody its greatest weakness, as well. Should this linked list become corrupted by an errant pointer assignment, all heap memory allocation can be jeopardized. Hence the need for the various consistency-checking services that are provided: **_heapchk()**, **_heapset()**, and **_heapwalk()**.

It should not be surprising that the C startup code itself and many other run-time library functions require dynamic memory-allocation services. The C startup code transforms the DOS command line passed in the PSP to a suitable and dynamically allocated memory space containing **argc** and **argv**. The environment passed from COMMAND.COM is dynamically allocated and its address passed in the PSP, from which the optional **main()** argument, **envp**, is constructed. Each of the run-time functions listed below relies on the **malloc()** function to fulfill its need for dynamic memory allocation.

calloc()	gets()
execvxx functions	**getw()**
execlxx functions	**printf()**
fgetc()	putc()
fgetchar()	putchar()
fgets()	putenv()
fprint()	puts()
fputc()	putw()

`fputchar()`	scanf()
`fputs()`	`_searchenv()`
`fread()`	`setvbuf()`
`fscanf()`	spawnl**xx** functions
`fseek()`	spawnv**xx** functions
`fsetpos()`	**strdup** functions
`_fullpath()`	system()
`fwrite()`	tempnam()
`getc()`	ungetc()
`getchar()`	vfprintf()
`getcwd()`	`vprintf()`
`_getdcwd()`	

Let's examine in more detail how the Near, Far, and recently introduced Based heap areas are supported by the run-time functions documented in this chapter.

Using the Near Heap

When the Tiny, Small, or Medium compiler memory model is employed, the term *heap* actually refers to the Near heap—that portion of unused memory within the address range of the DS register (see Figures 2.20, 2.21, 2.22). When the Standard run-time functions **malloc()**, **calloc()**, **free()**, and **realloc()** are used, they are actually replaced by calls to **_nmalloc()**, **_ncalloc()**, **_nfree()**, and **_nrealloc()**, respectively. The use of the standard function names noted above is recommended, however, because their substitution is performed automatically, should a different memory model be chosen. However, if explicit references are made to functions that begin with **_b** for Based heap, **_f** for Far heap, or **_n** for Near heap, no function substitutions ever occur.

When the Near heap space is exhausted, a **NULL** pointer value is returned. If the xVARSTCK.OBJ has been linked, an attempt will be made to satisfy the request against the unused portion of the stack before a **NULL** pointer is returned. It must be emphasized that when the Near heap space of a Tiny, Small, or Medium memory-model program is exhausted, alternatives are still available. Mixed memory-model programming can be employed by making explicit requests for heap space using the **_f..** or **_b..** memory allocation functions, or, in fact, allocation can be requested to occur directly on the stack using the **alloca()** function. An overall strategy that should be employed for Tiny, Small, and Medium memory-model programs is to exhaust the Near heap, then exhaust the Far heap, and finally resort to the stack.

Using the Far Heap

When the Compact, Large, or Huge compiler memory model is employed, the term *heap* actually refers to the Far heap—that portion of unused memory outside the address range of the DS register (see Figures 2.23, 2.24, 2.25). When the Standard run-time functions **malloc()**, **calloc()**, **free()**, and **realloc()** are used, they are actually replaced by calls to **_fmalloc()**, **_fcalloc()**, **_ffree()**, and **_frealloc()**, respectively. The use of the Standard function names noted above is recommended, however, because their substitution is performed automatically, should a different memory model be chosen. However, if explicit references are made to functions that begin with **_b** for Based heap, **_f** for Far heap, or **_n** for Near heap, no function substitutions ever occur.

When the Far heap space is exhausted, a **NULL** pointer value is returned. If the xVARSTCK.OBJ file has been linked, an attempt will be made to satisfy the request against the unused portion of the stack before a **NULL** pointer is returned. It must be emphasized that when the Far heap space of a Compact, Large, or Huge memory model program is exhausted, alternatives are still available. Mixed memory-model programming can be employed by making explicit requests for heap space using the **_n..** or **_b..** memory allocation functions, or, in fact, allocation can be requested to occur directly on the stack using the **alloca()** function. An overall strategy that should be employed for Compact, Large, and Huge memory-model programs is to exhaust the Far heap, then exhaust the Near heap, and finally resort to the stack.

The Huge memory model designates that all data object addressing is by **_huge** pointers, which use 20-bit address arithmetic (not 16-bit arithmetic as all other pointer types). However, if arrays of objects are to span segments, the **halloc()** and **hfree()** functions must be called explicitly for that purpose. Calls to **malloc()** and **free()** are not transformed into calls to **halloc()** and **hfree()**, respectively.

Using a Based Heap

The concept of a Based heap is new with QuickC version 2.5 and OptimizingC version 6.0. Unlike Near and Far heap segments, Based heap segments are not available for use automatically. Based heap segments must be created explicitly by using the **_bheapseg()** function, or by using the **_bheapadd()** function to establish Based heap areas in the predefined heap segment names **_CODE**, **_DATA**, **_CONST**, or **_STACK**, or, in fact, in any other named segment that may have been created using the **/ND** compiler option. A Based heap is also different in that the macros **_NULLSEG** and **_NULLOFF** are used instead of **NULL** as sentinels to indicate that segment or address allocation has failed. The **_bheapmin()** function does not release Based heap memory to DOS; the **_bfreeseg()** function must be used for that purpose. However, Based heap areas are automatically increased in **_amblksiz** increments, like the Near and Far heap.

ALLOCATING MULTIDIMENSIONED ARRAYS

The **calloc()**, **malloc()**, and **halloc()** dynamic memory allocation functions are prototyped to return a pointer to type void (**void ***), which implies that a one-dimensional array of objects was allocated. An interesting problem arises when multidimensioned arrays of objects are to be allocated to the heap. It is clear that such arrays are mapped to memory in row-major order (rightmost subscripts vary the fastest). See the discussion of multidimensioned arrays in Chapter 8. Since the prototypes of all dynamic memory allocation functions describe the space to be allocated in terms of the total number and individual size of the objects, the resolution to this problem must lie in casting the pointer return value of these functions.

Recall that aggregate types (see Figure 7.1) cannot be cast; however, pointers to arrays can be declared and cast as needed, and a pointer to type **void** is compatible with any other pointer type. Herein lies the answer to this problem.

First a pointer variable must be declared that describes the appropriate dimensioning of objects. Consider the following valid pointer declarations to one-, two-, and three-dimensioned arrays of type **int**:

```
int *ptr;            /* or ptr[] */
int (*ptr)[3];       /* or ptr[][3] */
int (*ptr)[3][4];    /* or ptr[][3][4] */
```

Recall that each level of subscripting **[]** can be replaced by one level of indirection (*****). The example program shown in Figure 24.1 combines the declaration and casting of such pointers to demonstrate how multidimensioned arrays of objects can be allocated to the heap.

The output produced by this example program, shown in Figure 24.2, confirms the storage mapping of multidimensioned arrays described in Chapter 8 and verifies that this technique is correct.

```
/* FILE: ch24e15.c */
#include <stdio.h>
#include <stdlib.h>
#include <malloc.h>

int main(void)
{
int i, j, k, val;
int *ptr_1d, (*ptr_2d)[3], (*ptr_3d)[3][4];
int dimen[3] = { 2, 3, 4 };
int elem[3] = { dimen[0], dimen[0] * dimen[1],
    dimen[0] * dimen[1] * dimen[2] };
/* allocate int array[2] */
ptr_1d = malloc(elem[0] * sizeof(int));
for (val=0, i=0; i<dimen[0]; i++, val++) ptr_1d[i] = val;
printf("\n\n1-D Array as 1-D:");
for (i=0; i<elem[0]; i++)
    printf("\n[%2d]=%2d", i, ptr_1d[i]);

/* allocate int array[2][3] */
ptr_2d = malloc(elem[1] * sizeof(int));
for (val=0, i=0; i<dimen[0]; i++)
    for (j=0; j<dimen[1]; j++, val++) ptr_2d[i][j] = val;
ptr_1d = (void *) ptr_2d;
printf("\n\n2-D Array as 1-D:");
for (i=0; i<elem[1]; i++)
    printf("\n[%2d]=%2d", i, ptr_1d[i]);

/* allocate int array[2][3][4] */
ptr_3d = malloc(elem[2] * sizeof(int));
for (val=0, i=0; i<dimen[0]; i++)
    for (j=0; j<dimen[1]; j++)
        for (k=0; k<dimen[2]; k++, val++) ptr_3d[i][j][k] = val;
ptr_1d = (void *)ptr_3d;
printf("\n\n3-D Array as 1-D:");
for (i=0; i<elem[2]; i++)
    printf("\n[%2d]=%2d", i, ptr_1d[i]);

exit(0);
}
```

FIGURE 24.1: Sample program ch24e15.c demonstrates allocation of multidimensioned arrays to the heap.

```
1-D Array as 1-D:
[ 0]= 0
[ 1]= 1
.
2-D Array as 1-D:
[ 0]= 0
[ 1]= 1
:
[ 4]= 4
[ 5]= 5

3-D Array as 1-D:
[ 0]= 0
[ 1]= 1
:
[22]=22
[23]=23
```

FIGURE 24.2: Output from sample program ch24e15.c.

MEMORY MANAGEMENT TASKS

The memory management functions that are documented in this chapter are summarized in Table 24.1 by tasks that highlight the operations that can be performed.

A complement of buffer management functions is available, which resembles those functions described in Chapter 26 for string handling. Buffer operations are not restricted to operate on strings and may be used to compare bytes of information anywhere in memory and of any data-object type. These functions do not attribute any special significance to the presence of the null character value (`'\0'`). The memory model independent versions of these functions begin with the non-Standard **_f** prefix.

To compare buffers, byte-by-byte, use either **memcmp()**, which is case-sensitive, or **memicmp()**, which is case-insensitive. Function **memchr()** can be used to locate the presence of a particular byte value.

TABLE 24.1: Memory Management Tasks

TASK	FUNCTION	
	STANDARD C ■ ANSI	MICROSOFT C ☐ ANSI
Buffer compare	`memcmp()`	`_fmemcmp()`
	`memchr()`	`_fmemchr()`
		`_fmemicmp()`
		`memicmp()`
Buffer copy	`memcpy()`	`_fmemccpy()`
	`memmove()`	`_fmemcpy()`
		`_fmemmove()`
		`memccpy()`
		`movedata()`
Buffer initialization	`memset()`	`_fmemset()`
DOS/BIOS memory allocation		`_bios_memsize()`
		`_dos_allocmem()`
		`_dos_freemem()`
		`_dos_setblock()`
Add/create heap space		`_bfreeseg()`
		`_bheapadd()`
		`_bheapseg()`
		`_heapadd()`

TABLE 24.1: Memory Management Tasks (continued)

TASK	FUNCTION	
	STANDARD C ■ ANSI	**MICROSOFT C** □ ANSI
Allocate a memory block (uninitialized)	`malloc()`	`_bmalloc()`
		`_fmalloc()`
		`_nmalloc()`
Allocate a memory block (initialized)	`calloc()`	`_bcalloc()`
		`_fcalloc()`
		`halloc()`
		`_ncalloc()`
Get heap memory block size		`_bmsize()`
		`_fmsize()`
		`_msize()`
		`_nmsize()`
Expand a heap memory block		`_bexpand()`
		`_expand()`
		`_fexpand()`
		`_nexpand()`
Free a heap memory block	`free()`	`_bfree()`
		`_bfreeseg()`
		`_ffree()`
		`hfree()`
		`_nfree()`
Interrogate the heap		`_bheapchk()`
		`_bheapset()`
		`_bheapwalk()`
		`_fheapchk()`
		`_fheapset()`
		`_fheapwalk()`
		`_heapchk()`
		`_heapset()`
		`_heapwalk()`
		`_nheapchk()`
		`_nheapset()`
		`_nheapwalk()`

TABLE 24.1: Memory Management Tasks (continued)

TASK	FUNCTION	
	STANDARD C ■ **ANSI**	**MICROSOFT C** □ **ANSI**
Near heap management		`_freect()`
		`_memavl()`
		`_memmax()`
Reallocate the heap	`realloc()`	`_brealloc()`
		`_frealloc()`
		`_nrealloc()`
Release unused heap		`_bheapmin()`
		`_fheapmin()`
		`_heapmin()`
		`_nheapmin()`
Stack allocation		`alloca()`
		`stackavail()`

To copy the contents of a buffer when buffers do not overlap, use the **memcpy()** or **memccpy()** functions. To accommodate overlapping buffers, use the **memmove()** functions. When buffers reside in different segments, use the **movedata()** function.

To initialize the bytes of a buffer to a particular value, use the **memset()** function.

To determine the amount of space remaining on the stack, use the **stackavail()** function, and to allocate memory space on the stack, use the **alloca()** function.

When direct access to the DOS/BIOS memory management interrupt services is necessary, use **_bios_memsize()** to determine the amount of installed memory, **_dos_allocmem()** to reserve a block of memory, **_dos_setblock()** to change the size of an existing memory block, and **_dos_freemem()** to release a block of memory back to DOS. Alternatively, issue an INT 0x21 for functions 0x48, 0x4A, and 0x49, respectively, using either run-time function **intdosx()** or **int86x()** (see Chapter 22).

The non-Standard functions used to manage the heap adhere to the following naming standard: the prefix **_b** for Based heap, **_f** for Far heap, and **_n** for Near heap; otherwise, each function allocates space to a heap area dictated by the compiler memory model selected: for the Tiny, Small, and Medium models, the Near heap is the default; for the Compact, Large, and Huge models, the Far heap is the default.

Only the Based heap must be allocated explicitly by the **_bheapseg()** function before heap allocation requests can be initiated, whereas, the Near heap, Far heap, and heap are available for use automatically. To add a specific amount of space to the heap, use the **_heapadd()** function; otherwise, all heap areas are expanded automatically in **_amblksiz** increments as needed.

To allocate a memory block in the heap, use a **malloc()** function for uninitialized space, or use a **calloc()** function for space that is initialized to zero (**'\0'**).

To get the size of a memory block that has been allocated, use an **_msize()** function; to expand the size of an existing memory block, use an **_expand()** function; and to free an existing block of memory for reuse by the heap, use a **free()** function.

To reallocate, and possibly relocate memory blocks, use a **realloc()** function; and to release unused heap space back to DOS, use a **_heapmin()** function, or the **_bfreeseg()** function for a Based heap.

A special set of functions is available that report only on the Near heap: **_freect()**, **_memavl()**, and **_memmax()**.

When working with **_huge** memory blocks in the Far heap, only the functions **halloc()** and **hfree()** may be used.

To interrogate the heap area (for debugging purposes), use a **_heapchk()** function to check for minimal consistency of the heap; use a **_heapset()** function to check for minimal consistency and to set all free heap entries to a fixed byte value; and, finally, use a **_heapwalk()** function to perform the most extensive checking of a heap area.

RUN-TIME LIBRARY FUNCTIONS FOR MEMORY MANAGEMENT

alloca() *Allocate memory on the stack*

Compatibility ☐ANSI ■OS/2 ■UNIX ☐XENIX

Specification

```
#include <malloc.h>
void *alloca(size_t size);
```

Arguments

size: The number of bytes to be allocated.

Return Value

If unsuccessful, a **NULL** pointer

Otherwise, a pointer to type **void**, which must be cast to an appropriate type before being dereferenced

Example

```
/* FILE: ch24e1.c */
#include <stdio.h>
#include <stdlib.h>
#include <malloc.h>
int main(void)
{
void *ptr;
size_t free_STACK, size=256;
while ((free_STACK = stackavail()) > (2*size)) {
    ptr = alloca(size);
    if (ptr) printf("\nfree=%4d addr=%lp",
        free_STACK, (void _far *)ptr);
    else exit(99);
    }
exit(0);
}
```

Output

```
free=1738   addr=0CE4:0C7A
free=1472   addr=0CE4:0B70
free=1206   addr=0CE4:0A66
free= 940   addr=0CE4:095C
free= 674   addr=0CE4:0852
```

Comments   The stack size is fixed at compile- or link-time, or subsequently by the use of the EXEHDR utility (see Chapter 3); the default size is normally 2048 bytes (2KB).

Notice in the example output that the blocks of memory are allocated on the stack (descending addresses), confirming the direction that the stack grows, and they are not treated as heap.

As an alternative to this function, you can link with the xVARSTCK.OJB module as described in the "Performance Considerations" section of Chapter 15. If this approach was used, the heap would grow from the bottom of the stack towards the top.

Because memory is allocated on the stack, to properly maintain the stack pointer (SP), the following precautions must be taken: a) always allocate one **auto** storage-class variable; b) do not free any pointer addresses returned by **alloca()**; and c) do not use **alloca()** as an argument value to a function.

_bcalloc() *Allocate initialized memory to Based heap*

Compatibility ☐ANSI ■OS/2 ☐UNIX ☐XENIX

Specification

```
#include <malloc.h>
void _based(void) *_bcalloc(_segment seg, size_t num, size_t size);
```

Comments See the **calloc()** entry for more information.

_bexpand() *Change the size of a memory block in Based heap*

Compatibility ☐ANSI ■OS/2 ☐UNIX ☐XENIX

Specification

```
#include <malloc.h>
void _based(void) *_bexpand(_segment seg, void _based(void) *memblock,
    size_t size);
```

Comments See the **expand()** entry for more information.

_bfree() *Deallocate a memory block in Based heap*

Compatibility ☐ANSI ■OS/2 ☐UNIX ☐XENIX

Specification

```
#include <malloc.h>
void _bfree(_segment seg, void _based(void) *memblock);
```

Comments See the **free()** entry for more information.

_bfreeseg() *Free a specified Based heap*

Compatibility ☐ANSI ■OS/2 ☐UNIX ☐XENIX

Specification

```
#include <malloc.h>
int _bfreeseg(_segment seg);
```

Arguments

seg: A Based heap segment returned by a prior call to **_bheapseg()**; the segment to be freed.

Return Value

Zero if successful

−1 if unsuccessful

Example   See: **_bheapseg()**.

Comments   Unlike the heap, Near heap, and Far heap, which are automatically available for use with each compiler memory model, Based heap areas must be created explicitly using **_bheapseg()** and ultimately relinquished using **_bfreeseg()**.

Unlike **_bfree()**, which releases previously allocated blocks of memory back to the pool of available Based heap space, **_bfreeseg()** releases the entire Based heap space that was allocated using **_bheapseg()** back to DOS, including any blocks of Based heap memory that may not have been released yet using **_bfree()**.

Once a Based heap is released to DOS using **_bfreeseg()**, it no longer exists. Another Based heap must be allocated using **_bheapseg()** if it is needed.

_bheapadd()   *Add memory to a specified Based heap*

Compatibility   □ ANSI   ■ OS/2   □ UNIX   □ XENIX

Specification

```
#include <malloc.h>
int _bheapadd(_segment seg, void _based(void) *memblock, size_t size);
```

Comments   See the **_heapadd()** entry for more information.

_bheapchk()   *Perform consistency checks on a specified Based heap*

Compatibility   □ ANSI   ■ OS/2   □ UNIX   □ XENIX

Specification

```
#include <malloc.h>
int _bheapchk(_segment seg);
```

Comments   See the **_heapchk()** entry for more information.

_bheapmin()   *Release unused memory to DOS from a specified Based heap*

Compatibility   ☐ ANSI   ■ OS/2   ☐ UNIX   ☐ XENIX

Specification

```
#include <malloc.h>
int _bheapmin(_segment seg);
```

Comments   See the **_heapmin()** entry for more information.

_bheapseg()   *Allocate a specified Based heap*

Compatibility   ☐ ANSI   ■ OS/2   ☐ UNIX   ☐ XENIX

Specification

```
#include <malloc.h>
_segment _bheapseg (size_t size);
```

Arguments

size: The initial number of bytes to allocate to a Based heap segment.

Return Value

If unsuccessful, **_NULLSEG** defined in **<malloc.h>**

Otherwise, a **_segment** type containing a segment address (on a paragraph or 16-byte boundary) with an implied offset of :0000

Example

```
/* FILE: ch24e2.c */
#include <stdio.h>
#include <stdlib.h>
#include <malloc.h>
#include <string.h>
#define SIZE 256

int main(void)
{
_segment seg1, seg2;
void _based(seg1) *bh1_ptr;
void _based(seg2) *bh2_ptr;
size_t bh_size = SIZE;
```

```
if ((seg1 = _bheapseg(bh_size)) == _NULLSEG) exit(91);
if ((seg2 = _bheapseg(bh_size)) == _NULLSEG) exit(92);

if ((bh1_ptr = _bmalloc(seg1, 20)) == _NULLOFF) exit(93);
_fstrcpy((char _far *)bh1_ptr, "test string");
if ((bh2_ptr = _bmalloc(seg2, 20)) == _NULLOFF) exit(94);
_fmemcpy((char _far *)bh2_ptr, (char _far *)bh1_ptr, 20);
printf("\nseg1 string = %Fs", (char _far *)bh1_ptr);
printf("\nseg2 string = %Fs", (char _far *)bh2_ptr);

if (_bfreeseg(seg1)) exit(95);
if ((bh1_ptr = _bmalloc(seg1, 20)) == _NULLOFF)
    printf("\nCannot allocate to seg1!");
_bfree(seg2, bh2_ptr);
if (_bfreeseg(seg2)) exit(96);
if ((bh2_ptr = _bmalloc(seg2, 20)) == _NULLOFF)
    printf("\nCannot allocate to seg2!");
exit(0);
}
```

Output

```
seg1 string = test string
seg2 string = test string
Cannot allocate to seg1!
Cannot allocate to seg2!
```

Comments   Each Based heap created by **_bheapseg()** is allocated to contain *size* bytes from the existing Far heap memory area; however, this Based heap is thereafter automatically increased in byte increments of global variable **_amblksiz**, unless **_bheapadd()** is used to add a specified amount of space to the Based heap.

In the example, notice the use of special Based heap macros **_NULLSEG** and **_NULLOFF**, which are used instead of the **NULL** pointer sentinel value used by the Near and Far heap.

Also notice how **_based** string pointers are cast to **_far** pointers for display by **printf()** using the control string format **%Fs**, not **%s**, because this program was run using the Small memory model.

_bheapset ()   *Check a specified Based heap for minimal consistency and set the free entries to a specified value*

Compatibility   □ ANSI   ■ OS/2   □ UNIX   □ XENIX

Specification

```
#include <malloc.h>
int _bheapset(_segment seg, unsigned int fill);
```

Comments   See the **heapset()** entry for more information.

`bheapwalk()`   *Traverse a specified Based heap and return information about the next heap entry*

Compatibility   ☐ ANSI   ■ OS/2   ☐ UNIX   ☐ XENIX

Specification

```
#include <malloc.h>
int _bheapwalk(_segment seg, _HEAPINFO *entry);
```

Comments   See the `_heapwalk()` entry for more information.

`_bios_memsize()`   *Invoke BIOS memory size services interrupt 0x12*

Compatibility   ☐ ANSI   ☐ OS/2   ☐ UNIX   ☐ XENIX

Specification

```
#include <bios.h>
unsigned _bios_memsize(void);
```

Return Value

The total amount of installed memory in 1KB (1024 byte) increments. A value of 640 represents 640KB.

Example   See: `_dos_allocmem()`.

`_bmalloc()`   *Allocate a memory block in a specified Based heap*

Compatibility   ☐ ANSI   ■ OS/2   ☐ UNIX   ☐ XENIX

Specification

```
#include <malloc.h>
void _based(void) *_bmalloc(_segment seg, size_t size);
```

Comments   See the `malloc()` entry for more information.

`_bmsize()`   *Return the size of a memory block allocated to a specified Based heap*

Compatibility   ☐ ANSI   ■ OS/2   ☐ UNIX   ☐ XENIX

Specification

```
#include <malloc.h>
size_t _bmsize(_segment seg, void _based(void) *memblock);
```

Comments   See the **_msize()** entry for more information.

_brealloc()   *Reallocate memory blocks in a specified Based heap*

Compatibility   □ANSI   ■OS/2   □UNIX   □XENIX

Specification

```
#include <malloc.h>
void _based(void) *_brealloc(_segment seg, void _based(void) *memblock, size_t
    size);
```

Comments   See **realloc()** functions for more information.

calloc() *Functions*   *Allocate an array of initialized objects to the heap*

Compatibility   ■ANSI   ■OS/2   ■UNIX   ■XENIX

See Also

```
halloc()
```

Specification

```
#include <stdlib.h> or <malloc.h>
void *calloc(size_t num, size_t size);
void _based(void) *_bcalloc(_segment seg, size_t num, size_t size);)
void _far *_fcalloc(size_t num, size_t size);
void _near *_ncalloc(size_t num, size_t size);
```

Arguments

num: A positive, nonzero number of array elements to allocate.

size: A positive, nonzero number of bytes per array element.

seg: The segment of the Based heap to be used that was returned by a prior call
to **_bheapseg()**.

Return Value

If unsuccessful, a **NULL** pointer (**_NULLSEG** for **_bcalloc()**)

Otherwise, a suitably aligned **VOID** pointer that must be cast to an appropriate
pointer type before being dereferenced

Example

```
/* FILE: ch24e3.c */
/* use the small memory model */
#include <stdio.h>
#include <stdlib.h>
#include <malloc.h>
int main(void)
{
_segment bseg;
void *ptr;
void _near *n_ptr;
void _far *f_ptr;
void _based(bseg) *bh_ptr;

if ((bseg = _bheapseg(256)) == _NULLSEG) exit(95);
if ((bh_ptr = _bcalloc(bseg, 1, sizeof(long))) == _NULLOFF) exit(96);
if ((ptr = calloc(1, sizeof(float))) == NULL) exit(97);
if ((n_ptr = _ncalloc(1, sizeof(int))) == NULL) exit(98);
if ((f_ptr = _fcalloc(1, sizeof(char))) == NULL) exit(99);
printf("\nptr = %lp float= %f", (void _far *)ptr,
    *(float *)ptr);
printf("\nn_ptr = %lp int = %d", (void _far *)n_ptr,
    *(int *)n_ptr);
printf("\nf_ptr = %lp char = %x", f_ptr, *(char _far *)f_ptr);
printf("\nbh_ptr= %lp long = %ld", (void _far *)bh_ptr,
    *(long _far *)bh_ptr);
exit(0);
}
```

Output

```
ptr   = 1136:117A  float= 0.000000
n_ptr = 1136:1180  int  = 0
f_ptr = 0B81:0016  char = 0
bh_ptr= 2137:0016  long = 0
```

Comments   The size of the largest array object that can be allocated is determined by **_HEAP_MAXREQ** (0xFFE8 or 65,512 bytes) defined in **<malloc.h>**; the largest sized array element is also **_HEAP_MAXREQ**.

Unlike **malloc()**, **calloc()** functions initialize the entire heap area to a null character value (**'\0'**), which explains the type values displayed in the example.

Since the example program used the Small memory model, it is consistent that the **ptr** and **n_ptr** addresses reside in the same segment (1136:), and **bh_ptr** is located in a segment (2137:) well above the Near heap.

The address of **f_ptr** (0B81:), which represents a lower memory address than **n_ptr**, is perhaps surprising. Because memory allocation always proceeds from low to high memory (except for the stack), the Far heap normally appears above the Near heap; however, the Far heap can represent any available DOS memory space that is outside of the data segment (DS). Since the allocation request was small, a memory block of sufficient size was found to lie below (0B81:) the data segment (1136:), and represents an anomaly.

Use a **malloc()** or **realloc()** function followed by a corresponding **_heapset()** function.

dos_allocmem()   *Invoke DOS interrupt 0x21 for memory allocation function 0x48*

Compatibility   □ANSI   □OS/2   □UNIX   □XENIX

See Also

alloca(), _bheapseg(), _bheapadd(), calloc(), _heapadd(), malloc()

Specification

```
#include <dos.h>
#include <errno.h>
unsigned _dos_allocmem(unsigned size, unsigned *seg);
```

Arguments

size: A positive, nonzero number of paragraphs (16-byte blocks) to allocate.

seg: Pointer to an **unsigned** type object containing the starting segment address (with an implied offset of :0000) of the memory block allocated.

Return Value

Zero if successful

Otherwise, the DOS error code, and **errno** set to **ENOMEM**

Example

```
/* FILE: ch24e4.c */
#include <stdio.h>
#include <bios.h>
#include <dos.h>
#include <stdlib.h>
#include <string.h>
/* 1KB = 1024 bytes = 64 paragraphs */
#define KB *64

int main(void)
{
unsigned mem_size, segment, maxsize;
char *ptr;

mem_size = _bios_memsize();
printf("\nTotal Installed Memory= %dKB", mem_size);
```

```
if (!_dos_allocmem(2KB, &segment))
    printf("\nInitial Segment Allocated= %u bytes", (2KB * 16));
else exit(96);
if (!_dos_setblock(1KB, segment, &maxsize))
    printf("\nSegment Resized to %u bytes", 1KB * 16);
else exit(97);
if (!_dos_freemem(segment)) printf("\nSegment Released to DOS");
else exit(98);

/* try to resize an invalid segment */
segment = -1;
errno=0;
if (_dos_setblock(1KB, segment, &maxsize)) {
    ptr = strerror(errno);
    printf("\nResize Failed: %s", ptr);
    }
exit(0);
}
```

Output

```
Total Installed Memory= 640KB
Initial Segment Allocated= 2048 bytes
Segment Resized to 1024 bytes
Segment Released to DOS
Resize Failed: Not enough core
```

Comments   The basic unit of memory allocation using **_dos_allocmem()** is in paragraph (16-byte) increments, not byte increments used by the **calloc()** and **malloc()** functions.

The memory size requested must be available as contiguous memory space if it is to be allocated successfully.

Notice the object-like macro definition of KB as *64, which acts as a multiplier to appropriately size each memory request, when expressed as 2KB (2*64) for example.

The global variable **_amblksiz** is not used to provide an automatic increment of memory by **_dos_allocmem()**.

Notice in the example that even though an invalid segment value was used, the message *Not enough memory* is generated because **_dos_allocmem()** only sets the macro **ENOMEM** if an error occurs.

_dos_freemem()   *Invoke DOS interrupt 0x21 for memory release*
function 0x49

Compatibility   □ANSI   □OS/2   □UNIX   □XENIX

See Also

`_bfreeseg(), free(), _heapmin`

Specification

```
#include <dos.h>
#include <errno.h>
unsigned _dos_freemem(unsigned seg);
```

Arguments

seg: The starting segment address (with an implied offset of :0000) of the memory block previously allocated using **_dos_allocmem()**.

Return Value

Zero if successful

Otherwise, the DOS error code, and **errno** set to **ENOMEM**

Example   See: **_dos_allocmem()**.

Comments   If any block of memory has been successfully released using **_dos_freemem()** it is entirely released and is thereafter available for reassignment by DOS.

_dos_setblock()   *Invoke DOS interrupt 0x21 for change memory segment size function 0x4A*

Compatibility   □ ANSI   □ OS/2   □ UNIX   □ XENIX

See Also

`_expand()`

Specification

```
#include <dos.h>
#include <errno.h>
unsigned _dos_setblock(unsigned size, unsigned seg, unsigned *maxsize);
```

Arguments

size: A new (not additional) positive, nonzero number of paragraphs (16-byte blocks) to allocate.

seg: The starting segment address (with an implied offset of :0000) of the memory block previously allocated using **_dos_allocmem()**.

maxsize: A pointer to an **unsigned int** that will contain the maximum possible size that was allocated, if the allocation request failed.

Return Value

Zero if successful

Otherwise, the DOS error code *maxsize* set accordingly, and **errno** set to **ENOMEM**

Example

See: **_dos_allocmem()**.

Comments

Only existing memory blocks are rescaled to the requested size by allocating additional contiguous memory space if available, or deallocating a portion of an existing memory block.

_expand() *Functions*   *Change the size of a memory block in the heap*

Compatibility   □ANSI   ■OS/2   □UNIX   □XENIX

See Also

_dos_setblock()

Specification

```
#include <malloc.h>
void *_expand(void *memblock, size_t size);
void _based(void) *_bexpand(_segment seg, void _based(void) *memblock,
     size_t size);
void _far *_fexpand(void _far *memblock, size_t size);
void _near *_nexpand(void _near *memblock, size_t size);
```

Arguments

memblock: Pointer to a previously allocated memory block.

size: A nonzero, positive new (not additional) block size in bytes (not paragraphs).

seg: The starting segment address (with an implied offset of :0000) of a Based heap allocated using **_bheapseg()**.

Return Value

If unsuccessful, a **NULL** pointer (**_NULLSEG** for **_bexpand()**)

Otherwise, a pointer to **void** corresponding to that of the original memory block

Example

```
/* FILE: ch24e5.c */
/* use the Small memory model */
#include <stdio.h>
#include <stdlib.h>
#include <malloc.h>
#define SIZE 256

_segment bseg;
void *ptr;
void _near *n_ptr;
void _far *f_ptr;
void _based(bseg) *bh_ptr;

void display(void)
{
printf("\n\nptr = %lp size= %d",
    (void _far *)ptr, _msize(ptr));
printf("\nn_ptr = %lp size= %d",
    (void _far *)n_ptr, _nmsize(n_ptr));
printf("\nf_ptr = %lp size= %d",
    f_ptr, _fmsize(f_ptr));
printf("\nbh_ptr= %lp size= %d",
    (void _far *)bh_ptr, _bmsize(bseg, bh_ptr));
}

int main(void)
{
if ((bseg = _bheapseg(4*SIZE)) == _NULLSEG) exit(91);

if ((ptr = calloc(2, SIZE)) == NULL) exit(93);
if ((n_ptr = _ncalloc(2, SIZE)) == NULL) exit(94);
if ((f_ptr = _fcalloc(2, SIZE)) == NULL) exit(95);
if ((bh_ptr = _bcalloc(bseg, 2, SIZE)) == _NULLOFF) exit(92);
display();

if ((ptr = _expand(ptr, 2*SIZE)) == NULL) exit(97);
if ((n_ptr = _nexpand(n_ptr, SIZE)) == NULL) exit(98);
if ((f_ptr = _fexpand(f_ptr, 4*SIZE)) == NULL) exit(99);
if ((bh_ptr = _bexpand(bseg, bh_ptr, SIZE)) == _NULLOFF) exit(96);
display();
exit(0);
}
```

Output

```
ptr   = 0D3B:0EBA  size= 512
n_ptr = 0D3B:10BC  size= 512
f_ptr = 1D7F:0016  size= 512
bh_ptr= 1D3C:0016  size= 512

ptr   = 0D3B:0EBA  size= 512
n_ptr = 0D3B:10BC  size= 256
```

```
f_ptr = 1D7F:0016  size= 1024
bh_ptr= 1D3C:0016  size= 256
```

Comments Only the size of existing memory blocks can be changed using **_expand()** functions.

_expand() functions are successful only if the memory block can be expanded without relocating its starting memory address.

Note in the example program that all **_expand()** function calls were successful in changing memory block sizes—making them first smaller, then the same size and, finally, larger—because sufficient memory existed to permit the expansions without moving the memory blocks.

Notice that the Far heap begins just beyond the 64KB reach of the DS register (DS=0D3B, Far heap=1D3C), which confirms the memory-model maps portrayed in Chapter 2 (Figures 2.20 through 2.25).

Notice from the addresses shown in the example output how the 1KB Based heap was "carved" from the available Far heap by the **_bheapseg()** function call.

_fcalloc() *Allocate initialized memory to Far heap*

Compatibility □ANSI ■OS/2 □UNIX □XENIX

Specification

```
#include <malloc.h>
void _far *_fcalloc(size_t num, size_t size);
```

Comments See the **calloc()** entry for more information.

_fexpand() *Change the size of a memory block in the Far heap*

Compatibility □ANSI ■OS/2 □UNIX □XENIX

Specification

```
#include <malloc.h>
void _far *_fexpand (void _far *memblock, size_t size);
```

Comments See the **_expand()** entry for more information.

_ffree() *Deallocate a memory block in Far heap*

Compatibility □ANSI ■OS/2 □UNIX □XENIX

Specification

```
#include <malloc.h>
void _ffree(void _far *memblock);
```

Comments   See the **free()** entry for more information.

_fheapchk()   *Perform consistency checks on a specified Far heap*

Compatibility   ☐ ANSI   ■ OS/2   ☐ UNIX   ☐ XENIX

Specification

```
#include <malloc.h>
int _fheapchk(void);
```

Comments   See the **_heapchk()** entry for more information.

_fheapmin()   *Release unused memory to DOS from Far heap*

Compatibility   ☐ ANSI   ■ OS/2   ☐ UNIX   ☐ XENIX

Specification

```
#include <malloc.h>
int _fheapmin(void);
```

Comments   See the **_heapmin()** entry for more information.

_fheapset()   *Check Far heap for minimal consistency and set the free entries to a specified value*

Compatibility   ☐ ANSI   ■ OS/2   ☐ UNIX   ☐ XENIX

Specification

```
#include <malloc.h>
int _fheapset(unsigned int fill);
```

Comments   See the **_heapset()** entry for more information.

_fheapwalk() *Traverse Far heap and return information about the next entry*

Compatibility □ANSI ■OS/2 □UNIX □XENIX

Specification

```
#include <malloc.h>
int _fheapwalk(_HEAPINFO *entry);
```

Comments   See the **_heapwalk()** entry for more information.

_fmalloc() *Allocate a memory block in Far heap*

Compatibility □ANSI ■OS/2 □UNIX □XENIX

Specification

```
#include <stdlib.h>
#include <malloc.h>
void _far *_fmalloc(size_t size);
```

Comments   See the **malloc()** entry for more information.

_fmemccpy() *Copy characters between buffers, memory-model independent*

Compatibility □ANSI ■OS/2 □UNIX □XENIX

Specification

```
#include <memory.h> or <string.h>
void _far * _far _fmemccpy(void _far *dest, const void _far *src,
    int c, unsigned int count);
```

Comments   See the **memccpy()** entry for more information.

_fmemchr() *Find characters in a buffer, memory-model independent*

Compatibility □ANSI ■OS/2 □UNIX □XENIX

Specification

```
#include <memory.h> or <string.h>
void _far * _far _fmemchr(const void _far *buf, int c, size_t count);
```

Comments   See the `memchr()` entry for more information.

_fmemcmp()   *Compare characters in two buffers, memory-model independent*

Compatibility   ☐ ANSI   ■ OS/2   ☐ UNIX   ☐ XENIX

Specification

```
#include <memory.h> or <string.h>
int _far _fmemcmp(const void _far *buf1, const void _far *buf2, size_t count);
```

Comments   See the `memcmp()` entry for more information.

_fmemcpy()   *Copy characters between buffers, memory-model independent*

Compatibility   ☐ ANSI   ■ OS/2   ☐ UNIX   ☐ XENIX

Specification

```
#include <memory.h> or <string.h>
void _far * _far _fmemcpy(void _far *dest, const void _far *src, size_t count);
```

Comments   See the `memcpy()` entry for more information.

_fmemicmp()   *Case-insensitive comparison of characters in two buffers, memory-model independent*

Compatibility   ☐ ANSI   ■ OS/2   ☐ UNIX   ☐ XENIX

Specification

```
#include <memory.h> or <string.h>
int _far _fmemicmp(const void _far *buf1, const void _far *buf2, unsigned int
    count);
```

Comments   See the `memicmp()` entry for more information.

_fmemmove()   *Move one buffer to another, memory-model independent*

Compatibility   ☐ ANSI   ■ OS/2   ☐ UNIX   ☐ XENIX

See Also

```
memmove()
```

Specification

```
#include <string.h>
void _far * _far _fmemmove(void _far *dest, const void _far *src, size_t count);
```

Comments

See the **memmove()** entry for more information.

_fmemset() *Set buffers to a specified character, memory-model independent*

Compatibility □ANSI ■OS/2 □UNIX □XENIX

Specification

```
#include <memory.h> or <string.h>
void _far * _far _fmemset(void _far *dest, int c, size_t count);
```

Comments

See the **memset()** entry for more information.

_fmsize() *Return the size of a memory block allocated to Far heap*

Compatibility □ANSI ■OS/2 □UNIX □XENIX

Specification

```
#include <malloc.h>
size_t _fmsize(void _far *memblock);
```

Comments

See the **_msize()** entry for more information.

_frealloc() *Reallocate memory blocks in the Far heap*

Compatibility □ANSI ■OS/2 □UNIX □XENIX

Specification

```
#include <malloc.h>
void _far *_frealloc(void _far *memblock, size_t size);
```

Comments

See the **realloc()** entry for more information.

free() *Functions*   *Deallocate a memory block in the heap*

Compatibility   ■ANSI   ■OS/2   ■UNIX   ■XENIX

See Also

`_bfreeseg(), _dos_freemem(), _heapmin`

Specification

```
#include <stdlib.h> or <malloc.h>
void free(void *memblock);
void _bfree(_segment seg, void _based(void) *memblock);
void _ffree(void _far *memblock);
void hfree(void _huge *memblock);
void _nfree(void _near *memblock);
```

Arguments

memblock: A pointer to a memory block previously allocated using a **calloc()**, **halloc()**, **malloc()**, or **realloc()** function.

seg: The starting segment address (with an implied offset of :0000) of previously allocated Based heap using **_bheapseg()**.

Example   See: **_bheapseg()**, **halloc()**, **malloc()**.

Comments   The **free()** functions release previously allocated memory blocks back to the heap, not DOS. These blocks are then flagged as free, not used, and immediately become available for reuse as demonstrated in the **malloc()** example.

In order to release heap space back to DOS, either the **_heapmin()** functions or **_bfreeseg()** function must be used.

Functions **_ffree()** and **_nfree()** have the same effect as **free()**, shown in the **malloc()** example, but upon the Far and Near heap areas, respectively.

freect()   *Return the number of times an object can be allocated to the remaining Near heap*

Compatibility   □ANSI   ■OS/2   □UNIX   □XENIX

See Also

`_memavl()`

Specification

```
#include <malloc.h>
unsigned int _freect(size_t size);
```

Arguments

size: A nonzero, positive number of bytes describing the size of the array element to be allocated subsequently using **calloc()**, **malloc()**, or **realloc()** functions.

Return Value

The number of *size* objects that can yet be allocated to the Near heap

Example   See: **_heapmin()**.

Comments   From the example program, notice that the number of 1-byte sized objects that can be allocated (15,299) is considerably less than the approximate amount of remaining Near heap space (61,200), because the **_freect()** function accounts for the overhead associated with allocating each memory block to the heap.

Because the overhead (heap data structure) is a fixed size for each memory block allocated, more efficient use of the heap is made when larger objects are allocated.

halloc()   *Allocate an initialized _huge memory block in the Far heap*

Compatibility   ☐ ANSI   ■ OS/2   ☐ UNIX   ☐ XENIX

Specification

```
#include <malloc.h>
void _huge *halloc(long num, size_t size);
```

Arguments

num: A positive, nonzero number of array elements to allocate.

size: A positive, nonzero number of bytes per array element. If the total array size is greater than 128KB (131,072 bytes), then *size* must be a power of 2.

Return Value

If unsuccessful, a **NULL** pointer

Otherwise, a suitably aligned *VOID* pointer that must be cast to an appropriate pointer type before being dereferenced

Example

```
/* FILE: ch24e6.c */
/* use the small memory model */
#include <stdio.h>
```

```
#include <stdlib.h>
#include <malloc.h>
#define ELEMENTS 10000

int main(void)
{
long double _huge *h_ptr;
int i;
if (!(h_ptr = halloc(ELEMENTS, sizeof(long double)))) exit(99);
for (i=0; i<ELEMENTS; i++) h_ptr[i] = i*10.0L;

for (i=0; i<ELEMENTS; i+=1000)
    printf("\naddr= %lp [%4d]= %Le",
        (void _far *)(h_ptr+i), i, h_ptr[i]);

hfree(h_ptr);
exit(0);
}
```

Output

```
addr= 211B:0006  [0]= 0.000000e+000
addr= 211B:2716  [1000]= 1.000000e+004
addr= 211B:4E26  [2000]= 2.000000e+004
addr= 211B:7536  [3000]= 3.000000e+004
addr= 211B:9C46  [4000]= 4.000000e+004
addr= 211B:C356  [5000]= 5.000000e+004
addr= 211B:EA66  [6000]= 6.000000e+004
addr= 311B:1176  [7000]= 7.000000e+004
addr= 311B:3886  [8000]= 8.000000e+004
addr= 311B:5F96  [9000]= 9.000000e+004
```

Comments   The size of the largest array object that can be allocated is limited only by the amount of free memory—arrays can therefore span segment boundaries; however, the maximum array element size is still **_HEAP_MAXREQ** (0xFFE8 or 65,512 bytes).

The execution time of the example above is slow because **long double** (10-byte) floating-point math is being performed.

Notice that the one-dimension array of **long double** objects spans segment addresses (211B, 311B); this is a unique property of **_huge** pointer addressing. For segments to be spanned, 20-bit address arithmetic is used, 16-bit arithmetic is used with **_near**, **_far**, and **_based** pointers.

_heapadd () *Functions*   **Add memory to the heap**

Compatibility   ☐ ANSI   ■ OS/2   ☐ UNIX   ☐ XENIX

Specification

```
#include <malloc.h>
int _heapadd(void _far *memblock, size_t size);
int _bheapadd(_segment seg, void _based(void) *memblock,
size_t size);
```

Arguments

memblock: A pointer to a previously declared or allocated data object, which is to be reused by adding it to the pool of available heap space.

size: The size of the memblock object in bytes.

seg: The starting segment address (with an implied offset of :0000) of previously allocated Based heap using **_bheapseg()**.

Return Value

Zero if successful

−1 if unsuccessful

Example

```
/* FILE: ch24e7.c */
/* use the small memory model */
#include <stdio.h>
#include <stdlib.h>
#include <malloc.h>

void heap_report(char *msg, struct _heapinfo *hi_ptr)
{
hi_ptr->_pentry=NULL;
printf("\n%s\n", msg);
while (_heapwalk(hi_ptr) == _heapOK )
    printf("\t%s block addr= %Fp size %u bytes\n",
        (hi_ptr->_useflag == _USEDENTRY ? "USED" : "FREE"),
        hi_ptr->_pentry, hi_ptr->_size);
printf("End of Report");
}

int main(void)
{
static int i_ary[500];
float f_ary[100];
static struct _heapinfo hi;

heap_report("Heap-1", &hi); /* initial Heap */

_heapadd(f_ary, sizeof(f_ary) );
heap_report("Heap-2", &hi); /* after SS add */

_heapadd(i_ary, sizeof(i_ary) );
heap_report("Heap-3", &hi); /* after DS add */
```

```
_heapmin();
heap_report("Heap-4", &hi); /* after release to DOS */
exit(0);
}
```

Output

```
Heap-1
    USED block addr= 0D26:11EC  size 142 bytes
    USED block addr= 0D26:127C  size 12 bytes
    USED block addr= 0D26:128A  size 512 bytes
    FREE block addr= 0D26:148C  size 2930 bytes
End of Report
Heap-2
    FREE block addr= 0D26:1036  size 396 bytes
    USED block addr= 0D26:11C4  size 38 bytes
    USED block addr= 0D26:11EC  size 142 bytes
    USED block addr= 0D26:127C  size 12 bytes
    USED block addr= 0D26:128A  size 512 bytes
    FREE block addr= 0D26:148C  size 2930 bytes
End of Report
Heap-3
    FREE block addr= 0D26:0402  size 996 bytes
    USED block addr= 0D26:07E8  size 2124 bytes
    FREE block addr= 0D26:1036  size 396 bytes
    USED block addr= 0D26:11C4  size 38 bytes
    USED block addr= 0D26:11EC  size 142 bytes
    USED block addr= 0D26:127C  size 12 bytes
    USED block addr= 0D26:128A  size 512 bytes
    FREE block addr= 0D26:148C  size 2930 bytes
End of Report
Heap-4
    FREE block addr= 0D26:0402  size 996 bytes
    USED block addr= 0D26:07E8  size 2124 bytes
    FREE block addr= 0D26:1036  size 396 bytes
    USED block addr= 0D26:11C4  size 38 bytes
    USED block addr= 0D26:11EC  size 142 bytes
    USED block addr= 0D26:127C  size 12 bytes
    USED block addr= 0D26:128A  size 512 bytes
    FREE block addr= 0D26:148C  size 2 bytes
End of Report
```

Comments   The **_heapadd()** functions provide an alternative method for allocating additional heap space that does not rely upon the automatic incrementation of the heap by the value of global variable **_amblksiz**.

If the address of the memory block being added is within the **DGROUP** (DS register range), it is added to the Near heap; otherwise, it is added to the Far heap, unless a Based heap is specifically specified.

In the example program, some stack space (**auto float f_ary[100]**) is added to the Near heap, and some data segment space (**static int i_ary[500]**) is added to the Near heap.

See **_bheapchk()** for an example of using the **_bheapadd()** function with the predefined segment name macros, **_CODE**, **_CONST**, **_DATA**, and **_STACK**.

As an alternative, you can change the size of the global variable **_amblksiz** (see Appendix C).

_heapchk() *Functions*   *Perform consistency checks on the heap*

Compatibility ☐ANSI ■OS/2 ☐UNIX ☐XENIX

See Also

```
_heapset(), _heapwalk()
```

Specification

```
#include <malloc.h>
int _heapchk(void);
int _bheapchk(_segment seg);
int _fheapchk(void);
int _nheapchk(void);
```

Arguments

seg: The starting segment address (with an implied offset of :0000) of previously allocated Based heap using **_bheapseg()**.

Return Value

One of the following object-like macros defined in **<malloc.h>**

_HEAPBADBEGIN	Initial header information bad
_HEAPBADNODE	Subsequent bad node
_HEAPEMPTY	Heap has not been initialized
_HEAPOK	Heap appears to be consistent

Example

```
/* FILE: ch24e8.c */
/* use the small memory model */
#include <stdio.h>
#include <stdlib.h>
#include <malloc.h>

int main(void)
{
```

```
char *names[] = { "_CODE", "_CONST", "_DATA", "_STACK" };
int i, j, status;
static int ary1[100], ary2[100], ary3[100], ary4[100];

for (i=0; i<3; i++) {
    for (j=0; j<4; j++) {
        printf("\n%6s Segment: ", names[j]);
        switch (j) {
            case 0: status = _bheapchk(_segname("_CODE"));  break;
            case 1: status = _bheapchk(_segname("_CONST")); break;
            case 2: status = _bheapchk(_segname("_DATA"));  break;
            case 3: status = _bheapchk(_segname("_STACK")); break;
        }
        switch (status) {
            case _HEAPOK:        printf("Heap OK");          break;
            case _HEAPEMPTY:     printf("Heap Empty");       break;
            case _HEAPBADBEGIN:  printf("Bad Heap Begin");   break;
            case _HEAPBADNODE:   printf("Bad Heap Node");    break;
            case _HEAPBADPTR:    printf("Bad _pentry field");break;
        }
    }
    if (i==0) {
        printf("\n\nStart Segment Add");
        if(_bheapadd(_segname("_CODE"), ary1, sizeof(ary1)))
            printf("\n%6s Segment Add Failed!", names[0]);
        if(_bheapadd(_segname("_CONST"), ary2, sizeof(ary1)))
            printf("\n%6s Segment Add Failed!", names[1]);
        if(_bheapadd(_segname("_DATA"), ary3, sizeof(ary1)))
            printf("\n%6s Segment Add Failed!", names[2]);
        if(_bheapadd(_segname("_STACK"), ary4, sizeof(ary1)))
            printf("\n%6s Segment Add Failed!", names[3]);
        printf("\nEnd Segment Add\n");
    }
    if (i==1) {
        printf("\n\nStart Segment Release");
        if(_bheapmin(_segname("_CODE")))
            printf("\n%6s Segment Release Failed!", names[0]);
        if(_bheapmin(_segname("_CONST")))
            printf("\n%6s Segment Release Failed!", names[1]);
        if(_bheapmin(_segname("_DATA")))
            printf("\n%6s Segment Release Failed!", names[2]);
        if(_bheapmin(_segname("_STACK")))
            printf("\n%6s Segment Release Failed!", names[3]);
        printf("\nEnd Segment Release\n");
    }
}
exit(0);
}
```

Output

```
_CODE Segment: Bad _pentry field
_CONST Segment: Bad _pentry field
```

```
_DATA Segment: Bad _pentry field
_STACK Segment: Bad _pentry field

Start Segment Add
End Segment Add

_CODE Segment: Heap OK
_CONST Segment: Heap OK
_DATA Segment: Heap OK
_STACK Segment: Heap OK

Start Segment Release
End Segment Release

_CODE Segment: Heap OK
_CONST Segment: Heap OK
_DATA Segment: Heap OK
_STACK Segment: Heap OK
```

Comments **_heapchk()** functions perform what is referred to as minimal consistency checking of the heap, which verifies the basic integrity of the heap, and unlike **_heapwalk** cannot detect any **_HEAPEND** and **_HEAPBADPTR** errors.

The first portion of the example program output demonstrates that the predefined segment names, **_CODE**, **_CONST**, **_DATA**, and **_STACK**, do not automatically have a valid heap associated with them, but do so subsequent to calling a **_heapadd()** function.

The use of the functions **_heapchk()**, **_fheapchk()**, and **_nheapchk()** parallels that of **_bheapchk()**, shown in the example above, but they are performed against the heap, Far heap, and Near heap areas respectively.

_heapmin() *Functions* *Release unused memory to DOS from the heap*

Compatibility ☐ANSI ■OS/2 ☐UNIX ☐XENIX

See Also

```
_dos_freemem()
```

Specification

```
#include <malloc.h>
int _heapmin(void);
int _bheapmin(_segment seg);
int _fheapmin(void);
int _nheapmin(void);
```

Arguments

seg: The starting segment address (with an implied offset of :0000) of previously allocated Based heap using **_bheapseg()**.

Return Value

Zero if successful

−1 if unsuccessful

Example

```
/* FILE: ch24e9.c */
#include <stdio.h>
#include <stdlib.h>
#include <malloc.h>
int main(void)
{
int i;
printf("\nNear Heap Statistics");
for (i=0; i<2; i++) {
    printf("\nTimes a byte can be allocated = %u", _freect(1));
    printf("\nRemaining space in bytes      = %u", _memavl());
    printf("\nLargest contiguous object     = %u", _memmax());
    if (!i) {
        printf("\n\nReleasing unused Heap to DOS");
        if (_nheapmin()) printf("\n_heapmin() unsuccessful");
        printf("\n");
        }
    }
exit(0);
}
```

Output

```
Near Heap Statistics
Times a byte can be allocated = 15299
Remaining space in bytes      = 61200
Largest contiguous object     = 61202

Releasing unused Heap to DOS

Times a byte can be allocated = 0
Remaining space in bytes      = 2
Largest contiguous object     = 2
```

Comments   From the example program above, notice that once contiguous free heap space is released to DOS, it is no longer available for allocation by the heap manager.

The use of a **_heapmin()** function does not prevent subsequent heap requests from being fulfilled, because any subsequent request that exceeds the memory space available to the heap manager is fulfilled automatically by requesting **_amblksiz** blocks of memory from DOS.

In the **_heapadd()** example program, the **_heapmin()** function releases only that portion of the Near heap that is contiguous with the top of the data segment (DS=0D26).

In the **_heapchk()** example program, the **_bheapmin()** function releases any free entries that are contiguous with the top of the Based heap.

The **_fheapmin()** function has the same effect as **_nheapmin()**, shown in the example above, but it works upon the Far heap.

_heapset() *Functions*   *Check heap for minimal consistency and set the Tree entries to a specified value*

Compatibility   □ ANSI   ■ OS/2   □ UNIX   □ XENIX

See Also

```
calloc(), _heapwalk(), halloc()
```

Specification

```
#include <malloc.h>
int _heapset(unsigned int fill);
int _bheapset(_segment seg, unsigned int fill);
int _fheapset(unsigned int fill);
int _nheapset(unsigned int fill);
```

Arguments

fill: The character value used to initialize the free space in the heap.

seg: The starting segment address (with an implied offset of :0000) of previously allocated Based heap using **_bheapseg()**.

Return Value

One of the following object-like macros defined in **<malloc.h>**

_HEAPBADBEGIN	Initial header information bad
_HEAPBADNODE	Subsequent bad node
_HEAPEMPTY	Heap has not been initialized
_HEAPOK	Heap appears to be consistent
_HEAPBADPTR	Invalid _pentry field

Example

```
/* FILE: ch24e10.c */
/* use the small memory model */
#include <stdio.h>
```

```c
#include <stdlib.h>
#include <malloc.h>

void heap_report(char *msg, struct _heapinfo *hi_ptr)
{
char _far *ptr;
int i;
hi_ptr->_pentry=NULL;
printf("\n%s", msg);
while (_heapwalk(hi_ptr) == _heapOK ) {
    printf("\n %s block addr= %Fp size %5u bytes [0]-[3]: ",
        (hi_ptr->_useflag == _USEDENTRY ? "USED" : "FREE"),
        hi_ptr->_pentry, hi_ptr->_size);
    ptr = (char _far *) hi_ptr->_pentry;
    for (i=0; i<4; i++) printf("%2x ", (char) *(ptr+i));
    }
printf("\nEnd of Report\n");
}

int main(void)
{
static struct _heapinfo hi;

heap_report("Heap-1", &hi); /* initial Heap */

switch (_heapset(0x7F)) {
    case _heapOK: printf("\nHeap OK\n"); break;
    case _heapEMPTY: printf("\nHeap Empty\n"); break;
    case _heapBADBEGIN: printf("\nBad Heap Begin\n"); break;
    case _heapBADNODE: printf("\nBad Heap Node\n"); break;
    case _heapBADPTR: printf("\nBad _pentry field\n");break;
    }

heap_report("Heap-2", &hi); /* after _heapset() */
exit(0);
}
```

Output

```
Heap-1
    USED block addr= 0D08:0E4C  size    142 bytes  [0]-[3]: 43 4f 4d 53
    USED block addr= 0D08:0EDC  size     12 bytes  [0]-[3]: 4c  e 63  e
    USED block addr= 0D08:0EEA  size    512 bytes  [0]-[3]:  a 48 65 61
    FREE block addr= 0D08:10EC  size   3858 bytes  [0]-[3]: 27  a 32 4d
End of Report

Heap OK

Heap-2
    USED block addr= 0D08:0E4C  size    142 bytes  [0]-[3]: 43 4f 4d 53
    USED block addr= 0D08:0EDC  size     12 bytes  [0]-[3]: 4c  e 63  e
    USED block addr= 0D08:0EEA  size    512 bytes  [0]-[3]: 32 20 62 79
    FREE block addr= 0D08:10EC  size   3858 bytes  [0]-[3]: 7f 7f 7f 7f
End of Report
```

Comments   The **_heapset()** functions are useful in debugging problems with the heap and for controlling the assignment of values other than zero to free heap areas.

In the example program above, **_heapset()** is used to initialize the 3858-byte free heap entry with the character value of 0x7F.

The **_bheapset()**, **_fheapset()**, and **_nheapset()** functions have the same effect as **_heapset()**, shown in the example above, but they work upon the Base heap, Far heap, and Near heap, respectively.

_heapwalk *Functions*   *Traverse the heap and return information about the* **next entry**

Compatibility   ☐ANSI   ■OS/2   ☐UNIX   ☐XENIX

Specification
```
#include <malloc.h>
int _heapwalk(_HEAPINFO *entry);
int _bheapwalk(_segment seg, _HEAPINFO *entry);
int _fheapwalk(_HEAPINFO *entry);
int _nheapwalk(_HEAPINFO *entry);
```

Arguments

entry: Pointer to a non-Standard structure (see Appendix E) containing the following members which describe a memory block allocated to the heap.

_pentry	heap entry pointer
_size	size of heap entry in bytes
_useflag	either _FREEENTRY or **_USEDENTRY**

seg: The starting segment address (with an implied offset of :0000) of previously allocated Based heap using **_bheapseg()**

Return Value

One of the following object-like macros defined in **<malloc.h>**

_HEAPBADBEGIN	Initial header information bad
_HEAPBADNODE	Subsequent bad node
_HEAPBADPTR	Bad heap structure pointer
_HEAPEND	End of heap not reached
_HEAPEMPTY	Heap has not been initialized
_HEAPOK	Heap appears to be consistent

Example   See: **_heapadd()**, **_heapset()**, **malloc()**, and **realloc()**.

Comments   The **_heapwalk()** functions are useful in debugging heap related problems, which can occur easily with C programs because of the lack of array (address) bounds checking and the inherent inability of DOS to provide any degree of memory protection.

   _heapwalk() functions provide a convenient mechanism to provide a comprehensive report on the integrity of the heap.

   The use of the **_bheapwalk()**, **_fheapwalk()**, and **_nheapwalk()** functions parallels that of **_heapwalk()**, demonstrated in the program example references noted above.

hfree()   *Deallocate a *_huge* memory block in Far heap*

Compatibility   ☐ANSI   ■OS/2   ☐UNIX   ☐XENIX

Specification

```
#include <malloc.h>
void hfree(void _huge *memblock);
```

Comments   See the **free()** and **halloc()** entries for more information.

malloc() *Functions*   *Allocate a memory block in the heap*

Compatibility   ■ANSI   ■OS/2   ■UNIX   ■XENIX

See Also

```
calloc(), realloc(), halloc()
```

Specification

```
#include <stdlib.h> or <malloc.h>
void *malloc(size_t size);
void _based(void) *_bmalloc(_segment seg, size_t size);
void _far *_fmalloc(size_t size);
void _near *_nmalloc(size_t size);
```

Arguments

size: A positive, nonzero number of bytes per array element.

seg: The segment of the Based heap to be used that was returned by a prior call to **_bheapseg()**.

Return Value

If unsuccessful, a **NULL** pointer (**_NULLSEG** for **_bcalloc()**)

Otherwise, a suitably aligned **void** pointer that must be cast to an appropriate pointer type before being dereferenced

Example

```
/* FILE: ch24e11.c */
/* use the small memory model */
#include <stdio.h>
#include <stdlib.h>
#include <malloc.h>
#define KB *1024

void heap_report(char *msg, struct _heapinfo *hi_ptr)
{
hi_ptr->_pentry=NULL;
printf("\n%s", msg);
while (_heapwalk(hi_ptr) == _heapOK )
    printf("\n    %s block addr= %Fp size %5u bytes",
        (hi_ptr->_useflag == _USEDENTRY ? "USED" : "FREE"),
        hi_ptr->_pentry, hi_ptr->_size);
printf("\nEnd of Report\n");
}

int main(void)
{
static struct _heapinfo hi;
void *ptr1, *ptr2, *ptr3;

if (ptr1=malloc(1KB)) printf("\nAllocated= %lp size= %5d",
    (void _far *)ptr1, 1KB);
if (ptr2=malloc(2KB)) printf("\nAllocated= %lp size= %5d",
    (void _far *)ptr2, 2KB);
if (ptr3=malloc(1KB)) printf("\nAllocated= %lp size= %5d\n",
    (void _far *)ptr3, 1KB);
heap_report("Heap-1", &hi); /* after malloc() */
free(ptr1);
free(ptr3);
heap_report("Heap-2", &hi); /* after free() */
exit(0);
}
```

Output

```
Allocated= 0D00:0EEA size=  1024
Allocated= 0D00:14EE size=  2048
Allocated= 0D00:1CF0 size=  1024

Heap-1
    USED block addr= 0D00:0E4C  size    142 bytes
    USED block addr= 0D00:0EDC  size     12 bytes
```

```
    USED block addr= 0D00:0EEA  size  1024 bytes
    USED block addr= 0D00:12EC  size   512 bytes
    USED block addr= 0D00:14EE  size  2048 bytes
    USED block addr= 0D00:1CF0  size  1024 bytes
    FREE block addr= 0D00:20F2  size  7948 bytes
End of Report

Heap-2
    USED block addr= 0D00:0E4C  size   142 bytes
    USED block addr= 0D00:0EDC  size    12 bytes
    FREE block addr= 0D00:0EEA  size  1024 bytes
    USED block addr= 0D00:12EC  size   512 bytes
    USED block addr= 0D00:14EE  size  2048 bytes
    FREE block addr= 0D00:1CF0  size  1024 bytes
    FREE block addr= 0D00:20F2  size  7948 bytes
End of Report
```

Comments   The size of the largest array object that can be allocated is determined by the object-like macro **_HEAP_MAXREQ** (0xFFE8 or 65,512 bytes), defined in **<malloc.h>**; the largest array element size is also **_HEAP_MAXREQ**.

Unlike **calloc()**, **malloc** functions do not initialize the entire heap area to a null character value (**' \0'**).

Since the example program used the Small memory model, it is consistent that all memory blocks reside in the same segment (DS=0D00).

Refer to the example program for **_bheapseg()** for an example of using **_bmalloc()** with the Based heap.

The use of the **_fmalloc()** and **_nmalloc()** functions parallels that of **malloc()**, as shown in the example above, but the memory block allocation is directed to the Far heap and Near heap, respectively.

A list of the various C run-time library functions that utilize the **malloc()** function, and therefore allocate memory blocks to the heap, is presented earlier in this chapter in the section "Basic Heap Concepts."

_memavl ()   *Return the size in bytes of the remaining Near heap*

Compatibility   ☐ANSI   ■OS/2   ☐UNIX   ☐XENIX

See Also

_freect(), _memmax()

Specification

```
#include <malloc.h>
size_t _memavl(void);
```

Return Value

The size in bytes of the total available (free) Near heap

Example

See: `_heapmin()`.

Comments

`_memavl()` returns the approximate total amount of free space that remains in the Near heap (DS range), not the largest contiguous space available reported by `_memmax()`.

memccpy ()   *Copy characters from one buffer to another*

Compatibility   □ANSI   ■OS/2   □UNIX   □XENIX

See Also

```
memcpy(), memmove()
```

Specification

```
#include <memory.h> or <string.h>
void *memccpy(void *dest, void *src, int c, unsigned int count);
void _far * _far _fmemccpy(void _far *dest, const void _far *src,
    int c, unsigned int count);
```

Arguments

dest: Pointer to a destination buffer area.

src: Pointer to a source buffer area.

c: The first occurrence of character value **c** in **src** is the last character to be copied, unless count is reached.

count: The maximum number of characters to copy from **src** to **dest**.

Return Value

If **c** is copied, a pointer to the next character in **dest**

Otherwise, a **NULL** pointer

Example

See: `memcpy()`.

Comments

`_fmemccpy()` is the memory-model independent version of function `memccpy()`.

`memccpy()` does not correctly handle buffer areas that may overlap; only `memmove()` and `fmemmove()` do so.

In the example, notice how the return value is used to display the remaining characters in a string.

Unlike string-handling functions, memory buffer-handling functions do not inherently rely upon the detection of a null character (`'\0'`), but simply treat each memory address as a byte value.

memchr ()   *Find characters in a buffer*

Compatibility ■ANSI ■OS/2 ■UNIX ■XENIX

See Also

memcmp(), memicmp()

Specification

```
#include <memory.h> or <string.h>
void *memchr(const void *buf, int c, size_t, count);
void _far * _far _fmemchr(const void _far *buf, int c, size_t count);
```

Arguments

buf: Pointer to a buffer area.

c: Character search value.

count: The number of byte (character) positions to search in **buf**.

Return Value

Pointer to the first occurrence of **c** within **buf**

Otherwise, a **NULL** pointer

Example   See: memcmp().

Comments   _fmemchr() is the memory-model independent version of function memchr().

As demonstrated in the example program, the **memchr()** functions always perform case-sensitive comparisons of byte values, regardless of the underlying array type elements that may be specified.

Only the first occurrence (at the lowest memory address) of a byte value is located by **memchr()** or **_fmemchr()**.

memcmp ()   *Case-sensitive character comparison of two buffer areas*

Compatibility ■ANSI ■OS/2 ■UNIX ■XENIX

Specification

```
#include <memory.h> or <string.h>
int memcmp(const void *buf1, const void *buf2, size_t count);
int _far _fmemcmp(const void _far *buf1, const void _far *buf2, size_t count);
```

Arguments

buf1: Pointer to one buffer area.

buf2: Pointer to a second buffer area.

count: The number of byte (character) positions to compare.

Return Value

A signed value that is interpreted as follows:

    < 0   **buf1** less than **buf2**

    ==0   buf1 equal to **buf2**

    > 0   **buf1** greater than **buf2**

Example

```
/* FILE: ch24e12.c */
#include <stdio.h>
#include <stdlib.h>
#include <memory.h>

int main(void)
{
union { unsigned char ch_ary[40];
    int int_ary[20];
    long long_ary[10];
    double dbl_ary[5];
    long double ldbl_ary[4]; } types[2] =
        {"abcdEFGHijklMNOPqrstUVWX0123456789",
        "ABCDefghIJKLmnopQRSTuvwx0123456789" };
char _far *ptr;

printf("\nch_ary[0]= %s\nch_ary[1]= %s\n",
    types[0].ch_ary, types[1].ch_ary);

printf("\nmemcmp() test: ");
if (memcmp(types[0].ch_ary, types[1].ch_ary, 40))
    printf("\n    ch_ary   !=");
else printf("\n    ch_ary   ==");
if (_fmemcmp(types[0].ldbl_ary, types[1].ldbl_ary, 40))
    printf("\n    ldbl_ary !=");
else printf("\n    ldbl_ary ==");

printf("\n  \nmemicmp() test: ");
```

```
if (memicmp(types[0].ch_ary, types[1].ch_ary, 40))
    printf("\n      ch_ary   !=");
else printf("\n      ch_ary   ==");
if (_fmemicmp(types[0].dbl_ary, types[1].dbl_ary, 40))
    printf("\n    dbl_ary  !=");
else printf("\n      dbl_ary  ==");

printf("\n   \nmemchr() test: ");
if (ptr = memchr(types[0].dbl_ary, 'q', 40))
    printf("\n      dbl_ary   == %c at %lp", *ptr, ptr);
else printf("\n    dbl_ary NO MATCH");
if (ptr = _fmemchr(types[0].ldbl_ary, 'q', 40))
    printf("\n      ldbl_ary == %c at %lp", *ptr, ptr);
else printf("\n      ldbl_ary NO MATCH");

exit(0);
}
```

Output

```
ch_ary[0]= abcdEFGHijklMNOPqrstUVWX0123456789
ch_ary[1]= ABCDefghIJKLmnopQRSTuvwx0123456789

memcmp() test:
    ch_ary   !=
    ldbl_ary !=

memicmp() test:
    ch_ary   ==
    dbl_ary ==

memchr() test:
    dbl_ary  == q at 0D22:0EB2
    ldbl_ary == q at 0D22:0EB2
```

Comments **_fmemcmp()** is the memory-model independent version of function **memcmp()**.

As demonstrated in the example program, the **memcmp()** functions always perform case-sensitive comparisons of byte values, regardless of the underlying array type elements that may be specified.

The **memcmp()** and **_fmemcmp()** functions are not restricted for use with strings and, therefore, do not terminate when a null character (**'\0'**) is encountered; they terminate only when a byte value difference is detected, or the count of bytes to be compared is completed.

memcmp() and **_fmemcmp()** can be used to reliably compare arrays of data-object types that do not include pad bytes.

As an alternative, use either the function or **#pragma intrinsic** form; the intrinsic form does not support **_huge** pointers.

`memcpy ()`   *Copy characters between buffers, ignoring overlap*

Compatibility   ■ANSI   ■OS/2   ■UNIX   ■XENIX

See Also

```
memmove(), movedata()
```

Specification

```
#include <memory.h> or <string.h>
void *memcpy(void *dest, const void *src, size_t count);
void _far * _far _fmemcpy(void _far *dest, const void _far *src, size_t count);
```

Arguments

dest: Pointer to a destination buffer area.

src: Pointer to a source buffer area.

count: The number of byte (character) positions to copy.

Return Value

Pointer to the destination buffer **dest**

Example

```
/* FILE: ch24e13.c */
#include <stdio.h>
#include <stdlib.h>
#include <memory.h>
#include <string.h>
#include <dos.h>

int main(void)
{
static char *msg = "abcdefghijklmno";
static char string1[20], _far *ptr_str1=string1;
static char string2[20], _far *ptr_str2=string2;
char _far *ptr1 = &(string1[10]);

printf("\nmemcpy() test    :");
strcpy(string1, msg);
printf("\nInitial String   : %s", string1);
printf("\nCopy/No Overlap : %s",
    memcpy(string2, string1, sizeof(string1)));
printf("\nCopy/Overlap     : %Fs",
    _fmemcpy(ptr1, string1, strlen(string1)));

printf("\n\nmemccpy() test   :");
memccpy(string1, msg, '\0', sizeof(string1));
printf("\nComplete string : %s", string1);
```

```
    printf("\nString remainder: %Fs",
        _fmemccpy(string1, msg, 'g', sizeof(string1)));

    printf("\n\nmemmove() test   :");
    strcpy(string1, msg);
    strcpy(string2,"");
    printf("\nInitial String  : %s", string1);
    printf("\nMove/No Overlap : %s",
        memmove(string2, string1, sizeof(string1)));
    printf("\nMove/Overlap    : %Fs",
        _fmemmove(ptr1, string1, strlen(string1)));

    printf("\n\nmovedata() test :");
    memset(string1, 'X', sizeof(string1));
    memset(string1+10, 'Z', 10);
    _fmemset(string2, '\0', sizeof(string2));
    printf("\nInitial String  : %s", string1);
    movedata(FP_SEG(ptr_str1), FP_OFF(ptr_str1),
        FP_SEG(ptr_str2), FP_OFF(ptr_str2), sizeof(string1) );
    printf("\nMove/No Overlap : %Fs", ptr_str2);
    movedata(FP_SEG(ptr_str1), FP_OFF(ptr_str1),
        FP_SEG(ptr1), FP_OFF(ptr1), strlen(string1)+1 );
    printf("\nMove/Overlap    : %Fs", ptr_str1);
    exit(0);
}
```

Output

```
memcpy() test   :
Initial String  : abcdefghijklmno
Copy/No Overlap : abcdefghijklmno
Copy/Overlap    : abcdefghijabcde

memccpy() test  :
Complete string : abcdefghijklmno
String remainder: hijklmno

memmove() test  :
Initial String  : abcdefghijklmno
Move/No Overlap : abcdefghijklmno
Move/Overlap    : abcdefghijklmno

movedata() test :
Initial String  : XXXXXXXXXXZZZZZZZZZZklmno
Move/No Overlap : XXXXXXXXXXZZZZZZZZZZ
Move/Overlap    : XXXXXXXXXXXXXXXXXXXXXXXXXXXXXXXXXXXXXXXX
```

Comments **_fmemcpy()** is the memory-model independent version of function
memcpy().

Notice that the example program output demonstrates that only the **mem-move()** and **_fmemmove()** functions properly accommodate buffer areas that overlap when duplicating arrays.

If buffer areas do not overlap, any of the buffer copy functions listed in Table 24.1 can be used to duplicate an array in memory properly.

Only the **movedata()** function can be used to copy buffers that span segment boundaries.

As an alternative to calling this function, you can use its **#pragma intrinsic** form; the intrinsic form does not support **_huge** pointers.

memicmp()   *Case-insensitive character comparison of two buffer areas*

Compatibility   □ANSI   ■OS/2   ■UNIX   ■XENIX

See Also

memcmp()

Specification

```
#include <memory.h> or <string.h>
int memicmp(const void *buf1, const void *buf2, unsigned int count);
int _far _fmemicmp(const void _far *buf1, const void _far *buf2,
        unsigned int count);
```

Arguments

buf1: Pointer to one buffer area.

buf2: Pointer to a second buffer area.

count: The number of byte (character) positions to compare.

Return Value

A signed value that is interpreted as follows

< 0	**buf1** less than **buf2**
==0	buf1 equal to **buf2**
> 0	buf1 greater than **buf2**

Example   See: **memcmp()**.

Comments   **_fmemicmp()** is the memory-model independent version of function **memicmp()**.

The **memicmp()** and **fmemicmp()** functions work in the same way as **memcmp()** and **_fmemcmp()**, except that their byte comparisons are case-insensitive; upper- and lowercase alphabetic characters are considered identical.

memmax () *Return the size of the largest contiguous memory block in the Near heap*

Compatibility ☐ ANSI ■ OS/2 ☐ UNIX ☐ XENIX

See Also

```
_freect(), _memavl()
```

Specification

```
#include <malloc.h>
size_t _memmax(void);
```

Return Value

The size of the largest free contiguous remaining memory area in the Near heap

Example   See: **_heapmin()**.

Comments   Unlike **_memavl()**, **_memmax()** returns the largest contiguous memory block in the Near heap, not the total available memory space.

memmove () *Move one buffer to another, accommodating overlap*

Compatibility ■ ANSI ■ OS/2 ☐ UNIX ☐ XENIX

See Also

```
memcpy(), movedata()
```

Specification

```
#include <string.h>
void *memmove(void *dest, const void *src, size_t count);
void _far * _far _fmemmove(void _far *dest, const void _far *src, size_t count);
```

Arguments

dest: Pointer to a destination buffer area.

src: Pointer to a source buffer area.

count: The number of byte (character) positions to copy.

Return Value

Pointer to the destination buffer, **dest**

Example   See: **memcpy()**.

Comments **_fmemmove()** is the memory-model independent version of function **memmove()**.

As demonstrated in the example program, only the **memmove()** and **_fmemmove()** functions correctly accommodate overlapping buffer areas when copying bytes of information.

memset () *Set buffers to a specified character*

Compatibility ■ANSI ■OS/2 ■UNIX ■XENIX

Specification

```
#include <memory.h> or <string.h>
void *memset(void *dest, int c, size_t count);
void _far * _far _fmemset(void _far *dest, int c, size_t count);
```

Arguments

dest: Pointer to a destination buffer area.

c: The character value used to initialize the buffer area.

count: The number of byte (character) positions to initialize.

Return Value

Pointer to the destination buffer, *dest*

Example See: **memcmp()**.

Comments **_fmemset()** is the memory-model independent version of function **memset()**.

Use **memset()** and **_fmemset()** to set the byte value associated with any memory address.

As an alternative to this function, use the **#pragma intrinsic** form; the intrinsic form does not support **_huge** pointers.

movedata () *Move characters between memory segments, ignoring overlap*

Compatibility □ANSI ■OS/2 □UNIX □XENIX

See Also

```
memcpy(), memmove()
```

Specification

```
#include <memory.h> or <string.h>
void movedata (unsigned int srcseg, unsigned int srcoff, unsigned int destseg,
        unsigned int destoff, unsigned int count);
```

Arguments

srcseg: The segment (macro **FP_SEG** or **_segment** type) of the source buffer area.

srcoff: The offset (macro **FP_OFF** or **unsigned** type) of the source buffer area.

destseg: The segment (macro **FP_SEG** or **_segment** type) of the destination buffer area.

destoff: The offset (macro **FP_OFF** or **unsigned** type) of the destination buffer area.

count: A positive, nonzero number of bytes (characters) to be moved.

Example   See: **memcpy()**.

Comments   The **movedata()** function copies bytes of information between buffer areas in the same or different segments, but each buffer area itself may not span a segment boundary.

As demonstrated in the example program, **movedata()** does not correctly handle the duplication of buffer areas that overlap; only the **memmove()** and **movedata()** functions do so.

`msize()` *Functions*   *Return the size of a memory block allocated to*
The heap

Compatibility   □ ANSI   ■ OS/2   □ UNIX   □ XENIX

See Also

```
_heapwalk
```

Specification

```
#include <malloc.h>
size_t _msize(void *memblock);
size_t _bmsize(_segment seg, void _based(void) *memblock);
size_t _fmsize(void _far *memblock);
size_t _nmsize(void _near *memblock);
```

Arguments

memblock: A pointer to a memory block previously allocated using a **calloc()**, **malloc()**, or **realloc()** function.

seg: The starting segment address (with an implied offset of :0000) of previously allocated Based heap using **_bheapseg()**.

Return Value

The size in bytes of the memory block described by *memblock*

Example   See: **_expand()**.

Comments   This function cannot be used to return the size of a **_huge** memory block allocated using **halloc()**.

_ncalloc()   *Allocate initialized memory to Near heap*

Compatibility   □ ANSI   ■ OS/2   □ UNIX   □ XENIX

Specification

```
#include <malloc.h>
void _near *_ncalloc(size_t num, size_t size);
```

Comments   See the **calloc()** entry for more information.

_nexpand()   *Change the size of a memory block in the Near heap*

Compatibility   □ ANSI   ■ OS/2   □ UNIX   □ XENIX

Specification

```
#include <malloc.h>
void _near *_nexpand(void _near *memblock, size_t size);
```

Comments   See the **_expand()** entry for more information.

_nfree()   *Deallocate a memory block in Near heap*

Compatibility   □ ANSI   ■ OS/2   □ UNIX   □ XENIX

Specification

```
#include <malloc.h>
void _nfree(void _near *memblock);
```

Comments   See the **free()** entry for more information.

_nheapchk()   *Perform consistency checks on a specified Near heap*

Compatibility ☐ ANSI   ■ OS/2   ☐ UNIX   ☐ XENIX

Specification

```
#include <malloc.h>
int _nheapchk(void);
```

Comments   See the **_heapchk()** entry for more information.

_nheapmin()   *Release unused memory to DOS from Near heap*

Compatibility ☐ ANSI   ■ OS/2   ☐ UNIX   ☐ XENIX

Specification

```
#include <malloc.h>
int _nheapmin(void);
```

Comments   See the **_heapmin()** entry for more information.

_nheapset()   *Check Near heap for minimal consistency and set the free entries to a specified value*

Compatibility ☐ ANSI   ■ OS/2   ☐ UNIX   ☐ XENIX

Specification

```
#include <malloc.h>
int _nheapset(unsigned int fill);
```

Comments   See the **_heapset()** entry for more information.

_nheapwalk() *Traverse Near heap and return information about the next entry*

Compatibility □ ANSI ■ OS/2 □ UNIX □ XENIX

Specification

```
#include <malloc.h>
int _nheapwalk(_HEAPINFO *entry);
```

Comments See the **_heapwalk()** entry for more information.

_nmalloc() *Allocate a memory block in Near heap*

Compatibility □ ANSI ■ OS/2 □ UNIX □ XENIX

Specification

```
#include <malloc.h>
void _near *_nmalloc(size_t size);
```

Comments See the **malloc()** entry for more information.

_nmsize() *Return the size of a memory block allocated to Near heap*

Compatibility □ ANSI ■ OS/2 □ UNIX □ XENIX

Specification

```
#include <malloc.h>
size_t _nmsize(void _near *memblock);
```

Comments See the **_msize()** entry for more information.

_nrealloc() *Reallocate memory blocks in the Near heap*

Compatibility □ ANSI ■ OS/2 □ UNIX □ XENIX

Specification

```
#include <malloc.h>
void _near *_nrealloc(void _near *memblock, size_t size);
```

Comments   See the **realloc()** entry for more information.

`realloc()` *Functions*   *Reallocate memory blocks in the heap*

Compatibility   ■ANSI   ■OS/2   ■UNIX   ■XENIX

See Also

_bheapadd(), _heapadd(), _expand(), free(), _heapmin

Specification

```
#include <stdlib.h> or <malloc.h>
void *realloc(void *memblock, size_t size);
void _based(void) *_brealloc(_segment seg, void _based(void) *memblock,
    size_t size);
void _far *_frealloc(void _far *memblock, size_t size);
void _near *_nrealloc(void _near *memblock, size_t size);
```

Arguments

memblock: A pointer to a memory block previously allocated using **calloc()** or **malloc()**.

size: A new (not additional) positive, nonzero number of bytes in **memblock**.

seg: The starting segment address (with an implied offset of :0000) of previously allocated Based heap using **_bheapseg()**.

Return Value

If unsuccessful, a **NULL** pointer (**_NULLSEG** for **_bcalloc()**)

Otherwise, a suitably aligned **void** pointer that must be cast to an appropriate pointer type before being dereferenced

Example

```
/* FILE: ch24e14.c */
/* use the small memory model */
#include <stdio.h>
#include <stdlib.h>
#include <malloc.h>
#define KB *1024

void heap_report(char *msg, _segment segvar, struct _heapinfo *hi_ptr)
{
hi_ptr->_pentry=NULL;
printf("\n%s", msg);
while ( _bheapwalk(segvar, hi_ptr) == _heapOK )
    printf("\n    %s block addr= %Fp size %5u bytes",
        (hi_ptr->_useflag == _USEDENTRY ? "USED" : "FREE"),
```

```
            hi_ptr->_pentry, hi_ptr->_size);
    printf("\nEnd of Report\n");
    }


    int main(void)
    {
    static struct _heapinfo hi;
    _segment bseg;
    void _based(bseg) *ptr1, _based(bseg) *ptr2, _based(bseg) *ptr3;
    if ((bseg = _bheapseg(8KB)) == _NULLSEG) exit(98);

    if (ptr1= _bmalloc(bseg, 1KB)) printf("\nAllocated= %lp size= %5d",
        (void _far *)ptr1, 1KB);
    if (ptr2= _bmalloc(bseg, 2KB)) printf("\nAllocated= %lp size= %5d",
        (void _far *)ptr2, 2KB);
    _bfree(bseg, ptr1);
    printf("\nReleased = %lp size= %5d", (void _far *)ptr1, 1KB);
    if (ptr3= _bmalloc(bseg, 2KB)) printf("\nAllocated= %lp size= %5d",
        (void _far *)ptr3, 2KB);
    _bfree(bseg, ptr2);
    printf("\nReleased = %lp size= %5d", (void _far *)ptr2, 2KB);
    if (ptr1= _bmalloc(bseg, 4KB)) printf("\nAllocated= %lp size= %5d\n",
        (void _far *)ptr1, 4KB);

    heap_report("Heap-1", bseg, &hi); /* after allocation() */
    if (_bheapmin(_NULLSEG)) exit(99);
    heap_report("Heap-2", bseg, &hi); /* after minimizing the Heap */
    _brealloc(bseg, ptr2, 3KB);
    heap_report("Heap-3", bseg, &hi); /* after reallocating the Heap */
    exit(0);
    }
```

Output

```
    Allocated= 1D51:0016 size=  1024
    Allocated= 1D51:0418 size=  2048
    Released = 1D51:0016 size=  1024
    Allocated= 1D51:0C1A size=  2048
    Released = 1D51:0418 size=  2048
    Allocated= 1D51:141C size=  4096

    Heap-1
        FREE block addr= 1D51:0016  size  3074 bytes
        USED block addr= 1D51:0C1A  size  2048 bytes
        USED block addr= 1D51:141C  size  4096 bytes
        FREE block addr= 1D51:241E  size  7136 bytes
    End of Report

    Heap-2
        FREE block addr= 1D51:0016  size  3074 bytes
        USED block addr= 1D51:0C1A  size  2048 bytes
        USED block addr= 1D51:141C  size  4096 bytes
        FREE block addr= 1D51:241E  size     0 bytes
    End of Report
```

```
Heap-3
    USED block addr= 1D51:0016  size   3072 bytes
    FREE block addr= 1D51:0C18  size      0 bytes
    USED block addr= 1D51:0C1A  size   2048 bytes
    USED block addr= 1D51:141C  size   4096 bytes
    FREE block addr= 1D51:241E  size      0 bytes
End of Report
```

Comments   The size of the largest array object that can be allocated is determined by the object-like macro **_HEAP_MAXREG** (0xFFE8 or 65,512 bytes) defined in `<malloc.h>`.

The **realloc()** functions differ from **_expand()** functions in that the starting address of the memory block may be relocated to satisfy the reallocation request.

The program example uses a Based heap and demonstrates how **_brealloc()** reassigned the starting address of pointer variable **ptr2** to satisfy the request for 3KB of space, after the **ptr2** variable had been allocated 2KB and then subsequently freed.

If program variables or other data structures contain memory address of objects allocated to the heap, the **realloc()** functions should not be used unless the other program variables and data structures are updated to reflect the relocation of heap objects.

The **_frealloc()**, **_nrealloc()**, and **realloc()** functions work in the same way as the **_brealloc()** function, demonstrated in the example above, except that they allocate memory directly to the Far heap, Near heap, and heap, respectively.

stackavail()   *Return the size of the free (unused) stack space*

Compatibility   □ANSI   ■OS/2   □UNIX   □XENIX

Specification

```
#include <malloc.h>
size_t stackavail(void);
```

Return Value

The approximate size in bytes (within 256) of the unused stack available for use by **alloca()**

Example   See: **alloca()**.

Comments   For additional discussion of the stack and another sample use of **stackavail()**, as well as alternatives to this function, see "Sizing the Stack" in Chapter 15.

Process Control Functions

Process Control Functions

Every .COM or .EXE program file that is executed by DOS must first be transformed into a *process*. A process is a program that has been assigned, and exercises control over, such computer resources as memory, disk storage, and peripheral devices. With DOS the terms program and process are often used interchangeably, because DOS is a single-tasking environment, meaning that it can execute only one process at a time. But in a multitasking environment such as OS/2, UNIX, or Xenix, a process represents one of perhaps several *threads of execution*, or series of instructions, that may be executing concurrently.

Process control—initiating, executing, and terminating—is normally the sole responsibility of the DOS command processor, COMMAND.COM. The run-time library functions discussed in this chapter, however, permit C application programs to perform process control activities as well. We will first examine the sequence of events that transform program files into processes, and then how C programs can be written that initiate other processes.

PROGRAMS VERSUS PROCESSES

Unlike multitasking operating systems, which support such fundamental units of execution as screen groups, tasks, and threads, DOS only supports the execution of processes. For this reason, process control services under DOS are relatively simple to use and require only that variations of the techniques used to initiate and terminate processes be mastered.

The DOS command processor, COMMAND.COM, first described in Chapter 1, is the best example of a process control program. It is designed to accept a command line and then interpret it either as a request to execute an internal (memory resident) DOS command or an executable file (.COM or .EXE), or as a batch file of other command requests.

COMMAND.COM attempts to locate the executable file in the default/current directory, in a path specified on the command line, or in a list of directories specified in an earlier SET PATH command. If no matching directory entry is found, the message *Bad command or filename* results; otherwise, the program file is loaded to memory and executed.

The execution of all programs under DOS involves the following steps, which are required to transform a program file into an executable process:

1. Request DOS for the contiguous memory space that will be necessary to load a process consisting of a program segment prefix (PSP), text (Code), data, and stack (see Chapter 1). Insufficient space prevents a program from being executed.

2. Request DOS for the contiguous memory space required to pass a copy of the environment table to the process. Insufficient space prevents a program from being executed.

3. Build the PSP (see Table 1.6). The key components are as follows: (a) The normal program termination address INT 0x22 identifies where control (CS:IP) is returned upon normal program termination; (b) the Ctrl-Break and (c) critical error addresses represent copies of INT 0x23 and INT 0x24 from the interrupt vector table of the parent process; (d) the environment table address is that returned by step 2 above; (e) the file handle table is optionally inherited from the parent process, depending upon the value of global variable **_fileinfo** and the use of the **O_NOINHERIT** file attribute; and (f) the DOS command line represents the command line stripped of all piping and redirection symbols and related tokens.

4. Load the PSP and the program (text and data) to the allotted memory in Step 1, and adjust all relocation table addresses in .EXE files. Tiny memory model (.COM) programs are loaded intact.

5. Transfer CPU control (CS:IP, Code Segment:Instruction Pointer) either by assigning the CS and IP values passed by the linker for .EXE files, or by assigning CS to the **_psp** segment address and IP to offset 0x100 (offset 256, size of the PSP) for .COM files.

In process terminology, COMMAND.COM acts as a *parent* process, which initiates (spawns) another process called a *child*. A child may in turn act as a parent process and initiate (spawn) other child processes. The run-time functions documented in this chapter enable C application programs, as well as the DOS command processor, to initiate processes.

THE PROCESS ENTITY

When a C program is viewed as a process, the importance of the program segment prefix (PSP) emerges. The PSP encapsulates everything that DOS deems essential for a program to be assigned resources and begin execution. The PSP also ensures that, regardless of whether the process terminates normally or abnormally, ultimately DOS will regain control over the computer resources that have been assigned to a process.

Processes are created, assigned resources, and processed, and then, in an orderly fashion, they relinquish all assigned resources and return control. Once a DOS process has begun execution, it maintains control of its assigned resources until completion, whether that be in a normal or abnormal manner. External events (interrupts, critical hardware error, signals, loss of power, and so on) or the logic of a program itself can cause abnormal process termination to occur and, as we will see, there are even variations in the manner in which normal process termination can occur.

Let's examine the initiation, execution, and termination phases in the life of every DOS process to gain better insight into the services provided by the many process control run-time library functions that are available.

Process Initiation

Steps 1 through 5 above highlight the tasks involved in transforming a program file into a DOS process. Some additional comments are in order regarding step 3, building the PSPs, as they relate to application programs developed using the C language.

The process environment table address noted in step 3(d) identifies a memory block of the size specified by default (160-bytes) or optionally by the **/E:xxxx** parameter of the DOS commands COMMAND or SHELL (see Chapter 1). It contains a copy of the environment table from the parent process. The DOS command processor always passes a copy of the present environment, while C programs that initiate processes using the **exec..()** and **spawn..()** family of functions can customize the copy of the environment table passed to a child process. Subsequent changes to the child process environment table, using the **getenv()** and **putenv()** functions, alter only the value of its environment copy, not that of a parent or grandparent.

The process file handle table noted in step 3(e) consists of up to 20 files, numbered elements [0]–[19]. All unused file entries assume a value of 0xFF. If the parent process either set the global variable **_fileinfo = 1**, or linked the application program using the special FILEINFO.OBJ module, then all files of the parent process that have not explicitly been opened using the **O_NOINHERIT** attribute will be passed to the child process.

DOS, however, automatically assigns only the first five entries in this table: **stdin**, **stdout**, **stderr**, **stdaux**, and **stdprn**. Any remaining open user-defined files that are to be passed from one C process to another (inherited) are handled in the following manner: First the parent process creates an environment variable, **_C_FILE_INFO**. Then the C startup code (**crt0.asm**, see Chapter 15) uses this binary environment string to update the PSP of the child process before function **main()** assumes control. The following example program demonstrates how the **_C_FILE_INFO** environment variable is created when this occurs.

```
/* FILE: ch25e12.c */
#include <stdio.h>
#include <stdlib.h>
#include <process.h>
/* execute this program, then when the secondary command
** processor is installed, enter a SET command to see the
** _C_FILE_INFO variable, and then enter an EXIT command
** to return and complete this program
*/
int main(void)
{
_fileinfo=1;
spawnlpe(P_WAIT, "command.com", NULL, environ);
printf("\nEnding ch25e12.c !");
exit(0);
}
```

The global variable **_fileinfo**, by default, is set equal to zero (false), and no **_C_FILE_INFO** environment variable is created. Therefore, the PSP file handle table contains entries only for elements [0] through [4], representing the five files that are automatically opened for use by DOS. The **_C_FILE_INFO** variable is deleted from the environment table immediately after it has been used by the child process's C startup code to update the file handle table entries in its PSP. The program example above captures the presence of the **_C_FILE_INFO** variable at an instance of time after being created by a parent process and before being deleted by a child process.

Step 3(f) described the process's copy of the DOS command line, which is used by the C start-up code to construct the **argc** and **argv** arguments that are optionally accessible by function **main()** (see Chapter 15) if defined as

```
int main(int argc, char *argv[]) { .. }
```

Process Execution

While a process is being executed, certain actions may be taken that can alter its normal outcome. Such actions involve nonlocal branching, signal processing, queued termination functions, and process initiation.

Nonlocal branching embodies any unconditional branch (jump) between functions that does not involve the use of the keyword **return**.

Normal unconditional branching (**goto**, **break**, **continue**) is restricted to occur within a function. From the discussion of stack frames in Chapter 15, which detailed the underlying mechanism that supports all function calling sequences, it is clear that for an unconditional branch to occur between functions, the context of the stack frame corresponding to the function being branched to must be preserved. The **setjmp()** function saves the context of the stack frame in a **jmp_buf** type variable (see Chapter 6, **<setjmp.h>**), which can be used subsequently to restore the state of the machine when a **longjmp()** occurs using that **jmp_buf** variable. Normally, this technique is used to accommodate error conditions and facilitate recovery procedures (see Chapter 23, floating-point exception handling).

Signal processing services are provided to handle certain common interrupts (asynchronous events) in a standard manner, as discussed in Chapter 22. The functions **signal()** and **raise()** are Standard C functions and, therefore, are available for use regardless of the operating system being employed. DOS recognizes the following signals:

SIGABRT	Abnormal termination
SIGFPE	Floating-point exception (Chapter 23)
SIGINT	Ctrl-Break or Ctrl-C (Chapter 27)

For other signals, you must write and install a non-Standard interrupt handler, as described in Chapter 27. A relatively simple custom signal function can be written that conforms with the minimal function prototype declaration **void func(void)**. Unlike an Interrupt Service Routine (ISR), however, a signal-handling function, once invoked, remains in effect only until the first signal of that type is encountered. After the first such signal occurs, subsequent signals of that type are handled in the default manner, unless the **signal()** function again registers a custom signal handler for use. As with ISRs, significant restrictions are placed upon the DOS/BIOS services that may be accessed from within a signal handling function.

The outcome of a process can also be altered by the use of the **atexit()** and **onexit()** functions. Up to 32 function pointers may be queued for processing (LIFO—last-in, first-out) by **atexit()** or **onexit()** if the process terminates in a normal manner; that is, each function pointer that has been queued for processing is executed before process resources or control is relinquished. For more about function pointers, see Chapter 14.

Finally, processes are also free to initiate other processes using the **execxx()** and **spawnxx()** families of functions, or by using the **system()** function to invoke the DOS command processor. The **execxx()**

functions always overlay the parent process, while the **spawnxx()** functions permit the child process either to overlay (**P_OVERLAY**) or to coexist (**P_WAIT**) with the parent process. When processes are spawned, the process initiation steps described above are repeated, thus permitting customized environments, file handle tables, and command-line arguments to be passed to a child process. Refer to Chapter 15 for additional explanation and further examples of process initiation using the **execxx()** and **spawnxx()** family of functions.

Process Termination

Process termination can be described as either normal, subnormal, or abnormal. Because processes are transitory (initiated, executed, terminated), process termination is intended to maintain and restore the integrity of the overall computing environment (hardware and operating system). In many respects, processes are handled in much the same way as interrupts (see Chapters 22 and 27). Both processes and interrupts represent asynchronous events and, ideally, both should be initiated, executed, and terminated without any undesirable side effects.

Termination activities involve more than just the reversal of the steps taken to initiate the process, for during a process's execution, additional computer resources may have been requested (files opened, dynamic memory allocated, termination functions queued, and so on) that must also be released.

If we define normal process termination as the set of termination tasks necessary to relinquish all assigned resources and return control to a parent process, subnormal and abnormal termination perform subsets of such services. To better understand the run-time functions that terminate processes, let's first analyze the complete set of tasks that are performed when a process terminates in a normal manner.

1. Perform any queued functions (**atexit()**/**onexit()**).
2. Optionally check for null pointer assignment (DS:0000).
3. Flush all file buffers.
4. Close all open files and remove all temporary files.
5. Perform all "quick" termination procedures:
    a. Floating-point termination
    b. Resetting divide by zero (INT 0x00)
    c. Restore overlay interrupt
    d. Restore INT 0x22, 0x23 and 0x24 from the PSP

6. Terminate the process (INT 0x21 function 0x4C):

   a. Free all memory assigned to the process, except memory dynamically allocated by the process itself.

   b. Return an exit status code to the parent process.

Of the run-time functions available to control process termination (see Table 25.1), only **exit()** provides normal termination (the full set of services described above). The abnormal termination performed by **abort()** and **assert()** includes only the "quick" services described in step 5; and the subnormal-termination functions (**_dos-keep()**, **_exit()**, **_cexit()**, and **_c_exit()**) perform larger subsets of the above-mentioned services. For more about how functions are terminated, refer to Chapter 15, Table 15.1, and the individual function documentation in this chapter.

PROCESS CONTROL TASKS

The process control functions that are documented in this chapter are summarized in Table 25.1 by the three stages in the life of every process: initiation, execution, and termination.

To retrieve the entries, or customize the environment table that is passed to a child process, use the **getenv()** and **putenv()** functions before initiating a child process.

To initiate a child process, which always overlays the parent when it is loaded into memory for execution, use the **execxxx()** family of functions. The **execxxx()** functions have been broken into two separate groups for documentation purposes: **execlxx()** and **execvxx()** functions. All **execlxx()** functions pass the command-line arguments to the child process by specifying them individually; the **execvxx()** functions pass an array of pointers to such command-line argument strings. The **execxxx()** family of functions is equivalent to using the **spawnxxx()** family of functions with a mode argument value of **P_WAIT**.

To initiate a child process that optionally may overlay or coexist with the parent, use the **spawnxxx()** family of functions. If the mode argument is assigned the value of **P_OVERLAY**, the child process overlays the parent; otherwise, specify **P_WAIT** for the child process to coexist with the parent. The **spawnxxx()** functions have also been broken into two separate groups for documentation purposes: **spawnlx()** and **spawnvx()** functions. All **spawnlx()** functions pass the command line arguments to the child process by specifying them individually; the **spawnvx()** functions pass an array of pointers to such command-line argument strings.

TABLE 25.1: Process Control Tasks

TASK		FUNCTION	
		STANDARD C ■ **ANSI**	**MICROSOFT C** ☐ **ANSI**

Process Initiation	Environment table
	Overlay the parent
		`getenv()`	`putenv()`
			`execl()`
			`execle()`
			`execlp()`
			`execlpe()`
			`execv()`
			`execve()`
			`execvp()`
			`execvpe()`

	Overlay/coexist w/parent		`spawnl()`
			`spawnle()`
			`spawnlp()`
			`spawnlpe()`
			`spawnv()`
			`spawnve()`
			`spawnvp()`
			`spawnvpe()`

	Invoke COMMAND.COM	`system()`	

Process Execution	Get the process ID
	Nonlocal branching
	
	Queue functions
	Signal processing
		`longjmp()`
		`setjmp()`
		`atexit()`
		`raise()`
		`signal()`
			`getpid()`
			
			`onexit()`

Process Termination	Normal
	Subnormal
	
	Abnormal
		`exit()`
		
		`abort()`
			
			`_cexit()`
			`_c_exit()`
			`_dos_keep()`
			`_exit()`
			`_assert()`

To invoke the DOS command processor from within a C program, issue a **system()** function call with an argument string that represents any valid DOS command-line entry.

The unique process ID that is assigned to every process by DOS can be retrieved using the **getpid()** function.

All nonlocal (function-to-function) branching is supported by the functions **setjmp()** and **longjmp()**. Nonlocal branching cannot otherwise be performed using the Standard C keywords **break**, **continue**, and **goto**.

To queue (defer) functions for processing when only normal process termination occurs, use either **atexit()** or **onexit()**. Function **atexit()** is preferred because it is now a Standard C function.

Use the **signal()** and **raise()** functions to enable a process to maintain control when an abnormal event occurs. The **SIGABRT** argument handles abnormal termination; **SIGFPE**, floating-point exceptions; and **SIGINT**, Ctrl-Break or Ctrl-C keystrokes.

To ensure that all normal termination tasks are performed, use the **exit()** function. Other subnormal process termination modes perform a subset of the tasks performed by **exit()**, and include **_exit()**, **_cexit()**, **_c_exit**, and **_dos_keep()**. Function **_dos_keep()** is unique in that it is used to install TSR (Terminate Stay Resident/Ready) programs (see Chapter 27).

Abnormal program termination is initiated by function calls either to **abort()** or **_assert()**. The function-like macro **assert()** is normally used in place of run-time function **_assert()**.

RUN-TIME LIBRARY FUNCTIONS FOR PROCESS CONTROL

abort () *Abort the current process and return an error code*

Compatibility ■ANSI ■OS/2 ■UNIX ■XENIX

See Also

```
_assert(), exit(), _exit()
```

Specification

```
#include <stdlib.h> or <process.h>
void abort(void);
```

Example

```
/* FILE: ch25e1.c */
```

```
#include <conio.h>
#include <io.h>
#include <stdlib.h>
#include <signal.h>

static int event;

static void my_abort(int sig)
{
cprintf("\n\rmy_abort action/message #%1d", ++event);
}

int main(void)
{
dup2(1,2);
signal(SIGABRT, my_abort);
raise(SIGABRT);

signal(SIGABRT, my_abort);
raise(SIGABRT);

signal(SIGABRT, my_abort);
abort();
}
```

Output

```
my_abort action/message #1
my_abort action/message #2
abnormal program termination
my_abort action/message #3
```

Comments This function performs no normal termination procedures (flushing buffers, closing files, **atexit()/onexit()** processing); instead, **raise (SIGABRT)** is called, a standard message is displayed to **stderr**, and an exit status code of <3> is returned to DOS (see Table 15.1).

In the example, the **abort()** function displays the standard **abort()** message *abnormal program termination,* then, when **raise (SIGABRT)** is issued, **my_abort()** is performed, and finally the program is terminated with an exit status code of <3>.

Recall that exit status codes can be interrogated within DOS batch (.BAT) files by using the IF ERRORLEVEL command (see Chapter 15).

Refer to the **signal()** and **raise()** entries in this chapter for an explanation of their proper use for "trapping" **SIGABRT**.

_assert ()   *Display an error message and* abort () *the current process*

Compatibility   ☐ANSI   ■OS/2   ☐UNIX   ☐XENIX

See Also

```
abort(), exit(), _exit()
```

Specification

```
#include <assert.h>
#include <stdio.h>
void _assert(void *expr, void *file, unsigned int line);
```

Arguments

expr: A pointer to the expression used as the argument to the assertion macro, or any descriptive string.

file: The name of the current source code file in which the assertion macro failed; normally the Standard C predefined macro **__FILE__**, or any descriptive string.

line: The line number within the file of the assertion statement that failed; normally the Standard C predefined macro **__LINE__**, or any unsigned integer value.

Example

```
/* FILE: ch25e2.c */
#include <stdio.h>
#include <io.h>
#include <string.h>
#include <assert.h>

int main(void)
{
int i;
char string[] = "sample string";

dup2(1,2);
printf("\n");
for (i=0; i<25; i++) {
    if (i > strlen(string)) _assert("index out-of-bounds",
        __FILE__, __LINE__);
    printf("%c", string[i]);
    }
}
```

Output

```
Assertion failed: index out-of-bounds, file ch25e2.c, line 16
abnormal program termination
```

Comments   The **_assert()** function is used to implement the **assert()** function-like macro, defined in **<assert.h>** and discussed in Chapter 29.

The format of the **_assert()** error message takes the following form: *Assertion failed: expression, file filename, line linenumber.*

In the example program above, the run-time function is called, not the function-like macro; normally the macro is used.

Notice that both assertion formats invoke the **abort()** function, which displays the **stderr** message *abnormal program termination.*

atexit() *Queue a function pointer for processing upon normal program termination*

Compatibility ■ANSI ■OS/2 □UNIX □XENIX

See Also

```
onexit()
```

Specification

```
#include <stdlib.h>
int atexit(void (*func)(void));
```

Arguments

func: A pointer to a function having no arguments and no return value; no other **func** pointer type is supported for use by **atexit()**.

Return Value

Zero (0) if successful

Otherwise, a nonzero value

Example   See also: **_cexit()**, **_exit()**

```
/* FILE: ch25e3.c */
#include <stdio.h>
#include <stdlib.h>
#include <process.h>

static void exit_1(void)
{
printf("\nexit_1 action");
}

static void exit_2(void)
{
printf("\nexit_2 action");
}
```

```
static void exit_3(void)
{
printf("\nexit_3 action");
}

int main(void)
{
int i;
atexit(exit_1);
onexit(exit_2);
atexit(exit_3);
exit(0);
}
```

Output

```
exit_3 action
exit_2 action
exit_1 action
```

Comments   Up to 32 function pointers may be stacked for processing, LIFO (last in, first out) as demonstrated in the example above.

Use of **atexit()** is preferred over **onexit()** because it conforms with Standard C.

atexit() can be used only to schedule function pointers of the type **void (*func)(void)**; no function argument or return value is permitted.

If functions that have argument and return values must be scheduled for termination processing using **atexit()**, include them as function call statements within a function of type **void func(void)**.

_cexit()   *Perform normal termination procedures and return, rather than Terminating a process*

Compatibility   □ ANSI   ■ OS/2   □ UNIX   □ XENIX

See Also

```
_c_exit()
```

Specification

```
#include <process.h>
void _cexit(void);
```

Example

```
/* FILE: ch25e4.c */
#include <stdio.h>
#include <stdlib.h>
#include <process.h>
```

```
static void exit_1(void)
{
printf("\nexit_1 action");
}

static void exit_2(void)
{
printf("\nexit_2 action");
}

int main(void)
{
int i;
atexit(exit_1);
onexit(exit_2);
_cexit();
exit(0);
}
```

Output

```
exit_2 action
exit_1 action
exit_2 action
exit_1 action
```

Comments   **_cexit()** performs the equivalent of **exit(0)** (flush buffers, close files, **atexit()/onexit()** processing), but returns to the caller rather than terminating the process.

The example program above demonstrates that **_cexit()** performs any scheduled **atexit()/onexit()** functions in LIFO order and then returns, whereas **exit(0)** repeats the **atexit()/onexit()** processing and terminates the process (see Table 15.1).

"Quick" tasks, involving floating-point termination, resetting the divide-by-zero (INT 0x00) interrupt vector, and restoring the overlay interrupt vector, are not itemized in Table 15.1, but are performed by all termination functions.

c exit()   *Perform only "quick" termination procedures and return without Terminating the process*

Compatibility   ☐ANSI   ■OS/2   ☐UNIX   ☐XENIX

See Also

```
_cexit()
```

Specification

```
#include <process.h>
void _c_exit(void);
```

Example   See: **_cexit()**.

Comments   **_c_exit()** only performs the "quick" termination procedures that are common to all termination functions. (See Table 15.1.)

Only the "quick" procedures for floating-point termination, resetting the divide by zero (INT 0x00) interrupt vector, and restoring the overlay interrupt vector are performed by all process termination functions.

_dos_keep()   *Installs a TSR program by calling DOS interrupt 0x21, service 0x31 and terminates the calling process*

Compatibility   ☐ANSI   ☐OS/2   ☐UNIX   ☐XENIX

Specification

```
#include <dos.h>
void _dos_keep(unsigned retcode, unsigned memsize);
```

Arguments

retcode: The low-order byte of *retcode* is returned to the parent of the calling process as an exit status code <n>.

memsize: The number of paragraphs (16-byte blocks) allocated for the TSR program; all excess space is returned to DOS.

Example   See the **_enable()** example TSR program in Chapter 27.

Comments   Unlike INT 0x27, **_dos_keep()** permits programs larger than 64KB to remain resident (see Chapter 22).

_dos_keep() performs all **exit()**-like program termination, except that files are not automatically closed and process memory is not released. Explicit closure of files is required.

If floating-point math must be performed within a TSR, use the alternate floating-point library, not the emulation library.

Do not execute programs that call **_dos_keep()** from within the integrated QuickC (QC) or OptimizingC (PWB) environments, or subsequent memory allocation problems will result.

execl*xx* *Functions*   *Load and execute a child process by overlaying the parent process and passing individual command-line arguments*

Compatibility   □ANSI   ■OS/2   ■UNIX   ■XENIX

Specification
```
#include <process.h>
#include <stdlib.h>
#include <errno.h>
int execlxx(const char *cmdname, const char *arg0, ...);
```

Arguments

xx: Omit or **e, p, pe**.

cmdname: Partial or complete pathname of an executable file (.COM or .EXE).

arg0: The first of a variable number of individual command-line arguments to be passed to **cmdname**, which must be terminated by a **NULL** argument value; and for **execle()** and **execlpe()**, followed by an argument that is a pointer to a **NULL**-terminated array of pointers to environment strings (**char **envp** or ***envp[]**).

. . .: A variable number of arguments may follow.

Return Value

execl*xx* functions do not return to the calling process if they are successful

If unsuccessful, a value of (−1) is returned, and the global variable **errno** is set as follows:

E2BIG: Argument list exceeds 127 bytes or environment table exceeds 32KB (see Chapter 1)

EACCES: The specified file has a file sharing or locking violation (see Chapter 16)

EMFILE: Too many files open (20 maximum)

ENOENT: File or path name not found

ENOEXEC: The file specified is not executable

ENOMEM: Insufficient memory available to load/execute the file

Example
```
/* FILE: ch25e5.c */
#include <stdio.h>
#include <stdlib.h>
#include <process.h>
```

```
static void display(char *cpy_argv[], char *cpy_envp[])
{
int i;
for(i=0; cpy_argv[i]; i++) printf("\nargv[%1d]=%s", i, cpy_argv[i]);
for(i=0; cpy_envp[i]; i++) printf("\nenvp[%1d]=%s", i, cpy_envp[i]);
printf("\n");
}

static char *arg[] = { "ch25e5", "val-1", "val-2", "val-3", "val-4" };
static char *my_envp[] = { "COMSPEC=C:\\COMMAND.COM", "PROMPT=$P$G",
    "PATH=C:\\", NULL, NULL };

int main(int argc, char *argv[], char *envp[])
{
char *envp_var, *program = arg[0];
int sw_flag;

envp_var = getenv("FLAG");
if (!envp_var) sw_flag = 0;
else sw_flag = atoi(envp_var) + 1;

switch (sw_flag) {
    case 0: printf("\nSetting-up execution of execl functions");
        display(argv, envp);
        putenv("FLAG=0");
        my_envp[3]="FLAG=0";
        execl(program, arg[0], arg[1], NULL);
    case 1: printf("\nExecuting execl()");
        display(argv, envp);
        putenv("FLAG=1");
        my_envp[3]="FLAG=1";
        execle(program, arg[0], arg[1], arg[2], NULL, my_envp);
    case 2: printf("\nExecuting execle()");
        display(argv, envp);
        putenv("FLAG=2");
        my_envp[3]="FLAG=2";
        execlp(program, arg[0], arg[1], arg[2], arg[3], NULL);
    case 3: printf("\nExecuting execlp()");
        display(argv, envp);
        putenv("FLAG=3");
        my_envp[3]="FLAG=3";
        execlpe(program, arg[0], arg[1], arg[2], arg[3],
            arg[4], NULL, my_envp);
    case 4: printf("\nExecuting execlpe()");
        display(argv, envp);
        printf("\nEnding execl function test!");
        break;
    }
exit(0);
}
```

Output

```
Executing execlpe()
argv[0]=ch25e5.exe
argv[1]=val-1
argv[2]=val-2
argv[3]=val-3
argv[4]=val-4
envp[0]=COMSPEC=C:\COMMAND.COM
envp[1]=PROMPT=$P$G
envp[2]=PATH=C:\
envp[3]=FLAG=3

Ending execl function test!
```

Comments   The **execl*xx*** functions differ from the **execv*xx*** functions in that the command-line arguments must be specified individually, rather than being passed as an array of pointers to such strings.

The aggregate size of the command-line argument strings must not exceed 127 characters; and the environment table must not exceed the environment space allocated (see Chapter 1).

In the example program, notice how the custom environment variable **FLAG** is used to control the successive execution of the **ch25e5.exe** program.

Notice that **break** statements have been omitted within the **switch** statement to emphasize that normally **execl*xx*** functions do not return. In practice, it is recommended that the return value of the **execx*xx*** function be tested in case the function call itself is unsuccessful.

The partial program output shown displays the values of all command-line arguments and environment strings passed to the **execl*xx*** function noted.

As an alternative to these functions use the **spawnl*xx*()** functions with a mode of **P_OVERLAY**.

execl ()   *Load and execute a child process, passing individual command-line arguments*

See Also

```
execlxx functions
```

Specification

```
#include <process>
#include <stdlib.h>
#include <errno.h>
int execl(const char *cmdname, const char *arg0, ...)
```

execle ()   *Load and execute a child process, passing command-line arguments individually and an array of pointers to environment variables*

See Also

```
execlxx functions
```

Specification

```
#include <process.h>
#include <stdlib.h>
#include <errno.h>
int execle(const char *cmdname, const char *arg0, ...);
```

execlp ()   *Load and execute a child process, passing command-line arguments individually, using the environment variable* PATH *to locate the program*

See Also

```
execlxx functions
```

Specification

```
#include <process.h>
#include <stdlib.h>
#include <errno.h>
int execlp(const char *cmdname, const char *arg0, ...);
```

execlpe ()   *Load and execute a child process, passing command-line arguments individually, and an array of pointers to environment variables, using the environment variable* PATH *to locate the program*

See Also

```
execlxx functions
```

Specification

```
#include <process.h>
#include <stdlib.h>
#include <errno.h>
int execlpe(const char *cmdname, const char *arg0, ...);
```

execv*xx* *Functions*   *Load and execute a child process by overlaying the parent process and passing command-line arguments as an array of pointers*

Compatibility   ☐ ANSI   ■ OS/2   ■ UNIX   ■ XENIX

Specification

```
#include <process.h>
#include <stdlib.h>
#include <errno.h>
int execvxx(const char *cmdname, const char * const *argv, ...);
```

Arguments

xx: Omit, or **e**, **p**, **pe**.

cmdname: Partial or complete pathname of an executable file (.COM or .EXE).

argv: A **NULL**-terminated array of pointers to the command-line argument strings (**char **argv** or ***argv[]**).

envp: A **NULL**-terminated array of pointers to environment strings (**char **envp** or ***envp[]**)

. . .: A variable number of arguments may follow.

Return Value

execvxx functions do not return to the calling process if they are successful

If unsuccessful, a value of −1 is returned, and the global variable **errno** is set as follows:

E2BIG: Argument list exceeds 127 bytes or environment table exceeds 32KB (see Chapter 1)

EACCES: The specified file has a file-sharing or locking violation (see Chapter 16)

EMFILE: Too many files open (20 maximum)

ENOENT: File or path name not found

ENOEXEC: The file specified is not executable

ENOMEM: Insufficient memory available to load/execute the file

Example

```
/* FILE: ch25e6.c */
#include <stdio.h>
#include <stdlib.h>
#include <process.h>

static void display(char *cpy_argv[], char *cpy_envp[])
{
int i;
for(i=0; cpy_argv[i]; i++) printf("\nargv[%1d]=%s", i, cpy_argv[i]);
for(i=0; cpy_envp[i]; i++) printf("\nenvp[%1d]=%s", i, cpy_envp[i]);
printf("\n");
}
```

```
static char *arg[] = { "ch25e6", "val-1", "val-2",
    "val-3", "val-4", NULL };
static char *my_envp[] = { "COMSPEC=C:\\COMMAND.COM", "PROMPT=$P$G",
    "PATH=C:\\", NULL, NULL };

int main(int argc, char *argv[], char *envp[])
{
char *envp_var, *program = arg[0];
int sw_flag;

envp_var = getenv("FLAG");
if (!envp_var)  sw_flag = 0;
else sw_flag = atoi(envp_var) + 1;
switch (sw_flag) {
    case 0: printf("\nSetting-up execution of execv functions");
        display(argv, envp);
        putenv("FLAG=0");
        my_envp[3]="FLAG=0";
        arg[2] = NULL;
        execv(program, arg);
    case 1: printf("\nExecuting execv()");
        display(argv, envp);
        putenv("FLAG=1");
        my_envp[3]="FLAG=1";
        arg[2] = "val-2";
        arg[3] = NULL;
        execve(program, arg, my_envp);
    case 2: printf("\nExecuting execve()");
        display(argv, envp);
        putenv("FLAG=2");
        my_envp[3]="FLAG=2";
        arg[3] = "val-3";
        arg[4] = NULL;
        execvp(program, arg);
    case 3: printf("\nExecuting execvp()");
        display(argv, envp);
        putenv("FLAG=3");
        my_envp[3]="FLAG=3";
        arg[4] = "val-4";
        arg[5] = NULL;
        execvpe(program, arg, my_envp);
    case 4: printf("\nExecuting execvpe()");
        display(argv, envp);
        printf("\nEnding execv function test!");
        break;
    }
exit(0);
}
```

Output

```
      .
      .
Executing execvpe()
argv[0]=ch25e6.exe
argv[1]=val-1
argv[2]=val-2
argv[3]=val-3
argv[4]=val-4
envp[0]=COMSPEC=C:\COMMAND.COM
envp[1]=PROMPT=$P$G
envp[2]=PATH=C:\
envp[3]=FLAG=3

Ending execv function test!
```

Comments   The **execvxx** functions differ from the **execlxx** functions in that the command-line arguments are specified as an array of pointers to strings, rather than individually with a terminating **NULL** entry.

The aggregate size of the command-line argument strings must not exceed 127 characters, and the environment strings must not exceed the environment space allocated (see Chapter 1).

In the example program, notice how the custom environment variable **FLAG** is used to control the successive execution of the **ch25e6.exe** program.

Notice that **break** statements have been omitted within the **switch** statement to emphasize that normally **execvxx** functions do not return. In practice, it is recommended that the return value of the **execxxx** function be tested in case the function call itself is unsuccessful.

The partial program output shown displays the values of all command-line arguments and environment strings passed to the **execvxx** function noted.

As an alternative to these functions, use the **spawnvxx** functions with a mode of **P_OVERLAY**.

execv()   *Load and execute a child process, passing command-line arguments as an array of pointers*

See Also

```
execvxx functions
```

Specification

```
#include <process.h>
#include <stdlib.h>
#include <errno.h>
int execv(const char *cmdname, const char * const *argv);
```

execve ( ) *Load and execute a child process, passing command-line arguments as an array of pointers and an array of pointers to environment variables*

See Also

```
execvxx functions
```

Specification

```
#include <process.h>
#include <stdlib.h>
#include <errno.h>
int execve(const char *cmdname, const char * const *argv,
       const char * const *envp);
```

execvp ( ) *Load and execute a child process, passing command-line arguments as an array of pointers, using the environment variable PATH to locate the program*

See Also

```
execvxx functions
```

Specification

```
#include <process.h>
#include <stdlib.h>
#include <errno.h>
int execvp(const char *cmdname, const char * const *argv);
```

execvpe ( ) *Load and execute a child process, passing command-line arguments as an array of pointers and an array of pointers to environment variables, using the environment variable PATH to locate the program*

See Also

```
execvxx functions
```

Specification

```
#include <process.h>
#include <stdlib.h>
#include <errno.h>
int execvpe(const char *cmdname, const char * const *argv,
       const char * const *envp);
```

`exit ()`   *Perform normal termination operations, terminate the process, and return an exit status code*

Compatibility   ■ANSI   ■OS/2   ■UNIX   ■XENIX

Specification

```
#include <stdlib.h> or <process.h>
void exit(int status);
```

Arguments

status: The low-order byte is returned to the calling process as a status code; normally zero indicates a normal exit, while a nonzero value indicates an error condition.

Example   Most program examples throughout this book

Comments   `exit()` performs all normal C library termination procedures (flush buffers, close files, `atexit/onexit` processing), terminates the process, and returns an exit status code to DOS. (See Table 15.1.)

The "quick" tasks involving floating-point termination, resetting the divide by zero (INT 0x00) interrupt vector, and restoring the overlay interrupt vector are performed by all termination functions.

`_exit ()`   *Terminate the process and return an exit status code without performing normal termination operations*

Compatibility   □ANSI   ■OS/2   □UNIX   □XENIX

See Also

`exit()`

Specification

```
#include <process.h>
void _exit(int status);
```

Arguments

status: The low-order byte is returned to the calling process as a status code; normally zero indicates a normal exit, while a nonzero value indicates an error condition.

Example

```
/* FILE: ch25e7.c */
#include <stdio.h>
#include <stdlib.h>
#include <process.h>

static void exit_1(void)
{
printf("\nexit_1 action");
}

static void exit_2(void)
{
printf("\nexit_2 action");
}

int main(void)
{
int i;
atexit(exit_1);
onexit(exit_2);
_exit(0);
}
```

Comments **_exit()** performs no normal C library-termination procedures (flush buffers, close files, atexit/onexit processing), terminates the process, and returns an exit status code to DOS. (See Table 15.1.)

The example program produces no output because **_exit()** does not perform **atexit()/onexit()** termination-processing.

The "quick" tasks involving floating-point termination, resetting the divide by zero (INT 0x00) interrupt vector, and restoring the overlay interrupt vector, are performed by all termination functions.

getenv()   *Get the string value of a variable in an environment table*

Compatibility   ■ANSI   ■OS/2   ■UNIX   ■XENIX

Specification

```
#include <stdlib.h>
char *getenv(const char *varname);
```

Arguments

varname: The case-sensitive name of any environment table variable entry, for example, "PATH", "LIB" (see Chapter 1, Table 1.9).

Return Value

If **varname** does not exist, a **NULL** pointer

Otherwise, a pointer to its corresponding assigned string value

Example   See the programs in the "Accessing the Environment Table" section of Chapter 15.

Comments   Use **getenv()** and **putenv()** to maintain the environment table variables for a process. These functions will always ensure that the environment table entries are always current, even if the environment table must be relocated in memory to accommodate any table editing activity that has taken place. Refer to the discussion in Chapter 15.

getpid()   *Get the process ID of the calling (parent) process*

Compatibility   □ANSI   ■OS/2   ■UNIX   ■XENIX

Specification

```
#include <process.h>
int getpid(void);
```

Return Value

A unique integer-type process identifier

No error return codes

Example   See the "**spawnl**xx functions" entry.

Comments   When **spawn**xxx**()** is used, the process ID (PID) is always that of the parent or calling process.

longjmp()   *Perform a nonlocal jump to a prior stack and processor state preserved by setjmp()*

Compatibility   ■ANSI   ■OS/2   ■UNIX   ■XENIX

See Also

```
setjmp()
```

Specification

```
#include <setjmp.h>
void longjmp(jmp_buf env, int value);
```

Arguments

env: A **jmp_buf** type variable that contains a processor "state" that was saved earlier by a call to function **setjmp()**. See Chapter 6, **<setjmp.h>**.

value: A nonzero value to be returned to **setjmp()**

Example   See: **setjmp()**.

Comments   **longjmp()** restores the register settings found in **jmp_buf env**, and readjusts the stack so that program control passes to the statement following the corresponding **setjmp()** statement that created **jmp_buf env**; refer to the comments for function **setjmp()**.

onexit()   *Queue a function pointer for processing upon normal program termination*

Compatibility   ☐ANSI   ■OS/2   ■UNIX   ■XENIX

See Also

```
atexit()
```

Specification

```
#include <stdlib.h>
onexit_t onexit(onexit_t func);
```

Arguments

func: A pointer to a function having no arguments and no return value; no other **func** pointer type is supported for use by **onexit()**.

Return Value

If unsuccessful, a **NULL** pointer

Otherwise the function pointer described by **func**

Example   See: **atexit()**, **_cexit()**, and **_exit()**.

Comments   Up to 32 function pointers may be stacked for processing. As demonstrated in the examples, the order is last in, first out (LIFO).

Use of **atexit()** is preferred over **onexit()** because it conforms with Standard C.

onexit() can only be used to queue function pointers of the type **onexit_t**, a **typedef** for **int (*func)(void)**; no function argument is permitted.

If functions that have arguments and return values must be scheduled for termination processing using **onexit()**, include them as function call statements within a function of type **onexit_t** defined in **<stdlib.h>**.

putenv()   *Create or update a variable in an environment table*

Compatibility   □ ANSI   ■ OS/2   ■ UNIX   ■ XENIX

Specification

```
#include <stdlib.h>
int putenv(const char *envstring);
```

Arguments

envstring: Any environment string conforming to the syntax described by **varname=string**, as discussed in Chapter 1 (Table 1.9) for the SET command; may add or change an environment table entry.

Return Value

Zero (0) if successful

Otherwise −1, indicating an error condition

Example

See the **execlxx**, **execvxx**, **spawnlxx**, and **spawnvxx** functions.

Comments

putenv() alters only the environment table of the current process (**_psp** offset 0x2C–0x2D), which may subsequently be passed to a child process created using an **execxxx**, **spawnxxx**, or **system()** function.

getenv() and **putenv()** alter the global variable **environ** (see Chapter 15 or Appendix C), not the **main()** formal argument ***envp[]**. Refer to the comments for **getenv()**.

raise() *Send a signal to the active process (program)*

Compatibility
■ANSI   ■OS/2   ■UNIX   ■XENIX

Specification
```
#include <signal.h>
int raise(int sig);
```

Arguments
sig: The signal to be raised; if **signal(sig)** has been called, the signal interrupt handler is processed; otherwise, the default signal handling actions are taken. Only the following object-like macros defined in **<signal.h>** are supported by DOS:

SIGABRT: Abnormal termination.

SIGFPE: Floating-point exception (see Chapter 23).

SIGINT: Ctrl-Break or Ctrl-C (see Chapter 27).

Return Value
Zero (0) if successful

Otherwise a nonzero value

Example   See: **abort()**.

Comments   Unless the **signal()** function has been called to install a custom signal handling function, raising the following signals generates the default actions shown:

SIGABRT: Terminate process exit code <3>

SIGFPE: Terminate the process

SIGINT: Issue an INT 0x23

Note in the **abort()** example that the **signal()** function is called to invoke the custom signal-handler **my_abort()** repeatedly, because the default actions are assumed once a **raise()** function is called for that signal.

As an alternative, issue a software interrupt (refer to Chapters 22, 23, and 27).

setjmp() *Preserve the current stack and processor state for a subsequent nonlocal jump by* longjmp()

Compatibility   ■ANSI   ■OS/2   ■UNIX   ■XENIX

Specification

```
#include <setjmp.h>
int setjmp(jmp_buf env);
```

Arguments

env: A **jmp_buf**-type variable that contains the current processor "state"; it establishes a pseudo-label that subsequently can be returned to from anywhere within the program environment by using a corresponding **longjmp()** function call.

Return Value

Zero upon saving the stack and processor "state" in a **jum_buf**-type buffer

Otherwise, a nonzero value that represents the **value** argument of function **longjmp()**

Example

```
/* FILE: ch25e8.c */
#include <stdio.h>
#include <stdlib.h>
#include <setjmp.h>

static jmp_buf jbuf0, jbuf1, jbuf2, jbuf3;

static void fn_1(void)
{
if (setjmp(jbuf1)) {
    printf("\nlongjmp() to fn_1");
    longjmp(jbuf0, 1);
    }
printf("\nnormal fn_1() call");
}

static void fn_2(void)
{
if (setjmp(jbuf2)) {
    printf("\nlongjmp() to fn_2");
    longjmp(jbuf1, 1);
    }
printf("\nnormal fn_2() call");
}

static void fn_3(void)
{
if (setjmp(jbuf3)) {
    printf("\nlongjmp() to fn_3");
    longjmp(jbuf2, 1);
    }
```

```
    printf("\nnormal fn_3() call");
    longjmp(jbuf3, 1);
    }

int main(void)
{
if (setjmp(jbuf0)) {
    printf("\nlongjmp() to main()");
    exit(0);
    }
fn_1();
fn_2();
fn_3();
printf("\nError condition");
}
```

Output

```
normal fn_1() call
normal fn_2() call
normal fn_3() call
longjmp() to fn_3
longjmp() to fn_2
longjmp() to fn_1
longjmp() to main()
```

Comments **setjmp()** marks the location to which a subsequent call to **longjmp()** returns to complete a nonlocal (between function) jump.

Recall that the unconditional **goto** statements can only transfer control to labels within a single function. Whenever branches must occur between functions, **setjmp()** and **longjmp()** are used.

From the example program, it is clear that **setjmp()** and **longjmp()** may be used within the same function (see **jbuf3** in **fn_3()**).

longjmp() functions return nonzero (true) values to the corresponding **setjmp()** function that established the pseudo-label for unconditional branching.

signal() *Install a custom signal handler function*

Compatibility ■ANSI ■OS/2 ■UNIX ■XENIX

Specification

```
#include <signal.h>
void (*signal(int sig, void (*func)(int sig, [int subcode])))
(int sig);
```

Arguments

sig: The identifier of the signal to be handled by custom interrupt function **func**; only the following object-like macros defined in **<signal.h>** are supported for use by DOS:

SIGABRT: Abnormal termination.

SIGFPE: Floating-point exception (see Chapter 23).

SIGINT: Ctrl-Break or Ctrl-C (see Chapter 27).

func: The signal-handling function that is to be installed for **sig**, or one of the following DOS function-like macros:

SIG_DFL: The system default response (equivalent to calling **abort()**).

SIG_IGN: Ignore any subsequent such interrupt signals; do not use with **SIGFPE**.

All signal-handling functions have one argument, **sig**, and return type **void**, except **SIGFPE**, which uses an additional argument, **subcode**.

[subcode]: An optional argument used by **SIGFPE**, the floating-point exception signal (see Chapter 23).

Return Value

If unsuccessful, −1, and **errno** is set to **EINVAL**

Otherwise, the previous function pointer associated with the **sig**

Example   See: **abort()**.

Comments   Unless the **signal()** function has been called to install a custom signal-handling function, raising the following signals generates the default actions shown:

SIGABRT: Terminate process exit code <3>

SIGFPE: Terminate the process

SIGINT: Issue an INT 0x23

Notice in the **abort()** example that the **signal()** function is called to invoke the custom signal-handler **my_abort()** repeatedly, because the default actions are assumed once a **raise()** function is called for that signal.

Because signals represent asynchronous events, the same restrictions apply to the development of signal-handling functions as for Interrupt Service Routines (ISR); see Chapter 27.

Additional discussion and examples of signal handling are provided in Chapter 29.

As an alternative, issue a software interrupt (refer to Chapters 22, 23, and 27).

spawnl*xx* *Functions* *Create, load, and execute a child process by optionally overlaying the parent process and passing individual command-line arguments*

Compatibility □ANSI ■OS/2 □UNIX □XENIX

See Also

execl*xx* Functions

Specification

```
#include <process.h>
#include <stdlib.h>
#include <errno.h>
int spawnlxx(int mode, const char *cmdname, const char *arg0, ...);
```

Arguments

xx: Omit or **e, p, pe**.

mode: One of the following execution modes for the parent (calling) process with DOS:

P_OVERLAY: Same effect as an **execl*xx*** function call; the parent process is overlaid (destroyed) by the child (called) process.

P_WAIT: Suspends the parent process until the execution of the child process is complete and loads the child process in an available portion of memory.

cmdname: Partial or complete pathname of an executable file (.COM or .EXE).

arg0: The first of a variable number of individual command-line arguments to be passed to **cmdname**, which must be terminated by a null argument value; and for **spawnle()** and **spawnlpe()**, followed by an argument that is a **NULL**-terminated array of pointers to environment strings (**char, **envp**, or *****char[]**).

. . . : A variable number of arguments may follow.

Return Value

If the **P_OVERLAY** mode is specified, **spawnl*xx*** functions do not return to the calling process if they are successful

If unsuccessful, a value of −1 is returned, and the global variable **errno** is set as follows:

E2BIG: Argument list exceeds 127 bytes or environment table exceeds 32KB (see Chapter 1)

EACCES: The specified file has a file sharing or locking violation (see Chapter 16)

EMFILE: Too many files open (20 maximum)

ENOENT: File or path name not found

ENOEXEC: The file specified is not executable

ENOMEM: Insufficient memory available to load/execute the file

If the **P_WAIT** mode is specified, **spawnl*xx*** functions return the child process exit status to the calling process

If the child process was successful, a value of zero is returned

Otherwise, a value of (−1) is returned, and the global variable **errno** is set as noted above for **P_OVERLAY**

Example

```
/* FILE: ch25e9.c */
#include <stdio.h>
#include <stdlib.h>
#include <process.h>

static void display(char *cpy_argv[], char *cpy_envp[])
{
int i;
printf("\nParent ProcessID= %d", getpid());
for(i=0; cpy_argv[i]; i++) printf("\nargv[%1d]=%s", i, cpy_argv[i]);
for(i=0; cpy_envp[i]; i++) printf("\nenvp[%1d]=%s", i, cpy_envp[i]);
printf("\n");
}

static char *arg[] = { "ch25e9", "val-1", "val-2", "val-3", "val-4" };
static char *my_envp[] = { "COMSPEC=C:\\COMMAND.COM", "PROMPT=$P$G",
    "PATH=C:\\", NULL, NULL };

int main(int argc, char *argv[], char *envp[])
{
char *envp_var, *program = arg[0];
int sw_flag;

envp_var = getenv("FLAG");
if (!envp_var) sw_flag = 0;
else sw_flag = atoi(envp_var) + 1;

switch (sw_flag) {
    case 0: printf("\nSetting-up execution of spawnl functions");
        display(argv, envp);
        putenv("FLAG=0");
        my_envp[3]="FLAG=0";
        spawnl(P_OVERLAY, program, arg[0], arg[1], NULL);
    case 1: printf("\nExecuting spawnl()");
        display(argv, envp);
        putenv("FLAG=1");
        my_envp[3]="FLAG=1";
```

```
                 spawnle(P_OVERLAY, program, arg[0], arg[1], arg[2],
                     NULL, my_envp);
        case 2: printf("\nExecuting spawnle()");
                display(argv, envp);
                putenv("FLAG=2");
                my_envp[3]="FLAG=2";
                spawnlp(P_OVERLAY, program, arg[0], arg[1], arg[2],
                    arg[3], NULL);
        case 3: printf("\nExecuting spawnlp()");
                display(argv, envp);
                putenv("FLAG=3");
                my_envp[3]="FLAG=3";
                spawnlpe(P_OVERLAY, program, arg[0], arg[1], arg[2],
                    arg[3], arg[4], NULL, my_envp);
        case 4: printf("\nExecuting spawnlpe()");
                display(argv, envp);
                printf("\nEnding spawnl function test!");
                break;
        }
    exit(0);
    }
```

Output

```
        .
        .
Executing spawnlpe()
Parent ProcessID= 2998
argv[0]=ch25e9.exe
argv[1]=val-1
argv[2]=val-2
argv[3]=val-3
argv[4]=val-4
envp[0]=COMSPEC=C:\COMMAND.COM
envp[1]=PROMPT=$P$G
envp[2]=PATH=C:\
envp[3]=FLAG=3

Ending spawnl function test!
```

Comments   The **spawnlxx** functions differ from the **spawnvxx** functions in that the command-line arguments must be specified individually, rather than being passed as an array of pointers to strings.

The aggregate size of the command-line argument strings must not exceed 127 characters; and the environment strings must not exceed the environment space allocated (see Chapter 1).

In the example program, notice how the custom environment variable **FLAG** is used to control the successive execution of the **ch25e9.exe** program.

Notice that **break** statements have been omitted within the switch statement because when the **P_OVERLAY** mode is specified with **spawnlxx** functions, they behave like **execlxx** functions. In practice, it is recommended that the return value of the **spawnxxx** function be tested in case the function call itself is unsuccessful.

The partial program output shown displays the values of all command-line arguments and environment strings passed to the **spawnlxx** function noted.

spawnl ()   *Create, load, and execute a child process, and passing individual command-line arguments*

See Also

spawnlxx Functions

Specification

```
#include <process.h>
#include <stdlib.h>
#include <errno.h>
int spawnl(int mode, const char *cmdname, const char *arg0, ...);
```

spawnle ()   *Create, load and execute a child process, passing command-line arguments individually and an array of pointers to environment variables*

See Also

spawnlxx Functions

Specification

```
#include <process.h>
#include <stdlib.h>
#include <errno.h>
int spawnle(int mode, const char *cmdname, const char *arg0, ...);
```

spawnlp ()   *Create, load, and execute a child process, passing command-line arguments individually, using the environment variable* PATH *to locate the program*

See Also

spawnlxx Functions

Specification

```
#include <process.h>
#include <stdlib.h>
#include <errno.h>
int spawnlp(int mode, const char *cmdname, const char *arg0, ...);
```

spawnlpe () *Create, load, and execute a child process, passing command-line arguments individually and an array of pointers to environment variables, using environment variable* PATH *to locate the program*

See Also

spawnl*xx* Functions

Specification

```
#include <process.h>
#include <stdlib.h>
#include <errno.h>
int spawnlpe(int mode, const char *cmdname, const char *arg0, ...);
```

spawnv*xx Functions* *Create, load, and execute a child process by optionally overlaying the parent process and passing command-line arguments as an array of pointers*

Compatibility　□ANSI　■OS/2　□UNIX　□XENIX

See Also

execv*xx* Functions

Specification

```
#include <process.h>
int spawnvxx(int mode, const char *cmdname, const char * const *argv, ...);
```

Arguments

xx: Omit or **e, p, pe**.

mode: One of the following execution modes for the parent (calling) process with DOS:

> **P_OVERLAY**: Same effect as an **execv*xx*** function call; the parent process is overlaid (destroyed) by the child (called) process.

> **P_WAIT**: Suspends the parent process until the execution of the child process is complete, and loads the child process in an available portion of memory.

cmdname: Partial or complete pathname of an executable file (.COM or .EXE).

argv: A NULL-terminated array of pointers to the command-line argument strings (**char**, ****argv**, or ***argv[]**).

envp: A NULL-terminated array of pointers to environment strings (**char**, ****envp**, or ***envp[]**).

. . .: A variable number of arguments may follow.

Return Value

If the **P_OVERLAY** mode is specified, **spawnvxx** functions do not return to the calling process if they are successful

If unsuccessful, a value of −1 is returned, and the global variable **errno** is set as follows:

E2BIG: Argument list exceeds 127 bytes or environment table exceeds 32KB (see Chapter 1)

EACCES: The specified file has a file sharing or locking violation (see Chapter 16)

EMFILE: Too many files open (20 maximum)

ENOENT: File or path name not found

ENOEXEC: The file specified is not executable

ENOMEM: Insufficient memory available to load/execute the file

If the **P_WAIT** mode is specified, **spawnvxx** functions return the child process exit status to the calling process

If the child process was successful, a value of zero is returned

Otherwise, a value of (−1) is returned, and the global variable **errno** is set as noted above for **P_OVERLAY**

Example

```
/* FILE: ch25e10.c */
#include <stdio.h>
#include <stdlib.h>
#include <process.h>

static void display(char *cpy_argv[], char *cpy_envp[])
{
int i;
for(i=0; cpy_argv[i]; i++) printf("\nargv[%1d]=%s", i, cpy_argv[i]);
for(i=0; cpy_envp[i]; i++) printf("\nenvp[%1d]=%s", i, cpy_envp[i]);
printf("\n");
}

static char *arg[] = {"ch25e10", "val-1", "val-2",
    "val-3", "val-4", NULL};
static char *my_envp[] = {"COMSPEC=C:\\COMMAND.COM", "PROMPT=$P$G",
    "PATH=C:\\", NULL, NULL};
```

```
int main(int argc, char *argv[], char *envp[])
{
char *envp_var, *program = arg[0];
int sw_flag;

envp_var = getenv("FLAG");
if (!envp_var) sw_flag = 0;
else sw_flag = atoi(envp_var) + 1;

switch (sw_flag) {
    case 0: printf("\nSetting-up execution of spawnv functions");
        display(argv, envp);
        putenv("FLAG=0");
        my_envp[3]="FLAG=0";
        arg[2] = NULL;
        spawnv(P_WAIT, program, arg);
        break;
    case 1: printf("\nExecuting spawnv()");
        display(argv, envp);
        putenv("FLAG=1");
        my_envp[3]="FLAG=1";
        arg[2] = "val-2";
        arg[3] = NULL;
        spawnve(P_WAIT, program, arg, my_envp);
        break;
    case 2: printf("\nExecuting spawnve()");
        display(argv, envp);
        putenv("FLAG=2");
        my_envp[3]="FLAG=2";
        arg[3] = "val-3";
        arg[4] = NULL;
        spawnvp(P_WAIT, program, arg);
        break;
    case 3: printf("\nExecuting spawnvp()");
        display(argv, envp);
        putenv("FLAG=3");
        my_envp[3]="FLAG=3";
        arg[4] = "val-4";
        arg[5] = NULL;
        spawnvpe(P_WAIT, program, arg, my_envp);
        break;
    case 4: printf("\nExecuting spawnvpe()");
        display(argv, envp);
        printf("\nEnding spawnv function test!");
        break;
    }
exit(0);
}
```

Output

```
.
.
Executing spawnvpe()
argv[0]=ch25e10.exe
argv[1]=val-1
argv[2]=val-2
argv[3]=val-3
argv[4]=val-4
envp[0]=COMSPEC=C:\COMMAND.COM
envp[1]=PROMPT=$P$G
envp[2]=PATH=C:\
envp[3]=FLAG=3

Ending spawnv function test!
```

Comments   The **spawnvxx** functions differ from the **spawnlxx** functions in that the command-line arguments are passed as an array of pointers to strings rather than being specified individually.

The aggregate size of the command-line argument strings must not exceed 127 characters; and the environment strings must not exceed the environment space allocated (see Chapter 1).

In the example program, notice how the custom environment variable **FLAG** is used to control the successive execution of the **ch25e10.exe** program.

Notice that **break** statements have necessarily been included within the **switch** statement because when the **P_WAIT** mode is specified with **spawnvxx** functions, they return to the calling process.

The partial program output shown displays the values of all command-line arguments and environment strings passed to the **spawnvxx** function noted.

spawnv ()   *Create, load, and execute a child process, and passing command-line arguments as an array of pointers*

See Also

spawnvxx Functions

Specification

```
#include <process.h>
#include <stdlib.h>
#include <errno.h>
int spawnv (int mode, const char *cmdname, const char * const *argv,
```

spawnve ()   *Create, load, and execute a child process, passing command-line arguments as an array of pointers, and an array of pointers to environment variables*

See Also

spawnv*xx* Functions

Specification

```
#include <process.h>
#include <stdlib.h>
#include <errno.h>
int spawnve (int mode, const char *cmdname, const char * const *argv,
       const char * const *envp);
```

spawnvp ()   *Create, load, and execute a child process, passing command-line arguments as an array of pointers, using the environment variable PATH to locate the program*

See Also

spawnv*xx* Functions

Specification

```
#include <process.h>
#include <stdlib.h>
#include <errno.h>
int spawnvp (int mode, const char *cmdname, const char * const *argv);
```

spawnvpe ()   *Create, load, and execute a child process passing command-line arguments as an array of pointers, and an array of pointers to environment variables, using the environment variable PATH to locate the program*

See Also

spawnv*xx* Functions

Specification

```
#include <process.h>
#include <stdlib.h>
#include <errno.h>
int spawnvpe (int mode, const char *cmdname, const char *
       const *argv, const char * const *envp);
```

system()   *Invoke COMMAND.COM to process a command line*

Compatibility   ■ANSI   ■OS/2   ■UNIX   ■XENIX

Specification

```
#include <stdlib.h> or <process.h>
int system(const char *command);
```

Arguments

command: Any valid DOS command-line entry (see Chapter 1); if **NULL**, then only a test is made whether COMMAND.COM exists.

Return Value

If a **NULL** *command* string was specified, then either true (nonzero; COMMAND.COM exists) or false (0; COMMAND.COM does not exist) is returned

If *command* is not **NULL**, then zero (0) is returned if COMMAND.COM is successfully loaded

Otherwise, a value of −1 is returned and **errno** is set as follows:

E2BIG: Argument list exceeds 127 bytes or environment table exceeds 32KB (see Chapter 1)

EMFILE: Too many files open (20 maximum)

ENOENT: File or path name not found

ENOEXEC: The file specified is not executable

ENOMEM: Insufficient memory available to load/execute the command processor

Example

```
/* FILE: ch25e11.c */
#include <stdio.h>
#include <stdlib.h>
#include <io.h>

char *dos_commands[] = {
    "x.bat",
    "y.com",
    "z.exe",
    NULL };
```

```
int main(void)
{
int i=0;
dup2(1,2);
while (dos_commands[i]) system(dos_commands[i++]);
exit(0);
}
```

Output

```
Bad command or file name
Bad command or file name
Bad command or file name
```

Comments   The **system()** function accepts any internal DOS command, executable file (.COM or .EXE), or batch file (.BAT), together with redirection and piping, just as if entered at the DOS command line.

    In the example above, the standard DOS command processor response *Bad command or file name* was generated by the three commands that were processed.

String-Handling Functions

String-Handling Functions

███████████ Since strings are not a fundamental data type in the C language, none of the C operators are designed to handle the manipulation of string objects. Instead, all such operations, even the common concatenation operation, must be accomplished using functions from the C run-time library. This chapter discusses all of the Microsoft C string-handling functions, exclusive of any I/O operations which are discussed in Part VI, Chapters 16-19, and the conversion between strings and other fundamental types, which is covered in Chapter 20.

As discussed in Chapter 8, a string represents a subset of an array of type **char** (character), which by convention is terminated with a null (`'\0'`) character. The length of a string is understood to represent the number of characters up to, but exclusive of, the first null character. Because strings are represented as arrays, when strings are passed as function arguments, they must be passed as a pointer to a character, since arrays are never passed as function arguments in C. Given the address (pointer) of a **char** type object, a string is then implied to consist of all consecutive bytes (ascending addresses) thereafter, until the first null (`'\0'`) character is encountered. Therefore, care must be taken to ensure that the terminating null character of a string is not inadvertently overwritten with a non-null value.

By default, the ASCII character set is used for representing strings in C; however, with the impending implementation of locales and multibyte character sets into Microsoft C, other character sets and, hence, collating sequences are possible (see Chapter 27). Presently, only the "C" locale is available for use, and in fact represents the default locale, upon which all string-I/O, data-conversion, and string-handling functions are dependent. As other locales are made available and, eventually, when multibyte character sets are supported by Microsoft C, greater care will need to be taken when working with strings in the C language; but for now, "a string is a string is a string."

The most noticeable enhancement to the run-time library with OptimizingC version 6.0 and QuickC version 2.5 is the newly introduced **_fxx** family of functions. The **_fxx** functions represent *memory-model independent versions* of those string-handling functions traditionally provided in Microsoft's run-time library. These functions are useful with mixed-memory-model programming, in which both **_near** and **_far** pointers are employed. Because the prototypes of the **_fxx** functions always utilize **_far** pointers, they are compatible for use with any memory model selected for use.

For example, if the Small memory model is selected and **_far** pointers are used as function arguments with traditional string-handling functions, the segment address component is truncated, and the default data segment (DS) is assumed. Obviously this produces incorrect program results. By using the new **_fxx** versions of the run-time string handling functions, **_far** pointer arguments are always passed, which supports the use of both **_near** and **_far** pointers as function arguments. Any **_near** pointers are cast to **_far** pointers thereby preserving the implied DS segment address component, while all **_far** pointers are preserved intact.

If you know the string-handling operation you want to perform, let Table 26.1 help you select which run-time function is available and best suited for that purpose.

Never forget that because string-handling functions always work with pointers as arguments and not copies of the strings themselves, the rules

TABLE 26.1: String-Handling Tasks

TASK	FUNCTION	
	STANDARD C ■ ANSI	MICROSOFT C ☐ ANSI
Append	`strcat()`	`_fstrcat()`
	`strncat()`	`_fstrncat()`
Compare (case-insensitive)		`_fstricmp()`
		`_fstrnicmp()`
		`strcmpi()`
		`stricmp()`
		`strnicmp()`
Compare (case-sensitive)	`strcmp()`	`_fstrcmp()`
	`strcoll()`	`_fstrncmp()`
	`strncmp()`	
Construct an error message	`strerror()`	`_strerror()`
Copy	`strcpy()`	`_fstrcpy()`
	`strncpy()`	`_fstrncpy()`
Duplicate		`_fstrdup()`
		`_nstrdup()`
		`strdup()`

TABLE 26.1: String-Handling Tasks (continued)

TASK	FUNCTION	
	STANDARD C ■ ANSI	MICROSOFT C ☐ ANSI
Find (character)	`strchr()`	`_fstrchr()`
	`strpbrk()`	`_fstrpbrk()`
	`strrchr()`	`_fstrrchr()`
Find (substring)	`strcspn()`	`_fstrcspn()`
	`strspn()`	`_fstrspn()`
	`strstr()`	`_fstrstr()`
Find (token)	`strtok()`	`_fstrtok()`
Initialize		`_fstrnset()`
		`_fstrset()`
		`strnset()`
		`strset()`
Length of	`strlen()`	`_fstrlen()`
Transform	`strxfrm()`	`_fstrlwr()`
		`_fstrrev()`
		`_fstrupr()`
		`strlwr()`
		`strrev()`
		`strupr()`

of address arithmetic apply—no array and, therefore string, bounds-checking is enforced! Be certain that sufficient space has been allocated to contain the result of the selected string-handling task; otherwise, memory addresses will be overwritten, and thus corrupted.

STRING-HANDLING TASKS

To append a string implies the nondestructive addition of characters to a string. If **strcat()** or **_fstrcat()** is used, all the characters of one string are added to the end of another, thereby creating a new string that equals the sum of the lengths of the initial strings. Use function **strncat()** or **_fstrncat()** to append a fixed number of characters to a string, not another entire string of characters.

String comparison functions must be chosen based upon whether case-sensitive or insensitive results are desired. Case sensitivity applies only to the alphabetic characters [a-z, A-Z]. For case-sensitive comparisons of entire strings, use **strcmp()** or **_fstrcmp()**; for a designated number of string characters, use **strncmp()** or **_fstrncmp()**; and for a locale-specific string comparison, use **strcoll()**. For case-insensitive comparisons of entire strings, use **strcmpi()**, **stricmp()**, or **_fstricmp()**; for a designated number of string characters, use **strnicmp()** or **_fstrnicmp()**. String comparisons by these functions all yield an integer result that represents the first character comparison value difference. For example, if **string1** were "catch" and **string2** were "category," and a case-sensitive comparison function was used, a return value of −2 would result, indicating that **string1** was lexicographically less than **string2**. This difference reflects that the fourth characters of these strings ('c' versus 'e') differ by their ASCII character equivalents (99–101 = −2). All characters up to and including the null character of the shorter string are compared if they are of unequal length. In this case, since the null character always has an ASCII codeset value of zero, string comparison functions always return another signed ASCII codeset value.

Error display messages can be constructed using **strerror()** and **_strerror()**; however, such messages are not automatically displayed. Function **perror()**, described in Chapter 17, uses function **_strerror()** and automatically displays the message to the standard error output stream, **stderr**.

String copying implies the duplication of all string characters, but does not provide for the automatic allocation of storage space. Use **strcpy()** or **_fstrcpy()** for a complete string copy including the terminating null, and use either **strncpy()** or **_fstrncpy()** to copy a portion of a string. With **strncpy()** and **_fstrncpy()**, if the number of characters specified exceeds the length of the string, null characters are padded to the number of characters specified.

String duplication combines string memory allocation with a string copy operation. The function chosen controls which heap (Near or Far; see Chapter 2) is used for the storage allocation of the string being duplicated. When **_nstrdup()** is used, allocation is always made to the Near heap, regardless of the memory model being used; with **_fstrdup()**, the Far heap is always used. When **strdup()** is used, allocation is always made to the heap, and is controlled by the memory model being employed.

To find an individual character in a string, use **strchr()** or **_fstrchr()** to locate the first occurrence of the character; use **strrchr()** or **_fstrrchr()** to locate the last occurrence; and use **strpbrk()** or

_fstrpbrk() to locate the first occurrence of any character found in another string. These functions are all case-sensitive.

Within a larger string, three pairs of case-sensitive functions can be used to locate a substring or a group of characters. They are **strstr()** and **_fstrstr()**, **strcspn()** and **_fstrcspn()**, and **strspn()** and **_fstrspn()**. Their reference entries summarize the different values returned by these functions.

Tokens differ from substrings in that tokens are always separated by a delimiting character, string comparisons are not performed, and tokens never contain other tokens. To strip tokens from a string, use **strtok()** or **_fstrtok()**.

All of the characters of an existing string may be initialized or set to a specific character value by using **strset()** or **_fstrset()**; whereas, a specific number of characters may be initialized using **strnset()** or **_fstrnset()**. Each of these functions replaces the characters of a string up to the first terminating null character encountered.

The length of a string, or the count of characters exclusive of the terminating null, is found using the **strlen()** or **_fstrlen()** functions, not the **sizeof** operator.

The characters of a string, exclusive of the terminating null, may be transformed in several different ways. To convert all characters to lowercase, use either **strlwr()** or **_fstrlwr()**; to uppercase, use **strupr()** or **_fstrupr()**; and to transform all characters according to a specified locale (once the new ANSI concept of locale is fully implemented), use **strxfrm()**. To reverse the characters within a string, use either **strrev()** or **_fstrrev()**.

RUN-TIME LIBRARY FUNCTIONS FOR STRING-HANDLING

_fstrcat()   *Append a string, memory-model independent*

Compatibility ☐ANSI ■OS/2 ☐UNIX ☐XENIX

See Also

```
strcat()
```

Specification

```
#include <string.h>
char _far * _far _fstrcat(char _far *string1, const char _far *string2);
```

_fstrchr() *Find a character in a string, memory-model independent*

Compatibility ☐ ANSI ■ OS/2 ☐ UNIX ☐ XENIX

See Also

```
strchr()
```

Specification

```
#include <string.h>
char _far * _far _fstrchr(const char _far *string, int c);
```

_fstrcmp() *Case-sensitive string comparison, memory-model independent*

Compatibility ☐ ANSI ■ OS/2 ☐ UNIX ☐ XENIX

See Also

```
strcmp()
```

Specification

```
#include <string.h>
int _far _fstrcmp(const char _far *string1, const char _far *string2);
```

_fstrcpy() *Copy a string, memory-model independent*

Compatibility ☐ ANSI ■ OS/2 ☐ UNIX ☐ XENIX

See Also

```
strcpy()
```

Specification

```
#include <string.h>
char _far * _far _fstrcpy(char _far *string1, const char _far *string2);
```

_fstrcspn() *Find a substring in a string, memory-model independent*

Compatibility ☐ ANSI ■ OS/2 ☐ UNIX ☐ XENIX

See Also

```
strcspn()
```

Specification

```
#include <string.h>
size_t _far _fstrcspn(const char _far *string1, const char _far *string2);
```

_fstrdup() *Duplicate a string using the Far heap, memory-model independent*

Compatibility ☐ANSI ■OS/2 ☐UNIX ☐XENIX

See Also

```
strdup()
```

Specification

```
#include <string.h>
char _far * _far _fstrdup(const char _far *string);
```

_fstricmp() *Case-insensitive string comparison, memory-model independent*

Compatibility ☐ANSI ■OS/2 ☐UNIX ☐XENIX

See Also

```
stricmp()
```

Specification

```
#include <string.h>
int _far _fstricmp(const char _far *string1, const char _far *string2);
```

_fstrlen() *Get the length of a string, exclusive of the terminating null, memory-model independent*

Compatibility ☐ANSI ■OS/2 ☐UNIX ☐XENIX

See Also

```
strlen()
```

Specification

```
#include <string.h>
size_t _far _fstrlen(const char _far *string);
```

_fstrlwr()   *Convert a string to lowercase, memory-model independent*

Compatibility   □ANSI   ■OS/2   □UNIX   □XENIX

See Also

```
strlwr()
```

Specification

```
#include <string.h>
char _far * _far _fstrlwr(char _far *string);
```

_fstrncat()   *Append characters of a string, memory-model independent*

Compatibility   □ANSI   ■OS/2   □UNIX   □XENIX

See Also

```
strncat()
```

Specification

```
#include <string.h>
char _far * _far _fstrncat(char _far *string1, const char _far *string2,
    size_t count);
```

_fstrncmp()   *Case-sensitive comparison of string characters, memory-model independent*

Compatibility   □ANSI   ■OS/2   □UNIX   □XENIX

See Also

```
strncmp()
```

Specification

```
#include <string.h>
int _far _fstrncmp(const char _far *string1, const char _far *string2,
    size_t count);
```

_fstrncpy()   *Copy characters from one string to another, memory-model independent*

Compatibility   □ANSI   ■OS/2   □UNIX   □XENIX

See Also

```
strncpy()
```

Specification

```
#include <string.h>
char _far * _far _fstrncpy(char _far *string1, const char _far *string2,
    size_t count);
```

_fstrnicmp() *Case-insensitive comparison of string characters, memory-model independent*

Compatibility   ☐ ANSI   ■ OS/2   ☐ UNIX   ☐ XENIX

See Also

```
strnicmp()
```

Specification

```
#include <string.h>
int _far _fstrnicmp(const char _far *string1, const char _far *string2,
    size_t count);
```

_fstrnset() *Initialize characters of a string to a given value, memory-model independent*

Compatibility   ☐ ANSI   ■ OS/2   ☐ UNIX   ☐ XENIX

See Also

```
strnset()
```

Specification

```
#include <string.h>
char _far * _far _fstrnset(char _far *string, int c, size_t count);
```

_fstrpbrk() *Scan a string for characters in a set, memory-model independent*

Compatibility   ☐ ANSI   ■ OS/2   ☐ UNIX   ☐ XENIX

See Also

```
strpbrk()
```

Specification

```
#include <string.h>
char _far * _far _fstrpbrk(const char _far *string1, const char _far *string2);
```

`_fstrrchr()`   *Scan a string for the last occurrence of a character, memory-model independent*

Compatibility   ☐ ANSI   ■ OS/2   ☐ UNIX   ☐ XENIX

See Also

```
strrchr()
```

Specification

```
#include <string.h>
char _far * _far _fstrrchr(const char _far *string, int c);
```

`_fstrrev()`   *Reverse characters of a string, memory-model independent*

Compatibility   ☐ ANSI   ■ OS/2   ☐ UNIX   ☐ XENIX

See Also

```
strrev()
```

Specification

```
#include <string.h>
char _far * _far _fstrrev(char _far *string);
```

`_fstrset()`   *Set characters of a string to a value, memory-model independent*

Compatibility   ☐ ANSI   ■ OS/2   ☐ UNIX   ☐ XENIX

See Also

```
strset()
```

Specification

```
#include <string.h>
char _far * _far _fstrset(char _far *string, int c);
```

_fstrspn() *Find the first substring, memory-model independent*

Compatibility ☐ANSI ■OS/2 ☐UNIX ☐XENIX

See Also

    strspn()

Specification

    #include <string.h>
    size_t _far _fstrspn(const char _far *string1, const char _far *string2);

_fstrstr() *Find a substring, memory-model independent*

Compatibility ☐ANSI ■OS/2 ☐UNIX ☐XENIX

See Also

    strstr()

Specification

    #include <string.h>
    char _far * _far _fstrstr(const char _far *string1, const char _far *string2);

_fstrtok() *Find the next token in a string, memory-model independent*

Compatibility ☐ANSI ■OS/2 ☐UNIX ☐XENIX

See Also

    strtok()

Specification

    #include <string.h>
    char _far * _far _fstrtok(char _far *string1, const char _far *string2);

_fstrupr() *Convert a string to uppercase, memory-model independent*

Compatibility ☐ANSI ■OS/2 ☐UNIX ☐XENIX

See Also

    strupr()

Specification

```
#include <string.h>
char _far * _far _fstrupr(char _far *string);
```

_nstrdup() *Duplicate a string using the Near heap*

Compatibility   ☐ANSI   ■OS/2   ☐UNIX   ☐XENIX

See Also

```
strdup()
```

Specification

```
#include <string.h>
char _near * _far _nstrdup(const char _far *string);
```

strcat() *Append a string*

Compatibility   ■ANSI   ■OS/2   ■UNIX   ■XENIX

See Also

```
_fstrcat(), strncat()
```

Specification

```
#include <string.h>
char *strcat(char *string1, const char *string2);
```

Arguments

string1: The destination string.

string2: The source string.

Return Value

The destination string

Example

```
/* FILE: ch26e1.c */
/* use the SMALL memory model */
#include <stdio.h>
#include <stdlib.h>
#include <string.h>

static char buffer[0x80];
```

```
static void display(void)
{
printf("\n%4d %4d %-40s", sizeof(buffer), strlen(buffer), buffer);
}

int main(void)
{
char *ptr1 = "SYBEX";
char *ptr2 = "Books";
char *ptr3 = "> <";
display();
strncat(buffer, ptr3, 1);
strcat(buffer, ptr1);
_fstrncat(buffer, ptr3+1, 1);
display();
_fstrcat(buffer, ptr2);
strncat(buffer, ptr3+2, 1);
display();
exit(0);
}
```

Output

```
128     0
128     7   >SYBEX
128    13   >SYBEX Books<
```

Comments   No error conditions are detected; **string1** should be declared large enough to contain the appended string.

Notice that the memory-model independent **_fxx** functions work correctly when the Small memory model is used. The function prototypes included for these functions ensure that each actual argument is cast to the argument type specified by the prototype before it is pushed to the stack (see the "Stack Frames" section in Chapter 15).

As an alternative to calling this function, you can use its **#pragma intrinsic** form.

strchr()   *Find a character in a string*

Compatibility   ■ANSI   ■OS/2   ■UNIX   ■XENIX

See Also

```
_fstrchr(), memchr(), strpbrk(), strrchr()
```

Specification

```
#include <string.h>
char *strchr(const char *string, int c);
```

Arguments

string: String to be searched.

c: Character value to be located in **string**.

Return Value

If unsuccessful, a **NULL** pointer

Otherwise, a pointer to the first occurrence of character **c** in **string**

Example

```
/* FILE: ch26e2.c */
/* use the SMALL memory model */
#include <stdio.h>
#include <stdlib.h>
#include <string.h>

static char buffer[0x80];
static char *ptr1 = "          ";
static char *ptr2 = "1234567890";

static void index(char *ch, char *ptr)
{
if (!ptr) printf("\nNo match for |%s|", ch);
else printf("\nMatch for |%s| at column %-2d", ch, ptr-buffer+1);
}

int main(void)
{
int i, ntimes, pos;
char *ptr, _far *fptr;
char *vowels = "aeiouAEIOU";
char *whitespace = "\n\r\t\v\f ";
while (1) {
    printf("\n\n\nEnter a sentence or END to Quit: ");
    gets(buffer);
    if (!strcmpi(buffer, "END")) break;
    printf("\n\n");
    ntimes = (strlen(buffer) / 10) + 1;
    for (i=0; i<ntimes; i++) printf("%s%1d", ptr1, i+1);
    printf("\n");
    for (i=0; i<ntimes; i++) printf("%s", ptr2);
    printf("\n%s\n", buffer);

    /* find first letter 'a' Left->Right */
    ptr = strchr(buffer, 'a');
    index("a", ptr);
    /* find first letter 'A' Left->Right */
    ptr = _fstrchr(buffer, 'A');
    index("A", ptr);
```

```
    /* find first letter 'a' Right->Left */
    ptr = strrchr(buffer, 'a');
    index("a", ptr);
    /* find first letter 'A' Right->Left */
    ptr = _fstrrchr(buffer, 'A');
    index("A", ptr);

    /* find all vowels */
    ptr = buffer;
    while (1) {
        ptr = strpbrk(ptr, vowels);
        if (!ptr) break;
        index("vowels", ptr);
        ptr++;
        }

    /* find all whitespace characters */
    fptr = buffer;
    while (1) {
        fptr = _fstrpbrk(fptr, whitespace);
        if (!fptr) break;
        index("whitespace", fptr);
        fptr++;
        }
    }
exit(0);
}
```

Output

```
Enter a sentence or END to Quit: A sample sentence

          1         2
12345678901234567890
A sample sentence

Match for |a| at column 4
Match for |A| at column 1
Match for |a| at column 4
Match for |A| at column 1
Match for |vowels| at column 1
Match for |vowels| at column 4
Match for |vowels| at column 8
Match for |vowels| at column 11
Match for |vowels| at column 14
Match for |vowels| at column 17
Match for |whitespace| at column 2
Match for |whitespace| at column 9

Enter a sentence or END to Quit: end
```

Comments   If every occurrence of a character within a string must be found, call `strchr()` successively until a **NULL** pointer value is returned, and redefine the starting address of **string** as the function return value address plus one each time.

`strcmp()`   *Case-sensitive string comparison*

Compatibility   ■ANSI   ■OS/2   ■UNIX   ■XENIX

See Also
`_fstrcmp()`, `memcmp()`, `strcoll()`, `strncmp()`

Specification
```
#include <string.h>
int strcmp(const char *string1, const char *string2);
```

Arguments
string1: String to compare.

string2: String to compare.

Return Value
A signed value that is interpreted as follows:

        <0 **string1** less than **string2**

        =0 **string1** equal to **string2**

        >0 **string1** greater than **string2**

Example
```
/* FILE: ch26e3.c */
/* use the SMALL memory model */
#include <stdio.h>
#include <stdlib.h>
#include <string.h>

static char buf1[20] = "abc123DEF321cba", buf2[20];

static void _display(char *fname, int result)
{
if (result) printf("\n%-20s\"!=\"", fname);
else printf("\n%-20s\"==\"", fname);
}

static void display(void)
{
printf("\n\n%-20s        %-20s", buf1, buf2);
_display(" strcmp()",    strcmp(buf1, buf2));
```

```
    _display("_fstrcmp()",   _fstrcmp(buf1, buf2));
    _display(" strncmp()",    strncmp(buf1, buf2, strlen(buf2)));
    _display("_fstrncmp()", _fstrncmp(buf1, buf2, _fstrlen(buf2)));
    _display(" strcoll()",    strcoll(buf1, buf2));
    printf("\n");
    _display(" stricmp()",    stricmp(buf1, buf2));
    _display("_fstricmp()",  _fstricmp(buf1, buf2));
    _display(" strnicmp()",   strnicmp(buf1, buf2, strlen(buf2)));
    _display("_fstrnicmp()", _fstrnicmp(buf1, buf2, _fstrlen(buf2)));
    _display(" strcmpi()",    strcmpi(buf1, buf2));
    }

int main(void)
{
strcpy(buf2, buf1); display();
strlwr(buf2);       display();
strupr(buf2);       display();
strupr(buf1);       display();
exit(0);
}
```

Output

```
        .
        .
abc123DEF321cba          abc123def321cba
strcmp()          "!="
_fstrcmp()        "!="
strncmp()         "!="
_fstrncmp()       "!="
strcoll()         "!="

stricmp()         "=="
_fstricmp()       "=="
strnicmp()        "=="
_fstrnicmp()      "=="
strcmpi()         "=="
        .
        .
```

Comments   String comparison is performed character by character, including the terminating null, until a character value difference results, which becomes the return value of the function.

If the string lengths being compared differ, the comparison is stopped when the first terminating null character is encountered.

As an alternative to calling this function, you can call its **#pragma intrinsic** form.

`strcmpi()`   *Case-insensitive string comparison*

Compatibility □ANSI   ■OS/2   □UNIX   □XENIX

See Also

```
memicmp(), stricmp(), strnicmp()
```

Specification

```
#include <string.h>
int strcmpi(const char *string1, const char *string2);
```

Arguments

string1: String to compare.

string2: String to compare.

Return Value

A signed value that is interpreted as follows:

<0 **string1** less than **string2**

=0 **string1** equal to **string2**

>0 **string1** greater than **string2**

Example   See: **strcmp()**, **strchr()**, **strcspn()**, **strlwr()**.

Comments   Case-insensitive comparisons compare each alphabetic character array element without regard to whether it is in upper- or lowercase.

There is no "**_fxx**" counterpart function for **strcmpi()**; use **stricmp()** or **_fstricmp()**.

`strcoll()`   *Case-sensitive string comparison using locale-specific information*

Compatibility ■ANSI   ■OS/2   □UNIX   □XENIX

Specification

```
#include <string.h>
int strcoll(const char *string1, const char *string2);
```

Arguments

string1: String to compare.

string2: String to compare.

Return Value

A signed value that is interpreted as follows:

<0 **string1** less than **string2**

=0 **string1** equal to **string2**

>0 **string1** greater than **string2**

Example

See: **strcmp()**.

Comments

Differs from **strcmp()** in that a locale-specific collating sequence is used (see **strxfrm()** and **setlocale()** described in Chapter 27).

Because only one locale ("C") is available for use presently, **strcoll()** produces identical results to that of **strcmp()**.

When other locales become available, the transformation will be controlled by the **LC_COLLATE** component of the designated locale (see Chapter 27).

strcpy() *Copy a string*

Compatibility ■ANSI   ■OS/2   ■UNIX   ■XENIX

See Also

_fstrcpy(), memcpy(), strncpy()

Specification

```
#include <string.h>
char *strcpy(char *string1, const char *string2);
```

Arguments

string1: Destination string.

string2: Source string.

Return Value

Destination string

Example

```
/* FILE: ch26e4.c */
/* use the SMALL memory model */
#include <stdio.h>
#include <stdlib.h>
#include <string.h>

static char buf1[20] = { "this is a test" };
```

```
static void display(char *name, char *ptr, int size)
{
int i;
printf("\n\n%-10s", name);
for (i=0; i<size; i++) printf("%-2c ", ptr[i]);
printf("\n%-10s","");
for (i=0; i<size; i++) printf("%02X ", (unsigned char) ptr[i]);
}

int main(void)
{
char buf2[20];
display("buf1", buf1, sizeof(buf1));
display("buf2", buf2, sizeof(buf2));

strncpy(buf2, buf1, strlen(buf1));
display("buf2", buf2, sizeof(buf2));

strcpy(buf2, buf1);
display("buf2", buf2, sizeof(buf2));

_fstrncpy(buf2, buf1+10, 4);
display("buf2", buf2, sizeof(buf2));

_fstrcpy(buf2, buf1+10);
display("buf2", buf2, sizeof(buf2));
exit(0);
}
```

Output

```
buf1       t  h  i  s     i  s     a     t  e  s  t
           74 68 69 73 20 69 73 20 61 20 74 65 73 74 00 00 00 00 00 00

buf2       t  e                             u
           74 65 EB 13 D3 80 00 00 D9 7F D3 80 75 00 80 00 00 00 A1 00

buf2       t  h  i  s     i  s     a     t  e  s  t
           74 68 69 73 20 69 73 20 61 20 74 65 73 74 80 00 00 00 A1 00
```

.
.

Comments   No error conditions are detected; **string1** therefore should be declared large enough to contain the result.

From the example program it is clear that **strcpy()** differs from **strncpy()** in that the terminating null character is not copied unless the number of characters specified by **strncpy()** is larger than the actual length of **string2**.

As an alternative to calling this function, you can call its **#pragma intrinsic** form.

`strcspn()`   *Find a substring*

Compatibility   ■ANSI   ■OS/2   ■UNIX   ■XENIX

See Also

```
_fstrcspn(), strspn(), strstr()
```

Specification

```
#include <string.h>
size_t strcspn(const char *string1, const char *string2);
```

Arguments

string1: String to search.

string2: Matching set of characters.

Return Value

The index position (0–n) of the first character in **string1**, which belongs to the set of characters defined by **string2**

Equivalent to the length of the initial substring in **string1**, which consists entirely of characters *not* in **string2**

Example

```
/* FILE: ch26e5.c */
/* use the SMALL memory model */
#include <stdio.h>
#include <stdlib.h>
#include <string.h>

static char buffer[0x80];
static char substr[0x80];

int main (void)
{
char *ptr;
int index;
while (1) {
    printf("\n\nEnter a string to search: ");
    gets(buffer);
    if(!strcmpi(buffer,"END")) break;
    printf("\nEnter a substring sequence: ");
    gets(substr);

    index = strcspn(buffer, substr);
    printf("\nstrcspn: %c at %d", buffer[index], index);
    index = strspn(buffer, substr);
    printf("\nstrspn : %c at %d", buffer[index], index);
    if(ptr = strstr(buffer, substr)) printf("\nstrstr : %s", ptr);
```

```
        index = _fstrcspn(buffer, substr);
        printf("\n_fstrcspn: %c at %d", buffer[index], index);
        index = _fstrspn(buffer, substr);
        printf("\n_fstrspn : %c at %d", buffer[index], index);
        if(ptr = _fstrstr(buffer, substr)) printf("\n_fstrstr : %s", ptr);
        }
    exit(0);
    }
```

Output

```
Enter a string to search: This is a sample string
Enter a substring sequence: is
strcspn: i at 2
strspn : T at 0
strstr : is a sample string
_fstrcspn: i at 2
_fstrspn : T at 0
_fstrstr : is a sample string

Enter a string to search: end
```

Comments   The index position values returned originate at zero, representing the first element of the array of characters.

strdup ()   *Duplicate a string*

Compatibility   □ ANSI   ■ OS/2   □ UNIX   □ XENIX

See Also

```
_fstrdup(), memccpy(), memcpy(), memmove(), movedata()
```

Specification

```
#include <string.h>
#include <stdlib.h>
char *strdup(const char *string);
```

Arguments

string: Source string to be duplicated.

Return Value

If unsuccessful, a **NULL** pointer

Otherwise, a pointer to a dynamically allocated (heap) string copy

Example

```
/* FILE: ch26e6.c */
/* use the SMALL memory model */
#include <stdio.h>
#include <stdlib.h>
#include <string.h>

static char buffer[0x0400];

int main(void)
{
char *ptr, _far *fptr;
int i, size;

for (i=0; i<sizeof(buffer); i++) buffer[i] = 'x';
buffer[sizeof(buffer)-1] = '\0';

ptr = strdup(buffer);
printf("\n strdup addr  = %lp  %d",
    (void _far *)ptr, strlen(ptr), ptr);

ptr = _nstrdup(buffer);
printf("\n_nstrdup addr = %lp  %d",
    (void _far *)ptr, strlen(ptr), ptr);

fptr = _fstrdup(buffer);
size = _fstrlen(fptr);
printf("\n_fstrdup addr = %lp  %d", fptr, size);
exit(0);
}
```

Output

```
 strdup addr  = 0E55:128A  1023
_nstrdup addr = 0E55:188E  1023
_fstrdup addr = 1E56:0016  1023
```

Comments The example program output confirms that when either the Tiny, Small, or Medium memory models are employed, **strdup()** and **_nstrdup()** allocate duplicated strings to the Near heap; when the Compact, Large, or Huge memory models are employed, **strdup()** and **_fstrdup()** allocate duplicated strings to the Far heap.

By assuming a maximum offset of 0xFFFF to DS segment 0x0E55, and converting the address values shown into absolute memory addresses, we get an **_fstrdup()** address of 0x1E576, which is greater than 0E55:FFFF (0x1E44F), confirming that **_fstrdup()** has allocated the string to the Far, not the Near, heap.

As an alternative, use a **malloc()** function in concert with **strcpy()**.

strerror() *Get a standard system error message*

Compatibility   ■ANSI   ■OS/2   □UNIX   □XENIX

See Also

_strerror()

Specification

```
#include <string.h>
char *strerror(int errnum);
```

Arguments

errnum: An error number in the range of value from [0] to [sys_nerr-1], where **sys_nerr** is a global variable (see Appendix C).

Return Value

Pointer to an error message string located in array of error messages defined by the global variable **sys_errlist[]** (see Appendix C)

Example

```
/* FILE: ch26e7.c */
/* use the SMALL memory model */
#include <stdio.h>
#include <stdlib.h>
#include <string.h>
#include <math.h>

int main(void)
{
char *ptr;

errno = 0;
acos(2.0);
ptr = strerror(errno);
printf("\n strerror() = %s ", ptr);

errno = 0;
acos(2.0);
ptr = _strerror("custom message ");
printf("\n_strerror() = %s ", ptr);
exit(0);
}
```

Output

```
 strerror() = Math argument
_strerror() = custom message : Math argument
```

Comments Notice that since error messages are dependent upon the value of global variable **errno**, care must be taken to ensure that **errno** is current when **strerror()** is invoked.

In the example, the math function **acos**(2.0) fails because the argument value must represent a cosine value between −1.0 and 1.0.

_strerror() *Construct a combined user and system error message*

Compatibility □ANSI ■OS/2 □UNIX □XENIX

See Also

```
strerror()
```

Specification

```
#include <string.h>
char *_strerror(const char *string);
```

Arguments

string: User-supplied message string; use **NULL** if no user message is supplied; otherwise, a message string up to 94 characters long may be specified.

Return Value

Pointer to an error message string consisting of string, a colon, a space, and the system error (**errno**), located in array of error messages defined by the global variable **sys_errlist[]**, defined in Appendix C

Example See: **strerror()**.

Comments The **perror()** function described in Chapter 17 uses **_strerror()** and automatically displays a combined error message to the standard error output stream, **stderr**.

stricmp() *Case-insensitive string comparison*

Compatibility □ANSI ■OS/2 ■UNIX ■XENIX

See Also

```
_fstricmp(), memicmp(), strcmpi(), strnicmp()
```

Specification

```
#include <string.h>
int stricmp(const char *string1, const char *string2);
```

Arguments

    string1: String to compare.

    string2: String to compare.

Return Value

    A signed value that is interpreted as follows:

        <0 **string1** less than **string2**

        =0 **string1** equal to **string2**

        >0 **string1** greater than **string2**

Example   See: **strcmp()**.

Comments   Case-insensitive comparisons compare each alphabetic character array element without regard to whether it is in upper- or lowercase.

strlen()   *Get the length of a string, exclusive of the terminating null*

Compatibility ■ANSI ■OS/2 ■UNIX ■XENIX

See Also

    _fstrlen()

Specification

```
#include <string.h>
size_t strlen(const char *string);
```

Arguments

    string: Any string.

Return Value

    The length of the string in characters, exclusive of the terminating null. A value from 0–n

Example   See: **strcat()**, **strchr()**, **strcmp()**, **strcpy()**, and **strdup()**.

Comments   The string length of a null string ("") is zero.

    As an alternative to calling this function, you can call its **#pragma intrinsic** form.

`strlwr()` *Convert a string to lowercase*

Compatibility ☐ANSI ■OS/2 ☐UNIX ☐XENIX

See Also

`_fstrlwr(), tolower(), _tolower()`

Specification

```
#include <string.h>
char *strlwr(char *string);
```

Arguments

string: String to be converted.

Return Value

Pointer to the converted string

Example

```
/* FILE: ch26e8.c */
/* use the SMALL memory model */
#include <stdio.h>
#include <stdlib.h>
#include <string.h>

static char buf1[0x80], buf2[0x80];

int main(void)
{
while (1) {
    printf("\n\nEnter a string: ");
    gets(buf1);
    if (!strcmpi(buf1,"END")) break;
    strxfrm(buf2, buf1, sizeof(buf2));
    printf("\n   strxfrm() = %s", buf2);
    printf("\n   strlwr()  = %s", strlwr(buf1));
    printf("\n   strupr()  = %s", strupr(buf1));
    printf("\n_fstrlwr()   = %s", _fstrlwr(buf1));
    printf("\n   strrev()  = %s", strrev(buf1));
    printf("\n_fstrrev()   = %s", _fstrrev(buf1));
    printf("\n_fstrupr()   = %s", _fstrupr(buf1));
    }
exit(0);
}
```

Output

```
Enter a string: abc123DEF123cba
 strxfrm() = abc123DEF123cba
 strlwr()  = abc123def123cba
 strupr()  = ABC123DEF123CBA
_fstrlwr() = abc123def123cba
 strrev()  = abc321fed321cba
_fstrrev() = abc123def123cba
_fstrupr() = ABC123DEF123CBA

Enter a string: end
```

Comments   Only uppercase [A–Z] letters are converted to lowercase; all other characters remain unchanged.

strncat()   *Append characters of a string*

Compatibility   ■ANSI   ■OS/2   ■UNIX   ■XENIX

See Also

```
_fstrncnt(), strcat()
```

Specification

```
#include <string.h>
char *strncat(char *string1, const char *string2, size_t count);
```

Arguments

string1: Destination string.

string2: Source string.

count: The number of characters from **string2** to append to **string1**; if count is greater than **strlen(string2)**, then **strlen(string2)** is assumed.

Return Value

The destination **string1**

Example   See: **strcat()**.

Comments   No error conditions are detected; **string1** should be declared large enough to contain the result.

strncmp ()   *Case-sensitive comparison of string characters*

Compatibility   ■ANSI   ■OS/2   ■UNIX   ■XENIX

See Also

```
_fstrcmp(), strcmp(), strcoll()
```

Specification

```
#include <string.h>
int strncmp(const char *string1, const char *string2, size_t count);
```

Arguments

string1: String to compare.

string2: String to compare.

count: The number of characters from **string2** to compare with **string1**; if count is greater than **strlen(string2)**, then a count of **strlen(string2)** is assumed.

Return Value

A signed value that is interpreted as follows:

<0 **string1** less than **string2**

=0 **string1** equal to **string2**

>0 **string1** greater than **string2**

Example   See: **strcmp()**.

Comments   Case-sensitive comparisons treat each alphabetic character as a distinct ASCII codeset value.

strncpy ()   *Copy characters from one string to another*

Compatibility   ■ANSI   ■OS/2   ■UNIX   ■XENIX

See Also

```
_fstrncpy(), memccpy(), strcpy()
```

Specification

```
#include <string.h>
char *strncpy(char *string1, const char *string2, size_t count);
```

Arguments

string1: Destination string.

string2: Source string to copy.

count: The number of characters from **string2** to copy from **string1**; if count is greater than **strlen(string2)**, then **string1**is padded with null characters to a length of **count**.

Return Value

Destination string

Example　　See: **strcpy()**.

Comments　　With **strncpy()**, the terminating null character is not copied if **count** is less than **strlen(string2)**.

strnicmp() *Case-insensitive comparison of string characters*

Compatibility　□ANSI　■OS/2　□UNIX　□XENIX

See Also

　_fstrnicmp(), memicmp(), strcmpi(), strnicmp()

Specification

```
#include <string.h>
int strnicmp(const char *string1, const char *string2, size_t count);
```

Arguments

string1: String to compare.

string2: String to compare.

count: The number of characters from **string2** to compare with **string1**; if count is greater than **strlen(string2)**, then **strlen(string2)** is assumed.

Return Value

A signed value that is interpreted as follows:

　　　<0 **string1** less than **string2**

　　　=0 **string1** equal to **string2**

　　　>0 **string1** greater than **string2**

Example　　See: **strcmp()**.

Comments   Case-insensitive comparisons compare each alphabetic character array element without regard to whether it is in upper- or lowercase.

`strnset()`   *Initialize characters of a string to a given value*

Compatibility   ☐ ANSI   ■ OS/2   ☐ UNIX   ☐ XENIX

See Also

```
_fstrnset(), memset(), strset()
```

Specification

```
#include <string.h>
char *strnset(char *string, int c, size_t count);
```

Arguments

string: String to be initialized.

c: The character value used to fill the string.

count: The number of character (byte) positions to initialize; if count is greater than **strlen(string)**, then a count of **strlen(string)** is assumed.

Return Value

The initialized string

Example   See: `strset()`.

Comments   Only those characters up to the terminating null character are set to the specified character value.

The length of a string cannot be altered by using **strset()**.

`strpbrk()`   *Scan a string for characters in a set*

Compatibility   ■ ANSI   ■ OS/2   ■ UNIX   ■ XENIX

See Also

```
_fstrpbrk(), strchr(), strrchr()
```

Specification

```
#include <string.h>
char *strpbrk(const char *string1, const char *string2);
```

Arguments

string1: String to be searched.

string2: Matching set of characters.

Return Value

If unsuccessful, a **NULL** pointer

Otherwise, a pointer to the first character in **string1** that belongs to the set of characters defined by **string2**

Example   See: **strchr()**.

Comments   Notice in the **strchr()** example program how successive calls to **strpbrk()** are made to find all occurrences of the set of characters (**string2**) in **string1**.

strrchr()   *Scan a string for the last occurrence of a character*

Compatibility   ■ANSI   ■OS/2   ■UNIX   ■XENIX

See Also

```
_fstrrchr(), strchr(), strpbrk()
```

Specification

```
#include <string.h>
char *strrchr(const char *string, int c);
```

Arguments

string: String to be searched.

c: The character value to be located in string.

Return Value

If unsuccessful, a **NULL** pointer

Otherwise, a pointer to the last character in **string** that matches character **c**

Example   See: **strchr()**.

Comments   **strrchr()** performs a search identical to **strchr()**, except that the search is performed from the end of the string to the beginning.

strrev ()   *Reverse characters of a string*

Compatibility   □ ANSI   ■ OS/2   □ UNIX   □ XENIX

See Also

```
_fstrrev()
```

Specification

```
#include <string.h>
char *strrev(char *string);
```

Arguments

string: String to be reversed.

Return Value

The reversed character string

Example   See: `strlwr()`.

Comments   Use `strrev()` to construct a mirror image of a string. The length of a string is never altered by `strrev()`.

strset ()   *Set characters of a string to a value*

Compatibility   □ ANSI   ■ OS/2   □ UNIX   □ XENIX

See Also

```
_fstrset(), memset(), strnset()
```

Specification

```
#include <string.h>
char *strset(char *string, int c);
```

Arguments

string: String to be initialized.

c: The character value used to fill the string.

Return Value

The initialized string

Example

```
/* FILE: ch26e9.c */
/* use the SMALL memory model */
#include <stdio.h>
#include <stdlib.h>
#include <string.h>

static char buf1[] = "buf1 sample string";

int main(void)
{
char buf2[] = "buf2 sample string";

printf("\nbuf1 = %s", buf1);
strnset(buf1, 'x', 5);
printf("\nbuf1 = %s", buf1);
strset(buf1, 'x');
printf("\nbuf1 = %s", buf1);

printf("\nbuf2 = %s", buf2);
_fstrnset(buf2, 'y', 5);
printf("\nbuf2 = %s", buf2);
_fstrset(buf2, 'y');
printf("\nbuf2 = %s", buf2);
exit(0);
}
```

Output

```
buf1 = buf1 sample string
buf1 = xxxxxsample string
buf1 = xxxxxxxxxxxxxxxxxx
buf2 = buf2 sample string
buf2 = yyyyysample string
buf2 = yyyyyyyyyyyyyyyyyy
```

Comments   Only those characters up to the terminating null character are set to the specified character value.

The length of a string cannot be altered by using **strset()**.

As an alternative to calling this function, use the **#pragma intrinsic** form.

strspn()   *Find the first substring*

Compatibility   ■ ANSI   ■ OS/2   ■ UNIX   ■ XENIX

See Also

```
_fstrspn(), strcspn(), strstr(), strtok()
```

Specification

```
#include <string.h>
size_t strspn(const char *string1, const char *string2);
```

Arguments

string1: String to be searched.

string2: Matching set of characters.

Return Value

The index position (0–n) of the first character in **string1** that does not belong to the set of characters defined by **string2**

Equivalent to the length of the initial substring in **string1**, which consists entirely of characters in **string2**

Example

See: **strcspn()**.

Comments

strspn() has the opposite effect of using **strcspn()**.

strstr()   *Find a substring*

Compatibility   ■ANSI   ■OS/2   ☐UNIX   ☐XENIX

See Also

```
_fstrstr(), strcspn(), strspn(), strtok()
```

Specification

```
#include <string.h>
char *strstr(const char *string1, const char *string2);
```

Arguments

string1: String to be searched.

string2: Exact substring to find.

Return Value

If unsuccessful, a **NULL** pointer

Otherwise, a pointer to the first occurrence of **string2** in **string1**

Example

See: **strcspn()**.

Comments   Unlike `strcspn()` and `strspn()`, `strstr()` finds an exact substring match, where the character order and values must agree, not just the values.

`strtok()`   *Find the next token in a string*

Compatibility   ■ANSI   ■OS/2   ■UNIX   ■XENIX

See Also

`_fstrtok()`

Specification

```
#include <string.h>
char *strtok(char *string1, const char *string2);
```

Arguments

string1: String containing tokens.

string2: Set of delimiting characters.

Return Value

If no (no more) tokens exist, a **NULL** pointer

Otherwise, a pointer to the next token delimited by one or more characters from **string2** in **string1**

Example

```
/* FILE: ch26e10.c */
/* use the SMALL memory model */
#include <stdio.h>
#include <stdlib.h>
#include <string.h>
#define MAX_TOKEN 6

int main(int argc, char *argv[])
{
FILE *file;
char buffer[0x80], *ptr;
char _far *fptr = buffer;
char delimiter[] = " ,()=;{}!\t\r\n\f\v";
int token_nbr;

printf("\n%s", argv[0]);
ptr = strstr(argv[0],"EXE");
strcpy(ptr,"C");
printf("\n%s", argv[0]);
```

```
file = fopen(argv[0],"r");
if (!file) abort();
printf("\n\n==1st File Pass==");
token_nbr=0;
while (fgets(buffer, 0x80, file)) {
    if (!(ptr = strtok(buffer, delimiter))) continue;
    printf("\n%4d %-40s", ++token_nbr, ptr);
    while (ptr = strtok(NULL, delimiter))
        printf("\n%4d %-40s", ++token_nbr, ptr);
    if (token_nbr >= MAX_TOKEN) break;
    }
rewind(file);
printf("\n\n==2nd File Pass==");
token_nbr=0;
while (fgets(buffer, 0x80, file)) {
    if (!(fptr = _fstrtok(buffer, delimiter))) continue;
    printf("\n%4d %-40s", ++token_nbr, fptr);
    while (fptr = _fstrtok(NULL, delimiter))
        printf("\n%4d %-40s", ++token_nbr, fptr);
    if (token_nbr >= MAX_TOKEN) break;
    }
exit(0);
}
```

Output

```
C:\QC25\BIN\CH26E10.EXE
C:\QC25\BIN\CH26E10.C

==1st File Pass==
   1 /*
   2 FILE:
   3 ch26e10.c
   4 */
   5 /*
   6 use
   7 the
   8 SMALL
   9 memory
  10 model
  11 */

==2nd File Pass==
   1 /*
   2 FILE:
   3 ch26e10.c
   4 */
   5 /*
   6 use
   7 the
   8 SMALL
   9 memory
  10 model
  11 */
```

Comments   An initial call to **strtok()** with a non-**NULL string1** skips any leading delimiters from **string2**; to locate additional tokens in **string1**, call **strtok()** repeatedly with a **NULL** pointer for **string1**, until a **NULL** pointer value is returned by **strtok()**.

strupr()   *Convert a string to uppercase*

Compatibility   □ANSI   ■OS/2   □UNIX   □XENIX

See Also

```
_fstrupr(), toupper(), _toupper()
```

Specification

```
#include <string.h>
char *strupr(char *string);
```

Arguments

string: String to be converted.

Return Value

Pointer to the converted string

Example   See: **strlwr()**.

Comments   Only lowercase [a–z] characters are converted to uppercase; all other characters remain unchanged.

strxfrm()   *Transform a string based upon locale-specific information*

Compatibility   ■ANSI   ■OS/2   □UNIX   □XENIX

Specification

```
#include <string.h>
size_t strxfrm(char *string1, const char *string2, size_t count);
```

Arguments

string1: String in which the transformed version of **string2** is returned.

string2: The string to transform.

count: The maximum number of characters to be placed into **string1**.

Return Value

strlen(string1)

If greater than *count*, the contents of **string1** are unpredictable

Example
See: **strlwr()**, **setlocale()**.

Comments
Since presently only one locale, "C," is provided by Microsoft, function **strxfrm()** is presently equivalent to the use of **strcpy()**.

When other locales become available, the transformation will be controlled by the **LC_COLLATE** component of the designated locale (see Chapter 27).

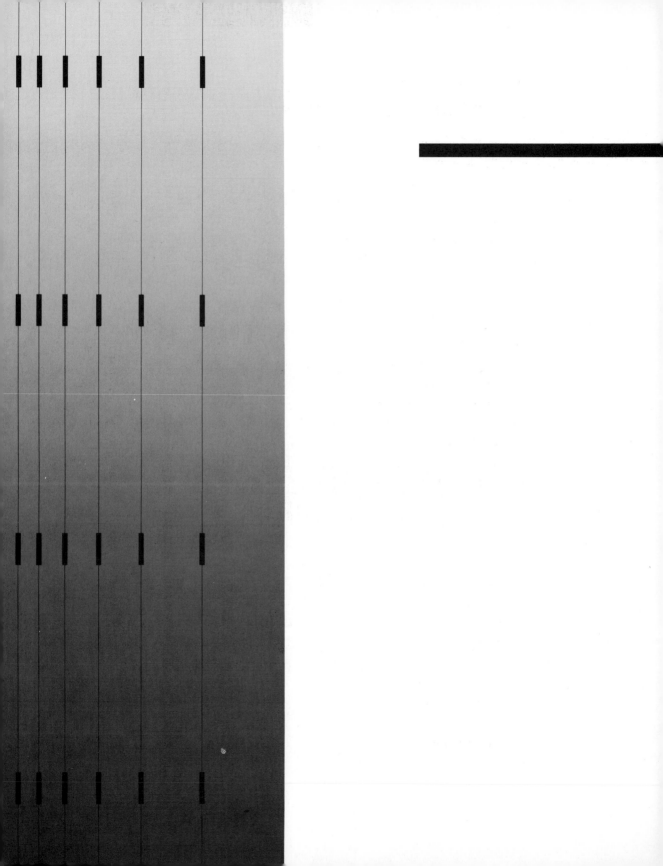

Miscellaneous Functions

Miscellaneous Functions

This chapter presents all the run-time library functions not covered elsewhere in this book (except for the graphics functions, omitted for space reasons) and discusses the programming issues related to their use. These issues include locale, searching and sorting, critical hardware-error handling, interrupt service routines, and library anomalies.

The concept of locale is new with Standard C, and as discussed in Chapter 4, it represents (together with trigraphs and multibyte (wide) character sets) an attempt to "internationalize" the C language and facilitate the adoption of the American National Standards Institute (ANSI) C by the International Standards Organization (ISO). Although it provides the locale functions mandated by Standard C, Microsoft C version 6.0 does not yet fully implement these features.

The search and sort functions of the run-time library are often overlooked because of their perceived complexity. They should be utilized, however, because of their power and speed. The example programs included in this chapter will demonstrate how easy it is to exploit the power of these functions to search and sort arrays of fundamental types, as well as arrays of pointers to fundamental and aggregate type objects.

This chapter next explains how critical hardware errors can be trapped by an application program, rather than simply defaulting to the DOS INT 0x24 error message *Abort, Retry, Ignore?*. By using the **_harderr()**, **_hardresume()**, and **_hardretn()** functions, an application program can avert abnormal program termination and either initiate recovery or perform controlled program termination.

Another programming technique that is often misunderstood and thus avoided involves writing and installing interrupt handlers, which are commonly referred to as ISRs (Interrupt Service Routines) and TSRs (Terminate-and-Stay-Resident routines). The use of TSRs makes DOS behave as if it were a multitasking operating system. The fundamental concepts involved in writing and installing interrupt functions are reviewed. A sample TSR, which you can customize and install on your computer, is included in this chapter as well.

To conclude the discussion of the run-time library, a summary of noteworthy run-time library anomalies is presented; and a task-oriented summary of the functions discussed in this chapter can be found in Table 27.1.

TABLE 27.1: Miscellaneous Function Tasks

TASK	FUNCTIONS	
	STANDARD C ■ ANSI	**MICROSOFT C □ ANSI**
Establish the locale	`localeconv()`	
	`setlocale()`	
Searching and Sorting	`bsearch()`	`lfind()`
	`qsort()`	`lsearch()`
Critical error handling		`_harderr()`
		`_hardresume()`
		`_hardretn()`
Interrupt Service Routines		`_chain_intr()`
		`_disable()`
		`_dos_getvect()`
		`_dos_setvect()`
		`_enable()`

LOCALE

The concept of locale is new with Standard C and is implemented by the **`<locale.h>`** header file (see Chapter 6). Until now, the accommodation of different regional and cultural display conventions for dates, times, and currency depended entirely on the conventions of the host operating system. By introducing a set of standard function calls in C, the ANSI committee has sought to ensure the portability of application software, regardless of the operating system in use.

Although Microsoft C now implements only one locale (named "C"), in the future it will provide other locales to provide choices to establish conventions that will apply to application programs under development for particular geographic or cultural settings. Every locale is designed to consist of the following five control components:

LC_COLLATE	Collation: **`strcoll()`** and **`strxfrm()`**
LC_CTYPE	Character handling: **`<ctype.h>`**
LC_MONETARY	Monetary: **`localeconv()`** formatting standards
LC_NUMERIC	Nonmonetary: **`localeconv()`** decimal display
LC_TIME	Time: **`strftime()`**

Application-specific locales can be customized for a component mix selected from the set of available locales by using the function **setlocale()**.

Programmers for whom international portability is an issue should track Microsoft's (and other C compiler vendors') implementation of other locales and begin writing programs that utilize **localeconv()** and **setlocale()**. This would be preferable to relying on the DOS configuration file **COUNTRY** command (see Chapter 1) and the non-Standard interrupt 0x21 function 0x38 (see **intdos()** in Chapter 22) to retrieve country-specific display conventions.

See the reference entries for functions **setlocale()** and **localeconv()** for complete details and example programs.

SEARCHING AND SORTING

A cursory review of the prototype descriptions for the run-time functions **bsearch()**, **lfind()**, **lsearch()**, and **qsort()** might convince you that these functions are too slow and complicated to sort an array of objects. They are, on the contrary, powerful, fast, and easy to use. A review of the program examples for these functions demonstrates how to use them with an array of structures (**qsort()**, ch27e7.c), an array of pointers to strings (**bsearch()**, ch27e1.c, filter program), and a multi-dimensional array of strings (**lfind()**, ch27e5.c, filter program). In each example, an array of objects is sorted and searched. Two of the examples are constructed as filter programs that rely upon **stdin** and **stdout** for their I/O, and are designed to have their input piped from the DOS command CHKDSK and their output redirected as desired.

The key to understanding and using these functions is the fact that each works with a user-defined array of objects and a corresponding user-defined comparison function that compares the array elements. A memory address is used to describe the starting point (*base*) of an array of *num* elements, each of which is *width* bytes in size. A search *key* is specified as the address of an object of the type specified.

It might appear that when a user-defined array of objects is sorted, that the array elements will always be ordered. This is true except when the array elements themselves are pointers. When an array of pointers is sorted, the user-defined comparison function compares the objects pointed to, not the array elements themselves. Herein lies the hidden power of these run-time functions. Not only contiguous arrays of objects, but discontiguous objects as well, may be sorted and searched when an array of pointers to such objects is specified together with an appropriate comparison function.

The examples in this chapter demonstrate three different types of array elements: a structure, a string, and a pointer to a string. Run the programs and see for yourself how quickly such arrays can be sorted and searched.

The only practical limitation on the use of these functions lies in the argument prototype definitions of the number (**num**) and size (**width**) of array elements, which are specified as type **size_t**. For Microsoft C, type **size_t** is synonymous with **unsigned int**, which establishes a maximum value of 65,535 (64KB). Neither the number of array elements (**num**) or size of an array element (**width**) may exceed 65,535. Because an array's total size may not exceed 64KB for the Tiny, Small, Medium, Compact, and Large memory models, the product of (**num**) times (**width**) may not exceed 65,535 bytes. If the Huge memory model is employed, arrays may span segments (exceed 64KB), but the maximum number of array elements is still restricted to 65,535 elements when these functions are employed.

To maximize the number and size of the array elements that may be searched and sorted by these run-time functions, always specify an array of pointers. In this manner, the pointed to objects may be discontiguous (allocated to the heap) and, in the aggregate, exceed the typical 65,535-byte space limitation on the array itself.

CRITICAL HARDWARE-ERROR HANDLING

This chapter addresses the detection and handling of still another special class of errors that are detected as interrupts and referred to as critical hardware errors. (See also floating-point exception handling in Chapter 23 and signal processing in Chapter 25.) We will see how to avoid the familiar *Abort, Retry, Ignore?* DOS error message and permit an application program to intervene and remedy the problem and continue processing, or to terminate processing normally (flushing buffers, closing files, and so on), rather than abnormally (via INT 0x23).

A critical hardware error represents any peripheral device abnormality that prevents the CPU from continuing until the device error condition is resolved. Critical errors include such events as having an open floppy disk gate, being out of printer paper, or encountering a cyclic-redundancy-check (CRC) disk read or write error. Whenever a critical hardware error occurs, DOS generates an INT 0x24. The default function pointed to by entry 0x24 in the interrupt vector table displays the message *Abort, Retry, Ignore?* and awaits a user response. If the error cannot be circumvented, the application program being executed must be abnormally terminated (INT 0x23 or Ctrl-C).

Herein lies the advantage of utilizing the **_hard** functions described in this chapter. With their use, the default INT 0x24 interrupt function can be altered to permit an application program to retain control over how processing is to continue or be terminated whenever an INT 0x24 occurs. The adverse consequences of abnormal program termination on an application program can thus be averted.

As discussed in Chapter 1, a copy of the INT 0x24 pointer is included in the Program Segment Prefix (**_psp**) of every program loaded for processing by DOS. Normal program termination processing always restores the copy of the INT 0x24 address from the **_psp** to the interrupt vector table to ensure that the default INT 0x24 address is restored.

By using the run-time functions **_harderr()**, **_hardresume()**, and **_hardretn()**, we can alter INT 0x24 and avert the need to write and install an interrupt handler. Instead, the function **_harderr()** is used to install a user-defined function in the logic path of INT 0x24. This function must satisfy the following prototype definition:

```
void _far handler(unsigned deverror, unsigned errcode,
    unsigned _far *devhdr)
```

For complete descriptions of the arguments shown above, see the **_hard** function entry in the alphabetic function list at the end of this chapter. Notice that the user-defined **handler()** function does not utilize the C keyword **_interrupt**.

From within the **handler()** function described above, either function **_hardresume()** or **_hardretn()** is called to control how process continuation or termination is to occur. If **_hardresume()** is used, control passes to DOS; otherwise, **_hardretn()** returns control to the application program. Normally, only interrupt 0x21 functions 0x01 through 0x0C, 0x30, and 0x59 may be used from within a **handler()** function, because these DOS services are reentrant (capable of being called more than once without disastrous side-effects), while nearly all the other DOS/BIOS services are not.

INTERRUPT SERVICE ROUTINES (ISR)

All interrupts, whether initiated by a hardware or software event, represent an asynchronous disruption of the normal processing activities of the CPU. Normally, when an interrupt event occurs (and is acknowledged), the context (register state) of the machine is saved, a branch to the assigned interrupt service function occurs, interrupt processing is performed and, finally, the context of the machine is restored, so the CPU can continue processing as if the interruption had not occurred. Interrupt service routines direct the processing performed by the CPU when such events take place.

This section extends the discussion of interrupt processing introduced in Chapter 22 with the **bdos()**, **intdos()**, **intdosx()**, **int86()**, and **int86x()** functions. It explains how interrupt service functions may be written in C, and be installed either temporarily or permanently as a terminate-and-stay-resident program (TSR), by using the **_dos_getvect()**, **_dos_setvect()**, and **_dos_keep()** run-time functions.

ISR Design Considerations

Although interrupt-handling functions written in C are simply functions, they also represent a special category to which certain unique design considerations apply. The following constraints are not imposed on any other C functions:

- They must be a **_cdecl** type function to ensure that a fixed order of register value placement is maintained when they are pushed to the stack.
- They must always be identified by a **_far** address that represents a compatible interrupt vector table entry and can be loaded anywhere in memory and remain accessible.
- They are invoked in response to asynchronous events that may occur and they compete with other maskable and nonmaskable interrupts for the CPU's resources.
- When an INT (interrupt) occurs, the processor context must be preserved, and upon exit, the processor context must be restored (IRET) so that the CPU can continue as if the interruption had not occurred.
- Ideally, all interrupt function code should be reentrant (pure code, no static variable dependency); however, DOS itself is not reentrant. Reentrant code can be processed by more than one task without error; non-reentrant code cannot. Since DOS was not designed as a multitasking operating system, its code is non-reentrant, and improperly designed interrupt functions that call non-reentrant DOS/BIOS interrupt services will cause DOS to crash (hang).
- Therefore, interrupt functions developed for DOS must ensure that reentrancy is maintained if system crashes are to be avoided. To do this, interrupt functions should normally disable all interrupt

processing by using the **_disable()** function while an interrupt function is being executed and avoid calling non-reentrant functions (DOS services) altogether.

- Because the INT instruction disables (**_asm cli**) the recognition of subsequent interrupts (unless interrupt recognition is explicitly enabled using the **_enable()** function), other interrupts may be ignored if they occur while an interrupt function is being processed.

- Interrupt functions that consume significant periods of time should selectively enable (**_enable()**, **_asm sti**) interrupt recognition for any noncritical sections of code, thereby permitting the CPU to process other interrupts should they occur.

Although the design constraints imposed on interrupt functions in C are complicated, learning to accommodate them requires patience and experimentation. The material presented in this chapter will clarify your understanding of the issues controlling the development of interrupt functions and, by example, demonstrate how to approach writing and installing such routines.

Let's first review how interrupt functions are declared. Then let's examine how to write interrupt functions intended either to remain installed only for the duration of a program, or to remain installed permanently (TSR), or until the DOS is rebooted.

Declaring an ISR

Three basic variations of interrupt function declaration are possible using Microsoft C. The first declaration format is expressed as follows:

```
void _cdecl _interrupt _far int_handler(void)
{
/* code */
}
```

When this form is used, no access to the register values pushed to the stack is possible from within the interrupt function itself. The function may be invoked by an INT instruction or a direct C function call, as discussed in the section that follows. The second declaration format is the following:

```
void _cdecl _interrupt _far int_handler(
    unsigned _es, unsigned _ds
    unsigned _di, unsigned _si,
    unsigned _bp, unsigned _sp,
    unsigned _bx, unsigned _dx,
    unsigned _cx, unsigned _ax,
```

```
        unsigned _ip, unsigned _cs
        unsigned flags)
{
/* code */
}
```

This form should be used by functions initiated by an INT instruction, when access to all of the register values pushed to the stack is required from within the interrupt function itself. This is necessary when an existing interrupt service that accepts register input is to be replaced. The flags, **_cs** (code segment), and **_ip** (instruction pointer) arguments are placed on the stack when an INT instruction is encountered. The remaining register values are pushed to the stack because the **_interrupt** keyword is specified for the function. It is important to note that because the **_cdecl** keyword is specified, the arguments shown are pushed to the stack, rightmost (last) to leftmost (first). To maintain a correspondence with the values on the stack, the order of arguments shown above must be maintained. The names of the formal arguments shown above are not reserved C identifiers, but their use is recommended for clarity.

The third possible declaration format is intended for use by functions that are called directly from within an interrupt function and are to be passed additional arguments (**arg1, .. argn**):

```
void _cdecl _interrupt _far int_handler(
    unsigned _es, unsigned _ds
    unsigned _di, unsigned _si,
    unsigned _bp, unsigned _sp,
    unsigned _bx, unsigned _dx,
    unsigned _cx, unsigned _ax,
    type arg1, .. type argn)
{
/* code */
}
```

Because interrupt functions initiated by an INT instruction are never passed actual arguments, this form is usable only when called directly from C. The use of the **_interrupt** keyword ensures that this function will still have the **_ax** through **_es** registers pushed to the stack, but the **flag**, **_cs**, and **_ip** register values and IRET return will be omitted because the INT instruction is not used to invoke the function call.

Calling an ISR

Interrupt functions can be invoked by three different methods. The first calling method involves the standard use of an INT instruction. When this occurs, the **flags**, **_cs**, and **_ip** register values are pushed to the stack; the function saves the **_ax** through **_es** registers because the **_interrupt** keyword was specified; the code of the function is processed; the **_es** through **_ax** register values are restored; and then an IRET rather than a RET instruction is performed, which pops and restores the **_ip, _cs**, and **flags** from the stack.

The second calling method is employed from within an interrupt function to invoke another interrupt function (**other_int_handler()**) and return to continue processing. In this case, an INT instruction cannot be issued because normally interrupt recognition is disabled within interrupt functions. Therefore, the **other_int_handler()** function is invoked using function pointer indirection (see Chapter 14):

```
void _cdecl _interrupt _far int_handler()
{
/* code */
(*other_int_handler)();
/* code */
}
```

The **other_int_handler()** function pushes only the additional registers (**_ax** through **_es**) to the stack, processes its code, restores (pops) the **_es** through **_ax** registers from the stack, and returns to the next instruction in **int_handler()** function above, using a normal RET instruction to pop the return address from the stack (see Chapter 15). Notice that this method avoids the normal INT function-calling and return conventions. The **flags, _cs**, and **_ip** are not pushed to the stack, and a corresponding IRET instruction to restore these values is not executed.

The third calling method is used when an interrupt handler wants another interrupt handler to complete the interrupt call, as if the second handler were called directly:

```
void _cdecl _interrupt _far int_handler()
{
/* code */
_chain_intr(other_int_handler);
/* code ignored, _chain_intr() never returns */
}
```

In this example, the **other_int_handler()** function is called using the run-time function **_chain_intr()**, and performs an IRET that returns as if **int_handler()** had terminated normally. This is useful for intercepting an interrupt such as the keyboard, for example, to check for a "hot key" sequence used to initiate a TSR. If the "hot key" has not been pressed, the keyboard interrupt function is called using **_chain_intr()** to perform its normal operation.

Installing an ISR

An interrupt function may be installed only for the duration of a program or permanently, as a TSR.

To replace an interrupt vector table entry for the duration of a program, use the **_dos_getvect()** function as follows:

```
void (_cdecl _interrupt _far *old_handler)(void);
old_handler = _dos_getvect(intnum);
```

This will get and save the current interrupt vector associated with interrupt number (**intnum**) in the function pointer, **old_handler**. Next, the new interrupt function must be installed using function **_dos_set-vect()** as follows:

```
_dos_setvect(intnum, new_handler);
```

This places the address of interrupt function **new_handler** into the **intnum** entry of the interrupt vector table. Just before terminating, the **old_handler** interrupt vector (**_far** address) must be restored to the interrupt vector table using the following statement:

```
_dos_setvect(intnum, old_handler);
```

If for any reason the program above should terminate abnormally (Ctrl-C or Ctrl-Break), and the address of **old_handler** is not restored to the **intnum** entry of the interrupt vector table upon program termination, the interrupt vector for **intnum** will point to a memory address that will become invalid when another program is loaded into memory. See the example program included with the **_dos_getvect()** function documentation.

To install an interrupt function permanently, it is necessary to load and execute a program that ends, but never relinquishes its assigned memory. Because it is not possible to load a function by itself, an entire program must be loaded, and it must remain intact to preserve its assigned memory address space and that of the interrupt function itself. The run-time function **_dos_keep()** is used for this purpose. A TSR program installs the address of an interrupt function it defines using a **_dos_setvect()** function call, and then it calls the **_dos_keep()** function, rather than terminating normally. See the example program included with the documentation of the **_enable()** function.

Either .EXE or .COM files may be loaded as TSRs, using the **_dos_keep()** function; however, the program size in paragraphs (16-byte blocks) must be provided as an argument value.

To determine the size of an .EXE file, use the EXEHDR utility program (see Chapter 3). To determine the size of a .COM file created using the

Tiny memory model (64KB maximum), use the **_psp** offset 6–7 value (Chapter 1, Table 1.6) to calculate the number of bytes remaining in the segment.

```
#include <stdlib.h>
_segment segvar = _psp;
size_t seg_bytes_free, prog_size_bytes, prog_size_para;
size_t _based(void) *ptr_free = (size_t _based(void) *)0x06;

seg_bytes_free = *(segvar:>ptr_free);
prog_size_bytes = 0xFFFF - seg_bytes_free + 1;
prog_size_para = (prog_size_bytes >> 4) + 1;
```

To conserve even more space, it is possible to free the environment space of a TSR program before calling the **_dos_keep()** function, by using the address in the **_psp** at offset 44–45 (Chapter 1, Table 1.6) and the **_dos_freemem()** function.

```
#include <stdlib.h>
#include <dos.h>
_segment segvar = _psp;
_segment _based(void) *ptr_envp =
    (_segment _based(void) *)0x2C;

segvar = *(segvar:>ptr_envp);
_dos_freemem(segvar);
```

Because all programs executed by DOS are loaded into the lowest available memory, TSR programs normally are invoked from the AUTOEXEC.BAT file (Chapter 1), so that memory does not become fragmented, but rather is tightly layered with TSRs in low memory.

RUN-TIME LIBRARY ANOMALIES

Although 426 different run-time library functions are documented in Chapters 16–27, this number does not include any graphics-related run-time functions, which are included in the library (**<graph.h>** and **<pgchart.h>**). It is easy to be overwhelmed by the sheer number of functions in the run-time library. The discussion presented in this section is intended to highlight some noteworthy anomalies that might otherwise become lost in the accompanying run-time library documentation.

Three notable run-time library anomalies are discussed below: function-like macros that do not have counterparts in the run-time library; run-time library functions that are provided but for which no application use is intended or supported; and Standard C functions that are specified but not yet available with Microsoft C.

Function-like Macros

Each run-time function that has a function-like macro counterpart is noted as such in the "Comments" section of its reference entry in this book. However, several common function-like macros are not available as functions and, therefore, are not included in Chapters 16–27. The following function-like macros fall into that category.

MACRO	HEADER FILE	DESCRIPTION
assert()	<assert.h>	Assertion statements
FP_OFF()	<dos.h>	Offset component of an address
FP_SEG()	<dos.h>	Segment component of an address
max()	<stdlib.h>	Maximum of two items
min()	<stdlib.h>	Minimum of two items
offsetof()	<stddef.h>	Structure/union member offsets
va_arg()	<stdarg.h>	Next variable argument from list
va_end()	<stdarg.h>	Restart variable argument list
va_start()	<stdarg.h>	First variable argument from list

For a description of the **assert()** macro, refer to Chapter 25 (**_assert()** function). Also see Chapter 29 for a description of the role that assertions can play in debugging a C program.

The **FP_SEG()** and **FP_OFF()** macros provide a means of splitting a **_far** memory address into its segment and offset components. It is also possible to use **_based()** pointers for this purpose.

The **min()** and **max()** macros have not been discussed elsewhere in this book, but provide a convenient way of selecting a minimum or maximum value for use, assuming they have not been expressed using a side-effects operator ++ or -- (see Chapter 5).

The **offsetof()** macro was discussed in Chapter 9 and is used to locate the exact byte-offset from the start of a structure of any addressable member of the structure.

Processing the arguments of a function that have been described in a prototype using the ellipsis (...) notation is implemented by Standard C using the **va_start()**, **va_arg()**, and **va_end()** function-like macros. A complete discussion of their use is found in Chapter 14.

Unsupported Functions

One function that was available in Microsoft's run-time library is no longer supported for use nor available. It is

void *sbrk(int);

whose prototype was found in **<malloc.h>**.

Prototypes for two functions found in the **<stdio.h>** header file distributed by Microsoft are not documented nor intended for application program use. They are

```
int _filbuf(FILE *);
int _flsbuf(int, FILE *)
```

Oddly enough, these run-time functions support the implementation of two function-like macros: **_filbuf()** is referenced by the **getc()** function-like macro, and **_flsbuf()** is referenced by the **putc()** function-like macro found in **<stdio.h>**.

Five additional functions, which can be found in the run-time library but are restricted for use with the OS/2 Operating System and *not DOS*, are the following:

FUNCTION	HEADER FILE	DESCRIPTION
_beginthread()	<process.h>	Begin a thread in an OS/2 process
cwait()	<process.h>	Wait for a child process to terminate
_endthread()	<process.h>	Terminate an OS/2 thread
_pclose()	<stdio.h>	Wait/close a pipe
_pipe()	<io.h>	Create a pipe for read/write
_popen()	<stdio.h>	Create a pipe
wait()	<process.h>	Suspend the calling process

Unavailable Functions

The Microsoft C 6.0 compiler does not yet implement multibyte (wide) character sets as mandated by Standard C. For this reason the following functions, normally defined in **<stdlib.h>**, are not provided in the run-time library:

FUNCTION	DESCRIPTION
mblen()	Length of a multibyte character string
mbstowcs()	Convert a multibyte character string to a wide-character string
mbtowc()	Convert a multibyte character to a wide character
wcstombs()	Convert a wide-character string to a multibyte character string
wctomb()	Convert a wide character to a multibyte character

MISCELLANEOUS RUN-TIME LIBRARY FUNCTIONS

bsearch() *Perform a binary search of a sorted array for a specified element value*

Compatibility ■ANSI ■OS/2 ■UNIX ■XENIX

See Also

    lfind(), lsearch()

Specification

    #include <stdlib.h> or <search.h>
    void *bsearch(const void *key, const void *base, size_t num, size_t width,
        int (*compare)(const void *elem1, const void *elem2));

Arguments

key: Pointer to a type object value to be searched for in the sorted array.

base: Pointer to first element of a sorted array.

num: The number of elements in the sorted array (up to 64KB).

width: The size of each array element in bytes (up to 64KB).

compare: A pointer to a user-defined function that compares two array elements and returns one of the following values:

>   <0 **elem1** less than **elem2**
>
>   =0 **elem1** equal to **elem2**
>
>   >0 **elem1** greater than **elem2**

elem1: Pointer to the key of the search.

elem2: Pointer to an array element to be compared with **elem1** by function compare.

Return Value

If no matching key is found, a **NULL** pointer

Otherwise, a pointer to the first matching occurrence of *key* in the sorted array

Example

```
/* FILE: ch27e1.c */
#include <stdio.h>
#include <stdlib.h>
#include <search.h>
#include <string.h>
#include <malloc.h>
#define LIMIT 2499

/*
** filter utility: query for filename.ext; report duplicates
** execute this program from the DOS command line as shown
** chkdsk [drive:] /v | ch27e1
** pipe the output from chkdsk to ch27e1.exe
*/

int size_ptrch;

int comp_1(char **arg1, char **arg2)
{
/* compare entire filename */
return(strcmpi(*arg1, *arg2));
}

int comp_2(char **arg1, char **arg2)
{
/* compare n-characters of filename */
return(strnicmp(*arg1, *arg2, size_ptrch) );
}

int main(void)
{
static char *name[2500];
static unsigned int idx, svidx, i, j;
size_t cntws;
```

```
char *ptrln, *ptrch, *ptrws, *ptrfile, **found, buffer[0x80];
char *svname, *svptrch, svptr, *svfound, strbuf[0x80];
FILE *in;

/* build complete file list with duplicates */
while (ptrln = fgets(buffer, sizeof(buffer), stdin)) {
    if (ptrch = strrchr(ptrln, '\\')) {
        ptrfile = ++ptrch;
        if (!strchr(ptrch, '.')) continue;
        if (ptrws = strpbrk(ptrch, " \n\r\t\f\v") )
            *ptrws = '\0';
        if (cntws = strspn(ptrln, " \n\r\t\f\v") )
            ptrch = ptrln + cntws;
        if (!strlen(ptrch) ) continue;
        svptrch = (char *) malloc(strlen(ptrch)+2);
        if (!svptrch) abort();
        name[idx++] = svptrch;
        strcpy(strbuf, ptrfile);
        strcat(strbuf, " ");
        *ptrfile = '\0';
        strcat(strbuf, ptrch);
        strcpy(svptrch, strbuf);
        if (idx > LIMIT) abort();
        }
    else continue;
    }

/* sort filenames */
qsort((void *)name, (size_t)idx, sizeof(char *), comp_1);

/* prompt user for a filename.ext ; list all occurrences */
in = fopen("CON", "r");
while (1) {
    printf("\n\nenter Filename.Ext (or part), END to Quit): ");
    if (!(ptrch = fgets(buffer, sizeof(buffer), in))) break;
    if (ptrws = strpbrk(ptrch, " \n\r\t\f\v") ) *ptrws = '\0';
    strupr(ptrch);
    if (!strcmp(ptrch,"END")) break;
    size_ptrch = strlen(ptrch);

    /* use bsearch() for quick check, cannot find duplicates */
    found = (char **) bsearch((char *)&ptrch, (char *)name, idx,
        sizeof(char *), comp_2);
    if (!found) {
        printf("\n\tNO MATCH: %s", ptrch);
        continue;
        }
    else {
        i=1;
        printf("\n\tMATCH %1d: %s", i, *found);
        svfound = *found;
        svname = (char *)name;
        svidx = idx;
```

```
        /* find/display any duplicates */
        while (1) {
            found = (char **)lfind((char *)&ptrch, (char *)svname,
                &svidx, sizeof(char *), comp_2);
            if (!found) break;
            svidx = (((char *)found - (char *)name)/sizeof(char *)) + 1;
            svname = (char *)&(name[svidx]);
            if (strcmp(*found, svfound) )
                printf("\n\tMATCH %ld: %s", ++i, *found);
        }
    }
}
exit(0);
}
```

Output   FOR: chdsk a: /v | ch27e1 >con

```
enter Filename.Ext (or part), END to Quit): XXX.XXX
    NO MATCH: XXX.XXX

Enter Filename.Ext (or part), END to Quit): TABLE 1.1
    MATCH 1: TABLE-1.1 A:\DIR-3\
    MATCH 2: TABLE-1.1 A:\DIR-1\
    MATCH 3: TABLE-1.1 A:\DIR-2\

enter Filename.Ext (or part), END to Quit): END
```

Comments   The array must be sorted in ascending order; otherwise the binary search will not work properly; use **qsort()** to sort the array if unordered.

If duplicate key values exist in the array, it cannot be predicted which duplicate will be returned.

The example above builds an array of pointers to all of the filenames on a volume that is piped to this program from the DOS utility CHKDSK, and then the user is queried for a filename and extension to list all occurrences of that filename.

qsort() is used to sort an array of pointers to strings that have been allocated to the heap using **malloc()**.

bsearch() is used to quickly find whether the filename exists and, because **bsearch()** cannot locate duplicates, **lfind()** is used to check for any such occurrences.

_chain_intr()   *Relinquish control from one interrupt handler to another*

Compatibility   ☐ANSI   ☐OS/2   ☐UNIX   ☐XENIX

Specification

```
#include <dos.h>
void _chain_intr(void(_interrupt _far *target)());
```

Arguments

target: Any pointer to an interrupt-handler function.

Example   See: **_enable()**.

Comments   Control is passed from one interrupt handler to another, as if the other interrupt handler had been called originally.

The stack and register values of the first interrupt handler are passed to the other interrupt handler.

Use **_chain_intr()** to ensure that a new interrupt function passes control to the old interrupt function that it replaced; in this way, newly installed interrupt functions can filter the input that is directed to an existing interrupt function.

As an alternative to using this function, invoke another interrupt function using function pointer indirection.

_disable()   *Disable interrupt acknowledgment (cli instruction)*

Compatibility   □ANSI   □OS/2   □UNIX   □XENIX

Specification

```
#include <dos.h>
void _disable(void);
```

Example   See: **_dos_getvect()**.

Comments   Explicitly use **_disable()** to suspend interrupt recognition by the processor; when interrupts are disabled, any interrupts that occur are ignored.

By default, interrupt functions initiated by an INT instruction always disable interrupt processing.

Use **_enable()** to restore interrupt recognition.

As an alternative to calling the function, use the **#pragma intrinsic** form or use an inline assembly $80x86$ cli instruction (see Chapter 28).

_dos_getvect()   *Get the current interrupt vector (_far address) for a given interrupt number (0x00–0xFF)*

Compatibility   □ANSI   □OS/2   □UNIX   □XENIX

Specification

```
#include <dos.h>
void (_interrupt _far *_dos_getvect(unsigned intnum))();
```

Arguments

intnum: Any installed interrupt number from 0x00 through 0xFF.

Return Value

A **NULL** pointer if no interrupt handler is installed

Otherwise, a **_far** pointer to an interrupt function, which may be cast if necessary

Example

```
/* FILE: ch27e2.c */
#include <stdio.h>
#include <dos.h>
#include <stdlib.h>
#define INT_VIDEO 0x10
#define INT_TICKS 0x1C
#define INT_CTRLC 0x23

unsigned long vt, dvt, testt;
void (_cdecl _interrupt _far *save_1C)(void);
void (_cdecl _far *save_23)(void); /* not _interrupt */
union REGS ir, or;
char display[8];

void _cdecl _interrupt _far my_intr(void)
{
vt++;
}

void _cdecl _far my_ctrl(void)
{
_dos_setvect(INT_TICKS, save_1C);
_dos_setvect(INT_CTRLC,
    (void (_cdecl _interrupt _far *)(void)) save_23);
printf("\a\a");
exit(0);
}

void wr_time (unsigned long seconds)
{
sprintf(display, "%6lu%$", seconds);

/* set the cursor */
ir.h.ah = 0x02;
ir.h.bh = 0;
ir.h.dh = 0;
ir.h.dl = 72;
int86(INT_VIDEO, &ir, &or);
```

```
/* write the attribute */
ir.h.ah = 0x09;
ir.h.al = ' ';
ir.h.bh = 0;
if (seconds > 10 ) ir.h.bl = 0x70;
else if (seconds <= 10 && seconds > 0 ) {
    ir.h.bl = 0x70;
    printf("\a");
    }
else if (seconds == 0) {
    strcpy(display, " STOP $");
    ir.h.bl = 0xF8;
    }
ir.x.cx = 6;
int86(INT_VIDEO, &ir, &or);

/* write the time */
ir.h.ah = 0x09;
ir.x.dx = (unsigned) display;
intdos(&ir, &or);
}

int main(void)
{
unsigned long ticks;
float min, factor = 1193180.0/65536.0;

printf("\nCountdown for xx.xx minutes: ");
fflush(stdin);
scanf("%f", &min);
ticks = (min * 60.0f * factor);

save_1C = _dos_getvect(INT_TICKS);
save_23 = (void (_cdecl _far *)(void)) _dos_getvect(INT_CTRLC);
_disable();
_dos_setvect(INT_TICKS, my_intr);
_dos_setvect(INT_CTRLC,
    (void (_cdecl _interrupt _far *)(void)) my_ctrl);
_enable();
wr_time((ticks/factor)+0.5F );
do {
    testt = ((float) vt) / factor;
    if (dvt != testt) {
        dvt = testt;
        wr_time((ticks/factor) - dvt );
        }
    } while (vt < ticks);
_disable();
_dos_setvect(INT_TICKS, save_1C);
_dos_setvect(INT_CTRLC,
    (void (_cdecl _interrupt _far *)(void)) save_23);
_enable();
exit(0);
}
```

Output   Execute ch27e2.exe to see the countdown timer.

Comments   Always save an interrupt vector table entry before replacing it with a custom interrupt handler. This ensures that the original interrupt handler address can be restored if necessary.

Notice in the example that if Ctrl-C or Ctrl-Break occurs while this program is running, the original interrupt vector table entries are restored; otherwise, the interrupt vector addresses would no longer point to a valid function in memory.

As an alternative, construct an address using a **_based()** pointer with a segment of 0x0000 and an offset of the interrupt number; then use indirection to retrieve the address.

For more information about timer interrupts, see Chapter 21.

_dos_setvect()   *Set the current interrupt vector (_far address) for a given interrupt number (0x00–0xFF)*

Compatibility   ☐ANSI   ☐ S/2   ☐UNIX   ☐XENIX

Specification

```
#include <dos.h>
void _dos_setvect(unsigned intnum, void( _interrupt _far *handler)());
```

Arguments

intnum: Any interrupt number from 0x00 through 0xFF.

handler: A pointer to an interrupt function.

Example   See: **_dos_getvect()**.

Comments   Always save an interrupt vector table entry before replacing it with a custom interrupt handler. This ensures that the original interrupt handler address can be restored if necessary.

Always restore the interrupt vectors that point to functions that are not permanently installed in memory.

The casting of the function pointers in the example program reflects the fact that INT 0x23 is not an interrupt function pointer, simply a function pointer; however, **_dos_setvect()** expects its argument to be an interrupt function pointer.

As an alternative, construct an address using a **_based()** pointer with a segment of 0x0000 and an offset of the interrupt number; then use indirection to assign the address.

_enable () *Enable interrupt acknowledgment (sti instruction)*

Compatibility ☐ANSI ☐OS/2 ☐UNIX ☐XENIX

Specification

```
#include <dos.h>
void _enable(void);
```

Example

```
/* FILE: ch27e3.c */
#include <time.h>
#include <dos.h>
#define INT_TICKS 0x1C

long int vt;
union {unsigned int u_int[8];
    unsigned char u_chr[16]; } v_display;
int i, _based(void) *vptr;
_segment segvar = 0xB000;    /* MONO; use 0xB800 for COLOR */
void (_cdecl _interrupt _far *save_intr)(void);

void _cdecl _interrupt _far my_intr(void)
{
vt++;
/* update display every 5 seconds or 18.2 x 5 = 91 ticks */
if (!(vt % 91L)) {
    _enable(); /* or _asm sti */
    while (1) {
        /* update the seconds [00-59] display */
        if ((v_display.u_chr[14] += 5) <= '9' ) break;
        else {
            v_display.u_chr[14] -= 10;
            (v_display.u_chr[12])++;
            }
        if (v_display.u_chr[12] <= '5' ) break;
        else {
            v_display.u_chr[12] -= 6;
            (v_display.u_chr[8])++;
            }
        /* update the minutes [00-59] display */
        if (v_display.u_chr[8] <= '9' ) break;
        else {
            v_display.u_chr[8] -= 10;
            (v_display.u_chr[6])++;
            }
        if (v_display.u_chr[6] <= '5' ) break;
        else {
            v_display.u_chr[6] -= 6;
            (v_display.u_chr[2])++;
            }
        /* update the hours [00-23] display */
```

```
        if (v_display.u_chr[0] == '1' ) {
            if (v_display.u_chr[2] <= '9' ) break;
            else {
                v_display.u_chr[2] -= 10;
                (v_display.u_chr[0])++;
                }
            }
        if (v_display.u_chr[0] == '2' ) {
            if (v_display.u_chr[2] <= '3' ) break;
            else (v_display.u_chr[0])++;
            }
        if (v_display.u_chr[0] <= '2' ) break;
        else {
            v_display.u_chr[0] = '0';
            v_display.u_chr[2] = '0';
            v_display.u_chr[6] = '0';
            v_display.u_chr[8] = '0';
            v_display.u_chr[12] = '0';
            v_display.u_chr[14] = '0';
            break;
            }
        }
    for (i=0, vptr=(int _based(void) *)144; i<8; i++,vptr++)
        *(segvar:>vptr) = v_display.u_int[i];
    }
_chain_intr(save_intr);
}

int main(void)
{
char display[9];
save_intr = _dos_getvect(INT_TICKS);

/* start at an even 5-second interval */
while (1) {
    _strtime(display);
    if (display[7] == '0') break;
    if (display[7] == '5') break;
    }

/* install the custom interrupt handler */
_dos_setvect(INT_TICKS, my_intr);

/* display/save the initial timestamp in reverse video */
for (i=0, vptr=(int _based(void) *)144; i<8; i++,vptr++) {
    v_display.u_int[i] = *(segvar:>vptr);
    v_display.u_chr[2*i] = display[i];
    v_display.u_chr[(2*i)+1] = 0x70; /* RV see ch22e6.c */
    *(segvar:>vptr) = v_display.u_int[i];
    }
/* install as TSR (permanent interrupt) */
_dos_keep(0x0000, 0x0180); /* 6KB = 0x0180 paragraphs */
    /* use the EXEHDR utility */
}
```

Output This is a TSR for a monochrome display; execute ch27e3.exe to install the time-stamp display permanently; for more about the timer interrupt, see Chapter 21. Modify the program as noted to use with a color display.

Comments Care must be exercised when interrupts are enabled within an interrupt function; all critical sections of code within an interrupt function must be performed with interrupts disabled.

Because no critical code sections exist in this interrupt function, **_enable()** is used to restore interrupt recognition.

No DOS/BIOS calls are made to write to the video because they are not reentrant; rather, the video memory addresses are updated directly using a **_based()** pointer.

_dos_keep() ensures that **my_intr()** interrupt function remains permanently installed in memory and in effect until INT 0x1C is replaced or the DOS is rebooted.

As an alternative to calling the function, use the **#pragma intrinsic** form; use an inline assembly 80*x*86 STI instruction (see Chapter 28).

_hard *Functions* *Handle critical hardware error conditions normally processed by INT 0x24*

Compatibility ☐ANSI ☐OS/2 ☐UNIX ☐XENIX

Specification
```
#include <dos.h>
void _harderr(void (_far *handler)(unsigned deverror, unsigned errcode,
    unsigned _far *devhdr));
void _hardresume(int result);
void _hardretn(int error);
```

Arguments

handler: Function pointer to which control passes when an INT 0x24 occurs.

deverror: The AX register value passed by DOS to the INT 0x24 handler; high-order bit-15 will be Off (0) if a disk device error has occurred, and the remaining bit positions are set as follows:

bit-15	Off	Disk error
bit-13	Off	*Ignore* response not allowed
	On	*Ignore* response permitted
bit-12	Off	*Retry* response not allowed
	On	*Retry* response permitted
bit-11	Off	*Fail* response not allowed
	On	*Fail* response permitted

bit-10/9	Off/Off	DOS error
	Off/On	File allocation table (FAT) error
	On/Off	Directory error
	On/On	Data area error
bit-8	Off	Read error
	On	Write error

For all other device error types, bit-15 will be On (1).

errcode: The DI register passed by DOS to the INT 0x24 handler; the low-order byte of **errcode** can be one of the following values:

0	Attempt to write to a write-protected disk
1	Unknown unit
2	Drive not ready
3	Unknown command
4	Cyclic-redundancy-check error in data
5	Bad drive-request structure length
6	Seek error
7	Unknown media type
8	Sector not found
9	Printer out of paper
10	Write fault
11	Read fault
12	General failure

devhdr: A pointer to the nondisk device header; if the attribute word, located at offset 4 in this header, has bit-15 Off (0), the error is a bad memory image of the file allocation table (FAT); otherwise, bit-15 is On (1) indicating a character device error, and the following bit positions are set On (1) to indicate the following:

bit-0	Current standard input
bit-1	Current standard output
bit-2	Current null device
bit-3	Current clock device

result: Only one of the following object-like macros defined in **<dos.h>**:

_HARDERR_ABORT	Abort the program using INT 0x23
_HARDERR_FAIL	Fail the system call that is in progress
_HARDERR_IGNORE	Ignore the error
_HARDERR_RETRY	Retry the operation

error: A DOS error code, not a XENIX-style error normally set in global variable, **errno**.

Example

```
/*FILE: ch27e4.c */
#include <stdio.h>
#include <dos.h>
#include <time.h>

void delay_sec(int nbr_sec)
{
clock_t wait, goal;
wait = nbr_sec * CLK_TCK;
goal = wait + clock();
while(goal > clock()) ;
}

void _far hard_msg(unsigned deverror,
    unsigned errcode,
    unsigned _far *devhdr)
{
char *ptr;
unsigned bit_10, bit_9, bits, drive;
unsigned hdr_attrib;
cprintf("\n\rDisk Device in error: ");
if (!(deverror & 0x8000)) {
    cprintf("Disk Drive ");
    drive = deverror & 0x000F;
    cprintf("%c: in the ", ('A' + drive));
    bit_10 = (deverror & 0x0400) >> 10;
    bit_9 = (deverror & 0x0200) >> 9;
    bits = 10 * bit_10 + bit_9;
    switch (bits) {
        case 0:     cprintf("DOS area"); break;
        case 1:     cprintf("File Allocation Table"); break;
        case 10:    cprintf("Directory"); break;
        case 11:    cprintf("Data Area"); break;
        }
    }
}

void _far resume(unsigned deverror,
    unsigned errcode,
    unsigned _far *devhdr)
{
hard_msg(deverror, errcode, devhdr);
_hardresume(_HARDERR_ABORT );
}

void _far retn(unsigned deverror,
    unsigned errcode,
    unsigned _far *devhdr)
{
```

```
hard_msg(deverror, errcode, devhdr);
_hardretn(0);
}

int main(void)
{
FILE *floppy;

printf("\n\n\aOpen the Gate on Drive A: !!");
delay_sec(2);
printf("\nRespond R to the Error Message, After Closing the Gate");
floppy = fopen("A:\\sample1.doc", "w");

printf("\n\n\aOpen the Gate on Drive A: Again !!");
delay_sec(3);
printf("\nAfter several Error Messages, Close the Gate");
_harderr(retn);
while (!(floppy = fopen("A:\\sample2.doc", "w")));

printf("\n\n\aOpen the Gate on Drive A: Again !!");
delay_sec(3);
_harderr(resume);
floppy = fopen("A:\\sample3.doc", "r");
}
```

Output

```
Open the Gate on Drive A: !!
Respond R to the Error Message, After Closing the Gate
Not ready error reading drive A
Abort, Retry, Ignore? R

Open the Gate on Drive A: Again !!
After several Error Messages, Close the Gate
Disk Device in error: Disk Drive A: in the File Allocation Table
Disk Device in error: Disk Drive A: in the File Allocation Table

Open the Gate on Drive A: Again !!
Disk Device in error: Disk Drive A: in the File Allocation Table
```

Comments **harderr()** schedules the handler to be called when a critical error (INT 0x24) occurs.

Either **hardresume()** or **hardretn()** is called from within the handler to control how handler is terminated; if **hardresume()** is called, control passes to DOS and the program is abnormally terminated; if **hardretn()** is called, control is passed to the application program, where either corrective action or normal termination may occur.

The example program above demonstrates all three possible outcomes: first, a default 0x24 interrupt message; next, a **_hardretn()**; and finally, a **_hardresume()**.

To execute this example program, insert a formatted scratch floppy disk in Drive A: and respond to the program prompts as directed.

_harderr ()   *Install a new critical-error handler for INT 0x24*

Compatibility ☐ANSI   ☐OS/2   ☐UNIX   ☐XENIX

See Also

    _hard functions

Specification

```
#include <dos.h>
void _harderr(void (_far *handler)( unsigned deverror, unsigned errcode,
    unsigned _far *devhdr));
```

_hardresume ()   *Function used by the installed critical error-handler to Return to DOS*

Compatibility ☐ANSI   ☐OS/2   ☐UNIX   ☐XENIX

See Also

    _hard functions

Specification

```
#include <dos.h>
void _hardresume(int result);
```

_hardretn ()   *Function used by the installed critical error-handler to return To an application program*

Compatibility ☐ANSI   ☐OS/2   ☐UNIX   ☐XENIX

See Also

    _hard functions

Specification

```
#include <dos.h>
void _hardretn(int error);
```

`lfind()` *Perform a linear search of a sorted/unsorted array for a specified element value*

Compatibility □ANSI ■OS/2 ■UNIX ■XENIX

See Also

```
bsearch(), lsearch()
```

Specification

```
#include <search.h>
void *lfind(const void *key, const void *base, unsigned int *num, unsigned int
    width, int (*compare)(const void *elem1, const void *elem2));
```

Arguments

key: Pointer to a type object value to be searched for in a sorted/unsorted array.

base: Pointer to first element of a sorted/unsorted array.

num: Pointer to the number of elements in the sorted/unsorted array (up to 64KB).

width: The size of each array element in bytes (up to 64KB).

compare: A pointer to a function that compares two array elements and returns one of the following values:

  !=0   Elements are different

  =0   Elements are identical

elem1: Pointer to the key of the search.

elem2: Pointer to an array element to be compared with **elem1** by function compare.

Return Value

If no matching key is found, a **NULL** pointer.

Otherwise, a pointer to the first matching occurrence of key in the sorted/unsorted array.

Example

```
/* FILE: ch27e5.c */
#include <stdio.h>
#include <stdlib.h>
#include <search.h>
#include <string.h>
#define LIMIT 2499
```

```c
/*
** filter utility: list duplicate files; unique files
** execute this program from the DOS command line as shown:
**      CHKDSK [drive:] /v | ch27e5 > [dev or file]
** pipe the output from chkdsk to ch27e5.exe
*/

int compare(char *arg1, char *arg2)
{
return(strcmpi(arg1, arg2));
}

int main(void)
{
static char name[2500][14];
static unsigned int idx, i;
char *ptrln, *ptrch, *ptrws, *found, buffer[0x80];
int col, row, rem;

printf("\f\rDuplicate filenames:\n");
while (ptrln = fgets(buffer, sizeof(buffer), stdin)) {
    if (ptrch = strrchr(ptrln, '\\')) {
            if (!strchr(ptrch, '.')) continue;
            if (ptrws = strpbrk(ptrch, " \n\r\t\f\v") ) *ptrws = '\0';
            if (!strlen(++ptrch) ) continue;

            found = lfind(ptrch, (char *)name, &idx, (size_t)14, compare);

            if (!found) strcpy(&(name[idx++][0]), ptrch);
            else printf("\n%s", ptrln);
            if (idx > LIMIT) break;
            }
    else continue;
    }

/* sort/display the non-duplicated filenames */
qsort((char *)name, idx, (size_t)14, compare);

printf("\f\rUnique filenames:\n");
col = 4;
row = idx/col;
rem = idx % col;
for (i=0; i<row; i++)
    printf("\n%-14s %-14s %-14s %-14s",
        &(name[i][0]), &(name[row+i][0]),
        &(name[(2*row)+i][0]), &(name[(3*row)+i][0]));
if (rem) for (i=row*col+1; i<=idx; i++)
    printf("\n%-14s %-14s %-14s %-14s",
    "","","",&(name[i][0]));
printf("\f");
exit(0);
}
```

Output   FOR: chkdsk a: /v | ch27e5 >prn

```
Duplicate filenames:
    A:\DIR-2\TABLE-1.1
    A:\DIR-2\TABLE-1.6
    A:\DIR-2\TABLE-1.2
    A:\DIR-2\TABLE-1.4
    A:\DIR-2\TABLE-1.3
    A:\DIR-2\TABLE-1.5
    A:\DIR-3\TABLE-1.1
    A:\DIR-3\TABLE-1.6
    A:\DIR-3\TABLE-1.2
    A:\DIR-3\TABLE-1.4
    A:\DIR-3\TABLE-1.3
    A:\DIR-3\TABLE-1.5

Unique filenames:
COMMAND.COM      TABLE-1.1      TABLE-1.3      TABLE-1.5
DPATH.COM        TABLE-1.2      TABLE-1.4      TABLE-1.6
```

Comments   Unlike **bsearch()**, the array specified for **lfind()** may be in sorted or unsorted order.

If duplicate key values exist in the array, the first occurrence encountered will be returned.

Checks for duplicates can be made by setting **base** to the address of the next array element, adjusting the number of array elements to search (**num**), and reissuing a call to **lfind()** as shown in the example above. This builds a two-dimensional array of characters from the filenames on a volume, piped to it from the DOS utility CHKDSK (entered on the command line that invokes the program). The example program then filters out all duplicate complete filenames (*filename.ext*) and produces an alphabetical list of unique *filename.ext* entries.

The example program uses **lfind()** to detect whether a filename is a duplicate or must be added to the array of filenames, and uses **qsort()** to sort the filenames contained in the contiguous array of characters for reporting purposes.

localeconv()   *Retrieve locale-specific information settings*

Compatibility ■ANSI   ■OS/2   ☐UNIX   ☐XENIX

See Also

setlocale()

Specification

```
#include <locale.h>
struct lconv *localeconv(void);
```

Return Value

Pointer to standard structure, **lconv**, described in Appendix E, which contains the "C" locale conventions established by default, or by the explicit use of **setlocale()**

Example

```
/* FILE: ch27e6.c */
#include <stdio.h>
#include <stdlib.h>
#include <locale.h>
#include <limits.h>

void message_1(int ch)
{
switch (ch) {
    case 0:        printf("repeat previous");     break;
    case CHAR_MAX: printf("no further grouping"); break;
    default:       printf("%d", ch);
    }
}

void message_2(int ch)
{
switch (ch) {
    case 0: printf("(qty sym)");     break;
    case 1: printf("sign qty sym"); break;
    case 2: printf("qty sym sign"); break;
    case 3: printf("qty sign/sym"); break;
    case 4: printf("qty sym/sign"); break;
    default: printf("%d", ch);
    }
}

int main(void)
{
char *ptr;
struct lconv *c_loc;

ptr = setlocale(LC_ALL, "C");
printf("\nLocale: %s", ptr);

c_loc = localeconv();
printf("\nNon-monetary decimal : %s", c_loc->decimal_point);
printf("\nNon-monetary thou-sep: %s", c_loc->thousands_sep);
printf("\nNon-monetary grouping: ");
    message_1(*(c_loc->grouping) );
printf("\n");
printf("\nInt'l currency symbol: %s", c_loc->int_curr_symbol);
printf("\nLocal currency symbol: %s", c_loc->currency_symbol);
printf("\nMonetary decimal    : %s", c_loc->mon_decimal_point);
printf("\nMonetary thou-sep   : %s", c_loc->mon_thousands_sep);
```

```
    printf("\nMonetary grouping     : ", *(c_loc->mon_grouping));
        message_1(*(c_loc->mon_grouping) );
    printf("\nMonetary positive     : %s", c_loc->positive_sign);
    printf("\nMonetary negative     : %s", c_loc->negative_sign);
    printf("\n");
    printf("\nInt'l monetary dec-pl: %d", c_loc->int_frac_digits);
    printf("\nLocal monetary dec-pl: %d", c_loc->frac_digits);
    printf("\nPositive currency sym: ");
        if (c_loc->p_cs_precedes) printf("precedes");
        else printf("follows");
    printf("\nPositive currency sep: ");
        if (c_loc->p_sep_by_space) printf("space separation");
        else printf("no space separation");
    printf("\nNegative currency sym: ");
        if (c_loc->n_cs_precedes) printf("precedes");
        else printf("follows");
    printf("\nNegative currency sep: ");
        if (c_loc->n_sep_by_space) printf("space separation");
        else printf("no space separation");
    printf("\nPositive sign pos    : ");
        message_2(c_loc->p_sign_posn);
    printf("\nNegative sign pos    : ");
        message_2(c_loc->n_sign_posn);
    printf("\n\nValue 127 indicates not meaningful to this locale");
    exit(0);
    }
```

Output

```
    Locale: C
    Non-monetary decimal : .
    Non-monetary thou-sep:
    Non-monetary grouping: repeat previous

    Int'l currency symbol:
    Local currency symbol:
    Monetary decimal     :
    Monetary thou-sep    :
    Monetary grouping    : repeat previous
    Monetary positive    :
    Monetary negative    :

    Int'l monetary dec-pl: 127
    Local monetary dec-pl: 127
    Positive currency sym: precedes
    Positive currency sep: space separation
    Negative currency sym: precedes
    Negative currency sep: space separation
    Positive sign pos    : 127
    Negative sign pos    : 127

    Value 127 indicates not meaningful to this locale
```

Comments Use the **setlocale()** function to establish the current locale settings which consist of the following components: **LC_COLLATE**, **LC_CTYPE**, **LC_MONETARY**, **LC_NUMERIC**, and **LC_TIME**; then use **localeconv()** to retrieve the **lconv** structure information noted above to use throughout an application program.

Presently Microsoft offers only one locale, named "C"; in the future, other locales will be available from which components may be chosen to construct a custom locale setting for use by an application program.

Get DOS-specific (**COUNTRY=xxx**) date, time, and currency conventions using INT 0x21 function 0x38 (see Chapter 22, function **intdos()**).

lsearch() *Perform a linear search of a sorted or unsorted array for a specified element value, and add the element to the end of the array if a match is not found*

Compatibility ☐ANSI ■OS/2 ■UNIX ■XENIX

See Also
    bsearch(), lfind()

Specification
    #include <search.h>
    void *lsearch(const void *key, const void *base, unsigned int *num,
        unsigned int width, int (*compare)(const void *elem1, const void *elem2));

Arguments
key: Pointer to a type object value to be searched for in the sorted/unsorted array.

base: Pointer to first element of a sorted/unsorted array.

num: Pointer to the number of elements in the sorted/unsorted array (up to 64KB).

width: The size of each array element in bytes (up to 64KB).

compare: A pointer to a function that compares two array elements and returns one of the following values:.

    !=0   Elements are different

    ==0   Elements are identical

elem1: Pointer to the key of the search.

elem2: Pointer to an array element to be compared with **elem1** by function compare.

Return Value

If no matching key is found, element *key* is added to the end of the array, and a pointer to that element is returned; otherwise, a pointer to the first occurrence of *key* in the array

Example   See: **bsearch()**, **lfind()**.

Comments   Unlike **bsearch()**, the **lsearch()** function can accept an array in sorted or unsorted order.

Duplicate key value entries will not be created by **lsearch()**; however, if duplicates already exist, they will not be removed.

qsort() *Perform a quick sort of array elements*

Compatibility   ■ANSI   ■OS/2   ■UNIX   ■XENIX

Specification

```
#include <stdlib.h>
#include <search.h>
void qsort(void *base, size_t num, size_t width, int (*compare)
    (const void *elem1, const void *elem2));
```

Arguments

base: Pointer to first element of an array to be sorted.

num: The number of elements in the array (up to 64KB).

width: The size of each array element in bytes (up to 64KB).

compare: A pointer to a function that compares two array elements and returns one of the following values:

    <0   **elem1** less than **elem2**

    =0   **elem1** equal to **elem2**

    >0   **elem1** greater than **elem2**

elem1: Pointer to an array element.

elem2: Pointer to an array element to be compared with **elem1** by function compare.

Example   See also: **bsearch()**, **lfind()**.

```
/* FILE: ch27e7.c */
#include <stdio.h>
#include <stdlib.h>
```

```
#include <search.h>
#define ASCEND     1
#define EQUAL      0
#define DESCEND   -1

static struct tagname {
    char ch;
    int iv;
    char id[11];
    float fv; } str[] = {
        { 'C', 1, "ELEMENT-1", 100.0 },
        { 'C', 26, "ELEMENT-2", 260.0 },
        { 'A', 2, "ELEMENT-3", 20.0 },
        { 'A', 25, "ELEMENT-4", 250.0 },
        { 'B', 3, "ELEMENT-5", 300.0 },
        { 'B', 24, "ELEMENT-6", 240.0 } };

static int width = sizeof(str[0]);
static int num   = sizeof(str)/sizeof(str[0]);

int comp_1(struct tagname *arg1, struct tagname *arg2)
{
/* member iv (ascending) within ch (ascending) */
if (arg1->ch > arg2->ch) return (ASCEND);
else if (arg1->ch == arg2->ch) {
    if (arg1->iv == arg2->iv) return (EQUAL);
    if (arg1->iv >  arg2->iv) return (ASCEND);
    else return(DESCEND);
    }
else return (DESCEND);
}

int comp_2(struct tagname *arg1, struct tagname *arg2)
{
/* member fv (descending) within ch (descending) */
if (arg1->ch > arg2->ch) return (DESCEND);
else if (arg1->ch == arg2->ch) {
    if (arg1->fv == arg2->fv) return (EQUAL);
    if (arg1->fv >  arg2->fv) return (DESCEND);
    else return(ASCEND);
    }
else return (ASCEND);
}

void display_str(struct tagname *ptr)
{
int i;
printf("\n\n");
for (i=0; i<num; i++, ptr++)
    printf("\nch= %c iv= %2d id= %s fv= %f",
        ptr->ch, ptr->iv, ptr->id, ptr->fv);
}
```

```
int main(void)
{
/* sort/display the array of structures using comp_1 */
qsort(str, num, width, comp_1);
display_str(str);

/* sort/display the array of structures using comp_2 */
qsort(str, num, width, comp_2);
display_str(str);
exit(0);
}
```

Output

```
ch= A  iv=  2  id= ELEMENT-3  fv= 20.000000
ch= A  iv= 25  id= ELEMENT-4  fv= 250.000000
ch= B  iv=  3  id= ELEMENT-5  fv= 300.000000
ch= B  iv= 24  id= ELEMENT-6  fv= 240.000000
ch= C  iv=  1  id= ELEMENT-1  fv= 100.000000
ch= C  iv= 26  id= ELEMENT-2  fv= 260.000000

ch= C  iv= 26  id= ELEMENT-2  fv= 260.000000
ch= C  iv=  1  id= ELEMENT-1  fv= 100.000000
ch= B  iv=  3  id= ELEMENT-5  fv= 300.000000
ch= B  iv= 24  id= ELEMENT-6  fv= 240.000000
ch= A  iv= 25  id= ELEMENT-4  fv= 250.000000
ch= A  iv=  2  id= ELEMENT-3  fv= 20.000000
```

Comments   The elements of the array are sorted into ascending order as defined by the compare function; to sort in descending order, reverse the sense of the comparison function as shown in the example program above.

setlocale()   *Establishes a locale for use by an application program*

Compatibility   ■ANSI   ■OS/2   ☐UNIX   ☐XENIX

Specification

```
#include <locale.h>
char *setlocale(int category, const char *locale);
```

Arguments

category: The selected category or subgroup of the items defined for locale, expressed as one of the following object-like macros defined in **<locale.h>**:

LC_ALL	All locale categories
LC_COLLATE	Collation: strcoll() and **strxfrm()**
LC_CTYPE	Character handling: <ctype.h>

LC_MONETARY	Monetary: **localeconv()** formatting standards
LC_NUMERIC	Nonmonetary: **localeconv()** decimal display
LC_TIME	Time: strftime()

locale: The name of the locale that will control the specified category; presently "C" is the only locale provided by Microsoft; if a **NULL** pointer is specified, the category values are not changed, but only retrieved.

Return Value

A pointer to a string that may be used later to restore that part of the locale's information; subsequent calls to **setlocale()** will overwrite the string

Example   See: **localeconv()**.

Comments   By using **setlocale()**, an application program will be able to dynamically reassign the locale setting in effect; this is unlike the present DOS facility which requires that the CONFIG.SYS file commands be revised, and the system rebooted to reflect the revisions. Both of these facilities coexist, but they do not interact. One does not affect the other.

Establish DOS-specific date, time, and currency conventions by using the DOS configuration command **COUNTRY=** and the other **NLSFUNC**-related DOS commands.

8

Extending Microsoft C

Part VIII will assist you in completing software projects that meet not only their design objectives, but the performance targets that were envisioned for those projects as well. The advanced topics include inline assembly programming (Chapter 28) and debugging strategies (Chapter 29).

At times, in spite of the advances that have been made to optimize the code generation capabilities of Microsoft's C compilers, even better program performance is needed. When this situation arises, source-code portability may have to be sacrificed and inline assembly programming utilized on a select basis as remedies. Because the use of inline assembly code is non-Standard, you should document carefully the restrictions and limitations applying to all such code.

Chapter 28 discusses how inline assembly instructions can be embedded within C source-code programs by using the non-Standard C keywords **_asm** and **_emit**. Because inline assembly instructions are interpreted by the C compiler, a separate assembler, such as Microsoft's QuickAssembler or MacroAssembler (MASM), is not required. Only a subset of the capabilities provided by MASM, however, is supported by the inline assembly feature of the QuickC and OptimizingC compilers.

This chapter is not intended as a tutorial on assembly language programming, but rather as an overview of how inline assembly programming can supplement the development of C programs and provide for improved program performance. In Chapter 28, we will present an interesting coding comparison that dramatizes how selective use of inline assembly programming can improve the performance of optimized C code.

Perhaps the most challenging aspect of working with the C language concerns the issue of debugging. The difficulty in debugging C programs is rooted in the basic design philosophy of the C language itself, which "trusts the programmer" and permits the programmmer "to do what needs to be done." Because of this philosophy, the subject of debugging C programs is heightened in importance and is discussed more suitably within the context of an overall strategy, rather than as an afterthought, as in other high-level languages.

Chapter 29 is intended to provide an overview of the CodeView, CV Pack, and QH tools and techniques available to make debugging C programs easier. Any overall debugging strategy starts with mastery of the C language itself. It is hoped that the information presented thus far has provided you with the framework to understand the concepts governing C program development. This framework will serve as the best source of insight to solve the problems that inevitably will be encountered when testing C programs. To remove some of the mystique associated with the art of debugging software, Chapter 29 presents a strategy for debugging C programs consisting of three major components: defensive programming techniques, interactive debugging tools, and third-party debugging utilities.

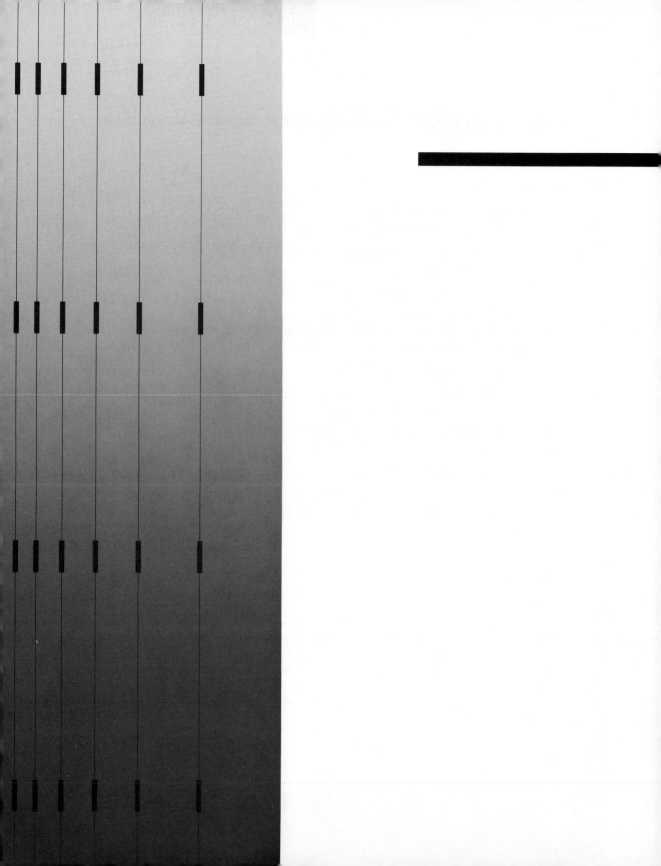

Inline Assembly Programming

Inline Assembly Programming

This chapter shows how to incorporate $80x86/87$ assembly-language code into Microsoft C programs. It is not, however, a tutorial on assembly-language programming.

Let's begin by reviewing the assembly-language programming options that are available for use with the Microsoft family of language products. The inline assembly features supported by both the QuickC and OptimizingC compilers are identical and represent a subset of the recently released Microsoft QuickAssembler and the mainstay MacroAssembler (MASM) products. This chapter features program examples that illustrate how inline assembly instructions are typically used within C programs.

Inline assembly has a number of distinct advantages over MASM when programming in the C language; however, when inline assembly blocks of code are incorporated into a C function, certain restrictions are placed on existing C coding conventions within that function. A code-timing example program demonstrates how the use of inline assembly code can improve the performance of the optimized code generated by either the QuickC or OptimizingC compiler.

When the performance requirements of an application outweigh the need to maintain source-code portability, and the recommended standard coding techniques described in this book are not sufficient, inline assembly-language programming should be used judiciously and documented carefully. Compiler options available only with the OptimizingC compiler (**/Fa**, **/Fc**, and **/Fl**) produce .COD files, which reveal the source, assembly, and corresponding object code generated by the OptimizingC compiler. Close scrutiny of .COD files can reveal sections of C source code that warrant improvement by replacement with inline assembly instructions. (As discussed in Chapter 29, the CodeView debugger can also be used to examine the assembly-language code generated by Microsoft's C compilers.)

The chapter concludes with a series of program examples that demonstrate some of the ways that inline assembly programming can be used to replace and improve upon the performance of existing C code.

ASSEMBLY LANGUAGE VERSUS C

Computer languages often are classified according to their level of abstraction away from the minutely detailed instructions of machine code. The closer it corresponds to machine instructions, the more "low-level" a language is said to be. C typically is described as a high-level language, but compared to BASIC, Fortran, and Pascal it more accurately might be called a mid-level language. Compared to assembly language, C provides partial but not complete control over machine registers and access to $80x86/87$ machine instructions. As discussed in Chapter 22, the REGS and SREGS structures (described in Appendix E) allow us to control the setting of some register values when used in conjunction with the **intdos()**, **intdosx()**, **int86()**, and **int86x()** run-time functions; segment register values can be retrieved using the **segread()** function. These services, however, do not offer complete access to and control over all machine register settings.

The non-Standard inline assembly feature of Microsoft C is designed to fill this void and permit C programs to access and alter machine register values directly, and to perform any instruction available for use with the $80x86/87$ processor in use. Even instructions not supported by the Quick-C and OptimizingC compilers may be performed by using the non-Standard keyword **_emit**.

Inline assembly instructions inherit the current values of all registers (see Table 22.2) and flags (see Figure 9.13). It is not necessary to preserve the AX, BX, CX, DX, ES, and Flag registers; however, all other register values should be preserved (DS, SS, DI, SI, SP and BP). If your inline code changes the direction flag (DF) by using the **std** or **cld** assembly instructions, be sure to restore the DF flag to its original value. Note that the C compiler uses the SI and DI registers to store **register** storage-class variables; however, there is no way to know which registers are used to store such variables.

Just as the C++ extensions to C are transforming C into a hybrid structured- and object-oriented programming language, the inline assembly extensions to C have transformed C into a hybrid high- and low-level language as well. For these reasons, it should not be surprising that C, which satisfies a wide range of software development needs, is rapidly becoming the industry language of choice.

Inline versus Stand-Alone Assembly

Before focusing on the details of coding inline assembly instructions, it is important to understand how inline assembly differs from stand-alone assembly programming.

Microsoft's MacroAssembler (MASM) product is designed for use as a stand-alone assembler and is marketed as a separate, full-service language product (list $150). Every assembly procedure (module) created for MASM must be edited into a separate .ASM source-code file and assembled to produce a corresponding .OBJ file, which subsequently must be linked to produce a .COM or .EXE file (see Chapter 3).

The inline assembly features supported for use with Microsoft's QuickC and OptimizingC compilers represent a subset of those features available with MASM. In particular, using MASM has the following advantages over inline assembly:

- MASM can declare data; inline assembly cannot.
- MASM has extensive macro-substitution capabilities; inline assembly has none.
- MASM accommodates source code written to comply with earlier versions of Microsoft's assembly language; inline assembly does not do so.
- MASM modules can be interfaced with other high-level language (BASIC, Fortran, Pascal) programs easily; inline assembly cannot.
- MASM assembles large files of source code more quickly than inline assembly.
- MASM provides a more comprehensive set of warning and error messages than inline assembly.

Inline assembly, however, does maintain a distinct advantage over MASM for the performance of certain programming tasks:

- Inline assembly instructions may be embedded within C source-code files, while MASM procedures must be edited into a separate .ASM file.
- Inline assembly instructions do not always represent a complete procedure (function), whereas MASM instructions always represent a complete procedure.
- Inline assembly instructions do not always involve the overhead of a function call (stack frame), whereas MASM procedures always use function calling conventions.

- Inline assembly supports spot-optimization with small sections of assembly code, whereas MASM does not.

In addition to the inline assembly features of the QuickC version 2.5 (list $99) and OptimizingC (list $495), Microsoft also markets an integrated C and assembly-language product called QuickC w/Quick-Assembler (list $199), which provides for the development of C programs, C programs with inline assembly instructions, and stand-alone assembly programs that have all the features of MASM, except for the protected-mode 80286 and 80386 instructions.

This chapter discusses only the inline assembler that is integrated with the QuickC and OptimizingC compilers and does not require the separate purchase of Microsoft's QuickAssembler or MacroAssembler. If you need assembly-language capabilities that exceed what inline assembly can provide, consider purchasing either the QuickAssembler or Macro-Assembler products and focus on mastering 80x86/87 assembly language.

Consequences of Using Inline Assembly

The use of inline assembly code within a C function affects the way the C code within that function is interpreted by the C compiler and, therefore, modifies the manner in which the C source code is normally interpreted in the following ways:

- The introduction of inline assembly instructions makes a C program non-Standard by the use of the non-Standard C keywords **_asm** and **_emit**.
- Inline assembly instructions may not be acceptable to other C compilers nor applicable to processor instruction sets that are not Intel-conforming.
- Inline assembly instructions are never optimized by the QuickC or OptimizingC compilers. The presence of inline code inhibits (1) the use of loop optimization (**/Oi**), (2) global register allocation (**/Oe**), and (3) the elimination of common subexpressions (**/Og**) for the remaining code within a function.
- To utilize 80286/87 inline assembler instructions, you must specify the C compiler option **/G2** or use the **_emit** keyword.
- Because assembly language recognizes the semicolon as the beginning of a comment and C recognizes it as the termination of a statement, restrict commenting in inline assembly blocks to use the C commenting style of **/* .. */**.

- When an inline assembly instruction is defined as a C object-like macro, certain restrictions apply to the expression of the inline code.
- Although C compiler directives may be used within inline assembly blocks of code, the inline assembler is not a MacroAssembler and does not support MASM macro-substitution directives.
- The use of **register** storage-class variables within a function containing inline assembly instructions is assured only if the **register** keyword is used.
- The use of the qualifier **_fastcall** is not recommended for functions that contain inline assembly instructions.
- The nesting of inline assembly instructions does not affect the visibility (scope) of variables as the use of braces does in C.
- Inline assembly instructions recognize all operators as assembly operators, not as C operators.
- Labels defined within inline assembly blocks are not case-sensitive, whereas, all labels within C source code are case-sensitive.
- Structure and union tags are not recognized within **_asm** blocks.
- Integer constant values within **_asm** blocks recognize the C decimal, octal, and hexadecimal notation formats, as well as the radix notation 10h which is equivalent to 0x10.

It must be emphasized that the restrictions noted above apply only to the functions in which the **_asm** keyword is used to introduce inline assembly code, not to the entire program that is produced by the linker.

PERFORMANCE COMPARISON

The example program shown in Figure 28.1 compares three alternative coding methods of getting the DOS system time:

1. Using the **int86()** function to access the DOS INT 0x21 function 0x2C as described in Chapter 22
2. Using the **_dos_gettime()** function described in Chapter 21
3. Using inline assembly code to generate a 0x21 interrupt

The program compares these three alternatives from a performance point of view by using the **START()** and **STOP** timing macros developed in Chapter 5.

```
/* FILE: ch28e1.c */
#include <stdio.h>
#include <stdlib.h>
#include <dos.h>
#define TIMER
#include "timer.h"
#define NTIMES 10000

int main(void)
{
struct dostime_t time;
union REGS ir, or;
int i, hours, minutes, seconds;

START(int86());
for (i=0; i<NTIMES; i++) {
  ir.h.ah=0x2C;
  int86(0x21, &ir, &or);
  hours = or.h.ch;
  minutes = or.h.cl;
  seconds = or.h.dh;
  }
STOP;

START(_dos_gettime());
for (i=0; i<NTIMES; i++) {
  _dos_gettime(&time);
  hours = time.hour;
  minutes = time.minute;
  seconds = time.second;
  }
STOP;

START(_asm);
for (i=0; i<NTIMES; i++) {
  _asm {
      mov ah, 2Ch
      int 21h
      mov al, ch
      cbw
      mov hours, ax
      mov al, cl
      cbw
      mov minutes,ax
      mov al, dh
      cbw
      mov seconds,ax
      }
  }
STOP;
exit(0);
}
```

FIGURE 28.1: Sample program ch28e1.c demonstrates how inline assembly programming can improve program performance.

When this program was compiled using the QuickC compiler (using **/Ox** optimization) and executed on an IBM/XT-compatible machine, the following output was produced:

```
for  : int86()
time :   16.20 sec
```

```
for  :  _dos_gettime()
time :     13.84 sec

for  :  _asm
time :     13.24 sec
```

Notice that the inline assembly version netted about a 5 percent improvement over using the **_dos_gettime()** function, and about a 20 percent improvement over using the **int86()** function.

The best way to understand these results is to examine the assembly listings that are generated when the **/Fa**, **/Fc**, or **/Fl** compiler options are specified with OptimizingC, or by using the CodeView debugger described in Chapter 29. An edited version of the .COD file produced for the program when the **/Fc** compiler option was used with OptimizingC is shown in Figure 28.2.

Examine the relative differences of the assembly code generated by the three alternatives in the combined source, assembly, and object code listing file (.COD). Notice that the biggest saving that resulted from using inline assembly code in this instance was the elimination of the function-calling sequence that requires a stack frame to be built (see Chapter 15).

Clearly, whenever function calls can be eliminated, performance will improve. Similarly, if functions must be used, those with fewer and smaller arguments will be faster and, if those arguments can be passed in registers rather than on the stack, additional time savings will result. This explains the attractiveness of declaring function arguments as **register** storage class and, when possible, using the **_fastcall** function qualifier. A similar line of reasoning applies to evaluating the tradeoffs of using **#pragma intrinsic** and macro versions of functions, rather than standard function-calling sequences.

Whenever performance considerations outweigh the need for source-code portability, examine the assembly code produced by Microsoft's C

```
;|*** START(int86());
;|*** hours=seconds=minutes=0;
;|*** for (i=0; i<NTIMES; i++) {
;|***     ir.h.ah=0x2C;
         *** 000036     c6 46 df 2c     mov     BYTE PTR [bp-33],44
;|***     int86(0x21, &ir, &or);
         *** 00003a     8d 46 f0        lea     ax,WORD PTR [bp-16]
         *** 00003d     50              push    ax
         *** 00003e     8d 46 de        lea     ax,WORD PTR [bp-34]
         *** 000041     50              push    ax
         *** 000042     b8 21 00        mov     ax,33
         *** 000045     50              push    ax
         *** 000046     e8 00 00        call    _int86
         *** 000049     83 c4 06        add     sp,6
```

FIGURE 28.2: Edited version of the .COD file for program ch28e1.c, compiled with option /Fc.

```
;|***    hours = or.h.ch;
         ***  00004c      8a 46 f5       mov     al,BYTE PTR [bp-11]
         ***  00004f      2a e4          sub     ah,ah
         ***  000051      89 46 fe       mov     WORD PTR [bp-2],ax
;|***    minutes = or.h.dh;
         ***  000054      8a 46 f7       mov     al,BYTE PTR [bp-9]
         ***  000057      89 46 ee       mov     WORD PTR [bp-18],ax
;|***    seconds = or.h.dl;
         ***  00005a      8a 46 f6       mov     al,BYTE PTR [bp-10]
         ***  00005d      89 46 dc       mov     WORD PTR [bp-36],ax
;|***    )

;|***    START(_dos_gettime());
;|***    hours=seconds=minutes=0;
;|***    for (i=0; i<NTIMES; i++) {
;|***        _dos_gettime(&time);
         ***  0000ee      8d 46 d8       lea     ax,WORD PTR [bp-40]
         ***  0000f1      50             push    ax
         ***  0000f2      e8 00 00       call    __dos_gettime
         ***  0000f5      83 c4 02       add     sp,2
;|***        hours = time.hour;
         ***  0000f8      8a 46 d8       mov     al,BYTE PTR [bp-40]
         ***  0000fb      2a e4          sub     ah,ah
         ***  0000fd      89 46 fe       mov     WORD PTR [bp-2],ax
;|***        minutes = time.minute;
         ***  000100      8a 46 d9       mov     al,BYTE PTR [bp-39]
         ***  000103      89 46 ee       mov     WORD PTR [bp-18],ax
;|***        seconds = time.second;
         ***  000106      8a 46 da       mov     al,BYTE PTR [bp-38]
         ***  000109      89 46 dc       mov     WORD PTR [bp-36],ax
;|***    )

;|***    START(_asm);
;|***    for (i=0; i<NTIMES; i++) {
;|***        _asm (
;|***            mov ah, 2Ch
         ***  000178      b4 2c          mov     ah,44
;|***            int 21h
         ***  00017a      cd 21          int     33
;|***        mov al, ch
         ***  00017c      8a c5          mov     al,ch
;|***        cbw
         ***  00017e      98             cbw
;|***        mov hours, ax
         ***  00017f      89 46 fe       mov     WORD PTR [bp-2],ax
;|***        mov al, cl
         ***  000182      8a c1          mov     al,cl
;|***        cbw
         ***  000184      98             cbw
;|***        mov minutes,ax
         ***  000185      89 46 ee       mov     WORD PTR [bp-18],ax
;|***        mov al, dh
         ***  000188      8a c6          mov     al,dh
;|***        cbw
         ***  00018a      98             cbw
;|***        mov seconds,ax
         ***  00018b      89 46 dc       mov     WORD PTR [bp-36],ax
;|***            )
;|***    )
```

FIGURE 28.2: Edited version of the .COD file for program ch28e1.c, compiled with option /Fc (continued).

compilers. Given the dependency of C upon the run-time library and function calls in general, it should not be surprising that whenever the use of standard function-calling conventions can be minimized, performance improvements result. If you are not convinced of this, review the discussion of stack frames in Chapter 15. Stack frames hold the answer to many performance and debugging problems that are experienced when working with C.

WRITING INLINE ASSEMBLY CODE

Now that the justification for using inline assembly code has been established, the optional ways in which assembly-language programming can be implemented have been reviewed, and the major impacts of electing to use inline assembly code have been highlighted, let's proceed to examine the rules that apply to the expression of inline assembly code.

C Keywords for Inline Assembly

The non-Standard keyword **_asm** invokes the inline assembler and can appear wherever a C statement can be used within a C source-code file. Two formats are possible when the **_asm** keyword is used. One uses the **_asm** keyword with each assembler instruction as follows:

```
_asm  mov ah, 3
_asm  mov bh, 0
_asm  int 10h
```

The second format uses an equivalent **_asm** block syntax as follows:

```
_asm {
    mov ah, 3
    mov bh, 0
    int 10h
    }
```

You may recognize that the instruction sequence above invokes the BIOS Video Interrupt 0x10 to get the current cursor position (see Chapter 22).

The first format above is convenient when individual assembly-language instructions must be inserted within C source code. For example, the **_disable()** and **_enable()** run-time functions can be replaced as follows:

```
_asm cli  /* disable interrupts */
_asm sti  /* enable interrupts  */
```

It is also possible to code more than one assembler instruction on a line of input (up to a newline character) as follows:

```
_asm  mov ah, 3  _asm  mov bh, 0  _asm  int 10h
```

This is not recommended, however, because the CodeView debugger (Chapter 29) can set breakpoints and watchpoints only at line boundaries, not for individual statements within a line. Therefore, when more than one assembly (or C) statement must be coded, use the **_asm {** .. **}** format shown above. By using this approach, you also can avoid the compilation errors that may arise by incorrectly intermingling C statements, assembly instructions, and any documenting comments.

The only exception to this recommendation arises when an **_asm** block of instructions is to be expressed as a C object-like macro, because object-like macro substitution is always treated as a contiguous line of input. For this reason, the correct expression of the example noted above would be as follows.

```
#define ASM _asm {          \
    _asm mov ah, 3          \
    _asm mov bh, 0          \
    _asm int 10h            \
    }
```

This expression is expanded by the C preprocessor to the following line of input:

```
_asm { _asm mov ah, 3 _asm mov bh, 0 _asm int 10h }
```

Notice that for the proper substitution to occur, we must use the backslash-newline convention to continue a macro definition (see Chapter 5) and preface each inline assembly instruction with the **_asm** keyword. Because of the reasons stated above concerning the CodeView debugger, it is not recommended that object-macro definitions be used to perform inline assembly programming.

The **_emit** keyword provides the mechanism to introduce machine instructions that are not supported by the C compiler and hence the inline assembler itself. For instance, you can use **_emit** to perform 80286/87 protected-mode or 80386/87 instructions, which are not presently supported by the QuickC and OptimizingC compilers.

The **_emit** keyword allows you to introduce a single immediate byte at the current location in the current text segment. This byte becomes the byte pointed to by the IP (Instruction Pointer) register and is the start of the next instruction to be executed. For instance, to define the 80386 CWDE (Convert Word to Double Word Sign Extended) instruction, which is not supported for use by either the QuickC or OptimizingC compiler, use one of the following sets of inline assembly instructions:

```
_asm _emit 0x66
_asm _emit 0x98
```

or

```
_asm {
    _emit 0x66
    _emit 0x98
    }
```

The 80386 CWDE instruction extends the sign bit of the AX register into the upper 16 bits of the 32-bit EAX register when the conversion is performed. The processor interprets the inline instructions above as the CWDE instruction. The 0x66 byte represents an implicit operand length prefix byte (double word), and the 0x98 byte represents the opcode of CWDE. Notice that the **_emit** keyword must be used in conjunction with the **_asm** keyword as demonstrated in the examples above; **_emit** is never used by itself.

Other Inline Assembly Restrictions

Now that we understand how to introduce inline assembly instructions into a C source-code file, let's consider some of the restrictions that apply to the use of inline versus stand-alone assembly programming.

Although an **_asm** block can reference C data types and objects, it cannot define data objects with MASM directives or operators. Neither the directives DB, DW, DD, DQ, DT, DF, STRUC, RECORD, WIDTH, or MASK, nor the operators DUP or THIS can be used; however, the directives EVEN and ALIGN are supported, together with the operators TYPE, LENGTH, and SIZE. If we had a C array declared as

```
int array[6];
```

then the TYPE, LENGTH, and SIZE operators could be used within an **_asm** block and would yield the values shown below for **array**:

TYPE	2
LENGTH	6
SIZE	12

Also, remember that the inline assembler is not a macro assembler; therefore the familar MASM macro directives MACRO, REPT, IRC, IRP, and ENDM cannot be used, nor can the macro operators **<>**, **!**, **&**, **%**, or **.TYPE** be used.

Finally, registers must always be specified to express the segment component of a memory address within an **_asm** block. The predefined names **_TEXT**, **_DATA**, **_CONST**, and **_STACK** cannot be used. When brackets are used with an **_asm** block, they are interpreted as the MASM index operator, which yields an unscaled byte offset value from any data object or label. This means that the subscript values coded are not scaled by the type of the object, but instead always assume a type size of 1 byte. To scale offset values within an **_asm** block and correctly assign the value of one to array[5], express the index as

```
_asm mov array[5 * TYPE int], 1
```

TYPICAL USES OF INLINE ASSEMBLY CODE

This section presents a series of example programs that demonstrate a variety of possible inline assembly uses. Their purpose is to spur your interest and curiosity to explore the uses of Microsoft's inline assembler, QuickAssembler, or MacroAssembler (MASM).

Review the following example programs to get a sense of how assembly language can be integrated with C programs when it is necessary to enhance overall program performance beyond the performance obtained by varying the selection of available C compiler and linker options.

Calling a Run-Time Function

By following the rules that govern the manner in which stack frames are constructed, **_asm** blocks can be used to push run-time function arguments to the stack (rightmost to leftmost for **_cdecl**) and then issue the assembly language **call** instruction, as demonstrated in the program listed in Figure 28.3.

The program generates this output:

```
str= sample st
```

Notice that the arguments for the **strncpy()** function are pushed to the stack to conform with the **_cdecl** function-calling convention. The variables (array, string, format) have been declared externally to force their segment addresses to be the DS register, rather than declaring them as **auto** storage class, in which case addressing would have been from the BP register (negative offset). Notice in the **_asm** block how pointer variables are handled differently than arrays.

Since function **strncpy()** returns a **_near** pointer (Small memory model), its return value is found in the AX register (see Chapter 15, Table 15.2). Because we cannot use a C assignment statement to capture the

```
/* FILE: ch28e2.c */
/* use the small memory model */
#include <stdio.h>
#include <string.h>

char array[20], *ptr_array;
char *string = "sample string";
char format[] = "\nstr= %s";

int main( void)
{
_asm {
        mov ax, 9
        push ax
        mov ax, string
        push ax
        mov ax, offset array
        push ax
        call strncpy
        mov ptr_array, ax
        }
printf(format, ptr_array);
exit(0);
}
```

FIGURE 28.3: Sample program ch28e2.c demonstrates how to call a C run-time function using in-line assembly.

return value of **strncpy()**, we have saved the contents of the AX register in program variable **ptr_array** immediately after returning from the call to **strncpy()**. Since only a portion (9 characters) of the entire string was copied by the **strncpy()** run-time function, the terminating null character was not copied, but its presence was guaranteed by the fact that the variable, **array[20]**, is of **extern** storage class, and therefore each of its character positions is automatically initialized to null ' **\0**' .

Replacing a C Function

The entire body of a C function can be replaced with an **_asm** block as demonstrated by the program listed in Figure 28.4. The function **rev_str()** accepts a pointer to a string as an argument, and returns a pointer to the same string whose characters have been reversed.

The output for a typical interactive session of running this program is shown below:

```
Enter a string to reverse (or END): SYBEX BOOKS
SYBEX BOOKS
SKOOB XEBYS

Enter a string to reverse (or END): end
```

```
/* FILE: ch28e3.c */
/* use the small memory model */
#include <stdio.h>
#include <stdlib.h>
#include <string.h>

char *rev_str(char *str_ptr)
{
_asm {
        mov bx, str_ptr
        sub cx, cx
  put:  push cx
        mov cl, [bx]
        jcxz rev
        inc bx
        jmp put
  rev:  mov bx, str_ptr
  get:  pop cx
        mov [bx], cl
        jcxz end
        inc bx
        jmp get
  end:  mov ax, str_ptr
        }
}

int main(void)
{
static char array[0x80];
while (1) {
     printf("\n\nEnter a string to reverse (or END): ");
     gets(array);
     if (!stricmp(array,"END")) break;
     printf("\n%s", array);
     printf("\n%s", rev_str(array));
     }
exit(0);
}
```

FIGURE 28.4: Sample program ch28e3.c demonstrates how to replace the body of a C function with inline assembly.

This example demonstrates that C function argument names serve as labels within **_asm** blocks and, when objects are pushed to the stack, they are popped from the stack in a LIFO (last in, first out) manner. This technique is used to reverse the characters of the string. Because we pushed a null character (AX=0) to the stack first, a count of characters pushed to the stack did not have to be maintained; rather, characters are simply popped off the stack until the null character value is encountered. In keeping with the C convention of using registers to return all function return values, the **_near** pointer, **str_ptr**, is returned in the AX register (see Chapter 15, Table 15.2).

Handling Interrupt Processing

Normally DOS and BIOS interrupts are processed by using run-time function **int86()** or **int86x()** (Chapter 22), or directly by initiating an interrupt from within an **_asm** block as demonstrated in Figure 28.1. The program listed in Figure 28.5 uses a hybrid approach, in which the register setup is performed using an **_asm** block and the actual function call is performed using indirection.

A representative copy of the output displayed by this program would be as follows:

```
DOS system time 14:25:30
```

Note that the interrupt function pointer, **vid_ptr**, is retrieved from the interrupt vector table by using the **_dos_getvect()** function (Chapter 27). Since the function pointer **vid_ptr** has no arguments, none are pushed to the stack and the **_cdecl** keyword has no effect; however, the keywords **_interrupt** and **_far** have distinct effects. When **_interrupt** is specified, additional register values are preserved on the stack (see Chapter 27). Because **_far** is used, both the CS and IP register values are set to reflect the branch (**jmp**) that is to occur. If **_near** were used, only the IP register value would be set and CS would remain unchanged.

```
/* FILE: ch28e4.c */
/* use the small memory model */
#include <stdio.h>
#include <stdlib.h>
#include <dos.h>
#include <time.h>
#define INT_VIDEO 0x10

int main(void)
{
int i;
char disp_ch, sys_time[9];
void (_cdecl _interrupt _far *vid_ptr)(void);

vid_ptr = _dos_getvect(INT_VIDEO);
_strtime(sys_time);

setbuf(stdout,NULL);
printf("\nDOS system time ");
for (i=0; i<9; i++) {
    disp_ch = sys_time[i];
    _asm {
        mov ah, 0Eh
        mov al, disp_ch
        mov bh, 0
        mov bl, 0
        }
    (*vid_ptr)();
    }
exit(0);
}
```

FIGURE 28.5: Sample program ch28e4.c demonstrates how to issue DOS interrupts using inline assembly.

Working with Far Pointers and Arrays

The example program listed in Figure 28.6 provides a comprehensive look at how both **_far** and **_based** pointers are handled in assembly language as argument and return values, and shows how register and array element values are accessed.

```c
/* FILE: ch28e6.c */
/* use the small memory model */
#include <stdio.h>
#include <stdlib.h>
#include <string.h>
#define LIM 25

/* return the address of the array
   element with the largest integer value */

int _far *maxval(int _far *st_addr, int nbr_elem)
{
int test_val;
_asm {
        les cx, st_addr
        mov di, cx
        mov cx, nbr_elem
        mov bx, es:[di]
        mov test_val, bx
    br1: mov bx, es:[di]
        cmp test_val, bx
        jg  br2
        mov test_val, bx
        mov ax, di
    br2: add di, TYPE nbr_elem
        loop br1
        mov dx, es
        }
    }

int main(void)
{
static int _based(_segname("_CODE")) array[LIM];
int _far *ptr_int;
_segment data_seg, code_seg;
int i, nbr_elem= sizeof(array)/sizeof(array[0]);

_asm {
    mov data_seg, ds
    mov code_seg, cs
    }
printf("\nData Segment= %04X", data_seg);
printf("\nCode Segment= %04X", code_seg);

for (i=0; i<nbr_elem; i++) array[i] = 10 + (i*10);
ptr_int = maxval( array, nbr_elem);
printf("\nArray Starting Address : %lp", (void _far *)array);
printf("\nMaximum Element Address: %lp", ptr_int);
printf("\nMaximum Element Value  : %d", *ptr_int);
exit(0);
}
```

FIGURE 28.6: Sample program ch28e6.c demonstrates how to work with arrays and _far pointers with inline assembly.

The output that was produced by this program is as follows:

```
Data Segment= 0CEC
Code Segment= 0BC6
Array Starting Address : 0BC6:0054
Maximum Element Address: 0BC6:0084
Maximum Element Value  : 250
```

The program demonstrates some interesting aspects of both C and assembly-language programmming. The **maxval()** function is designed to return a **_far** pointer and, conforming with C return conventions (see Table 15.2), places the segment in the DX register and the offset in the AX register.

The assembler TYPE operator is used to determine the size of an integer object, which is in turn used to increment the DI register, representing the offset portion of the address associated with each array element from its starting segment address stored in the ES register.

Notice in function **main()** that by declaring the integer array with **_based** addressing, we allocate the data array to the code segment (CS). Although every effort is made to segregate code and data, it is possible to place data within the code segment when **_based** addressing is used. Notice how the DS and CS register values are retrieved using an **_asm** block rather than using the run-time function **segread()**, and how the display of their respective values confirms the Small memory model map depicted in Figure 2.21. The segment addresses shown for the integer array confirm that the allocation occurred in the code segment.

Also note that although **_based** pointer variables themselves occupy only two bytes of storage, when they are passed as function arguments or returned by a function they are treated as **_far** pointer types, which reflects the fact that both the segment and offset of the memory address is passed and returned. In a similar fashion, notice how the cast (**void _far ***) is used to change the **_based** pointer (array) to a form suitable to the **printf()** function.

Working with Structures

The only restriction in working with structures (and unions) within an **_asm** block is that tag names are not recognized. The example program listed in Figure 28.7 demonstrates how to access the members of a structure (**str2**) that contains another structure as a member (**str1**).

```
/* FILE: ch28e5.c */
/* use the small memory model */
#include <stdio.h>
#include <stdlib.h>

int main(void)
{
static struct tag1 {
     char ch1;
     int iv1;
     struct tag1 *ptag1;
     } str1 = { 'C', 77, NULL };

static struct tag2 {
     char ch2;
     struct tag1 str1;
     } str2 = { 'B', { 'A', 99, &str1 } };

static struct tag1 *pstr2_str1, *pstr2_str1_ptag1;
static char str2_ch2, str2_str1_ch1;
static int str2_str1_iv1;

_asm {
     mov bx, offset str2
     sub cx, cx
     mov cl, [bx].ch2
     mov str2_ch2, cl

     mov bx, offset str2.str1
     mov pstr2_str1, bx

     sub cx, cx
     mov cl, [bx].ch1
     mov str2_str1_ch1, cl

     mov cx, [bx].iv1
     mov str2_str1_iv1, cx

     mov cx, [bx].ptag1
     mov pstr2_str1_ptag1, cx
     }
printf("\nstr2_ch2           = %c", str2_ch2);
printf("\nstr2_str1_ch1      = %c", pstr2_str1->ch1);
printf("\nstr2_str1_iv1      = %d", pstr2_str1->iv1);
printf("\nstr2_str1_ptag1    = %p", pstr2_str1->ptag1);

printf("\nstr2_str1_ch1      = %c", str2_str1_ch1);
printf("\nstr2_str1_iv1      = %d", str2_str1_iv1);
printf("\nstr2_str1_ptag1    = %p", pstr2_str1_ptag1);
printf("\nstr2_str1_ptag1_ch1 = %c", pstr2_str1_ptag1->ch1);
printf("\nstr2_str1_ptag1_iv1 = %d", pstr2_str1_ptag1->iv1);
printf("\nstr2_str1_ptag1_ptag1= %p", pstr2_str1_ptag1->ptag1);
exit(0);
}
```

FIGURE 28.7: Sample program ch28e5.c demonstrates how to work with members of structures using inline assembly.

The output produced by this program is shown below:

```
str2_ch2          = B
str2_str1_ch1     = A
str2_str1_iv1     = 99
str2_str1_ptag1   = 0042
str2_str1_ch1     = A
str2_str1_iv1     = 99
str2_str1_ptag1   = 0042
str2_str1_ptag1_ch1   = C
str2_str1_ptag1_iv1   = 77
str2_str1_ptag1_ptag1= 0000
```

In the example above, extensive use of the offset directive is made to determine an address of a member, as well as the period (.) member operator. Notice the differences between returning the value of a member object and its address. The addressing mechanism shown works only because the structures are declared to be of storage-class **static** (DS register). Whereas, had they been declared as **auto** storage class, they would have been located on the stack using negative offsets relative to the BP register (see Chapter 15, stack frames). To refresh your memory about the alignment of members within structures (and unions), refer to Chapter 9. Notice that a **NULL** pointer entry is indicated by an offset value of 0x0000, which is the equivalent of (**(void *)0**).

Using Labels and Branching

It is important to remember that all labels (identifiers) created within **_asm** blocks are case-insensitive, whereas all labels (identifiers) created elsewhere within a C program are always case-sensitive. The program listed in Figure 28.8 illustrates this point.

The output produced by this program appears as follows:

```
Ending asm_1 = 01
Ending asm_2 = 02
Ending asm_3 = 03
Ending asm_4 = 04
Ending asm_1 = 15
Ending asm_2 = 16
Ending asm_3 = 17
Ending asm_4 = 18
```

Notice that whenever a reference is made to a label defined by a C statement, whether from within an **_asm** block or not, it must always be specified exactly as it was created, because all C identifiers are case-sensitive. On the other hand, all labels created within an **_asm** block are always case-insensitive and may be referenced either within the **_asm** block or from a C statement using any case-insensitive equivalent identifier.

In Figure 28.8, all C label references to **main_1**, **Main_2**, **MaIn_3**, or **MAIN_4** must be expressed identically, because these labels are case-sensitive, whereas, the **_asm** block labels, **asm_1**, **Asm_2**, **aSm_3**, or **ASM_4**, may be referenced using any equivalent (case-insensitive) identifier.

Notice how the **exit()** run-time function is called to ensure that the argument value shown is returned to the DOS (parent) process (Chapter 25) as an exit status code.

```
/* FILE: ch28e7.c */
/* use the small memory model */
#include <stdio.h>
#include <stdlib.h>

int main(void)
{
static int label_val, flag;

start:  goto asm_1;

main_1: printf("\nEnding asm_1 = %1d%1d", flag, label_val);
        goto asm_2;
Main_2: printf("\nEnding asm_2 = %1d%1d", flag, label_val);
        goto asm_3;
MaIn_3: printf("\nEnding asm_3 = %1d%1d", flag, label_val);
        goto asm_4;
MAIN_4: printf("\nEnding asm_4 = %1d%1d", flag, label_val);
        if (flag) goto end;
        else flag++;
        goto start;
  end:    _asm mov ax, 99
          _asm push ax
          _asm call exit

   _asm {
          asm_1:  inc label_val
                  jmp main_1
          Asm_2:  inc label_val
                  jmp Main_2
          aSm_3:  inc label_val
                  jmp MaIn_3
          ASM_4:  inc label_val
                  jmp MAIN_4
          }
   }
```

FIGURE 28.8: Sample program ch28e7.c demonstrates how to use labels and perform branching with inline assembly.

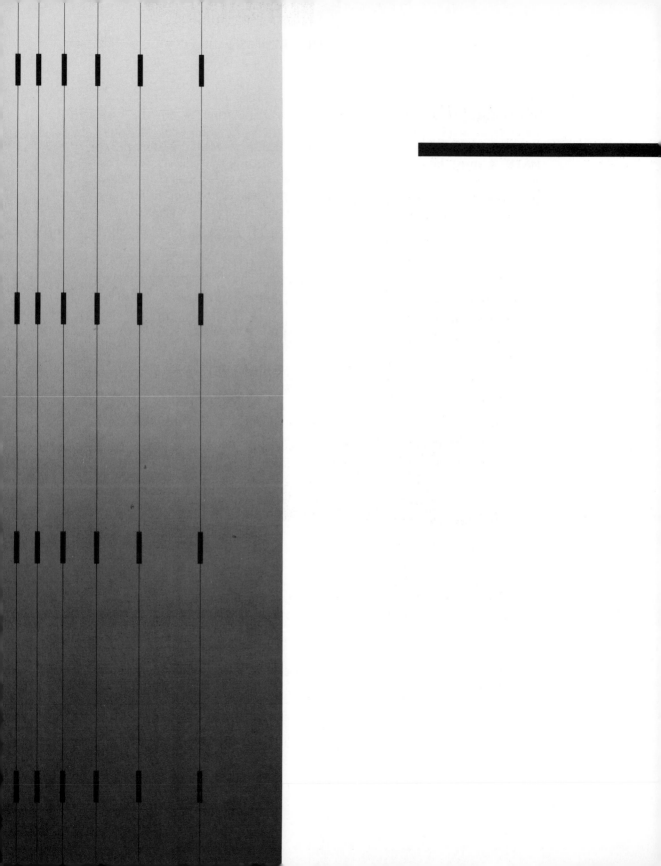

Debugging Strategies

Debugging Strategies

■■■■■■ The most challenging aspect of working with the C programming language involves debugging. This chapter provides a summary of alternative coding techniques and establishes a basis for developing a project-specific debugging strategy. The techniques described in this chapter are grouped into three categories: defensive programming techniques, interactive debugging tools, and third-party debugging utilities. These categories can help you to structure your approach to debugging C programs. First, consider programming techniques that can alter the formation of executable files; then examine techniques that permit the instructions of executable files to be dynamically monitored; and, finally, examine other techniques that can analyze and report upon both the structure of a C source-code program and the performance of the corresponding executable file.

By taking this approach, you will be able to devise a strategy for debugging C programs that complements your level of programming experience and is appropriate to the complexity of the application program itself.

DEFENSIVE PROGRAMMING TECHNIQUES

Debugging is the art of knowing what can go wrong with a program. Once a problem is identified, it is usually easy to fix. If you don't know what can happen, you are fishing without bait, so to speak, hoping to get a bite. This section summarizes the many useful error-prevention techniques presented throughout this book and introduces some additional approaches that merit attention. Use this section as both a checklist and cross-reference to the detailed explanations found elsewhere in the book, and as a reminder of what can go wrong. When it comes to programming in C, the adage "an ounce of prevention is worth a pound of cure" still applies.

Avoiding DOS Pitfalls

The various commands that can be used within the DOS CONFIG.SYS and AUTOEXEC.BAT files were summarized in Chapter 1. The most important command in CONFIG.SYS is FILES. If the FILES command is omitted, a default value of FILES=8 is assumed, which is quite restrictive for C programs, because five files are predefined. This permits only three additional files to be opened before the DOS *Too many files open* error message results. Remember to use the recommended FILES=20 command in CONFIG.SYS (see Chapter 1).

In AUTOEXEC.BAT, the DATE and TIME commands are essential if your application requires accurate date- and time-stamp information. Using the SET command to assign the appropriate environment variables is also essential for most of the Microsoft products to work properly, and can be important to the proper functioning of many application programs as well (see Chapter 1).

Finally, because DOS does not support the command-line redirection of **stderr** (OS/2 and UNIX do this by using 2>), supporting only **stdin** and **stdout**, special steps must be taken to redirect the **stderr** stream. It is because **stdout** and **stderr** share the console device by default that the problem arises. Although **stdout** can be redirected, **stderr** messages are always directed to the console (CON:). This can result in the loss of such messages if an error log file is being maintained. Earlier versions of Microsoft's C compilers were distributed with a utility program, **ERROUT**, which supported the command-line redirection of **stderr**, but this utility is no longer provided by Microsoft. The command-line redirection of **stderr** would be a valuable addition to DOS. For examples of redirecting **stderr**, see the "Redirection of **stderr**" section below (see also Chapter 18).

Microsoft Product Error Messages

The first line of defense against program errors involves the proper interpretation of the many error codes generated by Microsoft's products. There are three possible message categories (fatal errors, nonfatal errors, and warnings). Perhaps the most commonly made mistake is to assume that warnings can be ignored because they do not prevent the compilation and link steps from proceeding. Although warnings signify only possible errors, most if not all warnings should be investigated and resolved, producing what is referred to as a "lint-free" program. To emphasize this point, OptimizingC now offers option **/W5**, which treats all warnings as if they were fatal errors.

Table 29.1 summarizes Microsoft's **<error>** code naming standards by product (see Chapters 2 and 3).

Other Microsoft errors trap incorrect or inappropriate command-line entries:

D2*xxx*   Command-line errors

D4*xxx*   Command-line warnings

TABLE 29.1: Microsoft Error-Code Naming Conventions

PRODUCTS	ERROR CODE	DESCRIPTION
QC, QCL, PWB, CL	C1*xxx*	Fatal errors: compiler terminates abnormally
	C2*xxx*	Nonfatal errors: compiler finishes, but produces no .OBJ
	C4*xxx*	Warnings: compiler indicates possible problems, but an .OBJ is produced
LINK, QLINK	L*xxxx*	Errors and warnings
ILINK	L12*xx*	Errors and warnings
	L42*xx*	Errors and warnings
LIB	U11*nx*	Errors and warnings
	U41*nx*	Errors and warnings (n >= 5)
NMAKE	U10*xx*	Errors and warnings
	U14*xx*	Errors and warnings
	U40*xx*	Errors and warnings
EXEHDR	U11*nx*	Errors for (n < 5)

Any floating-point exceptions ($80x87$ or emulation) that are detected (see Chapter 23) are trapped with

> **M61*xx*** Floating-point math errors

and the code for run-time errors that may result from the execution of a C program is

> **R60*xx*** Run-time errors

Detailed explanations of these **<error>** codes can be found in Microsoft's documentation, both in printed and online Help form. The command-line version of Microsoft's Help Advisor, called QH (Quick Help), can be used (see Interactive Debugging Tools), or the online Help equivalent of QH (HELP Option or Function Key F1) can be used from within the integrated QC or PWB environments to retrieve explanations of the **<error>** codes mentioned above.

Preprocessor Tips

Although Chapter 5 examined in detail the features of the preprocessor, this section highlights the important role that the preprocessor can play when debugging C programs. As described in Chapter 5, use the compiler options (**/E**, **/P**, or **/EP**) to generate the intermediate file (.I) called the unit of translation. Recall that the unit of translation is the C source-code file that actually is translated by the C compiler.

Take the guesswork out of the actual interpretation of compiler **#directives** by examining the resulting (.I) intermediate file. Use (.I) files rather than (.C) files to port C programs between different machines and compilers.

Commenting-Out Code

Whenever it is necessary to "comment out" sections of C source code for debugging purposes, it is preferred that the following compiler directive be used to eliminate statements rather than the standard /* .. */ comment convention, because comments cannot be nested.

```
#if 0
( commented-out statements )
#endif
```

When the directive approach shown above is used, all intervening statements are removed from the (.C) file. Be sure you are not splitting another #if..#endif pair; however, the nesting of #if..#endif statements is permitted.

Conditional Compilation

A variation of the preceding example is to make temporary or debugging output dependent on the definition of an object-like macro; hence the term *conditional compilation*. Establish a command-line macro definition, such as **/DNDEBUG**, to indicate that no debugging is to occur (see Chapters 6 and 25, and the "Assertions" section below). If the object-like macro, **NDEBUG**, is defined, then any of the debugging statements shown below can be removed by the preprocessor using the following directives:

```
#ifndef NDEBUG
( debugging statements )
#endif
```

or

```
#if !defined(NDEBUG)
( debugging statements )
#endif
```

Typically, the debugging statements noted above generate the output of intermediate results for testing purposes, using the **printf()** family of functions (see Chapter 17). With this approach, the source code for an application retains all debugging statements for later use should a problem arise with the subject source code.

Redirection of `stderr`

The selection of an appropriate **`printf()`** function for the display of intermediate test output merits further comment. Using the **`fprintf()`** function is often preferred because then all test (debug) output can be directed to another output stream than **`stdout`**, if desired. This approach would, however, prevent command-line redirection from being used, since only the predefined streams, **`stdin`** and **`stdout`**, may be redirected from the DOS command line. It might be preferable to use the predefined **`stderr`** stream and redirect **`stderr`** using **`dup2()`**, so that all normal program output and error output can be separated or combined if desired. Consider the following example:

```
#ifndef NDEBUG
    #include <stdio.h>
    #include <io.h>
    {
    FILE *err;
    err = fopen("C:\\prognam.err", "a");
    dup2(fileno(err), fileno(stderr));
    }
#endif
```

Notice the introduction of the block **`{  ..  }`** to permit the stream pointer **`err`** to be defined, thereby permitting this compiler directive to be placed anywhere in the source code of a function. From this point on in a program, the predefined output stream, **`stderr`**, would be redirected and appended to a disk file of error output called C:\prognam.err. The runtime function, **`dup2()`**, reassigns **`stderr`** to **`err`**.

Embedded Test Drivers

Another variation of the conditional compilation approach can be used to embed a **`main()`** function within a source-code file that conditionally can serve as the test program for the function(s) within the source-code file itself. In the following example, the object-like macro **DRIVER** is used for this purpose:

```
void func1(void)
{
    /*   !! function code here !! One external storage-class
```

```
              function or a group of closely-related functions
              per source-code file
       */
}
static void sfunc1(void)
{
       /*   !! function code here !! Any number of static (file
              scope) functions per source-code file.
       */
}
#ifdef DRIVER
int main(int argc, char *argv[])
{
       /*   !! test code here !!
              func1();
              sfunc1();
       */
}
#endif
```

In this manner, the test program that was used when **func1()** and **sfunc1()** were developed can be retained within the same file for later use, should a problem arise. Only when the object-like macro **DRIVER** is defined from the command line will a test program be generated; otherwise, the compiler will create an .OBJ file that must be linked with another **main()** function before it can be executed.

Assertions

Chapter 6 introduced the **<assert.h>** header file, and Chapter 25 the function **_assert()**. Assertions represent logical expressions that are intended to be true and, if found to be false, abnormally terminate the execution of the program. One advantage to using the function-like macro **assert()** is that once assertions are placed into your source code, they may be conditionally included or excluded by the preprocessor, based on the definition of the object-like macro **NDEBUG**. Another advantage is that both the **assert()** macro and **NDEBUG** are features of Standard C, defined by all C compilers in the **<assert.h>** header file. If **NDEBUG** is not defined, the assertions remain in your source code; if **NDEBUG** is defined, they are removed.

The program listed in Figure 29.1 represents some typical uses of assertions.

When this program was executed, its output was directed to **stderr**:

```
Assertion failed: i >= 0 && i < size, file ch29e1.c, line 13
abnormal program termination
```

With Microsoft C, the **assert()** function-like macro must appear as shown in this example. That is, it must be semicolon-terminated and appear as if it were, in fact, a function, and not a macro.

A closer examination of how the **assert()** macro is defined in **<assert.h>** reveals why this is so:

```
#define assert(exp) \
    ( (exp) ? (void) 0 : _assert(#exp, __FILE__, __LINE__) )
```

Use of the ternary **?:** operator does not permit the use of embedded semicolons. Also note that the **assert()** function-like macro actually calls the run-time library function **_assert()**, described in Chapter 25. As we will see in the last example program of this section, it might have been better had Microsoft chosen to define the **assert()** macro differently.

The first assertion in the preceding example expresses a true integer expression; namely, that there is at least one command-line argument passed to every C **main()** function. (This argument represents the complete executable file pathname.) Likewise, the second assertion expresses a true statement—the first entry in **argv**, the array of pointers to characters, must not be a **NULL** pointer. The last assertion statement is violated when the variable **i** becomes equal to 10. The corresponding output shown above is directed to **stderr**, and the program is abnormally terminated at that point.

The major disadvantage of using assertions for debugging is that the execution of the program is terminated when the first assertion violation is encountered. The program example listed in Figure 29.2 is intended to demonstrate how a custom **_assert()** function can be written that is linked with your executable file to overcome this problem.

Notice that the **main()** function logic is identical to that of program ch29e1.c, and the custom **_assert()** function demonstrates some of the

```
/* FILE: ch29e1.c */
#include <stdio.h>
#include <assert.h>
#include <stdlib.h>

int main( int argc, char *argv[])
{
int i, array[10];
int size = sizeof(array)/sizeof(array[0]);

assert(argc >= 1 );
assert(argv[0] != NULL);
for (i=0; i<=10; i+=10) assert(i >= 0 && i < size );
exit(0);
}
```

FIGURE 29.1: Sample program ch29e1.c demonstrates how to use assertions.

programming tips discussed earlier in this chapter. By entirely replacing the run-time **_assert()** function called by the **assert()** macro, we can permit the execution of the program to continue when assertion violations occur. Also note the conditional redirection of **stderr** to a disk file to facilitate the debugging process.

The following output was produced by the ch29e2.c program:

```
Assertion failed: i >= 0 && i < size
    file ch29e2.c, line 29  [Sat Jun  9 16:24:48 1990]
    Program continuing..
```

Notice the use of the non-Standard predefined object-like macro, **__TIMESTAMP__**, which also can be used selectively to report on the performance of an application program.

One last improvement could be made by defining the **assert()** macro in a different manner from that found in the Microsoft **<assert.h>** header file. The program shown in Figure 29.3 represents a variation of the ch29e2.c program, modifying how the custom **_assert()** function is expressed, redefining the **assert()** macro, and demonstrating some alternative forms of expression that are possible when the **assert()** macro is defined in this manner.

```
/* FILE: ch29e2.c */
#include <stdio.h>
#include <assert.h>
#include <stdlib.h>

void _assert(void *expr, void *file, unsigned int line)
{
#ifndef NDEBUG
    #include <stdio.h>
    #include <io.h>
    {
    FILE *err;
    err = fopen("C:\\ch29e2.err", "a");
    dup2(fileno(err), fileno(stderr));
    }
#endif
fprintf(stderr, "\nAssertion failed: %s\n\tfile %s, line %d  [%s]",
    expr, file, line, __TIMESTAMP__);
fprintf(stderr, "\n\tProgram continuing..");
}

int main( int argc, char *argv[])
{
int i, array[10];
int size = sizeof(array)/sizeof(array[0]);

assert(argc >= 1);
assert(argv[0] != NULL);
for (i=0; i<=10; i+=10) assert(i >= 0 && i < size);
exit(0);
}
```

FIGURE 29.2: Sample program ch29e2.c demonstrates how to write a custom assert() function.

Notice that the **assert()** macro is first undefined, and then redefined without the **?:** operator by using a simple **if** statement. This change permits assertion statements in your program to be expressed with or without a trailing semicolon and permits a statement to follow on the same line as shown in Figure 29.3.

The following output is produced by the ch29e3.c program:

```
Assertion failed: i >= 0 && i < size
    file ch29e3.c, line 25   [Sat Jun  9 17:04:28 1990]
    Program continuing..
Assertion failed: i >= 0 && i < size
    file ch29e3.c, line 26   [Sat Jun  9 17:04:28 1990]
    Program continuing..
    Testing..
```

This output confirms that the redefined **assert()** function-like macro is correctly expressed and demonstrates how the redefinition of the **assert()** macro accommodates other ways of coding assertions.

```
/* FILE: ch29e3.c */
#include <stdio.h>
#include <assert.h>
#include <stdlib.h>
#include <io.h>

void _assert(void *expr, void *file, unsigned int line)
{
dup2(1,2);
fprintf(stderr, "\nAssertion failed: %s\n\tfile %s, line %d  [%s]",
    expr, file, line, __TIMESTAMP__);
fprintf(stderr, "\n\tProgram continuing..");
}

#undef assert
#define assert(exp) \
    if (!(exp)) _assert(#exp, __FILE__, __LINE__);

int main( int argc, char *argv[])
{
int i=0, array[10];
int size = sizeof(array)/sizeof(array[0]);

assert(i >= 0 && i < size )
for (i=0; i<=10; i+=10) assert(i >= 0 && i < size);
assert(i >= 0 && i < size ) fprintf(stderr, "\n\tTesting..");
exit(0);
}
```

FIGURE 29.3: Sample program ch29e3.c demonstrates how to redefine the assert() macro and write a custom assert() function.

Compiler and Linker Options

Of the many compiler options available for use with the QuickC and OptimizingC compilers, the following compilation options are particularly useful when debugging:

/c	Compile only, produce an .OBJ file, do not link.
/Zs	Syntax check only, do not produce an .OBJ file.
/C	Preserve comments during preprocessing.
/E	Preprocess to **stdout** with line numbers.
/EP	Preprocess to **stdout** without line numbers.
/P	Preprocess to an .I file.
/Fa	Produce an .ASM file only, not a .COD file.
/Fc	Produce a .COD file with source and object code.
/Fl	Produce a .COD file with object code only.
/Fr	Produce an .SBR standard browser file.
/FR	Produce an .SBR extended browser file.
/Od	Disable optimizations to prepare for CodeView.
/W4	Produce lint-like warning messages.
/W5	Treat all warnings as fatal errors.

The use of option **/C** passes all comments to the intermediate file (.I), which makes them visible when the CodeView debugger is used; otherwise, all comments are removed from the (.C) source code file. Refer to Chapter 28 for complete details of working with the **/Fa**, **/Fc**, and **/Fl** options. The **/Fr** and **/FR** options are useful only when the Browser (BROWSE option) is used with the PWB compiler. Although CodeView debugging can be performed upon optimized source code, generally, it is recommended that the option **/Od** be used when **/Zi** is specified, so there is a direct correspondence between your source code and the assembly and object code that is displayed by the CodeView debugger. Remember, when optimization options are specified, the compiler is free to alter the translation of your source code. The compiler warning options **/W4** and **/W5** are new with QuickC and OptimizingC and provide additional controls that assist the debugging process by reporting "lint-like" errors, and treating all warnings as fatal errors, respectively.

The following compiler options can set linker options that are used when a successful compilation is automatically followed by a link step.

/Fm   Produce a linker .MAP file.

/Zi   Prepare for CodeView debugging.

When the compiler option **/Fm** is specified, the link step is passed the linker option **/MAP**; likewise, when **/Zi** is specified, the option **/CO** also is passed.

The following linker options control the link step of the software development cycle:

/CO   Prepare an .EXE file for CodeView debugging.

/EXE   Remove CodeView information from an .EXE file.

/NOI   Treat identifiers with upper /lowercase sensitivity.

To use an .EXE file (not .COM files) with the CodeView debugger, the linker option **/CO** must be specified. To remove the CodeView debugger information from an existing .EXE file, use the **/EXE** option. Do not confuse the linker **/EXE** option with the CVPACK utility program described in the "Interactive Debugging Tools" section of this chapter. CVPACK does not remove debugging information from an .EXE file, it only reorganizes it so that a smaller .EXE file results, effectively permitting Code-View to debug a larger C program. Typically, C programs are case-sensitive and should be linked using the **/NOI** option. When the special keywords **_pascal** and **_fortran** are used, it may be necessary to link a C program without the **/NOI** option, effectively treating all identifiers without regard to case.

Microsoft Language Extensions

All of Microsoft's extensions to Standard C make your code less portable. As discussed throughout this book, many are essential for exploiting the power and performance of the Intel $80x86/87$ microprocessors and DOS services; others such as those listed below, however, are not essential and their use is not recommended. The default compiler option **/Ze** enables the recognition of the features described below; however, if compiler option **/Za** is specified, recognition of these features is disabled, and the Microsoft predefined macro **NO_EXT_KEYS** is defined (Chapter 5).

- Non-Standard keywords prefixed with an underscore (_) character (Appendix B)

- Use of a cast expression as an lvalue (Chapter 13)
- Redefinition of **extern** items as **static** (Chapter 7)
- Use of trailing comma (**,**) in a function prototype instead of the ellipsis (**, . . .**) (Chapter 14)
- Benign **typedef** redefinitions within the same scope (Chapters 7–11, and 14)
- Mixing character and string constants within a single initialization expression (Chapters 7–8)
- Use of bit-fields with base types other than **unsigned int** or **signed int** (Chapter 11)
- Casting between data pointers and function pointers (Chapter 14)
- Function declarator given file scope (Chapter 14)
- Nameless structures and unions (Chapter 9)
- Zero-sized arrays (incomplete) in structures and unions (Chapter 9)
- Single line, C++ style comments (**//**) (Chapter 4)

The fact that these non-Standard Microsoft extensions can be disabled only as a group presents a problem in developing project coding standards. The non-Standard keywords cannot be replaced with Standard C keywords; however, the non-Standard language extension features can be replaced using Standard C features. If non-Standard keywords must be used, then to detect use of the non-Standard constructs noted above, you either must use the QuickC and OptimizingC **/W4** compiler option, which produces lint-like warning messages, or purchase a third-party "lint-like utility," as described later in this chapter. Otherwise, these non-Standard extensions may inadvertently mask a violation of the coding standards established for a project.

Exception Handling

There are several categories of hardware and software exceptions (possible bugs) common to all programs, including DOS and BIOS software. The methods of handling these exceptions have been described elsewhere in this book, but are summarized here for your convenience. In addition, we will extend the discussion of signals to explain how they can serve as tools for debugging programs.

Hardware Errors

When hardware failure and operations-related errors occur with DOS, the familiar *Abort, Retry, Ignore?* message is displayed and, usually, abnormal program termination results. By using the **_harderr()** function, a custom function may be written to replace this fundamental hardware exception handling procedure, which either can terminate the program in a controlled manner, using the **_hardretn()** function, or permit processing to continue using the **_hardresume()** function. For complete details see Chapter 27.

Abnormal Program Termination

Many situations that arise can be resolved only by the abnormal termination of a process; however, when the normal termination sequence (described in Chapter 25) does not occur, the integrity of an application program's data is jeopardized. Whenever abnormal events occur, it is essential to try to preserve the integrity of an application's data (memory and disk storage), or if this cannot be done, to record in some manner exactly which data has been compromised. For complete details about normal, subnormal, and abnormal process termination, see Chapter 25 and the other exception handling sections of this chapter.

Floating-Point Exceptions

Whenever floating-point type calculations are performed, whether using an $80x87$ processor or a software emulation, a special set of exceptions can arise that is handled as interrupts or signals (**SIGFPE**). For a complete explanation of the alternatives available to handle floating-point exceptions, see Chapter 23.

Interrupt Services

Interrupts are asynchronous events that disrupt the normal sequence of instructions scheduled to be performed by a processor. Since bugs themselves often precipitate asynchronous events, they are sometimes handled directly or indirectly as interrupts. Because all interrupts are handled in a standard manner, it is possible to install custom ISRs (interrupt service routines) to handle such events. Chapter 22 shows how the interrupt vector table is constructed, and the mechanism by which DOS and BIOS interrupt services are accessed; Chapter 27 discusses declaring, calling, and installing custom ISRs.

Signal Processing

As discussed in Chapter 25, signals provide a Standard C approach to the handling of certain common interrupts that otherwise could be handled only in a non-Standard fashion. Whereas up to 256 possible interrupts can be handled by the interrupt vector table under DOS, only three interrupts can be handled in a Standard C manner using the run-time functions **signal()** and **raise()**: **SIGABRT** (Chapter 25), **SIGFPE** (Chapter 23), and **SIGINT** (Chapter 27). In this section we will focus on the use of **SIGINT**, which is raised when either Ctrl-C or Ctrl-Break is keyed, for debugging purposes.

Application programs that are designed to loop endlessly to perform monitoring or watchdog activities are usually difficult to debug. Often they maintain tables or data structures of information that record statistics about the activity under surveillance. From a debugging point of view it is convenient to press either Ctrl-C or Ctrl-Break to request such a program to produce a report on the status of these tables and data structures. In this manner, reports can be generated asynchronously, at the discretion of the person debugging the program, rather than having the program produce reports at fixed intervals.

Although many coding restrictions apply to the development of such signal handlers (see Chapter 23 for **SIGFPE**), sufficient services are available to fulfill all necessary I/O services. The program example shown in Figure 29.4 demonstrates the capability of a program being debugged to discover why a counter is overflowing.

A representative sample of the output directed to **stderr** is shown below.

```
.
.
Looping.. 10000
^C
cnt10=1000  cnt100=100  brkcnt=2
Looping.. 11000
Looping.. 12000
.
.
```

This program will terminate after six Ctrl-C or Ctrl-Break interrupts are issued from the keyboard. This basic approach of defining an **int_handler()** function can be used to display test results for any program that can be triggered by the Ctrl-C or Ctrl-Break keyboard interrupt. The **signal()** function is used to replace **sigint** with the custom **int_handler()** function. Notice how **SIGINT** signal recognition is disabled by the use of the predefined **SIG_IGN** function.

Memory and Addressing

Without question, the single largest source of bugs in C programs is the errant use of pointers (memory addresses). The inadvertent use of a **NULL** pointer value can be pinpointed either by specifying compiler option **/Zr** for QC, QCL, PWB, or CL, or including the directive **#pragma pointer_check(on|off)** for QC and CL. Either will terminate a program at the point of error with an **R6012** or **R6013** run-time error; otherwise, only the **R6001** run-time error message is displayed on program termination, indicating that the **NULL** segment has been altered at some point during the execution of the program. For more on **NULL** pointers, see Chapter 10.

```
/* FILE: ch29e4.c */
#include <stdio.h>
#include <signal.h>
#include <stdlib.h>

static int flag, brkcnt;

static void int_handler( void)
{
flag=1;
brkcnt++;
signal(SIGINT, SIG_IGN);
}

int main( void)
{
int cnt=1, cnt10=0, cnt100=0;
signal(SIGINT, int_handler);
while (1) {
    if (!(cnt % 10)) cnt10+=1;
    if (!(cnt % 100)) cnt100+=1;
    if (flag) {
        fprintf(stderr, "\ncnt10=%d  cnt100=%d  brkcnt=%d",
            cnt10, cnt100, brkcnt);
        flag=0;
        signal(SIGINT, int_handler);
        }
    if (!(cnt % 1000)) fprintf(stderr, "\nLooping.. %d", cnt);
    if (brkcnt > 5) break;
    cnt++;
    }
exit(0);
}
```

FIGURE 29.4: Sample program ch29e4.c demonstrates how to use the signal() function to debug a program.

Another common source of error is a stack overflow, which generates an **R6000** run-time error and terminates the program because the available stack space is exhausted. Refer to Chapter 15 for a discussion of how to resolve this problem. Normally, this error is generated because compiler option **/Ge** is automatically defaulted, thereby enabling stack checking upon entry to every C function. If the **/Gs** option is specified, stack checking is disabled, and if the alloted stack space is exceeded, then the data area of the program is clobbered (see Figures 2.20–2.25), and execution proceeds. To selectively enable and disable stack checking, use the directive **#pragma check_stack(on|off)**.

One common way to initiate the improper use of a **NULL** pointer using the **malloc()** family of functions previously described (see Chapter 24) is to perform dynamic memory allocation. Because the heap itself relies solely upon a dynamically allocated data structure, the integrity of the heap can be jeopardized easily by an errant pointer. To debug the heap, the run-time family of functions **_heapchk()**, **_heapset()**, and **_heapwalk()** must be employed. For complete details about the heap, refer to Chapter 24.

Run-Time Error Codes

Some of the run-time library functions described in Chapters 16–27 indicate that an error occurs, not by the assignment of a particular return value, but rather by assigning a value to global variable **errno**. The **E..** object-like macros defined in **<error.h>** are used for this purpose. Whenever DOS I/O interrupt services are utilized, a more detailed set of error codes unique to DOS can be accessed by using the global variable **_doserrno**. These extended error descriptions can be accessed using the **dosexterr()** run-time function; see Chapter 22, Table 22.6.

The example program shown in Figure 29.5 shows the relationship between **errno** values and the corresponding descriptions found in the global **sys_errlist[]** array. The **sys_errlist[]** array is used by the **perror()** function, discussed in Chapter 17, and by the **strerror()** and **_strerror()** functions, discussed in Chapter 26.

The output generated by this example program lists only those **sys_errlist[]** entries for which a nonblank description exists. The numbers shown correspond to the **E..** object-like macro values defined in **<errno.h>** (see Chapter 6).

```
0   Error 0
2   No such file or directory
7   Arg list too long
8   Exec format error
```

```
 9   Bad file number
12   Not enough core
13   Permission denied
17   File exists
18   Cross-device link
22   Invalid argument
24   Too many open files
28   No space left on device
33   Math argument
34   Result too large
36   Resource deadlock would occur
```

To use both **errno** and **_doserrno** properly, initialize these variables to **EZERO** or zero just prior to a run-time function call, and then immediately test their values after the function calls are completed. Neither **errno** nor **_doserrno** is automatically initialized or reset to zero.

```
/* FILE: ch29e5.c */
#include <stdio.h>
#include <stdlib.h>

int main( void)
{
int i;
for (i=0; i<sys_nerr; i++)
    if (*sys_errlist[i]) printf("\n%2d   %s", i, sys_errlist[i]);
exit(0);
}
```

FIGURE 29.5: Sample program ch29e5.c demonstrates the relationships that exist between global variables errno and sys_errlist[].

INTERACTIVE DEBUGGING TOOLS

In this section we will survey the features of the powerful interactive debugging tools that Microsoft provides with the purchase of a C compiler. With the purchase of QuickC, the QC integrated Debug and Help options are provided. With the purchase of OptimizingC, the PWB integrated Debug and Help options are augmented by the Browse option, and separate command-line versions of the CodeView debugger (CV), the CodeView Pack utility (CVPACK), and QuickHelp (QH) are provided. (See Table 2.7.)

The QuickC Debug, OptimizingC Debug, and CodeView debugger work only with .EXE files, not .COM files (Tiny memory model), and they require that **/Zi** compiler and **/CO** linker options be specified. Incrementally compiled (**/Gi**) and linked (**/Li**) programs may be debugged and, although it is recommended that compiler option **/Od** be used to disable optimization, optimized programs also may be debugged.

When the Browser is used with the CL compiler, the **/Fr** compiler option must be specified to produce a standard information .SBR file, while the **/FR** option can produce an extended information .SBR file. With the PWB compiler, use the Options menu to turn on the Browser and select either the **/Fr** or **/FR** option.

The online Help features rely on the presence of .HLP files, which are copied when the QuickC or OptimizingC compiler is installed. If you find that you do not use the online Help feature and wish to save disk storage space, delete the .HLP files.

Let's examine the major features of these tools to understand how they are used to debug C programs.

The QC Debug Option

The debugging features integrated with the QuickC compiler represent a subset of those provided by the CodeView debugger described in a section below. Basically, the QC Debug feature permits you to monitor select data variables of an executing program by specifying watchpoints and breakpoints, and either recording the session for replay or not. Watchpoints are used to stop a program conditionally; breakpoints are used to stop a program unconditionally. Both of these techniques return control to the user so program variable values can be monitored, or to single-step the program one instruction at a time to locate a logic error. These capabilities eliminate the need to intersperse **printf()** statements that display intermediate values of program variables throughout a program.

After a program has been compiled using the **/Od** and **/Zi** options, and linked using the **/CO** option, perform the following three steps to initiate QC Debug. First, choose the Run/Debug Bar of the QC Options menu, and select the Animate Speed, Screen Swap, and Debug History options that you want to be in effect as shown in Figure 29.6.

Next, pull down the Debug menu as shown in Figure 29.7, and establish the breakpoints and watchpoints for the program you are going to debug.

Finally, pull down the Run menu as shown in Figure 29.8, and control the execution of the program with the options shown.

The Trace Into option (highlighted) permits all the statements of a function to be traced when that function is called, whereas, the Step Over option can be used to omit a function call.

To master using the QC Debug option, review the online Help screens that are provided, or run the LEARN program exercises that are distributed and optionally installable with QuickC.

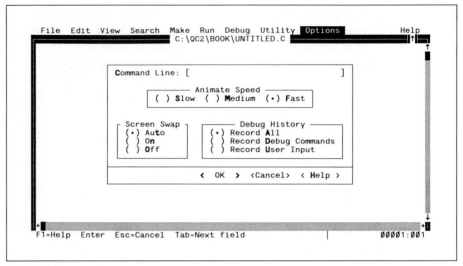

FIGURE 29.6: QC Options menu for debugging.

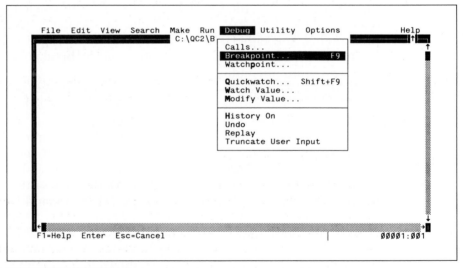

FIGURE 29.7: QC Debug menu.

The PWB Browse Option

For a closer look at the Browser, refer to the "OptimizingC Integrated (PWB)" section of Chapter 2. The Browser is available only with the PWB compiler, and is helpful in tracking down where program variables and

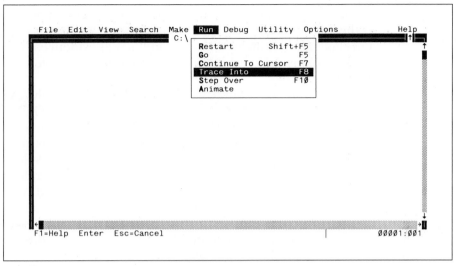

FIGURE 29.8: QC Run menu for debugging.

functions are referenced throughout the source code of an application program. Unlike CodeView, the Browser is a source code, not an object-code analyzer. Often, debugging a program requires the ability to quickly locate identifiers, and to make consistent changes to source code once the fix to a problem has been devised.

To master using the PWB Browser, review the online Help screens provided, and experiment using the available options for an application program you are working on.

The CodeView (CV) Debugger

The CodeView debugger is rapidly becoming the industry standard for interactive program debugging. It is presently bundled for use with all of Microsoft's language products. CodeView can be used only with .EXE (not .COM) files, and requires that compiler option **/Zi** and link option **/CO** be specified. Incrementally compiled and linked programs are acceptable for use with CodeView. Although it is recommended that compiler option **/Od** (disable Optimizations) be specified with CodeView, the use of other **/O..** options does not prevent CodeView use. Since CodeView is a line-oriented debugger, when more than one executable statement is expressed on the same source-code line (up to the first newline character), the statements are treated as a unit and cannot be separated when breakpoints and watchpoints are specified.

The basic approach described for the QC Debug option above applies to the CodeView debugger as well; however, a broader range of features and capabilities is included with CodeView as evidenced by the number of menu options and output windows that are available as shown in Figure 29.9.

In this figure, one source window depicts the assembly (.ASM) code and another depicts the C (.C) source-code file of the COUNTRY.EXE program being debugged. The watch window depicts the watch variables that have been selected; the register window displays the current status of all 80x86 registers and flags; and the memory window displays the contents of Data Segment for the program. Other possible windows that can be opened include: a command window for entering CodeView commands, a local window displaying the current values of all local variables to the current block or function, and an 80x87 math coprocessor register window. Notice the number of pulldown menus that are displayed at the top of Figure 29.9.

To master using the CodeView debugger, review the written and online documentation, and the tutorial that can be copied when OptimizingC is installed. When you master CodeView, you have a tool that can be applied to BASIC, Fortran, and Pascal as well.

The CodeView debugger can be invoked either from the DOS command line, or from the PWB integrated environment. The syntax of the DOS command line used to execute the CodeView debugger is as follows:

```
CV [cvoption..] exefile [argument..]
```

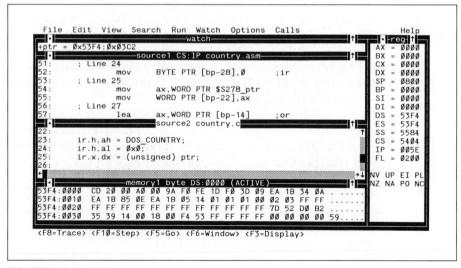

FIGURE 29.9: CodeView windows.

The following descriptions apply to the components:

[cvoption..]   The only options recognized by CodeView (CV) are described below and are case-insensitive.

exefile   Any existing .EXE file. The **exefile** should be in the current directory; otherwise, a complete pathname must be specified. If the file extension is omitted from **exefile**, then .EXE is assumed.

[argument..]   Any case-sensitive DOS command-line arguments that would normally be specified for the **exefile** being debugged.

   The Codeview options are described below:

/2   Use two video monitors. The program output will appear on the default monitor, while the CodeView output will appear on the other. Useful for debugging graphics programs.

/25   CodeView output to utilize a standard 25-line by 80-column video monitor.

/43   Codeview output to utilize a 43-line by 80-column text mode of an EGA/VGA graphics adaptor. **/25** used if unavailable.

/50   Codeview output to utilize a 50-line by 80-column text mode of a VGA graphics adaptor. **/25** used if unavailable.

/B   Forces CodeView to use only two colors for better readability, even if an EGA/VGA graphics adaptor is available.

/C<command>   Used when CodeView is invoked from a batch (.BAT) or make (.MAK) file to initiate a series of CodeView command-window commands on startup. Enclose everything in double quotes and separate command with spaces.

/D<size>   To optimize the performance of CodeView when neither expanded nor extended memory is used, specify the disk overlay <size> in 16K increments from **/D16** to **/D128**.

/E   Enables the use of expanded memory (LIM Lotus/Intel/Microsoft memory). Unnecessary because CodeView uses expanded memory if the expanded memory-module (EMM) driver is installed.

/F Do not swap video pages between CodeView and the application being debugged. This is the default for CodeView. See **/S**.

/G Use this option if you are using CodeView with a CGA monitor.

/I Equivalent to the **/I1** option described below.

/I0 Have CodeView trap Intel 8259 interrupts. This option enables the use of Ctrl-C and Ctrl-Break on non-IBM compatible computers.

/I1 Have CodeView ignore Intel 8259 interrupts. This option disables the use of Ctrl-C and Ctrl-Break on non-IBM compatible computers.

/K Prevents CodeView from intercepting (hooking) the keyboard interrupt to install a keyboard monitor. Use of this option permits CodeView commands to be recorded for reply, but not for user input.

/L For use with OS/2 only, not DOS. Tells the protected-mode Code-View debugger (CVP) to search a dynamic-link library (DLL) for symbolic information.

/M Have CodeView ignore the mouse that is installed. Use this option to disable a non-Microsoft mouse that conflicts with CodeView, or when debugging mouse application programs.

/N Equivalent to the **/N1** option described below.

/N0 Have CodeView trap Intel 8259 nonmaskable (NMI) interrupts.

/N1 Have CodeView ignore Intel 8259 nonmaskable interrupts.

/O For use with OS/2 only, not DOS. Tells the protected-mode Code-View debugger (CVP) to enable the debugging of multiple processes.

/R Tells CodeView to use the four debug registers that are available with the 80386 processor; otherwise ignored.

/S Swaps video pages between CodeView and the application being debugged. Use this when the application you are debugging uses video page zero, which is normally used by Codeview (unless **/2** specified). See **/F**.

/TSF   Toggles the Statefileread switch in the [CodeView] section of TOOLS.INI which controls whether CURRENT.STS (CodeView's current state file) is to be read or not.

/X   Enables the use of extended memory, the memory above 1MB on 80286, 80386, 80486 machines. Unnecessary because CodeView uses extended memory if the XMM driver is installed.

The PWB Debug Option

The PWB Debug option initiates a CodeView debugging session, just as if CodeView were executed from the DOS command line. This is unlike the QC Debug option, which is fully integrated with the QC compiler.

After a program has been compiled using the **/Od** and **/Zi** options, and linked using the **/CO** option, then perform the following two steps to initiate the use of the PWB Debug or the CodeView option. First, choose the CodeView Bar of the PWB Options menu and select the options described above for the DOS command-line version of CodeView that you wish to apply to the debugging session you are about to initiate, as shown in Figure 29.10.

Next, pull down the Run menu as shown in Figure 29.11 and select the Debug Bar as shown (highlighted) to execute the CodeView debugger.

At this point, use CodeView as if it had been executed from the DOS command line.

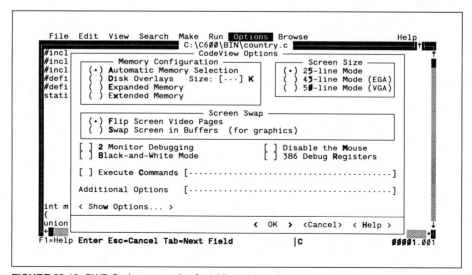

FIGURE 29.10: PWB Options menu for CodeView debugging.

```
      File  Edit  View  Search  Make  Run  Options  Browse            Help
                              C:\           Execute: country.exe
#include <dos.h>                            Command Line...
#include <stdio.h>                          Debug: country.exe
#include <string.h>
#define INT_DOS 0x21                        Run DOS Command...
#define DOS_COUNTRY 0x38                    Customize Menu...
static struct { unsigned date;
                char currency_s
                char thousands_sep[2];
                char decimal_sep[2];
                char date_sep[2];
                char time_sep[2] ;
                unsigned char currency_fmt;
                unsigned char currency_dec;
                unsigned char time_fmt;
                unsigned fill_1[2];
                char data_sep[2];
                unsigned fill_2[5]; } buffer, *ptr=&buffer;

int main (void)
{
union REGS ir, or;

Debug current program                              |C            00001.001
```

FIGURE 29.11: PWB Run menu for CodeView.

The CVPACK Utility

The CVPACK utility compresses an executable file (.EXE only, not .COM) by reducing the size of the CodeView debugger information stored within the file when the **/Zi** compiler option or **/CO** linker option is used. Because of the memory constraints that apply when CodeView is running, packing a file effectively allows us to debug a larger program.

Do not confuse the role of the CVPACK utility with the **/EXE** option. Unlike CVPACK, the **/EXE** option removes all CodeView debugging information from an .EXE file, rendering it unable to be debugged at the source level using CodeView.

The syntax of the DOS command line used to execute the CVPACK Utility is as follows:

`CVPACK [/p] [/?] [/help] exefile`

The following descriptions apply to the components:

[/p]   Packs the .EXE file to the smallest possible size.

[/?]   Displays command-line syntax help only; does not invoke Quick-Help (QH) for the CVPACK topic.

[/help]   Invokes QuickHelp (QH), if available, to display the online Help available for the topic, CVPACK.

exefile   Any existing .EXE file. The **exefile** should be in the current directory; otherwise a complete pathname must be specified. If the file extension is omitted from **exefile**, then .EXE is assumed.

Example   The following DOS command-line entry instructs DOS to execute the CVPACK utility upon the executable file COUNTRY.EXE, and to compress the file to the smallest possible size:

```
CVPACK /p COUNTRY.EXE
```

Help Alternatives

Both QuickC (QC) and OptimizingC (PWB) now provide an online Help feature called the C Advisor. When either product is installed, a series of .HLP files is copied that contains a complete hypertext reference that can be accessed by topic or index entries, or simply by placing the cursor on any desired text and pressing F1 (Function Key 1).

When not working from the DOS command line, comparable services are provided by invoking the C Advisor to execute the QH (QuickHelp) command that is bundled with the OptimizingC compiler (but not with QuickC).

Both the integrated and command-line version of the C Advisor permit portions of the online Help information, including example programs, to be printed as well as edited, using a cut-and-paste approach to copy the information directly into your own files.

For more about installing your QuickC and OptimizingC compiler, and the Help features of QC and PWB, refer to Chapter 2.

QuickHelp QH

The QuickHelp (QH) Utility provides access to the online C Advisor databases of information when working from the DOS command line, not from either QC or PWB. QH is provided only when you purchase OptimizingC, not QuickC.

The syntax of the DOS command line used to execute QH is as follows:

```
QH [qhoption..] topic
```

The following descriptions of the components apply:

[qhoption..]   The only options recognized by QH are described below and are case-insensitive.

`topic`   Any case-insensitive description to be searched for in a Help .HLP database file.

`/d<filename>`   Enter filename as a specific .HLP database filename; simply enter a path and all .HLP files found will be loaded for use; or specify an environment variable such as $INCLUDE:*.HLP, for example.

`/l<number>`   The number of lines the QuickHelp window should occupy.

`/m<number>`   Changes the screen mode to the specified number of lines. Enter a value in the range 25–50.

`/p<filename>`   Sets the name of the paste file. The default is PASTE.QH which is placed in the TMP directory. Enter filename as a complete file pathname.

`/pa[filename]`   Specifies that all paste operations are to be appended to the paste file, rather than being overwritten. An optional filename may be entered as described above for `/p`.

`/q`   Prevents the version box from being displayed when QuickHelp is installed as a keyboard monitor.

`/r<command>`   Specifies the command that QuickHelp is to perform when the right mouse button is clicked. Enter one of the following commands: **l** (display last topic viewed); **i** (display history of last topics viewed); **w** (temporarily hide the QuickHelp window); **b** (display the historically previous topic); **e** (continue to search for a topic); **t** (display the table of contents for the current topic).

`/s`   Indicates that clicking the mouse above or below the scroll box causes QuickHelp to scroll by lines rather than pages.

The following DOS command-line entries demonstrate some valid examples of using QuickHelp:

```
QH /l20 null
QH NULL
QH R6000
```

The first example above instructs QuickHelp to use only 20 lines of the video display and to search for information about **NULL** pointers. The second example permits QuickHelp to use the entire video screen and also searches for information about **NULL** pointers. The last example searches for information about the run-time error message **R6000**, corresponding to stack overflow.

THIRD-PARTY DEBUGGING UTILITIES

Although Microsoft provides a comprehensive set of programming tools, other useful tools are available for purchase from other vendors. In Table 29.2 you will find a summary of some of the available products that complement Microsoft's tools and that have been designed specifically for debugging purposes. These products have been grouped into six different categories. This table was prepared by reviewing the advertisements in the publications listed in Appendix A. The order of presentation is alphabetical within each category, and no effort has been made to evaluate, rank, or recommend the products shown.

Diagrammers and Documentors

This category describes those products that are designed to create flowcharts, block and tree diagrams, cross-reference listings, and other helpful reports by processing C source-code files directly. These tools are useful for documenting source code and understanding source code that has been purchased or "inherited." The features offered by these products are not yet available from Microsoft.

Interactive Debuggers

Although Microsoft's CodeView debugger is rapidly becoming the most widely used interactive debugger, others are commercially available and, generally, offer a set of unique features. Consider purchasing another interactive debugging product if your requirements exceed the features supported by the CodeView debugger.

Lint-like Utilities

These comprehensive C syntax analyzers are derived from the original UNIX lint utility, which was intended to supplement the level of syntax checking performed by the C compiler. The lint utility was designed for use as a C precompiler.

A new compiler option, **/W4**, is now available with QuickC and OptimizingC and provides lint-like reporting for your source code. Generally speaking, the available commercial products perform an even more exhaustive analysis, which is intended to root out probable erroneous conditions.

Source code that is "lint-free" has a better chance of remaining error-free when subject to exhaustive testing and execution. Any C source code that you consider for purchase should be lint-free.

TABLE 29.2: C Debugging Product Summary

PRODUCT CATEGORY	PRODUCT NAME	VENDOR	LIST PRICE
Diagrammers and Documentors	C-Clearly	V Communications	$130
	C-DOC	Software Blacksmiths	$149
	Clear version 1.0 for C	Clear Software	$200
	Codan	Implements	$395
	C Programmers Toolbox/PC	MMC/AD Systems	$175
	EasyFlow	HavenTree Software	$150
	Sbrowse	Computer Enterprises	$245
	Source Print	Powerline Software	$99
	Tree Diagrammer	Powerline Software	$99
Interactive Debuggers	MultiScope DOS Debugger	Logitech/MultiScope	$179
	Periscope..	Periscope	$145-$2595
	Sherlock	Sherlock Software	$195
LINT-like Utilities	C Programmers Toolbox/PC	MMC/AD Systems	$175
	PC-LINT	Gimpel Software	$139
Profilers	DOSTRACE	Alien Software	$95
	INSIDE!	Paradigm Systems	$125
	PC-METRIC	Set Laboratories	$199
	The PROFILER	DWB Associates	$125
Automated Testing	Auto Function Tester	Talis Computer Service	$199
	SMARTS/TCAT	Software Research	$800/$1400
Other UNIX-like Tools for DOS	Berkeley Utilities	OPENetwork	$125
	MKS Toolkit	Mortice Kern Systems	$249

Profilers

This category of utility is particularly useful for application software that is complete, but does not meet performance expectations. These tools monitor the performance of an executable file, and provide various reports that summarize, for instance, the number of times each function is called, and the total elapsed time spent in each function.

With this information, a priority list of functions that are critical to the performance of the entire application emerges, thereby identifying where effort should be expended to improve the overall performance of the program (See Chapter 28). Such tools are presently not available from Microsoft, but they are extremely helpful for gaining insight into the performance characteristics of software that you create, purchase, or "inherit."

Automated Testing

This category of tools is extremely helpful in reducing the time, and improving the quality of the testing that is performed on application software. Rather than relying on a trial and error approach, use these programs to develop, execute, and report on a test suite of program input. Such features are not presently available from Microsoft. Use these tools to provide a final exhaustive level of testing that would be prohibitively expensive if done manually.

Other UNIX-like Tools for DOS

The UNIX-based tools that have been used to help develop, test, and debug C programs are being made available in equivalent form for DOS. Most of these text-processing tools perform helpful services such as pattern matching, file differentiation, and text formatting, which can be useful in the debugging process. These tool are not presently available from Microsoft for DOS.

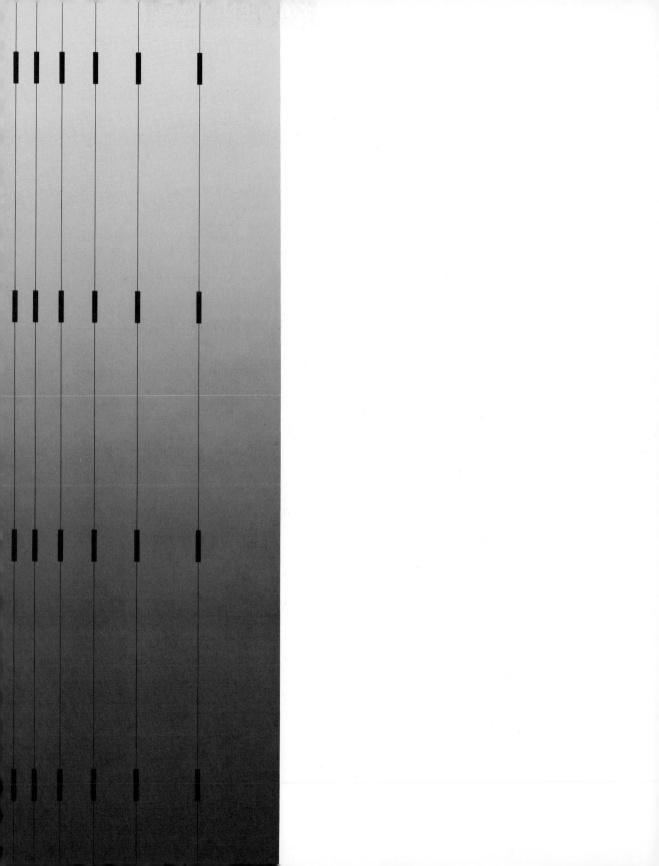

Bibliography

BOOKS

Anderson, P., and G. Anderson. *Advanced C Tips and Techniques.* Indianapolis, IN: Hayden Books, 1988. Excellent coverage of arrays, debugging, and the run-time memory mapping used by C compilers, $24.95.

Boillot, M. *Understanding Fortran 77.* Second edition. St. Paul, MN: West Publishing Company, 1987. Textbook style coverage of Fortran/77, price unknown.

Christopher, Jr., K.W., B.A. Feigenbaum, and S.O. Saliga. *DOS 4.0 Reference.* New York, NY: John Wiley & Sons, Inc., 1989. Overview and command summary of DOS V4.0, $10.95.

Jaeschke, R. *Mastering Standard C.* Horsham, PA: Professional Press, Inc., 1989. A self-paced, training-style workbook on Standard C, $39.95.

Jaeschke, R. *Portability and the C Language.* Indianapolis, IN: Hayden Books, 1989. Detailed look at programming techniques that ensure maximum program portability, $24.95.

Kernighan, B.W., and D.M. Ritchie. *The C Programming Language.* Englewood Cliffs, NJ: Prentice-Hall, Inc., 1978. The original K&R C "standard" document. $31.80, subsequently updated.

Kochan, S.G., and P.H. Wood. *Topics in C Programming.* Indianapolis, IN: Hayden Books, 1989. Excellent coverage of structures and pointers, with emphasis on programming for UNIX, $24.95.

Meyer, B. *Object-Oriented Software Construction.* New York, NY: Prentice Hall, 1988. Overview of OOP emphasizing the EIFFEL language, companion to Meyer's seminar "Object-Oriented Design and Programming," $39.00.

Microsoft Press. *Microsoft C Runtime Library Reference, Version 6.0,* Redmond, WA: 1990. Alphabetic run-time library documentation—not provided with the purchase of either QuickC v2.5 or OptimizingC v6.0, $22.95.

Morse, S.P., E.J. Isaacson, and D.J. Albert. *The 80386/387 Architecture.* New York, NY: John Wiley & Sons, Inc., 1987. Detailed look at and explanation of the design characteristics of the 80386/80387 chips, $24.95.

Norton, P., and R. Lafore. *Inside OS/2*. New York, NY: Brady Books, 1988. Excellent overview of the major features of OS/2, $24.95.

Plauger, P.J., and J. Brodie. *Standard C*. Redmond, WA: Microsoft Press, 1989. Authoritative summary of the ANSI C Standards document, a bargain at $7.95.

Radcliffe, R.A., and T.J. Raab. *Data Handling Utilities in Microsoft C*. Alameda, CA: SYBEX, Inc., 1988. A structured methodology for handling I/O when working with C, $24.95.

Robbins, J. *DOS User's Desktop Companion*. Alameda, CA: SYBEX, Inc., 1988. Comprehensive summary and explanation of DOS, $24.95.

Shammas, N. *Introducing C to Pascal Programmers*. New York, NY: John Wiley & Sons, Inc., 1988. A helpful bridge for Pascal programmers moving to C, $22.95.

Ward, R. *A Programmer's Introduction to Debugging C*. Lawrence, KS: R&D Publications, Inc., 1989. To understand how elusive C bugs can be, and some techniques for averting problems, $19.95.

Weiner, R.S., and L.J. Pinson. *An Introduction to Object-Oriented Programming and C++*. Reading, MA: Addison-Wesley Publishing Company, 1988. Overview of OOP with C++, $31.25.

PERIODICALS

The C Gazette. Pacific Data Works, 1341 Ocean Avenue, Suite 257, Santa Monica, CA 90401. Dedicated to using C and C++ with DOS, $21.00/year (4 issues).

The C Users Journal. R&D Publications, Inc., 2601 Iowa, Lawrence, KS 66046. Essential reading for anyone serious about C and C++, $28.00/year (12 issues).

The C++ Report. JPAM, Inc., SIGS Publishing Group, 588 Broadway, New York, NY 10012. Premier newsletter on the latest developments with C++, $69.00/year (10 issues).

Computer Language. Miller Freeman Publications, 500 Howard Street, San Francisco, CA 94105. Interesting selection of programming topics mostly illustrated in C, $34.95/year (12 issues).

Dr. Dobb's Journal. M&T Publishing, Inc., 501 Galveston Drive, Redwood City, CA 94063. The mainstay publication and diet for many over the years, $29.97/year (12 issues).

Embedded Systems Programming. Miller Freeman Publications, 500 Howard Street, San Francisco, CA 94105. New guy on the block, dedicated to embedded system topics illustrated in C and assembly language programming, $47.00/year (12 issues).

Inside Microsoft C. The Cobb Group, Inc., 9420 Bunsen Parkway, Suite 300, Louisville, KY 40220. Newsletter targeted exclusively at exploiting the capabilities of Microsoft's C compilers, $69.00/year (12 issues).

Microsoft Systems Journal. Microsoft Corporation, 666 Third Avenue, New York, NY 10017. The latest on Microsoft's products, by Microsoft's experts. $50.00/year (6 issues).

UNIX Review. Miller Freeman Publications, 500 Howard Street, San Francisco, CA 94105. UNIX systems and solutions, articles with commentary on C programming, $47.00/year (12 issues).

DOCUMENTATION

American National Standards Institute. ANSI X3J11 Committee. *Programming Language C.* Document X3.159-198x, 14 November 1988. This document is available for purchase only from Global Engineering Documents, Washington, DC. Call (800) 854-7179. Last price quote $75.00 + shipping.

IBM Corporation. *AT Technical Reference,* Boca Raton, FL, 1984. Essential source for IBM PC/AT hardware diagrams and BIOS assembly listings.

IBM Corporation. *BASIC Handbook,* Boca Raton, FL, 1984. General information about getting started with BASIC.

IBM Corporation. *BASIC Reference,* Boca Raton, FL, 1984. Encyclopedia style alphabetic BASIC command summary.

IBM Corporation. *Disk Operating System Reference,* version 3.3, Boca Raton, FL, 1987. Information about using, not programming with, DOS.

IBM Corporation. *Disk Operating System Technical Reference,* version 3.3, Boca Raton, FL, 1987. Detailed programming information about DOS internal structures and register usage for all DOS 0x21 interrupt functions.

INTEL Corporation. *iAPX286 Programmer's Reference Manual,* Santa Clara, CA, 1985. Essential source of design specifications and instruction set summary for the 80286/80287 chips.

Microsoft Corporation. *C For Yourself, Version 2.0,* Redmond, WA, 1988. Helpful C language introduction and overview distributed with QuickC v2.0—superseded by *Microsoft QuickC V2.5 Up and Running.*

Microsoft Corporation. *Microsoft C: Advanced Programming Techniques, Version 6.0,* Redmond, WA, 1990. Excellent resource for insight into selected C topics, distributed with OptimizingC v6.0.

Microsoft Corporation. *Microsoft C: Installing and Using the Professional Development System, Version 6.0,* Redmond, WA, 1990. Overview of how to install and use the integrated PWB compiler.

Microsoft Corporation. *Microsoft C Reference, Version 6.0,* Redmond, WA, 1990. Spiral-bound, alphabetic DOS command and run-time library summary distributed with OptimizingC v6.0.

Microsoft Corporation. *Microsoft QuickC Toolkit, Version 2.0,* Redmond, WA, 1988. Summaries of Microsoft utilities that supplement C program development distributed with QuickC v2.0—superseded by *Microsoft QuickC V2.5 Up and Running.*

Microsoft Corporation. *Microsoft QuickC Up and Running, V2.5,* Redmond, WA, 1990. Comprehensive documentation of the C language and utilities distributed with QuickC v2.5.

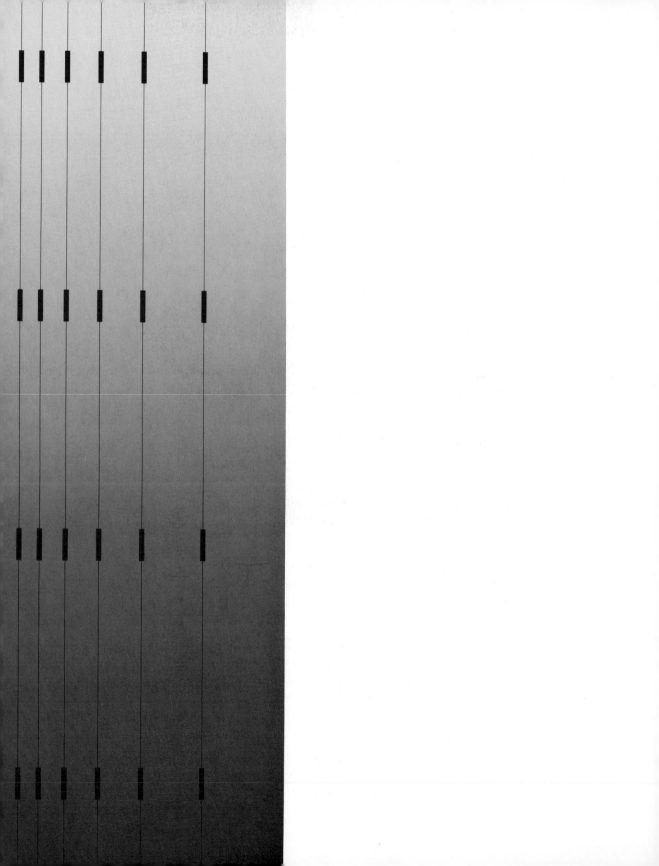

C Keywords

_asm   Non-Standard. Invokes the inline assembler and can appear wherever a C statement is permitted. See Chapter 28.

auto   Standard. The default storage-class specifier for variables that are declared within braces (internal) and only have the lifetime and visibility of the block in which they are declared. See Chapter 7.

_based(..)   Non-Standard. A data-object and pointer qualifier, like **_near**, **_far**, and **_huge**, that permits explicit control over the segment to which a memory allocation or pointer refers. A **_based (..)** pointer always consists of two bytes (:offset), and must be preceded by a two-byte (segment) base expression. See Chapters 7 and 10.

break   Standard. Terminates the current innermost **while**, **for**, **do**, or **switch** statement and passes control to the statement immediately following the one being terminated. See Chapter 13.

case   Standard. A special form of the label statement used within a **switch** statement that cannot be used as the target for a **goto** statement. See Chapter 13.

_cdecl   Non-Standard, supersedes using **cdecl**. A data-object qualifier that implements the C language identifier naming standards (case-sensitive, length), or function-type qualifier that additionally controls the order in which arguments are placed on the stack (rightmost first). See Chapters 7 and 14.

char   Standard. A fundamental integral-type data object that is at least eight bits, or large enough to hold the target system character set, and by default is considered to be signed. See Chapter 7.

const   Standard. A data-object type qualifier that restricts the object to become a nonmodifiable lvalue, and does not permit it to be assigned to, incremented, or decremented. May be specified together with keyword **volatile**. See Chapter 7.

continue   Standard. Terminates the current innermost **while-**, **for-**, or **do**-loop and initiates a branch to the beginning of the loop. Unlike the **break** statement, loop control is not terminated. See Chapter 13.

default   Standard. A special form of the label statement used within a **switch** statement to which control is transferred if no other **case** statements are performed, but which cannot be used as a target for a **goto** statement. See Chapter 13.

do   Standard. Used with keyword **while** to construct a **do-while** loop that is performed at least once and utilizes a post-loop test. See Chapter 13.

double   Standard. A fundamental floating-point type data object that is represented in IEEE format as eight bytes, and is the default type of all floating-point constants not explicitly qualified by the suffix characters F or L. When a variable is declared to be of type **long double**, or a floating-point constant is suffixed with L, the $80x87$ 10-byte real format is utilized. See Chapters 7 and 23.

else   Standard. Used in conjunction with keyword **if** to indicate the false path of the associated **if** (test). See Chapter 13.

_emit   Non-Standard. A pseudo MASM instruction, which is restricted for use within an inline assembly instruction specified by **_asm**. Used to insert bytes within the text (code) segment and circumvent the restricted instruction set recognized by the inline assembler. See Chapter 28.

enum   Standard. A fundamental integral data-object type comprised of a set of identifiers that are initialized by default and individually implemented as type **int**. See Chapter 7.

_export Non-Standard. Restricted for creating functions that will reside in Dynamic Link Libraries (DLL). See Chapter 14.

extern Standard. The default storage-class specifier for variables that are declared outside of braces (external) and have a lifetime and visibility of the program, and is initialized to zero. When explicitly specified, it signifies that the referenced object has been defined (allocated storage) elsewhere. See Chapters 7 and 14.

_far Non-Standard, supersedes using **far**. A data-object, pointer, and function qualifier, like **_near**, **_huge**, and **_based**, which always consists of four bytes (segment:offset), but unlike **_based**, the segment location is controlled by the memory model used. See Chapters 7 and 10.

_fastcall Non-Standard. A new function qualifier keyword with Microsoft C version 6.0 that implements the automatic use of up to three registers, if they are available, for passing arguments, rather than using the stack. This qualifier is incompatible with **_cdecl**, **_export**, **_fortran**, **_interrupt**, **_pascal**, and **_saveregs**. See Chapter 14.

float Standard. A fundamental floating-point type data object that is represented in IEEE format as four bytes, and is the type of a floating-point constant only if the suffix F is explicitly stated. See Chapter 7.

for Standard. A looping construct that involves a preloop test that may prevent the loop from being performed at all. The **for**-loop syntax involves initialization, testing, and incrementation, each of which may be omitted. If testing is omitted, a true condition is implied. See Chapter 13.

_fortran Non-Standard, supersedes using **fortran**. A data-object qualifier, which implements the Fortran language identifier naming standards (case-insensitivity, length), or function-type qualifier, which automatically controls the order in which arguments are placed on the stack (leftmost first). See Chapters 7 and 14.

goto   Standard. An unconditional branch to any label in the current function except **case** or **default**. If a branch to another function must be made, functions **setjmp()** and **longjmp()** must be employed. See Chapters 13 and 25.

_huge   Non-Standard, supersedes using **huge**. A data-object or pointer qualifier, like **_near**, **_far**, and **_based**, which always consists of four bytes (segment:offset), but the address arithmetic performed supports address ranges that span segments. See Chapters 7 and 10.

if   Standard. Used to construct a conditional branching statement that performs a logical test, which if true performs the associated statement or block of statements or, if false, the optional associated **else** statement or block of statements. **If-else** statements may be nested. See Chapter 13.

int   Standard. A fundamental integral-type data object that is at least 16 bits, which by default is considered **signed** by Microsoft. Typically sized to match the machine's word or register size. When a variable is declared to be of type **long int** or an integer constant is suffixed with L, then four bytes are allocated. See Chapter 7.

_interrupt   Non-Standard, supersedes using **interrupt**. Used to qualify a function for use as an interrupt handler by pushing all registers to the stack and setting up the DS register for that function, and by using the instruction IRET, not RET, to restore the machine "state" from the stack. This qualifier is incompatible with **_saveregs** and requires that the function always be qualified as **_cdecl** and **_far**. See Chapters 14 and 27.

_loadds   Non-Standard. Used to qualify a function and control setting for the DS register to a specific value upon function entry either to the compiler **/ND** data segment name or the default DGROUP. This has an effect identical to that which would occur if the **/Au** compiler option were used. See Chapter 14.

long   Standard. Synonymous with **long int** (integral, **signed**, four bytes), or used to qualify **int** or **double** data-object types. See Chapter 7.

_near   Non-Standard, supersedes using **near**. A data-object, pointer, and function qualifier, like **_far**, **_huge**, and **_based**, which always consists of two bytes (:offset), with the segment implied to be the current CS or DS register value. See Chapters 7 and 10.

_pascal   Non-Standard, supersedes using **pascal**. A data-object qualifier, which implements the Pascal language identifier naming standards (case-insensitivity, length), or function-type qualifier, which additionally controls the order in which arguments are placed on the stack (leftmost first). See Chapters 7 and 14.

register   Standard. A storage-class specifier for variables that are declared within braces (internal), have a lifetime and visibility of that block, are assigned to a register, if one is available for use, and are not allocated on the stack. If register allocation cannot be made, then storage-class **auto** is assumed. See Chapter 7.

return   Standard. An unconditional branch that terminates a function and initiates transfer of control to the calling function. Any non-**void** type function may optionally return a value. Function **main()** exhibits special properties because it returns to DOS or another parent process. See Chapters 14 and 15.

_saveregs   Non-Standard. Used to qualify a function so that all registers are pushed to the stack upon entry and restored upon returning. This qualifier is incompatible with **_interrupt**. See Chapter 14.

_segment   Non-Standard. A new keyword with Microsoft C version 6.0 that describes a fundamental **unsigned int** type object (**SEGvar**) that contains a segment address, and can serve as the argument of the keyword **_based(SEGvar)**. See Chapters 7 and 10.

_segname("..") Non-Standard. A new keyword with Microsoft C version 6.0 that identifies a string argument as the segment name that is converted by **_segname** into its equivalent segment address, thus serving as the argument of the keyword **_based(_segname(".."))**. See Chapters 7 and 10.

_self Non-Standard. A new keyword with Microsoft C version 6.0 that identifies for pointers only, the segment in which they reside to be the base segment they address, thus serving as the argument of the keyword **_based((_segment) _self)** when used in conjunction with the **(_segment)** type cast. See Chapters 7 and 10.

short Standard. Synonymous with **short int** (integral, **signed**, 16-bit minimum), or used to qualify the **int** data-object types. See Chapter 7.

signed Standard. Synonymous with **int** (integral, **signed**, 16-bit minimum), or used to qualify the **char**, **short**, **int**, or **long** data-object type and ensure that **signed** arithmetic is performed (see: **unsigned**). Created to clarify type **char**, which is considered plain (without the **signed** or **unsigned** keywords) and subject to implementation definition. See Chapter 7.

sizeof Standard. A compile-time (not preprocessor) operator that returns the size in bytes of its operand, but may not be used with type **void**, bit-fields, or function types. When used with structure and union-type objects, the size returned includes any necessary "pad" bytes. See Chapter 12.

static Standard. A storage-class specifier that restricts the visibility of a data object, pointer, or function type to the source-code file in which it is declared, has a lifetime for the duration of the program, and is initialized to zero unless specified otherwise. See Chapters 7 and 14.

struct Standard. Defines a structure-type object (analogous to a record), that represents the aggregation of dissimilar type objects called members. The **sizeof** a structure equals the sum of the size of its member components plus any necessary "pad" bytes. See Chapter 9.

switch   Standard. A multiway conditional branching statement-type that performs an integral test (qualified type **int** or **long**), and branches (**goto**) to the labels identified within the statement block identified by the keywords **case** and **default**. See Chapter 13.

typedef   Standard. A storage-class (**auto**, **register**, **static**, **extern**) incompatible keyword that defines a synonym for complex incomplete-type declarations. Considered a derived type, it does not convey any lifetime or visibility properties, and simply defines a new type name, which may subsequently be used to define objects. Useful when program portability is of paramount concern. See Chapter 7 and Appendix D.

union   Standard. Defines a union-type object that is analogous to a structure; however, the **sizeof** a union only equals the size of its largest member plus any necessary "pad" bytes. Only one member at a time is current, since all members share the same memory address space. See Chapter 9.

unsigned   Standard. Synonymous with **unsigned int** (integral, **unsigned**, 16-bit minimum), or used to qualify the **char**, **short**, **int**, or **long** data-object type and ensure that **unsigned** arithmetic is performed (see: **signed**). See Chapter 7.

void   Standard. A fundamental type that describes an object with no storage (memory) allocation. Data objects may not be declared to be of type **void**; however, pointers may be declared to type **void** objects, functions may return **void** (nothing), and functions may pass **void** as an argument (nothing). See Chapters 7, 10, and 14.

volatile   Standard. A data-object type qualifier describing an object that may be subject to change by actions outside of the current program. Necessary to prevent compiler optimizations from inadvertently eliminating accesses to the object. May be specified together with keyword **const**. See Chapter 7.

while   Standard. A looping construct that involves a preloop test that may prevent the loop from being performed at all. See Chapter 13.

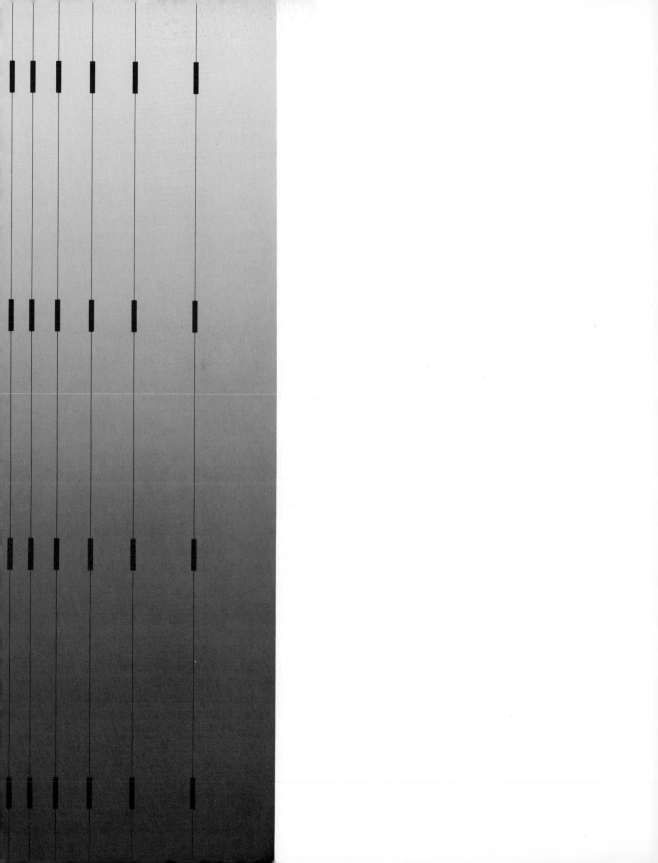

C Global Variables

TABLE C.1: C Global Variables

CATEGORY	DECLARATION	DESCRIPTION
Standard C	`extern volatile int        errno;`	System error, not `_doserrno`
Non-Standard C	`extern unsigned int    _amblksiz;`	Unit of heap allocation
	`extern unsigned char    _ctype[];`	Character classification
	`extern int            daylight;`	1=DST otherwise 0
	`extern int            _doserrno;`	Actual DOS error codes
	`extern char *          environ[];`	Environment table strings
	`extern int            _fileinfo;`	**spawn*xxx*** open file information
	`extern int            _fmode;`	0=text or `O_BINARY`, `O_RAW`
	`extern double           HUGE;`	`double` error value
	`extern FILE            _iob[];`	stream I/O buffers
	`extern long double      _LHUGE;`	`long double` error value
	`extern unsigned char    _osmajor;`	X of DOS X.yy
	`extern unsigned char    _osminor;`	yy of DOS X.yy
	`extern unsigned char    _osmode;`	Real/protected addressing
	`extern unsigned int    _osversion;`	Complete DOS X.yy version
	`extern int            _p_overlay;`	Process **modeflag** value
	`extern unsigned int      _psp;`	Program segment address
	`extern char *      sys_errlist[];`	System, not DOS messages
	`extern int            sys_nerr;`	`sys_errlist[0..sys_nerr]`
	`extern long            timezone;`	Seconds diff GMT and Local time
	`extern char *          tzname[2];`	[1]=timezone; [2]=DST

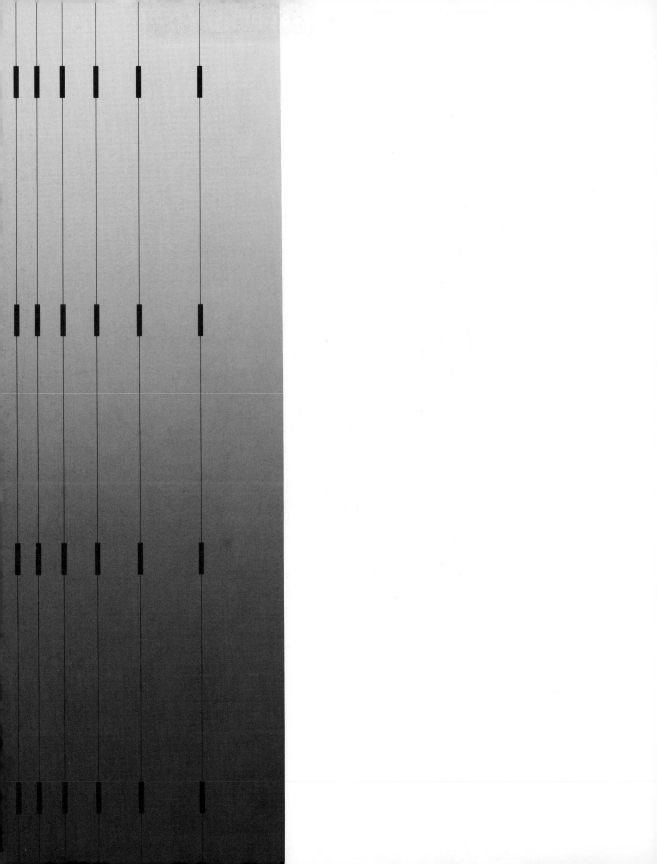

C Type Definitions

TABLE D.1: C Type Definitions

CATEGORY	*typedef*	HEADER FILE	DESCRIPTION
Standard C	clock_t	\<time.h\>	Elapsed processor time value
	div_t	\<stdlib.h\>	Return value of **div**()
	FILE	\<stdio.h\>	Stream file buffer
	fpos_t	\<stdio.h\>	File position indicator
	jmp_buf	\<setjmp.h\>	Machine state buffer
	ldiv_t	\<stdlib.h\>	Return value of **ldiv**()
	ptrdiff_t	\<stddef.h\>	Result of pointer subtraction
	sig_atomic_t	\<signal.h\>	Object never suspended in computation
	size_t	\<stddef.h\>	Return value of **sizeof** operator
	time_t	\<time.h\>	Calendar time value
	va_list	\<stdarg.h\>	Data type of all variable arguments
	wchar_t	\<stddef.h\>	Wide character (unsupported)
Non-Standard C	dev_t	\<sys\types.h\>	Device code
	_HEAPINFO	\<malloc.h\>	Heap control structure
	off_t	\<sys\types.h\>	File offset value
	onexit_t	\<stdlib.h\>	Function pointer for **onexit**()

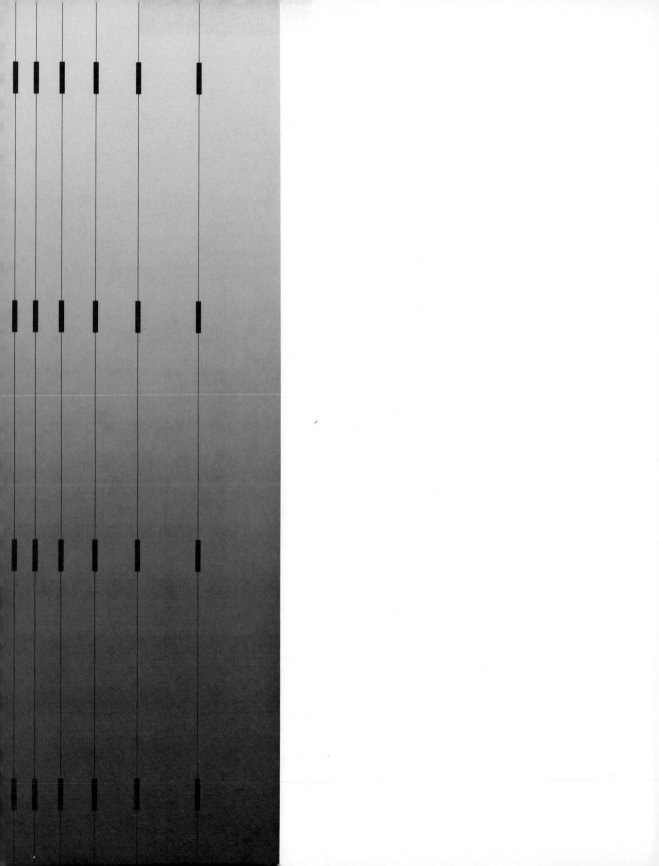

C Structure Tags and Union Declarations

STANDARD C

```
typedef struct _div_t {
        int quot;          /* quotient */
        int rem;           /* remainder */
        } div_t;

struct lconv {
        char *decimal_point;            /* nonmonetary dec. point */
        char *thousands_sep;            /* nonmonetary group separator */
        char *grouping;                 /* nonmonetary digit groups */
        char *int_curr_symbol;          /* international currency symbol */
        char *currency_symbol;          /* local currency symbol */
        char *mon_decimal_point;        /* monetary decimal point */
        char *mon_thousands_sep;        /* monetary group separator */
        char *mon_grouping;             /* monetary digit groups */
        char *positive_sign;            /* monetary positive sign */
        char *negative_sign;            /* monetary negative sign */
        char int_frac_digits;           /* international number of */
                                        /* decimal places */
        char frac_digits;               /* monetary number of */
                                        /* decimal places */
        char p_cs_precedes;             /* positive currency placement */
        char p_sep_by_space;            /* positive cs separator */
        char n_cs_precedes;             /* negative currency placement */
        char n_sep_by_space;            /* negative cs separator */
        char n_sign_posn;               /* parentheses for negative */
        char p_sign_posn; };            /* parentheses for positive */

typedef struct _ldiv_t {
        long quot;         /* quotient */
        long rem;          /* remainder */
        } ldiv_t;

struct tm {
        int tm_sec;        /* seconds after the minute - [0,59] */
        int tm_min;        /* minutes after the hour - [0,59] */
        int tm_hour;       /* hours since midnight - [0,23] */
        int tm_mday;       /* day of the month - [1,31] */
        int tm_mon;        /* months since January - [0,11] */
        int tm_year;       /* years since 1900 */
```

```
        int tm_wday;          /* days since Sunday - [0,6] */
        int tm_yday;          /* days since January 1 - [0,365] */
        int tm_isdst; };      /* daylight savings time flag */
```

NON-STANDARD C

```
struct BYTEREGS {
        unsigned char al;        /* accum register low-order 8 bits */
        unsigned char ah;        /* accum register high-order 8 bits */
        unsigned char bl;        /* base register low-order 8 bits */
        unsigned char bh;        /* base register high-order 8 bits */
        unsigned char cl;        /* count register low-order 8 bits */
        unsigned char ch;        /* count register high-order 8 bits */
        unsigned char dl;        /* data register low-order 8 bits */
        unsigned char dh; };     /* data register high-order 8 bits */

struct complex {
        double x;       /* real part x of (x + yi) */
        double y; };    /* imaginary part y of (x + yi) */

struct _complexl {
        long double x;       /* real part x of (x + yi) */
        long double y; };    /* imaginary part y of (x + yi) */

struct diskfree_t {
        unsigned total_clusters;         /* total clusters */
        unsigned avail_clusters;         /* available clusters */
        unsigned sectors_per_cluster;    /* sectors per cluster */
        unsigned bytes_per_sector; };    /* bytes per sector */

struct diskinfo_t {
        unsigned drive;         /* drive number */
        unsigned head;          /* head number */
        unsigned track;         /* track number */
        unsigned sector;        /* start sector number */
        unsigned nsectors;      /* number of sectors to rd,wr,cm */
        void _far *buffer; };   /* memory addr to rd,wr,cm */

struct dosdate_t {
        unsigned char day;               /* 1-31 */
        unsigned char month;             /* 1-12 */
        unsigned int year;               /* 1980-2099 */
        unsigned char dayofweek; };      /* 0-6, 0=Sunday */

struct DOSERROR {
        int exterror;     /* extended error-no DOS call 59H */
        char class;       /* error class */
        char action;      /* suggested action */
        char locus; };    /* locus */
```

```
struct dostime_t {
        unsigned char hour;           /* 0-23 */
        unsigned char minute;         /* 0-59 */
        unsigned char second;         /* 0-59 */
        unsigned char hsecond; };     /* 0-99 */

struct exception {
        int type;             /* DOMAIN, SING, OVERFLOW, PLOSS, TLOSS */
                              /* or UNDERFLOW from <math.h> */
        char *name;           /* function where error originates */
        double arg1;          /* first argument to function */
        double arg2;          /* second argument (if any) to function */
        double retval; };     /* value to be returned by function */

struct _exception1 {
        int type;             /* DOMAIN, SING, OVERFLOW, PLOSS, TLOSS */
                              /* or UNDERFLOW from <math.h> */
        char *name;           /* function where error originates */
        long double arg1;     /* first argument to function */
        long double arg2;     /* second argument (if any) to function */
        double retval; };     /* value to be returned by function */
struct find_t {
        char reserved[21];    /* reserved for DOS use */
        char attrib;          /* attribute byte for matched file */
                              /* _A_xxxxx object-like macros */
        unsigned wr_time;     /* time of last write to file */
        unsigned wr_date;     /* date of last write to file */
        long size;            /* length of file in bytes */
        char name[13]; };     /* filename w/o path */

typedef struct _heapinfo {
                int _far * _pentry; /* FAR heap entry pointer */
                size_t _size;       /* size of heap entry */
                int _useflag;       /* entry "in-use" flag */
                } _HEAPINFO;        /* get entry w/ _heapwalk */
or
typedef struct _heapinfo {
                int * _pentry;      /* NEAR heap entry pointer */
                size_t _size;       /* size of heap entry */
                int _useflag;       /* entry "in-use" flag */
                } _HEAPINFO;        /* get entry w/ _heapwalk */

extern struct _iobuf {
                char *_ptr;
                int   _cnt;
                char *_base;
                char  _flag;
                char  _file;
                } _iob[];           /* Microsoft global variable */
```

```
union  REGS {
       struct WORDREGS x;        /* 16-bit registers */
       struct BYTEREGS h; };     /* 8-bit registers */

struct SREGS {
       unsigned int es;          /* extra segment register */
       unsigned int cs;          /* code segment register */
       unsigned int ss;          /* stack segment register */
       unsigned int ds; };       /* data segment register */

struct stat {
       dev_t st_dev;             /* drive number or handle */
       ino_t st_ino;             /* unused by DOS */
       unsigned short st_mode;/* file information bit mask */
       short st_nlink;           /* always 1 */
       short st_uid;             /* unused by DOS */
       short st_gid;             /* unused by DOS */
       dev_t st_rdev;            /* drive number or handle */
       off_t st_size;            /* size of file in bytes */
       time_t st_atime;          /* time of last modification */
       time_t st_mtime;          /* time of last modification */
       time_t st_ctime; };       /* time of last modification */

struct timeb {
       time_t time;              /* GMT in seconds */
       unsigned short millitm;/* millisecond fraction */
       short timezone;           /* GMT → Local Time in minutes */
       short dstflag; };         /* =1 if DST in effect */

struct utimbuf {
       time_t actime;            /* access time */
       time_t modtime; };        /* modification time */

struct WORDREGS {
       unsigned int ax;          /* accum register 16 bits */
       unsigned int bx;          /* base register 16 bits */
       unsigned int cx;          /* count register 16 bits */
       unsigned int dx;          /* data register 16 bits */
       unsigned int si;          /* stack index register 16 bits */
       unsigned int di;          /* dest index register 16 bits */
       unsigned int cflag; }; /* flags */
```

Index

In the following index, **boldface** page numbers show where to find the formal reference entry for a given run-time library function. Consult the other page numbers for topical discussions and further information.

C

C

Selections from The SYBEX Library

LANGUAGES

The ABC's of GW-BASIC
William R. Orvis
320pp. Ref. 663-4
Featuring two parts: Part I is an easy-to-follow tutorial for beginners, while Part II is a complete, concise reference guide to GW-BASIC commands and functions. Covers everything from the basics of programming in the GW-BASIC environment, to debugging a major program. Includes special treatment of graphics and sound.

The ABC's of Quick C
Douglas Hergert
309pp. Ref. 557-3
This is the most unintimidating C language tutorial, designed especially for readers who have had little or no computer programming experience. The reader will learn programming essentials with step-by-step instructions for working with numbers, strings, arrays, pointers, structures, decisions, and loops. For Version 2.0.

The ABC's of Turbo C
Douglas Hergert
310pp. Ref. 594-8
This unintimidating C language tutorial was written especially for those with little or no experience with computer programming. The ABC's teaches fundamental programming concepts and techniques with lots of program examples for working with numbers, strings, arrays, pointers, loops, decisions, and more. For Version 2.0.

BASIC Programs for Scientists and Engineers
Alan R. Miller
318pp. Ref. 073-3

The algorithms presented in this book are programmed in standard BASIC code which should be usable with almost any implementation of BASIC. Includes statistical calculations, matrix algebra, curve fitting, integration, and more.

FORTRAN Programs for Scientists and Engineers (Second Edition)
Alan R. Miller
280pp. Ref. 571-9
In this collection of widely used scientific algorithms—for statistics, vector and matrix operations, curve fitting, and more—the author stresses effective use of little-known and powerful features of FORTRAN.

Introduction to Pascal: Including Turbo Pascal (Second Edition)
Rodnay Zaks
464pp. Ref. 533-6
This best-selling tutorial builds complete mastery of Pascal—from basic structured programming concepts, to advanced I/O, data structures, file operations, sets, pointers and lists, and more. Both ISO Standard and Turbo Pascal.

Introduction to Turbo Prolog (Second Edition)
Carl Townsend
325pp. Ref. 611-1
Written with beginning and intermediate users in mind, this thorough guide covers practical techniques for I/O, string and arithmetic operations, windows, graphics, sound, expert systems, natural language interfaces, and simulation systems. Includes exercises. For Version 2.0.

Mastering C
Craig Bolon

437pp. Ref. 326-0

This in-depth guide stresses planning, testing, efficiency and portability in C applications. Topics include data types, storage classes, arrays, pointers, data structures, control statements, I/O and the C function library.

Mastering QuickBASIC
Rita Belserene

450pp. Ref. 589-1

Readers build professional programs with this extensive language tutorial. Fundamental commands are mixed with the author's tips and tricks so that users can create their own applications. Program templates are included for video displays, computer games, and working with databases and printers. For Version 4.5.

Mastering QuickC
Stan Kelly-Bootle

602pp. Ref. 550-6

This extensive tutorial covers C language programming and features the latest version of QuickC. Veteran author Kelly-Bootle uses many examples to explain language and style, covering data types, storage classes, file I/O, the Graphics Toolbox, and the window-oriented debugger. For Version 2.0.

Mastering QuickPascal
Michael Yester

581pp. Ref. 653-7

Ideal for QuickPascal programmers who want a general reference to the language, as well as for experience Turbo Pascal programmers who are interested in how object-oriented programming can be used.

Includes a complete tutorial on the Pascal language.

Mastering Turbo C
(Second Edition)
Stan Kelly-Bootle

609pp. Ref. 595-6

With a foreword by Borland International President Philippe Kahn, this new edition has been expanded to include full details

on Version 2.0. Learn theory and practical programming, with tutorials on data types, real numbers and characters, controlling program flow, file I/O, and producing color charts and graphs. Through Version 2.

Mastering Turbo Pascal 5
(Second Edition)
Douglas Hergert

628pp. Ref. 647-2

Explore the potential of the fast and efficient programming environment offered by Turbo Pascal 5 Version 5.5. Discover the powerful new advanced object-oriented programming, in addition to all the essential elements of a professional programming language; file-handling procedures; recursion; support for the 8087 numeric coprocessor chip; and user-defined units.

QuickC Instant Reference
SYBEX Prompter Series
J. Daniel Gifford

394pp. Ref. 586-7, 4 ¾" × 8"

This concise guide to QuickC key words and library functions should be on every programmer's desk. Organized alphabetically for quick and easy access, it covers all the essential information such as format, syntax, arguments, and usage.

Systems Programming in
Microsoft C
Michael J. Young

604pp. Ref. 570-0

This sourcebook of advanced C programming techniques is for anyone who wants to make the most of their C compiler or Microsoft QuickC. It includes a comprehensive, annotated library of systems functions, ready to compile and call.

Systems Programming in Turbo C
Michael J. Young

365pp. Ref. 467-4

An introduction to advanced programming with Borland's Turbo C, and a gold-mine of ready-made routines for the system programmer's library: DOS and BIOS interfacing, interrupt handling, windows, graphics, expanded memory, UNIX utilities, and more.

Turbo Pascal Toolbox
(Second Edition)
Frank Dutton
425pp. Ref. 602-2

This collection of tested, efficient Turbo Pascal building blocks gives a boost to intermediate-level programmers, while teaching effective programming by example. Topics include accessing DOS, menus, bit maps, screen handling, and much more.

OPERATING SYSTEMS

The ABC's of DOS 4
Alan R. Miller
275pp. Ref. 583-2

This step-by-step introduction to using DOS 4 is written especially for beginners. Filled with simple examples, *The ABC's of DOS 4* covers the basics of hardware, software, disks, the system editor EDLIN, DOS commands, and more.

ABC's of MS-DOS
(Second Edition)
Alan R. Miller
233pp. Ref. 493-3

This handy guide to MS-DOS is all many PC users need to manage their computer files, organize floppy and hard disks, use EDLIN, and keep their computers organized. Additional information is given about utilities like Sidekick, and there is a DOS command and program summary. The second edition is fully updated for Version 3.3.

DOS Assembly Language
Programming
Alan R. Miller
365pp. 487-9

This book covers PC-DOS through 3.3, and gives clear explanations of how to assemble, link, and debug 8086, 8088, 80286, and 80386 programs. The example assembly language routines are valuable for students and programmers alike.

DOS Instant Reference
SYBEX Prompter Series
Greg Harvey
Kay Yarborough Nelson
220pp. Ref. 477-1, 4 ¾" × 8"

A complete fingertip reference for fast, easy on-line help:command summaries, syntax, usage and error messages. Organized by function—system commands, file commands, disk management, directories, batch files, I/O, networking, programming, and more. Through Version 3.3.

DOS User's Desktop Companion
SYBEX Ready Reference Series
Judd Robbins
969pp. Ref. 505-0

This comprehensive reference covers DOS commands, batch files, memory enhancements, printing, communications and more information on optimizing each user's DOS environment. Written with step-by-step instructions and plenty of examples, this volume covers all versions through 3.3.

Encyclopedia DOS
Judd Robbins
1030pp. Ref. 699-5

A comprehensive reference and user's guide to all versions of DOS through 4.0. Offers complete information on every DOS command, with all possible switches and parameters -- plus examples of effective usage. An invaluable tool.

Essential OS/2
(Second Edition)
Judd Robbins
445pp. Ref. 609-X

Written by an OS/2 expert, this is the guide to the powerful new resources of the OS/2 operating system standard edition 1.1 with presentation manager. Robbins introduces the standard edition, and details multitasking under OS/2, and the range of commands for installing, starting up, configuring, and running applications. For Version 1.1 Standard Edition.

Programs Available on Disk

The more than 200 comprehensive example programs included in this book that are identified with a figure description such as chxxeyy.c, or by a source code comment such as /* FILE: chxxeyy.c */, are available on disk.

One additional file is provided (which could not be included in this book) that represents a comprehensive alphabetical list of more than 1000 identifiers used by Standard C, Microsoft C and C++, including the location where the identifier is defined and what type of identifier it is (i.e., function, macro, keyword, etc.). This file, called MS-ID.DOC, is invaluable for creating global project identifiers that do not conflict with the Microsoft C compiler, header files, and run-time library (see Chapter 5).

You can order a copy of these files directly from the author, instead of keying-in the program examples, or struggling with identifier naming. Simply complete and mail the order form below. Include a check or money order (sorry, no credit cards) in the amount of:

$12.50   Continental U.S. orders
$15.00   Other orders

There are no additional postage or handling charges. To expedite delivery, you can call the author at (215) 988-9378.

- -

Computer Application Engineers, Inc.
c/o Robert A. Radcliffe
517 North 19th Street
Philadelphia, PA 19130

Name: _____

Address: _____

City/State/Zip: _____

Country: _____

Telephone: _____

Enclose your check or money order payable in U.S. dollars to Computer Application Engineers, Inc. for the Encyclopedia C disk formatted as follows (circle choice below):

Disk: 5-1/4" (360KB)   or   3-1/2" (720KB)

SYBEX

TO JOIN THE SYBEX MAILING LIST OR ORDER BOOKS
PLEASE COMPLETE THIS FORM

NAME _____ COMPANY _____

STREET _____ CITY _____

STATE _____ ZIP _____

☐ PLEASE MAIL ME MORE INFORMATION ABOUT **SYBEX** TITLES

ORDER FORM (There is no obligation to order)

PLEASE SEND ME THE FOLLOWING:

TITLE	QTY	PRICE
_____	____	____
_____	____	____
_____	____	____
_____	____	____

TOTAL BOOK ORDER   ____ $____

CUSTOMER SIGNATURE _____

SHIPPING AND HANDLING PLEASE ADD $2.00 PER BOOK VIA UPS   _____

FOR OVERSEAS SURFACE ADD $5.25 PER BOOK PLUS $4.40 REGISTRATION FEE   _____

FOR OVERSEAS AIRMAIL ADD $18.25 PER BOOK PLUS $4.40 REGISTRATION FEE   _____

CALIFORNIA RESIDENTS PLEASE ADD APPLICABLE SALES TAX   _____

TOTAL AMOUNT PAYABLE   _____

☐ CHECK ENCLOSED   ☐ VISA
☐ MASTERCARD   ☐ AMERICAN EXPRESS

ACCOUNT NUMBER _____

EXPIR. DATE _____   DAYTIME PHONE _____

CHECK AREA OF COMPUTER INTEREST:

☐ BUSINESS SOFTWARE

☐ TECHNICAL PROGRAMMING

☐ OTHER: _____

THE FACTOR THAT WAS MOST IMPORTANT IN YOUR SELECTION:

☐ THE SYBEX NAME

☐ QUALITY

☐ PRICE

☐ EXTRA FEATURES

☐ COMPREHENSIVENESS

☐ CLEAR WRITING

☐ OTHER _____

OTHER COMPUTER TITLES YOU WOULD LIKE TO SEE IN PRINT:

_____

_____

OCCUPATION

☐ PROGRAMMER   ☐ TEACHER

☐ SENIOR EXECUTIVE   ☐ HOMEMAKER

☐ COMPUTER CONSULTANT   ☐ RETIRED

☐ SUPERVISOR   ☐ STUDENT

☐ MIDDLE MANAGEMENT   ☐ OTHER:

☐ ENGINEER/TECHNICAL   _____

☐ CLERICAL/SERVICE

☐ BUSINESS OWNER/SELF EMPLOYED

CHECK YOUR LEVEL OF COMPUTER USE

☐ NEW TO COMPUTERS

☐ INFREQUENT COMPUTER USER

☐ FREQUENT USER OF ONE SOFTWARE

   PACKAGE:

   NAME _____

☐ FREQUENT USER OF MANY SOFTWARE

   PACKAGES

☐ PROFESSIONAL PROGRAMMER

OTHER COMMENTS:

_____

_____

_____

_____

_____

_____

_____

PLEASE FOLD, SEAL, AND MAIL TO SYBEX

– –

SYBEX, INC.

2021 CHALLENGER DR. #100

ALAMEDA, CALIFORNIA USA

              94501

SYBEX

FUNCTION	PAGE	FUNCTION	PAGE	FUNCTION	PAGE
_fmemset(NS)	1050	getc()	768	jn(NS)	1004
fmod()	1000	getch(NS)	825	_jnl(NS)	1004
fmodl()	1000	getchar()	770	kbhit(NS)	830
fmsbintoieee(NS)	852	getche(NS)	826	labs()	1004
_fmsize(NS)	1050	getcwd(NS)	709	ldexp()	1005
fopen()	757	_getdcwd(NS)	709	ldexpl()	1005
_fpreset(NS)	1002	_getdrive(NS)	710	ldiv()	1005
fprintf()	758	getenv()	1108	lfind(NS)	1200
fputc()	759	getpid(NS)	1109	localeconv()	1202
fputchar(NS)	759	gets()	771	localtime()	903
fputs()	760	getw(NS)	772	locking(NS)	711
fread()	761	gmtime()	900	log()	1006
_frealloc(NS)	1050	halloc(NS)	1052	logl()	1006
free()	1051	_harderr(NS)	1199	log10()	1007
_freect(NS)	1051	_hardresume(NS)	1199	log10l()	1007
freopen()	761	_hardretn(NS)	1199	longjmp()	1109
frexp()	1002	_heapadd(NS)	1053	_lrotl(NS)	860
frexpl()	1002	_heapchk(NS)	1056	_lrotr(NS)	861
fscanf()	762	_heapmin(NS)	1058	lsearch(NS)	1205
fseek()	763	_heapset(NS)	1060	lseek(NS)	809
fsetpos()	763	_heapwalk(NS)	1062	ltoa(NS)	862
_fsopen(NS)	764	hfree(NS)	1063	_makepath(NS)	715
fstat(NS)	707	hypot(NS)	1003	malloc()	1063
_fstrcat(NS)	1134	hypotl(NS)	1003	matherr(NS)	1008
_fstrchr(NS)	1135	inp(NS)	826	_matherrl(NS)	1008
_fstrcmp(NS)	1135	inpw(NS)	829	_memavl(NS)	1065
_fstrcpy(NS)	1135	int86(NS)	950	memccpy(NS)	1066
_fstrcspn(NS)	1135	int86x(NS)	953	memchr()	1067
_fstrdup(NS)	1136	intdos(NS)	955	memcmp()	1067
_fstricmp(NS)	1136	intdosx(NS)	958	memcpy()	1070
_fstrlen(NS)	1136	isalnum()	855	memicmp(NS)	1072
_fstrlwr(NS)	1137	isalpha()	856	_memmax(NS)	1073
_fstrncat(NS)	1137	isascii(NS)	856	memmove()	1073
_fstrncmp(NS)	1137	isatty(NS)	711	memset()	1074
_fstrncpy(NS)	1137	iscntrl()	856	mkdir(NS)	715
_fstrnicmp(NS)	1138	iscsym(NS)	857	mktemp(NS)	717
_fstrnset(NS)	1138	iscsymf(NS)	857	mktime()	904
_fstrpbrk(NS)	1138	isdigit()	857	modf()	1010
_fstrrchr(NS)	1139	isgraph()	857	modfl()	1010
_fstrrev(NS)	1139	islower()	858	movedata(NS)	1074
_fstrset(NS)	1139	isprint()	858	_msize(NS)	1075
_fstrspn(NS)	1140	ispunct()	858	_ncalloc(NS)	1076
_fstrstr(NS)	1140	isspace()	859	_nexpand(NS)	1076
_fstrtok(NS)	1140	isupper()	859	_nfree(NS)	1076
_fstrupr(NS)	1140	isxdigit()	859	_nheapchk(NS)	1077
ftell()	766	itoa(NS)	859	_nheapmin(NS)	1077
ftime(NS)	899	j0(NS)	1004	_nheapset(NS)	1077
_fullpath(NS)	707	_j0l(NS)	1004	_nheapwalk(NS)	1078
fwrite()	767	j1(NS)	1004	_nmalloc(NS)	1078
gcvt(NS)	853	_j1l(NS)	1004	_nmsize(NS)	1078